THE WESLEYAN EDITION OF THE
WORKS OF HENRY FIELDING

THE JOURNAL OF A VOYAGE TO LISBON,
SHAMELA,
AND OCCASIONAL WRITINGS

HENRY FIELDING

The Journal of a Voyage to Lisbon, Shamela, and Occasional Writings

EDITED BY

MARTIN C. BATTESTIN

with the late

SHERIDAN W. BAKER, JR., and HUGH AMORY

CLARENDON PRESS · OXFORD

OXFORD
UNIVERSITY PRESS

Great Clarendon Street, Oxford OX2 6DP

Oxford University Press is a department of the University of Oxford.
It furthers the University's objective of excellence in research, scholarship,
and education by publishing worldwide in

Oxford New York

Auckland Cape Town Dar es Salaam Hong Kong Karachi
Kuala Lumpur Madrid Melbourne Mexico City Nairobi
New Delhi Shanghai Taipei Toronto

With offices in

Argentina Austria Brazil Chile Czech Republic France Greece
Guatemala Hungary Italy Japan Poland Portugal Singapore
South Korea Switzerland Thailand Turkey Ukraine Vietnam

Oxford is a registered trade mark of Oxford University Press
in the UK and in certain other countries

Published in the United States
by Oxford University Press Inc., New York

© Martin Battestin 2008

British Library Cataloguing in Publication Data

Data available

Library of Congress Cataloging in Publication Data

Data available

Typeset by RefineCatch Limited, Bungay, Suffolk
Printed in Great Britain
on acid-free paper by
Biddles Ltd, King's Lynn

ISBN 978-0-19-926675-3

1 3 5 7 9 10 8 6 4 2

PREFACE

THE publication of this volume marks the completion of the Wesleyan Edition of Fielding's non-dramatic writings. The project was conceived forty-five years ago at Wesleyan University, Middletown, Connecticut, where the present editor, in collaboration with W. B. Coley, proposed the edition jointly to the Wesleyan University Press and the Oxford University Press. Soon after, I accepted an appointment at the University of Virginia in 1961.

It was my good fortune—and as it proved that of the Fielding edition—that Fredson Bowers (1905–91), editor of *Studies in Bibliography* and the pre-eminent textual scholar of his time, was then chairman of the department at Virginia.[1] It was Bowers who schooled me, among many others of my generation, in the principles of editing. Having accepted the invitation to become Textual Editor of the project, Bowers provided for the inaugural volume, the edition of *Joseph Andrews* (1966), a Textual Introduction that declared in the opening paragraph the objectives and procedures that would inform the practice of the editors during his lifetime and after:

This edition offers a critical unmodernized text of *Joseph Andrews*. The text is critical in that it has been established by the application of analytical criticism to the evidence of the various early documentary forms in which the novel appeared. It is unmodernized in that every effort has been made to present the text in as close a form to Fielding's own inscription and successive revisions as the surviving documents permit, subject to normal editorial regulation. (p. [xxxix])

On Bowers's death in 1991, the role of textual adviser to the Edition passed to Hugh Amory (1930–2001), Rare Book Cataloguer of the Houghton Library at Harvard. As Textual Editor, Amory collaborated with Bertrand Goldgar in editing volumes II (1993) and III (1997) of Fielding's *Miscellanies* (1743), completing the three-volume set, of which Henry Knight Miller had published the first in 1972.

Before his own death ten years later, Amory had been reading drafts of the texts, introductions, and notes that Sheridan Baker (1918–2000), the first editor of the present volume, submitted to him as he neared the end of the long and exacting process of preparing this collection of odds and ends

---

[1] For a biography of Bowers and an assessment of his achievements in descriptive and analytical bibliography and scholarly editing, see G. Thomas Tanselle, *The Life and Work of Fredson Bowers*, The Bibliographical Society of the University of Virginia (Charlottesville, Va., 1993).

for publication. As for Amory's own contributions to the volume, he was chiefly responsible for editing two of the most complicated and demanding of the texts: namely, *Ovid's Art of Love*, for which his command of Latin and the scholia was indispensable; and *The Journal of a Voyage to Lisbon*, which posed the most perplexing textual problem of all. With the permission of Judith Amory, as well as the members of the Bibliographical Society of Australia and New Zealand who first published it, an abridgement of Amory's essay 'The Authority of the Two Versions of Fielding's *Journal of a Voyage to Lisbon*' serves as Textual Introduction to the principal work of the collection. May this valedictory volume serve as a fitting memorial to two of the best of Fielding scholars.

As for my own part in the edition, thanks to the Executive Editor of the Wesleyan Edition and to Judith Amory, I have had the benefit of consulting the unfinished work of both these scholars. Baker's contributions amounted to numerous drafts and photocopies of material relevant to every aspect of the edition. It should be understood, however, that unless otherwise stated,[2] I am responsible for the introductions and commentary to all the texts, as well as the front matter and the content of the three Appendices.

Because this is such an anomalous collection—except for the three epilogues and the prologue, and Fielding's contributions to his sister's novels, no two works here have any obvious relation to each other, either generic or topical—the organization of the volume departs, in some respects, from the established format of the Wesleyan Edition. The usual General Introduction, typically an expansive essay, placed the principal work of the title, as well as any 'related writings', in a biographical and literary, and on occasion a social or political, context. Substituting for it here are individual introductions to each of the eighteen texts. These briefer essays are, as it were, miniature versions of the established paradigm: also biographical and literary, they focus on the circumstances of the work's composition and (with the exception of course of the two manuscripts) on the printing, publishing, and, when possible, the reception of the text.

Except for the individuation of these introductions, the treatment of the texts themselves conforms to the usual practice of the Wesleyan Edition: the explanatory annotation is comprehensive, and with regard to substantives the copy-texts are the sources closest to the author's manuscripts, in most cases the first edition. Appendix B offers a full textual apparatus:

---

[2] Notes based chiefly on the work of Baker and Amory will be signed, respectively, SWB and HA. Sections or passages adopted in the introductions to the texts are also acknowledged in this way. When these signatures after a sentence are enclosed in square brackets '[SWB]' and '[HA]', the contribution is limited to that specific statement only.

emendations of the text are recorded; substantive variants and revisions are listed in a Historical Collation; and whenever possible a technical Bibliographical Description of the work is provided.

Besides making readily available pieces that now complete the Wesleyan Edition of the established canon of Fielding's non-dramatic writings,[3] this volume arranges the texts in chronological order, beginning with the first of his extant publications, *The Masquerade* (1728) and ending with the last of his major works, the posthumous *Journal of a Voyage to Lisbon* (1755). To read these texts in sequence is to follow an outline of Fielding's life of writing.

Note: Throughout this edition I have treated as Fielding's the essays in *The Craftsman* that I attributed to him in *New Essays* (1989), where the reader will find what I believe to be cogent reasons for Fielding's authorship presented in full (see below, the headnote to Appendix A). Though I am not by any means alone among students of Fielding in accepting his authorship of these essays, they have not yet been generally accepted as his. A case for rejecting the attribution of these essays to Fielding is made by Thomas Lockwood, 'Did Fielding Write for the *Craftsman?*', forthcoming in *RES*. Advance Access to this article, published online on March 6, 2007, with implications for other attributions as well, is available through *The Review of English Studies*, doi:10.1093/res/hgll58.

MCB

Charlottesville, Virginia
May 2005

[3] As they have yet to be generally accepted as Fielding's, the attributed pieces in Appendix A are exceptions.

ACKNOWLEDGEMENTS

THE greater part by far of the work that has resulted in this book was accomplished by Sheridan W. Baker, Jr., Professor of English at the University of Michigan, who was engaged in the project from the late 1960s to his death at the turn of the century. The fruits of his research were subsequently committed to W. B. Coley, Executive Editor of the Wesleyan Edition, who made them available to me when I undertook to prepare the volume for publication. Among the cartons of these papers were sheets of notes and collations of texts, drafts of the introductions and commentary on the texts, and bibliographical descriptions of the relevant editions; there were also sheaves of correspondence—decades of it—that Baker had conducted with librarians and archivists in America and the United Kingdom.

A roll-call of these institutions in alphabetical order would include the following: In the United Kingdom, Blickling Hall, Norwich; the Bodleian Library, Oxford; the Bristol Public Library; the British Library; the libraries of Cambridge University and Edinburgh University; the John Rylands Library, Manchester University; and the library of the University of Wales (Lampeter). In the United States, the University of Chicago Library; the William Andrews Clark Library (Los Angeles); the Folger Library (Washington, DC); Goucher College Library (Baltimore); Harvard University; the Huntington Library (San Marino, California); the University of Illinois (Urbana); the University of Iowa (Ames); the University of Michigan (Ann Arbor); the New York Public Library; Princeton University; the University of Virginia; the Lewis Walpole Library (Farmington, Connecticut); the R. W. Woodruff Library, Emory University (Atlanta); and Yale University.

In any list of individuals who assisted him in this work Baker would certainly have included Coley and Hugh Amory, both of whom read and criticized the drafts of copy he submitted to them; my own thanks are also due Coley for this same service. Among many others known only to Baker and Amory, who succeeded Baker as editor, a few of the correspondents who answered queries can be identified. They include Margaret T. Prior, Curator of Lake Village Museum, Glastonbury; Guy Holborn of Lincoln's Inn Library; and Janice L. Wood, Archivist of the Devon Record Office.

My own thanks are due to David Vander Meulen, who prepared the final draft of the bibliographical description of *The Journal of a Voyage to Lisbon*; and to Robert Denommé, who translated from the French of Matthew

Maty the most interesting, but previously unnoticed, review of the *Journal*.
Michael J. Bosson, Archivist of the Harrowby MSS Trust, Sandon Hall,
Stafford, provided the photocopies of the manuscripts of Fielding's
'Cantos' and his 'Epistle to Lyttleton' on which the texts in this edition are
based. The searches of Amanda Gibbs, Archivist of the Bath Museum, and
her colleagues prevented me from venting an insupportable hypothesis
about a puzzling reference in Fielding's 'Plain Truth'. Readers of this
volume will also be aware of how much I have benefited from the deep
research and sound scholarship of Dr Frederick Ribble, author, with his
wife, Anne, of *Fielding's Library: An Annotated Catalogue*, and of ground-
breaking articles on Fielding's life, works, and friends. And as my notes to
The Journal of a Voyage to Lisbon acknowledge, Tom Keymer's commentary
in his Penguin edition of that work has improved my understanding of it.

Here, too, as in all my work for the past forty-two years, I owe much to
my wife, Ruthe Rootes Battestin.

MCB

CONTENTS

LIST OF ILLUSTRATIONS

ABBREVIATIONS

Account	*An Account of the Conduct of the Dowager Duchess of Marlborough, From her first coming to Court, To the Year 1710* (1742)
Amelia	*Amelia* (1751), ed. Martin C. Battestin (Oxford and Middletown, Conn., 1983)
Amory, 'Lisbon Letters'	'Fielding's Lisbon Letters', *Huntington Library Quarterly*, 35 (1971), pp. 65–83
—— 'Two Versions of *Voyage to Lisbon*'	'The Authority of the Two Versions of Fielding's *Journal of a Voyage to Lisbon*', in David Garrioch, Harold Love, Brian McMullin, Ian Morrison, and Meredith Sherlock (eds.), *The Culture of the Book: Essays from Two Hemispheres in Honour of Wallace Kirsop* (Melbourne, 1999), pp. 182–200
—— 'Fielding's Ovid'	'The Texts of Fielding's Ovid', Bibliographical Society of Australia and New Zealand, *Bulletin*, 23 (1999), pp. 11–26
Battestin, *Fielding's Art*	Martin C. Battestin, *The Moral Basis of Fielding's Art* (Middletown, Conn., 1959)
—— 'Four New Attributions'	'Four New Fielding Attributions', *Studies in Bibliography*, 36 (1983), pp. 69–109
—— '*Universal Spectator*	'Fielding's Contributions to the *Universal Spectator* (1736–1737)', *SP*, 83 (1986), pp. 88–116
BL	British Library
BLR	Bodleian Library Record
Burnet's *History*	Bishop Gilbert Burnet's *History of His Own Time*, 2 vols. (1724)
Burrows and Dunhill	*Music and the Theatre in Handel's World: The Family Papers of James Harris 1732–1780*, ed. Donald Burrows and Rosemary Dunhill (Oxford, 2002)
'Cantos'	Untitled MS of HF's unfinished burlesque of *The Dunciad* (1729–30). Text and pagination from the present volume
CGJ	*The Covent-Garden Journal and a Plan of the Universal Register-Office* (1752), ed. Bertrand A. Goldgar (Oxford and Middletown, Conn., 1988)

C-H	Chadwyck-Healey online database *Eighteenth-Century Fiction* (Cambridge, 1996), <http://www.chadwyck.co.uk>
Champion	*Contributions to 'The Champion' and Related Writings*, ed. W. B. Coley (Oxford and Middletown, Conn., 2003)
Charge	*A Charge Delivered to the Grand Jury . . . for the City and Liberty of Westminster* (1749). Text and pagination from *Enquiry*
Companion	Martin C. Battestin, *A Henry Fielding Companion* (Westport, Conn., and London, 2000)
Complete Letters	*The Complete Letters of Lady Mary Wortley Montagu*, 3 vols. (Oxford, 1965)
Correspondence	*The Correspondence of Henry and Sarah Fielding*, ed. Martin C. Battestin and Clive T. Probyn (Oxford, 1993)
Cross	Wilbur L. Cross, *The History of Henry Fielding*, 3 vols. (New Haven, 1918)
DA	*Daily Advertiser*
Dacier	Mme Dacier's *Le Plutus et les nuées d'Aristophane* (Lyons, 1696)
David Simple	Sarah Fielding, *The Adventures of David Simple* (1744)
Dobson	*Fielding's Journal of a Voyage to Lisbon*, ed. Austin Dobson (1907)
DP	*Daily Post*
Dudden	F. Homes Dudden, *Henry Fielding: His Life, Works, and Times*, 2 vols. (Oxford, 1952)
Eaves and Kimpel	T. C. Duncan Eaves and Ben D. Kimpel, *Samuel Richardson: A Biography* (Oxford, 1971)
EB	*Encyclopaedia Britannica*, 11th edn. (1910)
ECS	*Eighteenth-Century Studies*
ELH	*ELH: A Journal of English Literary History*
Enquiry	*An Enquiry into the Causes of the late Increase of Robbers and Related Writings* (1751), ed. Malvin R. Zirker (Oxford and Middletown, Conn., 1988)
Essays and Poems	Lady Mary Wortley Montagu, *Essays and Poems and Simplicity, A Comedy*, ed. Robert Halsband and Isobel Grundy (Oxford, 1977)

ESTC	*English Short Title Catalogue*
Familiar Letters	Sarah Fielding, *Familiar Letters between the Principal Characters in David Simple* (1747)
Fragment	*A Fragment of a Comment on L. Bolingbroke's Essays* (1755). Text and pagination from the present volume
GM	*The Gentleman's Magazine*
Goldgar	Bertrand A. Goldgar, *Walpole and the Wits: The Relation between Politics and Literature, 1722–1742* (Lincoln, Nebr., 1976)
Grose	Francis Grose, *A Classical Dictionary of the Vulgar Tongue* (1963)
Grundy	Isobel Grundy, *Lady Mary Wortley Montagu* (Oxford and New York, 1999)
HA	Hugh Amory
Halsband	Robert Halsband, *Lord Hervey: Eighteenth-Century Courtier* (Oxford and New York, 1974)
HF	Henry Fielding
HOOT	Thomas Lockwood, *The History of Our Own Times* (1741), attributed to HF; facs. (New York, 1986)
Hume	Robert D. Hume, *Henry Fielding and the London Theatre 1728–1737* (Oxford, 1988)
JJ	*The Jacobite's Journal and Related Writings*, ed. W. B. Coley (Oxford and Middletown, Conn., 1974–5)
Jonathan Wild	*The History of the Life of the late Mr. Jonathan Wild the Great* (1743). Text and pagination from *Miscellanies* iii
Joseph Andrews	*Joseph Andrews* (1742), ed. Martin C. Battestin (Oxford and Middletown, Conn., 1966–7)
Journal	*The Journal of a Voyage to Lisbon* (1755). Text and pagination from the present volume
JWN	*Journey from this World to the Next* (1743). Text and pagination from *Miscellanies* ii
Keymer, *Fielding's Journal*	*Fielding's Journal of a Voyage to Lisbon*, ed. Tom Keymer (Harmondsworth, 1996)
—— 'Fielding's Amanuensis'	'Fielding's Amanuensis', *N & Q*, NS 43 (1996), pp. 303–4
Küster	Ludolf Küster, ed. *Aristophanis Comædiæ* (Amsterdam, 1710)

LE	*The London Encyclopaedia*, ed. Ben Weinreb and Christopher Hibbert (London, 1983)
LEP	*London Evening Post*
Life	Martin C. Battestin with Ruthe R. Battestin, *Henry Fielding: A Life*, 2nd edn. (London and New York, 1993)
Lillywhite	Bryant Lillywhite, *London Coffee Houses* (London, 1963)
Loeb	The Loeb Classical Library
London Stage	*The London Stage, 1660–1800*, ed. A. H. Scouten, 5 pts. in 11 vols. (Carbondale, Ill., 1960–8)
MCB	Martin C. Battestin
Miller, *Essays*	Henry Knight Miller, *Essays on Fielding's Miscellanies: A Commentary on Volume One* (Princeton, 1961)
Miscellanies i, ii, iii	*Miscellanies by Henry Fielding, Esq; Volume One*, ed. Henry Knight Miller (Oxford and Middletown, Conn., 1972); *Volume Two*, ed. Bertrand A. Goldgar and Hugh Amory (Oxford and Middletown, Conn., 1993); *Volume Three*, ed. Bertrand A. Goldgar and Hugh Amory (Oxford and Middletown, Conn., 1997)
MLN	*Modern Language Notes*
MP	*Modern Philology*
N & Q	*Notes and Queries*
New Essays	Martin C. Battestin, *New Essays by Henry Fielding: His Contributions to The Craftsman (1734–1739) and Other Early Journalism* (Charlottesville, Va., 1989)
OED	*Oxford English Dictionary*
Opposition	*The Opposition, A Vision* (1742 [1741]). Text and pagination from *Champion*
Oxford DNB	*Oxford Dictionary of National Biography* (Oxford, 2004)
PA	*Public Advertiser*
Pamela Controversy	Thomas Keymer and Peter Sabor (eds.), *The Pamela Controversy: Criticisms and Adaptations of Samuel Richardson's Pamela*, 6 vols. (London, 2001)
Partridge	Eric Partridge, *Dictionary of Slang and Unconventional English*, 7th edn. (London, 1970)
Paulson	Ronald Paulson, *Hogarth: His Life, Art and Times*, 2 vols. (New Haven and London, 1971)

Paulson and Lockwood   Ronald Paulson and Thomas Lockwood (eds.), *Henry Fielding: The Critical Heritage* (London and New York, 1969)

Phillips, *Thames*   Hugh Phillips, *The Thames about 1750* (London, 1951)

—— *Mid-Georgian London*   Hugh Phillips, *Mid-Georgian London* (London, 1964)

Plays   Henry Fielding, *Plays, Volume I, 1728–1731*, ed. Thomas Lockwood (Oxford and Middletown, Conn., 2004)

Plomer   H. R. Plomer, *Dictionary of Printers and Booksellers who were at work in England, Scotland and Ireland from 1726–1775* (Oxford, 1932)

Plutus   *Plutus, the God of Riches* (1742). Text and pagination from the present volume

PMLA   *Publications of the Modern Language Association*

Potter   John Potter, *Archæologiæ Græcæ: or, The Antiquities of Greece* (1697)

PQ   *Philological Quarterly*

Probyn   Clive T. Probyn, *The Sociable Humanist: The Life and Letters of James Harris, 1709–1780* (Oxford, 1991)

Proper Answer   *A Proper Answer to a Late Scurrilous Libel* (1747). Text and pagination from *JJ*

Remarks   *Remarks upon the Account of the Conduct of a certain Dutchess* (1742)

Ribbles   Frederick G. Ribble and Anne G. Ribble, *Fielding's Library: An Annotated Catalogue* (Charlottesville, Va., 1996)

Rocque   John Rocque, Map of London (1747), in *The A to Z of Georgian London*, introd. Ralph Hyde (Lympne Castle, Kent, 1981)

Rothstein   Eric Rothstein, 'The Framework of *Shamela*', *ELH*, 35 (1968), pp. 381–402

SB   *Studies in Bibliography*

Shamela   *An Apology for the Life of Mrs. Shamela Andrews* (1741). Text and pagination from the present volume

Sommerstein   *Comedies of Aristophanes*, trans. Alan H. Sommerstein, 11 vols. (Warminster, 2001), xi: *Wealth*

SP   *Studies in Philology*

SWB   Sheridan W. Baker, Jr.

Theobald   Lewis Theobald, *Plutus: or, the World's Idol. A Comedy. Translated from the Greek of Aristophanes* (1715)

Tilley   Morris Palmer Tilley, *A Dictionary of the Proverbs of England in the Sixteenth and Seventeenth Centuries* (Ann Arbor, 1950)

Tom Jones   *The History of Tom Jones, a Foundling* (1749), ed. Martin C. Battestin and Fredson Bowers (Oxford and Middletown, Conn., 1974–5)

TP   *The True Patriot and Related Writings*, ed. W. B. Coley (Oxford and Middletown, Conn., 1987)

Vernoniad   *The Vernon-iad. Done into English, from the original Greek of Homer* (1741). Text and pagination from *Champion*

Vindication   *A Full Vindication of the Dutchess Dowager of Marlborough* (1742). Text and pagination from the present volume

Woods   Charles B. Woods, 'Fielding and the Authorship of *Shamela*', *PQ*, 25 (1946), pp. 248–72

Works   *The Works of Henry Fielding, Esq; with The Life of the Author* (1762)

Yale Walpole   *The Yale Edition of Horace Walpole's Correspondence*, ed. W. S. Lewis (New Haven, 1937–83)

TEXTUAL INTRODUCTION

THE copy-text for each work is its first edition, or first appearance in print, these being the printings closest to the manuscript and therefore most likely to transmit the author's accidentals[1]—that is, the spelling, punctuation, capitalization, word-division, and such typographical matters as the use of italicized words, and such deliberate manipulation of type sizes and spacing as Fielding used for comic effect at the close of the Dedication of *The Masquerade* (below, p. 14). Exceptions, of course, are the 'Cantos' and the 'Epistle to Mr. Lyttleton', manuscripts never published in Fielding's lifetime. Variant readings in subsequent editions or printings are admitted to the text only when probability suggests such emendations are Fielding's own. All emendations of the copy-text are listed in Appendix B.1, and when necessary are explained in B.2 (Textual Notes). Special considerations concerning word-division are treated in B.3 and in B.4 (Historical Collation) substantive variants in authoritative editions are recorded. Appendix B.5 offers bibliographical descriptions of the texts.

Though alterations of accidentals as well as substantives are recorded in the textual apparatus, in a few merely formal matters the policy of the Wesleyan Edition is to make the following editorial changes silently. (1) Typographical errors such as turned letters or wrong font are not recorded and have been corrected. (2) Initial capital letters, at times the value of four printed lines and enclosed in factotums, have been equalized to plain capitals the value of two lines of print. (3) According to modern Wesleyan practice, double quotation marks in the original become single. The running quotation marks in the left margin have been omitted and quotations have been indicated according to the modern custom. Throughout, necessary opening or closing quotation marks in dialogue have been supplied silently. (4) When the apostrophe and roman 's' follow an italicized name, the roman is retained only when it indicates the contraction for 'is' (e.g. '*Tom*'s going') but is normalized to italic when the possessive case is required ('*Tom*'s hat' becomes '*Tom's*'). (5) The font of punctuation is normalized without regard for the variable practice of the original. Pointing

---

[1] See Sir Walter Greg, 'The Rationale of Copy-Text', *Studies in Bibliography*, 3 (1950), pp. 19–36, the main authority on the subject. Also Fredson Bowers, 'Current Theories of Copy-Text, with an Illustration from Dryden', *MP*, 48 (1950), pp. 12–20, and 'Established Texts and Definitive Editions', *PQ*, 41 (1962), pp. 1–17. These authoritative essays were cited by Bowers in the Textual Introduction to the volume that launched the Wesleyan Edition: *Joseph Andrews*, ed. Battestin (Oxford, 1966), p. [xxxix].

within an italic passage is italicized; but pointing following an italicized word that is succeeded by roman text is silently placed in roman. (6) The long eighteenth-century ∫ becomes 's'.[2]

---

[2] This Textual Introduction is based on Bowers's original (see the Preface above) and Baker's copy adapted for the present edition.

I

OCCASIONAL
VERSE

1

THE MASQUERADE (1728)

IN September 1742 as he assembled various odds and ends of the compositions that would comprise his *Miscellanies*, Fielding wrote to thank James Harris for forwarding to him a copy of some verses he had written fourteen years earlier in 1728, and which their friend the Revd John Hoadly had preserved.[1] Commenting on the manuscript, Fielding revealed just how casually he regarded the craft of versifying and how well he understood that his talent as a writer was in prose:

As to the Verses . . . I sincerely think both the Chancelor [Hoadly was Chancellor of the Diocese of Winchester] & y^r self have over-valued y^m; he in so long preserving, & y^o in comenting on what was originally writ with the Haste & Inaccuracy of a comon Letter, & wch I shall be sorry if any Scarcity of Matter under the *Poetical* Article should oblige me to publish. To confess a Truth, I wish that long Word had never been inserted in my Proposals: for my Talents (if I have any) lie not in Versification. My Muse is a free born Briton & disdains the slavish Fetters of Rhyme. (*Correspondence*, pp. 23–4)

Also the product of this earliest period of Fielding's literary career—indeed, issued pseudonymously on 29 or 30 January 1728,[2] it is his earliest extant publication[3]—*The Masquerade*, a sixpenny pamphlet, is a satire

---

[1] *Correspondence*, Letter 14, written from Bath to Harris at Salisbury, 24 September 1742. Thanks to Frederick Ribble's research, we now know that the verses in question were HF's 'A DESCRIPTION OF U[pto]n G[rey]', (alias *New Hog's Norton*) in *Com. Hants*. Written to a young Lady in the Year 1728', published in *Miscellanies* i, pp. 53–5. (See Ribble, 'New Light on Henry Fielding from the Malmesbury Papers', *MP*, 103 [2005], pp. 63–4. For HF's residence at Upton Grey, see *Life*, pp. 47–8 and 631 n. 115.)

[2] *The Craftsman* for Saturday 27 January 1728 announced publication of *The Masquerade* 'On Monday next' (the 29th); in its 'Register of Books', however, the *Monthly Chronicle* (January 1728) gives the publication date as 30 January.

[3] The earliest of HF's publications appears to have been a pair of poems, on the coronation (11 October 1727) and the king's birthday (30 October). The following advertisement was carried in the *Daily Post* and *Daily Journal* for 10 November 1727: 'The Coronation. A Poem. And an Ode on the Birthday. By Mr. *Fielding*. Printed for *B. Creake* in *Jermayn-street*; and sold by *J. Roberts* near *Warwick-lane*. Price 6*d.*' No copy of this work has come to light; nor did HF include either poem in the *Miscellanies* (1743). See *Life*, pp. 57–8; for additional references Thomas Lockwood, 'Early Poems by—and not by—Fielding', *PQ* 73 (1994), pp. 177–8, and Frederick G. Ribble, 'Fielding's Lost Poems "The Coronation" and "An Ode on the Birth-Day" ', *N & Q*, NS 45 (December 1998), pp. 456–9.

in Hudibrastic verse of nearly 400 lines; its targets are the popular, and licentious, Venetian entertainment of the title and its notorious impresario, John James (by courtesy called 'Count') Heidegger, to whom the poem is ironically dedicated. The title-page attributes the work to the celebrated 'author' of Swift's recently published masterpiece (1726): 'By *LEMUEL GULLIVER*, Poet Laureat to the King of *LILLIPUT*'. The publisher, whose name also appears in the advertisements for the lost poems *The Coronation* and *Ode on the Birthday*,[4] was James Roberts (*c.*1670–1754), a master printer who in the 1720s was among London's principal 'trade publishers'.[5] The imprint also credits Ann Dodd (d. 1739), a prosperous 'mercury',[6] as retailer of the work.

It is unlikely, however, that *The Masquerade* sold well. It was ignored in the journals and no mention of it has been found in the private correspondence of the period. Fielding himself was dissatisfied with the work, perhaps sharing the opinion of it offered a century and a half later by Austin Dobson, who first claimed it for the canon: 'As verse this performance is worthless, and it is not very forcibly on the side of good manners.'[7] *The Masquerade* heads the list of pieces Fielding excluded from the *Miscellanies*, despite wanting copy enough to pad out the three volumes. It remained for his friend and publisher Andrew Millar posthumously to publish a second edition in 1755. (For discussion of editions and reprints of *The Masquerade*, see below, the Textual Introduction.)

CIRCUMSTANCES OF COMPOSITION

The spring of 1727 marks the moment when Fielding, in his twentieth year, began seriously to aspire to the career of dramatist and 'Poet' (as he in those days called himself). Earlier, as a schoolboy at Eton, he is said, in an anecdote recorded by Horace Walpole, to have drafted 'a Comedy, in which

---

[4] See above, n. 3.

[5] A 'trade publisher' was a subsidiary to the actual publisher: for a fee he lent his name and shop to anonymous works, and managed sales and promotion (see Michael Treadwell, 'London Trade Publishers 1675–1750', *Library*, 6th ser., 4 [1982], pp. 99–134). Roberts regularly acted in this capacity for John Watts, who owned the copyright to HF's plays (see *Plays*, pp. 13–14); Roberts also appeared in the imprint of HF's pamphlet *A Full Vindication of the Dutchess Dowager of Marlborough* (below, pp. 196–237). On Roberts, see Treadwell, 'James Roberts, *The British Literary Book Trade, 1700–1820*, ed. James K. Bracken and Joel Silver, *Dictionary of Literary Biography*, 154 (Detroit, 1995), pp. 248–9.

[6] A 'mercury' was an established dealer in newspapers, pamphlets, and books who was engaged by publishers and trade publishers to provide an additional outlet in another part of town. Ann (Barnes) Dodd, widow of Nathaniel Dodd (d. 1723), maintained her husband's shop until her death in 1739, after which the business was carried on by her daughter Ann, whose name appears in the imprint of later works by HF, including, in the present volume, *Shamela* (1741) and *Ovid's Art of Love Paraphrased* (1747). (See Treadwell, above, n. 5.)

[7] Austin Dobson, *Fielding* (1883), p. 13.

he had drawn the characters of his Father and Family';[8] and before he was 20 he had written a rude burlesque of Juvenal's *Sixth Satire* as 'the Revenge' he took as 'an injured Lover'.[9] But it was not until the spring of 1727, when he sent to his brilliant cousin Lady Mary Wortley Montagu for her advice the first three acts of his comedy *Love in Several Masques*,[10] that he made his commitment to the theatre. By September Fielding would be involved in the production of the play, which was announced as part of the new season at the Theatre Royal in Drury Lane.[11] It was an extraordinary triumph for a 20-year-old neophyte author, and one for which he could probably thank his influential cousin Lady Mary, to whom he dedicated the play. In October the king's coronation and birthday elicited from Fielding, as mentioned above, the two lost poems published on 10 November.

He appears to have begun writing *The Masquerade* some time after 24 November 1727, the date on which a pantomime *Burlesque upon the Ceremonial Coronation of Anna Bullen, as perform'd at the Theatre in Drury-Lane*,[12] was staged at Lincoln's Inn Fields by John Rich, who acted Harlequin under the name of Lun. At line 32 of the poem, Fielding alludes to this burlesque, which, under the title *Harlequin Anna Bullen*, Rich performed as an afterpiece from 11 to 19 December.

But what prompted Fielding to write a satire on Heidegger and his masquerades? The sequence of relevant events that began with the new season would certainly have made the time right. On 16 October the first of the masquerades was held, and proved to be so dissolute the *Daily Journal* reported the next day that the Queen had requested 'there be no more Entertainments of that Kind this Season'. The masquerades continued, however, provoking a sterner rebuke from Her Majesty, as announced in the *Daily Journal* of 12 December: 'It is confidently reported there will be no more Masquerades permitted; on which Occasion, we see a humorous Print in the Print-Shops, call'd Hei! Deger; or, The Masquerade destroy'd.' But the report, however confident, was false. On 19 January notices began announcing the first masquerade ball of the new year, to be held at the Royal Opera House in the Haymarket on Thursday the 25th. Nor did Fielding's satire, published the following Monday, succeed in shaming the revellers: on Thursday 8 February Heidegger produced another of the popular entertainments.

---

[8] See W. B. Coley, 'Henry Fielding and the Two Walpoles', *PQ*, 45 (1966), p. 166 n. 45.

[9] Preface to *Miscellanies* i, p. 3.

[10] *Correspondence*, Letter 1. See also Lockwood's account of the circumstances in which HF composed the play (*Plays*, pp. 1–3).

[11] *British Journal* (23 September 1727).

[12] *Daily Journal* (24 November 1727).

There was nothing novel about Fielding's choice of Heidegger's masquerades as a worthy target for ridicule or indignation. Since he became
manager of the Royal Opera House in 1713, Heidegger on off nights had
used the theatre to hold subscription balls and masquerades. In 1724, to go
no further back in time, Edmund Gibson, Bishop of London, preached
against the masquerades in a sermon before the Societies for the Reformation of Manners;[13] and Fielding's subject and title, '*The Masquerade. A
Poem*', as well as his publisher James Roberts, were adopted before him by
an anonymous versifier who rendered the event in a series of twenty-five
mildly amusing sestets, of which the conclusion may serve as a sample:

> 'Tis hard, from what we know, to say
> What Man went the worst pleas'd away,
>   That wondrous merry Night;
> But he who says, that *Heydegger*
> Was pleas'd the best, bids very fair
>   For being in the Right.

In 1725 Ned Ward's *The Amorous Bugbears: or, The Humours of the Masquerade* could well serve as a gloss for Fielding's poem. In 1726 George II
issued a royal proclamation against masquerades, which was circumvented
by calling them 'ridottos' or 'balls'.[14] In 1727 Hogarth's *Large Masquerade
Ticket*, depicting the lewd scene at Heidegger's Opera House, would have
made a perfect frontispiece for Fielding's satire.[15]

   The Masquerade was the first of many of Fielding's satiric indictments yet
to come of 'Count' Heidegger, 'the great High-Priest of Pleasure', as he
calls him in *Tom Jones* (XIII. vii), and of the dissolute entertainments he
presided over at the Royal Opera House, his 'Temple' in the Haymarket
(p. 712). *The Masquerade* can also be taken as a kind of prologue to the
subtler theme of *Love in Several Masques*, the five-act comedy in which, at
the Theatre Royal, Fielding a few days later made his debut as a playwright.
The 'Masques' of the play's title are metaphors in a deeper reading of the
human character. This is the theme of the following passage from Fielding's
'Essay on the Characters of Men', where by dissembling and hypocrisy,

the whole World becomes a vast Masquerade, where the greatest Part appear disguised under false Vizors and Habits; a very few only shewing their own Faces, who
become, by so doing, the Astonishment and Ridicule of all the rest.

---

[13] L. P. Goggin, 'Fielding's Masquerade', *PQ*, 36 (1957), p. 477; and Paulson, i. 116.
[14] Arthur Freeman, Introduction to *Heydegger's Letter to the Bishop of London* (1724), Garland Series
(1973), p. 5.
[15] Paulson, i. 172, pl. 58.

But however cunning the Disguise be which a Masquerader wears: however foreign to his Age, Degree, or Circumstance, yet if closely attended to, he very rarely escapes the Discovery of an accurate Observer; for Nature, which unwillingly submits to the Imposture, is ever endeavouring to peep forth and shew herself; nor can the Cardinal, the Friar, or the Judge, long conceal the Sot, the Gamester, or the Rake.

In the same Manner will those Disguises which are worn on the greater Stage, generally vanish, or prove ineffectual to impose the assumed for the real Character upon us, if we employ sufficient Diligence and Attention in the Scrutiny.[16]

Fielding's ridicule of Heidegger and the masquerades colours, in 1734, the revised version of *The Author's Farce* (15 January), where 'Count Ugly' makes a cameo appearance in the 'Puppet Show' (*Play*, p. 352), as well as an essay on 'Screens' in *The Craftsman* No. 403 (23 March);[17] and again, in 1742, the farce *Miss Lucy in Town* (see below, p. 21 n. 32). Later, as a magistrate, Fielding's attitude towards these targets changed from amusement at folly to indignation at the pernicious influence they were having on the manners and morals of the public. In *Tom Jones* (1749) Lady Bellaston begins her affair with Tom by luring him to a masquerade at Heidegger's Opera House (XIII. vi–vii). In *Amelia* (1751) Colonel James similarly means to debauch the heroine by enticing her to a masquerade (x. i–vi); and Dr Harrison describes these entertainments as 'Scenes of Riot, Disorder, and Intemperance, very improper to be frequented by a chaste and sober Christian Matron' (p. 423). In the social tracts *A Charge delivered to the Grand Jury* (1749) and *An Enquiry into the Causes of the Late Increase of Robbers* (1751) the places that house masquerades are generally denounced as 'Temples of Iniquity' (*Enquiry*, pp. 24–5, 79). Except that with Heidegger now dead, Fielding chose to make an exception of the Royal Opera House: 'As to the Masquerade in the *Hay-market*, I have nothing to say; I really think it a silly rather than a vicious Entertainment' (p. 84).

TEXTUAL HISTORY

The publishing history of *The Masquerade* is puzzling. No record of the printing of the original pamphlet survives; and the date of its publication is known today from just two contradictory sources: first is Roberts's

---

[16] *Miscellanies* i, p. 155.

[17] In this paragraph: 'The *Beaumonde* must give me Leave to observe that a *Masquerade* is, properly speaking, no better than a *Screen*, which gives the polite of both Sexes an Opportunity of conversing with more Freedom and Unreservedness than They might care to do, without some Disguise. The *worthy Gentleman* [Heidegger], who presides over these Assemblies, is therefore a Person of great Importance; and nobody can wonder at the Honours, which are paid Him by all Sorts of People' (*New Essays*, p. 23). See also *Craftsman*, No. 612 (1 April 1738), p. 288.

advertisement in *The Craftsman* of Saturday 27 January 1728, which promises publication the following Monday, the 29th; next, the 'Register of Books' in the *Monthly Chronicle* for January gives the date of publication as '30', a Tuesday.[18] Of this first edition, Baker was aware of only the three copies at Yale; at Blickling Hall, Norwich, Norfolk; and at the Founders' Library, University of Wales, Lampeter—of which only the last-mentioned is listed in the *ESTC*, which, however, identifies six additional copies, making a total of eight.[19] During Fielding's lifetime, not only was *The Masquerade* never attributed to him so far as is known; the poem itself vanished from the scene until 1750, when John Carlile of Glasgow included a reprint of the first edition in his posthumous publication, in two volumes, of *The Miscellaneous Works of the Late Dr. Arbuthnot*.[20]

The story of the second edition of *The Masquerade* is very much a puzzle. The poem appears, anomalously, in the three-volume collection of Fielding's *Dramatic Works* published posthumously in 1755 by Andrew Millar— a circumstance that established Fielding's authorship of the poem. Opening volume II is a separate publication, having the following title-page:

THE | GRUB-STREET | OPERA. | As it is Acted at the | THEATRE in the HAY-MARKET. | [rule] | By SCRIBLERUS SECUNDUS. | [rule] | . . . . | To which is added, | THE | MASQUERADE, | A | POEM. | Printed in MDCCXXVIII. | [rule] | LONDON, | Printed, and sold by J. ROBERTS, in Warwick-lane. | MDCCXXXI. | [Price One Shilling and Six-pence.][21]

Though considered individually the title-pages of the two works that comprise the 'volume' give for *The Grub-Street Opera* the date of 1731 and for

---

[18] In his notes the late Professor Charles Woods also cites a third contemporary reference: in John Wilford's *Monthly Catalogue of Books* (January 1728), p. 7, *The Masquerade* is listed among the works sold by J. Roberts.

[19] The *ESTC* lists the following copies: (1) Washington University Library, St Louis, Missouri, SpD PR3454 M3 1728; (2) the Founders' Library, University of Wales, Lampeter, Bowdler Tract Collection, T269; (3–4) BL, C.116.e.7 and E/03098; (5) Henry E. Huntington Library, San Marino, California, 125937; (6) Columbia University Libraries, New York (unverified); (7) New York University, Fales Collection, New York (2 copies).

[20] Dated 1751 on the title-page, the work was actually issued in September 1750. *The Masquerade*, for the most part a faithful reprint of the first edition, occupies pp. 5–18 of volume II. Despite George Arbuthnot's warning at the time of publication that the collection should not be accepted as 'the works of my late father', a second edition ('Printed for' W. Richardson, L. Urquhart, and J. Knox) was published in 1770, *The Masquerade* appearing in volume II, pp. 1–14. On George Arbuthnot, see Lester M. Beattie, *John Arbuthnot* (Cambridge, Mass., 1935), pp. 308–9.

[21] In addition to the copies of this work examined for the Wesleyan Edition at the British Library, Yale, Harvard, and the Huntington Library (see Appendix B.5, p. 735, 'NOTES' 3), the *ESTC* lists locations of the following four copies: (1) University of California Los Angeles, William Andrews Clark Library, Los Angeles, *PR3452. D55; (2) Trinity College Library, Watkinson Collection, Hartford, Connecticut, PR3451.5 1755; (3) Henry E. Huntington Library, San Marino, California, 77647; (4) University of Florida Libraries, Gainsville, PR3451, A2 1755.

The Masquerade the date of 1728, and though each work has its own independent pagination, the two texts were in fact set at the same time, the signatures being consecutive: $A^4 B-E^8 F^4$.

NOTE: What follows is a redaction of Sheridan Baker's account of this, as he well called it, 'strange edition'.

Edgar V. Roberts pointed out the essential oddity of this edition: it is printed in modern lower-case typography, belying the '1731' on its title-page.[22] Furthermore, L. J. Morrissey discovered in the ledger of the printer William Strahan an entry for June 1755 charging Andrew Millar's account for printing *The Grub-Street Opera*.[23] The '1731' publication, a separate 'volume' containing *The Grub-Street Opera* and *The Masquerade*, was apparently not published by Roberts and not in 1731, but by Millar in 1755 as the first item in the second volume of the *Dramatic Works of Henry Fielding*.[24]

No advertisements, either in 1731 or 1755, announce a dual publication of *The Grub-Street Opera* and *The Masquerade*. In 1731 publication of the *Opera* itself, aside from two pirated versions, was never advertised, because Fielding, under pressure from the authorities, suppressed it.[25] Baker reasons that the date '1731' of the unpublished dual 'volume', and the separate title-pages that introduce the texts of the two works it includes, suggest that Millar, while twenty-four years later resetting the two in modern type,[26] otherwise reprinted the 'volume' exactly as it had been prepared for publication in 1731.

To support this hypothesis, Baker had to answer the question who in fact had 'rights' to the play and to *The Masquerade*. Since John Watts (d. 1763)

---

[22] Fielding's *The Grub-Street Opera*, ed. Roberts (Lincoln, Nebr., 1968), p. xi and n. 1.

[23] See the authoritative account of the publishing history of the play in *The Grub-Street Opera*, ed. Morrissey (Edinburgh, 1973), pp. 13 ff., esp. pp. 18–21.

[24] This three-volume collection of the *Dramatic Works* prints plays of different editions and dates. The separate 'volume' of *The Grub-Street Opera* and *The Masquerade* dated 1731 is probably not an independent publication but one 'disbound' from the collection in the nineteenth and twentieth centuries for separate sale: see [Hugh Amory], *New Books by Fielding: An Exhibition of the Hyde Collection* (Cambridge, Mass.: Houghton Library, 12 January–6 March 1987), item 38.

[25] For an account of the circumstances that led to HF's suppression of *The Grub-Street Opera*, see *Life*, pp. 112–23.

[26] Regarding the shift in typographical practice at mid-century, from capitals and italics in nouns and names to lower-case and roman, Bertrand Bronson noted 'a quite abrupt shift of convention just at the midpoint of the century. Before 1750 poetry was likely to be generously capitalized; after 1750 it was likely to be given a modern capitalization. There are exceptions on either side of the line but they do not conceal the fact that 1750 is the Great Divide. And prose seems to have followed roughly the same course' (*Printing as an Index of Taste in Eighteenth Century England* [New York, 1958], p. 17). Baker remarks that in the 1730s Roberts's publications consistently followed the older convention. He further observes that with *The Covent-Garden Journal* (1752) Millar began adopting the new style by romanizing proper names; by 1755, with Fielding's *Journal of a Voyage to Lisbon*, he modernized completely.

owned the publishing rights to all other plays by Fielding, while using Roberts as 'trade publisher' for the irregular pieces of 1730 (*Tom Thumb* and *The Author's Farce*) and 1731 (*The Tragedy of Tragedies* and *The Letter Writers*, both published on 24 March), Baker assumed that Watts also owned the rights to *The Grub-Street Opera*. It is clear, certainly, that the book of the play was meant for publication at the opening: on 21 May 1731 the *Daily Post* announced that the *Opera* would 'be perform'd within a Fortnight' and 'is now in Press, and will be sold at the Theatre with the Musick prefix'd to the Songs (being about sixty in Number) on the first Night of Performance'. Fielding, as he had done before and would continue to do to the end of his career as dramatist, had no doubt arranged with Watts, and his agent Roberts, to publish the book of the play when it was staged, to the eager expectations of the town, on Friday 11 June.[27]

But the play was never staged; and the book of the play was not published until 1755, when, together with *The Masquerade*, it opened the second volume of Millar's *Dramatic Works of Henry Fielding*. In 1755 both Fielding and Roberts were dead, and Millar had acquired from Watts the right to reprint Watts's editions of the plays. Baker, noting the integrity of the little 'volume', dated 1731, which contained both *The Grub-Street Opera* (imprint Roberts 1731) and *The Masquerade* (imprint Roberts 1728), inferred that what Millar had reprinted was the original publication suppressed by Fielding. To account for the inclusion of the poem on the occasion of the *Opera*'s first night, Baker suggests that Watts in 1727, having acquired the rights to Fielding's first play, *Love in Several Masques*, might well have agreed to publish *The Masquerade* as well. If so, he soon found he had acquired a drug in the market; the occasion of the eagerly awaited publication of *The Grub-Street Opera* offered an opportunity to rid himself of the remaindered copies of the poem while adding sixpence to the price of the book.

As far as the mystery of the 'strange' second edition of *The Masquerade* is concerned, Baker's solution cannot be proved definitively, but it is more plausible, and more coherent, than any other proposed to date.

The only other reprint of *The Masquerade* was published two centuries later in Claude E. Jones's edition of *The Female Husband and Other Writings* (Liverpool, 1960). Except that it can be credited with having made Fielding's first extant publication—or, rather, an inaccurate travesty of it—available to modern readers, this edition and the accompanying commentary are rife with errors and cannot be recommended.

---

[27] *Daily Post* (9 June 1731) announced the play for Friday 11th.

THE

MASQUERADE.

A

POEM.

INSCRIB'D TO

C-----T H----D-----G----R.

————*Velut ægri ſomnia, vanæ*
————*Species*————   Hor. Art. Poet.

By *LEMVEL GVLLIVER*, Poet Laureat to the
King of *LILLIPVT.*

LONDON,

Printed: and Sold by *J. Roberts* in *Warwick-Lane*, and
A. Dodd at the *Peacock* without *Temple-Bar.* 1728.

[Price Six Pence.]

'C—T *H—D—G—R*': John James Heidegger (d. 1749), called 'Count', Master of the Revels to George II. A Swiss immigrant reputed to be the ugliest man in England, by promoting masquerades and other fashionable entertainments he became manager of the Royal Opera House in the Haymarket, over which he presided until his death. In 1729 he was presented by the grand jury of Middlesex as 'the principal promoter of vice and immorality' in the metropolis. In the revised version of *The Author's Farce* (1734) HF would ridicule him as 'Count Ugly'; and there are facetious references to him in *The Champion* (1 January and 19 February 1740), pp. 102, 188. In *Tom Jones* (XIII. vii) the hero begins his affair with Lady Bellaston at a masquerade held at the Opera House, 'that Temple, where *Heydegger*, the great *Arbiter Deliciarum*, the great High-Priest of Pleasure presides' (p. 712).

'*Velut . . . Species*': Horace, *De Arte Poetica*, lines 7–8: *velut aegri somnia, vanae | fingentur species* ('idle fancies shall be shaped like a sick man's dreams'; Loeb). Cf. text below, line 332: 'An idle, trifling, feverish Dream' (p. 26).

THE
DEDICATION.

SIR,

I *Believe no one will dispute your Right to this little Poem, any more than your* *presiding over that Diversion it celebrates; therefore I shall, without Excuse, lay it at your Feet.*

The Flattery of Dedications has been often exploded: to avoid the most distant Imputation of which I shall omit several things that (perhaps) might not be justly so called: And that the more readily, since your Merit is so well known, it wou'd be only publishing what is in every one's Mouth.

I cannot however help congratulating you on that Gift of Nature, by which you seem so adapted to the Post you enjoy. I mean that natural Masque, which is too visible a Perfection to be here insisted on—and, I am sure, never fails of making an Impression on the most indifferent Beholder.

Another Gift of Nature, which you seem to enjoy in no small Degree, is that modest Confidence supporting you in every Act of your Life. Certainly, a great Blessing! For I always have observ'd, that Brass in the Forehead draws Gold into the Pocket.

As for what Mankind calls Virtues, I shall not compliment you on them: Since you are so wise to keep them secret from the World, far be it from me to publish them; especially since they are Things which lie out of the way of your Calling.

Here I beg Leave to contradict two scandalous Aspersions which have been spread against you.

First, *That you are a B—d.*[1]

Secondly, *A Conjurer.*

Whoever has seen you at a M—sq—r—de, cannot believe the first—and you have given several Instances at White's,[2] *that you are not the other.*

---

[1] i.e. a bawd: as impresario of the licentious entertainments of masquerade balls, Heidegger had earned honorary membership in that profession. Charles B. Woods cites the following passage from a leader in the *Weekly Journal* (April 1725), where Heidegger, a native of Switzerland, is accused of injuring the trade of such true British madams as the notorious Elizabeth Needham (d. 1731) and 'Mother' Haywood (d. 1743): 'Mother N——am, Mother J——y, and some others, have taken as much Pains for the Diversion of Mankind as Mother Heyd——r, and in the same way; but as I am informed, they are eternally murmuring that Foreigners should come hither to take the Bread out of other People's Mouths, and that they are not suffered quietly to follow their honest Employments, whilst this Interloper, by being wink'd at, runs away with all the Business, and they give out, that it is very hard that Mother H——d should suffer the Pillory, whilst Mother Heyd——r rides in a Coach.'

[2] Founded in 1693, White's Chocolate House, in St James's Street near the Palace, was the resort of fashionable gamesters (Lillywhite, No. 1511). HF frequently alludes to it, as in *Tom Jones* (XIII. vi, p. 710) and *Amelia* (III. x, p. 139).

But what signifies attempting to confute what needs no Confutation?—Besides, you have so great a Soul, that you despite all Scandal—and live in the World with the same Indifference, that People have at a Masquerade where they are not known.

Smile then (if you can smile) on my Endeavours, and this little Poem, with Candour³—for which the Author desires no more Gratuity than a Ticket for your next Ball, and is,

SIR,

Your most Obedient,

From my Garret in
Grub-Street   Humble Servant,

*Lemuel Gulliver.*⁴

THE

MASQUERADE.

A

POEM.

SOME call *Curiosity* an Evil,
 And say 'twas that, by which the Devil
With *Eve* succeeded, in his Suit,
To taste the dear forbidden Fruit.
Others, (allowing this) yet wou'd   5
Prove it has done less Harm than Good.
To this (say They) whate'er we know
In Arts or Sciences, we owe.
To this, how justly are attributed

---

³ '*Candour*': i.e. with openness of mind, sweetness of temper (*OED*, s.v. 3–4).

⁴ Noting the unusual spacing and eccentric typography of this five-line valediction to the Dedication, in which the signature '*Lemuel Gulliver*' is in large italic type and the address in Lilliput 'From my Garret in | *Grub-Street*' is in minuscule, Baker offered the following delightful interpretation: 'HF spaces-out his five-line [valediction] to emphasize, through its pauses, his mocking deference to Heidegger. The tiny print of his address reflects the amusing Lilliputian cast of mind that the "giant" Gulliver acquired from his tiny countrymen, and the "Garret" again points up the mock humility of Heidegger's "Humble Servant".' HF was perfectly capable of this iconographic ingenuity: cf. *Tom Jones* (XI. i), where he rebukes those critics who, 'without assigning any particular Faults, condemn the whole . . . by the Use of the Monosyllable "Low"; a Word which becomes the Mouth of no "Critic" who is not RIGHT HONOURABLE' (p. 570); the type becomes a visual emblem of HF's meaning. See Battestin, 'Fielding's Novels and the Wesleyan Edition: Some Principles and Problems', in G. E. Bentley, Jr. (ed.), *Editing Eighteenth Century Novels* (Toronto, 1975), pp. 9–30, esp. p. 17.

What *W—st—n, H—l—y*,[5] have exhibited!   10
From this, we borrow Hopes of greater
Discoveries of Madam *Nature*.
Hence, is our Expectation gain'd,
To see the *Longitude* explain'd.
'Tis this, which sets the Chymist on,   15
To search that secret-natur'd Stone,
Which the Philosophers have told,
When found, turns all things into Gold:
But being hunted, and not caught,
Oh! sad Reverse! turns Gold to Nought.   20
Britain may hence her Knowledge brag,
Of *Lilliput* and *Brobdingnag:*
This Passion dictated that Voyage,
Which will be parallel'd in no Age.
'Twas this which furl'd[6] my swelling Sails,   25
And bid me trust uncertain Gales;
Gave me thro' unknown Seas a Lift,
And, spight of Dangers, made me *Swift*.
'Tis this, which sends the *British* Fair
To see *Italians* dance in Air.[7]   30
This crowds alike the Repr'sentation
Of *Lun's* and *Bullen's* Coronation.[8]

---

[5] William Whiston (1667–1752), natural philosopher, mathematician, and heterodox theologian; Edmond Halley (1656–1742), astronomer. In the present context (lines 10–14), HF refers to their involvement with the Longitude project. Both were instrumental in the passage of the Longitude Act of 1714, which offered a reward for the discovery of a method for calculating longitude accurate to one degree at sea. Whiston, with Humphrey Ditton, published that year *A New Method for Discovering the Longitude both at Sea and Land*, and in the 1720s he published further schemes for solving the problem of the longitude by 'dipping needle' (1721), by solar eclipses (1724). He was the target of ridicule by Swift and the Scriblerians (see Bertrand A. Goldgar, *The Curse of Party* [Lincoln, Nebr., 1961], pp. 8–10). In a leader written shortly after Whiston's death and signed 'W.W.' in *The Covent-Garden Journal*, No. 65 (7 October 1752), the author refers to 'an Oddity' in an otherwise excellent character, 'which I can no more account for, than I can find out the Longitude' (p. 344 and n. 1).

[6] The *OED* (s.v. 'furl' 6) cites only one instance (in 1798) of 'furl' misused, as here, for 'unfurl'.

[7] Signora Violante's company of rope dancers and acrobats was in its second season at the little Haymarket Theatre when *The Masquerade* was published.

[8] Two weeks after the coronation of George II on 11 October 1727, the Drury Lane company revived Shakespeare's *Henry VIII*, the bills promising that 'the Procession to the Coronation of Queen Anne Bullen will be performed with greater Order and Magnificence than has ever yet been seen on the English Stage' (*Daily Post*, 23 October). This scene received the approval of the Royal Family and became so popular that it was elaborated to include such features as 'the Ceremony of the Champion in Westminster Hall' (see below, p. 25 and n. 40); it was even attached to plays with which it had no logical connection. At Lincoln's Inn Fields on 24 November John Rich, whose stage name was Lun, inserted a new scene into

By this embolden'd, tim'rous Maids
Adventure to the Masquerades.
And, to confess the Truth, 'twas this,   35
Which sent me there, as well as Miss.
Now, for the Benefit of those,
Whose Curiosity oppose
Or Parents strict, or jealous Spouses,
(Rogues! who make Prisons of their Houses,)   40
The Sequel all its Joys unravels,
Plain as th' Adventures in my Travels.
    The Criticks wou'd be apt to bark,
Was I to leave them in the Dark
As to my Dress—Faith! I appear'd,   45
In the strange Habit of a Bard.
My shabby Coat you might have known
To have been black—tho' now 'twas brown.
My Breeches (old Tradition says)
Were new in Queen *Eliza's* Days;   50
And to inforce our Faith, we're told
They ne'er were worn with weighty Gold.[9]
My Goat-skin-aping Wig (I've heard)
Was made of *Hudibrass's* Beard;[10]
Its Hairs in Quantity and Hue   55
Declare its Ped'gree to be true.
The Laurel did my Temples grace,
As did a Masque my uglier Face.
Thus when equipp'd, I call'd a Chair,

---

one of his pantomimes, 'being a Burlesque upon the Ceremonial Coronation of Anna Bullen, as perform'd at the Theatre in Drury-Lane' (*Daily Journal*); on 11 December he made it into a separate 'Burlesque Farce' called *Harlequin Anna Bullen* [Charles Woods].

    In the original production of *The Author's Farce* (III. i) HF explains the scene of ghosts in the under-world: 'I can't say but I took the hint of this Thing from the old House [Drury Lane], who observing that every one could not see the real Coronation brought a Representation of it upon their Stage' (*Plays*, p. 258).

    [9] The absence of gold on the Elizabethan knee breeches indicates a Protestant protest against Catholic luxury.

    [10] In his burlesque epic *Hudibras* (1663) Samuel Butler offers a forty-line excursus on the beard of his Puritan hero, opening: 'His tawny *Beard* was th'equall grace | Both of his wisdome and his face; | In Cut and Dy so like a tile, | A sudden view it would beguile: | The upper part thereof was Whey, | The nether Orange mixt with Gray' (ed. J. Wilders [Oxford, 1967], I. i, pp. 239–44). A 'Goat-skin-aping Wig' would be of poorest quality; in Pope's *Odyssey* Ulysses finds the impoverished King Laertes wearing 'a double cap of goatskin hair' (xxiv. 264).

Go, to th' *Hay-Market* Theatre.[11]   60
　O Muse, some Simile indite,
To shew the Oddness of the Sight.
As in a Madman's frantick Skull,
When pale-fac'd *Luna* is at full,
In wild Confusion huddled lies   65
A Heap of Incoherencies;
So here, in one Confusion hurl'd,
Seem all the Nations of the World:
Cardinals, Quakers, Judges dance;
Grim *Turks* are coy, and Nuns advance.   70
Grave Churchmen here, at Hazard play;
Cinque-Ace ten Pound—done, Quater-tray.[12]
Known Prudes there, Libertines we find,
Who masque the Face, t'unmasque the Mind.
Here, Running Footmen[13] guzzle Tea;   75
There, Milkmaids Flasks of *Burgundy*.[14]
I saw two Shepherdesses dr–nk,
And heard a Friar call'd a P–nk.[15]
Lost in Amazement, as I stood,
A Lady in a Velvet Hood,   80
(Her Mein[16] St *James's* seem'd t'explain,
But her Assurance—*Drury-Lane*,[17]
Not *Hercules* was ever bolder,)
Came up and slapp'd me on the Shoulder.[18]

---

[11] The Royal Opera House, where Heidegger held his masquerades.

[12] Hazard, a two-dice game similar to modern craps. Here the first player bets £10 that the dice will show a five and a one; the other calls a four and a three. In *Jonathan Wild* (I. viii, p. xii) the Count, a sharper, is particularly fond of the game (*Miscellanies* iii, pp. 29, 41). To illustrate its addictive allure Bertrand Goldgar (p. 29 n. 6) quotes Charles Cotton, who calls it 'the most bewitching Game that is play'd on the Dice; for when a Man begins to play, he knows not when to leave off, and having once accustomed himself to play at *Hazzard*, he hardly ever after minds any thing else' (*The Compleat Gamester*, 5th edn. [1725], p. 123).

[13] A footman who ran ahead of his master's coach to announce his approach to the innkeeper, or to lend assistance if it threatened to overturn (*OED*, s.v. 'footman' 3).

[14] A much favoured red wine from France: cf. *Tom Jones* (XVIII. xii), where Squire Western, overjoyed at the engagement of Tom and Sophia, cries, 'wut ha? Wut ha Burgundy, Champaigne, or what?' (p. 976).

[15] 'P–nk': punk, a whore.

[16] Obsolete form of 'mien', the air, bearing, or manner of a person, as expressive of character (*OED*, s.v. 'mien').

[17] The extremes of upper- and lower-class neighbourhoods: St James's near the palace; Drury Lane, the theatre district and the haunt of prostitutes and pickpockets.

[18] Cf. *Tom Jones* (XIII. vii), where Jones attends a masquerade at the Opera House: 'a Lady in a Domino [Lady Bellaston] came up to him, and slapping him on the Shoulder, whispered him, at the same Time, in the Ear' (p. 713).

Why how now, Poet! pray, how fare   85
Our Friends who feed on *Grubstreet* Air?
For, be assur'd, we all shall dub
Thy Laureat Brow with Name of *Scrub*.[19]
No Man of any Fashion wou'd
Appear a Poet in a Crowd.   90
A Poet in this Age we shun,
With as much Terror as a Dun:
Both are receiv'd with equal Sorrow,
Who wou'd be paid, and who wou'd borrow.
And tho' you never speak—we spy   95
The craving Beggar in your Eye.
For Poverty rules all your Host,
And Sin against the———————.[20]
Madam, to understand we're giv'n
That Poverty's the Road to Heav'n.   100
Why ay (says she) so Churchmen say,
But still they chuse the other Way.
Well, Madam (if it will allure you)
I am no Poet, I assure you.
Tho' in this Garb—I'm, in Reality,   105
A young, smart, dapper Man of Quality.
No Lawrels—but a smart *Toupet*,[21]
In Drawing-Rooms, distinguish me.
I often frisk it to the Play,
To *Norfolk's*, *Kemp's*, and *Strafford's* Day.[22]   110

---

[19] '*Scrub*': a mean insignificant fellow (*OED*, s.v. II. 5, citing *Tom Jones*, VIII. iii: 'He is an arrant Scrub'). For HF's use of the same term in a different context, see *Journal of a Voyage to Lisbon*, below, p. 576 and n. 107.

[20] For the dashes, read 'Holy Ghost'. The sin against the Holy Ghost is the only unforgivable sin: see Matthew 12: 31–32.

[21] '*Toupet*': 'A curl or artificial lock of hair ... esp. as a crowning feature of a periwig' (*OED*, 3rd edn., s.v. 'toupee', citing HF's *Grub-Street Opera* [III. xv]: 'Love in his lac'd coat lies, And peeps from his toupee'). Also in the *OED*, s.v. 'toupet' 1b, citing HF's *Love in Several Masques*, Epilogue: 'From you then—ye toupets—he hopes defence' (cf. also *Love in Several Masques* (I. i) re beaux: 'Gentlemen Proprietors of the Toupet, Snuff-box, and Sword-knot'; *Plays*, p. 25); and 'toupet' 3, citing HF's *Modern Husband* (I. ix): 'I met with nothing but a parcel of toupet coxcombs, who plaster up their brains upon their periwigs.'

[22] The couplet is perplexing. Woods: 'Presumably the names of people of fashion who would frequently bespeak plays'; Baker: 'Prominent people would appoint a "day" on which they would hold an open house or an assembly without invitations.' (But neither of these assertions is documented.) '*Norfolk*' would be Thomas Howard (1683–1732), eighth Duke, who resided in London at Norfolk House, St James's Square (Phillips, *Mid-Georgian London*, p. 65). '*Kemp*' may be Sir Robert Kemp (d. 1734), MP for Suffolk, a wealthy man who 'had four wives' (*Gentleman's Magazine*, iv [1734], p. 703). '*Strafford*' would be Thomas Wentworth (1672–1739), first (third) Earl (*Oxford DNB*). Cf. HF's poem 'To Celia': 'I Hate the Town, and

An Opera I never miss:
To shew my Teeth—I sometimes hiss.
I'm seen where-e'er the Ladys flock;
My Conversation's—*What's a Clock?*
Then of the Weather I complain;   115
No matter whether Wind or Rain,
Or hot or cold: For in a Breath,
I'm sometimes scorch'd, and froze to Death.
Rain has been often the Creation
Of a dry frozen Conversation.   120
No Wind e'er rages—but it blows
In Sympathetick Mouths of Beaus.
Enough! (the Lady cry'd:) I see
You are, indeed, the Man for me:
For all our wiser Part despise   125
Those little apish Butterflies;
And if the Breed ben't quickly mended,
Your Empire shortly will be ended:
Breeches our brawny Thighs shall grace,
(Another *Amazonian* Race.)   130
For when Men Women turn—why then
May Women not be changed to Men?
　　But come, we'll take a Turn, and try
What Mysteries we can descry.
　　Hold, Madam, pray what hideous Figure   135
Advances? Sir, that's C——t H——d—g–r.
How cou'd it come into his Gizard,[23]
T' invent so horrible a Vizard?
How cou'd it, Sir! (says she) I'll tell you:
It came into his Mother's Belly;   140
For you must know, that horrid Phyz is
(*Puris naturalibus*)[24] his Visage.
Monstrous! that humane Nature can
Have form'd so strange Burlesque a Man.

---

all its Ways; | . . . Where Beauties lie in Ambush for Folks, | Earl *Straffords*, and the Duke of *Norfolks*'
(*Miscellanies* i, p. 63). The Countess of Strafford (d. 1754) subscribed to the *Miscellanies*. Amory's identification (i, p. 342) is mistaken: she was Anne (*née* Johnson), the only daughter and heir of a wealthy
shipbuilder; she married the Earl in 1711 (*Oxford DNB*).

[23] *OED*, s.v. 'gizzard' 2, citing Johnson's *Dictionary* (1755), s.v. 2: 'It is proverbially used for apprehension or conception of mind; as, he *frets his gizzard*, he harasses his imagination.'

[24] '*Puris naturalibus*': completely natural.

Why, Sir, (says she) there are who doubt   145
That Nature's self ne'er made it out:
For there's a little Scrip which resteth[25]
Of an Old Register, attesteth,
That *Amadis* being convey'd,
By Magick, to th' infernal Shade;[26]   150
By Magick there begot, upon
The fair *Tysiphone*, a Son:[27]
And that, as *Mulciber* was driv'n
Headlong for his Ugliness from Heav'n;[28]
So, for's Ugliness more fell,   155
Was H—d—g–r toss'd out of Hell.
And, in Return, by *Satan* made,
First Minister of's Masquerade.
Now this his just Preferment bears,
'Mongst Wits, the Name of *Kick-up-Stairs*.[29]   160
Madam, (says I) I am inclin'd,
(Tho' of no Superstitious Mind)
To think some Magick-Art is us'd,
By which our Senses are abus'd:
For what can here this Crowd pursue,   165
Where they all Nothing have to do?
Nothing! why see at yonder Side-board
What Sweet-meats Miss does in her Hide hoard.
A little farther take your Eye,

[25] 'Scrip': a scrap of paper with writing on it (*OED*, s.v. sb.³ obs.); 'resteth': to remain, be left, still undestroyed (*OED*, s.v. 'rest' v.² 1c. now rare).

[26] Woods was inclined to accept the view of Goggin that in lines 149–58 HF 'probably' alludes to Handel's *Amadigi di Gaula*, which was produced in May 1715 at the Royal Opera House by Heidegger, who signed the dedication to the Earl of Burlington and may have written the book (see L. P. Goggin, 'Fielding's *The Masquerade*', *PQ*, 36 [1957], p. 481). Baker, however, objected that HF was only 8 years old and living in Dorset in 1715, and that before 1728 there was no revival of the opera at a time when HF was likely to have seen it; he instead cites the original romance by Garcia de Montalvo while noting that Amadis never in that work descends to the underworld. One may add that HF, as far as we know, does not elsewhere in his writings refer to *Amadis de Gaul*.

[27] Tisiphone was one of the three Furies.

[28] Mulciber, among the Roman gods a name for Vulcan, was the counterpart of Hephaestus, the Greek god of fire and the arts. Born lame, he was thrown out of heaven for his deformity. Cf. Milton in *Paradise Lost*, where from 'Heav'n', with the rebellious angels, he 'was headlong sent | With his industrious crew to build in hell' (i. 740–50).

[29] An audacious allegory which puts Satan in the role of George II, who upon his coronation in October 1727 had appointed Heidegger Master of the Revels, promoting him from his former role as merely manager of entertainments for the Prince of Wales. The phrase in italics is presumably a current witticism on Heidegger's elevation.

And see how fast the Glasses fly.   170
Again survey the Inner-Room,
There trembling Gamesters wait their Doom.
Here, the gay Dance the Fair employs;
There, *Damon* sues[30] forbidden Joys,
Whilst *Sylvia* listening to his Pray'r,   175
Gives him no Reason to despair.
See, where poor *Doris*[31] tries t'asswage
The haughty *Laura's* fiery Rage;
Who caught him with a Rival Mistress,
(The sad Occasion of her Distress.)   180
For drinking, gaming, dancing—and
Contriving to—You understand—
(What well-bred Spouses must connive at)
Are the chief Bus'nesses they drive at.
Some indeed, hither sends Good-nature,   185
To vent their o'er-grown Wit in Satyr:
Some spend their Time in Repartee;
Others (rare Wits!) in Ribaldry:
Whilst others rally all they fee,
With that smart Phrase—*Do you know me?*[32]   190
Below Stairs,[33] hungry Whores are picking
The Bones of Wild-fowl, and of Chicken;
And into Pocket some convey
Provisions for another Day;
Preparing thus for future Wants,   195
They've both the Sting and Care of Ants.

---

[30] 'sues': chases, pursues (*OED*, s.v. 'sue' v. 3, obs., the latest example being Spenser's *Faerie Queene* (1596): 'I left him [Calidore] last | Sewing the Blatant Beast' (VI. ix. 2).

[31] '*Doris*': not in this case a woman's name. HF presumably meant 'Dorus', the legendary founder of Doris, one of the four great divisions of ancient Greece.

[32] In the Introduction to *A Compleat Collection of Genteel and Ingenious Conversation* (1738), Swift has Simon Wagstaff describe the 'whole Dialogue' which occurs at masquerades as 'being summed up in one sprightly (I confess, but) single Question and as sprightly an Answer. Do you know me? Yes, I do. And do you know me? Yes, I do' (*Prose Works*, ed. Herbert Davis, 14 vols. (Oxford, 1939–68), iv, p. 116). Cf. HF's *Miss Lucy in Town* (1742), where Tawdry, a prostitute, tells the heroine what people do at a masquerade: 'they dress themselves in a strange Dress, and they walk up and down the Room, and they cry, *Do you know me?* and then they burst out a laughing' (p. 7), which leads Lucy to sing a song: '*With a Mask on my Face,* | *I'll ask all I see* | *Do you know me?* | *Do you know me?*' (p. 7). Later, in *Tom Jones* (XIII. vii), Tom, hoping to find Sophia at the masquerade, accosts every woman he sees who resembles her; some answer 'in a squeaking Voice, *Do you know me?* Much the greater Numbers said, *I don't know you, Sir;* and nothing more' (p. 713).

[33] In Hogarth's *Large Masquerade Ticket* (1727), signs on either side of the room read 'Supper below'.

But see *Loretta* comes, that Common—
Madam, how from another Woman
Do you a Strumpet masqu'd distinguish?
Because that thing which we, in *English*,   200
Do Virtue call, is always took
To hold its Station in the Look.
Poet, quoth she, (first having shaken
Her Sides with Laughter) you're mistaken.
Your Brother Bards have often sung,   205
That Virtue's seated in the Tongue:
With you, nor them, can I agree;
For Virtue's unconfin'd and free;
Is neither seated here nor there,
A Perfect Shadow, light as Air,   210
It rambles loosely, every where.
In Miss's Heart, at Ten, it lies;[34]
At Twenty, mounts into her Eyes;
'Till Forty, how it does dispose
Of its dear self, no Mortal knows.   215
The Tongue is then its certain Station,
And thence it guards the Reputation.
Again (says she) some others ask,
They'll tell you Virtue is a Masque:
But it wou'd look extremely queer   220
In any one, to wear it here.
Madam, says I, methinks you ramble;

---

[34] Goggin ('Fielding's *The Masquerade*', p. 485) proposed that the passage beginning here, tracing the site of Virtue from the heart at age 10 to the tongue at 40, is a variation on the following theme, also in hudibrastics, from Prior's *Alma: or, The Progress of the Mind* (1718), which traces the progress of the mind from the toes in infancy upward to, finally, the head:

> My simple *System* shall suppose,
> That ALMA enters at the Toes;
> That then She mounts by just Degrees
> Up to the Ancles, Legs, and Knees:
> Next, as the Sap of Life does rise,
> She lends her Vigor to the Thighs:
> And, all these under-Regions past,
> She nestles somewhere near the Waste:
> Gives Pain or Pleasure, Grief or Laughter;
> As We shall show at large hereafter.
> Mature, if not improv'd, by Time
> Up to the Heart She loves to climb:
> From thence, compell'd by Craft and Age,
> She makes the Head her latest Stage.   (i. 252–65)

What need we this your long Preamble?
Well then, as in the different Ages,
So Virtue in the different Stages   225
Of Female Life, its Station alters:
It in the Widow's Jointure shelters;
In Wives, 'tis not so plain where laid;
But in the Virgin's Maidenhead.
A Maidenhead now never dies,   230
'Till, like true *Phoenix*, it supplies
Its Loss, by leaving us another:
For she's the Maid who is no Mother.
And she may be—we see in Life,
A Mother, who is not a Wife.   235
Now 'tis this Café, which in the Trumpet
Of Fame, distinguishes a Strumpet:
This, having been *Loretta's* Fate,
Did to the World her Loss relate.
So, poor *Calistho* it befel,   240
With secret Injuries, to swell;[35]
But had *Diana* through her Clan,
(To try how far th' Infection ran)
Forc'd all her Followers to Tryal
Of, Chastity, by *Ordeal*;[36]   245
Who knows (tho' it had rag'd no higher)
What pretty Feet had swell'd by Fire?
   But see that Knot[37] of Shepherdesses,
And Shepherds—well—they're pretty Dresses.
Such the *Arcadian* Shepherds were,   250
When Love along could charm the Fair:
Such the *Arcadian* Nymphs, when Love
Beauty alone in Men cou'd move.
How happy did they sport away,
In fragrant Bow'rs, the scorching Day;   255
Or, to the *Nightingale's* soft Tune,
Danc'd by the Lustre of the Moon!

---

[35] Callisto was a nymph in the train of the goddess Artemis (Diana), the virgin huntress and a goddess of childbirth. She was seduced by Zeus and gave birth to Arcas, the legendary ancestor of the Arcadians.

[36] The 'ordeal by fire'—once a test to prove a wife's fidelity by having her walk unscathed through flames or over glowing ploughshares—does not appear to have been, as here, a test to determine a woman's virginity (*EB*, s.v. 'ordeal').

[37] 'Knot': a small group of persons gathered together in one place (*OED*, s.v. 18).

Beauteous the Nymphs, the Swains sincere,
They knew no Jealousy, no Fear:
Together flock'd, like Turtle-Doves,   260
All constant to their plighted Loves.
How different is now their Fate!
Both equally conspire to cheat.
Florus, with lying *Billet-doux*
The charming *Rosalind* pursues;   265
Follows her to the Play—to Court,
Where-ever the *Beau-Monde* resort.
Some half a Year he's made that Tool,
The wise yclepe a Woman's Fool:
At last the pitying Fair relents,   270
And to his utmost Wish consents.
No sooner is the Nymph enjoy'd,
Than *Florus*, fickle Youth, is cloy'd.
He leaves her for another Toast;[38]
She laughs and crys—Pray—who has lost?   275
    Madam, said I, a Simile
Of mine will with your Tale agree.
So have I seen two Gamesters meet,
(Both ignorant that both wou'd cheat)
Throw half an Hour of Life away,   280
Cheating by turns in fruitless Play.
At last each other's Tricks discover,
And wisely give their throwing over:
At one another laugh, as Fools,
And run away to seek new Culls.[39]   285
    Poet, your Simile is just.
But what comes here? quoth I—A Ghost;
I hope the Fantom does not scare you?
O no; says she: But see what's near you.
Oh hideous! what a dreadful Face!   290
Worse than the Master's of the Place!
Has Nature been so very sparing

[38] 'Toast': According to Richard Steele in *The Tatler* Nos. 24 and 31 (2, 18 June 1709), this now familiar name for a belle, to whom the company is asked to drink a toast, was 'new' in the first decade of the eighteenth century (*OED*, s.v. sb.[2] and v.[2] 1–2; for both noun and verb the earliest citation is Congreve's *Way of the World* [1700]).
[39] 'Culls': dupes. Cf. *Tom Jones* (VIII. xii), where the sharper Watson, producing a pair of dice, assures the Man of the Hill: 'I will shew you a Way to empty the Pockets of a *Queer Cull*' (p. 464).

Of Ugliness, to th'Age we are in;
That our Deformity by Nature
Art must contrive to render greater?   295
Quoth she, for different Reasons here,
In different Masques, we all appear.
Some ugly Vizards are design'd
To raise Ideas in the Mind;
Which may, like Foils, conspire to grace   300
The lesser Horrors of the Face.
Others in beauteous Masques delight,
To be thought *Belles* for half a Night;
As proud of this short Transformation,
As Justice *D——k* at C–r–n–t—n.[40]   305
For know, (tho' 'tis by few believ'd)
Most go away from hence deceiv'd:
Error, (strange Goddess!) ruleth here,
And from her Castle in the Air,
Carefully watches o'er our Motions,   310
Receives our Off'rings and Devotions.
    Behold, aloft, the Goddess sit,
In her Appearance a Coquette;
Six *Beaus*, as many *Belles*, are shown,
On Right, and Left-hand of her Throne.   315
See *Venus, Bacchus, Fortune* there;
So, at this Distance, they appear:
But all are Pictures, view them near.
The Goddess these, with subtle Art,
Has Plac'd, to captivate each Heart.   320
For whilst you with a vain Entreaty,
Attack the Favourite painted Deity,
You fall into an unseen Net;
(By *Error* on that Purpose set.)
Thus caught, you are oblig'd to wander   325

[40] Lewis Dymoke, or Dymmok (d. 1760), whose family since the fourteenth century had performed the office of king's Champion at a coronation, as he had recently done at the coronation of George II (October 1727) by appearing well armed on horseback at the banquet in Westminster Hall, to prove against any challenger that the king who was crowned that day is the rightful heir of the kingdom. (See above, p. 15 n. 8.) This service was last performed by Sir Henry Dymoke at the coronation of George IV (1821). As lord of the manor of Scrivelsby, Lincolnshire, when not basking in this momentary glory, he would have acted the humble part of a country Justice of the Peace. (On the Dymoke family, see the *Oxford DNB*.) In *Craftsman* No. 618 (13 May 1738) HF spelled the name '*Dimmock*' (*New Essays*, p. 302); other examples, not in the Wesleyan Edition, are *Champion* (15 April ['Puffs'] and 18 October 1740).

Through a mysterious wild *Meander*:[41]
Wearied, at last you find the Door,
Then hey to Wine, or Wife, or W——e.
Of these, no matter which, a Dose
Your Senses does in Sleep compose;   330
Waking, all your Adventures seem
An idle, trifling, feverish Dream.[42]
This Fate, indeed, does not befal
(Tho' much the greater Numbers) all:
For some o'er-leap with nimble Feet;   335
Others, with stronger, break the Net:
Then kneeling at the favourite Shrine,
They make the Deity benign.
    Now that a G–d may be entreated,
By Prayers to Images related;   340
'Twill not be credited by some
In *England*, but by all at *Rome*.[43]
    Thus *Fortune* sends the Gamesters Luck,
Venus her Votary a—
——Mistress—Oh! Criticks, spare the Crime,   345
Of one who cou'd not find a Rhyme.
Bacchus, that Jolly Power Divine,
To his Petitioner sends Wine.
    The Lucky Gamester, when Repose
No longer will his Eye-lids close,   350
With Triumph feels his loaded Breeches.
That bend beneath the weighty Riches.
That happy Lover, when he wakes,
And a Survey of *Celia* takes,
As sleeping by his Side she lies,   355
Kisses, in Ecstasie, her Eyes,
Her Lips, her Breast; devours her Charms,
And dies in Raptures, in her Arms.
The honest Sot, disdaining Rest,
Finds Joy imperial in his Breast;   360
As great an Emperor as any

---

[41] '*Meander*': a labyrinth or maze (*OED*, s.v. 2c).

[42] HF paraphrases his epigraph from Horace (see above, notes to the title-page).

[43] In *Tom Jones* (XIII. ix) as Tom and Lady Bellaston continue their affair, which began after the masquerade, HF doubts he could please the reader by describing the event: 'unless', that is, 'he is one whose Devotion to the Fair Sex, like that of the Papists to their Saints, wants to be raised by the Help of Pictures' (p. 722).

In *Bedlam, Russia,* or *Germany.*[44]
  But tho' each Godship kindly grants
To some Petitioners their Wants:
Each does refuse (I know not why)   365
With Some Petitions to comply;
And oft requites a hearty Prayer,
(Instead of Joys) with Woes and Care:
For view the young unseason'd Drinker,
Oh L—d! methinks I smell him stink here;   370
Welt'ring, he in his *Pigsty* lies,
And curses all Debaucheries.
The undone Gamester wakes, and tears,
From his ill-fated Head, his Hairs.
The Lover, who has now possess'd,   375
From unknown *Flora*, his Request;
(Who with a pretty, modest Grace,
Discover'd all things but her Face:)
Pulls off her Masque in am'rous Fury,
And finds a gentle Nympth of *Drury*,[45]   380
Curses his Lust—laments his Fate,
And kicks her out of Bed too late.
From different Springs, of equal Pain,
The Gamester and Gallant complain;
The Gamester mourns his losing Lot,   385
The Lover fears—that he has got.
  These are the Scenes—wherein engage
The Numbers now upon this Stage.
These are the different Ends, which all
In different Degrees befal.   390
Now I'll discover who I am:
A Muse—*Calliope* my Name.[46]
I stood surpriz'd, whilst from my Sight
She vanish'd, in a sudden Flight.

[44] An emperor in Bedlam (Bethlehem Hospital) would be a deluded madman, as later depicted by Hogarth in the last scene of *A Rake's Progress* (1735), where, glimpsed in a cell, a naked lunatic squatting on a throne of straw wears a makeshift crown and flourishes a sceptre. The current Emperor of Russia was Peter II (1727–30); HF probably had in mind Peter's grandfather, Peter the Great (1672–1725). The 'Emperor' of Germany was Frederick William I (1688–1740), King of Prussia.

[45] A prostitute from Drury Lane (see above, line 82 and n. 17), from whom he will have contracted a venereal disease.

[46] So, the 'Muse' whom the poet summoned to his aid (line 61) proves to be Calliope, Muse of epic poetry. Disguised as the 'Lady in a Velvet Hood', she has been his companion ever since making her appearance (line 80).

2

'CANTOS': AN UNFINISHED
BURLESQUE OF *THE DUNCIAD* (1729–30)

IN 1968 Isobel Grundy discovered, preserved among the papers of Fielding's cousin Lady Mary Wortley Montagu, the manuscript of an unfinished poem comprising three 'Cantos' totalling 607 lines. Untitled and unsigned but written throughout in Fielding's hand,[1] the work is in the form of a mock-heroic burlesque of *The Dunciad* satirizing Pope and his Tory associates—chiefly the Scriblerians: Swift, Gay, Arbuthnot, Bolingbroke, and Bolingbroke's tool Nicholas Amhurst, editor of *The Craftsman*. Professor Grundy subsequently edited the 'Cantos' (as we will call them), with introduction and notes, in *PMLA* 87 (1972), pp. 213–45.

Though undated, the draft, as internal evidence suggests, was probably written some time after Fielding returned from the Continent in the summer of 1729; apparent references to *The Grub-Street Journal* make it likely that as late as January 1730 he had not yet put the work aside.[2] What provoked him to undertake the 'Cantos', however—in scope the most ambitious poem he ever attempted—was events that took place more than a year earlier while he was abroad in Holland.[3] On 8 March 1728 Pope and Swift had published volume III of their *Miscellanies*, in which Lady Mary found herself the subject of 'The Capon's Tale', an indecent lampoon in verse on which the authors appear to have collaborated; this was followed on 18 May by the publication of *The Dunciad*, in which Pope, alluding to Lady Mary's alleged affair with a certain Frenchman, compares her to a common prostitute who is presented to madam's clients as a woman of quality:

---

[1] Though the MS is unsigned, at the top of the first page of Canto 2 Lady Mary has written the initials 'H.F.'

[2] In Canto 3, line 81, HF alludes to the publication of the astronomer John Machin's 'Laws of the Moon's Motion, according to Gravity', appended to Andrew Motte's translation of Newton's *Principia*, published on 23 May 1729 (*Monthly Chronicle*). At 1. 98 and 3. 52–3, however, HF appears to allude to Pope's connection with *The Grub-Street Journal*, which began publication on 8 January 1729/30. (See below, 1. 98 n. 23; 3. 52–3 n. 133, and 81 n. 138; *Life*, pp. 79 and 634 n. 60.)

[3] It is unlikely that HF began the Cantos in 1728. He left England to attend the University of Leiden soon after his comedy *Love in Several Masques* closed in February and did not return until summer; in July and early August he was poking fun at Walpole, Lady Mary's friend, in the Opposition press; and the early autumn found him regretting his rustication in a farm his father had rented for him in Upton Grey, Hants.; by February 1729 he had returned to Leiden. (*Life*, pp. 62–72.)

> As the sage dame experience'd in her trade,
> By names of Toasts retails each batter'd jade,
> (Whence hapless Monsieur much complains at *Paris*
> Of wrongs from Duchesses and Lady *Marys*)[4]

Insults as rude as these were meant to wound, and, cited from this time forward by the pamphleteers who attacked Pope's character, they were not forgotten.[5] Moreover, in revising the poem for the Variorum edition, published a year later (10 April 1729), Pope, unabashed, had compounded the offence by letting the passage stand.

That Fielding resented these affronts to his cousin enough to risk the probable consequences of satirizing her tormentors, the most devastating wits of the day, attests to the closeness of their relationship. Lady Mary, herself remarkable as wit and poet, was not only family; she was his good friend and patron. He had solicited her opinion of his first play, *Love in Several Masques*, and it was probably owing to her influence that it was staged in Drury Lane, at the Theatre Royal, in February 1728; it ran for just four nights, with Lady Mary loyally attending half the performances. To her, Fielding gratefully dedicated the book of the play. Though, on returning from Holland in the summer of 1728, Fielding appears to have indulged in anonymous literary high jinks at the expense of the Prime Minister, Sir Robert Walpole,[6] the 'Cantos' show that a year later he had thoroughly adopted the political views of Lady Mary, a close friend of Walpole, against the opposition party led by Bolingbroke and Pulteney.

Fielding's ridicule of Pope in the 'Cantos' is tame compared to the spate of abuse directed at him in the pamphlets—more than thirty of them published by the end of 1729.[7] But the features of the character he draws are essentially those of the caricatures to be found in what J. V. Guerinot calls the literature of 'Popiana'.[8] The litany of complaints against Pope was long and ran as follows. In his religion, he was that hated thing, a papist, and therefore must also be a Jacobite. Though it could not be that he knew Greek, he had nevertheless made a fortune from his Homer while paying the real translators, William Broome and Elijah Fenton, a mere pittance. All could see that Lewis Theobald, having in *Shakespeare Restored* exposed

---

[4] *Dunciad* (1728), ii. 113–16.

[5] See J. V. Guerinot, *Pamphlet Attacks on Alexander Pope 1711–1744: A Descriptive Bibliography* (London, 1969).

[6] For HF's authorship of 'The Norfolk Lanthorn', a popular ballad ridiculing this ostentatious fixture in Walpole's house published in *The Craftsman* (20 July 1728), see Battestin, 'Four New Fielding Attributions: His Earliest Satires of Walpole', *Studies in Bibliography*, 36 (1983), pp. 69–109.

[7] Guerinot, *Pamphlet Attacks on Alexander Pope*, p. xxiii.

[8] See Guerinot's Introduction, ibid., sect. III.

the errors of Pope's edition, had for his pains been spitefully installed in *The Dunciad* as prince of Dulness. Pope, they said, was furthermore the worst of ingrates, having rewarded those who rescued him from obscurity when he first came to town by ridiculing them in his satires—Addison and Wycherley were the usual examples. No wonder, then, that Pope's stunted stature and deformed body were declared to be the symptoms of an inhuman viciousness of mind; he was called a toad, a monkey, a cur. And of course he was proud—so proud that he presumed to arrogate to himself the role of literary dictator, consigning to the dungeon of *The Dunciad* all authors but those of his own circle.

As Pope's sounder biographers have shown,[9] his true character bears little resemblance to these caricatures, but they served to define him for many in his own time and, indeed, for generations to come. For Fielding, too, in the 'Cantos' and later in the verse epistles to Lyttelton and John Hayes (*Miscellanies* i. 51–3), this would also be the image of Pope—and, turning against him Pope's own joke against Theobald in the Preface to *The Dunciad* (1728), Fielding would give him the name of Juvenal's poor poet, Codrus.[10] In time, his opinion of Pope's character would soften as he came to know him personally through the good offices of their common friend Ralph Allen. And in cooler moments, when he was not incensed by Pope's rudeness to Lady Mary—and on occasion even when he was, as the *Epistle to Lyttleton* attests—he expressly acknowledged the poet's genius. Later, indeed, in *The Champion* (27 November 1739), he would declare Pope to be no less than 'the greatest Poet of his Time', whose 'Works will be coeval with the Language in which they are writ'.

In one respect, however, Fielding—despite the evidence of his own poems to the contrary—seems never to have given up a prejudice, plainly expressed in the 'Cantos', against the verse form that Dryden and Pope had perfected: the form, that is, of the rhymed couplet. In the 'Cantos', Fielding presents Codrus as the offspring of both the goddess Dulness and the god Rhime. Given that Pope's verse form was the approved standard of the age, this would seem an unlikely complaint in a satire, but it is a recurrent theme among the pamphleteers, who followed Dennis in characterizing Pope as being 'neither a Poet nor Versifier, but only an eternal Rhimer'.[11] The three

---

[9] See George Sherburn, *The Early Career of Alexander Pope* (Oxford, 1934), and Maynard Mack, *Alexander Pope: A Life* (New York and New Haven, 1985).

[10] See Pope's Preface: 'Had the Hero, for instance, been called *Codrus*, how many would have affirm'd him to be Mr. *W[elsted]* Mr. *D[ennis]* Sir *R[ichard] B[lackmore]*, &c. but now, all that unjust scandal is saved, by calling him *Theobald*, which by good luck happens to be the name of a real person' (p. vii; italics reversed).

[11] John Dennis, *Remarks on Mr. Pope's 'Rape of the Lock'* (1728), p. ix.

satires that appear to have influenced the 'Cantos' directly—Lady Mary's own unpublished burlesque of *The Dunciad* (1729),[12] Welsted and Moore-Smythe's *One Epistle to Mr. A. Pope* (1730),[13] and most particularly James Ralph's *Sawney* (1728)—all echo the charge that Pope, the greatest poet of his time, was nothing more than a rhymer.

In joining the chorus of Pope's detractors on this point, Fielding, with his new-found friend Ralph, could at least offer as an excuse his conviction that Milton's blank verse was superior to Pope's rhymes because it was more natural and more amenable to the exact expression of thought— closer, indeed, to prose, the medium Fielding would make his own. Some years later, when preparing the *Miscellanies* for the press, he wrote to his friend James Harris regretting that the 'Scarcity of Matter' made it necessary to include his poetry in the collection:

my Talents (if I have any) lie not in Versification. My Muse is a free born Briton & disdains the slavish Fetters of Rhyme. And must not y° or the greatest Admirer of Numbers allow that, even in the Hands of the best Versifier, a noble Sentiment, or a noble Expression at least, may be sometimes lost by the unfortunate length or shortness of a Word? for the Poet must imitate the Recruiting Officer who rejects Strength & Symmetry for a long ill-made Fellow of 6 Foot. . . . how common is it with the Poets to admit a *shabby* word, as y° Lovers of Music do sometimes a shabby Treble only for being musical: nay amongst those who write in Rhime one Line is often introduced only to chime to the other, according to the Poetical Observaĉon,

> For one for Sense & one for Rhime
> I think is fairest at one Time[14]

wĉh is likewise an Example of the Practice, half the last Line being superfluous.[15]

Many passages in the 'Cantos' reflect the friendly rivalry in which, during the latter months of 1729, Fielding and Lady Mary vied with one another in attempting to turn Pope's *Dunciad* into a satire on himself and fellow Scriblerians. Bound in with Fielding's verses in volume 81 of the

---

[12] Lady Mary Wortley Montagu, *Essays and Poems and Simplicity, A Comedy*, ed. Robert Halsband and Isobel Grundy (Oxford, 1977), pp. 247–51.

[13] Leonard Welsted and James Moore-Smythe, *One Epistle to Mr. A. Pope*, introd. Joseph V. Guerinot, Augustan Reprint Society 114, (William Andrews Clark Memorial Library, University of California, Los Angeles, 1965). Though not published until April 1730, the poem was in preparation more than a year earlier (*Universal Spectator*, 1 February 1728/9) and had been circulating in manuscript since at least October. (See *The Correspondence of Alexander Pope*, ed. George Sherburn [Oxford, 1956], iii. 59 n. 3, and Guerinot, Introduction to Welsted and Moore-Smythe, *One Epistle*, p. iii.)

[14] Misquoted from Samuel Butler's *Hudibras* (1663), II. i. 27–30: 'But those that write in *Rhime*, still make | The one *Verse*, for the other's sake: | For, one for *Sense*, and one for *Rhime*, | I think's sufficient at one time.' HF alludes to this passage in Canto 1, line 142.

[15] HF to Harris (Bath, 24 September 1742), in *The Correspondence of Henry and Sarah Fielding*, ed. Martin C. Battestin and Clive T. Probyn (Oxford, 1993), pp. 23–4.

Harrowby manuscripts are drafts of two of his cousin's poems that develop independently the themes of the 'Cantos'.[16] The first opens with a rhyming triplet (a form Fielding also uses from time to time in the 'Cantos') depicting the 'Palace' of Dulness as Pope's grotto at Twickenham, 'Adorn'd within by Shells of small expence | (Emblems of tinsel Rhime, and triffleing Sense)' (lines 6–7). A passage paralleling Fielding's opening theme celebrates the beneficial effects of Henry VIII's break with the Catholic Church: 'From Reformation, Learning shall be born,' freeing Britain from 'the thraldom of Monastic Rhimes' and allowing Milton to 'free Poetry from the Monkish Chain' (lines 35–41). As in the 'Cantos', the rest of the Scriblerians make an appearance at the Court of Dulness. Swift is the 'darling Son' of 'Prophanation' (lines 65–80); Gay is the proselytizing subject of 'fair Obscœnity' (lines 80–8); Arbuthnot is the favourite of (in a deleted line) Cloacina, his verse full of 'foul Description' (lines 89–97). But it is Pope of course, in whom all vices combine, that Dulness names her 'Captain':

> A Soul where all these several gifts are joyn'd,
> Bold in Obscoenity, prophanely dull,
> With smooth unmeaning Rhime the Town shall lull.   (lines 105–7)

In the second set of mock-heroic verses Lady Mary's target is Pope's friend the Tory politician Bolingbroke, whom Fielding introduces in Canto 2.

For other details Fielding appears to have drawn upon an autograph copy of the pamphlet *One Epistle to Mr. A. Pope*, a verse satire which, though not published until April 1730, had been circulating in manuscript for months. The *Epistle* is now accepted as the work of Leonard Welsted and James Moore-Smythe. Pope, however, who had seen a copy, was certain the handwriting was Lady Mary's, and in October 1729 Arbuthnot, Lady Mary's physician, was deputed to tell her so. Vehemently denying the allegation, she made inquiries as to its source and wrote to inform Arbuthnot of the result: 'I am told Pope has had the surprizing Impudence to assert, he can bring the Lampoon when he pleases to produce it under my own hand', which she dared him to do that she might see him hanged for counterfeiting.[17] Though Lady Mary was not in fact author of the *Epistle*, it is nevertheless possible, as *The Grub-Street Journal* (21 May 1730) stated, that

---

[16] *Essays and Poems*, pp. 247–55. On the friendly rivalry in which HF and Lady Mary engaged as they composed their separate burlesques of Pope's *Dunciad*, see Grundy, pp. 331–2.

[17] Lady Mary to Dr Arbuthnot (29 October 1729), in *The Correspondence of Alexander Pope*, ed. George Sherburn (Oxford, 1956), iii. 60.

she had 'some hand in this piece'.[18] Pope might well have thought so, as a footnote to a line in the satire referring to him as one 'Who lets not Beauty base Detraction 'scape' refers the reader specifically to his treatment of 'Lady *M. W. M.*' (p. 12). Whatever Fielding knew, or thought he knew, about the authorship of the *Epistle*, it is likely that, in addition to more general thematic parallels, he was indebted to it, in particular, for his ridicule of the phrase 'Fights of Stand' (2. 36), an obscure allusion to Pope's *Iliad* (xiii. 890, deleted after 1736) cited in the *Epistle* (p. 18) among other infelicities of Pope's phrasing. Welsted's Preface, in which he refers to *The Dunciad* as 'these Cantos' (p. vii), may also explain Fielding's curious decision to divide his poem into 'Cantos' instead of 'Books', as in Pope's original.

Another likely influence on the poem was James Ralph, with whom Fielding that autumn was beginning a long and literary relationship.[19] The first sure sign of their friendship came during the theatrical season when Fielding, having been rebuffed by Colley Cibber at Drury Lane, took his new comedy, *The Temple Beau*, to Thomas Odell at Goodman's Fields: it opened there on 26 January, with a Prologue provided by Ralph. A year or two older than Fielding and the prolific author of a variety of unremarkable works, it was Ralph who introduced Fielding to the life of writing in London, and whose innovative ideas—set forth in *The Touch-Stone* (1728), a comprehensive review of the diversions of the Town—may well lie behind the experiments Fielding was about to undertake in a new kind of comedy, *The Author's Farce* and *Tom Thumb*, both produced at the Haymarket to great applause in the spring of 1730.[20]

In Ralph, Fielding had a friend who happened to share Lady Mary's political views and who disliked Pope and his circle. After the publication of *The Dunciad* in May 1728 he had rashly attacked Pope, as well as Swift and Gay, in *Sawney*, a 'Heroic' satire written in imitation of Milton's blank verse, except, that is, for the speeches of the eponymous hero, votary of the Muse of Rhyme. With the publication of Pope's Variorum edition a year later, Ralph, for his trouble, found that he had earned a place with Lady Mary among the dunces. The insult to his friend gave Fielding another reason to retaliate. In its sustained ridicule of Pope for his slavish devotion to feeble 'Rhime' despite the superior example of 'Milton's Strength' (1. 167), Ralph would recognize in the author of the 'Cantos' a champion of a cause he had made his own.

---

[18] Guerinot, *Pamphlet Attacks on Alexander Pope*, p. 189.

[19] On HF's relationship with Ralph in this period, see John Burke Shipley, 'James Ralph: Pretender to Genius', Ph.D. diss. (Columbia University, 1963), pp. 206–7, 211–14; *Life*, pp. 80–2.

[20] See Helen Sard Hughes, 'Fielding's Indebtedness to James Ralph', *MP*, 20 (1922–3), pp. 19–34; *Life*, pp. 80–1.

Textual Note: The 'Cantos'

THE unfinished 'Cantos' represent the only extant example of a poem by Fielding in the early stages of composition. Because the manuscripts themselves are not readily accessible and cannot be photographed, it has seemed preferable—because the method acquaints the reader with certain distinctive features of Fielding's writing style—to render the text in what Vander Meulen and Tanselle define as a 'transcription' of the original: that is, 'to report—insofar as typography allows—precisely what the textual inscription of a manuscript consists of'. The aim has been 'to record every ink . . . marking of textual significance on the manuscript—all letters, punctuation, superscripts, canceled matter . . . and so on'.[1] For the convenience of the reader, however, the transcription is presented in the form of a 'clear', rather than 'inclusive', text in which, in order to free the text itself from intrusive commentary, the record of revisions is relegated to footnotes to the text page.

Inconsistency in the treatment and form of accidentals is a notable feature of the holograph, which is an early draft not meant for the eyes of a compositor. The reader will notice, for example, both commas and periods used indiscriminately (or at times not used at all) where apostrophes would normally be expected, with the letters that follow raised in superscript: 'cry,^{d}' but 'Shatter^{d}' (2. 61); 'grov,^{ling}' (3. 39) but 'gen^{ral}' (3. 138). The most salient example of this inconsistency occurs in the inscription of letters meant for upper and lower case. Fielding often neglects to capitalize substantive nouns, a convention of the period that he followed in the fair copy of his poem 'An Epistle to Mr. Lyttleton', and which is characteristic of most of his printed works. The form he gives certain letters is constant, whether he intends them for upper or lower case: this is true of his *m, o, s, u, v, w*, and often his *a, c, g, y*. When he means to capitalize these letters, he simply writes them larger; and size being a relative thing, his intention is not always clear. Because the present text is, as defined above, a transcription of the holograph, no attempt has been made to impose conventional usage in the matter of capitals (except at the beginning of the lines of verse[2]), or in other features of the text. Square brackets [ ] signal editorial intervention, necessary in a few instances where the reading of the MS

---

[1] David M. Vander Meulen and Thomas Tanselle, 'A System of Manuscript Transcription', *Studies in Bibliography*, 52 (1999), p. 201.

[2] Twice in the Cantos, however, HF began lines with forms he generally reserved strictly for lower case: see 1. 130 ('from') and 2. 105 ('rather').

would otherwise be unclear or confusing. Angle brackets < > signal a word or letter that is uncertain.

The MSS are bound in volume 81, Harrowby MSS Trust, Sandon Hall, Stafford: ['Canto 1st'] is inscribed in fos. 182–5; 'Canto 2^{d}' and 'Canto 3^{d}' in fos. 172–80.

— & to look o'er ye old Records of time
The wondrous days! those glorious days of Rhime!
when not a Bard durst draw his labring Quill
Unbid by me — ungovern'd by my Will:
When tedious Histories in verse were writ,
with E——'s truth, S——'s metre and thy wit:
Latin was then a Tongue perplexing [?]
and reading Greek Heretical was deem'd.
Then to be learn'd was to have left [?] Lunch
Their doting Mother, whom Men call the Church.
The Deathless Fame which Home our Coast
How nearly was it in Oblivion lost
Virgil and Cicen in Shelves [?] read
None durst prophane the hallow'd [?] [?]
Moth's Homer eat on the neglected Shelf
Bards then were scarce more learned then thy self:
But soon as Reformation first prevail'd.
~~together~~ my Cause
and Popery together fail'd.
Popery still my nearest dearest friend
To the same purpose both our Efforts tend
To lull the Mind in that serene Repose
which those who think or those who study lose
All the Credenda of her faith survey,
How dull! how monstrous! how absurd are they!
Such! (were the Wretches whom her Priests deceive
allow'd to think) they never could believe

182

Opening leaf, 'Cantos' MS

AN UNFINISHED
BURLESQUE OF *THE DUNCIAD*

[CANTO 1st]¹

——O to look oer yᵉ old Records of Time²
The Monkish days! those glorious days of Rhime!³
When not a Bard durst draw his lab,ʳⁱⁿᵍ Quill
Unbid by me—ungovernᵈ by my Will:

References to lines of verse in the three Cantos cite the Canto number first followed by the number(s) of the line(s), e.g. 2. 161 = Canto 2, line 161. Cross-references to the notes are to page and note number, e.g. p. 100 n. 86.

¹ The MS opens without title, section heading, or exordium; presumably a leaf is missing.

² Cf. below, 'Look through the long Record of Ages past' (p. 57 n. 86).

³ The goddess Dulness addresses her son Codrus (Pope). The implication is misleading, however, that Pope, though a Catholic, shared her admiration of the 'Monkish days'. HF disregards the passage in the *Essay on Criticism* (1711, lines 685–92) in which Pope incurred the resentment of his co-religionists by depicting the Church as responsible for the Dark Ages: 'With *Tyranny* . . . *Superstition* join'd, | As that the *Body*, this enslav'd the *Mind*'; 'A *second* Deluge Learning thus o'er-run, | And the *Monks* finish'd what the *Goths* begun' (see the notes to the Twickenham edn., i. 317 nn. 687 ff. and 691 ff.). The same satiric theme occurs in the vision of the progress of Dulness in *The Dunciad* (iii. 91–114).

In praising the triumph of ignorance, 'popery' and superstition in Britain during the Dark Ages before the Protestant Reformation began under Henry VIII, when the monastic orders were abolished and, under the influence of the humanists, the teaching of Greek and Latin was accepted, Dulness takes a contrary view from that of such Whig historians as John Oldmixon (1673–1742). HF indeed appears to have drawn specifically on Oldmixon's *Critical History of England, Ecclesiastical and Civil: Wherein the Errors of the Monkish Writers, and others before the Reformation, are Expos'd and Corrected* (1724–6), which he had in his library (Ribbles O1); a third edition was published in May 1728. As announced on the title-page, Oldmixon attacks in particular the Tory historians Clarendon and Echard (see 2. 167–8 n. 88 and 1. 6 n. 5, respectively) and defends *The History of his Time* (1724) by Gilbert Burnet, HF's favourite historian (Ribbles B56). With the general tenor of HF's opening lines, cf. this from pt. 1, ch. 6, '*Of the Church History of England, from the earliest Times of Christianity, to the Fifteenth Century*':

> The Monks were a pamper'd standing Force, always devoted to the Interest of the Papacy, and very serviceable to that Interest by the Influence of their Revenues and Absolutions. . . . Little enough was the Learning of the World, for Ten Centuries; and it was impossible but some of these Recluses must employ themselves in something else besides Luxury and Devotion. Books therefore lay in their Way, and little in the Way of any body else for many Ages. No wonder then, that there were Writers among them. But what Sort of Writings have they left behind them? Legends, Prophecies, Rhimes, and Histories, so confounded with Fables, that one cannot depend upon them . . . (pp. 81–2)

HF in later years mentions Oldmixon chiefly as a dull writer: see *Ovid's Art of Love Paraphrased* (1747; below, p. 415 n. 39), *Tom Jones* (1749; v. i, p. 214), and *The Covent-Garden Journal*, No. 3 (11 January 1752), p. 28; in that journal No. 17 (29 February, p. 120) the abstract of Humphrey Newmixon's history of Great Britain parodies Oldmixon's *Critical History* (see Pat Rogers, 'Fielding's Parody of Oldmixon', *PQ*, 49 [1970]), pp. 262–6.

When tedious Histories[4] in verse were writ, 5
With E———[s5] Truth, S———[s6] Metre and thy wit:
Latin was then a Tongue prophane esteem,[d]
And reading Greek Heretical was deem[d].[7]
Then to be learn,[d] was to have left i,th, Lurch
Their doting Mother, whom Men call the Church. 10
The Deathless Fame which Horace Ovid[8] boast
How nearly was it in Oblivion lost
Virgil and Cicero[9] in Schools now read

---

[4] Cf. *Dunciad* (1728), iii. 171–2: '*Hist'ry* with her comrade *Ale* | Sooths the sad series of her tedious tale.' HF imperfectly recalls the couplet in *Tom Jones* (1749; IV. i, p. 150).

[5] Laurence Echard (1670–1730), whose *History of England* (1707–18) was attacked by Oldmixon (see above, n. 3) for the 'Poyson' of its Tory bias (*Critical History*, p. v). A copy of the third edition (1720) was in HF's library (Ribbles E1). Though HF could on occasion cite Echard as an authority (*Champion* [6 December 1739], p. 49; *Charge Delivered to the Grand Jury* [1749], p. 7; *Enquiry into the Late Increase of Robbers* [1751], p. 85; *Covent-Garden Journal*, No. 68 [28 October 1752], p. 358), he usually considered the *History* unreliable. In *Joseph Andrews* (1742; III. i, pp. 185–6), criticizing historians for allowing political bias to colour their accounts of persons and events, HF pairs the Whigs Paul de Rapin and Bulstrode Whitelocke against Oldmixon's targets, Clarendon and Echard. For a full account of HF's opinion of Echard as a historian, including his *Roman History* (1695–8), see *Companion*, p. 60.

[6] Referring perhaps to Swift and Pope's *Miscellanies*, iii (1728), where, annoyed that (as Pope believed) Lady Mary had accused him of writing an offensive poem of her own, they collaborated in making her the subject of an indecent satire entitled 'The Capon's Tale: To a Lady *who father'd her Lampoons upon her Acquaintance.*' Pope had presented her with an inscribed copy of the poem in his own hand, 'purporting', as Isobel Grundy remarks, 'to be the work of two cocks'. Grundy suggests that Pope's accomplice in the prank was Gay (p. 274); but Swift seems the more likely candidate, as it is included among much other verse by him in the section of the *Miscellanies* devoted to 'Miscellanies in Verse', pp. 51–3.

[7] With HF's subject and phrasing, cf. the following excerpt from 'Verses occasion'd by the General History of PRINTING' included in James Ralph's *Miscellaneous Poems by Several Hands* (pub. 15 April 1729). Honouring the publication of the first number of the work by Samuel Palmer (March 1729), the anonymous author (said to be Thomas Birch by J. B. Shipley [p. 156 n. 19]), recounts the effects of the suppression of learning by the Church before the invention of printing:

> Mysterious Jargon then Devotion seem'd,
> *Greek*, pious Ideots *Heresy* esteem'd;
> Yet *Latin*, oft was read,—not understood;
> For none but Pray'rs in Sounds unknown were good.   (p. 36)

Though it is the invention of printing, not the advent of the Reformation, that in this poem heralds enlightenment after the Dark Ages, the treatment of the subject is close to HF's own.

[8] Horace (Quintus Horatius Flaccus, 65–8 BC) was perhaps HF's favourite classical author. Inscribing a copy of Horace's works as a gift to Jane Collier, HF called him 'the best of all the Roman Poets' (Ribbles H38). In his writings HF alludes to and quotes from Horace more frequently than any other author (Ribbles H34). On HF and Ovid (Publius Ovidius Naso, 43 BC–AD 18), see below, pp. 385–8.

[9] Virgil (Publius Virgilius Maro, 70–19 BC). HF owned three editions of Virgil's works as well as Dryden's translation (Ribbles V10–13). In *Amelia* (1751; VIII. v, p. 338) Booth, referring to the *Aeneid*, places Virgil 'in the first Rank' of poets, together with Homer and Milton. For HF's parody of a passage from the *Aeneid*, see below, 1. 85–90.

HF was well read in Cicero (106–43 BC)—for his personal collection, see Ribbles C29–32. He refers to him in a variety of contexts, but especially as the philosopher of an enlightened stoicism. See *Companion*, pp. 45–6.

Neere durst prophane the hallow^d Friar^s Head
Moths Homer^{10} eat on the neglected Shelf   15
Bards then were scarce more learned then thy self.
But soon as Reformation first prevail^d
My Cause and Popery^s together fail^d
Popery^{11} still my nearest dearest Friend
To the same purpose both our Efforts tend   20
To lull the Mind in that serene Repose
Which those who think or those who study lose
All the Credenda^{12} of her Faith survey
How dull! how monstrous! how absurd are they!
Such! (were the Wretches whom her Priests deceive   25
Allow,^{d} to think) they never could believe

                                                              [fo. 182^v]

That <u>Superstition</u> whom her Sons adore
(The great Supporter of the <u>Romish</u> Power)
From my big Womb a mighty Offspring came
Dull! dismal! Coward! void of Sense or Shame!   30
One Light alone does in his Face appear
And Sights of Terrour only enter there
To him Idolatry a Son was giv^n
Who chang^d the former Government of Heav,^{n}
And introduc,^{d} into the blest abodes   35
(Such was his Power) Democracy of Gods^{13}

18] My Cause *interlined above cancelled* Together

---

[10] HF regarded Homer as a great genius 'who, of all others, saw farthest into human Nature' (*Tom Jones*, 1749; IV. xiii, p. 202); his allusions to him are numerous (Ribbles H27). As he launched his career as novelist, HF, in the Preface to *Joseph Andrews* (1742), claimed descent for his 'comic Epic-Poem in Prose' from Homer's lost work the *Margites* (pp. 3–4). Grundy observes that the Cantos 'recall most strongly the opening books of the *Iliad*' ('New Verse by Henry Fielding', *PMLA*, 87 (1972), p. 213); they represent the earliest of his experiments in the mock-epic mode.

[11] Like many of his countrymen in Protestant England at the time, HF was strongly anti-Catholic—an attitude that colours certain of his works beginning with *The Old Debauchees* (1732) and to be found especially in his publications of the late 1740s occasioned by the Jacobite Rebellion.

[12] Discussing his religion in *The Champion* (25 December 1739), HF dismissed 'the *Credenda*, or Matters of Faith, regarding Doctrinal and Ceremonial Points', as having no authority in Scripture. What mattered to him in religion was 'the *Agenda*, or Matters of Morality' (pp. 85–6). In his anti-Jacobite writings HF often alludes scornfully to certain articles of the Roman Catholic Church, particularly the doctrines of transubstantiation and the supremacy of the Pope (e.g. *A Serious Address to the People of Great Britain* [1745], p. 5).

[13] Cf. HF's *Of True Greatness* (1741) referring to the multitude of 'contending Images' that men call 'Greatness': 'Not *Greece*, in all her Temples wide Abodes, | Held a more wild Democracy of Gods' (*Miscellanies*, 1743; i. 19). In making 'Idolatry', a form of polytheism, the offspring of '*Superstition*' (lines 27–36), HF appears to have in mind the Roman Catholic institution of sainthood and the practice, with the

But if more glaring Proofs must be apply,^{d14}
To shew how near our Empires are alli^d
View all the Kingdoms which her Power deny
And see how all from my Embraces fly   40
Equal in Europe^s East our Power arose
In Realms which once were my severest Foes¹⁵
The Sun of Learning in his mid Career
We routed down the Eastern Hemisphere.
By Popery that Phaeton was he hurl,^d   45
And peaceful Darkness long o̅erspread the World
Till after Ages have at length confest
That hated Sun arisen in the West¹⁶
That Sun whose Course if not prevented soon
(O fatal Thought!) must gain his highest Noon.   50
Look up, my Son, and see it^s Glories shine¹⁷
See <u>Pallas</u>¹⁸ boast the Smiles of <u>Caroline</u>
While George and She Wit^s brightest Patrons reign
Vain all our Efforts! all our Hopes are vain!

38] Empires are *interlined above cancelled* Welfare is
40] my *written over* her
50] O *written over* Oh

help of icons, of invoking the saints to intercede for supplicants. He ridicules the practice in *A Dialogue between the Devil, the Pope, and the Pretender* (1745), pp. 82–3, and mocks it in *Tom Jones* (1749), XIII. ix, p. 722.

¹⁴ Lines 37–46 epitomize *Dunciad*, iii. 65–110, where Elkanah Settle, the goddess's 'Sage' and erstwhile poet laureate, opens to her son Theobald a vision of the progress of Dulness through the ages.

¹⁵ The reference is elusive. Grundy believed HF meant Greece and Rome; but Rome was not an eastern realm. Amory, followed by Baker, proposed 'Poland, Hungary, and Bohemia, where the Counter-reformation triumphed' (unpublished papers); but these countries are not well described as 'Foes' of Dulness and Superstition before the onslaught of the Vandals, Huns, and Ostrogoths from eastern Europe.

¹⁶ Referring to the Protestant Reformation of the sixteenth century, sparked by Martin Luther in Germany and Henry VIII in England.

¹⁷ Here begins a panegyric (51–74) on the virtues of the Royal Family, echoing perhaps HF's odes (now lost) on the occasions of the King's coronation and birthday in 1727 (see *Life*, pp. 56–8). First in order is Queen Caroline (1683–1737), whom HF's uncle Charles served as Gentleman Usher to the Queen's Privy Chamber; followed by King George II (1683–1760); Frederick Louis, Prince of Wales (1707–51); Princess Anne (b. 1709); Princess Amelia (b. 1711); Princess Caroline (b. 1713); and William Augustus, Duke of Cumberland (1726–65). Soon HF's praise would turn to ridicule in *The Grub-Street Opera* (1731), which was suppressed, in part no doubt for its satire of George and Caroline's domestic relations and of Frederick's philandering. Cumberland, however—who later distinguished himself in battle against the French (1743–5) and defeated the Jacobites at Culloden (1746)—would become for HF 'the Glorious Duke . . . that *Fulmen Belli*' (*TP*, No. 26 [22–9 April 1746], p. 275).

¹⁸ Pallas Athene, patron goddess of Athens.

What Muse can cease (a Friend to Arms and Truth)   55
To sing the Martial Glories of his youth[19]
Is there a Muse delighting to rehearse
Piety, Goodness, in eternal Verse

[fo. 183]

And shall she not in Carolinaˢ mind
The fairest, noblest, greatest Subject find   60
What tuneful Muse but Frederick must fire
Or Anneˢ majestick lively Looks inspire
What Muse that Beauties softest Charms can move
Who ever strung her Harp to Tunes of Love
Whose joyful Numbers shall not rise to trace   65
The softest Sweetness of Ameliaˢ Face
Amelia! whom with equal Force to praise
The Power that made her must inspire my Lays
See lovely Carolina next appears
See William far superior to his years   70
See thro each rising Glory of yᵉ Line
Something that Ruin bodes to me and mine
Never shall England more my God head own
While such a Race expect the British Throne
Never to wear my heavy Chains submit   75
Till on itˢ Throne some drowsy Monarch sit
To whom or whose a Monument to raise
Shall be beyond the very God of Lays
Till fixᵈ upon some Brow itˢ Crown shall be
Learnᵈ, witty, pious, noble, great as thee   80
This to command you to Attempt—has been
The Cause which hither sent yʳ [*blank*] Queen
My Gouty Limbs saught[20] to despise the way
—you know my Will—and instantley obey

60] Su *written over* O *in* Object
62] lively *interlined above cancelled* noble
67] Force *interlined above cancelled* Lines
71–4] *These couplets, originally in reverse order, are switched in MS*
82] [*blank*] *space left for word to be added*

---

[19] In 1708 at Oudenarde, Belgium, George had fought bravely in Marlborough's victory against the French.
[20] 'saught': obsolete past participle of *seek* (*OED*).

She s^d and turning shew,^d her wrinckled Neck²¹   85
In scales and Colour like a Roach⁵ Back
Forth from her greezy Locks such Odours flow
As those who,ᵛᵉ smelt dutch-Coffee-houses- know
Above her Knees, her Petticoats were rear^d
And the true Slattern in her Gate appear^d   90

[fo. 183ᵛ]

The Bard then rubbing oft his Iron Scull
Impenetrably hard supremely dull²²
Reflects with Pain, on what his Mother said
Willing—but knows not how—to give her Aid
In dreamy Slumbers pass^d the silent Night   95
While visionary Glories court his Sight
Sometimes the Lawrels on his Temples spring
And Grubstreet Allies ecchoe to their King²³
Proposals for Subscription then arise
(A lovely Vision to Poetick Eyes)   100

85] s^d *written over* said
86] scales *interlined above cancelled* shew
88] houses- *sic.*
94] how *written over illegible letters*
99] ise *in* arise *written over* e *in* are *followed by cancelled* seen

---

²¹ This passage (85–90)—a parody of the *Aeneid* (i. 402–5), Aeneas' meeting with Venus—was later published in HF's *Miscellanies* (1743) i, p. 80, with the final couplet revised as follows: 'To her Mid-Leg her Petticoat was rear'd, | And the true Slattern in her Dress appear'd.' (HF may have considered moving the lines to Canto 2: see n. 66.) The parody also amused Lady Mary, who borrowed HF's opening couplet to conclude her satire of Bolingbroke (*Essays and Poems*, p. 255). Cf. Dryden's rendering of the Latin:

> Thus having said, she turn'd, and made appear
> Her Neck refulgent, and dishevel'd Hair;
> Which flowing from her Shoulders, reach'd the Ground,
> And widely spread Ambrosial Scents around:
> In length of Train descends her sweeping Gown,
> And by her graceful Walk, the Queen of Love is known.

> (*Aeneid*, i. 556–61; *Works of Virgil* [1697], p. 218)

HF's 'commentator' in *The Vernoniad* (1741) cites this passage in the *Aeneid* as authority for a rude interpretation of a line referring to Mammon (Walpole) (*Champion*, p. 568 n. [33] and n. 7).
²² Cf. *Dunciad*, iii. 16–18, where Old Bavius dips 'poetic souls' to 'blunt the sense, and fit it for a scull | Of solid proof, impenetrably dull'.
²³ Grundy notes HF's conflation of Pope's ' "God save King Tibbald!" Grubstreet alleys roar' (*Dunciad*, i. 256) and Dryden's 'Echoes from *Pissing-Ally*, Sh——— call, | And Sh——— they resound from A[ston] Hall' (*MacFlecknoe* [1682], pp. 47–8; *The Works of John Dryden*, ed. H. T. Swedenberg, Jr. (Berkeley, 1972), ii. 55). Unless the misspelling—Grubstreet 'Allies' for 'Alleys'—is a lucky coincidence, this apparent allusion to Pope's connection to *The Grub-Street Journal* places the date of composition (of this line at least) after 8 January 1730, when the first number of the journal was published. For another apparent allusion to *The Grub-Street Journal*, see below (3. 52–3).

Deluded Multitudes to L——————[24] flock
Willing once more to purchase S-sea stock
An Equal share of wisdom both betray
These purchase only Paper so did They.
Last, at one view his ravish^d Eyes behold   105
Whole Rheams of Rhimeing Nonsense—Heaps of Gold
Chang^d are those Times since Pallas could alone
Give Wealth and Glory to her Favour^d Son
While Dulness Bards in Grubstreet^s lofty Rooms
Were forc^d to feed and meditate on Brooms.[25]   110
  Now from his Mrs Bed Apprentice Crop[26]
Had sprung to ope his Absent Master,^{s} Shop
Sots with hot Heads to Rest by Day-light lurk
And Poets rise with cold dull Brains to work
When Codrus[27] in high Raptures first awoke   115

101] L<?>— *only the first letter after* L *written but struck through and illegible*
103] An *added in margin before* Equal; share *interlined above cancelled* their; wisdom *originally plural but the* s *and following words* and their <Lots> *cancelled*
109] Dulness *interlined above cancelled* Grubstreet
112] Had *written over* Arose

---

[24] Bernard Lintot (1675–1736), bookseller, who published Pope's Homer by subscription—the *Iliad* (1715–20) and *Odyssey* (1725–6). By this method Pope made what at the time was a considerable fortune (Maynard Mack, *Alexander Pope* (New York, 1986), pp. 267–8, 416–17). But HF no doubt refers chiefly to Pope's duplicity in concealing from subscribers to the *Odyssey* the fact that he had himself translated only twelve of the twenty-four books, the rest having been farmed out to William Broome and Elijah Fenton. The 'Deluded Multitudes', who had paid dearly for a translation by the great poet, found that half the work was a swindle, its pages—in terms of HF's analogy (lines 101–4)—as worthless as South Sea stock certificates when the Bubble burst in 1720.

[25] Playing on the title of Swift's *Meditation on a Broomstick* (1710), HF alludes to Pope's alleged exploitation of William Broome (1689–1745), to whom he allowed £600 for translating eight books of the *Odyssey* and most of the notes (see above, n. 24). In *Peri Bathous* (1728), Pope ridiculed Broome as a poet by placing him among the Parrots and Tortoises (*The Art of Sinking in Poetry*, ed. Edna Leake Steeves [New York, 1952], pp. 27–8), and in *The Dunciad* Variorum (1729) Pope made him a metaphor for drudgery: 'And Pope's, translating three whole years with Broome' (iii. 328). Quoting that line in reporting Broome's death in *True Patriot*, No. 4 (26 November 1745), HF hinted that Pope was the cause of Broome's having 'less Reputation in [the Learned World] than he deserved' (p. 354).

[26] Cf. Swift's 'Description of the Morning' (1709): 'Now *Betty* from her Masters Bed had flown, | And softly stole to discompose her own' (lines 3–4). Though odd, the name of HF's City apprentice is clear in the MS and cannot be 'Slop', as Grundy tentatively suggests ('New Verse by Henry Fielding', p. 223 n. 111). 'Crop' was a slang term for Presbyterians, who wore short hair (Grose)—as indeed did Pope, whom Charles Gildon described as a 'little *Aesopic* sort of animal in his own cropt Hair' (*Memoirs of Wycherly* [1718], p. 16; Guerinot, p. xxxv).

[27] 'Codrus', the name of Juvenal's poor poet in *Satires* iii. 203–11. For HF in *The Champion* (15 March 1740)—as indeed for Pope in the Preface to *The Dunciad* (see Introduction, p. 30)—he is the type of 'all bad Authors' (p. 236). Since Edmund Curll's satire *Codrus: Or, The Dunciad Dissected* (1728), the name had been attached to Pope. It is HF's name for him in the verse epistle 'To John Hayes, Esq.', published in *Miscellanies* (1743), but probably written much earlier.

Bernardus[28] call[d] and in these Words bespoke
'Resolv[d] this day some matters to debate
'Of great Importance to the Grubstreet state
'We will you, Bernard, in our Royal Name
'A Council of our Nobles to proclaim   120
'Ten be the Time—our Theatre the Place[29]
['] Our Royal Presence shall the Council grace.

[fo. 184]

Bernardus bowing does his Chief obey
And Codrus takes to Rhime[s] far Court his Way
Beneath a Russian Mountain where the Trees   125
Are ever whistling with a rougher Breeze
Where ev,[ry] Bird frequents that knows to sing
With whose sweet Pipes the sounding valleys ring
Where twice three Cataracts impetuous flow
From the high Hill into the Vale below   130
Whose Sound hoarse Echoe from her hollow Seats
With mimick voice eternally repeats.
A Gothick Structure! built in modern Time
Is seen the Palace and the Court of Rhime[30]
Here Codrus came—and at his Father[s] Throne   135
Kneeling thus pray[d] his Votary and Son.
O Rhime eternal if from thee I sprung
(As many Bards assuredly have sung[)]
Let kind Compliance to my wishes prove
My Merit, Birth and thy paternal Love   140

117–21] *Crosshatching in left margin of MS indicates quotation marks*
130] F *in* From *though beginning the line is HF's lower case form* f
137] s *written over* p *cancelled, a false start*

------

[28] Bernardus: Bernard Lintot (see above, l. 101 and n. 24).
[29] Probably John Rich's theatre at Lincoln's Inn Fields (see below, 3. 106–9 and n. 144).
[30] Though probably not by HF but his collaborator James Ralph, who influenced his preference for blank verse; cf. the 'Essay on Truth' in *The Champion* (3 April 1740): 'Away thou Gothick Tyrant! Foe confess'd | To Sense and Harmony! Delusive Rhime | Away!' Gothic is also the style of architecture appropriate to the Palace of Death in *A Journey from This World to the Next* (1743; I. iv): 'Its Outside . . . appeared extremely magnificent. Its Structure was of the Gothic Order: vast beyond Imagination, the whole Pile consisting of black Marble' (*Miscellanies* ii. 21). Later, however, in *Tom Jones* (1749; I. iv), this could also be the order of Paradise Hall, Allworthy's house: 'THE *Gothick* Stile of Building could produce nothing nobler . . . There was an Air of Grandeur in it, that struck you with Awe, and rival'd the Beauties of the best *Grecian* Architecture' (p. 42). Indeed, HF's attitude varied towards the Goths themselves: in *Of True Greatness* (1741) HF, deploring the folly and vulgarity of his own time, called it 'This *Gothick* Leaden Age' (*Miscellanies* i. 26); yet in *Liberty* (1743) the Goths of northern Europe are to be envied: 'Possess'd of thee [Liberty], the *Vandal*, and the *Hun*, | Enjoy their Frost, nor mourn the distant Sun' (*Miscellanies* i. 40).

Still have thy Smiles propitious been to those
Who one for thee one verse for Sense compose[31]
Shall on my Cause less Showers of Goodness fall
Who to thy Self have dedicated all.
To Grubstreet Thou hast ever prov,^d most kind   145
Thy smiles in————works we find
Who once hast been my Bark^s propitious Guide
From Grubstreet born on Thames^s silver Tide
Till tost at last to T————[32] flying Shore.[33]
Be all ye Gods, to Grubstreet Foes no more   150
For Grubstreet^s lofty Towers no more we see
⎱ Great Addison[34] has conquer^d spight of me
O give the banish^d Bards in J————^s Lanes[35]
Once to renew their long forgotten Strains
So will I Festivals and Altars raise   155
So annual Hecatombs of Books shall blaze

————

[fo. 184ᵛ]

Thy fond Assistance, God of Rhime, I knew
When Iliad by thy aid I overthrew[36]
And Gratitude will ever bid me tell

---

[31] For this echo of Butler's *Hudibras* (II. i. 29–30) in the context of HF's disapproval of rhymed verse, see the Introduction (p. 31 and n. 14).

[32] In January 1719 Pope had moved to his 'villa' on the banks of the Thames at Twickenham, Middlesex; that same year Lady Mary settled into her country house nearby (Grundy, pp. 185–7).

[33] 'flying Shore': An allusion to Aeneas' interrupted journey to Italy: 'Italiam sequimur fugientem' ('we chase a fleeing Italy'; trans. H. R. Fairclough [Loeb, 1916], v. 629). Cf. John Phillips, *Maronides: or, Virgil Travesty* (1678), C–H: 'in vain do hunt the flying shore' (v. 2182); and Edward Young, *The Instalment: To the Right Honourable Sir Robert Walpole, Knight of the Most Noble Order of the Garter* (1726): when ambition (the sail) is without the applause of fame (the gail) 'She toils, she pants, nor gains the flying shore' (line 126; *Complete Works*, 2 vols. [1854], C–H).

[34] Joseph Addison (1672–1719), whom HF will later call 'immortal': 'Sense and Religion taught his Skilful Pen | The best of Criticks, and the best of Men' (3. 57–9). In his series of Saturday papers on *Paradise Lost* in *The Spectator* (No. 267 [5 January 1712]–No. 369 [3 May 1712]) and in *Cato* (1713), his tragedy in blank verse, Addison might be said to have 'conquered' the advocates of rhyme. He plays the same part in Lady Mary's satire of Pope (*Essays and Poems*, p. 248).

[35] Perhaps, as Grundy suggests ('New Verse by Henry Fielding', p. 224 n. 153), Old Jewry (or Jury) is meant—a street running north from the east end of Cheapside—near which could be found Honey Lane, St Lawrence Lane, Ironmonger Lane, Pancras Lane (see Rocque [13Aa]).

[36] HF's later opinion of Pope's translation of the *Iliad* (1715–20) was very different. In *The Champion* (12 June 1740) he praised Pope's 'divine Translation of the *Iliad*,' which he had 'with *no Disadvantage to the Translator* COMPARED with the Original' (p. 371); in the *Journey from This World to the Next* (I. viii) he has Homer himself repeat the compliment (*Miscellanies* [1743], ii. 37). In *Amelia* (VIII. v), however, Booth cannot agree with an author's opinion that Pope's Homer is 'the best Translation in the World': 'Indeed, Sir . . . tho' it is certainly a noble Paraphrase, and of itself a fine Poem, yet, in some Places, it is no Translation at all' (p. 326).

How by thy Rhimes alone Odyssee fell³⁷   160
Why should I mention all their labour^d Strains
In W——— Forest or in Duncia^s Plains³⁸
Each Rhime like Hydra³⁹ murder^d oft nēere fails
Each Rhime can match her hundred Heads in Tails
Their sweet Theocritus⁴⁰ the Greecians boast   165
While Ovid^s Numbers please the Latins most
Let English Criticks Milton^s Strength commend⁴¹
But mayst thou ever be thy Codrus Friend
Still to my Muse thy Influence impart
For Sense and Wit are needless where thou art   170
By thee almost ye Realm of Wit^s undone
Oh aid the greatest Efforts of thy Son
Attend propitious to my strongest Hate
And teach me how to undermine the State
To him the God o best belov^d of mine   175
I read thy Mother strong in ev^{ry} Line
In Dryden^s and in Denham I appear⁴²

177] Denham *originally possessive form in MS but* ^{'s} *works are cancelled*; Dryden^{'s} *possessive remains uncorrected*

---

³⁷ Pope's *Odyssey* (1725–6). For Booth's judgement of Pope's Homer in *Amelia*, see above, n. 36. In *Tom Jones* (IV. xiii), after referring to the characterization of Penelope in the *Odyssey*, HF comments: 'The *English* Reader will not find this in the Poem: For the Sentiment is entirely left out in the Translation' (p. 202). (See also below, 2. 19–22.)

³⁸ The examples are inept. *Windsor Forest* (1713) is among the poems of Pope HF admires in the 'Epistle to Lyttleton' (1733), lines 59–60 (see below, p. 93). And in the *Journal of a Voyage to Lisbon* (1755) it is—together with Denham's *Cooper's Hill* (1642)—HF's standard for the poem of topographical description (see also below, 2. 15–16). No 'Plains', moreover, are celebrated in *The Dunciad*, which is set in London.

³⁹ One of the twelve labours of Heracles, the Hydra was a poisonous watersnake with many heads; when one was cut off another grew in its place.

⁴⁰ Theocritus (*fl. c.* 270 BC), poet of Idylls. Curiously, HF refers to him just twice in his writings, both times as a standard for measuring Pope's qualities as a poet. In the Preface to *Plutus* (1742) referring to the *Essay on Man* (1733–4), he credits its author with having 'taught me a System of Philosophy in *English* Numbers, whose Sweetness is scarce inferior to that of *Theocritus* himself' (see below, p. 256).

⁴¹ John Milton (1608–74), author of *Paradise Lost* (1667), which HF variously called 'the best Poem which perhaps [the World] hath ever seen' (*TP*, No. 1 [5 November 1745], p. 106); 'the noblest Effort perhaps of human Genius' (*Jacobite's Journal*, No. 8 [23 January 1748], p. 138); 'the finest Poem in our Language' (*Covent-Garden Journal*, No. 50 [7 March 1752], p. 274). With James Ralph and Lady Mary, and the pamphleteers who attacked Pope's translations of Homer, HF preferred Milton's 'Strength'—a quality Addison attributed to his command of blank verse, the more natural form (see above, n. 30)—and charges Pope with sacrificing 'Sense and Wit' (l. 170) in his obedience to the God of 'Rhime'. (See the discussion above, pp. 30–1.)

⁴² John Dryden (1631–1700), whom, in a metaphorical history of the progress of wit in England, HF crowns as 'King' of the period of the Restoration (*Covent-Garden Journal*, No. 23 [21 March 1752], p. 153). Sir John Denham (1615–69), whose *Works* (3rd edn., 1719) were in HF's library (Ribbles D12). The reference here is one of only two in HF's writings, the other being to Denham's *Cooper's Hill* (see above, n. 38).

But Sense bears off the greater Trophies there
Oh! that great Caleb[43] would my power Confess
His Nonsense and his Lies in Metre dress   180
W———[44] himself might then be taught to fear
And England view her fancied dangers near
Charm^d with sweet Sounds the world might give the Praise
(Which they deny his Politicks)—t,his Lays
Poetick License might a plea supply   185
We like (tho not believ^d) the Poet,s Lie
The Poet^s Praise by his Invention gains
Ill suits y^t word ye Politician^s Pains

                                                            [fo. 185]

But thou, my Son, by better stars decreed
In softest-sounding Nonsense to succeed   190
Enjoy thy Wish of my Assistance sure
Write boldly on, and Gold and Praise procure
    He spoke, and shook ye Palace with his Nod
The vocal Palace eccchoes to ye God.[45]

                                                            [fo. 172]

CANTO 2^d

Thrice did the palefac^d Moon her Horns renew
And thrice three thousand in the City grew[46]
Eere Dulness (such slow Voyages she makes)
Gain^d the lov^d Borders of her Grubstreet Lakes.

194] eccchoes *sic. This is the last of only six lines on MS leaf 185; the rest of the leaf is blank*
Canto 2^d] *Begins a fresh MS page (leaf 172), labelled at upper left* H. F.

---

[43] Nicholas Amhurst (1697–1742), political writer. Under the name Caleb D'Anvers from December 1726 to his death he edited the *The Craftsman*, a journal sponsored by Bolingbroke (see below, n. 56) and William Pulteney, the leaders of the Opposition to Walpole and his ministry (see below, n. 44). Though HF had adopted Lady Mary's pro-ministerial political attitudes during the period in which he composed the Cantos, there are, in the opinion of the present editor, reasons for attributing to him two anti-Walpole satires published in *The Craftsman*—one a ballad called 'The Norfolk Lanthorn' (20 July 1728), the other an essay comparing fox-hunters and politicians (10 October 1730); indeed, this editor has argued that later, from 1734 to 1739, HF would become a regular contributor to Amhurst's journal. (See above, Introduction, p. 29 and n. 6, and *New Essays*.)

[44] Sir Robert Walpole (1676–1745), Prime Minister from 1724 to 1742. He was Lady Mary's close friend.

[45] Cf. *Iliad*, i. 528–30, rendered by Pope: 'He spoke . . . and gives the Nod; | The Stamp of Fate, and Sanction of the God: | High Heav'n with trembling the dread Signal took, | And all *Olympus* to the Centre shook' (i. 683–7).

[46] Grundy, 'New Verse by Henry Fielding' (p. 225 nn. 1–2) notes an echo of *The Wits Paraphras'd* (1680), a burlesque version of Ovid's *Epistles*: 'Thrice did the Moon her horns renew' (p. 17); in that time, according to the following line, 4,500 cuckolds were made in the City.

In Grubstreet^s inmost Lane whose narrow Bound 5
Neere knew ye rattling Hackney Coach^s Sound
A Lofty Garret rears it^s shelvy Crest
And with superiour Height oerlooks ye rest
So some tall Oak oer all the Forest Shews
So some tall Beau o̅e̅rlooks the shorter Beaus 10
Six times the Staircase counts the rising Floor
~~The Seventh Story~~ shews th,approaching Door.
With J————⁴⁷ Paintings all the Walls were hung
Here Macheath rav^d and P~~oll~~y Peachum Sung⁴⁸
Here the bright sun o̅e̅r Windsor Forest shines 15
Green looks the Meadow as in Codrus Lines⁴⁹
There Eloise to Abelard complains
With Looks as moving as her former strains⁵⁰
There Homer Sings—a Likeness sure as strong
Lives in the Colours as in Codrus Song. 20
Ah! Codrus hadst thou never told the Town
Thy Song was Homer,^s t,had been thought thy own

[fo. 172^v]

Far in a Corner twice two Shelves are spread
With Books; such Books as pretty Fellows read
No Latin sham,^d the courtly Shelf, no Greek⁵¹ 25
Obsolete Tongues! Which Pedants only speak

5] Bound *plural* s *cancelled*   6] Sound *Plural* s *cancelled*   7] Crest *altered from* Chrest
8] Height *interlined above cancelled letters (illegible)*
9] Oak oer all ~~his Brethren~~ the Forest *interlined above cancelled* Beau his lofty Forehead
11] Six times *followed by cancelled* you tell
12] ~~The Seventh Story~~ *words struck through but not cancelled*
13] ~~Eere the Tir^d Visitant can reach the Door~~ *line struck through and cancelled*
14] oll *in* Polly *struck through*
15] H *written over* T *in* There; the bright sun oer *interlined above* Windsor
20] Lives *written over* T; Colours as *interlined above cancelled* Paint, as lives
24] Books; *altered from* Books!   26] Obsolete Tongues! *interlined above* Which

⁴⁷ Charles Jervas (*c.*1675–1739), from 1723 Principal Portrait Painter to the King. He was Pope's friend and teacher in the art of painting, and the subject of Pope's verse epistle (1716).
⁴⁸ The hero and heroine of Gay's *Beggar's Opera*, which opened at Lincoln's Inn Fields on 29 January 1728 and ran to great applause for sixty-two nights, its unprecedented popularity contributing to the close of HF's *Love in Several Masques* after only four performances.
⁴⁹ Cf. *Windsor Forest*, where Pope wishes that his verse might make the Forest, like Milton's 'Groves of Eden . . . look green in Song' (lines 7–8).
⁵⁰ Pope's *Eloisa to Abelard* (1717). Lady Mary would have known, since Pope led her to believe as much in a letter accompanying the poem he sent her to Turkey, that, at the conclusion, the imagined 'Bard' who shares Eloisa's grief at the loss of her lover is himself (see the introduction to the poem, Twickenham edn., ii. 311–13).
⁵¹ Pope's alleged ignorance of Greek was among the faults the pamphleteers, Lady Mary among them, found in him (Guerinot, pp. 13–14, 100–1, 225–6).

The French Romance, and English Poem there
With his own works the dusty Region share
Prodigious Heaps[52] of Rhime—then which no Dose
Of Opiates Sooner would each Sense compose.   30
The Youth just clasp^d in the lov^d Virgin^s arms
Or Wretch just sentenc^d—would confess their Charms
Hadst thou o Codrus liv^d in Argos Time
Hermes had us^d no Method but thy Rhime[53]
Three words woud thirty thousand Eyes command   35
He must have slumber^d at the Fights of Stand[54]
Such was their Force, the Bard himself in vain
Strove his small Stock of Senses to maintain
For as he now some favour^d Piece reviews
Which Lintot^s Shop[55] shall publish in the News   40
Fast was he caught, in his own leaden Gin
When Dulness as L B————————[56] came in

30] Sooner *written over illegible word;* each Sense compose *interlined above cancelled* to Sleep dispose

35] Three words woud [*sic*] thirty thousand Eyes command *interlined above cancelled* <Een> half a Line would all his Eyes command

39] now *followed by cancelled* review'^{d}

41] Fast *followed by cancelled* he; he *interlined before* caught; leaden *interlined above cancelled* Toiled (*See OED* toil v.^{2} *citing Dorset dialect in Hardy.*)

---

[52] Cf. Richard Blackmore's epic *Eliza* (1705), C–H, celebrating the British victory: 'Prodigious Heaps of slaughter'd *Spaniards* slain | Lay welt'ring in their Blood o'er all the Plain' (x. 495–6).

[53] Argos, a watchman with eyes all over his body, was lulled to sleep by Hermes playing on a pipe of reeds (Ovid, *Metamorphoses*, i. 625 ff.). Opening the sleeping contest in *The Dunciad*, Dulness promises the prize to whoever can listen to Henley's prose or Blackmore's verse and stay awake: 'Sleep's all-subduing charm who dares defy, | And boasts Ulyssey's ear with Argus' eye' (ii. 341–2).

[54] Borrowing the 'Three words . . . Fights of Stand' from Chapman's *Iliad* (1611; xiii. 290), Pope, though in a different context, refers to the 'Locrian' troops of Ajax: 'His brave Associates had no following Band, | His Troops unpractis'd in the Fights of Stand' (*Iliad*, xiii. 889–90). In *One Epistle to Mr. A. Pope*, Leonard Welsted ironically advised Pope that, since *The Dunciad* had brought him notoriety, he should turn from writing such pieces as *The Rape of the Lock* (1712–14) and his Homer to concentrate on lampoons: 'Forget awhile *Belinda* and the Sun; | Forget the *Fights of Stand*, and Flights of Run' (p. 18). (See above, p. 33.)

[55] For Lintot, see above, n. 24.

[56] Henry St John (1678–1751), first Viscount Bolingbroke. HF here parodies *Iliad* (ii. 56 ff.), where Nestor, as emissary of Zeus, visits Agamemnon in a dream to rouse him to battle; see also below, lines 92–5 and n. 67. Bolingbroke was Pope's close friend and a member of the Scriblerus circle. He had been Secretary of State in the Tory government during the last years of Queen Anne. Known for his Jacobite sympathies, he fled to France at the rebellion of 1715. On returning from exile in 1725, he, together with William Pulteney, founded *The Craftsman*, the principal journal of the opposition to Walpole under the editorship of Nicholas Amhurst (see above, n. 43). In the Cantos HF reflects Lady Mary's contempt for Bolingbroke, whom she ridicules in an unfinished satire of this same period (*Essays and Poems*, pp. 251–5). As it happened, however, Bolingbroke's political views would later colour HF's own contributions to *The Craftsman* (1734–9) and *The Champion* (1739–40). For his attack on Bolingbroke's religious scepticism, see below, pp. 661–80.

Thus in a Dream the Poet she addrest.
—Canst Thou o Son of Dulness canst thou rest⁵⁷

No Chains of Slumbers should thy Eye-Lids keep   45
Let it be still thy Readers Lot to sleep⁵⁸
But, ah! the open Page, discovers all
Fool that thou art by thy own Hand to fall
Which of my Doctors would with Safety kill
Should he not only write but taste his Bill   50
Yet can there even in thy Numbers be
A Power that may continue Sleep to thee
When Theatres resound with Cato's Praise
And ev^ry Voice gives Addison the Bays⁵⁹
Yet let this rouse—not terrifie thy Soul   55
For See what's writ in Fate,'s unerring Scroll
Behold—for from thy Eyes those Clowds I^ll take
Which wretched Mortals blind to Vision make.
Then Images shall of thy Fate appear
Forms which shall charm thy Eye, and, Sounds to charm thy Ear   60

Here are to be introduc^d some Lines from the other Cop<y>⁶⁰

43] Thus *written over* And
44] D̶u̶l̶n̶e̶s̶s̶ *cancelled before* Son
[45]] T̶h̶y̶ ̶w̶a̶k̶e̶f̶u̶l̶ ̶E̶y̶e̶s̶ ̶s̶h̶o̶u̶l̶d̶ ̶n̶e̶v̶e̶r̶ *line begun and cancelled*
45] Chains *written over illegible word*
47] all *written over illegible letters*
48] Fool that thou art by thy own Hand to fall *interlined above cancelled* Tis thy own. A second Look my Eyes too would enthrall
50] write *interlined above space after* only
53] with *written over* to
55] thy *written over scrawl*
56] See *written over* <lo>; writ *written over* <First>
59] Images *interlined above cancelled* any Forms; of thy Fate *interlined above cancelled* to thy Sight
60] to charm *interlined after* Sounds
[61]] *HF's direction to himself; not underlined in MS*

⁵⁷ With Dulness, disguised as Bolingbroke in a dream, chiding Codrus for sleeping when there is mischief to be done, cf. *Iliad* (ii. 20–4). HF echoes Pope's version: 'Canst thou, with all a Monarch's Care opprest, | Oh *Atreus*' Son! Canst thou indulge thy Rest?' (ii. 25–6). Grundy, 'New Verse by Henry Fielding', p. 227 nn. 42, 44.

⁵⁸ Cf. *Dunciad*, i. 91–2: 'While pensive Poets painful vigils keep | Sleepless themselves to give their readers sleep'. In *Tom Jones* (v. i, p. 215) HF quotes the second line while referring to the soporific works of such authors as Oldmixon (see above, n. 3).

⁵⁹ For HF's opinion of Addison, see above, n. 34, with reference to 3. 57–9. In the theatrical season of 1729–30 Addison's *Cato* (1713) was performed four times at Drury Lane—7, 27 October, 27 December (a command performance attended by the Prince of Wales and Princess Caroline), and 6 May, the latter perhaps prompted by the revival at Lincoln's Inn Fields on 20 April, which was repeated on 21 May. (See *London Stage*, pts. 2–3.)

⁶⁰ HF's own instruction in the MS; no 'other' copy survives (italics added).

But see (cry,^d Dulness) see that Shatter^d Dame⁶¹
(Sure none ēere took so low a Road to Fame)
A Bundle see beneath her Arm she brings
New Ballads that to former Tunes she sings
You too might hear the Soft enchanting sound   65
Were not it^s murmurs in applauses drown,^d

[fo. 173^r]

This, this is she of whom such things are told⁶²
Promis^d by Fate in earliest days of old.
She Newgate to St James^s shall compare,
And charm with Ribaldry, the great, the Fair.   70
While Beau, and Footman by the same applause,
Too true confess the Parallel She draws
Her Venus—(so in Heathen Bards tis Seen)
Shall patronize against Olympus Queen.⁶³
Till drivn to Cyprus down from Heavn,^s high Dome   75
Fog⁶⁴ the good-natur^d Goddess welcomes home.
And dost thou sleep—sleep at such sounds as these
Awake, my son, shake off all Thoughts of Ease

63] A *written over* That; *see* interlined above cancelled *which*
64] New *written over illegible word*
66] it *cancelled after* Were; it^s *written over* in; murmurs in *interlined above cancelled* such lowd
71] eau *in* Beau *written over* ow
73] in *written over* the; Heathen *originally followed by cancelled* Tales we read *which was then replaced by*
Prophets say; Bards tis <sd?> *interlined above cancelled* Prophets say; seen *written over* <sd>
75] n *in* drivn *written over* en *in* driven

---

⁶¹ Polly Peachum, heroine of Gay's *Beggar's Opera* (see above, n. 48). The passage that follows (lines 61–76) recounts—anachronistically, as in a dream—images depicting the resounding popular success of the play when it opened in January 1728, but does so within the context of the government's subsequent suppression of its sequel *Polly* in December. Hence Polly is here 'that shatter'd Dame' and, with her patroness the Duchess of Queensberry, deserving of the support of the anti-ministerial organ *Fog's Weekly Journal* (see below, nn. 63–4). For later references to *Polly* expressing HF's approval of the government's decision to suppress it, see below, 3. 86–9, 146–61.
⁶² Cf. *Dunciad*, iii. 317, as Settle presents a vision of George II, in whose reign the arts submit to Dulness: 'This, this is He, foretold by ancient rhymes, | Th' Augustus born to bring Saturnian times.'
⁶³ As when Venus incurred the wrath of Juno by enabling Aeneas to reach Italy, Gay's patroness, the beautiful Duchess of Queensberry (Catherine Douglas, *née* Hyde [1701–77]), was banished from the court on 27 February 1729 for soliciting subscriptions for printing *Polly* in defiance of the King and her mistress Queen Caroline.
⁶⁴ *Fog's Weekly Journal*, an anti-ministerial paper edited by Charles Molloy (d. 1767), succeeded *Mist's Weekly Journal* after the latter was suppressed by the government in September 1728 and its editor, Nathaniel Mist, had fled the country. Though the anti-ministerial press did not lose the opportunity to comment on the suppression of *Polly* (see Goldgar, pp. 80–4), Molloy in *Fog's* (26 April 1729) might well be thought to have taken the Duchess's part against the Queen by ironically wringing seditious implications from perfectly innocuous passages in the play.

Instant a writing Company erect[65]
And damn all Bards but those whom you elect   80
To proper Members I^{ll} direct your choice
Some fam^d like thee for Nonsense and for Noise
She s^d ε turning &c^a.[66]

   Now in the empty Church the Priest begins
T,avert the absent Congregation,^s sins   85
Now Coffee-houses throng^d with Statesmen see
All Ladies (but St James^s) at their Tea
When met the Chiefs in Council—Codrus rear^d
On his own works above the rest appear^d.[67]
Bernardus silenc^d all the buzzing Gang   90
Codrus stood up, and thus began th,Harangue.
                                                    _____
                                                    [fo. 174]

Last Night as slumbring o͞er my Works I lay
My Mother in L—— B——————[68] Array
Before my Eyes appear^d—oh! to unfold

81] ir *in* direct *written over* er   82] Some *written over* <Those>; like *written over* for
83] ε *Greek epsilon signifying 'and'; HF in later instances merely writes an 'e' with a long tail*
84] empty *interlined above cancelled* absent
94] oh! to unfold *interlined above cancelled and much she told*

  [65] It was a frequent charge of the pamphleteers that Pope meant to become a literary dictator at the head of a circle of like-minded Tory wits—namely, the Scriblerus group of Swift, Gay, and Arbuthnot, together with the journalists Nicholas Amhurst of *The Craftsman*, Charles Molloy of *Fog's Weekly Journal*, and by 1730 the authors of *The Grub-Street Journal*, Richard Russel and John Martyn. Cf. the anonymous author of *Characters of the Times* (29 August 1728), who placed Pope at the head of 'a little Juncto of Authors, who have set themselves up to be Dictators to the World in what ever relates to *Polite Letters*' (pp. iii–iv). 'What they would be at, and wish in their Hearts . . . is to get it enacted by publick Authority, that no Man shall presume under the severest Penalties to write better than themselves: And that nothing good or bad, shall be publish'd without their Licence' (pp. 11–12, quoted in Guerinot, pp. 151–2; see also Guerinot, pp. 184–5, 193–4).
  [66] HF may have thought here of transposing l. 85–90.
  [67] Cf. the opening of *Paradise Lost*, book II:

> HIGH on a Throne of Royal State, which far
> Outshone the wealth of *Ormus* and of *Ind*,
> Or where the gorgeous East with richest hand
> Show'rs on her Kings *Barbaric* Pearl and Gold,
> Satan exalted sat, by merit rais'd
> To that bad eminence . . .   (ii. 1–6)

Pope ridiculing Theobald (*Dunciad*, ii. 1–5) and Dryden, Flecknoe (*MacFlecknoe*, lines 106–7) provided precedents for HF's burlesque of Codrus, but the echo of Dryden is more exact: 'The hoary Prince in Majesty appear'd | High on a Throne of his own Labours rear'd.'
  [68] L[ord] B[olingbroke's]. HF resumes his parody of Agamemnon's dream of Nestor (see above, n. 56), as in Pope's translation: 'Late as I slumber'd in the Shades of Night, | A Dream Divine appear'd before my Sight; | Whose Visionary Form like *Nestor* came, | The same in Habit, and in Mien the same' (ii. 71–4).

The Glories which of Grubstreet she foretold.   95
Had I a thousand Tongues of sounding Brass[69]
As that of H———[s70] or of C———[s71] Face
Vain would be the Effort—by her commands
I summon[d] hither all the Grubstreet Bands
She bids us in a Company unite[72]   100
And suffer none besides our selves to write—
—Ah! with what Anguish, what a Secret shame
I recollect your base Neglect of Fame.
Of Fame [—] nay more of Meat—can Grubstreet chuse
Rather to starve then to exert the Muse.   105
The Want of Learning is a mean Excuse
All Men may write—for writing comes by Use.
Had Wit or Learning necessary been
What Comedies! since Congreve[s73] had we seen
What Poems! (Poems with applauses read)   110
Had Lintot sold, since Prior[s74] Muse was dead

98] vain *written after cancelled* In; the Effort *interlined above* be   99] *First* h *in* hither *written over to*
101] And *written over* Nor   105] R *in* Rather *though beginning the line is HF's lower case form* r
109] What Comedies! *interlined above cancelled* Few Plays,

---

[69] HF was fond of this Homeric formula (*Iliad*, ii. 489), where the poet could not describe a scene though he had ten tongues and ten mouths and a heart of bronze. In Pope's translation these become 'a thousand Tongues, | A Throat of Brass' (ii. 580–1). Cf. *Joseph Andrews* (II. xiii, p. 160 and n. 1) and *Jonathan Wild* (IV. x, p. 169 and n. 3 citing *Aeneid*, vi. 625–7).

[70] Probably John 'Orator' Henley (1692–1756), journalist and preacher. An eccentric priest and 'Zany', as Pope called him in *The Dunciad* (iii. 202), he left the Church in 1726 and in 1729 set up an 'Oratory' in Lincoln's Inn Fields, where he charged a shilling for declaiming in an absurd manner on a variety of topics. In 1730 he began editing *The Hyp-Doctor* in support of Walpole's ministry. In March of that year HF introduced him into Act III of *The Author's Farce* as the 'puppet' Dr Orator. In *The Champion* (29 January 1740, p. 148 and n. 5) he exemplifies the art of impudence. See also, among other allusions to him in HF's works, *Joseph Andrews* (III. vi, pp. 235–6).

[71] Colley Cibber (1671–1757), comedian, playwright, manager (until 1733) of the Theatre Royal at Drury Lane, and from November 1730 Poet Laureate. Cibber had given HF his start as a dramatist by staging *Love in Several Masques* in 1728 and acting the part of Rattle, for which HF praised him in the preface to the published version. He rejected HF's next piece, however, and, like Henley (above, n. 70), would be satirized in *The Author's Farce* (March 1730), where he appears as the vain and arrogant Marplay. From this time on, except for the period of HF's brief tenure as house playwright at Drury Lane (1732–3), Cibber would remain a target of HF's ridicule (see *Companion*, pp. 43–4).

[72] See above, n. 65.

[73] William Congreve (1670–1729), who died 19 January 1729, was arguably HF's favourite comic dramatist after Shakespeare and Ben Jonson. In the Preface to *Love in Several Masques* (1728), his first play, HF cites Congreve and Wycherley as the proven authors in the genre he hoped to succeed in; and later in *The Covent-Garden Journal*, No. 18 (3 March 1752), he serves as the standard of 'Wit' (p. 124).

[74] Matthew Prior (1664–1721), as Miller found in editing the *Miscellanies* (i, p. xxviii), was HF's own chief English master in love poetry; and in *The Covent-Garden Journal*, No. 18 (3 March 1752), Prior takes his place in a short list of 'the most celebrated Authors' including Addison, Dryden, and (in a no longer biased context) Pope and Swift (p. 127). Of Pope's poetry of any consequence Lintot, who was also Prior's publisher, had published since Prior's death the translation of the *Odyssey* (1725–6) and *The Dunciad* (1728–9).

What Mathematicks mighty Newton gone[75]
Or Criticism outliv^d Addison[76]
Surely, no Age would fewer Volumes score
And—Heav,n be prais^d—no Age can number more   115

[fo. 174^v]

So strangely does the scribbling Itch[77] succeed
Ten thousand Write—when scarce one hundred read
Then, Caleb. Can you who our Labours own,
Our Silence and our Indolence bemoan?
Let F————n^s[78] Riches to our Glory tell   120
What Floods of Ink have from our Goose-quill fell
Whatever Feuds in jarring Factions rage,
All, all arose from our exclaiming Page.
Squires thoughtless of their Hounds and Drink I,^{ve} made
Priests of the Gospel—Shop-keepers of Trade.   125
Not Orpheus (tho more tuneful was his song)
Could draw more stupid senseless things along[79]
For what each Saturday my Papers speak
The Realm my Eccho murmurs all the Week.
And can the Man who all this Service knows   130
Deny what Dulness to our Labour owes
To him then Ilar[80]—Thy Successes may
Sedition^s Goddess with Applauses pay
But what to thee from Dulness can be due.
For tho thy Stile be often dull tis true   135
Thy great Invention proves thee of another Crew.

117] Write *written over* read
118] Caleb. *interlined above cancelled* Codrus *written over original* Caleb; C *in* Can *written over lower case* c
124] I,^{ve} *written over illegible letters*
134] to thee from *interlined above cancelled* has
[134–6] *lines marked as triplet in margin*

---

[75] Sir Isaac Newton (1642–1727).
[76] On Addison, see above, nn. 34 and 59.
[77] Cf. *Covent-Garden Journal*, No. 40 (19 May 1752), alluding to Juvenal, *Satires*, vii. 52: 'that Disease commonly called scribendi Cacoethes, or in English the Itch of Writing'.
[78] Richard Francklin (d. 1765), printer of *The Craftsman*.
[79] When he played the lyre and sang, Orpheus by the power of his music drew everything, animate and inanimate, after him. Grundy cites an epigram from Lady Mary's Commonplace Book: 'Sure P[ope] like Orph[eus] was alike inspir'd | The Blocks, and Beasts flock'd round them and admir'd' ('New Verse by Henry Fielding', p. 230 nn. 127–8).
[80] 'Ilar': from the Greek *hilaros*, 'gay'—here John Gay (1685–1732), Pope's fellow Scriblerian, author of *The Beggar's Opera* (1728) and its sequel, *Polly* (1729).

On me the Goddess should her Bays bestow
My Thoughts, my Stile, my Subject all were low
Plain, open, Scandal spoke my New——[81] Muse.
My Satyr did not railly but abuse   140
Dull, senseless Libels level[d] at the Great
My Thoughts, and Language both from B——————[82]

[fo. 175]

Hence what advancement to my Goddess Cause!
A Nation all submitting to her Laws
What Facts for Dulness Service canst thou tell   145
Wit certainly might <stand> tho W——— fell[83]
Then Caleb—Ignorance as brightly shines
In that last Word, as all thy senseless Lines.
Were Popery once Master of the Ball
How soon must Learning, Wit, e Knowledge fall   150
Wit (like a Summer Flower) can only thrive
By Liberty,[s] warm Beams preserv[d] alive[84]
And should the star of Popery arise
The star of Liberty must quit The Skies
But ah! it labours to ascend in Vain   155
By G——[85] depress[d] beneath an Iron Chain.
So Satan—as the Sacred Stories tell

  139] S *in* Scandal *written over* B
  140] did *written over* does
  141] senseless *interlined above cancelled* common-place *which had replaced cancelled* heavy
  145] what *after cancelled* But; Facts *interlined above space before* for; S *in* Service *written over lower case* s
  146] certainly *interlined above cancelled word (illegible)*; <stand> *written over illegible word and after cancelled* flourish
  148] ll *in* all *written over cancelled* ny *in* any; thy *after cancelled* of; senseless *interlined above space between* thy *and* Lines
  151] Wit *before parenthesis emended from* Wit[s] *written over* for

---

  [81] Newgate prison, London, where *The Beggar's Opera* is set.
  [82] Billingsgate, one of the gates of the City of London and the site of the fish market—famous for the foul, abusive language of the porters and fishmongers. For HF's facetious derivation of the name from *bi-lingua*, see *Tom Jones* (XI. viii, p. 603).
  [83] Walpole (see above, n. 44).
  [84] Oddly in the present context, HF allows Caleb (Nicholas Amhurst, editor of *The Craftsman*) to express what was usually his own agreement with Shaftesbury's argument in *Characteristicks* (1711) for allowing 'the Freedom of Wit and Humour'—qualities which, when restrained under the censorship laws of a Catholic nation such as Italy, give way to mere buffoonery and burlesque. See, for example, the Preface to *Joseph Andrews* (p. 5 and n. 1).
  [85] The reference is ambiguous: in his unpublished notes, Baker preferred 'George', the King, to 'God', Grundy's choice. The couplet that follows—'So Satan—as the Sacred Stories tell | Howl[d] vainly, by th,almighty chain[d] in Hell'—might seem to support Grundy's reading; but, though 'Popery' has not succeeded in becoming 'Master of the Ball', HF cannot be claiming that the deity has suppressed Roman Catholicism globally.

Howl^d vainly, by th,almighty chain^d in Hell
Then knows not Ilar to what mightier End
All My seditious Lieing Writings tend   160
Look through the long Record of Ages past[86]
The M—— first falls the K——[87] at last
The Counsellors from M——y[88] to drive
Is an old Game by Me still kept alive
See Edw—d^{89} forc^d his Friends to put away   165
Gain^d a Reprieve but for a later Day
And Chas So one of his best Friends has shewn
In signing Str–ff—d^s Ruin sign^d his own.[90]

[fo. 175^r]

A Mob—like Fire once kindled may be blown
By Winds about till it destroys a Town[91]   170
May all the Powers! to send that day conspire
While we enjoy the Plunder of the Fire—
Let foolish Patriots for their Country Sweat.[92]
At the Expence of Life or Fortune, great

158] v *in* vainly *written over* h; by *written over* pres
160] All *added in margin before* My; seditious *interlined above space between* My *and* Lieing; ing *in* Lieing *written over* s *in* Lies
162] K—— *dash formed by line extended through illegible letters*
171] Powers *written over* Gods
172] e *in* While *written over* <st> *in* Whilst
173] Sweat *written over* <Toil>

[86] Cf. Prior, 'Carmen Seculare, For the Year 1700': 'THY elder Look Great JANUS, cast | Into the long Records of Ages past' (lines 1–2; *Literary Works*, ed. H. Bunker Wright and Monroe K. Spears [Oxford, 1959], i. 161). Other lines from Prior's poem serve as epigraph to *Champion* (15 July 1740, p. 400).
[87] M[inister] . . . K[ing].
[88] M[ajest]y.
[89] Edward II (1284–1327), King of England (1307–27). Forced by his political enemies to sacrifice his favourite, Gaveston, Edward was later deposed and murdered.
[90] In his *History of the Rebellion and Civil Wars in England* (1702–4), the Royalist historian Edward Hyde, first Earl of Clarendon (1609–74), who was friend and Privy Counsellor to both Charles I and Charles II, recounts the King's reluctant acquiescence in the execution of Thomas Wentworth, Earl of Strafford (1593–1641), which in due course contributed to his own downfall (1649). HF, who favoured the Whig historian Gilbert Burnet, regarded Clarendon and Echard (see above, n. 5) as the principal Tory historians (*Joseph Andrews*, III. i, p. 185).
[91] Perhaps an allusion to the great London fire of 1666, popularly believed to have been deliberately set by Catholics. In the *Epistle to Bathurst* (1732), Pope scornfully alludes to the monument commemorating the fire which was inscribed with this accusation: 'Where London's column, pointing at the skies | Like a tall bully, lifts the head, and lyes' (lines 339–40).
[92] Cf. Signior Opera's song in *The Author's Farce* (1730): 'Let . . . The Patriot sweat | To be thought Great' (Air viii). Grundy notes that the word 'patriot' had not yet come to denote a supporter of the Opposition.

Axes and Gibbets are the Gains of Merit   175
From publick Gratitude to publick Spirit.
The Man whom publick statues should reward
Against the Gibbet carefully should guard
For Scandal by the disaffected Mouth
Is Sown and Scatter^d like the Gree[cian]^{s93} Tooth   180
Wherever thrown it finds a friendly soil
And not one grain deludes the Sower^s Toil
These to sow thick be all our Care and Pain.
W———⁹⁴ thy Services shall all be vain
Thy Place will be our certain Prize—for that,   185
You know, my Friends, I^m chiefly aiming at
My Interest commands at that to try
None warmer in his Interest then I
    —Then Codrus, hasty from his Cushion sprung
Then flow^d the Opiates from his tuneful Tongue.   190
None here none any where a Bosom knows
Which warmer with the Love of riches Glows
Here, here, a Soul—that holding Fame at nought
Well thinks that Place with Reputation bought

                                                        [fo. 176]
Let Wits be caught with Baits of empty Praise   195
Give me the Gold—ye Gods!—and them the Bays
Shall Caleb then be thus allow^d to Boast
Let Dulness judge whose Pen has done the most
Has he at W———⁹⁵ struck—have not my Darts
Been boldly thrown at much superior Hearts⁹⁶   200
And has he Aim^d at one Religion,^s Fall
I by my Writings will extirpate all
He s^d Ochistes⁹⁷ then—o mighty Bards

175–6 *space between lines owing to ink blot*
182] one *interlined above space between* not *and* grain
186] Y *in* You *written over* F

[93] Cadmus, founder of Thebes, sowed the teeth of a dragon he had slain and from the teeth warriors sprang up. The story is also told of Jason.
[94] Walpole.
[95] Walpole.
[96] Grundy ('New Verse by Henry Fielding', p. 232 nn. 200–1) notes the similar metaphor in HF's 'Epistle to Lyttleton' (1733; see below, p. 97, lines 144–5) referring to Pope's alleged insult to the Duke of Chandos in the *Epistle to Burlington* (1731); but that charge came later.
[97] 'Ochistes': from the Greek *okistos*, superlative of *okys*, 'swift'—here Jonathan Swift (1667–1745), Pope's fellow Scriblerian and with him author of the *Miscellanies*, vol. iii (1728), with its offensive verses on Lady Mary (see above, p. 28).

Give diff,rent Talents different rewards
To Caleb[s] Lot P—— M————[98] is due   205
But Poet L————[99] shall devolve on you.
Our Self the S— of C————[100] fills
Physician be the Poet read in Bills[101]
Ilar and Fog—shall Sec————s[102] be
D—— W——n will with C————r[103] agree.   210
The rising Wrath no longer Codrus bore.
Shall Caleb then above my Title soar
Sooner then we by such a Lot abide
Our-self on winged Pegasus will ride.
Sooner shall virtuous Poverty be woo,[d]   215
Masculine S——n[104] beauteous be ∈ Good
Or H——y[s105] advertisements understood

204] *comma (for apostrophe) written over first* e *in* different; Talents *interlined above cancelled* Merits
216] eous *in* beauteous *interlined above cancelled* iful *in* beautiful; be *interlined above space after* eous; e *(for and) written over* or
217] Or *written over* As

---

[98] P[rime] M[inister].
[99] L[aureate].
[100] S[ee] of C[anterbury].
[101] Dr John Arbuthnot (1667–1735), author and Pope's fellow Scriblerian; he was Lady Mary's physician (see above, p. 32).
[102] John Gay and Charles Molloy, author of *Fog's Weekly Journal* (see above, nn. 80 and 64, respectively), are to be Sec[retarie]s.
[103] Philip, Duke of Wharton (1698–1731). A staunch Jacobite who was Lady Mary's neighbour at Twickenham until he moved abroad in 1725, he converted to Roman Catholicism and, for participating in the Spanish siege of Gibraltar in 1727, was declared an outlaw by the House of Lords on 3 April 1729. For printing a seditious paper of Wharton's in his *Weekly Journal* (24 August 1728), Nathaniel Mist was forced to flee the country. Perhaps it was Wharton's eloquent defence of the Jacobite bishop Atterbury in the House of Lords in 1723 that explains Caleb's preposterous promise to make him Lord Chancellor. Pope, whom Lady Mary believed to be jealous of her friendship with Wharton (Grundy, p. 274), drew his character in the *Epistle to Cobham* (1733/4), lines 180–209.
[104] Probably the wife of Ned Sutton, Champion of Kent, who took part with her husband in bouts of boxing and quarterstaff at Figg's amphitheatre. In his early burlesque of Juvenal's *Sixth Satire* (sketched out before he was 20), HF asks:

> Have you not heard of fighting Females,
> Whom you would rather think to be Males?
> Of Madam *Sutton*, Mrs. *Stokes*,
> Who give confounded Cuts and Strokes?

> (*Miscellanies* i. 111 and n. 4)

For HF's amusement at the spectacle of such manly women, see *The Craftsman*, No. 422 (3 August 1734; *New Essays*, pp. 39–40), and below, the battle of the orange wenches Moll and Sue (2. 245–52).
[105] Henley (see above, n. 70). Advertisements for his preposterous declamations at the Oratory appeared regularly in the newspapers: Charles Woods provides a specimen from the *Daily Post* (30 October 1728) in his biographical notes to the characters in *The Author's Farce* (1730; p. 105). In an exchange with Dr Orator, Luckless, HF's alter ego in the farce, declares: 'if she had understood your Advertisements, I will believe *Nonsense* to have more Understanding than Apollo' (*Plays*, p. 271).

Beaus shall be fam^d for something more then Dress
Or Belles shall slight them for their Emptiness
Wycherly Shakespear, Johnson Congreve^s scenes[106]   220
Triumph o͞er Nonsense, Shew and Harlequins[107]

[fo. 176^v]

—sooner cease to be divine
No Paint in — —[108] Faces shine.
Sooner shall y— ε Bedlam be thought Foes
Or T————[109] get to Helicon in Prose   225
Sooner shall Helicon at T<~~wnhm~~>[110] rise
And K——[111] boast her Sense as well as Eyes
More had he Spoke—but then Ochistes laid

219] Be *in* Belles *written over* La
[224] ~~Bedlam and you shall be~~ *false start on line 224*
226] wnhm *in* Twnhm *written above dash* T——

---

[106] As in the Preface to *Love in Several Masques* (1728) and *The Author's Farce* (1730; III. i), HF considered William Wycherley (1641–1715) and Congreve (see above, n. 73) the best of the witty comic dramatists of the Restoration period, as Shakespeare and his contemporary Ben Jonson (1572–1637) were supreme in the earlier period. For his opinion of the four in greater detail, see *Companion*.

[107] A reference to John Rich (1682?–1761), manager at Lincoln's Inn Fields (see below, n. 144) and after 1732 at Covent Garden. He was chiefly responsible for the great popularity of pantomimes and 'entertainments', in which he performed the part of Harlequin, astonishing audiences with spectacular tricks and special effects. From the beginning of his career as dramatist HF satirized Rich for corrupting the taste of the town. He is the 'puppet' Monsieur Pantomime in *The Author's Farce* (1730; Act III); and in *Tumble-Down Dick* (1736), the published version of which HF ironically dedicated to him, Rich is Machine, who presides over the inane entertainment he has devised; his harlequinades are ridiculed in *The Champion* (3 May 1740, p. 302), *Joseph Andrews* (I. vii, p. 36), and *Tom Jones* (V. i, pp. 213–14).

[108] Grundy suggests the blanks may stand for names or 'Duchesses' and 'Maids of Honour'.

[109] Not identified. Grundy ('New Verse by Henry Fielding', p. 233 n. 226) suggests Lewis Theobald (pronounced Tibbald; 1688–1744), noting, however, that he was, like HF at this time, a supporter of Walpole. But that did not stop HF from ridiculing Theobald as Don Tragedio in *The Author's Farce* (1730; Act III) or mocking his bombast tragedy *The Persian Princess* in *The Tragedy of Tragedies* (1731); and in later years he chose to attack Theobald for his incompetence as a translator of Aristophanes (see below, the Preface to *Plutus* [1742]) and for his arrogance and pedantry as an editor of Shakespeare (*Journey from This World to the Next* [*Miscellanies* ii. 40] and *TP*, No. 16 [11–18 February 1746], pp. 217–18). But here, in a satire of Pope, why would HF wish to join in the ridicule of Theobald? Indeed, in the 'Epistle to Lyttleton' (lines 124–31) HF would chide Pope for lashing Theobald, who, by criticizing Pope's edition in *Shakespeare Restored* (1726), had earned his place as 'hero' of *The Dunciad*. And why point particularly at Theobald's 'Prose' when there were more glaring defects to mock?

The deists Matthew Tindal (1653?–1733) and John Toland (1670–1722), whom Grundy also proposes, seem more likely possibilities. Besides owning a copy of the 1702 edition of Toland's *Christianity not Mysterious* (Ribbles T22), HF in *A Journey from This World to the Next* (*Miscellanies* ii. 44 and n. 1) alludes to Toland's correspondence with Leibniz published in 1726; and in *Joseph Andrews* (I. xvii) Parson Barnabas calls attention to the pernicious 'Principles of Toland . . . and all the Free-Thinkers' (p. 81). As for Tindal, HF in *The Champion* (27 March 1740, p. 254 and n. 1) rejects the thesis of his principal work, *Christianity as Old as the Creation* (1730) and in *The Covent-Garden Journal*, No. 46 (9 June 1752) he links Tindal with Bolingbroke as authors who mean 'to subvert the Religion of [their] Country' (p. 256).

[110] Twickenham (see above, I. 149 and n. 32).

[111] K[itty]. Probably the Duchess of Queensberry (see above, n. 63).

A mighty Hand beneath his Shoulder Blade[112]
And grasping fast, high lifted him in Air   230
(Then Dulness, say, how great was thy Despair)
So have I seen some Boy a Squirrel take
And spight of Grandmother[s] Entreaty shake.
So Gulliver in Lilliput would rear
The Pigmy Race half-dead with shivring Fear   235
And sure Ochistes was as strong as Gulliver
Now the vast chief, the Lilliputian Bard
To Squeeze to Death between his Thumbs prepar[d]
But Scorn, his tut,lar Goddess interpos[d]
Unbent his fiery Mind and fingers loos[d]   240
Her wrinckled Cheeks were to the Heroe known
He bow,[d] and set the trembling Poet down
Him Fear (pale Deity) had now possess[d]
And left no Tumult raging in his Breast
So in the Play-House Passage once I knew   245
A Fight twixt swinging Moll ε little Sue[113]

[fo. 177]

Su bawl,[d], and curs[d] in Dialect so bad
Tis possible she[d] read the D———.[114]
At length Gigantick Moll began to twist,
The swelling Sinews of her Manly fist   250
Till Fear did Su, Scorn, greater Moll appease
And both retir[d] to cry their Oranges.

228] Spoke *written over illegible word*   229] A *written over* His; his *written over illegible word*
230] him in *interlined above cancelled* in the
236] was *interlined above cancelled* is
237] Now *followed by cancelled* was; vast chief *interlined above cancelled* great Gigantick Chief; the Lilliputian Bard *interlined above cancelled* prepar[d]
239] his tut,lar *interlined above cancelled* the haughty
247] ect *in* Dialect *written over* ogue *in* Dialogue
252] cry their *interlined above cancelled* selling
253] Lon *indented, with letter* n *unfinished—false start at opening of* Canto 3[d]

[112] In his earliest extant work—*The Masquerade* (January 1728) by 'Lemuel Gulliver, Poet Laureat to the King of Lilliput'—HF had anticipated the analogy in this passage (lines 228–42) between the satirist and his targets and Gulliver and the Lilliputians. With Swift as Gulliver manhandling Pope, 'the Lilliputian Bard', cf. the conclusion to the 'Epistle to Lyttleton' (lines 165–77), where HF, metaphorically appearing as a 'gen'rous Mastiff', shakes the 'little Curr' (Pope) in the air for insulting his mistress (Lady Mary) and 'throws him in the Kennel on his Back'.
[113] Grundy ('New Verse by Henry Fielding', p. 234 n. 247) calls Moll 'a forerunner of other female pugilists' in HF's works, citing Susan the chambermaid in the 'Battle of Upton' (*Tom Jones*, IX. iii), to which should be added the country viragos who beset Molly Seagrim in IV. viii. Also see above, n. 104.
[114] D[unciad].

CANTO 3^d

Long Silence held the chiefs—while Murmurs lowd
Began to buzz among the vulgar Crowd
Ilar at length arose—what heavnly Spite
What Foe to Dulness could these Brawls incite
Is this the Way a Company to form¹¹⁵   5
Let me, o let me lay this raging storm.
Hear my Proposals—let us first obtain
The Conquest e̅e̅re we quarrel o̅e̅r the Gain.
Let Fortune then, by Lots, each Place bestow,
Alike adapted to each Place I kn[o]w   10
Our sev,^{ral} Wits—Ochistes thou mayst be
Commander in a Camp, as well as See.
Not what^s the Bus,ness—what the Profits are
Of ev,^{ry} Office, is the Statesman^s Care
This on the Part of Codrus I agree   15
Caleb^s not fitter for that Place then He.
—Ochistes then[:]¹¹⁶ let Fools to Fortune trust
To Men like Me, too oft she proves unjust

                                                                    _____
                                                                    [fo. 177^r]

Think you I will to Chance my Right resign
Or for an earthly, change a Post divine.   20
Shall I who R————¹¹⁷ have been so smart in
Who taught the World the Benefit of Farting
To Whom the History of B—— is due¹¹⁸

9] Then. *cancelled before* Let; each *written over illegible word*
10] t *in to* and e *in* Place *written over illegible letters*
11] Wits *substituted for cancelled* Talents *preceding*   12] C *in* Commander *written over* A
14] e *in* ev,^{ry} *written over illegible letter*   19] I *written over* <oc>

---

¹¹⁵ On the 'Company' of Scriblerians and their allies, see above, 2. 79–80 and n. 65, also 2. 100–1.

¹¹⁶ Intended no doubt to please Lady Mary, who disliked Swift, the following satire (lines 17–30) is wholly uncharacteristic of HF's own opinion of him. From *The Masquerade* (1728) to *The Covent-Garden Journal* (1752) he lauded, and at times imitated, the author whom he regarded as, in the words of Booth in *Amelia* (1751), 'the greatest Master of Humour that ever wrote' (p. 324). In his obituary for Swift in *The True Patriot* (5 November 1745) HF called him 'A Genius who deserves to be ranked among the first whom the World ever saw' and one who 'employed his Wit to the noblest Purposes' (p. 336).

¹¹⁷ R[ibaldry].

¹¹⁸ Separately bound in with certain copies of the fourth edition of Swift's *Miscellanies* (1722) are two extra pieces, *The Benefit of Farting* and *The Wonderful Wonder of Wonders*; the latter in a fifth edition (1722) has the subtitle *Or, The Hole-History of The Life and Actions of Mr. Breech, The Eighth Wonder of the World*. (See *A Bibliography of the Writings of Jonathan Swift*, 2nd edn. rev., ed. H. Teerink and Arthur H. Scouten [Philadelphia, 1963], pp. 131 and 398.)

And Meditations on a Broomstick too[119]
But for the oddness of whose Mind ε Pen   25
Brobdingnag, Lilliput unknown had been[120]
Then whom none ēēre more learned to disguise
In burlesque Shape of Truth—Politick L——[121]
Who was The merry-Andrew of the Age
And left the P—pit, for the dearer Stage[122]   30
—then Codrus now recover^d from his Fit—
Must I, o Bards rehearse what I have writ.
Why do I name those miscellaneous Flowers[123]
Trifling small Works—and scarce accounted ours
Ochistes might perhaps the D———[124] boast   35
But in the Il——[125] that small Glory^s lost
No, let Odyssee all my Trophies raise
Dulness, from thence, shall still resound my Praise
Where Nonsense, Fustian, grov,^ling Diction speak
Me scarce more skill^d in English then in Greek.   40
Hence, hence o Bards—as long as his great Name
Be known, who burnt Diana^s shrine for Fame[126]

25] Mind ε *interlined above space between* whose *and* Pen   27] more *interlined above cancelled* so
29] Who was *added in margin before* The merry-Andrew
31] ~~Shall I~~ *struck through at beginning of the line*
32] Must *added in margin before cancelled word (illegible)*
35] Ochistes might perhaps the D——— boast: *original word order =* The D——— might perhaps
Ochistes boast *rearranged in MS by interlined numbers* 4, 5, 2, 3, 1 *above the first five words*
36] that *written over illegible word*
39] Di *in* Diction *written over* Lan
40] ish *in* English *written over dash in* Engl——

---

[119] See above, 1. 110 and n. 25.
[120] Cf. *The Masquerade* (1728), where HF as Gulliver celebrates 'Curiosity': 'Britain may hence her knowledge brag | Of Lilliput and Brobdingnag' (lines 21–2; see above, p. 15).
[121] L[ies].
[122] P[ul]pit. HF may refer to Swift's essay in *The Intelligencer* (25 May 1728), in which he defended his friend Gay against the Revd Thomas Herring, a royal chaplain and later Archbishop of Canterbury, who had publicly condemned *The Beggar's Opera* from the pulpit, denouncing the play for encouraging vice by representing highwaymen as heroes. (See Irvin Ehrenpreis, *Swift: The Man, his Works, and the Age* [Cambridge, Mass., 1983], iii. 559–61.)
[123] Pope and Swift's *Miscellanies*, 3 vols. (1727–8).
[124] Probably 'Drapier', not *Dunciad*, as the meter requires just two syllables (*drapier* = *draper*). The *Letters* (1724–5) Swift wrote impersonating a Dublin woollen draper who protests the introduction of 'Wood's halfpence' into Ireland made him a national hero. In Pope's dedication of *The Dunciad* Variorum (1729) to Swift, it is one of four 'titles' Swift prefers: 'O thou! whatever Title please thine ear, | Dean, Drapier, Bickerstaff, or Gulliver!' (i. 17–18).
[125] Il[iad].
[126] Herostratus, who, in 356 BC at Ephesus, burnt down the temple of Artemis to make his name immortal. HF also refers to him in *The Champion* (27 November 1739, p. 34 n. 1, and 3 May 1740, p. 299 n. 3).

Long as Ravilliac[127] (spight of France) conveys
What Honours he deserv[d] to Distant Days
And La Motte[s] Name be read tho not his Lays[128]   45

[fo. 178]

While Hobbes (not understood) delights the Fool
And Blockheads dare Religion ridicule[129]
While Nonsense on the B——sh[130] Stage has Scope
~~And Ignorance and Malice live in~~ ——[131]
While vilest Zoilus[132] in Schools be known   50
And Folly be the Mistress of the Town
While Mævius, Bavius (Stinking Names)[133] survive
So long in Grubstreet Annals shall I live.
He s[d]—Scriblerus[134] then—nor do I claim

[43–5] *triplet unmarked in MS*
49] *words struck through before* dash *for word to rhyme with* scope

[127] François Ravaillac (1578–1610), a disgruntled lawyer who believed Henri IV intended to make war on the Pope, assassinated the King on 14 May 1610. He was tortured and executed, and, HF recalls in *The Champion* (7 June 1740), his family 'were obliged to change that Name, which was so odious in *France*, that a Writer of that King's History, whom I have read, never once mentions it, but when he speaks of that Assassin, does it only by the Appellation of *le Scélérat* [villain], or other Terms of Reproach' (p. 359).

[128] Without knowing Greek, Antoine Houdar de La Motte (1672–1731) published in 1714 an abridged version of the *Iliad* in rhymed French verse while treating Homer as a poet irreverently. For this he was attacked by the classical scholar Mme Dacier in her critical work *Des causes de la corruption du goust* (1714), to which La Motte replied in kind. HF, who admired Mme Dacier and agreed with her opinion of La Motte, would also allude to the quarrel in *Amelia* (1751; x. i, pp. 408–9 and notes) and *The Covent-Garden Journal*, No. 11 (8 February 1752), p. 83 and n. 1.

[129] Thomas Hobbes (1588–1679), author of *Leviathan* (1651), was reviled by most of his contemporaries as a materialist who argued that there was no absolute basis for morality and that man was motivated entirely by self-interest. Though HF here avers that this unsavoury reputation was owing to a misunderstanding of Hobbes's philosophy, elsewhere in his writings—e.g. *The Author's Farce* (1730; II. ix); *Plays* (p. 253 and n. 2); *The Champion* (22 January 1740, pp. 134–8); 'An Essay on Nothing' (sect. iii; *Miscellanies* i. 189); *Joseph Andrews* (III. iii, p. 212 n. 1[2]); *Tom Jones* (VI. i, pp. 268–9)—he invariably concurs with the general view.

[130] B[ritish].
[131] [Pope].
[132] Zoilus of Amphipolis, a rhetorician of the fourth century BC who attacked Homer at great length; prototype of the ultracrepidarian critic.
[133] The names of a pair of poetasters ridiculed in Virgil's *Eclogues* (iii. 90) adopted as pseudonyms by John Martyn (Maevius) and Richard Russel (Bavius) of *The Grub-Street Journal*, an anti-ministerial paper associated with Pope that began publication on 8 January 1730.
[134] Under the name Martinus Scriblerus, the supreme pedant invented by 'the Scriblerus Club', Pope published the *Peri Bathous: or, The Art of Sinking in Poetry* as part of the 'last Volume' (vol. iii) of the *Miscellanies* (1728). Scriblerus also serves as editor of the *The Dunciad Variorum* (1729), contributing the 'prolegomena' and commentary. HF clearly enjoyed the joke. In March 1730 he published *The Author's Farce* under the name Scriblerus Secundus and continued using the pseudonym for *Tom Thumb* (2nd edn., June 1730), *The Tragedy of Tragedies* (March 1731), *The Letter-Writers* (March 1731), and the several versions of *The Grub-Street Opera* (1731).

An equal Share of Merit—or of Fame.   55
Yet Something sure for Dulness have I done
I have abus^d immortal Ad————¹³⁵
Sense and Religion taught his Skilful Pen
The best of Criticks, and the best of Men.
With Censure him the Bathos doth pursue   60
To me—O Poets—is that Bathos due.
Then Eager Caleb, started from his Seat.¹³⁶
Since boasting is n<o> Scandal to the great
Hear all ye Bards—tho have I need to tell
What all the Realms of Dulness know so well.   65
By easy Arts Men may the World deceive
The World will still malicious Lies believe
To call the honest, Knaves, with Fool to brand
The Wise—are easy Tricks to understand.
But he who Contradictions can persuade   ⎫   70
That Knave and Fool one Man^s by Nature made   ⎬
He is indeed a Master of his Trade   ⎭
                                                   ————————
                                                   [fo. 178^v]
By Words—not things, the Vulgar are abus^d
Assertions without Proofs, I still have us^d
For many Facts which boldly I aver   75

[61] That Bathos wh *false start of line*
62] ed *in* started *written over* ing *in* starting
63] <o> *ink blot obscures letter after* n
64] e *in* ye *written over illegible letter(s)*
68] To *written over illegible letters*
70] Contradictions *interlined above space between* who *and* can; the [space] World *cancelled after* can
75] Facts *interlined above cancelled* Things

---

¹³⁵ Addison: see above, nn. 34 and 59. Lines 60–1 below allude to the 'Libel' of Addison (as Welsted called it [*One Epistle*, p. 12 n.]) in Pope's *Peri Bathous* (chs. xi–xii), where lines from *The Campaign* (1704) are quoted as illustrating the excesses of 'Macrology and Pleonasm', and the 'Perfection' of these faults, 'Tautology'; other verses are chosen as examples of inept 'Expression' (see Steeves's commentary (see above, n. 25), pp. 160–4).

¹³⁶ With this speech of 'Caleb' [i.e. Nicholas Amhurst], editor of the anti-ministerial journal *The Craftsman*, cf. *TP*, No. 14 (28 January–4 February 1746), where HF, also characterizing opposition journalists who 'darken and corrupt the Minds of Men, by dressing up Falshood in the Colours of Truth, and Vice in those of Virtue', are called '*Scriblers*': 'This Appellation likewise hath been applied with great Indifference and Impropriety; and Fools, who are always the Ecchoes of Knaves, have drivelled it out against some of the best and worthiest Members of Society' (p. 208); in No. 17 (18–25 February 1746), HF continued the theme: 'The wicked Man in Scripture is called a Fool*. . . . Knave and Fool are synonymous Terms' (p. 224). [True only in the Catholic Douay version of Proverbs 24: 8: 'he that deviseth to do evils, shall be called fool'.] Coley also cites an earlier example in *The Champion* (11 March 1740), where HF refers to those who 'assert that *Solomon* [author of Proverbs] by the Word *Fool* means every where a wicked Man or a Rogue; nay, they insist that the Words *Rogue* and *Fool* are convertible Terms' (pp. 228–9).

Not J—son—B————ge[137] would attempt to swear
No nor a Witness in all W——————[138]
The Vulgar still believe whateer we teach
Of what,^{s} above their Understanding^s Reach.
What P~~ope~~ of high Parnassus Mount declares   80
Or John M————[139] Professor, of the Stars.
(Ah! P~~o~~—[140] how good that Telescope must be
Which from thy Garret can Parnassus see)
—Him Codrus interrupted—Cease—for shame
Let us no longer talk—but act for Fame.   85
See, see, before your Eyes, what I display.
The Se—— to the B———— O——[141]
Soon as The Hero had the Title spoke
With loud Huzzas the Council chamber shook

                                                              [fo. 179]
By Ilar be it instantly convey^d 90
To Plutus[142] with an Order to be play^d
Hence we our Contest easily decide.

79] what,^{s} *interlined above cancelled* Men or things
80] ope *in* Pope *struck through to form dash*
82] o *after* P *struck through to form dash*
84] Codrus *interlined above cancelled* Ilar; Cease *interlined above cancelled* Bards
87] e *after* S *struck through to form dash*
89] *This is the last of seventeen lines on MS leaf 178^v, leaving about one-third of the leaf blank*
[90] *This line, with interlined revisions, was cancelled, reading originally as follows:* With this **to Plutus** be
Ilar **strait to Plutus** sent *(bold type indicates interlined revisions)*
91] an *written over* our; to *written over illegible word*

[137] In this context of duplicity and prevarication, probably 'J[an]son' and 'B[ambrid]ge': i.e. Sir Theodore Janssen (1658?–1748), a notoriously corrupt director of the South Sea Company (see above, I. 102) who, when the 'bubble' burst in 1720, was in January 1721 expelled from the House of Commons, committed to the Tower, and forced to pay a mulct of some quarter of a million pounds. (A less likely candidate is his son Sir Henry Jansen, a gamester [Grundy, 'New Verse by Henry Fielding', p. 236 n. 76].) Baker (unpublished notes) proposed the notorious smuggler Roger Johnson, whom HF in *Jonathan Wild* (1743) introduces as the hero's rival for power in Newgate (IV. iii); however, in that novel, as elsewhere in his writings, HF, when referring to convicted felons, makes no attempt to conceal their names by omitting letters. The infamous Thomas Bambridge (d. 1741), cruel and corrupt Warden of the Fleet Prison, was in March 1729 investigated by a special committee of the House of Commons (depicted in the painting by Hogarth) and in June was deprived of the wardenship.
[138] W[estminster], referring to Westminster Hall, site of the courts of justice.
[139] John Machin (d. 1751), Professor of Astronomy at Gresham College and Secretary to the Royal Society. His *Laws of the Moon's Motion according to Gravity* was published in May 1729, appended to Andrew Motte's translation of Newton's *Principia*.
[140] Pope.
[141] Se[quel] to the B[eggar's] O[pera].
[142] Plutus (Greek *ploutos* = wealth): John Rich (see above, n. 107), manager at Lincoln's Inn Fields, had staged Gay's immensely popular *Beggar's Opera* in January 1728 and was offered *Polly*, its sequel in December. It was suppressed (see below, lines 144–61).

And by the gen^{ral} Taste it will be try^d
As all in this have shewn our utmost Powers
So he—whose Song shall gain the most Encores   95
P—— M————¹⁴³ in future Times shall be.
And by his Name we call the ~~Company~~
He s^d—all gave a general assent
The Council rose—and ~~ready~~ Ilar went

So among School-boys, have I seen (confest   100
In Impudence Superiour to the rest)
A Blade (such worth^s in Impudence allow,^d)
Give Laws successful to the wiser Crowd.

    Between two Regions differently fam^d
For Lawyers this—and that for Butchers nam^d   105
A Building rises in the middle Street¹⁴⁴
Where the two Tribes oft in one Jury meet.
The Temple to the Muses heretofore
But Dulness Fane, was now the Name it bore.
The Goddess Here those Trophies now displays   110
Which Smithfield Booths¹⁴⁵ adorn^d in ancient Days

                                                          [fo. 179ᵛ]

Here <stor,^d> she kept her mighty Magazins
Here were her Dancers, Pipers, Harlequins.¹⁴⁶

97] ompa *in* Company *struck through to form dash*
99] ready *interlined and struck through between* and *and* Ilar
108] to *written over* of
109] Name *interlined above cancelled* Fane
110] The Goddess *interlined in margin before* Here—*the* ere *in* Here *written over* ither *in* Hither
112] <stor,^d> *written over illegible word*

¹⁴³ P[rime] M[inister].
¹⁴⁴ Until 1713 theatrical productions took place in a converted tennis court situated at the centre of Portugal Street, just south of Lincoln's Inn Fields in a 'Region' occupied by the Inns of Court; farther south towards the Strand was Butcher Row, Temple Bar. In 1713 Christopher Rich, the proprietor, replaced the tennis court with the Lincoln's Inn Fields Theatre, which opened in 1714 with his son John Rich as manager, delighting audiences as Harlequin in pantomimes (see above, nn. 107 and 142). For the history and location of the theatre, see Phillips, *Mid Georgian London* pp. 192–3; and Rocque, *The A to Z of Georgian London*, 3Cc, 11Ca.
¹⁴⁵ Cf. Pope's note to the opening of *The Dunciad* (1729)—'Books and the Man I sing, the first who brings | The Smithfield Muses to the Ear of Kings': '*Smithfield* is the place where Bartholomew Fair was kept, whose Shews, Machines, and Dramatical Entertainments, formerly agreeable only to the Taste of the Rabble, were, by the Hero of this Poem [Lewis Theobald] and others of equal Genius, brought to the Theatres of Covent-Garden, Lincolns-inn Fields, and the Hay-Market, to be the reigning Pleasures of the Court and Town.'
¹⁴⁶ See above, nn. 142 and 144.

For Plutus <finding> Wit was left i,th Lurch
His Theatre as empty as a Church   115
And seeing too wheneēr he look^d Abroad
That Dulness was to Wealth the only Road
Thus reason^d with himself—perhaps the Fare
Of Wits, may like their Castles, be in air
But I—who plainly in my self can read   120
My Heels are much—much lighter then my Head[147]
Must have a grosser Food—without a S<ow>se?
My Belly must be empty as my House.
Which would I fill—the Town I must delight
The Town has now no senses but the Sight.   125
To that Sense only then we will apply
And Dulness knows the Way to charm the Eye[148]
To her he instantly address^d his Prayer
Which Dulness heard with a propitious Ear
For She, good Queen to Mortals ever kind   130
As soon as ask^d possesses ev^{ry} Mind
Hence see the Gods descend—& Devils rise[149]
While Plutus round the Stage like Lightning flies
Hear from the Clowds the rattling Thunder sound
Which soon in general Applause is drown^d[150]   135
Ah! ah! How Plutus skips—so have I seen
A frisking Ass run nimbly round the Green
While all his Brethren in a gen^{ral} Bray
Proclaim their Approbation of his Play

114] <finding> *written over* <found>
120] who plainly in my self can read *interlined above cancelled* of whom it may justly said *[sic]*
122] S<ow>se *ink blot obscures probable* o *and part of probable* w
130] to *ink blot partly obscures probable* t
136] Ah! ah! *added in margin before* How; nimbly *struck through before* Plutus

---

[147] In dedicating the farce *Tumble-Down Dick* (1736) to Rich—addressing him as 'Mr. John Lun', the name Rich used when performing the part of Harlequin—HF wondered whether the great success of his entertainments was 'owing to your Heels or your Head'. Cf. also below (pp. 78–85), *A Dialogue between a Beau's Head and His Heels* (1730).

[148] Cf. above, 2. 60.

[149] Here HF's ridicule of Rich's performance as Harlequin (lines 132–9) draws on Pope's satire of him in *The Dunciad* (1729), iii. 229–68: e.g. with HF's line 132 cf. *Dunciad* lines 233 ('Hell rises, Heav'n descends, and dance on Earth'); with HF's lines 133–4 cf. *Dunciad* lines 249–52 ('In yonder cloud, behold! | Whose sarcenet skirts are edg'd with flamy gold, | A matchless youth: His nod these worlds controuls, | Wings the red lightning, and the thunder rolls.'

[150] Cf. above, 2. 66.

[fo. 180]

Now Plutus all his Company convenes   140
To read (o H———d)[151] thy ~~exalted~~ Scenes
(Sure none eēre writ a Tragedy so deep)
The second Act had seal[d] most Eyes in sleep
When Ilar came—and all the Crew addrest[152]
But thee, great Plutus, far above the rest   ·   145
—A Herald from the Company I come
The [blank] Company of [blank] Poets whom
Not Grubstreet only but the Realm obeys
And Pe———s[153] and Porters sing their tuneful Lays
To you they send, and order you to play   150
The S——— of the B——— O———[154]
He s[d]—and Plutus reaching out his Hand

140] his *written over* <this>
141] y *in* thy *written over* e *in* the*;* exalted *struck through before* Scenes
143] The *substituted for preceding cancelled* How*;* second *interlined above cancelled* third*;* seal[d] *interlined above cancelled* fix[d]
149] And *written over* Who*;* e *after* P *struck through and line extended*

[151] Eliza Haywood (1693?–1756). Her tragedy *Frederick, Duke of Brunswick-Lunenburgh* was staged by Rich at Lincoln's Inn Fields on 4 March 1729; in the Preface to the published version, Haywood regretted the 'indifferent Reception' the play had met with. She had been a target of Pope's in *The Dunciad* (1729), ii. 149–58 and iii. 145; and she would be HF's target as well in *The Author's Farce* (1730; Act III), where she is figured as Mrs Novel in the 'puppet show'. Later she collaborated with William Hatchett in producing *The Opera of Operas* (1733), a musical version of HF's *Tragedy of Tragedies*; and in 1737, as an actress, she was part of HF's 'Company of Comedians' in his final season at the Haymarket. In her novel *The History of Betsy Thoughtless* (1751), however, she would remember HF and his theatre with contempt.

[152] The final lines of the Cantos allude to the suppression of Gay's sequel to *The Beggar's Opera*. In December 1728 *Polly* was ready for rehearsal at Lincoln's Inn Fields when, on 12 December, Rich was ordered by the Lord Chamberlain to stop production; it would be fifty years before the play reached the stage. This oppressive action recoiled against the government by provoking an enormous public demand for the book of the play, 10,500 copies of which were printed at Gay's expense, netting him £1,200 from subscribers and a total profit, if Swift is to be trusted, of £3,000 (see Calhoun Winton, *John Gay and the London Theatre* [Lexington, Ky., 1993], p. 135). As Arbuthnot reported to Swift on 19 March 1729, the affair also made Gay the martyred hero of the Opposition:

> The inoffensive John Gay is now become one of the obstructions to the peace of Europe, the terror of Ministers, the chief author of the Craftsman & all the seditious pamphlets which have been published against the government. He has gott several turnd out of their places, the greatest ornament of the court [the Duchess of Queensberry] Banishd from it for his sake . . . he is the darling of the city; if he should travel about the country, he would have hecatombs of Roasted oxen sacrificd to him. Since he became so conspicuous Will poultny [Pulteney, leader of the Opposition] hangs his head; to see himself so much outdone in the career of Glory. (Swift's *Correspondence*, ed. Harold Williams [Oxford, 1963], iii. 326)

[153] Pe[er]s.
[154] S[equel] of the B[eggar's] O[pera].

Obedient to ye Company^s Command
The God of Pantomime his Hand compell,^d
Unseen by Ilar—Plutus him beheld   155
Trembling, his motly Form he saw and knew
Then thus the God—o do not so pursue
Our mutual Ruin—the Command avoid
Should you obey your Th————^s155 destroy^d
The Gods resolve no Nonsense shall be sung   160
In any but the soft Italian Tongue.^156

---

[153] ~~Was willing to obey the Bards Command~~ *line cancelled*
154] compell,^d *substituted after cancelled* withheld

---

155 Th[eatre]'s.

156 From the beginning of his career HF was critical of the Italian opera—a prejudice he shared with Addison, Pope, Gay, and many others. In the 'puppet show' in *The Author's Farce* (1730; Act III), Signior Opera mimics the popular castrato Senesino and wins the heart of Nonsense. In dedicating *The Intriguing Chambermaid* (1734) to Kitty Clive, HF denounced 'the Folly, Injustice, and Barbarity of the Town', who 'sacrifice our own native Entertainments to a wanton affected Fondness for foreign Musick . . . when our Nobility seem to rival each other, in distinguishing themselves in favour of *Italian* Theatres, and in neglect of our own'. (For details, see *Companion*, s.v. 'opera'.)

3

PLAIN TRUTH (c.1729–1730)

IN 1758, four years after Fielding's death, Robert Dodsley (1704–63), the eminent bookseller,[1] brought out volumes V and VI of his immensely popular *Collection of Poems by Several Hands*, which he had launched ten years earlier intending 'to preserve to the public those poetical performances, which seemed to merit a longer remembrance than what would probably be secured to them by the manner wherein they were originally published' (vol. i, pp. iii–iv). It was an anthology, as Dodsley's biographer observes, that 'set the canon for mid-eighteenth-century poetry'.[2] In volume V of that *Collection* were included a pair of poems attributed to Fielding: the first, 'A LETTER to Sir ROBERT WALPOLE', is a shorter, and therefore probably earlier, version of the poem to Walpole dated 1730 in Fielding's *Miscellanies* (1743); the second is 'PLAIN TRUTH'.[3] The latter was not included either by Fielding in the *Miscellanies* or by his publisher Andrew Millar in the *Works* of 1762. In 1903 it was reprinted without comment in William Ernest Henley's edition of the *Complete Works*; and in his biography of 1918 Wilbur Cross briefly mentions it, 'a rather pretty poem in Hudibrastic metre'.[4]

But lacking any known provenance for the manuscript, Dodsley's assignment of the piece to Fielding has remained questionable. Among other discoveries that have illuminated the Fielding canon, however, Dr Ribble's research in the Malmesbury papers has recently strengthened the

---

[1] Dodsley and HF would certainly have been acquainted. In 1736–7, when HF's dramatic satires against Walpole were in vogue, Dodsley, who in 1735 had opened his famous bookshop at the sign of Tully's Head, Pall Mall, was also attracting theatregoers with his own anti-ministerial play *The King and the Miller of Mansfield* (1737). In the list of subscribers to HF's *Miscellanies* (1743), he is down for six sets, though no doubt these were commissioned by clients. Later, with Andrew Millar and others, he was among the booksellers involved in publishing HF's *True Patriot* (1745–6; pp. lxv–lxvi); and again with Millar, Dodsley, together with Samuel Baker, sponsored the proposal for HF and William Young's abortive translation of Lucian (see *Covent-Garden Journal*, No. 52 [30 June 1752], p. 285 and n. 2).

[2] James E. Tierney, *Oxford DNB*, s.v. Dodsley, Robert. For the details of Dodsley's career, see Harry M. Solomon, *The Rise of Robert Dodsley: Creating the New Age of Print* (Carbondale and Edwardsville, Ill., 1996).

[3] See *Collection of Poems by Several Hands* (1758), v, pp. 117–18 and 302–5.

[4] Henley xii, pp. 345–7; Cross i, pp. 383–4.

case for Fielding's authorship of the poem.[5] In the summer of 1742 Fielding, in order to fill out the three volumes of his *Miscellanies*, appealed to his friends for copies of his unpublished writings. From Bath on 24 September 1742 he wrote to thank James Harris:

As to the Verses y° are so kind to transmit me, & so partial (for I suspect y° of nothing worse) to commend; I sincerely think both the Chancelor & y^r self have over-valued y^m; he in so long preserving, & y° in comenting on what was originally writ with the Haste & Inaccuracy of a comon Letter . . .[6]

It now appears that Fielding's obliging 'Chancelor' was not, as I had thought,[7] Lord Chancellor Hardwicke, but my less 'likely' candidate, the Revd John Hoadly (1711–76), Chancellor since 1735 of his father, Bishop Benjamin Hoadly's, diocese of Winchester. In a letter from Hoadly to James Harris of 10 August 1742, Ribble found that Hoadly had 'preserved' Fielding's poem 'A Description of U[pto]n G[rey]' and made it available to him for the *Miscellanies*. On this discovery, Ribble reasoned, 'the evidence that Hoadly possessed manuscripts of some of Fielding's verse helps support the attribution to Fielding' of 'Plain Truth'.[8] Further strengthening the case for Fielding's authorship is Hoadly's letter to Dodsley of 18 October 1757, which reveals that it was he who provided Dodsley with most of the copy in this part of the volume. Considering this evidence, Ribble concluded: 'it is very probable that [Hoadly] himself supplied both the manuscript of the poem and the attribution'.

That the Revd John Hoadly might play this part in Dodsley's post-humous publication of 'Plain Truth', and probably the 'Letter' to Walpole as well, should not be surprising. He and his elder brother Benjamin (1706–57), a physician and playwright, were Fielding's close friends. They both subscribed generously to his *Miscellanies*—two sets on 'royal' paper for John, three sets for Benjamin—and Fielding compliments them both in his writings. Benjamin's skill as a physician is applauded in *Juvenal's Sixth Satire* (*Miscellanies* i, p. 111) and his comedy on jealousy is paired with *Othello* in *The Covent-Garden Journal*, No. 55 (18 July 1752), pp. 300–1.

A more impressive example of Fielding's friendship with John Hoadly is his indebtedness to him for the idea of constructing *Pasquin* (1736), his most popular play, around contrasting rehearsals of a comedy and a tragedy. Assisted by his brother, John in 1731 had staged at John Rich's theatre in Lincoln's Inn Fields a play entitled *The Contrast: A Tragi-Comical Rehearsal of Two Modern Plays*; after a brief run, he withdrew it at the

---

[5] See 'New Light on Henry Fielding from the Malmesbury Papers', *MP*, 103 (2005), 51–94.
[6] *Correspondence*, Letter 14, p. 23.   [7] Ibid., p. 26 n. 4.   [8] See Ribble, 'New Light', 64.

instance of his father the bishop. Accused of plagiarism by Rich, Fielding responded with *Tumble-Down Dick* (1736), a satire of Rich's pantomime 'entertainments'. Ironically dedicating the book of the play to Rich, Fielding acknowledged the debt he owed his friend, who had left writing plays to pursue the more lucrative vocation of being a priest in his father's diocese. Addressing Rich, Fielding declares himself

obliged to you for discovering in my imperfect Performance the Strokes of an Author, any of whose Wit, if I have preserved entire, I shall think it my chief Merit to the Town. Tho' I cannot enough cure myself of Selfishness, while I meddle in Dramatick Writings, to profess a Sorrow that One of so superior a Genius is led, by his better Sense and better Fortune, to more profitable Studies than the Stage.

John Hoadly was close to Fielding's sister Sarah as well, and on her death in 1768 composed the memorial to her in Bath Abbey.

As to the poem itself that Hoadly preserved and provided for publication in Dodsley's *Collection*, 'Plain Truth' is very much of a piece with Fielding's early amatory verse, dating from the period 1728 to 1733—a time when he was singing the charms of one young lady after another: from 'Rosalinda' and 'Euthalia' (1728) to 'Clarissa', whom he celebrated in a verse engraved on a window pane, to 'Jenny', 'Gloriana', 'Vince's Eyes', 'fair Bennet', 'S[o]per', several 'Celias', and for a year or two in 1732–3 a certain 'Dorinda', whom he loved in vain.[9]

'Plain Truth' exemplifies Fielding's light verse in the same mode as the untitled 'The Queen of Beauty, t'other Day' in the *Miscellanies*—a poem also of eighty lines of Hudibrastic verse, which Henry Knight Miller identified as 'a literary *Kallisteia*, or competition of beauties', citing the anonymous *Callistia: or, The Prize of Beauty. A Poem* (1738).[10] In 'The Queen of Beauty', written at Salisbury *c.*1729–1730,[11] Venus summons her 'Privy-Council' to 'substitute Vice Regents; | To Canton out her Subject Lands' (lines 8–9). In 'Plain Truth', written at Bath at about the same time,[12] she invites the gods to tea. Here Fielding makes the genre serve a

---

[9] For 'Dorinda', see the verse epistles to Lyttelton below, p. 91, and Ellys below, p. 687. For the other fleeting sweethearts, see the verses in HF's *Miscellanies* i, Contents: nos. 6, 9–12, 14, 21–7, 30, 32, 35. For an account of HF's romantic interests during this period, see *Life*, pp. 71–2, 94–8.

[10] *Miscellanies* i, p. 78 n. 1.

[11] ibid., i, p. 80 n. 1.

[12] Cf. the opening line of both poems: 'The Queen of Beauty, t'other Day'; in 'Plain Truth', 'As Bathian Venus t'other day'. There are other similarities with HF's 'To Celia' of the same period. In both poems Cupid serves his mother, Venus: in 'To Celia' she misses 'that cunning Urchin's Look' (line 24); in 'Plain Truth' she calls him 'my wicked urchin' (line 52). In 'To Celia' Cupid boasts, 'I in a Dimple lay' (line 47); in 'Plain Truth' he savours the sweets of Betty's 'dear dimple' (line 53). On Matthew Prior as HF's probable source for these terms, see *Miscellanies* i, p. 72 n. 1.

double purpose: first, to compliment his friend John Dalton on a set of witty verses celebrating the beauties of Bath (Minerva, Venus' rival, preferring wit to beauty); and then to rebuke him for neglecting to include the fairest of them all, one Betty Dalston, presumably his friend's sister, whose face Venus herself wears when visiting Bath.

Though both Betty and the witty poet are named Dalston in the poem, Baker—citing Musgrave's *Obituary*, which refers readers looking for 'Dalston' to 'Dalton'[13]—proposed John Dalton (1709–63) as the poet in question.[14] At the time Fielding probably wrote 'Plain Truth', Dalton, who in the 1740s would become a priest in the Church of England, was fresh from Oxford and soon to be appointed tutor to the only son of the Earl of Hertford. He took the opportunity, according to Horace Walpole, to have an affair with his patron's wife, Frances (*née* Thynne) Seymour (1699–1754), the literary Countess of Hertford (from 1748 also Duchess of Somerset), and also with her friend Henrietta (*née* St John) Knight (1699–1756), the bluestocking Lady Luxborough.[15] Both Dalton and Lady Hertford were among a favoured few readers to receive advance copies of the first two volumes of *Tom Jones*, which both warmly recommended to their friends.[16] In *The True Patriot*, No. 13 (21–8 January 1746) Fielding had 'Abraham Adams' recommend Dalton's sermons 'on the Subject of educating Youth, lately preached . . . at the University of *Oxford*' (p. 206 and n. 2).[17]

PLAIN TRUTH.
By HENRY FIELDING, Esq;

A S Bathian Venus t'other day
Invited all the Gods to tea,
Her maids of honour, the miss Graces,
Attending duely in their places,

[13] Draft of an Introduction to 'Plain Truth'.

[14] A selection of his verse, chiefly descriptive, was included in *A Collection of Poems in Two Volumes by Several Hands*, published by George Pearch (1768), i, pp. 23–67.

[15] See W. P. Courtney and John Wyatt, *Oxford DNB*, s.v. Dalton, John. Helen Sard Hughes, however, in *The Gentle Hertford: Her Life and Letters* (New York, 1940), pp. 170–81, saw no impropriety in the relationship (p. 170).

[16] See *Life*, pp. 442 and 669 n. 315.

[17] As further evidence of HF's friendship with the Dalton family, in *Covent-Garden Journal* No. 20 (10 March 1752) he warmly recommended a recently published work—'Views and Antiquities of Greece and Egypt' entitled *Museum Graecum et Egyptiacum*—by Dalton's younger brother Richard (1715–91), librarian to the Prince of Wales and Keeper of the Royal Drawings and Medals (pp. 472–3).

Their godships gave a loose to mirth, 5
As we at Butt'rings[1] here on earth.
  Minerva[2] in her usual way
Raillied[3] the daughter of the sea.[4]
Madam, said she, your lov'd resort,
The city where you hold your court,[5] 10
Is lately fallen from its duty,
And triumphs more in wit than beauty;
For here, she cried; see here a poem—
'Tis Dalston's;[6] you, Apollo, know him.
Little persuasion sure invites 15
Pallas to read what Dalston writes:
Nay, I have heard that in Parnassus[7]
For truth a current whisper passes,
That Dalston sometimes has been known
To publish her words as his own. 20
  Minerva read, and every God
Approv'd—Jove gave the critic nod:
Apollo and the sacred Nine
Were charm'd, and smil'd at ev'ry line;
And Mars, who little understood, 25
Swore, d—n him, if it was not good.
Venus alone sat all the while
Silent, nor deign'd a single smile.
All were surpriz'd: some thought her stupid:
Not so her confident 'squire Cupid; 30
For well the little rogue discern'd
At what his mother was concern'd,
Yet not a word the urchin said,

---

[1] 'Butt'rings': No recorded sense of *butter* as a verb or *buttering* as a gerund seems intended in this context; nor has a search by archivists of the Bath Museum found reference to a coffee house or other resort of that name.

[2] Pallas Athena, goddess of wisdom, or 'wit', and therefore the antagonist of Venus, goddess of love and beauty.

[3] 'Raillied': rallied, teased, scoffed at (*OED*, s.v. 'railly' v. 1b, 2).

[4] Venus, the Roman name for the Greek goddess Aphrodite, who, according to Hesiod, sprang from the foam (*aphros*) of the sea near Cyprus or Cytheria.

[5] Bath, the fashionable spa.

[6] *i.e.* John Dalton, the poet: see the Introduction above, p. 74. Apollo, god of poetry, knows him; Athena (Minerva), goddess of wit, reads him willingly.

[7] 'Parnassus': a lofty mountain sacred to Apollo and the Muses.

But hid in Hebe's[8] lap his head.
At length the rising choler broke   35
From Venus' lips,—and thus she spoke.
   That poetry so cram'd with wit,
Minerva, shou'd your palate hit,
I wonder not, nor that some prudes
(For such there are above the clouds)   40
Shou'd wish the prize of beauty torn
From her they view with envious scorn.
Me poets never please, but when
Justice and truth direct their pen.
This Dalston—formerly I've known him;[9]   45
Henceforth for ever I disown him;
For Homer's wit shall I despise
In him who writes with Homer's eyes.[10]
A poem on the fairest fair
At Bath, and Betty's[11] name not there!   50
Hath not this poet seen those glances
In which my wicked urchin dances?
Nor that dear dimple, where he treats
Himself with all Arabia's sweets;
In whose soft down while he reposes   55
In vain the lilies bloom, or roses,
To tempt him from a sweeter bed
Of fairer white or livelier red?
Hath he not seen, when some kind gale
Has blown aside the cambric veil,[12]   60
That seat of paradise, where Jove
Might pamper his almighty love?
Our milky way less fair does shew:
There summer's seen 'twixt hills of snow.

---

[8] In Greek mythology the daughter of Zeus and Hera, Hebe was the handmaiden of the gods and associated with perpetual youth.

[9] No doubt only an amusing coincidence, but in 1734, some time after the likely date of this poem, Dalton joined the Countess of Hertford and her friend Lady Luxborough, both ten years his senior, in a flirtatious triangle, Dalton playing the role of Adonis, the beautiful youth with whom Aphrodite (Venus) fell in love. See Hughes, *Gentle Hertford*, p. 171.

[10] Homer was blind.

[11] For Betty Dalston (i.e. Dalton), presumably the poet's sister, see Introduction above, p. 74.

[12] 'the cambric veil': a fine linen handkerchief covering a lady's bosom, and removed in many scenes of HF's fiction: e.g. Lord Fellamar's attempt to ravish Sophia in *Tom Jones* (XV. v), in which he 'only disordered her Handkerchief, and with his rude Lips committed Violence on her lovely Neck' (p. 798).

From her lov'd voice whene'er she speaks,   65
What softness in each accent breaks!
And when her dimpled smiles arise,
What sweetness sparkles in her eyes!
Can I then bear, enrag'd she said,
Slights offer'd to my fav'rite maid,   70
The nymph, whom I decreed to be
The representative of me?
    The Goddess ceas'd—the Gods all bow'd,
Nor one the wicked bard avow'd,
Who, while in beauty's praise he writ,   75
Dar'd Beauty's Goddess to omit:
For now their godships recollected,
'Twas Venus' self he had neglected,
Who in her visits to this place
Had still worn Betty Dalston's face.   80

4

A DIALOGUE BETWEEN A BEAU'S
HEAD AND HIS HEELS (1730)

ON Tuesday 10 November 1730 John Watts (d. 1763), in the sixth and final volume of his *Musical Miscellany*, published an amusing song in ten stanzas entitled 'A DIALOGUE between a BEAU's Head and His Heels' and written 'By Mr. FIELDING' (pp. 170–3). Omitted from Fielding's *Miscellanies* (1743) and from Andrew Millar's edition of Fielding's *Works* (1762), it remained unnoticed until, in 1922, Helen Sard Hughes persuasively claimed it for the canon.[1]

The only other remotely possible candidate for authorship of the verse was one Timothy Fielding (d. 1739), an actor–dancer with the Drury Lane company who, when not performing on stage, divided his time between keeping a booth at Smithfield during Bartholomew Fair and keeping the Buffalo Head Tavern near Bloomsbury Square; he published nothing.[2] 'By Mr. Fielding', moreover, was the formula Watts used on the title-pages of all three of Fielding's 'regular' comedies that he had published, from the first of these in 1728 (*Love in Several Masques*) to this present year of 1730 (*The Temple Beau* and *The Coffee-House Politician*). It is also the formula by which authorship of these plays is designated in the advertisement of Watts's publications prefixed to the *Musical Miscellany*.[3] That Watts, furthermore, in 1730 was already well aware of Fielding's talent as a writer of lyrics is evident from his including, with the 'Beau's Head' in volume VI

[1] See Helen Sard Hughes, 'A Dialogue—Possibly by Henry Fielding', *PQ*, 1 (1922), pp. 49–55.
[2] On Timothy Fielding, see Hughes, 'A Dialogue', pp. 51–3; *London Stage*, pt. 2, pp. 985, 988; *Life*, pp. 86, 635 n. 72, 645–6 n. 303.
[3] In the advertisement, 'BOOKS *Printed for* J. WATTS', immediately preceding the text of Watts's *Musical Miscellany*, all five of HF's plays staged through the year 1730 are listed: *Tom Thumb. A Tragedy*, 2nd edn., *The Author's Farce and The Pleasures of the Town* (both published under the imprint of the 'mercury' J. Roberts); and the three five-act comedies: *Love in Several Masques*, *The Temple Beau*, and *The Coffee-House Politician: or, The Justice Caught in his own Trap*—like the 'Beau's Head', all three are announced as on their title-pages: 'Written by Mr. Fielding'. It is worth noting, considering that Watts's *Miscellany* was published on 10 November 1730, that HF's *Rape upon Rape*, which had opened at the Haymarket on 23 June 1730, was not staged under its new title, *The Coffee-House Politician*, until 4 December 1730 at Lincoln's Inn Fields.

of the *Musical Miscellany*, three other songs by Fielding: one from each of the three comedies.[4]

With these three comedies—as well as the popular innovative pieces *The Author's Farce* and *Tom Thumb* from the same period, which were 'Written by Scriblerus Secundus', and carry the imprint of 'J. Roberts', but were in fact published by Watts—Watts launched Fielding's career as dramatist; all told, he published twenty-three of the plays. Twice Fielding introduced Watts into his plays: in *Pasquin* (1736) Trapwit, when his Epilogue hasn't 'double Entendres enough in it', borrows all Watts's stock of plays to find more (Act III, p. 35); in *Eurydice Hiss'd* (1737), after witnessing the damning of the piece, '*John Watts*, | Who was this Morning eager for the Copy, | Slunk hasty from the Pit, and shook his Head' (p. 40). And in the *Miscellanies*, Fielding offered, in verse, a second glimpse of his publisher 'J—N W—TS at a PLAY':

> While Hisses, Groans, and Cat-calls thro' the Pit,
> Deplore the hapless Poet's want of Wit:
> *J—n W—ts*, from Silence bursting in a Rage,
> Cry'd, *Men are mad who write in such an Age.*
> *Not so*, reply'd his Friend, a sneering Blade,
> *The Poet's only dull, the Printer's mad.*
>
> (*Miscellanies* i, p. 65)

From time to time after the passage of the Licensing Act of 1737 ended Fielding's theatrical career, Watts issued 'nonce collections' of nineteen of the twenty-three plays, excluding *Tom Thumb* and *Eurydice Hiss'd* and the revised versions of *The Author's Farce* and *Old Debauchees*.[5]

As to when Fielding wrote the 'Beau's Head' and what prompted him to write it, there is no evidence. Sheridan Baker, citing the satire of John Rich's acrobatic harlequinades in Fielding's 'Cantos' (*c.*1729–1730), recalls the line spoken by his character Plutus: 'My Heels are much—much lighter than my Head' (3. 121)—a joke repeated by Fielding six years later when, ironically dedicating *Tumble-Down Dick* (1736) to 'John Lun' (Rich's stage name as harlequin), he wondered at the popular success of Rich's 'entertainments': 'whether owing to your Heels or your Head, I will not determine'. Baker also recalls Rich's role in Fielding's *Author's Farce*

---

[4] From *Love in Several Masques* (v. xiv) Watts took '*Ye Nymphs of* Britain, *to whose Eyes*'; from *The Temple Beau* (III), '*Vain*, Belinda, *are your Wiles*'; from *Rape upon Rape* (IV. vii), '*Let a Set of sober Asses*' (see, respectively, the *Musical Miscellany*, vi, pp. 152–3, 129–30, and 40–1 [the tune] 42–3 [the lyric]). For commentary and the music—the song from *Rape upon Rape* given under the play's revised title of *The Coffee-House Politician*—see, respectively, *Plays*, pp. 95 and 668–9, 669–71, and 482–4 and 703–4.

[5] For a succinct and graphic account of these publications, see Hugh Amory, *New Books by Fielding: An Exhibition of the Hyde Collection* (Cambridge, Mass., 1987), pp. 29–31.

(staged at the Haymarket on 30 March 1730), where in the 'Puppet-Show'
he is 'taken off' in the figure of silent 'Monsieur Pantomime', who, having
arrived in the underworld as a result of breaking his neck, cuts a caper
(*Plays*, pp. 262–3, 269). From these references—and from finding that, in
The Fashionable Lady: or, Harlequin's Opera, which opened at Lincoln's Inn
Fields on Thursday 2 April 1730, three days after *The Author's Farce*
opened at the Haymarket, Fielding's friend James Ralph had used for Air
XIX the same ballad-tune, 'Dear Catholick Brother', that Fielding chose for
the 'Beau's Head'[6]—Baker drew the following conclusion:

It seems likely that Fielding had intended the 'Beau's Head' song-and-dance to
accompany the appearance of Monsieur Pantomime, which remains dispropor-
tionately brief, but had then set it aside after he realized the virtual impossibility of
putting such an acrobatic one-man dialogue effectively on the stage. The best guess
for Fielding's writing of the 'Beau's Head' would thus be sometime in February or
March 1730, before his *Author's Farce* was performed on 30 March.[7]

As conjecture this is plausible, if not entirely persuasive; and there are
none better to rival it. If Fielding did write the 'Beau's Head' for the stage
only to find in production there was no place for it, he might well have
responded to Watts's advertisement in the *London Evening-Post* (6 June
1730): announcing that volumes III and IV of the *Musical Miscellany* were
'*Lately publish'd*'. Watts added a note informing readers that, because the
fifth and sixth volumes were 'in the Press, and in great Forewardness, all
Gentlemen and Ladies who are willing to contribute any Choice Songs, are
desired to send them as soon as possible'. Presumably, his sixth volume
required copy to fill it out. That Fielding may have answered this call could
account for the 'Beau's Head' location in the volume: after the three songs
from Fielding's comedies and towards the end of the collection.[8] Despite
the 'great Forewardness' with which the two last volumes were proceeding
through Watts's presses in early June, it would be five months before they
were published. In the *London Evening-Post* of Saturday 31 October 1730 he
announced, somewhat optimistically, '*Next week will be publish'd*' volumes
V and VI. On Tuesday 10 November the paper announced they were '*This
Day . . . publish'd*'.

---

[6] The tune, however, was a favourite of the period and could be heard in several other recent ballad
operas: e.g. Thomas Walker, *The Quaker's Opera* (1728), Air XVII; Charles Johnson, *The Village Opera*
(1729), Air XXXII; Edward Phillips, *The Chambermaid* (1730), Air XVI. Baker credited Edgar V. Roberts
for this information.

[7] Draft of Baker's Introduction to the 'Beau's Head'.

[8] For the location in volume VI of the songs from HF's comedies, see above, n. 4. The 'Beau's Head'
occupies pp. 170–3 of the 208 pages in the volume; it is the seventy-sixth of ninety-two songs.

The title-page of volume VI, in which Fielding's song 'A DIALOGUE between a BEAU's Head and his Heels' appears, reads as follows:

THE MUSICAL | MISCELLANY; | *Being a* COLLECTION *of* | CHOICE SONGS, | AND | LYRIC POEMS: | *With the* BASSES *to each* TUNE, *and* | *Transpos'd for the* FLUTE. | By the most Eminent MASTERS. | [rule] | [ornament] | [rule] | VOLUME *the* SIXTH. | [rule] | LONDON: | *Printed by and for* JOHN WATTS, *at the* Printing- | Office *in* Wild-Court *near* Lincoln's-Inn Fields. | [rule] | M DCC XXXI.

Though the title-page gives the year of publication as 1731, the practice among booksellers of the period was to forward-date works not ready for publication before November.[9] As indicated above, volumes V and VI of Watts's *Musical Miscellany* were published on 10 November 1730.

That balladeers and the musical public at large found the 'Beau's Head' appealing is suggested by its subsequent appearance in two unauthorized, and somewhat altered, reprints. The version appearing among 'Poetical Essays' in *The Gentleman's Magazine* for November 1732 omits the attribution to Fielding and the name of the tune, as well as changing the scene from St James's Coffee House and environs to Lucas's Coffee House and having the Beau, instead of walking 'up *Constitution*', walking 'up to the Bason' (*GM*, ii, p. 1074). About 1740 at York, one John Jackson—in *The Vocal Medley. Part the Second. Being a Collection of 241 of the Most Celebrated English and Scots Songs*[10]—also reprints Fielding's song, following the changes in *The Gentleman's Magazine* (it does, however, restore Fielding's quatrains) and unhelpfully giving the tune as 'Come take up, &c.', the opening words of the lyrics.

---

[9] See W. B. Todd, 'On the Use of Advertisements in Bibliographical Studies', in O. M. Brack, Jr., and W. Barnes (eds.), *Bibliographical and Textual Criticism* (Chicago, 1969), pp. 160–1.

[10] Baker credited Edgar V. Roberts with finding HF's song in Jackson's *Vocal Medley*; his text was BL, copy 1078.e.35, which tentatively gives 1740 as the date.

A DIALOGUE *between a* BEAU'S HEAD *and his* HEELS, *taken from their Mouths as they were spoke at St.* James's *Coffee-House.*[1]

By Mr FIELDING

To the Tune of, *Dear Catholick Brother.*[2]

[1] Situated on the west side of St James's Street near the Palace, the St James's Coffee House looked down Pall Mall. Throughout the century it was a favourite resort of prominent Whigs, such as Addison and Steele, and of the Palace Guards. (See B. Lillywhite, *London Coffee Houses* [London, 1963], No. 1131, and Phillips, *Mid-Georgian London*, pp. 66–7 and fig. 74.) HF mentions it in the Prolegomena to *The Covent-Garden Tragedy* (1732); Wilson in *Joseph Andrews* (III. iii, p. 205) and Booth in *Amelia* (V. i, p. 195) both take coffee there.

[2] An Irish ballad first published in Thomas D'Urfey's *Wit and Mirth; or, Pills to Purge Melancholy* (1714), v. 177; also BL, G. 307, sheet 146, and H. 1601, sheet 134. Sheila welcomes home her scarred lover: 'Dear Catholick Brother, are you come from the Wars[?]' See also the Introduction above, p. 80 and n. 6.

[3] Cf. *OED*, s.v. 'dog' sb. 3: a worthless, cowardly fellow.

[4] Constitution Hill: the direct road from the western end of St James's Park (now the Queen Victoria

slen - der Re - pair,   We   beg that your Ho - nor wou'd

go   in   a   Chair.[5]   Fa,—   la,   la,   la, &c.

HEAD.

Ye indolent Dogs! do you dare to refuse
So little a Walk, in a new Pair of Shoes?
My Legs too, methinks, might have gratefully gone,
Since a new Pair of Calves I this Morning put on.[6]
Fa, la, la, la, &c.

HEELS.

Do you call us ungrateful? the Favours you prize,
Were design'd not to gratify us, but your Eyes;
Is the Footman oblig'd to his Lordship, or Grace,
Who, to feed his own Pride, has equipp'd him with Lace?
We think we have very good Cause to complain,

Memorial before Buckingham Palace) to Hyde Park Corner and the entry to the park. In *Amelia* (v. v) Captain Booth and Colonel Bath proceed from St James's up '*Constitution-Hill* to *Hyde-Park*' (p. 209), where they have their duel.

⁵ A sedan chair, a vehicle for hire.

⁶ Thin calves are invariably features of HF's characterization of 'beaus': cf. *Joseph Andrews* (III. ii), where he warns his 'fair Countrywomen' not to match themselves 'with the spindle-shanked Beaus and Petit Maîtres of the Age' (p. 194); and his later description (IV. ix) of Beau Didapper: 'The Shape of his Body and Legs none of the best; for he had very narrow Shoulders, and no Calf' (p. 312). Shamela, referring to Booby, her husband, regrets having to go to bed 'to a spindle-shanked young Squire' (below, p. 191, line 24 and n. 136). The beau in the song appears to have followed the example of Pope, of whom Johnson reports: 'His legs were so slender that he enlarged their bulk with three pair of stockings' ('Life of Pope', in *Lives of the English Poets*, ed. George Birkbeck Hill [Oxford, 1905], iii, p. 197).

That you are exalted without any Brain;
As our Merits are equal, we justly may plead
A Title[7] sometimes to walk on our Head.
       Fa, la, la, la, &c.

HEAD

Very fine! at this rate all the Beaus in the Town
Wou'd fairly, like Tumblers, be turn'd up-side down;
But when I am dissected, to shew you my Brains,
May all the World cry—He's a Fool for his Pains!
       Fa, la, la, la, &c.

But if I may argue; Pray, Sir, who takes Snuff,
Who Ogles, who Smiles? I think Titles enough;
Can you Sing, can you Laugh, can you Speak, can you See?
Or what can you do, silly Dogs, without me?
       Fa, la, la, la, &c.

And to shew you how much your Ambition's my Scoff,
When next you rebel, I'll e'en shake you off;
Tho' I stand not without you, I'm sure I can sit,
In Parliament too, tho' bereft of my Feet.
       Fa, la, la, la, &c.

HEELS

Do you twit us with that? You have Reason, we hear:
We danc'd with the Wives, or you had not got there.
But to dash you at once, let us tell you, 'tis said
That some have fat there without any Head.
       Fa, la, la, la, &c.

HEAD

Gad's Curse! and that's true; so a Word in your Ear:
To oblige you at once,—Here, Boy, call a chair.
Let us henceforth together, like wise Men agree,

---

[7] 'plead a Title': in law, to litigate for a legal right or ownership.

I'll strive to set you off, you shall set off me.
   In the first Place, I'll sit very light on your Shoulder;
For, Nature revers'd, I grow lighter as older:
     Then you dance a Minuet, I'll smile my best;
    And do you cut a Caper, when I cut a Jest.[8]
        Fa, la, la, la, &c.

For the **FLUTE**

---

[8] Cf. 'if you have handsome Legs, cut Capers, or slide into the Minuet Step' (*Ovid's Art of Love*, below, p. 439).

5

AN EPISTLE TO MR. LYTTLETON (1733)

UNLIKE the 'Cantos', which is an early and fragmented draft of a more ambitious work (see above, pp. 28–70), the other manuscript found by Isobel Grundy among the papers of Lady Mary Wortley Montagu is a fair copy (with a few emendations) of a finished work.[1] Though for good and prudent reasons HF did not include the 'Epistle to Lyttleton'[2] with his other early poems in the *Miscellanies* (1743), he nevertheless took some pains with it; at 177 lines it is forty lines longer than 'Liberty', also addressed to Lyttelton, which is included in that collection. As Grundy suggests, Lady Mary Wortley Montagu may well have been 'the driving force behind'[3] the Epistle, as she had been with the 'Cantos'. Five years after slandering her in the *Miscellanies* (vol. iii) and *The Dunciad* of 1728, Pope again insulted her in his imitation of the *First Satire of the Second Book of Horace* (15 February 1733): 'From furious *Sappho* scarce a milder Fate, | P[o]x'd by her Love, or libell'd by her Hate' (lines 83–4).

Fielding at this time was at the peak of his career as dramatist at Drury Lane. *The Miser*, his adaptation of Molière's *L'Avare*, opened at the Theatre Royal to great applause on 17 February; the most successful of all his regular comedies, it would play twenty-three nights and bring him four lucrative benefits. The elation he must have felt at the success of the play was tempered, however, by his anger at Pope's affront to Lady Mary, which had been published two days earlier. By nature a passionate man and by birth a gentleman, he soon put aside thoughts of the theatre to retaliate: 'The injur,ᵈ Sappho,ˢ Wrongs to Verse provoke, | And bid me for a-while lay by the Sock' (lines 16–17). The theme of retribution declared at the beginning of the poem is heard again at the end:

> Yet Sapphoˢ Wrongs the Muse shall neere forget,
> Neere leave unpaid one Scruple of <Her> Debt,
> Till groveling in the Dirt thy Name shall lie,
> And Fools shall wonder whom they rais,ᵈ so high.   (lines 162–5)

---

[1] See 'New Verse by Henry Fielding,' *PMLA*, 87 (1972), pp. 213–45.
[2] HF invariably misspelled his friend Lyttelton's name by reversing the 'el'.   [3] Grundy, p. 340.

The poem concludes with a metaphorical vignette in which Pope is figured as an obnoxious 'little Curr' that 'barks, and snaps' at everyone, until 'the gen,^rous Mastiff' (Fielding himself), protecting his mistress, lifts the venomous creature in the air, shakes him, and 'throws him in the Kennel on his Back'. Unlike the 'Cantos', the 'Epistle to Lyttleton' is not so much a satire of Pope as it is a diatribe in verse: its purpose is to denounce the famous poet as a blackguard.

Fielding addressed the Epistle to George Lyttelton (1709–73) of Hagley Park, Worcester.[4] It was the first of his many tributes to Lyttelton, who had been his schoolmate at Eton (1719–24) and would remain his friend, and patron, for life: later in the 1730s Fielding dedicated the poem 'Liberty' to him, as he would also do *Tom Jones* (1749), his masterpiece. Besides being Fielding's friend, Lyttelton was in other ways an appropriate choice to receive the poem: he was himself a poet and recently, in *Advice to a Lady* (written in 1731 but published 10–12 March 1733[5]), had presented himself to the public as a man who understood women and valued their companion-ship. One of Fielding's themes in the Epistle is to assert, in his cousin's cause, the natural superiority of her sex: 'Nature with Beauty gave superiour Sence' (line 25). Lyttelton, to be sure, as Lady Mary plainly saw, was far from entertaining any such romantic notion. What she thought of his 'Advice' is clear from the couplet she inscribed on a copy of the poem: 'Be plain in Dress and sober in your Diet; | In short my Dearee, kiss me, and be quiet.'[6]

Lyttelton was also a close friend of Pope. How close they were is evident from Lyttelton's *The Progress of Love* (1732): Pope helped him revise the poem and to Pope he addressed the first of the four eclogues that comprise it. Fielding might well wonder how Lyttelton would receive this attack on Pope's character: 'Frown not, my Lyttelton, nor angry see | This Justice on thy Friend address,d to thee' (lines 52–3). He could, however, count on the fact that Lyttelton was not only a gentleman, but something of a prig with lofty ideals that did not permit the appreciation of satire. In the verse *Epistle to Pope*, written at Rome in 1730, Lyttelton relates his encounter with the shade of Virgil, who charges him to advise Pope to give up 'meaner' satire, 'the least attractive' of the muses (lines 55, 60). Friend though he was to Pope, Lyttelton could be expected to deplore the poet's abuse of a lady.

---

[4] On Lyttelton, see Rose Mary Davis, *The Good Lord Lyttelton: A Study in Eighteenth Century Politics and Culture* (Bethlehem, Pa., 1939).

[5] In *Essays and Poems* Grundy gives the date of publication as 12 March 1733, a Monday; earlier she cited publication in the *Universal Spectator* for Saturday 10 March ('New Verse by Henry Fielding', p. 240 nn. 1–2).

[6] *Essays and Poems*, p. 264 and Grundy, p. 308.

   As remarked above in the introduction to the 'Cantos', Fielding's opinion
of Pope's character would improve with time (p. 30); and even now, in
anger, he could acknowledge Pope's brilliance as a poet, confessing to
Lyttelton his admiration of works of the early period: *Windsor Forest, Eloisa
to Abelard*, and *The Rape of the Lock* (lines 58–61). The latter, though a
satire, was written when Pope's Muse was kinder—when his 'Satire glow,[d]
with no malicious Rage'. Fielding was himself a satirist of course, and
knowing Lyttelton's low opinion of the genre, he took the present
opportunity to argue at some length for its usefulness to society when
enlisted, without personal animus, in the cause of morality and justice:
'Satire, the Scourge of Vice, was sure design,[d] | Like Laws, to profit, not to
hurt Mankind' (lines 72–3). This was the same theme Pope had sounded in
the *Imitation of Horace*, in which, however, Fielding charged, he abandoned
the principles and purpose of the worthy genre he claimed to practise in
order to slander individuals.

   Unless Fielding read Lyttelton's *Advice to a Lady* shortly before it was
published he cannot have begun the Epistle before then as in the opening
paragraph he recalls lines from the conclusion of the poem (see below,
p. 90 n. 2). Certain parallels with Lady Mary and Lord Hervey's *Verses
Address'd to the Imitator of Horace*, published on 8 March, also point to a
period of composition in mid-March (see below, pp. 92–3, nn. 15, 18, 22).
This was a time, moreover, when, after the tenth performance of *The
Miser* on Saturday 17 March, the Theatre Royal closed for Passion Week,[7]
affording Fielding a respite from stage and green room.

   The MSS of the 'Epistle to Lyttelton' are bound in volume 81,
Harrowby MSS Trust, Sandon Hall, Stafford, fos. 57–8, 64–5. On the treatment of the MSS, see the Textual Note to the 'Cantos' (above, pp. 34–5).

---

[7] *Daily Post.*

An Epistle to Mr. Lyttleton occasioned by two
Lines in Mr. Pope's Paraphrase on the first
Satire of the 2d Book of Horace.

While thy Sweet Strains, dear Lyttleton, impart,
To matchless Beauty all the aids of art,
And teach the charming Virgin to devise
A stronger Claim than Cowper's Conquering Eyes;
While in thy flowing Verse such Strength is found,
That Swift might claim the Sense and Young the Sound.
~~O There~~ be the pleasing task to form the fair,
To join a Charmer's Soul with ~~the~~ ... air
To shew the unskill'd Maid the Charms that bind,
How Smiling Harvey captivates the Mind,
And Rickinson leads in triumph all Mankind.
To thee the Lover best shall Pleasures owe
Which uninstructed Beauty can't bestowe.
What they should prove, Coquettes and Prudes shall see;
And what she is, Dorinda read in thee.

The injur'd Sappho's wrongs to Verse provoke,
And bid me for awhile lay by the Sock
My Muse an unaccustom'd Path pursue,
A Path so nobly trod by Young and ...

Opening leaf, MS of 'An Epistle to Mr. Lyttleton'

An Epistle to Mr Lyttleton occasioned by two

Lines in Mr Pope,^{s} Paraphrase on the first

Satire of the 2^d Book of Horace.^{1}

While thy Sweet Strains, dear Lyttleton, impart,
To matchless Beauty all the Aids of Art,^{2}
And teach the charming Virgin to devise
A stronger Chain than Cowper^{s3} conqu,^{ring} Eyes;
While in thy flowing Verse such Strength is found,   5
That Swift might claim the Sence^4 and Young the Sound;^{5}
Thine be the pleasing Task to form the Fair,
To join a Chamber,^{s6} Soul with Shaftsb,ry,^{s} Air,^{7}

7] A *cancelled before* Thine *written over illegible word*

---

^{1} On HF's friendship with Lyttelton and Lyttelton's with Pope, see the Introduction (p. 87). Pope's *First Satire of the Second Book of Horace Imitated* was published on 15 February 1733. The 'two Lines' referred to in HF's title occur in a passage illustrating the natural fact that 'each Creature' has 'Its proper Pow'r to hurt'—bulls gore, asses kick, the infamous Judge Page hangs people, and so Lady Mary: 'From furious *Sappho* scarce a milder Fate, | P[o]x'd by her Love, or libell'd by her Hate' (lines 83–4).

^{2} In the opening paragraph of the poem, though the selection of contemporary figures chosen to illustrate his compliments is HF's own, the gist and phrasing of the passage recall lines from the conclusion of Lyttelton's *Advice to a Lady* (10–12 March 1732):

> Thus I, Belinda, would your charms improve,
> And form your heart to all the arts of love . . .
> For well you twist the secret chains that bind
> With gentle force the captivated mind . . . (lines 127–8, 131–2)

^{3} Henrietta, *née* de Auverquerque (d. 1747), married the second Earl of Cowper in 1732.

^{4} Jonathan Swift (1667–1745). This compliment contradicts the characterization of Swift in the 'Cantos' (1729–30), where HF obliged Lady Mary by satirizing him (as Ochistes) together with his associates among the Scriblerians (see Canto 3, line 17 n. 116). The compliment, however, more truly reflects HF's deep admiration of Swift, to whom, in the obituary published in *The True Patriot* (5 November 1745), he refers as 'A Genius who deserves to be ranked among the first whom the World ever saw' (p. 336). Nearer to the *Epistle*, Swift is probably the 'certain great Genius' whom HF extols in *Champion* (15 April 1740), p. 279 and n. 5.

^{5} Edward Young (1683–1765), to whom HF in the *Miscellanies* (1743) refers as the Muses' 'Darling' and for 'Excellence in Poetry' links him with Pope (see 'Of True Greatness' and 'An Essay on Conversation', *Miscellanies* i, pp. 26, 136). HF began complimenting Young and Pope together as early as 1729–30 in the untitled poem beginning 'The Queen of Beauty' (*Miscellanies* i, p. 78; for the date, see p. 80 n. 1); the pair also appear in *Champion* (10 January 1740, p. 119). On Young, see also below, n. 12.

^{6} Lady Mary (d. 1735), daughter of the second Earl of Berkeley and wife of Thomas Chambers. As here, in the *Epistle to Ellys* (1732) she is complimented in the company of the Countess of Shaftesbury and the Duchess of Richmond (see below, nn. 7 and 9).

^{7} Susanna Cooper, *née* Noel (d. 1758), wife of the fourth Earl of Shaftesbury, who, as first cousin to James Harris of Salisbury, was on friendly terms with HF. Later, in his poem 'Of Good Nature' (1743), '*Shaftsb'ry*'s Air' complements the Duchess of Richmond's snow-white breast (*Miscellanies* i. 35). The Countess returned HF's compliments by subscribing to two sets of the *Miscellanies* (1743) on royal paper. In his *Epistle to Ellys* (1732), as here, HF paid similar compliments to Shaftesbury, Chambers, Richmond,

To shew the unskill,[d] the Charms that bind,
How smiling Harvey[8] captivates the Mind,   10
And Richmond[9] leads in Triumph all Mankind.
To thee, the Lover blest shall Pleasures owe
Which uninstructed Beauty can[f] bestowe.
What they should prove, Coquettes and Prudes shall see;
And what She is, Dorinda[10] read, in thee.   15

   The injur,[d] Sappho,[s] Wrongs to Verse provoke,
And bid me for a-while lay by the Sock,[11]
My Muse an unaccustom,[d] Path pursue,
A Path so nobly trod by Young and you.[12]

   9–11] *triplet not marked by bracket in margin*

and Lady Mary. See also the *Vernoniad* (1741) in *Champion*, p. 575 n. 5, and HF's own n. [49], in which Shaftesbury is 'ONE *of the* GRACES'.

[8] Harvey: Mary, *née* Leppel (1700–68), wife of John (1696–1743), Lord Hervey, Baron Ickworth. This compliment is the only reference to Lady Hervey in HF's writings, where her husband, however—a favourite of Queen Caroline and Sir Robert Walpole—figures several times and is invariably ridiculed: as John the groom in *The Grub-Street Opera* (1731) and later as 'Miss Fanny' in the dedication to *Shamela* (1741) and as Beau Didapper in *Joseph Andrews* (1742). The compliment to Hervey's pretty wife may have been HF's oblique way of acknowledging Lady Mary's friendship with her husband, a fellow victim of Pope's satire. In his imitation of Horace, Pope first refers to Hervey—an effeminate courtier and poetaster—by the sobriquet HF adopted in *Shamela*: 'The Lines are weak, another's pleas'd to say, | Lord Fanny spins a thousand such a Day' (lines 5–6). Hervey and Lady Mary immediately retaliated for these insults, collaborating on the venomous *Verses Address'd to the Imitator of the First Satire of the Second Book of Horace*, published 8 March 1733, just three weeks after Pope's offending satire appeared. For a full discussion of these events, see Isobel Grundy, '*Verses Address'd to the Imitator of Horace*: A Skirmish between Pope and Some Persons of Rank and Fortune', *Studies in Bibliography*, 30 (1977), pp. 96–119.

[9] Sarah, *née* Cadogan, Duchess of Richmond (1706–51). Her husband, Charles Lennox (1701–50), the second Duke, was HF's patron, to whom he had recently dedicated his comedy *The Miser* (staged at Drury Lane on 17 February; published on 13 March 1733), as he would also do the poem 'Of Good Nature', included in the *Miscellanies* (1743). In the *Epistle to Ellys* (1732) HF anticipated the compliments paid here to the Duchess (and her husband), the Countess of Shaftesbury, Lady Mary Chambers, and his cousin Lady Mary (see below, pp. 687–8). In 'Of Good Nature' she appears again with Shaftesbury, and in 'The Queen of Beauty' she is the most beautiful woman at court (*Miscellanies* i, pp. 35, 79). The Duchess repaid these favours by subscribing to the *Miscellanies*, six copies on royal paper.

[10] As revealed in a footnote to the *Epistle to Ellys* (see below, p. 687), Dorinda is HF's name for a certain 'Miss D. W.', whom he appears to have courted at this time earnestly but in vain: '(Too lovely Nymph! and O! too much belov'd!)'. Here she replaces Belinda, the recipient of Lyttelton's *Advice to a Lady*. On this brief and disappointing love affair, see *Life*, pp. 161–2.

[11] The theatrical season of 1732–3 marked the acme of HF's career as a comic dramatist. As the house playwright at Drury Lane, the Theatre Royal, he produced no fewer than six new comedies, the series culminating with the opening of *The Miser* on Saturday 17 February, just two days after the publication of Pope's imitation of Horace, with its infamous 'two lines' insulting Lady Mary under the name of 'Sappho'.

[12] Grundy, citing an article by John Wilson Croker in the *Quarterly Review*, 78 (1846), p. 235, notes that Lyttelton 'is said to have modeled' *Advice to a Lady* on Young's *Universal Passion* (1725–8), Satires V–VI ('On Women'). Lyttelton's biographer, however, is sceptical, commenting that 'satire was uncongenial to Lyttelton's temperament' and that the title of his poem 'indicates that he intended to counsel and not reprove' (Rose Mary Davis, *The Good Lord Lyttelton* (Bethlehem, Pa., 1939), p. 96 n. 11).

Man claims o̅er Woman, by o̅erbearing Might,   20
A Pow,r which Nature never meant his Right.
If partial, She to either Sex inclin,ᵈ,
With partial Care, She form,ᵈ the female Mind.
To greater Wisdom Men make false Pretence
Nature with Beauty gave superiour Sence.   25
'Tis hard Antiquity,ˢ high Hill to climb,
And thence survey the vast Abyss of Time.
Where thousand Trophies to the Sex are seen,
From the Assyrian to the Russian Queen.¹³
Speak, Sappho, for thy Sex, assert it,ˢ Sway   30
And Man, proud Man, shall listen and obey.¹⁴
Shall blush, unless so left so lost by Shame
As he who durst assassinate thy Fame.¹⁵
Could not thy Sex, thy Birth, thy Wit, thy Eyes,
All guard thee¹⁶ from the cruel Sland'rer,ˢ Lies?   35
Eyes! Which like, Marius,¹⁷ thine, could Fate forbid
And do with Sweetness what their Fierceness did.
Say, Wretch, why should her Charms thy Anger move?
Too ugly thou! too impotent for Love!¹⁸
'Twere capital to suffer thy Embrace,   40
For thou art surely not of human Race.

21] , in Pow,r *written over* e

---

¹³ Semiramis (*c.*800 BC), the legendary warrior queen of Assyria; Catherine I (1683–1727), wife of Peter the Great, reigned after his death as Empress of Russia from 1724 to 1727.

¹⁴ Grundy suggests that HF may have read in manuscript Lady Mary's 'more feminist poems', citing as an apt example the *Epistle from Mrs. Y[onge] to her Husband* (1724), written to protest the injustice of penalties inflicted lawfully on an unfaithful wife by her equally unfaithful husband. Less likely is an alternative suggestion that HF had in mind *Verses to the Imitator of Horace* (8 March 1733), the purpose of which is to vilify Pope rather than to assert the superiority of women.

¹⁵ Cf. *Verses to the Imitator of Horace* in reference to Pope: 'whilst with Coward Hand you stab a Name, | And try at least t'assassinate our Fame' (lines 105–6).

¹⁶ Cf. HF's *Of True Greatness* (1741): 'Beauty betrays the Mistress it should guard' (*Miscellanies* i, p. 22, line 87). Lady Mary's 'Wit' and her 'Eyes' are featured in HF's frequent compliments to her, a trope first found in the Dedication to *Love in Several Masques* (1728): 'your Judgment keeps Pace with your Eye'. Her 'sparkling Wit' in 'The Queen of Beauty' (line 17) and 'Euthalia' (line 14) (*Miscellanies* i, pp. 78, 82); her 'radiant Eye' in the *Epistle to Ellys* (see below, p. 688). Pope before they fell out was dazzled by her 'eyes' (Twickenham edn., vi, pp. 158, 225, 236).

¹⁷ Gaius Marius (157–86 BC), Roman general. Defeated by Sulla at the end of a brilliant career he was condemned to death; but the trooper who was sent to strike off his head was awestruck at the fire of his eyes and fled, crying, 'I cannot kill Gaius Marius' (Plutarch's *Life of Marius*, ch. xxxix).

¹⁸ Cf. *Verses to the Imitator of Horace*: 'But how should'st thou by Beauty's Force be mov'd, | No more for loving made, than to be lov'd?' (lines 48–9). HF's insults—Pope is ugly, impotent, subhuman, satanic, a slanderer who murders reputations—were commonplace among the pamphleteers, but, in addition to the lines quoted, cf. lines 11–15, 54–9, 103–12.

An evil Sprite, like Satan, sent to tell
Those Lies on Earth, thy Brother spreads in Hell

[fo. 58]

Sworn Foe to Beauty: Yet, thy Form believe,
Thou hast no Fruit to tempt a Second Eve.[19]   45
Hard, and unequal are our Laws that give
Death to the Thief and let the Sland'rer live.
Yet draw not thou Advantage from that Plea,
Nor think thou canst retort that Name on me.
The Ax the Murd'rer lifts we justly dread   50
But praise that falling on the Murd,rer,ˢ Head.
Frown not, my Lyttleton, nor angry see
This Justice on thy Friend address,ᵈ to thee.[20]
To thee! Whose am,ʳᵒᵘˢ Soul was form,ᵈ to prove
All the dear Softness of a tender Love.[21]   55
What Man but feels the Wrongs to Beauty done!
Cowards themselves can Scarce look patient on.[22]
I too with thee and with the World admire
The Bard, in Windsor Groves who strung his Lyre.
When Eloise, when Fermor grac,ᵈ his Page   60
When Satire glow,ᵈ with no malicious Rage.[23]
Eēre Envy and Ingratitude broke forth

48] n *in* not *written over illegible letters*   49] on *interlined above cancelled* from

[19] In 1719 Thomas Burnet, later a friend of HF's, wrote a set of witty verses complimenting Lady Mary on her beauty and wit. The unscrupulous bookseller Edmund Curll acquired a copy and in March 1720 published it as Pope's under the title 'The Second Eve'. Though widely accepted as his, Lady Mary was not taken in; in her own copy she correctly assigned it to Burnet. The allusion nevertheless serves HF's purpose in context, where Pope is called 'An evil Sprite, like Satan' (line 42). (See Grundy's note to line 45, citing Robert Halsband, *The Life of Lady Mary Wortley Montagu*, (Oxford, 1956), pp. 99–100; and Twickenham edn., vi, p. 423.)

[20] On Lyttelton's friendship with Pope, see Introduction (p. 87).

[21] Lyttelton proved his amorous soul in a series of lyrics—odes, eclogues, elegies—addressed to Delia (Anne Pitt) from 1729 to 1735, the most notable being *The Progress of Love* (1732), in which he was assisted by Pope. Under the name of Belinda, Miss Pitt, as noted above, was also Belinda in *Advice to a Lady* (1733). (See Davis, *The Good Lord Lyttelton*, pp. 94–100.)

[22] Grundy was tempted to see in this line HF's opinion of Lord Hervey, who, though he personally had reason enough to attack Pope, collaborated with Lady Mary in *Verses to the Imitator of Horace*. For HF's ridicule of Hervey, see above, n. 8.

[23] In Canto 2, lines 15–18, HF had earlier exempted *Windsor Forest* (1713) and *Eloisa to Abelard* (1717) from his otherwise general deprecation of Pope's poetry. Here he also approves *The Rape of the Lock* (1712–17) for the genial, elegant way in which Pope makes fun of Arabella Fermor, the original of Belinda. Commenting on HF's choice of verb in the phrase 'When Satire glow'd', Grundy also detects a reference to a note in the *Dunciad* Variorum (ii. 175), where Scriblerus prefers 'glow'—'this *beautiful word*'—to 'burn', supporting the emendation with seven lines from Pope's *Iliad*. Not wishing to grow 'too luxuriant in examples', Scriblerus had reason to stop at only seven lines: the Chadwyck-Healey Database lists no fewer than fifty instances of 'glow' in Pope's *Iliad*; and forty-four more in his *Odyssey*.

And the bad Man eclips,^d the Poet,^s Worth.
But oh! can Homer,^s Fire, can Virgil^s Art,
Ballance the Horrours of an evil Heart.   65

[fo. 58ᵛ]

Can Wit for wild Barbarity attone?
What Swift has writ for half what E——[24] has done?
Me, the Benevolence that joys to please,
The Heart that triumphs in another^s Ease,[25]
The more one Action of a Wade[26] delights   70
Than all that Poultney speaks, or St John writes.[27]

  Satire, the Scourge of Vice, was sure design,^d
Like Laws, to profit, not to hurt Mankind.[28]
Nay gentler and more friendly is it^s Course.
It cures you by Persuasion, not by Force.   75
Laws, while the bad they slay, the good defend,
But Satire teaches ev,ⁿ the bad to mend.
The Poet, when Vice horrible he draws,
Prevents, not executes the Force of Laws.
But wanton Wit that only seeks to scar,   80

68] joys *written after cancelled* glad

---

[24] Not identified.

[25] This couplet is the earliest of many passages in HF's works in which he defines 'good nature', the distinguishing concept of his moral system. Cf. the poem 'Of Good-Nature' (1743), where he calls it 'the glorious Lust of doing Good'; 'The Heart that finds it Happiness to please, | Can feel another's Pain, and taste his Ease' (*Miscellanies* i, p. 31, lines 24–6). Cf. also HF's essay in *Champion* (27 March 1740, pp. 251–5). For discussion of the concept, see Battestin, *Fielding's Art*, and Miller, *Essays*.

[26] General George Wade (1673–1748). In 1715 Wade quelled the Jacobites in Bath, which he later (1722–48) represented in Parliament; from 1724 to 1740 he commanded the Army in Scotland and improved the system of roads there. HF greatly admired him. On the report of Wade's death, he commented in *The Jacobite's Journal*, No. 16 (19 March 1748): 'He was . . . in private Life, a Gentleman of the highest Honour, Humanity and Generosity, and hath done more good and benevolent Actions than this whole Paper can contain' (p. 463; italics reversed).

[27] William Pulteney (1684–1764). During Walpole's long tenure as Prime Minister, he was leader of the Opposition in the House of Commons. On Henry St John (1678–1751), first Viscount Bolingbroke, who with Pulteney in 1726 founded the anti-ministerial journal *The Craftsman*, see above, 'Cantos', p. 50 n. 56. HF's contemptuous reference to the two leaders of the anti-ministerial party is a clear indication that at the time he wrote these verses neither he nor Lyttelton were ready, politically, to turn against Walpole. A year later, as the present editor has argued in *New Essays*, HF would find himself writing for *The Craftsman*, and in 1735 Lyttelton would become a leader of the so-called Boy Patriots, who harassed Walpole in opposition during the last seven years of his ministry.

[28] Cf. 'Of True Greatness' (1741), where HF reproves Alexander the Great, Pope's namesake: 'Virtue' had 'Taught thee to save, and not to slay Mankind' (*Miscellanies* i, p. 21, lines 65–6). In developing an analogy between the beneficent purposes of 'Satire' and 'Laws', HF follows Pope, who framed the *Imitation of Horace* (*Satires*, II. i) as a dialogue between himself and William Fortescue, an eminent attorney, and, rejecting the name of slanderer or libeller, defends the satirist as the champion and friend of Virtue: 'Hear this, and tremble! you, who 'scape the Laws' (line 118).

Is not the Sword of Justice but of War.
It shocks me when I think, that what should raise
The Horrour of Mankind, still meets their Praise.
That Man, mistaking, Honour should afford
To the great Slandrer,ˢ Pen or Conq,ror,ˢ Sword!   85
To Philipˢ Son²⁹ behold the Columns rise,
While by his Arms, the World half ravag,ᵈ lies.
Thee too we,ᵛᵉ read amid the Rolls of Fame
While bleeding Reputations cursᵈ thy Name.

[fo. 64]

Yet know with just Contempt, the wiser few   90
The Poetˢ Bayes and Victorˢ Lawrels view
Take then the Praise (if any Praise it be)
That much severer Wounds are felt from thee:
The Body hurt soon dies, or heals again;
Maim,ᵈ Reputations live and live in Pain.³⁰   95
What but the Soul of Rancour and of Spite
Could unprovok,ᵈ unhurt thy Pen incite?
Could bid thee the unhappy Wretch defame,
And drag him from Obscurity to Shame?³¹
What hurts it thee that meaner Bards are read   100
Thy Stores encrease not from their little Bread.
Do others Sowrer Fates make thine more sweet?
Canst thou not feast while any others eat?
   Is this the Muse that Laws and Pow,ʳ defies!
This great Domitian! this sworn Foe to Flies!³²   105

95] P *in* Pain *written over illegible letter*   101] *. replacing cancelled* ?

²⁹ Alexander the Great (356–323 BC), son of Philip II of Macedon. In HF's 'Of True Greatness' (lines 59–98) he is the prime example of false greatness.
³⁰ Elsewhere, as in his essay on the subject in *The Champion* (6 March 1740), HF also likens the slanderer's (or libeller's) pen to a murderer's sword. In the Preface to the *Miscellanies* (1743): 'I look on the Practice of stabbing a Man's Character in the Dark, to be as base and as barbarous as that of stabbing him with a Poignard in the same Manner' (p. 14). Indeed, in *Tom Jones* (XI. i) as here, the pen is worse: 'For Slander is a more cruel Weapon than a Sword, as the Wounds which the former gives are always incurable' (p. 567). See also below, lines 133–5.
³¹ In 'A Letter to the Publisher' prefixed to *The Dunciad* Variorum (1729) Pope, under the name 'William Cleland', addressed this complaint, anticipating the answer he gives in the *Imitation of Horace* (*Satires*, II. i) to William Fortescue, that the satirist alone can punish vices that escape the laws : 'The first objection I have heard made to the Poem is, that the persons are too obscure for Satyre. . . . On the contrary, obscurity renders them more dangerous, as less thought of: Law can pronounce judgment only on open Facts, Morality alone can pass censure on Intentions of mischief; so that for secret calumny or the arrow flying in the dark, there is no publick punishment left, but what a good writer inflicts' (p. 14).
³² Domitian, Roman emperor (AD 81–96). Domitian is said to have amused himself by catching flies and stabbing them with a sharpened stylus (Suetonius, *The Lives of the Twelve Caesars*, trans. J. C. Rolfe, 2 vols. [Cambridge, Mass., 1920], ii. 345).

That Nature,ˢ worst Productions can deform;
And rake the Kennels³³ to tread out the Worm[!]
   Yet not confin,ᵈ to such inferiour Game,
Thy Muse has dar,ᵈ to take a higher Aim.
Has dar,ᵈ all fixt Distinction to annul   110
'Twixt high and low, the witty and the dul[l]
For thou alike hast bent thy little Rage,
Against the Shame and Glory of thy Age.

                                                   [fo. 64ᵛ]

Few 'mongst the worst are with no Virtues blest,
As few are free from Vices 'mongst the best.   115
Thou too dishonest, or too void of Art,
To the bad Head still join'st the vicious Heart.
As Florimel³⁴ to her enchanting Eyes
Complexion, Teeth and Brows and Shape supplies,
By Nature of a single Charm possest   120
Complete she shines, and owes to Art the rest,
So can thy Spite to Imperfection add,
And shew Men from one Speck completely bad.
Why, when thou lashest Tibbald,ˢ lifeless Lays,
Dost thou not give the solid Critick Praise?³⁵   125

106] ; *replacing cancelled* ?
107] [!] *binding obscures edge of page; exclamation point is consistent with punctuation of lines 104 and 105 in this same paragraph*
111] [l] *in* dul[l] *binding obscures edge of page*

---

³³ 'Kennels': gutters in the streets.
³⁴ In Spenser's *Faerie Queene* (III. viii. 5–8) a witch creates by her art a counterfeit image of the fair Florimell (the type of perfect virtue in woman) so as to disguise the wicked purposes of a devil who impersonates her.
³⁵ Lewis Theobald (1688–1744), editor, translator, playwright, and in 1730 Walpole's unsuccessful candidate for the poet laureateship. In *Shakespeare Restored* (1726) Theobald had exposed the faults of Pope's edition of Shakespeare (1725), and for his trouble was elevated to the throne of Dulness in *The Dunciad* (1728–9). When HF penned the compliments to him here (lines 124–31), Theobald was about to publish his own edition of Shakespeare (1733), to which HF subscribed. This rare gesture, together with these compliments and the epilogue HF had earlier contributed to Theobald's opera *Orestes* (see below, pp. 99–106), appear to define a brief interlude of amity between the two men. In HF's poem 'Advice to the Nymphs of New S[aru]m' (1730) the thought that 'T——b—ld shall blaze with Wit, sweet *Pope* be dull' (*Miscellanies* i, p. 69) is one of a series of impossibilities; and in the same period Theobald is mocked as Don Tragedio in *The Author's Farce* (1730; Act III), while in *The Tragedy of Tragedies* (1731) his bombast tragedy *The Persian Princess* is ridiculed. HF would resume his mockery of Theobald's entertainments in *Tumble-Down Dick* (1736), *The Champion* (25 March 1740), and *Shamela* (see below, p. 181 n. 110). His incompetence as a translator of Aristophanes is scored in HF's Preface to *Plutus* (see below, p. 258). And in *A Journey from This World to the Next* (1743; I. viii; *Miscellanies* ii, p. 40) and *The True Patriot*, No. 16 (11–18 February 1746), HF's present praise of Theobald as a restorer of Shakespeare has turned to sarcasm directed at his arrogance and pedantry as Shakespeare's editor.

His Name with Shakespeare,ˢ shall to Ages so[ar]
When thou shalt jingle in our Ears no more
Shakespeare by him restor,ᵈ again we see
Recover,ᵈ of the Wounds he bore from thee.
And sure much brighter must his Merit shine   130
Who gives us Sha[kes]peare's Works, than his who thine.
    Of Truth regardless, studious to abuse
The Knight of Post³⁶ is gentler than thy Muse
Less him who swears away my Life I blame
Than him who falsely writes away my Fame   135
Surer the Shield of Innocence repels
The Wounds his Oath, than those thy Slander deals

_____
                                                        [fo. 65]

Pity m[a]y oft a Jury,ˢ Verdict guide;
The World is still on the Accuserˢ Side.   \
Say, against Chandois³⁷ what thy Fury arm,ᵈ,   140
Was it what any other Breast had charm,ᵈ!
Did thy malicious Soul with Envy burst?
And did his Virtue make thy Vice more curst
Thy Darts when thrown at any noble Head,
Still fly where Honour, Virtue, Learning lead.   145
But shew me, thou, that wouldst support the Laws,
A single Arrow drawn in Virtue,ˢ Cause.³⁸
Shew me the Man above the Laws accus,ᵈ
The lawless Pow,ʳ which Laws defend abusᵈ

_____

126] [ar] *in* so[ar] *ditto. Grundy's conjecture, plausibly completing the rhyme (soar/more)*
[128] ~~For sure must brighter must~~ *false start of line 128 cancelled*
131] [kes] *MS reads* Shapeare's
133] gentler *follows cancelled* harmless
138] [a] *in* m[a]y *MS reads* my

_____

³⁶ 'Knight of [the] Post': a perjurer; one who gets his living by giving false evidence (*OED*). With this passage, cf. above, n. 30.

³⁷ James Brydges (1673–1744), first Duke of Chandos, a wealthy man and a liberal patron of the arts. Soon after the publication of Pope's *Epistle to Burlington* (13 December 1731) it was widely believed that he meant to satirize Chandos in the figure of Timon, an insult particularly egregious, it was said, because Chandos was Pope's friend and patron. Pope denied these charges, which Chandos himself never believed, and modern scholarship has proved them false (see the Twickenham edn., III. ii, pp. xxvi–xxx, 170–4). HF here, however, and Lady Mary in *Verses to the Imitator of Horace* (*Essays and Poems*, p. 267 and nn. 36 ff.), continued to accept the slander as fact.

³⁸ In the *Imitation of Horace* Pope presents himself as the champion of moral law—'arm'd for *Virtue* when I point the Pen' (line 105)—and he chose as his motto a line from Horace (II. i. 70): 'uni aequus Virtuti atque eius amicis', which he rendered 'To VIRTUE ONLY and HER FRIENDS, A FRIEND' (line 121). See also above, n. 28.

No, it is thine the little Wretch to hurt   150
Or else at virtuous Greatness throw thy Dirt.
Beauty, which still the Sword of War restrains,
Leads the Subduers of the World in Chains
In smiling Triumph governing at Will,
The Poet,ˢ Wit and Politician,ˢ Skill   155
From thy Attacks alone is insecure,
And must in comm<on> with the World endure.
    Go on, enjoy the Triumphs of thy Spite,
And curse thy Self, and curse the World, and write.
The great Reward of all thy Labours bear,   160
To be both fear,ᵈ and hated by the Fair.

[fo. 65ᵛ]

Yet Sapphoˢ Wrongs the Muse shall ne͞ere forget,
Ne͞ere leave unpaid one Scruple of <Her> Debt,
Till groveling in the Dirt thy Name shall lie,
And Fools shall wonder whom they rais,ᵈ so high.   165

    Thus runs some little Curr along the Streets
And barks, and snaps at ev,ʳʸ one he meets.
Too much despis,ᵈ to find or Friends or Foes,
At all alike it,ˢ little Venom throws.
No Looks, no Words, no Threats itˢ Anger stir;   170
Only incens,ᵈ because it is a Curr.
But if the gen,ʳᵒᵘˢ Mastiff chance to stray
Waiting his lovely Mʳˢ Steps that Way
Her to attempt should the curs,ᵈ Urchin dare,
Aloft the Mastiff lifts him in the Air;³⁹   175
Awhile he shakes him for his bold Attack
Then throws him in the Kennel on his Back.

157] <on> *MS reads* comm *with final letters illegible*
163] Her *written over illegible word*
169] it,ˢ *written over* his
177] *A bold stroke of the pen, spaced under* on his Back, *marks the end of the poem*

³⁹ Cf. Canto 2, lines 229–43, where Ochistes (Swift) emulates Gulliver, lifting Codrus (Pope), 'the Lilliputian Bard', in the air and shaking him.

EPILOGUES AND PROLOGUE

6

EPILOGUE TO THEOBALD'S *ORESTES:*

A DRAMATIC OPERA (1731)

AFTER Fielding's extraordinary success with *The Author's Farce* and *Tom Thumb* in the spring of 1730, when the new season began in September he was still on the theatrical fringe at the Little Haymarket with a troupe that rented the theatre night by night.[1] Opening on 18 September with Farquhar's *Beaux Stratagem*, they reopened a month later with *The Author's Farce* on Wednesday 21 October, adding *Tom Thumb* to the bill on Friday the 23rd. After yielding their stage to a group of actors from the three principal theatres who rented it for nearly a fortnight from 7 November, they returned to the Haymarket on the 18th with *The Author's Farce*, only to yield again to another mixed company of actors on the 27th.

At this juncture began Fielding's brief ascent to the established theatre at Lincoln's Inn Fields, John Rich's[2] house, to whom he had earlier read *The Wedding Day*, and possibly *The Modern Husband*, in vain.[3] It was the house,

---

For HF's relations with Lewis Theobald, see above, the Introduction and notes to 'Cantos' (p. 60 n. 109), the 'Epistle to Lyttleton' (p. 96 n. 35), and below, *Plutus* (p. 258).

[1] Robert Hume, *Henry Fielding and the London Theatre, 1728–1737* (Oxford, 1988), p. 57; William J. Burling and Robert Hume, 'Theatrical Companies at the Little Haymarket, 1720–1737', *Essays in Theatre*, 4 (1986), pp. 98, 104.

[2] For HF's relations with Rich, see above, 'Cantos' (p. 60 n. 107).

[3] See HF's Preface to the *Miscellanies* (i, p. 5) and *Plays*, p. 102. On the possibility that Rich turned down *The Modern Husband*, see *Life*, pp. 99–100.

too, where Lewis Theobald staged his own plays and improvised such entertainments for Rich as the profitable *Harlequin, a Sorcerer*. Considering that Fielding had satirized both these eminent figures in the 'Puppet Show' of *The Author's Farce*—Rich as 'Monsieur Pantomime', Theobald as 'Don Tragedio'[4]—his appearance at their theatre is surprising. Rich this time had agreed to produce Fielding's five-act comedy *The Coffee-House Politician: or, The Justice Caught in his own Trap*, only this new title for *Rape upon Rape* justifying the advertisement 'Revis'd by the Author'. Before Rich's company were ready to stage it, however, the Haymarket players, who in June had introduced the play under its former title, repaid Fielding for his defection by anticipating this event: on Monday 30 November they staged it under its new name with *Tom Thumb* as afterpiece—to which a certain 'Scriblerus Tertius' (Fielding had published his popular burlesque of heroic tragedy as 'Scriblerus Secundus') added a new act, *The Battle of the Poets: or, The Contention for the Laurel*, satirizing the three leading hopefuls for the poet laureateship: namely, Colley Cibber, Stephen Duck, and Lewis Theobald, whose colleague Fielding hoped to become at Lincoln's Inn Fields.

On the day the Haymarket actors played this prank on him, Fielding published in the *Daily Journal* the following denial that he had had any part in the production:

Whereas it hath been advertised That an entire New Act, called, THE BATTLE OF THE POETS, is introduced into the Tragedy of TOM THUMB; This is to assure the Town, that I have never seen this additional Act, nor am any ways concerned therein. *Henry Fielding*.

Four nights later, on Friday 4 December, Rich staged *The Coffee-House Politician* at Lincoln's Inn Fields, with John Hippisley, who had played Peachum in *The Beggar's Opera*, in the role of Justice Squeezum, and Elizabeth Younger, the company's most popular actress, as Hilaret. She would speak Fielding's Epilogue, and would later speak the Epilogue he wrote for Theobald's *Orestes*. The production also saw the debut of Charles Macklin[5] (spelled 'Maclean' in the cast list) in the roles of Porer and Brazencourt; he would become Fielding's close friend. Despite this excellent cast, the play left the stage after just four nights never to be seen again except in the form of Bernard Miles's popular musical *Lock up your Daughters* (1959) and a revival under its original title *Rape upon Rape* in New York (1983), when it

---

[4] See Charles B. Woods, 'Theobald and Fielding's Don Tragedio', *English Language Notes*, 2 (1965), pp. 266–71.

[5] For HF's relations with Macklin, see below, *Journal of a Voyage to Lisbon*, pp. 606 n. 191 and 635 n. 270.

ran for twenty performances. Fielding's third-night benefit brought him £54 13*s*.[6]

The Coffee-House Politician was the first of his plays Fielding staged for Rich at Lincoln's Inn Fields, and it would be the last. By March 1731 he had returned to the Little Haymarket, where on the 24th he produced a pair of new pieces, *The Tragedy of Tragedies* and *The Letter Writers*. Ten days later, on 3 April, Theobald's *Orestes: A Dramatic Opera* would open at Rich's theatre, with an Epilogue 'Written by *HENRY FIELDING*, Esq;'.[7] It is difficult to account for the friendship that began at this time between Fielding and Theobald, whom Pope had made the 'hero' of *The Dunciad*. A year earlier, Fielding, looking for a line to define impossibility, imagined a time when '*T——b–ld* shall blaze with Wit, sweet *Pope* be dull'.[8] Indeed, in *The Tragedy of Tragedies* just a few days earlier, he had mocked both Theobald's commentary on Shakespeare (1. i. 8, n. *c*) and his lame attempts to soar in verse in his tragedy *The Persian Princess*.[9] Nevertheless, this Epilogue signals the beginning of a period of amity between the two men when Fielding in the 'Epistle to Lyttleton' (1733) not only declared his preference for Theobald's scholarship over the works of Pope,[10] but was uncharacteristically willing to part with two guineas to subscribe to his edition of Shakespeare (1734).[11] From the time of *The Champion* (1739) on, Fielding's references to Theobald were anything but friendly, as, for instance, in *Plutus, the God of Riches*, where Fielding misses no opportunity to sneer at his translation of Aristophanes.[12]

Baker usefully describes the themes and targets of the Epilogue, as follows:

Fielding addresses himself chiefly to the conventions and ruses of epilogues: the twittings of beaux, virgins, matrons, and intrigues as the heroine now comes forward and 'stands confest | E'en One of Us,—her Virtue all a Jest'. Indeed, he pays virtually no attention to the 'Dramatic Opera' the audience has just experienced, with its theatrics in plot and staging, its three pairs of passionately entangled loves, its two dragons rising from the earth, its chariot descending from the heavens, its concatenation of captures and escapes in which '*A Ship appears here*

---

[6] For these details, see Lockwood's account of the play's 'Stage History' (*Plays*, pp. 415–17).

[7] HF's authorship of the Epilogue was unknown to scholars until the middle of the last century, when Charles B. Woods published his discovery of it: see 'Fielding's Epilogue for Theobald', *PQ*, 28 (1949), pp. 419–24.

[8] 'Advice to the Nymphs of New S[aru]m. Written in the Year 1730' (*Miscellanies* i, p. 69).

[9] See Woods, 'Fielding's Epilogue for Theobald', and Nancy A. Mace, 'Fielding, Theobald, and *The Tragedy of Tragedies*', *PQ*, 66 (1987), pp. 457–72.

[10] See above, pp. 96–7, lines. 124–31.

[11] *Life*, p. 110.

[12] See below, the Preface and notes to *Plutus*.

under Sail', and much song and dance—the very sort of thing his *Author's Farce* and *Tragedy of Tragedies* would be satirizing a few streets away at the Haymarket.[13]

Fielding has Mrs Younger close the Epilogue with a compliment to Theobald for offering the ladies in the audience 'English *Sounds, and Tragedy that's Sense*' at a time when they chiefly patronized the nonsense of Italian opera and the falderal of his own *Tom Thumb*.

Theobald's *Orestes* ran for five more nights (6, 10, 19, 20, 27 April). On the last night Rich, perhaps at last impatient at Fielding's less cordial characterization of the fare the play offered—'*Love for soft Hearts,—and Musick for soft Brains*'—dropped his Epilogue in favour of another. John Watts published the play, with Fielding's Epilogue, on the day of its third night, Saturday 10 April.

---

[13] From Baker's draft of an introduction to the Epilogue.

ORESTES.

A

DRAMATIC OPERA.

As it is Acted at the

THEATRE-ROYAL

IN

LINCOLN's-INN FIELDS.

Written by Mr. *THEOBALD.*

———*Pœnis agitatus Oreſtes.* Virg.

LONDON:

Printed for JOHN WATTS at the Printing-Office
in *Wild-Court,* near *Lincoln's-Inn Fields.*

MDCCXXXI.
[Price One Shilling and Six-pence.]

EPILOGUE;

Written by *HENRY FIELDING*, Esq;.

Spoken by Mrs. *YOUNGER*.[1]

OF all the Plagues, with which a Poet's curst,
This heavy Tax of *Epilogue*'s the worst:[2]
For tho' his Muse be jaded in his Play,
Still she must speak, tho' she has Nought to say.
In vain the worn-out Goddess he invokes,
No Husbands, grown quite weary of their Yokes,
Are so to put to't for Love,—as those for Jokes.

 To save himself, One would the Beaux condemn;
And shews his Wit, by shewing none in them.
Their Bodies, as their Minds, he ridicules;
Nor will allow 'em that sure Claim of Fools.
To be, at least, the Women's proper Tools.[3]

 Another, more inclin'd to Love than Satire,
Would dress his Wit up by undressing Nature.
The Virgin, whom his Lines can fail to *touch*,
Must either know too little, or too much.
Virtue by Theory taught in five dull Acts is,
The *Epilogue* reduces Vice to Practice.
Tho', in his Play, the *Greek* or *Roman* Dame
Shuns the least Hint of an indecent Flame;
Tho', rather than submit to naughty Wooing,
She laughs at Danger, and encounters Ruin;
Wait till the *Epilogue* she stands confest

---

[1] Elizabeth (*née* Finch) Younger (1699–1762), actress and dancer, played Hermione in Theobald's *Orestes*. She had joined Rich's company at Lincoln's Inn Fields in October 1725 playing Margery Pinchwife in Wycherley's *The Country Wife* and became one of his leading actresses, playing such parts as Desdemona in *Othello* and Cordelia in Nahum Tate's version of *King Lear*. She was Hilaret in Fielding's *The Coffee-House Politician* (December 1730). On 7 December 1732, at the opening of Rich's new theatre at Covent Garden, she would be Millamant in Congreve's *Way of the World*. (Moira Goff, *Oxford DNB*, s.v.)

[2] Cf. *Tom Jones* XVI. i, where HF, perhaps recalling Terence in *Andria*, sides with a similar complaint about prologues: 'I HAVE heard of a Dramatic Writer who used to say, he would rather write a Play than a Prologue' (p. 832 and n. 1).

[3] Cf. *Tom Jones* V. v, where the philosopher Square appears, 'among other female Utensils', in Molly Seagrim's makeshift closet (p. 229).

E'en *One of Us,*—her Virtue all a Jest:[4]
Laughs at her Lover, if he let her 'scape;
And shews, she was too brave to fear a *Rape.*
Where-e'er the *Tragic* Scene is laid, 'tis plain
The *Epilogue* still lies—in *Drury-Lane.*[5]
　　But 'tis, alike, each Author's darling Care
To recommend his Labours to the Fair.
Our Author this attempts by various Strains,
Love for soft Hearts,—and Musick for soft Brains.
　　Ladies, be kind, and let his Plea stand good;
Condemn not Both, because they're understood.
Once in an Age, at least, your Smiles dispense
To *English* Sounds, and Tragedy that's Sense.
These are Variety to you, who come
From the *Italian Opera,*[6] and *Tom Thumb.*[7]

---

[4] Cf. HF's Epilogue to *Pasquin* (1736): 'THE Play once done, the *Epilogue,* by Rule, | Should come and turn it all to Ridicule; | Should tell the Ladies that the Tragic-Bards, | Who prate of Virtue and her Rewards, | Are all in Jest, and only Fools should heed 'em; | . . . This is the Method *Epilogues* pursue' (p. [65]).

[5] The environs of the Drury Lane playhouse were notorious: according to Ned Ward's calculations no fewer than 107 brothels could be found there—among them the tavern where Shamela's mother resides (see below, p. 160 n. 52).

[6] HF's campaign against the Italian opera began with the unfinished Cantos (above, p. 70 and n. 156) and continued in the 'Puppet-Show' of *The Author's Farce,* where the 'Goddess of Nonsense' is infatuated by 'Signior Opera'.

[7] This unexpected stroke of self-deprecation is of a piece with HF's attempts, evident in the Prologues of *The Coffee-House Politician* and *The Modern Husband,* to shake off the reputation he had earned at the Little Haymarket as a playwright who could succeed only at farce, burlesque, and ballad opera. He was now experimenting with a new kind of drama, 'Heroick' comedy—comedy that not only eschews 'low Farce' and the 'loud Laugh', but dares to be 'serious', taking aim at 'Modern Vice'. In the Prologue to *The Modern Husband* he thus apologized for the youthful mistakes of 'his unskill'd Muse', who entertained audiences 'With unshap'd Monsters of a wanton Brain! | He taught *Tom Thumb* strange Victories to boast, | Slew Heaps of Giants, and then—kill'd a Ghost!'

7

THE EPILOGUE TO
'CHARLES BODENS'S'
THE MODISH COUPLE (1732)

EXCEPT for the Epilogue he wrote for Lewis Theobald's *Orestes* at Lincoln's Inn Fields, Fielding's theatrical compositions in 1731 were all produced at the Little Haymarket under the name 'Scriblerus Secundus', the pseudonym he adopted for all his 'irregular' plays of this early period. *The Tragedy of Tragedies: or, The Life and Death of Tom Thumb the Great* and as an afterpiece *The Letter-Writers: or, A New Way to Keep a Wife at Home* were staged together on Wednesday 24 March. A month later *The Welsh Opera: or, The Grey Mare the better Horse* opened as an afterpiece to *The Tragedy of Tragedies* on Thursday 22 April; it was Fielding's twenty-fourth birthday and his third 'benefit' during the run of the popular *Tragedy*. *The Welsh Opera* played for only four nights, but its reception was encouraging enough to prompt Fielding to write a much enlarged and revised version. More than doubling the number of songs (from thirty-one to sixty-five), *The Grub-Street Opera*, as he now called it, showed every promise of being one of his greatest 'hits': 'it is fair to say', observes Edgar Roberts, 'that *The Grub-Street Opera* is musically the most satisfactory of all the ballad operas written in the decade following *The Beggar's Opera*'.[1]

As it happened, however, *The Grub-Street Opera* was never staged. The reason for this disappointment was the second element in the successful theatrical formula Fielding had hit upon in *The Welsh Opera*: the play was not only musical; it was also political—and in a way far more flagrant than Gay's *Beggar's Opera*. When *The Welsh Opera* began its second run on 26 May, it was further contaminated politically by being yoked together on the same bill with William Hatchett's *Fall of Mortimer*, a play obnoxious to Walpole, whom the actor Mullart satirized in the title role as he did as Robin the Butler in Fielding's afterpiece. After three weeks of 'puffs' and fanfares

---

[1] *The Grub Street Opera*, ed. Edgar V. Roberts (Lincoln, Nebr., 1968), p. 75.

in the papers, and more time than that spent by Fielding and the players in writing and rehearsing the work, the opening of *The Grub-Street Opera* was announced for 11 June. On that day, though the performance was advertised as scheduled, the theatre was shut; indeed, Fielding's eagerly awaited ballad opera would never after reach the stage.

The story of the suppression of *The Grub-Street Opera* remains a mystery.[2] The actors insisted that it was Fielding himself who withdrew the play before it opened. It is certain that he never authorized its publication during his lifetime. Why? What other than the threat of prosecution from the authorities can reasonably explain Fielding's decision, in effect, to consign the play to oblivion? Fielding, who never had enough money even when he had a lot of it, and who had applied himself for weeks to converting a modest afterpiece into a major musical event, a full evening's entertainment? Was he to be compensated for this sacrifice? It was, at least, his surprising good fortune in the autumn when, while the Haymarket players were harassed by the government and their theatre was given over to exhibitions of prize-fighting and rope dancing, Fielding was beginning his tenure as house playwright of the Theatre Royal at Drury Lane, where Colley Cibber and his partners had spurned him ever since the disappointment of *Love in Several Masques* three years earlier.

On 1 January 1732 Fielding's *The Lottery*, a ballad opera of one act that included seven tunes from the ill-fated *Grub-Street Opera*, served as afterpiece to Addison's *Cato*. This new play became an immediate favourite; it was performed fifteen times before the month was out. One of these performances was by royal command of the Prince of Wales on the benefit night of Charles Bodens (d. 1753), the putative author of a new comedy, *The Modish Couple*, for which Fielding provided the Epilogue.

For reasons having little to do with its theatrical qualities, *The Modish Couple* was the most resounding failure of the season.[3] The play purported to be the improbable creation of Bodens, an ensign who held the brevet rank of captain[4] in the Coldstream Guards; he was also Gentleman Usher Quarter Waiter in ordinary to the King, but best known at court for his corpulence and his resourcefulness as pimp to the Prince of Wales. Horace Walpole summed him up as 'a man of some humour, and universal

---

[2] For a full account of the circumstances of HF's composition of *The Grub-Street Opera* and an interpretation of its suppression, see *Life*, pp. 112–23. For a detailed and more cautious discussion of the subject, see Hume, pp. 93–104.

[3] The following account of *The Modish Couple* and its author is based on *Life*, pp. 125–7.

[4] See Calhoun Winton, *Captain Steele: The Early Career of Richard Steele* (Baltimore, 1964), pp. 45–6 and n. 18.

parasite'.[5] But whatever useful qualities he may have possessed, Captain Bodens was no playwright. The author of *The Modish Couple* was the theatrical parson and translator of Molière, James Miller (1704–44), who struck a bargain with Bodens, knowing that only someone of the Captain's interest at Drury Lane and at court could get the play performed and ensure it a successful run.[6]

Long before the play opened on 10 January 1732 it was obvious that *The Modish Couple* was the darling of the court. In September it was presented privately at St James's for the entertainment of the Royal Family. By December a claque of courtiers had formed to support it: on the 6th of that month the *Daily Post* reported that the Duke of Richmond and his chum the Duke of Montagu,[7] who hugely loved a hoax such as this, were seen together at rehearsal along with many other 'Persons of Quality . . . and were very much diverted, desiring some of the Scenes to be rehearsed over again'. To guarantee (they supposed) a successful first night for Captain Bodens's play, these noble friends invited 200 of their acquaintance to dinner at the Bedford Head Tavern and The Rose, after which their parties converged on the theatre and were privately admitted before the doors were opened—a flagrant gesture of favouritism that incensed the general public. Though not itself a political play, *The Modish Couple* by these events became thoroughly politicized. The play opened to a crowded and polarized audience, one half of whom were determined to damn it with jeers and catcalls, the other half to save it with cheers and the flourishing of oaken clubs. And the din from the political quarters of the house was augmented by the clamorous protests of the critical beaux of the Temple, who found themselves ridiculed in the character of Grinly.

So remarkable was the occasion that Fielding commemorated it in *Joseph Andrews* (III. vi), where, if there had been room for it, 'the first Night of Captain B———'s Play' would have had the honour of being first of the 'Histories' engraved on the hero's cudgel 'where you would have seen Criticks in Embroidery transplanted from the Boxes to the Pit, whose ancient Inhabitants were exalted to the Gallery, where they played on

[5] See Walpole's note in the British Library copy of Lord Chesterfield's *Miscellaneous Works*, ed. M. Maty and J. O. Justamond (1777), ii, p. 361.

[6] See Calhoun Winton, 'Benjamin Victor, James Miller, and the Authorship of *The Modish Couple*', *PQ*, 64 (1985), pp. 121–30. Winton's discovery of Benjamin Victor's MS account of the play's authorship has negated Charles B. Woods's view, based on remarks in the diary of the Earl of Egmont, that the authors were Lord Hervey and the Prince of Wales (Woods, 'Captain B———'s Play', *Harvard Studies and Notes in Philology and Literature*, 15 [1933], pp. 243–57). Though HF continued to attribute the comedy to Bodens, he would in *Champion* (21 February 1740) re-create for his readers the first-night damnation of Miller's farce *An Hospital for Fools* (pp. 194–5).

[7] On the two dukes and HF's relationship with them, see *Familiar Letters* below, pp. 498–9 nn. 82–3.

Catcalls' (p. 240). The play's enemies prevailed. Though the Prince's royal presence, as well as that of a dozen Grenadier guardsmen with fixed bayonets on the stage, ensured that Captain Bodens (and through him James Miller) had his benefit, *The Modish Couple* was driven from the theatre when the curtain rose on the fourth night.

Though Fielding played a part in this calamitous production, his opinion of the play and the talent of its author (as he appears to have believed Bodens to be) is apparent in the Epilogue: 'As the First Fault, ye *Criticks*, spare what's past, | And spare him, *Wits*, in hopes 'twill be his last.' Later, in *Pasquin* (v. i) indeed, the Queen of Ignorance orders Harlequin to arrange the staging, at both the patent theatres, of one particular drama— her favourite because 'There is not in it either Head or Tail.'

> The *Modish Couple* is its Name; my self
> Stood Gossip to it, and I will support
> This Play against the Town.   (p. 55)

THE
MODISH COUPLE.

A
COMEDY.

As it is Acted at the

THEATRE-ROYAL

In DRURY-LANE.

By His MAJESTY's Servants.

LONDON:

Printed for J. WATTS at the Printing-Office in
Wild-Court near *Lincoln's-Inn Fields.*

MDCCXXXII.
[Price One Shilling and Six Pence.]

EPILOGUE.

Spoke by Mrs. *CIBBER*.[1]

Written By *HENRY FIELDING*, Esq;

I Hear some honest Citizens are humming,
Jogging their Wives—ay—now, my Dear! 'tis coming:
The Fans, I see, are marshall'd, Rank and File,
Some to hide Blushes, more to hide a Smile,
While spindle[2] Beaux their meagre Sides are straining
To raise a Laugh, tho' they scarce know one's Meaning.
Faith! you're all bit.[3] Let Tragedy still deal
Such whetting Acids at its palling Meal;
Where Virtue in such sad Extremes is drest,
That first they make her dreadful, then a Jest;
In painting Vice, so well they know to charm ye,
Our Poets make mere Cuckolds, than our Army:
They raise such Spirits in a Female Brain,
That the poor Husband toils to lay in vain.
She, who before was well enough contented,
Now told what Flames the *Greeks* and *Romans* vented;
Her fancy fir'd with *Hector* or with *Caesar*,
What can a *Haberdasher*[4] do to please her?
But Ways, like these, our Comic *Captain* scorns;
He swears no Souse to him shall owe his Horns.
Our *Captain*—Gad! I almost had forgot him,
To such sad Plight this sweating Night has brought him,
Nine Nights together shou'd he lessen so,
Our plump, round Bard will dwindle to a Beau;
His *Pegasus*, when next he mounts, will know it,
And wonder what's become of *half* the *Poet*.

---

[1] Jane (*née* Johnson) Cibber (1704–33), who played Clarissa in *The Modish Couple*. She had been with the company at Drury Lane since the season of 1724–5, when she played Mistress Dol Mavis in Ben Jonson's *Silent Woman*. She married Colley Cibber's son Theophilus (1703–58) in May 1725.

[2] On HF's characterization of beaux as 'spindle-shanked', see 'A Dialogue between a Beau's Head and his Heels' above (p. 83 and n. 6).

[3] HF recalls Sir Lubbardly Block's remark to his son Squire Chip in the last scene of the play: 'No, no, Boy, she's coupled already—we are all bit, and plaid the Devil with here' (pp. 73–4).

[4] 'Haberdasher': cf. *A New Canting Dictionary* (1725): 'HABBERDASHER [*sic*] *of Nouns and Pronouns,* a Schoolmaster'.

I' faith! I think he has shewn his Spirit bolder,
In listing *Poet*, than in listing *Soldier*:
To mount the Stage, who'd not be more afraid,
Than to *mount* Guard at *Court* or *Masquerade*!
Which is more dangerous? (What say you Sparks?)
To march around *Parnassus*, or the, *Parks*?
How happy were the Bard, how void of Fear,
Were he as sure to find no En'my here,
As he is sure to march in Safety there.
But here no Prowess serve's the brave Commander,
One *Critic Clerk*[5] wou'd rout an *Alexander*.
Soldiers, give *Quarter* to a valiant Brother,
Courtiers are too well bred to Dam each other.
As the First Fault, ye *Criticks*, spare what's past,
And spare him, *Wits*, in hopes 'twill be his last.

---

[5] HF's warning of the threat to Captain Bodens's play posed by the critical law clerks of the inns of court near the Inner and Middle Temple anticipated the 'Templars' damning *The Modish Couple* when they found themselves satirized in the character of Grinly (see the Introduction, p. 109). On the type, see Wilding of HF's *The Temple Beau* (1730); and *The Champion* (22 December 1739), where HF defines the three offices held by the 'Clerks' and characterizes them as 'chosen out of such Gentlemen of the Inns of Court, as having had too high Parts to confine themselves to the dull crabbed Study of the Law, have spent so much of their youthful Days in Dress, Amour, and other Diversions, that they get a very uncomfortable Subsistance at the Bar; and from their Want of other Employment, are generally to be seen in the Coffee-Houses about the *Temple* and the *Theatre*' (pp. 82–3).

EPILOGUE TO CHARLES JOHNSON'S
CÆLIA: OR, THE PERJUR'D LOVER (1732)

FIELDINGS belated return to the Theatre Royal at Drury Lane, the scene of his debut as a playwright, had energized and inspired him. In the course of six months from January to June 1732 he produced five new plays: *The Lottery. A Farce* in January; *The Modern Husband*, the last of his experiments in 'Heroick' comedy, in February; and in June *The Old Debauchees*, *The Covent-Garden Tragedy*, and *The Mock Doctor: or, The Dumb Lady Cur'd*, the last a version of Molière's *Le Médecin malgré lui*. He was indeed fast becoming, in the judgement of the leading theatre historian of the period, 'the most dominant professional playwright in London since Dryden'.[1] His theatre, however, was in crisis. Before the new season began, Drury Lane's veteran 'triumvirate' of actor–managers were no longer in charge: Barton Booth (1681–1733), ill and no longer acting, had sold half his share of the patent to the rich and callow enthusiast John Highmore; Colley Cibber delegated his share to his son Theophilus (1703–58); and on the death of Robert Wilks (*c.*1665–1732) in September, his widow assigned half her inherited share to Fielding's friend the painter John Ellys (see Appendix A.2).

As Robert Hume observed, the new management, in which Theophilus Cibber shared decision-making with a pair of devoted amateurs, 'was anxious to secure [Fielding's] favour and scripts'.[2] On 8 September, as the new season began, Fielding's revised *Mock Doctor*, 'By Command' of the Queen herself, who attended the performance, was paired as afterpiece to *The Rehearsal*, and it continued to be featured with several other plays through November; on the 16th of the month, indeed, when it was on the bill with Vanbrugh's *Relapse*, the managers awarded Fielding the lucrative proceeds of an author's benefit—for a mere afterpiece an unusual favour.

Signs that Drury Lane was not prospering under its new management were clear the following month when the first new play of the season failed

---

[1] Hume, p. ix.   [2] Ibid., p. 150.

dismally. This was *Cælia: or, The Perjur'd Lover*, a tragedy by the prolific Charles Johnson (*c*.1679–1748), playwright and poet, with the Epilogue furnished by Fielding. The play opened and closed on Monday 11 December 1732; the book, with Johnson 'concealing' his name,[3] was published by John Watts on Friday the 15th.[4] *Cælia* was Johnson's last play and, though the audience damned it, John Genest declared it to be 'by far his best', a play of 'singular merit—it will afford great pleasure to any one, who is a lover of simplicity and true pathos'.[5] And Genest's verdict has been more recently seconded by Robert Hume: 'it is without doubt one of the most impressive and interesting tragedies of the 1730s'.[6]

Cælia may be seen to be, as Baker saw it, 'an *Ur-Clarissa*, but with pregnancy and abandonment in a brothel disguised as a lying-in hospital. Cælia's mother dies of grief. Wronglove, the rake, mortally wounded in a duel as the noble Bellamy defends Cælia's honor, repents, declares Cælia his wife, and leaves all to her and their unborn child, while she, having been found by her father in a prison with the harlots, dies of shame.'

As Johnson makes clear in his anonymous 'Advertisement to the Reader', the cause of the fiasco was his decision to ignore Barton Booth's advice to drop the scenes in the brothel:

I Had the Mortification to see this Play acted the first Night, and to hear the Characters of Mother *Lupine* and her Women disapprov'd by several of the Audience, who, as if they thought themselves in bad Company, were very severe. . . . I had the Pleasure, however, to hear the serious Scenes applauded, and to see some of those very Spectators, who were offended at the lower Characters, join with *Cælia* in her Tears.[7]

Fielding's Epilogue follows the facetious formula defined by the 'Ghost' in the Epilogue to *Pasquin* (1736):

> *T*HE *Play once done, the* Epilogue, *by Rule,*
> *Should come and turn it all to Ridicule;*[8]
> *Should tell the Ladies that the Tragic-Bards,*

---

[3] In an anonymous 'Advertisement to the Reader' Johnson remarks, 'I think every one will allow I have acted with Judgment, in concealing my Name.'

[4] For the dates of production and publication, see the *Daily Post* for Monday the 11th and Wednesday the 13th, the latter announcing publication '*On Friday next*'; the *Daily Journal* (Friday 15 December) confirms the date. The imprint has 1733.

[5] John Genest, *Some Account of the English Stage*, 10 vols. (Bath, 1832), iii, p. 365.

[6] Hume, *Henry Fielding and the London Theatre*, p. 150.

[7] *Cælia*, sig. [A3ʳ].

[8] HF was not alone in insisting that an epilogue must ridicule the tragedy that preceded it. Mary E. Knapp describes 'the very reluctant abandonment of the comic epilogue', citing nothing earlier than John Home's *Douglas* (1756) as a forthright condemnation of the convention (see *Prologues and Epilogues of the Eighteenth Century* [New Haven, 1961], p. 277).

> *Who prate of Virtue and her vast Rewards,*
> *Are all in Jest, and only Fools should heed 'em.*
> *For all* wise Women *flock to* Mother Needham.[9]
> *This is the Method* Epilogues *pursue.*

Adding to Johnson's 'mortification' on the night would be the theme and
tone of the Epilogue, in which—as in his parody of Richardson's *Pamela*—
Fielding mocks the author's treating as tragic the loss of a woman's
'Virtue'.[10] Later, it should be said, he would himself weep at the rape of
Clarissa.[11]

---

[9]   On 'Mother' Needham, the notorious bawd, see above, *Masquerade*, p. 13 n. 1.

[10] Genest regrets that HF's Epilogue, though 'good in itself . . . absurdly turns the distress of
Cælia into ridicule' (*Some Account*, iii, p. 365); and Hume remarks, 'Fielding's view of [*Cælia*] is hard to
judge from his flippantly ironic epilogue' (p. 150).

[11] See HF's letter of 15 October 1748 to Richardson (*Correspondence*, Letter 41).

C Æ L I A:

OR, THE

PERJUR'D LOVER.

A

P L A Y.

As it is Acted at the THEATRE-ROYAL
in DRURY-LANE,

By His MAJESTY's Servants.

——Tragicus plerumque dolet sermone pedestri. Hor.

LONDON:

Printed for J. WATTS at the Printing-Office in
Wild-Court near *Lincoln's-Inn Fields.*

MDCCXXXIII. [Price 1 *s.* and 6 *d.*]

line 9: Horace, *Ars Poetica*, line 95: 'tragedians often grieve in the language of prose' (cf. Loeb).

EPILOGUE

Written by *HENRY FIELDING*, Esq;

And Spoken by Miss *RAFTOR*.[1]

LUD! what a Fuss is here! what Blood and Slaughter!
Because poor Miss has prov'd her Mother's Daughter.
This unknown Bard is some insipid Beast,
From *Cornwall*, or *Northumberland* at least;[2]
Where if a Virgin chance to step aside,
And taste forbidden Sweetmeats of a Bride,
The virtuous Ladies, like Infection, fly her;
But here, 'mongst us so famous for Good-nature,
Who thinks a Cuckold quite a Fellow-Creature:
Where Miss may take great Liberties upon her,
And have her Man, and yet may keep her Honour:
Here does the Wretch his stupid Muse invoke,
And turn to Solemn Tragedy—A Joke!
Had some Town-Bard this Subject undertaken,
He wou'd have match'd, not kill'd, the Nymph forsaken.
Wronglove, as now, had the first Favour carried,
And *Bellamy* been, what he is fit for, married.
What else are all your Comic Heroes fam'd for,
Than such Exploits as *Wronglove* has been blam'd for?
The Girl was in the Fault, who strove to smother

---

[1] Catherine ('Kitty') Raftor (1711–85), actress and singer. In 1733 she would enter into an unhappy marriage with George Clive (d. 1780), a barrister. In 1728 she joined the company at Drury Lane as prompter and became the close friend of Jane Cibber (who played the lead in *Cælia*). In the season of 1728–9 she began appearing regularly in important parts, especially in afterpieces, such as farces and musical comedies (K. A. Crouch, *Oxford DNB*, s.v.). HF greatly admired her: in this year of 1732 she played Chloe in *The Lottery*, Kissinda in *The Covent-Garden Tragedy*, Isabel in *The Old Debauchees*, and Dorcas in *The Mock Doctor*, in the Preface to which HF lauded her as one of 'the rising Glories of the Theatre'. Later he would dedicate *The Intriguing Chamber Maid* (1734) to her, for whom he created the lead role of Lettice; in the Dedication he characterizes her as 'the best Wife, the best Daughter, the best Sister, and the best Friend'. She continued to appear in HF's comedies, and he continued to praise her: e.g., in *Tom Jones* (IX. i), *Amelia* (I. vi), and *The Covent-Garden Journal* (8 February 1752).

[2] Charles Johnson (*c*.1679–1748), the author of eighteen plays and a number of poems, was certainly not 'unknown', nor was he an unsophisticated 'Beast' from either of these two remotest counties, the first south-westerly and the other north-easterly, in England. Though nothing is known of his parents or birthplace, Johnson claimed to be trained in the law, and he appears to have lived in London all his adult life. He was also for many years the close friend of Robert Wilks (*c*.1665–1732), whose influence at Drury Lane ensured that most of his plays were produced at the Theatre Royal. (James William Kelly, *Oxford DNB*, s.v.)

That Cafe she shou'd have open'd to her Mother;
All had been hush'd by the old Lady's Skill,
And *Caelia* prov'd a good Town-Virgin still;
For as each Man is brave, till put to rout,
So is each Woman virtuous, till found out:
Which, Ladies, here I make my hearty Prayer,
May never be the Case of any Fair,
Who takes unhappy *Caelia* to her Care.

9

PROLOGUE TO LILLO'S
FATAL CURIOSITY (1736–7)

FIELDING'S first play of 1736, his first season as theatrical manager at
the Little Haymarket, was the greatest 'hit' of his career as dramatist.
Opening on 5 March, '*Pasquin. A Dramatic Satire on the Times*: Being the
Rehearsal of Two Plays, viz. A Comedy call'd, *The Election*; and a Tragedy,
call'd *The Life and Death of Common-Sense*' ran for more than sixty performances—'a success', Robert Hume remarks, 'on the scale of *The Beggar's
Opera*'.[1]

Concluding that season was a production that reveals as much about
Fielding's capacity for friendship as about his professional judgement and
enterprise. This was the staging of *Guilt Its Own Punishment: or, Fatal
Curiosity*, a new domestic tragedy in blank verse by George Lillo (1691/
3–1739),[2] who, five years earlier with *The London Merchant: or, The History
of George Barnwell* (1731), had staged at Drury Lane what soon became the
most popular example of this genre in English theatre history. Despite this
triumph, and more recently the production at Drury Lane of *The Christian
Hero* (1735), Lillo failed to interest either the management at Drury Lane
or John Rich at Covent Garden in *Fatal Curiosity*—as became its title with
the publication of the book in April 1737.

Nothing about Fielding's theatrical career to date would suggest that he
relished the sublime pleasures of the tragic mode. On the contrary, the
hilarity of *The Tragedy of Tragedies*, which he had recently revived at the
Haymarket—not to mention *The Covent-Garden Tragedy* with its mockery
of Ambrose Philips's *Distrest Mother*, or in *Pasquin* the ludicrous efforts of
author Fustian to stage 'The Life and Death of Common Sense': such
mockery of the genre was Fielding's trademark. Yet in the *Daily Advertiser*
for Tuesday 25 May, just two days before *Fatal Curiosity* opened at the

---

[1] Hume, p. 215.
[2] For Lillo's biography, see James L. Steffensen's article in the *Oxford DNB*.

Haymarket, there appeared the following anonymous letter, certainly by
Fielding:[3]

SIR,

In an Age when Tragedy is thought so much out of Fashion, that the great establish'd
Theatres dare hardly venture to attempt it, an Author may probably seem bold who
hazards his Reputation with a Set of young Actors on a Stage hitherto in its Infancy;
where he is sure, besides the Judgment, to encounter the Prejudice of the Town; and
has not only the Chance of not being liked, but of not being heard.

But as to the ill Success of Tragedy in general, I shall not attribute it entirely to
the Audience; I cannot persuade myself that we are sunk into such a stage of Levity
and Childhood, as to be utterly incapable of any serious Attention; or are so entirely
devoted to Farce and Puppet Shew, as to abandon what one of the greatest Criticks
who ever liv'd has call'd the noblest Work of Human Understanding.[4]

I am afraid the Truth is, our Poets have left off Writing, rather than our
Spectators loving Tragedy. The Modern Writers seem to me to have quite mistaken
the Path: They do not fail so much from want of Genius as of Judgment; they
embellish their Diction with their utmost Art, and concern themselves little about
their Fable:[5] In short, While they are industrious to please the Fancy, they forget
(what should be their first Care) to warm the Heart.

Give me leave, Sir, to recommend to you, and by you to the Town, a Tragedy,
written in a different Manner, where the Fable is contriv'd with great Art, and the
Incidents such as must affect the Heart of every one who is not void of Humanity.
A tender Sensation is, I think, in one of a Humane Temper, the most pleasing
that can be rais'd; and I will venture to affirm, no such Person will fail of enjoying
it who will be present on Thursday next at the Hay-Market Theatre; where, without the bombast Stile of Kings and Heroes, he will see a Scene in common Life,
which really happen'd in King James I's Time; and is accompany'd with the most
natural, dreadful and tender Circumstances, and affording the finest Moral that can
be invented by the Mind of Man.

What in Fielding's view distinguished *Fatal Curiosity* from the 'bombast
Stile' of the tragedies he ridiculed was chiefly its 'Fable'.[6] Lillo based his

---

[3] Robert Hume and I independently found and attributed this letter to HF, as well as the anonymous
review of the first-night production in the *DA* for 28 May: Hume, *Fielding and the London Theatre*, app. IV
('Fielding on Tragedy: The Puff for *Fatal Curiosity*') and *Life*, pp. 204–5, 206.

[4] Aristotle, *Poetics*, xxvi. Cf. Addison, *Spectator*, No. 39 (14 April 1711): 'a perfect Tragedy is the
Noblest Production of Human Nature' (ed. Bond, 5 vols. (Oxford, 1965), i, p. 163).

[5] 'Fable': cf. Thomas Rymer, *The Tragedies of the Last Age, Considered and Examined* (1678), Ded. 4: 'I
have chiefly consider'd the Fable or Plot, which all conclude to be the Soul of a Tragedy' (cited in *OED*,
s.v. 'fable' sb. 3).

[6] What particularly impressed the classicist James Harris was Lillo's masterly conduct of the plot: 'in
this Tragedy . . . we find the model of A PERFECT FABLE', deserving comparison with Sophocles' *Oedipus
Tyrannus*, and indeed with *Othello*, *King Lear*, and Milton's *Samson Agonistes* as well (*Philological Inquiries*
[1781], pp. 154–8).

play on (supposedly) an actual incident that occurred at Penryn, Cornwall, in 1618: a young man, having made a fortune travelling in the East for many years, returns home without revealing his identity and is murdered by his father at the instigation of his stepmother. Lillo's drama was not fanciful, but true;[7] its incidents are genuinely affecting; it is constructed with economy and a sense of pace, and, as William McBurney observes, with a fidelity to the Aristotelian unities even greater than Addison could manage in *Cato*;[8] and in his dialogue Lillo kept up a powerful simplicity and vigour of style, achieving one of the rare triumphs of dramatic blank verse of his century.

In this production of *Fatal Curiosity*, Thomas Davies (*c.*1712–1785), actor—and future editor of Lillo's *Works*—in the character of the son Young Wilmot played his first role. He witnessed at first hand not only Fielding's relationship with Lillo and his belief in the play, but also the role Fielding played in preparing *Fatal Curiosity* to be acted, not at Drury Lane or Covent Garden, but 'at an inferior Play-house, and by persons not so well skilled in their profession'.[9] Fielding had always despised those genteel critics who sneered at *The London Merchant* 'because the subject was too low'. He recognized Lillo's genius, and behaved towards him 'with great politeness and friendship'. Indeed, Fielding personally 'took upon himself the management of the play', applying all his talents and resources to ensure its success. Fielding, Davies remembered, 'was not merely content to revise the FATAL CURIOSITY, and to instruct the actors how to do justice to their parts. He warmly recommended the play to his friends, and to the public. Besides all this he presented the author with a well written prologue.'

Fielding's Prologue, the only verse of its kind in the canon, is indeed 'well written'. As for its content, it is a distillation in iambic pentameter couplets of the notice in the *Daily Advertiser* in which Fielding 'warmly recommended the play . . . to the public'. The day after the opening the following report in the same paper (28 May) served the same purpose, assuring the public that *Fatal Curiosity* had been received

with the greatest Applause that has been shewn to any Tragedy for many Years. The Scenes of Distress were so artfully work'd up, and so well perform'd, that there scarce remain'd a dry Eye among the Spectators at the Representation; and during the Scene preceding the Catastrophe, an attentive Silence possess'd the whole

---

[7] Steffensen his biographer, however, refers to Lillo's story as a 'version' of an 'oft-told tale'. While it 'probably originated in a black-letter pamphlet, *Newes from Penrin in Cornwall* (1618)'; the playwright's source was an abbreviated account given in *Sanderson's Annals* (1656) and reprinted in *Frankland's Annals* (1681).

[8] See Lillo's *Fatal Curiosity*, ed. William H. McBurney, (Lincoln Nebr., 1967), p. xix.

[9] Quotations are from Davies's 'Account' of Lillo in his edition of the *Works* (1775), i, pp. xv–xvi, xvii.

House, more expressive of an universal Approbation than the loudest Applauses, which were given to the many noble Sentiments that every where abound in this excellent Performance, which must meet with Encouragement in an Age that does not want both Sense and Humanity.

Whatever impact Lillo's tragedy had upon the audience that first night, it enjoyed only a modest run of seven performances, a showing attributable in part to its having been introduced so late in the season. In a second effort to serve his friend, Fielding brought it on again in March 1737, when it ran for eleven nights coupled with his own *Historical Register*.

   Fatal Curiosity was never staged again before Lillo's death on 3 September 1739. Its reputation among certain knowledgeable critics, however, remained very high: Sarah Fielding took up her brother's cause by defending the play in *The Adventures of David Simple* (ii. ii); and Davies, for whom Lillo was matched only by Shakespeare as 'a painter of the terrible graces', believed that for sheer affective power only the murder scene in *Macbeth* could equal the third act of *Fatal Curiosity*.[10] But it remained for Fielding's friend the classicist James Harris, who warmly praised *Fatal Curiosity* in *Philological Inquiries* (1781), to spark a reappraisal of the tragedy that, as Lillo's biographer remarks, brought it 'long-deserved recognition'.[11] Recognition which it certainly received in the last century from the historian of English drama Allardyce Nicoll, for whom *Fatal Curiosity* was the only tragic masterpiece produced in England between 1700 and 1750, its author 'a genius of no common rank'.[12]

POSTSCRIPT

In a review of Lillo's posthumously staged tragedy *Elmerick* in *The Champion* (26 February 1740), Fielding paid the following tribute to his friend's genius, as well as to his qualities as a man:

His fatal Curiosity, which is a Master-Piece in its Kind, and inferior only to Shakespear's best Pieces, gives him a Title to be called the best Tragick Poet of his Age; but this was the least of his Praise, he had the gentlest and honestest Manners, and at the same time the most friendly and obliging. He had a perfect Knowledge of human Nature, tho' his Contempt for all base Means of Application, which are the necessary Steps to great Acquaintance, restrain'd his Conversation within very narrow Bounds; he had the Spirit of an old Roman, join'd to the Innocence of a

---

[10] Ibid., p. xxvii.

[11] Steffensen, *Oxford DNB*.

[12] Allardyce Nicoll, *A History of English Drama, 1660–1900* (Cambridge, 1952), ii, pp. 122, 124. See also C. F. Burgess, 'Lillo sans Barnwell, or the Playwright Revisited', *MP*, 66 (1968), pp. 5–29.

primitive Christian; he was content with his little State of Life, in which his excellent Temper of Mind gave him an Happiness beyond the power of Riches, and it was necessary for his Friends to have a sharp Insight into his Want of their Services as well as good Inclinations or Abilities to serve him; in short, he was one of the best of Men, and those who knew him best, will most regret his Loss.

FATAL CURIOSITY:

A TRUE

TRAGEDY

OF

THREE. ACTS.

As it is Acted at the

NEW THEATRE

IN THE

HAY-MARKET.

By Mr. *LILLO.*

LONDON:

Printed for JOHN GRAY at the *Cross-Keys* in the
Poultry near *Cheapside.* MDCCXXXVII.
[Price One Shilling.]

PROLOGUE,

Written by *Henry Feilding*, Esq;

Spoken by Mr. *Roberts*.[1]

T HE tragic Muse has long forgot to please
With *Shakespear*'s Nature, or with *Fletcher*'s Ease:[2]
No Passion mov'd, thro five long Acts you sit,
Charm'd with the Poet's Language, or his Wit.
Fine Things are said, no matter whence they fall;
Each single Character might speak them all.
  But from this modern fashionable Way,
To Night, our Author begs your Leave to stray
No fustian Hero rages here to Night;
No Armies fall, to fix a Tyrant's Right:
From lower Life we draw our Scene's Distress:
—Let not your Equals move your Pity less!
Virtue distrest in humble State support;
Nor think, she never lives without the Court.
  Tho' to our Scenes no Royal Robes belong,
And tho' our little Stage as yet be young,[3]
Throw both your Scorn and Prejudice aside,
Let us with Favour, not Contempt be try'd;

---

[1] John Roberts (*fl.* 1722–48), who played Old Wilmot, the father in the tragedy. In 1733 the playwright and critic Aaron Hill said of Roberts, 'nobody speaks with more weight and significance' (*Works* [1753], i, p. 169), a feature of his acting that made him right for the role of 'sombre characters' (C. S. Rogers, *Oxford DNB*, s.v.). Charlotte Charke, who played opposite Roberts as the stepmother Agnes, described him as 'a very judicious Speaker' who 'discovered a Mastership in the Character of the Husband', adding 'We were kindly received by the Audience' (*A Narrative of the Life of Mrs. Charlotte Charke* [1755], p. 65). In 1732 Roberts had appeared in several of HF's plays at Drury Lane; at the Haymarket in 1734 he had the title role in *Don Quixote in England*, and in the present season in *Pasquin* he was Trapwit, author of the 'Comedy', and in the 'Tragedy', Firebrand the Priest. In HF's final season of 1737 Roberts would be Medley in the *Historical Register* and Pillage in *Eurydice Hiss'd*.

[2] John Fletcher (1579–1625), best known for his collaboration with Francis Beaumont. In *The Covent-Garden Journal*, No. 23 (21 March 1752) HF included both playwrights in the 'Quadrumvirate' of wits who ruled 'the literary Government' in the reign of James I (pp. 152–3), the period in which Lillo's tragedy is set. In a similar context in *Plutus* he would include Fletcher but not Beaumont (see below, p. 257 and n. 27).

[3] When speaking this line the actor John Roberts no doubt gestured to the stage of the Little Haymarket theatre on which he stood; but HF, when he wrote these words, may already have been dreaming of the grander and more capacious theatre he hoped to build. He announced the project in the *Daily Advertiser* (4 February 1737), but it came to nothing. See Hume, *Fielding and the London Theatre*, pp. 224–8.

Thro' the first Acts a kind Attention lend,
The growing Scene shall force you to attend;
Shall catch the Eyes of every tender Fair,
And make them charm their Lovers with a Tear.
The Lover too by Pity shall impart
His tender Passion to his fair One's Heart:
The Breast which others Anguish cannot move,
Was ne'er the Seat of Friendship, or of Love.

II

OCCASIONAL
PROSE

1

AN APOLOGY FOR THE LIFE OF
MRS. SHAMELA ANDREWS (1741)

SOME sixty years ago, as he opened his article 'Fielding and the Authorship of *Shamela*', Charles B. Woods expressed the belief that, since the
beginning of the century, the contributions of his predecessors—particularly Austin Dobson, J. Paul de Castro, Wilbur Cross, and Alan Dugald
McKillop—had 'so strengthened the hypothesis of Fielding's authorship
that *Shamela* should eventually win an undisputed place in the Fielding
canon'.[1] The argument for Fielding's authorship Woods went on to make in
that essay accomplished the result he hoped for. Though Fielding never
acknowledged *Shamela* as his own, no one any longer doubts he wrote it—
a work, in Sheridan Baker's opinion, that 'may well be the best parody in
English literature'.[2]

---

[1] *PQ*, 25 (1946), pp. 248–72. It should be useful to repeat here, with a few additions, Woods's list of
modern scholars who, beginning in 1900 with Clara Linklater Thomson's remark that *Shamela* was 'not
improbably written by Fielding' (*Samuel Richardson* [London, 1900], p. 38), either simply declared their
opinion that HF wrote the work or added to the evidence that helped demonstrate his authorship: Ethel
M. M. McKenna, introduction to *Writings of Samuel Richardson*, 20 vols. (London, 1902), i, pp. xiv, xxviii;
Austin Dobson, *Samuel Richardson* (London, 1902), pp. 42–5, and 'Fielding', *EB*, p. 325; J. Paul de Castro,
'Did Fielding Write *Shamela*?', *N & Q*, 12th ser., 1 (8 January 1916), pp. 24–6, and the Introductory Note
to his edition of *Joseph Andrews* (London, 1929), pp. 9–11; Gerard E. Jensen, 'An Apology for the Life of
Mrs. Shamela Andrews, 1741', *MLN*, 31 (1916), pp. 310–11; Wilbur L. Cross, *The History of Henry
Fielding*, 3 vols. (New Haven, 1918), i, pp. 303–13; Aurélien Digeon, *Les Romans de Fielding* (Paris, 1923),
pp. 63–7 (Eng. trans. (London, 1925), pp. 44–9); R. Brimley Johnson, Introduction to his reprint of
Shamela (Waltham St Lawrence, 1926); Brian W. Downs, *Samuel Richardson* (London, 1928), pp. 65–8,
and Introduction to his reprint of *Shamela* (Cambridge, 1930); H. K. Banerji, *Henry Fielding: Playwright,
Journalist and Master of the Art of Fiction* (Oxford, 1929), pp. 105–8; Ernest A. Baker, *The History of the
English Novel* (1930), iv, pp. 87–8; Alan D. McKillop, 'The Personal Relations between Fielding and
Richardson', *MP*, 28 (1931), pp. 424–5, and *Samuel Richardson: Printer and Novelist* (Chapel Hill, NC,
1936), pp. 73–5; William M. Sale, Jr., *Samuel Richardson, a Bibliographical Record* (New Haven, 1936),
pp. 113–14; Archibald Bolling Shepperson, *The Novel in Motley: A History of the Burlesque Novel in
English* (Cambridge, Mass. 1936), pp. 19–28; Charles Richard Greene, 'A Note on the Authorship of
Shamela', *MLN*, 59 (December 1944), p. 571.

[2] Henry Fielding, *An Apology for the Life of Mrs. Shamela Andrews*, ed. Sheridan W. Berker, Jr.
(Berkeley and Los Angeles, 1953), p. xi.

Shamela, though different in kind, represents, as far as we know,[3] the first work of prose fiction Fielding wrote, and it led directly to *Joseph Andrews* (1742) and the founding of what he called in *Tom Jones* (II. i) 'a new Province of Writing': no less than the great tradition of the English comic novel as it evolved through Smollett to Thackeray and Dickens.[4] Fielding's immediate target was of course Samuel Richardson's first novel, *Pamela: or, Virtue Rewarded*, the story of a vulnerable but resolute young servant maid who withstands her master's inept attempts on her 'virtue' until she brings him at last to his knees at the altar. *Pamela* was a phenomenal success from the moment it appeared, anonymously, on 6 November 1740; indeed, there had never been a literary event to compare with the enthusiastic reception of Richardson's romance, told by the beleaguered heroine herself in letters and in vivid particularity. Five authoritative editions (as well as an Irish piracy) were called for in less than a year. What is more, in response to spurious sequels such as John Kelly's *Pamela's Conduct in High Life* (May 1741), Richardson, who had been posing as merely the editor of his heroine's correspondence, revealed himself as author of the work, reluctantly publishing his own continuation in December 1741.

But it was the events of the preceding winter—when, as Fielding saw it, 'an epidemical Phrenzy' of foolish praise greeted Richardson's book—that provoked him to write a parody of it. As author of *The Tragedy of Tragedies* (1731) and *The Covent-Garden Tragedy* (1732) he had shown a flair for burlesquing fustian in the theatre; in the unfinished 'Cantos' he had tried to parody Pope; now a new form beckoned: an epistolary novel. In town, according to a notice in *The Gentleman's Magazine* of January 1740/1, it was 'judged . . . as great a Sign of Want of Curiosity not to have read *Pamela*, as not to have seen the *French* and *Italian* dancers', while in the country the illiterate villagers of Slough gathered at the smithy to hear it read aloud and celebrated Pamela's marriage to Mr. B—— by ringing the church bells. That same winter Horace Walpole observed that, like the snow, Pamela covered everything with her whiteness; and from Bath, James Leake the eminent bookseller reported to Richardson, his brother-in-law, that no less sophisticated a critic than Alexander Pope had declared, the novel 'will do more good than many volumes of sermons'.[5] Indeed, despite its

---

[3] For the view that HF wrote *Jonathan Wild*, which was published with the *Miscellanies* (1743), well before he wrote *Joseph Andrews*, see *Life*, pp. 280–2 and 655 n. 37. This, however, is not the view taken by the editors of the Wesleyan Edition (*Miscellanies* iii, pp. xxxii–xxxviii).

[4] The story of the phenomenon of *Pamela*'s reception follows, for the most part, the present editor's account in *Life* (pp. 302–3).

[5] In his Introduction to volume I of *The Pamela Controversy* (see the following note), however, Thomas Keymer suspects that 'Leake had persuaded Pope to speak his little set-piece about *Pamela* publicly in

'inflammatory' scenes of attempted seduction and rape, Richardson's romance was lauded as morally edifying and recommended by the clergy from their pulpits. Scenes and characters from the novel were represented on fans and in waxwork, and were depicted in a series of a dozen paintings by Joseph Highmore. Pamela's story inspired several comedies and an opera. Eulogies, imitations, sequels, piracies, translations—*Pamela* was paid every kind of tribute.[6]

To some readers, however—Fielding in every respect first among them—the book was an egregious performance.[7] The writing was inept, the morality crass and mercenary, the piety it recommended only a mask for hypocrisy, and pernicious in emphasizing the doctrine of grace and faith over good works.

CIRCUMSTANCES OF COMPOSITION

The winter months of 1740/1 were a difficult time for Fielding. In November, when *Pamela* was published, he was bringing his active participation in *The Champion* to an end in a series of leaders meant to rally the electorate behind the opposition candidates in the election scheduled for the spring.[8] In November, too, his father, General Edmund Fielding, was committed to the Fleet Prison (to lodgings in 'the Rules') for a debt of nearly £1,000; and there, in March of the new year, he would marry for the fourth time, thereby ending whatever hopes his eldest son may have had of a legacy that might rescue him and his family from poverty. For in November actions were also being brought against Fielding himself for debts he could not pay. Like his alter egos in the novels he later wrote—Wilson in *Joseph Andrews* (1742) and Billy Booth in *Amelia* (1751)—he was facing the prospect of debtor's prison. Having been admitted to the Bar in June 1740, he

[his] bookshop, so ensuring that it would travel about town, and thereafter the country, with maximum speed' (p. xliii). And he quotes another version of Pope's compliment, more ambiguous than Leake's: on 12 February 1741 George Cheyne wrote Richardson that Pope had asked him 'to tell you that he had read Pamela with great Approbation and Pleasure, and wanted a Night's Rest in finishing it, and says it will do more good than a great many of the new Sermons' (p. xliii). Keymer comments: 'if Cheyne's report is word-perfect, one might detect a whiff of faint praise in Pope's phrasing, which leaves craftily open whether *Pamela* kept him awake or put him to sleep, and may say as much about the new sermons . . . as it does about Richardson's novel' (p. xliii n. 1).

[6] On the vogue of *Pamela*, see Eaves and Kimpel, ch. VII; also the excellent collection Thomas Keymer and Peter Sabor (eds.), *The Pamela Controversy: Criticisms and Adaptations of Samuel Richardson's 'Pamela'*, 6 vols. (London, 2001).

[7] For a review of the negative response to *Pamela* that followed HF's lead, see Bernard Kreissman, *Pamela-Shamela: A Study of the Criticisms, Burlesques, Parodies, and Adaptations of Richardson's Pamela* (Lincoln, Nebr., 1960).

[8] On the part HF appears to have played in *An Address to the Electors of Great Britain*, see Coley's General Introduction, *Champion*. pp. lxxiv–lxxxiii.

was a lawyer now and succeeded by a favourite delaying tactic, the filing of a Writ of Error, in postponing judgment on the action for a few months.

Except for the two sixteenth shares he had in *The Champion*, Fielding, to pay his debts and provide for his wife, Charlotte, and his daughter, could count only on his facility with a pen. The first of his miscellaneous productions of the new year was *Of True Greatness*, a verse epistle of 282 lines addressed to his patron George Bubb Dodington, whom ten years later in *Amelia* (XI. ii), Fielding, stretching the limits of hyperbole, would call 'one of the greatest Men this Country ever produced' (p. 462). The poem was published on 7 January 1741, less than a week after one of Fielding's creditors initiated an action against him in the Palace Court; the publisher, for a time an associate on *The Champion*, was Charles Corbett (1710–52), who later that month would bring out two further publications of his. The first of these, a measure of how desperately Fielding needed money, was a short-lived periodical, issued bi-weekly at four pence a copy, called *The History of Our Own Times*—the title taken from a favourite work by his favourite English historian, Gilbert Burnet (1643–1715), Bishop of Salisbury, a Whig in politics and latitudinarian in religion. The first of just four numbers of the magazine—in which Fielding appears to have been assisted by his Dorset friend the classicist William Young[9]—appeared on Thursday 15 January. A week later, on the 22nd, Corbett also published an anonymous mock-epic, *The Vernoniad*, a poem of 296 lines, complete with editorial commentary. Facetiously purporting to be a lost work of Homer, it is in fact, as Fielding explained, 'a Parody on the first Part of *Virgil*'s Aeneid',[10] with, one might add, allusions as well to his favourite Milton. The *Vernoniad* is Fielding's most successful poem in the mode he attempted as a young man in the unfinished 'Cantos' burlesquing *The Dunciad*; now, however, the verse is more accomplished, and the target no longer Walpole's enemies but Walpole himself, in the figure of Mammon the Corrupter, who conspires with Satan to bribe the god of the winds to negate the success of Admiral Vernon's victory at Porto Bello by preventing the fleet from reaching him in time to secure the West Indies for England.

Whatever the literary quality of this hurried writing might be—and it is remarkably readable considering the circumstances—the money it realized was not enough to satisfy Fielding's creditors—one of whom, a certain Hugh Allen, pursued him through the Palace Court in Southwark until, on 27 February, a bailiff was ordered to track him down and take him into

---

[9] See below, pp. 238–9 ff., and Lockwood, 'New Facts and Writings from an Unknown Magazine by Henry Fielding', *Review of English Studies*, NS 35 (1984), pp. 478–9, and Ribble, 'Fielding and William Young', *SP*, 98 (2001), pp. 468–72.

[10] *History of Our Own Times*, No. 2 (15–29 January), p. 48.

custody. Perhaps by employing the same devices that enabled Booth in *Amelia* to keep his liberty for a time, Fielding managed to remain at large for a week. On 6 March, the day on which the fourth and final number of his magazine appeared after a week's delay and without any apparent contribution from him, Fielding, together with his attorney, appeared before the Court in Southwark. With him were four friends who were willing to stand bail for him; among the four were his eldest sister, Catharine, who had recently inherited her great-aunt's estate, his publisher Charles Corbett, and his peruke-maker John Sangwine. Until the sheriff could be satisfied that the securities offered were sufficient and safe, however, Fielding 'cooled his heels' in a sponging house for a fortnight, regaining his liberty on 20 March. On 24 April a jury would determine that he must pay the debt, plus costs and charges, amounting to £35 9s. 8d., but he managed to put off payment for more than a year.[11]

If Booth in *Amelia* (XII. v) benefited from his sojourn in a sponging house by passing the time reading the sermons of Isaac Barrow, his author in the same situation amused himself profitably, it appears, by writing *Shamela*. Fielding was of course well aware of the extraordinary reception that had been accorded *Pamela* ever since the novel first appeared in November 1740—Parson Oliver, his spokesman in the parody, describes it as an 'epidemical Phrenzy now raging in Town' (p. 157). It was, however, the second edition, published in two volumes on 14 February, that prompted Fielding's uproarious response. This was the edition to which Richardson, as announced on the title-page, 'prefixed, EXTRACTS from several curious LETTERS written to the *Editor* on the Subject'; and, as Oliver remarks in replying to Tickletext, the latter's rapturous 'Expressions' of praise for the work were 'borrowed from those remarkable Epistles, which the Author, or the Editor hath prefix'd to the second Edition which you send me of his Book' (p. 157).[12]

The frenzy over *Pamela* was not, however, the only symptom of what Fielding seems to have considered a general social distemper manifest in virtually every area of public life, whether in letters or politics or religion. There was the popularity of Colley Cibber's self-conceited autobiography with its droll title, *An Apology for the Life of Mr. Colley Cibber, Comedian, and Late Patentee of the Theatre-Royal. Written by Himself.* When the *Apology* was published in April 1740, Fielding had found himself (in

---

[11] For these and other details, see *Life*, pp. 295–6.

[12] Fielding, it should be noted, appears also to have been aware of the third edition of the novel, which was published on 12 March during his incarceration: Tickletext closes his letter by advising Oliver and his fellow clergy to 'supply yourselves for the Pulpit from the Booksellers, as soon as the fourth Edition is published' (p. 156).

chapter viii) roasted as a 'broken wit' whose scurrilous satires had precipitated the Theatrical Licensing Act. In *The Champion* (15 April) he ironically
lauded the work as the very model of '*consummate imperfection*' in writing
(p. 280); '*the Ultra sublime*', he declared in the issue for 3 May, 'will in future
Ages be called the CIBBERIAN STILE' (p. 301). For more than a month in
The Champion he kept up the ridicule of Cibber, of his vanity and attachment to Walpole as well as his ineptitude in prose and verse; these, too,
would soon be the qualifications that earned Cibber the place of Prince of
Folly in Pope's *New Dunciad* (1742).

Similar literary and political offences affronted Fielding's sensibilities
when, on 2 February, the Revd Dr Conyers Middleton, Librarian of
Cambridge University, delivered to his subscribers (more than 1,800 of
them) his *Life of Cicero*, with its egregious Dedication. The Dedication was
florid in style and fulsome in its flattery of John, Lord Hervey, the favourite
of Queen Caroline and of Walpole, whose corrupt policies (as Fielding
saw them) Hervey championed in the House of Lords. Fielding also had a
more personal reason to mock Middleton, who had alluded condescend-
ingly to a work on the same subject by Fielding's patron: George
Lyttelton's *Observations on the Life of Cicero* (1731) would be issued in a
second edition in April 1741, the same month as *Shamela*.

Besides the mockery of *Pamela*, however, the most persistent theme of
Fielding's narrative—one far more prominent than the incidental hits at
Cibber and Middleton[13]—is the need to reform the clergy and so to remove
the only just cause of a widespread contempt of their order. 'The contempt
of the clergy' was a catchphrase heard for decades, and the problem had
been addressed by the divines in a number of tracts—by, among others,
John Eachard (1670), Lancelot Addison (1709), Thomas Stackhouse (1722),
and most recently by John Hildrop (1739). In his plays Fielding's characterization of parsons and priests such as Murdertext in *The Author's Farce*
(1730), Puzzletext in *The Grub-Street Opera* (1731), Father Martin in *The
Old Debauchees* (1732), and Firebrand, the favourite of Queen Ignorance
in *Pasquin* (1736), contributed to the general atmosphere of irreverent
obloquy. Fielding's depiction of the clergy in *Shamela*, however, is the
expression in narrative form of a radical change in his attitude from a
time in the 1730s when he flirted with freethinkers[14] such as Wilson's
'*Rule of Right-men*' in *Joseph Andrews* (III. iii) to a time, first evident in *The*

---

[13] Charles B. Woods first called attention to the importance of HF's treatment of religion and the
clergy in *Shamela* (Woods, pp. 256–72). For a general discussion of this theme in HF's works, see Battestin
(1959, ch. VII).
[14] See the account of HF's association in the 1730s with such freethinkers as Thomas Cooke and James
Ralph (*Life*, pp. 152–7, 199–200).

Champion, when he accepted the Christian religion and recognized its importance, and the importance of those who represented it, to the moral health and political order of society. This would be a recurrent theme in his works during the last fifteen years of his life. The earliest and most elaborate document in Fielding's programme to check the contempt of the priesthood is his 'Apology for the Clergy', a series of four essays published in *The Champion* in the spring of 1740 (the issues for 29 March and 5, 12, 19 April). In these essays he delineated the characters of the true and false priest, providing in discursive form what he would dramatize graphically in the figures of his fiction. Although they are outnumbered by their vicious or incompetent counterparts, the good priests of the novels become, in what they do and say, Fielding's spokesmen.

In *Shamela*, Parson Oliver disabuses the gullible Parson Tickletext as to the true characters of Richardson's heroine and her lover, the hypocritical priest Arthur Williams. Indeed, the most notable of the parody's few departures from the format of Richardson's novel is Fielding's decision to emphasize the message of his 'Apology for the Clergy' by enclosing Shamela's story within the frame of an exchange of letters between two priests, the fatuous Tickletext and his wiser friend the Revd 'J. Oliver', whose name recalls that of the Revd John Oliver, the Dorset curate who taught Fielding Latin as a child.[15]

The theme of the contemptible priest extends to Shamela's reading as well. Having in March returned from South Carolina to resume preaching in the fields near London, the Methodist George Whitefield, a fiery Calvinist whose theology Fielding detested, has won over Shamela with his confessional autobiography, 'that charming Book about the Dealings' (p. 164). And heading the list of inanities that comprise the catalogue of her library is one of the many tracts written by High Churchmen against Fielding's favourite contemporary divine, the latitudinarian bishop Benjamin Hoadly, and his mystery-dispelling treatise on the eucharist, *A Plain Account of the Nature and End of the Sacrament of the Lord's Supper* (1735). At best a contradiction still, Shamela may find the Methodist Whitefield charming, but she has also been taught by Parson Williams to approve the views of that complacent defender of the Established Church, Joseph Trapp, who, in a series of sermons on Ecclesiastes 7: 16, denounced Whitefield's criticism of the worldliness of the clergy as being 'righteous over-much' (p. 171 and n. 86).

Though a work as rude and bawdy and hilarious as any Fielding wrote, *Shamela* is informed from beginning to end by a moral, and indeed

---

[15] From 1707 to his death in 1750 Oliver was curate of St Mary's, Motcombe, near the Fielding farm at East Stour (*Life*, pp. 14 and 628 n. 53).

religious, intent: it is, in this sense, a sequel to Fielding's 'Apology for the Clergy' in *The Champion*. In his final letter to his now chastened colleague, Oliver makes the moral clear:

As to the Character of Parson *Williams*, I am sorry it is a true one. Indeed those who do not know him, will hardly believe it so; but what Scandal doth it throw on the Order to have one bad Member, unless they endeavour to screen and protect him? In him you see a Picture of almost every Vice exposed in nauseous and odious Colours, and if a Clergyman would ask me by what Pattern he should form himself, I would say, Be the reverse of *Williams*: So far therefore he may be of use to the Clergy themselves, and though God forbid there should be many *Williams's* amongst them, you and I are too honest to pretend, that the Body wants no Reformation. (p. 193)

And remembering the clergy who, like Tickletext, had been silly enough publicly to recommend reading *Pamela* as a morally edifying experience— the most notorious of these being Dr Benjamin Slocock, chaplain of St Saviour's, Southwark, who in January had praised the novel from his pulpit—Oliver deprecates 'The confederating to cry up a nonsensical ridiculous Book, (I believe the most extensively so of any ever yet published,) and to be so weak and so wicked as to pretend to make it a Matter of Religion' (pp. 193–4).

PUBLICATION

All the above targets—*Pamela*, Cibber, Middleton, the foolish clergy—were displayed on the title-page, either in plain view or thinly veiled, when Fielding's little book was published on Thursday 2 April 1741,[16] at a shilling and sixpence a copy. The title-page reads as follows (for a photographic reproduction, see p. 147):

AN APOLOGY FOR THE LIFE OF Mrs. SHAMELA ANDREWS. In which, the many notorious FALSHOODS and MISREPRSENTATIONS of a Book called *PAMELA*, Are exposed and refuted; and all the matchless ARTS of that young Politician, set in a true and just Light. Together with A full Account of all that passed between her and Parson *Arthur Williams*; whose Character is represented in a manner something different from what he bears in *PAMELA*. The whole being exact Copies of authentick Papers delivered to the Editor. | Necessary to be had in all FAMILIES. | By Mr. *CONNY KEYBER*.

---

[16] *Daily Post* (2 April 1741). Other advertisements appeared in *The Craftsman* and *Common Sense* for Saturday 4 April; the *Daily Gazetteer* (11, 13, 15 April).

According to the colophon, the work was 'Printed for A. DODD at the *Peacock*, without *Temple-bar*'.[17] But Ann Dodd 'was neither', to borrow Professor Goldgar's efficient phrase, 'a copy-owning bookseller nor a printer, but only one of the more important "mercuries" or distributors of newspapers and pamphlets'.[18] It is known, moreover, thanks to a document brought to light by A. D. McKillop,[19] that on 10 July 1746 Andrew Millar purchased, for 'a very low price', the half-interest in 'Shamela, by Fielding' owned by the bookseller Francis Cogan—one of the partners in Fielding's *Champion*—whose shop, like Ann Dodd's, was also located at Temple Bar. Could Millar have wanted Cogan's half-interest because he owned the other half? Sheridan Baker made the interesting suggestion 'that they both may have been the silent publishers of *Shamela* behind Mrs Dodd and the other mercuries. Millar', Baker reasoned, 'would probably not have bought Cogan's half had he not already owned a half and had he not intended republication of this work by the successful author of *Joseph Andrews*.'[20] Considering that Millar's later association with Mrs Dodd was exactly what Baker suggests (see above, n. 17), and considering as well that, except for the electioneering pamphlets *The Crisis: A Sermon* (April 1741), which may be his, and *The Opposition: A Vision* (December), Fielding's next published work would be that greater burlesque of *Pamela*, *Joseph Andrews* (February 1742), which publicly marked the beginning of his close association with Millar, Baker's suggestion is appealing.

When he wrote *Shamela*, Fielding almost certainly did not know the identity of the author of *Pamela*. That he did not is surprising; for, though the book itself does not carry Richardson's name either as author or printer, many of his contemporaries knew that he wrote it. Most of those 'in the know' were, to be sure, Richardson's close friends and relations: among them were such literary gossips as the bookseller James Leake, Richardson's

[17] Advertisements for *Shamela* in the *Daily Post* (2–4, 14 April) add the information that, in addition to being 'Printed for' Ann Dodd, the pamphlet was also 'sold at the Exchange [i.e. the Royal Exchange, situated in the City between Threadneedle Street and Cornhill], and by J. Jolliffe in St. James's Street [near the Royal Palace in the West End]'. Though Ann Dodd alone is mentioned in the colophon to the work, advertisements in *The Craftsman* (4 April and following)—to wit: 'Printed for A. Dodd, at the Peacock without Temple-Bar; E. Nutt at the Change; and J. Jolliffe, in St. James's-street.'—do not distinguish her part in the publication from that played by the others. 'E. Nutt' is Sarah Nutt, widow of Edward Nutt, book- and pamphlet-seller at the Royal Exchange; she continued at the shop using her husband's initial from about 1735 (see Plomer, pp. 183–5). Two weeks after *Shamela* appeared she was also associated with Ann Dodd in publishing *The Crisis: A Sermon* (16 April), a pamphlet attributed to HF; later she was briefly involved in publishing *The Jacobite's Journal* (December 1747; ed. Coley, pp. liii–liv). John Jollyffe (*fl.* 1731–76), a more prominent bookseller, later moved to Pall Mall (Plomer).
[18] *CGJ*, p. xxix. See also Michael Treadwell, 'London Trade Publishers, 1675–1750', *Library*, 6th ser., 4 (1982), pp. [99]–134, esp. pp. 123–4.
[19] Alan Dugald McKillop, *Samuel Richardson: Printer and Novelist* (Chapel Hill, NC, 1936), pp. 73–4.
[20] Quoted from a draft of Baker's introduction for the Wesleyan Edition.

brother-in-law at Bath, whose shop buzzed with news of this kind; Dr
George Cheyne, also at Bath, who wrote him that Pope and Ralph Allen
were praising the book; the author and critic Aaron Hill, who knew the
identity of the author soon after publication and furnished most of the
preliminary puffs that Fielding ridiculed; and many others, both known
to Richardson and unknown, from whom he received letters, most of them
full of praise.[21] On 7 April, for example, just days after *Shamela* was published, there appeared in the *Daily Advertiser* the following anonymous
epigram entitled 'ADVICE *to* BOOKSELLERS, (*After reading* PAMELA)',
which implicitly congratulates Richardson on his authorship:

> Since printers with such pleasing nature write,
> And since so aukardly your scribes indite,
> Be wise in time, and take a friendly hint;
> Let printers write, and let your writers print.[22]

One would expect Fielding to be in on such an open secret as this; he had
many friends at Bath, where the secret was out, and he was very much a part
of the London literary scene. But that he did not know, or even suspect, that
Richardson was the perpetrator of *Pamela* is surely the case: there is no
hint anywhere in *Shamela* that he thought the book had been written by
that well-known printer—a printer, for that matter, who was to become
Fielding's rival for recognition as the greatest novelist of the century.

It was not the author of *Pamela* but the book itself and what it revealed of
the taste and spirit of the times that Fielding meant to correct by ridicule.
The 'author' of such a book was merely the most recent member of a sort
of fellowship of literary dunces whom Pope had pilloried, and who could
most conveniently be represented by combining into the phantom 'Conny
Keyber' two of their number who would be recognized by any knowledgeable reader of the day. Such a reader would think first of the comedian
Colley Cibber, whose *Apology* for his life inspired Fielding's title and whose
surname had been rendered into Hanoverian German ('Keiber' or 'Keyber')
by his adversaries. But when the reader found the author dedicating the
work 'To Miss *Fanny*', the name Pope had given Walpole's creature the
effeminate courtier John, Lord Hervey, a second prominent figure would
have come into focus. For 'Conny' points to the Cambridge divine Conyers
Middleton and his dedication of the *Life of Cicero* to Hervey.[23]

---

[21] Eaves and Kimpel, pp. 121–2.

[22] The poem was reprinted in *The Gentleman's Magazine* for April (*Pamela Controversy*, i, pp. xxiii
and 177).

[23] For more on Fielding's treatment of Cibber, Middleton, and Hervey, see the notes to the text,
title-page, and Dedication below, pp. 148 and 149–52.

RECEPTION

Richardson, his friends, and admirers understandably bristled at Fielding's travesty of *Pamela*, soon to be resumed in *Joseph Andrews* (February 1742). In a letter to Lady Bradshaigh written in the year of *Tom Jones* (1749), Richardson expressed himself on the subject: 'The Pamela, which [Fielding] abused in his Shamela, taught him how to write to please, tho' his manners are so different. Before his *Joseph Andrews* (hints and names taken from that story, with a lewd and ungenerous engraftment) the poor man wrote without being read.'[24]

But most readers—an insignificant exception being John Kelly, author of a spurious continuation of Richardson's novel[25]—relished *Shamela*. Writing on 12 April to his brother in London, Charles Yorke, son of Lord Chancellor Hardwicke, reported the reception the book was enjoying at Cambridge, where Middleton was university librarian:

Shammela & the Dedications to it, the former as a ridicule on Pamela, & the latter on the Dedication to the Life of Cicero, meet with general Applause.—Your Embassador has not as yet seen the Book, and is credibly informed that it is in such universal Request at the Theatre coffee-house, that unless he were to purchase it for himself (which he has by no means any Intention of doing) it will be impossible for him to gain a sight of it these two months.

Yorke added that among his fellow Cantabrigians of the Water-gruel Club, who met regularly to pronounce on the merits of current best-sellers, *Pamela* was 'condemned without mercy': 'No Advocate appeared on it's behalf—The whole Assembly concurred in Determination.'[26]

A huge success among the sophisticates at Cambridge—as well as such literate judges as Thomas Dampier, Dean of Durham, and Horace Walpole, both of whom also appreciated the ridicule of Middleton's Dedication to Hervey[27]—*Shamela* obviously was favourably received by readers other than 'the Weak and Vicious' sort to whom Kelly consigned it. (Both

---

[24] *Selected Letters of Samuel Richardson*, ed. John Carroll (Oxford, 1964), pp. 133.

[25] In his Introduction to *Pamela's Conduct in High Life* (28 May 1741), Kelly, signing himself 'B.W.', dismissed *Shamela*, together with the anonymous *Pamela Censured*, as hack work, granting it only 'some low Humour adapted to the Standard of a *petit Maitre*'s Capacity; but, I believe, the Author, whoever he is, has not got much Reputation by this Production, except among the Weak and Vicious' (pp. xii–xiii).

[26] BL, Add. MS 35633, fos. 31–2.

[27] In a letter of 30 July 1741 to compatriots at Geneva, Dampier comments on *Pamela* and Middleton's *Life of Cicero*: 'The dedication to Lord Hervey has been very justly and prettily ridiculed by Fielding in a dedication to a pamphlet called "Shamela" which he wrote to burlesque the forementioned romance' (Paulson and Lockwood, No. 38). Among 'Anecdotes relating to Dr. Conyers Middleton' in Walpole's 'Commonplace Book' is the following: 'Lord Hervey got him an infinite number of subscribers [to the *Life of Cicero*]. The dedication to that Lord was extremely ridiculed, particularly by Fielding in his dedication to *Shamela*, an admirable burlesque of *Pamela*' (*Yale Walpole*, xv [1951], p. 296).

Dampier and Walpole, it should be noted, knew Fielding had written it.[28])
The work was also having the effect Fielding hoped for of calming the
frenzy of the *Pamela* enthusiasts, as appears from the anonymous verses 'To
the Author of Shamela' in the *London Magazine* for June:

> Admir'd *Pamela*, till *Shamela* shown,
> Appear'd in every colour—but her own:
> Uncensur'd she remain'd in borrow'd light,
> No nun more chaste, few angels shone so bright.
> But now, the idol we no more adore,
> *Jervice* a bawd, and our chaste nymph a w——
> Each buxom lass may read poor *Booby*'s case,
> And charm a *Williams* to supply his place;
> Our thoughtless sons for round-ear'd caps may burn,
> And curse *Pamela*, when they've serv'd a turn.

Popular demand for *Shamela* appears to have been brisk and widespread.
In Dublin an unauthorized reprint of the first edition was published by
Oliver Nelson on 15 April, not quite a fortnight after the original.[29] Since no
records concerning the printing of the pamphlet have come to light, nothing
is known about the number of copies published or whether other printings
were required before the second edition some seven months later; but after
a hiatus of advertising in the papers beginning in mid-April, a flurry of
advertisements in the *Daily Advertiser* beginning Friday 8 May 1741, and
continuing the following Monday and Wednesday, suggests that there may
well have been a second printing.

A second edition, for the most part merely a corrected reprint of
the original, was published under curious circumstances on Saturday
31 October 1741, not in London but in Norwich, more than a hundred
miles from Ann Dodd's shop at Temple Bar. That, at least, is the date of
the earliest advertisement in the *Norwich Gazette*, announcing that *Shamela*
'This Day is published. Price 1 s. 6 d.'; the same notice was carried again
in that weekly paper on 7 and 14 November. The advertisement quotes the
title-page, as usual; however, it follows the title-page of the first edition not
the second. In order to highlight the ridicule of Middleton, it also elaborates
the concluding text of the title-page: 'Necessary to be had in all Families;

---

[28] In addition to the attributions to Fielding quoted above, n. 27, Walpole wrote 'By Fielding' in his
copy of the second edition (see Cross, i, pp. 306–7; Walpole's copy is in the Lewis Walpole Library,
Farmington, Conn.). Another contemporary who apparently associated HF with *Shamela* was Bonnell
Thornton: ridiculing HF's last novel in *Have At You All: or, The Drury-Lane Journal*, No. 1 (16 January
1752), Thornton burlesqued Millar's advertisements for it, announcing the imminent publication of
'SHAMELIA, A NOVEL.'

[29] Faulkner's *Dublin Journal* (11–14 April 1741).

with a modern DEDICATION after the Manner of the Antients, especially CICERO. By Mr. CONNY KEYBER'. After quoting the colophon, the advertisement concludes by listing three other titles for sale at
Ann Dodd's shop for a shilling, the last of which is 'The Death of
M——l——n in the LIFE of CICERO, being a proper Criticism of that
marvellous Performance. By an Oxford Scholar'. In London this same
advertisement was carried in Fielding's *Champion*, which was published
three times a week, on Tuesday, Thursday, and Saturday: see the issues
beginning Tuesday 3 November, then 5, 10, 12, and 14 November.

Questions remain about this new edition that have no ready answers.
Why the decision to publish it first in Norwich, far off in Norfolk, Walpole's
county? Why, for that matter, the decision seven months after the first
edition to publish a second? What if Baker was right in thinking that Millar
owned a half-interest in *Shamela* from the beginning? And what if Millar
about this time, as might well be the case, knew Fielding was writing
Joseph Andrews, and also knew that he (Millar) was soon to publish it? The
moment perhaps seemed right to remind readers how much they had
enjoyed Fielding's first 'go' at *Pamela* now that his grander work on the
same theme was on the way.

Whatever the motive for producing it may have been, the second edition
of *Shamela* was the last edition of Fielding's brilliant parody to be published
for nearly two centuries. Though Millar owned at least a half-interest in the
work, he and his editor Arthur Murphy omitted *Shamela*, together with the
paraphrase of *Ovid's Art of Love*, all the poetry, and eleven other pamphlets,
from the *Works* of 1762, which, as Murphy assured the public, included
'every thing worthy of a place in this edition'. Not until 1926, after an
interval of 185 years, was there a reprint of the second edition, published by
the Golden Cockerel Press with an introduction by R. Brimley Johnson;
this was followed in 1930 by another, introduced by Brian W. Downs. Not
until 1946, however, with the publication of Charles B. Woods's definitive
article, was the case for Fielding's authorship irreversibly made. From that
watershed, beginning in 1953 with Sheridan Baker's transcription of the
first edition, there has been a spate of editions and reprints.[30]

---

[30] The list of editions since 1926, when the Golden Cockerel Press published R. Brimley Johnson's
reprint, is as follows: *An Apology for the Life of Mrs. Shamela Andrews*, introd. Brian W. Downs (Cambridge, 1930); [ditto], ed. Sheridan W. Baker, Jr. (Berkeley and Los Angeles, 1953) and *Joseph Andrews and
Shamela*, ed. Sheridan W. Baker, Jr. (New York, 1972); *Shamela* [photographic reproduction of 2nd edn.],
ed. Ian Watt, Augustan Reprint Society, No. 57 (Los Angeles, 1956); *Joseph Andrews and Shamela*, ed.
Martin C. Battestin, Riverside Editions (Boston, 1961); [ditto], ed. Douglas Brooks, Oxford English
Novels (Oxford, 1970); and rev., ed. Douglas Brooks-Davies, with introd. Thomas Keymer (Oxford,
1999); [ditto], ed. Homer Goldberg (New York, 1987); [ditto], ed. Judith Hawley, (Harmondsworth,
1999); *Shamela*: [photographic reproduction of 2nd edn.], introd. Thomas Keymer (2001) in *Pamela
Controversy*, i, pp. 49–118.

AN
APOLOGY
FOR THE
LIFE
OF
Mrs. Shamela Andrews.

In which, the many notorious Falshoods and Misreprsentations of a Book called

PAMELA,

Are expofed and refuted; and all the matchlefs Arts of that young Politician, fet in a true and juft Light.

Together with

A full Account of all that paffed between her and Parfon *Arthur Williams*; whofe Character is reprefented in a manner fomething different from what he bears in *PAMELA.* The whole being exact Copies of authentick Papers delivered to the Editor.

Neceffary to be had in all Families.

By Mr. *CONNY KEYBER.*

LONDON:
Printed for A. Dodd, at the *Peacock*, without *Temple-bar.*
M. DCC. XLI.

Lines 14–17: For the character of Williams as he appears in *Pamela*, see below, p. 168 n. 77.

Lines 18–19: As the title-page of *Pamela* makes clear, Richardson posed as the careful editor, not the author, of 'a Series of Familiar Letters from a Beautiful Young Damsel, to her Parents', which comprise the narrative.

Line 20: 'Necessary to be had in all FAMILIES': This phrase was commonly found on the title-page of works offering moral or religious instruction, such as Shamela's favourite *The Whole Duty of Man* (below p. 155 n. 30), which is recommended as '*Necessary for all Families*' (1717 edn.). But HF no doubt also recalls the flattery in letters from Richardson's friends prefixed to the second edition of *Pamela*: in the first of these, 'J.B.D.F.' [Jean-Baptiste de Freval] 'boldly say[s], that if [*Pamela*'s] numerous Beauties are added to its excellent Tendency, it will be found worthy a Place . . . in all Families (especially such as have in them young Persons of either Sex)' (i, p. viii); and Aaron Hill (anonymously) believes *Pamela*'s 'Excellencies cannot be long unknown to the World, and that there will not be a Family without it; so I make no Doubt but every Family that has it, will be much improv'd and better'd by it' (i, p. xiv).

Line 21: The author's name, '*CONNY KEYBER*', consists of a double joke at two targets of HF's satire: (1) Colley Cibber (1671–1757), comedian, playwright, Poet Laureate, and author of the self-congratulatory autobiography *An Apology for the Life of Mr. Colley Cibber, Comedian, and Late Patentee of the Theatre-Royal* (published 7 April 1740); and (2) the Revd Dr Conyers Middleton (1683–1750), Cambridge Librarian and author of *The History of the Life of M. Tullius Cicero* (published 2 February 1741). Both works were in HF's library (Ribbles C28, M19).

The joke would have been caught by any knowledgeable reader of the time. First to come to mind is Cibber, whose *Apology* for his life inspired HF's title and whose surname of Danish extraction (he was the eldest son of the sculptor Caius Gabriel Cibber) was mockingly rendered into German 'Keiber' or 'Keyber' in the opposition press after the production of his anti-Stuart play *The Non-Juror* (1717), which he dedicated to George I, who rewarded him with a present of 200 guineas and later, in 1730, with the laureateship. In the *Apology*, Cibber recalls how the Tory journalist Nathaniel Mist over the course of fifteen years 'scarce ever fail'd of passing some of his Party Compliments upon me: The State, and the Stage, were his frequent Parallels, and the Minister, and *Minheer Keiber* the Menager, were as constantly droll'd upon' (ch. xv, p. 303). In HF's *Author's Farce* (1730; I. iv), 'Mr. Keyber' is not interested in staging Harry Luckless's play. For more on HF's relationship with Cibber, see below, p. 157 n. 36.

'CONNY'—with its overtones (see Partridge) of 'coney' (a dupe) and 'cunny' (the female pudendum), the latter suiting the ribaldry of HF's burlesque—is just a letter away from 'Colly'. But it is closer still to 'Conyers'; and Middleton's *Life of Cicero* is also HF's target, chiefly for two reasons: Middleton had dedicated the work to Walpole's creature, Lord Hervey (see below, the Dedication to 'Miss Fanny', pp. 149–52); and in the Preface (i, p. xxx) he had devoted a paragraph to depreciating the rival biography by HF's friend and patron George Lyttelton (see above, 'Epistle to Lyttleton'), whose *Observations on the Life of Cicero* (1731) was issued in a second edition in April 1741, the month *Shamela* appeared.

Some months later in *Joseph Andrews* (1742; III. vi), HF, launching his career as novelist in another burlesque of *Pamela*, invoked the Muse of Biography: 'Thou who hadst no Hand in that Dedication, and Preface, or the Translations which thou wouldst willingly have struck out of the Life of *Cicero* . . . Thou who without the Assistance of the least Spice of Literature, and even against his Inclination, hast, in some Pages of his Book, forced *Colley Cibber* to write *English*' (p. 239).

To Miss *Fanny*, &c.[1]

MADAM,

IT will naturally be expected, that when I write the Life of *Shamela*, I should dedicate it to some young Lady, whose Wit and Beauty might be the proper Subject of a Comparison with the Heroine of my Piece. This, those, who see I have done it in prefixing your Name to my Work, will much more confirmedly expect me to do; and, indeed, your Character would enable me to run some Length into a Parallel, tho' you, nor like any one else, are at all like the matchless *Shamela*.[2]

You see, Madam, I have some Value for your Good-nature, when in a Dedication, which is properly a Panegyrick, I speak against, not for you; but I remember it is a Life which I am presenting you, and why should I expose my Veracity to any Hazard in the Front of the Work, considering what I

---

[1] 'To Miss *Fanny*, *&c.*': HF's Dedication parodies Conyers Middleton's in the *Life of Cicero*, which is headed: 'To the RIGHT HONORABLE | JOHN Lord HERVEY, | Lord Keeper of His Majesty's Privy Seal'. HF's travesty of this celebrates the effeminate Hervey's notorious bisexuality by substituting salacious vulgarisms for his name and (conveniently 'privy') office: 'Fanny' is slang for the female pudendum; and while the '*&c.*' after the name was a polite formula signifying that a person's titles are well known, the symbol for '*et cetera*' carries the same meaning as 'Fanny' (see Rothstein, pp. 382–3 and n. 3; also below, pp. 156 n. 31; 159 n. 45; 189 n. 129). HF's effeminizing of Hervey was echoed before the month was out by the author of *The Death of M——l——n in the Life of Cicero*, who also anatomizes the Dedication: 'For shame, for shame Doctor. What talk to *my Lord Privy-Seal*, as if you was tattling to a *pretty Miss*? Entertain a Peer of the Realm and a Privy-Counsellor with a *Lulla-by Baby-by!*' (p. 7). (This pamphlet was published on 27 April by the same booksellers who published *Shamela* [*Daily Post*].)

'Lord *Fanny*' was Pope's name for Hervey—the little, foppish, philandering courtier who was Queen Caroline's favourite and Walpole's chief instrument in the House of Lords. (See *First Satire of the Second Book of Horace Imitated* [1733], line 6; Twickenham edn., iv, p. 4 n. 6.) His sinecures at court included appointments as Vice-Chamberlain (1730) and as Lord Privy Seal (1740). His health always delicate, Hervey painted his face with cosmetics to disguise his ghastly pallor, and he observed a strict regimen, drinking no wine or strong liquor. He was also a poet of sorts, hence Pope's couplet: 'The Lines are weak, another's pleas'd to say, | Lord *Fanny* spins a thousand such a Day'; and by rashly indulging his talent for ridicule at Pope's expense, Hervey became the subject of Pope's most devastating satiric portrait, 'Sporus' in the *Epistle to Dr. Arbuthnot* (1734), lines 305–33. HF's parody alludes to all these features of Hervey's life and character. He had earlier satirized Hervey as John the Groom in *The Grub-Street Opera* (1731) and soon Hervey would serve as the model for Beau Didapper in *Joseph Andrews* (1742), esp. p. 313 and n. 1.

[2] Cf. Middleton: 'THE public will naturally expect, that in chusing a Patron for *the Life of* CICERO, I should address myself to some person of illustrious rank, distinguished by his parts and eloquence, and bearing a principal share in the great affairs of the Nation; who, according to the usual stile of Dedications, might be the proper subject of a comparison with the Hero of my piece. Your Lordship's name will confirm that expectation, and Your character would justify me in running some length into the parallel; but . . . Your Lordship knows, what a disadvantage it would be to any character, to be placed in the same light with that of CICERO . . . the following History will suggest a reason in every page, why no man now living can justly be compared with him' (i, pp. [i]–ii).

have done in the Body.[3] Indeed, I wish it was possible to write a Dedication, and get any thing by it, without one Word of Flattery; but since it is not, come on, and I hope to shew my Delicacy at least in the Compliments I intend to pay you.

First, then, Madam, I must tell the World, that you have tickled up and brightned many Strokes in this Work by your Pencil.[4]

Secondly, You have intimately conversed with me, one of the greatest Wits and Scholars of my Age.[5]

Thirdly, You keep very good Hours, and frequently spend an useful Day before others begin to enjoy it.[6] This I will take my Oath on; for I am admitted to your Presence in a Morning before other People's Servants are up; when I have constantly found you reading in good Books; and if ever I have drawn you upon me, I have always felt you very heavy.[7]

Fourthly, You have a Virtue which enables you to rise early and study hard, and that is, forbearing to over-eat yourself, and this in spite of all the luscious Temptations of Puddings and Custards, exciting the Brute (as Dr. *Woodward* calls it) to rebel.[8] This is a Virtue which I

---

[3] Cf. Middleton: 'YOU see, my Lord, how much I trust to your good nature, as well as good sense, when in an *Epistle dedicatory*, the proper place of Panegyric, I am depreciating your abilities, instead of extolling them: but I remember, that it is an History, which I am offering to Your Lordship, and it would ill become me, in the front of such a work, to expose my veracity to any hazard' (i, p. iii).

[4] Cf. Middleton: 'I cannot forbear boasting, that some parts of my present work have been brightened by the strokes of Your Lordship's pencil [i.e. an artist's paintbrush]' (i, p. v).

[5] Cf. Middleton: 'IT was the custom of those *Roman* Nobles, to spend their leisure, not in vicious pleasures, or trifling diversions, contrived, as we truly call it, *to kill the time*; but in conversing with the celebrated wits and Scholars of the age . . . and here Your Lordship imitates them with success' (i, pp. v–vi). HF's 'intimately conversed with me' plays on a secondary meaning of 'converse': to have sexual intercourse (*OED*, 2b, citing *Tom Jones* [VI. x]: 'that Wench, with whom . . . he yet converses' [p. 307]). See below, p. 189 and n. 128.

[6] Cf. Middleton: 'Your Lordship . . . in those early hours, when all around You are hushed in sleep, [you] seize the opportunity of that quiet, as the most favorable season of study, and frequently spend an usefull day, before others begin to enjoy it' (i, p. vii).

[7] Cf. Middleton: 'I AM saying no more, my Lord, than what I know, from my constant admission to Your Lordship in my morning visits, before good manners would permit me to attempt a visit any where else; where I have found You commonly engaged with the Classical writers of *Greece* or *Rome*. . . . I have seen the solid effects of Your reading . . . and have felt Your weight even in controversy, on some of the most delicate parts of their History' (i, pp. vii–viii).

[8] John Woodward FRS (1665–1728), physician and geologist. The phrase HF parodies is Middleton's (see below, n. 9), not Woodward's; but HF alludes to Woodward's treatise *The State of Physic and of Diseases, with an Inquiry into the Causes of the late Increase of Them* (1718), wherein he traces all the evils of civilization—sickness, stupidity, poverty, faction, rebelliousness, atheism—to one cause: the rich pastries and seasoned meats and sauces of 'the New Cookery' (sect. xlvii). But, as Rothstein observed, there is something 'odd' about HF's choice of Woodward in this passage. Though in 1731 Middleton had held the first annual Woodwardian Lectureship at Cambridge, Woodward had been dead for thirteen years and was now neither a timely target for satire nor, as far as Hervey's dietary regime is concerned, the most obvious one. That would be Dr George Cheyne of Bath (1671–1743), author, among other works, of *An Essay of Health and Long Life* (1724), which so impressed Hervey he adopted Cheyne as his personal physician

can greatly admire, though I much question whether I could imitate it.[9]

Fifthly, A Circumstance greatly to your Honour, that by means of your extraordinary Merit and Beauty; you was carried into the Ball-Room at the *Bath*, by the discerning Mr. *Nash*;[10] before the Age that other young Ladies generally arrived at that Honour, and while your Mamma herself existed in her perfect Bloom. Here you was observed in Dancing to balance your Body exactly, and to weigh every Motion with the exact and equal Measure of Time and Tune;[11] and though you sometimes made a false Step, by leaning too much to one Side;[12] yet every body said you would one Time or other, dance perfectly well, and uprightly.

(his 'AEsculapius' as he called him); like Woodward, Cheyne also recommended temperance and a meatless diet, with doses of ass's milk (Halsband, pp. 56–7). What is more, Cheyne, his ungrammatical English, and his dietary theories in *An Essay of Regimen* (1739) had recently been HF's targets in *The Champion* (15 November 1739, 17 May and 12 June 1740), and he would be mocked again in *Tom Jones* (XI. viii, p. 605). Woodward, on the other hand, appears nowhere else in HF's writings (with the possible exception of *The Covent-Garden Journal*, No. 70 [p. 373 n. 3]). But it may not have been Woodward's views on regimen that qualified him for a place in the Dedication to 'Miss *Fanny*, &c.'; more likely, it may well have been, as Rothstein reasons, Woodward's notorious reputation as a cross-dresser and pederast (pp. 383–4).

[9] With the first sentence of the above paragraph, cf. Middleton: 'THERE is another circumstance peculiar to Your Lordship, which makes this task of Study the easier to you, by giving You not onely the greater health, but the greater leisure to pursue it; I mean that singular temperance in diet, in which Your Lordship perseveres with a constancy, superior to every temptation, that can excite an appetite to rebel' (i. p. viii).

[10] Richard 'Beau' Nash (1674–1761), self-styled 'King' of Bath, where among his other polite offices he acted as master of ceremonies in the Guildhall ballroom. HF, who regularly visited Bath and very much enjoyed treading a minuet (*Life*, pp. 357–8), may well have witnessed Nash escorting the effeminate Hervey into the room. He found Nash amusing: in his correspondence with James Harris, he jokes about the 'King', calling him 'CNASH' or 'Snash' and according him all the deference due royalty (Letters 18–19); and in 1748, in tribute to Nash's promotion of Punch and Joan at Bath, HF launched a fashionable puppet show in Panton Street under the name 'Madame de la Nash'. See also *Ovid's Art of Love* (below, p. 417) and *Tom Jones* (XI. iv, p. 585).

[11] Young 'Fanny's' entrance into the ballroom, courtesy of Nash 'the King', while her 'Mamma' still flourishes there is HF's metaphor for Hervey's elevation to the House of Lords in 1733, aged 36, as Lord Hervey of Ickworth in his father's barony, while the Earl of Bristol (1665–1751) was still very much alive (see Halsband, p. 148). Fanny's 'Dancing' mimics Middleton's description of Hervey's political conduct in the Lords: 'In this august Assembly, Your Lordship displays those shining talents, by which You acquired a seat in it, in the defence of our excellent Establishment; in maintaining the rights of the people, yet asserting the prerogative of the Crown; measuring them both by the equal balance of the laws' (i, p. ix). This passage was mocked a month later by the author of *The Death of M——l——n in the Life of Cicero*: 'In one Place he tells his Patron, *that he measures both the Rights of the People, and the Prerogative of the Crown, by the equal* Balance *of the Laws.* I have heard of Things being *weigh'd in a Balance*, but 'tis the first Time I was ever informed of Things being *measured by a Ballance*; but the Doctor has discover'd a new Way of Mensuration, it seems, which proves his Skill in Mechanicks at least' (pp. 9–10).

[12] 'leaning too much to one Side': Alluding to Hervey's politics, presumably his loyalty to Walpole.

Sixthly, I cannot forbear mentioning those pretty little Sonnets, and sprightly Compositions, which though they came from you with so much Ease, might be mentioned to the Praise of a great or grave Character.[13]

And now, Madam, I have done with you; it only remains to pay my Acknowledgments to an Author, whose Stile I have exactly followed in this Life, it being the properest for Biography. The Reader, I believe, easily guesses, I mean *Euclid's Elements*; it was *Euclid* who taught me to write. It is you, Madam, who pay me for Writing.[14] Therefore I am to both,

> *A most Obedient, and obliged humble Servant,*
> Conny Keyber.[15]

LETTERS TO THE EDITOR.

The EDITOR to *Himself.*

Dear SIR,

HOWEVER you came by the excellent *Shamela*, out with it, without Fear or Favour, Dedication and all; believe me, it will go through many Editions, be translated into all Languages, read in all Nations and Ages, and to say a bold Word, it will do more good than the C——y have done harm in the World.[16]

> *I am, Sir,*
> *Sincerely your Well-wisher,*
> Yourself.

---

[13] Cf. Middleton: 'BUT I ought to ask Your Lordship's pardon for dwelling so long upon a character, which is known to the whole Kingdom . . . not onely by the high Office, which You fill, and the eminent dignity that You bear in it, but by the sprightly compositions of various kinds, with which Your Lordship has often entertained it. It would be a presumption, to think of adding any honor to Your Lordship by my pen, after You have acquired so much by Your own' (i, pp. xi–xii). Halsband characterizes Hervey as 'practising two separate roles' as a writer: 'a public one as a propagandist for the Administration, and a private one as a self-indulgent amateur versifier' (p. 161)—in the latter role, by collaborating with HF's cousin Lady Mary Wortley Montagu against Pope, he is chiefly remembered in literature as 'Lord Fanny' and 'Sporus'.

[14] Cf. Middleton: 'it was CICERO, who instructed me to write; Your Lordship, who rewards me for writing' (i, p. xiii). Euclid's *Elements*, the basic textbook of geometry since the third century BC, was known for 'the prolixity of the style' (*EB*, s.v. 'Euclid' [ix. 879b]).

[15] See above, note to title-page, line 20.

[16] 'C——y': *Clergy*. HF may have heard a version of Pope's (dubious) praise of *Pamela*, reported by Dr Cheyne at Bath in a letter of 12 February 1741 to Richardson in London: 'it will do more good than a great many of the new Sermons' (Eaves and Kimpel, p. 124). See also the Introduction, p. 134 n. 5.

JOHN PUFF, *Esq; to the* EDITOR.

SIR,

I have read your *Shamela* through and through, and a most inimitable Performance it is.[17] Who is he, what is he that could write so excellent a Book?[18] He must be doubtless most agreeable to the Age, and to *his Honour*[19] himself; for he is able to draw every thing to Perfection but Virtue. Whoever the Author be, he hath one of the worst and most fashionable Hearts in the World,[20] and I would recommend to him, in his next Performance, to undertake the Life of *his Honour*.[21] For he who drew the Character of Parson *Williams*, is equal to the Task; nay he seems to have little more to do than to pull off the Parson's Gown, and *that* which makes him so agreeable to *Shamela*, and the Cap will fit.

I am, SIR,

Your humble Servant,

JOHN PUFF.

Note, Reader, several other COMMENDATORY LETTERS and COPIES of VERSES will be prepared against the NEXT EDITION.

---

[17] Cf. the opening exclamation of the first 'puffing' letter, by Freval: 'I HAVE had inexpressible Pleasure in the Perusal of your PAMELA' (i, p. vii).

[18] Cf. Aaron Hill in his second 'puffing' letter, who praises 'the wonderful AUTHOR of PAMELA.— Pray, Who is he, Dear Sir? And where, and how, has he been able to hide, hitherto, such an encircling and all-mastering Spirit?' (i, p. xvii).

[19] '*his Honour*': a sarcastic sobriquet for Walpole among the anti-ministerial writers, as in HF's *Vernoniad* (January 1741) and a few months earlier in *The Champion* (9 October 1740) and the *Address to the Electors*: see *Champion*, pp. 475, 548, 564 [24]. Woods (pp. 254–6) notes the frequency with which the name occurs in *The Champion* and quotes the following letter from a correspondent in the issue for 14 June 1740: 'Your Distinction of HIS HONOUR is certainly very just and applicable; for who is more deserving of that Title, than *One* that never *prevaricated*, trifled, or *falsified* his *Word* in a *Public Assembly*, and is as *eminent* in all the *Courts* of *Europe*, as in his own Country, for his *Personal* and *Political Resolution*, *untainted Virtue*, and *Public Spirit*.' See also below, n. 21.

[20] Cf. Aaron Hill, who continues the vein of praise: 'what, above All, I am charm'd with, is the amiable *Good-nature* of the AUTHOR; who, I am convinc'd, has one of the best, and most generous Hearts, of Mankind: because, mis-measuring *other* Minds, by *His Own*, he can draw Every thing, to Perfection, but *Wickedness*' (i, p. xviii).

[21] In his Introduction to *The Champion* Coley, noting that this is HF's 'one shot' at Walpole in *Shamela*, wonders if 'Puff's' advice that the 'Author' next 'undertake the Life of *his Honour* [Walpole]' might imply 'the curious possibility that the "real" author's [Fielding's] next contemplated performance was indeed a sort of "Life" of the minister, namely, *Jonathan Wild*' (pp. xc–xci; see also Woods, p. 256 n. 28). For the argument that HF, perhaps influenced by Dodington, drafted *Jonathan Wild* during the period of his association with *The Champion*, see *Life*, pp. 280–5.

AN

APOLOGY

For the LIFE of

Mrs. SHAMELA ANDREWS

Parson TICKLETEXT *to Parson* OLIVER.[22]

Rev. SIR,

HEREWITH I transmit you a Copy of sweet, dear, pretty *Pamela*, a little Book which this Winter hath produced; of which, I make no Doubt, you have already heard mention from some of your Neighbouring Clergy; for we have made it our common Business here, not only to cry it up, but to preach it up likewise: The Pulpit, as well as the Coffee-house, hath resounded with its Praise,[23] and it is expected shortly, that his L———p will recommend it in a —— Letter to our whole Body.[24]

And this Example, I am confident, will be imitated by all our Cloth in the Country: For besides speaking well of a Brother, in the Character of the Reverend Mr. *Williams*, the useful and truly religious Doctrine of *Grace* is everywhere inculcated.[25]

This Book is the 'SOUL of *Religion*, Good-Breeding, Discretion, Good-Nature, Wit, Fancy, Fine Thought, and Morality. There is an Ease, a natural Air, a dignified Simplicity, and a MEASURED FULLNESS in it,

---

[22] On the thematic importance of the framing device of the exchange of letters between Tickletext and Oliver, which is not a feature of Richardson's novel, see the Introduction, pp. 138–40, esp. p. 139. Tickletext, a colloquial name for a parson (Grose, s.v.), joins other clergy in HF's plays whose names suggest abusing the scripture: namely, Murdertext in *The Author's Farce* (1730) and Puzzletext in *The Grub-Street Opera* (1731). Oliver, whose Christian name begins with 'J.' (below, p. 194) will serve as HF's spokesman in *Shamela*; he may be meant as a compliment to the Revd John Oliver, the Dorset curate who taught HF Latin as a boy (*Life*, p. 14).

[23] The most notorious instance of this was Dr Benjamin Slocock's praising *Pamela* from the pulpit of St Saviour's, Southwark (see Introduction, p. 140).

[24] Edmund Gibson (1669–1748), who from his appointment as Bishop of London in 1723 wrote frequent 'pastoral' letters to the clergy of the diocese.

[25] Richardson's heroine repeatedly attributes the preservation of her virtue to 'the Divine Grace', 'the same protecting Grace', and it is 'by God's Grace' that she is saved from suicide and damnation (2nd edn., i, pp. 62, 106, 288). In commending this 'truly religious Doctrine', Tickletext reveals himself as a member of the High Church party within the Church of England, which inculcated the orthodox Pauline doctrine of justification by faith only, whereas HF favoured the Low Church latitudinarian party, which, after St James, emphasized the importance of works (see the Introduction, p. 139). HF resumed the theme in *Joseph Andrews* (I. x), when Joseph, writing to his sister Pamela, hopes he 'shall have more Resolution and more Grace than to part with my Virtue', and is certain that she 'will have Grace to preserve your Virtue against all Trials' (p. 46); later in the novel, Pamela (IV. vii), then herself 'Lady' Booby, advises him against his relationship with the low-born Fanny Goodwill: 'It would become you better, Brother, to pray for the Assistance of Grace against such a Passion' (p. 302). Cf. also Thwackum, the morose and villainous clergyman in *Tom Jones* (III. iii), whose 'favourite Phrase . . . was the *divine Power of Grace*' (p. 126).

that RESEMBLING LIFE, OUT-GLOWS IT. The author hath reconciled the *pleasing* to the *proper*; the Thought is every where exactly cloathed by the Expression; and becomes its Dress as *roundly* and as close as *Pamela* her Country Habit; or *as she doth her no Habit*, when modest Beauty seeks to hide itself, by casting off the Pride of Ornament, and displays itself without any Covering';[26] which it frequently doth in this admirable Work, and presents Images to the Reader, which the coldest Zealot cannot read without Emotion.

For my own Part (and, I believe, I may say the same of all the Clergy of my Acquaintance) 'I have done nothing but read it to others, and hear others again read it to me, ever since it came into my Hands; and I find I am like to nothing else, for I know not how long yet to come: because if I lay the Book down *it comes after me*. When it has dwelt all Day long upon the Ear, it takes Possession all Night of the Fancy. It hath Witchcraft in every Page of it.'[27]—Oh! I feel an Emotion even while I am relating this: Methinks I see *Pamela* at this Instant, with all the Pride of Ornament cast off.

'Little Book, charming *Pamela*, get thee gone; face the World, in which though wilt find nothing like thy self.'[28] Happy would it be for Mankind, if all other Books were burnt,[29] that we might do nothing but read thee all Day, and Dream of thee all Night. Thou alone art sufficient to teach us as much Morality as we want. Dost thou not teach us to pray, to sing Psalms, and to honour the Clergy? Are not these the Whole Duty of Man?[30] Forgive me, O Author of *Pamela*, mentioning the Name of a Book so unequal to thine: But, now I think of it, who is the Author, where is he, what is he, that

[26] In this paragraph HF conflates passages from Hill's second and third letters (i, pp. xvi, xx), making only three mischievous alterations: (1) emphasizing with small caps Hill's 'measured Fullness . . . resembling Life, out-glows it' (i, p. xx); (2) adding 'or *as she doth her no Habit*' (i, p. xx); and (3) altering Hill's 'without a Covering' (i, p. xx) to 'without any Covering'.

[27] The quoted passage in this paragraph is from Hill's second letter (i, p. xvi), HF italicizing 'it comes after me'.

[28] Cf. the first of the complimentary letters, from Richardson's French friend Jean-Baptiste de Freval: 'Little Book, charming PAMELA! Face the World' most particularly decadent France, which it will reform (i, p. ix).

[29] In a letter to Richardson in January, Knightley Chetwood had declared of *Pamela*: 'if all the Books in England were to be burnt, this Book, next the Bible, ought to be preserved' (Eaves and Kimpel, p. 121).

[30] Cf. Ecclesiastes 12: 13: 'Let us hear the conclusion of the whole matter: Fear God, and keep his commandments: for this *is* the whole *duty* of man.' *The Whole Duty of Man* (1658), to which Tickletext refers, was a favourite devotional work defining the individual's duty to God and his neighbour; it was probably written by Richard Allestree (1619–81), Chaplain to the King and Provost of Eton, where for an hour every Sunday afternoon HF would have heard it read aloud (*Life*, p. 41). It is one of the 'good Books' Joseph Andrews has read (1. iii, p. 24); and Shamela finds it—or rather part of it, the sections on one's duty to one's neighbour having been torn out of her copy (below, p. 181, n. 110)—diverting (below, p. 175). For emphasizing moral and religious duties rather than justification by faith alone, it had been recently attacked by the Methodist Whitefield in *A Letter . . . Shewing the Fundamental Error of a Book Entituled The Whole Duty of Man* (1740).

hath hitherto been able to hide such an encircling, all-mastering Spirit, 'he possesses every 'Quality that Art could have charm'd by: yet hath lent it to and concealed it in Nature. The Comprehensiveness of his Imagination must be truly prodigious! It has stretched out this diminutive mere Grain of Mustard-seed (a poor Girl's little, *&c.*) into a Resemblance of that Heaven, which the best of good Books has compared it to.'[31]

To be short, this Book will live to the Age of the Patriarchs, and like them will carry on the good Work many hundreds of Years hence, among our Posterity, who will not HESITATE their Esteem with Restraint.[32] If the *Romans* granted Exemptions to Men who begat a *few* Children for the Republick, what Distinction (if Policy and we should ever be reconciled) should we find to reward this Father of Millions, which are to owe Formation to the future Effect of his Influence.[33]—I feel another Emotion.

As soon as you have read this your self five or six Times over (which may possibly happen within a Week) I desire you would give it to my little God-Daughter, as a Present from me. This being the only Education we intend henceforth to give our Daughters.[34] And pray let your Servant-Maids read it over, or read it to them. Both your self and the neighbouring Clergy, will supply yourselves for the Pulpit from the Booksellers, as soon as the fourth Edition is published.[35] I am,

> *Sir,*
>> *Your most humble Servant,*
>> THO. TICKLETEXT

[31] The passage in quotation marks that concludes this paragraph, together with the introduction to it beginning 'But, now I think of it', is taken from Hill's first letter (i, p. xvii), except HF romanizes the italic '*Grain of Mustard-seed*' and substitutes '*&c.*' for the two last words in the parenthesis '(a poor Girl's little, innocent, story)'; for the obscene meaning of '*&c.*' see above, p. 149 n. 1. The biblical reference is to Mark 4: 30–2.

[32] With the first sentence of this paragraph, cf. Hill's second letter: 'this Book.—It will live on, through Posterity, with such unbounded Extent of Good Consequences, that Twenty Ages to come may be the Better and Wiser, for its Influence. . . . And, let me abominate the contemptible *Reserves of mean-spirited Men*, who while they but *hesitate* their Esteem, with Restraint, can be fluent and uncheck'd in their *Envy*' (i, pp. xviii–xix).

[33] With the last sentence, cf. Hill's second letter: 'I was thinking, just now, . . . on that *Old Roman Policy*, of Exemptions in Favour of Men, who had given a few, bodily, Children to the Republic.—What superior Distinction ought *our* Country to find (but that *Policy* and *We* are at Variance) for Reward of this *Father, of Millions of* MINDS, which are to owe new Formation to the future Effect of his Influence!' (i, p. xix).

[34] Hill, in his letter of 17 December 1740 prefixed to the second edition, gratefully acknowledged receipt of a copy of *Pamela* Richardson had sent his daughters Astræa and Minerva: 'Though I open'd this powerful little Piece with more Expectation than from common Designs, . . . because it came from *your* Hands, for my *Daughters*, yet, who could have dreamt, he should find, under the modest Disguise of a *Novel*, all the *Soul* of Religion, Good-breeding, Discretion, Good-nature, Wit, Fancy, Fine Thought, and Morality?' (i, p. xvi).

[35] The third edition of *Pamela* appeared on 12 March, during HF's confinement for debt; the fourth would be published in May.

Parson OLIVER *to Parson* TICKLETEXT.

Rev. SIR,

I Received the Favour of yours with the inclosed Book, and really must own myself sorry, to see the Report I have heard of an epidemical Phrenzy now raging in Town, confirmed in the Person of my Friend.

If I had not known your Hand, I should, from the Sentiments and Stile of the Letter, have imagined it to come from the Author of the famous Apology, which was sent me last Summer;[36] and on my reading the remarkable Paragraph of *measured Fulness, that resembling Life out-glows it,*[37] to a young Baronet, he cry'd out, *C—ly C—b—r by G—.*[38] But I have since observed, that this, as well as many other Expressions in your Letter, was borrowed from those remarkable Epistles, which the Author, or the Editor hath prefix'd to the second Edition which you send me of his Book.[39]

Is it possible that you or any of your Function can be in earnest, or think the Cause of Religion, or Morality, can want such slender Support? God forbid they should. As for Honour to the Clergy, I am sorry to see them so solicitous about it; for if worldly Honour be meant, it is what their Predecessors in the pure and primitive Age, never had or sought.[40] Indeed the secure Satisfaction of a good Conscience, the Approbation of the Wise and Good, (which never were or will be the Generality of Mankind) and the extatick Pleasure of contemplating, that their ways are acceptable to the Great Creator of the Universe, will always attend those, who really deserve these Blessings: But for worldly Honours, they are often the Purchase of Force and Fraud, we sometimes see them in an eminent Degree possessed by Men, who are notorious for Luxury, Pride, Cruelty, Treachery, and the most abandoned Prostitution; Wretches who are ready to invent and maintain Schemes repugnant to the Interest, the Liberty, and the Happiness of Mankind, not to supply their Necessities, or even Conveniencies, but

---

[36] Cibber's *Apology* for his life was published in April 1740 and immediately became the target of ridicule in HF's *Champion*: see the Introduction, pp. 137–8.

[37] See above, p. 155 and n. 26.

[38] 'C[ol]ly C[ib]b[e]r by G[od]'.

[39] See the Introduction, p. 137.

[40] On HF's concern over 'the contempt of the clergy' and his efforts to reform their order by exposing the un-Christian conduct of worldly priests while honouring those, like Parson Oliver, who are a credit to their calling, see the Introduction, pp. 137–9). In *Joseph Andrews* (1. xvii) this is the one and only theme on which Parson Adams, like Oliver, sides with the Methodist George Whitefield: 'Sir,' answered *Adams*, speaking to Parson Barnabas, who rails against Whitefield for wanting to 'reduce us to the Example of the Primitive Ages forsooth!', 'if Mr. *Whitfield* had carried his Doctrine no farther than you mention, I should have remained, as I once was, his Well-Wisher. I am myself as great an Enemy to the Luxury and Splendour of the Clergy as he can be. I do not, more than he, by the flourishing Estate of the Church, understand the Palaces, Equipages, Dress, Furniture, rich Dainties, and vast Fortunes of her Ministers. Surely those things, which savour so strongly of this World, become not the Servants of one who professed his Kingdom was not of it' (p. 82).

to pamper their Avarice and Ambition. And if this be the Road to worldly Honours, God forbid the Clergy should be even suspected of walking in it.[41]

The History of *Pamela* I was acquainted with long before I received it from you, from my Neighbourhood to the Scene of Action. Indeed I was in hopes that young Woman would have contented herself with the Good-fortune she hath attained; and rather suffered her little Arts to have been forgotten than have revived their Remembrance, and endeavoured by perverting and misrepresenting Facts to be thought to deserve what she now enjoys: for though we do not imagine her the Author of the Narrative itself, yet we must suppose the Instructions were given by her, as well as the Reward, to the Composer. Who that is, though you so earnestly require of me, I shall leave you to guess from that *Ciceronian* Eloquence, with which the Work abounds; and that excellent Knack of making every Character amiable, which he lays his hands on.[42]

But before I send you some Papers relating to this Matter, which will set *Pamela* and some others in a very different Light, than that in which they appear in the printed Book, I must beg leave to make some few Remarks on the book itself, and its Tendency, (admitting it to be a true Relation,) towards improving Morality, or doing any good, either to the present Age, or Posterity: which when I have done, I shall, I flatter myself, stand excused from delivering it, either into the hands of my Daughter, or my Servant-Maid.

The Instruction which it convents to Servant-Maids, is, I think, very plainly this, To look out for their Masters as sharp as they can. The Consequences of which will be, besides Neglect of their Business, and the using all manner of Means to come at Ornaments of their Persons, that if the Master is not a Fool, they will be debauched by him; and if he is a Fool, they will marry him. Neither of which, I apprehend, my good Friend, we desire should be the Case of our Sons.

---

[41] In the first (29 March 1740) of the four leaders that comprise the 'Apology for the Clergy' in *The Champion*, HF ascribes 'superior Dignity and Honour' to those whose 'Office . . . concerns the eternal Happiness of the Souls of Men'; and, he continues, 'here I would not be understood to mean what we vulgarly call Honour and Dignity in a worldly Sense, such as Pomp or Pride, or Flattery, or any of this Kind to which indeed nothing can be so opposite' (p. 259).

[42] Oliver has Middleton in mind. In the Dedication to his *Life of Cicero* Middleton declares 'it was CICERO, who instructed me to write' (i, p. xiii). Like HF, the 'Oxford Scholar' who wrote *The Death of M——l——n in the Life of Cicero* criticized Middleton for making his subject 'a faultless Monster of his own creating' whereas he praised Lyttelton in his *Observations on the Life of Cicero* for 'draw[ing] him as he really was, a Man of great Abilities and Virtues, and yet subject to as great Infirmities and Failings' (pp. 24–5).

And notwithstanding our Author's Professions of Modesty,[43] which in my youth I have heard at the Beginning of an Epilogue,[44] I cannot agree that my Daughter should entertain herself with some of his Pictures; which I do not expect to be contemplated without Emotion, unless by one of my Age and Temper, who can see the Girl lie on her Back, with one Arm round Mrs. *Jewkes* and the other round the Squire, naked in Bed, with his Hand on her Breasts, *&c.*[45] with as much Indifference as I read any other Page in the whole Novel. But surely this, and some other Descriptions, will not be put in the hands of his Daughter by any wise Man, though I believe it will be difficult for him to keep them from her; especially if the Clergy in Town have cried and preached it up as you say.

But, my Friend, the whole Narrative is such a Misrepresentation of Facts, such a Perversion of Truth, as you will, I am perswaded, agree, as soon as you have perused the Papers I now inclose to you, that I hope you or some other well-disposed Person, will communicate these Papers to the Publick, that this little Jade may not impose on the World, as she hath on her Master.

The true name of this Wench was *SHAMELA*, and not *Pamela*, as she stiles herself. Her Father had in his Youth the Misfortune to appear in no good Light at the *Old-Baily*;[46] he afterwards served in the Capacity of a Drummer in one of the *Scotch* Regiments in the *Dutch* Service;[47] where being drummed out, he came over to *England*, and turned Informer against several Persons on the late Gin-Act;[48] and becoming acquainted with an

---

[43] In his Preface, Richardson, modestly presenting himself as merely the editor not the author of *Pamela*, claims, despite the pruriency of many scenes in the novel, that these are 'practical *Examples, worthy to be followed in the most* critical *and* affecting *Cases, by the modest* Virgin' (i, p. v).

[44] Perhaps, as Aurélien Digeon suggested (*Les Romans de Fielding* [Paris, 1923], p. 67 n. 1), the Epilogue Cibber wrote for HF's *The Miser* (1733): 'Nor would I in that lovely Circle raise | One Blush, to gain a thousand Coxcombs' Praise'. But affectations of modesty are to be found in many epilogues of the period.

[45] The episode Oliver describes occurs at Mr B's Lincolnshire estate, of which Pamela gives an account to her mother in a letter headed '*TUESDAY Night*' (i, pp. 266–79): 'the guilty Wretch [Mr B] took my left Arm, and laid it under his Neck, as the vile Procuress [Mrs Jewkes] held my Right; and then he clasp'd me round my Waist! . . . and then . . . he put his Hand in my Bosom' (i, pp. 272–3). (For the ribald meaning of '*&c.*', see above, p. 149 n. 1). This scene is parodied below, p. 177. Despite such scenes, Richardson on the title-page assured his readers that the novel was 'intirely divested of all those Images, which, in too many Pieces calculated for Amusement only, tend to *inflame* the Minds they should *instruct*'.

[46] '*Old-Bailey*': the central criminal court of London.

[47] In 1665, when war broke out between England and the Netherlands, the Dutch Republic compelled the British regiments that had been serving them to swear allegiance to Holland. The English refused and returned home, but the Scots remained in the Dutch service for a century—making Shamela's father a traitor to his country.

[48] In an effort to control widespread drunkenness among the lower classes, Parliament in 1736 passed the 'Gin Act' (9 Geo. II, c. 23), which imposed a prohibitive duty on all spirituous liquors. The Act was extremely unpopular and riots broke out against it; if seized by the mob, those who informed against violators of the law were in danger of their lives. The Act is the subject of a satire HF contributed to *The Craftsman*, No. 518 (5 June 1736), and it inspired a character called the Genius of Gin in his farce *Tumble-Down Dick* (1736).

Hostler at an Inn, where a *Scotch* Gentleman's Horses stood, he hath at last by his Interest obtain'd a pretty snug Place in the *Custom-house*.⁴⁹ Her Mother sold Oranges in the Play-House;⁵⁰ and whether she was married to her Father or no, I never could learn.

After this short Introduction, the rest of her History will appear in the following Letters, which I assure you are authentick.⁵¹

LETTER I.

SHAMELA ANDREWS *to* Mrs. HENRIETTA
MARIA HONORA ANDREWS *at her Lodgings at*
the Fan *and* Pepper-Box *in* Drury-Lane.⁵²

Dear Mamma,

THIS comes to acquaint you, that I shall set out in the Waggon on *Monday*, desiring you to commodate me with a Ludgin, as near you as possible, in *Coulstin's-Court*, or *Wild Street*,⁵³ or somewhere there-abouts; pray let it be handsome, and not above two Stories high: For Parson

---

⁴⁹ Situated west of the Tower between Thames Street and the river, the Custom House, where duties were levied on goods imported and exported, was notorious for jobbery: Roy Porter notes that 'by 1718 there were 561 full-time and another 1,000 part-time customs officers in the Port of London alone' and 'every post's official salary could be doubled by fees and perks' (*English Society in the Eighteenth Century* [London, 1982], pp. 122–3). As First Lord of the Treasury, Walpole controlled the departments of Customs and Excise. Since the Union in 1707, Scotland was rife with disloyalty and fractiousness, which he attempted to control by bribing the Scottish peers and the forty-five Scottish MPs with fat pensions. The Opposition claimed that the duties and taxes imposed by Parliament (from which Scotland was exempt) were owing chiefly to the votes of Walpole's 'hirelings—the Scottish members' (J. H. Plumb, *Sir Robert Walpole: The King's Minister* [Cambridge, Mass., 1961], pp. 104–5, 243–4).

⁵⁰ Orange women at the theatres were thought of as prostitutes. Cf. the genealogy of HF's Jonathan Wild (1. ii), whose spinster aunt—her name, Honour, recalling Mrs Andrews's 'Honora'—'was a great frequenter of Plays, and used to be remarkable for distributing Oranges to all who would accept of them' (p. 12). 'Orange' was also a slang term for 'the female pudend' (Partridge, s.v.). The 'Play-House' in question is Drury Lane (below, p. 161 n. 57).

⁵¹ In his Preface posing as editor of the book, Richardson repeated the claim of the title-page: '*the following Letters . . . have their Foundation in* Truth *and* Nature' (i, p. v).

⁵² Shamela's mother is named after Charles I's Catholic queen, Henrietta Maria, whom the Puritan William Prynne in *Histriomastix* (1632), a diatribe against stage plays, was supposed to have insulted for taking part with actresses in the rehearsal of a play. Mrs Andrews's association with the disreputable aspects of the theatre district of Drury Lane, which, according to Ned Ward, contained no fewer than 107 brothels (*A View of London and Westminster* [1725], i, pp. 13–14; ii, p. 48), is confirmed by the name HF gives the tavern she lives in: as in 'Fanny' (see above, p. 149, n. 1), 'Fan' is slang for the female sex organ (HF had played on the word this way in *Pasquin*, Act II); and 'peppered' is slang for one's being infected by venereal disease (Grose).

⁵³ Not far from the Theatre Royal, Coulstin's (or rather Colson's, according to Rocque's survey [11Ba]) Court ran between Drury Lane and Great Wild Street.

Williams hath promised to visit me when he comes to Town, and I have got a good many fine Cloaths of the Old Put[54] my Mistress's, who died a wil ago; and I beleve Mrs. *Jervis* will come along with me, for she says she would like to keep a House somewhere about *Short's-Gardens*, or towards *Queen-Street*;[55] and if there was convenience for a *Bannio*,[56] she should like it the better; but that she will settle herself when she comes to Town.— *O! How I long to be in the Balconey at the Old House*[57]—so no more at present from

Your affectionate Daughter,[58]

SHAMELA.

LETTER II.[59]

SHAMELA ANDREWS *to* HENRIETTA
MARIA HONORA ANDREWS.

Dear Mamma,

O WHAT News, since I writ my last! the young Squire hath been here, and as sure as a Gun[60] he hath taken a Fancy to me; *Pamela*, says he, (for so I am called here) you was a great Favourite of your late Mistress's; yes, an't please your Honour, says I; and I believe you deserv'd it, says he; thank your Honour for your good Opinion, says I; and then he took me by the Hand, and I pretended to be shy: Laud, says I, Sir, I hope you don't intend to be rude; no, says he, my Dear, and then he kissed me, 'till he took

---

[54] 'Put': a blockhead, a duffer (*OED*, s.v., sb.⁴). Cf. *Joseph Andrews* (III. xii), where an ill-mannered servant calls Parson Adams 'the Old Put' (p. 272). Having reported her mistress's death in her first letter, Pamela, in Letter VI, writes that Mr B. 'has given me a Suit of my late Lady's Cloaths, and half a Dozen of her Shifts, and Six fine Handerchiefs, and Three of her Cambrick Aprons, and Four Holland ones. The Cloaths are fine Silk, and too rich and too good for me, to be sure' (i, p. 11).

[55] From Drury Lane, Short's Gardens extended towards Queen Street, which continued directly to Seven Dials in the parish of St Giles, a poor neighbourhood and one of the so-called 'rookeries' (or crime quarters) of London (Phillips, *Mid-Georgian London*, pp. 218–19).

[56] i.e. 'Bagnio': A house for hot therapeutic baths serving also as a brothel. In *Amelia* (I. vi) HF relates an episode of his youth when he saw the notorious prostitute Betty Careless 'in Bed with a Rake at a Bagnio' (p. 47). In Letter XII, Pamela writes that Mrs Jervis 'wish'd it was in her Power to live independent; that then she would take a little private House, and I should live with her like her Daughter' (i, p. 22).

[57] Cf. Pamela's closing exclamation to her mother in Letter XII: 'O that I had never left my little Bed in the Loft' (i, p. 23). The '*Old House*': the Theatre Royal at Drury Lane, where Shamela's mother sold oranges (above, p. 160).

[58] Pamela's usual signature is '*Your dutiful Daughter*', varied, according to the occasion and her mood, with '*afflicted*', '*distressed*', '*honest*', etc.

[59] Cf. Pamela's Letter XI, describing for her mother the first of Mr B.'s frustrated attempts on her virtue in the summer-house.

[60] 'as sure as a Gun': proverbial as early as 1622, meaning beyond all question, a dead certainty (*OED*, s.v. 'gun' 6a), citing HF's *Intriguing Chambermaid* (1734): ''Tis as pure, and as sure, and secure as a Gun, | The young Lover's Business is happily done' (I. i). See also below, p. 183 n. 117.

away my Breath—and I pretended to be Angry, and to get away, and then he kissed me again, and breathed very short, and looked very silly; and by Ill-Luck Mrs. *Jervis* came in, and had like to have spoiled Sport.—*How troublesome is such Interruption!*[61] You shall hear now soon, for I shall not come away yet, so I rest,

Your affectionate Daughter,

SHAMELA.

LETTER III.

HENRIETTA MARIA HONORA ANDREWS

to SHAMELA ANDREWS.

Dear Sham,

YOUR last Letter hath put me into a great hurry of Spirits,[62] for you have a very difficult Part to act. I hope you will remember your Slip with Parson *Williams*, and not be guilty of any more such Folly. Truly, a Girl who hath once known what is what, is in the highest Degree inexcusable if she respects her *Digressions*; but a Hint of this is sufficient.[63] When Mrs. *Jervis* thinks of coming to Town, I believe I can procure her a good House, and fit for the Business; so I am,

Your affectionate Mother,

HENRIETTA MARIA HONORA ANDREWS.

LETTER IV.

SHAMELA ANDREWS *to* HENRIETTA

MARIA HONORA ANDREWS.

MARRY come up,[64] good Madam, the Mother had never looked into the Over for her Daughter, if she had not been there herself. I shall

---

[61] Cf. Pamela's rather different moralizing ejaculation, one of many such in the novel, after successfully resisting her master's assault: 'O how poor and mean must those Actions be, and how little must they make the best of Gentlemen look, when they offer such things as are unworthy of themselves, and put it into the Power of their Inferiors to be greater than they!' (i, pp. 19–20).

[62] Unwelcome surprises often throw HF's female characters into a 'hurry of Spirits': so it is with Mrs Heartfree in *Jonathan Wild* (IV. x; *Miscellanies* iii, p. 167); in *Tom Jones* Lady Bellaston (XIII. ix, p. 726; XIV. ii, p. 744) and Sophia (XVIII. ix, p. 954); and in *Amelia* Miss Mathews (I. vi, p. 42).

[63] '*Digressions*' for 'Transgressions': Mrs Andrews here anticipates the character of Mrs Slipslop, who in *Joseph Andrews* (I. vi: a chapter headed '*How* Joseph Andrews *writ a Letter to his Sister* Pamela') is introduced speaking malapropisms, among them the following: 'If we like a Man, the lightest Hint *sophisticates*' (p. 33).

[64] This phrase expressing indignant or amused surprise (*OED*, s.v. 'marry' d; citing Shakespeare as the earliest example) occurs in HF's fiction at least fourteen times, two of these cited by the *OED*: namely,

never have done if you upbraid me with having had a small One by *Arthur Williams*, when you yourself—but I say no more. *O! What fine Times when the Kettle calls the Pot.* Let me do what I will, I say my Prayers as often as another, and I read in good Books, as often as I have Leisure; and Parson *William* says, that will make amends.—So no more, but I rest

Your afflicted Daughter,

S——

LETTER V.

HENRIETTA MARIA HONORA ANDREWS

to SHAMELA ANDREWS.

Dear Child,

WHY will you give such way to your Passion? How could you imagine I should be such a Simpleton, as to upbraid thee with being thy Mother's own Daughter! When I advised you not to be guilty of Folly, I mean no more than that you should take care to be well paid before-hand, and not trust to Promises, which a Man seldom keeps. after he hath had his wicked Will. And seeing you have a rich Fool to deal with, your not making a good Market will be the more inexcusable; indeed, with such Gentlemen as Parson *Williams*, there is more to be said; for they have nothing to give, and are commonly otherwise the best Sort of Men. I am glad to hear you read good Books, pray continue so to do. I have inclosed you one of Mr. *Whitefield's* Sermons, and also the Dealings with him,[65] and am

Your affectionate Mother,

HENRIETTA MARIA, &c.

Slipslop in *Joseph Andrews* (IV. i), 'departed [from Lady Booby] tossing her Nose and crying "Marry come up! there are some People more jealous than I, I believe"' (p. 280); and in *Tom Jones* (x. iv) Susan the maid 'muttered many "marry-come-ups, as good Flesh and Blood as yourself," with other such indignant Phrases' (p. 540).

[65] The evangelist George Whitefield (1714–70), who, with John Wesley, founded the Methodist movement, which by the late 1730s was growing rapidly among the lower classes; he had recently returned from South Carolina. The demand for his sermons was so great that in a letter of 25 March 1741 he wrote that his bookseller had already 'got some *hundreds* by me' (*Works* [1771–2], i, p. 256). In his spiritual autobiography, *A Short Account of God's Dealings with the Reverend Mr. George Whitefield* (1740), he relates how he was rescued by the grace of God from a life of sin and depravity and directed into the priesthood. HF's satiric campaign against Whitefield's Calvinism and his appeals to the passions of the populace may have begun with a contribution to *The Craftsman*, No. 687 (8 September 1739); it continued in *Joseph Andrews* (I. xvii), where Parson Adams, while siding with Whitefield's critique of the worldliness of the clergy, attacks his 'detestable Doctrine of Faith against good Works' (pp. 82–3). But this is a theme of HF's writings that recurs throughout the canon up to and including *Tom Jones* (1749) and *Amelia* (1751). In the present volume, see *The Female Husband* (below, p. 366 and nn. 1–2). For succinct articles on HF's attitude towards Whitefield and Methodism, see *Companion*, pp. 160–1 and 241–2.

LETTER VI

SHAMELA ANDREWS *to* HENRIETTA
MARIA HONORA ANDREWS.

O Madam, I have strange Things to tell you! As I was reading in that charming Book about the Dealings, in comes my Master—to be sure he is a precious One. *Pamela*, says he, what Book is that, I warrant you *Rochester's* Poems.[66]—No, forsooth, says I, as pertly as I could; why how now Saucy Chops, Boldface, says he—Mighty pretty Words, says I, pert again.—Yes (says he) you are a d——d, impudent, stinking, cursed, confounded Jade, and I have a great Mind to kick your A——. You, kiss —— says I. A-gad, says he, and so I will; with that he caught me in his Arms, and kissed me till be made my Face all over Fire. Now this served purely you know, to put upon the Fool for Anger. O! What precious Fools Men are! And so I flung from him in a might Rage, and pretended as how I would go out at the Door; but when I came to the End of the Room, I stood still, and my Master cryed out, Hussy, Slut, Saucebox, Boldface, come hither- —— Yes, to be sure, says I; why don't you come, says he; what should I come for, says I; if you don't come to me, I'll come to you, says he; I shan't come to you I assure you, says I. Upon which he run up, caught me in his Arms, and flung me upon a Chair, and began to offer to touch my Under-Petticoat. Sir, says I, you had better not offer to be rude; well, says he, no more I won't then; and away he went out of the Room. I was so mad to be sure I could have cry'd.

Oh what a prodigious Vexation it is to a Woman to be made a Fool of.

Mrs. *Jervis*,[67] who had been without, harkening, now came to me. She burst into a violent Laugh the Moment she came in. Well, says she, as soon as she could speak, I have reason to bless myself that I am an Old Woman. Ah Child! if you had known the Jolly Blades of my Age, you would not have been left in the Lurch in this manner. Dear Mrs. *Jervis*, says I, don't laugh at one; and to be sure I was a little angry with her.—Come, says she, my dear Honeysuckle, I have one Game to play for you; he shall see you in Bed; he shall, my little Rosebud, he shall see those pretty, little, white, round,

---

[66] John Wilmot (1647–80), second Earl of Rochester, notorious libertine of the court of Charles II and the writer of lewd love lyrics and biting satires. When, near the end of the novel (XVIII. xii), Tom Jones wishes to convince Sophia that he will in future be faithful to her, he shows her her image in a mirror, declaring that her beauty 'would fix a *Dorimant*, a Lord *Rochester*' (p. 973)—Dorimant being the dissolute hero of Etherege's *The Man of Mode* (1676), a character modelled on Rochester.

[67] HF here attributes to the kindly Mrs Jervis of B.'s Bedford estate the character of the vile and manly Mrs Jewkes, his accomplice at Lincolnshire in schemes to ravish Pamela.

panting—and, offer'd to pull off my Handkerchief.—Fie, Mrs. *Jervis*, says I, you make me blush, and upon my Fackins,[68] I believe she did: She went on thus. I know the Squire likes you, and notwithstanding the Aukwardness of his Proceeding, I am convinced hath some hot Blood in his Veins, which will not let him rest, 'till he hath communicated some of his Warmth to thee my little Angel; I heard him last Night at our Door, trying if it was open, now to-night I will take care it shall be so; I warrant that he makes the second Trial; which if he doth, he shall find us ready to receive him. I will at first counterfeit Sleep, and after a Swoon; so that he will have you naked in his Possession: and then if you are disappointed, a Plague of all young Squires, say I.—And so, Mrs. *Jervis*, says I, you would have me yield my self to him, would you; you would have me be a second Time a Fool for nothing. Thank you for that, Mrs. *Jervis*. For nothing! marry forbid, says she, you know he hath large Sums of Money, besides abundance of fine Things; and do you think, when you have inflamed him, by giving his Hand a Liberty, with that charming Person; and that you know he may easily think he obtains against your Will, he will not give any thing to come at all—. This will not do, Mrs. *Jervis*, answered I. I have heard my Mamma say, (and so you know, Madam, I have) that in her Youth, Fellows have often taken away in the Morning, what they gave over Night. No, Mrs. *Jervis*, nothing under a regular taking into Keeping, a settled Settlement, for me, and all my Heirs, all my whole Life-time, shall do the Business—or else cross-legged, is the Word, faith, with *Sham*; and then I snapt my Fingers.

Thursday Night, Twelve o'Clock.[69]

Mrs. *Jervis* and I are just in Bed, and the Door unlocked; if my Master should come—Odsbobs![70] I hear him just coming in at the Door. You see I write in the present Tense, as Parson *Williams* says. Well, he is in Bed between us, we both shamming a Sleep, he steals his Hand into my Bosom, which I, as if in my Sleep, press close to me with mine, and then pretend to awake.—I no sooner see him, but I scream out to Mrs. *Jervis*, she feigns likewise but just to come to herself; we both begin, she to becall, and I to bescratch very liberally. After having made a pretty free Use of my Fingers, without any great Regard to the Parts I attack'd, I counterfeit a Swoon.

---

[68] 'upon my Fackins': Grose, *Provincial Glossary*, s.v. I'fakins: 'In faith'. Cf. in *Joseph Andrews*, Mrs Trulliber (p. 167) 'Ifacks', and Slipslop (p. 298) 'Ifaukins!'; in *Tom Jones*, Allworthy's housekeeper (p. 246), Sophia's maid Mrs Honour (p. 291) 'i-fackins!', and the landlady at an inn (p. 563) 'I'fackins'.

[69] The following episode burlesques B.'s unsuccessful attempt to ravish Pamela by bursting forth from his hiding place in a closet in her bedroom (see Letter XXV [misnumbered XII in the 2nd edn.], i, pp. 74–7).

[70] 'Odsbobs!': a corruption of 'ods bodikins' ('God's little body'; Partridge).

Mrs. *Jervis* then cries out, O, Sir, what have you done, you have murthered poor *Pamela*: she is gone, she is gone—.

O what a Difficulty it is to keep one's Countenance, when a violent Laugh desires to burst forth.

The poor Booby frightned out of his Wits,[71] jumped out of Bed, and, in his Shirt, sat down by my Bed-Side, pale and trembling, for the Moon shone, and I kept my Eyes wide open, and pretended to fix them in my Head. Mrs. Jervis apply'd Lavender Water, and Hartshorn,[72] and this, for a full half Hour; when thinking I had carried it on long enough, and being likewise unable to continue the Sport any longer, I began by Degrees to come to my self.

The Squire who had sat all this while speechless, and was almost really in that Condition, which I feigned, the Moment he saw me give Symptoms of recovering my Senses, fell down on his Knees; and O *Pamela*, cryed he, can you forgive me, my injured Maid? by Heaven, I know not whether you are a Man or a Woman, unless by your swelling Breasts.[73] Will you promise to forgive me: I forgive you! D—n you (says I) and d—n you, says he, if you come to that. I wish I had never seen your bold Face, saucy Sow, and so went out of the Room.

O what a silly Fellow is a bashful young Lover!

He was no sooner out of hearing, as we thought, than we both burst into a violent Laugh. Well, says Mrs. *Jervis*, I never saw any thing better acted than your Part: But I wish you may not have discouraged him from any future Attempt: especially since his Passions are so cool, that you could prevent his Hands going further than your Bosom. Hang him, answer'd I, he is not quite so cold as that I assure you; our Hands, on neither Side, were idle in the Scuffle, nor have left us any Doubt of each other as to that matter.

Friday Morning.

My Master sent for Mrs. *Jervis*, as soon as he was up, and bid her give an Account of the Plate and Linnen in her Care; and told her, he was resolved that both she and the little Gipsy (I'll assure him) should set out together. Mrs. *Jervis* made him a saucy Answer; which any Servant of Spirit, you know, would, tho' it should be one's Ruin; and came immediately in Tears to me, crying, she had lost her Place on my Account, and that she should be forced to take to a House, as I mentioned before; and that she hoped I

---

[71] This and the following paragraph parody the Lincolnshire episode so vividly recalled by Parson Oliver (above, p. 159 n. 45).

[72] 'Lavender Water': a perfume compounded, with alcohol and ambergris, from the distilled flowers of lavender; 'Hartshorn': smelling salts, made from carbonate of ammonia (*OED*).

[73] The morning after the assault, B. assures Pamela: 'I know not, I declare beyond this lovely Bosom, your Sex' (i, p. 276).

would, at least, make her all the amends in my power, for her Loss on my Account, and come to her House whenever I was sent for. Never fear, says I, I'll warrant we are not so near being turned away, as you imagine; and i'cod, now it comes into my Head, I have a Fetch[74] for him, and you shall assist me in it. But it being now late, and my Letter pretty long, no more at present from

Your Dutiful Daughter,

SHAMELA.

LETTER VII.

Mrs. LUCRETIA JERVIS *to* HENRIETTA
MARIA HONORA ANDREWS

Madam,

MISS *Sham* being set out in a Hurry for my Master's House in *Lincolnshire*, desired me to acquaint you with the Success of her Stratagem, which was to dress herself in the plain Neatness of a Farmer's Daughter, for she before wore the Cloaths of my late Mistress, and to be introduced by me as a Stranger to her Master. To say the Truth, she became the Dress extremely, and if I was to keep a House a thousand Years, I would never desire a prettier Wench in it.

As soon as my Master saw her, he immediately threw his Arms round her Neck, and smothered her with Kisses (for indeed he hath but very little to say for himself to a Woman.) He swore that *Pamela* was an ugly Slut (pardon, dear Madam, the Coarseness of the Expression) compared to such divine Excellence. He added, he would turn *Pamela* away immediately, and take this new Girl, whom he thought to be one of his Tenant's Daughters, in her room.[75]

Miss *Sham* smiled at these Words, and so did your humble Servant, which he perceiving looked very earnestly at your fair Daughter, and discovered the Cheat.

How, *Pamela*, says he, is it you? I thought, Sir, said Miss, after what had happened, you would have known me in any Dress. No, Huffy, says he, but after what hath happened, I should know thee out of any Dress from all thy

---

[74] 'Fetch': a contrivance or trick (*OED*, s.v. 2).

[75] These paragraphs burlesque the passage in Letter XXIV in which B. fails to recognize Pamela, who, preparing to return home to her parents, has put aside the fine clothes her mistress had given her and dressed herself simply. She insists she is '*Pamela, her own self!* | He kissed me for all I could do; and said, Impossible! you are a lovelier Girl by half than *Pamela*; and sure I may be innocently free with you, tho' I would not do her so much Favour' (i, p. 66).

Sex. He then was what we Women call rude, when done in the Presence of others; but it seems it is not the first time, and Miss defended herself with great Strength and Spirit.

The Squire, who thinks her a pure Virgin, and who knows nothing of my Character, resolved to send her into *Lincolnshire*, on Pretence of conveying her home; where our old Friend *Nanny*[76] *Jewkes* is Housekeeper, and where Miss had her small one by Parson *Williams* about a Year ago.[77] This is a Piece of News communicated to us by *Robin* Coachman, who is intrusted by his Master to carry on this Affair privately for him: But we hang together, I believe, as well as any Family of Servants in the Nation.

You will, I believe, Madam, wonder that the Squire, who doth not want Generosity, should never have mentioned a Settlement all this while, I believe it slips his Memory: But it will not be long first, no Doubt: For, as I am convinced the young Lady will do nothing unbecoming your Daughter, nor ever admit him to taste her Charms, without something sure and handsome before-hand; so, I am certain, the Squire will never rest till they have danced *Adam* and *Eve's* kissing Dance together. Your Daughter set out yesterday Morning, and told me, as soon as she arrived, you might depend on hearing from her.

Be pleased to make my Compliments acceptable to Mrs. *Davis* and Mrs. *Silvester*, and Mrs. *Jolly*, and all Friends, and permit me the Honour, Madam, to be with the utmost Sincerity,

> *Your most Obedient,*
> *Humble Servant,*
> LUCRETIA JERVIS.

If the Squire should continue his Displeasure against me, so as to insist on the Warning he hath given me, you will see me soon, and I will lodge in

---

[76] In this context, given the shameless character of Mrs Jewkes, her friend's name no doubt carries its slang meaning, signifying 'a whore' (Partridge). Perhaps remembering his reason for using the name here in this sense, HF in the 1754 edition of *Jonathan Wild* (III. i) altered the passage in which Heartfree's daughter calls herself 'your little *Nanny*' to 'your little *Nancy*' (*Miscellanies* iii, p. 94 and n. 6). In common parlance, however, either is a perfectly innocent pet name for 'Anne': in the original editions of *Tom Jones* they are used this way by HF, referring to a chambermaid (VIII. iv; Wesleyan Edition, Appendix I, p. 998: 416. 2); and by Mrs Miller, referring to her eldest daughter (XIII. vi; Appendix I, p. 1005: 707. 4).

[77] Richardson's Williams, whom Pamela finds 'a sensible, sober young Gentleman' (i, p. 142), is an unbeneficed young clergyman in Lincolnshire who keeps a small Latin school in the village, preaches occasionally for the village priest, and on weekends has rooms in B.'s house, where he serves as chaplain. Unknown to him, B., who has promised Williams a 'living' in his gift when the old and ailing incumbent dies, plans to marry Pamela to him as a cover for an adulterous liaison he means to have with her (i, p. 108). Williams risks B.'s patronage by openly taking her part with his family and the village priest, by secretly acting as the conduit of her forbidden correspondence with her parents, and by plotting with her to effect her escape from confinement in B.'s house.

the same House with you, if you have room, till I can provide for my self to my Liking.

LETTER VIII
HENRIETTA MARIA HONORA ANDREWS
to LUCRETIA JERVIS.

Madam,

I Received the Favour of your Letter, and I find you have not forgot your usual Poluteness, which you learned when you was in keeping with a Lord.

I am very much obliged to you for your Care of my Daughter, am glad to hear she hath taken such good Resolutions, and hope she will have sufficient Grace to maintain them.

All Friends are well and remember to you. You will excuse the Shortness of this Scroll; for I have sprained my right Hand, with boxing three new made Officers.—Tho' to my Comfort, I beat them all.[78] I rest,
Your Friend and Servant,
HENRIETTA, &c.

LETTER IX.
SHAMELA ANDREWS *to* HENRIETTA
MARIA HONORA ANDREWS.

Dear Mamma,

I Suppose Mrs. *Jervis* acquainted you with what past 'till I left *Bedford-shire*; whence I am after a very pleasant Journey arrived in *Lincolnshire*, with your old Acquaintance Mrs. *Jewkes*, who formerly helped Parson *Williams* to me; and now designs I see, to sell me to my Master; thank her for that; she will find two Words go to that Bargain.

The Day after my Arrival here, I received a Letter from Mr. *Williams*, and as you have often desired to see one from him, I have inclosed it to you; it is, I think, the finest I ever received from that charming Man, and full of a great deal of Learning.

O! What a brave Thing it is to be a Scholard, and to be able to talk Latin.

---

[78] Cf. HF's *Covent-Garden Tragedy* (II. ii), where Bilkum reminds the bawd Mother Punchbowl of the time 'I found thee with a base Apprentice boxing[.] | And tho' none better dart the clinched Fist, | Yet wast thou over-match'd.'

Parson WILLIAMS *to* PAMELA ANDREWS.

Mrs. Pamela,

HAVING learnt by means of my Clerk, who Yesternight visited the Rev^d. Mr. *Peters*[79] with my Commands, that you are returned into this County, I purposed to have saluted your fair Hands this Day towards Even: But am obliged to sojourn this Night at a neighbouring Clergyman's; where we are to pierce a Virgin Barrel of Ale, in a Cup of which I shall not be unmindful to celebrate your Health.

I hope you have remembered your Promise, to bring me a Leaden Canister of Tobacco (the Saffron Cut) for in Troth, this Country at present affords nothing worthy the replenishing a Tube[80] with.—Some I tasted the other Day at an Alehouse, gave me the Heart-Burn, tho' I filled no oftner than five Times.

I was greatly concerned to learn, that your late Lady left you nothing, tho' I cannot say the Tidings much surprized me: For I am too intimately acquainted with the Family; (myself, Father and Grandfather having been successive Incumbents on the same Cure,[81] which you know is in their Gift) I say, I am too well acquainted with them to expect much from their Generosity. They are in Verity, as worthless a Family as any other whatever. The young Gentleman I am informed, is a perfect Reprobate; that he hath an *Ingenium Versatile*[82] to every Species of Vice, which, indeed, no one can wonder at, who animadverts on that want of Respect to the Clergy, which was observable in him when a Child. I remember when he was at the Age of Eleven only, he met my Father without either pulling off his Hat, or riding out of the way. Indeed, a Contempt of the Clergy is the fashionable Vice of the Times;[83] but let such wretches know, they cannot hate, detest, and despise us, half so much as we do them.

However, I have prevailed on myself to write a civil Letter to your Master, as there is a Probability of his being shortly in the Capacity of rendring me a Piece of Service; my good Friend and Neighbour, the Rev^d. Mr.

---

[79] The parish priest who declines Williams's request that he intervene to protect Pamela from B.'s unwanted advances.

[80] A tobacco pipe (*OED*, s.v. 4, earliest citation 1736).

[81] 'Cure': a parish or other sphere of spiritual ministration (*OED*, s.v. I.4b).

[82] 'Versatile genius': an ironic allusion to Livy (59 BC–AD 17), HF's favourite Roman historian, who praised Cato: 'his genius was so equally suited to all things that you would say that whatever he was doing was the one thing for which he was born' (*Ab Urbe Condita*, XXXIX. xl. 5).

[83] On this important theme, see the Introduction, pp. 138–9.

Squeeze-Tithe[84] being, as I am informed by one whom I have employed to attend for that Purpose, very near his Dissolution.[85]

You see, sweet Mrs. *Pamela*, the Confidence with which I dictate these Things to you; whom after those Endearments which have passed between us, I must in some Respects estimate as my Wife: For tho' the Omission of the Service was a Sin; yet, as I have told you, it was a Venial One, of which I have truly repented, as I hope you have; and also that you have continued the wholesome Office of reading good Books, and are improved in your Psalmody, of which I shall have a speedy Trial: For I purpose to give you a Sermon next *Sunday*, and shall spend the Evening with you, in Pleasures which tho' not strictly innocent, are however to be purged away by frequent and sincere Repentance. I am,

> Sweet Mrs. Pamela,
> Your faithful Servant,
> ARTHUR WILLIAMS.

You find, Mamma, what a charming way he hath of Writing, and yet I assure you, that is not the most charming Thing belonging to him: For, tho' he doth not put any Dears, and Sweets, and Loves into his Letters, yet he says a thousand of them: For he can be as fond of a Woman, as any Man living.

Sure Women are great Fools, when they prefer a laced Coat to the Clergy, whom it is our Duty to honour and respect.

Well, on *Sunday* Parson *Williams* came, according to his Promise, and an excellent Sermon he preached; his Text was, *Be not Righteous over-much*;[86]

---

[84] Cf. the characters in HF's plays: Justice Squeezum in *Rape upon Rape* and Squeezepurse the attorney in *The Wedding Day*.

[85] Pamela writes of Williams: 'Poor Gentleman! all his Dependence is upon my Master, who has a very good Living for him, if the Incumbent die; and he has kept his Bed these four Months, of old Age and Dropsy' (i, p. 144).

[86] Ecclesiastes 7: 16: 'Be not righteous over-much; neither make thyself over wise; why shouldest thou destroy thyself?' HF thus has the debauched Williams ape Dr Joseph Trapp (1679–1747), the first Professor of Poetry at Oxford and complacent defender of the Church Establishment against the Methodist Whitefield's criticisms of the worldliness and hedonism of the clergy. In 1739 Trapp preached a series of sermons, *The Nature, Folly, Sin, and Danger of being Righteous over-much*, to which Whitefield replied in, among other works, *An Explanatory Sermon on that Mistaken Text, Be not Righteous over-much*. Whitefield's attack on the luxury of the clergy would be the single tenet of his programme with which HF—like Parson Adams in *Joseph Andrews* (i. xvii)—concurred (see above, p. 157 and n. 40). Defining the characters of the true and false clergyman in *The Champion* (5 April 1740), he regretted that some of the clergy do not receive Christ's injunction to poverty 'in a strict litteral practical Sense: But without *being righteous over-much*, we may, I think, conclude, that if the Clergy are not to abandon all they have to their Ministry, neither are they to get immense Estates by it; and I would recommend it to the Consideration of those who do, whether they do not make a Trade of Divinity?' (pp. 270–1); see also *Champion* (24 May 1740), p. 341. And so, in *Tom Jones* (XVIII. iv), Thwackum admonishes Allworthy that his 'Objection to Pluralities is being righteous over-much' (pp. 928–9).

and, indeed, he handled it in a very fine way; he shewed us that the Bible doth not require too much Goodness of us, and that People very often call things Goodness that are not so. That to go to Church, and to pray, and to sing Psalms, and to honour the Clergy, and to repent, is true Religion; and 'tis not doing good to one another, for that is one of the greatest Sins we can commit, when we don't do it for the sake of Religion. That those People who talk of Vartue[87] and Morality, are the wickedest of all Persons. That 'tis not what we have to do, but what we believe, that must save us,[88] and a great many other good Things; I wish I could remember them all.

As soon as Church was over, he came to the Squires' House, and drank Tea with Mrs. *Jewkes* and me; after which Mrs. *Jewkes* went out and left us together for an Hour and half—Oh! he is a charming Man.

After Supper he went Home, and then Mrs. Jewkes began to catechize me, about my Familiarity with him. I see she wants him herself. Then she proceeded to tell me what an Honour my Master did me in liking me, and that it was both an inexcusable Folly and Pride in me, to pretend to refuse him any Favour. Pray, Madam, says I, consider I am a poor Girl, and have nothing but my Modesty to trust to. If I part with that, what will become of me. Methinks, says she, you are not so mighty modest when you are with Parson *Williams*; I have observed you gloat at one another, in a Manner that hath made me blush. I assure you, I shall let the Squire know what sort of Man he is; you may do your Will, says I, as long as he hath a Vote for Pallament-Men, the Squire dares do nothing to offend him; and you will only shew that you are jealous of him, and that's all. How now,

[87] 'Vartue': Shamela's malapropism for 'virtue' (a word that occurs forty-seven times in the second edition of *Pamela*) as a euphemism for her virginity became a kind of signature term of HF's parody. From this point it runs through her narrative until Booby marries her, the most celebrated instance occurring when she realizes the prize she aims at is within reach: 'I thought once of making a little Fortune by my Person. I now intend to make a great one by my Vartue' (below, p. 178). Cf. John Cleland's *Memoirs of a Woman of Pleasure* (1748–9), where Fanny Hill's girlhood friend Esther Davis approves Shamela's example, telling her '*as how several maids out of the country had made themselves and all their kin for ever, that by preserving their* VARTUE, *some had taken so with their masters, that they had married them, and kept them coaches, and lived vastly grand, and happy*' (ed. Peter Sabor, World's Classics [Oxford, 1985], p. 3; and the comment, pp. xxii–xxiii). Cf. also Smollett's *Peregrine Pickle* (1751), where the draper's wife indignantly replies to her cuckolded husband: 'How fellor! . . . do you doubt my vartue?' (ch. LXXXVI).

[88] Though not a Methodist but a priest of the Church of England who expects to succeed to the benefice of the infirm Parson Squeezetext, Williams has wholly adopted HF's understanding of the Calvinist theology of Whitefield, who denounced, among others, the latitudinarian Archbishop Tillotson as little better than a deist for preaching mere morality rather than the doctrine of grace. (For an account of this controversy, see Battestin, *Fielding's Art*, pp. 22–5.) A perfect gloss on the present passage is Parson Adams's diatribe against Whitefield for 'set[ting] up the detestable Doctrine of Faith against good Works . . . can any Doctrine have a more pernicious Influence on Society than a Persuasion, that it will be a good Plea for the Villain at the last Day; *Lord, it is true I never obeyed one of thy Commandments, yet punish me not, for I believe them all?*' (*Joseph Andrews*, I. xvii, p. 82).

Mynx,[89] says she; Mynx! No more Mynx than yourself, says I; with that she hit me a Slap on the Shoulder, and I flew at her and scratched her Face i'cod, 'till she went crying out of the Room;[90] so no more at Present, from

Your Dutiful Daughter,

SHAMELA.

LETTER X.

SHAMELA ANDREWS *to* HENRIETTA

MARIA HONORA ANDREWS.

O Mamma! Rare News! As soon as I was up this Morning, a Letter was brought me from the Squire, of which I send you a Copy.

Squire BOOBY[91] *to* PAMELA.

Dear Creature,

I HOPE that you are not angry with me for the Deceit put upon you, in conveying you to *Lincolnshire*, when you imagined yourself going to *London*. Indeed, my dear *Pamela*, I cannot live without you; and will very shortly come down and convince you, that my Designs are better than you imagine, and such as you may with Honour comply with. I am,

My Dear Creature,

Your doting Lover,

BOOBY.

Now, Mamma, what think you?—For my own Part, I am convinced he will marry me, and faith so he shall. O! Bless me! I shall be Mrs. *Booby*, and be Mistress of a great Estate, and have a dozen Coaches and Six, and a fine House at *London*, and another at *Bath*, and Servants, and Jewels, and Plate, and go to Plays, and Opera's, and Court; and do what I will, and spend what I will. But, poor Parson *Williams*! Well; and can't I see Parson *Williams*, as

---

[89] A pert girl, hussy (*OED*, s.v. 'minx' 2; citing Slipslop in *Joseph Andrews* [IV. xiii], who calls Fanny 'a little ugly Mynx'; p. 327).

[90] Cf. Pamela, writing of Mrs Jewkes's retaliation for her name-calling: 'Why *Jezebel*, said I, (I could not help it) would you ruin me by Force?—Upon this she gave me a deadly Slap upon my Shoulder . . . and [I] said, at last rubbing my Shoulder . . . Alas! for me! am I to be beaten too? And so I fell a-crying, and threw myself upon the Grass-walk we were upon' (i, p. 163).

[91] Here Parson Oliver's authentic text supplies the name of Richardson's 'Mr. B', which is ever so apt: a 'Booby', according to Johnson, is 'a dull, heavy, stupid fellow; a lubber', to which the *OED* adds 'a clown, a nincompoop'. The name was commonly attached to 'squires', as in Richardson's *Clarissa* (3rd edn., 1751), Letter XXXI, Lovelace to Belford, referring to James Harlowe : 'Never was there a Booby Squire that more wanted [improvement]' (i, p. 205).

well after Marriage as before: For I shall never care a Farthing for my Husband. No, I hate and despise him of all Things.

Well, as soon as I had read my Letter, in came Mrs. *Jewkes*. You see, Madam, says she, I carry the Marks of your Passion about me; but I have received Order from my Master to be civil to you, and I must obey him: For he is the best Man in the World, notwithstanding your Treatment of him. My Treatment of him; Madam, says I? Yes, says she, your Insensibility to the Honour he intends you, of making you his Mistress. I would have you to know, Madam, I would not be Mistress to the greatest King, no nor Lord in the Universe. I value my Vartue more than I do any thing my Master can give me; and so we talked a full Hour and a half, about my Vartue; and I was afraid at first, she had heard something about the Bantling, but I find she hath not; tho' she is as jealous, and suspicious, as old Scratch.[92]

In the Afternoon, I stole into the Garden to meet Mr. *Williams*; I found him at the Place of his Appointment, and we staid in a kind of Arbour, till it was quite dark. He was very angry when I told him what Mrs. *Jewkes* had threatned—Let him refuse me for the Living, says he, if he dares, I will vote for the other Party; and not only so, but will expose him all over the Country. I owe him 150*l.* indeed, but I don't care for that; by that Time the Election is past, and I shall be able to plead the *Statue of Lamentations*.[93]

I could have stayed with the dear Man for ever, but when it grew dark, he told me, he was to meet the neighbouring Clergy, to finish the Barrel of Ale they had tapped the other Day, and believed they should not part till three or four in the Morning—So he left me, and I promised to be penitent, and go on with my reading in good Books.

As soon as he was gone, I bethought myself, what Excuse I should make to Mrs. *Jewkes*, and it came into my Head to pretend as how I intended to drown myself; so I stript off one of my Petticoats, and threw it into the Canal; and then I went and hid myself in the Coal-hole, where I lay all Night;[94] and comforted myself with repeating over some Psalms, and other good things, which I had got by heart.

In the Morning, Mrs. *Jewkes* and all the Servants were frighted out of

[92] HF forgets that Shamela had 'her small one' by Williams in the house where Mrs Jewkes was housekeeper. 'Old Scratch' is the Devil (Grose).

[93] i.e. the Statute of Limitations of 1623 (21 Jac. I, c. 16), whereby an action to recover a debt had to be brought within six years. Elections occurred every seven years.

[94] Pamela had planned to feign suicide by drowning in order to delay pursuit after she escaped B. by climbing the garden wall: 'So what will I do, but strip off my upper Petticoat, and throw it into the Pond, with my Neck-handkerchief!' (i, p. 223). Prevented by an accident from executing this scheme, she thinks of throwing herself into the pond, but, spared by 'Divine Grace', 'refug'd myself in the Corner of an Out-house, where Wood and Coals are laid up for Family Use' (i, p. 232).

their Wits, thinking I had run away, and not devising how they should answer it to their Master. They searched all the likeliest Places they could think of for me, and at last saw my Petticoat floating in the Pond. Then they got a Drag-Net, imagining I was drowned, and intending to drag me out; but at last *Moll* Cook coming for some Coals, discovered me lying all along in no very good Pickle.[95] Bless me! Mrs. *Pamela*, says she, what can be the Meaning of this? I don't know, says I, help me up, and I will go in to Breakfast, for indeed I am very hungry. Mrs. *Jewkes* came in immediately, and was so rejoyced to find me alive, that she asked with great Good-Humour, where I had been? and how my Petticoat came into the Pond. I answered, I believed the Devil had put it into my Head to drown my self; but it was a Fib; for I never saw the Devil in my Life, nor I don't believe he hath any thing to do with me.

So much for this Matter. As soon as I had breakfasted, a Coach and Six came to the Door, and who should be in it but my Master.

I immediately run up into my Room, and stript, and washed, and drest my self as well as I could, and put on my prettiest round-ear'd Cap, and pulled down my Stays, to shew as much as I could of my Bosom, (for Parson Williams says, that is the most beautiful part of a Woman) and then I practised over all my Airs before the Glass, and then I sat down and read a Chapter in the Whole Duty of Man.[96]

Then Mrs. *Jewkes* came to me and told me, my Master wanted me below, and says she, Don't behave like a Fool; No, thinks I to my self. I believe I shall find Wit enough for my Master and you too.

So down goes me I[97] into the Parlour to him. *Pamela*, says he, the Moment I came in, you see I cannot stay long from you, which I think is a sufficient Proof of the Violence of my Passion. Yes, Sir, says I, I see your Honour intends to ruin me, that nothing but the Destruction of my Vartue will content you.

O what a charming Word that is, rest his Soul who first invented it.

How can you say I would ruin you, answered the Squire, when you shall not ask any thing which I will not grant you. If that be true, says I, good your Honour let me go Home to my poor but honest Parents; that is all I have to ask, and do not ruin a poor Maiden, who is resolved to carry her Vartue to the Grave with her.

Hussy, says he, don't provoke me, don't provoke me, I say. You are

[95] Mrs Jewkes, in a frantic state, ordered the pond searched by dragnet; but the maid '*Nan* came into the Wood-house; and there lay poor I, so weak, so low, and dejected, and withal so stiff with my Bruises, that I could not stir nor help myself to get upon my Feet' (i, pp. 233–4).
[96] See above, p. 155 n. 30.
[97] Cf. Bayes in Buckingham's *Rehearsal* (1672): 'Well, sir, then what do me I, but make . . .' (v. i).

absolutely in my power, and if you won't let me lie with you by fair Means, I will by Force. O La, Sir, says I, I don't understand your paw[98] Words.— Very pretty Treatment indeed, says he, to say I use paw Words; Hussy, Gipsie, Hypocrite, Saucebox, Boldface, get out of my Sight, or I will lend you such a Kick in the —— I don't care to repeat the Word, but he meant my hinder part. I was offering to go away, for I was half afraid, when he called me back, and took me round the Neck and kissed me, and then bid me to go about my Business.

I went directly into my Room, where Mrs. *Jewkes* came to me soon afterwards. So Madam, says she, you have left my Master below in a fine Pet, he hath threshed two or three of his Men already: It is mighty pretty that all his Servants are to be punished for your Impertinence.

Harkee, Madam, says I, don't you affront me, for if you do, d—n me (I am sure I have repented for using such a Word) if I am not revenged.

How sweet is Revenge: Sure the Sermon Book is in the Right, in calling it the sweetest Morsel the Devil ever dropped into the Mouth of a Sinner.[99]

Mrs. *Jewkes* remembered the Smart of my Nails too well to go farther, and so we sat down and talked about my Vartue till Dinner-time, and then I was sent for to wait on my Master. I took care to be often caught looking at him, and then I always turn'd away my Eyes and pretended to be ashamed. As soon as the Cloth was removed, he put a Bumper of Champagne into my Hand, and bid me drink—O la I can't name the Health. Parson *Williams* may well say he is a wicked Man.

Mrs. *Jewkes* took a Glass and drank the dear *Monysyllable*;[100] I don't understand that Word but I believe it is baudy. I then drank towards his Honour's good Pleasure. Ay, Hussy, says he, you can give me Pleasure if you will; Sir, says I, I shall always be glad to do what is in my power, and so I pretended not to know what he meant. Then he took me into his Lap.—O Mamma, I could tell you something if I would—and he kissed me—and I said I won't be slobber'd about so, so I won't, and he bid me get out of the Room for a saucy Baggage, and said he had a good mind to spit in my Face.

Sure no Man ever took such a Method to gain a Woman's Heart.

I had not been long in my Chamber before Mrs. *Jewkes* came to me and told me, my Master would not see me any more that Evening, that is, if he

---

[98] 'paw': naughty, obscene.
[99] Robert South (1634–1716) in his sermon on 1 Samuel 25: 32–3 ('Prevention of Sin an unvaluable Mercy'): 'Revenge is certainly the most luscious Morsel that the Devil can put into the Sinner's Mouth' (*Twelve Sermons*, 6th edn. [1727], ii, p. 381). HF greatly admired South, in whose sermons he found 'perhaps more Wit, than in the Comedies of Congreve' (*Covent-Garden Journal*, No. 18 [3 March 1752], p. 124); and he was particularly fond of this passage, which he quotes in *The Mock Doctor* (1732), scene 1, p. 13; *Champion* (2 February 1740), p. 158; *Enquiry* (1751), sect. x, p. 161; and *Amelia* (IX. viii), p. 391.
[100] '*Monysyllable*': 'The female pudend' (Partridge, s.v. 'monosyllable').

can help it; for, added she, I easily perceive the great Ascendant you have over him; and to confess the Truth, I don't doubt but you will shortly be my Mistress.

What says I, dear Mrs. *Jewkes*, what do you say? Don't flatter a poor Girl, it is impossible his Honour can have any honourable Design upon me. And so we talked of honourable Designs till Supper-time. And Mrs. *Jewkes* and I supped together upon a hot buttered Apple-Pie;[101] and about ten o'Clock we went to Bed.

We had not been a Bed half an Hour, when my Master came pit a pat into the Room in his Shirt as before, I pretended not to hear him, and Mrs. *Jewkes* laid hold of one Arm, and he pulled down the Bed-cloaths and came into Bed on the other Side, and took my other Arm and laid it under him, and fell a kissing one of my Breasts as if he would have devoured it; I was then forced to awake, and began to struggle with him, Mrs. *Jewkes* crying why don't you do it? I have one Arm secure, if you can't deal with the rest I am sorry for you.[102] He was as rude as possible to me; but I remembered, Mamma, the Instructions you gave me to avoid being ravished, and followed them, which soon brought him to Terms, and he promised me on quitting my hold, that he would leave the Bed.

O Parson Williams, *how little are all the Men in the World compared to thee.*

My Master was as good as his Word; upon which Mrs. *Jewkes* said, O Sir, I see you know very little of our Sect,[103] by parting so easily from the Blessing when you was so near it. No, Mrs. *Jewkes*, answered he, I am very glad no more hath happened, I would not have injured *Pamela* for the World. And to-morrow Morning perhaps she may hear of something to her Advantage. This she may be certain of, that I will never take her by Force, and then he left the Room.

What think you now, Mrs. *Pamela*, says Mrs. *Jewkes*, Are you not yet persuaded my Master hath honourable Designs? I think he hath given no

---

[101] HF here may resume the ridicule of Dr Woodward (above, p. 150 n. 8). Rothstein notes that Woodward had 'called this dish, like the puddings and custards mentioned by Keyber, a stimulant'. He cites the satire *A Letter from the Facetious Dr. Andrew Tripe at Bath* (1718), which links Woodward's '*State of Physick and Diseases*, and an History of *butter'd Applepye and Custard*', warning that the 'custom of feeding School Boys with *Plumb-Cake* and *Applepye*, is certainly of the most pernicious Consequence' (p. 384 n. 6).

[102] This scene parodies the one Parson Oliver specifically complained of (above, p. 159 n. 45)—with Mrs Jewkes, no longer able to contain her impatience at B.'s ineptitude, exclaiming: 'What you do, Sir, do; don't stand, dilly-dallying. She cannot exclaim worse than she has done. And she'll be quieter when she knows the worst' (i, p. 273).

[103] HF enjoyed this malapropism: in *Joseph Andrews* (II. iv), when Horatio is taken in by Leonora's rebuffing his proposal of marriage, Slipslop declares, 'More Fool he . . . it is a sign he knew very little of our *Sect*' (p. 105); and later (IV. iv) she sides with Lady Booby's opinion of Fanny, placing her among 'those nasty Creatures who are a Scandal to our *Sect*' (p. 287).

great Proof of them to-night, said I. Your Experience I find is not great, says she, but I am convinced you will shortly be my Mistress, and then what will become of poor me.[104]

With such Sort of Discourse we both fell asleep. Next Morning early my Master sent for me, and after kissing me, gave a Paper into my Hand which he bid me to read; I did so, and found it to be a Proposal for settling 250*l.* a Year on me, besides several other advantagious Offers, as Presents of Money and other Things.[105] Well, *Pamela*, said he, what Answer you make me to this. Sir, said I, I value my Vartue more than all the World, and I had rather be the poorest Man's Wife, than the Richest Man's Whore. You are a Simpleton, said he; That may be, and yet I may have as much Wit as some Folks, cry'd I; meaning me, I suppose, said he; every Man knows himself best, says I. Hussy, says he, get out of the Room, and let me see your saucy Face no more, for I find I am in more Danger than you are, and therefore it shall be my Business to avoid you as much as I can; and it shall be mine, thinks I, at every turn to throw my self in your Way. So I went out, and as I parted, I heard him sigh and say he was bewitched.

Mrs. *Jewkes* hath been with me since, and she assures me she is convinced I shall shortly be Mistress of the Family, and she really behaves to me, as if she already thought me so. I am resolved now to aim at it. I thought once of making a little Fortune by my Person. I now intend to make a great one by my Vartue. So asking Parson for this long Scroll, I am,

Your dutiful Daughter,

SHAMELA.

LETTER XI.

HENRIETTA MARIA HONORA
ANDREWS *to* SHAMELA ANDREWS.

Dear Sham,

I RECEIVED your last Letter with infinite Pleasure, and am convinced it will be your own Fault if you are not married to your Master, and I

---

[104] Cf. the prescient Mrs Jewkes: 'I am sure you are to be our Mistress! And then I know what will become of me' (i, p. 285).

[105] Before the attempted rape just parodied, B. sent Pamela a set of 'Proposals', the purpose of which is 'to make me a vile kept Mistress' (i, p. 249). The articles of the proposals are rather more liberal than Shamela represents them to be: to wit, she is to receive 500 guineas outright and her parents an estate in Kent worth £250 a year; he offers to extend his favours to her relatives; he will bestow upon her rich clothes and jewels; and he offers the hope of marriage after a year's trial. In short, 'You shall be Mistress of my Person and Fortune, as much as if the foolish Ceremony had passed' (i, p. 255). Though he threatens her ruin if she refuses him, Pamela is resolute: 'I will make no Free-will Offering of my Virtue' (i, p. 254).

would advise you now to take no less Terms. But, my dear Child, I am afraid of one Rock only, That Parson *Williams*, I wish he was out of the Way. A Woman never commits Folly but with such Sort of Men, as by many Hints in the Letters I collect him to be: but, consider, my dear Child, you will hereafter have Opportunities sufficient to indulge yourself with Parson *Williams*, or any other you like. My Advice therefore to you is, that you would avoid seeing him any more till the Knot is tied. Remember the first Lesson I taught you, that a Married Woman injures only her Husband, but a Single Woman herself. I am, in hopes of seeing you a great Lady,

Your affectionate Mother,

HENRIETTA MARIA, &c.

The following Letter seems to have been written before *Shamela* received the last from her Mother.

LETTER XII.

SHAMELA ANDREWS *to* HENRIETTA

MARIA HONORA ANDREWS.

Dear Mamma,

I LITTLE feared when I sent away my last, that all my Hopes would be so soon frustrated; but I am certain you will blame Fortune and not me. To proceed then. About two Hours after I had left the Squire, he sent for me into the Parlour. *Pamela*, said he, and takes me gently by the Hand, will you walk with me in the Garden; yes, Sir, says I, and pretended to tremble; but I hope your Honour will not be rude. Indeed, says he, you have nothing to fear from me, and I have something to tell you, which if it doth not please you, cannot offend. We walked out together, and he began thus, *Pamela*, will you tell me the Truth? Doth the Resistance you make to my Attempts proceed from Vartue only, or have I not some Rival in thy dear Bosom who might be more successful? Sir, says I, I do assure you I never had a thought of any Man in the World.[106] How, says he, not of Parson *Williams*! Parson *Williams*, says I, is the last Man upon Earth, and if I was a Dutchess, and your Honour was to make your Addresses to me, you would have no Reason to be jealous of any Rival, especially such a Fellow as Parson

---

[106] Cf. *Pamela*: 'Well, then, said he, I may promise myself, that neither the Parson [Williams], nor any other Man, is any the least secret Motive to your stedfast Refusal of my Offers? Indeed, Sir, said I, you may; and, as you was pleased to ask, I answer, that I have not the least Shadow of a Wish, or Thought, for any Man living' (i, p. 291).

Williams. If ever I had a Liking, I am sure—but I am not worthy of you one Way, and no Riches should ever bribe me the other. My Dear, says he, you are worthy of every Thing, and suppose I should lay aside all Considerations of Fortune, and disregard the Censure of the World, and marry you. O Sir, says I, I am sure you can have no such Thoughts, you cannot demean your self so low. Upon my Soul, I am in earnest, says he—O Pardon me, Sir, says I, you can't persuade me of this. How Mistress says he in a violent Rage, do you give me the Lie? Hussy, I have a great mind to box your saucy Ears, but I am resolved I will never put it in your power to affront me again, and therefore I desire you to prepare your self for your Journey this Instant. You deserve no better Vehicle than a Cart; however, for once you shall have a Chariot, and it shall be ready for you within this half Hour; and so he flung from me in a Fury,

What a foolish Thing it is for a Woman to dally too long with her Lover's Desires; how many have owed their being old Maids to their holding out too long.

Mrs. *Jewkes* came to me presently, and told me, I must make ready with all the Expedition imaginable, for that my Master had ordered the Chariot, and that if I was not prepared to go in it, I should be turned out of Doors and left to find my way Home on Foot. This startled me a little, yet I resolved, whether in the right or wrong, not to submit nor ask Pardon: For that you know, Mamma, you never could your self bring me to from my childhood: Besides, I thought he would be no more able to master his Passion for me now, than he had been hitherto; and if he sent two Horses away with me, I concluded he would send four to fetch me back. So, truly, I resolved to brazen it out, and with all the Spirit I could muster up, I told Mrs. *Jewkes* I was vastly pleased with the News she brought me; that no one ever went more readily than I should, from a Place where my Vartue had been in continual Danger. That as for my Master, he might easily get those who were fit for his Purpose; but, for my Part, I preferred my Vartue to all Rakes whatever—And for his Promises, and his Offers to me, I don't value them of a Fig—Not of a Fig, Mrs. *Jewkes*; and then I snapt my Fingers.

Mrs. *Jewkes* went in with me, and helped me to pack up my little All,[107] which was soon done; being no more than two Day-Caps, two Night-Caps,

---

[107] Preparing to return home to her parents, Pamela scorns Mrs Jewkes's offer of help with her baggage: 'I'll have no Portmanteau, I'll assure you, nor any thing but these few Things that I brought with me in my Handkerchief, besides what I have on' (ii, p. 34). The parody then turns to a passage at the beginning of the novel, where in Letter VII Pamela catalogues the gifts B. made her of items belonging to his deceased mother: 'Two Suits of fine *Flanders* lac'd Headcloaths, Three Pair of fine Silk Shoes, two hardly the worse, and just fit for me, and the other with rich Silver Buckles in them (for my Lady had a very little Foot); and several Ribbands and Topknots of all Colours; Four Pair of white Cotton Stockens, and Three Pair of fine Silk ones; and two Pair of rich Stays' (i, p. 12).

five Shifts, One Sham,[108] a Hoop, a Quilted-Petticoat, two Flannel-Petticoats, two pair of Stockings, one odd one, a pair of lac'd Shoes, a short flowered Apron, a lac'd Neck-Handkerchief, one Clog,[109] and almost another, and some few Books:[110] as, *A full Answer to a plain and true Account*, &c. The *Whole Duty of Man*, with only the Duty to one's Neighbour, torn out, The Third Volume of the *Atalantis*. *Venus in the Cloyster: Or, the Nun in her Smock*. *God's Dealings with Mr. Whitefield*. *Orfus and Eurydice*. Some Sermon-Books; and two or three Plays, with their Titles, and Part of the first Act torn off.[111]

So as soon as we had put all this into a Bundle, the Chariot was ready, and I took leave of all the Servants, and particularly Mrs. *Jewkes*, who pretended, I believe, to be more sorry to part with me than she was; and then crying out with an Air of Indifference, my Service to my Master, when he condescends to enquire after me, I flung my self into the Chariot, and bid *Robin* drive on.

We had not gone far, before a Man on Horseback, riding full Speed, overtook us, and coming up to the Side of the Chariot, threw a letter into the Window, and then departed without uttering a single Syllable.

[108] 'Sham': 'shams, false sleeves to put on over a dirty shirt, or false sleeves with ruffles to put over a plain one' (Grose).
[109] 'Clog': a woman's wooden-soled shoe.
[110] The catalogue of Shamela's little library reveals her to be without taste, morals, or sound religion. (1) The first item, '*A full Answer to a plain and true Account*, &c.', is among the many heated replies to one of the most controversial treatises of the period: namely, *A Plain Account of the Nature and End of the Sacrament of the Lord's Supper* (1735), a mystery-dispelling analysis of the Eucharist by Benjamin Hoadly (1676–1761), latitudinarian Bishop of Winchester. Given the scores of attacks this work provoked, no certain identification of Shamela's favourite is possible; but Woods (pp. 260–2) makes a plausible case for Thomas Bowyer's *A True Account of the Nature, end and efficacy of the Sacrament of the Lords Supper; being a full answer to the Plain Account* (1736). For HF, who knew the Bishop and his sons Benjamin and John personally, Hoadly represented 'true greatness' in religion, as he declared both in the poem of that title published in January 1741 (*Miscellanies* i, p. 28) and in *Tom Jones* (II. vii), where he refers admiringly to Hoadly's 'great Reputation' in divinity (p. 105). In *Joseph Andrews* (I. xvii) Parson Adams declares that Hoadly's *Plain Account* was 'written . . . with the Pen of an Angel, and calculated to restore the true Use of Christianity, and of that Sacred Institution [the Eucharist]' (p. 83). On the theme of religion and the clergy in *Shamela*, see the Introduction, pp. 138–40. (2) On *The Whole Duty of Man* see above, p. 155 n. 30. (3) *Secret Memoirs and Manners of Several Persons of Quality of Both Sexes, From the New Atalantis* (1709) by Mary Delarivière Manley (1663–1724), a scandalous *roman-à-clef*, which for HF in *Joseph Andrews* (III. i) was the generic representative of all the unnatural and immoral fiction of the period (p. 187 and n. 4). A copy of the book is also in the library of Mrs Fitzpatrick in *Tom Jones* (XI. vii, p. 596). (4) *Venus in the Cloyster: or, The Nun in her Smock*, a notorious piece of pornography translated from the French in 1724 by one Robert Samber; for publishing it the unscrupulous bookseller Edmund Curll was imprisoned. (5) On Whitefield's spiritual autobiography, see above, p. 163 n. 65. (6) *Orpheus and Eurydice: with the Metamorphosis of Harlequin*, a musical pantomime with book by Lewis Theobald (above, p. 96 and n. 35) and the role of Harlequin played by John Rich (above, p. 60 n. 107) was first performed at Covent Garden in February 1740. HF thought it an asinine 'Entertainment' and ridiculed it in several issues of *The Champion*, especially the leader for 24 May 1740.
[111] The plays, presumably, have served a purpose in the privy.

I immediately knew the Hand of my dear *Williams*, and was somewhat surprized, tho' I did not apprehend the Contents to be so terrible, as by the following exact Copy you will find them.

Parson WILLIAMS to PAMELA

Dear Mrs. PAMELA,

THAT Disrespect for the Clergy which I have formerly noted to you in that Villain your Master, hath now broke forth in a manifest Fact. I was proceeding to my Neighbour *Spruce's* Church, where I purposed to preach a Funeral Sermon, on the Death of Mr. *John Gage*, the Exciseman; when I was met by two Persons who are, it seems, Sheriffs Officers, and arrested for the 150*l.* which your Master had lent me; and unless I can find Bail within these few Days, of which I see no likelihood, I shall be carried to Goal.[112] This accounts for my not having visited you these two Days; which you might assure your self, I should not have fail'd, if the *Potestas*[113] had not been wanting. If you can by any means prevail on your Master to release me, I beseech you so to do, not scrupling any thing for Righteousness sake. I hear he is just arrived in this Country, I have herewith sent him a Letter, of which I transmit you a Copy. So with Prayers for your Success, I subscribe my self.

Your affectionate Friend,
ARTHUR WILLIAMS.

Parson WILLIAMS to Squire BOOBY.

Honoured Sir,

I Am justly surprized to feel so heavy a Weight of your Displeasure, without being conscious of the least Demerit towards so good and generous a Patron, as I have ever found you: For my own Part, I can truly say,

Nil conscire sibi nullæ pallescere culpæ.[114]

And therefore, as this Proceeding is so contrary to your usual Goodness, which I have often experienced, and more especially in the Loan of this

---

[112] 'Goal': This spelling for 'gaol' or 'jail' was usual in the period: it occurs twenty-four times in HF's fiction, whereas 'gaol' appears just twice, both instances in *Jonathan Wild*. Cf. *Pamela*: Mr B. has discovered letters between Williams and Pamela discussing plans for her escape: 'I have order'd Mr. *Shorter*, my Attorney, to throw him instantly into Gaol [*sic*], on an Action of Debt, for Money he has had of me, which I had intended never to carry to account against him' (i, p. 214).

[113] Power or opportunity.

[114] 'To be conscious of no wrongdoing, to turn pale for no fault' (Horace, *Epistles*, 1. i. 61).

Money for which I am now arrested; I cannot avoid thinking some malicious Persons have insinuated false Suggestions against me; intending thereby to eradicate those Seeds of Affection which I have hardly[115] travailed to sowe in your Heart, and which promised to produce such excellent Fruit. If I have any ways offended you, Sir, be graciously pleased to let me know it, and likewise to point out to me, the Means whereby I may reinstate myself in your Favour: For next to him whom the great themselves must bow down before, I know none to whom I shall bend with more Lowliness than your Honour. Permit me to subscribe my self,

> *Honoured Sir,*
> *Your most obedient, and most obliged,*
> *And most dutiful humble Servant,*
> ARTHUR WILLIAMS.

The Fate of poor Mr. *Williams* shocked me more than my own: For, as the *Beggar's Opera* says, *Nothing moves one so much as a great Man in Distress.*[116] And to see a Man of his Learning forced to submit so low, to one whom I have often heard him say, he despises, is, I think, a most affecting Circumstance. I write all this to you, Dear Mamma, at the Inn where I lie this first Night, and as I shall send it immediately, by the Post, it will be in Town a little before me.—Don't let my coming away vex you: For, as my Master will be in Town in a few Days, I shall have an Opportunity of seeing him; and let the worst come to the worst, I shall be sure of my Settlement at last. Which is all, from

> *Your Dutiful Daughter,*
> SHAMELA.

P.S. Just as I was going to send this away a Letter is come from my Master, desiring me to return, with a large Number of Promises.—I have him now as sure as a Gun,[117] as you will perceive by the Letter itself, which I have inclosed to you.

This letter is unhappily lost, as well as the next which *Shamela* wrote, and which contained an Account of all the Proceedings previous to her Marriage. The only remaining one which I could preserve, seems to have been written about a Week after the Ceremony was perform'd, and is as follows:

---

[115] 'hardly': vigorously (*OED*, s.v. 1, obs).
[116] From *The Beggar's Opera* (1728) by John Gay (see above, 'Cantos', p. 155 n. 80): Lucy Lockit's lament for her lover Macheath, the condemned highwayman hero (III. xv).
[117] See above, p. 161 n. 60.

SHAMELA BOOBY *to* HENRIETTA
MARIA HONORA ANDREWS.

Madam,

IN my last I left off at our sitting down to Supper on our Wedding Night,* where I behaved with as much Bashfulness as the purest Virgin in the World could have done. The most difficult Task for me was to blush; however, by holding my Breath, and squeezing my Cheeks with my Handkerchief, I did pretty well. My Husband was extremely eager and impatient to have Supper removed, after which he gave me leave to retire into my Closet for a Quarter of an Hour, which was very agreeable to me; for I employed that time in writing to Mr. *Williams*, who, as I informed you in my last, is released, and presented to the Living, upon the Death of the last Parson. Well, at last I went to Bed, and my Husband soon leapt in after me; where I shall only assure you, I acted my Part in such a manner, that no Bridegroom was ever better satisfied with his Bride's Virginity. And to confess the Truth, I might have been well enough satisfied too, if I had never been acquainted with Parson *Williams*.

O what regard Men who marry Widows should have to the Qualifications of their former Husbands.

We did not rise the next Morning till eleven, and then we sat down to Breakfast; I eat two Slices of Bread and Butter, and drank three Dishes of Tea, with a good deal of Sugar, and we both look'd very silly. After Breakfast we drest our selves, he in a blue Camlet Coat, very richly laced, and Breeches of the same; with a Paduasoy[118] Wastecoat, lac'd with Silver; and I, in one of my Mistress's Gowns. I will have finer when I come to Town. We then took a Walk in the Garden, and he kissed me several Times, and made me a Present of 100 Guineas, which I gave away before Night to the Servants, twenty to one, and ten to another, and so on.[119]

---

* This is the letter which is lost.

[118] 'Camlet': a kind of stuff originally made by a mixture of silk and camel's hair; it is now made with wool and silk (*OED*, citing Johnson). 'Paduasoy': a strong corded or gros-grain silk fabric (*OED*), citing Jenyn's *Art of Dancing* (1730): 'Let him his active limbs display | In camblet thin, or glossy paduasoy.'

[119] After Mr B. gives Pamela fifty guineas to pay her parents' debts, she writes: 'To me he gave no less than One hundred Guineas more; and said, I would have you, my Dear, give Mrs. *Jewkes*, when you go away from hence, what you think fit, out of these, as from yourself!—Nay, good dear Sir, said I, let that be what you please. Give her then, said he, Twenty Guineas, as a Compliment on your Nuptials. Give *Colbrand* Ten Guineas: Give the two Coachmen, Five Guineas each; to the two Maids at this House, Five Guineas each: Give *Abraham* Five Guineas: Give *Thomas* Five Guineas; and give the Gardeners, Grooms and Helpers, Twenty Guineas among them' (ii, p. 188).

We eat a very hearty Dinner, and about eight in the Evening went to Bed again. He is prodigiously fond of me; but I don't like him half so well as my dear *Williams*. The next Morning we rose earlier, and I asked him for another hundred Guineas, and he gave them me. I sent fifty to Parson *Williams*, and the rest I gave away, two Guineas to a Beggar, and three to a Man riding along the Road, and the rest to other People. I long to be in *London* that I may have an Opportunity of laying some out, as well as giving away. I believe I shall buy every Thing I see. What signifies having Money if one doth not spend it.

The next Day, as soon as I was up, I asked him for another Hundred. Why my Dear, says he, I don't grudge you any thing, but how was it possible for you to lay out the other two Hundred here. La! Sir, says I, I hope I am not obliged to give you an Account of every Shilling; Troth, that will be being your Servant still. I assure you, I married you with no such view, besides did not you tell me I should be Mistress of your Estate? And I will be too. For tho' I brought no Fortune, I am as much your Wife as if I had brought a Million—yes but, my Dear, says he, if you had brought a Million, you would spend it all at this rate; besides, what will your Expenses be in *London*, if they are so great here. Truly, says I, Sir, I shall live like other Ladies of my Fashion; and if you think, because I was a Servant, that I shall be contented to be governed as you please, I will shew you, you are mistaken. If you had not cared to marry me, you might have let it alone. I did not ask you, nor I did not court you. Madam, says he, I don't value a Hundred Guineas to oblige you; but this is a Spirit which I did not expect in you, nor did I ever see any Symptoms of it before. O but Times are altered now, I am your Lady,[120] Sir; yes to my Sorrow, says he, I am afraid to my Sorrow too: For if you use me in this manner already, I reckon you will beat me before a Month's at an End. I am sure if you did, it would injure me less than this barbarous Treatment; upon which I burst into Tears, and pretended to fall into a Fit. This frighted him out of his wits, and he called up the Servants. Mrs. *Jewkes* immediately came in, and she and another of the Maids fell heartily to rubbing my Temples, and holding Smelling-Bottles to my Nose. Mrs. *Jewkes* told him she fear'd I should never recover, upon which he began to beat his Breasts, and cried out, O my dearest Angel, curse on my passionate Temper, I have destroy'd her, I have destroy'd her!—would she had spent my whole Estate rather than this had happened. Speak to me, my Love, I will melt my self into Gold for thy Pleasure. At last having pretty

---

[120] Cf. *Joseph Andrews* (IV. vii), where Pamela is quick to remind Joseph that, as Mr Booby's wife, she, unlike Fanny, is no longer of the servant class: 'She was my Equal . . . but I am no longer *Pamela Andrews*, I am now this Gentleman's Lady, and as such am above her' (p. 302).

well tired my self with counterfeiting, and imagining I had continu'd long enough for my purpose in the sham Fit, I began to move my Eyes, to loosen my Teeth, and to open my Hands, which Mr. *Booby* no sooner perceived than he embraced and kissed me with the eagerest Extacy, asked my Pardon on his Knees for what I had suffered through his Folly and Perverseness, and without more Questions fetched me the Money. I fancy I have effectually prevented any farther Refusals or Inquiry into my Expences. It would be hard indeed that a Woman who marries a Man only for his Money should be debarred from spending it.

Well, after all Things were quiet, we sat down to Breakfast, yet I resolved not to smile once, nor to say one good-natured, or good-humoured Word on any Account.

Nothing can be more prudent in a Wife, than a sullen Backwardness to Reconciliations; it makes a Husband fearful of offending by the Length of his Punishment.

When we were drest, the Coach was by my Desire ordered for an Airing, which we took in it. A long Silence prevailed on both Sides, tho' he constantly squeezed my Hand, and kissed me, and used other Familiarities, which I peevishly permitted. At last, I opened my Mouth first.—And so, says I, you are sorry you are married?—Pray, my Dear, says he, forget what I said in a Passion. Passion, says I, is apter to discover our Thoughts than to teach us to counterfeit. Well, says he, whether you will believe me or no, I solemnly vow, I would not change thee for the richest Woman in the Universe. No, I warrant you, says I; and yet you could refuse me a nasty hundred Pound. At these very Words, I saw Mr. *Williams* riding as fast as he could across a Field; and I looked out, and saw a Lease[121] of Greyhounds coursing a Hare, which they presently killed, and I saw him alight, and take it from them.

My Husband ordered *Robin* to drive towards him, and looked horribly out of Humour, which I presently imputed to Jealousy. So I began with him first; for that is the wisest way. La, Sire, says I; what makes you look so Angry and Grim? Doth the Sight of Mr *Williams* give you all this Uneasiness? I am sure, I would never have married a Woman of whom I had so bad an Opinion, that I must be uneasy at every Fellow she looks at. My Dear, answered he, you injure me extremely, you was not in my Thoughts, nor, indeed, could be while they were covered by so morose a Countenance; I am justly angry with that Parson, whose Family hath been raised from the Dunghill by ours; and who hath received from me twenty Kindnesses, and

[121] 'Lease' or 'Leash': a set of three hounds held together by a leash until released for coursing (*OED*, s.v. 'leash' 2).

yet is not contented to destroy the Game in all other Places, which I freely give him leave to do; but hath the Impudence to pursue a few Hares, which I am desirous to preserve, round about this little Coppice. Look, my Dear, pray look, says he; I believe he is going to turn Higler.[122] To confess the Truth, he had no less than three ty'd up behind his Horse, and a fourth he held in his Hand.

Pshaw, says I, I wish all the Hares in the Country were d——d (the Parson himself chid me afterwards for using the Word, tho' it was in his Service.) Here's a Fuss, indeed, about a nasty little pitiful Creature, that is not half so useful as a Cat. You shall not persuade me, that a Man of your Understanding, would quarrel with a Clergyman for such a Trifle. No, no, I am the Hare,[123] for whom poor Parson *Williams* is persecuted; and Jealousy is the Motive. If you had married one of your Quality Ladies, she would have had Lovers by dozens, she would so; but because you have taken a Servant-Maid, forsooth! You are jealous if she but looks (and then I began to Water) at a poor P-a-a-rson in his Pu-u-u-lpit, and then out burst a Flood of Tears.

My Dear, said he, for Heaven's sake dry your Eyes, and don't let him be a Witness of your Tears, which I should be sorry to think might be imputed to my Unkindness; I have already given you some Proofs that I am not jealous of this Parson; I will now give you a very strong One: For I will mount my Horse, and you shall take *Williams* into the Coach. You may be sure, this Motion pleased me, yet I pretended to make as light of it as possible, and told him, I was sorry his Behaviour had made some such glaring Instance, necessary to the perfect clearing my Character.

He soon came up to Mr. *Williams*, who had attempted to ride off, but was prevented by one of our Horsemen, whom my Husband had sent to stop him. When we met, my Husband asked him how he did with a very good-humoured Air, and told him he perceived he had found good Sport that Morning. He answered pretty moderate, Sir; for that he had found the three Hares tied on to the Saddle dead in a Ditch (winking on me at the same Time) and added he was sorry there was such a Rot[124] among them.

---

[122] 'Higler' or 'Higgler': an itinerant dealer; especially a carrier or huckster who buys up poultry and dairy produce, and supplies in exchange petty commodities from the shops in town (*OED*, s.v. 'higgler'). In *Tom Jones* (III. x) Black George, having poached a hare, sells it to a 'Higler' who then informs on him in order to avoid prosecution (pp. 147–8).

[123] Given the context, Brooks-Davies's recalling the hare as a traditional symbol of lust is persuasive. Cf. *Tom Jones* (V. xii), where, as he beats the bushes looking for Molly Seagrim, with whom Tom has had sex, Western turns her literally into a hare: 'He then began to beat about, in the same Language, and in the same Manner, as if he had been beating for a Hare, and at last cried out, "Soho! Puss is not far off. Here's her Form . . . I believe I may cry *stole away*." And indeed so he might, for he had now discovered the Place whence the poor Girl had . . . *stolen away*, upon as many Feet as a Hare generally uses in travelling' (p. 267).

[124] 'a Rot': a virulent disease affecting the liver of sheep (*OED*, s.v. 2a–b), not hares.

Well, says Mr. *Booby*, if you please, Mr. *Williams*, you shall come in and ride with my Wife.[125] For my own part, I will mount on Horseback; for it is fine Weather, and besides it doth not became me to loll in a Chariot, whilst a Clergyman rides on Horseback.

At which Words, Mr. *Booby* leapt out, and Mr. *Williams* leapt in, in an instant, telling my Husband as he mounted, he was glad to see such a Reformation, and that if he continued his Respect to the Clergy, he might assure himself of Blessings from above.

It was now that the Airing began to grow pleasant to me. Mr. *Williams*, who never had but one Fault, *viz.* that he generally smells of Tobacco, was now perfectly sweet; for he had for two Days together enjoined himself as a Penance, not to smoke till he had kissed my Lips. I will loosen you from that Obligation, says I, observing my Husband looking another way, I gave him a charming Kiss, and then he asked me Questions concerning my Wedding-night; this actually made me blush: I vow I did not think it had been in him.

As he went along, he began to discourse very learnedly, and told me the Flesh and the Spirit were two distinct Matters, which had not the least relation to each other.[126] That all immaterial Substances[127] (those were his very Words) such as Love, Desire, and so forth, were guided by the Spirit: but fine Houses, large Estates, Coaches, and dainty Entertainments were the

---

[125] HF parodies an episode (before Pamela's marriage) in which Mr B. takes Pamela and her father for an airing. Pamela and B. leave the coach for a walk across a meadow, sending the coach ahead to meet them. They come upon Williams strolling and reading Boileau's *Lutrin*. After discussing Williams's former hopes of winning Pamela, B. gives him Pamela's hand 'in Token of her Friendship and Esteem'; the parson kisses her hand, and B. invites him to dinner. When they come to the coach, B. 'kindly said, Pray, Mr. *Williams*, oblige *Pamela* with your Hand; and step in yourself. He bow'd, and took my Hand, and my Master made him step in, and sit next me, all that ever he could do, and sat himself over-against him, next my Father, who sat against me' (ii, pp. 118–23).

[126] In this paragraph Williams, a self-serving casuist, transmogrifies a recurrent theme of the Pauline Epistles, distinguishing between the Spirit and the Flesh, as in Galatians 5: 'This I say then, Walk in the Spirit, and ye shall not fulfil the lust of the flesh. | For the flesh lusteth against the Spirit, and the Spirit against the flesh: and these are contrary the one to the other.' Among 'the works of the flesh' are 'Adultery, fornication, lasciviousness'; among 'the fruit of the Spirit' are 'love, joy, temperance' (verses 16–7, 19–23).

[127] 'immaterial Substances': in *Leviathan* (1651) the materialist philosopher Thomas Hobbes had dismissed, as a contradiction in terms, the scholastic definition of the soul as an 'immaterial substance' (e.g. I. iv, v, xii). In his 'Essay on Nothing' HF cites 'The Great Mr. *Hobbes* . . . as an Enemy to that notable immaterial Substance' (*Miscellanies* i, p. 189). Earlier in that essay he had attributed the absurdity of the definition to an incompetent choice of words. The passage separates HF from the materialists and is worth quoting: 'For Instance,' he asks, 'is there any one who hath not an Idea of immaterial Substance?—Now what is immaterial Substance, more than *Nothing*? But here we are artfully deceived by the Use of Words: For were we to ask another what Idea he had of immaterial Matter, or of unsubstantial Substance, the Absurdity of affirming it to be Something, would shock him, and he would immediately reply, it was *Nothing*.' To the second question above HF attached the following footnote: 'The Author would not be here understood to speak against the Doctrine of Immateriality, to which he is a hearty Well-wisher; but to point at the Stupidity of those, who instead of immaterial *Essence*, which would convey a rational Meaning, have substituted immaterial *Substance*, which is a Contradiction in Terms' (ibid., p. 181 and n. 2). See also *Journey from This World to the Next* (*Miscellanies* ii, p. 9).

Product of the Flesh. Therefore, he says, my Dear, you have two Husbands, one the Object of your love, and to satisfy your Desire; the other the Object of your Necessity, and to furnish you with those other Conveniencies. (I am sure I remember every Word, for he repeated it three Times; O he is very good whenever I desire him to repeat a thing to me three times he always doth it!) as then the Spirit is preferable to the Flesh, so am I preferable to your other Husband, to whom I am antecedent in Time likewise. I say these things, my Dear, (said he) to satisfy your Conscience. A Fig for my Confidence, said I, when shall I meet you again in the Garden?

My Husband now rode up to the Chariot, and asked us how we did—I hate the Sight of him. Mr. *Williams* answered, very well, at your Service. They then talked of the Weather, and other things, I wished him gone again, every Minute; but all in vain, I had no more Opportunity of conversing[128] with Mr. *Williams*.

Well, at Dinner Mr. *Booby* was very civil to Mr. *Williams*, and told him he was sorry for what had happened, and would make him sufficient Amends, if in his power, and desired him to accept of a Note for fifty Pounds; which he was so *good* to receive, notwithstanding all that had past, and told Mr. *Booby*, he hop'd he would be forgiven, and that he would pray for him.

We make a charming Fool of him, i'fackins; Times are finely altered, I have entirely got the better of him, and am resolved never to give him his Humour.

O how foolish it is in a Woman, who hath once got the Reins into her own Hand, ever to quit them again.

After Dinner Mr. *Williams* drank the Church et cætera;[129] and smiled on me; when my Husband's Turn came, he drank et cætera and the Church; for which he was very severely rebuked by Mr. *Williams*, it being a high Crime, it seems, to name any thing before the Church. I do not know what *Et cætera* is, but I believe it is something concerning chusing Pallament Men; for I asked if it was not a Health to Mr. *Booby's* Borough, and Mr. *Williams* with a hearty Laugh answered, Yes, Yes, it is his Borough we mean.[130]

I slipt out as soon as I could, hoping Mr. *Williams* would finish the Squire, as I have heard him say he could easily do, and come to me; but it happened quite otherwise, for in about half an Hour, *Booby* came to me, and told me he had left Mr. *Williams*, the Mayor of his Borough, and two or

---

[128] 'conversing': i.e. having sexual intercourse (above, p. 150 n. 5).

[129] For the bawdy meaning of '*et cætera*', see above, p. 149 n. 1.

[130] Here no doubt a ribald pun is intended on 'borough', a town that sends a representative to Parliament, and 'burrow', a rabbit's (or cony's) hole in the ground (see above, note to line 21 of title-page, s.v. 'CONNY').

three Aldermen heartily at it, and asked me if I would go hear *Williams*
sing a Catch,[131] which, added he, he doth to a Miracle.

Every Opportunity of seeing my dear *Williams*, was agreeable to me,
which indeed I scarce had at this Time; for when we returned, the
whole Corporation[132] were got together, and the Room was in a Cloud of
Tobacco; Parson *Williams* was at the upper End of the Table, and he hath
pure round cheery Cheeks, and his Face look'd all the World to nothing
like the Sun in a Fog. If the Sun had a Pipe in his Mouth, there would be
no Difference.

I began now to grow uneasy, apprehending I should have no more of Mr.
Williams's Company that Evening, and not at all caring for my Husband,
I advised him to sit down and drink for his Country with the rest of the
Company; but he refused, and desired me to give him some Tea; swearing
nothing made him so sick as to hear a Parcel of Scoundrels roaring forth
the Principles of honest Men over their Cups, when, says he, I know most
of them are such empty Blockheads, that they don't know their right
Hand from their left; and that Fellow there, who hath talked so much of
Shipping,[133] at the left Side of the Parson, in whom their all place a
Confidence, if I don't take care, will sell them to my Adversary.

I don't know why I mention this Stuff to you; for I am sure I know
nothing about *Pollitricks*,[134] more than Parson *Williams* tells me, who says
that the Court-side are in the right on't, and that every Christian ought to
be on the same with the Bishops.[135]

---

[131] 'Catch': a round.

[132] 'Corporation': the civic authorities of a borough or incorporated town, including the mayor, aldermen, and councillors.

[133] In his copy of *Shamela* Horace Walpole noted that this was a reference to William Shippen (1673–
1743), leader of the Jacobite faction in the House of Commons. In February, Shippen, by leading his
supporters from the chamber before a vote was taken, had in effect defeated the Opposition's motion
to impeach the Prime Minister. Later this year, in an allegorical satire of his former party, *The Opposition:
A Vision*, HF would represent Shippen, who had a reputation for being incorruptible, as the 'honest
Gentleman' who abandons the coach driving '*through thick and thin*' to remove Walpole from office. (See
Champion, pp. 589–90; *Life*, p. 321; and F. G. Ribble, 'Fielding's Rapprochement with Walpole in Late
1741', *PQ*, 80 [2001], pp. 71–81.) Judith Hawley notes that HF's placing the 'Fellow' who talks so much on
this topic 'at the left Side of the Parson' alludes to the custom in Parliament of the Opposition sitting to
the left of the Speaker (p. 343 n. 13).

[134] '*Pollitricks*': HF's coinage, which he used again when satirizing Walpole in *Jonathan Wild* (II. v):
'those great Arts, which the Vulgar call Treachery, Dissembling, Promising, Lying, Falshood, &c. but
which are by GREAT MEN summed up in the collective Name of Policy, or Politicks, or rather *Pollitricks*'
(*Miscellanies* iii, p. 67).

[135] In his writings of this period, HF adopted the Opposition view that, from self-interested motives,
the bench of bishops in the House of Lords shamefully supported the measures of Walpole: see Coley's
Introduction and notes to *The Champion* (1739–40) and *Vernoniad* (1741), p. lxxi and index (s.v. 'bishops').
Attributed to HF by some scholars—the present editor among them—the anti-ministerial pamphlet
The Crisis: A Sermon was published a fortnight after *Shamela* on 16 April shortly before the election, its
title-page declaring it to be 'Humbly inscribed to the Right Reverend the Bench of BISHOPS' (see
Champion, p. xci n. 1, pp. cvi–cx, and Appendix V).

When we had finished our Tea, we walked in the Garden till it was dark, and then my Husband proposed, instead of returning to the Company, (which I desired, that I might see Parson *Williams* again,) to sup in another Room by our selves, which, for fear of making him jealous, and considering too, that Parson *Williams* would be pretty far gone, I was obliged to consent to.

O! what a devilish Thing it is, for a Woman to be obliged to go to Bed to a spindle-shanked[136] *young Squire, she doth not like, when there is a jolly Parson in the same House she is fond of.*

In the Morning I grew very peevish, and in the Dumps, notwithstanding all he could say or do to please me. I exclaimed against the Priviledge of Husbands, and vowed I would not be pulled and tumbled about. At last he hit on the only Method, which could have brought me into Humour, and proposed to me a Journey to *London*, within a few Days. This you may easily guess pleased me; for besides the Desire which I have of shewing my self forth, of buying fine Cloaths, Jewels, Coaches, Houses, and ten thousand other fine Things, Parson *Williams* is, it seems, going thither too, to be *instuted*.[137]

O! what a charming Journey I shall have; for I hope to keep the dear Man in the Chariot with me all the way; and that foolish Booby (for that is the Name Mr. Williams *hath set him) will ride on Horseback.*

So as I shall have an Opportunity of seeing you so shortly, I think I will mention no more Matters to you now. O I had like to have forgot one very material Thing; which is that it will look horribly, for a Lady of my Quality and Fashion, to own such a Woman as you for my Mother. Therefore we must meet in private only, and if you will never claim me, nor mention me to any one, I will always allow you what is very handsome. Parson *Williams* hath greatly advised me in this, and says, he thinks I should do very well to lay out twenty Pounds, and set you up in a little Chandler's Shop: but you must remember all my Favours to you will depend on your Secrecy; for I am positively resolved, I will not be known to be your Daughter; and if you tell any one so, I shall deny it with all my Might, which Parson *Williams* says, I may do with a safe Conscience, being now a married Woman. So I rest
     Your humble Servant,
          SHAMELA.

---

[136] Cf. *Joseph Andrews* (III. ii), where HF warns his female readers, who may on occasion need to rely on the strength of a man, not to match themselves 'with the spindle-shanked Beaus and Petit-Maîtres of the Age' (p. 194).

[137] '*instuted*': i.e. instituted by the bishop into the benefice formerly held by the deceased Squeeze-Tythe.

P.S. The strangest Fancy hath enter'd into my *Booby's* Head, that can be imagined. He is resolved to have a Book made about him and me; he proposed it to Mr. *Williams*, and offered him a Reward for his Pains; but he says he never writ any thing of that kind, but will recommend my Husband, when he comes to Town, to a Parson *who does that Sort of Business for Folks*,[138] one who can make my Husband, and me, and Parson *Williams*, to be all great People; for he *can make black white*, it seems. Well, but they say my Name is to be altered, Mr. *Williams* says the first Syllabub hath too comical a Sound, so it is to be changed into *Pamela*; I own I can't imagine what can be said; for to be sure I shan't confess any of my Secrets to them, and so I whispered Parson *Williams* about that, who answered me, I need not give my self any Trouble: for the Gentleman *who writes Lives*, never asked more than a few Names of his Customers, and that he made all the rest out of his own Head; you mistake, Child, said he, if you apprehend any Truths are to be delivered. So far on the contrary, if you had not been acquainted with the Name, you would not have known it to be your own History. I have seen a *Piece of his Performance*, where the Parson, whose Life was written, could he have risen from the Dead again, would not even suspected he had been aimed at, unless by the Title of the Book, which was superscribed with his name. Well, all these Matters are strange to me, yet I can't help laughing, to think I shall see my self in a printed Book.

So much for Mrs. *Shamela*, or *Pamela*, which I have taken Pains to transcribe from the Originals, sent down by her Mother in a Rage, at the Proposal in her last Letter. The Originals themselves are in my Hands, and shall be communicated to you, if you think proper to make them publick;

---

[138] HF no doubt had a specific life-writing parson in mind, but only two candidates have been proposed for the part and neither is entirely convincing—though one is more likely than the other. Woods (pp. 251–3) argued for the Revd Thomas Birch (1705–66), historian and biographer; indeed, in the 1730s Birch contributed no fewer than 618 biographies to the translation of Pierre Bayle, *A General Dictionary, Historical and Critical*, 10 vols. (1734–41), and in addition published a life of Milton (1738). Baker (*Shamela* [Berkeley and Los Angeles, 1953], p. xxvi), on the other hand, noting Parson Oliver's observation that the author of *Pamela* wrote with 'Ciceronian Eloquence' (above, p. 158), believed HF was here taking a parting shot at Conyers Middleton; Rothstein concurs (p. 388 n. 12). Birch was certainly a prolific writer of lives, but he is not otherwise a target of HF's satire; on the contrary, he was, by 1747 at least, HF's good friend. And, after all, the uncertainty about HF's target is chiefly owing to Shamela, whose use of the plural (she refers to the biographer as 'the Gentleman *who writes Lives*'), if one takes it as just another instance of her tendency to exaggerate, counts for nothing. Conyers Middleton may have written just a single 'Life'; but the *Life of Cicero*—with its flattery of Lord Hervey and Walpole, and its disparagement of Lyttelton's book—was the reason for his being satirized in *Shamela*, and indeed for his being squinted at on the title-page in the name of its hybrid 'author'. At least one contemporary reader thought he knew whom HF meant: in his copy of *Shamela* Horace Walpole wrote in the margin, 'Dʳ Middleton'.

and certainly they will have their Use.[139] The Character of *Shamela*, will make young Gentleman wary how they take the most fatal Step both to themselves and Families, by youthful, hasty and improper Matches; indeed, they may assure themselves, that all such Prospects of Happiness are vain and delusive, and that they sacrifice all the solid Comforts of their Lives,[140] to a very transient Satisfaction of a Passion, which how hot so ever it be, will be soon cooled; and when cooled, will afford them nothing but Repentance.

Can any thing be more miserable, than to be despised by the whole World, and that must certainly be the Consequence; to be despised by the Person obliged, which it is more than probable will be the Consequence, and of which, we see an Instance in *Shamela*; and lastly to despise one's self, which must be the Result of any Reflection on so weak and unworthy a Choice.

As to the Character of Parson *Williams*, I am sorry it is a true one. Indeed those who do not know him, will hardly believe it so; but what Scandal doth it throw on the Order to have one bad Member, unless they endeavour to screen and protect him?[141] In him you see a Picture of almost every Vice exposed in nauseous and odious Colours, and if a Clergyman would ask me by what Pattern he should form himself, I would say, Be the reverse of *Williams*: So far therefore he may be of use to the Clergy themselves, and though God forbid there should be many *Williams*'s amongst them, you and I are too honest to pretend, that the Body wants no Reformation.

To say the Truth, I think no greater Instance of the contrary can be given than that which appears in your Letter. The confederating to cry up a nonsensical ridiculous Book, (I believe the most extensively so of any ever

[139] As Richardson concludes *Pamela* with 'a few brief Observations' presented in a series of paragraphs, each specifying an edifying moral that the novel offers 'to the Minds of YOUTH of BOTH SEXES' (ii, pp. 392–7), so Parson Oliver follows by enumerating the pernicious examples set by the work's scenes and principal characters, thereby providing 'an Antidote to this Poison' (p. 194).

[140] Cf., from the Preface to the *Miscellanies*, HF's phrase for the importance to him of his wife, Charlotte: 'one from whom I draw all the solid Comfort of my Life' (i, p. 13).

[141] HF opened the series he called 'An Apology for the Clergy' in *The Champion* (29 March 1740) by reiterating his conviction that 'There is nothing so unjustifiable as the general Abuse of any Nation or Body of Men.' He 'condemn'd the Custom of throwing Scandal on a whole Profession for the Vices of some particular Members'. With what appeared to be a general 'contempt of the clergy' in mind, he asked, 'Can any thing be more unreasonable than to cast Odium on the Professions of Divinity, Law, and Physick, because there have been absurd or wicked Divines, Lawyers, and Physicians?' He would not, however, tolerate priests such as Parson Williams: 'the greater Honour which we entertain for our Creator, the greater Abomination we shall have for those who pervert his holy Institutions, and have the Impudence to wear the Livery of his more immediate Service, whilst they act against it' (pp. 256–7). For the confederacy of clergy who 'cry up' Richardson's novel in the next paragraph, see above, Introduction, p. 140.

yet published,) and to be so weak and so wicked as to pretend to make it a Matter of Religion; whereas so far from having any moral Tendency, the Book is by no means innocent: For,

First, There are many lascivious Images in it, very improper to be laid before the Youth of either Sex.

2dly, Young Gentlemen are here taught, that to marry their Mother's Chambermaids, and to indulge the Passion of Lust, at the Expence of Reason and Common Sense, is an Act of Religion, Virtue, and Honour; and indeed the surest Road to Happiness.

3dly, All Chambermaids are strictly enjoined to look out after their Masters; they are taught to use little Arts to that purpose: And lastly, are countenanced in Impertinence to their Superiours, and in betraying the Secrets of Families.[142]

4thly, In the Character of Mrs. *Jewkes* Vice is rewarded; whence every Housekeeper may learn the Usefulness of pimping and bawding for her Master.

5thly, In Parson *Williams*, who is represented as a faultless Character, we see a busy Fellow, intermeddling with the private Affairs of his Patron, whom he is very ungratefully forward to expose and condemn on every occasion.

Many more Objections might, if I had Time or Inclination, be made to this Book; but I apprehend, what hath been said is sufficient to perswade you of the use which may arise from publishing an Antidote to this Poison. I have therefore sent you the Copies of these Papers, and if you have Leisure to communicate them to the Press, I will transmit you the Originals, tho' I assure you, the Copies are exact.

I shall only add, that there is not the least Foundation for any thing which is said of Lady *Davers*,[143] and don't hear Mr. *Booby* hath such a Relation, or that there is indeed any such Person existing. I am,

Dear Sir,
Most faithfully and respectfully,
Your humble Servant,
J. OLIVER.

---

[142] Writing '*to his Sister* Pamela' an account of Lady Booby's attempt to seduce him, Joseph Andrews (I. vi) nevertheless assures her: 'you know, *Pamela*, I never loved to tell the Secrets of my Master's Family' (p. 31).

[143] Mr B.'s sister Lady Davers at first offers to take Pamela into her household to protect her. She tries to dissuade her brother from ruining Pamela by seducing her, or demeaning himself and his family by marrying her. After he marries her, she treats Pamela with contempt, but in the end joins the neighbouring ladies in praising her.

Parson TICKLETEXT *to Parson* OLIVER.

Dear SIR,

I Have read over the History of *Shamela*, as it appears in those authentick Copies you favour'd me with, and am very much ashamed of the Character, which I was hastily prevailed on to give that Book. I am equally angry with the pert Jade herself, and with the Author of her Life: For I scarce know yet to whom I chiefly owe an Imposition, which hath been so general that if Numbers could defend me from Shame, I should have no Reason to apprehend it.

As I have your implied Leave to publish, what you so kindly sent me, I shall not wait for the Originals, as you assure me the Copies are exact, and as I am really impatient to do what I think a serviceable Act of Justice to the World.

Finding by the End of her last Letter, that the little Hussy was in Town, I made it pretty much my Business to enquire after her, but with no effect hitherto: As soon as I succeed in this Enquiry, you shall hear what Discoveries I can learn. You will pardon the Shortness of this Letter, as you shall be troubled with a much longer very soon: And believe me,

Dear Sir,
Your most faithful Servant,
THO. TICKLETEXT.

P.S. Since I writ, I have a certain Account, that Mr. *Booby* hath caught his Wife in bed with *Williams*; hath turned her off, and is prosecuting him in the spiritual Court.[144]

---

[144] The Ecclesiastical Court, under the jurisdiction of a metropolitan bishop, had charge of all religious and ecclesiastical matters, the sacrament of marriage among them.

2

A FULL VINDICATION OF THE
DUTCHESS DOWAGER OF
MARLBOROUGH (1742)

ON Friday 2 April 1742 the anonymous pamphlet *A Full Vindication of the Dutchess Dowager of Marlborough* was published, 'Printed for J. ROBERTS, in *Warwick-Lane*'.[1] On 13 April Fielding assigned rights to the pamphlet to Andrew Millar, along with those to *Joseph Andrews*, published five weeks before, and to his farce *Miss Lucy in Town*.[2] Millar, who may have prompted his newly acquired author to seize a timely opportunity, had possibly used Roberts to shield him from the political heat generated by the Duchess's autobiographical *Account of the Conduct of the Dowager Duchess of Marlborough, From her first coming to Court, to the Year 1710. In a Letter from herself to My Lord——*, which had appeared on 2 March.[3] In her eighty-second year and recovering from a perilous illness, Sarah Churchill (1660–1744), the once intimate friend of Queen Anne and widow of the great Duke of Marlborough, wanted to clear her name, as she says in her Introduction, from aspersions cast thirty years earlier, on her dismissal from court, now that she was 'drawing near my end'.

---

[1] *Daily Advertiser* and *Daily Post* (Friday 2 April 1742): '*This Day at Noon will be publish'd*'. The now obsolete form 'Dutchess', repeated throughout, was still current in the eighteenth century (*OED*, s.v. 'duchess'). James Roberts, whose name also appears in the imprint of *The Masquerade*, *Shamela*, and *Ovid's Art of Love*, was serving as trade publisher for Andrew Millar, who held the copyright (see below, n. 2).

[2] For a transcript of the document, witnessed by the Revd William Young, HF's friend and collaborator, see the General Introduction to *Joseph Andrews* (pp. xxx–xxxi). For a discussion of the biographical context of HF's authorship, see *Life*, pp. 343–5. Millar was not to list the *Full Vindication* in any advertisement of HF's works until 1758, on the end-page of Sarah Fielding's *Lives of Cleopatra and Octavia*, 2nd edn.; and he omitted it from the *Works* (1762).

[3] *Daily Post* (Tuesday 2 March 1741/2). The unnamed nobleman to whom the Duchess addressed the *Account* was 'probably' the Earl of Chesterfield, her executor and political ally. Chesterfield, together with Alexander Pope, had been instrumental in introducing to her the historian (and friend of HF) Nathaniel Hooke, who edited and shaped the final version of the *Account*. (Frances Harris, 'Accounts of the Conduct of Sarah, Duchess of Marlborough, 1704–1742', *British Library Journal*, 8 [1982], p. 28.)

Although Samuel Johnson had anonymously reviewed the book for *The Gentleman's Magazine* on 9 March, with no '*Intention to please or offend any Party*', he declares, aware that it had already become '*the most popular Topic of Conversation*'.[4] A flood of hostile pamphlets had then begun on 12 March[5] with the anonymous *Remarks upon the Account of the Conduct of a certain Dutchess. In a Letter from a Member of the last Parliament in the Reign of Queen Anne to a Young Nobleman*, a Tory attack on the Duchess's outspoken Whig position. Against these *Remarks*, Fielding addressed his *Full Vindication*.[6]

The Duchess's long-projected, long-delayed *Account*, radiating political energy from old Whig-and-Tory battles, could hardly have appeared in a more highly charged political atmosphere. Robert Walpole had resigned the seals of office on 11 February 1742, after twenty-one years of power had ended in a tempestuous session of Parliament. In December, as the debates began, the Duchess, whose riches had served the Opposition well,[7] fell desperately ill.

On Wednesday 9 December 1741 the *Daily Gazetteer* had reported: 'Last Night her Grace the Duchess Dowager of Marlborough lay so dangerously ill at Marlborough-house St. James's, that her Life is despaired of.' On Thursday 10 December Horace Walpole had concluded a letter to Horace Mann:

---

[4] *GM*, 12 (March 1742), pp. 128–31. Johnson finds the Duchess's characterization of William, Mary, and Anne surprisingly just as they break through noble stereotypes; but that of Robert Harley, the prime lord, 'partially drawn' and biased. From the Duchess's book, he says, 'the polite Writer may learn an unaffected Dignity of Stile, and an artful Simplicity of Narration' (pp. 131, 129).

[5] On 11 March, having apprised his friend 'John Clerke, Esq.' of the state of politics after the fall of Walpole, the poet Thomas Edwards continued: 'As for Literary News, the Duchess of Marlborough has published her Memoirs in which she abuses K. William & Q. Mary and Ld Oxford [Harley] & his party too, they reach down to 1710 but there is not a word of Bolingbroke in them: there is now in the Press an answer to them written by Lady Masham and left at her death to be published if ever the Duchess should print hers, so that we are like to have a Female book-war, but her Grace has this advantage that as Lady Masham is dead she will have the last word' ('Letters, 1738–42', Bodleian Library, MS Bodl. 1009, pp. 222–3). Lady Abigail Masham (d. 1734), the Duchess's cousin, had replaced her as Queen Anne's favourite: see the notes to the text below, p. 210 n. 14.

[6] Two other attacks preceded HF's *Full Vindication*: 'Britannicus', *A Review of a Late Treatise* (23 March) and *Her Grace of M———h's Party-Gibberish explained* (27 March). *The Sarah-ad: or, A Flight for Fame*, a satire in Hudibrastic verse, was published simultaneously with HF's pamphlet on 2 April. Others followed after: Aquila, *The Old Wife's Tale* (24 April); *A Continuation of the Review of a Late Treatise* (30 April); *The Other Side of the Question*, a book of almost 500 pages by James Ralph, HF's friend and collaborator (12 May), who was paid to write it (John B. Shipley, 'James Ralph's Pamphlets, 1741–1744', *Library*, 5th ser., xix (1964), p. 133 and n. 3); and *Memoirs of the Four Last Years of the Reign of Queen Anne* (27 May). Cross (i, p. 361), followed by Dudden (i, p. 394), mistakenly states that 'Britannicus' wrote the *Remarks* that provoked HF's vindication, which alone rose to the Duchess's defence: the so-called 'Second Edition' of the pamphlet (3 May) is merely a page-for-page reprint of the first.

[7] William Coxe, *Memoirs of the Life and Administration of Sir Robert Walpole, Earl of Orford*, 3 vols. (1798), i, pp. 683–4.

Old Marlborough is dying—but who can tell? Last year she had lain a great while ill, without speaking; her physicians said, 'She must be blistered or she will die.' She called out. 'I won't be blistered, and I won't die.' If she takes the same resolution now, I don't believe she will.[8]

On Friday 11 December the *Daily Gazetteer* had announced:

The Report of her Grace the Duchess Dowager of Marlborough being dead, as mention'd in one of the Papers last Night, is groundless, her Grace being much better: And Yesterday her Grace order'd all her Servants to be call'd before her, and gave them Bank Notes and Specie to the amount of 3000 l. for their great [Dili]gence, Care and Attendance on her Grace during [their] Service with her, VIZ. . . . [a list of servants and amounts].

Why did Fielding raise his voice, the only one, to vindicate the Duchess against her antagonists? The answer is clear from a passage in the Preface to the *Miscellanies* (1743):

While I was last Winter laid up in the Gout, with a favourite Child dying in one Bed, and my Wife in a Condition very little better, on another, attended with other Circumstances, which served as very proper Decorations to such a Scene, I received a Letter from a Friend, desiring me to vindicate myself from two very opposite Reflections, which two opposite Parties thought fit to cast on me . . .[9]

Fielding no doubt wished to defend this old woman from the aspersions cast upon her by her enemies; she was widow of the great Marlborough, under whom his father had fought gallantly at Blenheim and whose character and victories he praised in his works. But there was a far stronger motive: his family was in distress and the Duchess was known for the munificence of the rewards she bestowed on those who served her.[10]

'To this Fortune', Fielding writes in his *Vindication*, 'many private Persons and Families, who have been relieved by her Grace's Generosity, owe their Preservation' (p. 236). Moreover, Fielding was related to the Duchess by marriage: his mother's cousin Mary Gould was the Duchess's sister-in-law, the wife of the Duke's brother General Charles Churchill.[11] More immediately relevantly, Fielding was acquainted with the Duchess's

---

[8]   *Yale Walpole*, xvii, p. 235.

[9]   Preface to *Miscellanies* i, p. 14.

[10]   She had given £1,000 towards settling poor families in Georgia. In 1736, for some £50,000, she had built and endowed an almshouse at St Albans for veterans of the Duke's armies and their widows. And on Nathaniel Hooke, for editing and shaping the versions of her *Account* that had evolved over decades, she had bestowed the astonishing honorarium of £5,000 (Harris, 'Accounts of the Conduct of Sarah, Duchess of Marlborough', pp. 10–22; *Life*, p. 343).

[11]   G. M. Godden, *Henry Fielding: A Memoir* (London, 1910), p. 137.

grandson Charles Spencer (1706–58), third Duke of Marlborough, to whom, praising his generosity, Fielding had dedicated *The Universal Gallant* (1735).[12] Indeed, there is reason to believe Fielding may have visited the Duchess at Blenheim at about the time he was courting her grandson. The author of an essay in *The Craftsman*, No. 469 (28 June 1735), attributed to Fielding by the present editor, admiringly recalls the tapestries and pillar at Blenheim commemorating the Duke's victories.[13] In his *A Journey from This World to the Next* (i. iv), Fielding's 'author', viewing Death's palace, examines 'various Battle-pieces in Tapestry' that remind him of 'those beautiful ones I had in my Life-time seen at Blenheim' (*Miscellanies* ii, p. 22). In his *Vindication*, Fielding seems to write of the Duchess from personal experience, saying that 'none can equal her Affability and Condescension' to 'those who have acknowledged themselves to be her Inferiours' (p. 236).

Although Fielding had every reason, personal and pecuniary, to rally to the Duchess's side, his political position had become questionable. His devotion to the Duchess's opposition party had wavered as he stopped writing for *The Champion* and he had declared political neutrality in *The History of Our Own Times* early in 1741. On 7 January 1741 he had complained that 'I have drawn my Pen in Defence of my Country, [and] have sacrificed to it the Interest of myself and Family.'[14] In *The Opposition*, on 15 December 1741, just two weeks after the rolling parliamentary attack on Walpole had opened, headed by the Duchess's favourite Chesterfield, Fielding had satirized the Opposition Patriots and commended the Duchess's hated Walpole, in exchange for some much-needed money.[15] But Walpole's fall from power in February 1742 had eclipsed any prospects in that direction. Andrew Millar had yet to pay him anything for *Joseph Andrews*, published on 22 February, and, though Charles Fleetwood of Drury Lane had submitted *Miss Lucy in Town* on 5 March for the Lord Chamberlain's approval, any money from it would have to wait until its production on 6 May.[16] Fielding had needed to borrow £197 on 27 March, a week before his *Vindication* appeared, and he had been staving off in court an impending judgment against him for his share of an old debt of £200.[17] When the attacks on the Duchess's *Account* had begun on 12 March, he had

---

[12] *Life*, p. 183.

[13] *New Essays*, p. 82.

[14] Preface to *Of True Greatness* (*Miscellanies* i, p. 248).

[15] On HF's changing politics and his rapprochement with Walpole late in 1741, see the Postscript to this Introduction below.

[16] Huntington Library, Larpent MS (LA33); *Life*, pp. 346, 660 n. 125.

[17] To be settled on 26 May by court order to pay £35 9s. 8d. (*Life*, pp. 289, 296, 341, 660 n. 114).

evidently seen opportunity dawning again. A new Opposition was forming around his Eton friend William Pitt and the Duchess's Chesterfield. But Fielding's hopes for some reward from the Duchess were in vain. Perhaps mindful of his recent shift to Walpole, the Duchess did nothing for the preservation of Fielding and his family.[18]

Fielding had rushed to support the Duchess in answering the first attack, the *Remarks*, which had appeared on Friday 12 March.[19] His *Vindication*, published on Friday 2 April, was thus written at some time during about two weeks, Monday to Monday, let us say, 15 to 29 March, the last date he could reasonably get his copy to the printer, weeks in which he must also have faced the annotating and polishing of his and William Young's *Plutus*, just another two weeks off.

Fielding defends the veracity of the Duchess's account of the early years in the reign of William and Mary, which *Remarks* repeatedly challenges, especially her narrative concerning their treatment of Anne, Mary's sister and the future queen, and of the Duchess, Anne's First Lady of the Bedchamber and custodian of her Privy Purse. The author of *Remarks*, as his title-page states, is a 'MEMBER | Of the last PARLIAMENT | In the Reign of Queen *ANNE*' writing a 'Letter' to a young lord just entering 'the great and important Scene of Life' to enlighten him against 'the Party Prejudices' of which the old MP sees an eminent example in the Duchess's *Account* (p. [3]). He reveals himself a Tory, commenting ironically on 'the Gratitude of her and her Party', the Whigs (p. 48). But he is chiefly concerned 'to vindicate the Memory of two Princes [William and Mary] that ought to be dear to the Nation; and to put it in such a Light as that no Party shall lay hold of the Facts contained in this Account of her Grace's Conduct to blacken them' (p. 40).

---

[18] Cross (i, pp. 361–2) first challenged the assumption among HF's biographers that the Duchess rewarded him for the *Vindication*. There is no evidence that she either commissioned him to write it or paid him a gratuity for his efforts on her behalf. From a note on the verso side of the copyright assignment of *Joseph Andrews* (see above, n. 2), we know only that Andrew Millar gave him five guineas for the pamphlet. HF seems for a time to have remained hopeful that the Duchess would eventually come to the relief of himself and family: in *Of Good Nature*, his verse epistle to the Duke of Richmond published in the *Miscellanies*, he repeated the praise of her benevolence in the *Vindication*: 'few with you [Richmond] or *Marlborough* can save | From Poverty, from Prisons, and the Grave' (i, pp. 31–2). It would not be long, however, before HF's flattery of the wealthy Duchess turned to sarcasm. Among the death notices published in the *True Patriot* of December 1745 is the following, with HF's comment: 'A Man, supposed to be a Pensioner of the late Dutchess of Marlborough—*He is supposed to have been poor*' (ed. Coley, p. 374 and n. 1).

[19] The publisher of *Remarks* was Thomas Cooper, who had been publisher of Walpole's propaganda organ the *Daily Gazetteer* from its first issue in 1735. In *The Champion* (16 October 1740) HF had labelled Cooper '*Publisher-General* to the *Ministerial Society*' (p. 482); it followed that *The Opposition* (December 1741), HF's electioneering pamphlet calculated to serve Walpole's cause, was published by Cooper. He also published four others of the attacks on the Duchess's *Account*.

Who this author was is now indiscernible. Fielding's title-page designates him as 'the NOBLE AUTHOR', and Fielding addresses him as 'MY LORD'. The advertisements, probably of Fielding's authorship or approval, multiply the epithets to 'the Noble, Old and Spiteful Author'. But Fielding ignores the obvious age of this elder statesman, as well as the elderly stance and the Tory allegiance within the pamphlet. Adopting a strategy calculated to please the Duchess, he opens the *Vindication* by addressing the author as if he were Walpole himself—or one of his unemployed hirelings who once wrote for the ministerial organ the *Daily Gazetteer*,[20] now defunct since the Great Man's fall from power:

WHETHER the Piece I shall endeavour to answer was your own Performance, or whether it was written on your Command, by one of that scribbling Gang, which the disbanding Mr. *P[ax] ton*'s late Regiment of Gazetteers hath cast destitute on the Public, I need not determine?

Walpole was indeed now notoriously a lord, having been created Earl of Orford on 9 February as part of a manoeuvre to ease him out of the House of Commons and the ministry. As a young man, he had also been a leader in Queen Anne's last Parliament. But Walpole, at 66, was hardly an old man and he was still much engaged in current politics, including his resistance to a gathering movement to investigate his ministry. He was not at all the Tory nobleman who chose to defend the names of William and Mary in his *Remarks*.

Remarks quotes extensively to defend the King and Queen against the Duchess's picturing them as coldly heartless and vindictive towards Anne and her court-in-waiting. Fielding, in rebuttal, effectively counters his opponent's quotations from Bishop Burnet, his own favourite historian. But the author of *Remarks* closes before coming to the Duchess's eventual dismissal by Queen Anne, the emotional centre of her whole self-justification. As a parting gesture, however, he promises a continuation, in which he will 'lay open some Particulars in the latter part of Queen *Ann*'s [*sic*] Reign, of a very different Nature from those represented by her Grace' (p. 50). To this, Fielding, in closing the *Vindication*, warns his 'Old and Spiteful' adversary of the consequences should he carry out his threat: in that event, 'you may depend on a second letter, tho' perhaps differing somewhat in gentleness' (p. 40). The noble lord's continuation was not forthcoming.

The 'Particulars' promised by *Remarks* would have concerned the Duchess's 'Conduct' in the service of Queen Anne. What the Duchess presents as frankness others saw as imperiousness. The girl who at 8 or 9 had

---

[20] For HF's long campaign against Walpole's *Daily Gazetteer*, see the text below, p. 207 n. 1.

befriended the plain and forlorn little Princess Anne, five years her junior, and had stood by her later through thick and thin, grew higher of hand as time went on. None of the attacking pamphleteers, nor Fielding, knew, or dared to use, the evidence that would begin to appear in letters and memoirs after her death two years later. Horace Walpole reported that the Duchess 'always behaved rudely & yet making Court by abusing Queen Anne' behind her back and referring to her as 'The Creature': 'her Insolence . . . had totally estranged and worn out the patience of the poor Queen her Mistress. The duchess was often seen to give her Majesty her fan & gloves & turn away her own head, as if the Queen had offensive smells.'[21]

In 1832, in a footnote to a new edition of Bishop Burnet's *History*, the Earl of Dartmouth wrote:

The duchess of Marlborough had been long out of favour, before either her husband or lord Godolphin knew of it, (she keeping it a secret from them as long as she could.) After the battle of Blenheim, she thought her foundation so broad, that she treated the queen with the utmost insolence and contempt. The last free conference she had with her was at Windsor, where Mrs. Danvers, who was then in waiting, told me, the duchess reproached her for above an hour with her own and her family's services, in so loud and shrill a voice, that the footmen at the bottom of the back stairs could hear her: and all this storm was raised for the queen's having ordered a bottle of wine a day to be allowed her laundress, without having acquainted her grace with it. The queen, seeing her so outrageous, got up, to have gone out of the room: the duchess clapped her back against the door, and told her she should hear her out, for that was the least favour she could do her, for having set and kept the crown upon her head. As soon as she had done raging, she flounced out of the room, and said, she did not care if she never saw her more: to which the queen replied very calmly, that she thought the seldomer the better.[22]

Fielding's work would have been cut out for him had the author of *Remarks* carried out the threatened continuation.

                                                                    SWB

Postscript: Fielding's Changing Politics, 1741–2

To his readers, HF's political loyalties during the winter of 1741–2 must have seemed oddly equivocal. His profitable, but ineffectual,

---

[21] *Reminiscences Written by Mr. Horace Walpole in 1788, For the Amusement of Miss Mary and Miss Agnes Berry*, ed. Paget Toynbee (Oxford, 1924), p. 87.

[22] *Bishop Burnet's History of His Own Time: With the Suppressed Passages of the First Volume, And Notes by the Earls of Dartmouth and Hardwicke*, 6 vols. (Oxford, 1832), v, p. 440 n. *k*.

accommodation with Walpole in December produced the electioneering pamphlet *The Opposition: A Vision*, a satire representing members of his former party as self-serving hypocrites. The Great Man's bungling conduct of the war with Spain, which Fielding had scored a year earlier in the *Vernoniad*, cost Walpole control of the House of Commons and forced his resignation in February; as a reward for twenty years in power, he was elevated to the Lords as first Earl of Orford. In March HF, depressed by his wife's illness and the death of his favourite daughter, as well as the dunning of his creditors, could not 'join the general Joy' his friends in Opposition took at the apparent success of their efforts to impeach Walpole.[23] But Walpole in the Lords made certain that their design came to nothing, and that they were excluded from the new administration—with the glaring exception, that is, of Carteret and Pulteney: Carteret, the king's favourite, was appointed Secretary of State for the Northern Department, and Pulteney was bribed with a peerage as first Earl of Bath. For their defection to the court these former leaders of the 'Patriots' at once replaced Walpole as the targets of a 'new Opposition', which included Fielding's friends and patrons: Dodington, Lyttelton, Chesterfield, and Pitt.

It is important to keep in mind that, with the exception of the general satire of the party in *The Opposition: A Vision* (15 December 1741), which we now know Walpole paid him to write,[24] when Fielding ridicules 'Patriots' during this period, he aims not at the party of his patrons, whom, as members of the 'Broad Bottom' government under Pelham, he would in due course serve as author of *The True Patriot* and *Jacobite's Journal*. He aims at the likes of Carteret and Pulteney, who, in order to enjoy the per-quisites and power of placemen at court, betrayed the idealistic principles they once advocated. Keeping this distinction in mind lends a certain consistency to the otherwise incoherent political attitudes to be found in Fielding's writings of the early months of 1742, when he first published *Joseph Andrews* (22 February), then revised it for a second edition (10 June); wrote *A Full Vindication of the Dutchess Dowager of Marlborough* (2 April); translated Aristophanes' *Plutus* (31 May); and continued assembling the pieces that would comprise the *Miscellanies* (April 1743).

In *Joseph Andrews* Walpole's spell in office is denounced in scornful reference to 'the Trade . . . of *Prime Ministring*' (II. i, p. 89) and in the characterization of Lord Hervey as Beau Didapper, who is the tool of 'a Fellow, whom they call a Great-Man', whose 'Commands' he slavishly executes 'at the Expence of his Conscience, his Honour, and of his Country' (IV. ix, p. 313).

But hypocritical 'Patriots' are treated with still greater contempt[25]—particularly in a trio of chapters in book II, in which Parson Adams encounters the allegorical figure of a false patriot, whose professions of courage and of selfless devotion to his country's welfare are shown to be hypocritical (II. vi, ix); and Parson Adams, appearing '*in a political Light*', reveals that his efforts on behalf of candidates of the Country Party were not only unwise, but unrewarded (I. viii). In a kind of coda to these three chapters, Fielding in the second edition,[26] intending a slap at the motives of Carteret and Pulteney, altered the opening of the following chapter, in which Fanny, whom Adams has rescued from a would-be rapist, 'began to fear as great an Enemey in her Deliverer, as he had delivered her from; . . . she suspected he had used her as some very honest Men have used their Country; and had rescued her out of the hands of one Rifler, in order to rifle her himself' (II. x, p. 140).

But without naming him, Fielding in *Joseph Andrews* reserved his highest praise for the leader of the 'new Opposition'—a man he considered a true patriot; the Earl of Chesterfield (III. i, p. 190). And it was Chesterfield to whom the Duchess of Marlborough, an implacable enemy of Walpole, probably addressed the *Account* of her conduct[27] which Fielding in March chose to defend against the slurs of a certain 'Noble' antagonist.

MCB

[25] For a treatment in greater detail of HF's political references in *Joseph Andrews*, see Battestin, 'Fielding's Changing Politics and *Joseph Andrews*', *PQ*, 39 (1960), pp. 39–55, esp. 49–55.

[26] For a study of HF's revisions of *Joseph Andrews*, see Battestin, *Studies in Bibliography*, 16 (1963), pp. 81–117; on the political passages, pp. 94–5.

[27] See Frances Harris, 'Accounts of the Conduct of Sarah, Duchess of Marlborough', *British Library Journal*, 8 (1982), pp. 7–35.

A FULL VINDICATION

OF THE
Dutchess Dowager
OF

MARLBOROUGH:

BOTH

With regard to the ACCOUNT lately
Publiſhed by

HER GRACE,

AND TO

Her CHARACTER in general;

AGAINST

The *baſe* and *malicious* Invectives contained
in a late *ſcurrilous* Pamphlet, entitled
REMARKS on the Account, &c.

In a Letter to the NOBLE AUTHOR
of thoſe *Remarks.*

LONDON:
Printed for J. ROBERTS, in *Warwick Lane.*
M.DCC.XLII.

Title: Sarah (1660–1744), relict of John Churchill (1650–1722), first Duke of Marlborough, the victorious commander of British forces against France (1702–11). Though she was once the intimate favourite of Queen Anne and her influential adviser, the Duchess's overbearing manner resulted in 1710 in the Queen's banishing her from her presence and in 1711 dismissing her from her court offices. Written in several drafts over the course of forty years as an apologia for herself and husband, *An Account of the Conduct of the Dowager Duchess of Marlborough, From her first coming to Court, To the Year 1710* was prepared for publication (2 March 1742) by the historian Nathaniel Hooke. It at once became a cause célèbre and precipitated a spate of hostile publications (see the Introduction, above, p. 197 and nn. 4–6).

REMARKS: *Remarks upon the Account of the Conduct of a Certain Dutchess. In a Letter from a Member of the last Parliament in the Reign of Queen Anne. To a Young Nobleman* (12 March 1742), the first of the attacks on the Duchess's book and HF's specific target in the *Vindication*.

J. ROBERTS: see Introduction, p. 196 and n. 1.

A full Vindication of her Grace the Dutchess Dowager of MARLBOROUGH.

MY LORD,[1]

WHETHER the Piece I shall endeavour to answer was your own Performance, or whether it was written on your Command, by one of that scribbling Gang, which the disbanding Mr. P—ton's[2] late Regiment of Gazetteers hath cast destitute on the Public, I need not determine? In either case, you are entitled to my Answer; which, however, you have not so much reason to be startled at, as you may justly apprehend: for I do not intend to imitate you in Invective, and shall abstain from any other Reflections than those I shall make on your Remarks, and which are necessary to refute the groundless Slanders you endeavour to throw on an innocent and injured Character.

The Observation with which you set out is strictly true; nay your whole Letter is one continued flagrant Example of it. You say,

'It has been often observ'd, that it is extremely hard to form a just Notion of the Characters of Mankind, from those who are personally interested in either justifying or blackening them. In this Country, where Party is so prevalent, that no Person can be supposed to be indifferent with regard to public Characters and Transactions, this Observation holds perhaps more strictly just than any other; and Time alone must discover the Motives of many Actions, and the true Colours of many Characters, which are now seen thro' the false glare that Passion or Prejudice throws upon them.'[3]

It was from this Party-Prejudice you mention, and the Falsehoods it daily propagates, that the Dutchess of *Marlborough* was induced to publish an

---

[1] Beyond representing himself as 'a MEMBER of the last PARLIAMENT in the Reign of Queen *ANNE*', who died in 1714, the author of *Remarks* is unknown. In his opening paragraph, however, HF affects to believe he is addressing none other than the former Prime Minister Sir Robert Walpole, who had recently been created Earl of Orford. In adopting this ploy, HF no doubt hoped to please the Duchess, Walpole's implacable enemy, whose financial support of the Opposition in the recent election had helped to bring him down. On the animosity between the two, see below, p. 235 and n. 113.

[2] As Solicitor to the Treasury in Walpole's administration, Nicholas Paxton (d. 1744) organized and financed his propagandists. In June 1735 Paxton consolidated the authors of the *Daily Courant*, *London Journal*, *Free Briton*, and others into a single organ, the *Daily Gazetteer*, which the Post Office distributed gratis throughout the country. In *The Craftsman* for 12 July and 2 August 1735—in which, anticipating the metaphor here of a 'Regiment of Gazetteers', Paxton is labelled '*Muster-Master* and *Provedior-General*' of an army of propagandists (*New Essays*, p. 108)—HF began a satirical campaign against the paper that lasted for the duration of Walpole's ministry. On 13 March 1742, about the time HF was beginning to write the *Vindication*, the Earl of Egmont wrote in his diary that a secret committee reported to the House of Commons 'discoveries of money paid to bribe elections, but because Mr. Paxton refused to give any account of 90,000 *l*. by him disposed of . . . he is now in Newgate' (Historical Manuscripts Commission, *Diary of the First Earl of Egmont*, 3 vols. [1923], iii, p. 264).

[3] *Remarks* (p. [3]), the author's opening paragraph.

Apology for a Conduct, which appears so truly great and worthy the highest
Applause; and it is this Prejudice alone which could instigate any one to
attempt to sully and blacken a Character, which that Apology hath placed in
so amiable a Light, that a very impartial Reader declared to me on perusing
it; 'Why, if this be true, the Dutchess of *Marlborough* is one of the best as
well as the greatest Women ever Born.'

In the Course of her own Justification hath unavoidably led her Grace to
expose some others in disadvantagious Colours, I am convinced she was sorry
for it; but sure it is a new Doctrine, and something unreasonable, that the
Innocent must suffer, rather than the Guilty should be blamed. I am certain
she hath no where departed from Delicacy,[4] as you accuse her; and I am as
well convinced, she hath not deviated from the Truth. Her Facts appear
most of them in Letters from the Parties themselves; which hath been always
accounted the best and most certain kind of History; and which, while the
Originals remain, must be always allowed to be undeniable Evidence.

But indeed your Opinion of History is pretty singular; for you say, 'Even
the high Station and Character of the Authoress ought to give an alarm to
your Lordship's caution; for the greater Opportunities her Grace had of
knowing, the more deeply must we suppose her to be interested in *acting*,
and therefore the more solicitous in *vindicating* or *blaming*, according as it
may set her own *Conduct* in the *fairest*, and that of her Enemies in the most
disadvantageous Light.'[5]

So that it seems the *higher* any Person's Station and Character is, the
lower their Credit, and the *more* they know of any Transaction, the *less*
capable are they of recording it.

Your Lordship is pleased to proceed thus: As to the first Reason of her
Grace's Ascendancy over the Princess of *Denmark*,[6] (*viz.* their playing
together when at School) 'it entirely rests upon her Grace's own Word,
that the Daughter of Mrs. *J*——*gs*,[7] who, if we believe the common

---

[4] 'departed from Delicacy': cf. HF's objection below (p. 209 n. 9), after quoting a passage in *Remarks*
(p. 5) in which the author insinuates, by three lines of asterisks, that the Duchess ('the Daughter of *Mrs.
J[ennin]gs*') was too poor and common to have been allowed, as she claims, such 'Familiarity with a
Princess of so strict and *delicate* an Education' (emphasis added).

[5] *Remarks*, p. 4.

[6] Anne Stuart (1665–1714), the future Queen Anne; in 1683 she married Prince George (1653–1708)
of Denmark. Her close friendship with Sarah Jenyns (later Duchess of Marlborough), began in 1670–1
when they were girls, Anne age 5, Sarah age 10.

[7] '*J*——*gs*': Jennings, a common spelling of Jenyns, the Duchess's maiden name. Her father, Richard
Jenyns (*c*.1618–1668), was a country squire of modest means and Member of Parliament for St Albans,
Hertfordshire. The family connection with the court was owing to Sarah's eldest sister, Frances (1648–
1731), later Lady Tyrconnell (see below, p. 224 n. 64), whom, in 1664, James, Duke of York and brother
to Charles II, appointed maid of honour to his wife. In 1673 James similarly appointed Sarah, at age 13,
maid of honour to the new Duchess, Mary of Modena, and Sarah's relationship with Anne, his youngest
daughter, was cemented. (James Falkner, *Oxford DNB*, s.v. Marlborough, Duchess of.)

Report   *   *   *   *   *   had   but   a   *   *   *   *   *   *   *   *
*   *   *   *   *   *   * very narrow Fortune, was admitted to so much
Familiarity with a Princess of so strict and delicate an Education, as that
which Princess *Anne* receiv'd.'[8]

What you would have the Reader supply in the Place of these Asterisks,
I cannot guess. You are pleased to call her Grace's Veracity in question;
and, if I mistake not, would insinuate that Miss *Jennings* had some Levity in
her Character, which rendered her unfit for the Company of so strict and
delicate[9] a Princess; indeed the same Reason is given a little afterwards, for
Lady *Clarendon's* Dislike to her.[10] Black and detestable Malice! Why did you
not assert, that her Grace was never her Lady of the bedchamber? A Fact
not less notorious, and which the same false Insinuations would have better
supported, unless the Princess had very early quitted that Strictness and
Delicacy of her Education: for surely the same Blemishes would have
rendered Miss *Jennings*, when a Girl, an improper Companion for the
Princess, would have made her, when a Woman, very unfit to fill the Post of
a Lady of the Bedchamber; nor would the prudent Countess of *Clarendon*,
then first Lady of the Bedchamber, have consented to her Admission. But
this is indeed the first time, that any Enemy of her Grace hath had the
impudence to insinuate the least Hint of such a nature.

As to the Characters of Lady *Clarendon*, and the Princess of *Denmark*, I
have nothing to say. Her Grace seems to draw a lively Picture of the former;
and the latter hath, in her Letters, drawn her own.[11]

But your Lordship seems to have forgotten some Passages in the Book
you are criticising on, when you affirm, That 'As her Grace has been
pleased to give us no manner of Insight into that part of the Character of
her Royal Mistress, which wrought this prodigious Alteration in her
Confidence, and no other Account of the Fact, but that she was wormed out
by an upstart Favourite, who was in every respect infinitely below her
Grace, the World is at liberty to make its own Conjectures.'[12]

---

[8] *Remarks*, p. 5.
[9] See above, p. 208 n. 4.
[10] 'Dislike to her': i.e. to the Duchess not the Princess. Jane (*née* Leveson-Gower) Hyde, Countess of
Clarendon and Rochester (*c.*1672–1725), Princess Anne's aunt by marriage and after 1710 her Lady of the
Bedchamber. HF refers to *Remarks* (p. 6): ''Tis true, that some part of Miss J[ennin]g's Conduct might
not be agreeable to that severe way of thinking, for which that Lady [Clarendon] was always remarkable.'
The Duchess's characterization of the Countess—she 'looked like a mad-woman, and talked like a scholar'
(*Account*, p. 10)—might well be considered indelicate.
[11] In her *Account* the Duchess, to prove Princess Anne's 'tender' affection for her, published a generous
selection of the 'many' such letters she had received from Anne—the Princess using the pet name 'Mrs.
Morley' and addressing the Duchess as 'Mrs. Freeman' (these are dispersed through pp. 62–100).
[12] *Remarks*, p. 8.

Sure, my Lord, this is not the only Account we have from the Dutchess, who hath shewn us her Disgrace (if an honest, upright, and faithful Servant dismissed, may be said to be disgraced) was owing to the Arts of a designing Politician, a great Master of his Profession,[13] assisted (if you please) by an upstart Favourite, the more dangerous as the least suspected;[14] to her Mistress's violent Inclination to the Tories, perhaps *Jacobites*, and in favour of some Schemes not necessary here to mention, as some of their Effects have been too fatally felt, and the Intention of the others plainly and undeniably known.

I shall take no other notice of that on which your Lordship hath been pleased to throw away so much of your Time and Paper, I mean the Dutchess's Assertion concerning my Lord *Clarendon*,[15] than that what the Bishop says *on his proposing to have King* James *sent to* Breda,[16] agrees better with her Grace's Account of *his having advised the sending him to the* Tower,[17]

---

[13] Robert Harley (1661–1724), first Earl of Oxford and Mortimer, and after 1710, when the Tories drove the Whigs from power, Queen Anne's principal minister. For his shrewd and devious ways as a politician he was known as Robin the Trickster. HF, himself a Whig who greatly admired the Duke of Marlborough, despised Harley. In *A Proper Answer to a Late Scurrilous Libel* (1747)—as earlier in *The Craftsman*, No. 431 (5 October 1734; *New Essays*, p. 63)—Harley is represented as chief among the 'wicked Ministers' who deluded Queen Anne into consenting to 'that detestable Treaty of *Utrecht* . . . by which *France* was again re-instated in almost every Thing she had lost, and relieved from all she had to fear from her victorious Enemies' (*JJ*, pp. 65–6). Harley, whose negotiations for the treaty Marlborough had opposed, was at the head of the Tory action to arraign the Duke on charges of peculation. In his political intrigues he was aided by his cousin Lady Masham (below, n. 14), who had replaced the Duchess of Marlborough as the Queen's favourite. On Harley, see also below, p. 233 n. 99.

[14] Abigail (*née* Hill; 1670?–1734), later Lady Masham; she was the Duchess's first cousin and second cousin of Robert Harley (above, n. 13). From a family who could not support her, she was befriended by the Duchess, who took her into her own household and introduced her to the court. When Anne became queen in 1702, Abigail, at the Duchess's instance, was appointed to the Queen's bedchamber; and as the Duchess's estrangement from Anne grew worse, Abigail replaced her as the Queen's favourite. Recognizing how useful his cousin could be in promoting his political programmes with the Queen, Harley enlisted Abigail in his plans to discredit the Duke and Duchess. (Frances Harris, *Oxford DNB*, s.v. Masham, Abigail.)

[15] Henry Hyde (1638–1709), second Earl of Clarendon. The son of the Lord Chancellor and historian, and brother of Anne Hyde, mother of Queen Mary and Queen Anne.

[16] In relating the events of the Revolution of 1688, Bishop Burnet recalls that one party recommended the deposed King James be imprisoned; cooler heads objected that 'because it might raise too much compassion, and perhaps some disorder, if the King should be kept in restraint within the Kingdom, therefore the sending him to *Breda* [the Netherlands] was proposed. The Earl of *Clarendon* pressed this vehemently, on the account of the *Irish* Protestants, as the King himself told me' (Burnet's *History*, i, p. 800; HF quotes the passage below, p. 211: HF owned this edition [Ribbles B56]). Burnet not only read the first draft of the Duchess's *Account*; recognizing its importance as a history of the court, he advised her to publish it (Harris, 'Accounts of the Conduct of Sarah, Duchess of Marlborough', p. 32). For HF's high opinion of Burnet as a historian, see below, *Journal of a Voyage to Lisbon*, p. 547 n. 10.

[17] In *Remarks* (p. 9), the author quotes the Duchess's comments on a letter she received from the Earl of Clarendon, as follows: 'It was full of Compliments, and at the same time full of Complaints, that she had not told him of a thing he lik'd so well, that he might have had a share in it. How well these Complaints and the Earnestness he shewed (in a Consultation held at *Windsor*, before the Prince of *Orange* came to *London*) to have King *James* sent to the Tower, agreed with his Conduct afterwards, I shall leave the World to judge' (*Account*, p. 18).

than with the Reasons for which you would have it believe impossible for any Man in his senses to have given such advice: Your Words are, 'It is sufficient to observe, that the Consultation which her Grace mentions to have been held at *Windsor*, was held at so critical a time that no Man in his Senses could be supposed to have given such an Advice: For King *James* by that time had return'd to *London* from *Feversham*, and remained at *Whitehall*. And to use Bishop *Burnet's* own Words,[18] "All the Indignation which the People of *London* had formerly conceived against him was turned into Pity and Compassion. Even the Privy-Council, in whose Hands the executive part of the Government appears at that time to* have been look'd upon by him to be as much their King as ever; *and*, continues the Bishop, *as he came back through the City he was welcomed with Signs of Joy by great Numbers.*" The Earl of *Clarendon* then must be suppos'd to have been void of common Sense, if while this Disposition of the People continued, he advis'd of sending the King to the *Tower of London*.'

Now, surely, this was as soon a Reason, who no Man of common Sense should propose sending the King to *Breda*, as why he should not propose sending him to the *Tower*. But what says the Bishop; 'because it might raise too much Compassion, and perhaps some Disorder, that the King should be kept in restraint within the Kingdoms; therefore the sending him to *Breda* was proposed. The Earl of *Clarendon* press'd this vehemently, on account of the *Irish* Protestants, as the King himself told me; for those that gave their Opinion in this Matter did it secretly, and in Confidence to the Prince: The Prince said he could not deny but that this might be good and wise Advice.'[19] Can any thing be more congruous, at least, less repugnant than these two Accounts? The Prince, whom his Enemies can send to one Place, may be by them sent to any other; and indeed, both these Proposals might very reasonably, in the same Debate, be supposed to have come from the same Person, who finding the Proposal of sending the King to the *Tower* rejected for the Reasons the Bishop gives, might advance or second that of sending him to *Breda*; so that here is no such *flat Contradiction*,[20] as your Lordship hath been pleased to observe.

I am come now to a most notable Paragraph indeed, wherein I may hope to shew your Lordship as flat a Contradiction as is to be found in any Writer

---

* *Burnet's* Hist. of his own Times, Vol. I. p. 799.

[18] HF quotes an abridged paraphrase—often not at all in Burnet's 'own Words'—of a passage from Burnet's *History*, i, p. 799, as he found it in *Remarks*, p. 11, where the passage from Burnet is followed by the author's comment, beginning 'The Earl of *Clarendon*' to the end of the paragraph.

[19] Quoted from Burnet's *History*, i, p. 800, to which HF refers above, n. 16.

[20] 'no such *flat Contradiction*': cf. *Remarks*, p. 12 ('an Incident that flatly contradicts').

whatever. It will be necessary to transcribe a good part of the Passage. Your Lordship after giving us Bishop *Burnet's* Opinion of King *William's* Designs, and some Anecdotes out of that Right Reverend Author, of the King's Behaviour before the Establishment of the Crown, proceeds thus:[21]

'Admitting this to be a true and genuine Account of what passed upon this important Occasion, it amounts to no more than that the Prince of *Orange* acted a very fair and open Part, by telling them he expected to be King, which he did not at all wish for, or that he would do a Thing that every wise Man ought to do if he was disappointed; which was to retire, and do all the Service he could in his own Station to his native Country. But if one take her Grace's Account of this Transaction, the Prince had no other Motive for coming over to *England*, but *meer Ambition of wearing a Crown.** Having never read*, continues her Grace, *nor employ'd my time in any thing, but playing at Cards, and having no Ambition myself, I imagin'd that the Prince of* Orange's *sole Design, was to provide for the Safety of his own Country, by obliging King* James *to keep the Laws of ours. And that he would get back as soon as he had made us all happy; and that there was no sort of Difficulty in the Execution of this Design, and that to do so much Good would be a greater Pleasure to him than to be King of any Country upon Earth. I was soon taught to know the World better.* I say, one who reads these Words, will be apt to conclude that King *William*, even upon the first Concert of his Expedition to *England*, was determin'd at all Events to dethrone his Father-in-Law, though *I am unwilling to believe that this was the Case*; I will only observe, that if it was, it is extreamly improbable that her Grace, notwithstanding all her Professions of Sincerity, was ignorant of the Design upon this Occasion. I cannot help laying before your Lordship a Fact, which I had from the late E. of N————m,[22] of a near Relation of your Lordship, who was very deep in the Concert, and too worthy a Man to impose either upon me or the World. He told me, that immediately upon the Prince of *Orange's* Landing, there was a visible Coldness and Backwardness in the Nobility and Gentry, to declare in his Favour; upon which, the Prince called a Meeting of those he could most depend upon, and told them in plain Terms, that as he had ventur'd so far, to support them, it was not to be expected, he was to do it for nothing, and that he never would have been so mad to have exposed himself and his Country to unavoidable Ruin, had he not had very strong

---

* Account, p. 21.

---

[21] The quotation that comprises the long paragraph that follows is from *Remarks*, pp. 14–16.

[22] Daniel Finch (1647–1730), second Earl of Nottingham and seventh Earl of Winchelsea, Secretary of State under William. See below, p. 227 n. 75.

Assurances from *England* before he set out, that he should be supported even to the utmost. That upon this he produced an Instrument signed by the most eminent Persons, who afterwards declared most eminently for the Revolution; in which they engage themselves to support his Highness in forming that very Plan of Government, by which the Crown was settled upon the Abdication of King *James*.[23] That the Names not only of the Subscribers themselves were signed to this Instrument, but of those whom they engag'd to bring over to the Prince; and that amongst others he saw that of the Lord *Churchill*, who by means of his Lady engag'd to bring over the Prince and Princess of *Denmark*. If this is fact, it is highly improbable, nay it is impossible, but that her Grace, considering the Ascendancy she always had over her Husband, should be so vastly supriz'd as she now affects to be at the News of the Prince of *Orange* accepting of the Crown.'

In the first place, I do not see, that whoever reads the Words, I WAS SOON TAUGHT TO KNOW THE WORLD BETTER, 'will be apt to conclude, that King *William*, even upon the first Concert of his Expedition to *England*, was determined at all Events to dethrone his Father-in-Law.'[24] This is such a Conclusion, as Dr. *South* says,[25] which may well be said to be *drawn* from the Words, since I am sure it never would *follow*.—But to the Fact itself, which is to impeach her Grace's Veracity. The late E. of N———— told somebody that told your Lordship, that somebody had told the Earl (for he was not then present) that King *William* immediately upon his Landing called a Meeting of the Nobility and Gentry. &*c*.

First, 'Till long after his Landing, he had no Nobility nor Gentry with him.

---

[23] This sentence is HF's target in the '3rd' objection, below, p. 214.

[24] The words in small capitals are from the Duchess's *Account* (p. 21); the quotation following is the author of *Remarks*' comment (p. 15).

[25] Robert South (1634–1716), one of the divines HF most admired, and without doubt the one whose works he most enjoyed reading: the Ribbles (S41–2) cite no fewer than thirty-four references to South and his writings in HF's works. In an essay on 'Wit and Humour' in *The Covent-Garden Journal*, No. 18 (3 March 1752), HF declared: 'in the Sermons of [South], there is perhaps more Wit, than in the Comedies of Congreve' (p. 124).

In the present reference, HF, changing South's 'flow' to '*follow*', recalls a passage from his sermon on Matthew 13: 52, 'The Scribe Instructed, &c.' Defining true wit in the writing of sermons and homilies, South characterizes the false wit of 'Mountebanks and Quacks . . . in Divinity' (iv, p. 29): 'First of all they seize upon some Text, from whence they draw something, (which they call a *Doctrine*) and well may it be said to be *drawn* from the Words; forasmuch as it seldom naturally flows, or *results* from them' (*Twelve Sermons Preached upon Several Occasions*, 6th edn. [1727], iv, p. 50). See also below, p. 225 and n. 67. Also in this volume, see above, *Shamela* (p. 176 and n. 99) and below, *Journal of a Voyage to Lisbon* (p. 628 and n. 249).

2dly, It is very improbable, indeed almost impossible to conceive,[26] that a Man of King *William*'s *phlegmatick and cool Temper*[27] should expose an Instrument of this Nature, which, if he had been successless in his Expedition, as he had then some Reason to doubt, would have hanged every one of those Friends who had set their Hands to it: for Anger itself could not move the hottest Mind to such a Step; (and King *William* is by this Writer truly represented as *slow in taking Revenge*)[28] since it was not the Gentlemen of the Country of whose Backwardness alone he could complain, whom he was to expose to the Vengeance of King *James*, but of his Friends above, who could not possibly have joined him so soon; and from most of whom, he was too good a Politician to expect so open and hasty a Declaration in his favour, though he was assured of their private Services.

3dly, If the Prince of *Orange* was so desirous to conceal his original Intentions of aiming at the Crown (admitting he had such) he cannot be supposed, without an entire Subversion of his Character, to expose an Instrument so openly and rashly, in which *it was engaged to support his Royal Highness in forming that very Plan of Government, by which the Crown was settled on the Abdication of King* James.[29]

4thly, If he had taken so rash and ill-advis'd a Step, he would never afterwards have been guilty of so preposterous a Conduct, as with the most manifest Chicanery to deny a Design he had publickly and openly avowed, and which, (if what this Some-body relates had been true) his Enemies could have so incontestably proved against him.

5thly, Bishop *Burnet*, who was present, would hardly have omitted such a notable Fact; or if it should be said, he omitted it from his Friendship to King *William*, a Motive which will, I believe, hardly gain Credit against so impartial an Historian; surely those who have written against King *William*, both at home and abroad, would have mentioned a Fact, which, if true, must have been so generally known.

But *Lastly*, If you really believe this to be fact, how can you assert, as you do in the preceding Page, that you believe he had no Design of procuring the Crown at the first Concert of his Expedition?[30] How can your Lordship assert in one Page (I say) that *you believe he had concerted no such Design*, and

---

[26] HF mocks the phrasing of *Remarks*, p. 16 ('it is highly improbable, nay it is impossible' that the Duchess should be surprised).

[27] In this paragraph the two italicized phrases characterizing King William's temperament echo *Remarks*, p. 32 (referring to 'King *William*'s cold phlegmatick Temper, and his Slowness and Insensibility of giving or resenting ill Usage').

[28] See above, n. 27.

[29] *Remarks*, p. 16.

[30] Ibid., p. 15 ('I am unwilling to believe that this was the Case').

in the next, *that he came over on these express Terms.* This sure, my Lord, is
very near a round, if not a flat Contradiction.

I shall not enter on the Character of King *William*; her Grace knew him
better than I, nor is there any reason to suspect her Partiality: But here your
Lordship is singular in an Opinion that *harsh Treatment*[31] obliges us to
conceal the Faults of an Enemy. This is indeed an extraordinary Flight of
Christianity.

The next Remark I shall trouble your Lordship with, is on your Conclusion in Page 19, which is likewise so lame, that your whole Strength is
required to draw it. Your Quotation is as follows:

' "I confess", says her Grace, "had I been in her Place, the Princess of
Denmark, I should have thought it more for my Honour to be easy in this
Matter than to shew an Impatience to get Possession of a Crown that had
been wrested from my Father." I believe no body ever either spoke or wrote
in this Manner, but with a Design of accusing the Person in whose Stead
they wish themselves to be. "And as it ought," continues her Grace, "to
have been a great Trouble to the Children of King *James* to be forced to act
the Part they did against him, so it seem'd to me that she who discover'd the
less Ambition would have the more amiable Character." There it is very
plain that by the Expression, *and as it ought to have been*, &c. her Grace
implies, that *the thing was not*; therefore her Grace speaking in the plural,
must mean that both the Children of King *James. viz.* Queen *Mary* and the
Princess of *Denmark, did shew an Impatience to get Possession of a Crown that
was wrested from her Father.*'[32]

I own, indeed, we are taught to confess *that we have done those things we
ought not to have done, and left undone those things we ought to have done;*[33]
but to say, that this is an eternal Obligation on our Nature, to affirm that
the bare supposing a Thing *ought to have been* done, is consequentially
affirming that it *was not*; this is to be a very strong Advocate for the
Necessity of human Actions. I shall make no Reflection on the Character of
Queen *Mary*; but why the Silence of the *Jacobites* or the Reverence of the
Whigs, should deter the Dutchess from attacking her, I can no more see,
than I can think the Obligations which she had to Queen *Anne* (which her
own faithful Conduct, and the immortal and barbarously and ungratefully

---

[31] *Remarks*, pp. 17–18 ('such a Reflection upon the Memory of King *William* comes with a very bad
Grace from a Person who owns and complains very loudly of *harsh Treatment* from that Quarter';
emphasis added).

[32] *Remarks* (p. 19), quoting *Account*, p. 21.

[33] From the Book of Common Prayer, HF adapts a passage from the liturgy of A General Confession in
the Order for Morning Prayer: 'We have left undone those things which we ought to have done, And we
have done those things which we ought not to have done, And there is no health in us.'

returned Services of her glorious Husband so well and nobly deserved)[34]
incapable of being obliterated by any future ill Treatment: Or why any
Attachment to the Characters of these Princesses should restrain her from
a just Vindication of her own. Your Arguments are indeed very curious, if
not strong. I will therefore quote the whole Passage, as well as that of the
Inscription, with your Observations on it. You say, it would be decent in
the Dutchess to conceal any thing which might cast a Reflection on Queen
Mary,[35] because her Character 'has never yet been attack'd by the most
bigotted Jacobite, and has always been had in great Veneration by the
greatest Whigs. As to that of Queen *Anne*, her Grace lies under so many
Obligations to support and defend it, against all Attempts to blacken it, that
it is the Height of Imprudence, to call it by no worse a Name, to attack it in
the Manner her Grace does in the above Passages. But the Matter does not
rest here; for we find that what her Grace insinuates, or rather asserts here,
is directly in contradiction to that solemn Inscription which her Grace
consign'd to Marble, sign'd by herself, as the Character of Queen *Anne*,
upon the Pedestal of the Statue erected to her Memory at *Blenheim*.[36] We
therefore see instead of shewing her Impatience to get Possession of her
Father's Crown, she look'd with the greatest Indifference upon that of

---

[34] John Churchill (1650–1722), first Duke of Marlborough, British hero of the War of the Spanish
Succession (1702–13). In his writings from the Dedication to *The Universal Gallant* (1735) to the
Introduction to the *Journal of a Voyage to Lisbon* (1755), HF, whose father had served gallantly under
Marlborough at Blenheim, was adulatory. In *A Proper Answer* (1747) he paid tribute to 'the
unparalell'd [*sic*] Successes of our Arms, under the Conduct of the Great, the Protestant, the Whig Duke
of *Marlborough*' (*JJ*, p. 65). In the present passage HF bitterly remembers the ingratitude and treachery of
Robert Harley (above, p. 210 n. 13) and the Tory ministry, who in 1710–11 disgraced the Duke by
charging him with peculation and dismissing him from his offices. In discussing the ministerial 'Art
of Lying, and Misrepresentation' in *The Jacobite's Journal*, No. 15 (12 March 1748), HF recalls this
outrageous insult to his hero: '"Twas by such Arts as these that the brave *Marlborough* . . . fell a Victim to
the Intrigues of *Harley* and [*Bolingbroke*]' (p. 190).

[35] Just before the paragraphs HF proceeds to quote from *Remarks* (pp. 20–1), the author criticizes the
Duchess for revealing too many 'important Truths' prejudicial to Queen Mary: she ought 'to have discov-
er'd no more than were barely necessary for the profess'd Design of her Undertaking: I mean the
Vindication of [her] own Conduct. This, I say, would have been decent, because the private Character of
Queen *Mary* has never yet been attack'd' etc.

[36] In 1734 the Duchess, for £300, commissioned John Michael Rysbrach to sculpt a statue of
Queen Anne; it was erected in the Great Gallery at Blenheim in 1738. (David Green, *Sarah Duchess of
Marlborough* [New York, 1976], p. 270.) The Duchess composed a 'Character' of Anne of some 450 words,
which was inscribed on the pedestal. The author of *Remarks*, presumably supplying his own typographical
features, paraphrases the first two sentences: 'Queen Anne had a person very graceful and majestic; she
was religious without affectation, and always meant well. Though she believed that King James had
followed such Counsells as endangered the religion and laws of her country, it was a great affliction to her
to be forced to act against him even for Security' (Frank Chancellor, *Sarah Churchill* [London, 1932],
p. 269, transcribing Sarah's holograph). In 1746, after the Duchess's death, the family replaced
the inscription with another: 'To | The Memory | of | *QUEEN ANNE* | Under Whose Auspices | *JOHN
DUKE* of MARLBOROUGH | Conquered | And to Whose Munificence | He and His Posterity | with
Gratitude | Owe the Possession | of | *BLENHEIM* | *A D MDCCXXXXVI*'. In her *Account* the
Duchess does not mention the statue. SWB

her Brother-in-Law, tho' he wore it in prejudice of her own Right. What are her Words?

'QUEEN *ANNE*—WAS RELIGIOUS WITHOUT AFFECTATION; SHE ALWAYS MEANT WELL; SHE HAD NO FALSE AMBITION; WHICH APPEARED BY HER NEVER COMPLAINING AT KING *WILLIAM*'s BEING PREFERRED TO THE CROWN BEFORE HER, WHEN IT WAS TAKEN FROM THE KING HER FATHER, FOR FOLLOWING SUCH COUNSELS AND PURSUING SUCH MEASURES AS MADE THE REVOLUTION NECESSARY. IT WAS HER GREATEST AFFLIC-TION TO BE FORCED TO ACT AGAINST HIM, EVEN FOR SECURITY.

'If any impartial Person should compare these Lines with the above Quotations from the Account of her Conduct, would he not draw one of these two Conclusions; either *that the Character is not drawn for the same Person*, or *that it was not the same Person who drew it?*'

The Character her Grace hath been pleased to inscribe on her Monu-ment, erected to the Memory of Queen *Anne*, is an Instance of the Good-ness and Gratitude of her Temper; and tho' perhaps these have inclined her to carry Truth as far as possible, yet there is nothing on this Marble inconsistent with what her Grace hath since committed to Paper: She hath not taxed her with Ambition, she hath not denied that it was her greatest Affliction to be forced to act against her Father; and so far from questioning her Religion, she hath imputed many of her Actions to a Fondness for even the Shadow of it, *the Church*.[37]

Your Lordship is facetious about Parsons and old Women;[38] nor can I think you much in earnest, when you represent the Revolution to be no instance of the People's electing a King. If my Lords of *Clarendon* and *Rochester*[39] advised the Princess to give up her Right of Blood in order to

---

[37] With HF's figure of '*the Church*' as 'the Shadow' of religion, cf. the Duchess's remarks on Anne's devotion to 'that phantom which she called *the church*: That *darling phantom* which the tories were for ever presenting to her imagination, and employing as a *will in the whisp*, to bewilder her mind, and entice her, (as she at last unhappily experienced) to the destruction of her quiet and her glory' (*Account*, p. 270).

[38] *Remarks* (p. 21), referring to Princess Anne's seeking advice from 'my Lady *Russel* of Southampton-*House* and Dr. *Tillotson* [Archbishop]': 'I cannot but think that the Expedient which her Grace fell upon to reconcile the Conduct of the Princess *Anne*, upon the Settlement of the Crown, to Decency and Safety, was a little extraordinary in one who had liv'd all her Life upon such Terms with *Parsons, and old Women*, as her Grace has ever done' (p. 21; emphasis added).

[39] The brothers Henry Hyde, second Earl of Clarendon (see above, p. 210 n. 15), the elder, and Laurence Hyde (1642–1711), first Earl of Rochester, were Anne's uncles. The author of *Remarks* (p. 22) represents them as advising Anne not to press her right to succeed Mary to the throne, thus retiring William from the scene, because William's supporters in Parliament were strong enough to give him the throne outright, with reversion then to Mary, then to Anne, on his death. This, they argued, would establish Parliament's power to elect kings, whereas giving William the crown through 'the *Matrimonial Right* which King *William* had by Queen *Mary*' would preserve the right of succession.

defend it, they were, I think, no great Logicians. I am sure they were no great Lawyers, if they imagined preferring King *William* to a joint Estate in the Crown, and afterwards to the Reversion of the whole before Queen *Anne*, was not an instance of their using the Right of Election. As such it was understood by all who wrote on the Subject on both sides; and if a Precedent could establish a Right, I think that Right of Election could never hereafter be called in question.

Whether my Lord *Marlborough's* Disgrace in King *William's* time[40] was owing to his being Husband to Lady *Marlborough*, as you say, I know not: but certain I am, that the Merits of her illustrious Husband should have protected the Dutchess from any Disgrace in Queen *Anne's* time, and should have endeared her to the whole Nation. If the Wives and Widows of great Men have been esteemed in all Countries: If I have seen in a very public Assembly a Respect paid to the Wife of a Man who lately took an undefended Town in the *West-Indies*;[41] what Honours should be paid to the Consort of that Glorious Man, who carried the Honour of our Arms so high, and by such a Series of Courage, Conduct and Success, preserved the Liberties of *Europe*?

As your Lordship is pleased to bring in Bishop *Burnet*, confirming almost every thing which her Grace hath said relating to the Quarrel between the two Sisters, I will likewise repeat his Words once more to you:[42]

'The Princess of *Denmark*,' says that Prelate, 'thought herself too much neglected by the King, whose cold way towards her was soon observed. After the King was on the Throne no Propositions were made to her of a Settlement, nor any Advances of Money. So she thinking she was to be kept in a necessitous Dependance on the Court, got some to move in the House

---

[40] On 4 May 1692 Queen Mary, suspecting that Marlborough had informed the Jacobites of William's plan to attack Dunkirk, ordered him arrested on suspicion of high treason and committed to the Tower. Though released on 15 June, he was still suspected of opposing William and was excluded from office as Privy Councillor. He remained out of favour until after the death of Mary in December 1694. (John Hattendorf, *Oxford DNB*, s.v. Churchill, John). See also below, pp. 223–4.

[41] Probably a reference to Sarah, the wife of Admiral Edward Vernon (1684–1757), hero of British action against Spain in the West Indies. With six ships only he captured Porto Bello, Panama, in two days (20–1 November 1739) and in May 1740, levelling the sole fort defending the port, he again took just two days to take Chagres, Panama. In England he was lionized as a national hero. Vernon was also an outspoken critic of Walpole's conduct of the war. For HF in *The Champion* (10 May, 3 and 24 June 1740) he was 'that Hero *Vernon*', 'the immortal *Vernon*', 'the brave Admiral *Vernon*' (pp. 317, 356, 386); and, though Vernon figures not at all in the poem, he is the eponymous hero of *The Vernoniad* (January 1741). Despite the defeat of the British forces at Cartagena, Columbia (April 1741), Vernon at home remained 'a symbol of liberty and patriotism' (Richard Harding, *Oxford DNB*, s.v. Vernon, Edward), and in the election of December 1741 he was chosen MP for Ipswich, Suffolk. The 'very public Assembly' at which HF saw 'Respect paid' to Vernon's wife may have been a gathering of partisan voters at the recent election. Vernon subscribed to HF's *Miscellanies* (1743), a copy on royal paper (iii, p. 347, no. 395).

[42] HF repeats the quotation in *Remarks* (pp. 23–4) from Burnet's *History* (1724–34), ii, pp. 90–1.

of Commons in the Year 1698;[43] when they were in the Debate concerning the Revenue, that she should have Assignments suitable to her Dignity. This both King and Queen took amiss from her.———[44] The Act pass'd allowing her a Settlement of Fifty Thousand Pounds. But upon this a Coldness follow'd between not only the King, but even the Queen and Princess. And the blame of this Motion was cast upon the Countess of *Marlborough*, as most in favour with the Princess: And this had contributed much to alienate the King from her husband, and had disposed him to receive ill Impressions of him.'

It is impossible to give a stronger Confirmation of the Truth of her Grace's Account.

Let us survey the next Paragraph, which hath any thing material in it. In Page 25[45] is the following:

'As to the different Character of the two Sisters, I believe your Lordship, upon reflecting a little upon the Nature of the Fair Sex in general, will agree with me, that no such Disagreement could ever have happen'd from the Causes assigned by her Grace.* *It was impossible*, says her Grace, *that they should ever be very agreeable Companions together, because Queen* Mary *grew weary of any body who would not talk a great deal, and the Princess was so silent that she rarely spoke more than was necessary to answer a Question.* I believe the World will allow, that Bishop *Burnet* was at least as good a Judge of Queen *Mary*'s private Character, as ever her Grace was, who, as would appear, had scarcely any opportunity of knowing it. But he gives her a Character, that with regard to her Quality, if I am not quite out of my Judgment as to Woman-kind, is quite the reverse of that given by her Grace. For the Prelate says, *that Queen* Mary *lov'd to talk a great deal:*[47] Now I may venture to appeal to all the Experience of that Sex, if there was ever found a Woman *who lov'd to talk a great deal herself*, and yet at the same time *grew weary of every body who did not talk a great deal too.* Admitting Bishop *Burnet*'s Character of Queen *Mary* in this respect to be the true one, because he knew her best; and likewise the Character which her Grace gives

---

* *Account*, p. 24.[46]

---

[43] HF repeats the error in *Remarks*: Burnet gives the date as 1690.

[44] HF, following *Remarks*, omits sixteen lines detailing the disagreement between Mary and Anne.

[45] i.e. *Remarks*, pp. 25–6.

[46] *Account*, pp. 24–5.

[47] Burnet nowhere says this, either in his *History*, which *Remarks* appears to quote, or in his *Essay on the Memory of the Late Queen* (1696). In his Conclusion to the *History* he contrasts the two sisters and comes closest to what *Remarks* prints as a quotation: 'Queen *Mary* was Affable, Cheerful and Lively, spoke much, and yet under great Reserves . . . Queen *Anne* is easy of Access, and hears every thing very gently; but opens herself to so few, and is so Cold and General in her Answers, that People soon find that the chief Application is to be made to her Ministers and Favourites' (ii, p. 661).

of the Princess of *Denmark* to be a true one too, *viz.** *That the Princess was so silent that she rarely spoke more than was necessary to answer a Question:* I say, admitting these two Characters to be true in both respects, we have the very best reason in the World for wondering why a perpetual Harmony did not subsist betwixt the two Sisters; since no Person in the World can be so agreeable to *a Woman who loves to talk a great deal,* as another *who loves to talk very little.'*

Sure your Lordship hath too much insight into the Fair Sex, and into human Nature in general, to be in earnest. Indeed, it is true, that talkative Women, and talkative Men too, are sometimes fond of one who will be *Auditor tantum*;[48] but this listning must be with the greatest Attention, must be accompanied with frequent assenting Nods, Smiles, and Words too, and is what no one ever finds but amongst Inferiors and Dependents, and not in an Equal of a solemn and sullen Disposition, and of a different way of thinking; who would be very absent in Attention, and would not fail of betraying in Looks and Gestures sufficient Marks of Dislike, and perhaps Contempt; which silent People generally have for those of a loquacious Temper. Besides, doth not common Experience teach us, that Gossips always affect one another's Company? Nor is there the least inconvenience, since a dozen Women can talk all together, without the least Interruption or Disturbance one to another.

As to Queen *Mary*'s Behaviour, as the Dutchess relates it, on her first coming to *White-Hall*, I apprehend any Spectator of Humanity would have formed the same Conclusions with her Grace from it.[49] If it proceeded from the Prince's Orders, as Bishop *Burnet* tells us,[50] it doth indeed in some

---

* Account, p. 25.

[48] Juvenal, *Satires*, i. 1: *Semper ego auditor tantum? numquamne reponam?* ('What? Am I to be a listener only all my days? Am I never to get my word in?'; Loeb).

[49] The author of *Remarks* (pp. 26–7) charges the Duchess with an ill-natured bias against Queen Mary, quoting the following passage from *Account* (pp. 25–6): 'And here I cannot forbear saying, that whatever good qualities queen MARY had to make her popular, it is too evident by many instances *that she wanted bowels* [i.e. compassion]'. 'Of this she seemed to me to give an unquestionable proof the first day she came to Whitehall. I was one of those who had the honour to wait on her to her own apartment. She ran about it, looking into every closet and conveniency, and turning up the quilts upon the bed, as people do when they come into an inn, and with no other sort of concern in her appearance, but such as they express; a behaviour, which, though at the time I was extremely caressed by her, I thought very strange and unbecoming. For, whatever necessity there was of deposing king JAMES, he was still her father, who had been so lately driven from that chamber, and that bed; and, if she felt no tenderness, I thought she should at least have looked grave, or even pensively sad, at so melancholy a reverse of his fortune.'

[50] In pressing his defence of Queen Mary against the Duchess, the author of *Remarks* (p. 27), though omitting the part in which Burnet confesses he, too, thought Mary's behaviour inappropriate, quotes the following passage from the *History*: discussing the events of 1689, Burnet writes that, on hearing that a rumour had been spread that Mary was unhappy about her father's deposition and the settlement of the crown on her husband, 'The Prince wrote to her, that it was necessary she should appear at first so

measure justify the Queen; but lays no imputation on the Dutchess, who knew not of those Orders.

In Page 28, you proceed as follows: '* Her Grace next relates upon hearsay, an angry Conversation that pass'd between the two Royal Sisters, upon the Subject of the Princess's Settlement, which went so well in the House of Commons, that their Friends being *encouraged to propose a much larger Revenue, the King, in order to prevent it, prorogu'd the Parliament.* But her Grace, tho' she takes care to let us know that the whole of this Affair lay upon herself, leaves us entirely in doubt by what means it happen'd, that the Intention of augmenting the Settlement was defeated. All we can learn is, that the King thought proper to compound the matter with the Princess's Friends; at the same time we don't learn by her Grace's Account that the Princess had any other Friend but herself; nay, it would appear from the† Applications made to her by my Lady *Fitzharding*,[52] and my Lord *Shrewsbury*,[53] the two Persons of the greatest Credit at Court, that she was consider'd as the Manager of the whole on the side of the Princess. I shall therefore offer an Insinuation which I have heard made to the Disadvantage of her Grace by the Tories, who certainly were at that time strong enough in Parliament to have carried a large Settlement for the Princess, and were heartily inclined to have done it, had they not been deceiv'd by a secret Collusion betwixt the Courts and those in whom the Princess put her chief confidence.'

This, your Lordship justly indeed calls an Insinuation, you might have added a cruel one; for you found it only on the common Report of the

---

* Account, p. 27.[51]
† Account, p. 29.

---

cheerful, that no body might be discouraged by her looks, or be led to believe that she was uneasy by reason of what had been done. This made her put on a great air of gaiety when she came to *Whitehall*, and, as may be imagined, had great crouds of all sorts coming to wait on her. I confess, I was one of those that censured this in my thoughts. I thought a little more seriousness had done as well, when she came into her father's Palace, and was to be set on his Throne next day' (i, p. 825).

[51] HF repeats *Remarks'* (p. 28 n.) erroneous citation: the quotation is an abridgement of *Account*, pp. 29–31, 33–4.

[52] Lady Fitzharding (d. 1708), wife of Colonel John Berkeley, Lord Viscount Fitzharding of Beerhaven. She was 'greatly beloved' by Queen Anne, who settled £1,000 a year on her for services as governess to Anne's son, the Duke of Gloucester. Together with the Duchess of Marlborough she accompanied Princess Anne on her midnight flight from London during the Revolution. (Narcissus Luttrel, *A Brief Historical Relation of State Affairs from September 1678 to April 1714*, 6 vols. [Oxford, 1857], ii, p. 57; vi, p. 353.)

[53] Charles Talbot (1660–1718), Duke of Shrewsbury and twelfth Earl of Shrewsbury. A Catholic convert to the Church of England, he was one of the seven signatories of the letter (30 June 1688) inviting Prince William to England. A privy councillor to King William, Talbot was his Secretary of State for the Southern Department. He was one of the peers who escorted James out of England. (Stuart Handley, *Oxford DNB*, s.v. Talbot, Charles.)

Tories, who, on your own Principles, are not to be received as very credible Witnesses against her Grace; but as the Affirmative is not supported by any Proof or Pretence of Proof whatever, so I will venture to say the Negative may be demonstrated by all the Evidence of Reason and Common Sense. For, can we suppose, if her Grace could be prevailed on to betray the Interest of the Princess to the King and Queen, that they would have desired her (as the Bishop, the World, and your Lordship agree they did) to part with a Servant who was so effectually their Spy and Tool? Or if she had afterwards disobliged them, might not this have been used as the certain means of destroying her with her Mistress? I omit the handsome Reflection cast on a Brother and Sister, who would be base enough to corrupt the Sister's Servant to betray her Interest. But can any thing equal your Lordship's Saying, that her Grace hath left us intirely in doubt by what means the Defeat happened, when she plainly and expressly tells us, it happen'd from the King's purposely proroguing the Parliament.

The Reason given by the Dutchess why the Prince of *Denmark* preferred the Sea to the Land Service, is a good and substantial one, and not to be overthrown by your Lordship's asserting, 'You cannot conceive why his Highness should have a Passion for going to Sea, merely because the King could not suffer him to go in a Coach with him in *Ireland*.'[54] A Neglect to which, I believe, few Princes so nearly affianced would submit.[55]

You will pardon me, my Lord, if I censure your Remark in the next Paragraph, as deficient in that Candour[56] which becomes a generous Adversary, especially a Writer who pretends to no more than an Enquiry after Truth, or a Refutation of Falshood. You say, 'You shall make no other Remark upon the Letter which her Grace has given us from Queen *Mary* to her Sister, than that it is plain, that the Queen thought that my Lord *M*————[57] had given his Majesty more Cause of Displeasure than what appears to the World, and that she had informed the Princess of it before. This appears from the following Passage: *I need not repeat, says the Queen, the Cause he has given the King to do what he has done, nor*

---

[54] *Remarks*, p. 29.
[55] The Duchess writes: 'The next difference that happened between the sisters, was upon the PRINCE's design of going to sea. He was carried to this resolution by his unwillingness to stay at home, while there was so much action abroad; and by the remembrance of the extreme ill usage he had met with, when, at a great expence, he attended his MAJESTY into Ireland. For the KING would not suffer his ROYAL HIGHNESS to go in the coach with him: An affront never put upon a person of that rank before. . . . You will allow, I believe, that it was very natural for the PRINCE to chuse a sea-expedition, rather than expose himself again to the like contemptuous usage' (*Account*, p. 38).
[56] 'Candour': fairness, impartiality (*OED*, s.v. 3).
[57] Marlborough.

his Unwillingness at all times to come to such Extremities, tho' People do deserve it.[58]

Now, my Lord, the Sense you here put upon the Word *repeat*, is what it will not in common Usage bear; for I will appeal to your Lordship's Reflection, and to the whole World, whether this Word in all epistolary Correspondence is not used to mean the inserting something in a Letter which hath happened, tho' not related by the Person who writes to the Correspondent. For Instance: *I will not repeat to you what happened at such a Place, or what was said by such a Person*, &c. And this in Writers of much greater Accuracy than Queens can generally be supposed. Queen *Mary* therefore means here by the Word *repeat*, no more than if she had writ, *I need not tell you:* for indeed if the Queen had communicated this before, I see no reason why she should even mention it again, unless with a Desire of insulting her Sister; a Censure I am unwilling to cast upon her.

I come now to the most notable Paragraph of all; to introduce which, indeed all the rest seems chiefly written; and yet pompous as this is, it is no more than the Repetition of an old thread-bare Falshood, invented by the *Jacobites*, and long since disbelieved and laughed out of the World. Let us see the whole Paragraph:[59]

'But, in justice to the Memory of this Princess, I cannot avoid acquainting your Lordship with a Fact which I had from a Person of the greatest Consideration in that and the succeeding Reign; who told me, upon my seeming surprized at the Motives that could induce King *William* to treat my Lord *M*————[60] with the Severity he did; that it was wholly owing to the Indiscretion of a Lady, whom I am unwilling to name, but whom your Lordship and the World will easily guess at.[61] He said, that a *French* Engineer, who had received some Disgust from his Officers, had come over at that time from *France*, and had laid before King *William* a Plan by which *Dunkirk* might be surpriz'd. That the Plan was examin'd and approv'd of by King *William*, who admitted nobody into the Secret but *Benthink*,[62]

---

[58] *Remarks*, p. 29. The italicized passage, except for variants in the accidentals, is from *Account*, p. 43.

[59] *Remarks*, pp. 29–31.

[60] In 1692 Marlborough was committed to the Tower on suspicion of treason (see above, p. 218 n. 40).

[61] The Duchess of Marlborough.

[62] Hans Willem Bentinck (1649–1709), first Earl of Portland, diplomat and politician. Of a noble Dutch family, he and William of Orange came of age together as close friends at The Hague. He was instrumental in negotiating William's marriage to Mary Stuart in 1677, and he was responsible for organizing the land and sea forces when William successfully invaded England in 1688, precipitating James's flight to France. It was Bentinck who convinced William that he and his wife should become joint sovereigns. Parliament, in April 1689, subsequently decreed that Bentinck and his children become naturalized citizens; he was created Earl of Portland, Viscount Woodstock, and Baron Cirencester. William's closest adviser and secretary, he held, among other honours, the offices of Privy Councillor and Keeper of the Privy Purse. (Hugh Dunthorne and David Onnekink, *Oxford DNB*, s.v. Bentinck, Hans Willem.)

Zulestein,[63] and my Lord *M*————————; but that before the Execution of
the Design such Orders came from the *French* Court, and such a Number of
Forces were pour'd into *Dunkirk*, as plainly shew'd that the Design was
discover'd. He said, that King *William* immediately suspected my Lord
M————————, but was unwilling to discover his Suspicions till he could
have Proofs, which he soon had by means of a Spy from the Court of
St. Germains, who was seiz'd here, and confess'd that he was employ'd as
an Agent betwixt my Lady *Tyrconnel*[64] and King *James's* Queen.[65] And
that this Person, upon hopes not only of Pardon but Reward, directed the
Government to a Packet from *France*, which discover'd that my Lady
Tyrconnel, by means of a certain Lady who gave her all her Confidence, and
to whom my Lord *M*———————— was so weak as to discover the Design.
That the King upon this sent for Lord *M*————————, and reproach'd him
with his Easiness; upon which the latter confess'd the whole. This Incident
accounts pretty well for the Insinuation which is dropp'd by Queen *Mary* in
this Letter, and it was no wonder afterwards if the King was a little too
susceptible of a Prejudice against the Earl when he was committed to the
Tower.'

Here is an Insinuation of the blackest and most heinous kind, against a
Person of the highest Dignity, thrown out without an Author, or any sort
of Proof whatever. Her Grace's high Station and Character surely require,
that the Name or Title of this Person of Consideration should be mention'd
at least, and even then we may doubt whether it came from him, or whether
he spoke truth if it did: Tho', by the way, admitting all true that is here

---

[63] Willem Frederic Nassau van Zuylestein (1649–1708), first Earl of Rochford, soldier and diplomat.
His mother was Mary (*née* Killigrew, b. 1627), maid of honour to Mary Stuart, Princess Royal of England
and Princess of Orange. Like Bentinck a close companion of William, he was instrumental in raising
support in England for the invasion, in which he sailed with William in the Dutch flagship. Like Bentinck
he was naturalized in 1689 a month after the coronation; and like Bentinck he took part in William's Irish
campaign and the victory at the Boyne (1690). In 1695 he was created Baron Enfield, Viscount Tunbridge,
and Earl of Rochford. (Hugh Dunthorne, *Oxford DNB*, s.v)

[64] Frances (*née* Jenyns) Talbot (1648–1731), Jacobite Duchess of Tyrconnell, and elder sister of the
Duchess of Marlborough. In her first marriage (1666), to George Hamilton (d. 1676), an Irish Roman
Catholic officer in the French army who was created a count by Louis XIV, she converted to Catholicism.
In 1681 in Paris she married Richard Talbot (1630–91), also a Roman Catholic and army officer. Talbot
moved to Dublin in 1684, and was created Earl of Tyrconnell by James II, who appointed him Lord
Deputy of Ireland and in 1689 Duke of Tyrconnell, Frances having witnessed, on 10 June 1688, the birth
at St James's Palace of the Prince of Wales, the future Pretender to the throne. She fled to France in 1690,
and was indicted in Ireland for high treason, but the charge was not proved and she was allowed to return
to England and Ireland in 1702, in the meantime living in France as a Lady of the Bedchamber to Mary of
Modena (below, n. 65) and supported by a pension from James II.

[65] Mary of Modena, Italy (1658–1718), who in 1673 married James, Duke of York, and on his accession
to the throne in 1685 became Queen of England, Scotland, and Ireland. On 10 June 1688 at St James's
Palace she gave birth to James Francis Edward, Prince of Wales and, on his father's death in 1701,
Pretender to the throne. Lady Tyrconnell (above, n. 64), sister to the Duchess of Marlborough, witnessed
the birth of Mary's son and lived with her in exile.

asserted, the Dutchess may nevertheless be innocent: Here were three more Persons, to wit, *Benthink, Zulestein,* and the Engineer himself in this Secret; and why none of them as capable of discovering it as the Earl of *Marlborough?* But can we believe, that if this had been the Reason of the King's prejudice against the Earl, as is asserted, that he would have concealed this Reason? or if the Discovery could have been brought home to the Dutchess; that the King and Queen, who (as is confest on all hands) were her Enemies, would have kept this Treachery in her a Secret? or that her other Enemies (of which I believe then as well as since, Envy and Malice had created her many) would not have promulgated, with the utmost diligence, a Story which would not only have justified their Resentment, but would have render'd it indecent even for the Princess to retain her longer in her Service. These things, I say, would almost inevitably follow the Belief of this pretended Fact; which, had it been true, it is impossible to conceive, should in so short a time be obliged to submit only on a Report which a nameless Author had from a nameless Person; a kind of Evidence which would not be admitted to blacken the Character of the lowest of Creatures, but which is admirably calculated to spread what *Cicero* calls *Contumelia*;[66] it is a Bow to shoot those Arrows of Detraction from, which (according to an excellent Writer of our Church)[67] are always flying about in the Dark, and against which no Power but of that God who sees and knows all things, can defend the greatest and best Characters.

You are pleased, my Lord, to say you will make no Remarks on the Difference 'that happen'd betwixt the Queen and the Princess, on account of the latter being obstinate in keeping my Lady C————[68] about her Person: Her Grace (you say) has prevented me in this,* by vindicating her Conduct, with regard to the important Points, that of the Succession, and that of the Pension, and that of the Prince's going to Sea'[69] You are right in

---

* Account, p. 49.

[66] Cicero, 'Pro Publius Sylla': *nullam contumeliam jacere potueris* ('you can throw no contumely' at him that would not also fit most of the citizenry; *Oratio*, xxv).

[67] Robert South (see above, p. 213 and n. 25) in a sermon preached on Isaiah 5: 20, '*The Fatal Imposture, and Force of* WORDS'. HF conflates two of his favourite passages: 'I say Detraction, that killing, poysoned *Arrow* drawn out of the Devil's *Quiver*, which is always flying abroad, and doing Execution in the *Dark*; against which no Virtue is a Defence, no Innocence a Security' and 'it is a Weapon forg'd in Hell, and formed by the prime Artificer, and Engineer of all Mischief, the *Devil*; and none but that God, who knows all Things, and can do all Things, can protect the best of Men against it' (*Twelve Sermons*, ii, pp. 353, 356–7). HF had quoted this same combination of passages in *The Champion* (6 March 1739/40), p. 222; and he would do so again in 'An Essay on the Knowledge of the Characters of Men' (*Miscellanies* i, p. 170, and *The Jacobite's Journal*, No. 28 (11 June 1748), p. 308.

[68] Lady Churchill, the Duchess of Marlborough.

[69] HF quotes *Remarks*, p. 31, which accurately cites *Account*, p. 49.

avoiding any such Remarks; the Account her Grace hath given is satisfactory to every impartial Reader, and is and will be unimpeached by the
Malice of Party and Prejudice.

Your Lordship says, 'But with regard to the two Letters given us from the
Princess of *Orange* to her Grace, I think nothing more can be said, but that
there was a time when the Princess of *Orange* thought very well of my Lady
C————, and a time when Queen *Mary* thought very ill of her. A Case
that happens every Day in private Life.'[70] Yes, my Lord, something more
may be said; and it is, *That there was a time when the Princess was Princess
of* Orange; *and a time when she was* Queen *Mary*: and then what follows will
be truly a Case that happens every day.

Your Lordship's next Fling,[71] agreeable to the Malice of the Party, is at
the Duke.

'Her Grace, in apologizing for her own and her Husband's Conduct, says,
that, "every one knows that my Lord *Marlborough* had great Employments
under King *James*, and might have hoped to be as great a Favourite as any
body.——It was highly improbable therefore that he who had done so
much, and sacrificed so much for the Preservation of the Religion and
Liberty of his Country, shou'd on a sudden engage in a Conspiracy to
destroy them." But this is, according to what her Grace herself seems to
own, but a poor Compliment to the Integrity and Disinterestedness of the
Earl of *M*————; for it seems to be not only the Opinion of her Grace,
but of the World, that the Designs of King *James* were so weakly laid, and
so foolishly carried on, that for a Man to have embark'd in them, was to
involve himself into unavoidable Ruin.'

The Colours which your Lordship throws on my Lord of *Marlborough's*
Conduct, in leaving King *James*, and adhering to the Prince of *Orange*,
are what may be, and generally are applied to every great Action, which
those who are strangers to the Motives of true Greatness[72] and Virtue,
always impute to mean, private, and mercenary Designs. It is easy to see into
Consequences, when they have happened; but I believe many then alive
apprehended more Danger in the Success of those weak Measures that your

[70] *Remarks*, p. 31, referring to letters from Mary to Sarah (the future Duchess), expressing her affection
for both Anne and Sarah (*Account*, pp. 50–2).

[71] The following paragraph is quoted verbatim from *Remarks*, pp. 32–3, which abridges a passage from
Account, pp. 61–2—the author changing 'considerable employments' to 'great Employments' and omitting, as signalled by the dash after 'any body', the following words: 'could he have assisted in bringing
about that unhappy PRINCE's scheme of fixing popery and arbitrary power in England', which of course
Marlborough refused to do.

[72] Another of the many compliments HF paid in his writings to the Duchess's 'glorious Husband'
(above, p. 216 n. 34). In his poem *Of True Greatness* (January 1741), lines 99–110, Marlborough serves to
define that ideal—'the *true Sublime* in Human Nature', as HF called it in the Preface to the *Miscellanies* (i,
pp. 12, 23).

Lordship seems to think they threatened: Nay, even at last, it hath been made a Doubt by many, if King *James* had not deserted the Crown, whether it would have been taken from him: and if he had retained it, let the Restraints under which he had been laid been what they will, the Duke of *Marlborough* cou'd have expected no Forgiveness, nor Restoration to his Favour.

You are pleased to say you will make no other Remark on those warm friendly Letters from the Princess of *Denmark* to her Grace, than what your Lordship hath made on those of Queen *Mary*; to which therefore I shall give the same Answer: You then ask a Question; 'But is there any thing wonderful, any thing unaccountable, any thing criminal in one's altering their Opinion of Woman-kind! Or are Princes oblig'd to give the World an Account of the Motives that induce them to do it?'[73] Perhaps, indeed, there is nothing *wonderful* in the Alteration of one's Opinion of another; but surely the Dismission of an old faithful Servant, after a long continued Execution of the greatest Trust with Integrity, conceiving a sudden Dislike after the highest Friendship and Familiarity with an Inferiour for many Years, removing and displacing such a Servant from her Office and Trust without any visible Reason, or condescending, even when ardently desired, to assign any; sure such Conduct is not so perfectly *accountable*, if clear from being *criminal*, as you would imagine. And *if Princes are not obliged to give the World an Account of the Motives* that induce them to such extraordinary Actions, surely the lowest Subjects, much more the highest, are at liberty to justify themselves if the malicious part of the World lays the Blame on their Misconduct.

I am desirous with the utmost caution to avoid Reflections on any Person's Character. I shall therefore take no more Notice of what you say concerning my Lord *Rochester*,[74] than to observe, that if he had the Queen wholly in his Hands at the time of the Order being sent by Lord *Nott———m*[75] to the simple Mayor of B*ath*, the Dutchess in imputing it to Lord *Rochester*,[76] deals no harder with his Lordship, than hath been ever done with all Favourites and Ministers, who must be contented to bear the Blame and Burthen or whatever is done, not only by their Sovereigns

---

[73] *Remarks*, p. 33.

[74] On Rochester, Queen Mary's uncle and adviser, see above, p. 217 n. 39.

[75] On Nottingham, see above, p. 212 and n. 22.

[76] The Duchess prints a letter from Nottingham, Secretary of State, to the Mayor of Bath, a tallow chandler, reprimanding him for according Anne 'the same respect and ceremony, as have been usually pay'd to the ROYAL FAMILY', and instructing him, as commanded by the Queen, not to do so again 'without leave from HER MAJESTY' (*Account*, pp. 97–8). The Duchess concluded that Rochester had advised the Queen in this petty matter. See HF's following quotation from *Account* (p. 98), which the author of *Remarks* (p. 36) had also quoted.

themselves, but by all their Inferiours in Office. Nor is it likely that any one without Orders from the Queen, or from him who govern'd the Queen, would have dared to attempt such a Measure with such a Person; nor indeed doth it appear that Lord *Nottingham* himself had any Motive for so doing: to which I shall beg leave to add the Dutchess's own Words:

'*The King being abroad when this Letter was writ, and the Queen being at that Time wholly in my Lord* Rochester'*s hands, every Body concluded, that it was done by his Advice: And I am myself the more fully persuaded of it, for the Fondness he discovered for such sort of Pageantry, when (in the Beginning of Queen* Anne'*s Reign) he made his Progress in those Parts, and took Pains in begging Treats, and Speeches from such Sort of People. But it must be own'd, that his Lordship had a singular Taste for trifling Ceremonies.*'[77]

The Character which her Grace gives the Earl of *Godolphin*,[78] your Lordship says requires Notice, and I readily agree with you it does: for it is an extraordinary and a true one. The Passage you quote is as follows:[79]

'The Princess, after this, continued at *Berkley-House*,[80] in a very quiet Way; for there was nothing more to be done, unless they would stop her Revenue, which doubtless they would have attempted, had they thought it practicable; but my Lord *Godolphin* was then first Commissioner of the Treasury, a Man esteemed very useful to the Service, and who they knew would quit upon any Orders; and they could not easily have found a Person with Qualities fit for that Employment.'

You are pleased to say: 'It is very surprizing that one who knows the World so well as her Grace does, should write in this Manner. Upon the Terms in which she represents the Princess of *Denmark* to have stood with King *William* and Queen *Mary*, can it be imagined that had these two Princes inclined to have stopt the Revenue of the Princess, they would have been frighten'd from the Attempt, merely because they conceived that one of their *own Servants* would oppose it? Is this agreeable to that positive determined Conduct for which King *William* was always remarkable.'[81]

---

[77] *Account*, p. 98.

[78] Sidney Godolphin (1645–1712), later (1706) first Earl of Godolphin. He was a skilful manager of the nation's finances; among the many offices he held over a period of thirty years were First Lord of the Treasury (1684–5, 1690–6, 1700–1). After the accession of Anne, he and the Duke of Marlborough—to HF they were 'the brave *Marlborough*, and the just *Godolphin*' (*Jacobite's Journal*, No. 15 [12 March 1748], p. 190)—later joined by Robert Harley (above, p. 210 n. 13), ran the government, with Godolphin as Lord Treasurer and Prime Minister until Harley succeeded in driving him from office in 1710.

[79] HF quotes a paragraph from *Remarks* (p. 37), which—omitting in line 9 the 'such' before 'Orders', however—the author had quoted from *Account* (p. 102).

[80] Berkeley House, a grand mansion with a spacious garden built on the north side of Piccadilly in 1665 for the first Lord Berkeley, a royalist commander in the Civil War. In 1692–5 Princess Anne lived there, having quarrelled with her sister Mary (*LE*, s.v.).

[81] *Remarks*, p. 37.

To be apprehensive of an Opposition from a great, able, and honest Minister, may stagger a Prince of King William's Understanding, and may well deter him from a Step of so extraordinary a Nature.

As to the Account of the Queen's Behaviour related by Bishop *Burnet*, and that given us by her Grace, I cannot observe any such Disagreement or Contradiction, as your Lordship mentions.[82] Indeed, that of the Dutchess is fuller and more particular, as she had undoubtedly more Opportunity of knowing the whole. The Bishop says, 'That the Queen when she was dying had received a kind Letter from, and had sent a reconciling Message to the Princess; and so that Breach was made up. It is true, the Sisters did not meet; it was thought, that might *throw the Queen into too great a Commotion*; so it was put off till it was too late.'[83]

Her Grace gives us the following Relation: 'As I knew', says she, 'that several People, and even one of the Princess's own Family, were allowed to see the Queen, I was fully persuaded, that the deferring the Princess's Coming, was only to leave room for continuing the Quarrel, in case the Queen should chance to recover, or for Reconciliation with the King, (if that should be thought convenient) in case of the Queen's death. During all the time of the Queen's Illness, to her Decease, the Princess sent every Day to enquire how she did; and once I am sure her Majesty heard of it, because my Lady *Fitzharding*,[84] who was charg'd with her Message, and who had more desire than ordinary to see the Queen, broke in whether they would or not, and delivered it to her, endeavouring to express in how much Concern the Princess was; to which the Queen returned no other Answer but a cold Thanks: Nor, though she received the Sacrament in her Illness, did she ever sent the least Message to the Princess, except that in my Lady *Derby's* Letter,[85] which perhaps her Majesty knew nothing of.'[86]

---

[82] The author of *Remarks* (pp. 38–9), after quoting the passages from Burnet and the Duchess's *Account* that follow, concludes with a sneer: 'This Account is so very contradictory to what we have seen from the Right Reverend Prelate, that there needs no Suggestion of the Causes from whence it proceeds' (p. 39).

[83] Burnet, *History*, ii, p. 149.

[84] See above, p. 221 n. 52.

[85] Elizabeth (*née* Butler) Derby (1660–1717), wife of William George Richard Stanley (1655–1702), ninth Earl of Derby. A close friend of Queen Mary, who appointed her Groomess of the Stole, she was buried in Westminster Abbey (John H. Rains III, *Oxford DNB*, s.v. Stanley, William George Richard). When Mary was fatally stricken with smallpox, Anne, who was herself confined at Berkeley House believing she was pregnant, wrote asking permission to visit her sister: she would '*run any hazard for that satisfaction*'. Lady Derby, who received and delivered the message to Mary, wrote Anne's messenger in reply: 'I am commanded by the KING and QUEEN to tell you, they desire you would let the PRINCESS know they both thank her for sending and desiring to come: But, it being thought so necessary to keep the QUEEN as quiet as possible, hope she will defer it' (*Account*, pp. 104–6).

[86] HF quotes *Remarks* (pp. 38–9), which quotes *Account*, pp. 106–7.

What Incongruity? The Bishop is a Confirmation of all the Dutchess says, and both agree in the material Points, That the Queen sent but one Message, and that she died without seeing her Sister.

I come now to a most wonderful Discovery indeed, no less, than *that Lord* Marlborough *and his Lady were the two staunchest Tories in the Kingdom.*[87]

The Proofs of this are;

1. That at Queen *Anne*'s coming to the Crown, notwithstanding the Favour in which the Dutchess then stood, she put herself (as the Dutchess complains) entirely into the Hands of the Tories. This is represented as a Contradiction, *viz.* that a Prince[88] should act contrary to the Opinion of her Favourite.

2. The Disfavour this Lord and Lady were in at Court, during all the time that King *William* employed the Whigs. Tho' this Disfavour hath been accounted for, so many other ways already.

3. The Earls of *Marlborough* and *Godolphin* were continued in their Posts, and caress'd and followed by the Tories.[89]

4. Were believed to be such by the Queen.

5. Were educated in those Principles.

It may indeed be probable, that the Tories, at the Beginning of the Queen's Reign, perceiving that her Love for the Church had not yet wormed my Lady *Marlborough* out of her Affections, and that it would be difficult to displace the two Earls in whom she placed so deserved a Confidence, might content themselves to unite with Persons who had no Violence of Party, nor were extremely zealous, unless in what they imagined to be the true Interest of their Country. This I say, is probable: for we have seen Whigs and Tories of later days, unite and agree in Place very well together. Nay farther, it is probable that the Earls, to engage the Favour of the Queen and to serve her effectually, as they afterwards DID, IN THE HIGHEST DEGREE, might, by their conversation and Intimacy with some Men, give the Tories, who are *good-natured Politicians*, Reasons to imagine they were better Tories in their Hearts, than they afterwards found them: But if they were really so, whence the Whig Ministry, under which those glorious Victories, the Defence and Preservation of *Europe's*

---

[87] *Remarks* (p. 41): 'it was the general Opinion at the Accession of Queen *Anne* to the Crown, that both my Lord M————— and his Lady were the staunchest Tories in the Kingdom.' Points 1 and 2 refer to *Remarks*, p. 41.

[88] 'Prince' used in reference to a female sovereign (here Queen Anne) was common usage in the sixteenth and seventeenth centuries, but was obsolete by the eighteenth; the latest example cited in the *OED* (s.v. 1b) is dated 1650.

[89] Points 3, 4, and 5 refer to *Remarks*, p. 42.

Liberties, were obtained? whence the Cry of the *Church in Danger?*[90] whence
that Opposition to those Earls, which ended in their being turned out, after
all their faithful and eminent Services? A black Spot in the History of that
Reign, which your Lordship will never be able to whiten.

Your Lordship is pleased to say, *that the Pains her Grace is at in vindicating
her Conduct from the Imputation of private View, is very studied:*[91] I do not
know what you would be understood to mean by *studied*: if you would say,
her Grace hath taken the Trouble to write several Sheets, containing an
Account of Matters of Fact, attested by the strongest and most undeniable
Evidence, (Letters and public Accounts of the Nature of Records,) to convince the World that she was a faithful, honest, upright and thrifty Servant
to her Mistress, both before and after she was Queen; I shall agree with you,
and so will the World. But I cannot so readily own, *that Truth and Sincerity
will always speak for themselves, and require no other Advocates but their own
good Effects.*[92] Daily Experience must convince the blindest of us of the Blots
which Malice, Envy and Ingratitude can throw on the whitest Name. Nay, I
wish that the very Paper now under my Consideration, did not afford Marks
of this kind; your Lordship will pardon me if the Sneers in the following
Paragraph savour to me of one of those Principles. I will quote the whole.

'In *p.* 136, we find a most exalted Sketch of her Grace's Character, both as
a Christian and a Politician. She could have forgiven even the Earl of *Rochester*, if she had *thought that he would have followed the Queen's true Interest*;
and she was a Whig, only because the *Principles of the Tories appeared
Gibberish*, and *those of the Whigs rational*, and no ways to the Prejudice of
the Church as by Law established.[93] Having thus discussed her Religious

---

[90] 'The Church in Danger' was a cry raised by High Churchmen, such as Henry Sacheverell and
Francis Atterbury, against the Whig government, which supported latitudinarianism within the Church of
England and toleration of Nonconformists and Dissenters. In 1709–10 the popular furore over the
impeachment of Sacheverell, who had denounced the liberal Whigs from the pulpit, accusing them of
undermining the Church and Constitution, resulted in the Tories under Harley, with Queen Anne's
blessing, turning out HF's idols, Godolphin and Marlborough. For HF's scornful references to this Tory
slogan, 'that ever-memorable Cant Phrase' (*A Dialogue between a Gentleman of London and an Alderman of
the Country Party* [1747], pp. 16–17), see from this period *The Champion* (1 January 1739/40, 29 March
and 13 September 1740), p. 101 n. 1, pp. 257, 463) and *Joseph Andrews* (1742; II. viii), where Parson Adams
advises his nephew to vote against the Court candidate in the election, 'for it was at a Season when the
Church was in Danger' (p. 133 and n. 1).

[91] *Remarks*, p. 44.   [92] Ibid.

[93] This paragraph is from *Remarks* (pp. 44–5), partly paraphrasing and partly quoting *Account* (p. 136),
where the Duchess writes: 'And I do assure you most sincerely, that I could so entirely have forgotten all
his lordship's [Rochester's] ill treatment of me, as to have acted in concert and friendship with him, if I
had thought he would have followed the QUEEN's true interest. But the gibberish of that party about non-
resistance and passive-obedience and hereditary right, I could not think to forebode any good to my
mistress, whose title rested upon a different foundation. On the other hand, the principles professed by
those called whigs seemed to me rational, entirely tending to the preservation of the liberties of the
subject, and no way to the prejudice of the church as by law established.'

and Political Character, we have in the same Page a Specimen of her Natural one; that so not one of all the Circle of amiable Qualities may be wanting in her Composition. "As this," says her Grace, "was really my Way of thinking concerning the two Parties, it would have been contrary to the Frankness of my Temper, and to the Obligation of that Friendship with which the Queen honoured me, not to have told her my Sentiments without Reserve." '[94]

These Sneers are not, I think, agreeable either to the Sex or the Dignity of the Person who is the Subject of them.

I am as unwilling as your Lordship to detract from Sir *George Rook's* Character.[95] He was a brave Man, and his Victory a signal one; but that *the taking* Gilbralta *doth as much credit to Queen* Anne*'s Reign, as any Action that happened in it*, I can no more concede that I can that his present M—— of P————[96] is as great a Soldier as *Charles* XII. of *Sweden*.[97] That we have indeed little to show for all those glorious Victories, which will render the Duke of *Marlborough's* Name equal to that of the greatest Commanders of Antiquity, besides the torn Colours in *Westminster-Hall*,[98] I am sorry to allow; but I believe no one will impute this to his Grace.

---

[94] *Remarks'* concluding quotation from *Account* (pp. 136–7) is accurate except that the singular form 'Obligation' is plural in the original ('obligations').

[95] Sir George Rooke (*c.* 1650–1709), Admiral. In the War of the Spanish Succession, Rooke, commanding a fleet of sixty-three English and Dutch ships with a large force of English and Dutch marines and several hundred Catalans from Barcelona, took Gibraltar on 24 July 1704 after an action lasting three days; the citizens, who had been allied to the Bourbon Philip V, were then obliged to recognize Charles III of Spain as their legitimate king. In August near Cape Malaga, in battle with a French fleet of equal strength but freshly supplied with ammunition, Rooke lost none of his ships, but nearly 3,000 officers and men were killed or wounded. The French retreated to Toulon, but, without sufficient supplies to pursue them, Rooke returned to Gibraltar. The 'victory', known as the Battle of Vélez-Malaga, occurred on the same day as Marlborough's victory at Blenheim. Rooke's biographer observes: 'This coincidence aroused the passions of party politics . . . and the tories declared Rooke to be the equal of Marlborough, while the duke's political friends were incensed to find Rooke raised to Marlborough's stature.' Though he was the pre-eminent seaman of the period, 'political efforts to turn Rooke into a popular hero failed miserably' (John B. Hattendorf, *Oxford DNB*, s.v. Rooke, George).

[96] Presumably the 'present M[ajesty] or M[onarch] of P[oland]', Augustus III (1696–1763), Elector of Saxony and King of Poland since 1733; an indolent and incompetent monarch, he was the very antithesis of the mighty warrior Charles XII of Sweden, to whom HF contrasts him (see below, n. 97). In 1706 Charles, invading Poland, forced Augustus's father, Augustus II 'the Strong' (1670–1733), to abdicate, though he regained the crown in 1709 when Charles was defeated at Poltava by Peter I's army.

[97] Charles XII (1682–1718), King of Sweden. In 1740 HF had published his translation of Gustaf Adlerfelt's *Military History of Charles XII, King of Sweden*, a work of 3 volumes. Charles was for HF, as for Pope, the modern counterpart of 'Macedonia's madman' Alexander the Great (*Essay on Man* [1733–4; iv, p. 220]). In *A Journey from This World to the Next* (1743; I. iv) the shades of these two ruthless conquerors flank the Emperor's throne in the Palace of Death, where they serve as foils to the magnanimity of HF's hero the Duke of Marlborough (*Miscellanies* ii, p. 23).

[98] As an anonymous correspondent to *The Craftsman*, No. 627 (15 July 1738), HF tells of touring Westminster Hall: 'I never omit shewing *this Place*; not only as it is the most spacious Room in the World, but likewise the Repository for the glorious Trophies of our *late English Hero* [Marlborough]. I am a very

What your Lordship says of Mr. *Harley*[99] shall not be controverted by me. I shall only observe, that what her Grace says both of him[100] and others, will require more Ink, more Eloquence, more Art and more Proofs too, to set aside than your Lordship hath been pleased to employ at present.

I shall now proceed to take notice of those general Slanders which, tho' your Lordship hath been pleased to disperse through the whole Letter, I shall endeavour to collect together. Page 8. Was not the Character of Her Grace's Mildness and Disinterestedness so well established, it would be natural to think that there must have been some secret Mismanagement; some Instances of flagrant Insolence and Rapaciousness, that could effect this wonderful Change.[101] Page 9. The Lye oblique is given.[102] Page 12. She

---

good *Ciceroni*, and have learnt to what Regiments many of the *Colours* and *Standards* belong'd, and by what *Corps* taken' (*New Essays*, p. 339). In *The Coffee-House Politician* (1730; IV. iii) Ramble remarks on the 'ragged . . . Colours' of 'our brave Soldiers' hanging in Westminster Hall (*Plays*, p. 474). HF blamed the Tories, and particularly Harley, for negotiating the disadvantageous Treaty of Utrecht (1713), which put an end to Marlborough's victorious campaigns against the French (see above, p. 210 n. 13).

[99] The author of *Remarks*, who 'knew him well', praises Harley, 'this great Man': 'His Character has been the Subject of great Censure and Panegyrick . . . He was a Man naturally a Philosopher, which led him, as a Politician, to very extended Notions of Government; at the Bottom he despised all the little Arts which his Enemies charged him with, and which they themselves practised. In his Notion, he embraced the safest and wisest Maxims, both of the Whigs and Tories; and tho' possessed of very great Power and Trust, died without making a Groat of his Places' (p. 49). For Harley and HF's different opinion of him, see above, p. 210 n. 13.

[100] Alleging that Harley and Lady Masham had driven her from court, and that Harley had convinced Queen Anne he should replace Godolphin as Prime Minister, the Duchess offers the following 'just character' of him drawn 'by a friend of mine, many years ago': 'He was a cunning and a dark man, of too small abilities to do much good, but of all the qualities requisite to do mischief, and to bring on the ruin and destruction of a nation. This mischievous darkness of his Soul was written in his countenance, and plainly legible in a very odd look, disagreeable to every body at first sight, which being joined with a constant, aukward motion or rather agitation of his head and body, betrayed a turbulent dishonesty within, even in the midst of all those familiar airs, jocular bowing and smiling, which he always affected, to cover what could not be covered. He had long accustomed himself so much to dissemble his real intentions, and to use the ambiguous and obscure way of speaking, that he could hardly ever be understood when he designed it, or be believed, when he never so much desired it. His natural temper led him to so expensive and profuse a way of living, that he had brought himself into great necessities, though he had long enjoyed the advantages of very great and profitable posts. One principal and very expensive piece of his art, in which he seems to have excelled all that went before him, was, to have in pay a great number of spies of all sorts, to let him into what was passing in all considerable families. It was remarkable, that when he came most into favour with the QUEEN, he was perhaps the only man, in whose ruin the two contending parties would have united, as one in whom there was no foundation to repose any confidence' (*Account*, pp. 261–2).

[101] Though without quotation marks, HF quotes the author's words. The 'wonderful Change' is Anne's coldness towards the Duchess, her friend from childhood.

[102] Presumably referring to the author's insinuation that in representing events and characters the Duchess's 'Aversion' to the Tories 'has a little influenced her Judgment, I won't say Veracity'. From time to time in this litany of the author's 'general Slanders' HF echoes Touchstone the clown in *As You Like It* (V. iv. 81 ff.): 'and so to the Lie Circumstantial and the Lie Direct'. Cf. *The Champion* (29 January 1739/40): 'Such Lies as these should, if possible, be avoided. But this regards only the Lie Scandalous, if you come to the Lie Panagyrical [*sic*] you need set no Bounds' (p. 146).

is accus'd of downright Affection.[103] Page 15. The Lye oblique.[104] Page 19.
She is upbraided with the little Capacity which Age and Infirmities have left
her for Enjoyments.[105] Page 29, her Grace's Doubt and Backwardness about
receiving a Pension of a thousand a Year, is so very agreeable to her known
Aversion to Money, that your Lordship can make no doubt of the Fact.[106]
Page 33. The Lye semidirect.[107] Page 34. A fresh Instance of her Grace's
known Disinterestedness and Generosity. *Ibid.* Her Grace's exaggerated
Account of her own Merits.[108] Page 37. Her forgiving Temper ironically.[109]
Page 39. Charged with treating King *William* with Indecency. Page 46.
Charged with Spite. Page 48. With Ingratitude. *Ibid.* With Cant. *Ibid.*
With Insolence. Page 49. She is represented as a Tyrant *Passim*, charged
with Ill-nature and governing her Husband.[110]

Will any Man say, my Lord, that this is a proper manner of treating a
Woman of her Grace's exalted Station and Character, one of her Age, who
hath lived upon such an intimate footing with her Sovereign, and who is the
Widow of so great a Man, one to whom this Nation in particular, and all
Europe in general, are so much obliged?

Many, indeed most of these Slanders are such as do no injury, but to the
Person who vents them. I shall only remark one, in Page 8, her Grace is
obliquely charged with Rapaciousness; as in another place, with inordinate
Love of Money.[111]

---

[103] 'downright Affection': the author's own phrase.

[104] The author referring to the Duchess's saying that she thought William, when he came to England,
had no ambition for the crown: 'it is extreamly improbable that her Grace, notwithstanding all her
Professions of Sincerity, was ignorant of the Design upon this Occasion'.

[105] 'the little Capacity . . . Enjoyments': the author's words.

[106] Quoting the author's own sarcasm.

[107] Referring to the author's mocking acceptance of the Duchess's caution that what she relates of
Queen Mary's callous behaviour to her sister will be hard to believe.

[108] [In *Remarks* page 34 is misprinted 43.] Both HF's references to p. 34 are verbatim quotations of the
author, whose sarcasm implying the Duchess's miserly nature was decidedly unjust. During her widow-
hood Sarah's gifts to charities totalled well over £250,000. She was generous to the poor on her numerous
estates, to struggling writers, and others in need. She built and amply endowed thirty-six almshouses at
St Albans and others at Woodstock. She sent £1,000 to help Swiss peasants emigrate to America. She
rescued an officer of Child's Bank, under pressure from the Bank of England, with a direct draft of
£100,000 (Chancellor, *Sarah Churchill*, pp. 232–3). HF, who extols the Duchess's open-handed liberality
(below, p. 236), appears to have been himself neglected by her (see the Introduction, above, p. 200 and
n. 18). SWB

[109] 'Her forgiving Temper': this further example of the author's sarcasm is misplaced. Though the
Duchess was not renowned for having a forgiving temper, in the passage referred to in *Remarks* (i.e.
Account, p. 104), she is illustrating not her own, but Princess Anne's, forgiveness of Mary's messengers,
who ignored her when her only son, the 11-year-old Duke of Gloucester, was dying.

[110] The author makes these and other charges against the Duchess as cited. 'Indecency' (*Remarks*, p. 39)
is HFs translation of the author's irony in praising the Duchess's 'decent manner' of recounting King
William's rude behaviour towards Anne.

[111] HF appears to forget that he included these particular insults above among the 'general slanders':
under 'Page 8' and 'Page 29'.

That her Grace is rich, is most undoubtedly certain. It is impossible to be otherwise; Extravagance itself, without other Vices, could not have prevented it. The many great and lucrative Employments, with which both her Grace and the late Duke were so long invested, and the vast Settlement on the Family by Act of Parliament,[112] sufficiently account for it.

But that her Grace discharged her Trust with Fidelity, and that she saved the Queen vast Sums of Money, which she might have visibly sunk into her own Pocket; that she never submitted to any mean or dishonest Arts of enriching herself, are Facts not asserted only, but proved, in the Account she hath been pleased to give of her own Conduct.

Nor do I remember to have ever heard her accused of any public Rapaciousness or private Exaction.

She is indeed rich, and if her Enemies accuse her of that, I believe she must plead guilty, at least I have nothing to say in her Vindication.

But, perhaps it may be some Alleviation even of this, that this Wealth was got in the greatest and most eminent Service of her Country; and if the Tears of Widows and Orphans attended it, they were the Widows and Orphans of those who were in open Arms against this Kingdom.

2ndly, That the Influence and Power, which her Grace from her great Fortune enjoys, hath been constantly exerted in Defence of the Liberties of her Country against the highest, most powerful, and most insolent Invaders of it. Had the Weight of the Dutchess of *Marlborough* been lately thrown into the Scale of Corruption, the Nation must have sunk under it: But, on the contrary, her whole Power hath been employed in Defence of our Liberties, and to this Power we in a very great measure owe their Protection; and this, the barbarous and inhuman Exultations of the Corruptor[113] and his

---

[112] After the victory at Blenheim (13 August 1704), Parliament unanimously requested the Queen to 'consider a proper means of perpetuating the memory of the great services performed by the Duke of Marlborough'. On 17 February 1705 the Queen reported that she would give Marlborough and his heirs the Royal Manor and Park of Woodstock, 15,000 acres valued at £6,000 per annum, and proposed to build there at her own expense a palace to be named Blenheim. Anne assigned crown monies directly from the Exchequer to Marlborough to build as he chose. By June 1710 Sir John Vanbrugh, Marlborough's architect, had spent £134,000. Parliament baulked. In June 1714, after numerous suspensions, Vanbrugh told Marlborough that the total costs, with all bills paid, would be £287,000. Marlborough settled some of the bills at major reductions and left in his will £50,000, with which Sarah, after his death in 1722, completed the building and grounds. See David Green, *Blenheim Palace* (London, 1951), pp. 37–44, 137; and Winston Churchill, *Marlborough: His Life and Times*, 6 vols. (New York, 1933–8), iv, pp. 169–70; vi, pp. 317, 608, 640, 651. SWB

[113] 'The Corruptor', of course, is Walpole, whom the Duchess despised. In the recent election the resources of her great fortune had ensured the success of the Opposition's campaign to put an end to his twenty-year tenure as Prime Minister. Here, HF's denunciation of Walpole and ministerial corruption might well have seemed awkward to those who knew that four months earlier Walpole had employed him to write *The Opposition: A Vision*, in which HF's former friends and patrons are ridiculed as self-serving hypocrites, the Minister is represented as a true patriot who blocks their way to power, and the corruption HF now deplores is dismissed as a necessary fact of political life. For an account of HF's changing politics, see the Postscript to the introduction.

chief Friends last Winter exprest on her Grace's dangerous Illness, and their eager Expectation of her Death, which they declared would do their Business, sufficiently testify.[114] So that this Nation may be truely said to have been twice saved within 40 Years by the glorious Conduct of this Illustrious Pair; and whoever considers this in a just light, must acknowledge, that no Name ought to be so dear to the People of *England*, as that of the Dutchess of *Marlborough*.

Lastly, To this Fortune many private Persons and Families, who have been relieved by her Grace's Generosity, owe their Preservation. Nor do I believe any Person in her time hath equalled her Donations of this kind: So your Lordship hath, I think, chosen a very improper Subject for so much Calumny, which, unless we could suppose this Nation to deserve a Character of the blackest Ingratitude, must be very distasteful to us all, when thrown on ONE, to whom so many in particular, and the whole People in general, are so greatly obliged.

But, before I quit this Glorious Woman, whose Character I have never contemplated but with Admiration, I shall just mention a Reflection interspersed through this mighty Performance, and which is agreeable to what hath been always reported by the lowest and most ignorant of her Grace's Enemies; I mean, the representing her as a Woman of great Pride and Haughtiness. That her Grace is superiour to all Meanness, that she knows her own great Consequence, that her vast Abilities are no more hid from herself, than from those who have the Honour of her Conversation, I agree readily. That these have produced an Elevation of Mind which can with Scorn look down on the pitiful Arts of her Adversaries, is as true. But, I suppose, your Lordship meant not this. Do you not rather mean, that Greatness of Mind with which the Dutchess hath asserted her Dignity to those who would falsely flatter themselves with the Imagination of being her Superiours, or as vainly pretend to be her Equals. I can truly affirm no such Pride hath been ever shewn to those who have acknowledged themselves to be her Inferiours, to whom none can equal her in Affability and Condescension.

I shall now take leave of your Lordship for this time, and I hope for ever; but if you should think proper to keep your Word (which I hardly think you will) in laying open those Particulars in the latter Part of Queen *Anne's* Reign, which you say are of a different nature from the Facts represented by

---

[114] As the December election drew near, the Duchess fell seriously ill, and Walpole's supporters apparently took heart. On 7 December 1741 Mary Godolphin, daughter of the Earl, wrote a certain Mrs Owen that Walpole's party had 'eager Expectations of her Death' (Frances Harris, *A Passion for Government: The Life of Sarah, Duchess of Marlborough* [Oxford, 1991], p. 332). This letter, and HF's remarks here, seem to be the only reports of such 'Exultations' in the ministerial camp.

her Grace, you may depend on a second Letter, tho' perhaps differing somewhat in gentleness with this,[115] from

> *Your Lordship's*
> *most Obedient Humble Servant.*

---

[115] Concluding his *Remarks* (pp. 49–50), the author promises that, if his critique meets the approval of the young lord to whom it is addressed, 'I shall, in a second Letter, take the Liberty to pursue those Remarks, and lay open some Particulars in the latter Part of Queen *Ann*'s Reign, of a very different Nature from those represented by her Grace.'

3

ARISTOPHANES' *PLUTUS,*

THE GOD OF RICHES (1742)

IN May 1742—two months after his first novel *Joseph Andrews* and a month after the pamphlet *A Full Vindication of the Dutchess Dowager of Marlborough*—*Plutus, the God of Riches*, a comedy translated from the Greek of Aristophanes by Fielding and William Young, was published by the obscure bookseller Thomas Waller. For some time Fielding had been trying to make a living with his pen, as journalist, as translator from French, as poet of an epistle on Greatness and a mock-epic, *The Vernoniad*, meant to please patrons in the Opposition, and as author of an allegory in prose satirizing those same patrons. Not so long before these hard times, Fielding had been producing plays at the Haymarket Theatre and, in the biting manner of Aristophanes, writing satires against the Walpole administration that the Town applauded. Indeed, as Robert Hume remarks in the authoritative study of Fielding's theatrical career, he had established himself as 'the most dominant professional playwright in London since Dryden': 'in the spring of 1737 any theatrical insider would have assumed that Fielding would soon control a major company of his own, and that he would go on to write a long string of hits'.[1]

But what the Town applauded, the Walpole administration did not find amusing. The Licensing Act of June 1737 put an end to Fielding's lucrative career in the theatre. He turned then to the law, his mother's family's profession, but, though in time he would earn fame as a magistrate and social publicist, for the present he lived in the shadow of debtor's prison.

CIRCUMSTANCES OF COMPOSITION:
FIELDING AND WILLIAM YOUNG

Owing to the scholarship of Frederick Ribble,[2] we can now fully appreciate for the first time the significant role played in Fielding's life and works by

---

[1] Robert D. Hume, *Henry Fielding and the London Theatre 1728–1737* (Oxford, 1988), p. ix.
[2] See Frederick G. Ribble, 'Fielding and William Young', *SP*, 98 (2001), pp. 457–501.

his neighbour the learned Dorset parson William Young (1689–1757). Young was not only the original of Fielding's most memorable character, the Revd Abraham Adams of *Joseph Andrews*; he also figured prominently in the conception and execution of the translation of *Plutus*.

The friendship between Fielding and Young, whom classicists at the time considered one of the most proficient contemporary scholars of Hebrew and Greek, was cemented during the decade of the 1730s, when Young, a native of nearby Gillingham, Dorset, served as curate of East Stour, where the Fieldings had their farm. (In the churchyard a few steps from their house, Young in June 1733 buried Fielding's grandmother Lady Sarah Gould.[3]) Fielding may well have given us a glimpse of the intimacy between Young and himself, of their love of scholarship and conviviality, in the Postscript to *The Craftsman*, No. 600 (7 January 1738), when the author is interrupted by 'an *honest, jovial Country Parson*' who drops in 'to quaff a Bottle' with him, and to solve an exegetical problem in the *Aeneid* by producing 'a mouldy Edition of *Virgil*'.[4]

In October 1740 Fielding, whose active association with *The Champion* was nearing an end, had finished his translation of Gustaf Adlerfelt's voluminous *Histoire militaire de Charles XII, Roi de Suède* and may have begun forming plans for a new magazine, to be called *The History of Our Own Times* (see below, Appendix A) after the title of his favourite work by his favourite English historian, Gilbert Burnet. We now know from Young's letter to James Harris of 3 October that Fielding was 'pressing [him] to hasten to London'.[5] Young soon left Dorset for the metropolis, and by January of the new year he was, for the four issues the magazine lasted, writing the reviews section ('The History of the Learned World') for Fielding.[6] In the spring of 1741 Young was assisting William Guthrie in a new translation of the *Orations of Cicero*; and in the final issue of the magazine (5 March) he took the opportunity to discredit Conyers Middleton's command of Latin in his *History of the Life of Marcus Tullius Cicero*: 'there is not a single Page of these Translations in which the plain obvious grammatical Meaning of *Tully* is not mistaken' (p. 116).[7] At the

[3] *Life*, pp. 168, 643 n. 268.
[4] *New Essays*, p. 277. Cf. the *Vernoniad* (1741), where Coley suggests that in HF's note [51] Young may be the 'facetious Friend of mine' who has offered an amusing 'Reading' of the Greek (*Champion*, p. 576 n. 3).
[5] Ribble, 'Fielding and William Young', p. 467.
[6] Thomas Lockwood, Introduction to *The History of Our Own Times (1741)* (New York, 1985), p. 15; and Ribble, 'Fielding and William Young', pp. 468–71.
[7] Cf. *Joseph Andrews* (III. vi), where Fielding, perhaps recalling Young's review, invokes the Muse of Biography: 'Thou who hadst no Hand in . . . the Translations which thou wouldst willingly have struck out of the Life of *Cicero*' (p. 239).

same time Young was assisting the bookseller Richard Manby by travelling
to Oxford to translate the manuscript, in Greek, of a certain scholiast's
interlined commentary on the tragedies of Sophocles, whom Young's
surrogate, Parson Adams in *Joseph Andrews* (III. ii), regards as 'the greatest
Genius who ever wrote Tragedy' (p. 199).[8]

FIELDING'S KNOWLEDGE OF GREEK

How important was the role Young played in the *Plutus* project? The answer
must surely be 'very'. Fielding was of course well educated by the rigorous
philological standards of the time, when to be called 'illiterate' meant
one was ignorant of the classical languages: he had been well birched at
Eton and he had studied literature, in a desultory way, at the University
of Leiden. But he was nevertheless aware that his command of Greek
was limited. In the first of his playful poems to Walpole (1730), he
facetiously declared his qualifications for the post of Foreign Secretary:
'*Tuscan* and *French* are in my Head; | *Latin* I write, and *Greek* I—read.'[9]
And when preparing his translation of Demosthenes' *First Olynthiac* for the
Miscellanies, he depended on James Harris to correct it: 'I am infinitely
obliged to yᵒ', Fielding wrote his friend, 'for yᵉ Trouble yᵒ have given yrself
on my incorrect and lame Translation.'[10]

Such evidence would appear to validate the view of scholars since
Cross—who 'safely assigned' the translation of *Plutus* to Young 'except for
some rephrasing here and there'.[11] Fielding's knowledge of Greek has been
thought inadequate to the task of translation.[12] But if Harris saw fit to
correct Fielding's translation of Demosthenes, Fielding himself felt
sufficiently competent in the language to undertake the project in the
first place. Henry Knight Miller conceded, with Cross, that it was 'likely'
Fielding's role in the *Plutus* translation was 'to give a literary gloss to his
scholarly partner's translation'. Yet, recalling Fielding's later description
of the role he would play in the projected translation of Lucian, Miller came
to a fairer judgement of the matter: 'Fielding, though deferring to Young's
greater mastery of the language, seemed to claim an equal role in the duties

---

[8] Ribble, 'Fielding and William Young', pp. 472–3.

[9] *Miscellanies* i, p. 58.

[10] *Correspondence*, Letter 16 (14 March 1743), pp. 29–30.

[11] Cross, i, pp. 364–5.

[12] See, for instance, Nancy A. Mace, *Henry Fielding's Novels and the Classical Tradition* (Newark, Del., 1996), p. 56; however, earlier in her study Mace cautions the reader: 'Because we have no way of knowing absolutely how they divided their responsibilities, the play offers little indication of Fielding's skill in Greek' (p. 45).

of the translation.'[13] In *The Covent-Garden Journal*, No. 52 (30 June 1752), Fielding assured prospective readers of the Lucian project that while Young was an acknowledged authority in Greek, he himself brought to the partnership a virtue that complemented his friend's mastery of philology: 'As to the Abilities of one of the Gentlemen who propose this Translation I shall be silent; I will only venture to say, that no Man seems so likely to translate an Author well, as he who hath formed his Stile upon that very Author' (pp. 288–9). Miller's observation on the passage makes the essential point: 'Even if this is an advertising "puff," the implication surely is that Fielding was well read in his great exemplar's original tongue.' After considering the question carefully, Dr Ribble, citing Miller, concurs: 'With *Plutus*, Fielding's function, even in rendering the Greek, must have been that of an informed colleague through whom Young's ideas were filtered and clarified.'[14]

GENESIS OF THE *PLUTUS* PROJECT

Dr Ribble's research in the Malmesbury papers also sheds light on Young's part in the genesis of the *Plutus* project. Thomas Waller, publisher of the translation, was also the publisher of Guthrie's translation *The Orations of Cicero*, to which Young contributed, and by June 1741 Young's address in London was 'Mr. Waller's Shop in the Temple'.[15] Young was so closely involved with Waller that, as Ribble suggests, it may well have been he, rather than Fielding, who initiated the project. The hypothesis certainly helps to explain Fielding's otherwise curious decision to abandon Millar as his publisher in this instance. In another letter to Harris of 6 April (1742), Young discloses the motive behind the translation:

Mr Fielding & I are employed by a Bookseller, Mr Waller, to translate Aristophanes—We have made some progress in the Plutus; as soon as we have finished that play, & 600 are Sold, we shall proceed to the rest.[16]

As for the question why, of Aristophanes' eleven comedies, Fielding and Young chose the *Plutus* as the most likely lure to attract the requisite 600 buyers, Charles A. Knight offers an answer:

---

[13] Henry Knight Miller, *Essays on Fielding's Miscellanies: A Commentary on Volume One* (Princeton, 1961), p. 343. Ribble, citing Miller, concurs: 'With *Plutus*, Fielding's function, even in rendering the Greek, must have been that of an informed colleague through whom Young's ideas were filtered and clarified' ('Fielding and William Young', p. 483).

[14] Ribble, 'Fielding and William Young', p. 483.

[15] Young's letter to Harris of 16 June 1741 (Ribble, 'Fielding and William Young', p. 469 n. 45, p. 499).

[16] Ribble, 'Fielding and William Young', p. 481.

In the eighteenth century it was the Greek comedy one would have been most likely to read in school, for its Greek is comparatively easy, it depends little on specific historical references, and it is relatively unobjectionable for the minds of susceptible youth. As the only extant example of Middle Comedy, it drops the *parabasis*, reduces the role of the Chorus, and is closer in form to the traditional 'five-act' structure of New Comedy and most Roman comedy. Hence it is no surprise that this, the most accessible of his plays, should be chosen to initiate a projected translation of Aristophanes.[17]

It is surprising, however, to find that Fielding so early in April had found time enough to work on the translation, as well as the *Full Vindication* of the Duchess of Marlborough, which was published on 2 April, not to mention the musical farce *Miss Lucy in Town*, which was staged at Drury Lane and published early in May. On 13 April, Young witnessed Fielding's signature on the formal assignment to Andrew Millar of the copyright of these two pieces and *Joseph Andrews*, which Fielding would revise in some detail for the second edition, published in June. For the novel, farce, and pamphlet Millar paid him the generous sum of £199 6s.,[18] most of which he owed his creditors.[19]

PUBLICATION AND RECEPTION

The translation of *Plutus* and the larger project it was meant to herald were first announced in *The Champion* (4 May):

> *In the Press, and speedily will be publish'd,*
> PLUTUS the God of Riches. . . .
> Translated. . . . With large Notes, Explanatory, Historical, and Critical.
> *By* HENRY FIELDING, *Esq; and the Reverend*
> *Mr.* YOUNG. . . .

This Play is publish'd as a Specimen of an intended Translation of all the Comedies, (being Eleven in Number) of *Aristophanes*, by the same Gentlemen who intend to proceed in the Work according to the Reception this Play meets with from the Public.

N.B. The Notes will contain, besides a full Explanation of the Author, a complete History of the Manners and Customs of the Alcient [*sic*] Greeks, particularly of the *Athenians*.

---

[17] Knight, 'Fielding and Aristophanes', *Studies in English Literature*, 21 (1981), p. 483.
[18] For a transcript of the document, see the General Introduction to *Joseph Andrews*, ed. Battestin (Oxford, 1966), pp. xxx–xxxi.
[19] On HF's dismal circumstances during this period, see *Life*, pp. 340–3.

On Saturday 29 May *The Champion* and the *Daily Post* both announced publication for Monday the 31st:[20] *'(With large Notes, Explanatory, Historical and Critical)* | PLUTUS, the God of Riches a Comedy. | Translated into English from the Original Greek of | ARISTOPHANES. | *By* HENRY FIELDING, *Esq; and* | *The Rev. Mr.* YOUNG. | Printed for T. Waller in the Temple Cloysters'. The advertisement concludes by repeating the information given in the preliminary announcement of 4 May.

The public's reception of the trial balloon that Fielding and Young hoped would launch a lofty and lucrative translation of the comedies of Aristophanes was decisively disappointing—except, that is, for a gratifying essay in *The Champion* for 29 June. Writing from 'Otter's Pool' three weeks after publication and signing himself 'Morpheus', the author was William Robinson, an attorney of the Inner Temple, Fielding's friend and a frequent contributor to the journal he once edited.[21] Robinson was delighted with the translation; indeed, he found it so irresistibly amusing he was unable to control his laughter: 'having been a Truant in my *Greek*, since I left School, [I] pull'd out of my Pocket the *new* Translation of *Plutus the God of Riches*, from *Aristophanes*, by *Fielding* and *Young*, which I read over for my Evening's Amusement'.

The Drollery [Robinson continues], the exquisites [*sic*] Strokes of Humour, Satire, and Ridicule, with the admirable Vein of Wit and Pleasantry, that run through that inimitable Piece, made me several Times burst out into a loud Laugh, tho' alone, insomuch that the People of the House, if they were not well accustomed to my way in such Cases, would certainly take me to be mad, at least for the Time, and indeed . . . I am so strongly agitated on such facetious Occasions that they might guess worse.

This experience induces a nightmare in which Plutus, having regained his sight, bestows riches on everyone according to his just deserts. Walpole and his brother, the double-dealing Patriots, self-serving kings, generals, lawyers, princes of the Church—none escapes Plutus' judgement, with one exception: 'in the midst of these Disasters, I was not a little comforted to see

---

[20] No notice of publication appeared, however, in any paper on Monday the 31st. The *Daily Post* for Tuesday and Wednesday (1–2 June) carried advertisements for *Plutus* headed '*This Day is publish'd*'. Advertisements for the work later appeared in *The Craftsman* (Saturday 5 June) and the *London Evening-Post* (10 June, 22 July, and 10 August).

[21] On Robinson, and his contributions to HF's *Champion*—six of which were published during HF's association with the journal—see Frederick G. Ribble, 'William Robinson, Contributor to Fielding's *Champion*', *Studies in Bibliography*, 43 (1990), pp. 182–9. (The article is available online: <http://www.etext.lib.virginia.edu/bsuva/sb>). Robinson was a subscriber to HF's *Miscellanies* (iii, p. 341).

my reverend and worthy Friend Mr. *Abraham Adams* translated from his Living of *twenty three Pounds per. Ann.* to the See of——'.[22]

William Young, whom Robinson recognized as the original of Fielding's Parson Adams, was not translated to a bishopric as a reward for his part in *Plutus*, though he is said to have reluctantly accepted a share of the five guineas of 'Aristophanic gold' that Fielding's Dedication elicited from Lord Talbot.[23] Indeed, as Dr Ribble observes, Young was not only Fielding's 'closest male associate from 1740 until the early 1750s', he was also his 'most important literary collaborator, assisting him in a number of ambitious publishing ventures'.[24] He may have assisted Fielding in editing *The True Patriot* (1745–6) and *The Jacobite's Journal* (1747–8); and his contemporaries represent him as Fielding's associate in *The Covent-Garden Journal* (1752), in which Fielding advertised their proposal for publishing by subscription a translation of Lucian's work—a plan similar to that of the Aristophanes project and equally abortive.[25]

Six months after *Plutus* was published, Waller devised a scheme to rid himself of the unsold copies. While Fielding was engaged in assembling the odds and ends of his writings for the *Miscellanies*, which in June he had promised for delivery to the subscribers by Christmas,[26] the following notice appeared in the *London Evening-Post* for 23 November, and was repeated a week later:

> *This Day is publish'd,*
> *(Translated into English, with Notes, Explanatory,*
> *and Critical)*

---

[22] Quotations are from the copy of *The Champion* (29 June 1742) in the Bodleian Library, Oxford (Don. c. 72), which, together with his other contributions to the journal, was reprinted in Robinson's *Essays* (1755), XII. See Ribble, above, n. 20.

[23] The anecdote, from a manuscript dated 18 December 1742, is found in J. Paul de Castro, 'Fielding's "Parson Adams" ', *N & Q*, 12th ser., 1 (18 March 1916), pp. 224–5. 'The following story shows him [Young] honest, simple, and without guile. Jointly with Fielding he translated Aristophanes' "Plutus" or God of Riches. Lord Talbot, to whom it is dedicated, sent Young five guineas, as a gratuity, but he for a long time refused it, because it did not belong to him, he having no hand in the dedication. At last he took it, but not for himself, but for Fielding, who writ the dedication. He saw him daily for five days, but still forgot the five guineas. At last, upon a dispute, he pulled out the money to lay a wager; being questioned about it, he said 'twas [Greek = Aristophanic gold] and belonged to Fielding: and so told the manner of his coming by it. 'Twas with great difficulty he could be persuaded to take any part of it, but at last, they, upon the judgment of the company, divided it; but he still insisted upon paying Fielding's reckoning out of his share.'

[24] Ribble, 'Fielding and William Young', p. 457 and nn. 2–3.

[25] See ibid., pp. 488–90, 492–4. The Wesleyan editor does not propose an author for the lead essays by 'Abraham Adams' in *The True Patriot*, Nos. 7 (17 December 1745) and 13 (21–8 January 1746); but the letter by 'Adams' in *The Jacobite's Journal*, No. 32 (9 July 1748), 'might have been written' by Young, who 'possibly' assisted HF in that journal (p. 330 n. 5); Goldgar finds the evidence insufficient to declare that Young assisted HF in *The Covent-Garden Journal* (1752), p. xxxi.

[26] See the advertisement in the *Daily Post* for 5 June 1742 (*Miscellanies* i, p. xlvi).

PLUTUS, the God of RICHES.
By HENRY FIELDING, *Esq; and*
The Rev. Mr. YOUNG.
PROPOSALS for printing by SUBSCRIPTION,
(No Money to be paid 'till the Work is deliver'd, which will be
put to the Press when there is 500 Subscribers)
All the Comedies of ARISTOPHANES, being eleven
in Number. By the same Gentlement [*sic*].

The Notes contain, besides a full Explanation of this very difficult Author, a complete History of the Manners and Customs of the antient Greeks, particularly of the Athenians, beautifully printed into two large Vols. Price 12 s. in Sheets. Those who have bought, or shall buy Plutus, to have them for 10 s. Gentlemen are desir'd to send their Names and Places of Abode to T. Waller, Bookseller, at the Crown and Mitre over-against Fetter-Lane, Fleet-Street.

Nothing came of Waller's plans for a handsome subscription edition of Aristophanes' comedies translated into English by Fielding and Young. In its own century the last sign of the *Plutus* project as originally conceived was an advertisement in the *London Evening-Post* for 30 April 1743. There would be no second edition of the 'Specimen'.

In the next century the *Plutus* of Fielding and Young fared better. It was reprinted in *Comedies of Aristophanes* (1812) and reviewed, together with the other translations, in the *Quarterly Review*, 9 (1813), pp. 139–61. Dr Ribble notes that it was treated respectfully by William James Hickie in the notes to his *Comedies of Aristophanes* (1853), and he refers readers to 'a detailed analysis' of the translation by Samuel Philip Hines, Jr., in his dissertation 'English Translations of Aristophanes' Comedies, 1655–1742'.[27]

POSTSCRIPT: FIELDING AND ARISTOPHANES

From the start of his career as playwright Fielding regarded Aristophanes (*c.*448–385 BC), greatest of the Greek comic dramatists, as his model. The Prologue to *Rape upon Rape: or, The Justice Caught in His Own Trap*,[28] the first of his 'Heroick' comedies, opens by implicitly invoking Aristophanes to sound the theme of Fielding's own satires:

IN *ancient* Greece, *the Infant* Muse's *School,*
Where Vice *first felt the Pen of* Ridicule,
With honest Freedom and impartial Blows
The Muse *attack'd each* Vice *as it arose.*[29]

---

[27] (University of North Carolina, 1967); Ribble, 'Fielding and William Young', p. 482 n. 86.
[28] Subsequently retitled *The Coffee-House Politician.*   [29] *Plays*, p. 426.

In 1734, on the eve of the general election, he dedicated *Don Quixote in England* to the Earl of Chesterfield, a leader of the Opposition, lamenting 'the Calamities brought on a Country by general Corruption' and recalling Aristophanes' comedies as testifying to 'the Force of Theatrical Ridicule' (sig. A3). In *The Craftsman*, No. 471 (12 July 1735), Fielding opens the theme of a satire on Walpole and the gazetteers with a passage from Aristophanes' *The Frogs* (*New Essays*, p. 97). And in the fateful spring of 1737, as the ministry moved to shut his theatre down and silence him by passing the Licensing Act, it was the Athenians' tolerance of Aristophanes that he invoked in each of the three essays he wrote in defence of his own rude satires and the liberty of the stage.[30]

When celebrating the 'Greatness of this Author's Genius' in the Dedication of *Plutus* to Lord Talbot, a 'Patriot' who supported the opposition party, it is still the Aristophanes of the 'Old Comedy' Fielding has in mind:

He exerted that Genius in the Service of his Country. He attack'd and expos'd its Enemies and Betrayers with a Boldness and Integrity, which must endear his Memory to every true and sincere Patriot. (below, p. 250)

But *Plutus*, the last of Aristophanes' extant plays, represents a radical departure from the political satires of the 'Old Comedy' which Fielding in such plays as *Pasquin* and *The Historical Register* took as his model. *Plutus* ushered in the 'New Comedy' that represented the beginning of the European comic tradition, turning from public satire to the exploration of character and a concern with private morality. In his introduction to the play (the title translated as '*Wealth*'), J. Michael Walton writes: 'a sense of character begins to dominate situation' and 'The comparative absence of coarseness, combined with a humanist message, led to the recovery of the play when little else of Aristophanes was thought to merit translation.' Walton cites a performance in Greek by the undergraduates at St John's College, Cambridge, in 1536, and in 1652 a private production of Thomas Randolph's adaptation at a time when all the theatres were closed.[31] In an essay on Wealth and Poverty in *The Spectator*, No. 464 (22 August 1712), Addison summarized the plot of the play[32] and derived from it a very Christian moral: 'This Allegory instructed the *Athenians* in two Points; first,

[30] See the following: *Some Thoughts on the Present State of the Theatres, and the Consequences of an Act to Destroy the Liberty of the Stage*, reprinted in the *Daily Journal*, No. 5955 (25 March 1737); and the leaders in *Common Sense*, No. 16 (21 May 1737), and *The Craftsman*, No. 569 (28 May 1737). All these essays, attributed to HF, are available in *New Essays*, respectively, at pp. 531–5, 536–9, and 202–7.

[31] The above remarks are indebted to Walton's helpful Introduction to *Aristophanes and Menander: New Comedy*, trans. and introd. Kenneth McLeish and J. Michael Walton (London, 1994), esp. pp. xxi–xxii.

[32] In the Preface to their translation HF and Young use Addison's summary as 'the Argument' of the play (see below, pp. 258–9 and n. 29).

as it vindicated the Conduct of Providence in its ordinary Distributions of Wealth; and in the next place, as it showed the great Tendency of Riches to corrupt the Morals of those who possessed them' (ed. Bond, iv, p. 141). Walton remarks: 'One small part of Aristophanes had become respectable.' And in reference to the Theatrical Licensing Act, which Fielding's satires provoked, 'It took until the abolition of censorship in Britain in 1968 to liberate the rest' (p. xxiii).

To the reasons offered by Charles Knight (above, pp. 241–2) for Fielding's choice of *Plutus*, rather than a 'specimen' from among the satires that defined for him Aristophanes' true 'Genius', we might add the influence of his collaborator, the Revd Mr Young. In *Joseph Andrews* (III. xi), at least, Young's alter ego Parson Adams gives vent to his impatience when Joseph recites a passage from *Macbeth*: 'Ay, there is nothing but Heathenism to be learn'd from Plays . . . I never heard of any Plays fit for a Christian to read, but [Addison's] *Cato* and [Steele's] the *Conscious Lovers*; and I must own in the latter there are some things almost solemn enough for a Sermon' (p. 267). Consider, too, *A Journey from This World to the Next* (I. x), where Julian tells of his incarnation as servant to St Chrysostom (*c*.347–407), Father of the Church in Greece, whose diatribes against the female sex were made more telling by the purity of style he reputedly learned from reading Aristophanes' comedies at bedtime.

He was, indeed, [Julian relates] extremely fond of that *Greek* Poet, and frequently made me read his Comedies to him: when I came to any of the loose Passages, he would smile, and say, *It was pity his Matter was not as pure as his Style*; of which latter, he was so immoderately fond, that notwithstanding the Detestation he expressed for Obscenity, he hath made me repeat those Passages ten times over. (*Miscellanies* ii, p. 49)

In the Preface to *Plutus*, Young's influence is surely apparent when, after relating this same tradition about St Chrysostom, the authors conclude by dismissing as 'ill-natured' the implication Fielding so plainly intends in Julian's account, that Aristophanes' '*Purity* of . . . Diction did not alone recommend him to the Father for a Bedfellow' (below, p. 253 and n. 14).

As late as *Tom Jones* (1749) Fielding placed Aristophanes at the head of a pantheon of comic writers inspired by 'Genius' (XIII. i, p. 686). Once into the period of his magistracy, however, Fielding adopted a moralistic bias of his own. In *The Covent-Garden Journal*, No. 10 (4 February 1752), he regrets that Aristophanes—together with Rabelais, another of the pantheon honoured in *Tom Jones*—had used his talents irresponsibly, indeed with a design 'to ridicule all Sobriety, Modesty, Decency, Virtue and Religion, out of the World' (p. 74). In the *Journal*, No. 52 (30 June 1752), now wishing to recommend his and Young's projected translation of Lucian, he disputes Dryden's view that the satirist might have formed his style from Aristophanes: Lucian would never have condescended 'to be the Imitator of a Writer, whose Humour is often extravagant, his Wit coarse, and his Satire unjust and immoral' (p. 286)—Fielding, with the last charge, has in mind 'the base and barbarous Abuse of Socrates' in *The Clouds*, which nearly thirty years earlier, in the Dedication to *Don Quixote in England*, he had condemned without otherwise denying the 'Genius' of the playwright who was then for him a 'Genius' and his own great model. In the last of his writings, the posthumously published *Fragment of a Comment on Lord Bolingbroke's Essays* (1755), Fielding again cited Aristophanes' abuse of Socrates as 'a flagrant instance' of the fallacy in the Shaftesburian doctrine that ridicule should be the test of truth.

PLUTUS,

THE

GOD *of* RICHES.

A

COMEDY.

Tranſlated from the Original *Greek* of

ARISTOPHANES:

With Large N O T E S Explanatory and
Critical.

By *HENRY FIELDING*, Eſq;

A N D

The Rev^d. Mr. *YOUNG*.

LONDON:

Printed for T. WALLER in the *Temple-Cloiſters.*

M DCC XLII.   [Price 2 s.]

To the Right Honourable the
LORD *TALBOT*.[1]

MY LORD,

IN an Age when Learning hath so few Friends, and fewer Patrons, it might require an Apology to introduce an Ancient *Greek* Poet to a Person of an exalted Station.

For could the Poet himself revive, and attend many such in his own Person, he would be esteem'd an unfashionable Visitor, and might, perhaps, find some Difficulty in gaining Admittance.

But when we reflect on the rever'd Name of the late Lord Chancellor of *Great Britain*,[2] who, at the Head of the greatest Excellences and Abilities, which ever warm'd the Heart, or embellish'd the Understanding of Man, preserv'd (which is, perhaps, the highest of human Perfections) the most tender Regard for the Distressed; when we recollect what manifest Tokens You have given that You inherit the Virtues of that truly Great and Amiable Person, we are embolden'd, rather than discourag'd, by this very Consideration, to address the following Attempt to Your LORDSHIP.

Permit us then, my LORD, to recommend *Aristophanes*;[3] and with him, the distressed, and at present, declining State of Learning to Your Protection.

The Greatness of this Author's Genius need not be mentioned to Your LORDSHIP; but there is a much stronger Recommendation to one of Your known Principles. He exerted that Genius in the Service of his Country. He attack'd and expos'd its Enemies and Betrayers with a Boldness and Integrity, which must endear his Memory to every True and Sincere Patriot.[4]

---

[1] William Talbot (1710–82), second Baron (1737) and Earl Talbot (1761). Son of the late Lord Chancellor (below, n. 2), he was a patron of letters and a supporter of the 'new opposition' that formed after the resignation of Walpole in February 1742. For a contemporary account of his acknowledging the Dedication with a gratuity of five guineas, see the Introduction (above, p. 244 and n. 23). Talbot also subscribed to Fielding's *Miscellanies* (1743), ordering two sets on royal paper.

[2] Charles Talbot (1685–14 February 1737), first Baron Talbot of Hensol, Glamorganshire (1733), was appointed Lord Chancellor (1734), an office in which he served for only three years. Though a ministerial appointment under Walpole, in 1736 Talbot—together with Philip Yorke, who would succeed him as Chancellor—supported the opposition amendments to the bill to protect excise officers. This and other divergencies from ministerial policy were appreciated by the Opposition, as reflected in his favourable obituary in *The Craftsman*: indeed, as his biographer observes, 'no-one seems to have had a bad word to say about him' (M. Macnair, *Oxford DNB*, s.v.).

[3] For an account of HF's ambivalent opinion of Aristophanes from the beginning of his career as dramatist to the period of his magistracy, see the Introduction (above, pp. 245–8).

[4] In the political context of the time a 'Patriot', or member of the 'Country Party', was one who opposed the government. On the complex matter of HF's political affiliations at this time, see the Introduction to *A Full Vindication of the Dutchess Dowager of Marlborough* (above, pp. 202–4), as well as

In presenting *Aristophanes* therefore, to Your LORDSHIP, we present him to One, whom he, had he been an *Englishman*, would have chosen for his Patron. Permit us, therefore, to make him this Amends for the Injury done him in our Translation, and to subscribe Ourselves,

> *My LORD,*
>> YOUR LORDSHIP'S
>>> *most Obedient,*
>>>> *most Humble Servants,*
>>>> HENRY FIELDING,
>>>> WILLIAM YOUNG.[5]

PREFACE.

*A*S *we intend, if we proceed in this Work, to prefix to it a very large Dissertation on the Nature and the End of Comedy, with an Account of its Original, Rise, and Progress to this Day; which will include a full View of the Grecian Stage: We shall at present confine ourselves to a very few Words, in Recommendation of our Author himself, and in Apology for this Translation.*

ARISTOPHANES *was born about 460 Years before* CHRIST, *most probably in an Island called Ægina near Athens, where it is certain he had an Estate.[6] He is one of the oldest Professors of the Comic Art, and indeed lived so very near the Original of the Drama, that, besides the Admiration due to his deep Discernment in Human Nature, to the incomparable Humour of his Characters, to his Wit, Style, Numbers, &c. which have received great Elogiums both from antient and modern Critics; we must be astonished at the Regularity and Order of his Comedies, to which in more than two thousand Years successive Poets have been able to add so little.*

We have not Room here to relate half, which hath been written in Praise of our Author, the Honours which he received not only from his own Countrymen, who ordered his Name to be enrolled above those of all his Cotemporaries; but from the Emperor of Persia, who considered him merely the Force of his Wit, and the Uses he applied it to, as a Person of the greatest Consequence in Athens.

HF's notes to the present text (below, p. 263 nn. [9] and 38, p. 300 nn. 136 and [155]). For a detailed examination of HF's political affiliations, see the General Introduction to the *Champion* (pp. xcii–cvi).

[5] On the relationship between HF and the Revd. William Young, see the Introduction (above, pp. 238–40 and *passim*.

[6] The year of Aristophanes' birth is uncertain; *EB* gives *c*.448 BC, stating that his father was a landholder in Aegina and that Aristophanes was an Athenian citizen.

But as the Esteem of one great, and wise, and good Man, is infinitely preferable to the giddy Shouts of the Rabble, or to the capricious Favour of Kings, we hasten to the Account given by Olympiodorus *in his Life of* Plato; *who tells us, that a very intimate Acquaintance subsisted between the Philosopher and the Poet; and that the former learnt from the Writings of the latter, the Art of adapting in his Dialogues the Diction to the Character of the Speaker.*[7] *Indeed it is impossible to read the Works of both with any Attention, without observing the most striking Similitude in their Expression; both being remarkable for that* Attic *Purity of Language, and the elegant Use of those Particles, which, though they give such an inexpressible nervous Force to the Diction of these Authors, have been represented as Expletives, and useless by the Ignorance of Posterity.*

The Affection of Plato *for* Aristophanes *is reported to have been so extremely strong, that after the Death of the Philosopher a Volume of the other's Comedies were found in his Bed. The following Epigram likewise is said to have been his:*

Ἀι Χάριτες τέμενός τι λαβεῖν ὅπερ οὐχὶ πεσεῖται
Ζητοῦσαι ψυχήν εὗρον Ἀριστοφάνους.

The *Graces* endeavouring to obtain a never-falling Temple, found one in the Genius of *Aristophanes.*[8]

We know that Plato, *in his* Phædon, *speaks against a Comic Poet with the utmost Vehemence;*[9] *and, in his Apology for* Socrates, *mentions* Aristophanes *among his false Accusers by Name;*[10] *and that* Ælian *ascribes the Death of* Socrates *to the Ridicule brought on him by the Comedy of the* Clouds;[11] *with*

---

[7] Olympiodorus of Alexandria, a Neoplatonist philosopher of the sixth century AD In his *Life of Plato* he states that Plato 'took likewise great delight in Aristophanes, the comic writer, and in Sophron [a mime]; from whom he benefited in his imitation of the characters in his dialogues' (George Burges, *Works of Plato* [1854], vi, p. 235).

[8] Copies of Aristophanes and Sophron were found on Plato's couch after his death. The epigram that HF and Young quote and translate follows immediately in Olympiodorus (ibid., vi, p. 235).

[9] 'I reckon, said Socrates, that no one who heard me now, not even if he were one of my old enemies, the comic poets, could accuse me of idle talking about matters in which I have no concern' (*Phaedon*, 70b, in Benjamin Jowett, *The Dialogues of Plato* [New York, 1914], iii, p. 203').

[10] In the *Apology* (19b–c), Socrates speaks of the charges against him: 'Well, what do the slanderers say? They shall be my prosecutors, and this is the information they swear against me: "Socrates is an evil-doer; a meddler who searches into things under the earth and in heaven, and makes the worse appear the better cause, and teaches the aforesaid practices to others." Such is the nature of the accusation: it is just what you have yourselves seen in the comedy of Aristophanes [*Clouds*, 225 ff.], who has introduced a man whom he calls Socrates, swinging about and saying that he walks on air, and talking a deal of nonsense concerning matters of which I do not pretend to know either much or little' (ibid. i, p. 343).

[11] Aelian (Claudius Aelianus) (*c.*AD 170–*c.*235). In *Varia Historia* ('Historical Miscellany'), 2. 13, drawing on Plato's *Apology* (see above, n. 10), Aelian relates at some length how Anytus and other enemies of Socrates persuaded Aristophanes 'to lampoon' the philosopher, accusing him of being an atheist who dishonoured the gods and taught others to follow his example. Aristophanes is said to have 'applied himself to the task with great energy', and in the *Clouds* made Socrates the target of destructive ridicule (trans. N. G. Wilson, Loeb [1997], pp. 79–85). The Loeb translator observes, however, that the story, though 'widely believed in antiquity', is 'chronologically absurd' as the *Clouds* was produced in 423 BC and

which Diogenes Laertius *seems to assent:* [12] *But we question not refuting this Story, if ever it be our Fortune to translate that Play.*

But farther, the Elegance of his Style, and the Justness of his Sentiments, recommended him, notwithstanding his Impurities, to the Primitive Fathers of the Church. Thus we find him several times quoted by Clemens Alexandrius;[13] *and there is a Tradition, that St.* Chrysostom *held him in so great Favour, as never to sleep without one of his Comedies under his Pillow, in order to begin the next Day's Reading with the Works of the most correct Writer.*[14] *And to this perhaps we may justly ascribe that Father's having surpassed all the rest in the Purity of his Diction; and hence likewise he probably drew that remarkable Acrimony of Style, in which he hath so severely exposed the Faults of the Fair Sex; which latter we the rather mention, as it takes off an ill-natured Observation, which might otherwise have been insinuated, that the Purity of our Author's Diction did not alone recommend him to the Father for a Bedfellow.*

To conclude this Part of our Preface, Longinus *gives the Character of* Sublime *to our Author's Diction;*[15] Horace *Commends the Freedom and Justice with which he lashed the Vices of his Times:* [16] *Indeed so great hath been always*

Socrates' trial took place in 399 BC (p. 81 n. *a*). In planning to refute Aelian's accusation if given the opportunity, HF and Young would have benefited from the scholiast Nicodemus Frischlin's 'Defense of Aristophanes against Plutarch's Accusations', prefixed to the Küster edition (pp. xix–xxv, esp. p. xxiv).

[12] Diogenes Laertius (*c.*AD 200–50), *Lives of Eminent Philosophers*, 2 vols.: 'Life of Socrates', I. ii. 19: 'And Aristophanes attacks him in his plays for making the worse appear the better reason' (trans. R. D. Hicks, Loeb [1972], p. 151). Also ii. 27–8 and 38.

[13] Clement of Alexandria (*c.*AD 150–*c.*215), Greek Father of the Church. *EB* (s.v.) remarks on Clement's broad familiarity with the Greek poets of every genre, and cites Johannes Albertus Fabricius, *Bibliotheca Graeca* (Hamburg, 1718); Baker notes in Fabricius six references to Aristophanes in Clement's works. HF owned a copy of Jacques Lect's edition *Poetae Graeci veteres*, in Greek and Latin (Geneva, 1614), which includes verse attributed to Clement (Ribbles L5). The reference in *Plutus* is the only mention of him in HF's writings.

[14] St John Chrysostom (*c.*345–407), most famous of the Greek Fathers of the Church and Archbishop of Constantinople, he was noted equally for his eloquence as a homilist and for his ascetic manner of life. Both these attributes are notable in his public castigation of the empress Eudoxia and her ladies for their loose and luxurious way of living—an offence which resulted in his deposition and exile. In *A Journey from This World to the Next* (1. x) HF would hint at an ulterior motive for Chrysostom's enjoyment of Aristophanes' bawdy comedies as 'his constant Bed-fellow' (p. 49). Here such an insinuation is pointedly dismissed as 'ill-natured', owing perhaps to the influence of HF's collaborator, the Revd Mr Young. (See the Introduction, above, p. 247.) In his note to the passage in *JWN* (p. 49 n. 5), Bertrand Goldgar identifies HF's source 'for the legend of the Saint's pillowbook' as Nicodemus Frischlin's life of Aristophanes (1586), reprinted in Küster's edition of 1710, p. xvii.

[15] Longinus, *On the Sublime* (xl. 4): 'many writers both in prose and poetry, who are not by nature sublime, perhaps even the very opposite, while using for the most part current vulgar language, which suggests nothing out of the common, yet by the mere force of composition and verbal carpentry have achieved dignity and distinction and an effect of grandeur; Philistus, for instance, among many others, Aristophanes occasionally, Euripides almost always' (trans. W. Hamilton Fyfe, Loeb [1965], p. 239).

[16] Horace, *Satires* (1. iv. 1–5); 'Eupolis and Cratinus and Aristophanes, true poets, and the other good men to whom Old Comedy belongs, if there was anyone deserving to be drawn as a rogue and thief, as a rake or cut-throat, or as scandalous in any other way, set their mark upon him with great freedom' (trans. H. Rushton Fairclough, Loeb [1961], p. 49). Horace, in such passages, served HF in defence of his own political satires.

his Reputation, that, as M. Dacier *observes, to deny his Merit, would be* to give the Lye to all Antiquity.[17]

It may seem therefore impossible, that the Works of such an Author should fail of Success in any Language, unless through the Fault of the Translation; to which our Reader will, I suppose, if he finds this Play disagree with his Taste, impute it.

There are some, I am told, protest *Admirers of* Aristophanes *in the* Greek, *who assert the Impossibility of translating him; which, in my Opinion, is asserting, in other Words, the Impossibility of understanding him: for sure a Man must have a very superficial Knowledge of his own Language, who cannot communicate his Ideas in it. If the Original conveys clear and adequate Ideas to me, I must be capable of delivering them to others in that Language which I am myself a perfect Master of.*[18] *I am deceived therefore, if the Complaints of Translators do not generally arise from the same Cause with those I have often heard made in Conversation by Men, who have mistaken some floating imperfect Images in their Minds for clear and distinct Conceptions, and bitterly lament that they* are unable to express themselves: *Whereas a Man who conceives clearly, will, I apprehend, always express himself so.*

I remember a Translation of a celebrated Line in Lucan *into* French, *which is thus:*

Victrix causa Deis placuit, sed victa Catoni.[19]

Les Dieux servent Cesar, mais Caton suit Pompée.

The Sense of the Latin *is,*

---

[17] Anne (Lefèvre) Dacier (1654–1720), eminent French classical scholar and wife of André Dacier (1651–1722), whom HF in *Tom Jones* (XI. i) ranks with René Le Bossu as the greatest of modern critics (p. 569). When revising *Joseph Andrews* for the second edition (published June 1742)—a time when he was also preparing the translation of *Plutus*—HF, excusing an inconsistency in the narrative, added a footnote to book III, ch. ii applying 'an Observation which M. *Dacier* makes in her Preface to her *Aristophanes*', preferring '*une Beauté médiocre*' to '*une Beauté sans défaut*' (p. 201 n.). (NB: in HF's own Preface, as well as this footnote and elsewhere in his works, he refers to Madam Dacier as 'M. *Dacier*'.) For other references to her, see *Champion* (4 December 1739), *A Journey from This World to the Next* (I. viii), *Tom Jones* (VII. xii), *Amelia* (VI. vii), and *Covent-Garden Journal*, No. 11 (8 February 1752) and No. 67 (21 October 1752).

HF had in his library (Ribbles A22) a copy of Mme Dacier's *Le Plutus et les nuées d'Aristophane, Comédies greques, traduites en François. Avec des remarques & un examen de chaque pièce selon les règles du théâtre* (Lyon, 1696); the first edition was 1684.

[18] Cf. Dryden in his 'Life of Lucian': 'The Qualification of a Translator worth Reading must be a Mastery of the Language he Translates out of, and that he Translates into; but if a deficience be to be allow'd in either, it is in the Original, since if he be but Master enough of the Tongue of his Author, as to be Master of his Sense, it is possible for him to express that Sense, with Eloquence, in his own, if he have a through Command of that' (*The Works of John Dryden: Prose 1691–1698*, ed. A. E. Wallace Maurer and George R. Guffey [Berkeley and Los Angeles, 1989], xx, pp. 226–7).

[19] From the epic poem *Pharsalia* (i. 128) by Marcus Annaeus Lucanus (AD 39–65) or Lucan. In *The Craftsman*, No. 600 (7 January 1737/8), HF comments on this line: 'The Criticks almost unanimously condemn that famous Turn of *Lucan*, *Victrix Causa* Diis *placuit, sed victa* Catoni, as at once both false and impious; since it advances *Cato* above the *Gods*, and sets *his Opinion* of the Cause in Opposition to *theirs*' (*New Essays*, p. 275)

The Gods embraced the Cause of the Conqueror, but *Cato* that of the Conquered.

The Sense of the French *is,*

The Gods preserved *Caesar,* but *Cato* followed *Pompey.*

Will any Man say, that this Frenchman *understood his Author, or that* Lucan *had conveyed the same Idea to him, which he himself had conceived when he wrote that excellent and beautiful Compliment to* Cato.

To mention no more Instances, (for Thousands occur in most Translations) I am convinced that the Complaint of the Difficulty of rendering an Author in the Translator's own Language, arises commonly from the Difficulty of comprehending him.

I do not, however, affect to say, that a Translation labours under no Disadvantage, or that it can be entirely alter & idem.[20]

On the contrary, I am sensible, that in this particular Undertaking we have three principal ones to encounter.

First, *We are to render a purer and more copious Language in that which is impurer and more confined. This drives us often from literally pursuing the Original, and makes a Periphrasis necessary to explain a single Word, or the concisest Expression.*

Secondly, *There is in* Aristophanes *a great deal of that Wit which consists merely in the Words themselves, and is so inseparable from them, that it is impossible to transfer it into any others: But this is a Species of Wit, which our Readers of the better Taste will not much repine at being deprived of. It is indeed sometimes found in good Authors, where it appears like a Tinsel-Ornament on a beautiful Woman, to catch the Admiration of vulgar Eyes, and to offend Persons of real Taste. However, that we might oblige all, and be as faithful to our Author as possible, where we have not been able to preserve such Facetiousness in our Text, we have generally remarked it in our Notes.*

The last Disadvantage I shall mention, is the Harmony which in many Places of the Original is excellently sweet. This, perhaps, I should have thought impossible to preserve, had not the inimitable Author of the Essay on Man[21]

---

[20] 'other and the same'.

[21] HF always acknowledged Pope's brilliance as a poet: in *The Champion* (27 November 1739) HF declared him to be one 'whose Works will be coeval with the Language in which they are writ' (p. 34). In the period 1728–33, however, Pope's cruel satires of Lady Mary Wortley Montagu, as well as Theobald, had earned HF's contempt for the poet as a person (for which, see the Introductions to HF's 'Cantos' and 'Epistle to Lyttleton', above, pp. 30, 86–7).

A radical change for the better in HF's relations with Pope may be dated from the late autumn of 1741, when he was entertained by Ralph Allen at Bath while Pope was a guest at Allen's new Palladian house at Prior Park. The first sign of the new friendship is in *Joseph Andrews* (III. vi), published in February 1742, where HF's footman hero recalls ' 'Squire *Pope,* the great Poet' celebrating Allen's benevolence at the dinner table (p. 235). And in March, when Pope published *The New Dunciad,* which he had completed at Prior Park, HF would have appreciated the compliment the 'great Poet' paid, implicitly, to *Pasquin* and

taught me a System of Philosophy in English *Numbers whose Sweetness is scarce inferior to that of* Theocritus *himself:* [22] *But*

Non omnia possumus omnes.[23]

These are indeed Objections which can only be made by our most learned Readers, whom perhaps our close Adherence to our Author, and particularly in the Simplicity of his Language, *may in some measure conciliate to us. The most dangerous and fatal Enemies we are to dread, are those whom this very Simplicity may offend; the Admirers of that pretty, dapper, brisk, smart, pert Dialogue, which hath lately flourished on our Stage. This was first introduced with infinite Wit by* Wycherley,[24] *and continued with still less and less by his Successors, till it is at last degenerated into such sort of Pleasantry as this, in the* Provoked Husband:[25]

The Historical Register, which alone had kept the comic Muse alive until the Licensing Act shut his theatre down: 'There sunk Thalia, nerveless, cold, and dead, | Had not her sister Satyr held her head' (*Dunciad*, iv. 41–2). In *A Journey from This World to the Next* (i. viii), which HF wrote this year, he would cement the relationship: Homer 'asked much after Mr. *Pope*, and said he was very desirous of seeing him: for that he had read his *Iliad* in his Translation with almost as much delight, as he believed he had given others in the Original' (*Miscellanies* ii, p. 37).

[22] Theocritus (*fl. c.*270 BC), Greek pastoral poet. In *Joseph Andrews* (II. ii) Parson Adams recites a verse from Idyll IV (p. 93).

[23] A favourite maxim of HF's, who in *Tom Jones* (IV. viii) translates it: 'All things are not in the Power of all' (p. 178); Partridge utters it twice (VIII. iv, p. 414, and X. v, p. 543). See also *The Champion* (14 February 1739/40), p. 178; *Joseph Andrews* (II. viii, p. 134).

[24] From the beginning of his literary career HF ranked William Wycherley (1641–1715) with the greatest dramatists in English. In the Preface to his first play, *Love in Several Masques* (1728), he granted 'the superior Force of a *Wycherly*, or a *Congreve*' (*Plays*, p. 20); and in the unfinished 'Cantos' (ii. 220) these two are mentioned in the same company with Shakespeare and Jonson as having set the standard for excellence in comedy (above, p. 60). And later, in *Tom Jones* (IX. i) though Otway replaces Congreve in the short list of dramatists who are capable of 'the nicest Strokes . . . of Nature' (p. 493), Wycherley remains.

[25] First staged at Drury Lane on 10 January 1728, *The Provok'd Husband* was Colley Cibber's genteel adaptation of *A Journey to London*, an unfinished comedy of 'low' humour by Sir John Vanbrugh (1664–1726). Cibber refined and moralized the original in an attempt, as he assured the Queen in dedicating the book to her, 'to Establish such [public diversions], as are fit to Entertain the Minds of a sensible Nation; and to wipe off that Aspersion of Barbarity, which the *Virtuosi* among our Neighbours, have sometimes thrown upon our Taste' (sig. A2ʳ). *The Provok'd Husband* was a huge success, running twenty-eight nights in succession (Hume, p. 36) and setting a sobering example for HF, a neophyte playwright whose *Love in Several Masques* followed it at Drury Lane. He wrote in the Prologue, 'Though it some Beauties has, it still must fall, | Compar'd to that, which has excell'd in All' (*Plays*, p. 22). Since then Cibber, having refused HF's next offering, had become a target of his satire (see the Introduction, above pp. 137–8, and the note to line 21 of the title-page of *Shamela*). But HF would reserve his best stroke against Cibber and his gentrification, as it were, of Vanbrugh's 'low' comedy for *Tom Jones* (XII. v–vi), where Tom and Partridge attend a 'Puppet-show' which 'was performed with great Regularity and Decency. It was called the fine and serious Part of the *Provok'd Husband*; and it was indeed a very grave and solemn Entertainment, without any low Wit or Humour, or Jests; or to do it no more than Justice, without any thing which could provoke a Laugh' (pp. 637–8). As for the edifying effect of this Cibberian production, the landlady's maid, moved by the example set by the Lady Townly puppet, is found on 'Stage in Company with the Merry Andrew, and in a Situation not very proper to be described' (p. 640). (The dialogue quoted by HF, though verbatim, is an abridgement of the exchange between Manly and Lady Grace in Act I, scene i.)

Manly. If that were my Case, I believe I should certainly sleep in another House.

L. Grace. How do you mean?

Manly. Only a Compliment, Madam.

L. Grace. A Compliment!

Manly. Yes, Madam, in rather turning myself out of Doors than her.

L. Grace. Don't you think that would be going too far?

Manly. I don't know but it might, Madam: for in strict Justice I think she ought rather go than I.

Again.

L. Grace. Can a Husband love a Wife too well?

Manly. As easily, Madam, as a Wife may love her Husband too little.

L. Grace. 'Tis Pity *but* your Mistress should hear your Doctrine.

Manly. Pity me, Madam, when I marry the Woman *that* won't hear it, *&c. &c. &c.*

This sort of Stuff, which is, I think, called genteel Comedy, and in which our Laureate[26] *succeeded so excellently well both as Author and Actor, had some Years ago taken almost sole Possession of our Stage, and banished* Shakespeare, Fletcher, Johnson,[27] *&c. from it; the last of whom, of all our* English *Poets, seems chiefly to have studied and imitated* Aristophanes, *which we have remarked more than once in our Notes. To such therefore of our Readers, whose Palates are vitiated with the theatrical Diet I have above-mentioned, I would recommend a Play or two of* Johnson's, *to be taken as a kind of Preparative before they enter on this Play; for otherwise the Simplicity of its Style, for want of being sweetned with modern Quaintness, may, like old Wine after Sugar-Plumbs, appear insipid, and without any Flavour. But our Readers of a purer Taste and sounder Judgment, will be able, we apprehend, to digest good Sense, manly Wit, just Satire, and true Humour, without those Garnishments which we could with infinitely greater Ease have supplied (as others have done) in the*

---

[26] Colley Cibber, comedian, author of *The Provok'd Husband* and principal patentee of the Theatre Royal at Drury Lane, was appointed Poet Laureate in 1730. Later, in *The Covent-Garden Journal*, No. 19 (7 March 1752), HF repeated this complaint against Cibberian comedy: 'What can we sometimes conceive of an Audience at a Play-House, where I have heard the dullest Chitchat between Gentlemen and Ladies called Humour, and applauded as such!' (p. 130).

[27] In *The Covent-Garden Journal*, No. 23 (21 March 1752), HF again included, with Shakespeare of course, the dramatists John Fletcher (1579–1625), with his collaborator Beaumont, and Ben Jonson (1572–1637) in the 'Quadrumvirate' of wits who ruled 'the literary Government' in the reign of James I (pp. 152–3). As satirist and playwright, HF felt a special kinship with Jonson, 'who', as he declared in the Preface to *Joseph Andrews*, 'of all Men understood the *Ridiculous* best' (p. 9); and, as he declares in this present context, HF recognized in Jonson's comedies of 'humour' the hand of a fellow follower of Aristophanes. In *The Covent-Garden Journal*, No. 55 (18 July 1752), quoting at length the Induction to Jonson's *Every Man Out of His Humour*, he defined 'the Term Humour' as 'a violent Bent or Disposition of the Mind to some particular Point' (pp. 299–300).

room of our Author's Meaning, than have preserved it in his own plain Simplicity of Stile.

It may be expected that we should here take some Notice of the other Translations of this Play, especially those two of M. Dacier *and Mr.* Theobald,[28] *which we have sometimes taken the Liberty of dissenting from in our Translation, and on which we have commented with some Freedom in our Notes; but if we are right on these Occasions, little Apology will be required; if wrong, we shall gladly embrace Correction, nor persist obstinately in Error. I own, we have more to answer to the Memory of the Lady than to Mr.* Theobald, *who being a Critic of great Nicety himself, and great Diligence in correcting Mistakes in others, cannot be offended at the same Treatment. Indeed there are some Parts of his Work which I should be more surprised at, had he not informed us in his Dedication, that he was assisted in it by M.* Dacier. *We are not therefore much to wonder, if Mr.* Theobald *errs a little, when we find his Guide going before out of the Way.*

We shall conclude our Preface with the Argument of this Play, as left us by Mr. Addison *in his 464th* Spectator.[29]

'*Chremylus*, who was an old and a good Man, and withal exceeding poor, being desirous to leave some Riches to his Son, consults the Oracle of *Apollo* upon the Subject. The Oracle bids him follow the first Man he should see upon his going out of the Temple. The Person he chanced to see was to Appearance an old sordid blind Man, but upon his following him from Place to Place, he at last found by his own Confession, that he was *Plutus* the God of Riches, and that he was just come out of the House of a Miser. *Plutus* further told him, that when he was a Boy, he used to declare, that as soon as he came to Age he would distribute Wealth to none but virtuous and just Men; upon which considering the pernicious Consequences of such a Resolution, took his Sight away from him, and left him to strole about the World in the blind Condition wherein *Chremylus* beheld him. With much ado *Chremylus* prevailed upon him to go to his House, where he met an Old Woman in a tatter'd Raiment, who had been his Guest for many Years, and whose Name was *Poverty*. The Old Woman refusing to turn out so easily as he would have her, he threatned to banish her not only from his own House, but out of all *Greece*, if she made any more Words upon the Matter. *Poverty* on this Occasion pleads her Cause very notably, and represents to her old Landlord, that should she be driven out of the Country, all their Trades, Arts and Sciences would be driven out with her; and that if every one was

---

[28] For an account of HF's relationship with Lewis Theobald, see the 'Epistle to Lyttleton' (above, p. 96 n. 35). Here HF's target is Theobald's translation, *Plutus: or, The World's Idol. A Comedy. Translated from the Greek of Aristophanes* (1715).

[29] Except for minor variants in accidentals, the 'Argument' that follows reprints the complete text of Addison's summary of the plot of *Plutus* (*Spectator*, No. 464 [22 August 1712], ed. Bond, iv, pp. 139–41).

Rich, they would never be supplied with those Pomps, Ornaments and Conveniencies of Life which made Riches desirable. She likewise represented to him the several Advantages which she bestowed upon her Votaries, in regard to their Shape, their Health, and their Activity, by preserving them from Gouts, Dropsies, Unwieldiness, and Intemperance. But whatever she had to say for herself, she was at last forced to troop off. *Chremylus* immediately consider'd how he might restore *Plutus* to his Sight; and in order to it conveyed him to the Temple of *Æsculapius*, who was famous for Cures and Miracles of this Nature. By this Means the Deity recover'd his Eyes, and begun to make a right use of them, by enriching every one that was distinguished by Piety towards the Gods, and Justice towards Men; and at the same time by taking away his Gifts from the Impious and Undeserving. This produced several merry Incidents, 'till in the last Act *Mercury* descends with great Complaints from the Gods, that since the Good Men were grown Rich they had received no Sacrifices, which is confirmed by a Priest of *Jupiter*, who enters with a Remonstrance, that since this late Innovation he was reduced to a starving Condition, and could not live upon his Office. *Chremylus,* who in the beginning of the Play was Religious in his Poverty, concludes it with a Proposal which was relished by all the Good Men who were now grown rich as well as himself, that they should carry *Plutus* in a solemn Procession to the Temple, and install him in the Place of *Jupiter*. This Allegory instructed the *Athenians* in two Points, first, as it indicated the Conduct of Providence in its ordinary Distributions of Wealth; and in the next Place, as it shewed the great Tendency of Riches to corrupt the Morals of those who possessed them.'

Dramatis Personæ.

MEN.

Plutus, the GOD of RICHES

Chremylus,
Blepsidemus, } Two old Yeomen in decayed Circumstances

Dicaeus, a just and honest Man.
Sycophantes, a Sycophant, or common Informer.
Neaniscus, a young Gallant.
Mercury.
Priest of *Jupiter.*
Cario, a Slave belonging to *Chremylus.*
Chorus of Yeomen.

WOMEN.

The *Wife* of *Chremylus.*
An *Old Woman.*

The SCENE is in *ATHENS.*

PLUTUS,

The GOD of RICHES.

ACT I. SCENE I.

SCENE, *the Street in Athens before the House of* Chremylus.
CARIO and CHREMYLUS *following* PLUTUS.

CARIO.

O *Jupiter*,[1] and all ye Gods! what a vexatious thing it is to be the Slave of a mad Master! for, be the Servant's Advice never so excellent, if his Master takes it into his Head not to follow it, the poor Domestic is by Necessity forced[2] to partake all the bad Consequences. Fortune permits not[3] the natural Lord to have any Power over his own Person; but transfers it all to the Purchaser. Well! these Things are all so. However, I do complain (and my Complaint is just) of that Oblique Deity, who sings forth his Oracles from his golden Tripod. Who, tho' he is both a Physician and a Prophet, a very good one too, as Folks say, hath sent my Master away in such a Fit of the Spleen, that with his Eyes open he follows behind a blind Fellow.[4] Doing thus, the very Reverse of what is agreeable to Reason: for, whereas the Blind are always led by us who can see, this Master of mine

---

[1] *And all ye Gods.*] Madam *Dacier* hath thought proper to degrade the rest of the Gods from the Text;[30] but Mr. *Theobald* hath piously *restored* them.[31] The Words are here a literal Translation from the *Greek*; and indeed we have endeavoured through the whole to stick as close to our Author as possible: We have not, however, thought it necessary to retain every Oath, unless where it gives a peculiar Energy to the Sentence: for as Swearing was no Crime among the *Greeks*, the Dialogues even of Plato are full of Oaths, and they occur in almost every Line of this Play; the constant Repetition of which would be tiresome to an *English* Reader.

[2] *To partake all the bad Consequences.*] Madam *Dacier* hath translated it, la moitié des maux, &c. which Mr. *Theobald* mistaking, hath given the Blame of half the Master's Miscarriages only to the Servant.[32]

[3] *The natural Lord.*] This is the *Greek*, and truly humorous in this Servant, which is a Character of Impertinence and Sauciness, and as well at least supported through the whole Play, as any such Character in any modern Comedy. There is indeed an Elegance in the *Greek* impossible to be entirely preserved: for the same Word signifies both Lord and Owner; we have therefore added the Word *natural*.

[4] *Doing thus,* &c.] The mock Dignity here, and the Solemnity with which this vulgar Observation is introduced, is highly suitable to the Person who delivers it, and would not fail of pleasing from the Mouth of a sensible Actor.

---

[30] Dacier (Lyon, 1696): 'Grands Dieux'. Theobald (1715): 'O *Jove*, and all you Herd of Gods!' Loeb: 'O Zeus and all ye Gods' (trans. Benjamin Bickley Rogers, 1991).

[31] Alluding to Theobald's *Shakespeare Restored* (1726 reissued 1740), an attack on Pope's edition (1725).

[32] Theobald: 'the poor Counseller is blam'd for half the Miscarriages' (p. 1). Loeb: 'must share the ill results'.

follows the Guidance of the Blind; nay, and compels me also to do the same: and all this without the blind Rascal's answering us a single Word.[5] There is, therefore, no Reason why I should be silent any longer; unless you will tell me, Sir, for what Purpose we follow this Fellow, I shall be very troublesome, indeed I shall—I know[6] you will not lift your Hand against a Man with a sacred Chaplet on his Head.

Chrem. By *Jupiter!* if you plague me, I will——first taking off your Chaplet, to punish you the more.

Cario.[7] This is trifling: I shall never leave off till you tell me who that Fellow there is. It is my great Affection to you, which makes me so extremely vehemently inquisitive.

Chrem. Well: I will not hide it from thee; for, of all my Domestics, I believe

---

[5] *Without his answering a single Word.*] All the Commentators and Translators too have ascribed this Silence to the wrong Person. The *French* and *English* Translators give it to the Servant; the *Latin* to the Master. *Girardus*[33] indeed saw the Grammatical Construction would not bear it, and therefore would have the Genitive Case, without any reason, to be put for the Nominative. Madam *Dacier* finds justly fault with the *Latin* Translation; but surely she is herself as wrong in referring it to *Cario*, from his saying *there is no reason why I should be silent any longer*: for can any thing be more humorous than these Words from a Servant, who hath been all this while walking and chattering before his Master? But the *Greek* Construction justifies and requires the Translation here given. Dr. *Bentley*[34] agrees with the *Latin* Translation, but not with the *Greek* Text, which, *more suo*,[35] he first corrected, alters into the Nominative Case, and then refers the Speech to *Chremylus*: for, says he, *Plutus* had yet been asked no Question. To confirm his Opinion, he quotes *Verses* 52, and 60, the former of which makes directly against him, and the latter is nothing to the purpose, as our learned Reader will observe.

[6] *You will not lift*, &c.] It was the Custom among the Antients, when they returned from consulting the Oracle, and received a favourable Answer, to wear Garlands on their Heads; otherwise not; as is expressly said in the *Oedipus Tyrannus* of *Sophocles*, *V.* 82. where the Priest concludes *Creon* to be returned with good News, on seeing him crowned with Laurel; for *otherwise*, says he, he would not wear it. The Scholiast,[36] on this Place, tells us, that the Slaves likewise were equally entitled to these Crowns; nor was any Mark of Pre-eminence allowed to their Masters. Madam *Dacier* makes a pretty Observation on this Custom: *It gave us to understand*, says she, *that in the Temples the whole World is on an equal Condition, and that there is no Distinction of Persons before God, who is no less the Father of Slaves than of Freemen; and while they were thus crowned, their Masters durst not beat nor chide them. And it was this Privilege which gave Cario so much Assurance.*

[7] *This is trifling.*] *Cario* knew his Master did not dare by Law to take his Chaplet from him; and thence he is emboldened to make this impudent Answer.

---

[33] Charles Girard (*fl.* 1534–49), French classicist, author of *Institutions de la langue Grecque* (1541–4) and *Plutus d'Aristophane* (1549). HF's Küster reprints in Latin the commentary from the latter.

[34] Richard Bentley (1662–1742), Master of Trinity College, Cambridge, classical scholar and editor. HF's Küster reprints his comments on *Plutus*. Today considered one of the great classicists, Bentley was, in the literary circles of his own time, regarded as a meddlesome pedant. He was ridiculed by Swift in *The Battle of the Books* (1697), by Pope in *The New Dunciad* (1742), and by HF in, for example, the Preface and notes to *The Tragedy of Tragedies* (1731), the notes to the *Vernoniad* (1741), *The Champion* (27 November 1739/40), and *Amelia* (1751; X. i). For HF's view of Bentley and other scholiasts, see Bertrand Goldgar, ' "The Learned English Dog": Fielding's Mock Scholarship', in Albert J. Rivero (ed.), *Augustan Subjects* (Newark, Del., 1997), pp. 192–206.

[35] 'as is his custom'.

[36] HF's Küster includes, in Latin, all the known scholiasts on Aristophanes, both ancient and modern.

thee to be the most faithful, and most[8] expert at concealing what thou canst of thy Master's! Thou knowest, that I a religious and upright Man as I am, have had very ill Success in the World——nay, have suffered extreme *Poverty*.

Cario. Ay, Ay, I know it very well.

Chrem. Whilst others have acquired great Riches, being at the same time guilty of Sacrilege,[9] public Incendiaries, Informers, and Villains of all Kinds.

Cario. I am persuaded of it.

---

[8] *Expert at concealing.*] The Commentators have puzzled on this Place.——The greater part of them would have this spoken *by way of surprize*, on *Cario*, who, after his Master had commended him as the most faithful, expecting he would go on praising him, was disappointed by his adding, after a Pause, a Word of a rascally Signification; a Method indeed usual enough among all the Comic Poets; but in my opinion, the meaning of *Aristophanes* is much pleasanter. There is an Ambiguity in the *Greek* Word [Κλεπτίστατον, line 27],[37] which properly signifies *hiding, concealing, secreting*. I do not indeed agree with *Girardus*, that this Word is used in a *good Sense* by the antient *Greek* Writers (for the Scholiast says no more than that it signified *cunning* in the common Conversation of the *Greeks* of his time, viz. above 1000 Years after our Poet.) The Meaning, I apprehend, is this: I know thou art very capable of concealing my Goods from me, why then not capable of concealing my Secrets from others? This Pleasantry is preserved in the Translation.

[9] *Public Incendiaries.*] Mr. *Theobald* gives here *Patriots*. *Girardus* hath this Note: 'The *Athenians*, as well as other Cities, had formerly their Orators, who reminded the People on all occasions of their real Interest; such were *Aristides, Nicias, Miltiades, Pericles*, and others, being Men of great Merit; against whom *Aristophanes* by no means inveighs, but against those, who regarding only their own Interest, and neglecting that of the Public, harangued the Populace on plausible rather than useful Subjects. *Demosthenes* lashes those latter in the following Words: *Some of these from Beggars are become rich; others from Obscurity are enobled. Some have erected* PRIVATE PALACES *more magnificent than the Publick Edifices. Their Wealth is increased in proportion to the Diminution of the Public Treasure.*'[38]

---

[37] Loeb (line 26) has, simply, 'I'll tell you'; Sommerstein, 'I won't keep it a secret from you' (Aristophanes, *Wealth*, trans. Alan H. Sommerstein [Warminster, 2001]).

[38] Demosthenes (*c.*384–322 BC), *Third Olynthiac*, 29, referring sarcastically to the 'men whose statesmanship' has resulted in the failure of Athens's 'foreign policy' and the enrichment of themselves at home: 'some of them were poor and now are rich, some were obscure and now are eminent, some have reared private houses more stately than our public buildings, while the lower the fortunes of the city have sunk, the higher have their fortunes soared' (Loeb). In his comments on HF's translation of *The First Olynthiac*, Henry Knight Miller, citing leaders in the anti-ministerial journal *Common Sense* in the winter of 1737-8, remarks that the Opposition exploited an analogy between Walpole's failure to take action against Philip of Spain for depredations against British shipping and Demosthenes' denunciation of the Athenian demagogues who doomed their state by failing to take action against Philip of Macedon (*Miscellanies* i, p. xlii and n. 4).

In the present passage HF's reference to 'PRIVATE PALACES' (emphasized in small capitals) is another of his hits at Walpole's bilking the public treasury in order to erect and furnish Houghton Hall, his '*great Palace*' in Norfolk, as HF calls it in the satirical ballad 'The Norfolk Lanthorn' (*New Essays*, pp. 510–11). See also *The Craftsman*, No. 569 (28 May 1737), Walpole's '*Country Palace*' (*New Essays*, p. 202 and n. 4); *The Champion* (16 February 1739/40), p. 185 and n. 4; *Vernoniad* (*Champion*, pp. 573 nn. [43] and 2; 583 and n. 3); and *Jonathan Wild* (I. v; *Miscellanies* iii, p. 23 and n. 1). On the resumption of HF's attacks on Walpole after praising him in *The Opposition: A Vision*, see the Introduction to *A Full Vindication of the Dutchess Dowager of Marlborough* (above, pp. 199–201).

Chrem. I went therefore to consult *Apollo*, concluding indeed[10] the Quiver of my miserable Days to be almost shot out, the enquire of him,[11] for the sake of my Son, who is my only Child, whether it was his Interest to depart from his Father's Morals, and to become crafty, unjust, entirely corrupt; for these seemed to me the necessary Qualifications for this World.

Cario. What from his Garlands[12] chatter'd forth the God?

Chrem. You shall hear. The God told me this[13] plainly. The first Person whom I should meet after I departed from the Temple, him he commanded me never to quit, till I had prevailed on him to accompany me to my House.

Cario. [14] And pray who was the first Person you met?

Chrem. Why, this very Person here before us?

---

[10] *The Quiver.*][39] The Metaphor here used is extremely beautiful, and we have ventured to preserve it; notwithstanding, Madam *Dacier* hath thought proper to drop it; and so hath her good Friend Mr. *Theobald*. This is a Metaphor in frequent use among the *Greek* Poets, particularly in the *Oedipus Tyrannus* of *Sophocles*, V. 1205. Horace hath likewise imitated it, Ode XVI. Book II.

> *Quid brevi fortes jaculamur aevo*
> *Multa?*———[40]

The Note of *Girardus* is so very ingenious, and so finely illustrates the Beauty of this Passage, that I cannot help translating it.

'Whilst Men, *says he*, are in their Vigour, one is ambitious of great Honours; another applies himself to the acquiring Riches; a third with the utmost Diligence aspires to immense Learning: but when once a Man finds himself broken with Old-Age, his Mind desponds; nor hath he a greater Incentive to these Pursuits, than an Archer hath to level his Bow at a Mark, when he sees his Quiver empty of Arrows.[41] 'Tis observable, that the same Word in *Greek* signifies both Life and a Bow.' Dr. *Bentley* hath shot his Arrow at this Place, and, being a good Marksman, hath hit the Word ἐκτετοξεῦσθαι[42] and struck it out of the Text. In the room of which he hath substituted ἐκτετολυπεῦσθαι, *i.e. spun out*; a Reading to which we have no other Objection than that it doth not come from *Aristophanes*.

[11] *For the sake of my Son.*] Ben *Johnson*, who hath founded two of his best Plays on the Passion of Avarice, seems to have an Eye to this; for he introduces every Man pursuing Riches, on the pretence of doing good to others, or the Public, and disclaiming all selfish Views; one wants to build Hospitals, another for the Propagation of Religion, &c.[43]

[12] *Chatter'd forth.*] We have translated this into a blank Verse; it is in the Original in the Tragic Stile, and an intended Burlesque on *Euripides* for the affected Use of this Word upon the same occasion.

[13] *Plainly.*] In opposition to his Character of LOXIAS, or the oblique God, of which kind were most of his Oracles, and to which *Cario* alludes in the first Speech.

[14] *And pray who.*] Madam *Dacier* and her Friend have mistaken the Original here. They translate it, *And was this the first*, &c. The Fault is indeed trivial, but Lovers of Accuracy will not be offended at the Observation.

---

[39] Loeb: 'the quiver of my life | Is well-nigh emptied of its arrows now' (line 35); Sommerstein: 'my own miserable life had already pretty well shot its bolt'.

[40] Horace, *Odes*, II. xvi. 17–18: 'Why do we, valiant fellows that we are, aim at so many targets in our short life?' (Loeb).

[41] [Küster, 'Notæ in Plutum', line 34, p. 19 (second pagination series).

[42] Bentley, 'Emendationes in Plutum', Küster, 'Notæ', line 34, p. 319.

[43] In *Volpone* (1605) and *The Alchemist* (1610) Ben Jonson ridiculed avarice in, respectively, the characters of Sir Epicure Mammon, who affects to want money to build hospitals; and the religious zealots Ananias and Tribulation Wholesome, who professedly seek gold in order to spread the faith.

Cario. And can you be so dull to misapprehend the God's Meaning, which declares to you in[15] the plainest manner,[16] that your Son should pursue the Manners of his Country.

Chrem. Whence do you infer this?

Cario. Most certainly. A blind Man may see into this Oracle, That it is extremely advantageous, to exercise all kind of Corruption at this present Season.

Chrem. The Oracle can by no means lean to this; it tends to something more important. And if this Fellow will but tell us, who he is, and for what Purpose, or on what Occasion, he is come hither with us, we may then understand what our Oracle means.

Cario to Plutus. Come on; you, Sir, first and foremost, tell us who you are,[17] or Consequences will follow. (*Laying his stick on* Plutus's *Shoulder.*)

Chrem. [18] It behoves you to speak to him immediately.

SCENE II.

Plutus, Cario, Chremylus.

Plutus. I then desire much Grief may attend thee.

Cario. Do you understand, Sir, whom he declares himself to be?

Chrem. It is to you, not me he speaks thus: for you questioned the Gentleman in an aukward and rude manner. (To *Plutus*) But Sir, if you delight in the Behaviour of[19] a Gentleman, declare yourself to me.

---

[15] *The Plainest.*] This Word which is here used in the Superlative Degree, seems to be retorted by *Cario* on his Master, for the Reason mentioned in our last Note but one.

[16] *That your Son should pursue.*] 'Nothing can be smarter, *says Madam* Dacier, than this Explanation of the Oracle. *Apollo* had order *Chremylus* to carry home with him the first Person he met: And as there were then no others but Caitiffs to be found, *Cario* draws this just Consequence, that the God had ordered him to follow the Torrent, and to educate his Son in the Manners then in vogue, The Scholiasts, says she, have not well comprehended all the Fineness of this Passage.'

[17] *Or consequences.*] This is the true Meaning of the *Greek*, and agreeable to the best Commentators, The *French* and the *English* Translators have dropt the Humour of the Original without any reason.[44]

[18] *It behoves you.*] Mr. *Theobald* hath addressed this Speech to *Cario* erroneously.[45]

[19] *A Gentleman.*] The *Greek* is *a Man who hath regard to his Oath.* In opposition to those scandalous Fellows, who are afterwards lash'd in this Play, the Informers and their Witnesses. The *Athenians* in common with the other *Greeks*, had so religious a Regard to an Oath, that Perjury was the most base and infamous Imputation with which any Character could be aspersed.[46] Ἔνορκον is the *Honnête Homme* of

---

[44] HF's criticism seems unwarranted. In Loeb (lines 56–7), Cario indeed threatens: 'Hallo, you sirrah, tell me who you are, | Or take the consequence! Out with it, quick!' But—after interjecting the stage direction: '*Laying his Stick on* Plutus's *Shoulder*' and moving Plutus' retort to open Scene ii—HF, without warrant from the text, follows Theobald in assigning Cario's final command ('Out with it, quick!') to Chremylus.

[45] Both Loeb and Sommerstein give the speech ('Out with it, quick!') to Cario.

[46] To his burlesque of Juvenal's Satire VI, published a year later in the *Miscellanies* (1743), HF would add the following footnote directing the reader to this note in *Plutus*: 'They [the Greeks] were so infamous

Plutus. I then declare, I wish much Wailing may attend thee.

Cario. The Gentleman, and the Omen, Sir, are both your own.

Chrem. By *Ceres*,[20] no Joy shall ever attend thee: for, if thou dost not unfold thyself, to a miserable End will I bring thee, thou miserable Wretch.

Plutus. Good Gentlemen, depart from me, I beseech you.

Chrem. No, by no Means.

Cario. Odso![21] Master, I will tell you the best Method in the World to deal with him, I will put this Fellow to the most execrable End imaginable: for, having led him up to the Top of some Precipice, there leaving him, away go I———that tumbling from thence, the Gentleman———may break his Neck.

Chrem. Away with him then immediately.

(Cario lays hold on Plutus.)

Plutus. O by no Means!

Chrem. Will you not tell then?

Plutus. Ay, but if you should know who I am, I am certain, you will still do me some Mischief, and not dismiss me.

Chrem. Not we, by all the Gods, if you will but———

Plutus. Take your Hands off from me.

Cario. There, you are at your Liberty.

Plutus. Hear me, then: for, it seems I must discover what I had so firmly resolved to conceal. Know then that I am PLUTUS.

Chrem. Of thou most accursed of all Mortals. What! Art thou *Plutus*, and wouldst thou conceal thyself?

Cario. What! you, *Plutus*? in such a miserable Pickle———O *Phoebus*, *Apollo*, and O ye Gods! and O ye Dæmons, and O *Jupiter*!———How say you! And art thou He indeed?[47]

Plutus. Indeed.

Chrem. What! He himself.

---

the *French*, a *Gentleman*. M. *Dacier* translates it *Homme de bien*.

[20] *No Joy*, &c.] The Compliment of Salutation among the *Greeks*, was to give one another Joy; but *Plutus* had wished Grief and Wailing only to attend *Chremylus* and *Cario*, to which *Chremylus* alludes in this Speech.

[21] *Master, I will tell you the best Method.*] Our Translation is literal, and there is great Humour in *Cario*'s pretending to have found out some extraordinary Method to make *Plutus* discover himself, and afterwards proposing to break his Neck. Madam *Dacier* hath dropt this. Mr. *Theobald* hath introduced in its stead a Facetiousness which I do not understand.———I will make the Devil go to the Wood with his Reverence.

---

for Perjury, that to have Regard to an Oath was a great Character among them, and sufficient to denote a Gentleman' (*Miscellanies* i, p. 87 n. 2). In *The Covent-Garden Journal*, No. 12 (11 February 1752), HF quotes Juvenal's Satire X to illustrate the notorious mendacity of the Greek historians (p. 86 and n. 1).

[47] 'O *Phoebus*, *Apollo* . . . art thou He indeed?': both Loeb (lines 80–2) and Sommerstein assign this speech to Chremylus.

Plutus. The very self-same He.

Chrem. Tell me then, whence comes it that thou art in[22] this dirty Condition?

Plutus. I come, Sir, from the House of one[23] *Patroclus*, who hath never been at the Expence of washing himself, from his Mother's Womb.

Chrem. But pray tell me, how came you by this Misfortune in your Eyes.

Plutus. *Jupiter*, out of Envy to Mankind, afflicted me thus: for, when I was a little Boy, I threatned, that I would only visit the just, and the wise, and the modest among them; whereupon he struck me with Blindness, that I might not distinguish those from others. To such a Degree doth this God envy good Men!

Chrem. And yet it is by the Good and Just only that he is honoured.

Plutus. I agree with you.

Chrem. Well, Sir, and if you should be restored to your Sight, would you now avoid the Habitations of the Wicked?

Plutus. I do promise it.

Chrem. And you would frequent the Just?

Plutus. Most certainly: for it is a long While since I have seen them.

Chrem. No Wonder, truly: for neither have I, who have my Eyes, seen any such lately.

Plutus. Well: now dismiss me; since you know every thing concerning me.

Chrem. No, by *Jupiter*, we will stick so much the closer to you.

Plutus. Did I not say, you would be troublesome to me?

Chrem. Be prevailed on, I beseech you, and forsake me not: for should you seek him never so diligently, you will not find an honester Man. No, by *Jupiter*, will you not;[24] for, indeed, there is no other honest Man besides myself.

---

[22] *This dirty Condition.*] *Aristophanes* here alludes to the Dirtiness of *Plutus*'s Person, and not to his Dress, as Madam *Dacier* hath in her Translation, and her Note on this Place would understand it.[48] This is plain from the Reason which he himself presently assigns, *viz.* that he could get no Water to wash himself; besides, the *Greek* Word signifies properly Drowth, Dirt for want of washing.

[23] *Patroclus.*] He was a very rich *Athenian*, and so sordid that he was frequently upbraided with it by his Acquaintance; on which Occasions he answered, that he *lived after the manner of the Lacedemonians*, whose Plainness and Temperance was proverbial in all *Greece*. The *Greek* Words literally translated, are, *who never washed from the time of his Birth*. One of the Commentators would have it, that the Poet insinuates the Dirt and Nastiness of this Fellow to be as it were innate.[49] But probably he meant no more, than that he never allowed himself a Bagnio; these were so universally used and so extremely cheap at *Athens*, that a total Abstinence of them must have indicated the last Degree of Avarice.

[24] *For indeed, there is no other.*] This is truly Comic, and displays a Vanity in *Chremylus*, with which a good Actor would not fail to charm an Audience.

---

[48] In a note Mme Dacier explains that since valets always judge persons by their clothes, Cario can't understand how one dressed in such '*méchant équipage*' could be the God of Riches (p. 96).

[49] Girardus (note to line 85): 'Aristophanes wants to indicate a congenital, innate avarice so deep in those like Patroclus that going to the bath has not been their custom since they were born' (trans. Baker): Küster, 'Notae in Plutum', p. 21.

Plutus. Ay, all of you say this: but when once you have Possession of me, and are become rich, you throw off the Mask, and grow rampant in Iniquity.

Chrem. It is indeed too commonly so: yet all Men are not Villains.

Plutus. Yes, by *Jove*, every Mother's Son of you.

Cario aside.[25] You shall roar aloud for this, Sir.

Chrem. That you may know then how many Advantages you will enjoy under my Roof, only lend me your Attention, and I will make you sensible. I flatter myself, indeed, I flatter myself, (with the Assistance of Heaven be it spoken) that I shall deliver you from this Infirmity of your Eyes, and restore you to perfect Sight.

Plutus. Indeed you shall not: for I have no Desire to see any more.

Cario. What doth the Fellow say! This is a miserable Dog in his own Nature.

Plutus. Should *Jupiter*, who so well knows the Follies of Mankind, hear I had recovered my Sight, he would pound me in a Mortar.

Chrem. Doth he less to you now, who suffers you to stroll about stumbling in this manner?

Plutus. I know not what he may do: but I dread him exceedingly.

Chrem. Indeed, thou art the greatest Coward of all Deities. Do you think the Power of *Jupiter*, and all his Thunderbolts, would be of a[26] *Triobolus* Consequence to you, if you could once recover your Sight, tho' it were for never so little Time.

Plutus. O miserable Wretch! utter not such Things.

Chrem. Be under no Concern: for I will demonstrate that your Power is much greater than that of *Jupiter*.

Plutus. [27] You demonstrate this of me!

Chrem. Yes, by Heavens! Instantly will I. By whose Means doth *Jupiter* reign over the Gods?

Cario. By the Means of Money: for he hath the most of it.

Chrem. Well, and who furnishes him with these Means?

Cario. This honest Gentleman here.

Chrem. And through whom do Men sacrifice to *Jupiter*————Is it not through him there?

---

[25] *You shall roar, &c.*] The Offence which *Cario*, a rascally Slave, takes at the universal Satire of *Plutus*, is extremely pleasant.

[26] Triobolus.] About a Groat of our Money. As the Scene is in *Athens*, we thought proper not to export our own Coin thither.

[27] *You demonstrate this of me.*] The literal Translation would be *Me, you!* a Conciseness in that Language inimitable in ours.

Cario. Ay, by *Jupiter,* for they[28] pray aloud for Riches.

Chrem. Most certainly he is the Cause, and if he pleased, could easily put an End to their Sacrifices.

Pluto. How so, pray?

Chrem. Because no Man could offer[29] an Ox, nor even a Barley-Cake, no, nor any other Thing, without your good Pleasure.

Pluto. How!

Chrem. [30] How! Why, he will not know how to purchase any thing; unless you are present, and give him the Money: So that if the Power of *Jupiter* be offensive to you, you alone will be able to demolish it.

Pluto. How say you? Do Men sacrifice to him through me?

Chrem. [31] I do say so. And by *Jupiter!* if there is any thing[32] splendid, or beautiful, or lovely among Men, it proceeds from you; for[33] to Money all Things pay Obedience.

Cario. Even I myself, for a small Piece of Money, am become a Slave:[34] because I was not so rich as some People.

[28] *Pray aloud.*] Here seems to be a Beauty in this Passage, which hath escaped Madam *Dacier,* and consequently Mr. *Theobald.*[50] The *Greek* Word is *aloud, openly, in express Terms. Cario,* I apprehend, means, that they are not ashamed *openly* to profess their putting up Prayers for Riches; whereas those, for Revenge on their Enemies, the Death of their Friends or Parents, or such like, are offered up more privately and secretly. With this agrees *the Aperto vivere voto of Persius.*[51]

[29] *An Ox nor a Barley-cake.*] Madam *Dacier* and Mr. *Theobald* add a Sheep, which I should not have mentioned but for their remarkable Agreement in this additional Sacrifice.

[30] *How! Why, he would not know how.*] In this Instance, as many others, we have with great Labour and Care preserved the *Greek* Ambiguity, which may give some Pleasure to our learned Readers.

[31] *I do say so. And by* Jupiter.] This is literal; M. *Dacier* hath added, and much more. Mr. *Theobald,* ——and I tell you further.

[32] *Splendid, beautiful, or lovely.*] Literal. M. *Dacier, rien de beau & d'agreeable*; Mr. *Theobald, nothing fine or agreeable.*

[33] *To Money, &c.*] This is *verbatim.* M. Dacier, *Aujourd'hui les Richesses font tout*; Mr. Theobald, *At this day Riches alone perform all things.*

[34] *Because I was not so rich.*] This is truly in the Character of *Cario*: he insinuates, the only Difference between him and his Master lies in their Purses. I am surprised M. *Dacier* passed this by. What Mr. *Theobald* means by *redeeming* a Slave bought in the Market, I know not.[52]

---

50 Mme Dacier: 'car les hommes ne font des Sacrifices à Jupiter que pour le prier de les enrichir' (p. 11); Theobald: 'For Men only Sacrifice to *Jove,* that they may put up a Prayer for Increase of Wealth' (p. 7).

51 Persius (AD 34–62), Satire II, line 7: 'to offer prayers such as all men may hear' (Loeb).

52 HF's complaint against his predecessors seems gratuitous. Loeb (lines 147–8): 'Hence for a little filthy lucre I'm | A slave, forsooth, because I've got no wealth.' Mme Dacier renders the Greek: 'Moi, par exemple, je suis exclave à cause d'un peu d'argent que mon Maître a donné pour moi, & parce que je non suis pas riche' (p. 12); Theobald: 'This dear Person of mine is a Slave to that Man, upon account of a few scurvy Pence he gave for me, and because I had not as many to redeem my self' (p. 8).

Chrem. They say too of[35] the *Corinthian* Courtesans, that, if a poor Lover attacks them, they will not even lend him an Ear: but when a rich Lover presents himself before them, they will themselves present any thing to him.[53]

Cario. They say that Boys will present too: not for the sake of their Lovers, but of Money.

Chrem. You speak of Prostitutes, not the worthier Sort: for those never ask for Money.

Cario: Why, what do these ask for?

Chrem. One will accept a fine Horse, another a Pack of Hounds.

Cario. O then it is probable they are ashamed to ask for the Money: they are pleased to cover their Iniquity with the Name of a Present.

Chrem. [36] All Arts, all Crafts known amongst Mankind, are invented

---

[35] *The* Corinthian *Courtesans.*] There was, according to *Strabo*,[54] at *Corinth* a Temple dedicated to *Venus*, in which were contained more than a thousand Women, who were prostituted to all Persons who would come up to their Prices, which at last grew so exorbitant, that it became proverbial. *Every Man is not capable of going to* Corinth. There are many Names of the more Famous remembred; but none equal to *Lais*, whose Story is well known. Perhaps there is something in this Passage, which the Commentators have not well understood; but which we shall be excused from explaining. Madam *Dacier* hath shewn great Art in her Translation of this Place. Mr. *Theobald* hath thought proper to change the Scene into *Drury-Lane*;[55] facetiously enough, perhaps, if we all him that Liberty.

[36] *All Arts, all Crafts*] The curious Reader may, perhaps, have some Pleasure in seeing the Trades in Use among the *Athenians*: The judicious one, and who is well versed in Human Nature, will not fail to observe how ingeniously our Poet hath blended all the Means of acquiring Riches together, whence we may conjecture that the fair Traders of his Days were not so honest as those of ours. As for Mr. *Theobald*, he hath here thought proper entirely to quit his Author; we shall, therefore, at present, quit him. The Conjecture of Madam *Dacier*, on the Action in this Place, is too pretty to be omitted. 'There is, *says she*, something more in this Speech of *Chremylus*, than the Translators and Scholiast have perceived. Under Pretence of running through the different Trades and Occupations of Men, he points with his Finger at certain Persons among the Spectators, whom he taxes with Theft, and whom he accuses of being caught in Adultery, and suffering a very severe Penance for it.'

---

[53] Cf. *The Vernoniad* (1741), where, expatiating in a note on Mammon's [Walpole's] regret that no 'Man will ever kiss my——again', HF cites *Plutus* (line 155 [for 152]), commenting: '*Aristophanes* shews us, that the *Corinthian* Ladies were wont to present another Part [than their mouth] to their Lovers. . . . And this too it seems was a very particular Favour, and conferr'd only on their rich Favourites' (*Champion*, p. 568 n. [33]).

[54] Strabo (*c*.63 BC–AD 24), *Geographica*, VIII. vi. 20; a copy of the 1707 edition was in HF's library (Ribbles S62). HF obviously enjoyed the story of Lais and the thousand Corinthian prostitutes of the fourth century BC, whose prices were so exorbitant they inspired the proverb HF recalls in this note: '*Every Man is not capable of going to* Corinth.' HF first found a place for it in *The Champion* (28 February 1739/40), pp. 208–9; and later in *The True Patriot*, No. 28 (6–13 May 1746), p. 288, and *The Covent-Garden Journal*, No. 2 (7 January 1752), p. 20. And for the second edition of *Joseph Andrews* (II. iv), which was published less than a fortnight after his and Young's translation of *Plutus*, HF contrived to have Young's surrogate, Parson Adams, exclaim at the shameless behaviour of Leonora: 'She must have then more than *Corinthian* Assurance . . . ay, more than *Lais* herself' (p. 113).

[55] Mme Dacier's elegant version: 'si un homme, qui n'a quere de bien, va chez les Courtisanes de Corynthe, elles ne l'écoutent pas seulement; mais que si un Partisan les aborde, il n'y a point de caresses qu'elles ne lui fassent' (p. 12). Theobald's rendition, in which the courtesan becomes 'a Side-box Mistress' (p. 8), evokes a common scene of flirtation at Drury Lane Theatre.

through thee. One sits down, and cuts out Leather; another hammers out
Brass, a third hammers up Wainscot, and a fourth casts the Gold he hath
received from thee. This filches away Clothes from the public Bagnio,
another breaks open Houses. One cleans Cloth, another skins, another tanns
them; one deals in Onions: Nay, through thee, that Gallant, when surprized
with another Man's Wife, is[37] stripped as naked as when he was born.

Plutus. Unhappy Wretch that I am! I never knew a Syllable of all this
before.

Chrem. to *Cario.* Doth not the mighty Emperor of *Persia* owe all his
Splendor to this Person?

Cario. Are not all[38] public Assemblies called together through him?

Chrem. What! dost not thou[39] man our Gallies? answer me.

Cario. Doth not he maintain the[40] foreign Troops in *Corinth.*

Chrem. Will not[41] *Pamphilus* owe many a Groan to thee?

Cario. And will not[42] *Belonopoles* together with *Pamphilus*?

[37] *Stripped.*] The *Greek* here alludes to a particular Punishment for this Crime, which we could not
literally translate into *English.*[56]
[38] *Public Assemblies.*] Parliaments in Mr. *Theobald*: It hath been disputed whether these were derived
from the *Saxons* or *Normans*; but Mr. *Theobald* hath now first shewn that they came from the *Athenians.*
[39] *Man our Gallies.*] In their Naval Wars their Gallies were commanded by the Rich, who were obliged
at their own Expence to man them.
[40] *Foreign Troops in Corinth.*] The *Athenians* were at this time engaged in Alliance with the *Corinthians*,
and Others, against the *Lacedemonians*, they supplied their Allies with Money instead of Men; for which
they are likewise accused by *Demosthenes.*[57]
[41] Pamphilus.] He was a rich Usurer at *Athens*, who had been in public Office, and robbed the Treasury;
of which being convicted, his Goods were confiscated: but the *Greek* Verb is, as we have translated it, in
the Future Tense; and it is a Denunciation of a future Judgment against him by the Poet. It is more than
probable that he might be detected, and under Prosecution at the Time of this Comedy. Madam *Dacier*
therefore, and her *English* Follower, have departed from the Original, in speaking of the Punishment of
Pamphilus as of a Thing already past.
[42] Belonopoles.] The Agent or Parasite of *Pamphilus.*

[56] In *The Covent-Garden Journal*, No. 67 (21 October 1752), HF refers to a particular 'corporal'
punishment at Athens for the 'Crime' of adultery that 'was a Mixture both of Pain and Shame' (p. 355). In
his note, Bertrand Goldgar explains that the Greek word means 'plucking out hair'; he describes the
punishment, quoting HF's source, John Potter's *Archaeologiae Graecae*, ii (1699), pp. 328–9: 'having
pluck'd off the Hair from their Privities, they threw hot Ashes upon the Place, and thrust up a *Radish*,
Mullet, or some such thing into their Fundament' (Goldgar, p. 355 n. 1). On Potter, whom HF cites
frequently in the notes to *Plutus*, see below, p. 280 n. 89.
[57] In his *First Philippic*, 24, Demosthenes, recalling that the Athenians had supplemented their own
forces by supplying Corinth, their allies, with mercenary troops in what proved to be a successful war
against the Lacedaemonians, warned them now against their present unsuccessful policy of relying
exclusively on mercenaries against Philip. HF's first readers would be reminded of the Opposition's
warnings against the pro-Hanoverian policy of Carteret, who was draining the public treasury by, as
Chesterfield complained, 'taking no less than *sixteen* THOUSAND HANOVERIANS into *British* Pay' (*The
Case of the Hanover Forces in the Pay of Great-Britain, Impartially and freely examined: with some Season-
able Reflections on the Present* [1742], p. 2). HF would later take the Opposition's position in his satires
Some Papers proper to be Read before the R[oya]l Society (February 1743) and *An Attempt towards a Natural
History of the Hanover Rat* (1744), which I take to be by HF; for the text, see *Champion*, pp. 657–68.

Chrem. Is it not through him that we support the F—ts of[43] *Argyrius?*
Cario. Ay, Sir, and is it not through him that we support the Stories
of[44] *Philepsius?*
Chrem. Do we not through thee send[45] Auxiliaries to the *Aegyptians?*

[43] Argyrius.] A rich *Athenian*, so insolent with his Wealth, that he used to indulge himself in all
Indecencies, and particularly that here mentioned. This is a fine Stroke on the *Athenians* for their mean
Submission to any Insult in their rich Men.

[44] *The Stories of* Philepsius.] The *Greek* is simply, Doth not *Philepsius*, through thee, tell Stories?
Philepsius says M. Dacier, *after having ruined himself by his Debauches, was at last reduced to tell Stories for his
Livelihood.* Mr. *Theobald* hath rendred this Note literally, and both in their Translations have understood
the Original in this Sense. The Scholiast and the Commentators all coincide with this Interpretation. We
have, however, ventured to give it another Turn. Had *Philepsius* been able to get his Livelihood in this
extraordinary Manner, he must have been excellent in his Way, and a properer Subject of Panegyric than
Satire. Besides, such a beggarly Instance would have been very improper to set forth the great Power of
Plutus, and very disagreeable to all the others; to omit the Anticlimax between the Example of *Argyrius* and
this of *Philepsius*. The Truth is, *Suidas*[58] seems to be the Ringleader of this Mistake, who, from no other
Authority than that of this single Line in *Aristophanes*, hath (*More suo*)[59] given us a short History of this
Person, who is, he says, mentioned by *Demosthenes* in his Oration against *Timocrates*.[60] Now the Account
given us by *Demosthenes* is, that he was a very considerable Person, and imprisoned for his ill Administration of the Affairs of the Republic. He mentions *Argyrius* in the same Place, and gives a very different
Character of him from that given by the Commentators and Translators of our Author. *Aristophanes*,
therefore, means in this Place, that People attended to the silly Stories of this wealthy Man, in order to get
a Supper, or some other Reward; that they submitted to the impertinent and tiresome Repetitions of
Philepsius, for the same Reason as to the Insolence of *Argyrius*. A very pregnant Satire, by which his
Stories are represented as more worthless and noisome than a F—t. This Custom of treating their
Acquaintance with the Repetition of their own Works, so common in *Athens* and *Rome*, is bitterly
inveighed against by many Classic Authors, particularly *Horace, Juvenal* and *Martial*.[61]

[45] *Auxiliaries to the* Egyptians.] The *Greek* Scholiast is very uncertain to what Fact the Poet alludes.[62]
He gives us our choice of four, not one of which was, as I apprehend, a true one. For as to *Amasis*, to omit
that he lived too long before the time of this Play, can we believe that *Aristophanes* would have thought
their sending for Corn in a time of Dearth, was any just Cause of Satire? The same Objection lies against
Psammitichus. The Objection of Antiquity holds good likewise against his third and fourth Conjectures.
Madam *Dacier*, and her literal Translator Mr. *Theobald*, have, in their learned Notes on this Place, been
misled into applying this Satire to a Transaction, which, as they say, happen'd 65 Years before:[63] a Method
very inconsistent with the Freedom of our Author. The Truth is, as the learned *Kuster* hath given us from
Palmerius, the Person here inveighed against, 'was *Chabrias*, who, *at that time*, without public Authority
had been induced, by the Greatness of the Presents made him by *Nectanebus* King of the *Aegyptians*, to

---

[58] '*Suidas*': The name of a Greek lexicon of the tenth century. HF's personal copy was *Suidae Lexicon*
(Cambridge, 1705), 3 vols. in Greek and Latin, ed. Ludolf Küster (1670–1716) (Ribbles S73); Baker cites
vol. iii, p. 599. HF cites *Suidas* in the head note to *The Vernoniad* (1741); it may also be HF's source in *The
Covent-Garden Journal*, No. 2 (7 January 1752), p. 20 n. 4.

[59] See p. 262 n. 35.

[60] Demosthenes, *Against Timocrates*, 134, where Philepsius of Lamptra, once known as a good man, is
imprisoned for malfeasance.

[61] Horace, *Ars Poetica*, 419–21, 472–6; *Satires*, I. iv. 78. Juvenal, *Satires*, i. 1–18. Martial, *Epigrams*, III.
xliv, VIII. lxxvi.

[62] Cf. Sommerstein's comment on *Plutus*, line 178: 'this passage, and its scholia, are our sole source for
the making of such an alliance at this time [cf. also Loeb, p. 379 n. c]. . . . In what sense this alliance is
being said to have been made "because of Wealth" is not clear; the scholia say that the Egyptians sent
Athens a large gift of corn, but their inability to distinguish between the fourth century and the sixth (they
name the Egyptian king Amasis or Psammetichus, and in one place the Persian king is identified as
Cambyses) does not inspire confidence here' (p. 148).

[63] Theobald, p. 9.

Cario. Is not[46] *Nais* through thee enamoured of[47] *Philonides?*
Chrem. Nay,[48] the Tower of *Timotheus.*————

strike up an Alliance with that King, and to assist him against *Artaxerxes*; on which account, *Artaxerxes* having complained to the *Athenians*, *Chabrias* was recalled by a public Decree.[64] *Cornelius Nepos* tells us, that a certain Day was prefixed for his Return, which if he did not observe, they threatned to condemn him to Death. On these Threats, he returned to *Athens*, but staid there no longer than was necessary; *for his splendid Living, and the Liberties in which he indulged himself, were regarded with an evil Eye, and created him the Envy of his Fellow-Citizens.*[65] This therefore was a very popular Subject for *Aristophanes* to fall upon, and his Satire must have been received with the greatest Applause by the Audience. *Chabrias* was Archon seven Years before this Play was acted.

[46] *Nais.*] The Original is *Lais*, which the Translators have all preserved; but the true Reading is *Nais*, who was likewise a Courtesan of *Corinth*, and whose Age very well agrees with the Time of this Play.[66] And this Mr. *Petit*[67] recommends from *Athenaeus*. The famous *Lais* was at this time no more than fourteen Years old; and tho' it is probable she was early enough in her Iniquity, we can hardly suppose her to have been then so famous a Harlot, that her Fame at *Athens* could be public enough to be used as the most eminent Example of her Profession. Mr. *Bayle*[68] agrees with *Athenaeus*, and suppose this *Nais* to have been the Courtesan with whom *Euripides* had his Conversation.

[47] *Philonides.*] He was an ugly and ignorant Fellow, but wealthy, and the Subject of much Invective. *Phyllius* says of him, alluding to his gigantic Size, that his Mother was a Camel. *Theopompus* will have him to have been born of an Ass.[69] It was likewise proverbially said, that such a one was more ignorant than *Philonides.*

[48] *The Tower of* Timotheus.] *Timotheus* was an *Athenian* General,[70] who, from his extraordinary Successes, became so much the Object of Envy, that he was exposed by the Painters in a sleeping Posture, with Fortune standing by him, and driving Cities into his Net. *Timotheus*, with true Greatness

---

[64] Küster, Latin commentary to line 178, pp. 3–4.

[65] Cornelius Nepos (*c*.99–*c*.24 BC), Roman historian and biographer. HF refers to his *De Viris Illustribus*, XII. iii. In *Joseph Andrews* (I. i, p. 6) and *Jonathan Wild* (I. i; *Miscellanies* iii, p. 8) HF, in a similar context, refers to Nepos in the company of Plutarch.

[66] Sommerstein has 'Nais' in the Greek text; Loeb, 'Lais'. Citing from the third-century Greek anecdotalist Athenaeus' *Deipnosophistai* (xiii. 592c–d), who cites 'a passage from Lysias' lost speech *Against Philonides* (Lys, fr. 82) in which it is stated that Philonides "says he is in love" with a courtesan named *Nais*', Sommerstein comments, 'it is easier to suppose that *ΝΑΙΣ* was early corrupted into *ΔΝΑΙΣ* in Aristophanes' text than to suppose that Philonides successively courted the only two top-class *hetairai* in Corinth who had almost identical names!' (p. 148 n. 179).

[67] The French scholar Samuel Petit (1594–1643). In his *Miscellaneorum* (Paris, 1630) he rendered in Latin the remarks of Athenaeus (above, n. 66) on Lais.

[68] Pierre Bayle (1647–1706), French rationalist philosopher and author of *Dictionnaire historique et critique* (1696–1702). A copy of the fifth edition (5 vols.; Amsterdam, 1734) was in HF's library (Ribbles B13). In his article 'Lais' (sect. s), Bayle recalls the anecdote of the courtesan's impudent conversation with Euripides: Lais asked the great dramatist what he meant by a line about 'a man who does filthy actions'; he answered her, '*You your self are one of those I mean.* She fell a laughing, and quoted a verse in which he said, that an action was not filthy, unless he who did it thought it so.' In his comment on the story Bayle reasoned that it could not have been Lais who made the clever retort because she was too young at the time (15 or 16), and had never been at the court of Archelaus, where Euripides resided. Referring to the passage in *Plutus*, which was acted at a time when Lais was not yet famous, Bayle remarks: 'The difficulty will vanish, if it be supposed, that it ought to be read Nais, and not Lais in that play . . . Perhaps it was with Nais, that Euripides entered into discourse' (*Dictionary Historical and Critical*, 2nd edn., 5 vols. [1734–8], iii, p. 705 [s]). HF had earlier drawn on Bayle's article on Lais in another context (*Champion* [28 February 1739/40], p. 208). His earliest reference to Bayle's *Dictionary* occurs in the revised version of the *Author's Farce* (1734), II. iv (*Plays*, p. 325). See also *Common Sense* (21 May 1737) in *Champion*, p. 3; *Champion* (14 February 1739/40), p. 178; *Tom Jones* (IV. xiii, p. 202); and *Amelia* (XII. iii, p. 504).

[69] This description paraphrases Girardus, line 179 (Küster, p. 5).

[70] HF, referring to Plutarch's *Lives* ('Sulla', vi. 5), without naming Timotheus (*fl.* 378–354 BC), alludes to this story in *The Champion* (6 December 1739); see p. 45 and n. 2.

Cario. O[49] may it fall on thy Head.

Chrem. Are not all Matters, in short, transacted through thee? For thou art the whole and sole Author of all Things whether evil or good[71]————— Assure yourself, Sir, you are.

Cario. This I am sure of————that in all Battles they obtain the Victory, into whose Scale this Gentleman throws himself.

Plutus. What I! who am but one; can I effect such might matters?

Chrem. Can you! Ay, by *Jupiter*, and many more too: For no man ever had his Fill of thee; of all other Things we may be[50] surfeited: Even with Love.

Cario. With Bread.

Chrem. With[51] Poetry.

Cario. With[52] Sweetmeats.

Chrem. With Honour.

Cario. With Cheese-cakes.

Chrem. With Bravery.

Cario. With Figs.

Chrem. With Glory.

---

of Mind, eluded their Malevolence, by saying, If I take such Cities in my Sleep, what do ye think I can do when I am awake? He built a Tower of a stupendous Height, which he boasted he had raised without the Assistance of Fortune; an Affront which that Deity so highly resented, that whereas she had been formerly represented to have held frequent Conversations with him in Person, she entirely forsook him, and never appeared to him more. By this Allegory perhaps we may understand, that he impoverished himself by the vast Expences laid out on this Work; the Vanity of which is probably here objected to him by the Poet.

[49] *May fall.*] This Freedom of *Cario* with his Master must be accounted for from the Chaplet, which we before remark'd to have been his Protection. Madam *Dacier's* Conjecture on this Interruption by the Slave, is very ingenious. Perhaps, says she, this Tower was the Prison in which the *Athenian* Slaves were confined, when they had committed any roguish Actions, and deserved Chastisement; which contributed not a little to the Pleasantry of this Passage.

[50] *Surfeited.*] The *Greek* is *sated.* Madam Dacier, *lasse*; *Mr.* Theobald, *weary*.

[51] *Poetry.*] M. *Dacier* speaks, I apprehend, too generally, where she says, that the *Greeks*, by the Word Μουσικῆς, mean the Liberal Arts.[72] The Antients opposed the *Artes Musicae,* or *Canorae,* to the *Artes Mutae.* In the first, they included Music, Oratory, Poetry, &c. In the latter, Grammar, Geometry, and other Sciences. And this appears clearly by *Socrates,* in *Plato's Phaedon, Sect. 4.* Indeed the Word is sometimes used in a more general Sense, and Ἄμουσος signifies commonly illiterate; but the purer and more confined Sense is only to the *Artes Canorae;* and these must be meant here; for the Sentiment is not otherwise just, since no Man can be surfeited with *Learning,* as Mr. *Theobald* hath rendred the *Belles Lettres of Dacier.*

[52] *Sweetmeats.*] What was brought to the Table at the end of the Entertainment; the *Greek* Scholiast calls it the Desert. The Old Woman, in the Fourth Act of this Play, says, she sent her Lover a Cake and other Sweetmeats. *M.* Dacier, *Confitures*; *Mr.* Theobald, *Sugar-Plumbs.* By which we may observe, how much the Palate of these Translators agrees.

---

[71] In *The Vernoniad,* in a note to lines describing Mammon, HF quotes this description from Aristophanes' *Plutus* (*Champion,* p. 579 n. [60]), translating: '*Thou art the* onliest *Cause of all Good or Evil.*'

[72] The Greek (line 189) that HF translates 'Poetry', Mme Dacier, 'belles Lettres' (p. 15), and Theobald, 'Learning' (p. 10), is in Loeb, 'literature' and in Sommerstein, 'culture'.

Cario. With[53] Hasty-Pudding.

Chrem. With the Command of Armies.

Cario. With[54] Pease-Porridge.

Chrem. Whereas of thee none ever had his Fill: For when any one hath acquired thirteen Talents, he becomes the more desirous of acquiring sixteen; and when he hath compassed these, he then desires forty; and if he fails in his last Wish, he complains he hath none of the Comforts of Life.

Plutus. You seem to me to speak very well; I apprehend only one thing.

Chrem. Tell me what.

Plutus. How I shall be able to[55] retain the Possession of this Power, which you represent me to have.

Chrem. By *Jove*, you need not fear it: but indeed, all Men agree that thou art a most[56] timorous Animal.

[53] *Hasty-Pudding.*] A Dish, saith *Erasmus*, composed of Wheat-Flower, in so great Request, that it gave occasion to a Proverb, whereby they reproached any one with dainty Living.[73] *M.* Dacier, *Bouillie*; *Mr.* Theobald, *Boil'd Beef.*

[54] *Pease-Porridge.*] The *Greek* is *boiled Lentils*, or Lentil-Broth. *Mr.* Theobald, *Stew'd Cabbage.* The Scholiast remarks that Contrast which the Poet hath here introduced between the Tastes of the Master and Slave; for while the one contemplates Love, Honour, &c. the Slave hath no regard but to his Belly. This is obvious to a very indifferent Reader; but there is here a more latent Beauty, and which still more humourously exposes the Grossness of the latter; for whereas *Chremylus* rises in a regular Climax from Love and Poetry to Military Glory, the highest Honour among the *Greeks*, the Slave, in as direct an Anticlimax, comes from Bread, Sweet-meats, Cheese-cakes, &c. down to Pease-Porridge, the greatest of Dainties in his Opinion.

[55] *Retain the Possession.*] In the *Greek*, *to become Master, Proprietor of.* M. Dacier, *Je crains fort de n'avoir jamais cet pouvoir*; *M.* Theobald, *I strongly suspect I shall never have this Power.* But *Plutus* had agreed with them before that he had it; his Fear therefore was how to retain it; and this is agreeable to the *Greek* Phrase, and to all that follows.

[56] *Timorous Animal.*] The Word is here in the Neuter Gender, as being more contemptuous; so *Virgil*:

———*Varium & mutabile semper*
Fœmina———

Which Mr. *Dryden* observes, is the severest Reflexion which hath been ever made on the Fair Sex.[74] M. *Dacier* says, the Scholiast reports this Verse from a *Comic* Poet; but indeed the *Comic* Poet mentioned

[73] '*Hasty-Pudding*': translates μάϛης (line. 192); Loeb has 'Barley-meal' and Sommerstein, 'barley-cake'. Erasmus' *Adagia* (Proverbs), citing Aristophanes' *Knights*, gives the following in Latin: 'Mazam pinsuit a me pistam' ('He baked the sponge cake I kneaded'), i.e. referring to one who takes credit for another's labours. Erasmus concludes in Latin: 'Maza cibi genus est ex lacte & farina, fermē panis instar confectumj' ('Maze is a kind of food confected from milk and meal into something almost like bread'). (*Collected Works of Erasmus*, trans. R. A. B. Mynors [Toronto, 1982], xxxiv: *Adages*, p. 129.)

[74] Cf. *Amelia* (x. i), where Dr Harrison, in an exchange with Mrs Atkinson, reminds her of a famous passage from Virgil's *Aeneid* (iv. 569–70): 'Varium et mutabile semper Foemina', which Dryden translated 'Woman's a various and a changeful Thing' (iv. 820), remarking that the Latin 'is the sharpest Satire in the fewest words that was ever made on Womankind; for both the Adjectives are Neuter, and *Animal* must be understood, to make them Grammar' (*Works of Virgil* [1697], sig. (c)3). In *A Journey from This World to the Next* (1. x) Julian recalls his incarnation as a slave, when he was abused by a maidservant 'who never called me by any other Names than those of *the Thing* and *the Animal*' (*Miscellanies* ii, p. 48). The verse Chremylus quotes (line 203) is from Euripides' *Phoenissae*, line 597: translating the line in *Plutus*, Loeb and Sommerstein have, respectively, 'Wealth is the cowardliest thing', 'the most cowardly thing'.

Plutus. Not in the least. This is no more than the Scandal of a House-breaker, who, when he had stolen into a House, and found every thing so cautiously locked up, that he was able to carry off no Booty; he, forsooth, called my Prudence Timidity.

Chrem. However, be under no Concern now: for, if you will but heartily enter into my Proposals, I will undertake to make you more quick-sighted[57] than *Lynceus* himself.

Plutus. But how will you be able to effect this, being but a Mortal?

Chrem. I have very good Hopes from what *Apollo* himself,[58] shaking his *Pythian* Laurel, communicated to me.

Plutus. Is he then privy to this?

Chrem. He is, I assure you.

Plutus. Be very cautious.

Chrem. Good Sir, give yourself no Trouble about it: for, be assured, tho' at the Expence of my Life, I will accomplish it.

Cario. And I promise you too, if you desire it.

Chrem. And many others will assist us, who are so honest, that they now want Bread.

Plutus. Alas! you promise me very sorry Assistants.

by the Scholiast, is *Euripides*, and the Verse mentioned is in the *Phoenissæ*, but not a Word of the Paleness of Gold.[75] I am rather apt to understand this allegorically of the Timidity of Rich Men, who are under eternal Fears of Designs against themselves and their Money; and this Allegory is extremely just and beautiful, which is well supported in the Answer of *Plutus*.

[57] *Than* Lynceus.] M. Dacier, a *Lynx*; *Mr.* Theobald, *an Eagle*. This *Lynceus* was a famous Discoverer of Mines in the Earth, which gave occasion to the Poets to feign, that his Eyes could penetrate into its Bowels, and see what was doing in the Lower World.[76]

[58] *Shaking his* Pythian *Laurel*.] The shaking the Laurel denoted the Presence of the God; according to *Callimachus*, in his Hymn to *Apollo*, and *Virgil*.

> ————*tremere omnia visa repentè,*
> *Liminaque laurusque Dei.*
> AEN. 3. ver. 90.[77]

There is something very humorous in the Endeavour of *Chremylus* to persuade *Plutus*, that *Apollo*, who presided over Physic, had communicated to him the Method of curing his Blindness, and no less Pleasantry in the Concern *Plutus* (from his Fear of *Jupiter*, which hath been mentioned before) expresses lest *Apollo* should be in the Secret.

---

[75] Dacier: 'C'estoit un proverbe … *Plutus est peureux*. Et cela revient à ce que le Scholiaste rapporte d'un Poëte Comique qui dit que l'or est pâle, parce que toute le monde lui dresse des embuches' (p. 103).

[76] *Lynceus'*: one of the Argonauts, whose eyesight was 'the sharpest of anyone on earth' (Pindar, *Nemeans*, x. 63; Apollonius Rhodius, *Argonautica*, i. 153–5). Sommerstein, p. 150 n. 210.

[77] Loeb: 'suddenly it seemed all things trembled, | the doors and laurels of the god' (*Aeneid*, iii. 90–1).

Chrem. Not at all,[59] provided you change their Circumstances, and make them rich: But, *Cario*, do thou run away with the utmost Expedition.

Cario. You will please to tell me what I am to do.

Chrem. Call hither my Brother-Farmers—you will find them, probably, in the Fields sweating at their hard Labour————bid them come hither, that every one may have his Share in this *Plutus*.

Cario. Well, I am going: but let some of your Family within take care of this[60] Beef-Steak here.

Chrem. That shall be my care—But[61] away, fly instantly—And now, *Plutus*, thou most excellent of all Deities, be pleased to go in with me; for this is the House, which you must this Day fill with Riches,[62] by all Methods whatsoever.

Plutus. Oh! Sir, I swear to you, I never enter another Man's House without the utmost Concern; for[63] I have never been dealt well with in any. If I enter the House of a Miser, he instantly buries me deep under Ground; and if a worthy Friend comes to ask him for a little Piece of Money, he

---

[59] *Provided you change their Circumstances.*] We have taken here a little Liberty with the Original, in order to give our Reader some Idea, which I think is not easy to gather from the other Translations of this Speech.[78]

[60] *Beef-Steak.*] The *Greek* Word is a Diminutive, and signifies literally a little Bit of Flesh, and is spoken contemptuously by *Cario.* This was a Piece of the Sacrifice, which the Antients used to bring home to those who did not assist at it.

[61] *Away, fly instantly.*] The Use of the Participle ἀνύσας is not to be rendered exactly in any other Language. The literal Translation here would be, *run, having dispatched it.* It may be expressed in *Latin* by *jamdudum curre*, which is more emphatical than Frischlin's *curre celeriter.*[79] M. Dacier, *cours & fais ce que je t'ai dit.* Mr. Theobald, *run and do as I have ordered you.*

[62] *By all Methods.*] The literal Translation is, *justly and unjustly.* In our Translation we have followed *Suidas*, who tells us, that the Words are not to be taken rigorously, and that they signify no more than *by every Method.*[80] M. *Dacier* says, *Chremylus* doth not speak there according to his real Sentiments; for this would not agree with the Probity of which he makes Profession; but he uses these Terms as the common Formulary of Prayers, which Men addressed to *Plutus.* This, says she, *is more beautiful than it appears at first sight. Girardus* likewise thinks this Expression foreign to the Character of *Chremylus* as we have done from *Suidas.* To say the truth, I think there is more beauty, than even M. *Dacier* herself apprehends, in this Passage. There is infinitely more Humour in suspecting the Veracity of *Chremylus* in his former Declaration, than here. But admitting that he had hitherto preserved an honest Character, there is nothing more natural than his abandoning it at this near and sudden Approach of Riches: To which we may add, that it is on his first being left *alone* with *Plutus*, and in the Rapture of his Devotion to him, that he throws off the Mask, and expresses his unbridled Eagerness to come at Wealth *by all Methods whatsoever.*

[63] *I have never been dealt well with.*] For the poor, who become rich all at once, are almost sure to fall either into excessive Prodigality, or into an extreme Avarice. *Dacier.* Nothing can be more just and fine than this Allegory.

---

[78] Dacier: 'Point du tout, si une fois ils sont riches' (p. 17); Theobald: 'Not when they shall once begin to grow rich' (p. 12).

[79] 'run quickly', Nicodemus Frischlin's Latin version of line 229 (Küster, p. 15).

[80] *Suidae Lexicon*, i, p. 587. Loeb and Sommerstein: 'by fair means or foul' (line 233).

denies me stoutly, says, that he never saw me: But, if I visit a mad-headed Fellow, I am exposed to Whores and Dice, and in a Moment turned naked out of Doors.

Chrem.[64] But you have never lighted on a moderate Man before: for my part, this was ever my Way. I rejoice in Frugality more than any Man alive; and so I do in Expence, whenever it is necessary to be expensive. But let us go in: for I am desirous that you should see my Wife, and my only Son, whom I love dearer than any thing——I mean, after you.

Plutus. I verily believe you.

Chrem. For why should any Man tell a Falshood to you?

ACT II. SCENE I.

SCENE, *The Open Country.*
C*ARIO*, C*HORUS.*

Cario. O Yes! All you that live upon[65] Grass-Sallets, as well as my Master, my good Friends, and Countrymen, and Lovers of hard Work; come,

---

[64] *But you have,* &c.] This whole Speech is admirable, and agreeable to the Character of *Chremylus,* in which there is a Mixture of Hypocrisy and Drollery. The Conclusion, in which this just and good Man professes to love his Wife and Child in Subordination to the Affection he bears for *Plutus* (or for Wealth) is a Stroke of Nature which every ordinary Reader cannot take. Had such a Sentiment dropt from one of a contrary Disposition, there would be no Humour in it; for true Humour arises from the Contention and Opposition of the Passions. Thus it is the fond, jealous and *Italian* Husband, who, in *Johnson's* Play of the *Fox*, sacrifices his *Wife* and his Honour to his Avarice.[81] The behaviour of *Chremylus* here, is an Instance of that Insight into Nature, which alone constitutes the true Comic Poet, and of which numberless Examples appear in this our Author.

[65] *Grass Sallets.*] The *Greek* Word is θύμον, Wild Thyme.[82] *M.* Dacier translates it *Onion*; which *Pliny* denies.[83] The Sense requires it should be some poor and vile Diet, whereas Onions were in much greater Repute among the *Greeks*; for *Homer* sets two of his Heroes to breakfast upon them.[84] The Scholiast calls it a worthless Plant.

---

[81] In Ben Jonson's *Volpone: or, The Fox* (1605), Corvino proposes to give his wife to Volpone in hopes of becoming his heir.

[82] Both Loeb and Sommerstein have 'thyme'. With HF's rendering this fare for the poor as 'Grass-Sallets', cf. *Joseph Andrews* (III. xiii), where the miser Peter Pounce scoffs at Parson Adams's plea for charity to the poor and hungry: 'How can any Man complain of Hunger . . . in a Country where such excellent Sallads are to be gathered in almost every Field?' (pp. 274–5).

[83] Pliny 'denies' that onions are the food of peasants: *Natural History*, XIX. xxxii. 101: 'In Egypt people swear by garlic and onions as deities in taking an oath' (Loeb).

[84] In the *Iliad* (xi. 630), Nestor brings the wounded Machaon to his tent, where his beautiful slave Hecamede serves them refreshments: 'And wholesome Garlick crown'd the sav'ry Treat' (Pope's trans., xi. 771).

come, hasten, hurry, the Time admits no Delay; it is, indeed, the very[66] Nick of Time, when your Assistance is required.

Chorus. You perceive we have been long bustling towards you with all our Might, making the best Haste in the Power of feeble old Men: But you would have me run as fast as yourself———besides, first tell me on what Account your Master hath sent for us.

Cario. I have been telling you a long time: but you don't hear me. My Master then says, that he will deliver you from that cold and comfortless Life you now lead, and make you all live pleasantly.

Chorus. What is all this? Whence doth this Fellow talk in such a manner?

Cario. Why, my good pains-taking Men, he hath brought home with him a certain old Gentleman, who is all dirty, crooked, wretched, wrinkled, bald, toothless———Nay, and by *Jupiter,* I believe he is circumcised into the Bargain.

Chorus.[67] O golden News! How say you! pray tell me, for you are proving he hath brought home a whole Heap of Money.

---

[66] *Nick of time.*] In *Greek, the Point*; alluding to the Picture of *Occasio* on the Point of a Razor.[85]

[67] *O golden News.*] M. *Dacier* hath understood this Passage as if the Chorus of Peasants had concluded from the Description given by *Cario* in his last Speech, that the old Man so brought home must have been immensely rich. Her Words are, 'By the Description which you have made of this Man, I find that he has Heaps of Gold; for, says she, in her Notes, he would say that no one would entertain such a sorry Guest, if he was not extremely rich.' This Translation and Note Mr. *Theobald* hath thought proper to embrace. I own there is something pretty enough in this Conceit; but I question whether it ever entred into the Head of *Aristophanes.* Our Translation is literal, and will not, I apprehend, convey any such Idea to the Reader. We must suppose, from many things in this Scene, that *Cario* had, before the opening it, given them Hints of his Master's Good-Fortune. Doth he not say, in the third Speech of this Scene, I have been telling you a long time?—and doth not the *Chorus* presently afterwards threaten him for imposing on them? which surely they could not have accused him of from the Description of this miserable old Man, whose Riches they could not, without the Gift of conjuring, have foretold, from what *Cario's* Words import. *Girardus,* who well knew that the *Greek* would not admit of the Construction which M. *Dacier* hath put on it, and not attending perhaps to that Method in use among the Dramatic Poets of carrying on part of the Business behind the Scenes, which *Horace* alludes to in his *Intus digna geri,*[86] hath advanced the most ridiculous

---

[85] Baker cites a relevant passage from Herodotus, *Historia,* VI. ii, where Dionysius speaks: 'Our affairs hang on the razor's edge, men of Ionia, either to be free or to be slaves.' But HF recalls 'the Picture of *Occasio*' in an iconographic tradition in emblem books that descends from Caesar Ripa's *Iconologia* (1593). The tradition, depicting 'Occasion' or 'Opportunity', is usefully explained in George Richardson's *Iconology* (1779, fig. 184, pl. XLVII), commenting on an epigram of Ausonius on '*occasio*': 'Opportunity, | Was considered by the ancients, as a divinity who presided over that *crisis or point of time* which could bring any action to a favourable conclusion. It is here represented according to Phidias the Greek sculptor, who expressed opportunity by the figure of a young woman, having a large tuft of hair on her forehead, and the hinder part bald, with wings at her feet, and a piece of drapery waving around her; with one arm leaning on a wheel, and *holding a razor in her hand; the razor denotes actual readiness to rescind or cut off every obstruction in the way*' (i, pp. 101–2; emphasis added). Among earlier examples, see R.B., *Choice Emblems Divine and Moral, Ancient and Modern* (1721), Emblem 41, pp. 161–5, where the figure stands upon the wheel and brandishes the razor.

[86] *Ars Poetica,* lines 182–3: 'what should be performed behind the scenes' (Loeb).

Cario. I think I prove that he hath brought home[68] a Heap of the Infirmities of Old-Age.

Chorus. And do you expect to escape in a whole Skin, after imposing on us thus, whilst I have this Cudgel in my Hand.

Cario. You think then that I am a Person naturally given to such Tricks; and nothing but what is stark naught, I warrant you, can come from my Mouth.

Chorus. Observe the Gravity of this Hang-Dog. Sirrah, your Shins cry out aloud for the Stocks and Fetters.

Cario.[69] Your Lot is to distribute Justice in the other World; yet you will not set out, tho' *Charon* hath delivered you your Staff.

Solution imaginable. Whence, says he, did the Chorus know this old Fellow, who was in so miserable a Condition, to have a Heap of Riches? Why, he conjectured it from no other Reason, than because *Cario* said he was an Old Man; for it is the Genius of Old Men not only to keep what they have, but to increase it more and more, &c.[87] The Exclamation, *Golden News*, is spoken ironically. We shall only add, that this Line is alluded to by *Julian* the Emperor, in an Epistle to *S. Basil.*[88]

[68] *A Heap of the Infirmities.*] This is literal from the *Greek*; and there is great Humour in the Repetition of the Word, which M. *Dacier* hath dropt, and, after her, Mr. *Theobald.* This Word in the Original, which properly signifies a Heap of Corn, is very pertinently put into the Mouth of these Rusticks.

[69] *Your Lot,* &c.] This Passage is by no means of itself intelligible to a mere *English* Reader. As the Learned Archbishop *Potter* in his excellent Discourse of the Civil Government of *Athens, Chap.* XX.[89] hath fully explained the Custom here alluded to, we shall give his Account at large in his own Words. 'The judges were chosen out of the Citizens, without Distinction of Quality; the very meanest being by Solon admitted to give their Voices in the Popular Assembly, and to determine Causes, provided they were arrived at the Age of Thirty Years, and had never been convicted of any notorious Crime.

'The Courts of Justice were Ten, besides that in *Areopagus*; four had Cognizance in Causes concerning Blood; the remaining fix of Civil Matters. These Ten Courts were all painted with Colours, from which Names were given them; and on each of them was engraven one of the ten following Letters, *A. B. Γ. Δ. E. Z. H. Θ. I. K.* Whence they are likewise called *Alpha, Beta,* &c. Such therefore of the *Athenians,* as were at leisure to hear and determine Causes, delivered in their Names, together with the Name of their Father and Borough inscribed upon a Tablet, to the *Thesmothetae,* who returned it to them with another

---

[87] Flavius Claudius Julianus (AD 331–63), known as Julian the Apostate. In 361 he was proclaimed emperor on the death of Constantine, his uncle; rejecting Christianity, he declared for Henotheistic polytheism. Friends from their student days in Athens, Julian corresponded with Basil (c.330–379), not yet a presbyter, and in 362 wrote inviting him to Constantinople. Julian opened the letter by quoting this phrase from *Plutus*: 'Oh thou whose words bring golden news' (Letter 26, *Works* [London, 1923], iii, pp. 80–1). Though Julian plays a major role in *A Journey from this World to the Next*, Bertrand Goldgar notes that this is the only other mention of him in HF's works (*Miscellanies* ii, p. xxxii n. 2).

[88] Unlike their predecessors Dacier and Theobald, HF and Young here follow the original at lines 269–70, repeating the sense of σωρὸν 'Heap [of Money]' and 'Heap [of the Infirmities of Old Age]'; they are followed by Loeb ('heap [of treasure]' and 'heap [of woes and wretchedness]'); and nearly verbatim by Sommerstein ('heap [of money]' and 'heap [of the miseries of old age]').

[89] John Potter (c.1674–1747), Archbishop of Canterbury from 1737, author of *Archaeologiae Graecae: or, The antiquities of Greece,* 2 vols. (1697–9), a copy of which was in HF's library (Ribbles P40). HF quotes from the opening paragraphs of vol. 1, ch. xx ('Of Some Other Courts of Justice'). See also above, p. 271 n. 56.

Chorus. Burst thy Guts, for an impudent Rascal as thou art, and a Cheat in Grain, that hast thus imposed on us—and hast had the Assurance not yet to tell us on what Account thy Master sent thee to call us from our Work, and made us hasten hither when we had so little Leisure, and pass by many good Herbs, without gathering any.

Cario. Well,[70] I will conceal the Matter no longer; *Plutus,* then, my good People, is the Person my Master hath brought home, *Plutus,* who will[71] make us rich.

Chorus. Indeed! and is it possible that we shall all become rich?

Cario. Ay, by the Gods, shall ye,[72] all be *Midas's,* if you can but each procure a Pair of Ass's Ears.

Chorus. How I am delighted! How I am transported, and[73] ready to dance for Joy—If all this is really true.

Tablet, whereon was inscribed the Letter of one of the Courts, as the Lot had directed. These Tablets they carried to the Crier of the several Courts signified by the Letters, who thereupon gave to every Man a Tablet inscribed with his own Name, and the Name of the Court which fell to his Lot, and a Staff or Scepter. Having received these, they were all admitted to sit in the Court.' M. *Dacier* hath, from *Girardus,* differed a little from this Account; for instead of Ten Courts, she hath made but one, beside the *Areopagus,* and called it the Court of Ten. She would have likewise not different Courts, but the Precedency of the Judges in the same Court to be decided by Lot; which would destroy the Beauty of the Allusion here. The Sense of this Passage, which I suspect none of the Translators nor Commentators have rightly *smelt out,*[90] is this:—Whereas one of the Old Fellows shook his Staff at *Cario,* and also threatned him with a judicial Punishment; he answers pleasantly, I see, Sir, you have the Staff of Authority in your Hand, but instead of being destined by your Lot to judge in one of our Courts of Justice, your Lot destines you a Court of Justice in the next World; and *Charon* is the Crier who delivered you that Staff.

[70] *I will conceal no longer.*] Tho' *Cario,* as we have said before, had given them a Hint of his Master's Riches; yet he had neither acquainted them with the manner of his acquiring his Wealth, nor that the Advantage would extend to his Neighbours.

[71] *Make us rich.*] Some Copies read, make you rich, less agreeably to the Character of this Slave, who is always with great Forwardness thrusting in himself as a Person of Consequence on every Occasion.

[72] *All be Midas's.*] So is the *Greek.* M. Dacier, *Vous allez tous étre* (Riches) *autant de Midas—vous en avez déja les oreilles; Mr.* Theobald, *You shall all be rich as* Midas, *and have his Asses Ears to boot.* In both which the excellent Humour of the Original is lost.[91]

[73] *Ready to dance for Joy.*] This is verbatim. *Mr.* Theobald, *I could dance till I kick the Moon almost.*

---

[90] Cf. *Vernoniad* (1741) in *Champion,* where the critic Bentley '*smells* the true Reading' of a 'Hiatus' (p. 568 n. [33]).

[91] The humour, that is, depends on the conditional conjunction: they will be rich as Midas *if* they first acquire ass's ears, as Apollo gave Midas when he foolishly judged Pan's performance on his pipes superior to Apollo's on the lyre.

Cario. And I myself[74] will dance like the *Cyclops*,[75] *Tantararara*—and capering thus with my Feet, I will lead up myself. Come on, my Boys, at every Turn bawl and bleat forth the Songs of Sheep and stinking Goats— Come, follow me, and dance as wantonly as ye can,[76] with all the qualifications of a Goat.

Chorus. We'll follow thee bleating, Mr. *Tantararara Cyclops*; and when we have caught thee, thou hungry Cur,[77] with thy Satchel full of wild Pot-herbs,[78] staggering before thy Flock; or perhaps, when thou art snoring

---

[74] *Will dance like the* Cyclops.] Madam *Dacier* has so well explained this Passage, that our Reader will be very well satisfied to see her entire Note on the Occasion. 'One of the Old Men having said, that he would dance *de toute sa Force* [which Words, by the way, are not in the Original] *Cario* lays hold on this Occasion, and says, that he will act the *Cyclops*, put himself at the Head of his Company, and lead them, as the *Cyclops* led his Rams and his Oxen. This *Cyclops* is *Polyphemus*, whose History we gave in *Homer's Odyssey*. The Passage is very lively and beautiful; but it will appear more so to those who know, that *Aristophanes* is here burlesquing a Tragedy of *Philoxenus*;[92] out of which he introduces whole Speeches. This *Philoxenus* fell in Love with a Mistress of *Dionysius* the *Sycilian* Tyrant. They say farther, that he was so well received by her, as to create a Jealousy in the Tyrant, who not understanding Rallery, caused the Poet to be seized and sent to the Quarries. Happily for him, he found Means to escape, he retreated to the Island of *Cerigo*, and produced a Play, which he entitled *The* Cyclops, *or the Loves of* Philoxenus *and* Galatea. This was a very lucky Subject; for, as on the one Side, *Galatea* was the Name of the *Cyclops's* Mistress, so was it likewise the Name of *Dionysius's*. On the other part, *Dionysius* himself was not unlike this Giant, in his enormous Stature, in his great Cruelty, and in the ugly Cast of his Eyes. Lastly, as *Polyphemus* crushed his Rival *Acis* under the great Rocks, which he threw on him, in the same manner this Tyrant had buried *Philoxenus* alive in his Quarries. Tho' this Play was far from being bad; it, nevertheless, fell under the Lash of *Aristophanes*, from the ridiculous Representation of the *Cyclops* with a Sack and a Guitar.

[75] Tantararara.] In the Original *Threttanelo*, which Word the *Greek* Scholiast tells us, without either Reason or Authority, *resembled the Sound of the Guitar when played upon*. Madam *Dacier* hath accordingly translated it, *Joüer de la* GUITARRE. Mr. *Theobald*, *dance to the Music of my own* GUITAR. Whereas the *Greek* mentions nothing of this Instrument, nor can we suppose *Cario* had any such in his Hand. The Word hath in no Language any Meaning, and was like that which we have rendered it, and many others in Songs in our own Language, used only as a Vehicle for the Music.[93]

[76] *With all the Qualifications.*] Our Reader is at Liberty here to guess what these are: We cannot, with Decency, render the *Greek* more literally.[94] M. *Dacier* and Mr. *Theobald* have modestly omitted it.

[77] *With thy Satchel full of wild Pot-herbs.*] 'This is also taken from Philoxenus his Tragedy, where the *Cyclops* carried a Bag full of Herbs, which he had provided. And *Aristophanes* condemns this very justly: for Probability should always be preserved, especially in Characters. And Herbs were by no means proper Diet for a *Cyclops*, who used to eat up two or three Men at a Breakfast.' *Dacier*: tho' *Homer*, in his *Odyssey*, says of the *Cyclops*, *That they plant not with their Hands, nor do they plow: but they feed on what the Earth produces without Seed, and without the Plough*.

[78] *Staggering before thy Flock.*] He supposes that *Cario* would be drunk, alluding to *Polyphemus*, into whose Cave *Ulysses* having entred, in order to avoid his Cruelty (for he had seen several of his Companions cut in pieces, and devoured by *Polyphemus*) invited him to drink a Cup of Wine sweet as Honey, and divine,

---

[92] Aristophanes' allusions to the Cyclops are in part to the *Odyssey* (books ix–x), but also to a quasi-dramatic dithyramb by Philoxenus of Cythera (435–380 BC), whose masterpiece was the *Cyclops*, a pastoral burlesque on the love of the Cyclops for Galatea (*EB*, s.v. Philoxenus).

[93] Cf. *Vernoniad*, where HF concludes a footnote 'with the Tag of an old song. | *Sing Tantararara Bribe all Bribe all,* | *Sing Tantararara B* [o] *bs all*' (*Champion*, p. 575 n. [47] and Coley's comment [n. 2]).

[94] The omitted word (line 295) ἀπεψωλημένοι·: 'with genitals denuded'. The scholia explain that rutting goats dance on their hind legs in this manner. For more expansive and explicit comment on this and other 'indecent' passages in the comedy, see Sommerstein's notes, keyed to the line numbers.

under some Hedge, then, Sirrah, we will take a swinging Staff, and burning it at one End, blind thee.

Cario.[79] I will in all Things imitate the *Circe,* who mixed up those Drugs, which formerly[80] persuaded the Retinue of *Philonides* at *Corinth,* as if they were really Swine, to eat well-kneaded Dung, which she herself kneaded for them; and do you, my little Pigs, grunting with Delight,[81] follow me your Dam.

Chorus. Well then,[82] and we, in our merry Mood, will take thee, Madam The *Circe,* mixing up those Drugs, enchanting and defiling that Retinue, and hang thee up by thy Virility; and[83] anoint thy Nostrils with thy kneaded

---

and so strong, that it required twenty times as much Water to mix with it. *Polyphemus* getting drunk with it, and falling into a sound Sleep, was deprived of his Sight by *Ulysses.*

[79] *I will imitate the* Circe.] As the old Fellows had said that they would imitate *Ulysses* and his Companions in the Punishment they inflicted on *Polyphemus, Cario* quits that Character, and says, that he will personate that of *Circe,* who changed *Ulysses's* Companions into Swine.

[80] *Persuaded the Companions of* Philonides.] *Circe* was a famous Courtesan of *Circei. Ulysses* coming on that Shore, sent *Eurylochus* with twenty-two Men to *reconnoitre* the Country; They arrived at the Palace of this Lady, who, by the Attraction of her Charms, made them forget their Companions, whom they had left in the Ship. *Eurylochus* alone returned to inform *Ulysses* of what had happen'd. *Homer* has dress'd up in this Matter of Fact in a very ingenious Fable; in which he says, that *Circe* transformed these Men into Swine. *Aristophanes* alludes to this Fable, but changes it; for, instead of saying the Companions of *Ulysses,* or *Eurylochus,* he says the Companions of *Philonides*; and, instead of laying the Scene at *Circei,* as *Homer* has done, he lays it at Corinth; by that means giving a terrible Stroke to that same *Philonides,* whom we have mentioned before, reproaching him, that *Lais* (*Nais*) the *Corinthian* Courtesan had entirely bewitched him; and that, with a Set of Parasites, whom he always had about him, he led an infamous Life in her Company. This requires no great Explanation, nor can any Satire be more ingenious. Or more bitter. *Dacier.*

Mr. *Pope,* in his Notes on the Tenth Book of the *Odyssey,* differs from this Learned Lady in her Account of this Fable. '*Homer,* (says he) was very well acquainted with the Story of Medea, and applies what is reported of that Enchantress to *Circe,* and gives the Name of *Aeaea* to the Island of *Circe,* in Remembrance to *Aeaea,* a City of *Colchis,* the Country of *Medea* and *Aeetes.* That *Homer* was not a Stranger to the Story of *Medea* is evident; for he mentions the Ship *Argo* in the Twelfth *Odyssey,* in which *Jason* sailed to *Colchis,* where *Medea* fell in Love with him; so that, tho' *Circe* be a fabled Deity, yet what *Homer* says of her was applicable to the Character of another Person; and consequently, a just Foundation for a Story in Poetry.'[95]

The Observation of *Girardus* is likewise worth mentioning. The Poet says, he makes this Courtesan worse than *Circe*; for she changed the Minds and internal Disposition of her Followers, whereas *Circe,* as *Homer* expressly remarks, metamorphosed only their outward Form.

[81] *Little Pigs, follow your Dam.*] This was a Proverb, and, as *Erasmus* tells us,[96] used to denote a great Degree of Ignorance and Stupidity; for the Sow was opposed to *Minerva.*

[82] *And we will take thee,* &c.] *Aristophanes* here alludes to the Punishment inflicted by *Ulysses* on *Melanthius,* in the 22d *Odyssey.*

[83] *Anoint their Nostrils.*] This Place is entirely misunderstood by the Scholiast. The Allusion is, indeed, none of the cleanliest, but may be easily guessed at, by those who have observed the Misfortunes which sometimes happen to the Noses of Rams and He-Goats, when they make Love.

---

[95] From Pope's *Odyssey,* 5 vols. (1725–6), book X, line 158 n. (iii, p. 20).

[96] Baker cites *Adagiorum Chilia* (Basel, 1546), xlii, p. 1002, s.v. index: *Matrem sequimini porci.* He remarks: 'Erasmus says that Aristophanes, here, may be quoting a proverb; it does not appear in earlier editions of Erasmus.'

Dung, till they have the Savour of a He-Goat; and thou, like gaping[84] *Aristyllus*, shalt say——Pigs, follow your Dam.

Cario. But, come——now a Truce with jesting. Do you return[85] to your former Shapes.[86] As for my part, I will steal some Bread and Meat from my Master, and employ the Remainder of my Leisure in eating; and, when I have filled my Belly, will set my Hands to the Work we are upon.

SCENE II.

Chremylus, Chorus.

Chrem. To bid you barely Welcome, my Countrymen,[87] is an old and fusty Salutation. I say, I receive you with open Arms, since you hasten to me with so much Alacrity, and[88] in such good Order. Now persevere, and lend me your Assistance, that we may be[89] the Preservers of this God.

---

[84] Aristyllus.] This *Aristyllus* was a Poet, who added to many other Vices that of Obscenity; for which Reason *Aristophanes* gives him here this nasty Entertainment. When he spoke, he screw'd up his Mouth, either thro' Affectation, or natural Impediment, and rather snorted out his Words thro' his Nose: so that, says *Erasmus*, he imitated the Sound of a Pig.[97] There can be nothing, therefore, more apposite and severe than this Satire. Our Poet mentions this *Aristyllus* again in his *Ecclesiazousai*, Ver. 643,[98] where *Praxagoras* objects to *Blepyrus*.

Prax. Ay, but there is a much greater Misfortune than this.
Blep. What can that be?
Prax. If *Aristyllus* should kiss you, and call you his Father?
Blep. He should roar for it, if he did &c.

[85] *To your former Shapes.*] This must be referred to those Transformations into Goats and Hogs, which *Cario* humourously supposed to have actually happened.

[86] *As for my Part.*] *Cario* leaves the *Chorus*, and goes in to his Master, to acquaint him with their Arrival. He securing *Plutus* in his House, comes forth to meet them.

[87] *Is an old and fusty Salutation.*] The Remark of Madam *Dacier* here is so very ingenious, that our Readers will be pleased to see it entire. *Aristophanes* touches on a Folly common to all Ages. For those who make their own Fortune, and arrive at Estates and Honours, which they could not hope for from the Meanness of their Birth, are eager all at once to change their former Manners, and imitate the Fashions and Manners of the polite World. So *Chremylus* the Moment he has got *Plutus* in his House, finds the Word Χαίρειν, the ordinary Term of Salutation, to be too obsolete and vulgar. He will now, therefore, say nothing less than ἀσπάζομαι, which signifies, *I kiss your Hands, I embrace you*; which was a Phrase peculiar to the *Beau Monde*, and used only among the Great.

[88] *In good Order.*] This was, probably, spoken Ironically, to ridicule the extreme Hurry and Confusion in which these Old Fellows advanced to see *Plutus*.

[89] *The Preservers.*] None of the Translators and Commentators have at all understood this Passage. The Title of Σωτήρ was ascribed to the Deity. The *Athenians* had dedicated a Temple to *Jupiter* by that Title, which they attributed also to *Apollo, Bacchus, Aesculapius*, and *Hercules*; and the Feminine of it to *Juno, Minerva, Venus*, and *Diana*. *Cicero*, in his Oration against *Verres*, observes, that the Word Σωτήρ is so emphatical that it cannot be adequately translated into the *Latin* Language: And this Remark he makes, the more effectually to exaggerate the Arrogance of *Verres* in assuming to himself that sacred Appellation. From this Hint, therefore, our sagacious Readers will admire the Beauty of this Passage. *M. Dacier*,

---

[97] See above, p. 283 n. 96.
[98] Both Loeb and Sommerstein have *Ecclesiazusae*, lines 646–8.

Chorus. Courage! Imagine you have in me a very *Mars* before your Eyes. It would be a Shame indeed, that we, who all of us wrangle so stoutly in our Assemblies for a[90] *Triobolus*, should tamely suffer any one to carry off *Plutus* from us.

Chrem. Odso! I see *Blepsidemus* too coming this Way: It is plain, by the Haste he is in, he hath heard something of this Business.

SCENE III.

Blepsidemus, Chremylus.

Blepsid. What can I make of this? Whence, and by what Means, hath *Chremylus* got all these Riches on a sudden? I will not believe it; and yet, by *Hercules*, it is the public Discourse of all the[91] Barbers Shops, that he is grown rich in an Instant: but to me it is a Prodigy, that a Man who hath

M'aidez à garder Plutus; *Mr.* Theobald, *Give me your Succour in the guarding* Plutus. Where, by the by, as the former is no Translation of the *Greek*; so the latter is a Translation neither of the *Greek* nor the *French.* The Occasion of this Mistake in the *Latin* and *French* Translators, was probably that the Chorus, in their Answer, take no notice of the Jest of *Chremylus*; who intimated, that, by restoring his Eyes, they should be the Preservers of the God, and so be to a God what Gods ought to be to Mortals.

[90] Triobolus.] This was the Reward of their Judges from the Time of *Cleon*, who increased it from two *Oboli* to three. The Greediness of the *Athenians* for these Offices, for the sake of this small Fee,[99] and again in his *Frogs*, in his *Birds*, in his *Wasps*, and in almost every one of the rest.[100]

[91] *Barbers Shops.*] These were the Coffee-Houses of the Antients.[101] *Theophrastus* calls them ἄοινα συμπόσια, i.e. Wineless Compotations.[102] They were Assemblies of all idle gossipping Fellows, who there assembled to vent their Malignity against their Betters. The Barbers themselves were likewise the most talkative and impertinent of all People. On this occasion we will tell a little Story out of *Plutarch's* Treatise of *Talkativeness.*[103] There happened once in a Barber's Shop a Discourse about *Dionysius*; in which it being asserted by one of the Company, that his Government was settled and firm as a Rock, the Barber answered with a Smile; 'Can we affirm this of *Dionysius*, at whose Throat I every day hold this Razor? These Words being carried to *Dionysius*, he ordered the poor Barber to be crucified.'

---

[99] '*Triobolus*': see above, p. 268 n. [26].
[100] Sommerstein (p. 162 nn. 329–30) cites no fewer than six passages on this theme in *Ecclesiazusae.*
[101] HF was amused by barbers, and by their shops as centres of gossipmongering. Cf. Partridge in *Tom Jones* and the following passage from that novel (II. iv):

Mankind have always taken great Delight in knowing and descanting on the Actions of others. Hence there have been, in all Ages, and Nations, certain Places set apart for public Rendezvous, where the Curious might meet, and satisfy their mutual Curiosity. Among these, the Barbers Shops have justly borne the Pre-eminence. Among the *Greeks*, Barbers News was a proverbial Expression, and *Horace*, in one of his Epistles [i.e. *Satires*, I. vii. 2–3], makes honourable Mention of the *Roman* Barbers in the same Light.

Those of *England* are known to be no wise inferior to their *Greek* or *Roman* Predecessors. You there see foreign Affairs discussed in a Manner little inferior to that with which they are handled in the Coffee-houses; and domestick Occurrences are much more largely and freely treated in the former, than in the latter. (p. 87)

Cf. also *The Craftsman*, No. 539 (30 October 1736); *New Essays*, pp. 172–9.
[102] Cf. Fredericus Wimmer, *Theophrasti Opera* (Paris, 1931), frag. 75, p. 433. On Theophrastus, see the Preface to *David Simple*, below, p. 353 and n. 17.
[103] Cf. Plutarch, 'Concerning Talkativeness', *Moralia*, vi. 508 f–509.

any good Luck, should send for his Friends to share it. Surely, he hath done a very unfashionable Thing.

Chrem. By the Gods! I will tell him the Truth, concealing nothing. O *Blepsidemus*, our Circumstances are finely altered since Yesterday; for you are at Liberty to share my good Fortune, since you are one of my Friends.

Blepsid. And are you indeed become rich, as the Report goes?

Chrem. I shall be so very suddenly,—[92] if our God pleases: for there is yet——there is some Hazard in the Matter.

Blepsid. What Hazard!

Chrem. Why, there is——

Blepsid. Tell me instantly, what is it?

Chrem. If we are successful, we are made for ever. If we miscarry, we are utterly ruined.

Blepsid.[93] This Concern of yours looks ill on your Side, and is far from pleasing me; for, to grow extremely rich all on a sudden, and at the same time to be so full of Apprehensions, betokens a Man who hath committed some[94] heinous Crime.

Chrem. How! some heinous Crime!

Blepsid.[95] If you have stolen something from *Delphos*, whence you are just arrived, either Gold or Silver belonging to the God, and you now repent of it——

Chrem. O *Apollo*, the Averter————[96] Not I indeed.

Blepsid. Leave trifling, good old Gentleman, I know very well————

Chrem. Do you suspect such a thing of me?

Blepsid. I know—[97] that there is no Man truly honest; we are none of us above the Influence of Gain.

[92] *If our God pleases.*] This is very pleasant; he acknowledges no other God than *Plutus*. Dacier.

[93] *This Concern.*] The *Greek* Word signifies a Burden; but here it is to be taken metaphorically. Our Translation is almost verbal; M. Dacier, *Voila des circonstances qui ne me plaisent nullement*; Mr. Theobald, *These are Circumstances which in no ways please me.*————This Translation doth in no ways please me.

[94] *Heinous Crime.*] The *Greek* is οὐδὲν ὑγιὲς, which is often used by our Author, to signify the extremest Degree of Turpitude;[104] in which Sense it occurs in *Plato's Phaedon*. M. Dacier, *Sent fort quelque méchante action*; Theobald, *Smells strong of some dishonest Action.*

[95] *If you have stolen.*] *Blepsidemus* is interrupted in his Speech by *Chremylus*, who loses all Patience at the Suspicion. He was probably proceeding to advise him, if *he repented*, to make Restitution of what he had stolen. Ours is the true and literal rendering of the *Greek*. M. Dacier, *Mon Dieu! vous avez derobez*, &c. Mr. Theobald, *My God! you may perhaps have stolen something*, &c.

[96] *Not I indeed.*] M. Dacier, *Je n'en ai jamais eu la pensée;* Mr. Theobald, *I never had a thought of that nature.*

[97] *That there is no Man truly honest.*] This Passage hath been hitherto misunderstood.—This Speech is to be connected with the former of *Blepsidemus*. The Meaning of it is this: *Don't trifle with me, by pretending to Honesty; for I know very well that there is no Man truly honest*, &c. He was interrupted by *Chremylus*;

---

[104] Loeb (line 355): 'some rotten thing'; Sommerstein: 'something dirty'.

Chrem.[98] By *Ceres*, you seem to me to be out of your Senses.

Blepsid. aside. How different is this poor Man's Behaviour from what it was?

Chrem. By Heavens, Friend, you are out of your Mind.

Blepsid. aside.[99] How his Eyes wander!————the certain Indication of a Man who hath committed some knavish Prank.

Chrem. I know what you are[100] croaking to yourself. You think I have stole something, and want to share in the Booty.

Blepsid. I want to share! In what, pray?

Chrem. But this is no such thing————it is an Affair of quite another Nature.

Blepsid. O! then you have not stolen, you have taken it away by Violence.

Chrem. The Man is possessed.

Blepsid. What, not even cheated any one?

Chrem.[101] Not I, truly.

Blepsid. O *Hercules*, which Way can a Man turn himself in this Affair: for I see you will not discover a Word of Truth.

Chrem. You accuse me, before you have informed yourself of the Nature of my Case.

Blepsid. Harkee, Friend; I will make this Matter up for you very cheap, before the Town knows any thing of it. A small Matter of Money will[102] stop the Orators Mouths.

for which he throws in that Particle of Impatience Φεῦ *i.e.* Pooh! Pshaw! and then proceeds to deliver his Opinion; upon which *Chremylus* conjectures he is out of his Senses. M. *Dacier* hath erred here with the rest, and mistranslated the *Greek*, and Mr. *Theobald* hath very strictly translated her.[105]

[98] *By* Ceres.] It is strange none of the Commentators should remark the Propriety of this Oath. *Ceres* was supposed by the Antients to be one of those Deities who deprived Men of their Senses. So *Horace*, *Cerritus*;[106] a distracted Man, a Man under the Wrath of *Ceres*.

[99] *How his Eyes wander.*] The *Greek* literally rendered is, *neither do his Eyes keep one Place.* The Behaviour of *Blepsidemus*, on the generous Communication of Wealth by his Friend *Chremylus*, first in thinking him a Rogue, and that he intends, instead of conferring a Benefit on him, to draw him into a Scrape; and afterwards, in concluding him a Madman, is, I am sorry to say it, as fine and just a Picture of Human Nature as ever was drawn.

[100] *Croaking.*] Literal from the *Greek*. M. *Dacier*, *Je vois bien pourquoy vous dites toutes ces sotises*; Mr. *Theobald*, *I know what you drive at by this Foollery.*

[101] *Not I truly.*] Literal. M. *Dacier*, *non assurement, jamais*; Mr. *Theobald*, *most certainly, never.*

[102] *Stop the Orators Mouths.*] M. *Dacier's* Note here is worth transcribing. 'This is extremely severe; *Aristophanes* would insinuate by it, that all the Orators at *Athens* were corruptible. And he had regard to what happened to *Demosthenes*: He had pleased one Day against the *Milesians*, and the Cause was adjourned to the next Morning. The Ambassadors found him in the intervening Night, and, to oblige him

---

[105] Dacier: 'Grands Dieux! comme il n'y a personne de sage, lors qu'il s'agit de richesses! faut-il que tout le monde absolument succombe a l'envie d'en amasser' (pp. 26–7). Theobald: 'Phu! Phu!—Is there no Integrity in the World? But must every individual Man be a Slave to Avarice and Sordid Passion?' (p. 18). Their predecessors read the speech as a question; HF and Young, with Loeb and Sommerstein, have it declarative.

[106] *Satires*, II. iii. 278.

Chrem. By *Jupiter*, you appear a very good Friend indeed; I suppose you will lay out[103] three *Minae*, and then charge me twelve.

Blepsid. Methinks, I see a certain Person standing at the Bar, with his Petition in his Hand, and his Wife and Children by him, extremely resembling the Picture of[104] the *Heraclidae*, as it was drawn by *Pamphilus*.

Chrem. I a Suppliant![105] No, thou Sot: but henceforward none but the good and worthy, and modest Part of Mankind, shall be enriched by me.

Blepsid. How say you! What, have you stolen such a prodigious Sum?

Chrem. O Villany![106] Thou wilt ruin—.

Blepsid. You will ruin yourself, or I'm mistaken.

Chrem. Not I: for I have *Plutus* in my Possession, you Wretch!

Blepsid. You[107] *Plutus*! What *Plutus*?

Chrem. *Plutus*, the God of Riches.

not to speak against them, they gave him the full sum he demanded. The next Morning *Demosthenes* appeared at the Bar, with his Neck wrapped with Wool and Linen, and pretended he was very much disordered with the Quincy, which obstructed his Breath; but it was well known that this Quincy was nothing more than the Gold which he had received. On which a Wit said, that it was not the Συνάγχη ἀλλ ἀργυράγχη, which is a Pun, untranslatable, and signifies that his Breath was stopt not with the Quincy, but with Money.'107 Mr. *Theobald* hath literally translated this Note. The Story is a true and pleasant one, and is related by *Plutarch*, in his Life of this Orator;108 but there is a Beauty in this Passage, which neither M. *Dacier* nor her Translator hath observed; and this is, that *Aristophanes* hath here shewn himself to be a true Prophet as well as a Satirist; for *Demosthenes* was not born when this Play was writ.

[103] *Three Minae.*] M. *Dacier* hath here transferred the Scene to *France*; Mr. *Theobald* to *England*; but they have both made another Mistake, by not preserving the Proportion between the Sums. A *Mina* answered to the Sum of Three Guineas; so that the first Sum answers to Nine, the latter to thirty-six.109

[104] *The* Heraclidae] After the Death of *Hercules*, *Eurystheus* persecuted his Descendants so fiercely, that they were obliged to fly to the Protection of the *Athenians*. They went therefore into the Senate with all the Marks of Suppliants, having *Alcmena* at their Head. *Chaerephon* made a Tragedy of this Subject, and *Pamphilus* a Picture, which was hung up in their Picture-Gallery. There is nothing pleasanter than this Comparison, which *Blepsidemus* draws between the Posture of *Chremylus* begging Mercy with his Wife and Son, and the posture of *Alcmena* and her Children, imploring the Protection of the *Athenians*, *Dacier*. To this we may add, that the Poet could use no more ingenious Artifice to ingratiate himself with his Audience, than by alluding to a Story which reflected so much Honour on the *Athenians*, and of which they were so vain.

[105] *No, thou Sot*, &c.] The *Greek* Scholiast explains this Place very ingeniously, by reducing the Answer of *Chremylus* into the following Argument: *If I had committed Sacrilege, as you say, I should be a wicked Man; and, if a wicked Man, I should not give any thing to another: but now, by choosing to bestow Riches on the Good, it is plain I am a good Man; and if so, it is plain I can have committed no Sacrilege.*

[106] *Thou wilt ruin.*] This is strictly literal. *Chremylus* is interrupted by *Blepsidemus*, imagining he was going to say, *You will ruin yourself and your Family by this Treatment of me, which will be the Occasion that I shall give you nothing*; or something of this kind, which was natural for him to suspect, from the Drift of his last Speech. M. *Dacier* hath translated, or rather alter'd it into, *Vous me faites mourir avec vos soupçons*; Mr. Theobald, *You distract me with these Calumnies.*

[107] *Plutus! What Plutus?*] There is a Double Meaning in the *Greek* impossible to be preserved, the same

107 In the quoted passage Dacier, without acknowledgement, translated Girardus' note to line 377 (Küster, p. 30).

108 Plutarch, *Lives* ('Demosthenes'), xxv–xxvi. HF had recently told this story at length in *The Vernoniad* (*Champion*, p. 574 n. [47]).

109 Dacier translates 'dix pistoles' (p. 28); Theobald, 'Ten Guineas' (p. 19).

Blepsid. And where is he?

Chrem. Within.

Blepsid. Where?

Chrem. Here in my House.

Blepsid. In your House!

Chrem. Even so.

Blepsid.[108] Go hang yourself——————*Plutus* at your House!

Chrem. Yes, by the Gods, is he.

Blepsid. And do you really tell Truth?

Chrem. I do.

Blepsid. Do you, by *Vesta*?

Chrem. Yes, and by *Neptune* too.

Blepsid.[109] What *Neptune*, do you mean the God of the Sea?

Chrem. Ay, and t'other *Neptune* too, if there be any other.

Blepsid.[110] What, keep *Plutus* to yourself,[111] and not send him over to us your Friends.

Chrem. Matters are not yet ripe enough for that.

Blepsid. What, not to communicate him to any one!

Word signifying Riches, and the God of Riches. We have therefore been obliged to deviate from the Original in the next Line, and give it a new Turn.

[108] *Go hang yourself.*] In the *Greek*, Go to the Ravens;[110] that is, to be hang'd on a Gibbet, where thou wilt be devoured by those Birds; a Curse frequent among the *Greeks*, and several times used by our Author. The same is mentioned by *Solomon* in the *Proverbs*.[111] So *Horace*:

$$\text{——————} \textit{non pasces in cruce corvos.}^{112}$$

Zenodotus gives a different Account of this, and says, that there was a Place in *Thessaly* named Κόρακες, into which Villains were thrown headlong.[113]

[109] *What* Neptune.] M. *Dacier* observes, that this was a Joke on the *Athenians*, for worshipping *Neptune* under different Names, as the Sea *Neptune*, the Horseman *Neptune*, &c. Indeed, our Poet omits no Occasion of taking the most particular Freedoms with the Deities of his Time; and one would scarce imagine he wrote in the same Age when the Divine *Socrates*[114] suffered Death for Atheism.

[110] *What, keep* Plutus *to yourself.*] We have added this for the sake of our Reader, the better to connect it with what preceded.

[111] *And not send him over,* &c.] Literal. *M.* Dacier, *Et vous ne m'envoyiés pas chercher*; *Mr.* Theobald, *And had not you sent to me?* This is neither the Letter nor Spirit of the Original.

---

[110] See below, p. 303 and n. 141.

[111] Proverbs 30: 17: 'The eye *that* mocketh at *his* father, and despiseth to obey *his* mother, the ravens of the valley shall pick it out, and the young eagles shall eat it.'

[112] Horace, *Epistles*, I. xvi. 48: 'You'll hang on no cross to feed crows' (Loeb).

[113] Zenodotus (*fl. c.*280 BC), Greek grammarian, the first superintendent of the library at Alexandria and the first critical editor of Homer. Baker notes that, whereas Girardus, commenting on the Greek οὐκ ἐς κόρακας (line 394; Küster, p. 30) has simply 'others say', HF and Young substitute '*Zenodotus* . . . says', 'probably from his scholium on the word in *Odyssey*, xiii. 408'.

[114] For HF the epithet 'Divine' when applied to Socrates was scarcely hyperbole. In the Preface to the *Miscellanies* (1743) Socrates represents 'the *true* Sublime in Human Nature. That Elevation by which the Soul of Man, raising and extending itself above the Order of this Creation, and brighten'd with a certain Ray of Divinity, looks down on the Condition of Mortals' (*Miscellanies* i, p. 12).

Chrem. No, by *Jupiter*—we must first——
Blepsid. What must we?
Chrem. Restore him to his Sight.
Blepsid. Restore whom! tell me.
Chrem. Plutus; and[112] by some Means or other, make him see as well as ever.
Blepsid. Is *Plutus* then really blind?
Chrem. Ay, by *Jove* is he.
Blepsid. O then it is no Wonder he never came near my House.
Chrem. But, by the Blessing of the Gods, he will come now.
Blepsid. Would it not be proper then to call in the Assistance of some[113] Physician?
Chrem. Pray, what Physician can there be in this City: for, as there are here no Fees for Physicians, there is, consequently, no such Art[114]
Blepsid. Let us see, however.
Chrem. But I tell you there is none.

---

[112] *By some means or other.*] This is the true Rendring of ἑνί γέ τῷ τρόπῳ; τῷ here is put for τινί. This is the same as ἀμωσγέπως, a Word used by our Author, *Thelm.* 436.[115] and well known to those who are conversant in the *Attic* Writers. M. *Dacier* hath, for I know not what reason, dropt this; *Mr.* Theobald, I suppose, *from Complacence to that Lady*.

[113] *Physician.*] Mr. *Theobald* hath confined this to *Oculists*, by which the Generality of the Satire is restrained to that one Branch.[116]

[114] *There is consequently no such Art.*] This is a twofold Stroke both against the Avarice of the Physicians, and against the Avarice of the *Athenians*. M. *Dacier* hath added here, *Ou leur Art est si meprisé*; Mr. *Theobald* in Complacence, *in a Town that contemns the Science*. In her Note on this Place, that Lady says, that in the time of *Aristophanes* Physicians *were neither esteem'd nor paid*. This little agrees with what the Learned Baron *Spanheim* writes on this Subject. 'There is at this Day extant amongst the Works of *Hippocrates*, a Decree of the *Athenians*, in which it is ordered, that he should be initiated into the Great Mysteries, presented with a Golden Crown, and be maintained in the *Prytaneum*, for having removed the Plague from that City, and for writing his Books in the Medicinal Art. We are told by *Hyginus*, that Slaves and Women were by Law forbidden to learn it, &c.—So that it appears, Physic was reckoned by the *Athenians* among the more noble Arts, and worthy to be profest by Gentlemen.'[117] And here I may add, that as *Hippocrates* was but fifty Years older than our Author, this Satire, in M. *Dacier's* Sense, is the more incredible. No Stage, except the *French*, hath taken more Liberties with the Faculty than our own;[118] yet God forbid that any Man who is sick, if he hath a Guinea in his Pocket, should conclude hence that we have no Physicians in this populous City.

---

[115] In *Plutus* (line 403) the phrase is translated by Loeb, 'by any means'; by Sommerstein, 'by hook or by crook'. In *Thesmophoriazusae* ('Priestesses of Demeter'), the word is rendered in Loeb (line 429) 'or [by] some other way'.

[116] Theobald: 'What d'ye talk of Oculists. Where shall we meet with one, in a Town that contemns the Science, and so ill rewards the Operator!' (p. 21). With HF and Young, both Loeb (line 406) and Sommerstein choose a general term, 'doctor'.

[117] Baron Ezekiel Spanheim FRS (1629–1710), numismatist and philologist; in 1702 he came to London as Ambassador Extraordinary from the King of Prussia to Queen Anne, and upon his death he was buried in Westminster Abbey. His commentary on Aristophanes' *Plutus* was available to HF in Küster, pp. 244–70; the passage in question is on line 408 at p. 253.

[118] In referring to the ridicule of 'the Faculty' on the French and English stage, HF would have had in mind, among others, Molière's farce *Le Médecin malgré lui* and his own version of it, *The Mock Doctor* (1732), with its Dedication to the quack Dr Misaubin.

Blepsid. Nay, I believe so too.

Chrem. By *Jupiter*, the best Way is to lay him in the Temple of *Aesculapius*, as I myself before intended.

Blepsid. You say true. Be not dilatory: but[115] do something or other immediately.

Chrem. I am going.

Blepsid. Well, make haste.

Chrem. I think of nothing else.

SCENE IV.

Poverty, Chremylus, Blepsidemus.

Poverty.[116] O ye Wretches, possessed with the Devil, who dare attempt this bold, wicked, and lawless Action———whither, whither do you fly? will you not stop?

Chrem. O *Hercules*!

Poverty. Be assured I will absolutely destroy you, ye wicked Wretches, who have dared conceive such an insufferable and audacious Attempt; an Attempt, which no one, at any time, either God or Man, hath ventured on: wherefore you may both[117] conclude yourselves already destroyed.

Chrem. Who, pray, are you with your terrible pale Countenance?

Blepsid. Perhaps, she is[118] a tragical Fury belonging to the Play-House: for she hath a wild and tragical Aspect.

---

[115] *Do something or other.*] Ἔν γέ τι M. *Dacier,* &c. Have dropt this Expression again, as a little before.[119]

[116] *O ye Wretches.*] 'Poverty, having learned that the Old Men were endeavouring to restore *Plutus* his Eyes, attempts to prevent them, This is very ingenious, and well conducted.' *Dacier.*

[117] *Conclude yourselves.*] This Manner of considering future Events as already past, is peculiar to the *Greek* and Oriental Tongues.[120]

[118] *A tragical Fury.*] *Aristophanes* here rallies the absurd Methods, which the Tragic Poets of his Time took to inspire Terror, or rather Horror, into their Audience. He particularly points here at *Aeschylus,* who introduced these dreadful Deities into many of his Plays, and chiefly in his *Eumenides,* where they made so frightful an Appearance, that it terrified many Women into Fits, Miscarriages, &c. The dreadful Apprehensions which the Antients had of these Infernal Divinities, gave good Advantage to the Poets: Our own, for want of those, are obliged to have recourse to the poor Assistance of Thunder and Lightning, and now and then a Ghost; which last hath seldom appeared of late Years on our Stage, without more reason to be afraid of the Audience, than they of him.[121]

---

[119] See above, p. 290 and HF's n. [112].

[120] 'Oriental Tongues': i.e. Hebrew and the languages derived from it (*OED,* s.v. 'oriental' B2 ['oriental languages']). In addition to Greek and Latin, Parson Adams, William Young's surrogate in *Joseph Andrews* (1. iii), has 'a great Share of Knowledge in the Oriental Tongues' (pp. 22–3).

[121] HF's own *Tragedy of Tragedies* (1731) usefully illustrates the 'modern' playwright's 'recourse to the poor Assistance of Thunder and Lightning' (as indicated in the stage directions for III. I; *Plays,* p. 586); 'and now and then a Ghost' (III. i, p. 579)—the entrance of the latter being accompanied in the published version by HF's note: 'Of all the Particulars in which the modern Stage falls short of the ancient, there is

Chrem. Ay, but she hath[119] no Torch in her Hand.

Blepsid. If she be no Fury,[120] she shall howl for this Behaviour.

Poverty. Whom, pray, do you imagine me to be?

Chrem. Why, some paltry[121] Hostess, or[122] Oister-Wench; for else you would not have scolded at us in this manner, without receiving any Affront.

Poverty. Indeed! Why, have you not done me the greatest Injury in the World, who have endeavoured to expel me out of this whole Country.

Chrem. Not out of the whole Country; there is still the[123] BARATHRUM left open to you.————————But seriously, you had best tell us this very Instant who you are?

Poverty. I am one, who will this Day punish you both, for having endeavoured to exterminate me hence.

Blepsid. Oho! is not this she, who keeps the Hedge-Tavern in our Neighbourhood, who is constantly ruining me with her bad Half-Pints.

Poverty. I am *Poverty* then, who have dwelt with you both these many Years.

Blepsid. O King *Apollo*, and yet Gods,[124] whither may one fly?

[119] *No Torch.*] This was as necessary an Ornament to the Tragical Furies of the Antients, as a lighted Taper is to the Tragical Ghosts of the Moderns.

[120] *She shall howl.*] The *Greek* is simply, *she shall weep then.* M. Dacier, *Il faut donc lui donner mille coups*; Mr. Theobald, *God so! she deserves to be whipt at the Cart's Arse, for forgetting that Part of her Furniture.*

[121] *Hostess.*][122] The *Greek* Word, by its Origination, signifies one that entertains all Guests; whence, in *Lycophron*, the Masculine of this Word is applied to *Hell*; ἄδης πανδοχεύ.

[122] *Oister-Wench.*][123] In the *Greek* an *Egg-seller*.

[123] *Barathrum.*] We could not adequately translate this Word. It was, says the Learned Archbishop *Potter*, a deep Pit belonging to the Tribe *Hippothoontis* at *Athens*, into which condemned Persons were cast headlong; a dark, noisome Hole, and had sharp Spikes at the Top, that no Man might escape out; others at the Bottom, to pierce and torment such as were cast in.[124] Madam *Dacier* has translated it, the *River*, and Mr. Theobald, *Hell*; imagining, I suppose, that the *French* Lady meant the River *Styx*.

[124] *Whither may one fly.*] There are few Scenes in any Play, whether antient or modern, which contain more exquisite Humour than this. Those Descriptions by which the Figure and Dress of this Character of *Poverty* are as visible to the Reader as they could be made to the Spectator, are Instances of quick Invention

none so much to be lamented, as the great Scarcity of Ghosts in the latter. Whence this proceeds, I will not presume to determine. Some are of opinion, that the Moderns are unequal to that sublime Language which a Ghost ought to speak. One says ludicrously, That Ghosts are out of Fashion' (p. 579 n. (*a*)). The probable source of this ludicrous declaration, Thomas Lockwood suggests, is HF himself in *The Author's Farce* (1730), 'where Dash observes that the business of ghosts and murders "is at a very low Ebb now" (II. iii)' (p. 605 n. 167). Cf. also *The Champion* (27 November 1739), where HF, having referred to 'the Style of the Author of *Tom Thumb*' (i.e. himself), comments in a footnote: 'An Author who dealt so much in Ghosts, that he is said to have spoiled the *Hay-Market* Stage, by cutting it all into Trap-Doors' (p. 33 and n. 6). Also *Joseph Andrews* (I. viii), where he recalls the surprise of the audience: 'You have seen the Faces, in the Eighteen-penny Gallery, when through the Trap-Door, to soft or no Musick, Mr. *Bridgewater*, Mr. *William Mills*, or some other of ghostly Appearance, hath ascended with a Face all pale with Powder, and a Shirt all bloody with Ribbons' (p. 40).

122 '*Hostess*': Loeb (line 426) has 'Some pot-house girl'; Sommerstein, 'an innkeeper'.

123 '*Oister-Wench*': Loeb has 'Or omelette-seller' (line 427); Sommerstein, 'or a porridge-vendor'.

124 Potter, *Archæologiæ Græcæ*, i, pp. 134–5; his note (*d*) refers specifically to this passage in *Plutus*. For the sense of the word given in Potter and HF the earliest instance given in *OED* (s.v. 'barathrum') is 1809 (see Philip Hines, Jr., *N & Q*, 22/1 (January 1975), p. 13. See also below, p. 331 and n. [273].

Chrem. What are you doing? What a cowardly Animal art thou?-
——————Why don't you stand your Ground!

Blepsid. Not by any means.

Chrem. How! not stay! Shall we two Men fly from one Woman?

Blepsid. But she is *Poverty*, thou miserable Man, than which a more[125] pernicious Creature was never produced.

Chrem. Stand firmly: I beseech thee, stand.

Blepsid. By *Jove*, but I won't.

Chrem. Why, I tell you, we shall be guilty of the absurdest of all Actions in the World, if we should run away, and leave the God destitute, for Fear for this Woman here, without daring to contend with her.

Blepsid. In what Arms, or what Strength shall we confide: for, is there a Breast-Plate, or even a Shield, which this old Hag[126] doth not carry to Pawn.

Chrem. Courage![127] This God alone (I am confident) will triumph over all the Tricks of this Woman.

Poverty. Do you presume to mutter, you[128] Refuse of Mankind, when you have been caught in this detestable Undertaking, caught in the very Fact.

and great Art. The dreadful Apprehension which *Blepsidemus* here expresses of *Poverty*, the Moment she declares herself, if well represented by a skilful Actor, would delight a very indifferent and cold Spectator: Nor can the Reason why *Chremylus* expresses so much greater Boldness escape the most ordinary Reader, who will only reflect that he hath *Plutus* in his House.

[125] *Pernicious Creature.*] 'Theognis, a very moral Poet, had said before *Aristophanes*, that, to avoid Poverty, a Man should throw himself into the Sea, or precipitate himself from a Rock.' *Dacier.* I cannot help adding, that this Old Man had shewn no Consternation when he apprehended he was in Company with one of the Furies, who is now so shock'd at the Presence of *Poverty*; a Circumstance which, if well attended to, as greatly heightens the Pleasantry of this Scene, as any which the Wit of Man can invent.

[126] *Doth not carry to Pawn.*] So is the *Greek*, in which, as the Scholiast observes, there is a remarkable Elegance; for the Verb is in the Present Tense, to indicate that poor People are constantly pawning their Goods. M. *Dacier* hath render'd it, *Ne nous a't'elle pas fait engager?* Mr. Theobald, *Hath she not forced us to pawn?* This is a Departure from the Letter, from the Allegory, and from the Humour of the Original; *Chremylus* is here drolling on *Poverty*, who had before said she had lived with them many Years; and he gives this as an Instance of the Service she had done them. The learned Reader will observe the Force of the Word ασπὶς, the *Shield.* Which as it was most scandalous for any *Greek* or *Roman* to be without, so we may suppose it was the last Piece of Furniture, and that she had before stripped the House of all the rest. M. *Dacier* hath a Note on this Place, which, as Mr. *Theobald* literally translates it, I shall give in his Words. *They had a Law at Athens, which forbade all sorts of People to pawn their Arms; but they did not scruple to violate this Prohibition; and 'tis on this account that* Aristophanes *reproaches them.* DACIER. Theobald. The only Author, which I can find, of this Law, is the Scholiast on this very Line; and even he says no more, than that it *seems to have been forbidden.* Our Learned Archbishop, in the Second Volume of his *Grecian Antiquities,* Page 35 says, *That to pawn their Arms was an indelible Disgrace, and scarce ever to be atoned for.*[125] But that it was forbidden at *Athens* by a LAW, I much question, there being, as I remember, no Authority for it; and the Text here seems rather to imply the Negative.

[127] *This God alone.*] The *Greek* is very emphatical, and seems to intimate that this is the only God who could get the better of her.

[128] *Refuse of Mankind.*] 'In *Greek* Καθάρματα, *i.e.* Rascals who, deserve to be sacrificed as Persons

---

125 HF cites Potter, *Archælogiæ Græcæ,* ii, p. 85, presumably a typo.

Blepsid. Why dost thou,[129] while the Rod hangs over thee, attack us with thy Reproaches, when thou hast not suffered the least Injury?

Poverty. How! in the Name of the Gods, do you think you have done me no Injury, in endeavouring to restore the Eyes of *Plutus*?

Chrem. What Injury do we do you in this, whilst we are doing so much Good to all Mankind?

Poverty. What great Good are you contriving?

Chrem. What Good![130] First, having expelled you out of Greece———

Poverty. Expelled me! and, pray, what greater Mischief can you imagine yourselves being able to bring on Mankind?

Chrem. What?———why, by delaying to expel you.

Poverty. But I am willing, first, to give you a satisfactory Account of this Matter: And if I demonstrate, that I am the only Cause of all the Good which happens to you; and it is[131] through me alone you live—Nay, if I don't, then do to me whatever is agreeable to your Pleasure.

Chrem. And, have you the Boldness, you Hag, to say this?

Poverty. Nay, be you undeceived: for I shall easily demonstrate you to be utterly mistaken, when you say that you will make honest Men rich.

Blepsid. O for some[132] Instruments of Torture for thee!

Poverty. You ought not to make this Outcry and Uproar before you know any thing of the Matter.

Blepsid. Who can forbear roaring out, when he hears all this?

loaded with the Iniquities of all the People, and who ought to be sacrificed to appease the Anger of the Gods.' *Dacier*

[129] *While the Rod*, &c.] The *Greek* is simply, *That art about to perish miserably.*

[130] *First, having expelled you out of* Greece.] So is the *Greek. Chremylus* was proceeding, but is interrupted by *Poverty.* M. Dacier, *C'est premierement que nous te chasserons de toute la Grece*; M. Theobald, *Why, first and foremost, that we shall send you out of all* Greece.

[131] *Through me alone you live—Nay if I don't.*] Here we are to suppose the Impatience of *Chremylus* was going to interrupt her, which will make this Passage more familiar to an *English* Reader, and will agree with the Custom of our own Theatres; but this Form of omitting the *Apodosis*, or second Part of the Sentence is to be met with frequently in the best Writers, not only in the *Greek*, but also in the Oriental Languages. Thus *Achilles, Hom. Il.* i. 135 says, *If the* Greeks *will give an Equivalent agreeable to my Mind*———*But if they will not give me one.* See *Eustachius* on the Place. *Daniel* iii. 15. *Now if ye be ready that at what time ye hear the Sound of the Cornet, Flute, Harp, Sackbut, Psaltery and Dulcimer, and all kinds of Musick, ye fall down and worship the Image which I have made.*———Here the *Apodosis* is omitted; and therefore our Translators have interpolated the Word *well.* The same may be observed, *Luke* xiii. 8, 9. *Let it alone this Year also, till I shall dig about it and dung it: And if it bear Fruit,* well: (which last Word is not in the Original).[126] *And if not, then after that, thou shalt cut it down,* &c.

[132] *Instruments of Torture.*] In the *Greek, Tympana & Cyphones.* The first of which were wooden Cudgels, with which Malefactors were beaten to Death, being handed upon a Pole; and the latter were Collars usually made of Wood, which constrained the Criminal to bow down his Head. *Potter's Antiquities.*[127]

---

[126] The parenthesis confirms HF's dependence here on Mme Dacier's note: the King James version authorized by the Church of England *does* read, 'And if it bear fruit, *well*' (Luke 13: 9).

[127] Potter, i, p. 134 (the cudgels and pole), p. 130 (the wooden collars).

Poverty. Every Man of Sense can forbear it.

Chrem. But, if you are cast,[133] what Penalty will you be bound to undergo?

Poverty. Whatever you please.

Blepsid. Now you talk to the Purpose.

Poverty.[134] For, if you are cast, you must submit to the same Terms.

Blepsid. I suppose[135] twenty Hangings will be sufficient.

Chrem. Ay, for her: but one a-piece will suffice for us.

Poverty. This you shall surely suffer, or find some very substantial Reply to my Allegations.

[136]SCENE V.

Chorus, Chremylus, Blepsidemus, and *Poverty*

Chorus. It now behoves you to say something very specious on your Side; if you will get the better of this Antagonist, it will require your utmost Abilities.

Chrem. First then, I am persuaded this is universally acknowledged, that good Men are justly entitled to Prosperity; and as certainly, that the base and[137] wicked should suffer a contrary Fate. We, therefore, having considered this, have, with great Difficulty, found out the Means to effect an Expedient in itself excellent, generous, and most effectual to this Purpose: for, if *Plutus* should be now restored to his Sight, instead of strolling blindly about the World, he will then go to the Habitations of the Good, and never again forsake them: at the same time he will fly the Dwellings of the

[133] *What Penalty.*] 'It was a Custom among those who had any Cause depending in a Court of Justice, that he who was cast, beside the Principal which was the Subject of the Suit, should pay, moreover, certain Damages to the successful Party, which was called Ἐπιγρφειν τίμημα, which are the Words here used by *Aristophanes.* This was adding to the Principal Sum in Dispute an arbitrary Satisfaction for the Benefit of him who carried the Cause. The *Greeks* took this Custom from the Orientals, and gave it to the *Romans.*' *Dacier.*

[134] *For if you are all cast, &c.*] This Speech is to be connected to the former, and we have translated it almost literally. M. Dacier, *Mais il est just aussi que si vous perdez vous paiéz la meme amende que je vous aurois paié, si j'avois perdu.* Mr. Theobald, *But then it is but Equity on the other hand, that if you lose the Day, you shall make me the same Satisfaction which you would have imposed if I had been worsted.*

[135] *Twenty Hangings.*] There is something very humorous, as M. *Dacier* remarks, in this Desire of killing *Poverty* twenty times over, as if a single Death was no sufficient Security to them.

[136] *Scene 5.*] The Sentiments in this Scene are inimitable, tho' the Air of it is something graver than the rest of the Play. Here, according to *Horace, Vocem Comoedia tollit.*[128] The Sweetness of the Numbers cannot be preserved in any modern Language.

[137] *Wicked.*] The Greek is Ἀθέους, which M. *Dacier* hath translated *Athées;* Mr. Theobald, *Atheists;* and *Girardus* imagines that this Word, in the Sense these Translators understand it, was introduced by *Aristophanes* to reflect on *Socrates.* But indeed the *Greeks* use this Word most commonly to signify a Man who, on account of his Crimes, was forsaken and deserted by the Gods; in which Sense I remember it is frequently used by *Sophocles.*

---

[128] Horace, *Ars Poetica,* line 93: 'Yet at times even Comedy raises her voice' (Loeb).

Wicked.[138] And thus he will, in the End, make all Men good, rich, and religious. And now, who can invent an Expedient more useful to Mankind than this?

Blepsid. No one, surely. I will attest all you say,[139] don't ask her Confirmation.

Chrem. For, as human Affairs are now circumstanced, who would not rather call the whole Phrenzy, and raving Madness! For, how many Villains flourish in Riches, notwithstanding the Injustice with which they have accumulated them; and how many of the best of Men are in the utmost Distress, nay, even starve, and are obliged to spend most of their time in thy Company. (To *Poverty*.)[140] There is a Way, therefore, I say, to stop this Mischief; and, if we put *Plutus* with his Eyes open into it, he will effect the greatest Advantages for Mankind.

Poverty. You two old Dotards, joint Companions in Folly and Madness; you, who of all Men are the most easily persuaded to quit the Road of sound Reason. Should this which you long for be accomplished, I say, it would not be conducive to your Happiness: for, should *Plutus* recover his Sight, and distribute his Favours equally, no Man would trouble himself with the Theory of any Art, nor with the Exercise of any Craft; and if these two should once disappear, who afterwards will become a Brasier, a[141] Shipwright, a Taylor, a Wheelwright, a Shoe-maker, a Brick-maker, a Dyer, or a Skinner? Or who will plough up the Bowels of the Earth,[142] in order

[138] *And thus in the end will make all Men good.*] For when *Plutus* visits only good Men, the whole World would become virtuous out of Desire of Riches. The Generality of Mankind seldom love Virtue on her own account; they then only seek her, when she rewards their Pursuit.

[139] *Do not ask her Confirmation.*] M. Dacier, *Ne l'interrogez pas d'avantage*; M. Theobald, *We need question the Matter no farther.* 'This, says M. *Dacier*, is very pleasant; *Blepsidemus* is afraid that *Poverty* will answer and overthrow all which *Chremylus* hath said; therefore he takes it up, and gives his Judgment, and would have the whole Dispute ended, as if it was already but too much decided.' I am surprised the Lady, who says this is a Beauty, should drop it in her Translation.

[140] *There is a Way.*] The Learned will observe with what Difficulty we have here preserved the very Phrase of the Original, which no other Translator hath endeavoured.

[141] *Shipwright.*] '*Poverty* here runs over the most necessary Trades to the Support of Human Life, and includes the Shipwright; for as *Athens* was a very sterile Country, she could not subsist without Commerce.' *Dacier*.

[142] *In order to reap.*] This is the Sense of the Original. Literally it would stand thus: *Who would reap the Fruits of Ceres, having first broken up the Earth with Ploughs?* The Ploughing and previous Toil of the Husbandman is always insisted on by those Poets who describe the laborious and painful Art of Husbandry, not the more joyful Employment of gathering the ripe Corn into the Garner. *Ovid*, in describing the Golden Age, doth not say they enjoyed the Fruits of the Earth without gathering them, but without Ploughing and Sowing.

> *Ipsa quoque immunis rastroque intacta, nec ullis*
> *Saucia vomeribus, per se dabat omnia tellus.*[129]

M. *Dacier* gives, *Qui labourera la Terre? Qui fera la maison?* Mr. Theobald, *Who will till your Earth, or lay*

---

[129] Ovid, *Metamorphoses*, i. 101–2: 'The earth herself, without compulsion, untouched by hoe or plow-share, of herself gave all things needful' (Loeb).

to reap the Fruits of *Ceres*, if it was once possible for you to live with the Neglect of all these Things.

Chrem. Ridiculous Trifler! our Slaves will with their Labour perform for us all you have enumerated,

Poverty. But whence will you have any Slaves?

Chrem. We will purchase them with Money, to be sure.

Poverty. But who will be the Seller, when he himself is in no want of Money?

Chrem. O! some[143] *Thessalian* Merchant, or other, amongst those numerous Slave-mongers, will be induced by the Lust of Gain.

Poverty. But, according to your Scheme, there will, in the first Place, be no such Slave-monger: for what rich Man would run the Hazard of Life in such Traffick? You yourself, therefore, will be obliged to plough and to dig, and to undergo all other laborious Tasks; so that you will pass your Time much worse than at present.

Chrem. May this Evil fall on your own Head.

Poverty. No more shall you sleep on downy[144] Beds, or repose on Carpets: for none such will be; since no Man with his Pockets full of Money will be a Weaver. Nor shall you be perfumed with liquid Sweets, not even on your Wedding-Day; nor adorn yourselves with sumptuous Embroidery. What then will avail your Riches, when you will be able to purchase none of these things with them: for,[145] as for the Necessaries of Life, these will be copiously supplied you by me: for I it is, who standing by the Handicraft, compel him, like a Mistress, thro' Poverty, and the want of Necessaries, to labour for his Sustenance.

Chrem. With what Good canst thou supply Mankind, except[146] Blisters

---

your Harvest into the Barn? However, the *French* Lady hath thought proper to understand the Passage with us in her Note, and gives the Character of Sublime to this Verse in the Original.

[143] Thessalian *Merchant.*] The *Thessalians* had formerly a very scandalous Character. *Demosthenes*, in his first *Olynthian* Oration, says of them, *That they are perfidious by Nature, and had behaved so to all Mankind.*[130] They were infamous likewise on many other Accounts, but especially in this Merchandize of Slaves; for they not only stole the Slaves of other Nations, but sometimes even kidnapped Freemen, and sold them into remote Countries. To this the Poet particularly alludes in the next Speech, where he says, *No one would run the Hazard of his Life in such Traffick.* Nothing can be more just or poignant than this Satire.

[144] *Beds or Carpets.*] In the Eastern Countries Beds were used only in the Winter, and Carpets in the Summer.

[145] *As for the Necessaries.*] This is a most noble Sentiment, and the Diction in the Original altogether as sublime.

[146] *Blisters on the Legs.*] In the Winter, the Poor used to get round the Fire-Places which heated the Public Bagnios; and as they wore no Stockings, these Spots on their Legs, which they contracted from the

---

[130] *First Olynthiac*, 22. In his own translation, HF renders the passage: 'these [Thessalonians] are by Nature the most perfidious of Mortals, and have always proved so' (*Miscellanies* i, p. 210).

on the Legs from the public Bagnio-Fires, and the Cries of half-starved Children and old Women! together[147] with an Army of Lice, Gnats, and Fleas, (too numerous to be muster'd) which humming round our Heads, torment us, awakening us, and saying, *Rise, or Starve*. Moreover, instead of Clothes we shall have Rags; instead of a Bed of Down we shall have one of Rushes full of Bugs, which will awaken us out of the soundest Sleep; instead of a Carpet we shall have a rotten Mat; and instead of a Pillow, we shall prop our Heads with a Stone. As to our Food, we shall exchange Bread for Mallow-Branches, and Furmety for the Leaves of Radishes. Our Seats will not be Chairs, but the Head of a broken Jar; and lastly, we shall be even compelled to use one Side of a broken Crutch, instead of a Kneading-Trough——Well, Madam, do not I demonstrate that you are the Author of many Blessings to Mankind?

Poverty. You have not been describing[148] my Life: but canting forth the Life of Beggars.

Chrem. Well: and we commonly say, that Poverty is the Sister of Beggary.

Poverty. Very well you may, who make[149] no Distinction between the Tyrant *Dionysius* and the Patriot *Thrasybulus*. But I never suffered any of

Scorching of the Fire, were visible to all. This was a scandalous Mark of extreme and abject Poverty, and is again mentioned in this very Play.

[147] *With an Army of Lice*, &c.] M. *Dacier* hath dropt the greater Part of this Speech as too indelicate for her Language, and perhaps it would not agree with the nice Ears of an *English* Audience, who are apter to consider what is spoke, than what is suitable to the Character that speaks. But surely our Poet hath not injudiciously chosen the lowest and vilest of Things, to expose the Inconveniencies and Miseries of Poverty. As therefore we conceive, the more sensible of our unlearned Readers will be pleased to see the particular Customs of the *Athenians*, as well of the poorer sort as the richer; we have here endeavoured, as nearly as possible, to preserve the Original.

[148] *My Life.*] So is the *Greek*. M. *Dacier* and Mr. *Theobald* have dropt the Allegory, and consequently the Humour of *Chremylus*'s Answer.[131]

[149] *No Distinction between the tyrant* Dionysius *and the Patriot* THRASYBULUS.] It is impossible to imagine a more severe Satire on the *Athenians* than this. *It implies*, says M. *Dacier*, *that they made no Distinction between Virtue and Vice*. *Thrasybulus* was an *Athenian*, a Patriot in the truest Sense and the greatest Defender of the Democratic Power. He had delivered his Country from Slavery, by the Expulsion of the Thirty Tyrants: Whereas *Dionysius*, on the contrary, had totally subverted the Liberties of the *Syracusans*, and erected an absolute Dominion, which he exercised with the utmost Cruelty. The confounding, therefore, these two together, and holding them both in an equal light, must be an Instance of the greatest Depravity in any People. But there is a Beauty in this Passage, so obvious, that I am surprised even the dullest Commentator should pass it by. *Poverty*, in the Person of *Dionysius*, characterizes *Plutus*, whose Tyranny over Mankind, subduing their Consciences, Passions and Affections, to his absolute Will, is finely represented by such an arbitrary Prince: Whereas *Poverty* likens herself to the Patriot, under whose Administration all Men may enjoy Safety and Freedom with a Competency; and, by adhering to whom, they are delivered from that Slavery which enormous Wealth exacts from its Possessors.

---

[131] Dacier: 'Ce n'est pas la vie des pauvres que tu viens de décrire, mais des gueux & des mendians' (p. 40); Theobald: 'It is not the Life of the poor you have labour'd to describe, but of Vagabonds and Beggars' (p. 27).

these Calamities; nor, by *Jupiter*, am I in any Danger of them. The Life of a Beggar, which you mention, is indeed exposed to every Want: but the State of Poverty is only confined to Frugality and Business; and neither wants, nor abounds.

Chrem. O *Ceres*! what a blessed Life you have described. If after all his Parsimony and Labour, he[150] shall not leave enough to bury him.

Poverty. You aim at Banter and Rallery, and are unwilling to be serious; not knowing that I make better Men, both in Body and Mind, than *Plutus*; for[151] about him are the Gouty, and the Tun-bellied, and the Dropsy-legged, and Men choked with their own Fat; but in my Train are only the slender,[152] the active, and the most terrible to their Enemies.

Chrem. Very probably! for by starving them you make them slender enough.

Poverty. Well, then, I proceed now to the Purity of Mens Manners, and I shall convince you, that[153] Good-Manners dwell entirely with me; for all Abuse belongs to Riches.

---

[150] *Shall not leave enough.*] M. *Dacier* and Mr. *Theobald* say, that he shall leave enough. This is a Departure from the *Greek*, and only lessens the Strength of the Original. I shall add, that our Poet seems here to have had his Eye on *Aristides*, who had such a great Contempt for Wealth, that when he died, not leaving enough to bury him, his Funeral Expences were defray'd by the Public; and *Aelian* tells us, that those who had espoused his Daughters, after his Death rejected the Marriage, on account of his extreme Poverty.[132] And this happened within the Memory of *Aristophanes*.

[151] *About him.*] Here M. *Dacier* and Mr. *Theobald* again drop the Allegory, and say, that *Plutus* gives Men the Gout, &c. A Reader of any Taste will easily see the Difference; which is far more easy to conceive than to express.

[152] *The active.*] Literally the *waspish*, referring as well to their Dispositions as to their Shapes.

[153] *Good-Manners dwell.*] The Deficiency and Corruption of our Language, by the Confusion introduced into it from our applying improper and inconsistent Ideas to Words, of which Mr. *Locke* so justly complains,[133] makes it exceeding difficult to render adequately so copious and exact a Language as the *Greek*; especially in what regards their Philosophy and Morals. The *Greek* Word here is Κοσμιότης, which properly signifies the good Order of the Mind, and in that Sense it is used in *Plato*. For the *Greek* Philosophers considered a Mind distracted with Passions, and polluted with Vices, to be in a maimed and distorted Condition. Hence Κοσμιοτης is used more at large, to signify the Behaviour arising from such a Disposition of Mind. When we translate this *Good-Manners*, we must be understood in the true and genuine, and not the corrupted Use of the Word. M. *Dacier*, *L'Honnêtéte & la Moderation, L'Orgeüil & l'Insolence*; Mr. *Theobald*, *Moderation and Honesty, Insolence and Injustice.* Whence we observe how much easier it is to translate *French* than *Greek*.

---

[132] Aelian, *Varia Historia*, 10. 15.

[133] John Locke (1632–1704) profoundly influenced HF's thought in many areas—in politics, in the theory of education, in religion; but in none more deeply than in his philosophy of language as set forth in *An Essay concerning Human Understanding* (1690), 11. xxix ('Of Clear and Obscure, Distinct and Confused Ideas') and at length in 111 ('Of the Abuse of Words'). As early as the Preface to *Tom Thumb*, 2nd edn. (1730), where 'Scriblerus' notes, 'Mr *Lock* complains of confused Ideas in Words' (*Plays*, p. 378) and as late as *The Covent-Garden Journal*, No. 4 (14 January 1752), where a quotation from Locke's 'Of the Abuse of Words' introduces 'A modern Glossary', HF recalls Locke in this context: e.g. *The Champion* (17 January 1739/40 and 27 March 1740). See also Glenn W. Hatfield, *Henry Fielding and the Language of Irony* (Chicago, 1968), esp. ch. 1 ('The Corruption of Language'), which cites the present passage (pp. 25–6).

Chrem. O certainly! for to steal, and to break open Houses, is, no Doubt, a very mannerly thing.

Blepsid. Yes, by *Jove*: it must be certainly very reputable,[154] if the Thief be obliged to conceal himself.

Poverty. Look round among the[155] Orators; whilst they are poor, how careful of conserving the Rights of the People : but, when they are once enriched with the publick Money, they immediately part with their

---

[154] *If the Thief be obliged to conceal himself.*] '*Blepsidemus* says this in Rallery;[134] but *Aristophanes*, in many Places, seems desirous to insinuate, that the *Athenians* imitated, in some Instances, the Customs of the *Lacedaemonians*, and that amongst them Theft passed for Gallantry, and as a Jest, provided the Thief was not taken in the Fact.' *Dacier. Theobald.* Perhaps other Nations differ from these, in requiring that the Theft, in order to be reputable, should be considerable as well as secret. But I am sorry, notwithstanding the Ingenuity of the above Note, we cannot agree with this Learned Lady and Gentleman in their Translation of the Passage, to which the Note relates. Ours is strictly literal, and the Meaning, if it wants Explanation, is, that it must be a very reputable Thing indeed, which a Man is obliged to hide himself for having done. We need not observe that this is spoke ironically. M. *Dacier* is thus: *Ouy sans doute, est-ce qu'il y a rien qui ne soit honnête dans le Vol? à moins que le Voleur ne soit allez sot pour se laisser surprendre.*

M. *Theobald, Doubtless, if he have but Policy enough to conceal his Knavery, what can be more commendable?* The most Learned *Bentley* hath given us the following Note on this Place. 'This is the Interpolation of some most stupid Blockhead, which ought to be sent packing, with a vengeance to the Place from whence it came. Here is not even the least Trace of Metre; not the least Sense. How can that be *reputable* which is *concealed?* What the Devil is the Meaning of δεῖ λαδεῖν?'[135] As to the Sense of this Passage, we hope we have already satisfied our Reader, and as to the Metre, with the utmost Deference to this exact Man, whose Objection, we suppose, (for he hath mentioned none) is, that the last Foot but two is a *Trochee.* That Objection lies equally against *Verse* 591. Whoever will consider the Numbers in this Scene, will find, that except ending them like *Hexameters*, with a *Dactyl* and *Spondee*, the Poet's chief Care hath been to have Thirty Times in each, two short Syllables being equal in Time to one long one.

[155] *Orators.*] In *Greek* Ῥήτορες. We have in the first Scene rendred this Word by *Public Incendiaries.* In neither Sense can it be made familiar to a meer *English* Reader. In all the little Cities of *Greece* there were certain Men, who undertook, on public Occasions, to harangue and advise People, sometimes honestly, and for their Good; but more frequently they stirred up the People to pursue their Disadvantage, in order to effect their own private Interests. There were many of these at *Athens*, against whom our Poet is very liberal of Invectives; in which he is surely worthy of Commendation, since TO MAKE USE OF POPULAR INTEREST, AND THE CHARACTER OF PATRIOTISM, IN ORDER TO BETRAY ONE'S COUNTRY, is perhaps the most flagitious of all Crimes.[136]

---

[134] 'Rallery': an obsolete variant of 'raillery' representing the older pronunciation (*OED*, s.v.).

[135] HF's translation of Bentley's note to line 566 (Küster, p. 320). Loeb: 'Such modesty too! In whatever they do | they are careful to keep out of sight.' Sommerstein omits this line entirely, offering the following explanation which helps to explain the difficulties HF addresses: 'Here the mss. have the following line, evidently to be spoken by Blepsidemus: "Yes, by Zeus, if he has to remain undetected, how is it not decent behaviour?" The line as transmitted is unmetrical, and it has not been convincingly emended: all emendations yet proposed introduce at least one particle that is worse than redundant. It is true that it could make an effective joke to say that thieves are modest, self-effacing fellows . . . but here the joke is so clumsily expressed as to be most unlikely to raise a laugh. Either the line has suffered early and irremediable corruption, or else it is an explanatory note that was mistaken for part of the text and expanded into a rough semblance of an anapaestic tetrameter' (pp. 176–7 n. [566]).

[136] Again HF's capitals highlight a political complaint, this time not a hit at Walpole (see above, p. 263 nn. [9] and 38), but at the former leaders of the Opposition, or 'Patriot' party, Carteret and Pulteney, who had 'betrayed their country' by selling out to the present administration. For an account of HF's politics at this time, see the Introduction to *A Full Vindication* (above, pp. 202–4).

Honesty; they form Designs against their City, and declare War with the People.

Chrem. Why, there is no great Falshood in this, as malicious a Witch as thou art; but you shall not suffer the less; so I would not advise you to swagger for[156] I will not forgive your Endeavour to deceive us into an Opinion that *Poverty* is superior to the God of Riches.

Poverty. Nor can you refute a Word of what I have said. You trifle only:[157] Your Wit, like an unfledged Bird, can but flutter; it is unable to rise.

Chrem. But[158] how comes it that all Men shun you as they do?

Poverty.[159] Because I make them better. This may be chiefly perceived in Children, who shun their Fathers, for advising them to pursue what is most excellent: so difficult is it to distinguish what is right,

Chrem. You will not, I hope, say that *Jupiter* doth not truly distinguish what is right, for he hath Riches: but he keeps them to himself, and[160] sends you only to us.

Poverty. O you Dotards, whose Minds are blinded with obsolete Opinions——*Jupiter* is most certainly poor——and I will convince you of it plainly: for, if he was rich, would he, when he celebrates the[161] *Olympic*

---

[156] *I will not forgive your Endeavour.*] We have ventured to add a Word or two here, the better to explain the Meaning of the Original, which is extremely concise, and from which M. *Dacier* and Mr. *Theobald* have deviated, and both the same way. The *Greek* is obscure, by the Collocation and false Pointing. The Learned Reader may not be displeased, if we insert the Passage pointed, as we apprehend, it ought to be. ἀτὰρ οὐχ ἧττόν γ' οὐδὲν κλαύσει (μηδὲν ταύτη γε κομήσης) ὅτι ζητεῖς τουτ' αναπειθειν ἡμᾶς ὡς εστιν ἀμείνων Πενια πλουτου. [lines 572–4]. The parenthetical Sentence relates to what he says in the foregoing Line: A Collocation usual among the *Greeks*.

[157] *Your Wit, like an unfledg'd Bird.*] We have taken a paraphrastical Licence with the Original here; of which, to explain the Meaning in *English*, we have been obliged to amplify a Metaphor into a Simile.

[158] *How comes it,* &c.] This is exactly from the *Greek*. M. Dacier hath added, '*S'il y a tant d'avantage à t'avoir*; Mr. Theobald, *If there are so many Advantages in the Possession of thee.*

[159] *Because I made them better.*] Verbatim. M. Dacier, *Les Hommes ne me fuient que parce qu'*, &c. Mr. Theobald, *Men only fly me for,* &c.

[160] *Sends you only.*] The *Greek* is ταύτην, in the third Person, which Dr *Bentley* well observes,[137] adds a Politeness to the Original. But this is an Instance of the Superiority of the *Greek* Language, which is not to be imitated, nor even explained to those that do not understand it.

[161] *Olympic Games.*] M. *Dacier* seems to understand the Ποιῶν ἀγῶνα to mean the original Institution of these Games, in which she follows *Nicodemus Frischlinus* the *Latin* Translator;[138] but indeed ποιεῖν ἀγῶνα doth not signify to institute, but to celebrate; of which the Learned Reader will not want any Examples. So, ποιεῖν γάμον to celebrate (not institute) a Marriage. So in *Latin*; *facio* is used for *celebro*: As,

Cūm faciam vitulâ pro frugibus————VIRG.[139]

Where, by the way, *rem sacram* is understood. Indeed *Jupiter* was not the Institutor of these Games; the

---

[137] Bentley's comment on line 579 (Küster, p. 320).

[138] Frischlin on line 583 renders the Greek as 'Olympiacum institutens' (Küster, p. 29). Loeb has, 'the games he was founding, | . . . on Olympia's plains to be holden'; Sommerstein, 'he himself holds the Olympic festival'.

[139] Virgil, *Eclogues*, iii. 77: 'When I sacrifice a heifer for the harvest' (Loeb).

Games, (for which Purpose he convenes all *Greece* every five Years) crown with wild Olive those whom he proclaims the Victorious Wrestlers. It would rather become him, if he was rich, to give them a Golden Crown.

Chrem. By this Instance you see he manifestly shews his Respect for Riches: for, with the utmost Frugality, and Hatred to Expence, he binds the Victors with Trifles, and keeps all the Riches to himself.

Poverty. You endeavour to fasten a much greater Scandal than Poverty on him, by saying he is rich; and at the same time so void of Liberality, and so tenacious.

Chrem. May *Jupiter* confound thee; but may he first crown thee with wild Olive.

Poverty.[162] For your presuming to contradict me, when I say that *Poverty* is the Authoress of all your blessings, may you————

Chrem. You need only[163] consult *Hecate*, to know whether Wealth or Poverty be preferable: she will tell you, that the Rich send her in every Month a Supper; but that the Poor snatch it away before it is laid on the Table————But go hang yourself, with out muttering another Word:

Original of which is, by different Authors, attributed to different Persons; but the better Opinion is, that they owe their Original to *Hercules* the Son of *Alcmena*, as we find it in *Diodorus, Solinus*, and others. They are said to have been first dedicated to the Honour of *Pelops*, and were perhaps, by one of those who revived them, (for they were more than once discontinued) dedicated to *Jupiter*; in which Sense the Poet is here to be understood, when he derives the Crown with which the Victors were rewarded from that God. There is a wonderful Beauty in this Passage. The pious *Chremylus*, who, notwithstanding his Piety, had lived in extreme Poverty, was incensed with *Jupiter* for keeping his Riches to himself. The Answer of *Poverty* to this, representing *Jupiter* to be poor, and consequently, that Riches were, in reality, of no Value, since the greatest of the Gods was destitute of them, is admirable; to which we may add the Reply of *Chremylus*, who concludes from the Instance of *Poverty*, that *Jupiter* was an avaricious, not a poor Deity. Perhaps no Poet hath ever outdone this.

[162] *For your presuming,* &c. *may you.*] Here *Poverty* was going to denounce some Vengeance on the Old Men, but is interrupted by *Chremylus*. These Interruptions are extremely frequent in all the Comic Poets, and give a great Life to the Action; for which reason I am surprised, that they are always dropt by M. *Dacier*; for Mr. *Theobald's* imitating her, we account from his wonderful Complaisance to that Lady.

[163] *Consult* Hecate.] 'The *Athenians* had a great Veneration for this Goddess, believing that she was Overseer of their Families, and protected their Children. Whence it was customary to erect Statues to her before the Doors of their Houses, which, from the Goddess's Name, were called *Hecataea*. Every New Moon there was a public Supper provided at the Charge of the richer Sort, which was no sooner brought to the accustomed Place, but the poor People carried all off, giving out that *Hecate* (the Moon) had devoured it; whence it was called *Hecate's* Supper. This was done in a Place where Three Ways met, because this Goddess was supposed to have a Threefold Nature, or three Offices. And the above-mentioned Sacrifices or Suppers, were expiatory Offerings to move this Goddess to avert any Evils which might impend by reason of piacular Crimes committed in the Highways, as we are informed by Plutarch.' *Potter's Antiquities*, Vol. I. p. 386.[140] The Reason why these Suppers were offered to her on the first Days of the Month, was, because they reckoned their Months by the Moon. The Beauty of this Passage in *Aristophanes* need not be remarked.

---

[140] Potter, i, p. 386. After 'or three Offices' HF omits ten lines explaining Hecate's names and functions, resuming with 'And the above-mentioned Sacrifices and Suppers' etc.

for,[164] tho' you should persuade us of the Truth, you shall not persuade us to believe you.

Poverty.[165] O City of Argos, hear, what he says.

Chrem. Call rather for your Mess-mate[166] *Pauson.*

Poverty. What shall I do? unhappy that I am!

Chrem. Go hang yourself[141] immediately,

Poverty. Whither shall I go?

Chrem. To the Pillory. Nay, loiter not—but away with you.

Poverty. Verily, verily, you will send for me hither again.

Chrem. When we send for thee thou shalt return: but, at present, go, and be d——d: for Riches seem to me much the more eligible; and[167] you may blubber, and tear your Hair off with Madness, if you please.

Blepsid. For my Part,[168] the Moment I have got the Riches which I have

---

[164] *Tho' you shall persuade us,* &c.] The *Greek* is, *Tho' you shall persuade me, you shall not persuade me.* *Straton,* the Comic Poet, hath a Line something like this, Whom *Persuasion* herself could hardly persuade. Where, by *Persuasion,* is meant the Goddess whom the *Greeks* called Πειπθώ *i.e.* Persuasion. We have in our own Language an hyperbolical Phrase like it, *viz. I would not believe my own Eyes.*[142]

[165] *O City of Argos.*] M. *Dacier* very justly reproves the Scholiast for having falsly quoted this Line from the *Phoenissae* of *Euripides;* but I know not for what reason she herself will have this taken from any other Tragedy. The Poet seems only to reproach the *Athenians* with the Frugality and Temperance of the *Argives.*[143]

[166] Pauson.] He was an *Athenian* Painter, whose Indigence became proverbial. Mr. *Theobald* will have him to have been an Acquaintance and Cotemporary with one Δοὺκ Οὑμφρει, of whom the *Greek* Historians, whom we have consulted, make no mention.[144]

[167] *You may blubber.*] We have here translated the Original, which is very concise, with a little Amplification. M. *Dacier* and Mr. *Theobald* agree in giving it a different Turn.[145]

[168] *The Moment I have got.*] The Conclusion of this Scene is excellent, and very much tends to convey that Instruction, which the Poet intended in this Play, to the *Athenians.* You have here a Man even on the Prospect of Riches, resolving before-hand to indulge himself not only in all Kinds of Luxury, but in the highest Insolence to those who were formerly either his Equals, or perhaps his Superiors. The Reader may collect from a Word in this Speech, not very decent to repeat, and which the Poet had before mentioned in the Character of *Argyrius;* a particular kind of Insolence in use among the *Athenians* towards their Inferiors.

---

[141] In *The Covent-Garden Journal,* No. 26 (31 March 1752), HF, deploring the insolent behaviour of a set of bullies called 'Bucks', wishes there were knight-errants 'to extirpate' them, 'to drive them from the Face of the Earth; to force them, after the Greek Phrase, ἐs κόρακαs, after the English, *to the Dogs*' (p. 170). Citing this expression in Aristophanes' works, including *Plutus* in this instance (line 604), Bertrand Goldgar comments: 'Literally, "to the ravens" or "to the crows": used proverbially in the sense Fielding indicates or in the sense of "go to hell" by Aristophanes' (n. 3). See also above, p. 289 n. [108]: '*Go hang yourself*'. Loeb here has, 'Be off to the ravens'; Sommerstein, 'Get the hell out of our sight.'

[142] In *Deipnosophistae* (ix. 28–9), Athanaeus praises Straton, 'a Poet of the Middle Comedy', and quotes an amusing passage from his *Phoenicides* about a cook whose master cannot get to speak plainly, concluding: 'Persuasion herself, I swear by Gaea, could not have shaken him.' Both Loeb and Sommerstein agree with HF and Young's sense of the Greek in their translations—Loeb: 'Persuade me you may, but I won't be persuaded'; Sommerstein: 'You won't persuade us, not even if you persuade us!'

[143] HF is also mistaken. Loeb (line 600) and Sommerstein note that the quotation is from Euripides' *Telephus (frag.* 713) and is also found in Aristophanes' earlier work *Knights* (813).

[144] HF seems confused. Theobald's note reads in full: 'He was a Painter, both vain and poor to Extremity: The *Athenians* made this Proverb on him, *More beggarly than* Pauson' (p. 30 n. (*c*)).

[145] Dacier: 'tu n'as qu'à aller quelque part pleurer tes malheurs' (p. 45); Theobald: 'and therefore go Nurse the Spleen, and Sing to the Tune of your Sorrows and Disappointments' (p. 30).

set my Heart upon, I will feast it with my Wife and Children; and then, having washed and perfumed myself, as I return from the Bagnio, I will f——t in the Faces of all the Handicraft-men, and this Hag *Poverty*, wherever I meet her.

SCENE VI.

Chremylus, Blepsidemus.

Chrem. Well, this Goal-Bird[146] is gone at last; and now we Two will, with the utmost Expedition, convey the God into the Temple of *Aesculapius*, and there lay him on a Bed.

Blepsid. Let us then lose no Time, lest we should meet with a second Interruption in our Business.

Chrem. Here, *Cario*, bring out the Blankets, and conduct *Plutus* himself[169] with all proper Ceremonies, and bring too all the other Things which are prepared within:

---

[169] *With all proper Ceremonies.*] The *Greeks*, whose Superstition our Poet here derides, were very ceremonious on all these Occasions; and, doubtless, there was at the End of this Act a ridiculous Procession made over the Stage from the House of *Chremylus* to the Temple; in which *Cario*, by performing some absurd Ceremonies, had an Opportunity of diverting the Audience. Madam *Dacier* hath applied these Ceremonies, contrary to the Reading in the Original, to the Preparations within, and not to the leading forth *Plutus*. I cannot here avoid mentioning a Conjecture which that ingenious and learned Lady makes in her Preface. 'As *Plutus*, says she, must pass the whole Night in the Temple, the Spectators could not wait for his Return. It was therefore absolutely necessary that this Comedy should be performed on two several Days; for it was not possible for *Aristophanes* to shorten this Time, the Spectators being too well apprized of the tedious Ceremonies used on such Occasions.' In another Part of her Preface, she enlarges on this Head, and says, 'Nothing can be more certain than this Division in the Times of the Representation; which, if we attend to it, will give a great Beauty to this Performance. And if it was taking a Liberty, it was no more than what the Festival in which this Play was exhibited, gave him. Moreover, the Novelty could not fail pleasing the *Athenians* in so extraordinary a Subject, and inspiring them with a very great Curiosity and Impatience of knowing to what so great a Preparation and such magnificent Promises tended.' I cannot forbear thinking, that this Lady hath a little too much indulged her Talent in conjecturing, in the present Instance. For, as I apprehend, it is founded on no Authority whatever; so neither is there, I conceive, any Reason for so extraordinary a Supposition. The Curiosity and Impatience which she mentions to have been raised in the Audience, seems not at all to favour her Opinion; but indeed I see no Cause to imagine, that the *Athenian*, any more than any other Stage, was confined to such Exactness, that the full Time must be allowed for the strict Performance of every thing supposed to be done behind the Scenes; or that the Imagination of the Spectators cannot as well fancy a Thing transacted in less than the real Time, as it can impose on us to believe that the Actors are performing their Parts behind the Scenes; or that the Imagination of the Spectators cannot as well fancy a Thing transacted in less than the real Time, as it can impose on us to believe that the Actors are performing their Parts behind the Scenes, as well as they had done on the Stage, when we know the contrary, and that they have dropt the Drama, and are conversing in their own Characters. If I had not a very particular Tenderness for the Sex, as well as Regard for the truly great Learning and Ingenuity of this Lady, I should, in any other, condemn an affected Nicety, which

---

[146] 'Goal': not a typo, this spelling for 'gaol' or 'jail' was usual in the period and with HF (see *Shamela*, above, p. 182 n. 112).

ACT III. SCENE I.

CARIO, CHORUS.

Cario. O Yes! All ye happy Old Men, who in the[170] Festivals of *Theseus*, have been contented with very scanty Meals of Bread; and all others, who have any Honesty in you.

Chorus. What is the Matter, thou best of all thy Gang; for thou seemest to be the Messenger of some good News.

Cario. My Master hath had some excellent good Fortune; or rather indeed, *Plutus* himself hath had it: for, from Blindness; he[171] hath recovered his Eyes; ay, not only the Sight, but the Beauty of them, by the favourable Assistance of *Aesculapius.*

Chorus. You give me Joy, you set me a huzza-ing.

Cario. Yes, Joy is come to you now, whether you will or no.

I may venture to call the Enthusiasm of a Critic.[147] This puts me in mind of a humorous Complaint (for I believe the Gentleman was not very serious in it) of a very nice Critic, who, some few Years ago, in his Remark on a Play, where the fine Gentleman carries off his Mistress into her Bed-chamber at the End of an Act, exclaims against the civil Office which the Poet imposed on his Audience, whom he intimates to be no better than Pimps on that Occasion.

[170] *Festivals of* Theseus.] The *Athenians*, upon the eighth Day of every Month, celebrated a Festival in Memory of *Theseus*, because he was the reputed Son of *Neptune*, to whom these Days were held sacred; or because in his first Journey from *Troezen*, he arrived at *Athens* upon the eighth of *Hecatombaeon*; or in Memory of his safe Return from *Crete*, which happen'd on the eighth of *Pyanepsion*, for which reason the Festival was observed with greater Solemnity upon that Day than at any other Times. Some also there are, that will have it to have been at first instituted in Memory of *Theseus's* uniting the *Athenians* into one Body, who before lay dispersed in little Hamlets up and down in *Attica*. It was celebrated with Sports and Games, with Mirth and Banquets; and such as were poor and unable to contribute to them, were entertained upon free Cost at the public Tables. *Potter's Antiquities*, Vol 1. pag. 404.[148] The Drollery in this Character of *Cario*, is admirably supported throughout the whole Play.

[171] *Hath recovered his Eyes.*] There is an Ambiguity in the *Greek* Word, which signifies *is blinded*, or *has all Obstructions and Disorders removed from his Eyes.*

The Scholiast says, that this Expression is taken from *Phineus*, a Tragedy of *Sophocles*, which is lost;[149] and we are to suppose it to be introduced here in order to burlesque it, which is much more likely than that he should intend so vile and senseless a Conundrum, as some of his Commentators have here with wonderful Labour hammered out for him.

---

[147] In a note to the passage in *A Journey from This World to the Next* (1. viii) where the narrator in Elysium discovers Mme Dacier sitting in Homer's lap, Goldgar cites HF's comment here, making the point that, though he greatly admired 'that ingenious and learned Lady', HF objected to her tendency to indulge 'her Talent in conjecturing', which he calls 'the Enthusiasm of a Critic' (*Miscellanies* ii, p. 37 n. 5).

[148] After rearranging the opening phrases, HF quotes Potter (i, p. 404) almost verbatim.

[149] Loeb translates these lines (634–6): 'no longer blind, | He hath relumed the brightness of his eyes, | So kind a Healer hath Asclepius proved', commenting that lines 635–6 are from Sophocles, *Phineus* (frag. 644). Sommerstein, much the same: 'having been blind till now | He has the bright orbs of his eyes restored, | Finding a friend and healer in Asclepius!', commenting, 'at least part, and probably all, of this is quoted from one of Sophocles' two plays about the blind seer Phineus (Soph. fr. 710)' (p. 180 nn. 634–6).

Chorus. I will hollow[150] forth the Praises of *Aesculapius*,[172] the Father of so fine and numerous a Progeny, and great Light to Mankind.

SCENE II.

Cario and the *Wife* of *Chremylus*.

Wife. What can be the Meaning of all this hollowing? will it bring us any good Tidings? for I have waited within for this *Cario*, a long time in Expectation of them.

Cario. Quickly, quickly, Mistress, give us some Wine; that you may drink yourself——(which is, I know what you dearly love to do) *aside*: for I bring all manner of Blessings to you in a Lump.

Wife. And where are they?

---

[172] *The Father,* &c.] Εὔπαιδα in the Original, a Word which may have various Significations; we here follow M. *Dacier,* who hath chosen the most humorous. By his fine and numerous Offspring, are meant the Physicians who were called (or, as M. *Dacier* says, called themselves) the Sons of *Aesculapius*; and those of *Athens* were, according to that Lady, *pas de trop beaux garçons. Those who have wrote Comments on this Play,* says she, *have not understood the Wit of it.* Indeed Mr. *Pope,* in his *Dunciad,* seems to have no inadequate Notion of these Learned Gentlemen, whose Business seems to be to

> ——*explain a Thing till all Men doubt it,*
> *And write about it, Goddess, and about it.*[151]

Mons. *Dacier,* in his Remarks on *Hierocles* his Comment on the Golden Verses of *Pythagoras,* says, that meeting with a very difficult Passage in that Author, he in vain sought the Assistance of Commentators, who are, says he, *very tedious in explaining what is most obvious to the Understanding, but seldom say one Word on any Place which is difficult and obscure.*[152] The Truth of which Observation is truly exemplified in the Comments on this Play, where, excepting a few Places perhaps in *Girardus,* there is scarce a Remark on any single Beauty. Their true Character, in short, is, that they are

> ——*Chartam consumere nati*[153]

---

150 To cry out loud, to shout (*OED*, s.v. 'hollo, hollow, holla').

151 *Dunciad* (1728), i. 159–60 (Twickenham edn., *Dunciad A,* i. 169–70). Whereas HF in the 'Epistle to Lyttleton' (1733) had praised Theobald's *Shakespeare Restored* (1726), a criticism of 'the Many Errors' in Pope's edition of Shakespeare (see above, p. 96 and n. 35), he now, having found a new friend in the poet, applies to the scholiasts on *Plutus* Pope's lines, in which Theobald, Prince of Dulness, boasts to the Queen about his own obfuscating pedantry in that work. Cf. *Champion* (15 March 1740), where these same lines characterize 'That laborious Tribe the Commentators' (p. 235).

152 Paraphrased from *The Life of Pythagoras, with his Symbols and Golden Verses. Together with the Life of Hierocles, and his Commentaries upon the Verses . . .* By M. Dacier (1707), p. 196 n. (*h*). André Dacier (1651–1722), husband of Mme Dacier, was an eminent French classicist. In *Tom Jones* (XI. i) HF names him and René Le Bossu, together with Aristotle, Horace, and Longinus, among those 'Critics, to whose Labours the learned World are so greatly indebted' (p. 596). Other references to him occur in *The Tragedy of Tragedies* (I. i; *Plays,* p. 579 n. (*a*)), *The Champion* (27 November 1739), p. 35, and *The Covent-Garden Journal,* No. 67 (21 October 1752), p. 352.

153 '*Chartam consumere nati*': 'Born to consume paper'. Here, as in *Tom Jones* (III. ii), HF plays with Horace's 'fruges consumere nati' (*Epistles,* I. ii. 27), which, after translating 'Born to consume the Fruits of the Earth', he adapts to describe the likes of Squire Western, '*Feras consumere nati*'—'Born to consume the Beasts of the Field' (p. 120). See also *Jonathan Wild* (I. viii; *Miscellanies* iii, p. 30 and n. 3) and *An Enquiry into the Late Increase of Robbers* (sect. I, p. 80 and n. 4).

Cario. You shall soon know them in what I am going to tell you.

Wife. Dispatch them immediately.

Cario. Hasten then: for I will deduce the whole Affair[173] from Foot to Head.

Wife. Deduce nothing on my Head, I beseech you.

Cario. What? not the good things which have just now happened.

Wife.[174] None of your Affairs, I desire.

Cario. As soon as we arrived[175] at the Temple,[176] conducting a Man, then in the most miserable Condition; but now happy and blessed, if any one is so: first, we led him to the Sea, and then washed him.

---

[173] *From Foot to Head.*] We have here preserved the Original as near as possible; tho' perhaps we might have been excused, if we had followed M. *Dacier's* Example,[154] and dropt it; nay, we might have pleaded the Authority of *Horace* likewise.

$$\text{————————————————}Et\ quae$$
$$Despere\ tractata\ nitescere\ posse,\ relinquas.^{155}$$

Unless, perhaps, this Advice was given rather to an Original Author than a Translator. To say the Truth, however cold this may appear in our Language, as M. *Dacier* complains it would be in hers, there is more Beauty in the Passage than even that Lady observed. *Aristophanes* here rallies the extravagant Superstition of the *Athenians*, who were afraid of hearing good News, when told in an ominous Manner. The Explanation of the Place is this: It was a Custom among the *Greeks*, when any one denounced[156] an Evil against them, to wish the Omen might fall on the Head of the Person who denounced it. *Cario*, therefore, by inverting the common Phrase, instead from the Head to Feet, or, as we express it, from Head to Tail, *says from the Feet to the Head*; and the Poet, by an apt Collocation of the Words, hath introduced the very Phrase ἐς κεφαλήν σοι, which was used by way of Imprecation,[157] which immediately frightens the Old Woman, and drives both *Plutus*, and what was perhaps stronger, her Curiosity out of her Head, with the Fear of the Omen.

[174] *None of your Affairs.*] There is a Pun in the Original, neither capable of being preserved, nor much worth it. We have endeavoured therefore to give another Turn to the Sentiment.

[175] *At the Temple.*] There were at *Athens* two Temples of *Aesculapius*, one within the City, the other without the *Piraean* Gate, near the Sea, in which diseased and polluted Persons used to be washed by way of Purification; a Custom which the *Greeks* had probably from the *Egyptians*.

[176] *Conducting a Man.*] As the Antients made their Gods of Men, so in their Discourse they applied to them not only the Passions and Vices incident to Mortals, but their Names likewise. Thus *Virgil, Divûm nemo*, i.e. *ne homo*, literally, not one Man of all the Gods.[158]

---

[154] Madam Dacier, not her husband: see the Preface, above, p. 254 n. 17.

[155] *Ars Poetica*, lines 149–50: 'and what he fears he cannot make attractive with his touch he abandons' (Loeb, with 'desperat' for 'Desperes' and 'relinquit' for 'relinquas').

[156] 'denounced': denounce = to give formal, authoritative, or official information of; to proclaim; to publish, promulgate (*OED*, s.v. obs.).

[157] Loeb ('Up from the foot on to the very head' [line 650]), and Sommerstein more precisely ('from the feet to the head' [p. 180 nn. 649–52]), confirm HF's reading of the Greek. Sommerstein notes that the wife misunderstands the statement 'as referring to troubles (a common meaning of "*pragmata*" ["business" or HF's "Affair"]) falling on her head'.

[158] *Aeneid*, ix. 6. Cf. *Joseph Andrews* (II. xv), where HF quotes the entire sentence: '*Turne, quod optanti Divûm promittere nemo | auderet, volvenda dies en attulit ultro*' (roman added for emphasis), 'Turnus, what none of the gods would have dared to promise you as you wished, lo! rolling time has brought unasked' (p. 170 and n. 1).

Wife. By *Jove*, he must be truly happy; a poor old Fellow, duck'd in the cold Water.

Cario. But when we came within the holy Precincts, and the Loaves, and[177] previous Sacrifices were placed on the Altar, together with a Cake well hardened with Fire, we laid *Plutus* down, and, according to the Custom, every one of us fell to[178] making his own Bed.

Wife. What, were there any more of you who wanted the God's Assistance?

Cario. There was only one,[179] *Neoclides* by Name; who is indeed blind, but in Thieving hath always outshot those who can see. There were likewise many others afflicted with various Diseases. At length the[180] SACRISTAN having put out the Lights[181] ordered us to fall asleep; and charged us, if we heard any Noise not to cry out. We then laid down all of us in a very orderly Manner: but I could not sleep. A Pot of Pease-Porridge, which lay at a little Distance from an Old Woman's Head, had a violent Effect on my Nostrils: indeed, I had a supernatural Motion to creep towards it; when looking up, I saw the Priest greedily snatching away the Cakes and Figs from the sacred Table: after which he took his Rounds about

---

[177] *Previous Sacrifices*.] There were many Ceremonies performed previous to their Sacrifices, too tedious to be here set down. Our curious Reader may find them accurately digested in the Fourth Chapter of the Second Book of *Potter's Antiquities*.[159]

[178] *Making his bed*.] This Custom of sleeping in the Temple was, on many Occasions, practised by the *Greeks* and *Romans*.

[179] Neoclides.] He was an *Athenian* Orator, and had embezzled the Public Money; he has also an Infirmity in his Eyes, for which he is aptly introduced here to be cured by *Aesculapius*. He is again mentioned as having this Blear-eyedness, *Ecclesiaz*. v. 254.[160]

[180] *Sacristan*.] The *Greek* is, *the Servant of the God*. 'These were Priests, says our learned Archbishop, waiting on the Gods, whose Prayers the People desired at Sacrifices, at which these seemed to have performed some other Rites distinct from the *Ceryces*, who were the Cooks of the Sacrifice.' *Potters Antiquities*, Vol. I. pag. 208.[161]

[181] *The Sacristan having put out the Lights*.] 'It is Matter of Astonishment, that *Aristophanes* took the Liberty of rallying their Religion and Priests, before a People so devoted to Superstition, and whom it was so dangerous to endeavour to undeceive. He very pleasantly here lays open the Cheats of these Priests, who presided over the Sacrifices; who, after having stoln away the Offerings in the Night, the next Morning imposed on the credulous Multitude, by telling them that the God had devoured the whole. There are many Examples of these Tricks of the Pagans recorded in Holy Writ.' *Dacier*. By Holy Writ, she means the *Apocrypha*.[162]

---

[159] Potter (II. iv ['*Of the* Grecian *Sacrifices, Sacred* Presents, *and* Tythes']), i, pp. 209–37.

[160] Aristophanes, *Ecclesiazusae*, line 254.

[161] Quoted, nearly verbatim, from Potter (II. iii ['*Of the* Grecian *Priests and their Offices*'], i, p. 208.

[162] The only example of such priestly trickery in the Apocrypha would appear to be 'The History of the Destruction of Bel and the Dragon', 1–22, in which Daniel exposes the 'fraud' of the seventy priests of Bel, a brazen idol: at night the priests, with their wives and children, secretly entered the temple of Bel and consumed the sacrificial food and wine, making it appear that the idol had consumed the sacrifice; by strewing the temple floor with ashes, Daniel exposed the deceit.

the Altars, to see if there was any Loaf left, and[182] consecrated all he found into a Wallet, which he carried for that Purpose; upon which, I thinking this was a great Act of Devotion, stood up in my Turn to the Porridge-Pot.

Wife. O thou Wretch, hadst thou no Apprehension of the God?

Cario. Yes, by all the Gods, had I, an Apprehension, that,[183] having his Garlands on, he would get to the Pot before me:[184] for that Priest had told me before-hand. As for the Old Woman, when she heard the Noise, she put out her Hand to secure her Porridge; I hissing like one of *Aesculapius's* Serpents, seized it in my Teeth; upon which she immediately drew it back into her Bed, and wrapping herself up close, very quietly laid down till she outstunk a Cat, f—ting with Fear: but then I fell to supping up the Pease-Porridge. When my Belly was full, I betook myself to my Repose.

Wife, But, did not the God appear to you?

Cario. No, not yet. After this I did a very merry thing: for, as the God was approaching, I let a loud F—t; for my Belly was cursedly puffed up with the Porridge.

Wife. For which he certainly held thee in[185] the utmost Abhorrence.

Cario. No, but[186] his Daughter *Jaso,* as she attended her Father,

---

[182] *Consecrated.*] This Expression is so humorous, that I am surprised that the other Translators have dropped it. The inimitable Pleasantry of this whole Scene need not be hinted even to an ordinary Reader.

[183] *Having his Garlands.*] The Images of the Pagan Deities were crowned with Garlands. The Ridicule here is exquisite.

[184] *For that the Priest had told me before-hand.*] M. *Dacier, Car ce que venoit de faire le Sacrificateur m'en disoit trop pour ne me donner point de peur. Mr.* Theobald, *For the Priest had done enough to give me Suspicions of that kind.* But the Meaning of *Aristophanes* is much finer and stronger than this. *Cario* would say, that he had great reason to fear the God would intercept his Meal, since the Priest had very gravely assured the Congregation, that the God himself would, whilst they were asleep, eat up whatever Eatables he found in the Temple. This he might well believe, for he had it from the Priest himself. As for what had past, it was without his Suspicion; for of that he had not been forewarned by the Priest. For a farther Illustration of this the Reader may consult the History of *Bel* and the *Dragon.*[163] There is still more latent Humour in this Place. The Old Woman's Mess was not designed for a Sacrifice, but for her own Supper; yet as the Priest had stoln every thing from the Altars, *Cario* had some reason to fear, that the God finding nothing else, would be forced, in his Hunger, to take up even with the Old Woman's Potage.

[185] *the utmost Abhorrence.*] There is a peculiar Propriety in the *Greek* Word, which properly signifies *to abhor a Man for f—t—g.* M. *Dacier* hath avoided these gross Expressions, which, as we have undertaken to give a Translation of *Aristophanes,* we do not think ourselves at liberty to do, unless where a literal Translation would offend the Chastity, as well as the Delicacy of our Readers; the former of which we shall always carefully avoid offending.

[186] *His Daughter* Jaso.] *Aesculapius* had three Daughters, *Hygeia, Jaso,* and *Panacea,* i.e. *Health, Cure, Universal Remedy.*[164] Madam Dacier's Note on this Place is very ingenious. 'There is more Satire, says she, in this, than the Translators or the Commentators have observed. *Aristophanes* would here insinuate that the Priests brought Courtesans by Night into the Temples, to feast with them on the consecrated Offerings. This could not have been touched in a more fine and delicate Manner.'

---

[163] See above, n. 162.

[164] In *A Journey from This World to the Next* (1. iii), as Bertrand Goldgar suggests, HF may have meant to contrast the three daughters of '*Maladie Alamode*' (i.e. syphilis)—namely, '*Lepra, Chœras,* and *Scorbutia*' (*Miscellanies* ii, p. 20 and n. 8)—with this present account of the three salubrious daughters of Aesculapius.

redden'd a little; and her Sister *Panacea* turned away her head, holding her Nose: for I assure you I fart no Frankincense.

Wife. But *Aesculapius* himself———what did he?

Cario. O by *Jove*, he never troubled his Head about it.

Wife. Surely, according to your Account, this God hath very little Regard to good Manners.

Cario. My Account!———I say[187] the Goldfinders and he live upon the same Commodity.

Wife. O Wretch!

Cario. After this, I presently covered myself up, out of Fear; and he very decently went his Rounds, and inspected all the Cases: Immediately afterwards his Apprentice brought him[188] his Stone-Mortar, and his Pestle, and his Box.

Wife. What! a Stone-Box?

Cario. No, by *Hercules*! not the Box, but the Mortar was of Stone.

Wife. Sure, some terrible Judgment will fall on thy Head: for, how could you see all these Things, when you say you had covered your Head in the Bed-Clothes?

Cario. I saw all through the Hole of my Cloke; and, by *Jupiter*, there are Windows enow in it. The first Operation was performed on *Neoclides*, for whom the God ordered his Apprentice to pound an Ointment in a Mortar, throwing in three Heads of Garlick of[189] *Tenos*; which being done, he

---

[187] *The Goldfinders and he.*] The *Greek* is σχατοφάγον, *one who lives on human Ord–re*. There is more Wit than Cleanliness in the Expressions. It was reported of both *Hippocrates* and *Aesculapius*, that they carried their Curiosity very far for the sake of their Patients.

Girardus is severe on the Learned Faculty here, in applying this Epithet too directly to them all, *who, in the Cure of Diseases*, says he, *are obliged to be familiar with P–ss, and more nasty things, by which Trade as they support themselves, they may in some Sense be called* σχατοφάγοι. We have introduced the Word *Goldfinders*,[165] not so much with Desire of adding any Pleasantry to *Aristophanes*, which is not in the Original, as from Necessity, that without the utmost Flatness we might preserve a little Decency in this Place, which the nice Reader hath already, I believe, had too much of. I cannot, however, quit it, without observing, that a certain *French* Translator hath rendred this Place by a Detour, in order to avoid the Grossness, and given an Idea ten times more strong than the Original.[166]

[188] *His Stone-Mortar, his Pestle, and his Box.* Wife. *What a Stone-Box?*] M. Dacier, *Une petite Boëte, un Pillon, & un Mortier de Marbre. Myrrhine, Quoi, une petite Boëte de Marbre?* Mr. Theobald, *A little Casket, Pestle and Mortar of Marble.* Every one perceives that the *French* Collocation, which is directly contrary to the *Greek*, makes the Woman's Answer entirely improper: Mr. Theobald hath therefore carried his Complaisance too far in imitating it. The ridiculous Exhibition of *Aesculapius*, in the Character and with the Implements of an Apothecary, cannot fail to strike.

[189] *Tenos.*] An Island, one of the *Cyclades*.

---

[165] '*Goldfinders*': a slang term for those who cleaned out latrines. See also *The Champion* (31 May 1740), p. 352, and *Tom Jones* (VI. i, p. 269).

[166] Dacier: 'Mais je dis que comme il est grand Médecin, il gouste volontiers aux viands que les hommes ont déja mangées & qu'il ne hait pas l'odeur dont je viens de parler' (p. 51).

himself mixed it with[190] Benjamin and[191] Mastic, and then adding some[192] Vinegar of *Sphettus*, he spread the Plaister, and put it on, having first turned his Eye-lids outwards, that he might[193] put him to the greater Torment. Poor *Neoclides* first squalled, then roared, then took to his Heels, and ran away full Speed: at which the God laughing heartily, said to him, Sit quietly down with your Plaister;[194] I will take care you shall keep your Oath, and abstain from the Courts of Justice.

[190] *Benjamin.*] A Gum of great Value among the Antients: *Pliny* says that it was sold for its Weight in Silver.[167]

[191] *Mastic.*] M. Dacier *and Mr.* Theobald, *Sea-Onions.*[168]

[192] *Vinegar of* Sphettus.] *Sphettus* was a Borough in the Tribe *Acamantis* in *Attica.* Some will have this to be a Satire on that particular Borough, alluding to their sharp or sour Disposition.

[193] *Put him to the greater Torment.*] This Stroke on the Physicians needs no great Explanation; *Moliere,* in one of his Comedies, introduces a Doctor asking his Patient how he does? To which the Patient answers, *Much Worse.* The Doctor replies, *So much the better.*[169]

[194] *I will take care,* &c.] This Passage is one of the most difficult in all *Aristophanes.* The *Latin* Interpreter hath explained it very ill, *Ut si jurejurando forte postules dilationes causarum, ego te liberem.*[170] This is neither intelligible nor just. The *Greek* Scholiasts have given other Explanations, which are no better. One says, the *Greek* signifies, *to the end that after your Oath, I may give you a true Pretence to keep out of the Court*; for it was the Custom, when they were desirous not to appear before the Judges, to swear that they had substantial Reasons to prevent them. Here then *Aristophanes* accuses *Neoclides* of having often forsworn himself, to avoid appearing to the Summons of the Citizens. This would be very good Sense, if it could agree with the Answer of *Myrrhina, that* Aesculapius *had the Public Interest at heart.*

Another Scholiast explains it thus: *To the end that I may give you a true Pretence of swearing that you can not come into Court*; and says, that *Aesculapius* alludes to the Custom of those, who well foreseeing that they must be condemned, counterfeited Sickness to obtain Delay of their Sentence; after which the whole Process was to be renewed from the Beginning. But this is still less agreeable to what follows. I am persuaded I have given the most natural Sense to this Passage. This *Neoclides* was a noted Informer, who went every Day into the Courts of Justice, in order to accuse some of the Citizens, and to inrich himself with their Spoil; and as he was very distemper'd, and had often need of the Assistance of *Aesculapius*, he was a great Frequenter of his Temple, where, to inforce his Prayers, he constantly swore that he would

---

[167] Pliny, *Natural History*, XII. liv. 117: 'duplo rependebatur argento' ('its price was twice its weight in silver' (Loeb). On Benjamin, see below, p. 322 n. [234].

[168] '*Mastic*': a gum or resin which exudes from the bark of *Pistacia lentiscus*; formerly much used in medicine (*OED*, s.v.).

[169] Molière, *Le Médecin malgré lui* (1666), III. v. 'Sganarelle [to the patient's father]: *Comment se porte la malade?* | Géronte: *Un peu plus mal depuis votre remède.* | Sganarelle: *Tant mieux: c'est signe qu'il opère.*' In *The Mock Doctor* (1732), HF's version of Molière's farce, he renders the scene (xvi) as follows: '*Gregory*: Well, Sir, how does my Patient? | *Sir Jasper*: Rather worse, Sir, since your Prescription. | *Gregory*: So much the better; 'tis a Sign that it operates' (2nd edn., p. 29). HF found this scene particularly amusing: in a letter to the *General Advertiser* (8 October 1751) promoting the efficacy of the Glastonbury Waters, he recalls: 'the Humour of Moliere, who introduces a Physician, saying, *tant mieux,* when his Patient declares he is worse' (Battestin, 'Fielding and the Glastonbury Waters', *Yearbook of English Studies*, 10 [1980], p. 208). In his *Charge to the Jury* (1745) he also recalls an earlier scene very like this one (*Mock Doctor*, sc. ix): 'the Doctor having asked his Patient how he does, he answers, *In great Pain*; to which the Doctor replies, *So much the better*' (*Champion*, pp. 611–12 and n. 1). This earlier scene plays as follows: '*Gregory*: Does this Distemper . . . oppress her very much? | *Sir Jasper*: Yes, sir. | *Gregory*: So much the better. Has she any great Pains? | *Sir Jasper*: Very great. | *Gregory*: That's just as I would have it' (p. 16).

[170] Frischlin's translation of lines 724–5: 'So if by taking oath you perhaps request delays, I will free you' (Küster, p. 35). The passage in question concerns the arcana of Hellenic jurisprudence: see the exegesis in Sommerstein (p. 183 n. 725).

Wife. What a wise Deity this is, and what a Lover of the People!

Cario. He then sat down by *Plutus.* And[195] first he stroked his Head; next, taking a clean Napkin, he wiped round his Eye-lids. *Panacea* now covered his Head and Face with a Scarlet Cloth, after which the God whistled; immediately[196] two Serpents of a supernatural Size rushed forth from the sacred Part of the Temple.

Wife.[197] O good God!

Cario. And these creeping softly under the Scarlet Cloth, fell a licking the Eye-lids; at least so it seemed to me: and in less time than you could drink off ten Half-pints of Wine, *Plutus,* (I assure you, Madam, it is true,) was started up with his Eyes open. I clapped my Hands for Joy, and wakened my Master; presently[198] the God disappeared, and the Serpents returned into

renounce his former way of Life; but no sooner had he left the Temple than he returned to the same Courses. *Aesculapius,* who had been too often deceived by him to confide any longer in his Oaths, takes care himself to oblige him to keep his Promise, by increasing his Distemper: on which account this good Woman answers, *that* Aesculapius *hath the public Interest at heart.* If we understand it in this manner, the Passage is full of Wit, and the Character so strong, that it is impossible to see it, without recollecting some such Person; for the Age of *Aristophanes* is not the only one which hath produced a *Neoclides.*' *Dacier.* This is indeed the better Sense, and we have accordingly embraced it.

[195] *First he stroked his Head.*] The Ridicule of this Ceremony is very apparent.

[196] *Two Serpents.*] The Poet hath already in this Scene alluded to these. Many Reasons are given why the Antients consecrated the Serpent to *Aesculapius,* as the God of Physic. First, that the Serpent doth in a manner renew his Youth, by casting his Skin every Spring and Autumn, which *Virgil* hath described in these beautiful Lines:

> *Cùm positis novus exuviis, nitidúsque juventâ*
> *Volvitur, aut catulos tectis aut ova relinquens,*
> *Arduus ad solem linguis micat ore trisulcis.* Georg.[171]

Secondly, from the Quick-sightedness of this Creature; whence the Eye of a Serpent was proverbially applied to very Quick-sighted Persons: So *Horace,*

> *Cur in amicorum vitiis tam cernis acutum,*
> *Quàm aut aquila, aut serpens Epidaurius.*[172]

Lastly, they were sacred to this God, as they afforded in themselves excellent Remedies for many Distempers. A huge Serpent was brought from *Epidaurus* to *Rome,* which the *Romans* worshipped, believing it to be *Aesculapius* himself. Our Apothecaries give a Serpent in their Arms, by which some conceive they intimate their true Descent from *Aesculapius*; others will have it to be in Commemoration of *Apollo's* killing the Serpent Python; for they are likewise of the Family of that Deity. For my own part, I imagine this to be only a kind of Sign, signifying that they have excellent Vipers in their Shops.

[197] *O good God!*] The Superstition of this Woman, which is so excellently plaid upon by *Cario,* must have afforded great Diversion to the Spectators.

[198] *The God disappeared.*] '*Aesculapius* had other Patients to visit; but on account of the great Noise which was occasioned by the Cure of *Plutus,* and the Hurry in which they all rose from their Beds, the God thought proper to retire, lest the whole Cheat should be discovered. All this is perfectly well conducted.' *Dacier.*

---

[171] *Georgics,* iii. 437–9: 'when, his slough cast off, fresh and glistening in youth, | he rolls along, leaving his young or eggs at home, | towering towards the sun, and darting from his mouth a three-forked tongue!' (Loeb).

[172] *Satires,* I. iii. 26–7: 'When you view the failings of your friends, are you as keen of sight | as an eagle or as a serpent of Epidaurus?' (Loeb).

the inmost Recesses of the Temple. Now several of[199] those who lay near him fell to embracing him with inexpressible Affection, and kept awake till it was broad Day-light. I uttered vehement Praises of the God, for having so suddenly restored *Plutus* his Eyes, and made *Neoclides* blinder than before.

Wife. O *Aesculapius*, what a powerful Deity art thou![200] but tell me what is become of *Plutus?*

Cario. He is coming: but there is a prodigious Crowd gathered about him. Those who had led honest Lives, and been poor, embraced him, and all received him with much Pleasure: but those who had dishonestly acquired great Substance, knitted their Brows, and[201] looked very sour. Whereas the former, crowned with Garlands, followed behind, laughing and shouting.[202] The Shoes of the Elders resounded as they went; for they advanc'd, beating Time, as it were, with their Feet: Come on, my Boys, with one Accord, every Man of you, dance and caper and[203] figure in; for no Man will hereafter tell us, when we enter his House, that there is no[204] Pudding in the Pot.

Wife. O *Hecate,*[205] I will crown thee————with a String of Buns for this good News.

Cario. Make no longer Delay; for the Men are near our Door.

---

[199] *Those who lay near him, fell to embracing him.*] There is great Spirit in this whole Passage. 'At the very moment that *Plutus* recovered his Sight, all the Sick Persons who lay in the Temple, in order to be cured, forgot all their Diseases, and the Deity himself from whom they expected their Cure, and thought of nothing more than making their Court to the God of Riches.' *Dacier.* To which I shall add, that there is a particular Beauty, as the Learned well know, in the Tenses used in this Speech, which we have endeavoured to preserve in the Translation.

[200] *But tell me what,* &c.] Notwithstanding the Religion and Superstition of this Old Woman, her Devotion cannot keep her Thoughts a Moment from *Plutus.*

[201] *Looked very sour.*] The *Greek* is, *Looked like* Scythians, whose fierce and savage Manners were well known.

[202] *The Shoes resounded.*] This Verse was probably taken from some Tragedy,[173] which it intends to burlesque. The literal Translation would be, *The Shoes of the Old Men resounded with their well-tuned Advances.*

[203] *Figure in.*] The *Greek* is χορεύετε, *dance in Chorus.* Our Translation agrees with the best and gravest Authors who have writ on the Subject of Country-Dances.

[204] *Pudding in the Pot.*] The *Greek* is *Meal in the Bag.*

[205] *I will crown thee with a String of Buns.*] We have before observed, that those who returned with good News from the Oracles, were crowned with Garlands. The Old Lady therefore tells *Cario*, that, as a Reward of the good News which he hath brought of *Plutus* from the Temple, she will crown him————but instead of adding, *with a Garland*, as the Spectators expected, she adds, with a *String of Buns.* This could not fail raising a Laugh in an *Athenian* Audience.

---

[173] Sommerstein on lines 758–9, 'and old men's shoes with rhythmic tread resounded': 'it is not clear whether the sentence is directly adapted from an actual tragedy (cf. Euripides' *Medea*, 1179–80, *Bacchae*, 1090–1, both from messenger speeches) or whether it is pastiche' (p. 184 n. 758–9).

Wife. Well, I go in, and will fetch the customary[206] Entertainment, to welcome his new-purchased Eyes.

Cario. And I will go and meet the Procession.

SCENE III.

Plutus, Chremylus, and his *Wife.*

Plutus.[207] First, I pay my Adoration to the Sun; then I salute the[208] illustrious Soil of the venerable *Pallas*,[209] and all the Country of *Cecrops*, which hath hospitably received me. I blush at my Misfortunes, when I recollect with what Men I have ignorantly passed my Time, and have shunned those who were only worthy of my Conversation. Unhappy as I was, who knew nothing of the Matter all this while. How wrong have I been in both; but, for the future, turning over a new Leaf, I will show all Mankind, that it was against my Will I gave up myself to the Wicked.

Chrem. Go, and be hang'd,[174] all of you—what troublesome things are Friends, who[210] immediately appear, when any good Fortune attends you! They tread on my Heels, and squeeze me to Death, every one expressing his Affection for me: for, who hath not spoke to me! with what a Crowd of Elders have I been surrounded in the *Forum*!

Wife. Your humble Servant, dear Sir, (*to* Plutus) and your's, Sir, (*to her Husband*)—Give me Leave,

Sir, according to our Custom, to welcome you with this Entertainment.

Plutus. By no Means: for, at my Entrance into your House, on the Recovery of my Sight, it becomes me better to make you a Present, than to receive one.

Wife. Will you be so unkind not to accept it?

---

[206] *Entertainment*.] At *Athens*, when a Slave was first brought home, there was an Entertainment provided to welcome him to his new Service, and certain Sweetmeats were *poured* on his Head. Which for that reason they called Καταχύσματα. *Potter's Antiquities*, Vol. I. pag. 7.[175] The Poet here uses the Word νεωνήτοισιν, new-bought or purchased. The Old Lady will therefore have *Plutus* entertain his new-purchased Eyes in the same manner as they entertained their new-purchased Slaves.

[207] *First, I pay my Adoration to the Sun*.] M. *Dacier* prettily remarks how well this is adapted to a Man who hath just recovered his Sight.

[208] *The illustrious Soil of the venerable* Pallas.] *Athens*, which was built by *Neptune* and *Pallas*, but took its Name from the latter, of whose Protection they were most vain: The Poet therefore takes this Occasion to flatter the Opinion of his Audience.

[209] *And all the Country of* Cecrops.] *Attica*, whose first King was *Cecrops*.

[210] *Immediately appear*.] This is literal from the *Greek*, and the Beauty of it need not be remarked. M. Dacier, *naissent*; Mr. Theobald, *spring up*. I apprehend this whole Speech may be tasted by an *English* as well as an *Athenian* Audience.

---

[174] See above, p. 303 n. 141.

[175] Potter, I. x ('*Of the* Sojourners *and* Servants *in* Athens'), i, p. 71.

Plutus. Not till I am[211] at your Fire-side: for there it is the Custom to receive it. After I have got clear of[212] this troublesome Crowd: for it becomes not our Poet to throw Figs and Sweetmeats among the Spectators, in order to bribe their Applause.

Wife. You say very true: for yonder I see stand up[213] *Xenicus* ready to scramble for the Figs.

ACT IV. SCENE I.
C ARIO.

HOW sweet it is, Sirs, to get Riches, without sending out any Ventures for them! How is a whole Heap of good Things rushed in upon us, without doing the least Evil! Riches so acquired are indeed a Blessing——Our Bin is full of fine Flour; our Vessels of black sweet flavoured Wine; our Trunks of Gold and Silver! Well, it is wonderful! Our Well is full of Oil, our Oil-Cruises are filled with precious Ointment! Our Garrett with Figs! Every Vinegar-Jar, and Tray, and Pot, are all become

[211] *At the Fire-side.*] This was among the Antients the most sacred Part of the House, where their Houshold-Gods were placed, and particularly the Goddess *Vesta*, who is called by the same Name, taken from a *Chaldean* Word signifying *Fire*.[176]

[212] *This troublesome Crowd, for it becomes not our Poet.*] *Aristophanes* here very pleasantly includes all the Spectators in the Number of the Followers of *Plutus*; a Liberty frequently taken by the Comic Poets. The latter Part of this Speech is a just Ridicule on the many absurd Methods which the Poets have taken to ingratiate themselves with their Audience. The Duke of *Buckingham*, in his *Rehearsal*, hath likewise very excellently ridiculed this Artifice; where Mr. *Bays* attempts to move the Compassion, and next to frighten the Spectators into applauding him.[177] The Method our Poet hath taken hath still a farther Beauty, from its being so well adapted to his Subject; intimating, that the *Athenians* were so very avaricious and corrupt, that their Voices were to be purchased even by Figs and Sweetmeats.

[213] Xenicus.] We have chosen to make this a proper Name, following the common Editions which place the Accent on the first, and not on the last Syllable. Dr. *Bentley* hath proposed an ingenious Correction, Εὖ πάνυ λέγεις ὀχλος δὲ ξενικὸς οὐσαὶ. *You say very well; but this Rabble of Strangers,* &c.[178]

[176] Baker comments: 'Latin *Vesta* derives from the Indo-European root *wes*, meaning "to dwell". The association with fire is owing to the hearth, the center of a dwelling, hence the perpetual fire the vestal virgins guarded in Vesta's temple' (*American Heritage Dictionary of Indo-European Roots* (Boston, Mass.), s.v.).

[177] In *The Rehearsal* (I. i) by George Villiers, second Duke of Buckingham (1628–87), Bayes the playwright, wishing to impress the critics Smith and Johnson with his devices for ensuring the audience's applause, reveals schemes for two prologues: in the first, calculated to move their compassion, 'I come out in a long black Veil, and a great huge hangman behind me, with a Furr'd-cap, and his Sword drawn; and there tell'm plainly, That if, out of good nature, they will not like my Play, I gad, I'll e'en kneel down, and he shall cut my head off. Whereupon they all clapping'; the second is meant to terrify them by bringing on stage, in dialogue, a pair of actors impersonating Thunder and Lightning: in Smith's opinion, ''Tis short indeed; but very terrible' (8th edn. [1711], pp. 6–8).

[178] Bentley's 'ingenious Correction' of line 800, as HF calls it ironically, is in Küster, p. 320. The original reads εὖ πάνυ λέγεις· ὡς Δεξίνικός γ' ὁντοσὶ: 'Well said indeed: for Dexinicus there' | [Is rising up, to scramble for the figs'] (Loeb, lines 800–1).

of shining Brass! Our Fish-Platters, which were of Wood, and something
rotten, are now all Silver! Our Dresser is of a sudden become Ivory! We
Servants now play at Even and Odd[179] with[214] Golden Staters, and are so
elegant, that we wipe our Posteriors with Garlic, instead of Stones. And
now my Master, with a Garland on his Head, is sacrificing within, a Hog, a
Goat, and a Ram;[215] the Smoke hath sent me out: for I was able to bear it no
longer, it so offended my Eyes.

SCENE II.

Dicaeus and *Cario*.

[216]*Dicaeus. (speaking to a Youth.)*[217] Follow me, my Child, and let us go
together to the God.

Cario. Hey day! who comes here?

Dicaeus. One, who was miserable: but is now fortunate.

Cario. O then,[218] certainly you are of the Number of good Men, as it
should seem.

Dicaeus. Most certainly.

Cario. And what do you want?

Dicaeus. I am going to the God; who is the Author of great Blessings to
me. You must know, that I, having inherited a very sufficient Fortune from
my Father, supplied my necessitous Friends with it: for I thought it the
surest way to secure to myself a comfortable Life.

Cario. No Doubt you soon[219] saw the Bottom of your Purse.

Dicaeus. You are in the right.

Cario. You was then certainly miserable.

Dicaeus. Even so. But I thought, when I assisted them in their Necessity,

---

[214] *Golden Staters.*] A Silver Stater is worth near Three Shillings; and consequently a Golden one must
be worth above Forty.

[215] *The Smoke hath sent me out.*] The Delicacy of Curio is admirable. He cannot bear what his Master
supports very well.

[216] *Dicaeus.*] The *Greek* is Δίκαιος, *a just Man*; but we judged the calling him by a proper Name, would
be more agreeable to an *English* Reader.

[217] *Follow me, my Child.*] Girardus well observes, that, by his manner of speaking, this Youth was his
Son, not his Servant.

[218] *Surely you are of the Number of Good Men, as it should seem.*] Here is a kind of Contrast in the
Original between them Words δῆλου [certainly, clearly] and ὡς ἔοικας [so seem], which we have
endeavoured to preserve.[180] M. *Dacier* had added, *Au moins en avez vous la mine*; Mr. Theobald, *Indeed
your Face speaks for you.*

[219] *Saw the Bottom of the Purse.*] Literally, Your Riches failed you.

---

179 'Even and Odd': a game of chance (*OED*, s.v. 'even' *a* 15 *d*).

180 Sommerstein (line 826) renders the 'Contrast' neatly: 'You *seem plainly* to be one of the good sort'
[emphasis].

that I should find them Friends indeed, if I should ever want any; whereas, when that Day came, they turned their Backs, and pretended not to see me.

Cario. Ay, and I make no Doubt laugh'd heartily at you into the Bargain.

Dicaeus. Very true. I was almost destroyed[220] by the Drought——of my Dishes.

Cario. But it is not so now with you?

Dicaeus. No: for which Reason I am come to the God to offer my Adoration, as I ought.

Cario.[221] But this old Cloke here——what, in the Name of *Jupiter*, is the Meaning of this old Cloke, which the Boy carries after you?——Pray tell me.

Dicaeus. I intend to dedicate it to the God.

Cario. I hope you was not[222] initiated into the great Mysteries in this——

Dicaeus. No, but I have shivered in it these thirteen Years.

Cario. And those old Shoes there?

[220] *By the Drought of my Dishes.*] M. Dacier, *Ils rioient de ce que j'avois vendu tous mes meubles*; Mr. Theobald, *Laughed at me for having sold my all.* But this is not the Meaning of the Original. Indeed Drowth may metaphorically signify *Scarcity*; but a Scarcity of Dishes would not indicate a Man's wanting Bread. The Poet uses here the Ἀπροσδόκητον [the unexpected—a rhetorical figure], and instead of expressing the Drought of the Season, or of his Lands, which ruins Farmers, and might be expected from the former Part of his Speech, when he said he was ruined by the Drought, he adds pleasantly, *of his Dishes.*[181] Among the lower sort of our own People, a Kitchin adorned with shining Plates and Dishes is thought no Sign of their good House-keeping; and among the Higher, *Will you foul a Plate with me?* is as much as to say, *Will you dine with me?*

[221] *But this old Cloke.*] We have been obliged to repeat this Word, to preserve the Force of the Original, which otherwise would have been lost by the *English* Collocation. The Antients, on their Delivery from Danger or Misfortune, used to consecrate some Memorial to the Gods. Thus *Horace*,

> ——— *me tabulâ sacer*
> *Votivâ paries indicat uvida*
> *Suspendisse potenti*
> *Vestimenta maris Deo,*[182]

Alluding to the Custom of hanging up in the Temple of *Neptune* the Garments in which they had escaped Shipwreck. This Old Man therefore having just escaped out of Poverty, very pleasantly proposes to consecrate this Emblem of it to the God who had delivered him.

[222] *Initiated into the great Mysteries.*] These were the *Eleusinian* Mysteries, which were celebrated at *Eleusis* a Town of *Attica.* They were of Two Sorts; the Great and the Little: The first were sacred to *Ceres,* and the latter to *Proserpina.* They were the most solemn of all their religious Ceremonies, and all the *Athenians* indifferently were initiated into them, unless such as had been convicted of any heinous Crime. The Manner of Initiation was very formal, and may be seen at large in *Potter's Antiquities*, Book II. Chap. 20.[183] The Garments in which they were initiated were held sacred, nor did they ever leave them off till worn to Rags. This Allusion therefore of *Cario*, while he rallies the mean Offerings which *Dicaeus* was carrying to the God, is full of Drollery.

---

[181] Loeb (line 839) has, 'The drought in all my vessels'; Sommerstein, 'a drought in my stores'.

[182] *Odes*, I. v. 13–16: 'As for me, a votive tablet on his temple wall records that I have dedicated my drenched clothes to the deity who rules the sea' (Loeb).

[183] Potter, II. xx ('Grecian *Festivals*'), I, pp. 389–93. In his burlesque of Juvenal's Sixth Satire, HF would soon again refer to the Eleusinian mysteries: 'Few worthy are to touch those Mysteries, | Of which

Dicaeus. And these have spent the Winter with me.

Cario. And do you dedicate these too?

Dicaeus. Yes, by *Jove*.

Cario. You have brought most grateful Offerings to the Deity, no Doubt.

SCENE III.

[223]*Sycophantes*, *Cario*, and *Dicaeus*.

Sycoph. O unhappy and undone Man that I am! O thrice unhappy, and four times, and five times, and twelve times, and ten thousand

---

[223] *Sycophantes*.] We have made a Proper Name of this; in the Original, it signifies an Informer, or, as Archbishop Potter says, a Common Barreter.[184] These Persons were very great Pests among the *Athenians*, and our Poet hath frequently lashed them; particularly here, where he introduces one on the Stage. The following short Account of these People, extracted from the learned Archbishop, may not be disagreeable to our unlearned Reader. 'Every Corner of the Streets was pester'd with Swarms of turbulent Rascals, that made it their constant Business to pick up Stories, and catch at every occasion, to accuse Persons of Credit and Reputation. These they called Συκοφάνται, which Word sometimes signifies *False Witnesses*, but is more properly taken for what we call *Common Barreters*, being derived ἀπο τοῦ συκοφαίνειν, *from indicting Persons that exported Figs*; for amongst the primitive *Athenians*, when the Use of that Fruit was first found out, or in the Time of a Dearth, when all Sorts of Provisions were exceeding scarce, it was enacted, That no Figs should be exported out of *Attica*; and this Law not being actually repealed, when a plentiful Harvest had rendred it useless, by taking away its Reason, gave occasion to ill-natured and malicious Men to accuse all Persons they caught transgressing the Letter of it; and from them all busy Informers have ever since been branded with the Name of *Sycophants*.' *Potter's Antiquities*, Vol. I. pag. 121.[185] We need not observe that the Use of the Word *Sycophant* is much perverted in our Language; and that we use it here, wherever it occurs, in the antient Sense.[186]

---

we lately know the Histories' (lines 79–80); this time, however, it was not Archbishop Potter he credited for illuminating them. For an explanation of the mysteries, written 'in a most masterly Stile, and with the profoundest Knowledge of Antiquity', HF advised his readers to turn to the Revd William Warburton's *Divine Legation of Moses vindicated* (*Miscellanies* i, p. 91 n. 3); and in *A Journey from This World to the Next* (I. viii), when a puzzled Addison, in Elysium, overhears the narrator acquaint Virgil 'with the Discovery made by Mr. *Warburton* of the *Eleusinian* Mysteries couched in his 6th Book', the poet himself confirms the fact (*Miscellanies*. ii, p. 38). In *The Champion* (31 May 1740) HF had mocked Warburton's scholarship; and in a letter of 24 September 1742 to James Harris from Bath, though he acknowledged Warburton's 'extraordinary' intellect, HF found the divine's other qualities quite another matter: 'Pride, Arrogance, Self Sufficiency and some other such Ecclesiastical Qualities compose his Character' (*Correspondence*, Letter 14, p. 25).

The change, from mockery to praise, in HF's attitude towards Warburton as publicly expressed—in *Tom Jones* (XIII. i) he asks the Muse of Learning, 'Give me awhile that Key to all thy Treasures, which to thy *Warburton* thou hast entrusted' (p. 687)—may be traceable to the time late in 1741 when, shortly before the publication of *Joseph Andrews*, HF's friendship with his patron Ralph Allen began at Prior Park, Bath, where Allen was also entertaining Pope and Warburton, who in 1745 would marry Allen's favourite niece.

[184] 'Barreter': i.e. 'Barrator': a person who buys or sells ecclesiastical preferment, a simoniac or simonist (*OED*, s.v. I. 1 obs.).

[185] Potter, I. xxi ('*Of Some Other* Courts *of* Justice, *their Judicial Process*, &c.'), i, pp. 121–2.

[186] '*Sycophant*': the original meaning in Greek was 'fig-shower', which was long explained, though unsubstantiated, as referring to one who was an informer against the unlawful exportation of figs. The term may have referred originally to the obscene gesture of 'making a fig' (*OED*, s.v.). By the eighteenth century, 'sycophant' generally had its modern meaning, 'an abject flatterer; a parasite, toady' (*OED*, s.v. 3).

times————O! O! of what a Variety of Ills is[224] my Fortune composed!

Cario. Apollo, and all propitious Deities defend us. What terrible Misfortune hath happened to this Man!

Sycoph. Have not the greatest Misfortunes fallen on me this Day; who am, by the Means of this God, stripped of every thing I had in the World? But, if there be any Justice upon Earth, I'll have him restored to his former Blindness again.

Dicaeus. I begin to smell the Matter. This Man is certainly in a very *bad Way*; but he hath[225] a very bad Stamp on his Countenance.

Cario. If he is a Rascal, I think, when he is in the Road to Destruction, he may be said to be in a very F A I R W A Y.[226]

Sycoph. Where is he? where is the Traitor! who promised to-day, that, when he had recovered his Eyes, he would alone[227] make us all rich; and now he hath them, he puts some of us into a worse Condition than we were in before!

Cario. Whom, pray, hath he served so?

Sycoph. Whom! why, me myself.

Cario. You! Ay, but you are a Rogue, and a Housebreaker.

Sycoph. No, Sirrah! But there is not a Grain of Honesty in such Fellows as you————nor is it possible but you must have robbed me of my Money.

Cario. Bless me! what a magisterial Air the Sycophant advances to us with.

Dicaeus. The Man is plainly perishing with Hunger.

Sycoph. (to *Cario*.) Come, you Sir,[228] this Instant, into Court: you

---

[224] *My Fortune composed.*] The Metaphor in the Original is taken from Wine quite dispirited by too great Infusion of Water.[187]

[225] *A very bad Stamp.*] This is literal from the *Greek*, and is a Phrase often used by our Author, to denote a vile and infamous Fellow. It was a Metaphor taken from their Money. We have a Proverb in *English* not unlike it, a *bad Penny.*

[226] *In a very fair Way.*] We have here preserved the Opposition between the κακῶς and καλῶς πράττων in the Original.

[227] *Make us all rich.*] This scandalous Fellow lays claim to those Promises which were made to good Men only; in which Number he impudently enrols himself. This is true Humour.

[228] *This Instant into Court.*] This is one of those Strokes of Nature, which, tho' they are Instances of the greatest Penetration in the Writer, are sure to escape all Readers, but those of accurate Judgment and strict Attention. This Informer, who hath been deprived of all his Wealth, as a Punishment for having procured it by Informations on Penal Laws against his Fellow-Citizens, still preserves his old Disposition, and is for haling into Court every Man he sees.

---

[187] Loeb (line 853): 'So strong the spirit of ill-luck that swamps me'; Sommerstein: 'what a voracious fate has swallowed me!'—commenting: 'lit. "with so concentrated (*poluphoros* 'capable of bearing a large admixture of water') a fate I have been blended!" In elevated poetry, a person who experiences misfortune or grief may be said to be mixed or blended (*sunkerannusthai*) with it . . . Aristophanes here in effect treats this as a live metaphor from the dilution of wine with water in a mixing-bowl, with the sufferer as the water and his fate as the wine, which in this case is so strong that it absorbs its victim at hardly any cost in potency' (p. 190 n. 853). HF and William Young appear to have misunderstood the metaphor.

shall be[229] put on the Wheel, and rack'd till you confess all your
Rogueries.

Cario. You be rack'd yourself!

Dicaeus. By *Jupiter* the Preserver; this God is worthy of the highest
Honour from all Greece; for exacting such just Vengeance of Sycophants.

Sycoph. What a Wretch am I!——Ha! do you too laugh at me, after
having a Share in the Plunder! for whence could you otherwise come by this
fine Coat; you, whom yesterday I saw wrapped up in a miserable old Cloke!

Dicaeus. I regard you not. See on my Finger[230] this Amulet-Ring, which
I bought of *Eudamus* for a *Drachma*.

Cario. There are no Charms in your Ring against the Bite of a
Sycophant.

Sycoph. I think this very injurious Treatment: you revile me, but will not
tell me what is your Business: for you are here on no good Design, I am
certain.

Cario. With no Design for your Good, you may be well assured of that.

Sycoph. By *Jupiter*, but you will sup to-night at my Expence.

Dicaeus. May this be true; and may you[231] and your Witness burst your
Bellies———but not with Meat.

Sycoph. Do you deny it, you Villains, when I smell such a Flavour of Fish
and Rost-meat from within? Phu, Phu, Phu. (*Sniffling.*)

Cario. What do you smell, Sirrah?

Dicaeus. I suppose he smells the Cold: for his Clothes are in a very
tatter'd Condition.

Sycoph. This is insufferable. O *Jupiter*, and all you Gods! are these Fellows to insult me! how my Indignation rises, that an honest Man, and a
Patriot, should be reduced to such a Condition.

---

[229] *Put on the Wheel, and rack'd.*] This, among the *Athenians*, was inflicted only on Slaves; it was a
Torture not inflicted to punish their Crimes, but rather to extort a Confession of them, agreeable to the
Question used by the Civil Law.

[230] *This Amulet Ring.*] The Antients superstitiously placed great Virtues in Rings. The Story of that
which *Gyges* King of *Lydia* wore, is well known.[188] *Eudamus* was a Professor of the Magic Art, and
pretended to make Rings which should be Preservatives against the Bites of Serpents; *Cario*, by his
Answer, implies that this Informer was a more venomous and pernicious Animal than a Serpent; and that
against his Malice there was no Guard whatsoever.

[231] *And your Witness.*] These Informers usually carried some profligate Fellow about with them, who
was by his Evidence to support their Informations.

---

[188] Gyges (687–652 BC), King of Lydia. In the *Republic* (ii. 359), Plato tells the story of Gyges, a
shepherd in the king's service, who descends into a chasm caused by an earthquake and finds a hollow
brazen horse wherein he sees a corpse, naked except for a gold ring, which he removes from its finger. He
finds that by turning the bezel of the ring he becomes invisible. Acting as a messenger to the court, he uses
this talisman to seduce the queen; with her help he murders the king and seizes the throne.

Dicaeus.[232] You an honest Man, and a Patriot!

Sycoph. Yes, no other comes near me.

Dicaeus. Answer me a few Questions.

Sycoph. What are they?

Dicaeus. Are you a Farmer?

Sycoph. Do you think me such a Madman?

Dicaeus. You are a Merchant then, I suppose.

Sycoph.[233] I pretend to be so, when I see Occasion.

Dicaeus. What then?——Have you learned any Handicraft?

Sycoph. No, by *Jove.*

Dicaeus. How do you live then, if you do nothing for your Livelihood?

Sycoph. I am a Superintendent of the Publick Weal, and of the Good of every private Person.

Dicaeus. You! and how came you, pray, to take this Office upon you?

Sycoph. Such is my Will and Pleasure.

Dicaeus. Thou Villain! dost thou pretend to be an honest Man, who art odious to every one, by doing what doth not belong to you?

Sycoph. Doth it not belong to me, thou Gull, to serve my Country with all my Might?

Dicaeus. Is an officious medling with every Man's Business serving your Country?

Sycoph. Yes, to assist the dead Letter of the Law; and not to suffer those who offend it to escape with Impunity.

Dicaeus. The Publick takes care to provide proper Judges.

---

[232] *You an honest Man, and a Patriot.*] Literally, M. Dacier, *Tu as preferé le Bien de la Patrie à tes Interests*; Mr. Theobald, *When did you e're prefer your Country's Good?*[189]

[233] *I pretend to be so.*] 'As the Country of *Attica* was very barren, the Inhabitants subsisted only by Commerce, on which account the *Athenian* Laws indulged their Merchants with great Privileges. They were exempted from going to War, and from paying Taxes. This gave occasion to very enormous Abuses; for there were always some, who, to avoid the Payment of these Taxes, or that they might not be obliged to list in their Armies, pretended to be in Partnership with the Merchants, who for a small Bribe lent their hand to the Imposition. This is what the Informer means, by answering that he pretended to be so when he saw occasion.' *Dacier.* This Method of perverting the Privileges which the Laws of a Country indulge to some particular Members or Bodies in it, hath not been confined to *Athens.* Such Instances, when they happen, fall very justly under the Lash of a Comic Poet. And it is by exposing such Persons and Things, that *unlicensed* Comedy will be found of great Use in a Society; and a Free Stage and a Free People will always agree very well together.[190]

---

[189] Another hit at former leaders of the 'Patriot' party such as Carteret and Pulteney, who, after the resignation of Walpole, joined the administration they had been denouncing. See above, p. 300 n. 136.

[190] By italicizing '*unlicensed*' HF recalls the event that put an end to his career as playwright: the Theatrical Licensing Act of 1737, which imposed censorship on the stage for 230 years (see V. J. Liesenfeld, *The Licensing Act of 1737* [Madison, Wis., 1984]). HF's comment epitomizes his arguments at that time in defence of the comic dramatist who, following the example of Aristophanes, serves the public by exposing corruption in high places: see the Introduction, above, p. 246 and n. 30.

Sycoph. But who will inform?

Dicaeus. Whoever pleases.

Sycoph. I am then that He, and thus the Affairs of the City devolve on me.

Dicaeus. The City hath indeed a sorry Protector. Would it not be better for thee to live quietly and peaceably, and intermeddle in no-body's Affairs?

Sycoph. You describe the Life of a silly Sheep: for such is the Life of a Man without Business.

Dicaeus. You are resolved then not to reform.

Sycoph. No, not if you would give me *Plutus* himself, and all[234] the *Benjamin* in *Cyrene.*

Dicaeus.[235] Off with your Cloke immediately.

Cario.[236] The Gentleman speaks to you, Sir.

Dicaeus. And your Shoes too.

Cario. It is all to you, Sir.

Sycoph. Touch me either of you, whoever pleases.

Cario.[237] *I am then that he. (Here* Cario *lays hold on the Informer, and strips him, at which his Witness runs away.)*

Sycoph. What a Wretch am I, to be thus stripp'd in open Day-light!

Dicaeus. This is your Punishment for seeking a scandalous Livelihood, by medling with what doth not belong to you.

Sycoph. Take care what you do; for I have a Witness present.

Cario. No, Sirrah, your Witness hath taken to his Heels.

Sycoph. Ha! Wo is me; am I then left alone?

Cario. What, now you roar?

Sycoph. Wo is me! I say again.

[234] *Benjamin in* Cyrene.] In the *Greek, all the Benjamin of Battus.* This Benjamin-Herb was a great Branch of the *Graecian* Commerce with *Cyrene,* a City built by *Battus,* who planted there a Colony from *Thera* an Island in the *Aegean* Sea.[191]

[235] *Off with your Cloke immediately.*] The last Words of the Informer, by which he testifies such an Abhorrence of Reformation, destroy all Patience in *Dicaeus.* The latter Part of this Scene consists chiefly in Action; nor could the Distress of the Informer fail of giving the greatest Delight to the *Athenians,* who held such Persons in the utmost Detestation.

[236] *The Gentleman speaks to you.*] It was customary to strip Slaves, when they were going to whip them; for which reason, the Speech of *Dicaeus* seem'd to be directed to *Cario,* to whom the Informer, by some Motion of his Hand, applied it: *Cario* therefore answers in Triumph, *It is not to me, Sir, but to you that he speaks.*

[237] *I am then that he.*] As the Informer ended his Speech with βουλόμενος *whoever pleases,* which were the Words *Dicaeus* had used a little before, when the Informer had asked, *Who should inform? Cario* here answers in the same Words, which the Informer had just before very haughtily made use of Ὁυκοῦν ἐκεῖνός ἐμ'ἐγώ. *I am then that he.*

[191] Sommerstein translates the line (925), 'all the silphium of Battus'; and Loeb has 'all Battus's silphium', commenting: 'Battus led the colony [in the latter part of the seventh century BC] from Thera to Cyrene . . . Silphium, a kind of giant fennel, was the wealth of the place, being used for human food, animals' fodder, and medicine.' The *OED* (s.v. 'silphium') cites a single instance (from 1820): 'The silphium, or herb Benjamin'; no such synonymous connection is given under 'Benjamin'.

Cario. Lend me your old Cloke then, that I may cover the Gentleman's Nakedness.

Dicaeus. By no Means. It is already sacred to *Plutus.*

Cario. How can it be offered more properly than of the Shoulders of this Rogue and Robber? *Plutus* should be adorned with rich Clothes.

Dicaeus. But tell me to what Use shall we put these old Shoes?

Cario. I will[238] nail them up to his Forehead, as you nail Offerings against the wild Olive-Tree.

Sycoph. I will depart; for I see you are too many for me: but, as soon as I find any of my Evidences, tho' never so bad a one, I will bring this God, stout as he is, to condign Punishment this very Day: for this single Fellow[239] manifestly subverts the Government, and all without obtaining any Authority from the Senate or People.

Dicaeus. Well, Sir, since you march in my Furniture, make as much Haste as you can to the Bagnio-Fire, that you may get the first Place, and warm yourself. It is a Post I myself have often stood Centry at.

Cario. The Master of the Bagnio will lug him out by the Heels: he will know him the Moment he sees him; for the Fellow hath Rogue written in his Face—But come, let us Two go in, that you may pay your Adoration to the Deity.

SCENE IV.

Old Woman, Chorus, Chremylus.

Old Woman. Tell me, honest Friends,[240] are we indeed arrived at[241] the House of this new Deity, or have we missed our Way?

---

[238] *Nail them up to his Forehead.*] We have before in our Notes on this Scene, mentioned the Custom of the Antients, of consecrating their Garments, &c. in their Temples. These were fastned to Posts, as *Virgil,* in his 12th *Aeneid.*

> ————*Figere dona solebant*
> *Laurenti Divo*—[192]

Cario therefore very pleasantly desires to make such a Post of the Informer.

[239] *manifestly subverts.*] The Poet here makes use of a *Delphic* Sword, *i.e.* one of two Edges; for this may be understood either as a Satire on the Informer, who hath the Impudence to accuse *Plutus* of manifestly intending to subvert the Democracy by those very Means, which were in reality the only ones of establishing it: Or, it may be applied to the Government, which, as he insinuates, gave no Countenance to any such good Measures.

[240] *Are we indeed arrived.*] This Translation is almost *verbatim,* and the Plural Number here used indicates this Old Lady to have brought her Retinue with her; whence we may conclude her to have been of some Consequence. M. *Dacier* and Mr. *Theobald* agree here in the Use of the Singular Number.

[241] *The House of this new Deity.*] This is contemptuously spoken by the angry Old Lady.

---

[192] *Aeneid,* xii. 768–9: referring to a certain wild olive, 'a tree revered of old by mariners, whereon, when saved from the waves *they were wont to fasten their gifts to the god of Laurentum* and hang up their votive raiment' (Loeb).

Chorus. Know, my pretty Miss, you ask in very good time for you are arrived at the very Door.

Old Woman. Well, then, shall I call some-body out?

Chrem. There is no need of calling any one; for I am just come out myself: but it will be necessary for you to tell me your Business.

Old Woman. O Sir! I have suffered very great and sad Mischiefs indeed; for ever since this God here hath recovered his Eye-sight, I have had a most uncomfortable Life.

Chrem. What is this? you are[242] an Informeress, I suppose.

Old Woman. Not I, by all that is sacred.

Chrem. What, I suppose, you never had[243] the good Fortune to be Tost-Mistress at your Club.

---

[242] *An Informeress.*] We have here taken the same Liberty with our Language, as M. Dacier hath taken with hers; and which indeed *Aristophanes* had authorized her to do by this Example.[193]

[243] *The good Fortune to be tost Mistress.*] The Antients used to cast Lots who should preside at their Compotations. The Prize-Lot, on this occasion, had a particular Mark or Letter on it; a Custom which they borrowed from the Methods used in electing their Judges, which we have touched on before.[194] Among the *Romans*, who derived this Custom from the *Greeks*, the Lot denoting the King or Master of the Feast, had the Name of *Venus* inscribed on it. Whence *Horace*,

> *Quem Venus arbitrum*
> *Dicet bibendi?*———[195]

He again mentions the same Custom in another Place,

> *Nec regna vini sortiere talis.*[196]

There is something not very unlike this in use even among us at Twelfth-tide, when the King and Queen of the Entertainment are chosen by Lot:[197] *Chremylus* therefore pleasantly supposes here, that the Old Lady's Complaint against this new Deity was, that she could not have the Good-Fortune to draw this Lot, of which it appears the Antients were extremely vain. M. *Dacier* and Mr. *Theobald* have alike misunderstood this Passage.[198]

---

[193] Aristophanes 'coined *sukophantria* [line 970] as a feminine equivalent of *sukophantes*' (Sommerstein [p. 199 n. 970], who follows HF in translating the word as 'informeress', whereas Loeb has 'she-informer'). Mme Dacier has '*Delatrice*' (p. 69) instead of *délateur*, in a note apologizing for the coinage (pp. 152–3).

[194] Above, p. 280 n. 89.

[195] *Odes*, II. vii. 25–6: 'Who will be declared toastmaster by Venus' throw [the highest throw with the dice]?' (Loeb).

[196] *Odes*, I. iv. 18: 'you will not throw dice to decide who directs the party' (Loeb).

[197] Cf. *The Champion* (6 December 1739), where HF, having mentioned 'our *Saxon* Ancestors' who 'used to decide all Controversies by Lot', continues: 'a Custom which seems to be preserved in an old *English* Play, or Gambol, celebrated yearly on the *Epiphany*, or *Twelfth-Day*, wherein a King, a Queen, a Knave, and a Fool are created by blind Chance' (p. 47).

[198] Dacier: 'Mais n'estes-vous point de ces bonnes commeres qui boivent volontiers le petit coup?' (p. 70); Theobald: 'Are you not then one of those sociable Damsels that cast Lots over their Cups, who shall be Queen of the Company?' (p. 46). Baker comments: 'Although Mme. Dacier omits it in her translation, she explains the custom of drawing lots in her notes (p. 153)'; and he suggests that HF objects to Theobald's translation 'apparently because it assumes a party for ladies only, whereas the Greeks and Romans drank in mixed company and accepted men and women equally as rulers of the feast, whoever drew the winning lot'.

Old Woman. You banter me: but, alas! I am[244] troubled with a terrible Itch.

Chrem. What Itch? Discover quickly, what Itch?

Old Woman. Listen then. I had a dear young Fellow, poor indeed he was, but a handsome well-shaped Lad, and good-natur'd; for he supplied all my Wants, in the modestest, and prettiest Manner: and I, on the other hand, supplied him with all these Necessaries——

Chrem. What were the Necessaries, pray, which he chiefly used to want of you?

Old Woman. Not many: for he was a bashful Youth, and had a most awful Respect for me——He would ask me twenty *Drachmas* to buy him a Coat, and eight to buy him a Pair of Shoes.

And he would ask me to buy a cheap Gown for his Sisters, and a poor Wrapper for his Mother. Sometimes he would beg four[245] *Medimni* of Wheat of me.

Chrem. By *Apollo*, what you tell me is no great Matter; it is indeed plain he had a most awful Respect for you.

Old Woman. And these Things, he constantly told me, he did not ask as the Reward of his Performances, but out of pure Friendship, that he might wear my Coat for my sake, and remember me by it.

Chrem. This young Fellow, by your Account, must have been most desperately in Love with you.

Old Woman. Ah! the impudent Varlet is not now of the same Mind, but is exceedingly altered; for, upon my sending him this Cheesecake, and a whole Saucer full of Sweetmeats, with an Assignation, that I would come to him in the Evening——

Chrem. What did he do?——tell me.

Old Woman.[246] He returned me the Cheesecake, intending, that I should come no more thither to him; nay, and besides all this, he ordered the Messenger to tell me, that the[247] *Milesians* were formerly stout Fellows.

---

[244] *Troubled with a terrible Itch.*] This is literal. *M. Dacier, C'est une passion bien plus honnête qui cause tout mon mal; Mr.* Theobald, *A Passion much more honourable has been my Ruin.*

[245] Medimnus.] The Name of a Measure used at *Athens*, containing six Bushels.

[246] *He returned me this Cheesecake.*] By the Word τουτουὶ, this appears to be the Cheesecake which she had mentioned before, and which she then held in her Hand, tho' the Words in the Original are different.

[247] *The* Milesians *were formerly stout Fellows.*] 'This Proverb was formerly applied to those who were sunk from their former Fortune, or had degenerated from the Manners of their Ancestors. And it will suit with all those who have ceased to be what they were, and are become worse, as Old Men from Youths, or Poor from having been Rich; or reduced to a private Station from a Throne, or into Obscurity from Eminence. The *Greeks* assigned various Accounts of the Original of this Proverb; some say, that the *Milesians* formerly excelled all other Nations in Military Glory, and conquered all those with whom they had any War. In after-times, *Polycrates* King of *Samos*, when he was entring upon a War, being desirous to call in the Assistance of the *Milesians*, sent to consult the Oracle on that Affair: The God answered,

Chrem. It is plain this young Fellow hath not[248] a depraved Taste; since now he is grown rich, he delights no longer in Lentils:

for, formerly his Poverty obliged him to take up with any Dish he could Procure.

Old Woman. And yet I swear to you,[249] by the Twin-Gods, he formerly used to walk every Day by my Door.

Chrem. What,[250] looking for your Corps!

Old Woman. No, only for the Pleasure of hearing my Voice.

Chrem.—[251] Bidding him take something, I suppose.

Πάλαι ποτ᾽ ἦσον ἄλκιμοι Μιλήσιοι.
The Milesians *were formerly stout Fellows.*

Others report another Story: when the *Carians* intended to attack some other Nation, and had decreed to employ Auxiliaries from the most powerful of their Neighbours, some were of opinion that the *Milesians* should be called in; others were for applying to the *Persians*: On which Occasion *Apollo* being consulted, returned the same Answer as we have mentioned before; the Fame of which was spread all over *Greece*; and the *Milesians* being afterwards almost all slain in a Battle with the *Persians*, the Oracle became a merry Proverb. Others again write, that the *Carians* being at War with *Darius*, according to an Oracle by which they were admonished to apply to the Assistance of the bravest People, went to the *Branchidae*, and consulted the God of that Place, whether they were to call in the Aid of the *Milesians*; and that he answered, that *the* Milesians *were formerly brave*, signifying, to wit, that they were now become weak and effeminate through Luxury. But this Story *Zenodotus* refutes from Chronology; if indeed this Verse be found in *Anacreon*, who flourished in the Age of *Cyrus* King of *Persia*, from whom *Darius* was the Third. *Politian* therefore chose rather to refer it to the Morals of the *Milesians*, which were corrupted with Effeminacy; as does *Athenaeus*. *Aristophanes* uses this Proverb in his *Plutus*, and puts it in the Mouth of a young Man, who was again sent for by an Old Lady, whose Company he had in his Poverty frequented for the sake of her Riches; but now being become rich, he despised her whose Treasures he had exhausted.' *Erasmus.*[199]

[248] *A depraved Taste.*] Whilst he was poor, the taking up with this Old Woman must have been imputed to his Necessity; now it would be referred to his Choice. M. Dacier, *Le jeune homme n'est pas sot*; Mr. Theobald, *The Youth has Sense.*

[249] *By the Twin-Gods.*] *Castor* and *Pollux*. This Oath is used even among our Vulgar, *By Gemini*.[200] The Women accustomed themselves peculiarly to swear by these Gods.

[250] *Looking for your Corps.*] This is the better Meaning, in which Sense our Author again uses the Word in his *Ecclesiazousai*; *Aeschylus* and *Euripides* use it in the same. Indeed it is the common understanding of it. The *Latins* used the Word *Essero* in like manner. M. *Dacier* and Mr. *Theobald* interpret it in another manner.[201]

[251] *Bidding him take something.*] The Original is literally, For the sake of taking something. M. Dacier, *Pour recevoir quelque petit Present à la fin de la visite*; Mr. Theobald, *To get some little Present for every Visit.*

---

[199] Baker notes that HF and Young 'here translate the Latin of Erasmus, "Chiliadis Primae, Centuria LXIX", *Adagiorum Chiliades Tres* (Venice, 1508), leaves 97ᵛ–98ʳ, indexed "FUERE QUONDAM STRENUI MILESII". [Baker continues] It also appears in its entirety in the Greek scholium to line 1003, Küster p. 43, but not attributed to Erasmus.'

[200] Cf. HF's *Love in Several Masques* (1728; III. ii), where Catchit, a servant girl, opens the scene by exclaiming to Malvil: 'O Gemini! Sir, what's the matter?' In his note, Thomas Lockwood quotes the *OED*: 'a mild oath or exclamation' (1664), and cites later instances from Congreve and Wycherley, as well as Chloe in HF's *The Lottery* (1732; sc. ii): see *Plays*, p. 50 and n. 38. Sommerstein, however, translates this as 'by the Two Goddesses', making it a reference to Demeter and Persephone (p. 202 n. 1006).

[201] '*Effero*' (to carry to the grave, to bury). Dacier: 'Pour en emporter quelque chose, sans doute?' (p. 72); Theobald: 'For the Convenience of assisting his Fortune, doubtless!' (p. 47).

Old Woman. And then, if ever he found me in a Fit of the Vapours, he would caress me by the fond Names of My little[252] Duck, and my little Dove.

Chrem. And then, perhaps, he would ask you for a Pair of Shoes.

Old Woman. When I have rode out in my Chariot, on the Day of cele-brating the[253] great Mysteries,

I have been sure of[254] a hearty thrashing, if any young Fellow took it into his Head to ogle me:[255] so violently jealous of me was this sweet Youth.

Chrem. It seems then he liked to eat alone.

Old Woman. My Hands were, he said, extremely beautiful.

Chrem. When they held out twenty *Drachmas* to him.

Old Woman. And my Skin, he said, had a most delicate Smell.

Chrem. Very probably while you poured forth[256] *Thasian* Wine.

Old Woman. That I had a soft and lovely Eye.

Chrem. This was no aukward Fellow, I find—he knows how to feed upon a Rampant Old Woman.

Old Woman.[257] The God, therefore, my good Friend, doth not do well; tho' he pretends that he will redress the Wrongs of the Injured.

Chrem. Tell me what you would have him do, and it shall be done immediately.

Old Woman. It is surely reasonable, that he should compel this young Man, to whom I have done so much Good, to return some good Offices to me, otherwise it is not just he should enjoy any Advantage whatever.

Chrem. What! did he not make you a suitable Return every Night?

Old Woman. Ay, but he promised never to leave me, whilst I was alive.

---

[252] *My little Duck and my Dove.*] The Original here is faulty. The true Reading is, as the learned *Bentley* and *Faber* have most ingeniously amended it,

Νηττάριου και φάττιον.

This Reading we have followed in our Translation.[202]

[253] *The great Mysteries.*] We have mentioned these before.[203]

[254] *A hearty thrashing.*] The Greek is ὅλην τὴν ἡμεράν, *thrashed me the whole Day.* This is used indefinitely.

[255] *So violently jealous.*] The Vanity of this Old Lady is extremely humorous and natural.

[256] *Thasian Wine.*] *Thasus.* An Island in *Thrace,* produced very excellent Wine of a sweet Savour.

[257] *The God doth not do well.*] The Allegory intends, that the young Fellow had devoured the Substance of this lascivious Old Woman; by which being enriched, he forsook her, and refused to bestow any Gratuities on her for former Favours. This teaches a Moral, which may be of use to my fair Readers who are upwards of Fifty.

---

[202] In his note to line 1012 [i.e. 1011], Bentley deletes *av* between *nettarion* and *kai* (Küster, p. 321), an emendation unacceptable to either Loeb or Sommerstein. Yet HF's translation is the same as theirs: Loeb has 'Calling me "little duck" and "little dove"'; Sommerstein, '"my little duck" and "my little dove"' (see his note, p. 203 n. 1011). HF's other authority is Tanneguy Lefebvre or Tanaquillus Faber (1615–72), father of Mme Dacier and an eminent classical scholar whose Latin translation of Aristophanes is included in Küster.

[203] See p. 317 nn. [222] and 183.

Chrem. True! but he now thinks you alive no longer.

Old Woman. Indeed, Friend, I am considerably pined away with Trouble.

Chrem. You seem rather to be pined away with Rottenmess.

Old Woman. You may draw me through a Ring.

Chrem. Ay, if it was as big as a Hoop.

Old Woman. As I live, here comes the very Youth I have been all this while accusing; he seems to be come[258] a revelling.

Chrem. He doth so; for he hath a Garland and a Torch with him.

SCENE V.

[259]*Neaniscus, Old Woman, Chremylus.*

Neaniscus.[260] Save you, good People.

Old Woman. What says he?

Neaniscus. My old Friend, you are grown grey all on a sudden.

Old Woman. What a Wretch am I, to be thus abused!

Chrem. It seems he hath not seen you a long while.

Old Woman. How long, Sirrah!—he was at my House but yesterday.

Chrem. I find Drink hath a contrary Effect on him to what it hath on others; it makes him see the clearer.

Old Woman. No: but[261] he is always saucy in his Behaviour.

Neaniscus.[262] O SEA-NEPTUNE, and all ye antique Gods, what a

---

[258] *A revelling.*] M. *Dacier* and Mr. *Theobald* translate it, *to pay a Visit to the God* Comus: but I apprehend ours is the Meaning of the Author.[204]

[259] *Neaniscus.*] In *Greek, a young Man*; we have given him a Proper Name in Conformity to our Stage.

[260] *Save you, good People.*] The *Greek* is ἀσπάομαί *I embrace*; a Word which hath a visible Effect on the Old Lady. This was likewise a polite Term of Salutation, as we have before remarked. We could not preserve this Pleasantry in the Translation.

[261] *He is always saucy.*] This is the Reverse of what the Old Lady had before said. But she is willing to impute his present Behaviour to any Cause, rather than to a Contempt of her Charms. This is extremely natural and humorous.

[262] *Sea-Neptune, and all ye antient Gods.*] We have before remarked the Propriety with which the Antients invoked their Gods. *Diogenes Laertius*, in his Life of *Thales*, whose Doctrine was at this time in vogue, tells us, that Philosopher asserted *Water to be the first Principle of all Things*, ἀρχὴν δὲ τῶν πάντωνὕδsρ ὑπεϛήσατο Homer, in his Thirteenth *Odyssey*, calls *Neptune* Πρεϛβύτατον, the most antient of the Gods. To which I will only add, that our Poet, in his *Birds*, ver. 702, makes the Ocean elder than the Earth.[205]

Sea-Neptune.] In our Notes on the second Act[206] we have shewn that the *Athenians* worshipped this Deity by many Names, the Horseman, the *Sea-Neptune*, &c.

---

[204] Both Loeb (line 1041) and Sommerstein concur.

[205] Diogenes Laertius, *Lives of Eminent Philosophers*, I. i. 27 (Thales): 'His doctrine was that water is the universal primary substance'; *Odyssey*, xiii. 140–3, where Zeus calls Poseidon 'the oldest and best' of the gods (Loeb).

[206] See Act II, scene iii, p. 289 n. [109].

Number of Wrinkles she hath in her Forehead! (*Holding his Torch up to her Face.*)

Old Woman. Ah! Oh! don't thrust your Torch in my Face.

Chrem. She is in the Right: for, if a single Spark should seize her, she will burn like[263] a dry Olive-Branch.

Neaniscus. Are you willing we should have a little Play together,[264] after this long Absence?

Old Woman. Where, Wretch?

Neaniscus. Here, with these Wall-Nuts.

Old Woman. What Play?

Neaniscus. How many Teeth have you?

Chrem. I will have my Guess. Perhaps, she hath three or four.

Neaniscus. Pay me: she[265] wears but one, and that is a Grinder.

Old Woman. Sure, you are out of your Senses, Villains, to endeavour before[266] so many Men to[267] besprinkle me thus with your Jests.

Neaniscus. Sprinkle you!——I am sure you would be the better for it, if you was well washed.

Chrem. No, truly: for she is now varnished over; but, should the Paint be once washed away, the Furrows of her Face will appear plain.

Old Woman. As old a Man as you are, you seem to me a very simple Fellow.

Neaniscus. Perhaps, he is tempting you. I suppose he doth not think I see him playing with your pretty Bubbies.

Old Woman. No, by *Venus*, you Rascal, he touches not mine.

---

[263] *A dry Olive-Branch.*] The *Greek* is Εἰρεσιώνη, *an Olive-branch covered with Wooll,* which the *Athenians* loaded with all Kinds of Fruits, and hung out before their Doors as an Antidote or Charm against the Plague. This Superstition is here squinted at by the Poet.

[264] *After this long Absence.*] The *Greek* is Παῖσαι Διά Χρόνου. The *Latin* Translation is, *Lusitare diutule;*[207] M. Dacier, *Joüer un moment*; Mr. Theobald, *Play a little.* All erroneously. Διᾱ before the Genitive Case of Nouns of Time signifies an Intermission; so Διᾱ πολλοῦ χρόνου, a few lines before, and in a thousand other instances.

[265] *Wears.*] So is the *Greek.* Perhaps it would be too fine to infer from hence, that even this was a false one.

[266] *So many Men.*] This must include either the *Chorus*, or the Spectators.

[267] *Besprinkle.*] M. *Dacier* hath declined this Passage, which she says cannot be render'd in her Language; we hope we have preserved it in ours.[208]

---

207 Frischlin's translation of this phrase (line 1055; Küster, p. 45).

208 Baker comments: Mme. Dacier translates, 'de me faire servir de divertissement à tout le monde' (p. 76), and explains in her note that the passage depends on the verb *laver*, which in Greek means both 'to wash' and 'to ridicule', the old woman meaning 'to ridicule me' and the young man punning literally that she could use a washing (p. 156). Cf. Theobald: 'to besprinkle me with Scandal? | *Neoch.* A good hearty Sprinkling, for ought I know, might be of singular Service' (p. 49).

Chrem. No I,[268] by *Hecate!* I am not so simple: but, harkee, young Gentleman, you must not have such an Aversion to this Lass.

Neaniscus. I! I dote on her!

Chrem. Why, she accuses you.

Neaniscus. Of what doth she accuse me?

Chrem. She says you are insolent, and have told her, that the *Milesians* were formerly stout Fellows.

Neaniscus. I will not fight with you for her.

Chrem. Why, pray?

Neaniscus. In Respect to your Age; for I should permit this in no other: but, as you are, you may go off safely, and carry the Lass along with you.

Chrem. I well know your Meaning——you will not now vouchsafe to converse with her, as you have.

Old Woman. Who is he, who is[269] so free to deliver me up?

Neaniscus. I do not choose a Conversation with one who hath been embraced by Thirteen Thousand Years.

Chrem. But, since you have drank the Wine, you ought to drink the Dregs also.

Neaniscus. Ay, but these are very old and fusty indeed.

Chrem. Well then,[270] a Strainer will cure all that.

Neaniscus. But go in: for I am desirous to consecrate these Crowns to the God.

Old Woman. And I too have something to say to him.

Neaniscus. But I will not go in.

Chrem. Courage, Man, never fear; she sha'n't ravish you.

Neaniscus. You speak very kindly: for I have sufficiently pitched up the old Vessel already.

Old Woman. Enter; and I will follow you behind.

Chrem. O King *Jupiter*, how closely the *Old Woman* sticks to the Youth, even as a Limpet doth to the Rock!

---

[268] *By* Hecate.] As the *Old Woman* had affectedly sworn by *Venus*, the Goddess of youthful Pleasure, the Old Fellow pleasantly swears by *Hecate*; intimating, that this was her proper Deity to swear by. This Goddess was otherwise called *Proserpina*, and presided over the Lower World, whither this Old Lady was shortly going.

[269] *So free to deliver me up.*] The *Greek* is simply, *Who is he who delivers me up?* M. Dacier, *Y-a-t'il au monde un autre homme qui voulût me ceder de la sorte?* Mr. Theobald, *Who but he would so shamefully resign me?*

[270] *A Strainer.*] *i.e.* The young Fellow might draw off all the Good of the *Old Woman*, namely, her Money, *&c.* and leave the rest behind.

ACT V. SCENE I.

CARIO, MERCURY.
(Mercury *knocks hard at the Door, and then retires.*)

Cario.[271] WHO knocks at the Door?——Heyday! What is the Meaning of this? Here is no-body.——What, hath the Door made all this Lamentation, when no-body hurt it!

Mercury. You, you, *Cario*; I speak to you, stay.

Cario. Pray tell me, Sir, was it you that knocked so heartily at our Door?

Mercury.[272] Not I, by *Jove*! but I should have knocked, had not you prevented me, by opening it: but run quickly, and call your Master hither; and then call his Wife and Children; then his Servants, then the Bitch, then yourself, and then the Sow.

Cario. Pray, what is the Meaning of all this?

Mercury. Jupiter, Sirrah, intends to make a Hotch-potch of you all together, and then souse you into the[273] Barathrum.

Cario. Such Criers as you, truly[274] deserve a Tongue cut out: but wherefore, pray, is he contriving this for us?

Mercury. Because you have committed the most horrible of all Facts: for, ever since *Plutus* hath recovered[275] a Glimpse of Sight, no one hath sacrificed to the Gods any Frankincense, or Laurel, or Cake, or any Victim; or, in short, any thing at all.

---

[271] *Who knocks at the Door? Here is no-body.*] '*Mercury* having knocked at the Door of *Chremylus*, hides himself, in order to make it apprehended, that the Door, at the Approach of a Deity, had made this Noise of its own accord' says M. *Dacier.* A religious Poet would have introduced the Servant in a Fright; but ours, by the Pleasantry of *Cario,* seems to insinuate, that the God miscarried in his Design. This whole Scene is indeed as delicate, and at the same time as severe a Ridicule on the Religion of the *Greeks,* as is possible to be invented.

[272] *Not I, by* Jove.] This is a direct Falshood, and intended to expose the Character of this Deity, of whom indeed the most superstitious of the Antients seem to have had no very honourable Opinion.

[273] *Barathrum.*] We have described this already.[209] M. Dacier, *la Riviere*; Mr. Theobald, *the River.*

[274] *Deserve a Tongue cut out.*] We have here preserved the original Ambiguity of this, which M. *Dacier* hath professedly declined, declaring her Inability, to which Mr. *Theobald* hath modestly subscribed. It was the Custom of the *Greeks* to give the Tongues of the Victims, as being an unclean Part, to the Crier (*Praeconi*) because, according to some, they admonished the People before the Sacrifice begun, *ut linguis faverent, to be favourable with their Tongues.* Others will have it to be, because the Crier gets his Livelihood by his Tongue. When *Cario* therefore says, *Such a Crier deserves a Tongue cut out,* it may be understood by *Mercury,* either to allude to this Custom; or, by way of Menace, to insinuate that, as a Reward for his ill News, he deserves to have his own Tongue cut out. It may likewise be observed here, that the Antients used to sacrifice a Tongue to *Mercury* on account of his Eloquence.

[275] *A Glimpse of Sight.*] The Expression in the Original is very emphatical. We have endeavoured to preserve it.

---

[209] See above, p. 292 and n. 124.

Cario. No, Faith! nor will not neither: for I am sure you have taken very little Care of us.

Mercury. Well, as for the other Gods, I trouble not myself much: but I myself am ruined and undone.

Cario. Why, this is modestly spoken.

Mercury. Formerly I received every Morning all kind of good Things from the[276] Tavern-Women, such as Wine-Cakes, Honey, Figs, as much as was decent for *Mercury* to eat: but now I go all Day hungry, and have nothing to do but stretch out my Legs, and sleep.

Cario. Very justly: Since, notwithstanding all these good Things,[277] you often made Losers of those who gave them you.

Mercury. O miserable Deity!—[278] O for that Cheese-cake, which used to be dressed for me on[279] the fourth Day of the Moon.

Cario.[280] You desire one who is absent, and call for him in vain.

Mercury. O! for a Gammon of Bacon, which I used to feed on.

Cario.[281] Leap upon the Bottle here in the open Air.

---

[276] *Tavern-Women.*] *Mercury* presided over all sorts of Roguery; wherefore the Tavern-keepers, who, it seems, understood the Use of bad Wine and scanty Measures in those early Days, were wont to sacrifice every Morning to this God, in order to obtain Success in their Knavery.

[277] *You often made Losers.*] This is extremely pleasant; *Cario* intimates, that notwithstanding their Dexterity in their Craft, they were often detected and punished for their Roguery.

[278] *Oh! for that Cheese-cake.*] Nothing can be exposed in a more ridiculous Light than *Mercury* in this Scene.

[279] *The fourth Day of the Moon.*] The Fourth of every Month was sacred to *Mercury*, as other Days were to other Gods. *Girardus* fancies that it is hence we call the fourth Day of our Week *Mercurii Dies*.[210]

[280] *You desire.*] The Reader, in order to taste this, must be acquainted with the Story to which it alludes. *Hercules* had the Misfortune to lose his Favourite Youth *Hylas*, in the Expedition to *Colchis*; nor would he be prevailed upon by the Importunities and angry Remonstrances of his Companions, to depart, till they all assisted him, in bellowing after him, *Hyla, Hyla!* At last one of the Company despairing to see the Youth any more, repeated to *Hercules* this Line, which probably was in some Play:[211]

$$\text{Ποθεῖς τὸν οὐ παρόντα καὶ μάτην καλεῖς.}$$

Cario therefore pronounced this Line in a ridiculous bemoaning Voice.

[281] *Leap upon the Bottle.*] This Leaping on the Bottle was an Exercise practised at a Festival celebrated in Honour of *Bacchus*, at which they sacrificed a He-Goat; because, as that Animal destroys the vine, they supposed him odious to the God. Of the Victim's Skin they made a Bottle, which they endeavour'd to leap upon with one Foot; which who first did, received it full of Wine as a Prize: This was called ἀσκωλίαζειν the Word here used. *Cario* attempts wretchedly to pun on the Word κωλῆ in the preceeding Line, which it is impossible to keep in our Language.[212] This indeed the *English* Reader hath little reason to regret; for the

---

[210] Girardus, note to line 1127 (Küster, p. 46).

[211] Elsewhere HF recalls the story of Hercules' infatuation with Hylas (among other sources, Apollonius Rhodius, *Argonautica*, i. 1207 ff.). In *Joseph Andrews* (IV. xiv) Parson Adams, having mistaken the incapable rapist Beau Didapper for a woman, protests: 'if I had suspected him for a Man, I would have seized him had he been another *Hercules*, tho' indeed he seems rather to resemble *Hylas*' (p. 333). In *Tom Jones* (X. viii), Squire Western, having discovered his daughter's flight from home, 'began to roar forth the Name of *Sophia* as loudly, and in as hoarse a Voice, as whileom did *Hercules* that of *Hylas*' (p. 556).

[212] Sommerstein translates line 1129, 'Up on *one* leg with you . . . and hop it!', commenting: 'the Greek says simply *askoliaze* "hop!", with an extremely feeble pun on *kole* (thigh)' (p. 210 n. 1129).

Mercury. O those Meals of Tripe, which I have made!

Cario. The Wind in your own Tripes turns your Meditations that Way.

Mercury. O those Cups of[282] Wine and Water equally mixed up!

Cario. You shall not stir till you have drank[283] this Cup also.

Mercury. Will you assist one, who hath a great Friendship for you?

Cario. Ay, if you want any thing within my Capacity of helping you to.

Mercury.[284] If you would but give me one of those well-baked Loaves, and a Piece of that Flesh you are sacrificing within.

Cario. But they[285] must not be conveyed out.

Mercury. Why, when you used to filch any Vessel from your Master, I always assisted you in concealing it.

Conceit is so poor in the Original, that I can hardly excuse *Aristophanes* for having put it even into the Mouth of a Slave.

[282] *Wine and Water.*] The Antients sacrificed pure Wine to the other Gods, but to *Mercury* an equal Mixture of Wine and Water.

[283] *This Cup also.*] This Place hath very much puzzled the Learned. M. Dacier hath translated it, *L'on auroit bien mieux fait de ne te donner que de l'eau, le vin n'est pas bon aux fous.* If this be a Translation at all, it is a Translation of some other Book; for it hath not the least Relation to this. *Mr. Theobald, If you could but meet with such a one here, you would scarce be in haste to return to your own Quarters.* This Interpretation is taken from the *Latin* of *Nicodemus Frischlinus; Hunc si imbibas, tu hinc nunquam mediteris fugam.*[213] Neither can this be deduced from the Original. The Interpretation of *Girardus* is not, in my opinion, much nearer the Truth. He would have *Cario*, while he says these Words, deliver a Cup of Wine to *Mercury*.[214] But, in the first Place, it doth not appear that *Cario* had any Cup in his Hand. *2dly,* It would be inconsistent with the Character of that Slave, who would have more naturally drunk off the Wine himself. *3dly,* This would be very disagreeable to the continued Raillery and Ill-treatment with which he behaves to *Mercury* through the whole Scene. Lastly, It would be repugnant to what immediately follows. *Bisetus,* in his *Greek* Annotations, seems to have approached nearer. 'Some, says he, refer ταύτην, not to the Cup, but to a Fart which *Cario* lets.'[215] This will be very consonant to the Character of *Cario*, and to the Manners, which, as we have remarked, our Poet hath so frequently reprehended in the *Athenians*, and was likely enough to raise a Laugh in the Audience. The Old Scholiast points, I apprehend, at the true Meaning of this Passage. *Cario* says, *You shall not run away till you have drunk this Cup also,* i.e. *You have not yet come to the End of your Misfortunes; you shall have no more Sacrifices nor Respect to your Deity, but shall suffer all the Indignities I think fit to offer you.* The suffering Misfortunes was frequently expressed by the Phrase of *drinking a Cup.* So *Aeschylus, Plautus,* &c. Not to mention any of those many Instances to be found both in the Old and New Testament.[216]

[284] *If you would but give me.*] 'This is very pleasant between two Servants; and *Aristophanes* here shews, that the Servants of his Time acted like those of ours; and that such as were in Place, supported those that were out of one.' *Dacier.* It may be necessary to acquaint our unlearned Reader, that *Mercury* was the Servant of the other Gods.

[285] *Must not be conveyed out.*] It was lawful to send their Friends a Part of some Sacrifices, as we have mentioned in the first Scene of this Play:[217] But of those which were consecrated to *Vesta* and their Houshold-Gods, it was not lawful to carry away the minutest Morsel.

---

213 'If you drink this, you will never consider fleeing from here' (Küster, p. 47).

214 Frischlin's translation of line 1134 (Küster, p. 47).

215 Édouard Biset de Charolais (*fl. c.*1607), French classicist and editor of *Aristophanis Comoedia* in Greek and Latin (1607). HF refers to his note to line 1134 (Küster, p. 47).

216 Cf. (King James version) OT: Psalms 11: 6; Isaiah 51: 17, 22; Jeremiah 25: 15–17; 49: 12; 51: 7; Ezekiel 23: 31–3. NT: Matthew 26: 42; Mark 14: 36; Luke 22: 42.

217 Cf. Act I, scene ii, p. 277 n. [60].

Cario. Ay, you Rascal; that you might partake in the Booty: for a well-baked Cake[286] came always to your Share.

Mercury. Ay, but you eat it afterwards yourself.

Cario. Well: for you had no Share in the Whipping, when I was taken in my Rogueries.

Mercury. No Remembrance of past Injuries[287] now *Phyle* is taken. So pray receive me into your House, in the Name of the Gods, and let me dwell with you.

Cario. What, will you leave the Gods to dwell with us?

Mercury. Yes indeed will I: for[288] your Affairs are in a much better Situation.

Cario. But in what Light do you esteem a Man who deserts from his Country?

Mercury.[289] That is every Man's Country, where he lives best.

Cario. Well, but what Advantage would you bring to us, if you were here?

Mercury.[290] I will be your Turnkey, and stand behind your Door.

Cario.[291] Turnkey! —No, we want none of your Turns.

---

[286] *Came always to your Share.*] This was the Sacrifice which *Cario* made to *Mercury* as the God of the Thieves, to protect and assist him in his Roguery, which the other answers with excellent Ridicule on their Sacrifices, *that he eat it all himself.* I think it is impossible for any one to be so stupid as not to taste this Pleasantry.

[287] *Now* Phyle *is taken.*] *Thrasybulus*, when he had resolved to endeavour the Extirpation of the Thirty Tyrants, suddenly took possession of *Phyle*, a Castle in *Attica*, where being attacked by the *Lacedaemonians*, who had imposed those Tyrants on the *Athenians*, he obtained a complete Victory.[218] After this, a Law was made, that none of the *Athenians* should for the future revive the Memory of former Quarrels or Animosities. *Mercury* therefore says to *Cario*, if you have taken *Phyle*, i.e. if you are become rich, and have obtained a more splendid Fortune, don't recall the Remembrance of the Evils you have formerly suffered.

[288] *Your affairs are in a much better Situation.*] Nothing can be stronger than this. He represents the Possession of *Plutus* to be of such Consequence, that it hath elated Men above the Gods. The Greediness of the *Athenians* for Riches, and their vast Estimation of them, is finely satyrized in this Instance.

[289] *That is every Man's Country.*] This perhaps alludes to that Saying of *Socrates*, that he was a *Citizen of the World*.

[290] *I will be your Turnkey*, &c.] In order to make an *English* Reader comprehend the beauty of this Place, he must be acquainted that all the following Occupations which *Mercury* professes himself ready to undertake, were drawn from the several Surnames which the *Greeks* gave to that God, supposing him to preside over these several Offices. We have with great difficulty preserved the Original throughout.

[291] *Turnkey.*] As Thieves generally used to lurk behind Doors, so they placed the Statue of *Mercury* there, that he might drive them away. The Answer of *Cario* to this is very pleasant, inferring, that he would rather encourage than expel them.

---

[218] Thrasybulus (*fl.* 411–388 BC), Athenian general. For supporting the democracy he was exiled to Thebes by the Thirty Tyrants of the oligarchy. In 403 BC, with only seventy men, he seized the hill fort of Phyle. After defeating a force sent to retake it, he ousted the Thirty and restored the democracy, declaring an amnesty. (See the notes to line 1146 in Loeb and Sommerstein.)

Mercury. Employ me then in my[292] mercantile Capacity.

Cario. But we are rich, what then should we do with such a[293] Huckster as *Mercury?*

Mercury. In my[294] crafty Vocation then.

Cario. We have done with Craft. Honestly is for our Purpose.

Mercury. You know me to be[295] a Conductor.

Cario. No, the God hath his Eyes now, and wants no Conductor.

Mercury. Odso! I will be[296] Master of your Sports—will not that do?— This is an Office, which I am sure will be very convenient for *Plutus*: for rich Men often make Matches between Musicians and Prize-Fighters.

Cario. How useful it is to have[297] various Occupations: for by one or the other this Fellow hath found out a Livelihood:

[292] *Mercantile Capacity.*] Hence, as *Festus* observes,[219] the *Latins* gave him the Name of *Mercurius.* By the *Greek* Word Ἐμπολαῖον, he was supposed to preside over all Manner of Merchandise; but *Cario* satyrically represents him as having to do only with the vilest and lowest Trades, with which *Chremylus*, being now rich, had no Concern.

[293] *Huckster.*] The *Greek* Παλιγχάπηλον, *a Retailer at the third Hand.* The Merchant was called Ἔμπορον, the Retailer Κάπηλον, and the Huckster or Sub-retailer Παλιγκάπηλον.

[294] *Crafty Vocation.*] Δόλιον in the Original. He was supposed to preside over all Craft and cunning Knavery.

[295] *A Conductor.*] Ἡγεμόνιον, a Conductor or Leader; so called, because on the Public Roads, where three Ways met, there were Statues set up to him, with three Heads, on each of which were written Directions, as we see on Crosses in *England.* To him likewise was assigned the Office of conducting Ghosts to the other World.

[296] *Master of your Sports.*] Ἐναγώνιος. By which Surname he is mentioned by *Pindar. Pyth. Ode* 2. and *Pausanias* tells us, that an Altar was set up to him by that Name, where the *Olympic* Games were celebrated.[220]

[297] *Various Occupations.*] In the Original, Titles, Surnames, of which no other God had so many as *Mercury.*

'The Surnames of *Porter*, (*Turnkey*) *Merchant*, and *Man of Business*, (*Craft*) and *Guide* (*Conductor*) had been useless to *Mercury*; and he must have starved, if the Surname of *Master of Sports* had not put him in mind, that he was proper to be an Intendant of Sports. This Passage is finer than it appeared to the Scholiasts and Translators. *Aristophanes* laughs very prettily at the great Number of Names which the Gods gave themselves, as if they took so many only to catch by the one what they could not catch by the other. *Homer* says of *Apollo*,

————ἐπεὶ πολυώνυμός ἐςι.
For he hath several Names.[221]

And *Callimachus*[222] introduces *Diana* praying to *Jupiter* to *suffer her to be always a Virgin, and to give her several Names.' Dacier.*

---

[219] On Sextus Pompeius Festus (late second century AD), whose epitome of the *De Verborum Significatu* of Verrius Flaccus is represented in an edition (1498) of three works on the Latin language, the only incunabulum in HF's library, see Ribbles, p. xxxv and N9.

[220] Pindar (582–438 BC), *Pythian Odes*, ii. 10: 'Hermes, lord of the games' (Ribble P21); Pausanias (*fl. c.*AD 150), *Description of Greece*, V. xxiv. 9: 'Quite close to the entrance to the stadium' is 'the altar of Hermes of the Games' (Ribble P8).

[221] Homeric *Hymn to Apollo*, line 82 (*polyonoumos*: 'many-named').

[222] Callimachus (*c.*305–*c.*240 BC), Hymn III ('To Artemis'), lines 6–7, addressing Zeus: 'Give me to keep my maidenhood, Father, for ever: and give me to be of many names, that Phoebus may not vie with me' (Loeb).

it is not without Reason, I find, that[298] our Judges put in as many Tickets with their Names as they can.

Mercury. Will nothing that I have said gain me Admittance?

Cario. Yes, yes; come to the Well, and[299] wash some Guts for me; then you will shew yourself to be a good Scullion.

SCENE II.

Priest of Jupiter, *Cario*.

Priest. Who can direct me to the very Door where *Chremylus* lives?

Cario. What is the Matter, honest Gentleman?

Priest. No Good, I assure you, Sir. Since this *Plutus* first recovered his Eyes, I have been perishing with Hunger: for, indeed,[300] I have not a Morsel to eat; and this, tho' I am[301] the Priest of *Jupiter* the Protector.

Cario. And what is the Reason of this, pray?

Priest. No Person thinks proper to sacrifice any longer.

Cario. On what Account?

Priest. Because they are all rich; whereas formerly, when they were poor, the Merchant returning from his Voyage offered up his Victim; the Rogue who escaped out of the Hands of Justice did the same; and when any one made a handsome Sacrifice, he invited the Priest to it: but now there is not one who sacrifices, no, not the least Matter in the World; nor even comes

---

[298] *Our Judges put in.*] See our Note on this Custom of electing their Judges in the first Act.[223] *Aristophanes* seems here to hint at a Piece of Knavery, which I do not remember any Traces of in the *Athenian* History, tho' similar Tricks have been plaid in all Countries; I mean, of putting several Tickets in, with the same Name inscribed on them, by which they had the better Chance of being drawn; for my own part, I cannot otherwise understand the *Greek* itself, nor apply it to the many Surnames of *Mercury*, as is here intended. M. *Dacier*, as I have already observed, seems to have misunderstood this Custom; for they drew the Court by Lot where they were to sit as Judges, and did not put their Tickets into several different Jurisdictions, as she conceives.

[299] *Wash some Guts.*] What can be more ridiculous than the Office to which he applies this God, who was admitted as an Inspector of Sports. Hence he secretly implies, that he is now entitled to another Surname, i.e. *Mercury* the *Scullion*.

[300] *I have not a Morsel to eat.*] Not a Morsel to put in my Head. Mr. Theobald.

[301] *The Priest of* Jupiter, *the Protector*.] 'There were at *Athens* six Temples of *Jupiter*. Amongst others, there was one of *Jupiter* the *Protector*. *Aristophanes* introduces the Priest of this Temple rather than any other on the Stage, because, if *Jupiter* the *Protector* had not wherewithal to maintain his Priest, the Priests of the other Temples could not expect any thing of the same *Jupiter* whom they served under other Names. All the Beauty of this Passage hath not been perceived.' *Dacier*.

---

[223] Above, Act II, sc. 1, p. 280 n. [69].

near the Temple, unless those Thousands who come there to lay their Cates.[224]

Cario. And have you not[302] your lawful Share of these?

Priest. As to *Jupiter* the Protector,[303] I think proper to take my Leave of him, and abide here with you.

Cario. Courage! all will be well, if the God pleases: for *Jupiter* the Protector is within already: he came hither of his own accord.

Priest. You now tell me delightful News indeed.

Cario. We shall presently place (bear it with Patience) *Plutus* where your *Jupiter* was formerly placed,[304] to preserve the Treasure which is behind the Temple of *Minerva.*————————But give me those lighted Torches there some-body————Here, Priest, do you take them, and carry them before the God.

Priest.[305] We are doing no more than we ought.

Cario. Now call *Plutus* out.

SCENE III.

Old Woman, Cario, Chorus.

Old Woman. What shall I do?

Cario. Take[306] these Pots, with which we are to place the God in the

---

[302] *Your lawful Share of these.*] The Pleasantry of thus Allusion needs not be explained.

[303] *I think proper to take my Leave of him.*] This making the Priest ready to forsake the Service of *Jupiter*, when he can no longer thrive by it, is perhaps as severe a Satire on the Ecclesiasticks of those Days, as could be easily imagined; but the Answer of *Cario*, intimating that *Jupiter* himself hath already inlisted himself in the Number of the Devotees of *Plutus*, is as fine a Piece of Pleasantry as ever was invented by the Wit of Man. I question whether M. *Dacier* hath not unjustly complained of this Place being misunderstood, and whether she herself hath rightly apprehended it; for the αὐτόματος ἥκων in the Original doth not agree with her Interpretation. Her Translation is, *Le veritable Jupiter faveur est chez nous*; meaning, as she tells us in her Notes, *that there is no other Protector than Riches.* Mr. *Theobald* hath embraced her literally. A judicious Reader will, we apprehend, see a visible Difference in these two Ways of understanding the Original.

[304] *To preserve the Treasure which is behind the Temple of Minerva.*] The dethroning *Jupiter*, to place *Plutus* in his stead, was, as M. *Dacier* very justly observes, a very bitter Invective on the Avarice of the *Athenians*; but there is still a farther Beauty in this Passage; for besides the Statue of *Jupiter* the Protector, the *Athenians* had actually erected one of *Plutus*, with his Eyes open, in this Place.

[305] *We are doing no more*, &c.] The Behaviour of this Priest requires no Comment.

[306] *These Pots, with which we are to place.*] 'When they consecrated Altars, or erected Statues to the Gods, they caused the young Women to carry Pots full of boiled Pulse, with which they made their first Offerings to the God, intending to signify that this was Mankind's first Food. The Girls who carried these Pots, wore Garments of various Colours. *Aristophanes*, with great Wit, rallies the Old Women on this

---

[224] 'Cates': choice viands, delicacies (*OED*, s.v.). Here, however, used ironically for faeces. Cf. Sommerstein's translation of the priest's complaint at the impiety of the times (lines 1183–4): '*now* no one sacrifices anything at all; they don't even come into the sanctuary—except that there's thousands on thousands who come in to have a crap!'

Temple, carry them on your Head with a grave Countenance. I see you
have already your Flower'd Gown on.

Old Woman. Ay, but of that which I came hither for————

Cario. All shall be immediately done for you. The young Fellow shall be
with you in the Evening.

Old Woman. Well, if you will be bound that the Youth shall visit me, I will
carry the Pots.

Cario [*turning to the Spectators.*] These Pots are the very Reverse of all
others: for in all others[307] the Scum used to be at the Top of the Pot, here
it is at the Bottom.

Chorus. There is no Reason why we should stay here longer, but follow
behind: for it is our Part to bring up the Rear with a Song.

Occasion, that forgetting the Decency suitable to their Age, they endeavoured, like the youngest Girls, to
engage the Affection of the young Men. This Passage is so much the pleasanter, as we see every day certain
Persons for whom it seems designed.' *Dacier.*

[307] *The Scum.*] There is a Pun in the Original not to be preserved; for γραῦς signifies both the Scum of
a Pot and an Old Woman.[225]

---

[225] Loeb comments on lines 1206–7: ' "γραῦς" means (1) "old woman," (2) "scum" on the surface of
milk, boiled vegetables, soup, etc. So "mother" is applied to scum on boiling liquids, mould on fermenting
jams, yeast, and the like' (*English Dialect Dictionary*, iv. 175).

4

PREFACE TO SARAH FIELDING'S *THE ADVENTURES OF DAVID SIMPLE* (1744)

ON 3 May 1744 Andrew Millar, Fielding's publisher, brought out *The Adventures of David Simple: Containing an Account of his Travels through the Cities of London and Westminster, in the Search of a Real Friend*, a novel in two volumes 'By a Lady'. Preferring in this way to remain anonymous, Sarah Fielding launched her career as a novelist, introducing herself in the following 'Advertisement to the Reader':

The following Moral Romance (or whatever Title the Reader shall please to give it) is the Work of a Woman, and her first Essay; which, to the good-natured and candid Reader will, it is hoped, be a sufficient Apology for the many Inaccuracies he will find in the Style, and other Faults of the Composition.

Perhaps the best Excuse that can be made for a Woman's venturing to write at all, is that which really produced this Book; Distress in her Circumstances: which she could not so well remove by any other Means in her Power.

If it should meet with Success, it will be *the only Good Fortune* she ever has known; but as she is very sensible, *That* must chiefly depend upon the Entertainment the World will find in the Book itself, and not upon what she can say in the Preface, either to move their Compassion, or bespeak their Good-will, she will detain them from it no longer. (italics reversed)

Sarah's poignant apology for having to stoop to the trade of authorship in order to survive is echoed in the novel itself in the complaint of Camilla, her heroine, to David Simple:

Alas, Sir . . . there is no Situation so deplorable, no Condition so much to be pitied, as that of a Gentle-woman in real Poverty. I mean by real Poverty, not having sufficient to procure us Necessaries; for good Sense will teach People to moderate their Desires, and lessen their way of living, and yet be content. Birth, Family, and Education, become Misfortunes, when we cannot attain some Means of supporting ourselves in the Station they throw us into; our Friends and former Acquaintance look on it as a Disgrace to own us.[1]

---

[1] *The Adventures of David Simple* and *Volume the Last*, ed. Peter Sabor (Lexington, Ky., 1998), book III, ch. ii, p. 132.

Until the close of the last century,[2] in all future editions of the novel
beginning with the second, which was called for two months later by brisk
public demand and published 13 July 1744, Sarah's 'Advertisement' would
be replaced, as the title-page declares, 'With a PREFACE | By HENRY
FIELDING Esq;'. The Preface is notable both for the place it holds in
the history of literary criticism and for what it reveals, for the biographer,
about Fielding's relationship with his sister. As Peter Sabor declares in his
admirable edition of the novel, the Preface is 'a major contribution to
eighteenth-century theoretical discussions of the novel':[3] with the Preface
to *Joseph Andrews* (1742), which it complements and develops, the essay is
the earliest attempt in English to define the new genre of the modern
novel. Critics of our own time, however, have regretted Fielding's tone and
manner—fairly characterized by Sabor as 'rebarbative' and 'tendentious';[4]
and they are inclined to resent the seemingly ambivalent attitude he
assumes towards Sarah and her book—affectionate, to be sure, yet condescending; at times adulatory, but more often patronizing. More typical of
critical opinion a generation ago was Malcolm Kelsall in the Oxford English
Novels edition of 1969, who, if allowing Fielding's claims for Sarah's 'deep
Knowledge of Human Nature', concurred in his appraisal of her limitations
as a writer and regarded his extensive revisions for the second edition as
beneficial.[5]

Kelsall can hardly be faulted for recognizing her brother's superiority as a
writer; but there is equity in the complaints of those like Sabor and Bree,
and feminist critics such as Dale Spender and Janine Barchas,[6] who wish to
restore Sarah's book to its author. In her anonymous contributions to *Joseph
Andrews* (1742) and *A Journey from This World to the Next* (1743),[7] she
had, as it were, served an apprenticeship under Fielding's tutelage; now,
presumably, she had invited his contributions to the second edition of her
first novel: namely, the Preface, as well as the revisions and corrections
announced on the title-page. Fielding took these duties seriously: though
he assured readers that 'the Share I have in this Book . . . amounts to

---

[2] In his edition Peter Sabor restored Sarah Fielding's 'Advertisement' to its original place at the
beginning of the novel, as does Linda Bree in the Penguin Classics edition (2002).

[3] Ed. Sabor, p. xxvii.

[4] Ibid., pp. xxvii–xxviii.

[5] See Kelsall's Introduction and note on the Text, and the Bibliographical Essay added to the 1994
reprint of this edition.

[6] See Dale Spender, 'Sarah Fielding and Misrepresentation', in her *Mothers of the Novel: 100 Good
Women Writers before Jane Austen* (London, 1986), pp. 180–93; and Janine Barchas, 'Sarah Fielding's
Dashing Style and Eighteenth-Century Print Culture', *ELH*, 63 (1996), pp. 633–56.

[7] It is now generally accepted that Sarah wrote the letter from 'Leonora to Horatio' in *Joseph Andrews*
(II. iv, pp. 106–7) and the 'History' of Anna Boleyn, which concludes the *Journey* (XIX. vii).

little more than the Correction of some small Errors', collation of the two original editions has revealed hundreds of alterations of Sarah's text.[8]

He also, moreover, used the occasion to confirm the theory of fiction he had advanced in *Joseph Andrews*. Though Sarah thought of her work as a 'Moral Romance', Fielding would have it 'that every Work of this kind is in its Nature a comic Epic Poem', as he had 'attempted . . . to prove' in the Preface to *Joseph Andrews*. The 'Precedent' for *David Simple* therefore must be Homer's lost work the *Margites*; its formal model in prose, Cervantes' *Don Quixote*, in verse the *Odyssey*. Its 'Fable' must be characterized by 'three difficult Ingredients', being 'at once amiable, ridiculous and natural'—the second of these, 'the Ridiculous', Fielding having declared to be his 'Province' in *Joseph Andrews* and defined it at some length in the Preface to that work (pp. 6–9). He hoped now to make it appear that Sarah had conformed to the model he had given her; but any attentive reader can see that she had not. As Peter Sabor remarks: 'Far from working in the same tradition . . . the Fieldings are writing very different kinds of fiction: *Joseph Andrews* is a comic satire, and *The Adventures of David Simple* a "Moral Romance" ' (p. xxviii).

Feminist criticism, however, has gone too far in taking the view that Fielding, instead of assisting Sarah in her debut as novelist, used the opportunity to depreciate her abilities and accomplishment. His opening remarks on *David Simple* are surely respectful and complimentary: 'the strongest Reason which hath drawn me into Print, is to do Justice to the real and sole Author of *this little Book*; who, notwithstanding the many excellent Observations dispersed through it, and the deep Knowledge of Human Nature it discovers, is *a young Woman*; one so nearly and dearly allied to me, in the highest Friendship as well as Relation' (p. 350; emphasis added). What critics now chiefly notice in the passage are the italicized phrases; *David Simple* is not, in number of pages at least, a 'little' book; nor was Sarah Fielding, at 33, a 'young' woman. In an age when only knowledge of Latin and Greek defined a 'literate' person—and most women therefore, like most modern critics, qualified as 'illiterate'—Fielding claims only to have corrected in Sarah's work 'some Grammatical and other Errors in Style'. The 'Imperfections of this little Book', he insists, 'arise, not from want of Genius, but of Learning'. The criticism, indeed, may well have had the helpful effect of motivating Sarah to master the classical languages; in

---

[8] For the more important of these alterations, some 600 of them, see Sabor's appendix II ('Substantive Variants between the First and Second Editions'). For discussions of the nature of these variants and their effect on the narrative, see Sabor (see n. 1 above), pp. xxvi–xxx; Bree (see n. 2 above), pp. xli–xliii; and Kelsall, pp. xix–xxiii.

1762 she would publish a translation of *Xenophon's Memoirs of Socrates* that was often reprinted until the middle of the last century.[9]

But Fielding clearly meant to pay Sarah the compliment of measuring her work by the highest standards. Besides the wishful illusion that *David Simple* conformed to the model of *Joseph Andrews*, he places it in a context of literary classics: Homer, Virgil, and Milton; Lucan, Silius Italicus, and Ariosto; Boileau and Pope; Butler and Cervantes. Not only are 'the Incidents' of her narrative 'every where natural'; they share 'one Beauty' attributed by Aristotle, 'the greatest of Critics to the greatest of Poets' (Homer, in the *Odyssey*): namely, 'that every Episode bears a manifest Impression of the principal Design, and chiefly turns on the Perfection or Imperfection of Friendship; of which noble Passion, from its highest Purity to its lowest Falshoods and Disguises, this little Book is, in my Opinion, the most exact Model'. He agrees with the view of an anonymous contemporary that the characters '*are as wonderfully drawn by the Writer, as they were by* Nature *herself*'—indeed, they deserve comparison with others that 'have shined' in Theophrastus, Horace, or La Bruyère. 'Nay', Fielding declares, 'there are some Touches, which I will venture to say might have done honour to the Pencil of the immortal *Shakespear* himself' (p. 353).

Earlier in the Preface, before he began this examination of Sarah's work according to the categories and rules of neoclassical criticism, Fielding identified the true source of her power as a novelist: 'the Merit of this Work consists in a vast Penetration into human Nature, a deep and profound Discernment of all the Mazes, Windings and Labyrinths, which perplex the Heart of Man to such a degree, that he is himself often incapable of seeing through them'; 'this', he avers, 'is the greatest, noblest, and rarest of all the Talents which constitute a Genius'. And bringing the Preface to a close, he paid tribute to the sister he loved, now a fellow novelist. As a keen 'Observer', she need not know much of 'the World' to know 'Evil'; and as for knowing its opposite, 'a short Communication with her own Heart, will leave the Author of this Book very little to seek abroad of all the Good which is to be found in Human Nature' (p. 354).

Can it really, fairly, be thought that Fielding meant in the Preface to *David Simple* to humble Sarah? He not only continued to assist her in her novel-writing;[10] he made this novel the favourite reading of Sophie Western in *Tom Jones* (VI. v, p. 286).

---

[9] See *Correspondence*, p. 173 n. 7.
[10] See HF's contributions to Sarah Fielding's *Familiar Letters*, below, pp. 462–513.

CIRCUMSTANCES OF COMPOSITION

It is not known where Sarah Fielding wrote *David Simple*, whether at Bath as local tradition has it;[11] or perhaps in London living with the rest of the 'sisterhood' in a house leased by Catharine, the eldest. Quite possibly, since they were near enough by his own account for him to offer her 'Hints which arose on reading' the manuscript, as well as 'some little Direction as to the Conduct of the second Volume' (books III–IV), Sarah may have been living with Fielding and his wife, Charlotte, whose health had been for many months in serious decline. After Charlotte's death in November of this year, Sarah was certainly living with Fielding and his family at Boswell Court; but he cannot be placed there with certainty, or anywhere else for that matter, until the autumn.

Indeed, Fielding's movements this year leave the impression of restlessness—of journeys between Bath and London interrupted en route by visits to Winchester and Salisbury and Gloucester. He writes in the Preface (p. 350) that his 'Absence from Town' prevented him from correcting the first edition of *David Simple* before it went to press in April, and it was not until after it was published (3 May) that he had seen 'much the greater Part' of the contents of the second volume (books III–IV). The Preface to the second edition, then, was written, and Fielding's corrections and revisions of the novel executed, some time in May or June before the second edition was published on 13 July.

Besides wishing to recommend his sister's book to the public, Fielding had an urgent personal motive for undertaking the Preface. Despite the promise he had 'solemnly made', a year before in the Preface to the *Miscellanies*, that he would in future set his name to anything he published, readers persisted in attributing to him anonymous works. One of these, despite the declaration 'By a Lady' on the title-page, was *David Simple* itself.[12] But, to use his own metaphor, he was more concerned

---

[11] Bree, *Sarah Fielding*, pp. 6–7.

[12] Even such knowledgeable literary gossips as Thomas Birch and Lady Grey were uncertain whether Sarah Fielding or her brother had written *David Simple*. Not long after the novel was published, Lady Grey, who had arrived at her country seat, Wrest, on 21 May 1744 accompanied by Birch, wrote the next day to another well-known bluestocking, Catherine Talbot: 'We follow'd your example, & amused ourselves upon the Road with David Simple, & it really did amuse me extreamly, but I think I could have spared or at least shorten'd some of the Stories for as the excellence of Mr. or Mrs. Feilding (whichever I am to call the Person) seems to be their Odd Original Characters, David's own Adventures gave more Scope for exercising that Genius than anything of the Novel Kind, & yet they are not half the Book' (Jemima, Marchioness Grey, Lady Lucas, to Catherine Talbot, Bedfordshire and Luton Archives and Records, Lady Lucas Collection, L30/9A/3, p. 107).

about the fathering upon him of works far more damaging: 'I have been
reputed', he protests, 'and reported the Author of half the Scurrility,
Bawdy, Treason and Blasphemy, which these last few Years have produced'
(p. 349). Though he had published nothing at all for more than a year, these
rumours were making it impossible for him to shake off his reputation
as an unprincipled satirist. At the time he wrote the Preface, the author
of the verse *Essay on Calumny* (June 1744) linked him with the notorious
Tory satirist Paul Whitehead as the very type of the vice that was his
subject:

> Whether the *nameless* or *fictitious* Page
> Convey the *printed* Venom thro' an Age,
> Where ceaseless *Strife*—and *Party-Rage* prevails,
> And best the Satire takes which wildest rails;
> Whether by Pr[e]l[a]te wrote, or garter'd P[ee]r
> By *F[ie]ld[in]g*, *Wh[i]t[e]h[ea]d*,—or the *G[a]z[e]tt[ee]r!*
> So Whores in Rags, or Velvet are the same,
> In *Fashion* only differ—not in *Name!*

Fielding feared one work in particular would ruin him professionally if
he did not put a stop to rumours he had written it. This was *The Causidicade*,
an outrageous satire on the legal profession that had been circulating in a
number of editions since it was published anonymously in June 1743; it is
now generally ascribed to Macnamara Morgan (d. 1762), an Irish lawyer
and hackney author who in the second and succeeding editions called himself 'Porcupinus Pelagius' on the title-page. Occasioned by the resignation
in 1742 of the Solicitor-General, Sir John Strange (1696–1754), and the
appointment in his place of William Murray (1705–93), later first Earl
of Mansfield, this flagitious performance fell foul of every person of any
eminence in the law: besides Strange and Murray, it hit the late Lord
Chancellor Talbot; the present Lord Chancellor, Hardwicke; the Attorney-
General, Dudley Ryder; Chief Justice Willes; the Master of the Rolls,
William Fortescue; and many others, including the Earls of Bath (Pulteney)
and Orford (Walpole). Small wonder that Fielding, who had given up
thoughts of novel-writing in order to devote his energies to proving his
competence at law, chose to use the Preface to disclaim any connection with
the work:

Among all the Scurrilities with which I have been accused . . . none ever raised my
Indignation so much as the *Causidicade*: this accused me not only of being a bad
Writer, and a bad Man, but with downright Idiotism, in flying in the Face of the
greatest Men of my Profession. I take therefore this Opportunity to protest, that I

never saw that infamous, paultry Libel, till long after it had been in Print; nor can any Man hold it in greater Contempt and Abhorrence than myself.[13]

Fielding used this occasion to disown the fickle Muses who inspired novel-writing. He meant now instead to continue applying himself to his profession as he had been doing for the past year 'with so arduous and intent a Diligence' (p. 348). Very likely, indeed, he had already formulated plans to publish the work he thought would establish him as an authority in the law. Entitled 'An Institute of the Pleas of the Crown' and in conception copious enough to require two folio volumes, this work was far enough advanced by February of the following year for Fielding to announce that its publication was imminent.[14]

---

[13] In *The Jacobite's Journal* HF would resume his complaint against the author of the 'infamous' *Causidicade* (and other satires), whom he identified with the writer of the anti-ministerial journal *Old England*: see *JJ*, No. 11 (13 February 1748), pp. 161–2 and n., and No. 15 (12 March 1748), p. 197.

[14] See W. B. Coley, 'Henry Fielding's "Lost" Law Book', *MLN*, 76 (May 1961), pp. 408–13.

THE
ADVENTURES
OF
DAVID SIMPLE:
Containing
An Account of his TRAVELS
Through the
CITIES of *LONDON* and
WESTMINSTER,
In the Search of
A REAL FRIEND.

By a LADY.

IN TWO VOLUMES.

VOL. I.

THE SECOND EDITION,
Revised and Corrected.

With a PREFACE
By HENRY FIELDING *Esq;*

LONDON:
Printed for A. MILLAR, opposite *Katharine-street,* in the *Strand.*
M. DCC. XLIV.

THE PREFACE

A S so many worthy Persons have, I am told, ascribed the Honour of this Performance to me,[1] they will not be surprized at seeing my name to this Preface: Nor am I very insincere, when I call it an Honour; for if the Authors of the Age are amongst the Number of those who have conferred it on me, I know very few of them to whom I shall return the Compliment of such a Suspicion.

I could indeed have been very well content with the Reputation, well knowing that some Writings may be justly laid to my charge, of a Merit greatly inferior to that of the following Work; had not the Imputation directly accused me of Falshood, in breaking a Promise, which I have solemnly made in Print, of never publishing, even a Pamphlet, without setting my Name to it:[2] A Promise I have always hitherto faithfully kept; and, for the sake of Men's Characters, I wish all other Writers were by Law obliged to use the same Method: but 'till they are, I shall no longer impose any such Restraint on myself.

A second Reason which induces me to refute this Untruth, is, that it may have a Tendency to injure me in a Profession,[3] to which I have applied with so arduous and intent a Diligence, that I have had no Leisure, if I had Inclination, to compose any thing of this kind. Indeed I am very far from entertaining such an Inclination; I know the Value of the Reward, which Fame confers on Authors, too well, to endeavour any longer to obtain it; nor was the World ever more unwilling to bestow the glorious, envied Prize of the Laurel or Bays, than I should now be to receive any such Garland or Fool's Cap. There is not, I believe, (and it is bold to affirm) a single *Free Briton*[4] in this Kingdom, who hates his Wife more heartily than I detest

---

[1] Soon after publication (3 May 1744), despite the declaration on the title-page that *David Simple* was 'By a Lady', even such knowledgeable literary gossips as Thomas Birch and Lady Grey were uncertain whether Sarah Fielding or HF was the author (see the Introduction, above p. 343 n. 12).

[2] In the Preface to the *Miscellanies* (1743) HF, annoyed at the false attribution to him of anonymous publications, protested: 'I will never hereafter publish any Book or Pamphlet whatever, to which I will not put my Name. A Promise, which as I shall sacredly keep, so will it, I hope, be so far believed, that I may henceforth receive no more Praise or Censure, to which I have not the least Title' (i, p. 15).

[3] The law: HF was a barrister.

[4] Malcolm Kelsall wondered if this might be 'a sly hit' at the *Free Briton*, from 1729 to 1735 a pro-Walpole journal edited by William Arnall (1700?–1736). That the words '*Free Briton*' are emphasized usually would signal an allusion in HF's writings, and he often ridiculed the paper and its author in *The Craftsman*—e.g. Nos. 423 (10 August 1734) and 471 (12 July 1735), the latter on the occasion of the clubbing of the ministerial authors of the *Daily Courant*, *London Journal*, and *Free Briton* to form the *Daily Gazetteer*; also Arnall as late as *The Champion* (6 September and 16 October 1740), pp. 450 n. 5 and 481 n. 5. But in 1744 Arnall had been dead and his paper defunct for years, and Walpole was no longer HF's target.

the Muses. They have indeed behaved to me like the most infamous Harlots, and have laid many a spurious, as well as deformed Production at my Door: In all which, my good Friends the Critics have, in their profound Discernment, discovered some Resemblance of the Parent; and thus I have been reputed and reported the Author of half the Scurrility, Bawdy, Treason and Blasphemy, which these few last Years have produced.[5]

I am far from thinking every Person who hath thus aspersed me, had a determinate Design of doing me an Injury; I impute it only to an idle, childish Levity, which possesses too many Minds, and makes them report their Conjectures as Matters of Fact, without weighing the Proof, or considering the Consequence. But as to the former of these, my Readers will do well to examine their own Talents very strictly, before they are too thoroughly convinced of their Abilities to distinguish an Author's Style so accurately, as from that only to pronounce an anonymous Work to be his: And as to the latter, a little Reflection will convince them of the Cruelty they are guilty of by such Reports. For my own part, I can aver, that there are few Crimes, of which I should have been more ashamed, than of some Writings laid to my charge. I am as well assured of the Injuries I have suffered from such unjust Imputations, not only in general Character, but as they have, I conceive, frequently raised me inveterate Enemies, in Persons to whose Disadvantage I have never entertained a single Thought; nay, in Men whose Characters, and even Names have been unknown to me.

Among all the Scurrilities with which I have been accused, (tho' equally and totally innocent of every one) none ever raised my Indignation so much as the *Causidicade*:[6] this accused me not only of being a bad Writer, and a bad Man, but with downright Idiotism, in flying in the Face of the greatest Men of my Profession. I take therefore this Opportunity to protest, that I never saw that infamous, paultry Libel, till long after it had been in Print; nor can any Man hold it in greater Contempt and Abhorrence than myself.

The Reader will pardon my dwelling so long on this Subject, as I have suffered so cruelly by these Aspersions in my own Ease, in my Reputation, and in my Interest. I shall however henceforth treat such Censure with the Contempt it deserves; and do here revoke the Promise I formerly made; so

---

[5] On HF's reputation as a scurrilous satirist at this time, see the Introduction, above, p. 344.

[6] Taking its name from the Latin *causidicus*, a contemptuous term for an incompetent lawyer who pleads for money, *The Causidicade: A Panegyri-Satiri-Serio-Comic-Dramatical Poem. On the Strange Resignation, and Stranger-Promotion* was published anonymously in June 1743; the three subsequent editions that year attributed the work to 'Porcupinus Pelagius', now taken to be the pseudonym of Macnamara Morgan (d. 1762), Irish lawyer and hackney author. It was attacked in July 1743 by one 'Flavius Flap-Bugg' in the shilling pamphlet *Causticks Applied to the Causidicade*, written 'To discharge the *Malignity* with which that *lawless Libel* is so redundant'. The author, however, makes no reference to HF. For discussion of the *Causidicade* and HF's reaction to it, see the Introduction, above, pp. 344–5.

that I shall now look upon myself at full Liberty to publish an anonymous
Work, without any Breach of Faith. For tho' probably I shall never make any
use of this Liberty, there is no reason why I should be under a Restraint, for
which I have not enjoyed the purposed Recompence.[7]

A third, and indeed the strongest Reason which hath drawn me into
Print, is to do Justice to the real and sole Author of this little Book; who,
notwithstanding the many excellent Observations dispersed through it and
the deep Knowledge of Human Nature it discovers, is a young Woman; one
so nearly and dearly allied to me, in the highest Friendship as well as
Relation, that if she had wanted any Assistance of mine, I would have been
as ready to have given it to her, as I would have been just to my Word in
owning it: but in reality, two or three Hints which arose on the reading it,
and some little Direction as to the Conduct of the second Volume, much the
greater Part of which I never saw till in Print, were all the Aid she received
from me. Indeed I believe there are few Books in the World so absolutely the
Author's own as this.

There were some Grammatical and other Errors in Style in the first
Impression, which my Absence from Town prevented my correcting, as I
have endeavoured, tho' in great Haste, in this Edition: By comparing the
one with the other, the Reader may see, if he thinks it worth his while, the
Share I have in this Book,[8] as it now stands, and which amounts to little
more than the Correction of some small Errors, which Want of Habit in
Writing chiefly occasioned, and which no Man of Learning would think
worth his Censure in a Romance; nor any Gentleman, in the Writings of a
young Woman.

And as the Faults of this Work want very little Excuse, so its Beauties
want as little Recommendation: tho' I will not say but they may sometimes
stand in need of being pointed out to the generality of Readers. For as the
Merit of this Work consists in a vast Penetration into human Nature, a deep
and profound Discernment of all the Mazes, Windings and Labyrinths,
which perplex the Heart of Man to such a degree, that he is himself often
incapable of seeing through them; and as this is the greatest, noblest, and
rarest of all the Talents which constitute a Genius; so a much larger Share

---

[7] Indeed—with the single exception of *The Debauchees: or, The Jesuit Caught* (October 1745), a version
of his comedy *The Old Debauchees* (1732)—and beginning with *An Attempt towards a Natural History of the
Hanover Rat* (November 1744) (which in my opinion is almost certainly by him)—HF subsequently
published, anonymously or pseudonymously, every other publication of any kind until *Tom Jones*
(February 1749).

[8] For discussion of the extent and nature of HF's corrections and revisions for the second edition, see
the Introduction, above, pp. 340–1 and n. 8. For a full record of the substantive variants between the first
and second edition, see Sabor's edn., appendix II.

of this Talent is necessary, even to recognize these Discoveries, when they are laid before us, than falls to the share of a common Reader. Such Beauties therefore in an Author must be contented to pass often unobserved and untasted; whereas, on the contrary, the Imperfections of this little Book, which arise, not from want of Genius, but of Learning,[9] lie open to the Eyes of every Fool, who has had a little *Latin* inoculated into his Tail; but had the same great Quantity of Birch been better employ'd, in scourging away his Ill-nature, he would not have exposed it in endeavouring to cavil at the first Performance of one, whose Sex and Age entitle her to the gentlest Criticism, while her Merit, of an infinitely higher kind, may defy the severest. But I believe the Warmth of my Friendship hath led me to engage a Critic of my own Imagination only: for I should be sorry to conceive such a one had any real Existence. If however any such Composition of Folly, Meanness and Malevolence should actually exist, he must be as incapable of Conviction, as unworthy of an Answer. I shall therefore proceed to the more pleasing Task of pointing out some of the Beauties of this little Work.

I have attempted in my Preface to *Joseph Andrews* to prove, that every Work of this kind is in its Nature a comic Epic Poem, of which *Homer* left us a Precedent, tho' it be unhappily lost.[10]

The two great Originals of a serious Air, which we have derived from that mighty Genius, differ principally in the Action, which in the *Iliad* is entire and uniform; in the *Odyssey*, is rather a Series of Actions, all tending to produce one great End. *Virgil* and *Milton* are, I think, the only pure Imitators of the former; most of the other *Latin*, as well as *Italian*, *French*, and *English* Epic Poets, chusing rather the History of some War, as *Lucan* and *Silius Italicus*; or a Series of Adventures, as *Ariosto*, &c. for the Subject of their Poems.[11]

---

[9] In *Tom Jones* (XIII. i), invoking the Muses whose assistance he requires in creating such a work, HF begins with 'First, Genius; thou Gift of Heaven' (p. 685), next 'Humanity', and then 'Learning, (for without thy Assistance nothing pure, nothing correct, can Genius produce'—the thought of which, as here, recalls his schooldays at Eton: 'To thee, at thy birchen Altar, with true *Spartan* Devotion, I have sacrificed my Blood' (p. 687).

[10] In the Preface, opening his argument that *Joseph Andrews* (1742) is not just another 'comic Romance' but something grander, 'a comic Epic-Poem in Prose', HF recalls Aristotle's *Poetics* (iv. 10–12): 'The EPIC as well as the DRAMA is divided into Tragedy and Comedy. *Homer*, who was the Father of this Species of Poetry, gave us a Pattern of both these, tho' that of the latter kind is entirely lost; which *Aristotle* tells us, bore the same relation to Comedy which his *Iliad* bears to Tragedy' (pp. 3–4). The lost work is the *Margites*, a satirical epic having a fool (*margos*) as hero. Though Aristotle is his principal source, HF in his last phrase echoes Pope's 'Martinus Scriblerus' in *The Dunciad* (1729), who speaks of the *Margites* as 'now unhappily lost' (Twickenham edn., v, p. 48).

[11] In this paragraph, in addition to Virgil's *Aeneid* and Milton's *Paradise Lost* (1667), both of which Booth in *Amelia* (VIII. v) places with Homer's epics 'in the first Rank' (p. 328), HF refers to Lucan's *Pharsalia* (*c.* AD 62–5), an unfinished epic of the war between Caesar and Pompey; the *Punica* by Silius Italicus, an epic of the Second Punic War with Hannibal (218–201 BC); and Ludovico Ariosto's great romance *Orlando Furioso* (1532).

In the same manner the Comic Writer may either fix on one Action, as
the Authors of *Le Lutrin*, the *Dunciad*, *&c*. or on a Series, as *Butler* in Verse,
and *Cervantes* in Prose have done.[12]

Of this latter kind is the Book now before us, where the Fable consists of
a Series of separate Adventures detached from, and independent on each
other, yet all tending to one great End; so that those who should object want
of Unity of Action here, may, if they please, or if they dare, fly back with
their Objection, in the Face even of the *Odyssey* itself.

This Fable hath in it these three difficult Ingredients, which will be
found on Consideration to be always necessary to Works of this kind, *viz.*
that the main End or Scope be at once amiable, ridiculous and natural.

It is to be said, that some of the Comic Performances I have above
mentioned differ in the first of these, and set before us the odious instead of
the amiable;[13] I answer, that is far from being one of their Perfections; and of
this the Authors themselves seem so sensible, that they endeavour to deceive
their Reader by false Glosses and Colours, and by the help of Irony at least
to represent the Aim and Design of their Heroes in a favourable and agreeable Light.

I might farther observe, that as the Incidents arising from this Fable,[14]
tho' often surprizing, are every where natural, (Credibility not being once
shocked through the whole) so there is one Beauty very apparent, which
hath been attributed by the greatest of Critics to the greatest of Poets,[15] that
every Episode bears a manifest Impression of the principal Design, and
chiefly turns on the Perfection or Imperfection of Friendship; of which

[12] HF refers to the mock-epics *Le Lutrin* (1674–83), a satire of a clerical quarrel over a lectern by
Nicolas Boileau Despréaux, and Pope's *Dunciad* (1728–43); to Samuel Butler's burlesque epic of the
Puritan party in the English Civil War, *Hudibras* (1663–78); and to HF's own great model Miguel de
Cervantes Saavedra, author of *Don Quixote* (1605–15). Though HF had in his library the *Œuvres de
Boileau*, 3 vols. (1717), this is his only known reference to him (Ribbles B30).

[13] Cf. the Preface to *Joseph Andrews*, where HF discusses the proper subjects of 'The Ridiculous', from
which he firmly excludes what he calls here 'the odious': namely, 'the blackest Villanies; and what is worse,
the most dreadful Calamities' (p. 7).

[14] 'Fable': one of the more elusive terms of neoclassical criticism: depending on the context it can mean
either the plot or story (including the episodes) of a narrative or a play; or the underlying moral of the
work. In defining the 'comic Epic-Poem in Prose' in the Preface to *Joseph Andrews*, HF, having in mind the
former meaning, states that 'It differs from the serious Romance in its Fable and Action, in this; that as in
the one these are grave and solemn, so in the other they are light and ridiculous' (p. 4). In the present
paragraph he would seem to prefer the latter sense when referring to 'the principal Design', which 'chiefly
turns on the Perfection or Imperfection of Friendship'.

[15] Cf. in *Joseph Andrews* (III. ii) Parson Adams's panegyric on Homer's *Iliad*, in which he quotes
Aristotle on 'his Action, termed by *Aristotle Pragmaton Systasis* [*Poetics*, iv. 12]; is it possible for the Mind
of Man to conceive an Idea of such perfect Unity', citing in particular 'the *Harmotton*, that agreement of
his Action to his Subject: For as the Subject is Anger, how agreeable is his Action, which is War? from
which every Incident arises, and to which every Episode immediately relates' (p. 198).

noble Passion, from its highest Purity to its lowest Falshoods and Disguises, this little Book is, in my Opinion, the most exact Model.

As to the Characters here described, I shall repeat the Saying of one of the greatest Men of this Age,[16] *That they are as wonderfully drawn by the Writer, as they were by* Nature *herself.* There are many Strokes in *Orgueil, Spatter, Varnish, Le-vif,* the *Balancer,* and some others, which would have shined in the Pages of *Theophrastus, Horace,* or *La Bruyere.*[17] Nay, there are some Touches, which I will venture to say might have done honour to the Pencil of the immortal *Shakespear* himself.

The Sentiments are in general extremely delicate; those particularly which regard Friendship, are, I think, as noble and elevated as I have any where met with: Nor can I help remarking, that the Author hath been so careful, in justly adapting them to her Characters, that a very indifferent Reader, after he is in the least acquainted with the Character of the Speaker, can seldom fail of applying every Sentiment to the Person who utters it. Of this we have the strongest Instance in *Cynthia* and *Camilla,* where the lively Spirit of the former, and the gentle Softness of the latter, breathe through every Sentence which drops from either of them.

The Diction I shall say no more of, than as it is the last, and lowest Perfection in a Writer, and one which many of great Genius seem to have little regarded; so I must allow my Author to have the least Merit on this Head: Many Errors in Style existing in the first Edition, and some, I am convinced, remaining still uncured in this; but Experience and Habit will most certainly remove this Objection; for a good Style, as well as a good Hand in Writing, is chiefly learn'd by Practice.

I shall here finish these short Remarks on this little Book, which have been drawn from me by those People, who have very falsely and

---

[16] Not identified. However, the extravagance of this particular compliment ('one of the greatest Men of this Age') HF usually reserved for his friend and patron George Bubb Dodington (1691–1762), later Baron Melcombe, to whom he refers in *Amelia* (XI. ii) as 'one of the greatest Men this Country ever produced' (p. 462 and n. 3). In the Preface to *Of True Greatness. An Epistle to the Right Honourable George Dodington, Esq;* (1741), HF declared, 'THIS Poem . . . could be so properly addressed to no other as to that illustrious Person from whose Conduct and Conversation I actually borrowed the first Hint of the Subject' (*Miscellanies* i, Appendix A, p. 247). On HF's association with Dodington during the period 1739–41 and the view that he may have sponsored *The Champion* and *Jonathan Wild the Great,* see *Life,* pp. 278–81; also Coley in *Champion,* pp. lxxx–lxxxi.

[17] Besides the *Satires* of Horace (35–30 BC), HF refers to the *Characters* (sketches of various types among his contemporaries) by the Greek philosopher Theophrastus (*c.*372–*c.*287 BC), Aristotle's pupil and successor as head of the Peripatetic school; it was widely imitated in England in the seventeenth century. And to Jean de La Bruyère (1645–96): appended to his translation of Theophrastus, La Bruyère published *Les Caractères ou les moeurs de ce siècle* (1688); it was translated into English as *The Characters, or the Manners of the Age* (1699). No copy of Theophrastus or La Bruyère is listed in the catalogue of HF's library; but in *The Jacobite's Journal,* No. 45 (8 October 1748), when recalling 'the Sentiment of some modern *French Theophrastus*' (p. 403), he refers to La Bruyère's *Characters.* In *David Simple* (II. vi), Sarah Fielding recalls La Bruyère's comment on 'Raillery' (ed. Sabor, p. 84 and n. 47).

impertinently called me it's Author. I declare I have spoken no more than my real Sentiments of it, nor can I see why any Relation or Attachment to Merit, should restrain me from its Commendation.

The true Reason why some have been backward in giving this Book its just Praise, and why others have sought after some more known and experienced Author for it, is, I apprehend, no other than an Astonishment how one so young, and, in appearance, so unacquainted with the World, should know so much both of the better and worse Part, as is here exemplified: But, in reality, as a very little Knowledge of the World will afford an Observer, moderately accurate, sufficient Instances of Evil; and a short Communication with her own Heart, will leave the Author of this Book very little to seek abroad of all the Good which is to be found in Human Nature.

HENRY FIELDING.

5

THE FEMALE HUSBAND (1746)[1]

The Female Husband, a sixpenny pamphlet of twenty-three pages, purports to be the biography of the infamous Mary Hamilton, lesbian and trans-vestite, who, in the summer of 1746 while masquerading in Somersetshire as a doctor of physic, deceitfully married one Mary Price. The pamphlet, published anonymously on 12 November 1746,[2] was 'Printed', as the title-page states, 'for M. COOPER, at the Globe in Pater-noster-Row'; but on this, as on other occasions, Mary Cooper was merely acting as 'mercury' (or distributor of the work) for Fielding's publisher Andrew Millar, who owned the copy and had ordered the printer William Strahan to cast off 1,000 copies, and then another 250, before the month was out.[3] Fielding's authorship of this scandalous catchpenny piece might well have been known as early as 1758, when Millar listed it among his known works on a flyleaf of his sister Sarah's *Lives of Cleopatra and Octavia* (second edition). The attribution, however, went unnoticed by Fielding scholars until 1918, when Wilbur Cross called attention to it, albeit reluctantly, granting only that 'this piece of hack-work . . . may have come from the pen' of the author of *Tom Jones*.[4] Soon after Cross, J. Paul de Castro entertained no doubts whatever about Fielding's authorship of the pamphlet, to the point, indeed, where he could imagine him 'seated among counsel' at Mary Ham-ilton's trial.[5] It remained, however, for Sheridan Baker, in an important article of 1959, to marshal the evidence and argue the case that won for *The Female Husband: or, The Surprising History of Mrs. Mary, alias Mr. George Hamilton* a permanent place in the canon.[6]

---

[1] In what follows the editor benefited from a draft of an Introduction to *The Female Husband* by the late Sheridan Baker, whose article, published nearly a half-century ago, established HF's authorship of the pamphlet: see below, n. 6.

[2] *General Advertiser* and *Daily Advertiser* (12 November 1746); advertisements were repeated in the *General Advertiser* (13, 29 November, 1 December; and 23, 25 February 1747).

[3] See Strahan's ledger for November 1746 (BL, Add. MS 48800, fo. 71ʳ).

[4] Cross, ii, p. 51.

[5] De Castro, 'Fielding's Pamphlet "The Female Husband" ', *N & Q*, ser. 8, 12 (5 March 1921), pp. 184–5.

[6] See Sheridan Baker, 'Henry Fielding's *The Female Husband*: Fact and Fiction', *PMLA*, 74 (1959), pp. 213–24.

CIRCUMSTANCES OF COMPOSITION

In October 1746, when Mary Hamilton was tried in Somerset for imposture, Fielding found himself, as usual, in need of money. Since the death of his wife, Charlotte, two years earlier, he had been living in an expensive house in Old Boswell Court,[7] a highly desirable residential area near Lincoln's Inn Fields and the Inns of Court. With him was his sister Sarah, who had taken Charlotte's place supervising the household, the cook–maid Mary Daniel (whom a year later Fielding would marry in the sixth month of her pregnancy), and his infant son and daughter, Henry and Henrietta (or Harriet), aged 2 and 1, respectively.

Like his more prosperous neighbours, Fielding was a lawyer. In April, before he discontinued *The True Patriot* in June, he successfully solicited his great patron the Duke of Bedford for the place of High Steward of the New Forest, the royal preserve in Hampshire. For more than a year, furthermore, Fielding, in the grandest case of his career, had been representing his friend Sir Charles Hanbury Williams, one of the polite Subscribers to the Italian opera who were being sued by the Directors to cover lavish expenses for which the Directors themselves were responsible.[8] Fielding had also been representing another friend, Dr Arthur Collier, who was besieged by creditors for debts totalling more than £1,500.[9] But the income from the Stewardship (an annual stipend of £5 plus whatever incidental fees might accrue in the course of executing the office) was inconsiderable; and not even a generous retainer from Hanbury Williams could have covered Fielding's notorious extravagance. As for the Collier affair, far from expecting to profit from it, Fielding feared that, having with James Harris posted the bail to save their friend from confinement, he could be held responsible for the debt—an anxiety he appears to have felt despite the understanding he had with Harris that, if Collier defaulted, Harris alone would pay the money.[10]

Frederick Ribble's research in the Malmesbury papers has revealed, surprisingly,[11] that Fielding had, as Cross surmised,[12] begun writing *Tom Jones* in the last months of this year. Such, at least, is the inference to be drawn from John Upton's letter to James Harris of 19 March 1746/7:

---

[7] *Life*, p. 664 nn. 204–5. [8] Ibid., pp. 391–2. [9] Ibid., pp. 392–5.
[10] See HF's letter to Harris of 13 May 1746 (*Correspondence*, Letter 30).
[11] Surprising, for reasons that would appear to preclude the possibility of HF's having *begun* the novel *after* the Jacobite Rebellion: see the General Introduction to the two-volume Wesleyan edition (Oxford, 1974), i, pp. xxxv–xlii.
[12] Cross, ii, p. 100.

Your friend Fielding [Upton writes] is about another kind of work than w^t relates to the Laws &c; He has finished one volume of a large humourous work, wch has a reference, I hear, to some particulars. I take the Completion of this work will depend, not so much on any of ye heathenish deities, as Clio &c; as on a modern Goddess, ycleped Necessity; deservedly called The mother of invention.[13]

No doubt it was a more immediately urgent impulse from 'Necessity', the muse Upton understood to have prompted Fielding to write *Tom Jones*, that moved him to set his masterpiece aside temporarily in order to write the two uncharacteristically prurient works in the canon: *The Female Husband* and his paraphrase of Ovid's *Art of Love*, both experiments, as Dr Ribble remarks, in the genre of 'soft pornography'.[14]

Fielding, the anonymous author, took some pains to represent *The Female Husband* as an authentic case history of Mary Hamilton's life and 'unnatural' sexual practices—an account, indeed, as the title-page proclaims, 'TAKEN FROM Her own MOUTH since her Confinement' after she had been tried before the General Quarter Sessions at Taunton, the county town of Somerset, on 7 October 1746. He may actually have been at Bath, as usual in the late summer after the assizes for the Western Circuit ended at Bristol on 6 September;[15] and if so, he would have heard of Mary Hamilton's arrest on the 13th at nearby Glastonbury, his birthplace, where at Sharpham Park his uncle resided. Though Fielding may have been at Bath when the first of Thomas Boddely's three articles on the case was published in the *Bath Journal* (Monday 22 September), he had left for London before the second appeared in the next issue (29 September). As Sheridan Baker demonstrated long ago (see above, n. 6), Fielding's account of Mary Hamilton is, by far, more fiction than fact, more a story than a true history. He was not present at her trial, nor did he personally consult the records of the court, which are collected here in the Supplement to the Wesleyan text (below, pp. 382–4).

So far as Fielding sought documentary evidence at all, he appears to have relied on two notices of the case excerpted from Boddely's *Bath Journal* (22 September and 3 November), the first of which was reprinted on 2 October in both the *General Advertiser* and the *General London Evening Mercury*, as follows:

Tuesday last a Woman, dress'd in Man's Apparel, was committed to Shepton-Mallet Bridewell. She was detected at Glastenbury [*sic*]; and has for some Time

---

[13] Frederick G. Ribble, 'New Light on Henry Fielding from the Malmesbury Papers', *MP*, 103 (2005), pp. 78–80.

[14] Ibid., p. 76.

[15] *Life*, pp. 410–11.

follow'd the Profession of Quack Doctor, up and down the Country. There are great Numbers of People flock to see her in Bridewell, to whom she sells a great Deal of her Quackery; and appears very bold and impudent. She seems very gay, with Perriwig, Ruffles, and Breeches; and it is publickly talk'd, that she has deceived several of the Fair Sex, by marrying them. As the Circumstances in general are somewhat remarkable, we shall make further Enquiry, and give our Readers the Particulars in our next.

From this brief article Fielding may have drawn the facts that his heroine masqueraded as a doctor and that her duplicity was 'detected' at Glastonbury. But the information was available to anyone with access to the record of the 'Examinations' of Mary Hamilton and her victimized 'wife' Mary Price before the Glastonbury justices John Masters and Thomas White on 13 September and 7 October, respectively (see below, pp. 382–4). And Fielding had close and influential family connections in Glastonbury who would have had access to the records and, for that matter, to Mary Hamilton herself: Davidge Gould (*c.*1684–1765), Fielding's uncle, was Master of the Bench at the Middle Temple; and his son Henry (1711–94), Fielding's first cousin, was already well launched on a career in the law that would lead to his appointments as king's counsel (1754), sergeant and Baron of the Exchequer (1761), and Judge of the Court of Common Pleas (1763). Henry Gould, indeed, was at this time directly involved in the case of Mary Hamilton, having been retained by the Corporation of Glastonbury on 9 October to 'advice [*sic*] and assist' in recommending 'the severest' possible punishment for the 'woman impostor' under the law (see below, p. 384).

Baker, however, was inclined to believe that Fielding, though he did not see Boddely's second article on the case, was chiefly dependent for his 'facts' on Boddely's third article, published at Bath on 3 November, more than a month later, and reprinted in London on 7 November, as follows in the *Daily Advertiser* for that date:

We hear from Taunton, that at a General Quarter Sessions of the Peace, for the County of Somerset, held there lately, *Mary Hamilton*, otherwise *George*, otherwise *Charles Hamilton*, was try'd for a very singular and notorious Offence: Mr. Gold, Council for the King, open'd to the Court, That the said *Mary*, *&c.* pretending herself a Man, had married fourteen Wives, the last of which Number was one Mary Price, who appeared in Court, and deposed, that she was married to the Prisoner, some little Time since, at the Parish Church of St. Cuthbert's in Wells, and that they were Bedded as Man and Wife, and lived as such for about a Quarter of a Year, during which Time she, the said Price, thought the Prisoner a Man, owing to the Prisoner's using certain vile and deceitful Practices, not fit to be mentioned.

There was a great Debate for some Time in Court about the Nature of her Crime, and what to call it, but at last it was agreed, that she was an uncommon notorious Cheat, and as such was sentenced to be publickly whipp'd in the four following Towns, Taunton, Glastonbury, Wells and Shipton-Mallet; to be imprisoned for six Months, and to find Sureties for her good Behaviour, for as long a Time as the Justices at the next Quarter-Sessions shall think fit.

Fielding, Baker observed (p. 222), would have found here details of the case not mentioned in the court records: the article, for example, 'gives Hamilton a plurality of wives'; for the first time in print it mentions 'George' as an alias for her,[16] as well as 'Charles', the latter alone to be found in the records; and it gives the duration of the couple's marriage as 'about a Quarter of a Year', or the 'three months' Fielding twice stipulates (pp. 378, 380), whereas the records make clear that the marriage lasted just two months (from 16 July to 13 September).

On 7 November Fielding may well have read this article in the *Daily Advertiser* in time to revise the manuscript before sending it to Millar for publication. But Baker's notion that Fielding was so dependent on Boddely he might have written the entire 6,900 words in time for Strahan to print 1,000 copies for publication five days later is very much a stretch. Most, if not all, of the information on which Fielding based his account of Mary Hamilton could have been communicated to him by his cousin Henry Gould in the latter weeks of October. Gould had every opportunity to take her story from her own mouth during her confinement, as the title-page has it. That Fielding, in writing the story, would have failed to draw on so useful and friendly a source is unlikely. His admiration of his cousin's abilities as a lawyer, and indeed his affection for him, are evident in the eulogy Fielding wrote in *The Jacobite's Journal*, No. 38 (20 August 1748), prompted by a (false) report of Gould's death: '*This young Gentleman (who was of the Middle-Temple) had great Parts, and had with great Diligence applied them to the Study of his Profession; in which he was arrived at a very extensive Knowledge, and had very early in Life acquired much Reputation*' (p. 481).

PUBLICATION AND RECEPTION

The ledger of the printer William Strahan for November 1746 records that Andrew Millar, Fielding's publisher, first ordered 1,000 copies of *The Female Husband*, and later that month another 250 copies, at a total cost of £4 15s. 1½ d.:

---

[16] To explain Fielding's choice of 'George' rather than 'Charles' for the alias, Baker noted the coincidental collocation in the *St. James's Evening Post* for Saturday 8 November of an article about Mary Hamilton preceded immediately by another reporting the trial and execution for treason, at York on 1 November, of the Jacobite George Hamilton, Captain of Hussars (Baker, 'Henry Fielding's *The Female Husband*', p. 222 n. 29).

Nov[r]. 1746	The Female Husband	1¾ Sheets Pica 8[vo].
	N[o]. 1000	2/2/—
	For 3½ Reams of Paper for D[o]. @ 11s.	1/18/6
	For Casting off 250 more of D[o]	/5/—
	For 17½ Quires of Paper for D[o]	9/7½[17]

In ordering a further printing within the month, Millar must have been pleased with the public's initial demand for the pamphlet; but this original supply had not been exhausted twelve years later when he advertised *The Female Husband* for sale in Sarah Fielding's *Lives of Cleopatra and Octavia*.

In a recent essay Bonnie Blackwell identified two audiences 'Fielding's text presupposes': 'young virginal readers, akin to the women Mary Hamilton pursues, and more knowing male and female readers who grasp the rampant innuendo. The knowing female reader [she continues] also has a place to identify within the text: she may see herself reflected in the widows, wives, and mothers who expose Hamilton and mock her insufficiency as a husband.'[18] A broad and numerous audience, to be sure, but despite its encouraging sale on publication, *The Female Husband* was ignored by reviewers and also, it appears, by the usual epistolizing literary gossips of the period. Fielding's title, at least, was later adopted in a miscellany of 1769 by the author of the tale of one Mary East, lesbian and transvestite, who lived with an 'intimate' friend many years as husband and wife; and it was also adopted in the final decade of the century by a frisky balladeer.[19]

More directly relevant is the anonymous spin-off of Fielding's pamphlet published in 1813, with the following synopsis for a title-page:

The Surprising Adventures of a FEMALE HUSBAND! *containing the whimsical Amours, curious Incidents, and* DIABOLICAL TRICKS, *of Miss M. Hamilton, alias Mr. G. Hamilton, alias Minister Bentley, Mr. O'Keefe, alias Mrs. Knight, the Midwife, &c. who* **Married Three Wives,** *And lived with each some time undiscovered,* FOR WHICH ACTS *she was tried at the Summer Sessions, in the County of Somerset, in the Year 1752,* FOUND GUILTY, *and whipped four several Times, in four Market Towns, and afterwards Imprisoned Six Months; notwithstanding which, On the Evening*

---

[17] BL, Add. MS 48800, fo. 71[v].

[18] ' "An Infallible Nostrum": Female Husbands and Greensick Girls in Eighteenth-Century England', *Literature and Medicine*, 21 (2002), pp. 58–9.

[19] See 'The FEMALE HUSBAND; *or a circumstantial Account of the extraordinary Affair which lately happened at* POPLAR; *with many interesting Particulars, relating thereto*', in *The Merry Droll, or Pleasing Companion* (1769), pp. 36–41; and *The Female Husband: A New Song* (1790?), a ballad of a single sheet (*ESTC*, T199729).

*of the first Day of her Exposure, she attempted to bribe the Goaler to procure her a fine young Girl to gratify her most monstrous and **Unnatural Propensity!***

This sixpenny potboiler equals Fielding's twenty-three pages in number and price if not in literary quality. For more immediate pornographic appeal than mere narrative could provide, it includes an illustration by George Cruikshank depicting the half-naked heroine being whipped in the town square.

More recently, Terry Castle has discussed *The Female Husband* from feminist and psychoanalytic perspectives.[20]

---

[20] See Terry Castle, *The Female Thermometer: Eighteenth-Century Culture and the Invention of the Uncanny* (Oxford, 1995), ch. 5 (' "Matters Not Fit to be Mentioned": Fielding's *The Female Husband*')— an essay originally published in *ELH*, 49 (1982), pp. 602–22. For Castle's helpful review of publications on HF's pamphlet and the related subjects of female transvestism and homosexuality from 1976, see her book, p. 223–4 n. 2.

THE
Female Husband:
OR, THE
SURPRISING
HISTORY
OF
Mrs. *Mary,* alias Mr. *George Hamilton.*

(Price Sixpence.)

THE
Female Hufband:
OR, THE
SURPRISING
HISTORY
OF
Mrs. *MARY*,
ALIAS
Mr GEORGE HAMILTON,

Who was convicted of having married a YOUNG
WOMAN of *WELLS* and lived with her as
her HUSBAND.

TAKEN FROM

Her own MOUTH fince her Confinement.

~~By Henry Fielding~~

—— *Quodque id mirum magis effet in illo;*
Fæmina natus erat. Monftri novitate moventur,
Quifquis adeft : narretque rogant. ——
OVID Metam. Lib. 12.

LONDON:
Printed for M. COOPER, at the Globe in Pater-
nofter-Row. 1746.

The epigraph is from Ovid's *Metamorphoses*, xii. 174–6. Nestor tells the Greeks of Caeneus, a great warrior of former times whose body was impervious to sword strokes: ' "and to enhance the marvel of him, he had been born a woman." All who heard were struck with wonder at this marvel and begged him to tell the tale' (Loeb). He then relates the story of the beautiful maiden Caenis, whom Neptune, having ravished her, granted her wish to be transformed into a man who could never be violated; she became the invulnerable Caeneus (xii. 195–209).

THE Female Husband

THAT propense inclination which is for very wise purposes implanted in the one sex for the other, is not only necessary for the continuance of the human species; but is, at the same time, when govern'd and directed by virtue and religion, productive not only of corporeal delight, but of the most rational felicity.

But if once our carnal appetites are let loose, without those prudent and secure guides, there is no excess and disorder which they are not liable to commit, even while they pursue their natural satisfaction; and, which may seem still more strange, there is nothing monstrous and unnatural, which they are not capable of inventing, nothing so brutal and shocking which they have not actually committed.

Of these unnatural lusts, all ages and countries have afforded us too many instances; but none I think more surprising than what will be found in the history of Mrs. *Mary*, otherwise Mr. *George Hamilton*.

This heroine in iniquity was born in the Isle of *Man*, on the 16th Day of *August*, 1721.[1] Her father was formerly a serjeant of grenadiers in the Foot-Guards, who having the good fortune to marry a widow of some estate in that island, purchased his discharge from the army, and retired thither with his wife.

He had not been long arrived there before he died, and left his wife with child of this *Mary*; but her mother, tho' she had not two months to reckon, could not stay till she was delivered, before she took a third husband.

As her mother, tho' she had three husbands, never had any other child, she always express'd an extraordinary affection for this daughter, to whom she gave as good an education as the island afforded; and tho' she used her with much tenderness, yet was the girl brought up in the strictest principles of virtue and religion; nor did she in her younger years discover the least proneness to any kind of vice, much less give cause of suspicion that she would one day disgrace her sex by the most abominable and unnatural pollutions. And indeed she hath often declared from her conscience, that no irregular passion ever had any place in her mind, till she was first seduced by one *Anne Johnson*, a neighbour of hers, with whom she had been acquainted

---

[1] HF's fabrication of the details of Mary Hamilton's life story begins at once. According to her deposition, given before the Glastonbury Justices on 13 September 1746, she was born in Somerset; and the inference from the same source, which does not record a date of birth, is that she was about 20 years old, not 25 (see below, p. 382). HF archly chose the Isle of Man as the birthplace for his subject, a lesbian transvestite.

from her childhood; but not with such intimacy as afterwards grew between them.

This *Anne Johnson* going on some business to *Bristol*, which detained her there near half a year, became acquainted with some of the people called *Methodists*, and was by them persuaded to embrace their sect.[2]

At her return to the Isle of *Man*, she soon made an easy convert of *Molly Hamilton*, the warmth of whose disposition rendered her susceptible enough of Enthusiasm,[3] and ready to receive all those impressions which her friend the *Methodist* endeavoured to make on her mind.

These two young women became now inseparable companions, and at length bed-fellows: For *Molly Hamilton* was prevail'd on to leave her mother's house, and to reside entirely with Mrs. *Johnson*, whose fortune was not thought inconsiderable in that cheap country.

Young Mrs. *Hamilton* began to conceive a very great affection for her friend, which perhaps was not returned with equal faith by the other. However, Mrs. *Hamilton* declares her love, or rather friendship, was totally innocent, till the temptations of *Johnson* first led her astray. This latter was, it seems, no novice in impurity, which, as she confess'd, she had learnt and often practiced at *Bristol* with her methodistical sisters.

As *Molly Hamilton* was extremely warm in her inclinations, and as those inclinations were so violently attached to Mrs. *Johnson*, it would not have

---

[2] HF's making Mary Hamilton a convert to Methodism had no basis in either the court records or the reports of the case in Boddely's *Bath Journal*. On his inveterate hostility towards Methodism from the time the movement began in the late 1730s under the leadership of the great evangelists John Wesley and George Whitefield (HF's particular target), see the Introduction to *Shamela* (above, p. 139). Among the earliest triumphs of Whitefield's evangelism were the many converts he won in Bristol. From Bristol, Tom Jones follows the road towards Gloucester, not far to the north, where he stays at the Bell Inn, Whitefield's former home. Keeper of the inn is 'the great Preacher's' brother, who, HF hastens to inform the reader, 'is absolutely untainted with the pernicious Principles of Methodism' (viii. viii, p. 430).

[3] Cf. *Joseph Andrews* (I. xvii), where, in a passage that sums up HF's objections to Whitefield's doctrines and his manner of appealing to the emotions of his followers, Parson Adams denounces the Methodist for calling 'Nonsense and Enthusiasm to his Aid' (p. 82). Like Swift in *The Mechanical Operation of the Spirit*, HF regarded religious 'enthusiasm' (that is, the delusion of being divinely inspired) as being, essentially, the sublimated expression of lust. The Blifil brothers in *Tom Jones*, which HF was writing at this time, illustrate the connection between the two emotions, religious and sexual. Dr Blifil excites Bridget Allworthy's interest by flaunting his knowledge of 'religious Controversies'; and though his approach proves unproductive, it resembles that of Mrs Johnson in her more successful seduction of Mary Hamilton. HF comments on Blifil's appeal: 'As Sympathies of all Kinds are apt to beget Love, so Experience teaches us that none have a more direct Tendency this Way than those of a religious Kind between Persons of different Sexes' (I. x, p. 62). Captain Blifil, who supplants his brother in Bridget's affection, adopts a similar strategy: betaking 'himself to studying the Scriptures', he is 'not a little suspected of an Inclination to *Methodism*' (p. 63). Bridget weds the Captain when she considers this appealing spiritual qualification together with his physical endowments, which promise a 'much more solid Satisfaction' (I. xi, p. 66). At the denouement, their son, the villain of the novel, turns 'Methodist, in hopes of marrying a very rich Widow of that Sect' (xviii. xiii, pp. 979–80).

been difficult for a less artful woman, in the most private hours, to turn the ardour of enthusiastic devotion into a different kind of flame.

Their conversation, therefore, soon became in the highest manner criminal, and transactions not fit to be mention'd past between them.

They had not long carried on this wicked crime before Mrs. *Johnson* was again called by her affairs to visit *Bristol*, and her friend was prevail'd on to accompany her thither.

Here when they arrived, they took up their lodgings together, and lived in the same detestable manner as before; till an end was put to their vile amours, by the means of one *Rogers*,[4] a young fellow, who by his extraordinary devotion (for he was a very zealous *Methodist*) or by some other charms, (for he was very jolly and handsome) gained the heart of Mrs. *Johnson*, and married her.

This amour, which was not of any long continuance before it was brought to a conclusion, was kept an entire secret from Mrs. *Hamilton*; but she was no sooner informed of it, than she became almost frantic, she tore her hair, beat her breasts, and behaved in as outrageous a manner as the fondest husband could, who had unexpectedly discovered the infidelity of a beloved wife.

In the midst of these agonies she received a letter from Mrs. *Johnson*, in the following words, or as near them as she can possibly remember:

'DEAR MOLLY,

I Know you will condemn what I have now done; but I condemn myself much more for what I have done formerly: For I take the whole shame and guilt of what hath passed between us on myself. I was indeed the first seducer of your innocence, for which I ask GOD's pardon and yours. All the amends I can make you, is earnestly to beseech you, in the name of the Lord, to forsake all such evil courses, and to follow my example now, as you before did my temptation, and enter as soon as you can into that holy state into which I was yesterday called. In which, tho' I am yet but a novice, believe me, there are delights infinitely surpassing the faint endearments we have experienc'd together. I shall always pray for you, and continue your friend.'

This letter rather increased than abated her rage, and she resolved to go immediately and upbraid her false friend; but while she was taking this resolution, she was informed that Mr. *Rogers* and his bride were departed from *Bristol* by a messenger, who brought her a second short note, and a bill for some money from Mrs. *Rogers*.

---

[4] 'Mr. *Rogers*': cf. *OED*, 2nd edn., in eighteenth-century slang, 'roger' as a verb: 'To copulate with (a woman)'; 'roger' as a noun: 'A Man's Yard' (i.e. penis).

As soon as the first violence of her passion subsided, she began to consult what course to take, when the strangest thought imaginable suggested itself to her fancy. This was to dress herself in men's cloaths, to embarque for *Ireland*, and commence Methodist teacher.

Nothing remarkable happened to her during the rest of her stay at *Bristol*, which adverse winds occasioned to be a whole week, after she had provided herself with her dress; but at last having procured a passage, and the wind becoming favourable, she set sail for *Dublin*.

As she was a very pretty woman, she now appeared a most beautiful youth. A circumstance which had its consequences aboard the ship, and had like to have discovered her, in the very beginning of her adventures.

There happened to be in the same vessel with this adventurer, a Methodist, who was bound to the same place, on the same design with herself.

These two being alone in the cabin together, and both at their devotions, the man in the extasy of his enthusiasm, thrust one of his hands into the other's bosom. Upon which, in her surprize, she gave so effeminate a squawl, that it reached the Captain's ears, as he was smoking his pipe upon deck. Hey day, says he, what have we a woman in the ship! and immediately descended into the cabin, where he found the two Methodists on their knees.

Pox on't, says the Captain, I thought you had had a woman with you here; I could have sworn I had heard one cry out as if she had been ravishing, and yet the Devil must have been in you, if you could convey her in here without my knowledge.

I defy the Devil and all his works, answered the He Methodist. He has no power but over the wicked; and if he be in the ship, thy oaths must have brought him hither: for I have heard thee pronounce more than twenty since I came on board; and we should have been at the bottom before this, had not my prayers prevented it.

Don't abuse my vessel, cried the Captain, she is as safe a vessel, and as good a sailer as ever floated, and if you had been afraid of going to the bottom, you might have stay'd on shore and been damn'd.

The Methodist made no answer, but fell a groaning, and that so loud, that the Captain giving him a hearty curse or two, quitted the cabbin, and resumed his pipe.

He was no sooner gone, than the Methodist gave farther tokens of brotherly love to his companion, which soon became so importunate and troublesome to her, that after having gently rejected his hands several times, she at last recollected the sex she had assumed, and gave him so violent a blow in the nostrils, that the blood issued from them with great Impetuosity.

Whether fighting be opposite to the tenets of this sect (for I have not the honour to be deeply read in their doctrines) or from what other motive it proceeded, I will not determine; but the Methodist made no other return to this rough treatment, than by many groans, and prayed heartily to be delivered soon from the conversation of the wicked; which prayers were at length so successful, that, together with a very brisk gale, they brought the vessel into *Dublin* harbour.

Here our adventurer took a lodging in a back-street near *St. Stephen's Green*,[5] at which place she intended to preach the next day; but had got a cold in the voyage, which occasioned such a hoarseness that made it impossible to put that design in practice.

There lodged in the same house with her, a brisk widow of near 40 Years of age, who had buried two husbands, and seemed by her behaviour to be far from having determined against a third expedition to the land of matrimony.

To this widow our adventurer began presently to make addresses, and as he[6] at present wanted tongue to express the ardency of his flame, he was obliged to make use of actions of endearment, such as squeezing, kissing, toying, &c.[7]

These were received in such a manner by the fair widow, that her lover thought he had sufficient encouragement to proceed to a formal declaration of his passion. And this she chose to do by letter, as her voice still continued too hoarse for uttering the soft accents of love.

A letter therefore was penned accordingly in the usual stile, which, to prevent any miscarriages, Mrs. *Hamilton* thought proper to deliver with her own hands; and immediately retired to give the adored lady an opportunity of digesting the contents alone, little doubting of an answer agreeable to her wishes, or at least such a one as the coyness of the sex generally dictates in the beginning of an amour, and which lovers, by long experience, know pretty well how to interpret.

But what was the gallant's surprize, when in return to an amorous epistle, she read the following sarcasms, which it was impossible for the most sanguine temper to misunderstand, or construe favourably.

'SIR,

I Was greatly astonished at what you put into my hands. Indeed I thought, when I took it, it might have been an Opera song, and which for certain

---

[5] Dublin's central park. Whitefield had often preached in the open fields near Bristol and London, but by 1746, when HF wrote *The Female Husband*, he had visited Dublin just once, on returning from America in 1738, and then briefly, preaching twice in churches: see Whitefield's *Short Account of God's Dealings with the Reverend Mr. George Whitefield* (1740), and his *Two First Parts of his Life, with his Journals* (1756).

[6] From this point HF refers to Mary (alias George) Hamilton by either the male or the female pronoun, as in the next paragraph, where he uses both.

[7] For the bawdy implications of '&c.', see *Shamela* (above, p. 149 n. 1).

reasons I should think, when your cold is gone, you might sing as well as *Farinelli*,[8] from the great resemblance there is between your persons. I know not what you mean by encouragement to your hopes; if I could have conceived my innocent freedoms could have been so misrepresented, I should have been more upon my guard: but you have taught me how to watch my actions for the future, and to preserve myself even from any suspicion of forfeiting the regard I owe to the memory of the best of men, by any future choice. The remembrance of that dear person makes me incapable of proceeding father.——'

And so firm was this resolution, that she would never afterwards admit of the least familiarity with the despairing Mrs. *Hamilton*; but perhaps that destiny which is remarked to interpose in all matrimonial things, had taken the widow into her protection: for in a few days afterwards, she was married to one *Jack Strong*, a cadet in an *Irish* regiment.

Our adventurer being thus disappointed in her love, and what is worse, her money drawing towards an end, began to have some thoughts of returning home, when fortune seemed inclined to make her amends for the tricks she had hitherto played her,[9] and accordingly now threw another Mistress in her way, whose fortune was much superior to the former widow, and who received Mrs. *Hamilton's* addresses with all the complaisance she could wish.

This Lady, whose name was *Rushford*,[10] was the widow of a rich cheesemonger, who left her all he had, and only one great grand-child to take care of, whom, at her death, he recommended to be her Heir; but wholly at her own power and discretion.

---

[8] Carlo Broschi (1705–82), called Farinelli, the most celebrated of the castrati who sang in the Italian opera, which HF, like his literary contemporaries Addison, Gay, and Pope, considered an inferior and effeminate form of entertainment. In *Joseph Andrews* (I. ix) Mrs Slipslop hates the sight of 'a Sett of *Mophrodites* . . . singing in an Opera' (p. 43). Farinelli was a favourite target of HF's dramatic satires: in *Pasquin* (1736i; II. i) he is 'Faribelly, the strange man-woman'; in *Eurydice* (1737) he is ridiculed in the character of Orpheus, or Signior Orpheo; and in *The Historical Register* (1737; II. i) he is 'Farinello', in whom the ladies find 'almost everything one could wish'.

[9] A favourite formula of HF's narratives is the notion of an event or act that 'makes Amends' for some unpleasantness (C-H lists fifty-eight instances in the fiction). With the present phrasing cf. *Amelia* (XII. ix): 'As to *Booth* and *Amelia*, Fortune seems to have made them large Amends for the Tricks she played them in their Youth' (p. 532); also *Tom Jones* (XII. ii): 'Whether Fortune . . . in her wantonest Tricks . . . might not resolve to make [Squire Western] Amends some other Way, I will not assert' (pp. 622–3).

[10] Given the sexually charged name games HF plays in the narrative (e.g. Isle of Man, Mr Rogers, Jack Strong), and the recurrence in his comedies and fiction of lusty ladies past their prime from Lady Booby and Mrs Slipslop to Bridget Allworthy and Lady Bellaston, Mrs Rushford ('Rush-forward'/'Rush-for-it'?) appears to belong to the company of female characters of the Restoration stage: e.g. Etherege's 'Mrs Loveit' (*The Man of Mode*) and, especially, Congreve's 'Lady Wishfort'.

She was now in the sixty eighth year of her age and had not, it seems, entirely abandoned all thoughts of the pleasures of this world: for she was no sooner acquainted with Mrs. *Hamilton*, but, taking her for a beautiful lad of about eighteen, she cast the eyes of affection on her,[11] and having pretty well outlived the bashfulness of her youth, made little scruple of giving hints of her passion of her own accord.

It has been observed that women know more of one another than the wisest men (if ever such have been employed in the study) have with all their art been capable of discovering. It is therefore no wonder that these hints were quickly perceived and understood by the female gallant, who animadverting on the conveniency which the old gentlewoman's fortune would produce in her present situation, very gladly embraced the opportunity, and advancing with great warmth of love to the attack, in which she was received almost with open arms, by the tottering citadel, which presently offered to throw open the gates, and surrender at discretion.[12]

In her amour with the former widow, Mrs. *Hamilton* had never any other design than of gaining the lady's affection, and then discovering herself to her, hoping to have had the same success which Mrs. *Johnson* had found with her: but with this old lady, whose fortune only she was desirous to possess, such views would have afforded very little gratification. After some reflection, therefore, a device entered into her head, as strange and surprizing, as it was wicked and vile; and this was actually to marry the old woman, and to deceive her, by means which decency forbids me even to mention.

The wedding was accordingly celebrated in the most public manner, and with all kind of gaiety, the old woman greatly triumphing in her shame instead of hiding her own head for fear of infamy, was actually proud of the beauty of her new husband, for whose sake she intended to disinherit her poor great-grandson, tho' she had derived her riches from her husband's family, who had always intended this boy as his heir. Nay, what may seem very remarkable, she insisted on the parson's not omitting the prayer in the matrimonial service for fruitfulness; drest herself as airy as a girl of eighteen, concealed twenty years of her age, and laughed and promoted all the jokes which are usual at weddings; but she was not so well pleased with a repartee of her great-grandson, a pretty and a smart lad, who, when somebody jested on the bridegroom because he had no beard, answered smartly:

---

[11] Cf. *Joseph Andrews* (I. vi), where Mrs Slipslop 'had long cast the Eyes of Affection on *Joseph*' (p. 32); and *Tom Jones* (IV. vi), where Tom at 19 'began first to cast the Eyes of Affection upon Sophia' (p. 174).

[12] Cf. *Tom Jones* (I. xi), where Captain Blifil at last succeeds in his courtship of Bridget Allworthy: 'the Captain made his Advances in Form, the Citadel was defended in Form, and at length, in proper Form, surrendered at Discretion' (pp. 68–9).

There should never be a beard on both-sides: For indeed the old lady's chin was pretty well stocked with bristles.[13]

Nor was this bride contented with displaying her shame by a public wedding dinner, she would have the whole ceremony completed, and the stocking was accordingly thrown[14] with the usual sport and merriment.

During the three first days of marriage, the bride expressed herself so well satisfied with her choice, that being in company with another old lady, she exulted so much in her happiness, that her friend began to envy her, and could not forbear inveighing against effeminacy in men; upon which a discourse arose between the two ladies, not proper to be repeated, if I knew every particular; but ended at the last, in the unmarried lady's declaring to the bride, that she thought her husband looked more like a woman than a man. To which the other replied in triumph, he was the best man in *Ireland*.

This and the rest which past, was faithfully recounted to Mrs. *Hamilton* by her wife, at their next meeting, and occasioned our young bridegroom to blush, which the old lady perceiving and regarding as an effect of youth, fell upon her in a rage of love like a tygress, and almost murdered her with kisses.[15]

*One of our *English* Poets remarks in the case of a more able husband than Mrs. *Hamilton* was, when his wife grew amorous in an unseasonable time.

> *The doctor understood the call,*
> *But had not always wherewithal.*[16]

---

* *Prior*.

[13] Cf. *Joseph Andrews* (IV. xiv), where, in the dark, Parson Adams mistakes Slipslop's sex: 'laying hold on *Slipslop's* Chin . . . he found a rough Beard' (p. 332).

[14] Cf. *Champion* (5 August 1740), where, in his travels, Job Vinegar describes the marriage customs of the 'Ptfghsiumgski': 'At Night as soon as the married Couple are in Bed together, they use a very extraordinary Piece of Merriment, which they call THRWNG the STCKNG, by which Means the Bride is exposed in the Arms of her Husband, to the whole Company'. At which moment, Coley's note explains, the bride 'throws her stocking among them, the superstition being that whoever is hit by the stocking will be the first of the company to be married' (pp. 415–16 and n. 1). The custom continues today at weddings, the bride throwing her bouquet instead of her stocking.

[15] Again cf. *Joseph Andrews* (I. vi), where the same simile renders the passion of Slipslop: 'As when a hungry Tygress, who had long traversed the Woods in fruitless search, sees within the Reach of her Claws a Lamb, she prepares to leap on her Prey . . . so did Mrs. *Slipslop* prepare to lay her violent amorous Hands on the poor *Joseph*' (pp. 33–4).

[16] From *Paulo Purganti and His Wife: An Honest, but a Simple Pair* (1708; lines 82–3), HF's favourite poem by Matthew Prior (1664–1721), one of his favourite poets (see Canto 2, lines 110–13, above, p. 54 and n. 74). The passage is apt in the present context; for Paulo Purganti, a physician, cannot always rise to the occasion of his wife's ardour. HF quotes from the poem, or alludes to it, in *Tom Jones* (XV. x, p. 823), *Amelia* (IV. ii, p. 160; XII. ii, p. 496), and *The Covent-Garden Journal*, No. 57 (1 August 1752), p. 307.

So it happened to our poor bridegroom, who having not at that time *the wherewithal* about her, was obliged to remain meerly passive, under all this torrent of kindness of his wife; but this did not discourage her, who was an experienced woman, and thought she had a cure for this coldness in her husband, the efficacy of which, she might perhaps have essayed formerly. Saying therefore with a tender smile to her husband, I believe you are a woman, her hands began to move in such direction, that the discovery would absolutely have been made, had not the arrival of dinner, at that very instant, prevented it.

However, as there is but one way of laying the spirit of curiosity, when once raised in a woman, *viz.* by satisfying it, so that discovery, though delayed, could not now be long prevented. And accordingly the very next night, the husband and wife had not been long in bed together, before a storm arose, as if drums, guns, wind and thunder were all roaring together. Villain, rogue, whore, beast, cheat, all resounded at the same instant, and were followed by curses, imprecations and threats, which soon waked the poor great-grandson in the garret; who immediately ran down stairs into his great-grandmother's room. He found her in the midst of it in her shift, with a handful of shirt in one hand, and a handful of hair in the other, stamping and crying, I am undone, cheated, abused, ruined, robbed by a vile jade, impostor, whore.—What is the matter, dear Madam, answered the youth; O child, replied she, undone! I am married to one who is no man. My husband? a woman, a woman, a woman.[17] Ay, said the grandson, where is she?—Run away, gone, said the great-grandmother, and indeed so she was: For no sooner was the fatal discovery made, than the poor female bridegroom whipt on her breeches, in the pockets of which, she had stowed all the money she could, and slipping on her shoes, with her coat, waiste-coat and stockings in her hands, had made the best of her way into the street, leaving almost one half of her shirt behind, which the enraged wife had torn from her back.

As Mrs. *Hamilton* well knew that an adventure of that kind would soon fill all *Dublin*, and that it was impossible for her to remain there undiscovered, she hastened away to the Key, where by good fortune, she met with a ship just bound to *Dartmouth*, on board which she immediately went, and sailed out of the harbour, before her pursuers could find out or overtake her.

She was a full fortnight in her passage, during which time, no adventure

---

[17] Though the circumstances differ, this episode is a version of the 'Night-Adventures' in *Joseph Andrews* (IV. xiv), where Slipslop, pretending the effeminate Beau Didapper has attempted to rape her, tears his nightshirt, screaming 'Murther! Murther! Rape! Robbery! Ruin' (pp. 331–2).

occurred worthy remembrance. At length she landed at *Dartmouth*,[18] where she soon provided herself with linnen, and thence went to *Totnes*,[19] where she assumed the title of a doctor of physic, and took lodgings in the house of one Mrs. *Baytree*.[20]

Here she soon became acquainted with a young girl, the daughter of one Mr. *Ivythorn*, who had the green sickness; a distemper which the doctor gave out he could cure by an infallible *nostrum*.

The doctor had not been long intrusted with the care of this young patient before he began to make love to her: for though her complexion was somewhat faded with her distemper, she was otherwise extreamly pretty.

This Girl became an easy conquest to the doctor, and the day of their marriage was appointed, without the knowledge, or even suspicion of her father, or of an old aunt who was very fond of her, and would neither of them have easily given their consent to the match, had the doctor been as good a Man as the niece thought him.

At the day appointed, the doctor and his mistress found means to escape very early in the morning from *Totnes*, and went to a town called *Ashburton*[21] in *Devonshire*, where they were married by a regular Licence which the doctor had previously obtained.

Here they staid two days at a public house, during which time the Doctor so well acted his part, that his bride had not the least suspicion of the legality of her marriage, or that she had not got a husband for life. The third day they returned to *Totnes*, where they both threw themselves at Mr. *Ivythorn's* feet, who was highly rejoic'd at finding his daughter restor'd to him, and that she was not debauched, as he had suspected of her. And being a very worthy good-natur'd man, and regarding the true interest and happiness of his daughter more than the satisfying his own pride, ambition, or obstinacy, he was prevailed on to forgive her, and to receive her and her husband into his house, as his children, notwithstanding the opposition of the old aunt, who declared she would never forgive the wanton slut, and

---

[18] An important harbour town in Devon at the mouth of the River Dart; since 1905 the site of the Royal Naval College. In her deposition before the Justices, Mary Hamilton said that, after travelling from Scotland through several counties in England, she returned to her native Somerset from Devon (see Supplement, p. 382).

[19] Totnes, a town in Devon, upriver from Dartmouth.

[20] Cf. Psalm 37: 36, sung at Evening Prayer (Book of Common Prayer): 'the ungodly' flourish 'like a green bay-tree'. In her article on *The Female Husband*, however, Bonnie Blackwell connects the names of both 'Mrs. *Baytree*' and Miss '*Ivythorn*' (in the next paragraph) with the anaemic condition of 'the green sickness', which affects girls at puberty: Miss Ivythorn's 'name puns expressly on the greenness of her complexion and the stinging problem concealed in the conflicted interior of this young woman'; whereas 'baytree berries' are a contemporary 'remedy for disordered appetite . . . caused by greensickness' (*Literature and Medicine*, 21 [2002], pp. 62).

[21] Ashburton is some 10 miles north-west of Totnes.

immediately quitted the house, as soon as the young couple were admitted into it.

The Doctor and his wife lived together above a fortnight, without the least doubt conceived either by the wife, or by any other person of the Doctor's being what he appeared; till one evening the Doctor having drank a little too much punch, slept somewhat longer than usual, and when he waked, he found his wife in tears, who asked her husband, amidst many sobs, how he could be so barbarous to have taken such advantage of her ignorance and innocence, and to ruin her in such a manner? The Doctor being surprized and scarce awake, asked her what he had done. Done, says she, have you not married me a poor young girl, when you know, you have not——you have not——what you ought have. I always thought indeed your shape was something odd, and have often wondred that you had not the least bit of beard; but I thought you had been a man for all that, or I am sure I would not have been so wicked to marry you for the world. The Doctor endeavoured to pacify her, by every kind of promise, and telling her she would have all the pleasures of marriage without the inconveniences. No, no, said she, you shall not persuade me to that, nor will I be guilty of so much wickedness on any account. I will tell my Papa of you as soon as I am up; for you are no husband of mine, nor will I ever have any thing more to say to you. Which resolution the Doctor finding himself unable to alter, she put on her cloaths with all the haste she could, and taking a horse, which she had bought a few days before, hastened instantly out of the town, and made the best of her way, thro' bye-roads and across the country, into *Somersetshire*, missing *Exeter*, and every other great town which lay in the road.

And well it was for her, that she used both this haste and precaution: For Mr. *Ivythorn* having heard his daughter's story, immediately obtained a warrant from a justice of peace, with which he presently dispatch'd the proper officers; and not only so, but set forward himself to *Exeter*, in order to try if he could learn any news of his son-in-law, or apprehend her there; till after much search being unable to hear any tidings of her, he was obliged to set down contented with his misfortune, as was his poor daughter to submit to all the ill-natured sneers of her own sex, who were often witty at her expence, and at the expence of their own decency.

The Doctor having escaped, arrived safe at *Wells* in *Somersetshire*, where thinking herself at a safe distance from her pursuers, she again sat herself down in quest of new adventures.

She had not been long in this city, before she became acquainted with one *Mary Price*, a girl of about eighteen years of age, and of extraordinary beauty. With this girl, hath this wicked woman since her confinement declared, she was really as much in love, as it was possible for a man ever to be with one of her own sex.

The first opportunity our Doctor obtain'd of conversing closely with this new mistress, was at a dancing among the inferior sort of people, in contriving which the Doctor had herself the principal share. At that meeting the two lovers had an occasion of dancing all night together; and the Doctor lost no opportunity of shewing his fondness, as well by his tongue as by his hands, whispering many soft things in her ears, and squeezing as many soft things into her hands, which, together with a good number of kisses, &c. so pleased and warmed this poor girl, who never before had felt any of those tender sensations which we call love, that she retired from the dancing in a flutter of spirits, which her youth and ignorance could not well account for; but which did not suffer her to close her eyes, either that morning or the next night.

The Day after that the Doctor sent her the following letter.

'*My Dearest Molly*,

Excuse the fondness of that expression; for I assure you, my angel, all I write to you proceeds only from my heart, which you have so entirely conquered, and made your own, that nothing else has any share in it; and, my angel, could you know what I feel when I am writing to you, nay even at every thought of my *Molly*, I know I should gain your pity if not your love; if I am so happy to have already succeeded in raising the former, do let me have once more an opportunity of seeing you, and that soon, that I may breathe forth my soul at those dear feet, where I would willingly die, if I am not suffer'd to lie there and live. My sweetest creature, give me leave to subscribe myself

Your fond, doating,

Undone SLAVE.'

This letter added much to the disquietude which before began to torment poor *Molly's* breast. She read it over twenty times, and, at last, having carefully survey'd every part of the room, that no body was present, she kissed it eagerly. However, as she was perfectly modest, and afraid of appearing too forward, she resolved not to answer this first letter; and if she met the Doctor, to behave with great coldness towards him.

Her mother being ill, prevented her going out that day; and the next morning she received a second letter from the Doctor, in terms more warm and endearing than before, and which made so absolute a conquest over the unexperienc'd and tender heart of this poor girl, that she suffered herself to be prevailed on, by the intreaties of her lover, to write an answer, which nevertheless she determin'd should be so distant and cool, that the woman of the strictest virtue and modesty in *England* might have no reason to be asham'd of having writ it; of which letter the reader hath here an exact copy:

'*SUR*,

I Haf recevd boath your too litters, and sur I ham much surprise hat the loafe you priten to haf for so pur a garl as mee. I kan nut beleef you wul desgrace yourself by marring sutch a yf as mee, and Sur I wool nut be thee hore of the gratest man in the kuntry. For thof mi vartu his all I haf, yit hit is a potion I ham rissolv to kare to mi housband, soe noe moor at presant, from your umble savant to cummand.'[22]

The Doctor received this letter with all the ecstasies any lover could be inspired with, and, as Mr. *Congreve* says in his *Old Batchelor*, Thought there was more eloquence in the false spellings, with which it abounded, than in all Aristotle.[23] She now resolved to be no longer contented with this distant kind of conversation, but to meet her mistress face to face. Accordingly that very afternoon she went to her mother's house, and enquired for her poor *Molly*, who no sooner heard her lover's voice than she fell a trembling in the most violent manner. Her sister who opened the door informed the Doctor she was at home, and let the impostor in; but *Molly* being then in dishabille, would not see him till she had put on clean linnen, and was arrayed from head to foot in as neat, tho' not in so fine a manner, as the highest court lady in the kingdom could attire herself in, to receive her embroider'd lover.

Very tender and delicate was the interview of this pair, and if any corner of *Molly's* heart remain'd untaken, it was now totally subdued. She would willingly have postponed the match somewhat longer, from her strict regard to decency; but the earnestness and ardour of her lover would not suffer her, and she was at last obliged to consent to be married within two days.

Her sister, who was older than herself, and had over-heard all that had past, no sooner perceiv'd the Doctor gone, than she came to her, and wishing her joy with a sneer, said much good may it do her with such a husband;

[22] HF, it appears, corresponded with members of the opposite sex whose letters, like this of Mary Price, were as illiterate as they were illegible. Cf. the narrator of the *Journey from This World to the Next*, who has 'a surprising Curiosity to read every thing which is almost illegible; partly, perhaps, from the sweet Remembrance of the dear *Scrawls, Skrawls*, or *Skrales*, (for the Word is variously spelt) which I have in my youth received from that lovely part of the Creation for which I have the tenderest Regard' (p. 3). Cf. *Champion* (4 September 1740), where, when illustrating deficiencies in the education of female Ptfghsiumgskis, Job Vinegar triples the number of misspellings of the same word (p. 447).

[23] In the opening scene of *The Old Batchelor* (1693) by William Congreve (1670–1729) Bellmour reacts to a letter of assignation Vainlove throws down: 'I have a Hawks Eye at a Womans hand—There's more Elegancy in the false Spelling of this Superscription than in all *Cicero*.' Besides misquoting the speech, HF exaggerates the degree of the lady's illiteracy. In *Tom Jones* (IV. vi, p. 174) he quotes another passage from the play. On Congreve, who was HF's favourite modern dramatist, see Canto 2, line 109 (above, p. 54 n. 73).

for that, for her own part, she would almost as willingly be married to one of her own sex, and made some remarks not so proper to be here inserted. This was resented by the other with much warmth. She said she had chosen for herself only, and that if she was pleased, it did not become people to trouble their heads with what was none of their business. She was indeed so extremely enamoured, that I question whether she would have exchanged the Doctor for the greatest and richest match in the world.

And had not her affections been fixed in this strong manner, it is possible that an accident which happened the very next night might have altered her mind: for being at another dancing with her lover, a quarrel arose between the Doctor and a man there present, upon which the mother seizing the former violently by the collar, tore open her waistcoat, and rent her shirt, so that all her breast was discovered, which, tho' beyond expression beautiful in a woman, were of so different a kind from the bosom of a man, that the married women there set up a great titter; and tho' it did not bring the Doctor's sex into an absolute suspicion, yet caused some whispers, which perhaps might have spoiled the match with a less innocent and less enamoured virgin.

It had however no such effect on poor *Molly*. As her fond heart was free from any deceit, so was it entirely free from suspicion; and accordingly, at the fixed time she met the Doctor, and their nuptials were celebrated in the usual form.

The mother was extremely pleased at this preferment (as she thought it) of her daughter. The joy of it did indeed contribute to restore her perfectly to health, and nothing but mirth and happiness appeared in the faces of the whole family.

The new married couple not only continued, but greatly increased the fondness which they had conceived for each other, and poor *Molly*, from some stories she told among her acquaintance, the other young married women of the town, was received as a great fibber, and was at last universally laughed at as such among them all.

Three months past in this manner,[24] when the Doctor was sent for to *Glastonbury* to a patient (for the fame of our adventurer's knowledge in physic began now to spread) when a person of *Totnes* being accidentally present, happened to see and know her, and having heard upon enquiry, that the Doctor was married at *Wells*, as we have above mentioned, related the whole story of Mr. *Ivythorn*'s daughter, and the whole adventure at *Totnes*.

---

[24] According to the court records, the couple were married at St Cuthbert's, Wells, on 16 July, two months before Mary Hamilton was arrested (see Supplement, pp. 382–3).

News of this kind seldom wants wings; it reached *Wells*, and the ears of the Doctor's mother before her return from *Glastonbury*. Upon this the old woman immediately sent for her daughter, and very strictly examined her, telling her the great sin she would be guilty of, if she concealed a fact of this kind, and the great disgrace she would bring on her own family, and even on her whole sex, by living quietly and contentedly with a husband who was in any degree less a man than the rest of his neighbours.

Molly assured her mother of the falsehood of this report; and as it is usual for persons who are too eager in any cause, to prove too much, she asserted some things which staggered her mother's belief, and made her cry out, O child, there is no such thing in human nature.

Such was the progress this story had made in *Wells*, that before the Doctor arrived there, it was in every body's mouth; and as the Doctor rode through the streets, the mob, especially the women, all paid their compliments of congratulation. Some laughed at her, others threw dirt at her, and others made use of terms of reproach not fit to be commemorated. When she came to her own house, she found her wife in tears, and having asked her the cause, was informed of the dialogue which had past between her and her mother. Upon which the Doctor, tho' he knew not yet by what means the discovery had been made, yet too well knowing the truth, began to think of using the same method which she had heard before put in practice, of delivering herself from any impertinence; for as to danger, she was not sufficiently versed in the laws to apprehend any.

In the mean time the mother, at the solicitation of some of her relations, who, notwithstanding the stout denial of the wife, had given credit to the story, had applied herself to a magistrate, before whom the *Totnes* man appeared, and gave evidence as is before mentioned. Upon this a warrant was granted to apprehend the Doctor, with which the constable arrived at her house, just as she was meditating her escape.

The husband was no sooner seized, but the wife threw herself into the greatest agonies of rage and grief, vowing that he was injured, and that the information was false and malicious, and that she was resolved to attend her husband wherever they conveyed him.

And now they all proceeded before the Justice, where a strict examination being made into the affair, the whole happened to be true, to the great shock and astonishment of every body; but more especially of the poor wife, who fell into fits, out of which she was with great difficulty recovered.

The whole truth having been disclosed before the Justice, and something of too vile, wicked and scandalous a nature, which was found in the Doctor's trunk, having been produced in evidence against her, she was committed to *Bridewell*,[25] and Mr. *Gold*,[26] an eminent and learned counsellor at law, who lives in those parts, was consulted with upon the occasion, who gave his advice that she should be prosecuted at the next sessions, on a clause in the vagrant act, *for having by false and deceitful practices endeavoured to impose on some of his Majesty's subjects.*[27]

As the Doctor was conveyed to *Bridewell*, she was attended by many insults from the mob; but what was more unjustifiable, was the cruel treatment which the poor innocent wife received from her own sex, upon the extraordinary accounts which she had formerly given of her husband.

Accordingly at the ensuing sessions of the peace for the county of *Somerset*, the Doctor was indicted for the abovementioned diabolical fact, and after a fair trial convicted, to the entire satisfaction of the whole court.

At the trial the said *Mary Price* the wife, was produced as a witness, and being asked by the council, whether she had ever any suspicion of the Doctor's sex during the whole time of the courtship, she answered positively in the negative. She was then asked how long they had been married, to which she answered three months; and whether they had cohabited the whole time together? to which her reply was in the affirmative. Then the council asked her, whether during the time of this cohabitation, she imagined the Doctor had behaved to her as a husband ought to his wife? Her modesty confounded her a little at this question; but she at last answered she did imagine so. Lastly, she was asked when it was that she first harboured any suspicion of her being imposed upon? To which she answered, she had not the least suspicion till her husband was carried before a magistrate, and there discovered, as hath been said above.

[25] After Bridewell Hospital in London, the name given to any house of correction, wherein minor offenders, such as prostitutes and vagabonds, were set to work and supported on a penny loaf of bread a day. In *Tom Jones* (1. ix) Squire Allworthy refuses to commit Jenny Jones to a Bridewell, where she would have been 'sacrificed to Ruin and Infamy by a shameful Correction' (p. 59). Later, during HF's tenure as magistrate, he refused to commit any but the most hardened offenders to such prisons, which, in *An Enquiry into the Causes of the Late Increase of Robbers* (sect. IV), he denounced as 'Schools of Vice, Seminaries of Idleness, and Common-shores of Nastiness and Disease' (p. 121).

[26] On Henry Gould of Glastonbury, HF's first cousin, who was involved in the prosecution of Mary Hamilton, see the Introduction, (above, pp. 358–9) and the Supplement (below, p. 384).

[27] Mary Hamilton was convicted under a provision of the Vagrancy Act of 1744 (17 Geo. II, c. 5), by which all persons convicted of 'using any subtil craft to deceive or impose on any of his Majesty's subjects' were, as HF summarizes it (*Enquiry*, p. 121 n.), 'to be whipt OR sent to the House of Correction'. In sentencing Hamilton to be both whipped (four times) *and* imprisoned (for six months), the justices appear to have far exceeded their authority (see Supplement, below, p. 384). According, however, to a standard guide to their office—Theodore Barlow's *The Justice of Peace* (1745), which HF had in his library (Ribbles B8)—their more severe sentence was in fact authorized: after waiting, under arrest, until the next quarter sessions, a vagrant could then be 'detained and kept in the House of Correction to hard Labour for any further Time not exceeding six Months . . . such Person in the mean Time to be corrected by Whipping, and may after be sent away by Pass' (p. 560).

The prisoner having been convicted of this base and scandalous crime, was by the court sentenced to be publickly and severely whipt four several times, in four market towns within the country of *Somerset*, to wit, once in each market town, and to be imprisoned, &c.[28]

These whippings she has according undergone, and very severely have they been inflicted, insomuch, that those persons who have more regard to beauty than to justice, could not refrain from exerting some pity toward her, when they saw so lovely a skin scarified with rods, in such a manner that her back was almost flead:[29] yet so little effect had the smart or shame of this punishment on the person who underwent it, that the very evening she had suffered the first whipping, she offered the goaler[30] money, to procure her a young girl to satisfy her most monstrous and unnatural desires.

But it is to be hoped that this example will be sufficient to deter all others from the commission of any such foul and unnatural crimes: for which, if they should escape the shame and ruin which they so well deserve in this world, they will be most certain of meeting with their full punishments in the next: for unnatural affections are equally vicious and equally detestable in both sexes, nay, if modesty[31] be the peculiar characteristick of the fair sex, it is in them most shocking and odious to prostitute and debase it.

In order to caution therefore that lovely sex, which, while they preserve their natural innocence and purity, will still look most lovely in the eyes of men, the above pages have been written, which, that they might be worthy of their perusal, such strict regard hath been had to the utmost decency, that notwithstanding the subject of this narrative be of a nature so difficult to be handled inoffensively, not a single word occurs through the whole, which might shock the most delicate ear, or give offence to the purest chastity.[32]

---

[28] For a transcript of the order for Hamilton's punishment, see the Supplement (below, p. 384).

[29] 'flead': flayed. Cf. Swift in *A Tale of a Tub* (sect. IX): 'Last week I saw a woman flayed, and you will hardly believe how much it altered her person for the worse.'

[30] For HF's preference for this then common spelling of 'gaol' or 'jail', see *Shamela* (above, p. 182 n. 112).

[31] HF in fact considered 'modesty' essential to the female character; it distinguishes his heroines from Fanny Goodwill to Amelia. C-H lists no fewer than seventy-two occurrences of the word in his fiction.

[32] Cf. the similar assurances of propriety addressed to readers of HF's other literary productions of these months: in his paraphrase of *Ovid's Art of Love*, 'there is nothing capable of offending the nicest Ear' (below, p. 397); in *Tom Jones* (Dedication), the reader 'will find nothing inconsistent with the strictest Rules of Decency, nor which can offend even the chastest Eye in the Perusal' (p. 7).

Supplement

NOTE: Transcribed here [courtesy of Margaret T. Prior, Curator, Lake Village Museum, Glastonbury, 2 January 1956], are extracts from the Somerset Quarter Sessions Rolls of 1746 relating to the case of Mary Hamilton. Included are (1) The 'Examination' on 13 September of Mary Hamilton by John Masters, Mayor, and Thomas White, Justices of the Peace for Glastonbury; (2) The 'Examination' on 7 October of Mary Price by John Masters, Mayor, and Thomas White of Glastonbury; (3) The Statement of the punishment ordered for Mary Hamilton, taken from the General Calendar of Prisoners at the General Quarter Sessions, Taunton Castle, 7 October; (4) Letter of 9 October to HF's cousin Henry Gould at Taunton from Thomas Hughes, concerning Gould's part in the prosecution of Mary Hamilton.

1. [Ref. No. 314.7(5)]

Borough & Town	The Examination [*written above* Information *deleted*] of
of Glaston in ye	Mary Hamilton daughter of Wm Hamilton & Mary his
County of Somerset	wife, taken and sworn before us two of his Majesties
	Justices of the Peace for the Borough and Town afores^d,
	this thirteenth day of September 1746

This Examinant saith that she was Born in the County of Somerset afores^d but doe not know in what parish and [but *deleted*] went from thence to the shire of Angus in Scotland and there continued till she [I *deleted*] was about fourteen years of age, and then put on her [my *deleted*] Brothers Cloaths and travelled for England, and in Northumberland entered into the service of Doctor Edward Green, a Mountebank and continued with him between two and three years, & then entered into the service of Doctor Finly Green & continued with him near a twelve month and then set up for a Quack doctor herselfe [my *deleted*], and travelled through several counties of England, and at length came to the County of Devonshire, and from thence into Somersetshire aforesd in the Month of May Last Past where she [I *deleted*] have followed [m *deleted*] ye afores^d business of a Quack doctor, continueing to wear mans apparell ever since she [I *deleted*] put on her [my *deleted*] brothers, before she [I *deleted*] came out of Scotland

This Examinant further saith that in the course of her travels in mans apparel she came to the City of Wells in ye County afores^d and went by the Name of Charles Hamilton, and quartered in the house of Mary Creed, where lived her Neice Mary Price, to whome she [I *deleted*] proposed Marraige and the s^d Mary Price consented, and then she [I *deleted*] put in the Banes of Marrige to Mr Kinston Curate of St Cuthberts in the City of Well afores^d and was by ye s^d Mr Kingstone Married to the s^d Mary Price, in ye parish church of St Cuthberts afores^d, on the sixteenth day of July last past and have since travell^d as a husband with her in severall parts of ye County to the day of the date above mentioned and further this Examinant saith not

ye mark of Mary Hamilton

['Mary Hamon' *in different hand*]

Endorsed:

The within Examination taken and sworn before us—

John Masters & Thos White two of his Majesties Justices of ye Peace for the Town within Mentioned this thirteenth day of September 1746

J Masters Mayor

Thos White

2. [Ref. No. 314. 7(6)]

Town and Corporation of Glaston in the County of Somersett	The Examination of Mary Price of Glaston aforesaid taken before us Two of his Majestyes Justices of the Peace for the said Town and Corporation this 7th day of October 1746

Who on her Oath saith that in the Month of May last past a Person who called himself by the name of Charles Hamilton introduced himself into the company of this Examinant and made his Addresses to her, and prevailed on this Examinant to be married to him, which she accordingly was on the Sixteenth day of July last by the Revd Mr Kingstone Curate of the Parish of St Cuthbert in Wells in the said county—And this Examinant Further saith that after their Marriage they lay together several Nights, and that the said pretended Charles Hamilton (who had married her as aforesaid) [Did *deleted*] entered her Body several times, which made this Examin^t beleive, at first, that the said Hamilton was a real Man, but soon had reason to judge [otherwise *deleted*] that the said Hamilton was not a Man but a Woman, and which the said Hamilton [own *deleted*] acknowledged and confessed afterwards (on the Complaint of this Examin^t [before *deleted*] to the Justices) when brought before them that she was such to the Great Prejudice of this Examinant

Taken and Sworn before— us Two of his Majestyes Justices of the Peace for the Town & Corporation afs^d the day & year aforesaid—	The Mark of Mary Price

J Masters   May^r

Thos: White

Endorsed: 'Glastonbury affair'

3. [REF. 314. 6(53)]
Extract from the General Calendar of Prisoners at the General Quarter Sessions
held at Taunton Castle 7 Oct. 1746
                          Shepton Mallett House of Correction.

Mary Hamilton—Continued as a vagrant for Six Months to hard Labour, and to
                          be whipped publickly as follows (that is to say) at Taunton afore-
                          said the Eleventh instant as usual; At Glastonbury in ye said
                          County the first day of November next from the Higher Conduit
                          to ye Market House there: At ye City of Wells in ye said County
                          the Twenty Second day of November aforesaid as usual there:
                          And at Shepton Mallett afores[d] the Nineteenth day of December
                          then next ensuing also as usual there.

4. [Ref. No. 314. 7(3)]
Letter addressed   To Henry Gould Esq[re.]   at Taunton
D[r] S[r]
    The Genll' of the Corporation of Glaston as well as the principal Inhabitants, are
Desirous that the woman impostor who was sometime since committed, sho[d] be
punished in the severest manner the Quarter Sessions can, have sent you a Fee to
advice and assist therein; My Clerk will shew you the Informations and the wench
imposed on attends if necessary, to give Evidence of the Imposition—If she be well
whipt, will be satisfactory; I hope to hear from you soon after the Sessions and am
S[r]. with the greatest respect
                                        Yo[r]. m[t]. ob[t]. Serv[t]:
                                        Tho Hughes
                                        1746
                                        9th Oct—

6

OVID'S ART OF LOVE PARAPHRASED

(1747)

On 25 February 1747,[1] some three months after the publication of *The Female Husband* (see above, pp. 355–84), there appeared, again anonymously, the second of Fielding's curious experiments in a genre Dr Ribble aptly calls 'soft pornography':[2] this was book I of *Ovid's Art of Love Paraphrased, and Adapted to the Present Time*, 'With NOTES. and A most CORRECT Edition of the Original'. Priced at two shillings, it was an ambitious little book of nearly a hundred pages octavo, with the Latin text at the left of each opening and at the right Fielding's prose paraphrase, adapting Ovid's context of Augustan Rome to suit analogous themes and characters of mid-Georgian England. The publisher was as usual Andrew Millar, who also chose to remain anonymous; the colophon reads 'Printed for M. COOPER, in *Pater-Noster-Row*; A. DODD, without *Temple-Bar*; and G. WOODFALL, at *Charing-Cross*'.

In the Preface, Fielding, somewhat disingenuously surely, gave his reason for returning now to this modern version of Ovid's manual of seduction and erotic technique, which he had 'begun many Years ago': 'What inclined the Author to publish it now, was that Passage so justly applicable to the Glorious Duke of CUMBERLAND.' The passage in question, in which Ovid celebrates the heroism of Augustus's grandson Gaius Caesar (see below, p. 413 and n. 36), no doubt offered Fielding a welcome opportunity to flatter the Royal Family; but sex, not military heroics, is Ovid's theme and it is Fielding's as well.

---

[1] See the *General Advertiser* for that date, a Wednesday; the advertisement was repeated in that paper for 26, 27, 28 February and 2, 3 March. See also *London Evening-Post* (19, 21, 24, 28, 31 March and 2 April); *St. James's Evening Post* (21, 24, 26 March). In these notices Dodd's address, 'opposite Clements-Church', though seemingly different from that given in the colophon of the title-page, 'without *Temple-Bar*', is simply another way of placing her shop just west of Temple Bar.

[2] Frederick G. Ribble, 'New Light on Henry Fielding from the Malmesbury Papers', *MP*, 103 (2005), p. 76.

386 *Occasional Prose*

CIRCUMSTANCES OF COMPOSITION

In the winter of 1746–7, only two literary projects of his own interrupted Fielding's progress on his masterpiece *Tom Jones*: *The Female Husband* and his paraphrase of Ovid's *Ars Amatoria*. The first of these by modern example, the perversion of the lesbian Mary Hamilton, and the latter by classical authority attest to his fascination during this period with subjects illustrating the rawest sexuality, especially the sexuality of women. In the Ovid, Fielding lingers over a long catalogue of lewd women such as Byblis, 'who being in love with her Brother, punished her Crime with her own Hands, and hanged herself in her Garters', and Pasiphae, who 'conceived a Passion worse, if possible, than that of Mrs. *Mary Hamilton*, for [a] Bull' (p. 419). 'All these', Fielding's version concludes, 'have been the Effects of Womens raging Desires, which are so much more violent and mad than ours' (p. 421).

In the Preface, after quoting Dryden's defence of Ovid's poem against the charge of indecency, Fielding assured his readers 'that if the Objection of Impurity lies against any part of this Work, it is only against the two latter Books, for in that which we have here paraphrased, there is nothing capable of offending the nicest Ear' (p. 397). Such assurances notwithstanding, the preoccupation in Fielding's two publications of these three months with eroticism, of a kind perverse and degrading, represents thematically a remarkable aberration even in the eccentric course of his literary career. Might this odd phenomenon find an explanation in Fielding's personal circumstances of the moment? It was a time when, his sister Sarah having taken his deceased wife's place as mistress of the house at Boswell Court, Fielding began a relationship with the maid, Mary Daniel, that, in November, would lead to his marrying her in the sixth month of her pregnancy with his son.[3]

Fielding's financial circumstances at this time were not cheering. He hoped to sell the 'Reversion' of exchequer annuities which he had inherited from a favourite uncle nine years earlier, a legacy worth more than £120, but it remained stalled in the courts. Promising these phantom proceeds from the sale as security, he wrote his friend James Harris on 19 February, a week before the Ovid was published, touching him for yet another loan: 'If you dare venture fifty Pounds more on the same bad Bottom to wch y° have trusted a hundred, it will be of very particular service to me at this Time.'[4] As with his hope that his and Young's translation of *Plutus* would

---

[3] These remarks are an abridgement of the discussion of the topic in *Life*, pp. 410–12.
[4] *Correspondence*, p. 59.

lead to the public's demand for translations of Aristophanes' other plays, he would be disappointed in supposing that the reception accorded *Ovid's Art of Love* might lead to a whole series of similar works 'carried on with other *Latin* Poets'.[5] From London on 3 March, within a week of publication, Thomas Harris wrote his elder brother James at Salisbury with news of the event and a sound forecast of the work's unrewarding reception: 'Fielding has just publishd Ovids first book of ye art of love, with a paraphrase in prose, in wch I think there is humour, but I should not think it a work likely to be very profitable.'[6]

But Fielding was irrepressibly sanguine when it came to money-making schemes, even though most of them came to nothing;[7] and Dr Ribble's research in the Malmesbury papers has brought to light the most delightful, and preposterous, of them all. In this same letter of 3 March 1747 Thomas Harris described his friend's latest, zaniest project:

Fielding . . . has formed a Scheme for getting above a hundred thousand pound in about two years time: He is so Sanguine in it, y^t if he were to write in any treatise a chapter concerning Projectors, what he himself now says & does would furnish matter of ye highest humour, & would form a perfect character of y^t kind. The grand Scheme is to take Mountagu house, & exhibit during ye winter half year Tea drinking, dining, auctioneering, puppet shews, balls, music, & (what seems a little foreign) pawnbroking: all ye world are to be there from morning to night, & I already address him by ye title of Petronius. He has actually bin with ye D. of Mountagu to take ye house, & has I think offerd 3000^ll a year: ye Duke took time to consider, & I don't hear yet what his answer is.[8]

There is no obvious hint in Thomas Harris's letter that Fielding was 'biting' him or he his brother. But the 'Scheme' described is so outré and represents Fielding playing parts he loved to ridicule—not to mention the unlikely possibility that even he, as prodigal as he was with money he never had, could think of paying rent of £3,000 a year—that it invites dubiety. Not least because the principals involved famously loved a joke: Fielding, according to Lyttelton, 'had more wit and humour' than Swift, Pope, and the other wits of his time put together; and the Duke of Montagu, soon to perpetrate the famous 'bottle-conjuror' hoax at the Haymarket Theatre, was a notorious prankster.[9] If Harris's account of this amazing enterprise is

---

[5] Preface, p. 397; font reversed.

[6] This letter, as Ribble observes, 'provides the earliest recorded attribution of this anonymous work to fielding' ('New Light on Fielding', p. 76).

[7] On HF as entrepreneur, see Lance Bertelsen, *Henry Fielding at Work: Magistrate, Businessman, Writer* (New York, 2000).

[8] Ribble, 'New Light on Fielding', pp. 77–8.

[9] See *Life*, pp. 150–1, 464–5.

true, moreover, Fielding would himself be standing in for contemporary figures he loved to ridicule—for Samuel Foote, who this year on the pretext of 'giving tea' began staging 'diversions' at the Haymarket Theatre; for Christopher Cock, the fashionable auctioneer; for 'Beau' Nash of Bath, who sponsored puppet shows and presided over balls and concerts; for William Deards, toyman and pawnbroker, whom Fielding indeed had scored in his Ovid (see below, p. 427 n. 54); and not least for 'Count' Heidegger, Master of the King's Revels, to whom Fielding had ironically dedicated *The Masquerade* (above, pp. 13–14) and whom in *Tom Jones* (XIII. vii), using the very allusion to Petronius that Harris here applies to Fielding, the narrator calls 'the great *Arbiter Deliciarum*, the great High-Priest of Pleasure' (p. 712).[10]

Improbable as it may seem that Fielding should aspire to the vocations of those he laughed at, other details in Harris's account ring true enough. Fielding, through his friend and patron the Duke of Richmond, might well have known Montagu, Richmond's inseparable companion. And Montagu House, Bloomsbury, might well have been available to lease: badly in need of repair, it had been abandoned by the Duke; in 1755 it would become the first home of the British Museum. Fielding of course never realized his dream of renting this 'grandiose palace'[11] for a small fortune and earning £100,000 (a 'plum' as that sum was called) by playing Petronius in the Age of George Augustus. In a year's time, however, he would appear on Panton Street as 'Madame de la Nash', impresario of a fashionable puppet show.[12]

MCB

---

[10] For HF's attitude towards each of these figures, see the articles under their names in *Companion*, 'Others in the Life'.

[11] Ben Weinreb and Christopher Hibbert, *The London Encyclopaedia* (London, 1983), p. 524.

[12] See Battestin, 'Fielding and "Master Punch" in Panton Street', *PQ*, 45 (1966), pp. 191–208; *Life*, pp. 434–9.

Textual Introduction[1]

Though his authorship was known to his friends from the beginning (above, p. 387), the first edition of Fielding's paraphrase of Ovid's *Ars Amatoria* (book I), published on 25 February 1747, was anonymous; his name did not appear on the title-page until the Dublin reprint of 1756. The work was also published anonymously by Andrew Millar, who, however, began advertising it as his own a year later in *The Jacobite's Journal*, No. 15 (12 March 1748),[2] an issue in which Fielding, introducing his own 'Parody on the first Book of *Ovid's Art of Love*' (entitled *De Arte Jacobitica*), openly puffed the earlier paraphrase:

we recommend a new Translation of that Book to the unlearned Reader, where he will find all the Precepts of the Original modernized, and rendered agreeable to the present Times, and where he will be better enabled to relish the Beauties of this Performance. (p. 189)

Despite such clues to Fielding's authorship, and the fact of the work's having been recorded in classical bibliographies at least since an 'Index Editionum' in the second Bipontine edition of Ovid (1807), it was forgotten by those it most concerned, and had to be rediscovered by W. L. Cross in 1918, and Claude E. Jones in the 1960s.[3] Only the first edition is of any textual importance; the second London edition corrects some obvious typos, but is otherwise a straightforward reprint.

Composition allegedly goes back in places to Fielding's youth ('many Years ago' [Preface]), but the historical references have been systematically modernized, if so. By the date of the advertisement in *The Jacobite's Journal* (above) the parallel between the Duke of Cumberland and Augustus's grandson Gaius had been rendered more exact by Cumberland's defeat at Lauffeld. The puff in the *Journal*, in which Fielding hinted at publishing 'the Translation of the second Book' if suitably encouraged, contrasts with the original Preface, where he confessed that 'the Objection of Impurity' lay

---

[1] Except for a few corrections and additions by the present editor, the Textual Introduction is by the late Hugh Amory, whose essay 'The Texts of Fielding's Ovid' is the authoritative study (Bibliographical Society of Australia and New Zealand, *Bulletin*, 23 [1999], pp. 11–26).

[2] The advertisement also ran in the *London Evening-Post* (31 March, 5 April 1748). Coley suggests that Millar 'may have been trying to "remainder" the original issue' (*JJ*, p. 189 n. 2). Millar later listed the Ovid among HF's other works advertised in the 1754 edition of *Jonathan Wild*, and again in the 1758 edition of Sarah Fielding's *Lives of Cleopatra and Octavia*.

[3] See Cross, ii, pp. 52–4, iii, 313–14; and Jones's edition of the reprint of the Dublin edition entitled *The Lover's Assistant, or, New Art of Love* (1760), Augustan Reprint Society, No. 89 (Los Angeles, 1961), reviewed by W. B. Coley, *PQ*, 41 (1962), pp. 587–8. The *ESTC* lists five known copies of the first edition: at the British Library; Trinity College, Cambridge; Harvard; Yale; and Princeton.

'against the two latter Books' and proposed instead to continue with translations of 'other *Latin* Poets'. In both promotions, however, there is an affinity with some other abortive projects, such as Fielding's translation of Aristophanes, launched with the *Plutus* (1742), or his never-realized Lucian (1752): prose versions for the unlearned that are quite unlike the metrical paraphrases of Juvenal (annotated in Latin) and others characteristic of his juvenilia and collected in the *Miscellanies* (1743). We need not doubt that Fielding had translated the *Ars* at some earlier date, but the version of Ovid that he printed cannot have been composed much before 1743: *none* of the many English equivalents of classical *realia* in his version can be certainly assigned to Fielding's youth, and despite Fielding's confirmed habit of quoting himself, there is only one earlier verbal echo of his Ovid. A date of composition around 1745, then, makes good sense: conceivably, the dating 'many Years ago' is an attempt to deflect criticism of a youthful effort; Fielding had made the same claim for his poems, which he also updated before publishing them in the *Miscellanies*.

The filiation of Fielding's Latin text is uncertain, in part because, as in the apparatus of many early editions of the classics, his paraphrase follows a different text from the one he prints,[4] in part because the Latin descends from more than one printed authority. Renaissance spellings like Aemonia, Phyllirides, and Sidoniaeque may derive from the innumerable school editions of Ovid's *Amatoria* printed for the Stationers' Company (1583–1694); these essentially reproduce the Aldine edition (1514–15, etc.) of Andrea Navagero ('Nauigerius', or 'Naugerius', 1483–1529), the best text before Nicolaas Heinsius' (1652, etc.). Such a cheap, vulgate edition, marked up with corrections from later editions, may have provided the printer's copy, but the ancestry of the text is mixed ('contaminated'), and the original or originals can no longer be identified by stemmatic analysis.

In his life of Fielding, James Harris noted his friend's 'particular' study of 'Terence, Virgil, and Horace and Ovid'.[5] Only a single volume from a broken set of an unidentified edition of Ovid appears in the catalogue of Fielding's library (Ribbles O14), but Ovid is his third most frequently cited Latin author (often from memory), according to Nancy Mace.[6] He would have used Navagero's text under Parson Oliver's tutelage, and Heinsius' in the *Electa Minora* (1697, etc.) at Eton, which includes selections from the *Ars Amatoria*, book I (lines 177–218, 527–64). Schrevel (1662), Cnipping

---

[4] Cf. E. J. Kenney, *The Classical Text* (Berkeley, 1974), ch. 3.

[5] Clive T. Probyn, *The Sociable Humanist: The Life and Works of James Harris 1709–1780* (Oxford, 1991), p. 305.

[6] Nancy A. Mace, *Henry Fielding's Novels and the Classical Tradition* (Newark, Del., 1996), p. 53.

(1670, etc.), and Crespin ('Crispinus') *In Usum Delphini* (1689, etc.) reprint selections of Heinsius' notes and emendations in their popular editions. Fielding's footnotes refer to Micyllus (Jakob Molsheym, 1508–58; see n. *qq*), and to 'Scaliger and others' (see n. *n*), but all this information was reprinted and easily available in Burmann. He also owned and praised the Abbé Banier's *Mythology and Fables of the Ancients* (1739–40; Ribbles B6), whose euhemerist readings of Ovid had been anticipated in Banier's translation of and commentary on the *Metamorphoses* (1732); none of these readings seem to have influenced Fielding's translation, however.

As a student of literature at the University of Leiden, 1728–9, Fielding must have encountered Pieter Burmann ('Burmannus', 1668–1744), Professor of History, eloquence, Greek, and poetry. Burmann's editions of Petronius, Quintilian, and Valerius Flaccus were in his library (Ribbles P11, Q1, and V1), and Fielding was probably familiar with his Variorum edition of Ovid (1727; cf. below, apparatus criticus, lines 114 and 236; text, lines 91–2 and 601 nn.), which sets forth a nearly exhaustive conspectus of post-incunabular Ovidian scholarship. Though in the *Tragedy of Tragedies* (1731) and the *Vernoniad* (1741) Fielding parodied Burmann's scholarship, as well as Bentley's, he did so in part certainly because they were the most distinguished classicists of the age.[7] His own scholarship never rose above the standard of his age and there was nothing personal of course in his mockery. In *Ovid's Art of Love Paraphrased* and the *Plutus*, Fielding takes learned annotation for granted, as a necessary adjunct to understanding the ancient world of the classics; his satire, like Pope's, falls heaviest on those who require such an apparatus to explain the moderns—just such an apparatus, indeed, as will be provided here.

TREATMENT OF THE COPY-TEXT

In the classic 'rationale of copy-text' followed by the Wesleyan Edition, the editor conserves the 'accidentals' or presentation (spelling, punctuation, italicization, etc.) of the earliest printed or manuscript representative of his author's text, but emends the 'substantives' to accord with the author's latest revisions. This rationale is obviously inapplicable where the author has revised the 'accidentals', or where, as in a parallel text, the 'accidentals' appear in two different versions, or function to maintain parallelism. Thus the compositors of Fielding's Ovid often broke up his English into brief

---

[7] On HF's view and treatment of scholarship and of pedantry, see Bertrand A. Goldgar, ' "The Learned English Dog": Fielding's Mock Scholarship', in Albert J. Rivero (ed.), *Augustan Subjects* (Newark, Del., 1997).

paragraphs, sometimes corresponding to a single Latin couplet, in order to achieve more exact parallelism with the facing Latin. In the longer lines and smaller, more closely set type of the Wesleyan Edition, these brief paragraphs would become visually intrusive and dysfunctional, and I have freely combined them in the edited text, spacing out the Latin into verse blocks that correspond to my larger paragraphs. When my English paragraph runs over to a new page, but the Latin verse block does not, I have also spaced out the beginning of the next, parallel English page. None of these devices are found in the copy-text, but it did not seem worthwhile to record the differences.

Fielding extensively annotated his version, cuing the footnotes to a twenty-four-letter alphabet, omitting j and v, but occasionally inserting extra notes with asterisks. In the present edition the latter are treated as footnotes to the text as in his other writings, whereas those cued alphabetically are relegated to an appendix, as endnotes, with their own critical apparatus. In these notes, Fielding provided literal translations, potted mythography, and a little Roman archaeology, and signalled occasional corrections of Ovid's logic or morality. Such annotations add little to the English text, whose modern equivalents for classical *realia* are more immediately intelligible than the notes. Exasperatingly, too, the notes themselves require annotation. A fourfold commentary on two parallel texts is forbiddingly cumbersome, however, not only to print, but also to read. It would be possible to present Fielding's text as he originally intended it, for the 'unlearned reader', but it would not be a critical edition, nor, I feel, would it find much of an audience today.

The title-page advertises the Latin as 'A most CORRECT Edition of the Original'. Nevertheless, for the most part it simply reprints a vulgate text descending from Navagero (1514), with a few corrections from Heinsius and Burmann. Fielding's English, indeed, also translates yet another, eclectic text, with many more corrections from these authorities, but also retaining earlier readings that they corrected or rejected, and in at least one instance proposing his own emendation. I have therefore aimed at bringing the sense of the Latin and English together as closely as possible, short of printing an unmetrical Latin.

The presentation of the Latin is hideously overpunctuated, often marking the end of a line with a semicolon or colon even where the sense runs on, and in frequent disagreement with the sense and punctuation of Fielding's English. A complete recasting of the Latin to agree with modern standards seemed inappropriate, however: the treatment of ij and uv, the diacritics, and the capitalization of divine names, even when they stand for their province (Ceres = wheat, Bacchus = wine, Venus = sex), are part of the history of the text as Fielding knew it. Since Fielding's hand is only occasionally visible in the Latin, a full record of emendation in such matters would be of little interest, I feel. I have therefore compromised, silently emending the punctuation to agree, so far as Latin's different syntax permits, with Fielding's English, but recording any changes in spelling or wording.

The font of quoted speech is silently reversed, and the capitalization of *deus* (or *dea*, etc.) is retained only where some particular god is meant; so, too, *Urbs* = *the* city, or Rome. *Amor* is often ambiguous, but I have made him small, in cases of doubt. In a language that lacks the definite article such devices remain useful: *Zephyr* = the West wind, but *zephyr* may be any breeze. As a result, my Latin text often jumbles together Renaissance presentation with sophisticated seventeenth- or eighteenth-century emendations, but it has a better chance of representing what Fielding translated, I feel, than a completely revamped text based on Burmann or Heinsius. If some day we can definitely identify either the edition that Fielding's compositor reprinted, or the Ovids that he owned and used, we may hope for more precise criteria.

The editor must ponder four questions: has Fielding accurately translated or paraphrased the Latin text that accompanies his version? If not, does his translation reflect readings or interpretations from other printed sources available to him? May the Latin be emended to accord with his translation? Or may we adjust the English to accord with the Latin? The appropriate allocation of the notes to the Latin or English text, or to their apparatus, is a matter of some perplexity. Annotation of the Latin is confined to pointing out the places where the Latin text departs from the vulgate to follow Bersmann, Heinsius, or Burmann, and to a few notes of palmary emendations and inveterate corruptions. The focus of the commentary is on the English, and the problems of translation.

HA

BIBLIOGRAPHY

AMORY, HUGH, 'The Texts of Fielding's Ovid', Bibliographical Society of Australia and New Zealand, *Bulletin*, 23 (1999), pp. 11–26.

COLEY, W. B., Review of *The Lover's Assistant*, ed. Claude E. Jones (1961), *PQ*, 41 (1962), pp. 587–8.

GOLDGAR, BERTRAND A., ' "The Learned English Dog": Fielding's Mock Scholarship', in Albert J. Rivero (ed.), *Augustan Subjects* (Newark, Del., 1997).

GOOLD, G. P., 'Amatoria Critica', *Harvard Studies in Classical Philology*, 69 (1965), pp. (1)–107.

KENNEY, E. J., *The Classical Text* (Berkeley, 1974).

MACE, NANCY A., *Henry Fielding's Novels and the Classical Tradition* (Newark, Del., 1996).

OVID, *Pvb. Ovidii Nasonis Svlmonensis poetæ Opervm tomvs primvs[-tertivs]* (Frankfurt: Typis Wechelianis apud Claudium Marnium & heredes Ioannis Aubrij, 1601). Prints the text and commentary of Bartolomeo Merula (1st edn., 1494), with emendations and additional commentary by Jacob Micyllus (1549), Ercole Ciofano, and Gregor Bersmann.

—— *P. Ovidii Nasonis Heroidvm epistolæ . . .; De arte amandi, libri III . . . aliaque huius generis . . .* omnia ex . . . Andreæ Nauigeri castigatione . . . (London: Ex typographia Societatis Stationariorum, 1631). With summaries of the *Heroides* by Guy Morillon; forms vol. III of an edn. of Ovid's works, licensed to T. Vautrollier for ten years in 1574, and afterwards part of the Company's English Stock.

—— *Totum opus (nunc demūm, 1694) optimis exemplaribus collatum, & ab innumeris ferē mendis repurgatum* (Cambridge: Ex officinā J. Hayes . . ., 1694). Copy at the Bodleian Library. Adds a marginal apparatus of variants and commentary from Heinsius and Schrevel; next reprinted in 1705 (copy at Cambridge University Library) and 1709 (copy at Rutgers).

—— *Operum P. Ovidii Nasonis editio nova*, ed. Nicolaas Heinsius, 3 vols. in 6 (Amsterdam: Ex officina Elzeviriana, 1658–61; 1st edn. (text only), 1652).

—— *Publii Ovidii Nasonis Opera omnia*, ed. Pieter Burmann, *cum notis variorum*, 5 pts. in 4 vols. (Amsterdam: Apud R. & J. Wetstenios & G. Smith, 1727). Issued on large and small papers; also issued with Changuion or Janssonius van Waesberge imprints (all three imprints are at Harvard, on OP; L. P. Wetsten-Smith and Changuion imprints at BL; L. P. Waesberge imprint at the Bodleian); v. 3, sig. Vvv3, and v. 4, sig. T4, are cancels in all copies seen. ¶ Reprints the full annotation of Micyllus, Ciofano, and Heinsius (1658–61), and selected notes of other commentators, adding the prefatory material of earlier editions, unpublished notes from Heinsius' MSS, and indices rerum, verborum, et auctorum by H. Dreux. ¶ A brief preface dated 'Kal. Octob. MDCCXXVI', found in most copies, is censored; the full *Præfatio* ([10] leaves, dated 'Kal. Novembribus MDCCXXVI'), excoriating Burmann's booksellers, was first published in 1757, according to the *Nieuw Nederlandsch Biografisch Woordenboek*, ed. Molhuysen and Blok, iv. 354–8 (copy at BL, bound in Grenville G.9739).

—— *Ars Amatoria, Book I*, ed. [E. J. Kenney], with introd. and comm. A. S. Hollis (Oxford, 1977).

—— *The Art of Love and Other Poems*, trans. J. H. Mozley; 2nd edn., rev. G. P. Goold, Loeb Classical Library (Cambridge, Mass., 1979).

REEVE, M. D., 'Heinsius's Manuscripts of Ovid', *Rheinisches Museum für Philologie*, n.F., 117 (1974), pp. 133–66; 119 (1976), pp. [65]–78.

SCHWEIGER, F. L. A., *Handbuch der classischen Bibliographie*, 2 vols. (Leipzig, 1834).

STEINER, GRUNDY, 'The Textual Tradition of the Ovidian Incunabula', *Transactions of the American Philological Association*, 83 (1952), pp. 312–18.

OVID's
ART of LOVE
PARAPHRASED,
AND
ADAPTED to the Prefent Time.
With NOTES.
AND
A moft CORRECT Edition of the Original.

BOOK I.

LONDON:
Printed for M. COOPER, in *Pater-Nofter-Row*;
A. DODD, without *Temple-Bar*; and G.
WOODFALL, at *Charing-Crofs*. (Price 2*s*.)
M.DCC.XLVII.

PREFACE

THIS work was begun many Years ago,[1] *although altered in some Places, as will appear by the modern Instances introduced in it. What inclined the Author to publish it now, was that Passage so justly applicable to the Glorious Duke of* CUMBERLAND,[2] *which cannot fail of pleasing every good Briton.*

As to any Exception which may be made to the Impurity of this Work, we shall transcribe what was written long ago in its Defence, from the Preface prefixed to Mr. Dryden's *Translation of this Poem.*[3]

'A great many People are mistaken in these Books; and tho' they were made use of as a Pretence to drive the Author from the Court of *Augustus*, and confine him to *Tomos* on the Frontiers of the *Getæ* and *Sarmatæ*, yet they were not the true Cause of his Confinement. They are very far from being so licentious as the Writings of several other Poets, both *Greek* and *Latin*. However we must own he might have been a little more discreet, especially in some Places.*

'That which hath offended the *Romans* most in this Work, cannot touch us. It has always been more dangerous in *Italy* to converse with Women of Honour, and frequent their Houses, than 'tis with us; where there is more Liberty, and what in that Country may be an Occasion of Debauchery, would not at all be so in ours.

'Notwithstanding all that has been said against these Books of *the Art of Love*, by some over-scrupulous Persons, whose Discretion has too much of Affectation in it: they are not only necessary for the Knowledge of the *Latin* Tongue, and the *Roman* History, concerning which they contain several things very particular; but for the noble Sentiments we find in them, which the *Gravest* and *Learnedest* Writers have thought worthy to be quoted for authorities.

'In a word, there's nothing in them that comes near the *Licence* of some Epigrams of *Catallus*, *Martial*, and *Ausonius*, of some Satires of *Horace* and *Juvenal*, and several other Pieces of *Ancient* and *Modern* Authors, which are

---

* He means in the other two Books.

[1] See Textual Introduction, p. 389.

[2] William Augustus (1721–65), Duke of Cumberland, younger son of George II. Cumberland distinguished himself in victory against the French at the Battle of Dettingen (1743) and in defeat at Fontenoy (1745); and on 16 April 1746 he put an end to the Jacobite uprising by defeating the rebels at Culloden, for which HF in *The True Patriot*, Nos. 26–7, praised 'the Glorious Duke of CUMBERLAND, that *Fulmen Belli* [thunderbolt of war]' (pp. 275). See also below, pp. 413, 415. For later compliments to him in *Tom Jones* (1749), *An Enquiry into the Causes of the Late Increase of Robbers* (1751), and *The Covent-Garden Journal* (1752), see below, *Voyage to Lisbon* (p. 579, n. 115).

[3] Dryden's translation of *Ovid's Art of Love*, book I only, was published posthumously in 1709; he may not have written the Preface.

read and commented upon; and about which even celebrated *Jesuits* and other religious Persons, as eminent for their Piety as their Erudition, have employed their Studies. Yet who has condemn'd or complain'd of them? We must confess, such things should be managed with Address: and those of them who have meddled with any of the Authors I have named, have shewn that it may be done so, by their succeeding so happily in it.

'As for this Treatise of the *Art of Love*, for which the Author has also prescrib'd a *Remedy*,[4] as it is liable to be ill interpreted by those whose Pens poison every thing they touch; so it may bear a good Construction, by such as know how to turn every thing to Advantage.

'I will yet say, this *Art* may be apply'd to those that intend to marry. There is nothing sure against Decency in all that. I agree, if you will have it so, that it extends so far as to direct one to the Means to gain a Mistress. If this was not lawful heretofore in *Italy*, on account of the jealous Humour of the *Italians*, we cannot, for the same Reason only, say it ought to be forbidden in our Country, any more than in several others, provided we could be sure the Ladies Modesty would not be offended before whom Youth should always be careful not to exceed the Bounds of the Respect that's due to them.'

To this I may add, that if the Objection of Impurity lies against any part of this Work, it is only against the two latter Books, for in that which we have here paraphrased, there is nothing capable of offending the nicest Ear.

With regard to the Merit of this Paraphrase, which is entirely a new Undertaking, and might perhaps, if properly encouraged, be carried on with other Latin Poets, we shall only observe, that the utmost Care hath been taken to preserve the Spirit and true Sense of the Author, and where we have been obliged to deviate, we have given the literal Translation in the Notes.

Upon the whole, we cannot suppress what one of the most learned Men of this Age[5] *said upon perusing the Paraphrase, viz.* That he thought it would serve better to explain the Meaning of *Ovid* to a Learner, than any other Translation, or all his numerous Commentators.

---

[4] Ovid's *Remedia Amoris*, written, it would seem, to atone for the immorality of the *Ars Amatoria*, which had offended the Emperor and resulted in Ovid's exile. A poem in elegiacs, it offers advice on how to overcome unrequited love, in part by ignoring the strategies recommended in the *Ars Amatoria*.

[5] In their notes Amory ('possibly') and Baker ('most probably') suggest that HF here refers to James Harris, whom he and his sister Sarah occasionally consulted on their translations from the Greek. As appears, however, from Thomas Harris's letter of 3 March 1747 (see Introduction, p. 387), his brother James knew nothing of HF's Ovid. The compliment here is most likely meant for the Revd William Young, HF's collaborator on the *Plutus* (above, pp. 238–338), and also 'a possible collaborator' on the *Vernoniad* (Coley in *Champion*, p. lxxxix), with whom he later hoped to join again in a translation of Lucian. In a premature announcement of that abortive project in *The Covent-Garden Journal*, No. 52 (30 June 1752) HF refers to Young in much the same terms: 'I believe, I shall have the universal Concurrence of those learned Men of this Age to whom he is known, that no Man now alive is better versed in that Language [Greek] in which the Wit of Lucian lies as yet concealed' (p. 289).

S I quis in hoc artem populo non novit amandi,
    Me legat; & lecto carmine doctus amet.
Arte citæ veloque rates remoque reguntur:
    Arte leves currus, arte regendus amor.
Curribus Automedon lentisque erat aptus habenis;   5
    Tiphys in Æmonia puppe magister erat.
Me Venus artificem tenero præfecit amori:
    Tiphys & Automedon dicar amoris ego.
Ille quidem ferus est, & qui mihi sæpe repugnet;
    Sed puer est, aetas mollis & apta regi.   10
Phyllirides puerum citharâ perfecit Achillem,
    Atque animos molli contudit arte feros.
Qui toties socios, toties perterruit hostes,
    Creditur annosum pertimuisse senem.
Quas Hector sensurus erat, poscente magistro,   15
    Verberibus jussas præbuit ille manus.
Æacidae Chiron, ego sum præceptor Amoris.
    Sævus uterque puer; natus uterque deâ.
Sed tamen & tauri cervix oneratur aratro,
    Frænaque magnanimi dente teruntur equi.   20
Et mihi cedet Amor; quamvis mea vulneret arcu
    Pectora, jactatas excutiatque faces.
Quo me fixit Amor, quo me violentius ussit,
    Hoc melior facti vulneris ultor ero.

Non ego, Phœbe, datas à te mihi mentiar artes;   25
    Nec nos aëriae voce monemur avis:

IF in so learned an Age as this, when Arts and Sciences are risen to such Perfection,[6] there be any Gentleman unskilled in the Art of Loving, let him come to my School; where, if he hath any Genius, he will soon become an Adept: For I would by no means have any young Gentleman think, that Erudition is unnecessary upon this Occasion. It is well known that the (a)[7] Rules of Art are necessary to the Conduct of a Ship; for which reason, none but able and experienced Seamen are preferred to the Command of one. Rules are necessary even to make a good Coachman, as those Gentlemen who have the Ambition to excel this way very well know. In the same manner is Art required to drive the Chariot of Love well. Now it hath pleased *Venus* to place me in the Coach-Box: What a Captain is to a Ship, or the Driver to his Chariot, that am I to Love; I own indeed Master *Cupid* is a little wild, and often stubborn; but he is only a Child, and of an Age to be disciplined: And however fierce the Disposition of a Lad may be, a judicious Schoolmaster knows very well how to correct it: For many a Boy who hath afterwards turned out a Hero, hath when at School very patiently submitted to the Lash, and quietly, at the Word of Command, held out his Hands to be whipt (b). Duke *William* (c) himself,[8] when a Lad, very possibly submitted to Correction; and he (d) who was hereafter to become the Terror of his Enemies, may on his Youth have been afraid of his Tutor. Mr. *Pointz* was his Preceptor:[9] I am the Preceptor of Love. Both these Youths were of a fierce Disposition, both elevated (e) in their Birth. But as the stoutest Ox submits himself to the Yoke, and the most fiery Horse to the Bridle, so shall Love to me. Though he may bend his Bow against my Breast, and shake his Torches at me; no matter: nay, the more he pierces me with his Arrows, the more he burns me, the more severely will I be revenged of him.

But here, Master *Apollo*, I will tell no lyes to my Readers. I do not pretend to have received any Inspiration from you, any more than from Parson

---

[6] Cf. the surely ironic compliment in *The Journal of a Voyage to Lisbon*, admiring 'the spirit of improving arts and sciences, and of advancing useful and substantial learning, which so eminently distinguishes this age' (below, p. 571). And for his openly satiric attitude towards the natural—or rather '*unnatural*', as he calls them in *Tom Jones* (XIII. v, p. 701)—philosophers of the Royal Society, see below, HF's Letter XL of Sarah Fielding's *Familiar Letters* (pp. 484–5). For a comprehensive discussion of the subject, see Miller, *Essays*, pp. 315–31.

[7] For HF's notes, signalled by letters of the alphabet in parentheses as here, see the appendix to the text (below, pp. 454–6).

[8] HF assigns two parallels for Cumberland (see above, n. 2): that of Ovid's Achilles, as here, which better suits the Duke's military position on the Continent; and that of Gaius Caesar, grandson of Augustus (p. 413 and n. 36), which better suits his domestic situation.

[9] Stephen Poyntz (1685–1750), scholar and diplomat; he was appointed steward of William's household when the Duke was 9, and acted as his adviser.

Nec mihi sunt visae Clio Cliusque sorores,
    Servanti pecudes vallibus, Ascra, tuis.

Usus opus movet hoc; vati parete perito:
    Vera canam; coeptis, mater Amoris, ades.   30
Este procul, vittæ tenues, insigne pudoris;
    Quæque tegis medios, instita longa, pedes.
Nos Venerem tutam, concessaque furta canemus;
    Inque meo nullum carmine crimen erit.

Principio, quod amare velis, reperire labora,   35
    Qui nova nunc primum miles in arma venis.
Proximus huic labor est, placitam exorare puellam.
    Tertius, ut longo tempore duret amor.
Hic modus; hæc nostro signabitur area curru;
    Hæc erit admissâ meta terenda rotâ.   40

Dum licet, & loris passim potes ire solutis,
    Elige, cui dicas, *Tu mihi sola places.*
Hæc tibi non veniet tenues delapsa per auras:
    Quærenda est oculis apta puella tuis.
Scit bene venator cervis ubi retia tendat;   45
    Scit bene quâ frendens valle moretur aper.
Aucupibus noti frustices. Qui sustinet hamos,
    Novit quae multo pisce nanentur aquae.
Tu quoque, materiam longo qui quæris amori,
    Antè frequens quo sit disce puella loco.   50

Non ego quærentem ventis dare vela jubebo;
    Nec tibi, ut invenias, longa terenda via est.
Andromedan Perseus nigris portârit ab Indis,
    Raptaque sit Phrygio Graia puella viro,

Whitefield (*f*):[10] And as for Miss *Clio* (*g*) and her eight Sisters, I never visit them; nor have I even a Cap-Acquaintance with them.[11] I write from Experience only; and *Experto crede Roberto*[12] is my Motto. I promise my Readers that I will tell them truth; and if I must, for form sake, invoke any Muse, *Venus* herself shall be the Person (*h*). Sweet Goddess! then be thou present, and smile at my Undertaking. But as for you who cannot smile, I mean you, Prudes, with your screw'd Faces, which may be considered as Signs hung forth before the Door of Virtue, and which perhaps, like other Signs, promise what is not to be found in the House; I desire neither your Favour nor your Company, Good natur'd Girls (*i*) are all I write to; and such I promise them may read my Works without a blush.

Know then, my good Scholar, that art unexperienced in the Art of Love, that this Art consists of three principal Points: First, to select a proper Mistress: Secondly, to win her Affections: And, Thirdly, to preserve your mutual Affection. Of all these therefore we will treat; or, to speak metaphorically, through these three Roads we will drive the Chariot we have undertaken to guide.

First then as to the Choice of a Mistress, to whom you may say, *In Thee along my Choice is fixed*. Do not believe such a one will fall into your Lap. It will become you to look about sharp for her, and with all your Eyes, I do assure you. And here my first Instruction shall be, where she may most probably be found: For he is a bad Huntsman who would beat about the *Royal-Exchange*[13] for a Hare of a Fox; and not a much better Gunner or Fisherman, who goes a shooting in *Somerset-Gardens*, or attempts to angle in the magnificent Bason there.[14] As these all know the Places where their Game resort, so must you.

Here then, I by no means advise you to make a long Voyage after a foreign Mistress, as *Perseus* did, who fetched *Andromeda* (*k*) from the *Indies*; or *Paris*, whom nothing would serve but a *Grecian* Mistress. Your own

---

[10] The Methodist evangelist George Whitefield (1714–70) was a favourite target of HF's ridicule: see above, the Introduction and notes to *Shamela*; also the *Female Husband* (above, p. 366 and nn. 2–3). By 'Inspiration' HF refers to Whitefield's appealing to the emotions of the crowds assembled in the fields to hear him preach, what Parson Adams in *Joseph Andrews* (I. xvii) denounces as 'Nonsense and Enthusiasm' (p. 82).

[11] As the Latin shows, 'Cap-Acquaintance' means 'slightly acquainted' (Partridge, s.v.).

[12] 'Trust Robert, who knows from experience'—a proverbial expression (H. Walther, *Proverbia sententiaeque Latinitatis Medii Aevi* [Göttingen, 1963–7], no. 8531), used by HF in *The Champion* (4 October 1740) as a signature for Walpole (p. 474 and n. 5).

[13] The financial centre of the City of London, founded by Sir Thomas Gresham in 1570 and rebuilt between Threadneedle Street and Cornhill after the Fire of London. (*LE*).

[14] This passage ('For he is a bad Huntsman . . . so must you') is quoted verbatim in HF's parody of Ovid's book I in *The Jacobite's Journal* (12 March 1748), p. 192. The water gardens at Somerset House on the Strand were located on the Thames side; for a view of Somerset Gardens in 1720 showing the 'Bason' and fountain, see Phillips, *Thames*, p. 101.

Tot tibi tamque dabit formosas Roma puellas;   55
   Hæc habet, ut dicas, quicquid in orbe fuit.
Gargara quot segetes, quot habet Methymna racemos,
   Æquore quot pisces, fronde teguntur aves,

Quot cœlum stellas, tot habet tua Roma puellas;
   Mater & Æneæ constat in urbe sui.   60
Seu caperis primis & adhus crescentibus annis,
   Ante oculos veniet vera puella tuos.
Sive cupis juvenum, juvenes tibi mille placebunt;
   Cogêris voti nescius esse tui.
Seu te forte juvat sera & sapientior ætas,   65
   Hoc quoque (crede mihi) plenius agmen erit.

Tu modo Pompeïâ lentus spatiare sub umbrâ,
   Cum sol Herculei terga Leonis adit:
Aut ubi muneribus nati sua munera mater
   Addidit, externo marmore dives opus.   70

59–60] With most modern edns., HF retains these lines, which Heinsius considered spurious.

Country, my Friend, will produce Women which the World cannot equal. Beauties are as plenty in the City of *London* as Apples in (*l*) *Herefordshire*, or Grains of Wheat (*m*) in *Hampshire*; they are indeed as plenty as Fish in the Sea, or Birds in the Air; nay, the Sky hath not more Stars than *London* hath Beauties: for *England* (*n*), not *Cyprus*, is the Queen of Love's favourite Island.[15] Whether you love green Fruit, and which is in the Bud only, or Beauty in its fuller Bloom, or that which is arrived to perfect Ripeness; nay, if nothing but Wisdom or Sagacity will serve your turn, of these too Old *England* will afford you a sufficient Plenty.

In the pleasant Month of *May*, repair to *Vaux-Hall* (*o*).[16] Here take your Evening Walk, either round the verdant Scenes, where Nightingales, the only Foreigners who give us their Songs for nothing,[17] warble their most delicious Notes. When your Limbs demand Repose, you may enjoy it in an Alcove, from whence the embattl'd Troops of *Venus* will pass in review before you. Again, the lofty Dome of *Ranelagh* invites your Steps.[18] Whether the illustrious Artist took his Model from that House, which as a Reward for their Industry, or for some little regard for their Honey, the benevolent Nature of Man hath conferred on that laborious Animal the Bee: Or whether a more pious Disposition chose this Form from the musical Instrument which summons the whole Paris to Church: Or whether the wondrous Force of Genius, unassisted by any Model, did not of itself strike out this wondrous Architecture; let *Kent*[19] or

[15] Cf. HF's untitled poem 'The Queen of Beauty': 'Thou *Britain*, on my Labours smile, | The Queen of Beauty's favour'd Isle; | Whom she long since hath priz'd above | The *Paphian*, or the *Cyprian* Grove' (*Miscellanies* i, p. 79 and nn. 2–3).

[16] HF's friend Jonathan Tyers (d. 1767) opened Vauxhall to the public in 1732; in *Amelia* (IX. ix) HF takes his heroine to the pleasure gardens there and takes the opportunity to pay the proprietor a compliment: 'To delineate the particular Beauties of these Gardens, would, indeed, require as much Pains and as much Paper too, as to rehearse all the good Actions of their Master' (pp. 393–4).

[17] Cf. *True Patriot*, No. 13 (21–8 January 1746), where HF decries the vogue of the Italian opera: 'a Diversion in which a prodigious Sum of Money, more than is to be collected out of twenty Parishes, is lavish'd away on foreign Eunuchs and Papists' (p. 202). For an account of HF's attacks on the opera from the beginning to the end of his career, see *Companion*, pp. 242–3.

[18] In 1742 a syndicate led by HF's friend James Lacy (d. 1774), the actor and from 1747 the manager with Garrick of the Drury Lane Theatre, opened the fashionable pleasure gardens and large rococo Rotunda at Ranelagh, just east of the Chelsea Royal Hospital (*LE*). Though in *Amelia* (1751) HF has the dissolute Noble Lord use the masquerades at Ranelagh as stalking grounds for seduction, in the *Enquiry* (sect. i) he represented both Vauxhall and Ranelagh as places where 'a strict Regard to Decency is preserved' and 'Persons of Fashion and Fortune' amuse themselves in an 'idle, though otherwise innocentWay' (pp. 83–4).

[19] William Jones, the architect of the lavish Rotunda at Ranelagh, was a follower of William Kent (1684–1748), artist, sculptor, architect, and pioneer of the English 'natural' garden. Kent was responsible for laying out the gardens at Henry Pelham's estate at Esher, Surrey (on Pelham, see below, *Voyage to Lisbon*, p. 562 and n. 58); at Viscount Cobham's celebrated Stowe, and at the Earl of Pembroke's Wilton, near Salisbury—all three of which HF compliments in a passage in *Tom Jones* (XI. ix, p. 612 and nn. 1–3).

Nec tibi vitetur quae, priscis sparsa tabellis,
  Porticus auctoris Livia nomen habet.
Quâque parare necem miseris patruelibus ausæ
  Belides, & stricto stat ferus ense pater.
Nec te prætereat Veneri ploratus Adonis,   75
  Cultaque Judæo septima sacra Syro.
Neu fuge linigerae Memphitica sacra juvencæ;
  Multas illa facit, quod fuit ipsa Jovi.

Et fora conveniunt (quis credere possit?) amori;
  Flammaque in arguto saepe reperta foro.   80

Benson[20] inquire. Hither, from every Corner of the Town, repair the loveliest Nymphs. Here too thou may'st survey them, either walking or reposed on Benches at thy Ease.

Nor is the *Mall* to be neglected, where once the brawny Arm of *Charles* displayed its Strength, and beat his subtle Courtiers at the Play, whence it derives its Name.[21] Nor, *Kensington*, must thy Gardens be passed by, once the Delight of mighty *Caroline*, and to the future Age a Monument of her Taste.[22] Here the Charmers draw in sweet Air, and send it forth again in sweeter Sighs, as Tributes to the loved Memory of that mighty Queen. As for the Ring, formerly the Scene of Beauty's many Triumphs, it is now become a lonely deserted Place: Brilliants and brilliant Eyes no longer sparkle there: No more the heedless Beau falls by the random Glance, or well-pointed Fan. The Ring is now no more:[23] Yet *Ruckholt, Marybone* and *The Wells* survive;[24] Places by no means to be neglected by the Gallant: for Beauty may lurk beneath the Straw Hat, and *Venus* often clothes her lovely Limbs in Stuffs.[25]

Nay, the very Courts of Law are not excluded; and the Scenes of Wrangling are sometimes the Scenes of Love. In that Hall where *Thames*

[20] William Benson (1682–1754), Surveyor-General and pioneer of the new Palladian movement in architecture; in 1710 he built Wilbury Park in Wiltshire after a design (unpublished) by Inigo Jones (James Lees-Milne, *Earls of Creation* [London, 1962], p. 116).
[21] Originally created by Charles II as an alley for the game of Pall Mall (a game resembling croquet), the broad straight walk called The Mall ran, as the thoroughfare of that name does today, eastward for about a half-mile from Buckingham House between St James's Palace and the Park. It soon became a crowded promenade for the beau monde and remained so for 150 years. (*London Encyclopaedia*) Cf. HF's poem 'To Celia' (*Miscellanies* i, p. 63).
[22] In 1728 Queen Caroline (1683–1737) engaged Charles Bridgeman to devise a new layout for the gardens at Kensington Palace, which included the Broad Walk and the Round Pond, and the extension of the Serpentine into Hyde Park. The gardens were open to the public on weekends.
[23] A circle enclosed in a square of trees and situated in Hyde Park north of the Serpentine (see the map in *Amelia*, p. [596]), the Ring had been a fashionable place to ride or promenade (cf. 'To Celia', above, n. 21). By the mid–1730s, however, after the extension of the Serpentine (above, n. 22), it was no longer a favoured resort of the gentry (Peter Willis, *Charles Bridgeman and the English Landscape Garden* [London, 1977], pp. 97–8).
[24] In 1742 William Barton opened Ruckholt House, Leyton (Essex), for breakfast and concerts. Since it opened in 1650, Marylebone Gardens, in the fields north of Oxford Road, had become the resort of sharpers and thieves such as the highwayman Macheath in Gay's *Beggar's Opera* (1728). In 1738, however, the beginning of a change for the better took place when the gardens were enlarged, music played in the evenings, the refreshments improved, and assembly rooms were built for balls and concerts; the enterprise prospered until it closed in 1778. '*The Wells*' may be Hampstead, Lambeth, or Sadler's Wells, but HF probably refers to New Wells, Clerkenwell, a spa which became popular after a theatre was built in 1737, featuring performances by acrobats, musicians, clowns, freaks of nature, etc.; it was demolished in 1756. (*LE*.)
[25] 'Stuff': a woollen fabric (*OED*, s.v. II. 5. c).

Subdita quâ Veneris facto de marmore templo
    Appias expressis aëra pulsat aquis.
Illo sæpe loco capitur consultus Amori;
    Quique aliis cavit, non cavet ipse sibi.
Illo sæpe loco desunt sua verba diserto,   85
    Resque novæ veniunt, causaque agenda sua est.
Hunc Venus è templis, quæ sunt confinia, ridet;
    Qui modò patronus, jam cupit esse cliens.

Sed tu præcipue curvis venare theatris;
    Hæc loca sunt voto fertiliora tuo: 90
Illic invenies, quod ames, quod ludere possis,
    Quodque semel tangas, quodque tenere velis.
Ut redit, itque frequens longum formica per agmen,
    Granifero solitum cum vehit ore cibum;
Aut ut apes, saltúsque suos & olentia nactae   95
    Pascua, per flores & thyma summa volant;
Sic ruit ad celebres cultissima foemina ludos;
    Copia judicium sæpe morata meum.
Spectatum veniunt, veniunt spectentur ut ipsæ.
    Ille locus casti damna pudoris habet.   100

Primus sollicitos fecisti, Romule, ludos,
    Cùm juvit viduos rapta Sabina viros.
Tunc neque marmoreo pendebant vela theatro,
    Nec fuerant liquido pulpita rubra croco.
Illic, quas tulerant nemorosa palatia, frondes   105
    Simpliciter positæ; scena sine arte fuit.
In gradibus sedit populus de cespite factis,
    Qualibet hirsutas fronde tegente comas.
Respiciunt oculisque notant sibi quisque puellam
    Quam velit; & tacito pectore multa movent.   110

101–2] 'Thou first, Romulus, didst disturb the dames, when the rape of Sabine women consoled the wifeless men' (Loeb). HF's translation assumes a different, unmetrical Latin, apparently understanding *sollicitatos* ('instigated' = 'acted by his Command') for *sollicitos* ('disturbed'), and reading (?) *Cùm jussit viduis raptam Sabinam viris* for line 102.

sometimes overflowing, washes the Temple of *Venus Lucy*,[26] the grave
Serjeant becomes a Victim to the Fair; and he who so well knows how to
defend others, cannot defend himself. Here the Special Pleader loses all
Power to Demurr, and finds beyond his Expectation a novel Assignment
spring up in the Cause.[27] Him *Venus Lucy* (*p*) laughs at from her neighbouring Temple; for the Council is now become the Client, and squeezes an
empty Hand harder that he ever did a full one.

But above all, the Theatres are the Place of Sport: for these will be most
fruitful to your Wishes. Here you will find one Object to love, and another
to toy with. Some, of whom a single Touch will suffice, and others, in whom
you will desire a stronger Tenure. Neither do the Ants in pursuit of
Grain, or the Bees in quest of Flowers, swarm in greater Numbers than the
Beauties to the Theatres. The Variety of Charmers here have often distracted my Choice. Hither they come to see, and to be themselves seen; and
many are the Love-Bargains here made.

And now, Friend, I will tell you a Story. *Romulus* was the first Person who
ever made this use of the Theatre, when he ordered his Soldiers to fall
foul on the *Sabine* Ladies, whom he invited to a Play acted by his Command.
Not that I would have you think, that Theatre was like the Play-house in
Covent-Garden, enriched with Scenes, Machines, and other Decorations.[28]
To say the truth, it was no better than a Barn, or Booth. Here he assembled
the *Sabine* Girls, and ordered his *Romans* to chuse every Man his Miss.
They did so, and while the poor Girls thought no Harm, those Fellows felt
strange Emotions within. Now while a certain Dancer, called, *The Ludio*,

[26] Westminster Hall, the site of the Law Courts, was periodically flooded before the construction of the
Thames Embankment. One such flood occurred on 16 February 1736 and featured in the speech of
the Lawyer in HF's *Pasquin* (IV. I): 'A mighty Deluge swam into our Hall, | As if it meant to wash away
the Law'. The 'Temple' presumably is St Margaret's, Westminster, nearby, the ex officio parish church of
members of the Commons; but '*Venus Lucy*' is puzzling. HF conflates both Venus Genetrix (the ancestress
of Augustus and the Julian *gens*) and Juno as Lucina (the goddess who 'brings to light', and presides over
childbirth), but substituting St Lucy, who brings light to the blind. Whatever the witticism he intended
may have been, it is lost today.

[27] HF wittily adapts Ovid (literally, 'often there does the glib speaker fail for words: a new case comes
on' [Loeb]). A 'Special Pleader' is a lawyer who frames highly technical evasions (e.g. 'You did'; 'You did it
first'): a 'demurrer' accepts the truth of a complaint, but denies the plaintiff's legal right to relief; a 'novel
Assignment' removes an ambiguity of time or place in the plaintiff's original declaration, forcing the
defendant to a more specific reply (e.g. 'You did'; 'I didn't [sc. On Monday]'; 'You did on Tuesday' (Giles
Jacob, *A New Law-Dictionary* [1743]). Metaphorically, HF's lawyer cannot evade the 'legality' of his
feelings, and his ambiguous response to them 'springs up' in its proper place. For similar legal–sexual
'Gibbrish', cf. *Joseph Andrews* (I. xii, p. 54). HA

[28] A pun ('enriched') on the name of John Rich (1692–1761), manager of the Covent Garden Theatre,
where, acting the part of Harlequin himself, he staged pantomime 'entertainments' with spectacular stage
effects. At the Little Haymarket Theatre in 1736 HF dedicated to Rich (using his stage name of 'Lun') his
farce *Tumble-Down Dick: or, Phaeton in the Suds*, a burlesque of Rich's productions in which he is 'taken
off' in the character of Machine. On Rich, who was a recurrent target of HF's ridicule, see above, 'Cantos',
p. 60n. 107.

Dumque, rudem præbente modum tibicine Thusco,
    Ludius æquatam ter pede pulsat humum,
In medio plausu (plausus tunc arte carebat)
    Rex populo prædæ signa repente dedit.
Protinus exiliunt, animum clamore fatentes,   115
    Virginibus cupidas injiciuntque manus.

Ut fugiunt aquilas, timidissima turba, columbæ;
    Utque fugit visos agna novella lupos;
Sic illæ timuêre viros sine lege ruentes;
    Constitit in nulla, qui fuit ante color.   120
Nam timor unus erat, facies non una timoris:
    Pars laniat crines; pars sine mente sedet;
Altera mœsta silet, frustra vocat altera matrem;
    Hæc queritur, stupet hæc; hæc manet, illa fugit.
Ducuntur raptæ, genialis præda, puellæ;   125
    Et potuit multas ipse decere pudor.
Siqua repugnabat nimium, comitemque negabat;
    Sublatum cupido vir tulit ipse sinu.
Atque ità, *Quid teneros lacrymis corrumpis ocellos?*
    Quod matri pater est, hoc tibi, dixit, *ero.*   130
Romule, militibus scisti dare commoda solus;
    Hæc mihi si dederis commoda, miles ero.
Scilicet ex illo sollenia more theatra
    Nunc quoque formosis insidiosa manent.

Nec te nobilium fugiat certamen equorum: 135
    Multa capax populi commoda Circus habet.
Nil opus est digitis, per quos arcana loquaris,
    Nec tibi per nutus accipienda nota est.
Proximus à dominâ, nullo prohibente, sedeto:
    Junge tuum lateri, quàm potes, usque latus.   140
Et bene, quod cogit, si nolit, linea jungi;
    Quod tibi tangenda est lege puella loci.
Hic tibi quæratur socii sermonis origo;
    Et moveant primos publica verba sonos,

was performing a *Tambourine*,[29] which I suppose took greatly at that time, *Romulus* on a sudden gave the Signal for falling on. This was instantly obeyed. They all rushed in, laid their Hands upon the Girls, and soon gave them sufficient Tokens of their Purpose.

As the Doves, who are the most timorous of Birds, fly from Eagles; or as the young Lamb runs from the Wolves, as soon as she sees them, so terrified were these Ladies, at the Men rushing upon them, in this unlawful manner. The Colour forsook their Cheeks at once. All were equally in a Fright, though they discovered their Fear by different Symptoms. Some of them tear their Hair, others sit in Amazement, Terror strikes some dumb, others call in vain for the Assistance of their Mammas. One cries out, another is shocked to death; one stands still, another endeavours to get out of the House. But all their Endeavours are vain; and perhaps indeed their Blushes heightened their Beauty; they were all led off, and those who would not go were carried. Methinks, I hear one of their Gallants thus addressing his weeping Fair. *Why, my Dear, will you spoil those lovely Eyes with Tears? I promise you, you shall be served no worse than your Mother hath been before. I will only do to you what your Father did to her.* Ah *Romulus! Romulus!* no General ever better knew how to reward his Soldiers; I promise you, that when I hear your Drum beating up for Voluntiers, I will enlist under your Command.

Ever since that time, the Theatre hath been consecrated to Love, and many a pretty Girl, since the *Sabines*, hath owed the Loss of her Maidenhead to it.

Other Places of publick Meeting may likewise be frequented, as Horse-Races (*q*) and the like. And especially public Shews, which never fail of Women. Here get upon a crouded Scaffold, and sit next to the Girl you like. Squeeze yourself as close to her as you can; for Custom here countenances such squeezing whether the pretty Creatures will or no. Here find some Opportunity to begin a Discourse; you will not be driven to talk upon your Fingers, or by Signs, but may use your Tongue*. Begin then with News, or the Chitchat of the Town. Nay, the Shew itself will afford a Subject: for instance supposing it was my Lord Mayor's Shew,[30] you may ask her what

---

* These Verses are transposed from the Place in which they stand in the Original, and this, I think, with Advantage to the Connection.

[29] French dancers performing the 'Tambourin', a Provençal dance performed to the beat of a drum (first cited in the *OED* from 1797), were popular in the London theatres from 1736 to 1746 (*London Stage*, pt. 3, index).

[30] The annual installation of the new Lord Mayor of London in late October entailed a pompous procession of City dignitaries by barge to Westminster Hall, where the oaths of office are taken, returning by water to Blackfriars, and from there by coach to Guildhall, where a magnificent feast awaited them. Cf. *Tom Jones* (IV. i, p. 153 and n. 1).

Cujus equi veniant, facito, studiose, requiras;   145
　　Nec mora, quisquis erit, cui favet illa, fave.
At cum pompa frequens cœlestibus ibit eburnis;
　　Tu Veneri dominæ plaude, favente manu.

Utque fit, in gremium pulvis si forte puellæ
　　Deciderit, digitis excutiendus erit;   150
Et, si nullus erit pulvis, tamen excute nullum.
　　Quælibet officio causa sit apta tuo.
Pallia si terræ nimium demissa jacebunt,
　　Collige, & immundâ sedulus effer humo.
Protinus officii pretium, patiente puellâ,   155
　　Contingent oculis crura videnda tuis.
Respice præterea, post vos quicumque sedebit,
　　Ne premat opposito mollia terga genu.
Parve leves capiunt animos; fuit utile multis
　　Pulvinar facili composuisse manu.   160
Profuit & tenui ventum movisse tabella,
　　Et cava sub tenerum scamna dedisse pedem.

Hos aditus Circusque novo præbebit amori,
　　Sparsaque sollicito tristis arena foro.
Illa sæpe puer Veneris pugnavit arenâ,   165
　　Et qui spectavit vulnera, vulnus habet.
Dum loquitur, tangitque manum, poscitque libellum,
　　Et quærit, posito pignore, vincat uter,
Saucius ingemuit, telumque volatile sensit,
　　Et pars spectati muneris ipse fuit.   170

Quid? modo cum belli navalis imagine Cæsar
　　Persidas induxit, Cecropidasque rates?
Nempe ab utruoque mari juvenes, ab utroque puellæ
　　Venêre: atque ingens orbis in Urbe fuit.

Alderman that Coach, or those Liveries belong to; and be sure to admire the same with herself: Do not omit moreover, to give her an early Intimation of your Gallantry, and that you are a Woman's Man. If it should happen that any one of the Aldermen should be a greater Cuckold that the rest of his Brethren; take care to titter at his Appearance; and while the Pageants (*r*) are passing by, endeavour to find out a Resemblance of Horns in some of them. All those Things have a remote Tendency to this great Point.

If a Grain of Snuff should happen to fall on the Lady's Bosom, wipe it off with your Fingers; and if none fall, wipe off that none.[31] Take every Opportunity to be as officious in her Service as possible. If she drop her Fan or Gloves, presently take them up; for this you will have sure Reward in the very Fact, for you may at the same time lift up her Petticoat and see her Legs. Be careful that the Person who sits behind her doth not press her tender Back with his Knee. Small Matters captivate light Minds.[32] Many a Man hath drawn considerable Advantage from handing (*s*) a Lady to her Coach, by gallanting her Fan,[33] or even by taking up her Clog (*t*).

Nor will (*u*) *Tower-hill*, when the Tragic Scaffold is strewed with Saw-Dust,[34] be an improper Place to begin your Intrigue: for *Cupid* himself always attends, and acts the Part of an Executioner on such Occasions; many a poor Man having lost his Heart, while he hath attended to another's losing his Head. While the Fair-One carelessly laying her Hand on his,[35] argues concerning the Criminal's Guilt, and offers to lay a Wager that he will die well; the wounded Lover feels a sudden Stroke, and is not better able to bear the Smart without a Sigh.

If it was the Custom of *England* to imitate the *Romans* in insulting over the Conquered, what Spectacles might have formerly been exhibited (*w*)! How many *French* Youths and Virgins might have followed the Chariot-Wheels of our Monarchs! In that Case many a poor *English* Heart must have

---

[31] HF substitutes 'Snuff'—as in *Tom Jones* (v. viii) he does 'Tears'—for Ovid's *pulvis* (dust). In *Tom Jones* he quotes the Latin (line 151, omitting *pulvis*), translating it: 'If there be none then wipe away that none' (p. 250).

[32] In *Tom Jones* (IV. v) HF quotes the Latin (line 159), translating it: 'Small Things affect light Minds' (p. 165).

[33] 'gallanting her Fan': 'to break it with Design, on Purpose to have the . . . Favour to Present a better' (*OED*, s.v. 'gallant', v. 6, quoting *A New Dictionary . . . of the Canting Crew* [1699]; also citing Addison, *Spectator*, No. 102 [27 June 1711]: 'I teach young Gentlemen the whole Art of Gallanting a Fan'). Cf. *Champion* (15 May 1740), p. 320.

[34] This was the scene of the execution of the 'Jacobite Lords', the Earl of Kilmarnock and Lord Balmerino, on 18 August 1746—'Tragic' because only nobility were beheaded there for treason or some other crime of state; common criminals were hanged at Tyburn. So, in *Jonathan Wild* (I. v) HF's hero asks: 'where is the essential Difference if the one ends on *Tower-Hill*, and the other at *Tyburn*? Hath the Block any Preference to the Gallows, or the Ax to the Halter' (*Miscellanies* iii, p. 21).

[35] Cf. Lady Booby to the hero in *Joseph Andrews* (I. viii): 'Consider, Child, (*laying her Hand carelessly upon his*) you are a handsome young Fellow' (p. 39).

Quis non invênit turba quod amaret in illa?   175
  Eheu, quàm multos advena torsit amor!
Ecce parat Caesar domito, quod defuit, orbi
  Addere: nunc, oriens ultime, noster eris.
Parthe, dabis pœnas, Crassi gaudete sepulti,
  Signaque barbaricas non bene passa manus;   180
Ultor adest, primisque ducem profitetur in armis;
  Bellaque non puero tractat agenda puer.
Parcite natales, timidi, numerare deorum:
  Cæsaribus virtus contigit ante diem.
Ingenium cœleste suis velocius annis   185
  Surgit, & ignavæ fert male damna moræ.
Parvus erat, manibusque duos Tirynthius angues
  Pressit; & in cunis jam Jove dignus erat.
Nunc quoque qui puer es, quantus tum, Bacche, fuisti;
  Cum timuit thrysos India victa tuos!   190
Auspiciis animisque patris, puer, arma movebis,
  Et vinces animis auspiciisque patris.
Tale rudimentum tanto sub nomine debes,
  Nunc juvenum princeps, deinde future senum.
Cum tibi sint fratres, fratres ulciscere læsos: 195
  Cumque pater sibi sit, juta tuere patris.

Induit arma tibi genitor patriæque tuusque:
  Hostis ab invito regna parente rapit.
Tu pia tela feres, sceleratas ille sagittas;
  Stabit pro signis jusque piumque tuis.   200
Vincuntur Parthi causà, vincantur & armis:
  Eoas Latio dux meus addat opes.
Marsque pater, Cæsarque pater, data numen eunti:
  Nam deus è vobis alter es, alter eris.
Auguror en, vinces: votivaque carmina reddam,   205
  Et magno nobis ore sonandus eris.
Consistes, aciemque meis hortabere verbis:
  O desint animis ne mea vera tuis!
Tergaque Parthorum, Romanaque pectora dicam;
  Telaque ab averso quae jacet hostis equo.   210

191–2] HF reads *animis* with Burmann against *annis* with Merula, Heinsius, the Eton *Electa minora*,
and modern edns. ('With the authority and *experience* of thy sire . . .', Loeb).

submitted to a *French* Conquest, and Beauty would have been triumphant in Chains. Nay, I prophesy we shall again see those victorious Times. Our Mighty GEORGE now meditates new Triumphs, and *France* (*x*) shall be punished as she ought. Rejoice, O ye Shades (*y*), whose Bodies lie buried in the Plains of *Fontenoy*, where *British* Colours were polluted by *Gallic* Hands. WILLIAM your Avenger comes.[36] The General in him shone forth in his first Campaign, and while a Youth, he managed War beyond his Years. Let not his Age therefore deter us from ranking him among our greatest Commanders. His Warlike Genius springs forth and out-runs his Years, impatient of the sluggish Pace of Time. The *Swedish Charles* (*z*) was scarce beyond a Child when he crushed two mighty Enemies at once; *Charles* (*a*) the *German* Prince, yet but a Youth, what was he when he past the *Rhine* and terrified the Host of *France*?[37]

Thy Father's Genius, WILLIAM, and his Courage shall inspire thy youthful Arms. With that Genius and that Courage shalt thou conquer. Such Beginnings dost thou owe to the mighty Name of thy Illustrious Sire; that thou who art the Noblest of all young Commanders mayst hereafter become the first among the old. 'Tis time to avenge the Injuries attempted to thy House, and to maintain thy glorious Father's Rights.

Thy Country's Father and thy own, girts on thy Sword, and thy Cause is no less glorious than thy Arms. In both is *France* inferiour, and to both shall yield. I prophesy, that thou shalt conquer, and to thy Conquest I dedicate my votive Prayers, prepared hereafter to resound thy Praise; when we shall

[36] Cf. '*William* the Avenger is abroad' (*JJ* [12 March 1748]), p. 193 and n. 1). After his final victory over the Jacobites at Culloden (16 April 1746), British hopes were high that the Duke of Cumberland would avenge the earlier defeat of the allied armies at Fontenoy (May 1745). In *A Dialogue between a Gentleman . . . and an Alderman* (23 June 1747), HF hoped that Cumberland, 'whose very Name is dreaded' by the French, would 'add to the Palm of *Culloden*, a still nobler Wreath' (*JJ*, pp. 44–5). Such hopes, however, were soon dashed by the defeat of the allies at Lauffeld (2 July 1747) in the Netherlands: see below, *Voyage to Lisbon*, p. 579 nn. 114–15.

[37] In 1700, at 18, Charles XII of Sweden (1682–1718) defeated both the Danes at Humelback (4 August) and a coalition of Poland and Russia at Narva (19 November). (HF had translated Gustaf Adlerfelt's *Military History* of him in 1740.) Though at 32 hardly a youth, Charles-Alexandre (1712–80), Prince of Lorraine and Marshal of the allied Austrian army, crossed the Rhine in July 1744.

Qui fugis, ut vincas? quid victos, Parthe, relinquis?
   Parthe, malum jam nunc Mars tuus omen habet.
Ergo erit illa dies, quâ tu, pulcherrime rerum
   Quatuor in niveis aureus ibis equis?
Ibunt ante duces onerati colla catenis: 215
   Nè possint tuti, quâ prius, esse fugâ
Spectabunt juvenes læti, mistæque puellæ,
   Diffundetque animos omnibus ista dies.

Atque aliqua ex illis, cum regum nomina quæret,
   Quæ loca, qui montes, quæve ferantur aquæ,   220
Omnia responde, nec tantum siqua rogabit:
   Et quæ nescieris, ut bene nota, refer.
Hic est Euphrates præcintus arundine frontem:
   Cui coma dependet cærula, Tygris erit.
Hos facito Armenios: hæc est Danëia Persis: 225
   Urbs in Achæmeniis vallibus ista fuit.
Ille, vel ille, duces. Et erunt quae nomina dicas:
   Si poteris, vere; si minus, apta tamen.
Dant etiam positis aditum convivia mensis;
   Est aliquid, præter vina, quod inde petas.   230
Sæpe illic positi teneris adducta lacertis
   Purpureus Bacchi cornua pressit Amor.
Vinaque cum bibulas sparsere Cupidinis alas,
   Permanet, & capto stat gravis ille loco.
Ille quidem pennas velociter excutit udas;   235
   Sed tamen et spargi pectus amore docet.
Vina parant animos, faciuntque caloribus aptos,
   Cura fugit, multo diluiturque mero.
Tunc veniunt risus, tunc pauper cornua sumit:
   Tunc dolor & curæ, rugaque frontis abit.   240
Tunc aperit mentes aevo rarissima nostro
   Simplicitas, artes excutiente Deo.

Illic sæpe animos juvenum rapuêre puellæ:
   Et Venus in vinis, ignis in igne fuit.
Hic tu fallaci nimium ne crede lucernæ;   245
   Judicio formae noxque merumque nocent.
Luce deas cœloque Paris spectavit aperto,
   Cum dixit Veneri, *Vincis utramque, Venus.*

225] MSS have *facit/facis/fac* for *facito*; HF's text follows Heinsius' emendation.

see thee, most lovely Prince, returning, thy Glories far outshining the Gold in which thou art attired. Thee shall Crouds of Youths and beauteous Virgins hail from their crouded Windows as thou passest, and universal Joy shall overspread each *British* Face on that blest Day.

If then, my Scholar, thou shoulds't happen to be placed in a Window near some lovely Girl, who fired with the Glories of the young Conqueror should enquire into all his matchless Labours (*b*), his Wound at *Dettingen*; his Danger and Intrepidity at *Fontenoy*; his Toils at home, in defiance of Cold and Fatigue; his Pursuit to *Carlisle*; his Victory at *Culloden*;[38] and many more which will then be as well known; repeat all if thou canst, and if thy Memory fails, go on nevertheless: for Invention cannot here outdo the Reality, and thy Fictions shall recommend thee equal with Truth to her Ears.

Again, when thou dost sit down at table among the Women, thou may'st reap other Pleasures besides those of Wine: For to speak figuratively, *Cupid* with glowing Cheeks often presses the Horns of *Bacchus* in his tender Arms; and the Wings of the little God of Love being wetted with Wine, he is unable to fly off: And if he happens to shake his wet Wings, he may possibly sprinkle the Bosom of your Mistress with Love.

In more intelligible Language, Wine fills our Minds with Courage, and makes them susceptible of other warm Passions. Care flies away, and is dissolved in much Liquor. Then comes Laughter; the poor Man becomes bold, and Grief and Solicitude, and knitted Brows vanish. Then it is that Simplicity, a rare Virtue in our Age, opens our Hearts, Wine having divested us of Cunning.

At this Season, many a watchful young Fellow hath gained the Heart of his Mistress (*c*). And Love hath sprung from Wine, as the Flame doth from Fire. However, do not confide too much at this time to the Light of a

---

[38] The Jacobite forces surrendered Carlisle to Cumberland on 30 December 1745; for Dettingen, Fontenoy, and Culloden, see above, n. 2.

Nocte latent mendæ, vitioque ignoscitur omni;
   Horaque formosam quamlibet illa facit.   250
Consule de gemmis, de tinctâ murice lanâ,
   Consule de facie corporibusque diem.

Quid tibi fœmineos coetus venatibus aptos
   Enumerem? numero cedet arena meo.
Quid referam Baias, prætextaque littora velis,   255
   Et, quæ de calido sulphure fumat, aquam?
Hinc aliquis vulnus referens in pectore dixit,
   Non hæc, (ut fama est) unda salubris erat.
Ecce suburbanæ templum nemorale Dianæ,
   Partaque per gladios regna nocente manu.   260
Illa quod est virgo, quod tela Cupidinis odit,
   Multa dedit populo vulnera, multa dabit.
Hactenus, unde legas quod ames, ubi retia tendas,
   Præcipit imparibus vecta Thalia rotis.
Nunc tibi quæ placuit, quas sit capienda per artes,   265
   Dicere præcipuae molior artis opus.
Quisquis ubique, viri, dociles advertite mentes,
   Pollicitisque favens, vulgus, adeste meis.

Prima tuæ menti veniat fiducia, cunctas
   Posse capi; capies: tu modo tende plagas.   270

Candle: for Night and Wine obstruct us in forming a true Judgment of Beauty. *Paris* beheld the Goddesses in open Day-light, when he gave the Preference to *Venus*. Indeed by Candle-light and in a Side-Box, almost every one is a Beauty: Jewels, Clothes, and Women, are all best discerned by the Light of the Sun.

And here if I should recount all the rural Haunts in which a Lover may find his Game, I might write more Volumes than *Oldmixon*.[39] *Tunbridge*, and *Scarborough*, and *Cheltenham*, and *Holt*,[40] and many other Places shall be therefore omitted; but Bath (*d*), thy sulphurous Waters must not be past by. Hence Master *Dapperwit*[41] bringing home the Wounds made by fair Eyes in his Bosom, cries out, on his Return, *The Waters are not so wholesome as they are reported; I have received more Harm than Good at this Place.* Here rises the Temple (*e*) of the God (CNASH),[42] whose Walls are hung round with the Portraits of Beauties. The Apotheosis of this God hath cost many a poor Man his Heart.

Thus far, my Scholar, I have endeavoured to instruct thee in what Places thou art to hunt for thy Game, and where to spread thy Net. I will now proceed to shew thee by what means Puss is to be taken, when you have found her Sitting.[43] *Mind all*, as my old Schoolmaster used to say: for I assure you my Instructions will be worthy the Attention of both the Great Vulgar and the Small.

My first Lesson then is: Be confident. Believe every Woman is to be come at. Do but spread your Net, and I warrant she runs into it. Sooner shall the

[39] John Oldmixon (1673–1742), journalist and historian, was for HF the very type of the tedious, long-winded hackney author (cf. *Tom Jones* [V. i, p. 214 and n. 3]). In *The Covent-Garden Journal*, No. 3 (11 January 1752), HF asks: 'If I delight in a Slice of Bullock's Liver or of Oldmixon, why shall I be confined to Turtle or to Swift'? (p. 28). Among Oldmixon's voluminous works are *The Secret History of Europe* (1712–15), the *Critical History of England* (1724–6), and *The History of England* from the time of the Stuarts until the reign of George I (1729–35).

[40] Spas: Tunbridge Wells (Kent) enjoyed a vogue second only to Bath; Scarborough (Yorks.) had been renovated in 1738, after an earthquake destroyed it; Cheltenham (Glos.) opened in 1739; Holt (Leics.) had recently been promoted in *A Discourse on the Nature and Uses of Neville-Holt-Water* (1742).

[41] Cf. Pope in *The Rape of the Lock* (v. 61–2): 'O cruel Nymph! a living Death I bear, | Cry'd Dapperwit, and sunk beside his Chair'.

[42] Richard 'Beau' Nash (1674–1762), self-appointed master of ceremonies and 'King of Bath', who presided over polite society at the Guildhall and Pump Room. As early as 1743 HF in corresponding with his friend James Harris amused himself by playing with Nash's name, calling him 'Reg: CNASH', assimilating the name (as Amory notes) to the inscriptional form ('Cn.') of the Roman 'Gnaeus'—though on another occasion he called him the 'Great Snash' (*Correspondence*, pp. 33, 37). See also above, *Shamela*, p. 151 and n. 10.

[43] Cf. *Tom Jones* (VI. x), Squire Western's angry comment on Tom and Sophia: 'The Son of a Bitch was always good at finding a Hare sitting . . . I little thought what Puss he was looking after' (p. 305). On the bawdy connotations of hare-hunting, see above, *Shamela*, p. 187 n. 123.

Vere prius volucres taceant, æstate cicadæ,
  Mænalius lepori det sua terga canis,
Fœmina quam juveni blande tentata, repugnet:
  Hæc quoque, quam poteris credere nolle, volet.
Utque viro furtiva Venus, sic grata puellæ: 275
  Vir male dissimulat: tectius illa cupit.
Conveniat maribus, ne quam nos ante rogemus,
  Fœmina jam partes victa regantis agat.
Mollibus in pratis admugit fœmina tauro:
  Fœmina cornipedi semper adhinnit equo.   280

Fortior in nobis, nec tam furiosa libido est:
  Legitimum finem flamma virilis habet.
Byblida quid referam, vetito quæ fratris amore
  Arsit, & est laqueo fortiter ulta nefas?
Myrrha patrem, sed non ut filia debet, amavit,   285
  Et nunc obducto cortice pressa latet.
Illius & lacrymis, quas arbor fundit odora,
  Ungimur, & dominæ nomina gutta tenet.

Forte sub umbrosis nemorosæ vallibus Idæ
  Candidus armenti gloria taurus erat,   290
Signatus tenui media inter cornua nigro:
  Una fuit labes, cætera lactis erant.
Illum Gnossiadesque Cydoneæque juvencæ
  Optârunt tergo sustinuisse suo.
Pasiphaë fieri gaudebat adultera tauri: 295
  Invida formosas oderat illa boves.
Nota cano: non hoc, quæ centum sustinet urbes,
  Quamvis sit mendax, Creta negare potest.

281] The MSS divide, *Fortior/Parcior* ('lust is *stronger/soberer* in us'). HF seems to follow Crespin's gloss on *Fortior*, 'Men are not so powerless as women, who are more susceptible to lust' (trans. HA).

Birds be silent in the Spring, or the Frogs in the Winter:[44] Sooner shall the Greyhound run away from the Hare, than a Woman shall resist the Youth who gently assails her. Though she skrews up her Face ever so demurely, she will at length yield to his Persuasions. A dark Corner is as agreeable to a Girl, as to one of us, though we cannot so well dissemble our Desires as she can; but if we should once enter into a Confederacy against the Sex to leave off courting them, they would soon begin to act the Part of Lovers, and come a wooing us. And what is this but a natural Affection, common to the Females of every other Species, who often make love to the Males?

And give me leave to tell the Ladies, that we are more able to command our Affections, nor are our Desires so furious, and exceeding all Bounds, as theirs. The Story of *Byblis* (*f*) is too well known to be related, who being in love with her Brother, punished her Crime with her own Hands, and hanged herself in her Garters. Miss *Myrrhe* (*g*) loved her Papa with an Affection improper for a Daughter; for which she was turned into a Tree. I do assure you the Story is true; and the Tree now drops continual Tears for her Offence, which we use as a Perfume; and they retain the Lady's Name.

In the shady Valleys of *Ida* (*h*), there was a white Bull, which was the Glory of the Farmer to whom he belonged. This Bull had a beautiful black Speck between his Horns, all the rest of his Body being as white as Milk. With him the *Gnossian* and *Cydonian* Heifers were all in love, and eagerly longed to be embraced by him in the tenderest manner in which Bulls embrace the Fair Sex of Cows. *Pasiphaë*, I am very sorry to say it, conceived a Passion worse, if possible, than that of Mrs. *Mary Hamilton*,[45] for this Bull. Lady——is not more envied in the Drawing-Room than was every handsome Heifer by this unfortunate Woman. The Story is so well-known, that there is not a Freethinker (*i*) in the Age who can refuse his Credit to it, though they believe nothing which they cannot see and account for.[46]

---

[44] Amory, remarking that frogs hibernate in winter and citing *OED*, s.v. 'frog' 4b, suggests that HF, wanting a parallel for Ovid's line 271 (*aestate cicade* = cicadas in summer) plays on the sense of a 'frog' as a hacking cough.

[45] The sensational heroine of HF's *Female Husband* (above, pp. 355–81).

[46] Cf. the definition by 'Philomath' (probably HF) in *The Covent-Garden Journal*, No. 62 (16 September 1752): 'by a Freethinker I mean a Man who in the Old Testament, as well as in all other Writings, makes use of his Reason as a Guide, and will believe nothing contradictory to that or common Sense, and who does not put faith in Matters he does not comprehend' (p. 335). In *Amelia* (I. iii) HF characterizes Robinson as 'what they call a Freethinker, that is to say, a Deist, or, perhaps, an Atheist; for tho' he did not absolutely deny the Existence of a God; yet he entirely denied his Providence: A Doctrine which, if it is not downright Atheism, hath a direct Tendency towards it' (p. 30). Indeed, deism is a topic in all three of HF's major novels: see *Joseph Andrews* (III. iii) and *Tom Jones* (III. iii, XVIII. iv). See also below, HF's *Fragment of a Comment on Bolingbroke's Essays*, pp. 667–80.

Ipsa novas frondes, & prata tenerrima tauro
    Fertur inadsuetâ subsecuisse manu.   300
It comes armentis, nec ituram cura moratur
    Conjugis: & Minos à bove victus erat.
Quò tibi, Pasiphaë, pretiosas sumere vestes?
    Iste tuus nullas sentit adulter opes.
Quid tibi cum speculo montana armenta petenti?   305
    Quid toties positas fingis, inepta, comas?
Crede tamen speculo, quod te negat esse juvencam:
    Quàm cuperes fronti cornua nata tuæ!
Sive placet Minos, nullus quæratur adulter:
    Sive virum mavis fallere, falle viro.   310

In nemus & saltus thalamo regina relicto
    Fertur, ut Aonio concita Baccha Deo.
Ah quoties vultu vaccam spectavit iniquo,
    Et dixit, *Domino cur placet ista meo?*
Aspice ut ante ipsum teneris exsultet in herbis!   315
    Nec dubito, quin se stulta decere putet.
Dixit; & ingenti jamdudum de grege duci
    Jussit, & immeritam sub juga curva trahi;
Aut cadere ante aras commentaque sacra coëgit,
    Et tenuit lætâ pellicis exta manu.   320
Pellicibus quoties placavit numina cæsis?
    Atque ait exta tenens, *Ita, placete meo!*

Et modo se Europam fieri, modo postula Io,
    Altera quod bos est, altera vecta bove.
Hanc tamen implecit vaccâ deceptus acernâ   325
    Dux gregis; & partu proditus auctor erat.

Cressa Thyestæo si se abstinuisset amore,
    (O quantum est, uni posse placere viro!)
Non medium rupisset iter, curruque retorto
    Auroram versis Phœbus adisset equis.   330
Filia purpureos Niso furata capillos,
    Pube premit rabidos inguinibusque canes.

303] HF follows Heinsius' conjecture, *Quò*, though 'contrary to the [reading of the] codices' (*Quod/Quid*; trans. HA).

332] Some spurious verses found in the MSS and early editions, explaining the difference between the two Scyllas, are silently omitted here; see note (below, p. 458 n. (m)).

This poor Girl is reported to have mowed the sweetest Grass with her own Hands for her beloved Bull. She likewise wandered about among the Cows, without the least Regard to Mr. Alderman *Minos* her Husband; for a Bull had totally supplanted him in her Esteem. Alas! *Pasiphaë*, to what purpose are these brocaded Petticoats? Your Gallant is not sensible of your Finery. Why do you consult your Looking-Glass, in order to pursue the Mountain-Herds? Or why with so much Art do you set your *Tête*?[47] If you will consult your Glass, let it inform you you are no Heifer. Ah! how desirous are you to have those Horns on your own Forehead, which you intend to graft on your Husband's! It would be better to preserve your Virtue, and be constant to the Alderman, if you can like him: But if you must make a Cuckold of him, do it at least with a young Fellow.

No; nothing but a Bull will suffice. She leaves the Alderman's House, and flies away to the Groves and Mountains. To say the truth, I believe she used to drink away her Senses; and that is the best Excuse for her. Ah! how often hath she cast a jealous Eye on some Heifer! and cried out, *Why should that Vixen please my Love? Behold*, says she, *how the Slut dances a Minuet on the Grass before him: Let me die, but she is silly enough to think her Airs become her in my Love's Eyes*. At length she resolved to punish her Rivals. One Heifer she ordered barbarously to be yoked to the Plough; another she condemned to be sacrificed, and held the Entrails of the poor Victim in her Hand with all the insulting Triumph of a Rival: *Now*, says she, having the Entrails in her Hand, *now go and make yourself agreeable to my Dear*.

At one time she wishes to be *Europa* (*k*), at another *Io*: for one of these was herself the Wife of a Bull, and the other made her Horse of one. Filled with these Thoughts, she contrived the strangest Method of compleating her Desires. She sent for a Joiner of great Ingenuity, and ordered him to make her a large Cow of Wood. Into this she conveyed herself, and thus deceived Master Bull into her Embraces. She conceived by this monstrous Coition, and brought forth an Offspring, which by his partaking equally of the human and taurine Form, betrayed her horrid Passion.

If the *Cretan* Lady (*l*) had abstained from the Love of *Thyestes*, (O! how Women disdain Constancy to their Husbands!) the Sun had not stopt in the middle of his Career, and turned about his Face to the East, that he might avoid the bloody Banquet. God be praised! the Cuckolds of our Age are not so bloody in their Revenge. The Daughter of *Nisus* (*m*), who stole her Papa's Hair, feeds hungry Dogs in those Parts which first set her a longing for

---

[47] '*Tête*': 'A woman's head of hair . . . dressed high and elaborately ornamented' (*OED*).

Qui Martem terrâ, Neptunum effugit in undis,
  Conjugis Atrides victima dira fuit,
Cui non defleta est Ephyrææ flamma Creüsæ?   335
  Et nece natorum sanguinolenta parens?
Flevit Amyntorides per inania lumina Phœnix:
  Hippolytum pavidi diripuistis equi.
Quid fodis immeritis, Phineu, sua lumina natis?
  Pœna reversura est in caput ista tuum.   340
Omnia fœmineâ sunt ista libidine mota,
  Acrior est nostrâ, plúsque furoris habet.

Ergo age, nè dubita cunctas superare puellas:
  Vix erit è multis quæ neget una tibi.
Quae dant, quæque negant, gaudent tamen esse rogatæ: 345
  Ut jam fallaris, tuta repulsa tua est.
Sed cur fallaris, cum sit nova grata voluptas
  Et capiant animos plus aliena suis?
Fertilior seges est alienis semper in agris,
  Vicinumque pecus grandius uber habet.   350

Sed prius ancillam captandae nôsse puellæ
  Cura sit: accessus molliet illa tuos.
Proxima consiliis dominæ sit ut illa videto:
  Neve parum tacitis conscia fida jocis.
Hanc tu pollicitis, hanc tu corrumpe rogando: 355
  Quod petis, è facili, si volet illa, feres.
Illas legat tempus (medici quoque tempora servant)
  Quo facilis dominæ mens sit, & apta capi.
Mens erit apta capi tunc, cùm lætissima rerum,
  Ut seges in pingui luxuriabit humo.   360
Pectora dum gaudent nec sunt adstricta dolore,
  Ipsa patent; blandâ tum subit arte Venus:

Minos. *Agamemnon*, after returning safe from so many bloody Campaigns, and from the dangerous Seas which he crossed, fell at last a dreadful Victim to the Whore his Wife (*n*).

Who hath not wept at the sad Story of *Creüsa*? consumed by the Flames of a Sorceress, who afterwards drenched her Hands in the Blood of her own Children (*o*). *Phoenix* (*p*), the Son of *Amyntor*, hath often paid many a Tear for his Amours, though he had not the wretched Fate of *Hippolytus* (*q*), to be torn in pieces by wild Horses. And thou, O *Phineus* (*r*)! Why dost thou indulge that Jade *Harpalice*, by digging out the Eyes of thy Children? Believe me, Divine Vengeance will hereafter inflict the same Punishment on thyself. All these have been the Effects of Womens raging Desires, which are so much more violent and mad than ours.

Come on then, and doubt not the Conquest of any Girl whatever: There is not one in a thousand who will deny you. And even those who will deny you, love to be put to the Question; if you are disappointed therefore, your Repulse will be attended with no Danger. But why should you apprehend any Disappointment, when every new Amour pleases them, and they all hanker after the Lovers and Husbands of other Women? This I am afraid is too natural in all things. The Corn in our Neighbour's Field seems always to flourish beyond our own;[48] and we think our own Cow gives less Milk than his.

However, before you attack any Lady, make first sure of her Maid; for she will pave the Way to your Addresses. If the Lady have many Females about her Person, take care to secure her who is most in the Confidence of her Mistress; and who will faithfully betray to you all her private Conversation. When you have found this Confidant out, corrupt her with Promises and Intreaties; for she can soon bring you to the End of your Desires, if she pleases. Let her watch the Opportunity, (Physicians will tell you the Use of attending proper Seasons) when the Mind of your Mistress is easy, and apt for your Purpose. This Season, I apprehend, is when she is in the best Humour; for Love then becomes luxuriant in her Mind, as Corn doth in a rich Soil. When the Heart is full of Gladness, and bound up by no Vexation, it is open; and then the Compliments of a Lover will easily find an Admission. Remember, *Troy* was defended while it remained in a sullen Mood, and opened its Gates to the armed Horse, when it was full of Good-Humour, and drunk with Joy.

Yet every Vexation should not deter you; for if your Mistress should be uneasy at the Falshood of her Husband, then is a proper time to attack her,

---

[48] Tilley, N115.

Tum, cùm tristis erat, defensa est Ilios armis:
  Militibus gravidum læta recepit equum.

Tum quoque tentanda est, cum pellice læsa dolebit: 365
  Tunc facies operâ nè sit inulta tuâ.
Hanc matutinos pectens ancilla capillos
  Incitet: & et velo remigis addat opem.
Et secum tenui suspirans murmure dicat,
  Ut puto, non poteris ipsa referre vicem.   370
Tunc de te narret: tunc persuadentia verba
  Addat: & insano juret amore mori.
Sed propera, ne vela cadant, iræque residant:
  Ut fragilis glacies, interit ira morâ.

Quæris, an hanc ipsam prosit vitiare ministram?   375
  Talibus admissis alea grandis inest.
Hæc à concubitu fit sedula: tardior illa:
  Hæc dominæ munus comparat, illa sibi:
Causus in eventu est: licet hæc indulgeat ausis,
  Consilium tamen est abstinuisse meum.   380
Non ego per præceps & acuta cacumina vadam:
  Nec juvenum quisquam, me duce, captus erit.

Si tamen ill tibi, dum dat recipitque tabellas,
  Corpore, non tantùm sedulitate, placet,
Fac dominâ potiare priùs, comes illa sequetur.   385
  Non tibi ab ancilla est incipienda Venus.
Hoc unum moneo (si quid modo creditur arti,
  Nec mea dicta rapax per mare ventus agit)
Aut numquam tentes, aut perfice: tollitur index,
  Cùm semel in partem criminis illa venit.   390
Non avis utiliter viscatis effugit alis:
  Non bene de laxis cassibus exit aper.

373–4 'But be speedy, lest the sails sink and the breezes fail: like brittle ice, so perishes anger by delaying' (Loeb, reading *auraeque* with Heinsius). Did HF perhaps read *Ut friget glacies*? He does not translate *fragilis*, at any rate, transfers the mistress's *ira* to the lover, and renders *interit* etymologically as 'intervene', though its usual sense is 'perishes'.

and to assist her in revenging the Injury. When your Mistress is in this Humour, let *Abigail*[49] while combing her Hair at the Toilette in a Morning, stir her up to Vengeance. This will under-hand promote your Voyage: for while you openly manage your Sails, she works under the Water with her Oars. Now let *Abigail* with a soft Sigh mutter to her self: *Ah! poor Lady, I am afraid it is not in your power alone to revenge your Husband's Perfidy!* Then let her introduce a Discourse of you; let her say something in your Favour, and swear that you are gone distracted and dying for Love. But no Time must be lost; lest the Passions she hath raised should again subside; and Resentment intervene by Delay, and freeze up her Love as Ice doth Water.

And here perhaps you will ask a Question, Whether it is prudent to kiss the Agent herself. This is not easy to answer: for it is a mere Cast of the Dye, whether you succeed the better or the worse for it. One Woman is by Enjoyment made a more industrious Solicitor, another becomes just the reverse. One thinks of procuring the Pleasures she hath tasted for her Mistress, another of securing them herself. The Event is doubtful; and though she may be easy enough to be had, my Advice is, abstain from the Confidant: for I will not imitate the Empyric in striking bold Strokes;[50] nor will I lead my Scholars over a Precipice. I give no Advice but what is safe, nor shall any Youth by following my Precepts run himself into *Rosamond's Pond*.[51]

If therefore the Girl who goes between you and your Mistress, pleases you in her Person as well as in her Diligence; enjoy the Mistress first, and the Maid falls of course; but never begin with the latter. One thing however I must admonish you, (if my Art deserve any Credit, and my Words are to be regarded as any thing better than Wind) EITHER NEVER ATTEMPT THE CONFIDANT, OR GO THOROUGH STITCH WITH HER: for by making her *particeps criminis* you take away her Evidence.[52] This Doctrine you may learn from all other Sportsmen: for if a Bird escapes with Birdlime on his Wings, or a Boar breaks through the Toils, or a Fish gets off from the Hook; they are all sure to alarm their Companions, and spoil the Sport of the Fowler, the Hunter, or the Fisher. If once therefore you attempt her, press

---

[49] A conventional name for a lady's maid.

[50] Cf. *The Wedding Day* (IV. v), where Millamour says of physicians schooled at a university: 'Not one in fifty of them ever ventures to strike a bold stroke' (*Miscellanies* ii, p. 201).

[51] Situated near the south-west corner of St James's Park, Rosamond's Pond was 'long consecrated to disastrous love, and *elegiac* poetry' (*Rape of the Lock*, ed. Geoffrey Tillotson, citing Warburton's *Letters* [1805], Twickenham edn., ii, p. 400).

[52] To carry an action out completely (*OED*, s.v. 'thorough-stitch' B), thereby by making her an accomplice.

Saucius arrepto piscis retinetur ab hamo;
  Perprime tentatam, nec, nisi victor, abi.
Tunc neque te prodet communi noxia culpâ,   395
  Factaque erunt dominæ, dictaque nota tibi.
Sed bene celetur: bene si celabitur index,
  Notitiæ suberit semper amica tuæ.

Tempora qui solis operosa colentibus arva,
  Fallitur, & nautis aspicienda putat.   400
Nec semper credenda Ceres fallacibus arvis,
  Nec semper viridi concava puppis aquæ;
Nec teneras semper tutum est captare puellas:
  Sæpe dato meliùs tempore fiet idem.
Sive dies suberit natalis, sive calendæ,   405
  Quas Venerem Marti continuâsse juvat,
Sive erit ornatus, non ut fuit ante, sigillis,
  Sed regum expositas Circus habebit opes,
Differ opus: tunc tristis hyems, tunc Pleiades instant,
  Tunc tener æquoreâ mergitur Hœdus aquâ.   410
Tunc bene desinitur: tunc, si quis creditur alto,
  Vix tenuit laceræ naufraga membra ratis.
Tu licet incipias, quâ flebilis Allia luce
  Vulneribus Latiis sanguinolenta fuit,
Quâque die redeunt rebus minùs apta gerendis   415
  Culta Palaestino septima festa Syro.

Magna superstitio tibi sit natalis amicæ:
  Quâque aliquid dandum est, illa sit atra dies.
Cùm bene vitâris, tamen auferet: invenit artem
  Fœmina, quâ cupidi carpat amantis opes.   420
Institor ad dominam veniet discinctus emacem,
  Expediet merces teque sedente suas;
Quas illa, inspicias, sapere ut videare rogabit:
  Oscula deinde dabit: deinde rogabit, emas.
Hoc fore contentam multos jurabit in annos.   425
  Nunc opus esse sibi, nunc bene dicet emi.

her to it with all your Vigour, and never leave her till you have enjoyed her. For when once she is involved in the same Guilt with yourself, you are sure she will not betray you. Nay, you may be assured further, that she will betray every Word and Action of her Mistress to you. But take particular care not to blab any of the Secrets she discloses to you: for while her Mistress hath no Suspicion of her Confidant, she will be able to lay her entirely open to your Knowledge.

And now, to resume that Matter, believe me, he is deceived, who thinks that none but the Farmer and Mariner are obliged to regard the Seasons: for as it is not proper at all times to commit the Corn to the fallacious Fields, nor to trust your Vessel at all times to the green Ocean; so neither is it always safe to attack a tender Girl, for she will be taken at one time who will resist at another. If it be for instance her Birth-day (*s*), perhaps her Grand-mother hath instructed her to be particularly cautious on that day; so if it be the Day of the Week on which *Childermas* hath happened to fall that Year; or King *Charles's* Martyrdom:[53] defer the attack at all such Seasons. For to speak in Sea-Language, then is dirty Weather (*t*), then it blows a Hurricane; and if you weigh Anchor at that Season, you will be scarce able to keep your Keel downwards.

Above all avoid your Mistress's Birth-day; nor will it be more prudent in you to visit her first on the Morning of *Valentine's* Day (*u*), you will pay more for being her Valentine than it is worth. Indeed all Seasons which give them any Hint of receiving Presents should be carefully avoided: for be never so cautious and sneaking, have it of you she will. They all very well know the Art of squeezing a Lover who longs to squeeze them.

Mr. *Deards* will make his Appearance in his Silk Night-Gown,[54] and unbundle his Packet in your Presence. The Lady will then desire you to look over his Trinkets, (she can do no less, you know, in Compliment to your Taste:) then she will make you a Present of a Kiss, and afterwards desire you to buy it. *I promise you, my Dear*, says she, *if you will but buy me this single Jewel, I will not ask another of you the Lord knows how long; but I have really a present Occasion for this, and besides it is the cheapest Thing I ever saw.*

---

[53] Childermas (28 December), the festival of the Holy Innocents, commemorating the slaughter of the children by Herod (Matthew 2: 16), was considered an unlucky day (*OED*, s.v. 2, citing Swift's *Directions to Servants*). The anniversary (30 January) of the execution of Charles I in 1649, a holy day in the Church of England: cf. *Joseph Andrews*, (I. xvii, pp. 80–1).

[54] William Deards (d. 1761), fashionable jeweller, toyman, and pawnbroker in the Strand. References to Deards, who traded in elegant vanities and lent money at unconscionable rates of interest, begin in HF's writings with *The Miser* (1732; II. i) and after HF brought suit against him in November 1739 for some

Si non esse domi, quos des, causabere nummos,
   Littera poscetur—ne didicisse juvat.
Quid, quasi natali cùm poscit munera libo,
   Et quoties opus est, nascitur illa sibi?   430
Quid cùm mendaci damno mœstissima plorat,
   Elapsusque cavâ fingitur aure lapis?
Multa rogant reddenda dari, data reddere nolunt.
   Perdis, & in damno gratia nulla tuo est.
Non mihi, sacrilegas meretricum ut persequar artes,   435
   Cum totidem linguis sint satis ora decem.
Cera vadum tentet rasis infusa tabellis:
   Cera tuæ primum nuncia mentis eat.
Blanditias ferat illa tuas, imitataque amantum
   Verba, nec exiguas, quisquis es, adde preces.   440
Hectora donavit Priamo prece motus Achilles:
   Flecitur iratus, voce rogante, deus.

Promittas facito; quid enim promittere lædit?
   Pollicitis dives quilibet esse potest.

If you pretend to have no Money about you, the Answer is, *O, my Dear, you may give your Note: Mr.* Deards *will take your Note.* So that you may repent having learnt to write your Name. Then she adds, *O la, I had almost forgot, it is my Birth-day I am sure you will make me a Present on my Birth-day:* for they can be born every Day in the Year to serve their Purpose. Or else she pretends to have lost a Drop from her Ear-Ring; this Loss makes her miserable, and *Sure*, says she, *if you loved me, you would repair that Loss.*

Nay, some are not so honest as to desire a Present, they only borrow; but they are sure never to restore. By this means you lose the Thing without having the Merit of bestowing it. In short, if I had ten Mouths with ten Tongues in each,[55] all would not suffice to display all the Arts by which Harlots pick the Pockets of their Cullies.

Begin then your Amour with an Epistle; let that break the Ice for you, and make the first Discovery of your Flame. In this you may insert all your little Blandishments, and Expressions of Fondness, nor be ashamed, how-ever high your Quality[56] is, to add the strongest Entreaties. Remember that many a Rebel's Son hath had his Life spared at the Supplication of his Father; nay, the Wrath of Heaven itself is often averted by Prayer.[57]

It is moreover my Advice to you to be liberal of your Promises: for what Injury can you receive by Promising? This is a Treasure in which any Man

---

grievance (the nature of which is unknown but was probably financial) Deards became a regular target: in the *Vernoniad* (1741) he is a tradesman of the sort who, 'as we read in Scripture were driven out of the Temple' (*Champion*, p. 579); in *Joseph Andrews* (III. vi) he is the 'Artificer' whose workmen made the hero's cudgel (p. 239); there are satiric references to him in *A Journey from This World to the Next* (I. i; *Miscellanies* ii, p. 9), *Jonathan Wild* (II. iii; *Miscellanies* iii, p. 61), and *Tom Jones* (XII. iv, p. 632); and in *The Covent-Garden Journal*, No. 1 (4 January 1752) he is ironically labelled 'THE GREAT Mr. DEARD' (p. 16).

[55] A favourite topos of Latin poetry, ultimately derived from *Iliad* (ii. 489), where Homer wishes for ten tongues and ten mouths; in the *Aeneid* (vi. 625–7), the Sibyl declares that even if she had 'a hundred tongues, a hundred mouths, and voice of iron' she could not describe the torments of sinners in the underworld. HF also alludes to these passages in *Joseph Andrews* (II. xiii, p. 160), *Jonathan Wild* (IV. x; *Miscellanies* iii, p. 169), and *Tom Jones* (IV. v, p. 169).

[56] i.e. social rank or status.

[57] HF alters the sense of the original: 'Entreaty moved Achilles to give Hector back to Priam' (Loeb); but Hector was not a rebel, and it was his dead body that was returned to his father. Perhaps HF had in mind the case of the Jacobite rebel who was pardoned when his kinsman, an earl, interceded for him (Rupert C. Jarvis, *Collected Papers on the Jacobite Risings*, 2 vols. [Manchester, 1972], ii, pp. 295–9). The most remarkable case of clemency, however, was that of the third Earl of Cromarty (*c*.1703–1766), who, together with the Earl of Kilmarnock and Lord Balmerino (see above, n. 34), was sentenced to death on 1 August 1746; but, owing to the intercession of his wife and several influential Scottish nobles, he alone of the Jacobite lords received a 'respite' on 9 August (*Oxford DNB*). Cromarty was later exiled to Devon in February 1748, a judgment HF considered so lenient it deserved facetious comparison with the harshness of Ovid's banishment from Rome (*JJ*, No. 37 [13 August 1748], p. 480); see also below, Appendix C, p. 765 and n. 13).

Spes tenet in tempus, semel est si credita, longum: 445
  Illa quidem fallax, sed tamen apta dea est.
Si dederis quisquam, poteris ratione relinqui:
  Præteritum tulerit, perdideritque nihil.
At quod non dederis, semper videare daturus:
  Sic dominum sterilis sæpe fefellit ager.   450
Sic nè perdiderit, non cessat perdere lusor,
  Et revocat cupidas alea blanda manus.
Hoc opus, hic labor est, primò sine munere jungi:
  Ne dederit gratis quæ dedit, usque dabit.
Ergo eat, & blandis peraretur littera verbis,   455
  Exploretque animos, primaque tentet iter.
Littera Cydippen pomo perlata fefellit:
  Insciaque est verbis capta puella suis.

Disce bonas artes (moneo,) Romana juventus;
  Non tantùm trepidos ut tueare reos: 460
Quàm populus, judexque gravis, lectusque senatus,
  Tam dabit eloquio victa puella manus.
Sed lateant vires, nec sis in fronte disertus:
  Effugiant ceræ verba molesta tuæ.
Quis, nisi mentis inops, teneræ declamat amicæ?   465
  Sæpe valens odii littera causa fuit.

may be rich.[58] Nor can your Mistress complain that she is absolutely cheated, if you can bring her to believe your Promises. A lively Faith hath supported many a Man for a long time: for though our Faith may sometimes deceive us, it is however a great and commodious Virtue.

Beware of giving: for once your Mistress hath the Present in her Clutches, she may answer jilting you to her Prudence. She hath gained at least what she is in possession of, and cannot be said to have lost any thing by the Bargain. On the contrary, keep her still in Expectation. Seem always about to give, but never part with a Shilling: for in this manner doth a barren Soil often deceive its Owner. Thus, that he may not be a Loser, the Gamester pushes on his ill Luck, and one flattering Throw makes him eager to have the Box again in his Hands.

Indeed the great Business is to enjoy your Mistress before she hath touched you.[59] If she once yield to you gratis, she will continue to bestow her Favours still gratis, in hopes of being at last rewarded for all her past Favours. Epistolize therefore first;[60] flatter and sooth her with tender Lines. Let these probe her Mind, and open the Way for your Addresses. You know the Story of *Cydippe* (*w*), who was outwitted by a Letter inclosed in an Apple; by which means she was made to speak Words she never intended.

I would advise the young Gentlemen of the *Temple*[61] to study the Arts of Persuasion, on other accounts besides that of defending Sheep-stealers at an Assizes:[62] For a pretty Girl may be as easily captivated by Eloquence as a Judge or Jury; and surely she is a much nobler Prize. But here conceal your Art, and do not carry your Eloquence in your Face: And above all things, beware of hard Words; for who but an empty Coxcomb ever made a verbose Declamation to his Mistress? By such Methods you may raise her

---

[58] To exposing the character of the false 'PROMISER' HF devoted a pair of monitory paragraphs in 'An Essay of the Knowledge of the Characters of Men' (*Miscellanies* i, pp. 166–7) and a chapter and more in *Joseph Andrews* (II. xvi–xvii).

[59] 'touch': to 'tap' (a person) for money (*OED*, s.v. 'touch' v. 16b).

[60] HF appears to have heeded this advice in pursuing his own affairs. In a letter from Bath to James Harris (8 September 1741) he recalls a time when 'explaining' to his friend 'the clear Distinction between Love and Lust', he was 'interrupted by several fair Objects of both those Passions. Had I then proceeded, I should have told y°, as perhaps one Instance of their distinct Existence in my Mind, that nothing was ever more irksome to me than those Letters which I had formerly from the latter Motive written to Women, nor any thing more agreeable and delightful than I have always found this Method of conversing with the absent beloved Object. . . . For my own Part, I solemnly declare, I can never give Man or Woman with whom I have no Business (which the Satisfaction of Lust may well be called) a more certain Token of a violent Affection than by writing to them' (*Correspondence*, p. 11).

[61] i.e. those preparing at the Inner or (as in HF's case) Middle Temple for admission to the Bar.

[62] i.e. a county court, held twice a year before the circuit judges outside of London. Cf. the apprehension of the band of 'Sheep-stealers' in *Joseph Andrews* (III. ii, pp. 192–5); for anecdotes of horse-stealers before judges at an assize, see *Tom Jones* (VIII. xi, pp. 458–60) and below, *Voyage to Lisbon* (p. 560 and n. 54).

Sit tibi credilibis sermo consuetaque verba,
   Blanda tamen, præsens ut videare loqui.

Si non accipiet scriptum, illectumque remittet,
   Lecturam spera, propositumque tene.   470
Tempore difficiles veniunt ad aratra juvenci,
   Tempore lenta pati fræna docentur equi.
Ferreus assiduo consumitur annulus usu:
   Interit assiduâ vomer aduncus humo.
Quid magis est saxo durum? quid mollius unda?   475
   Dura tamen molli saxa cavantur aquâ.
Penelopen ipsam perstes modo, tempore vinces:
   Capta vides sero Pergama, capta tamen.

Legerit, & nolit rescribere, cogere noli:
   Tu modo blanditias fac legat ipsa tuas.   480
Quæ voluit legisse, volet rescribere lectis:
   Per numeros venient ista gradusque suos.
Fortisan & primo veniet tibi littera tristis,
   Quæque roget ne se sollicitare velis.
Quod rogat illa, timet: quod non rogat, optat ut instes: 485
   Insequere, & voti postmodo compos eris.

Interea sive illa toro resupina feretur,
   Lecticam dominæ dissimulanter adi.
Neve aliquis verbis odiosas afferat aures,
   Quàm potes ambiguis callidus abde notis.   490
Seu pedibus vacuis illi spatiosa teretur
   Porticus, hic socias tu quoque junge moras.
Et modo præcedas facito, modo terga sequaris;
   Et modo festines, & modo lentus eas.
Nec tibi de mediis aliquot transire columnis   495
   Sit pudor, & lateri continâsse latus.

Nec sine te curvo sedeat speciosa theatro:
   Quod spectes, humeris afferet illa suis.
Illam respicias, illam mirêre licebit:
   Multa supercilio, multa loquare notis.   500

Abhorrence more probably than her Love. Let your Passion appear credible, and disclose it in easy and common Language; it may be as tender and warm as you please; but preserve the Stile of Conversation.[63]

If she should not receive your Letter, but send it back unopened, hope for better Success another time, and maintain your Purpose. Time brings the stubborn Steer to bend his Neck to the Yoke, and the Horse to endure the Bridle. Iron Bonds and Ploughshares are worn out by constant Use. What is harder than a Rock? or what is softer than Water? And yet hard Rocks are hollowed by soft Water. *Penelope* herself in time might have been conquered. You see *Troy*, though it defended itself so long, was however taken at last.

If she reads your Letters, but is unwilling to answer them, do not attempt to compel her. If she but reads your Fondness, it is sufficient. If she will read, in time she will answer what she reads. All these Matters will be brought about in their own good time. Perhaps the first Answer she sends you will be a cruel one, and may desire you to quit all future Solicitations. She fears to be taken at her word, and hopes you will not grant her Request. Follow her, and in time you will obtain your Wishes.

If you meet her Chair, and the Curtains should be drawn, approach it as it were by accident; and when you discover her there, whisper something tender in her Ear; but whisper softly, lest the Chairman, or any other impertinent Person, should over-hear you. When she walks in the *Mall*, dangle after her, and interrupt her Walk with your Conversation. Here you will have an opportunity of seeing her Shape, and shewing yours, by sometimes walking behind, and sometimes before her. But for the most part keep even pace with her, whether she trips along briskly, or only saunters. Sometimes she will take a longer walk, as far perhaps as the second or third Stone. Hither follow her, and take every Opportunity of getting up close to her side.

Never let her go to the Play without attending her: No matter what the Play is, she will bring sufficient Entertainment for you with her. Here keep your Eyes always intent on her only, and admire every thing about her. By your Eyes, and by Signs, you may inform her of many things. Be sure to applaud greatly any amorous wanton Dance; and be no less favourable to those Scenes where the Business of Love is transacted, and almost brought to a Conclusion on the Stage: Many of which occur in *Congreve*, *Vanbrugh*

---

[63] Cf. HF's Preface to Sarah Fielding's *Familiar Letters*, where HF quotes this same 'Rule' of Ovid's (below, p. 475 and n. 3).

Et plaudas aliquam mimo saltante puellam:
 Et faveas illi, quisquis agatur amans.
Cum surgit, surges: donec sedet illa, sedebis;
 Arbitrio dominae tempora perde tuæ.
Sed tibi nec ferro placeat torquere capillos, 505
 Nec tua mordaci pumice crura teras.
Ista jube faciant, quorum Cybeleïa mater
 Concintur Phrygiis exululata modis.
Forma viros neglecta decet. Minoïda Theseus
 Abstulit, à nulla tempora comptus acu. 510
Hippolytum Phædra, nec erat bene cultus, amavit;
 Cura Deæ sylvis aptus Adonis erat.

Munditiæ placeant; fuscentur corpora campo;
 Sit bene conveniens & sine labe toga.
Linguaque ne rigeat, careant rubigine dentes; 515
 Nec vagus in laxâ pes tibi pelle natet.
Nec malè deformet rigidos tonsura capillos;
 Sit coma, sit doctâ barba resecta manu.
Et nihil emineant, & sint sine sordibus ungues;
 Inque cavâ nullus stet tibi nare pilus 520
Nec male ordorati sit tristis anhelitus oris;
 Nec lædat nares virque paterque gregis.
Cætera lascivæ faciant concede puellæ,
 Et si quis malè vir quaerit habere virum.

Ecce suum vatem Liber vocat, hic quoque amantes 525
 Adjuvat, & flammæ, quâ calet ipse, favet.
Gnossis in ignotis amens errabat arenis,
 Quà brevis æquoreis Dia feritur aquis.
Utque erat è somno tunicâ velata recinctâ,
 Nuda pedem, croceas irreligata comas; 530
Thesea crudelem surdas clamabat as undas,
 Indigno teneras imbre rigante genas:
Clamabat, flebatque simul (sed utrumque decebat)
 Nec facta est lacrymis turpior illa suis.
Jamque iterum tundens mollissima pectora palmis, 535
 Perfidus ille abiit, quid mihi fiet? ait.
Quid mihi fiet? ait: sonuerunt cymbala toto
 Littore, & attonitâ tympana pulsa manu.

501] MSS have *aliqua / aliquo* for *aliquam*; HF's text follows Heinsius' emendation.
515] The Latin is probably corrupt, and may refer to the 'tongue' or strap (*lingula*) and 'clasp' (*dens*) of footwear (cf. Goold, 'Amatoria', pp. 65–6).

and *Wycherly*.[64] If she rises between the Acts, rise also; if she sits, as sometimes Ladies do, to express their Contempt for the Audience, do you likewise keep your Seat. In a word, conduct yourself entirely according to her Example and Pleasure.

Now with regard to your Person: Do not imitate some finical *Petit Maître* in his *Toupet*,[65] much less in more detestable Effeminacies. Tuck your Hair rather under your Hat, like the rough Fox-Hunter, who traverses Hill and Dale to the Musick of the Horn. A careless Air in Dress becomes a Man. Colonel *Theseus* (x) carried off Miss *Ariadne* in a Campaign Wig without a single Curl in it.[66] In the same manner did Captain *Hippolytus* march off with Miss *Phædra*, though his Shock Head[67] of Hair never had any Powder in it: nay, Lady *Venus* herself chose your *Jack Adonis* in a Jockey Coat and Buckskin Breeches.

Cleanliness however is agreeable: Let your Face be burnt with the Sun; but let your Clothes be well made, and without a Spot on them. Wash your Mouth, and clean your Teeth often; let your Beard be close shaved, and your Nails short and free from Dirt. Observe these Documents,[68] and leave all other Niceties to the Women, and to Men who desire to supply their Places.

But now *Bacchus* summons his Poet. He likewise assists Lovers, and favours the Flame which warms himself. The *Cretan* Lady having jumped out of Bed in a raving Fit, wandered on the foreign Shore of *Dia*. She had nothing on but a loose wrapping Gown, without Stockings or Cap; and her Hair hung dishevelled over her Shoulders. She complained of the Cruelty of *Theseus* to the deaf Waves, whilst an unworthy Shower of Tears ran down her Cheeks. She wept, and lamented aloud, and both became her; nor did her Tears diminish her Beauty. Once and again, she beat her delicious Breasts with her Hands, and cried aloud, *The perfidious Man hath abandoned me; What will become of poor* Ariadne? *What will become of poor* Ariadne? On a sudden a vast Multitude was heard, while many kinds of strange

---

[64] The comic dramatists William Congreve (1670–1729), Sir John Vanbrugh (1664–1726), and William Wycherley (1641–1715). Though HF here appears to approve the complaints against their alleged indecency lodged by Jeremy Collier in *A Short View of the Immorality and Profaneness of the English Stage* (1698), he in fact regarded them as the best of the modern dramatists and indeed as models for his own plays. For his opinion of Congreve and Wycherley, see above, 'Cantos': p. 54 and n. 73, and p. 60 n. 106, respectively. For Wycherley as innovator of the comedy of wit whose example has proved to be inimitable, see above, Preface to *Plutus* (p. 256 and n. 24). In *Tom Jones* (XIV. i), HF praised Vanbrugh, together with Congreve, as a dramatist who 'copied Nature' (p. 742). For fuller accounts of HF's view of these three masters of comedy, see the articles on each in *Companion* (pp. 50, 150–1, 166).

[65] 'Toupet': a tuft of hair, esp. over the forehead (*OED*, s.v.).

[66] A campaign wig is plain, often named for one of Marlborough's battles (e.g. a 'Ramillies' wig).

[67] 'Shock Head': a head covered with a thick crop of hair (*OED*, s.v.).

[68] 'Documents': instructions (*OED*, s.v., obs.).

Excidit illa metu, rupitque novissima verba;
    Nullus in exanimi corpore sanguis erat.   540
Ecce Mimallonides sparsis in terga capillis;
    Ecce leves satyri, prævia turba Dei.
Ebrius ecce senex pando Silenus asello
    Vix sedet, & pressas continet arte jubas.
Dum sequitur Bacchus, Bacchæ fugiuntque petuntque,   545
    Quadrupedem ferulâ dum malus urget eques,
In caput aurito cecidit delapsus asello;
    Clamarunt satyri, *Surge, age, surge, pater.*
Jam Deus è curru, quem summum texerat uvis,
    Tigribus adjunctis aurea lora dabat.   550
Et color, & Theseus, & vox abiêre puellæ;
    Terque fugam petiit, terque retenta metu est.
Horruit ut steriles, agitat quas ventus, aristæ;
    Ut levis in madidâ canna palude tremit.
Cui Deus, *En adsum tibi cura fidelior*, inquit;   555
    Pone metum; Bacchi, Gnossias, uxor eris.
Munus habe cœlum; cœlo spectabere sydus;
    Sæpe reges dubiam, Cressa corona, ratem.

Dixit, & è curru, ne tigres illa timeret,
    Desilit: imposito cessit arena pede;   560
Implicitamque sinu (neque enim pugnare valebat)
    Abstulit; ut facilè est omnia posse deo.

Pars *Hymenæe* canunt; pars clamant *Evie, Evoe!*
    Sic coëunt sacro nupta Deusque toro.

557] HF seems to assume that Ariadne herself, not just her crown, was stellified, ignoring Heinsius'
emendation of *spectabere* to *spectabile*; and cf. *Jacobite's Journal*, No. 1 (5 December 1747): '*Ariadne's* Crown
in among the Constellations' (p. 94).

Instruments, like those of the miserable Masons,[69] accompanied the Voices. The poor Lady sunk with Fear, and suppressed her last Words; nor did the least Blood remain in her Countenance.

And now behold the *Bacchanalian* Women, with their Hair about their Ears, and the light Satyrs, who are always Forerunners of the God. Behold old Master *Silenus* (*y*) as drunk as a Piper,[70] riding on an Ass, which he is hardly able either to sit or guide. The old Gentleman, endeavouring to follow the *Bacchanalians*, who fly from him and towards him, sets spurs to his Ass, which being a vicious Beast, kicked up, and threw him over his Ears: upon which all the Satyrs set up a loud Shout, crying out, *Rise, Father, rise and be d——n'd to you.* And now the God himself, high mounted on his Four-Wheel Chaise, the top of which was adorned with Grapes, and which he drove himself, flung his golden Reigns over the Backs of his Pair of Tygers. Poor *Ariadne's* Colour forsook her Cheeks, and *Theseus* and her Voice at once deserted her Lips. Thrice she attempted to fly, and thrice being retained, she grew stiff with Fear, and stood trembling as Corn waves in the Field, or Reeds on the River Bank, when fanned by the Wind. To whom the God: *Behold, Madam, a more faithful Lover at your Feet: Fear nothing, Lady fair, you shall be the wife of* Bacchus. *The sky shall be your Dowry, where shining in a bright Constellation, by the Name of* Ariadne's *Crown, you shall often direct the doubtful Mariner's Passage.*

He said; and leaping from his Chariot, lest *Ariadne* should be afraid of the Tygers, the Sand sunk under the Weight of his Feet; and catching her instantly in his Arms, he carried her, who was incapable of scratching, directly off; (for every thing, we know, is in the power of a Deity). And now, whilst Part of his Train sing the *Hymenaeum*, and others cry *Evie, Evoe*, two very mysterious Words, and full of Masonry,[71] the God and his new-ravished Bride go together between a Pair of sacred Sheets.

---

[69] 'The Scald-Miserable Masons' ('scald miserable' having the sense of 'despicable wretch' [*OED*, s.v. 'scald' adj. 2]) were the invention of the virulent Tory satirist Paul Whitehead (1710–74) and a certain Squire Carey (1710–56), surgeon and political agent, who in March 1741 mocked the Freemasons' annual parade by staging a burlesque procession of ragamuffins, notable for loud, wild music and ridiculous costumes. See BL, *Catalogue of Political and Personal Satires*, by F. S. Stephens *et al.*, nos. 2494, 2546, and 2548–9; also HF's comment in *JJ*, No. 4 (26 December 1747), p. 449.

[70] Very drunk, with reference esp. to a Scots bagpiper (*OED*, s.v. 'piper' 1b).

[71] From the first number of *The Jacobite's Journal* (5 December 1747) HF will liken the 'Mysteries' of Jacobitism to those of 'Free Masonry' (p. 95). In No. 6 (9 January 1748), recalling the present passage from Ovid, he likens the Jacobites, wild *'Highlanders'*, to 'ancient *Bacchanalians*' and their 'mysterious . . . Rites': 'The *Iacchites* are said to have made the Air resound with the Words EVOHE IACCHE: Now do not the modern *Jackites*, or *Jacobites*, at all their Meetings, make the Air ring with the same Word *Evohe*, or *Evoy*' (p. 125).

Ergo, ubi contigerint positi tibi munera Bacchi,   565
   Atque erit in socii fœmina parte tori,
Nycteliumque patrem, nocturnaque sacra precare,
   Ne jubeant capiti vina nocere tuo.
Hic tibi multa licet sermone licentia ficto
   Dicere, quæ dici sentiat illa sibi;   570
Blanditiasque leves tentui prescribere vino,
   Ut dominam in mensâ se legat illa tuam;
Atque oculos oculis spectare fatentibus ignem,
   Sæpe tacens vocem verbaque vultus habet.
Fac primus rapias illius tacta labellis   575
   Pocula; quaque bibit parte puella, bibas.
Et quemcumque cibum digitis libaverit illa,
   Tu pete: dumque petes, sit tibi tacta manus.
Sint etiam tua vota, viro placuisse puellæ;
   Utilior votis factus amicus erit.   580
Huic, si forte bibas, sortem concede priorem:
   Huic detur capiti dempta corona tuo.
Sive sit inferior, seu par, prior omnia sumat:
   Neu dubites illi verba secunda loqui.

Tuta frequensque via est, per amici fallere nomen: 585
   Tuta frequensque licet sit via, crimen habet.
Inde propinator nimium quoque multa propinet,
   Et sibi mandatis plura bibenda putet.
Certa tibi à nobis dabitur mensura bibendi:
   Officium præstent mensque pedesque suum.   590
Jurgia præcipuè vino stimulata caveto,
   Et nimium faciles ad fera bella manus.
Occidit Eurytion stulte data vine bibendo:
   Aptior est dulci mensa merumque joco.

Si vox est, canta; si mollia brachia, salta: 595
   Ut quacunque potes dote placere, place.

Whenever therefore you happen to be in company with a pretty Girl over a Bottle, pray heartily to *Bacchus*, and invoke his nocturnal Rites, that the Wine may not get into your Head. You may now take an opportunity to toast some Nymph by a fictitious Name, of whom you may say an hundred amorous things; all which, with the least Assistance, she will readily apply to herself. Double Entendres likewise may be used. You may moreover draw certain Figures in Wine on the Table; and after having spoken of your Mistress in the third Person, you may take this Method of writing her Name, and convincing her, that she herself is the Goddess. But let your gloating Eyes inform her of your Passion: for an expressive Countenance often finds both Words and Utterance. When she drinks, receive the Cup from her; and let her see you industrious to find out the Place before pressed by her Lips; and then drink eagerly at the same. And whatever Part of the Meat she shall touch with her Fingers, do not fail to give the preference to that: if in catching at it, you touch her Hand into the bargain, it is the better.

But above all things, let it be your Endeavour to please her Keeper, if she have any: for to make a Friend of him will be very useful to you both. When you are at Table, let him be always helped first, and to the most elegant Tid-Bit; and when you drink together, offer him always the Place of Toast-maker; whether he be your Inferiour or your Equal, let him always choose before you, and be not ashamed to trowel him well over with Flattery.

It is a safe and common way to deceive under Pretence of Friendship; I must own, however safe and common it is, it is not altogether blameless. This is indeed a Dishonesty not very unlike that of a Major Domo, who under the Colour of Friendship empties your Cellars of your Wine by pushing the Bottle further than is necessary.

Now to fix a certain Stint to your Cups, I allow you never to drink till your Head becomes giddy, and your Feet begin to totter. Beware of Quarrels, which are often occasioned by Wine. Let not your Hands be too ready to strike in your Cups. Remember the old Story of the Wedding of *Pyrithous* (*z*), and many more where drunken Fools by being quarrelsome in their Liquor have come short home.[72] A drinking Bout is in reality a properer Scene for Joke and Mirth, than for Fighting.

I proceed to other Lessons (*a*). If you have a Voice, then sing; if you have handsome Legs, cut Capers, or slide into the Minuet Step. In short, endeavour to please your Mistress, by exerting those Talents in which Nature hath given you to excel. Now, as real Drunkenness may be hurtful to

---

[72] 'come short home': come to grief (*OED*, s.v. 'home' adv., 7c).

Ebrietas ut vera nocet, sic ficta juvabit;
  Fac titubet blæso subdola lingua sono.
Et quicquid dicas faciasve protervius aequo,
  Credatur nimium causa fuisse merum.   600
Et bene dic dominæ, bene, cum quo dormiet illa;
  Sed male sit, tacitâ mente precare viro.
At cum discedet mensâ conviva remotâ,
  Ipsa tibi accessus turba, locumque dabit.
Insere te turbæ, leviterque admotus eunti   605
  Velle latus digitis, & pede tange pedem.
Colloquio jam tempus adest. Fuge rustice longe
  Hinc pudor; audacem Forsque Venusque juvant.
Non tua sub nostras veniet facundia leges;
  Fac tantum incipias, sponte disertus eris.   610
Est tibi agendus amans, imitandaque vulnera verbis:
  Haec tibi quæratur qualibet art fides.

Nec credi labor est; sibi quæque videtur amanda;
  Pessima sit, nulli non sua forma placet.
Sæpe tamen vere coepit simulator amare;   615
  Sæpe, quod incipiens finxerat esse, fuit.
Quo magis ô faciles imitantibus este, puellæ;
  Fiet amor verus, qui modo fictus erat.

Blanditiis animum furtim deprendere fas sit,
  Ut pendens liquidâ ripa subitur aquâ.   620
Nec faciem, nec pigeat laudare capillos,
  Et teretes digitos, exiguumque pedem.
Delectant etiam castas præconia formæ:
  Virginibus curæ grataque forma sua est.
Nam cur in Phrygiis Junonem & Pallada sylvis   625
  Nunc quoque judicium non tenuisse pudet?

601] Heinsius: 'I think we should write *dominam*, even contrary to the [reading of the] codices [i.e. *dominae*]; Burmann: 'I will not budge contrary to the [reading of the] codices' (HA trans.). Whether *benedicere* takes the accusative or the dative only slightly affects the sense: 'Here's luck . . . to the lady' (Loeb), with the dative; 'Your health, lady' with the accusative (*dominam*); HF seems to favour the dative, following Burmann.

620] Both HF and Dryden give the requisite sense, though the right reading (*subestur*) was only recovered in the twentieth century (Axelson, *Hermes*, 86 (1958), pp. 127–8).

you, so you may sometimes reap Advantages by pretending yourself in Liquor, by Stammering or Lisping a little slyly: for then if you should descend to some Expressions of the grosser kind, it will be imputed to your having taken a Cup too much. Drink Bumpers to the Health of your Mistress, and of the Gentleman with whom she is obliged to sleep; but I do not insist on your being extremely sincere on this Occasion: for you may heartily wish him hanged at the same time, if you please. When the Company rises to go away, there is always a Confusion in the Room, of which you may take advantage. You may then creep close up to your Mistress, may perhaps palm her,[73] and gently tread on her Toes.

Whenever you have an Opportunity of speaking to her privately, be not bashful like a Country Boobily[74] Squire. Remember Fortune and Love both favour the Bold. I do not intend to lay down any Rules for your Oratory on this Occasion. Do but begin boldly, and you will be Eloquent of course: Set this only before you, that you are to act the part of a Lover, to talk of Wounds and Darts, and Dying and Despair, and all that, as Mr. *Bayes* says:[75] for if you can once make her believe you are in love, your Business is done. To create therefore this Faith in her, you must employ every Art of which you are Master.

Nor is this indeed so difficult a Task: for every Woman believes herself to be the Object of Love; be she never so ugly, she is still amiable in her own Eye. Sometimes indeed no Deceit is in the End put on the Woman, for her pretended Lover becomes often a real one, and is the very Creature which he before personated. And by the way, young Ladies, let me tell you this is no small Encouragement to you, to countenance such Pretences; for if you manage well, you may often inspire a Man with Love in earnest, while he is endeavouring to impose a fictitious Passion upon you.

But to return to my Scholars. Flatter with all your might: for the Mind is taken as it were by Stealth, by Flattery, even as the Bank which hangs over a River is undermined by the liquid Waves. Never be weary therefore of commending her Face, or her Hair; her taper Arm, or her pretty little Foot. The chastest Matrons are fond of hearing the Praises of their Beauty; and the purest Virgins make the Charms of their Persons at once their Business and their Pleasure. What else is meant by that ancient Fable of *Juno* and *Pallas*, whom the *Greek* Poets represent as yet ashamed of the Conquest obtained by *Venus*? This Vanity seems to extend itself to Animals, in many

---

[73] Stroke with the hand (*OED*).

[74] Boobyish, booby-like (*OED*, s.v., obs.).

[75] The hero of the Duke of Buckingham's farce *The Rehearsal* (1672): Bayes's simile 'alludes to passion, to consuming, to dying, and all that, which, you know, are the natural effects of an amour' (II. iii).

Laudatus ostendit avis Junonia pennas:
   Si tacitus spectes, illa recondit opes.
Quadrupedes inter rapidi certamina cursus,
   Depexæque jubæ, plausaque colla juvant.   630
Nec timide promitte: trahunt promissa puellas.
   Pollicitis testes quoslibet adde deos.
Jupiter ex alto perjuria ridet amantum,
   Et jubet Æolios irrita ferre notos.
Per Styga Junoni falso jurare solebat   635
   Jupiter: exemplo nunc favet ipse suo.
Expedit esse deos; &, ut expedit, esse putemus;
   Dentur in antiquos thura merumque focos.
Nec secure quies illos similisque sopori
   Detinet; innocui vivite, numen adest.   640
Reddite depositum; pietas sua fœdera servet:
   Fraus absit; vacuas cædis habete manus.
Ludite, si sapitis, solas impune puellas;
   Hac minus est unâ fraude pudenda fides.
Fallite fallentes; ex magna parte profanum   645
   Sunt genus; in laqueos, quos posuere, cadant.

Dicitur Ægyptos caruisse juvantibus arva
   Imbribus, atque annos sicca fuisse novem;
Cum Thrasius Busirin adit, monstratque piari
   Hospitis effuso sanguine posse Jovem;   650

644] Most MSS read *magis . . . pudenda*. HF partially adheres to the reading of Navagero, *minus . . . tuenda* (i.e. 'keep faith save for this one deceitfulness', Loeb).

of which we may observe some Traces of it. The Peacock, if you seem to admire her, spreads forth her Golden Plumes, which she never displays to an indifferent Spectator. The Race-Horse, while he is running for a Plate, enjoys the Beauties of his well-combed Mane, and gracefully turned Neck.

Secondly, to Flattery add Promises, and those not timorous nor sneaking ones. If a Girl insists upon a Promise of Marriage, give it her, and bind it by many Oaths*: for no Indictment lies for this sort of Perjury. The Antients vented horrid Impieties on this Occasion, and introduced *Jupiter* shaking his Sides at the Perjuries of Lovers, and ordering the Winds to puff them away: Nay, he is said to have forsworn himself even by *Styx* to *Juno*; and therefore, say they, he encourages Men to follow his Example.[76] But though a *Christian* must not talk in this manner, yet I believe it may be one of those Sins which the Church of *Rome* holds to be venial, or rather venal.[77]

I would here by no means be suspected of Infidelity or Profaneness. It is necessary there should be a God; and therefore we must believe there is; nay, we must worship him: for he doth not possess himself in that indolent State in which the Deities of *Epicurus* are depictured. If we live innocent Lives, we may depend on the Care of his Providence.[78] Restore faithfully whatever is deposited in your Hands: Be just in all your Contracts: Avoid all kind of Fraud, and be not polluted with Blood. A wise Man will be a Rogue only among the Girls: for in all other Articles a Gentleman will be ashamed of breaking his Word. And what is this more than deceiving the Deceivers? The Sex are for the greatest part Impostors; let them therefore fall into the Snares which they have spread for others.

Perhaps you have never read the Justice of *Busiris*; when *Egypt* was burnt up nine Years together for want of Rain, one *Thrasius* a Foreigner came to Court, and being introduced to the King by *Clementinus Cotterelius*,[79] he acquainted his Majesty, that *Jupiter* was to be propitiated by

---

* This is the most exceptionable Passage in the whole Work. We have endeavoured to soften it as much as possible; but even as it now stands, we cannot help expressing our Detestation of this Sentiment, which appears shocking even in a Heathen Writer.

---

[76] '*Jupiter* shaking his Sides . . . his Example' is paraphrased in *JJ*, No. 15 (12 March 1748), pp. 190–1.

[77] Protestants rejected the distinction between mortal sins, which entail damnation if not confessed, and venial sins, which may be expiated by temporal penalties (*New Catholic Encyclopedia*). By the pun, HF appears to allude to the Roman Catholic doctrine of Indulgences, allegedly the granting of remission of sins for a pecuniary contribution.

[78] HF adapts Ovid's 'gods' to the Christian context of 'a God' and 'his Providence'. The Greek philosopher Epicurus (341–270 BC), a materialist, taught that if the gods exist, they do not concern themselves with the affairs of mankind.

[79] Sir Clement Cotterel (d. 1758), Master of the Ceremonies of the King's Household. In *Jonathan Wild* (II. xii), he is featured in Proverb II (*Miscellanies* iii, p. 84).

Illi Busiris, Fies *Jovis hostia primus*,
    Inquit, *& Ægypto tu dabis hospes aquam.*
Et Phalaris tauro violenti membra Perilli
    Torruit; infelix imbuit auctor opus.
Justus uterque fuit; neque enim lex æquior ulla est,   655
    Quàm necis artifices arte perire suâ.
Ergo (ut perjuras merito perjuria fallant)
    Exemplo doleat fœmina laesa suo.

Et lacrymæ prosunt; lacrymis adamanta movebis;
    Fac madidas videat, si potes, illa genas.   660
Si lacrymæ (neque enim veniunt in tempore semper)
    Deficient, uda lumina tange manu.
Quis sapiens blandis non misceat oscula verbis?
    Illa licet non det, non data sume tamen.
Pugnabit primo fortassis, *& Improbe!* dicet;   665
    Pugnando vinci se tamen illa volet.
Tantum ne noceant teneris male rapta labellis,
    Neve queri possit dura fuisse, cave:

Oscula qui sumpsit, si non & cætera sumet,
    Hæc quoque, quae data sunt, perdere dignus erat.   670
Quantum defuerat pleno post oscula voto!
    Hei mihi, rusticitas non pudor ille fuit.
Vim licet appellent; grata est vis ista puellis;
    Quod juvat, invitae sæpe dedisse volunt.
Quæcunque est subitâ Veneris violata rapinâ   675
    Gaudet, & improbitas muneris instar habet:
At quæ, cum posset cogi, non tacta recessit,
    Ut simulet vultu gaudia, tristis erit.

Vim passa est Phœbe; vis est illata sorori:
    Et gratus raptis raptor uterque fuit.   680

the Blood of a Stranger. The King answered him, *Then thou thyself shalt be the first Victim, and with thy foreign Blood shalt give Rain to* Egypt. To the same purpose is the Story of *Phalaris*, who roasted the Limbs of *Perillus* in his own Bull: Thus making proof of the Goodness of the Work by the Torments of the unhappy Maker. Now there was great Justice in both these Examples; for nothing can be more equitable than that the Inventors of Cruelty should perish by their own Art. To apply this to our present Purpose: As there is no Deceit or Perjury which Women will stick at putting in use against us, let them lament the Consequence of their own Examples.

Thirdly, Tears are of great Service. The Proverb tells you, *Tears will move Adamant.*[80] If you can bring it about therefore, let your Mistress see your Cheeks a little blubbered upon occasion. If Tears should refuse to come (as they sometimes will) an Onion in your Handkerchief will be of great use.[81]

Fourthly, Kisses. What Lover of any Sense doth not mix Kisses with his tender Expressions! Perhaps she will not give them easily: No matter, take them without her leave. Perhaps she will scratch, and say you are rude: notwithstanding her Scratches, she will be pleased with your getting the better. Do this, however, in so gentle a manner, that you may not hurt her tender Lips; nor let her complain of being scrubbed with your Beard.

Now when you have proceeded to Kisses, if you proceed no farther, you may well be called unworthy of what you have hitherto obtained. When you was at her Lips, how near was you to your Journey's End! If therefore you stop there, you rather deserve the Name of a bashful 'Squire than of a modest Man. The Girls may call this perhaps Violence; but it is a Violence agreeable to them: for they are often desirous of being pleased against their Will: For a Woman taken without her Consent, notwithstanding her Frowns, is often well satisfied in her Heart, and your Impudence is taken as a Favour; whilst she who, when inclined to be ravished, hath retreated untouched, however she may affect to smile, is in reality out of humour.

Ravishing is indeed out of fashion in this Age; and therefore I am at a loss for modern Examples; but ancient Story abounds with them.[82] Miss (*b*) *Phœbe* and her Sister were both ravished, and both were well pleased with the Men who ravished them. Though the Story of *Deidamia* was formerly

---

[80] HF's 'Proverb' seems to have originated with Ovid: 'lacrymis adamanta movebis'; it has eluded a search in the usual sources.

[81] The Latin merely advises, 'touch your eyes with a wet hand' (Loeb). HF may recall *The Taming of the Shrew* (Induction, lines 125–6): 'To rain a shower of commanded tears, | An onion will do well.'

[82] Cf. *Tom Jones* (xv. iv), as Lady Bellaston mocks Fellamar for baulking at her proposal that he ravish Sophia: 'Fie upon it! Have more Resolution. Are you frightened by the Word Rape? . . . Well, if the Story

Fabula nota quidem, sed non indigna referri,
  Scyrias Hæmonio juncta puella viro.
Jam Dea laudatæ dederat sua præmia formæ,
  Colle sub Idæo vincere digna Venus;
Jam nurus ad Priamum diverso venerat orbe,   685
  Graiaque in Iliacis mœnibus uxor erat;
Jurabant omnes in læsi verba mariti,
  Nam dolor unius publica causa fuit.
Turpe, nisi hoc matris precibus tribuisset, Achilles
  Veste virum longâ dissimulatus erat.   690
Quid facis, Æacide? non sunt tua munera lanae;
  Tu titulos aliâ Palladis arte petas,
Quid tibi cum calathis? clypeo manus apta tenendo ;
  Pensa quid in dextrâ, quâ cadet Hector, habes?
Rejice succintos operoso stamine fusos;   695
  Quassanda est ista Pelias hasta manu.

in all the *Trojan* News-Papers, yet my Reader may be pleased to see it better told. *Venus* had now kept her word to *Paris*, and given him the Beauty she had promised, not as a Bribe, but as a Gratification for his having made an Award in her favour, in the famous Cause between *Juno* and others against *Venus*, in *Trover*[83] for a Golden Apple; which was referred to him at the Assizes at *Ida*. *Paris*, every one knows, no sooner had received Mrs. *Helen*, than he immediately carried her off to his Father's Court. Upon this the *Grecians* entered into an Association; and several Noblemen raised Regiments at their own Expence, out of their Regard to the Public:[84] For Cuckoldom was a public Cause, no one knowing whose Turn it would be next.

Lieutenant-General *Achilles*, who was to command a large Body of Grenadiers, which the *Greeks* call *Myrmidons*, did not behave handsomely on that Occasion, though he got off afterwards at a Court-Martial by pleading, that his Mother (who had a great deal in her own power) had insisted on his acting the Part he did; for, I am ashamed to say, he dressed himself in Womens Clothes, and hid himself at the House of one *Lycomedes*, a Man of good Fortune in those Parts. *Fie upon it, General, I am ashamed to see you sit quilting among the Girls; a Sword becomes your Hands much better than a Needle. What can you mean by that Work-Basket in a Hand by which Count* Hector *is to fall? Do you carry that Basket with you to put his Head in? For shame, then, cast away your Huswife,*[85] *and all those effeminate Trinkets from a Fist able to wield* Harry the Fifth's Sword.[86]

of *Helen* was modern, I should think it unnatural. I mean the Behaviour of *Paris*, not the Fondness of the Lady; for all Women love a Man of Spirit. There is another Story of the *Sabine* Ladies,—and that too, I thank Heaven, is very ancient. . . . I fancy few of my married Acquaintance were ravished by their Husbands' (pp. 794–5).

[83] Amory comments: Trover is a highly fictionalized form of action, in which 'the Plaintiff in his Declaration surmises, that he lost such and such Goods, and that the Defendant found them, and at such a Place converted them to his own Use: But here the losing is only a mere Suggestion, and in no Respect material'—indeed, neither the loss nor the finding might be contested in court (Giles Jacob, *New Law-Dictionary* [1743]). In 'trover', however, the plaintiff sues for the *value* of the apple, not for the fruit itself; by rights, Juno should have proceeded in 'detinue'. The fiction of 'finding' (= Law French *trover*) clearly amused HF, who later wondered whether an actual finder, though not the true owner, may bring trover to recover damages from a third party who detains the goods (*Tom Jones* [XII. iv, p. 632]; see also *Amelia* [1. xi, p. 61]). The leading case, *Armory* v. *Delamirie*, decided by Chief Justice Pratt in 1722, held for the finder, but Sir John Strange's report of it was not published until 1755 (*English Reports: Full reprint*, 178 vols. [1900–32], xliii, p. 664).

[84] HF alludes to the irregular regiments mustered by County associations and individual noblemen in September–October 1745, following the Jacobite victory at Prestonpans; they never saw action, however (W. A. Speck, *The Butcher* [Oxford, 1981], 778).

[85] 'Huswife': a pocket-case for needles, pins, thread, scissors, etc. (*OED*, s.v. 'housewife' 3, earliest citation is 1749).

[86] HF continues the analogy between Achilles and the Duke of Cumberland, 'William the Avenger' (above, p. 413 and n. 36), who, after the British defeat at Fontenoy, is to repeat, in a contemporary setting, Henry V's victory over the French at Agincourt (1415).

Forte erat in thalamo virgo regalis eodem;
  Hæc illum strupro comperit esse virum.
Viribus illa quidem vincta est; (ita credere oportet)
  Sed voluit vinci viribus illa tamen.   700

Sæpe, *Mane!* dixit, cum jam properaret Achilles;
  Fortia nam posita sumpserat arma colo.
Vis ubi nunc illa est? Quid blanda voce moraris
  Auctorem stupri, Deidamia, tui?

Scilicet, ut pudor est, quiddam cœpisse priorem;   705
  Sic alio gratum est incipiente pati.
Ah nimia est propriæ juveni fiducia formæ!
  Expectet si quis, dum prior illa roget.
Vir prior accedat; vir verba precantia dicat;
  Excipiet blandas comiter illa preces.   710
Ut potiare, roga; tantùm cupit ill rogari:
  Da causam voti principiumque tui.
Jupiter ad veteres supplex heroïdas ibat;
  Corripuit magnum nulla puella Jovem.

Si tamen à precibus tumidos accedere flatus   715
  Senseris, incepto parce, referque pedem.
Quod refugit, multæ cupiunt: odêre quod instat,
  Lenius instando tædia tolle tui.
Nec spec est Veneris semper profitenda roganti;
  Intret amicitæ nomine tectus amor.   720

It happened, that at the same time when the General, at the House of 'Squire *Lycomedes*, performed this Feat, Miss *Deidamia*, one of the Maids of Honour, was visiting at the same Place. This young Lady soon discovered that the General was a Man; for indeed he got her Maidenhead. He ravished her, that is the truth o'nt; that a Gentleman ought to believe in favour of the Lady: but he may believe the Lady was willing enough to be ravished at the same time.[87]

When the General threw away his Needle, and grasped the Armour, (you must remember the Story, for it was in the *Trojan Alamain*[88]) the young Lady began to change her Note, and to hope he would not forsake her so. *Ah! little* Mia! *is this the Violence you complained of? Is this the Ravisher you are afraid of? Why with that gentle Voice do you solicit the Author of your Dishonour to stay with you?*

To come at once to the Moral of my Story; as they are ashamed to make the first Advances, so they are ready to suffer whatever a pushing Man can do unto them. As for those pretty Master-Misses,[89] the *Adonis's* of the Age, who confide in their own Charms, and desire to be courted by the Girls, believe me, they will stay long enough before they are asked the Question. If you are a Man, make the first Overtures: Remember, it is the Man's Part to address the Fair; and it will be her's to be tenderly won. Be bold then, and put the Question; she desires no more than to have the Question put; and sure you will not deny your own Wishes that Favour. *Jupiter* himself went a courting to the Heroines of old: for I never heard of any Girl who courted him.

But if you find Madam gives herself any immoderate Airs at your Proposal, it will then be good to recede a little from your Undertaking, and to affect to steer off: for many of them, according to the Poet,

Pursue what flies, and fly what doth pursue.[90]

A short Absence will soon cure her Disdain. It may be proper likewise to conceal your Intentions a little at first, and make your first Advance under the Pretence of *Platonic* Friendship. I have known many a Prude taken

---

[87] Cf. *Jonathan Wild* (III. vii), where Fireblood lusts after Laetitia: 'he in a few Minutes ravished this fair Creature, or at least would have ravished her, if she had not, by a timely Compliance, prevented him' (p. 109).
[88] Short for 'nouvelles à la main', newsletters (usually scandalous): *Trésor de la langue française*, s.v. 'main', I.H.1.b. The Paris *alamain* was often cited in London newspapers.
[89] Cf. William Pulteney's characterization of the effeminate Lord Hervey, HF's target in *Shamela* (above, p. 149 n. 1), as 'a pretty, little, *Master-Miss*' (*A Proper Reply to a Late Scurrilous Libel* [1731], p. 6), echoed in Pope's portrait of Hervey as 'Sporus' (*Epistle to Dr. Arbuthnot* [1735], line 324).
[90] Cf. the lesson Ford has learned in Shakespeare's *Merry Wives of Windsor* (II. ii. 215–16): 'Love like a shadow flies when substance love pursues, | Pursuing that that flies, and flying what pursues.'

Hoc aditu vidi tetriæ data verba puellæ;
  Qui fuerat cultor, factus amator erat.

Candidus in nautâ turpis color; æquoris undâ
  Debet & à radiis syderis esse niger.

Turpis & agricolæ, qui vomere semper adunco   725
  Et gravibus rostris sub Jove versat humum.

Et tu, Palladiæ petitur cui fama coronæ,
  Candida si fuerint corpora, turpis eris.

Palleat omnis amans; color hic est aptus amanti;
  Hic decet; hoc vultu non valuisse putent.   730

Pallidus in Lyrice sylvis errabat Orion;
  Pallidus in lentâ Naïde Daphnis erat.

Arguat & macies animum; nec turpe putâris
  Palliolum nitidis imposuisse comis.

Attenuant juvenum vigilatæ corpora noctes,   735
  Curaque &, è magno qui sit amore, dolor.

Ut voto potiare tuo, miserabilis esto;
  Ut qui te videat dicere possit, *Amas.*

Conquerar, an moneam, mistum fas omne nefasque?
  Nomen amicitia, nomen inane fides.   740

Hei mihi, non tutum est, quod amas, laudare sodali:
  Cum tibi laudanti credidit, ipse subit.

At non Actorides lectùm temeravit Achillis;
  Quantum as Pririthoum, Phædra pudica fuit.

Hermionam Pylades, qua Pallada Phœbus amabat;   745
  Quodque tibi geminus, Tyndari, Castor erat.

Si quis idem sperat, jacturas poma myricas
  Speret, & è medio flumine mella petat.

730] The Latin is corrupt, with most MSS reading *multi . . . putant*: HF's text follows the emendation
of Heinsius, who glosses, 'From this [pale] face girls may conclude and believe that you are not well and
languish for excessive love of them' (HA trans.).

under these false Colours; and the *Platonic* Friend hath soon become a happy Lover.

And now as to your Complexion; for, believe me, this is a matter of some Consequence: though I would not have you effeminate, yet I would have you delicate. A fair Complexion in a Tar is scandalous, and looks more like a Borough Captain, or one of those fresh-water Sailors, who have so much dishonoured our Navy.[91] The Skin of a Seaman ought to be rough, and well battered with Winds and Waves. Such likewise ought to be the Face of a Fox-hunter, who ought not to fear Rain or Easterly Winds: and the same becomes the Soldier. But let the Soldier of *Venus* look fair and delicate; nay, if your Complexion inclines to Paleness, so much the better; for this will be imputed by every young Girl to Love.

Young *Orion* (c) with a pale Countenance wandered through the Groves, being sick with the Love of *Lyrice*: and the sane Effect had the Love of *Naïs* upon the Countenance of *Daphnis* (d); two Lovers very famous in Antiquity. Leanness is another Token of a Lover; to obtain which, you need not take Physick; sitting up all Night, and writing Love-Letters, will bring this about. Be sure to look as miserable as possible; so that every one who sees you, may cry, *There goes a Lover.*

And here shall I lament the Wickedness of Mankind, or only simply observe it to you? But in reality all Friendship and Integrity are nothing more than Names. Alas! it is dangerous to be too prodigal in the Praises of your Mistress, even to your Friend; for if he believes you, he becomes your Rival. It is true, there are some old Stories of faithful Friends: *Patroclus* never made a Cuckold of *Achilles*; and *Phaedra's* Chastity was never tempted by *Pirithous. Pylades* loved *Hermione*, who was his Friend's Wife; but it was with the pure Love of a brother:[92] and the same Fidelity did *Castor* preserve towards his Twin-Brother *Pollux.*

But if you expect to find such instances in these degenerate Days, you may as well have Faith enough to expect a Pine-Apple from a Pear-Tree, or

---

[91] The distinction between sea-bred officers ('tarpaulins') and lubberly 'gentlemen' goes back to the Restoration (J. D. Davis, *Gentlemen and Tarpaulins* [Oxford, 1991], chs. 1–2). A 'Borough Captain' (not in the *OED*) is presumably one who owes his commission to political influence, like those MPs who, 'by their attendance in the House, are prevented from ever going to sea' (*Voyage to Lisbon*, below, p. 631; and see N. A. M. Rodger, *The Wooden World: An Anatomy of the Georgian Navy* [New York, 1986], ch. 8). The discomfiture of the British fleet under Admiral Thomas Mathews in the Battle of Toulon (19 February 1744), and the recent escape of two French ships from a superior British force under Captain Savage Mostyn (6 January 1745) had brought public opinion of the Navy to an all-time low, with 'court martials in abundance' (HMC, *Du Cane MSS* [1905], pp. 54, 113, 130; [Edward Vernon], *An Enquiry into the Conduct of Capt. M[osty]n* [1745]). HA

[92] Literally, 'as Phoebus [loved] Pallas' (Loeb), his 'sister'.

Nil nisi turpe juvat; curae est sua cuique voluptas;
    Hæc quoque ab alterius grata dolore venit.   750
Heu facinus non est hostis metuendus amanti!
    Quos credis fidos, effuge, tutus eris.
Cognatum fratremque cave, carunque sodalem:
    Præbebit veros hæc tibi turba metus.

Finiturus eram, sed sunt diversa puellis   755
    Pectora: mille animos excipe mille modis.
Nec tullus eadem parit omnia: vitibus illa
    Convenit; hæc oleis; hac bene farra virent:
Pectoribus mores tot sunt, quot in orbe figuræ;
    Qui sapit, innumeris moribus aptus erit,   760
Utque leves Proteus modo se tenuabat in undas;
    Nunc leo, nunc arbor, nunc erat hirtus aper.
Hic jaculo pisces, illi capiuntur ab hamis;
    Hos cava contento retia fune trahunt.

Nec tibi conveniet cunctos modus unus ad annos: 765
    Longius insidias cerva videbit anus.
Si doctus videare rudi, petulansve pudenti,
    Diffidet miseræ protinus illa sibi.
Inde fit, ut quae se timuit committere honesto,
    Vilis in amplexus inferioris eat.   770

759] 'Hearts have as many fashions as the face has features' (Loeb; reading *ore* for *orbe*, with Bentley).

to hope to fill your Bottle with *Burgundy* from the River. I am afraid we are grown so bad, that Iniquity itself gives a relish to our Pleasures; and every Man is not only addicted to his Pleasures, but those are the sweeter, when seasoned with another's Pain. It is in short a terrible Case, that a Lover ought to fear his Friend more than his Enemy. Beware of the former, and you are safe. Beware of your Cousin, and your Brother, and your dear and intimate Companions. These are the sort of Gentry from whom you are to apprehend most Danger.

Here I intended to have finished; but one Rule more suggests itself. You are to note then, that there is a great Variety in the Tempers of Women; for a thousand different Women are to be wooed a thousand different Ways. Mr. *Miller* will tell you, that the same kind of Soil is not proper for all Fruits. One produces good Carrots, another Potatoes, and a third Turneps.[93] Now there is as great a Variety of Dispositions in the human Mind, as there are Forms in the World: for which reason a Politician is capable of accommodating himself to innumerable kinds of Tempers: Not *Proteus* could indeed diversify himself more Ways than he can.[94] Nay, you may learn this Lesson from every Fisherman; for some Fish are to be taken with one Bait, and some with another; others will scarce bite at any, but are however to be drawn out of the Water by a Net.

One good Caution under this Head, is to consider the Age of your Mistress: Old Birds are not taken with Chaff; and an old Hare will be sure to double.[95] Again, consider Circumstances. Do not frighten an ignorant Woman with Learning, nor a poor Country Girl with your fine Clothes; for by these means you will create in them too great an Awe of you. Many a Girl hath run away frightned from the Embraces of the Master, and afterwards fallen into the Clutches of his Footman.

---

[93] Philip Miller FRS (1691–1771), gardener to the Company of Apothecaries at the Botanic Garden, Chelsea, and author of *The Gardener's Dictionary* (1731–9), where he advises that carrots need 'a warm sandy Soil', potatoes, a soil 'rather moist than dry, and of a rich soft loose Texture', and turnips, 'a light sandy Soil, which must not be rich' (4th edn., s.v., respectively: 'Daucus, Solanum *tuberosum*', and 'Rapa'). HF owned a copy of Miller's *Gardener's Calendar* (7th edn., 1745), an abridgement of the *Dictionary* (Ribbles M20). Preferring practical experience to mere book learning in *Tom Jones* (IX. i), HF cites 'the ingenious Mr. *Miller*' as his authority (pp. 492–3).

[94] HF omits two lines: 'Proteus will now resolve himself into light waves, and now will be a lion, now a tree, now a shaggy boar' (Loeb, lines 761–2). In the parody of Ovid's book I in *The Jacobite's Journal*, No. 15 (12 March 1748), however, he renders the passage: '*Proteus* . . . transformed himself into what monstrous Appearance he pleased: He roar'd a Lion, he grinn'd a Wolf, he flash'd a Fire, he flow'd a River' (p. 191).

[95] Cf. the parody in *The Jacobite's Journal*: 'Old Birds are not to be caught with Chaff [proverbial, Tilley, B396]; and an old Hare will be sure to double' (p. 192). For the latter maxim, cf. Squire Western on his sister in *Tom Jones* (XVI. vii): 'I can no more turn her, than a Beagle can turn an old Hare' (p. 862).

Pars superat cœpti, pars est exhausta laboris;
 Hic teneat nostras anchora jacta rates.

And here we will now cast our Anchor, having finished the first Part of our intended Voyage.[96]

FINIS

---

[96] The parody in *The Jacobite's Journal* renders Ovid's conclusion more closely: 'Part of our Undertaking still remains, and Part is finish'd: Here, then, let us cast Anchor, and moor the Ship' (p. 193). HF's specifying this as 'the first Part of our intended Voyage' suggests that he originally meant to continue the paraphrase with books II and III. By the time he wrote the Preface, however, he had had second thoughts; there he insists that 'the Objection of Impurity' often brought against Ovid's work could fairly obtain 'only against the two latter Books'. By then he was entertaining a different plan: 'if properly encouraged' he 'might perhaps' extend this 'new Undertaking' not to books II and III of Ovid's poem, but to 'other *Latin* Poets' (above, p. 387). The encouragement he looked for, however, never came.

FIELDING'S NOTES

[Commentary by Amory]

Pages 399–401:

(a) Here *Ovid* uses the Examples of *Automedon*, who was the Coachman of *Achilles*; and of *Tiphys*, who was Pilot or Steersman to the *Argonauts*.

(b) This is a literal Translation: by which it appears this barbarous Custom of whipping Boys on the Hands, till they look as if they had the Itch, was used by the *Roman* Schoolmasters as well as by ours.

(c) The Original introduces *Achilles*, who was the Pupil of *Chiron*.

(d) In the Original, —*held forth at his Master's Command those Hands to be whipt, which* Hector *was hereafter to feel.* The Indelicacy of which Image we have avoided applying to our *British* Hero.

(e) *Both born of a Goddess.*

(f) This is transferred, we hope not improperly, from *Roman to British* Superstition. The Latin alludes to Augury, and very justly ridicules the Folly of Divination by the Flight of Birds.

(g) *Nor were* Clio *or her Sisters seen by me, while I tended a Flock in the Valleys of* Ascra. This *Ascra* was a Valley near the *Helicon*, which was the Residence of the Parents of *Hesiod*. Now *Hesiod* was fabled, whilst he was keeping his Father's Sheep, to have been led by the Muse to the Fountain *Hippocrene*; and being, I suppose, well ducked in that Water, commenced Poet.

Pages 401–56:

(h) This whole Passage is a manifest Burlesque on the Invocations with which the Ancients began their Poems. Not very different is that Sneer at the Beginning of the *Metamorphosis*,

> —*Dii, coeptis,* (NAM VOS MUTASTUS ET ILLAS)
> *Adspirate—*[97]

But the strongest Piece of Burlesque of this kind is the Invocation to *Venus* at the Beginning of *Lucretius*: For what can be more so than a solemn Application to a Deity for her Assistance in a Work, the professed Intention of which is to expose the Belief of any Deity at all; and more particularly of any Concern which such superior Beings might be supposed to take in the Affairs of Men. For my own part, I must confess, I cannot perceive *that graceful Air of Enthusiasm* which a noble Author observes in the Invocation of the Ancients;[98] many of them indeed seem to have been too apparently in jest, to endeavour to

---

[97] 'Ye gods, for you yourselves have wrought the changes, breathe on these my undertakings' (Loeb).

[98] Anthony Ashley Cooper, 3rd Earl of Shaftesbury, *A Letter concerning Enthusiasm* (1708): 'You have wondered, perhaps, why that air of enthusiasm, which sits so gracefully with an ancient, should be so spiritless in a modern.' HF refers to this passage again in *Tom Jones* (VIII. i, pp. 398–9).

impose on their Readers, and in reality to apply to the Muses with less Devotion than our modern Poets, many of whom perhaps believe as much in those Deities as in any other.

(i) *Ovid* would here insinuate, that the Courtezans only were the Subjects of the ensuing Poem; and in his *Tristibus* he cites these Lines, and pleads them in his Defence:[99] But he is not over-honest in this Profession: for in many Parts it appears, that his Instructions are calculated for much more than *concessa furta*.

(k) *Andromeda* was the Daughter of *Cepheus* King of *Aethiopia*, and of *Cassiope*. Her Mother having offended the *Nereids*, by contending with them for Superiority in Beauty, *Neptune*, at their Petition, sent a Sea-Monster, which greatly annoyed the *Aethiopians*. Upon this they consulted the Oracle of *Jupiter Ammon*, who ordered them to expose one of the Progeny of *Cepheus* and *Cassiope* to be devoured by the Monster. *Andromeda* was accordingly ty'd to a Rock, where she was espied by *Perseus*, who killed the Monster, and rescued the Lady; for which he received her at the hands of her Parents as his Reward. The Story is told in the 4th Book of the *Metamorphosis* [662–751].

(l) *Bunches of Grapes in* Methymna: a City of *Lesbia*, the Wine of which Country was famous among the Ancients.

(m) *Ears of Corn in* Gargara; which was in *Mysia*, A Province of the *Hellespont*.

Page 403:

(n) The Original is, *And the Mother of Æneas resides in the City of her Son, Æneas*, from whom the *Romans* derived their Original, was the Son of *Venus* by *Anchises*.

(o) The Original, rendered as literally as possible, is as follows: *Walk at your ease under the* Pompeian *Shade, when the Sun enters the* Herculean *Lion; or where the Mother hath added her Benefactions to those of her Son; a Work rich in foreign Marble: Nor avoid that Portico adorned with ancient Pictures, which is called* Livia, *from the Name of its Founder; nor that adorned by the Statues of the* Belides, *who attempted the Lives of their unfortunate Cousins; and where you see the cruel Father standing with his drawn Sword: Nor pass by the Temple of* Venus *and her lamented* Adonis; *nor omit the Seventh-Day Festivals of the* Jews; *nor the* Egyptian *Temples of the* Linnen-clad *Heifer: She makes many Women to be that which she herself was to* Jupiter.

To explain these several Particulars to an *English* Reader, it must be known, that the Portico's in *Rome* were the publick Walks; and here Persons of both Sexes used to assemble. Among these was one built by *Pompey*. The second Portico mentioned, is by the best Commentators understood of the *Octavian*, which was built by *Octavia*, Sister to *Augustus*, and Mother to *Marcellus*; and this adjoined to a Temple built by the same *Marcellus*. The third Portico was built by *Livia* the Wife of *Augustus*, and called from her Name. The fourth,

---

[99] *Tristia*, ii. 249–50. The reason for Ovid's exile, which he attributed to 'a poem and an indiscretion', remain mysterious; see Peter Green, 'Carmen et Error', *Classical Antiquity*, 1 (1982), 202–20.

where the Picture of the *Belides* was,[100] is to be understood of the Portico of Apollo *Palatinus*, in which were the Statues of the fifty Daughters of *Danaus* and Grand-daughters of *Belus*. These being married to the fifty sons of their Uncle *Ægyptus*, every one, by her Father's Command, slew her Husband on the first Night, save only *Hypermnestra*. For this they were punished in the lower World, by being obliged to fill a Barrel full of Holes with Water. *Scaliger* and others have here made a mistake, supposing the Picture of the *Belides* was here hung up: But the contrary appears by many Authorities, particularly by this in *Ov. Trist.* 3.

> *Signa peregrinis ubi sunt alterna columnis,*
> *Belides, & stricto barbarus ense pater.*[101]

It appears that the Number of Pillars was equalled by the number of Statues.[102] 5thly, The Temple of *Venus*, in which she was worshipped, together with *Adonis*, after the *Assyrian* manner. This *Adonis* was the Son of *Cinyras* King of *Cyprus*, begotten by him on his own Daughter *Myrrha*. The Fame of his Beauty, and the Passion which *Venus* bore towards him, are well known. 6thly, the *Jewish* Synagogues. The *Jews* having been encouraged by *Julius Cæsar*, were very numerous in *Rome* at that time; and the Strangeness and Pomp of their Ceremonies inviting the Curiosity of the *Roman* Ladies, their Synagogues became famous Places of Intrigue. 7. The Temple of *Isis*. This Goddess, when a Woman, was called *Io*: She was the Daughter of *Inachus*; and being beloved by *Jupiter*, was by him, to preserve her from his Wife's Jealousy, turned into a Heifer. *Juno* suspecting the Fact, obtained this Heifer of her Husband, and set *Argus* to watch over her. *Jupiter* wanting to visit his old Friend, sent *Mercury* to kill *Argus*; in revenge of which, *Juno* ordered a Gad-Bee[103] to sting the poor Heifer; which thereupon growing mad, ran to *Egypt*, where she was again restored to the Shape of a Woman, and married to *Osiris*. The Feast of *Isis* was celebrated in *Rome* ten Days together by the Women, and was a time of Carnival among them.

Page 407:
(p) In *Cæsar's* Forum, which was built on the *Appian* Way, was the Temple of *Venus Genetrix*.

Pages 409–11:
(q) Races were run at *Rome* in *April* in the *Circus Maximus*, which was likewise the Scene of many other public Exercises and Shews.

[100] Or wasn't, as HF will shortly argue.
[101] 'where alternating with the columns of foreign marble stand the figures of the Belids, the barbaric father with a drawn sword' (Loeb, *Tristia*. 3. i. 60–1).
[102] HF follows Heinsius' correction of Joseph Scalliger 'and others' whose error arose from the corrupt reading *spatium* (for *speciem*) in *Fasti*, 3. 529. See also Samuel B. Platner and T. Ashby, *A Topographical Dictionary of Ancient Rome* (Oxford, 1929), s.v. Apollo Palatinus, *aedes*.
[103] i.e. a gadfly (*OED*).

(r) *And when the Procession shall pass on with the Ivory Deities, do you applaud most the Statue of* Lady *Venus.* Thus the Original. The Paraphrase preserves the same Sense, though in other Circumstances. These Statues were carried in Procession on many Occasions, particularly at the *Megalesian* Games.

(s) *Adjusting her Cushion.*

(t) *Putting a Foot-stool under her.*

(u) The Original mentions the Fights of the *Gladiators.* The Paraphrase comes as near as our Customs admit; for *British* Ladies never attend to see Men kill one another in jest.

Pages 411–13:

(w) *Augustus Cæsar* among other rich Shews, with which he entertained the People, exhibited to them a Sea-Fight in a Place dug on purpose near the Banks of the *Tyber.* The Poet takes this Occasion of introducing many Compliments to the Grandson of this Prince. We have done little more than altered Names in this Place; and as we are assured all here said is as properly applicable to the noble Person to whom we have transferred it, the learned Reader will admire that any Passage in an antient Author can be so apposite to the present Times, and the true *English* Reader will be no less delighted to see *Ovid* introduced as singing forth the Praises of the *British* Hero.

(x) *Parthia*

(y) The *Crassi*

(z) *Hercules*

(a) *Bacchus*

Page 413:

(b) The Original here describes the many Nations who are led Captives.

Pages 415–17:

(c) Here we have inverted the Original; but sure the Sense upholds us in so doing.[104]

(d) *Baiæ,* a Place not far from *Naples,* famous for wholesome as well as pleasant Baths. It is described very largely by *Diodorus*; and *Horace* mentions it as the pleasantest Place in the World.[105]

(e) In the Original, the Temple of *Diana* in the Suburbs. It stood in a Grove not far from *Rome.* The next Line, *Partaque per gladios, &c.* alludes to a very singular Custom, by which the Priests of this Temple succeeded to each other, *viz.* by Conquest in single Combat, for which every Slave or Fugitive was admitted to contend, and the Victor was rewarded with the Priesthood. This Practice

---

[104] In the original, the girls 'ravished' (*rapuêre*) the boys, but the boys are Ovid's primary audience here, and HF senses an inconsistency.

[105] Diodorus Siculus does not mention Baiae; HF may be thinking of Strabo, v. C425. According to Horace, 'nullus in orbe sinus Bais praelucet amoenis' ('No bay in the world outshines Baiae', Loeb, *Epistles*, I. i. 83).

Occasional Prose

was renewed every Year, and was, as *Strabo* informs us, originally taken from the *Scythians*.[106]

Pages 417–21:

(f) *Byblis* fell in love with her Brother *Caunus*; and upon his rejecting her Addresses, hanged herself. The Poets feign she was afterwards turned into a Fountain. See *Metam.* IX [453–665].

(g) *Myrrha* was the Daughter of *Cinyras*, who being in love with her Father, took an Opportunity, while her Mother was employed in the Sacrifices to *Ceres*, to supply her Place. Her Father discovering the Imposture, ran after her with a drawn Sword to kill her: But she escaped by means of the Night, and fled into *Sabæa*. She was changed into a Myrrh-Tree. The Story of which is in *Metam.* X [298–502]. But though the Poets have subjoined Fable to this Fact, it is related by *Pliny* as a true History.[107]

(h) *Pasiphaë* was the Daughter of the Sun, married to *Minos*, King of *Crete*. The Poets feign that being in love with a Bull, she employed *Dædalus*, a famous Artist, to make her a wooden Cow, into which she conveyed herself, in order to enjoy her monstrous Desires. From this unnatural Coition sprung the *Minotaur*, a Monster half Man and half Bull, which was inclosed in a Labyrinth, and afterwards destroyed by *Theseus*.

(i) The Original alludes to the *Cretans*, who were famous among the Antients for the Vice of Lying.

(k) *Europa* was the Daughter of *Agenor* King of *Cddon*, beloved by *Jupiter*, and by him run away with in the Shape of a Bull.

(l) *Ærope* was the Wife of *Atreus*. She committed Adultery with her Husband's Brother *Thyestes*, by whom she had two Sons, whom *Atreus* caused to be killed, and served up to his Brother's Table. To avoid this Sight, the Sun is said to have gone backward.

(m) *Scylla* the Daughter of *Nisus*, King of the *Megarensians*, fell in love with *Minos*, while he was besieging her Father's City. She stole away her Father's Hair, on which the Fate of the City depended, and carried it to *Minos*; for which Fact she was rewarded by her Lover with Contempt only. She is said by some to have been changed into a Lark: But *Ovid*, who here seems to confound two Stories together,[108] makes her Transformation to have been into a Rock, which

---

[106] Strabo, v. C239. HF's note closely follows Micyllus' commentary: 'The poet alludes to the story and custom by which the priests at Aricia succeeded one another. For freeborn persons did not strive for this prize, but slaves and fugitives alike contending with one another in single combat, acquired the priesthood by conquest: each victor always succeeded by the next. Thus by *regnum* ["kingdom"] you should understand the priesthood; for the priest himself was styled "king of the wood", to wit the wood of Aricia, where the goddess's temple was' (Amory's trans.).

[107] Neither the Elder nor the Younger Pliny touch on the myth; HF is probably thinking of Plutarch, *Parallela* 22 (*Moralia*, iv. 310f–311a).

[108] The confusion lies less between two different stories than between two different Scyllas: the daughter of Nisus who was changed into a bird; and the daughter of Phorcus, changed into a navigational hazard; see Charles Estienne, *Dictionarium historicum, geographicum, poeticum* (1671), s.v. 'Scylla' and 'ciris'.

lies between *Sicily* and *Italy*; where the dashing of the Waves against the Rock, representing the Sound of the Barking of Dogs, gave rise to the Fable which is here hinted at.

(*n*) *Clytemnestra*, the Wife of *Agamemnon*, who in the Absence of her Husband committed Adultery with *Ægysthus*, and with him afterwards murdered *Agamemnon*, at his Return from *Troy*.

Pages 421, 425:

(*o*) *Creüsa* was the Daughter of *Creon* King of *Corinth*, and second Wife to *Jason*; to whom *Medea*, enraged with *Jason*, who had forsaken her, sent a Casket in which Wild-Fire was inclosed, and by which she was burnt as soon as it was opened. This *Medea* afterwards, on account of the same Anger with *Jason*, tore to pieces her two Sons which she had bore to him.

(*p*) This *Phœnix* having incensed his Father, by lying with a Woman who was beloved by the latter, fled to the Protection of *Peleus* the Father of *Achilles*, and was by him made Preceptor of that young Hero.[109]

(*q*) *Hippolytus* being beloved by his Stepmother *Phædra*, and refusing to gratify her Desires, was by her falsely accused to his Father *Theseus*; upon which account he was obliged to fly, and the Chariot Horses being frighted by Sea-Calves, dashed the Chariot to pieces, and him also.

(*r*) *Phineus* King of *Arcadia*, having repudiated his Wife *Cleopatra*, married *Harpalice*; by whose Instigation he put out the Eyes of his Son: for which he was afterwards punished by Divine Vengeance with the Loss of his own.

(*s*) The *Romans* paid a Religious Regard to their Birth-Day, as appears from many Passages in their Poets. At this time they used to receive Presents from their Relations and Acquaintance. We have here given the Sense of the Original, only varying the Customs (*Kalendæ Martii*). *Ovid* advises the Lover to abstain from visiting his Mistress in the Kalends of *March*. At which time the *Matronalia* were celebrated to *Juno Lucina*, and the Husbands used to pray to that Goddess to protect the Chastity of their Wives. *Horace* likewise Lib. III. Ode 8. hints that this was not the proper Season for Bachelors to give a Loose to their Gaieties. (*Sive erit ornatus Circus*, &c.). A Third Caution *Ovid* gives, is not to visit on those Days when the Wealth of the *Roman* Conquests were exposed to the *Circus*, in admiring which, as *Micyllus* observes, the Girls were too much taken up, to attend to the Desires of their Lovers.[110] To say the truth, some Custom seems to be alluded to here, which is not sufficiently preserved from the Ruins of Antiquity.

---

[109] Estienne, *Dictionarium*, adds that Phoenix's mother instigated the affair, and that Amyntor blinded his son, though you would never know it from HF's muted translation (literally, 'Phoenix, son of Amyntor, shed tears from empty eyes', Loeb).

[110] 'The poet hints that when the Circus is so variously and beautifully adorned that the girls spend more time admiring those ornaments than the lover would wish, he should abstain' (trans. HA).

Page 425:
(*t*) *Then the* Pleiades *are at hand. Then the Goat is merged in the Sea, viz.* in the Months of *October* and *November.*

(*u*) The Original points at the Day in which the *Romans* were overthrown by the *Gauls* on the Banks of the River *Allia.* This was the 15th Day of the Kalends of *August* A.U.C. 363, and it was marked as a black Day in the Kalendar. As this Nation is too happy to produce any such Day, we have been obliged to give it a different Turn in our Paraphrase.

Page 431:
(*w*) *Cydippe* was a beautiful Virgin of the Island of *Delos.* She was celebrating the Rites of *Diana* when she was seen by *Acontius,* who falling in love with her, and not daring openly to declare his Passion, contrived to drop an Apple at her feet, in which were inclosed these two Lines:

> *I swear to you by the mystical Rites of* Diana,
> *That I will attend you as a Companion, and become your Bride.*[111]

Cydippe took up the Apple, and read the Lines; by repeating which Words they became her own; and she was ignorantly betrothed to her Lover: For it was a Law, that whatever Persons said in *Diana's* Temple, they were obliged to perform.

Page 433:
(*x*) *Ariadne* was the Daughter of *Minos* King of *Crete.* She fell in love with *Theseus,* and with a Clew of Thread helped him out of the Labyrinth into which he went to kill the *Minotaur.* He afterwards basely deserted the poor Lady, of which our Poet will presently tell the Story.

Page 435:
(*y*) Silenus was the Pedagogue of *Bacchus,* and his Foster-Father: He was likewise his Companion on all Occasions; and is often introduced in his drunken Mood by our Poet.

Pages 437, 439:
(*z*) At this Wedding *Eurytion* the *Centaur* getting drunk attempted to ravish *Hippodamia* the Bride of *Pyrithous,* but *Theseus* knocked his Brains out with a Bowl. Upon this a Battle ensued between the *Centaurs* and the *Lapithæ,* who defending the Cause of their Prince Pyrithous, destroyed almost all the Centaurs. Horace Lib. I. Ode 18. mentions this Story likewise, as a Caution to Men not to be quarrelsome in their Cups.

---

[111] A translation of some verses by Scriverius, 'Juro tibi sane per mystica sacra Dianæ, | Me tibi venturam comitem nuptamque futuram'; cit. Burmann, at *Heroides* 20. II, and Estienne, *Dictionarium.*

(a) Here and in many other Places, we have been obliged to supply that Connection which is greatly wanting in the Original.[112]

Page 445:

(b) *Phœbe* and *Ilaira* were two pretty Girls, the Daughters of *Leucippus*, and by their Father betrothed to two Brothers *Idas* and *Lynceus*; but before the Celebration of their Nuptials, were ravished by *Castor* and *Pollux*. This ended in the Death of *Castor*, by the Hands of *Lynceus*; and of *Lynceus*, by *Pollux*, whose Death while *Idas* was attempting to revenge, he was struck dead by Thunder at the Feet of *Pollux*.

Page 449:

(c) *Orion* the *Theban* was in love with *Merope* the Daughter of *Œnopion*; but who this *Lyrice* was, is not so plain, no mention being made of her in any other Place.[113]

(d) *Daphnis* was the Son of *Mercury*; for his Love for this *Naïs*,[114] we have here *Ovid's* Authority.

---

[112] For some other instances, cf. 'And now, Friend, I will tell you a Story' (p. 5); 'In more intelligible Language' (p. 9); 'This I am afraid is too natural in all things' (p. 12); 'Now with regard to your Person' (p. 17); 'But to return to my Scholars' (p. 20); and 'It is true, there are some old Stories of faithful Friends' (p. 25).

[113] The MSS have wildly variant and implausible readings for the name of Orion's beloved. Merope (or Ærope) is also described as the wife of Œnopion (cf. Estienne, *Dictionarium*, and Natalis Comes, *Mythologia*). HF's note follows Mycillus: '[*Lyricen*] is the reading of the Aldine editions . . . Merula indeed argues we should read *Lyncem*: as though the poet implies that Orion chased the lynxes in the woods as a means of quenching the passion of love. But the poet's language will not bear it: for Orion was not wan for love of lynxes, but for love of a woman. Again, says the poet, he was *wandering* in the woods—not, pursuing lynxes. So I prefer the earlier reading, except that I have nothing to add in favour of Lyrice . . . perhaps [one should read] *Meropen*' (my trans.). Heinsius adds that 'Orion the Theban' had a number of loves, including his wife, Side, and Merope, daughter of Oenopion, and proposes to read in *Dirces sylvis* ('in the woods of Dirce'). Modern editions read *Side*.

[114] HF takes *Naïs* as a proper name, though it might equally well be rendered 'the naiad' (Loeb).

PREFACE AND LETTERS XL–XLIV

OF SARAH FIELDING'S *FAMILIAR*

LETTERS BETWEEN THE PRINCIPAL

CHARACTERS IN DAVID SIMPLE (1747)

FOR some time, since the death of Charlotte in the autumn of 1744, Fielding and his sister Sarah (1710–68) had been sharing the comfortable house at Old Boswell Court, together with Mary Daniel, Charlotte's maid and cook, and the children Henry and Harriet. In May of that same year Sarah, who had first tested her talent as a writer of fiction by contributing pieces to her brother's *Joseph Andrews* (1742) and *Journey from This World to the Next* (1743),[1] published her first novel, *The Adventures of David Simple*. In the Preface he wrote for the second edition (13 July 1744) Fielding refers to her as 'a young Woman . . . so nearly and dearly allied to me, in the highest Friendship as well as Relation', whose heart contains 'all the Good which is to be found in Human Nature'.[2]

Notwithstanding the success of *Joseph Andrews* and *Jonathan Wild*, Fielding opened his remarks on that occasion by declaring that he had given up novel-writing in order to devote himself to the law, and, in particular as it proved, to writing an ambitious treatise on Crown Law in which he was indebted to the manuscript notes and reports of his grandfather Sir Henry Gould. He made such progress on this work that in February 1745 he advertised it as 'Shortly' to be published.[3] He continued advertising it for a month, but he never finished it. In the summer of 1745 Fielding was

---

[1] Sarah probably wrote the letter from Leonora to Horatio in *Joseph Andrews* (II. iv) and in the *Journey* the concluding chapter, '*Wherein* Anna Boleyn *relates the History of her Life*'.

[2] See above, p. 354 (italics removed).

[3] *General Evening Post* (26–8 February 1745). See W. B. Coley, 'Henry Fielding's "Lost" Law Book', *MLN*, 76 (May 1961), pp. 408–13. For an edition of the extant fragments of the MS, see *Henry Fielding: An Institute of the Pleas of the Crown: An Exhibition of the Hyde Collection at the Houghton Library, 1987*, ed. Hugh Amory, introd. Charles Donahue ([Cambridge, Mass.], 1987).

occupied with legal business: defending his friend Arthur Collier from actions brought against him by his creditors, representing his friend Sir Charles Hanbury Williams in a suit brought by the Directors of the Opera against the Subscribers, and as usual riding the Western Circuit.[4] In the autumn of the year, his writings against the Jacobite rebels would engage him—three pamphlets published in October in less than a fortnight,[5] and in November the launching of his periodical *The True Patriot*, published weekly until, the danger past, it closed with No. 33 (17 June 1746).

Though her brother, as promised in the Preface to *David Simple*, appears to have abandoned the Muses during this period,[6] the success of her novel had encouraged Sarah to undertake a sequel, *Familiar Letters between the Principal Characters in David Simple*. This work, however, unlike its predecessor (as Fielding, at least, chose to represent it in the Preface), would not be written 'in the Manner of Cervantes' he had adopted in *Joseph Andrews*, but in the epistolary mode favoured by his rival, her new-found friend Samuel Richardson, with whom she probably became acquainted soon after coming to London in 1744.[7]

Perhaps remembering Fielding's lucrative success in publishing the *Miscellanies* (1743) by subscription, Sarah arranged with Andrew Millar to do the same. That she had begun the book well before the crisis of the rebellion intervened is clear from the following advertisement she placed in *The True Patriot*, No. 16 (11–18 February 1746):

THE *Author of* David Simple *hopes her Subscribers will not take it amiss, that she is obliged to defer the Publication of* Familiar Letters between the principal Characters in David Simple, *as her Friends were totally prevented by the late Public Confusion, to favour her with their Interest, as they kindly intended; nor could she herself think it decent to solicit a private Subscription, in a Time of such Public Danger.*

This Book will be ready to deliver to the Subscribers in January *next; in the mean Time Subscriptions will be taken in, and Receipts deliver'd, by Mr. A. Millar, opposite* Katherine-Street *in the* Strand.

---

[4] For an account of HF's activities as a lawyer during this period, see *Life*, pp. 390–6.

[5] These were *A Serious Address to the People of Great Britain* (3 October), *The History of the Present Rebellion in Scotland* (7 October), and *A Dialogue between the Devil, the Pope, and the Pretender* (12–15 October), published in the Wesleyan Edition of *The True Patriot*, ed. W. B. Coley.

[6] The hypothesis, based necessarily on internal and circumstantial evidence, that HF began writing *Tom Jones* in the spring of 1745 and continued with it until interrupted by the Jacobite Rebellion in September (see the Wesleyan Edition, i, pp. xxxv–xlii) has been convincingly contradicted by Dr Ribble's discovery of a letter of 19 March 1746/7 from HF's friend John Upton to James Harris, reporting that HF had 'finished one volume of a large humourous work'. (See Ribble, 'New Light on Henry Fielding from the Malmesbury Papers', *MP*, 103 (2005), p. 79.) Cross's hypothesis (ii, pp. 100–8) that HF began his masterpiece in the summer of 1746 after the rebellion had been put down would seem to be confirmed.

[7] Linda Bree, *Sarah Fielding* (New York, 1996), p. 13.

Whatever the conditions of Sarah's arrangement with Millar may have been, he took no obvious part in promoting the subscription until 23 November 1746, when, as the ledger of Henry Woodfall records, he ordered 500 proposals printed.[8] Though conducted privately by the Fieldings and their friends, the subscription was nevertheless extraordinarily successful: the List of Subscribers published with the first edition on 10 April 1747 runs to 506 names—ordering 403 sets on plain paper at ten shillings each, and 149 sets on royal paper at a guinea, together amounting to a gross sale of £357 9s. Among those who ordered sets on royal paper are Fielding's patrons Ralph Allen (five sets), the Duke of Bedford, the Duke and Duchess of Richmond, the Duchess of Montagu, Mrs George Bubb Dodington, and James Harris and his wife; others included the Earls of Burlington and of Bath (William Pulteney), Henry Gould (the Fieldings' first cousin, who had recently played a part in the story of *The Female Husband*), Lady Mary Wortley Montagu and her husband, and Richard 'Beau' Nash. Among those who chose the cheaper set were the Duchess of Bedford, the Earl of Chesterfield and the Countess, the Countess of Orford (Robert Walpole's widow), Edward Cave (editor of *The Gentleman's Magazine*), the publishers Robert Dodsley (six sets) and John Watts (publisher of Fielding's plays), and the Bath bookseller James Leake (six sets); there, too, are Samuel Richardson, and '*The Reverend Mr.* Warburton' (Pope's friend and editor, who recently married Ralph Allen's niece). All these, as well as others listed but not mentioned here, played a part in the story of Fielding's life. There are, however, a few surprising omissions in this impressive company: missing, for example, are David Garrick and William Hogarth, George Lyttelton and the Duke of Somerset, all of whom Fielding compliments in the Preface or the Letters he contributed. But on the whole, Sarah's 'Friends' and his own rallied to support her.

CIRCUMSTANCES OF COMPOSITION

Interrupted by the rebellion, Sarah had much to do if the work was to be ready for delivery to the subscribers in January 1747, as promised. But this was a novel that had no plot that might be spun out indefinitely; it consisted instead in unrelated groups of letters concerning manners and morals, or stories about eccentric characters or unfortunate ladies, and she found it difficult to fill out the requisite two volumes. She needed 350 pages in volume II to pair with volume I, but she was 125 pages short of that

---

[8] P.T.P., 'Woodfall's Ledger, 1734–1747', *N & Q*, 1st ser., 11 (2 June 1855), p. 419: the entry reads '500 8vo. page proposals for Miss Fielding, 6s.'.

goal when she had to call for help. James Harris, the Fieldings' friend in Salisbury, answered the call by contributing a couple of light satirical dialogues called 'Much Ado' and 'Fashion',[9] which together account for pages 225–93; and Fielding, who also wrote the Preface, carried the text to page 351 by contributing Letters XL–XLIV. In a headnote introducing them, Sarah left no doubt as to his authorship and her readiness to defend him from detractors:

The following five Letters were given me by the Author of the Preface. I should have thought this Hint unnecessary, had not much Nonsense and Scurrility been unjustly imputed to him by the Good-Judgment *or* Good-nature *of the Age. They can know but little of his Writings, who want to have them pointed out; but they know much less of him, who impute any such base and scandalous Productions to his Pen.*

If this was anything more than an echo of Fielding's earlier complaint in the Preface to *David Simple* (above, pp. 348–50), the 'base and scandalous Productions' being attributed to him have not been identified, though his authorship of *The Female Husband*, published last November, may well have been suspected.

   As for the five letters, Fielding, who was at this time not only in the early stages of writing *Tom Jones* but also in the midst of preparing his paraphrase of Ovid's *Ars Amatoria* for publication, must somehow have found the time to dash them off even as the first volume of the *Familiar Letters* was committed to the press. The first of the letters (Letter XL), in which Valentine comments on contemporary politics and the taste of the town, is dated 'Decem. 20', but must have been written no earlier than January 1747; for in complaining that Rowe's *Fair Penitent* and *Jane Shore* had 'furnished the Entertainment of a Month this Winter at *Covent Garden*', he refers to runs of those plays that took place during 14–29 November 1746 and 2–16 January 1747, respectively. His subjects allow Fielding, on the political scene, to compliment the 'Broad Bottom' administration in general and the Earl of Chesterfield in particular; and in matters of taste, Handel's neglected oratorios, and in the theatre, several of his favourite actors—chief among them Garrick, 'one who never had, nor, I believe, ever will have an Equal' and 'the vast Genius of Mrs. *Clive* (inimitable in all Humour'). In Letter XLI, a French visitor to London comments on places of interest along the Thames from Whitehall to Putney and back, giving Fielding opportunities to remark on the statesmanship of Bolingbroke and to compliment the Dukes of Richmond, Montagu, and Somerset. Letters

---

[9] Samuel Johnson ascribed these pieces to Harris: see *Diary and Letters of Madame D'Arblay*, ed. Charlotte Barrett (1904), i, p. 86.

XLII and XLIII are an exchange between Miss Prudentia Flutter and Miss Lucy Rural, the one spoiled by the vanities of the town, the other sensibly preferring the pleasures of the country. Considering Fielding's recent flagrant preoccupation with less edifying aspects of sexual relations, Sarah must have welcomed the theme of his closing contribution: in Letter XLIV, Valentine writes his wife in praise of romantic love, true and chaste—a sort of saccharine preview of the chapter 'Of Love' in *Tom Jones* (VI. i).

There are signs in the Preface, however—in the testy, defensive anatomy of Sarah's choice of narrative form, the genre of 'those Writings that are called Letters', and in the patronizing attitude towards female authors (his cousin Lady Mary excepted)—signs that Fielding was bitterly disappointed in Sarah's defection to Richardson's camp. His judgement in the matter is absolute: 'And sure no one will contend, that the epistolary Style is in general the most proper to a Novelist, or that it hath been used by the best Writers of this kind' (p. 476). Now he presents himself coolly as her 'Relation' and 'Friend' who cannot praise her book warmly for fear of drawing upon himself 'the Censure of Partiality' (p. 477). No such scruple tempered the compliments he paid Sarah as a woman and a writer in the Preface to *David Simple*. But even here, despite his injured pride, he cannot ignore the qualities of her book. He admires her genius at perceiving 'the nicest and most delicate Touches of Nature'—a genius, indeed, worthy of comparison with Cervantes and Hogarth: 'I cannot control myself from averring, that many Touches of this kind appear to me in these Letters; some of which I cannot help thinking as fine, as I have ever met with in any of the Authors, who have made Human Nature their Subject' (p. 477).

There was a bond of affection between brother and sister that nothing, it seems, could weaken. There was a time when Sarah could come first in the order of Fielding's friends—as the moment at Boswell Court in January 1746 when she surprised him writing to his benefactor James Harris and he abruptly closed the letter: 'Farewell I am prevented from saying more by the Company of the Woman in the world whom I like best.'[10] In October of that same year, Joseph Warton, recalling for his brother Thomas a visit with the Fieldings, gave us the only glimpse we have of their companionship: 'I wish you had been with me last week, when I spent two evenings with Fielding and his sister, who wrote David Simple, and you may guess I was very well entertained.'[11]

---

[10] *Correspondence*, Letter 28, p. 56. Writing to his fastidious friend, HF could not have meant Harris to think this perfect female companion was the only other woman in the household, the cook–maid Mary Daniel, however much he later enjoyed her company.

[11] Letter of 29 October 1746 from Basingstoke: see J. Wooll, *Biographical Memoirs of the late Rev. Joseph Warton* (1806), p. 215; *Life*, pp. 412–13.

But now, certainly by the spring of 1747 if not earlier, Fielding had entered into a sexual relationship with their servant Mary Daniel, a woman of 25 or 26, that Sarah must have thought a crueller and more humiliating defection from loyalty than her own recent experiment with Richardson's way of telling a story. Her brother's affair with his 'cook–maid', as Lady Mary called his mistress,[12] was soon the topic of sarcastic gossip among their friends. On 16 May 1747 Thomas Harris, who had tried in vain to find Fielding in town in order to ask where he bought his snuff, wrote Mrs James Harris in Salisbury that 'he was gone to visit his Lady at his country seat', Fielding the year before having acquired a house at Mortlake, Surrey, that served as a summer retreat.[13] On 27 November of this year, at St Benet's, Paul's Wharf, with his friend Lyttelton attending to give away the bride, Fielding would marry Mary Daniel in the sixth month of her pregnancy with his son William.

The scandal, and what Sarah might well have considered a kind of betrayal of her friendship with her brother, drove her from the house at Boswell Court to join her sisters living in Duke Street, Westminster. But the bond between the two, though no doubt strained by the episode, was never broken. A year later, if she was indeed the author of a letter to *The Jacobite's Journal*, No. 30 (25 June 1748) signing herself 'Honoria Hunter',[14] the unpleasantness associated with Fielding's marriage had become for his sister merely a topic to tease him about: commending the 'Humanity' that gave him 'a Concern for any domestic Distress', she was sure he 'could find a Time for Attention to the reasonable Complaints even of a Cookmaid'. Moreover, she represents herself as being 'quite happy in the Friendship of an only Brother, somewhat older than myself, a Man of Virtue, Sense, and

[12] Lady Mary to the Countess of Bute (22 September 1755), in *Complete Letters*, iii, p. 87.

[13] Ribble, 'New Light on Henry Fielding', pp. 79–80, 84. His friend Thomas Harris places HF at his country house in June 1746, much earlier than we have previously supposed (*Life*, p. 507); but Harris probably mistook Mortlake for Barnes, the adjacent village. As tradition has it, HF wrote much of *Tom Jones* at 'Milbourne House' in Barnes; this new evidence makes it entirely possible that he did.

[14] Cross (ii, p. 92) was first to suggest that the letter from 'Honoria Hunter' in the *Journal* 'may have been written by Sarah Fielding'. The editor of the Wesleyan Edition, while not offering an opinion, calls attention to a similarity between a mistake in the letter ('Mrs. *Hartly*' instead of 'Mrs. *Heartfree*' of *Jonathan Wild*) and Sarah Fielding's 'slip' in *David Simple* (iv. vi), 'Heartwell' in Congreve's *Old Batchelor* misnamed '*Heartfree*' (ed. Kelsall, pp. 284 and 435 n.). Sarah's biographer finds the attribution 'plausible' [my adjective for Bree's adverb, p. 14]).

I believe a careful analysis of the letter using Sarah Fielding's novels in the C-H database will support the attribution. My own cursory trial—choosing only the letter-writer's unusual use of 'huge' ('my huge Mortification', 'my huge Satisfaction') and her preference for 'Creature' rather than 'person' or 'man/woman' ('the worthy Creature')—produced for the former one match in *David Simple* (ii. iii), '*huge Forests*' and another in *The Cry* (i. x), 'what a huge man was this *Alexander*'; more striking were the results for the writer's use of 'Creature': no fewer than 174 matches for all Sarah's fiction in the C-H program: including 77 in *David Simple* and 61 in *The Cry*.

Honour' (p. 317)—three attributes that, in the context of the scandal, could be taken seriously only in reference to Fielding's having chosen to humiliate himself by making an honest woman of the servant he got with child.

Sarah's next work of fiction, *The Governess: or, Little Female Academy* (1749), illustrates perfectly both her admiration of Richardson and her affection for her brother. It was Richardson she now turned to for advice on the manuscript and it was Richardson, not Fielding's publisher Millar, who published the work. But in the novel itself, which is based on her experience of Mary Rookes's boarding school at Salisbury, she has her heroine declare her love for her older brother 'Harry', her friend and protector.[15] Indeed, that the compliment to her brother passed Richardson's scrutiny of the manuscript may be owing to Fielding's efforts during 1748 to close the wounds he had inflicted in *Shamela* and *Joseph Andrews*: in *The Jacobite's Journal* (2 January and 5 March) he had cordially recommended *Clarissa* to the public; and on 15 October, in a famous letter to his rival, he expressed at length his admiration of Richardson's masterpiece.[16] Adding to the mood of reconciliation, in *Tom Jones* (VI. v), published a month after *The Governess*, Sarah would appreciate Sophia's defence of *David Simple* and its author: 'It is the Production of a young Lady of Fashion, whose good Understanding . . . doth Honour to her Sex, and whose good Heart is an Honour to Human Nature' (p. 286).

The known facts concerning Fielding's continuing relationship with Sarah are few. A pair of entries in his bank account record payments to her of £10 on 29 August 1750 and £9 on 19 March 1750/1—the latter date corresponding to the time when she was being sued for debt.[17] By 1750 Sarah was sharing lodgings in London with her friend and fellow novelist Jane Collier, and both were prominent among the circle of Richardson's female admirers, his 'daughters' as he called them. But Sarah was also often at Bath, where in June 1754 illness prevented her from joining her friend Jane Collier among the company of Fielding's friends who bade him farewell as he left England on the voyage to Lisbon. Testimony to her continuing affection for him, however, is to be found in her fiction in a number of complimentary allusions to his novels (and to *Tom Thumb*);[18] and it is plain

[15] *The Governess*, ed. J. E. Grey (London, 1968), pp. 124–8.
[16] *Correspondence*, Letter 41.
[17] *Life*, p. 509.
[18] Allusions to HF in *The Cry* (1754): i, p. 16 (invoking the authority of 'the author of *Tom Jones*'); i, p. 169 (HF in *Joseph Andrews* commenting 'very judiciously' on high people and low people); ii, p. 1 (quoting HF in *Tom Jones* on 'invention', 'an ingenious author'); ii, pp. 99–100 (mocking 'The Cry' by comparing them to Noodle and Doodle in *Tom Thumb*); ii, p. 297 (mocking 'The Cry' by quoting *Tom Thumb*: 'a country dance of joy was in their eyes'); iii, p. 118 (HF in *Tom Jones*, 'an ingenious author'); iii, p. 122–4 (defending HF's parson Adams against detractors). *The Lives of Cleopatra and Octavia* (1757),

in her correspondence with James Harris on their unsuccessful attempt to collaborate on an essay celebrating Fielding's life and genius that would serve to introduce Millar's edition of his *Works* (1762).[19]

On 9 April 1768 in her fifty-seventh year Sarah died at Bath, where a handsome memorial to her graces a wall of the Abbey Church. She chose to be buried, however, two miles away, in the little church of St Mary the Virgin, Charlcombe—where in November 1734 Henry had married Charlotte Cradock.

PRINTING AND PUBLICATION

In January 1747 the *Familiar Letters* were not ready to deliver to the subscribers, as Sarah had promised; Fielding, indeed, had then only begun writing his five letters. The work was, however, far enough along for Millar to announce in the *General Advertiser* of 24 January that it was 'in the PRESS' and would be published 'in March'.[20] Harris's two dialogues had been written some time ago,[21] and Fielding was perfectly capable of producing his contributions in a few days. But Sarah, presumably, caused a delay by writing a forty-one-page supplement to volume II called 'A Vision', a moral allegory depicting the deceitful ways that lead to Wealth, Power, Pleasure, and Virtue.[22] On 20 March in the *General Advertiser* Millar announced a new date of publication:

On the 10th of April *next will be delivered to* | *the* SUBSCRIBERS, | FAMILIAR LETTERS, &c. | BY THE AUTHOR OF DAVID SIMPLE. | The Books will be delivered at the Shop of *A. Millar*, Bookseller, | opposite Catherine-Street in the Strand; to whom those Persons who | intend to favour the Author by Subscribing, are desired to send in their | Names *by the last Day of this Month*; or they cannot be

---

pp. ii–iii (together with Sidney's *Arcadia, Don Quixote*, and *Sir Charles Grandison, Joseph Andrews* is a model for fiction). *The History of the Countess of Dellwyn* (1759): i, p. 6 (in *Tom Jones* 'the moral Philosopher *Square*, appeared to be so fully acquainted with the *Fitness of Things*'); i, pp. 53–4 (citing 'King *Arthur*, and Queen *Dollalolla*, in the Tragedy of *Tom Thumb*'); i, p. 97 ('swallowed up, like *Tom Thumb*, by a Cow'); i, p. 249 n. ('the *Slip-slops*' used as a generic name for 'Waiting-maids'); i, p. 258 (reference to *Tom Thumb*); i, p. 282 ('*The Life of Jonathan Wild . . . that renowned great Man*'); ii, p. 162 (recalling *Tom Jones*, Lady Dellwyn 'may, as Mrs. *Western* says, *Comfort herself that it is her own Fault*').

[19] See *Correspondence*, Letters 87–92.

[20] The notices continued in that paper for 26–30 January.

[21] 'Much Ado' was written in October 1744 and 'Fashion' in 1746 (Probyn, p. 82).

[22] I once thought it 'likely' that HF had written this piece ('Henry Fielding, Sarah Fielding, and "the dreadful Sin of Incest" ', *Novel*, 13 [1979], p. 14 n. 21), a view that was independently supported by computer-assisted analysis, in J. F. Burrows and A. J. Hassall, '*Anna Boleyn* and the Authenticity of Fielding's Feminine Narratives', *ECS*, 21 (1988), pp. 427–53. With Sheridan Baker, however—see Baker, 'Did Fielding Write "A Vision"?' and Burrows, ' "A Vision" as a Revision?', *ECS*, 22 (1989), pp. 548–65—I now take the piece to be Sarah Fielding's (see *Life*, p. 414). For an account of the work, see Bree, *Sarah Fielding*, pp. 53–6.

inserted in | the Printed List, which will then go to the Press. | *Where may be had,* | The Adventures of *David Simple*. The Second Edition, 2 Vols. | Price bound Six-Shillings.[23]

The work was duly published on Friday 10 April;[24] but subscribers were in no hurry to claim their copies. As late as November Sarah felt it necessary to make the following appeal in the *General Advertiser*: 'The SUB-SCRIBERS . . . are desired to send for their Books to Mr. Millar, Bookseller, opposite Katherine-street in the Strand, before the 1st of February next, it being a great Inconvenience to the Author to keep them so long, when they might be otherwise dispos'd of to her Advantage.'[25]

Except for an unauthorized Dublin edition also published in 1747,[26] the initial supply of subscription copies of *Familiar Letters* was sufficient to satisfy demand for five years before Millar believed the public would welcome a second edition. It was published on 7 April 1752[27] as volumes III and IV of a four-volume set in duodecimo, volumes I and II being unsold copies of the second edition of *David Simple*. On the day of publication an advertisement, appearing only in Fielding's *Covent-Garden Journal*, No. 28, confirms the date and explains the new format:

This Day is published, | (In four Volumes 12mo, Price bound 12s.) | THE | ADVENTURES | OF | DAVID SIMPLE, | The two first Volumes containing an account of | his Travels through the Cities of London and | West-minster, in the Search of a real Friend: | and the two last containing Lettters [*sic*] between | David Simple and others. | By a LADY. | The Second Edition, revised and corrected. | With a Preface by HENRY FIELDING, esq; | Printed for A. Millar, in the Strand. | N.B. *The Third and Fourth Volumes containing the* | *Familiar Letters, were formerly printed by Sub-* | *scription, in Two Volumes Octave, and* *are now re-* | *printed in Two Volumes* 12mo (*and will be sepa-* | *rate*) *to compleat those Gentlemen's Setts who have* | *already purchased those Two Volumes of David* | *Simple in the Size.*[28]

[23] This notice was repeated in the *General Advertiser* (21, 23 March). It also ran in the *St. James's Evening Post* (21, 24, 26 March), with a shorter version in the *London Evening-Post* (31 March, 2, 4 April).
[24] Notices appeared in the *General Advertiser*: 9 April ('*To-morrow will be publish'd, in Two Vols. 8vo.* | *And ready to be delivered to the Subscribers*'), 10 April ('*This Day is publish'd*'), repeated 11, 13, 15–16 April. See also *St. James's Evening Post* (9, 14, 18 April), *London Evening-Post* (9, 11, 14, 16, 18, 21 April).
[25] *General Advertiser*, 20, 23, 25 November 1747.
[26] The imprint reads '*DUBLIN*: | Printed for E. and J. Exshaw, at the *Bible* on | *Cork-hill*, M,DCC,XLVII'. The *ESTC* lists five copies as follows: University of Arizona Library, Tucson, PR3459. F3F3 1748; Cambridge University Library, Hib. 7. 747. 33; BL, C.175.bb.8 (on the end flyleaf are drawn crude sketches of a man and a woman in profile, presumably meant for HF and Sarah); Dalhousie University Library, Halifax, Nova Scotia, PR3459. F3F3. 1747 RB; and New York University Library, Fales.
[27] The *General Advertiser* (28 March 1752) and *London Evening-Post* (31 March): '*Tuesday, April 7, will be published*'.
[28] The advertisement was repeated in *The Covent-Garden Journal* for 11, 14, 28 April; 12, 19 May 1752.

The following entry in Strahan's ledger for March 1752 shows that Millar ordered 1,000 copies of the second edition printed: 'Simple's Familiar Letters 20 Sheets N° 1000 @ 1:6:–p Sheet', the total charge being £26.[29] With reference to HF's contributions, the claim of the advertisement that the edition was 'revised and corrected' is borne out in a very few instances, only five of them involving slight changes in phrasing (see Appendix I). The 1762 edition of Fielding's *Works* includes his Preface, but not the five letters.

[29] BL, Add. MS 48800.

FAMILIAR

LETTERS

BETWEEN THE

Principal Characters

IN

DAVID SIMPLE,

And SOME OTHERS.

To which is added,

A VISION.

By the AUTHOR of

DAVID SIMPLE.

IN TWO VOLUMES.

VOL. I.

LONDON:

Printed for the AUTHOR:

And Sold by A. MILLAR, oppofite
Katharine-Street in the *Strand.*
M.DCC.XLVII.

PREFACE:

Written by a Friend of the Author.

THE Taste of the Public, with regard to Epistolary Writing, having been much vitiated by some modern Authors,[1] it may not be amiss to premise some short matter concerning it in this Place, that the Reader may not expect another Kind of Entertainment than he will meet with in the following Papers, nor impute the Author's designed Deviation from the common Road, to any Mistake or Error.

THOSE Writings which are called Letters, may be divided into four Classes. Under the first Class may be ranged those Letters, as well antient as modern, which have been written by Men, who have filled up the principal Characters on the Stage of Life, upon great and memorable Occasions. These have been always esteemed as the most valuable Parts of History, as they are not only the most authentic Memorials of Facts, but as they serve greatly to illustrate the true Character of the Writer, and do in a manner introduce the Person himself to our Acquaintance.[2]

A SECOND Kind owe their Merit not to Truth, but to Invention; such are the Letters which contain ingenious Novels, or shorter Tales, either pathetic or humorous; these bear the same Relation to the former, as Romance doth to true History; and, as the former may be called short Histories, so may these be styled short Romances.

---

[1] A reflection on Samuel Richardson, whose epistolary novel *Pamela* (1740)—followed in December 1741 by a sequel—had been received by the public with such enthusiasm Parson Oliver, HF's spokesman in the parody *Shamela*, calls the phenomenon an 'epidemical Phrenzy' (above, p. 157); HF had continued his ridicule of the book in *Joseph Andrews* (above, p. 143). His criticism here of Richardson's narrative mode might well be thought 'tactless' (Bree, *Sarah Fielding*, p. 13), considering that Richardson had subscribed to *Familiar Letters* and the book itself that he is introducing for his sister is an epistolary novel. With the publication of *Clarissa*, beginning in December 1747 with the first two volumes, HF's attitude towards its author changed (for a year at least) from one of scorn and ridicule to unmitigated praise (see the Introduction, above, p. 468).

[2] In his life of Pope, Samuel Johnson rejects this commonly held view of the biographical value of personal correspondence: 'It has been so long said as to be commonly believed that the true characters of men may be found in their letters, and that he who writes to his friend lays his heart open before him. But the truth is that such were simple friendships of the *Golden Age*, and are now the friendships only of children. Very few can boast of hearts which they dare lay open to themselves, and of which, by whatever accident exposed, they do not shun a distinct and continued view; and certainly what we hide from ourselves we do not show to our friends. There is, indeed, no transaction which offers stronger temptations to fallacy and sophistication than epistolary intercourse' (*Lives of the English Poets*, ed. George Birkbeck Hill [Oxford, 1905], iii, pp. 206–7). On another occasion, when initiating a correspondence with James Harris in September 1741, HF anticipated Johnson in appreciating how reluctant we are to 'expose' our private selves to view: 'I believe it is not in the Power of three Persons to expose my epistolary Correspondence' (*Correspondence*, No. 10, p. 11).

IN the next Branch may be ranked those Letters, which have past between Men of Eminence in the Republic of Literature. Many of these are in high Estimation in the learned World, in which they are considered as having equal Authority to that, which the political World allows to those of the first Class.

BESIDES these three Kinds of Letters, which have all their several Merits, there are two more, with which the Moderns have very plentifully supplied the World, tho' I shall not be very profuse in my Encomiums on either: These are Love-Letters, and Letters of Conversation, in which last are contained the private Affairs of Persons of no Consequence to the Public, either in a political or learned Consideration, or indeed in any Consideration whatever.

WITH these two Kinds of Letters the *French* Language in particular so vastly abounds, that it would employ most of the leisure Hours of Life to read them all; nay, I believe indeed, they are the principal Study of many of our fine Gentlemen and Ladies, who learn that Language.

AND hence such Readers have learnt the critical Phrases of a *familiar easy Style*, a *concise epistolary Style*, *&c.* and these they apply to all Letters whatever.

NOW, from some polite modern Performances, written I suppose by this Rule, I much doubt, whether these *French* Readers have any just and adequate Notion of *this epistolary Style*, with which they are so enamoured. To say the truth, I question whether they do not place it entirely in short, abrupt, unconnected Periods; a Style so easy, that any Man may write it, and which, one would imagine, it must be very difficult to procure any Person to read.

TO such Critics therefore I would recommend *Ovid*, who was perhaps the ablest Writer of *les Lettres Galantes*, that ever lived. In his *Arte amandi* they will find the following Rule,

$$\text{---}praesens \ ut \ videare \ loqui.^3$$

viz. that these Letters should preserve the Style of Conversation; and in his Epistles they will see this excellently illustrated by Example. But if we are to form our Idea of the Conversation of some modern Writers from their Letters, we shall have, I am afraid, a very indifferent Opinion of both.

BUT in reality, this Style of Conversation is only proper, at least only necessary to these, which I have called Letters of Conversation; and is not at

---

[3] *Ars Amatoria*, i. 468: 'So that you seem to be speaking in her presence' (Loeb). HF here repeats the paraphrase he gave in *Ovid's Art of Love*, published a few weeks earlier: 'preserve the Stile of Conversation' (above, p. 431).

all requisite, either to Letters of Business, which in After-ages make a Part of History, or to those on the Subject of Literature and Criticism.

MUCH less is it adapted to the Novel or Story-Writer; for what difference is there, whether a Tale is related this or any other way? And sure no one will contend, that the epistolary Style is in general the most proper to a Novelist, or that it hath been used by the best Writers of this Kind.[4]

IT is not my Purpose here to write a large Dissertation on Style in general, nor to assign what is proper to the Historian, what to the Romance, and what to the Novel-Writer, nor to observe in what manner all these differ from each other; it is sufficient to have obviated an Objection, which, I foresaw, might be made to these little Volumes by some, who are in truth as incapable of knowing any of the Faults, as of reaping any of the Beauties of an Author; and I assure them, there is no Branch of Criticism, in which Learning, as well as Good-sense is more required, than to the forming an accurate Judgment of Style, tho' there is non, I believe, in which every trifling Reader is more ready to give his Decision.

INSTEAD of laying down any Rules for the use of such Tyros in the critical Art, I shall recommend them to one, who is a Master of Style, as of every other Excellence. This Gentleman in his *Persian* Letters,[5] many of which are written on the most important Subjects in Ethics, Politics, and Philosophy, hath condescended to introduce two or three Novels: in these they will find that inimitable Writer very judiciously changing the Style which he uses on other Occasions, where the Subjects of his Letters require the Air and Style of Conversation; to preserve which, in relating Stories that run to any length, would be faulty in the Writer, and tiresome to the Reader.

TO conclude this Point, I know not of any essential Difference between this, and any other way of writing Novels, save only, that by making use of Letters, the Writer is freed from the regular Beginnings and Conclusions of Stories, with some other Formalities, in which the Reader of Taste finds no less Ease and Advantage, than the Author himself.

AS to the Matter contained in the following Volumes, I am not perhaps at

---

[4] Another hit at Richardson (see above, p. 474 n. 1).

[5] George Lyttelton (1709–73), later first Baron Lyttelton (1757), author of *Letters from a Persian in England, to his Friend at Ispahan* (1735). HF's friendship with Lyttelton was formed when they were schoolfellows at Eton. It is evident as early as 1733 in his unpublished verse 'Epistle to Mr. Lyttelton' (above, pp. 86–98) and in the poem 'Liberty' (*Miscellanies* i, pp. 36–41), which HF dedicated to him, as he would soon do *Tom Jones* (1749), which he was now writing. In the Dedication, HF acknowledged not only that he had undertaken his masterpiece at Lyttelton's urging, but that, as he put it, 'I partly owe to you my Existence during great Part of the Time which I have employed in composing it' (pp. 3–4); Lyttelton, together with Ralph Allen, would serve as the model for Squire Allworthy. In the work itself (VIII. i), borrowing a metaphor from another work by Lyttelton, HF calls him 'a most excellent Writer' (p. 405).

liberty to declare my Opinion: Relation and Friendship to the Writer may draw upon me the Censure of Partiality, if I should be as warm, as I am inclined to be in their Commendation.

THE Reader will however excuse me, if I advise him not to run them over with too much Haste and Indifference; such Readers will, I promise them, find little to admire in this Book, whose Beauties (if it have any) require the same Attention to discover them, with which the Author herself hath considered that Book of Nature, whence they are taken. In Books, as well as Pictures, where the Excellence lies in the Expression or Colouring only, the first Glance of the Eyes acquaints us with all the Perfection of the Piece; but the nicest and most delicate Touches of Nature are not so soon perceived. In the Works of *Cervantes* or *Hogarth*,[6] he is, I believe, a wretched Judge, who discovers no new Beauties on a second, or even a third Perusal.

AND here I cannot controll myself from averring, that many Touches of this kind appear to me in these Letters; some of which I cannot help thinking as fine, as I have ever met with in any of the Authors, who have made Human Nature their Subject.

As such Observations are generally supposed to be the Effects of long Experience in, and much Acquaintance with Mankind, it may perhaps surprize many, to find them in the Works of a Woman; especially of one, who, to use the common Phrase, hath *seen so little of the World*: and I should not wonder on this account, that these Letters were ascribed to another Author, if I knew any one capable of writing them.

BUT in reality the Knowledge of Human Nature is not learnt by living in the Hurry of the World. True Genius, with the help of a little Conversation, will be capable of making a vast Progress in this Learning; and indeed I have observed, there are none who know so little of Men, as those who are placed in the Crouds, either of Business or Pleasure. The Truth of the Assertion, that Pedants in Colleges have seldom any Share of this Knowledge, doth not arise from any Defect in the College, but from a Defect in the Pedant, who would have spent many Years at *St. James's*[7] to as little Purpose: for

---

[6] Miguel de Cervantes Saavedra (1547–1616), author of *Don Quixote* (1605–15), the work, as HF declared on the title-page, which served him as the model for *Joseph Andrews*, the novel that introduced a 'new species of writing' into England. William Hogarth (1697–1764), HF's close friend and the pre-eminent artist of mid-Georgian England. In the Preface to *Joseph Andrews*, the works of 'the Ingenious *Hogarth*' serve to illustrate the distinction between 'Comic History' painting and what 'the *Italians* call Caricatura', as HF in fiction distinguished between the Comic and mere Burlesque. In *Tom Jones*, rather than attempting to describe the physical appearance of his characters—Bridget Allworthy (I. xi, p. 66), Mrs Partridge (II. iii, p. 82), and Thwackum (III. vi, p. 138)—HF refers the reader to specific prints by Hogarth.

[7] The royal palace.

daily Experience may convince us, that it is possible for a Blockhead to see much of the World, and know little of it.[8]

THE Objection to the Sex of the Author hardly requires an Answer: It will be chiefly advanced by those, who derive their Opinion of Women very unfairly from the fine Ladies of the Age; whereas, if the Behaviour of their Counterparts the Beaus, was to denote the Understanding of Men, I apprehend the Conclusion would be in favour of the Women, without making a Compliment to that Sex. I can of my own Knowledge, and from my own Acquaintance[9] bear Testimony to the Possibility of those Examples, which History gives of Women eminent for the highest Endowments and Faculties of the Mind. I shall only add an Answer to the same Objection, relating to *David Simple*, given by a Lady of very high Rank, whose Quality is however less an Honour to her than her Understanding. *So far*, said she, *from doubting* David Simple *to be the Performance of a Woman, I am well convinced, it could not have been written by a Man.*

IN the Conduct of Women, in that great and important Business of their Lives, the Affair of Love, there are Mysteries, with which Men are perfectly unacquainted: their Education being on this head in Constraint of, nay, in direct Opposition to, Truth and Nature, creates such a constant Struggle between Nature and Habit, Truth and Hypocrisy, as introduce often much Humour into their Characters; especially when drawn by sensible Writers of their own Sex, who are on this Subject much more capable than the ablest of ours.

I REMEMBER it was the Observation of a Lady, for whose Opinion I have a great Veneration, that there is nothing more generally unnatural, than the Characters of Women on the Stage,[10] and that even in our best

---

[8] A variation on the theme of *Joseph Andrews* (II. xvii), where Parson Adams, who has *seen* nothing of the world but is well read in classical literature, insists he *knows* more of the world and human nature than the innkeeper, formerly 'a Sea-faring Man' who had seen many countries: 'the travelling I mean is in Books, the only way of travelling by which any Knowledge is to be acquired' (pp. 181–2).

[9] The lady HF has particularly in mind throughout this paragraph is no doubt his cousin Lady Mary Wortley Montagu (1689–1762), his friend and mentor as he began his career as a playwright. (On HF and Lady Mary, see above, the Introduction and notes to 'Cantos' and the 'Epistle to Lyttleton', pp. 28–33 and 86–8.) Lady Mary and her husband each subscribed to the *Familiar Letters*, on royal paper. In *Tom Jones* (VIII. i) she is also probably the lady 'of the first Rank . . . very eminent for her Understanding' who, in similar circumstances—when 'the unanimous Voice of a very large Assembly of Clerks and Apprentices' had condemned as 'unnatural' the character of Lady Charlotte in HF's *Modern Husband* (1732)— 'declared it was the Picture of half the young People of her Acquaintance' (p. 407). Earlier, recalling this same episode in *The Champion* (1 July 1740), HF refers to her as 'a Lady of great Sense and Knowledge of the World' (pp. 394–5). HF dedicated to her his first play, *Love in Several Masques* (1728), referring to her, as in the present context, as 'a living Confutation of those morose Schoolmen who wou'd confine Knowledge to the Male Part of the Species' (*Plays*, 19).

[10] The lady whose opinion HF venerates is again his cousin Lady Mary Wortley Montagu, who once assured him that *his* characterization (of Lady Charlotte in *The Modern Husband*) was *not* 'unnatural' (above, n. 9).

Plays: If this be fact, as I sincerely believe it is, whence can it proceed, but from the Ignorance in which the artificial Behaviour of Women leaves us, of what really passes in their Minds, and which, like all other Mysteries, is known only to the Initiated?

MANY of the foregoing Assertations will, I question not, meet with very little Assent from those great and wise Men, who are not only absolute Masters of some poor Woman's Person, but likewise of her Thoughts. With such Opposition I must rest contented; but what I more dread, is, that I may have unadvisedly drawn the Resentment of her own lovely Sex against the Author of these Volumes, for having betrayed the Secrets of the Society.

To this I shall attempt giving two Answers: First, that these nice Touches will, like the Signs of Masonry,[11] escape the Observation and Detection of all those, who are not already in the Secret.

SECONDLY, if she should have exposed some of those nicer Female Foibles, which have escaped most other Writers, she hath at the same time nobly displayed the Beauties and Virtues of the more amiable Part, which abundantly over-balances in the Account. By comparing these together, young Ladies may, if they please, receive great Advantages: I will venture to say, no Book extant is so well calculated for their Instruction and Improvement. It is indeed a Glass, by which they may dress out their Minds, and adorn themselves with more becoming, as well as more lasting Graces, than the Dancing-Master, the Manteau-Maker,[12] or the Millener can give them. Here even their Vanity may be rendered useful, as it may make them detest and scorn all base, mean, shuffling Tricks, and admire and cultivate whatever is truly amiable, generous and good: Here they must learn, if they will please to attend, that the Consummation of a Woman's Character, is to maintain the Qualities of Goodness, Tenderness, Affection and Sincerity, in the several social Offices and Duties of Life; and not to unite Ambition, Avarice, Luxury, and Wantonness in the Person of a Woman of the World, or to affect Folly, Childishness and Levity, under the Appellation of a fine Lady.

---

[11] Incidental satire directed against the esotericism of Freemasonry occurs in HF's publications of 1747, as in *Ovid's Art of Love Paraphrased* (above, pp. 435–7 nn. 69, 71) and *The Jacobite's Journal*, Nos. 1–3, as well as the early books of *Tom Jones* (II. iv, V. vi), which he was writing at this time: e.g. 'matrimonial Concerns, well known to most Husbands . . . which, like the Secrets of Free Masonry, should be divulged to none who are not Members of that honourable Fraternity' (pp. 85–6); and 'nor have [Knaves], like Free Masons, any common Sign of Communication' (p. 236). For the signs to which HF refers, see *The Secret History of the Free-Masons. . . . With a Short Dictionary of private Signs, or Signals* (2nd edn., 1725).

[12] 'Manteau-Maker': a dressmaker, specializing in the *manteau* (French)—a loose upper garment that early in the century replaced the straight-bodied gown in women's fashions (*OED*, s.v. 'manteau' and 'manteau-maker', obs.). The name of the style of garment (*manteau*) was superseded by 'mantua' and 'mantua-maker' from the Italian silk it was often made of (see *OED*, s.v. 1–3).

To conclude, I hope, for the Sake of my fair Country-Women, that these
excellent Pictures of Virtue and Vice, which, To my Knowledge, the Author
hath bestowed such Pains in drawing, will not be thrown away on the World,
but that much more Advantage may accrue to the Reader, than the Good-
nature and Sensibility of the Age have, to their immortal Honour, bestowed
on the Author.[13]

---

[13] HF's sarcasm would seem to be uncalled for, considering that *David Simple* had sold well enough to
have called for a second edition within two months in 1744, and then the present sequel—to which,
however, though more than 500 subscribed, many failed to claim their copies (see Introduction, p. 470).

FAMILIAR
LETTERS

BETWEEN THE

Principal Characters

IN

DAVID SIMPLE,

And SOME OTHERS.

To which is added,

A VISION.

By the AUTHOR of

DAVID SIMPLE.

VOL. II.

LONDON
Printed for the AUTHOR:
And Sold by A. MILLAR, oppofite
Katharine-Street in the *Strand.*
M.DCC.XLVII.

Note. *The following five Letters were given me by the Author of the Preface. I should have thought this Hint unnecessary, had not much Nonsense and Scurrility been unjustly imputed to him by the* Good-Judgment *or* Good-nature *of the Age. They can know but little of his Writings, who want to have them pointed out; but they know much less of him, who impute any such base and scandalous Productions to his Pen.*[14]

LETTER XL.
VALENTINE *to* DAVID SIMPLE.

Dear DAVID,   [London, Decem. 20.[15]

IN Compliance with your Request, I sit down to write you my Sense of the present State of the Town, tho' I fear what I have to say will serve but as little Inducement to you, to give us your Company here.

To begin then with Politics, on which head I shall be extremely short; The Administration, at present in the Hands of the very Men, whom you, and every honest Person would wish to be intrusted with it.[16] Amongst those, tho' there is no absolute Prime Minister, yet there is one, whose Genius must always make him the superior in every Society, as he hath joined to the most penetrating Wit, the clearest Judgment both in Men and Things, and the profoundest Knowledge of them, of any Man, whom, perhaps the World ever saw.[17]

---

[14] For a comment on these curious remarks by Sarah Fielding, see the Introduction (above, p. 465).

[15] HF's reference to the productions of Rowe's *Jane Shore* and *Fair Penitent* at Covent Garden puts the date of composition of this letter no earlier than January 1747 (see below, p. 486).

[16] In February 1746, with the rebellion not yet quelled, Henry Pelham, his brother the Duke of Newcastle, and Lord Chancellor Hardwicke combined with HF's friends and patrons—Dodington, Lyttelton, William Pitt, and Chesterfield—to form a new 'Broad Bottom' government. In *The True Patriot*, No. 17 (18–25 February 1746) HF celebrated his party's triumph: 'the Administration of Affairs is now in the Hands of Men who have given such Proofs of their Integrity, that have at once convinced us we are free Men, and may depend on being so under their Protection. It is indeed the rare Blessing of the Public, in the present Age, to be convinced that their Friends are in Power; that the greatest Men in the Kingdom are at the same time the honestest; that the very Person to whose Councils it is to be attributed, that the Pretender hath not been long since in Possession of this City, is at the Head of the Ministry' (pp. 227–8). Pelham was then the person 'at the Head of the Ministry' HF so warmly praised. Now, a year later in *Familiar Letters*, it will be the Earl of Chesterfield (see the following note).

[17] Here, and in the paragraph after next, the 'Genius' HF has in mind is his great patron Philip Dormer Stanhope (1694–1773), fourth Earl of Chesterfield. This would be the last of HF's many compliments to Chesterfield that began thirteen years before with the Dedication of *Don Quixote in England* (1734). In *Joseph Andrews* (III. i) HF anticipated the present tribute, calling Chesterfield 'a Peer no less elevated by Nature than by Fortune, who whilst he wears the noblest Ensigns of Honour on his Person, bears

THIS is indeed *multum in parvo*,[18] and will be abundantly sufficient to cheer you in that Love, which I know you sincerely bear your Country: for this will thrive in every different Branch, as the several Branches are governed and directed by Men of proper and adequate Ability.

AND, if Arguments *a posteriore*[19] may corroborate the Opinion I have above given, surely we are furnished with great Plenty. What but a Genius of the highest kind could have preserved *Ireland* in a perfect State of Tranquillity and Obedience during the late Troubles![20] Or what could have restored this Nation from that drooping and languid Fit of Despair, which so lately appeared in every honest Countenance, to those chearful Expectations, which the present Prospect of Things affords us?

FROM the abovementioned Reason, I suppose you will conclude, that the great and important Article of Religion is in the most flourishing Situation; and, to say the Truth, as to the external Part, which most properly belongs to the Heads of the Church to regulate, there is no apparent Deficiency; but with regard to Morality, which may be considered as the internal Part, I freely own, I believe no Age or Nation was ever sunk to a more deplorable State.

ONE great Cause of this, I conceive, may be that Luxury which of late Years hath rolled in like a Deluge upon us:[21] For the greatest Estates being

the truest Stamp of Dignity on his Mind, adorned with Greatness, enriched with Knowledge, and embellished with Genius' (p. 190). When the 'Broad Bottom' government came to power in 1744, Chesterfield, who had been a leader of the Opposition since 1733, was appointed Lord Lieutenant of Ireland, and in October 1746 he became Secretary of State for the Northern Department. When he resigned that office in February 1748, his place would be taken by the Duke of Bedford, who proved to be for HF a more attentive patron. (For an account of HF's sudden disaffection from Chesterfield, see Coley's Introduction to *The Jacobite's Journal*, pp. xxii–xxiii, xlix–l, lxiii.) HF's abrupt change in attitude from fulsome panegyric to total silence may well be explained by Chesterfield's unwillingness to correct the 'Mistake' he would make in June 1747 when he recommended HF for a commission in the Middlesex magistracy for which he lacked the property qualification of £100 (*Correspondence*, Letter 39, p. 68). For that favour he depended on the Earl's successor, Bedford, his 'princely' benefactor, as HF called him in the Dedication to *Tom Jones* (p. 5).

[18] 'much in little': a compendium (proverbial).

[19] '*a posteriori*': from what comes after; in logic, arguing from the effect to the cause (Black, *Law Dictionary*, 6th edn. [1990]).

[20] Referring to Chesterfield's masterly tenure as Lord Lieutenant of Ireland during the period of the rebellion, when he managed to conciliate and control the Orange and Roman Catholic factions. See above, n. 17.

[21] That the 'Deluge' of luxury, rife among the upper classes, was undermining the social order in general is a recurrent theme in HF's writing: e.g. his burlesque of Juvenal's Sixth Satire: 'Money's the Source of all our Woes; | Money! Whence Luxury o'erflows, | And in a Torrent, like the *Nile*, | Bears off the Virtues of this Isle' (*Miscellanies* i, p. 117); or the *Enquiry into the Causes of the Late Increase of Robbers*, sect. 1: 'the vast Torrent of Luxury . . . hath poured itself into this Nation' (p. 77). Indeed, as a magistrate addressing the Grand Jury in 1749, he declared: 'This Fury after luxurious Pleasures is grown to so great a Height, that it may be called the Characteristic of this present Age' (*Enquiry*, p. 25). For a study of the attack on luxury by moralists of the period, see John Sekora, *Luxury: The Concept in Western Thought, Eden to Smollett* (Baltimore, 1977), chs. 2–3.

barely sufficient to satisfy the Demands of so outrageous a Monster, the Hearts of the Opulent are of necessity shut to the Wants of their Fellow-Creatures, and Liberality, nay even Hospitality, are banished from among us; while men of smaller Fortunes are pushed on to all Acts of Meanness and Miscreantism, in order to supply themselves with the Means of imitating their Superiors. Hence arises a total Disregard to all true Honour and Honesty; hence every kind of Corruption and Prostitution, no Man being ashamed of any thing but the Appearance of Poverty.

NOW whence doth this proceed, but from our Morals being in wrong Hands? true Wit and Genius being in a manner deposed, and Impostors advanced in their Place.

IN reality, what the Ministry are to the State, the Bishops to the Church, the Chancellor and Judges to the Law, the Generals to the Army, and the Admirals to the Fleet; that is a great and good Writer over the Morals of his Countrymen.

THE Truth of this Observation will appear, if it be considered, that there is a strict Analogy between the Taste and Morals of an Age; and Depravity in the one always induces Depravity in the other.

TRUE Taste is indeed no other than the Knowledge of what is right and fit in every thing.[22] It cannot be imagined therefore, that one capable of discerning this in all lesser Matters, should be unable to perceive it in that highest and noblest Object the Human Mind.

WHEN therefore we see a false Taste prevail in all things else, we may naturally conclude it exists here likewise.

THE first great Corrupters of our Taste are the Virtuoso's,[23] a sort of People with which we abound to so prodigious a degree, that their Dexterities engross almost our whole Conversation. These are a kind of burlesque natural Philosophers, whose Endeavours are not to discover the

---

[22] Cf. *Amelia* (IX. ix), where HF has 'read in some Ethic Writer, that a truly elegant Taste is generally accompanied with an Excellency of Heart; or in other Words, that true Virtue is, indeed, nothing else but true Taste' (p. 394 and n. 2). The idea is commonplace among moralists of the period, especially in Shaftesbury's *Characteristicks* (1711), the likely source in *Tom Jones* (III. iii) of the philosopher Square's 'favourite Phrase . . . *the natural Beauty of Virtue*' (p. 126). Cf. also Hume in *Philosophical Essays concerning Human Understanding* (1748): 'MORALS and Criticism are not so properly Objects of the Understanding as of Taste and Sentiment. Beauty, whether moral or natural, is felt, more properly than perceived' (p. 255); and Hume credits Francis Hutcheson, in his *Inquiry into the Original of our Ideas of Beauty and Virtue* (1725), with having 'taught us, by the most convincing Arguments, that Morality is nothing in the abstract Nature of Things, but is entirely relative to the Sentiment or mental Taste of each particular Being. . . . Moral Perceptions therefore, ought not to be class'd with the Operations of the Understanding, but with the Tastes or Sentiments' (p. 15 n.).

[23] In *The True Patriot*, No. 22 (25 March–1 April 1746) 'Torricelli, Jun.', himself one of the virtuosi, describes HF's own attitude when he represents that of 'the Generality of Mankind', who 'entertain a low and contemptible Opinion of us, as an useless Sett of People' (p. 250). On the virtuosi and HF's opinion of them, see *The Journal of a Voyage to Lisbon* (below, p. 573 n. 98).

Beauties, but the Oddities and Frolicks of Nature. They are indeed a sort of natural Jugglers, whose Business it is to *elevate* and *surprize*, not to satisfy, inform, or entertain.

THE next great Business of the Age is Musick; of our Taste in which I need say no more, to give you an adequate Idea, than barely to inform you we have Operas, in which Mr. *Handel* is totally silent.[24]

ARCHITECTURE, Painting and Sculpture cannot fail of Encouragement in an Age devoted to Luxury. In these therefore we imitate the Extravagance of the *Romans*, and the Delicacy of the *Goths*.[25]

THESE however assist in forming the Subjects of our Conversation; and it is difficult to find a single Person who is not a Connoisseur in them all; and this often without knowing the common Rules of the Art in which he affects to be a Judge.

I COME now to the Theatres, of which you will doubtless expect a more favourable Account. And indeed our Actors promise no less; many of these being equal to any of their Predecessors, and some, I believe, superior to any who have ever been.[26] But so artfully[27] is the Theatre conducted in

---

[24] George Frederick Handel (1685–1759), whom HF considered in music 'the greatest Master in *Europe*'; 'that great Man', he called him while praising 'the enchanting Harmony of *Handel*'s Compositions' (*Champion* [15 March and 10 June 1740], pp. 237, 365). In *The True Patriot*, No. 1 (5 November 1745) Handel is to music what Shakespeare is to poetry (p. 104; see also n. 3, in which Coley first proposed that HF may have been personally acquainted with Handel through their connection with James Harris). Here, as in *Tom Jones* (IV. v), HF alludes to the all too effective opposition to Handel and his oratorios organized by the opera party led by the Earl of Middlesex and Lady Margaret Brown (on the latter, see HF's letter to James Harris of 14 November 1743, *Correspondence*, pp. 37–8 and n. 8). On 2 April 1745 Mrs Elizabeth Carter summarized the situation in a letter to Catherine Talbot: 'Handel, once so crowded, plays to empty walls in that opera house [i.e. the King's Theatre in the Haymarket], where there used to be a constant *audience* as long as there were any dancers to be seen. Unfashionable that I am, I was I own highly delighted the other night at his last oratorio' (see O. E. Deutsch, *Handel: A Documentary Biography* [London, 1955], p. 610). Like Mrs Carter, HF's Amelia (IV. ix), who delights in Handel's music, attends one his oratorios. During the rebellion Handel refrained from putting on concerts until his 'New Occasional Oratorio' (14 February 1746).
[25] Like HF's own birthplace at Sharpham Park, near Glastonbury, Squire Allworthy's house in *Tom Jones* (I. iv) is in 'the *Gothic* Stile' and 'rival'd the Beauties of the best *Grecian* Architecture' (p. 42)—the latter, in the present passage referred to as '*Roman*', being the predominant Palladian style favoured in the first half of the century notably by the Earls of Burlington and Pembroke (see James Lees-Milne, *Earls of Creation* [London, 1962], chs. 2–3). The preference given to the '*Goths*' here, however, would have pleased Lyttelton (see HF's Preface, above, p. 476 and n. 5) and their mutual friend Sanderson Miller (1717–80), amateur architect and pioneer of the vogue of the Gothic getting under way at just this time. In 1747–8 Lyttelton was erecting at Hagley Park a ruined castle and rotunda of Miller's design, and he hoped that Miller would build him a Gothic house (see R. M. Davis, *The Good Lord Lyttelton* [Bethlehem, Pa., 1939], p. 256).
[26] Cf. Horace Walpole (5 December 1746): 'at one house [Covent Garden] the best company that perhaps ever were together, Quin, Garrick, Mrs. Pritchard, Mrs. Cibber; at the other [Drury Lane] Barry, a young favourite actor' (*Yale Walpole*, xix, pp. 342–3).
[27] 'artfully': cunningly, craftily (*OED*, s.v. 'artful' 3). In 1737, anticipating the evil of the Theatrical Licensing Act, HF warned of the stultifying 'Stage Tyranny' that would ensue if the London stage 'were reduced . . . to two Theatres under two Managers with a Cartel between them'. He then—as in the present

the Choice of Plays, and the Casting of Parts, that I have seldom sufficient Inticement to visit it.

HALF a dozen Tragedies, two of which were *Jane Shore* and the *Fair Penitent*, furnished the Entertainment of a Month this Winter at *Covent-Garden*: So that we were obliged either to visit the Theatre seldom, or to be dieted with the same Dish.[28] Nor did *Drury-Lane* give us any Relief; for that Theatre, instead of treating us with another kind of Dramatical Food, very wisely attempted to emulate the best Actors of *Covent-Garden* in their best Parts; and vainly endeavoured to rival one who never had, nor, I believe, ever will have an Equal.[29]

How much more judicious would it have been in that House to have applied themselves to the Revival of several of our old Comedies, to which their Company is so well adapted. Mr. *Barry*,[30] who seems to have all the Materials of a good Actor, might then have gained Applause, without the Danger of a disadvantageous Comparison. Mr. *Cibber*[31] and Mr.

passage referring to the effects of the same duopoly of the stage—reminded his readers how, with only Covent Garden as their rival, the management at Drury Lane had 'forced upon the Town whatever Performance it pleased . . . it was a Maxim with the Triumvirs who directed it, That if the Town disliked a Thing at first, they must have it till they did like it: and thus, with the constant Repetition of thirty or at the most forty Plays, they dieted the Town' (*Some Thoughts on the Present State of the Theatres, and the Consequences of an Act to destroy the Liberty of the Stage*: see T. Lockwood, 'A New Essay by Fielding', *MP*, 78 [1980], pp. 48–58).

[28] During the winter season of 1746–7 *The Fair Penitent* (1703) and *Jane Shore* (1714)—tragedies by Nicholas Rowe (1674–1718)—ran at Covent Garden, respectively, 14 November–16 December and 2–16 January. In *Tom Jones* (IX. i), alluding to *Jane Shore*, HF would ridicule Rowe's belief, declared on the title-page, that he had successfully imitated Shakespeare's 'Style' (p. 488 and n. 2). Later in this letter he will dismiss the rhetorical mannerisms of Rowe, and Nathaniel Lee, as mere 'Fustian' (below, p. 487). Of Rowe's tragedies he appears to have admired most *The Fair Penitent*, particularly the characterization of Lothario, whom Nightingale quotes in *Tom Jones* (XIV. iv, pp. 754–5), and Calista, with whom Miss Mathews identifies in *Amelia* (III. ix, p. 134; IV. ii, p. 157). HF's complaint about being 'dieted with the same Dish' presumably refers to Covent Garden's not having produced a *new* play for four seasons (*London Stage*, pt. 3, ii, p. 1247 and *passim*).

[29] No doubt another of HF's extravagant, but eminently well-deserved, compliments to his friend David Garrick (1717–79), whom, in *Tom Jones* (VII. i), he declares to be 'in Tragedy the greatest Genius the World hath ever produced' (p. 327) and in *The Covent-Garden Journal*, No. 3 (11 January 1752), without any generic qualification, 'the best Actor the World could have ever produced' (p. 31). Later this year Garrick would leave Covent Garden to become, with James Lacy, patentee of Drury Lane, where he was joined by 'Kitty' Clive (see below, n. 33).

[30] Spranger Barry (1719–77), from Dublin, had made his debut in London on 4 October 1746 as Othello at Drury Lane, receiving 'as great Applause as could be express'd' (*General Advertiser*, quoted in *London Stage*, pt. 3, ii, p. 1253). He continued as tragedian at Drury Lane that season, in HF's opinion, subjecting himself to 'a disadvantageous Comparison' with Garrick.

[31] Theophilus Cibber (1703–58), Colley Cibber's disreputable son, a gifted comedian who at Drury Lane in 1732–3 had important parts in every production of HF's plays. In 1733, however, he led the actors' successful mutiny against the management of the theatre, which put an end to HF's lucrative tenure as house playwright. Before leaving Drury Lane, HF satirized the two Cibbers as Marplay Junior and Senior in the revised version of *The Author's Farce* (1734); and later in *The Historical Register* (1737) with son as Shakespeare's blustering Pistol (his signature role as a comedian) and father as Ground-Ivy. In *The Champion* (1739–40) HF regularly ridiculed both Cibbers, and in *Joseph Andrews* (III. x) the Player sneers at 'that face-making Puppy young *Cibber*' (p. 262).

Macklin[32] could not have failed to pleasing; nor would the vast Genius of Mrs. *Clive*[33] (inimitable in all Humour) have been lost and forgotten by the Folly and Ingratitude of the Town.

IT is pity, I think, that the Legislature do not interfere,[34] and put the Conduct of this so noble, so rational, and so useful a Diversion, into Hands more capable of conducting it; by which means public Entertainment and Example might be rather considered in Theatrical Performances, than the acquiring immense Fortunes to private Persons, who will make it more their Business to indulge, than to correct a vicious or bad Taste, when such prevails.

'TILL something of this kind is done, the Theatre can never truly flourish, nor the World reap so much either of the Useful or the Delightful from it, as it is capable of affording; but the Fustian of *Lee*[35] and *Rowe*,[36]

---

[32] Charles Macklin (1697–1797), comedian. At the beginning of his career he played Porer in HF's *Coffee-House Politician* (1730), and in the revival of *The Author's Farce* (1734) it was Macklin who as Marplay, Jr., 'took off' Theophilus Cibber. With HF at the Haymarket he played Squire Badger in *Don Quixote in England* (1734). From these early days, their association in the theatre continued and grew into an amusing friendship, still remembered by HF at the end of his life: see *Journal of a Voyage to Lisbon* (below, p. 606 n. 191, p. 635 n. 270).

[33] Catherine 'Kitty' Clive (1711–85), actress, who had a pleasant singing voice and excelled at comedy. As a dramatist in the 1730s, HF claimed to have been first to recognize her talents: in the Preface to *The Mock Doctor* (1732), in which she played Dorcas, he lauds her as one of 'the rising Glories of the Theatre', and he dedicated *The Intriguing Chambermaid* (1734) to her. In *Tom Jones* (IX. i) she is praised with Garrick for being a 'judicious' actor (p. 493) and in *Amelia* (I. vi) she is to acting what Shakespeare is to poetry and Hogarth to painting (p. 43). By the late 1740s, however, her fortunes were in decline. One writer observed that she, though once 'esteemed the Phaenix [*sic*] of the Age, seems now to be of little Consequence; her Laurels are all wither'd; her Friends grown cold; and the repeated Acclamations that us'd to welcome her Appearance, are now no more' ('J.T.', *A Letter of Compliment to the Author of a Treatise on the Passions* [1747?], p. 33). But however critical of her others might have become, HF remained her champion, as in *The Covent-Garden Journal*, No. 11 (8 February 1752): '*Mrs. Clive in her Walk on the Stage is the greatest Actress the World ever saw; and if as many really understood true Humour as pretend to understand it, she would have nothing to wish, but that the House was six Times as large as it is*' (p. 467).

[34] A curious volte-face in HF's thinking about governmental regulation of the theatres. In 1737 passage of the Theatrical Licensing Act put an end to his career as a dramatist. On the eve of that event, his views on the subject are evident, in the opinion of the present editor, in the essay *Some Thoughts on the Present State of the Theatres, and the Consequences of an Act to Destroy the Liberty of the Stage* (March 1737), where he insists that public taste, not 'the Legislature', is the only appropriate check on the 'Tyranny' of the playhouse managers: see Lockwood, 'A New Essay by Fielding', *MP*, 78 [1980], pp. 48–58; the essay is reprinted in *New Essays*, pp. 531–5.

[35] Nathaniel Lee (*c.*1649–1692), prolific author of tragedies in the high heroic mode. In the notes to the hilarious burlesque *The Tragedy of Tragedies* (1731) HF's persona, the pedant 'H. Scriblerus Secundus', quotes from no fewer than eight of Lee's plays. In *The Champion* (28 August 1740), p. 440, HF, as a sample of 'the Language of Mr. *Lee*', quotes a line from *Sophonisba* (1676); in *The Champion* (15 November 1740), p. 520, but in a less ironic vein, HF offers a passage from Lee's *Junius Brutus* (1681). In *Joseph Andrews* (III. x, p. 262) the Player quotes a passage from Lee's *Theodosia* (1680); and in *Tom Jones* (VI. xii) the same play provides the narrator with an inflated metaphor of 'the gigantic Poet *Lee*' (p. 312).

[36] On Rowe, see above, p. 486 n. 28.

with *French* and *Italian Buffoonry*,[37] will in a great measure monopolize the Stage.

THIS Regulation is then to be wished; but I am afraid it is to be despaired of: For as to the few truly Great Men[38] whom this Age hath produced, either the Necessity of the Times, or their own Inclinations, have totally diverted them from any Thoughts of this kind. They are themselves far from wanting Taste, (for none can be in reality a Great Man without it) but they will give themselves no trouble to reform that of the Public; thinking it probably of much less consequence to the Good of Society than it hath always appeared to the Wise of former Times.

AND if the Theatres be totally over-looked by them, it is no wonder that every other Branch of the Republic of Letters should meet with equal Disregard. This is notoriously the Case; for I think I may affirm with Truth, that there is no one Patron of true Genius, nor the least Encouragement left for it in this Kingdom.[39]

IF I was writing to a Sneerer, I might apprehend he would answer, by inverting the Complaint, and say, that there was no true Genius at present to patronize.

THIS in fact is not the Case; but admit that it was, the Reason would still be the Want of Encouragement; and indeed I may here apply the Answer of a Gardener to his covetous Master, who was angry that he had no Cucumbers in his Garden: *How should you have Cucumbers, Sir*, said the Gardener, *when you know you would not afford a Hot-Bed*[40] *to raise them in?*

PLANTS of this tender kind should be carefully watched when they first appear, and placed in warm Situations, if we expect any ripe and good Fruit

[37] Both Covent Garden and Drury Lane featured French dancers and ballet masters; the Italian opera was a favourite target of HF's ridicule.

[38] Cf. HF's verse epistle *Of True Greatness* (1741), dedicated to Dodington, his patron (*Miscellanies* i, pp. 19–29).

[39] In the closing paragraphs of his Introduction to *The True Patriot* (pp. cv–cvi) W. B. Coley offers a plausible explanation of HF's disappointment at not having been rewarded for his service to the government. Pelham, as HF remarked affecting disdain, took no interest in such services: 'Those who have the Honour to know him better than myself, assure me he hath the utmost Indifference for all Writers, and the greatest Contempt for any Good or Harm which they can do him' (*True Patriot*, No. 14 [28 January–4 February 1746], p. 209). His friends in the government—Lyttelton, Pitt, and Dodington—as yet lacked sufficient influence to serve him. Chesterfield remained aloof, above such pragmatics; and Bedford's benefactions were yet to come. A plausible explanation for the most part, but we now know that in April 1746 Bedford had begun acting as HF's patron by appointing him High Steward of the New Forest, Hants. (*Life*, pp. 408–9). And since it now also appears that HF had completed the first three books of *Tom Jones* by the time he wrote this Letter for his sister (see the Introduction, above, p. 463 n. 6), he was also, as the Dedication declares, enjoying Lyttelton's patronage. HF was indeed a 'true Genius', but it was not because he lacked patrons that he was seldom solvent.

[40] 'A bed of earth heated by fermenting manure, and usually covered with glass, for raising or forcing plants' (*OED*). The importance of hot beds in growing cucumbers in kitchen gardens is emphasized in Philip Miller's *Gardener's Kalendar*, 7th edn. (1745), p. 18 and *passim*, a copy of which was in HF's library (Ribbles M20). HF appears to have invented the anecdote to suit his present purpose.

from them. The cold Air of Neglect nips and destroys them; nor can their Shoots be ever strong and flourishing in a poor hungry Soil, which denies them Nourishment at the Root.

THERE have been indeed some Instances of Men of a very rare and singular Strength of Genius, which (to resume my Allegory) have flourished in the poorest Soil,[41] and bid defiance to the frosty Breath of the World; but they make a very thin Appearance in History: and even of these few or none perhaps ever arrived at the full Perfection of which they were capable.

'TILL some Patron then of the Muses shall again arise in this Nation, you will not be very curious in inquiring after their Productions. When I meet with any Performance untainted with Profaneness, Indecency, Slander, or Dulness, I will certainly send it to you.

ONE Particular, I think, now only remains to be spoken to; namely, the private Amusement of Persons in their own Houses. This, my Friend, consists of one Article only, *viz.* Whisk,[42] a Game so universally in vogue, that there are few Persons who do not play two or three Rubbers[43] every Day.

SEVERAL get a Livelihood, and others of consequence injure their Fortunes by these means; but much the larger Number play with such equal Success, and for such inconsiderable Stakes, that they lose nothing more than the Card-Money and their Time.

OF which latter, I am afraid, you will think I have already borrowed too much from you. I shall therefore conclude, by assuring you

I am, &c.

VALENTINE.

---

[41] In a similar 'Allegory' in *Ovid's Art of Love*, published a few weeks earlier, HF cites Philip Miller's *Gardener's Dictionary* on the different soils required for different plants (above, p. 451 and n. 93).

[42] 'Whisk' is the earlier name of the card game called whist (*OED*, sb.²). The rage for whisk, or whist (HF used both names), amused him, as it did Hogarth (see *Marriage à la Mode* [1745], pl. II). 'Whisk-Learning' would be among the 'Comical Humours of the Town' satirized at HF's puppet theatre in the spring of 1748 (see Battestin, 'Fielding and "Master Punch" in Panton Street', *PQ*, 45 [1966], p. 201) and in *The Covent-Garden Journal*, No. 56 (25 July 1752), 'the Whist Master' is necessary to form the character of 'the Town-Lady' (p. 305). In *Tom Jones* (XIII. v, p. 704) Nightingale is distressed at an accident that has spoiled his copy of the chief authority on the game, Edmond Hoyle's *A Short Treatise on the Game of Whist, containing the Laws of the Game* (1742), which sold for a guinea and had gone through nine editions by 1748; and later in the novel (XV. iii), Tom and Sophia, Lady Bellaston, and Lord Fellamar are found 'at Whist . . . in the last Game of their Rubbers' (p. 791). References to this fashionable card game are frequent in HF's writings from at least *The Champion* (25 March 1739/40), p. 247.

[43] A 'rubber' is a set of three games, won by the partners who take two out of three (*OED*, sb.²).

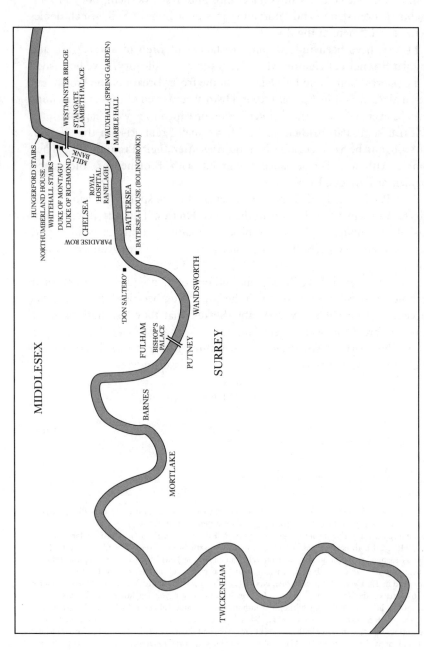

MIDDLESEX

HUNGERFORD STAIRS
NORTHUMBERLAND HOUSE
WHITEHALL STAIRS
DUKE OF MONTAGU
DUKE OF RICHMOND
MILL BANK
WESTMINSTER BRIDGE
STANGATE
LAMBETH PALACE
VAUXHALL (SPRING GARDEN)
MARBLE HALL

CHELSEA
ROYAL HOSPITAL
RANELAGH
BATTERSEA
PARADISE ROW
BATERSEA HOUSE (BOLINGBROKE)

'DON SALTERO'

BARNES

FULHAM

BISHOP'S PALACE

PUTNEY

WANDSWORTH

SURREY

MORTLAKE

TWICKENHAM

Map of the journey, Letter XLI. Based on Hugh Phillips, *The Thames about 1750* (1951), fig. 195A, which was compiled from Rocque's map of 1741–5

LETTER XLI.

A LETTER *from a* French *Gentleman to his Friend at* Paris; *in Imitation of* Horace,[44] Addison, *and all other Writers of travelling Letters.*[45]

Done into ENGLISH.

Monsieur,

AT *Whitehall* we took a Pair of Oars for *Putney.*[46] These we had indeed some Difficulty to procure; for many refused to go with us farther than *Foxhall* or *Ranelagh* Gardens.[47] At last we prevailed with two Fellows for three Half-Crowns to take us on board.

I HAVE been told there was formerly a Law regulating the Fares of these People; but that is to be sure obsolete. I think it pity it was not revived.[48]

As the Weather was extremely fine, we did not regret the Tide's running against us, since by that means we had more Opportunity of making Observations on the finest River in the World except the *Seine.*

[44] Quintus Horatius Flaccus (65–8 BC). In his *Satires*, I. v, Horace, whom HF called 'the best of all the Roman Poets' (Ribbles H38), describes a journey he took to Brundisium (today Brindisi), a harbour on the Adriatic coast of Italy connected with Rome by the Via Appia. Horace's farewell to the reader in that poem would later serve HF as he brought to a close his own *Journal of a Voyage to Lisbon* (see below, p. 659).

[45] In the Preface to the *Journal of a Voyage to Lisbon* HF exempts only Joseph Addison (1672–1719), author of *Remarks on Several Parts of Italy* (1705), and Gilbert Burnet from his general complaint against travel writers (see below, p. 547 and nn. 10–11). He also alludes to Addison's *Remarks* in *The Craftsman*, No. 539 (30 October 1736), *New Essays*, p. 175 and n. 6.

[46] See p. 490 for a map illustrating their journey up the Thames from Whitehall, Westminster, along the Surrey shore some 6 miles to Putney and then, crossing the river to Fulham, returning to London along the Middlesex shore to their destination at Hungerford Stairs, a short distance beyond Whitehall, with more convenient access to Charing Cross and the Strand.

[47] The two most fashionable pleasure gardens within a short distance upriver from town: Vauxhall, across the river on the Surrey shore (see below, pp. 492–3 nn. 55–6), and Ranelagh on the north shore in Middlesex (below, p. 498 n. 78). In *Amelia* (IX. ix) HF praises the 'extreme Beauty and Elegance' of the Vauxhall Gardens, as well as the 'Taste' and 'Virtue' of his friend Jonathan Tyers, who from 1732 to his death in 1767 was 'Master' of the resort (pp. 393–4 and n. 1). Ranelagh also figures in *Amelia* (VI. v), where the masquerades there serve the Noble Lord's schemes of debauching women (p. 247 and n. 1).

[48] Laws intended to regulate the watermen were enacted in 1514 (7 Hen. VIII, c. vi) and 1555 (2 and 3 P. & M., c. xvi); most recently, in 1737 (10 Geo. II, c. 31), a law had defined the conditions for apprenticeships. But rates for watermen on the Thames were fixed by the Lord Mayor and aldermen of London at 3*d.* for carrying a passenger a mile from London Bridge downriver to Wapping or upriver to Westminster. A waterman demanding or taking more than this rate 'lies liable to pay forty Shillings, and to suffer half a Year's Imprisonment' (*Universal Pocket Book* [1745]). In an essay on 'the fourth Estate' or 'Mob' in *The Covent-Garden Journal*, No. 49 (20 June 1752)—an essay, Bertrand Goldgar notes, written after the watermen's rates had been 'fixed by statute (*e.g.* 23 George II, c. 26)'—HF remarks that they continued to accept passengers 'only upon Suffrance; for which they pay whatever [the watermen] are pleased to exact of them' (p. 270 and n. 3). Complaining in *The Journal of a Voyage to Lisbon* (below, p. 589) about the gouging practices of the watermen of Deal, HF similarly regarded as extortionate the same charge of 'three half crowns' (i.e. a sum of 7*s.* 6*d.*).

AFTER taking a Survey of the *New Bridge*,[49] which must be greatly admired by all who have not seen the *Pontneuf*,[50] we past by a Row of Buildings, not very remarkable for their Elegance, being chiefly built of Wood, and irregular.[51] Many of them are supported by Pillars; but of what Order we could not plainly discern.[52]

WE came now to *Lambeth*, where is a Palace of the Archbishop of *Canterbury*, the Metropolitan of *England*. This is a vast Pile of Building, not very beautiful indeed in its Structure, but wonderfully well calculated, as well to signify, as to answer the Use for which it was, I suppose, originally intended; containing a great Number of little Apartments for the Reception of travelling and distressed Christians.[53]

Lambeth is perhaps so called from *Lamb*, which is the Type of Meekness.[54]

THE next Place of Note, as we ascend this River, is *Fox-Hall*, or rather *Fox-Hole*, the first Syllable of which is corrupted into *Vaux* by the Vulgar, who tell a foolish Story of one *Vaux* who resided here, and attempted to blow up the *Thames*.[55] But the true Reading is *Fox-Hole*, as appears by an antient Piece of Painting, representing that Animal whence it takes its

---

[49] i.e. Westminster Bridge; later the view of the city from it would inspire Wordsworth's sonnet. Begun in 1738 under the direction of the Swiss engineer Charles Labelye, it was opened to the public in November 1750. Before its completion the only means of crossing the Thames between London Bridge and Putney (see below, p. 494 n. 63) was by boat or horse ferry (*LE*, s.v.). Four paintings by Canaletto show the bridge under construction, as HF's traveller would have seen it: see David Bindman, *Complete Paintings of Canaletto* (London, 1970), nos. 265–7 and pls. LII–LIII.

[50] The Pont-Neuf, crossing both arms of the Seine at the west end of the Île de la Cité, is, despite its name, the oldest bridge in Paris, completed in 1603.

[51] Referring to Stangate, buildings situated on the south bank just past Westminster Bridge—the site now occupied by St Thomas's Hospital. See Rocque, 19Ba, and Phillips, *Thames*, p. 134, fig. 148A.

[52] A facetious reference to the orders of columns in classical architecture: three in Greek = Doric, Ionic, Corinthian; two in Roman = Tuscan and Composite.

[53] Lambeth Palace: the official residence of the Archbishop of Canterbury, metropolitan of the Church of England. Built originally as a house for Premonstratensian canons (*c*.1200), the chapel was added soon after, the Lollard's Tower in 1432—so called from a legend that followers of Wyclif were imprisoned there, though it was built as a water tower—and the gatehouse in 1486–1501 (*LE*, s.v. Lambeth Palace).

[54] Though spiritual rather than economic, HF's conjectural etymology for Lambeth is close to correct: the *Domesday Book* (1086) records *Lambehythe*, indicating 'a bay from which lambs are shipped', i.e. shipped from the Surrey meadows across the Thames to the City. In his series 'An Apology for the Clergy' in *The Champion* (29 March 1740) HF, defining the true character of a clergyman, quotes Christ's injunction to the disciples in Luke 10: 3: 'Go your ways: behold, I send you forth as lambs among wolves.' HF continues by declaring 'Humility' the essential 'Virtue' of his followers (pp. 259, 260).

[55] The French gentleman's claim that 'Vauxhall' is a sophistication of 'Fox-Hall' appears to have merit. According to the *London Encyclopaedia*, 'Vauxhall Derived its name from Falkes de Breauté (second husband of Margaret, widow of Baldwin de Redvers) who built a house here in the reign of King John. It was formerly known as Fulke's Hall, Faukeshall and Foxhall.' Citing Owen Manning and William Bray, *The History and Antiquities of Surrey* (1814), iii, p. 489; and Thomas Allen, *The History and Antiquities of the Parish of Lambeth* (1826), pp. 359, 370–1, Baker, in his MS note to the passage, recalls a local tradition attributing the name to Guy Fawkes because, at some time before he joined them, the conspirators of the plot to blow up Parliament on 5 November 1605 had met somewhere in the vicinity.

Name, and which is now to be seen on a high wooden Pillar, *Anglicè* a Sign-Post, not far from the Landing-Place.[56]

A VERY little further stands *Marble-Hall*,[57] of which we had a full View from the Water. This is a most august Edifice, built all of a rich Marble, which reflecting the Sun-Beams, creates an Object too dazling for the Sight.

HAVING passed this, we were entertained with a most superb Piece of Architecture of white, or rather yellow Brick. This belongs to one of the *Bourgeois*, as do indeed most of the Villas which border on both sides this River, and they tend to give as magnificent an Idea of the Riches which flow in to these People by Trade,[58] as the Shipping doth, which is to be seen below the Bridge of *London*.

HENCE a Range of most delicious Meadows begins to open, which, being richly enamelled with Flowers of all kinds, seem to contend whether they shall convey most Pleasure to your Sight or to your Smell. Our Contemplation was however diverted from this Scene by a Boat, in which were two young Ladies extremely handsome, who accosted us in some Phrase which we, who thought ourselves pretty good Masters of the *English* Tongue, did not understand. They were answered however by our Watermen, who afterwards told us, that this is called Water-Language; and consequently, I suppose, not to be learn'd on Shore.[59]

THE next Place which presents itself on the *Surry* Side (for I reserve the other Shore for my Return) is the pleasant Village of *Battersea*; the true Reading of which we conjectured to be *Bettersee*; and that it was formerly a

---

[56] As for the French gentleman's 'Fox-Hole', if the alleged 'Sign-Post' belonged to a tavern there is no record of it in Bryant Lillywhite, *London Signs* (London, 1972), s.v. 'fox'. HF, however, who was in general amused by the iconography of signposts, may simply have taken this opportunity to invent one (see his essay on the subject in *The Craftsman*, No. 623 [17 June 1738] and the introduction to it: *New Essays*, pp. 311–22).

[57] 'Marble Hall' is shown in Rocque's map as situated at riverside on a walk leading directly to Vauxhall Spring Gardens (Rocque, 19Ac). Entered as 'Marble Hill' in the *London Encyclopaedia*: 'It was opened in 1740 by Joseph Crosier who enlarged and illuminated the gardens and provided a "Long Room" for dancing.' From 1752 to 1756 it was a dancing school, and later a coffee house and tavern.

[58] In his Introduction to the Wesleyan Edition of the *Enquiry*, Malvin Zirker comments on HF's 'ambiguous remarks on the benefits of trade', which at once enriches the nation and corrupts it by introducing luxury' (p. lxiv). For what Zirker calls HF's 'most enthusiastic encomium on trade' (p. 70 n. 7), see *The Journal of a Voyage to Lisbon* (below, p. 586 and n. 135).

[59] Cf. *The Champion* (28 August 1740), where a female correspondent complains of 'that Licentiousness used on the River of *Thames*, and which, if I am not mistaken, is called *Water-Language* . . . Language which I cannot repeat the least Syllable of' (p. 443). In *The Covent-Garden Journal*, No. 49 (20 June 1752) HF remarks how the watermen express their resentment of better-dressed passengers, whom 'they never fail to attack . . . with all Kind of scurrilous, abusive and indecent Terms, which indeed they claim as their own, and call Mob Language' (p. 270). In the present case, of course, the 'handsome' young ladies are no doubt to be numbered among the well-dressed prostitutes who ply their trade among the gentry who flock to the pleasure gardens at Vauxhall, as noticed by Addison in *The Spectator*, No. 383 (20 May 1712).

Bishoprick,[60] and had the Preference to *Shelsee*, of which we shall speak anon. It is chiefly famous at present for affording a Retreat to one of the greatest Statesmen of his Time, who hath here a magnificent Palace.[61]

FROM *Bettersee*, verging to the South-West, stands *Wansor*,[62] as it is vulgarly called; but its true Name was undoubtedly *Windmill-Shore*, from whence it is a very easy Corruption; and several Windmills are yet to be found in its Neighbourhood. Here are to be seen a Parish-Church, and some Houses; but it is otherwise little worth the Curiosity of Travellers.

As you sail from hence, two lofty Towers at once salute your Eyes from opposite Shores of the River, divided by a magnificent wooden Bridge.[63] That on the *Surry* Shore is called *Putney*[64] or *Putnigh*, a fair and beautiful Town, consisting principally of one vast Street, which extends from North to South, and is adorned with most beautiful Buildings.

HERE we went ashore, in order to regale ourselves in one of their Houses of Entertainment, as they are called; but in reality there is no Entertainment at them. Here were no Tarts nor Cheesecakes, nor any sort of Food but an *English* Dish called *Breadandcheese*, and some raw Flesh.

---

[60] HF puns on 'sea' and 'see' (the seat or diocese of a bishop), but Battersea was never a bishopric. The earliest record is a charter of AD 693 granting to the Abbess of Barking 'Batrices Ege' (i.e. 'Badric's Island', the site being surrounded by water) (*LE*).

[61] A compliment to Henry St John, first Viscount Bolingbroke (1678–1751), who served under Queen Anne as Secretary of State (1710–14) and, fleeing to France after the accession of George I, served the Pretender in the same capacity. More recently, after an absence of ten years, Bolingbroke had returned from France in 1744 and retired to Battersea House (the Manor House). Situated on the river near St Mary's Church, where he was baptized and buried, the house, having forty rooms on a floor, might well be called a 'Palace' (Charles Petrie, *Bolingbroke* [London, 1937], H. T. Dickinson, *Bolingbroke*, [London, 1970]).

The compliment here may well puzzle readers of HF's posthumously published *Fragment of a Comment on L. Bolingbroke's Essays* (below, pp. 667–80). At this time, however, though he scorned Bolingbroke's early association with the Jacobites, HF remained his admirer, an attitude first evident in his writings for *The Craftsman* (1734–9), an anti-ministerial journal founded by Bolingbroke (see headnote to Appendix A, below). Bolingbroke's political ideology of disinterested patriotism became the programme of the Opposition to Walpole, adopted by HF and his friends Lyttelton and Dodington. Once back in England, Bolingbroke had worked behind the scenes to assure the rise to power of the 'Broad Bottom' government, whose interests HF promoted in *The True Patriot* at the time of the rebellion. When introducing that journal to the public, he teasingly hinted it was 'very probable' the author was 'Lord B———ke. This I collect from my Stile and Knowledge in Politics' (pp. 108–9).

[62] i.e. the borough of Wandsworth, which takes its name from the River Wandle, a small tributary of the Thames. Known for its industries, it was occupied chiefly by fullers, who bleached cloth, by hatters, and by Huguenots renowned for their iron and copperware (*LE*).

[63] In 1727–9 a toll bridge built of timber was built across the Thames connecting Putney and Fulham. Until 1750, when Westminster Bridge opened (see above, p. 492 n. 49), it was the only bridge across the river west of London Bridge. For views of the bridge, see Phillips, *Thames*, p. 171 (figs. 193–4).

[64] The name derives from Anglo-Saxon and means 'Putta's landing-place'. Putney was long considered a desirable suburban locale and by the eighteenth century it had become fashionable; in 1720 the Duchess Dowager of Marlborough (see above, pp. 196–237) purchased the manor, which after her death in 1744 remained in the Spencer family (*LE*). Adjacent to Putney upriver is Barnes, where in 1746–7, as he began writing *Tom Jones*, HF lived during the summer at Milbourne House (see the Introduction, above, p. 467 n. 13).

BUT if it be difficult to find any thing to allay Hunger, it is still more so to quench your Thirst. There is a Liquor sold in this Country which they call Wine, (most of the Inhabitants indeed call it *Wind*.)[65] Of what Ingredients it is composed I cannot tell; but you are not to conceive, as the Word seems to import, that this is a Translation of our *French* Word *Vin*, a Liquor made of the Juice of the Grape; for I am very well assured there is not a Drop of any such Juice in it. There must be many Ingredients in this Liquor, from the many different Tastes; some of which are sweet, others sour, and others bitter; but though it appeared so nauseous to me and my Friend, that we could not swallow it, the *English* relish it very well; nay, they will often drink a Gallon of it at a Sitting; and sometimes in their Cups (for it intoxicates) will wantonly give it the Names of all our best Wines.

HOWEVER, though we found nothing to eat or drink, we found something to pay. I send you a Copy of the Bill produced us on this Occasion, as I think it a Curiosity:

	s.	*d.*
For Bread and Bear —	0	8
Eating — —	2	0
Wind — —	5	0
Watermens Eating and Lickor	1	6
	9	2

So that, with the Drawer, we were at the Expence of ten Shillings; though no Catholic ever kept an *Ash-Wednesday* better.[66]

THE Drawers here may want some Explanation: You must know then, that in this Country, in whatever House you eat or drink, whether private or public, you are obliged to pay the Servants a Fee at your Departure, otherwise they certainly affront you.

THESE Fees are called Vails;[67] and they serve instead of Wages: for though in private Houses the Master generally contracts with his Servant to give him Wages, yet these are seldom or never paid; and indeed the Vails commonly amount to much more.

FROM *Putnigh* we crossed over to the other Shore, where stands the fair

---

[65] For HF's amusement at this peculiarly English drink, see *Journal of a Voyage to Lisbon* (below, p. 601 and n. 175).

[66] Ash Wednesday marks the beginning of the Christian season of Lent, a period of fasting and penitence lasting forty weekdays before Easter.

[67] In the eighteenth century a vail was 'a gratuity . . . given by a visitor on his departure to the servants of the house in which he has been a guest' (*OED*, s.v. 'vail' II. 5). Cf. *The Champion* (26 February 1740), where the 'Servants . . . seemed to look on their Vails as a surer Subsistence than their Wages' (p. 201).

and beautiful Town of *Full home*, vulgarly called *Fulham*.[68] It is principally
remarkable for being the Residence of a Bishop; but a large Grove of Trees
prevented our seeing his Palace from the Water.[69]

THESE two Towns were founded by two Sisters; and they received their
Names from the following Occasion. These Ladies being on the *Surry*
Shore, called for a Boat to convey them across the Water. The Watermen
being somewhat lazy, and not coming near enough to the Land, the Lady
who had founded the Town which stands in *Surry*, bid them *put nigh*; upon
which her Sister immediately cried out, *A good Omen; let* Putnigh *be the
Name of the Place.* When they came to the other Side, she who had founded
the other Town, ordered the Watermen to push the Boat *full home*; her
Sister then returned the Favour, and gave the Name of *Full home* to the
Place.

HERE stands a most stately and magnificent Bridge.[70] We inquired of
the Watermen by whose Benefaction this was built. *Benefaction, do you call
it?* says one of them with a Sneer; *I heartily wish it had been by mine; there
hath been a fine Parcel of Money got by that* JOB;[71] a Name which the *English*
give to all Works of a public Nature: For so grateful are these People, that
nobody ever doth any thing for the Public, but he is certain to make his
Fortune by it.

WE now returned by the Shore of *Middlesex*, and passed by several
beautiful Meadows where the new-mow'd Hay would have wonderfully
delighted our Smell, had it not been for a great Variety of dead Dogs, Cats,
and other Animals, which being plentifully bestrewed along this Shore, a good
deal abated the Sweetness which must have otherwise impregnated the Air.

WE at length arrived at *Shelsee*,[72] a Corruption from *Shallow See*; for the

---

[68] The name 'Fulham' is 'said to be derived from a personal name and to mean Fulla's settlement in a
low-lying bend of the river'. The town of Fulham, to which the bridge leads from Putney, is the centre of
the manor of Fulham, which was granted to the Bishops of London in the eighth century. From about the
eleventh century it was their summer home, and the Bishop's Palace was their manor house (*LE*).

[69] HF's observation in 1747 that the Palace was hidden by 'a large Grove of Trees', supports the view
that the grove, which today consists of 'many rare trees', was planted not by the nineteenth-century
bishops Howley, Blomfield, and Jackson (as seemed probable to the author of the *London Encyclopaedia*
[s.v. Fulham Palace]), but instead (as seemed less likely to him) by Edmund Grindal and Henry Compton,
Bishops of London in, respectively, 1559–70 and 1675–1713.

[70] HF repeats the observation already made (above, p. 494 and n. 63).

[71] 'JOB': a public service or trust turned to private gain (*OED*, s.v. 'job' 3). Cf. Pope, *The Fourth Satire
of Dr. John Donne* (1733): 'Who makes a *Trust*, or *Charity*, a Job, | And gets an Act of Parliament to rob?'
(lines 142–3; Twickenham edn., iv, p. 37). The building of the Putney–Fulham Bridge was undertaken by
an Act of 1726 urged through Parliament by Walpole.

[72] i.e. Chelsea, a metropolitan borough west of the city of Westminster. Like the others in this letter, the
etymology proposed by HF's Frenchman is silly. The origin of the name is disputed: citing 'Cealchythe'
and 'Chelcith' in the earliest records, the *Encyclopedia Britannica* (11th edn., p. 24b) suggests the meanings
'a gravel bank thrown up by the river' or 'a haven'; the *London Encyclopaedia*, citing forms of the name
such as 'Chelcheya' and 'Chelchythe', prefers 'Chalk Wharf'. It was never a bishopric.

Word shallow signifies *empty, worthless*. Thus a *shallow Purse* and a *shallow Fellow* are Words of Contempt. This, formerly, was doubtless a small Bishoprick, and inferior to that on the other Side the Water, which was called *Bettersee*.

HERE are many things worthy the Curiosity of Travellers. This Place is famous for the Residence of *Don Saltero*, a *Spanish* Nobleman, who hath a vast Collection of all sorts of Rarities;[73] but we had not time to see them.

HERE is likewise a Walk called *Paradise-Row*,[74] from the delightful Situation, and the magnificent Buildings with which it is adorned. We had certainly gone on shore to admire the Beauty of this Walk; but here being no Landing-Place, we must have spoiled our Stockings, by stepping into the Mud; and were besides informed, that the Road was so abominably dirty, that it would be difficult to cross; the latter, as it seemed entirely stopped up by a great Number of Dust-Carts.[75]

A LITTLE farther stands an Hospital, or rather a Palace, for the Reception of old and wounded Soldiers.[76] A Benefaction of so noble a kind, that it really doth honour to the *English* Nation. Here are some very beautiful Apartments, which they told us belonged to the Officers; a Word

[73] 'Don Saltero' was not in fact 'a *Spanish* Nobleman' but one James Salter (d. 1728), a versatile Irishman who, having served as valet and barber in the household of Sir Hans Sloane (1660–1753), collector of curiosities and specimens of natural history, opened a coffee house in Cheyne Walk, Chelsea, *c.*1697. Given the sobriquet 'Don Saltero' by Admiral Sir John Munden, whose voyaging to the coast of Spain had resulted in a weakness for Spanish titles, Salter and the Chelsea Coffee-House, 'where the *Literati* sit in Council', were introduced to the general public by Richard Steele in *The Tatler*, No. 34 (28 June 1709). Benefiting from his association with Sloane, who from 1712 lived in Chelsea, 'Don Saltero' filled the coffee house with curiosities; by Steele's estimate there were 'Ten thousand Gimcracks round the Room and on the Sieling'—among them a straw hat said to have been 'Pontius Pilate's *Wife's Chamber-Maid's Sister's Hat*' (quotations are from *Tatler*, ed. Donald F. Bond, 3 vols. [Oxford, 1987], i, pp. 252, 254). But Don Saltero speaks for himself in the *Weekly Journal* (23 June 1723): 'Monsters of all sorts here are seen, | Strange things in nature as they grew so, | Some relicks of the Sheba Queen, | And fragments of the fam'd Bob Crusoe. | Knick-knacks, too, dangle round the wall, | Some in glass cases, some on the shelf; | But what's the greatest sight of all, | Your humble servant shows himself. | On this my chiefest hope depends, | Now if you will the cause espouse, | In journals pray direct your friends | To my Museum Coffee House.' From 1718 Don Saltero's Chelsea Coffee-House was located at 18 Cheyne Walk; after Salter's death, his daughter and her husband continued it as a tavern until 1758. In 1867 it became a private residence. (Henry C. Shelley, *Inns and Taverns of Old London* [Boston, 1909], pt. II: 'Coffee-Houses of Old London'; Lillywhite, p. 194.)

[74] A street in Chelsea running between Dilke Street near the river and Royal Hospital Road, Paradise Row (now Paradise Walk) was formerly lined with neat small Georgian houses (*LE*, s.v. Paradise Walk).

[75] A tumbrel or cart for conveying refuse. The only example in the *OED* is from 1776 (2nd edn., s.v. 'dust' 8, comb.).

[76] Founded in 1682 by Charles II, who appointed Christopher Wren as architect, Chelsea Hospital for veteran soldiers was finished in 1692. The handsomest of institutional buildings, it was well described by Thomas Carlyle as 'quiet and dignified and the work of a gentleman'. In 1719 HF's father, General Edmund Fielding (1680–1741), was commissioned Colonel of a new Regiment of Invalids raised from the out-pensioners of the Hospital, a command he kept for the rest of his life. Later, HF's friend and collaborator the Revd William Young (see above, pp. 238–9), who had served as chaplain in the Army during the War of the Austrian Succession, would reside at the Hospital during the last years of his life; he died and was buried there in 1757. (*LE* and *Life*, pp. 18, 189–90.)

which led us into a Mistake, as we afterwards discovered: For we imagined that these Apartments were allotted to those Gentlemen who had borne Commissions in the Army, and who had, by being disabled in the Service, entitled themselves to the public Favour; but on further Inquiry, we were surprized to find there was no Provision at all for any such; and that these Officers were a certain Number of Placemen,[77] who had never borne Arms, nor had any military Merit whatever.

BEYOND this stands *Ranelagh*, of which we shall say no more, than that it is a very large round Room, and will contain abundance of People.[78] This is indeed a sufficient Recommendation to the *English*, who never inquire farther into the Merit of any Diversion, when they hear it is very much frequented. A Humour, of which we saw many Instances: all their publick Places being either quite empty of Company, or so crouded, that we could hardly get to them.

HENCE sailing by a Shore where we saw little very remarkable, save only the Carcasses of Animals, which were here in much greater plenty than we had before found them, we arrived at a Place called *Mill-Bank* or *Mile-Bank*;[79] and soon after we passed, as we were informed, by the Senate-Houses: but though we went within a few Yards of them, we could not discern with any Certainty which were they.[80]

HAVING again shot (as they call it) the *New Bridge*,[81] we saw the Palace of a Nobleman, who hath the Honour to be a Duke of *France* as well as of *England*, and the Happiness to be greatly esteemed in both Countries.[82]

---

[77] 'One who holds an appointment in the service of the sovereign or the state ... appointed to such a position from motives of interest, without regard to fitness' (*OED*, s.v. 'placeman'; earliest citing 1741).

[78] At Ranelagh Gardens, which opened to the public in 1742 just east of Chelsea Hospital, the most prominent feature was a large rococo Rotunda 150 feet in diameter. Into it for a shilling was admitted 'everybody that loves eating, drinking, staring or crowding' (*LE*). See also *Ovid's Art of Love* (above, p. 403 n. 18).

[79] Millbank by the 1740s—after Sir Robert Grosvenor, in order to build a house, had demolished the Westminster Abbey mill that gave the place its name—had become a lonely riverside road stretching about a mile from Westminster to Chelsea (*LE*).

[80] The 'Senate-Houses', presumably, are what remained of the Palace of Westminster, the residence of the kings and home of the court from the time of Edward the Confessor and William the Conqueror until Henry VIII, who abandoned it for Whitehall Palace in 1512. Chief among the remaining buildings were Westminster Hall and St Stephen's Chapel, which served as the House of Commons.

[81] See above, p. 492 n. 49.

[82] Charles Lennox (1701–50), second Duke of Richmond, grandson of Charles II by his mistress Louise de Keroualle, Duchess of Portsmouth; upon her death in 1734, he also became Duke of Aubigny, France. HF greatly admired Richmond, his friend and patron: to Richmond he dedicated both *The Miser* (1733), his version of Molière's comedy *L'Avare*, and the verse epistle *Of Good-Nature* (*Miscellanies* i [1743]). Richmond's house was in Privy Gardens, Whitehall, overlooking the river just east of Westminster Bridge. In 1746 he commissioned Canaletto to paint views of the Thames and Whitehall from his house, the former including the house of his friend the Duke of Montagu (see Phillips, *Thames*, figs. 133–4; also figs. 130–2). Richmond and the Duchess each subscribed to *Familiar Letters* on royal paper.

NEAR this Palace stands that of another Duke, who, among other great and good Qualities, is reputed the most benevolent Man in the World.[83]

A LITTLE further we saw the Palace of an Earl, of a very high Character likewise among his Countrymen; and who, in Times of Corruption, hath maintained the Integrity of an old *Roman*.[84]

THE Palaces of these three Noblemen, who do a real Honour to their high Rank, and who are greatly beloved and respected by their Country, are extremely elegant in their Buildings, as well as delightful in their Situation; and, to be sincere, are the only Edifices that discover any true Taste, which we saw in all our Voyage.

WE now approached to *Hungerford-Stairs*,[85] the Place destined for our landing; where we were entertained with a Sight very common, it seems, in this Country: This was the ducking a Pickpocket.[86] When we were first

---

[83] John (1688?–1749), second Duke of Montagu, the inseparable companion of the Duke of Richmond (above, n. 82), lived next to him on the riverside. Montagu is chiefly remembered for the practical jokes he played, assisted by Richmond. Theirs, for example, was the scheme of causing a riot by politicizing the Revd James Miller's comedy *The Modish Couple* (1732), for which HF wrote the Epilogue (see above, p. 109). In 1749, the year Montagu died, they were also behind the famous 'Bottle Conjuror' hoax that resulted in the destruction of the Little Theatre in the Haymarket (*Life*, pp. 464–5). But Montagu, as HF here declares, was also known for his benevolence. He kept a home for superannuated cows and horses, and left a bequest for his 'dogs, cats and creatures'. Upon his death Horace Walpole wrote: 'His loss will be extremely felt! He paid no less than £2,700 a year in private pensions, which ought to be known, to balance his immense history of places . . . In short with some foibles, he was a most amiable man, and one of the most feeling I ever knew' (*Yale Walpole*, xx, p. 79). The Duchess of Montagu subscribed to *Familiar Letters* on royal paper.

[84] HF refers to the only 'Palace' between Whitehall and the Hungerford Stairs: Northumberland House, Charing Cross, which, facing the Strand, had views to the south over gardens and the river. It was not, however, occupied by an earl, but by Charles Seymour (1662–1748), sixth Duke of Somerset. HF may have assumed that Seymour, through his marriage in 1682 to the heiress Elizabeth Percy, daughter of the Earl of Northumberland, had assumed the title when the male line became extinct with the death of her father; however, in 1687 James II denied him that honour because he had refused to introduce the papal nuncio at court. Upon the Duke's death in 1748, his son Algernon (1684–1750), the seventh Duke, became Earl of Northumberland by maternal descent.

In praising Somerset's 'very high Character' HF may have had in mind his acting from Whig–Protestant principles in defying James II by refusing to introduce the papal nuncio; or in 1708 his siding with the Whigs Marlborough and Godolphin against Harley, the Tory Prime Minister under Queen Anne—both acts that cost him honours those monarchs had bestowed on him. More important than these examples, moreover, was the role Somerset played in 1714 when Anne was dying: by joining with other Whig lords in insisting on their right to be present at the meeting of the Privy Council, he was instrumental in securing the Hanoverian Succession. (*EB*, s.v. 'Somerset, Earls and Dukes of'; *Oxford Companion to British History*, ed. John Cannon [Oxford, 1997].)

[85] The next landing upriver after Whitehall Stairs, from which the travellers began their journey (above, p. 491 and n. 46), Hungerford Stairs led from the river directly to Hungerford Market and the Strand (see map, above, p. 490).

[86] Cf. *The Covent-Garden Journal*, No. 68 (28 October 1752), where HF recommends that a magistrate or a clergyman who commits adultery be 'esteemed as infamous as he who picks his Neighbour's Pocket, and therefore might with no Impropriety suffer that same Punishment which the Mob inflict on the latter Crime, viz. Ducking in a Horsepond' (p. 361).

told this, we imagined it might be the Execution of some legal Sentence; but we were informed, that his Executioners had been likewise his Judges.

To give you some Idea of this, (for it is impossible for any one who doth not live in what they call a free Country, to have an adequate Notion of a Mob)[87] whenever a Pickpocket is taken in the Fact, the Person who takes him calls out *Pickpocket.* Upon which Word, the Mob, who are always at hand in the Street, assemble; and having heard the Accusation, and sometimes the Defence, (though they are not always very strict as to the latter, judging a good deal by Appearances) if they believe the Accuser, the Prisoner is sentenced to be ducked; and this Sentence is immediately executed with such Rigour, that he hardly escapes with his Life.

The Mob take Cognizance of all other Misdemeanors which happen in the Streets,[88] and they are a Court, which generally endeavours to do Justice, tho' they sometimes err, by the Hastiness of their Decisions. Perhaps it is the only Court in the World, where there is no Partiality arising from Respect of Persons.

They are great Enemies to the Use of Swords, as they are Weapons with which they are not intrusted. If a Gentleman draws a Sword, tho' it be only *in terrorem* to defend himself, he is certain to be very severely treated by them; but they give great Encouragement to their Superiors, who will condescend to shew their Courage in the way which the Mob themselves use, namely, Boxing, of which we shall presently shew you an Instance.

Our Boat was now with some difficulty close to the Landing-place; for there was a great Croud of Boats, every one of which, instead of making way for us, served to endeavour to keep us out. Upon this occasion many hundred Curses passed between our Watermen and their Fellows, and not a few Affronts were cast on us, especially as we were drest after the manner of our Country.

---

[87] Before becoming a magistrate, HF, as in the present case, could look upon the rough justice meted out by the London mob with a certain amused detachment. More typical of his later attitude, which owed much to such experiences as the riots of July 1749, when thousands of angry sailors looted brothels in the Strand and set fire to the furniture in the street, are essays in *The Covent-Garden Journal*, Nos. 47 and 49 (13, 20 June 1752), in which he refers sarcastically to 'the Mobility' as the nation's 'fourth Estate' and declares that it is 'entirely owing' to their fear of the law and of the Army that the rabble 'have not long since rooted all the other Orders out of the Commonwealth' (p. 273). See also HF's reflections on 'the mob and their betters' in *The Journal of a Voyage to Lisbon* (below, p. 610 and nn. 200–1). For discussion of contemporary attitudes towards the 'mob', see the following: G. Rudé, 'The London "Mob" of the Eighteenth Century', *Historical Journal*, 2 (1959), pp. 1–18; id., *The Crowd in History: A Study of Popular Disturbances in France and England, 1730–1848* ([New York], 1964); and Herbert M. Atherton, 'The "Mob" in Eighteenth-Century Caricature', *ECS*, 12 (1978), pp. 47–58.

[88] Cf. *Amelia* (XII. vi), where 'the frequent Cry of "stop Thief" . . . presently drew together a large Mob, who began, as is usual, to enter immediately upon Business, and to make strict Enquiry into the Matter, in order to proceed to do Justice in their summary Way' (p. 519).

AT last we arrived safe on shore, where we paid our Watermen, who grumbled at our not giving them something to drink, (for all the labouring People of this Country apply their Hire only to Eatables, for which reason they expect *something over and above* to drink.)

As we walked towards the *Strand*, a Drayman[89] run his Whip directly into my Friend's Face, perhaps with no Design of doing this, but at the same time, without any Design of avoiding it. My Friend, who is impatient of an Affront, immediately struck the Carter with his Fist, who attempted to return the Favour with his Whip; but Monsieur *Bellair*, who is extremely strong and active, and who hath learnt to box in this Country, presently closed in with him, and tript up his Heels.

THE Mob now assembled round us, and being pleased with my Friend for not having drawn his Sword, inclined visibly to his side, and commended many Blows which he gave his Adversary, and other Feats of Activity[90] which he displayed during the Combat, that lasted some Minutes; at the End of which, the Drayman yielded up the Victory, crying with a Sneer—*D—n you, you have been on the Stage, or I am mistaken.*[91]

THE Mob now gave a Huzza in my Friend's favour, and sufficiently upbraided his Antagonist, who, they said, was well enough served for affronting a Gentleman.

MONSIEUR *Bellair* had on the Beginning of the Scuffle, while the Enemy lay on the Ground, delivered his Sword to one of the By-standers; which Person had unluckily walked off in the Croud, without remembring to restore it.

UPON this the Mob raged violently, and swore Vengeance against the Thief, if he could be discovered; but, as this could not be done, he was obliged at length to submit to the Loss.

WHEN we began to depart, several of our Friends demanded of us something to drink; but, as we were more out of humour with the Loss, than pleased with the Glory obtained, we could not be prevailed with to open our Purses.

---

[89] Dray: a low cart without sides used for carrying heavy loads; usually a brewer's cart (*OED*, s.v. 3).

[90] 'Feats of Activity': the *OED* (s.v. 'activity' 3) gives the obsolete meaning 'Physical exercise, gymnastics, athletics', quoting Steele, *Tatler* (1709), No. 51: 'A great deal of good Company of us were this Day to see or rather to hear an artful Person do several Feats of Activity.'

[91] Cf. *Tom Jones* (XIII. v), where the footman Tom has knocked down exclaims, 'I'll nothing more to do with you, you have been upon the Stage, or I am d—nably mistaken' (p. 703). In that context (p. 702 and n. 1) the stage HF has in mind is that of the champion prize-fighter John Broughton (1705–89), at whose Amphitheatre in Oxford Road from 1743 until it was closed by the legislature in 1750, bloody combats were staged in boxing, cudgel-playing, and at broadsword. Cf, *The Champion* (1 April 1740), where one 'Vander Bruin' (i.e. HF on April Fool's Day) remarks on HF's frequenting such events (p. 262 and n. 2).

THE Company were incensed at this. We were saluted with the Titles of *Mounshire*, and other contemptuous Appellations; several missile Weapons, such as Dirt, *&c.* began likewise to play on us, and we were both challenged to fight by several, who told my Friend, tho' he beat the Drayman, he was not above half a Man.

WE then made the best of our way, and soon escaped into a Hackney-Coach.

THUS I have sent you a particular Account of this Voyage, from some Parts of which you may perhaps conclude, that the meanest Rank of People are in this Country better provided for, than their Superiors; and that the Gentry, at least those of the lower Class of that Order, fare full as well in other Places: for, to say the truth, it appears to me, that an *Englishman* in that Station, is liable to be opprest by all above him, and insulted by all below him.

I am, &c.

LETTER XLII.

From Miss PRUDENTIA FLUTTER

to Miss LUCY RURAL

Sunday *Morning, Seven o'Clock, just out of Bed.*

Dear LUCY,

I SHOULD have writ to you sooner, according to my Promise, but I have not had one moment's Time since I came to Town, till now; and, if I had not taken the opportunity of a Sunday, I don't believe I should have been able to write till I had seen you, which I hope,[92] my Dear, will be a long Time hence, unless you can persuade your Papa to let you come to Town.

WELL then, to begin. After a tedious Journey of five Days, my Papa and Mamma, and myself and *Alice*, arrived safe in charming *London*. Poor Mamma was sick upon the Road, and could not eat; so we brought half our Cake, almost a whole Turkey, great Part of a Ham, and a Mutton-Pye quite through.

---

[92] 'hope': expect or anticipate (without implication of desire); suppose (*OED*, v. 4, obs.—the latest example given is 1632).

AND now, my Dear, I must tell you, we have taken a Lodging in *Pall-Mall*, which is to serve us for the present; but my Mamma says it won't do, for she wants a whole House to herself in Thingamy-Square.[93] Papa looks a little grim, but I believe Mamma will get the better, for she has cryed about it twice already.

I HAVE been only at four Plays yet, so I can't give you much Opinion about them; but the Play-House is a charming Place, I can assure you; such a many Candles makes one look so grim;[94] and there is such a Number of fine Gentlemen, I never saw. And the Player-Men are fine Men too, and prodigiously well drest: There is one sweet Man among them; I wanted to hear him talk; but, tho' he came upon the Stage several times, he never once opened his Mouth. He is a sweet Man; but this is not he, that all the Ladies are in love with; for there is one Mr. *Grick*,[95] by almost a Foot, I warrant you: I ask'd a young Lady, who sat by me, his Name, and she answered me, he was nobody; I assure her he was handsomer than any body.[96]

O, BUT, my Dear, I must tell you; there is one Colonel *Sprucely*, who is got so well acquainted with Mamma already, that they are almost always together, especially when Papa's not at home. I am always sent out of the Room when he comes; but if I had my handsome Player-Man with me, I should not envy her his Company.

I WARRANT you will stare, to hear me own I think a Man handsome; but it is all the Fashion, and there is no harm in it here: I was a little ashamed the

[93] Mrs Flutter scorns lodging in rooms even though they are in the fashionable street of Pall Mall near the royal palace of St James; she prefers a house in the recently developed and still more fashionable residential areas of Mayfair: Hanover or Grosvenor Square. When Tom Jones reaches London (XIII. ii), he arrives in 'a Quarter of the Town, the Inhabitants of which have very little Intercourse with the Housholders of *Hanover* and *Grosvenor* Square' (p. 689). As for 'Thingamy'—or 'Thingummy' in the *OED*, where it is synonymous with 'what-you-may-call-it'—Miss Flutter, having just used the verb 'hope' in an obsolete sense more than 200 years after the last example cited in that dictionary, now uses 'Thingamy' fifty years before the earliest example cited (Fanny Burney's *Camilla* [1796]).

[94] 'gim': spruce, smart (*OED*, s.v. obs. except in dialect; pronounced 'jim').

[95] A tall man himself, HF enjoyed teasing his friend David Garrick about his height—by Garrick's own measurement he was 5 feet 4 inches (Margaret Barton, *Garrick* [London, 1948], p. 53). To Partridge watching a performance of *Hamlet* in *Tom Jones* (XVI. v), Garrick is 'that little Man', 'the little Man' (p. 854). For an essay (probably by HF) ridiculing Samuel Foote for arguing that Garrick's smallness of stature detracted from his effectiveness in heroic parts, see 'On the Standards of Modern Criticism' (Appendix A, pp. 702–5).

[96] In her reply to this letter, Lucy Rural supposes that the tall actor was 'one of the Gentleman Ushers to *Alexander the Great*, or some other Hero' (p. 506). In annotating this passage, Baker pointed out that no play including Alexander (e.g. Lee's *Rival Queens*) was staged this season, and that Garrick never played the part. 'Miss Prue's handsome mute', he suggested, 'is evidently a supernumerary to Garrick's Lord Hastings in *Jane Shore*' (see above, p. 486).

first day or two, but good Company soon teaches us better. Dear *Lucy*, do, come to Town; for a Country Girl is a horrible aukward Creature.

O, DEAR *London*, it is quite another World. Was I to mention half our Diversions to you, you would not even know the Names of them. Here are Drums, and Routs, and Hurricanes.[97] Mamma intends to have a Drum, as soon as we get into a tolerable House; for we have but one poor nasty Dining-Room, were we are, and a Drum can't be made without three, at least.

I WARRANT now, I have set you a guessing what a Drum is; nay, I'll leave you a thousand Years to guess what it is made of.—To satisfy your Curiosity then, it is made of a great many Rooms, and a great many Tables, and a great many Candles, and a great many People—O, 'tis a charming thing: and, as Mamma told Papa, we had better be out of the World, than not have a Drum.

O, BUT I promised to write about the Court; ay, but we have not been able to go there yet: for, tho' Mamma laid out so much Money in Clothes last Year, every thing must be pulled to pieces, before it will do. Would you believe it, Child, my best Hoop wants above three Yards of being any thing decent.[98] Not one Rag of our Laces will do, for they are not fine enough

---

[97] In *The True Patriot*, No. 13 (21–8 January 1746), 'Abraham Adams', the good 'Parson' of *Joseph Andrews*, decries the fashionable pastimes of 'Drums and Routs': 'These are, it seems, large Congregations of Men and Women, who, instead of assembling together to hear something that is good; nay, or to divert themselves with Gambols, which might be allowed now and then in Holiday Times, meet for no other Purpose but that of Gaming, for a whole Guinea and much more at a Stake. At this married Women sit up all Night, nay sometimes till one or two in the Morning, neglect their Families, lose their Money, and some . . . have been suspected of doing even worse than that' (pp. 202–3). In *Tom Jones* (XVII. vi) Adams's author offers his own description of a drum (which holds as well for the synonymous 'Rout'): 'A Drum . . . is an Assembly of well dressed Persons of both Sexes, most of whom play at Cards, and the rest do nothing at all; while the Mistress of the House perform the Part of the Landlady at an Inn, and like the Landlady of an Inn prides herself in the Number of her Guests, though she doth not always, like her, get any Thing by it' (p. 898). For further nuances of meaning, see *The True Patriot*, No. 1 (5 November 1745), p. 108 n. 2; and *The Covent-Garden Journal* (1752), index, s.v. 'drums and routs'. A 'Hurricane' is much the same: 'A large and crowded assembly of fashionable people at a private house, of a kind common during part of the 18th century' (*OED*, s.v. 2b).

[98] At its widest in the 1740s, the fashionable 'great hoop' projected 7 feet and more in either direction (for illustrations, see Anne Buck, *Dress in Eighteenth-Century England* [London, 1979], pp. 17, 26–7). It provoked a flurry of satires, such as *The Enormous Abomination of the Hoop-Petticoat, as the Fashion Now is, And has been for about these Two Years Fully Display'd* (1745). In *The True Patriot*, No. 15 (4–11 February 1746) chief among 'the strutting Articles of Luxury' flaunted by the ladies are 'their Hoop-petticoats, which have of late grown to so very enormous, and indeed portentous a Size, that should they increase as they have done within these last ten Years, our Houses must be soon pulled down, and built with Gates instead of Doors to admit them' (pp. 212–13). In the spring of 1748 'Hoops'—together with such other targets in these letters as 'Drums, Routs, Hurricanes, Criticizing, and Whisk-Learning'— would be among the 'Comical Humours of the Town' ridiculed in HF's puppet theatre (*Life*, p. 436). In *Tom Jones* (XIII. iv) Lady Bellaston enters a room 'pushing in her Hoop sideways before her' (p. 697 and n. 2).

to be seen in; so we have thrown away a fine deal of Money as well as Time, to no purpose in the Country; but Mrs. *Modish* the Millener, and Mrs. *Tabby* the Manteau-Maker,[99] have promised to remedy all soon; so, that in about a Week more, we hope to be fit to appear in the best Company. My Mamma's Clothes will be prodigiously handsome: the Silk cost above three Pounds a Yard. Papa was at first a little out of humour at the Price, but three Ladies happening to come in just at the Time, made all that matter easy, by telling him, it was the cheapest Thing they ever saw in their Lives. She has bespoke two other Gowns and Petticoats, which Papa knows nothing of; for Mamma says, she may very likely win Money enough to pay for them. I have new Clothes bespoke too, but they are so shockingly plain, I am ashamed to mention them. But now I must tell you a Secret. I was at the Opera last Night, and more fine Gentlemen talked to me, than to any of the finest drest Ladies there—I assure you, Miss; nay, they admired my Clothes too, I promise you, and yet I had only the old *Shocker*[100] on: thinks I to myself, you will like me better soon. As for the Opera itself, I did not understand a Word of it, and I had rather hear you sing the *Lass by the Brow of the Hill*;[101] but Mamma says, every body likes it, and so I like it too; for, to be genteel, you must do what every body does.

I BELIEVE I had more to tell you; but the Colonel is just gone, and Mamma has sent for me—and just this minute there is a great Rap at the Door.[102] I believe some People of Quality are coming up, so in haste, I conclude,

Your affectionate,
Humble Servant,
PRUDENTIA FLUTTER.

---

[99] See above, p. 479 n. 12).

[100] '*Shocker*': the italics suggest a term from fashionable slang, from *shock* in the sense of French *choquer*: 'In early use, to wound the feelings of, to offend, displease; to affect with a painful feeling of intense aversion or disapproval; to scandalize, horrify; to outrage a person's sentiments, prejudices, etc.' (*OED*, s.v. 'shock' v.² 4), citing Swift, *Abolishing Christianity* (1708): 'The Gentlemen of Wit and Pleasure are apt to murmur, and be choqued at the sight of so many daggled-tail Parsons.'

[101] '*Lass by the Brow of the Hill*' eluded a thorough search by Baker, who, however, notes the similarity with '*The Lass of Loch Royal* concerning a hilltop seduction with tragic consequences. One version repeats the phrase "the lass of Ruchlaw hill" (Francis J. Child, *English and Scottish Popular Ballads* [Boston, 1882–98] 76c, ii. 219).'

[102] HF elsewhere remarks on the deafening rap of a London footman at the door. In *Joseph Andrews* (IV. ix) Parson Adams and his guests are thrown into confusion when Beau Didapper 'mimicked the Rap of a *London* Footman at the Door' (p. 312); in *Tom Jones* (XIII. iv) HF despairs of attempting to describe the phenomenon when Lady Bellaston's footman announces her arrival: 'a most violent Knock shook the whole House. . . . In short a Footman knocked, or rather thundered at the Door' (p. 697).

LETTER XLIII.

From Miss LUCY RURAL *to Miss* PRUDENTIA FLUTTER.

Dear PRUE,

I HAVE been detained from reading your agreeable Letter the whole Evening, by being in some very merry Company, where we have had a Game of *Christmass* Gambols: *Jack Bonny* was with us; and you know his comical Humour never fails of making every body happy where he is. And to say the truth, my Dear, I believe you have not spent so pleasant an Evening since you left us.

INDEED, dear *Prue*, so far from having my Opinion raised of the Town Pleasures, by what you write, I am the more convinced of the Impertinence and Stupidity of a Town-Life; and that we are not only more innocent, but much more merry and happy in the Country.

AS to Plays, which are the only rational Amusement you mention, you know I am very fond of them, and have often an Opportunity of seeing them within two Miles of our House. I confess, they are probably better acted in *London*; but don't be angry if I say, this Circumstance seems to have added very little to your Entertainment. I dare swear, we have as good Actors as that dumb Gentlemen you mention, whom I suppose to have been one of the Gentlemen Ushers to *Alexander the Great*,[103] or some other Hero; and am very sorry, he has made so deep an Impression on your Mind, which I impute to the notorious Demerit of the Beaus, of whom, from the Accounts I have received, I have no very high Opinion. Sure the Opera must be a very wretched Entertainment, or you would never suffer such Animals to divert your Attention from it.[104]

I OWN, my Dear, I have not much Idea of a Drum;[105] and you'll pardon me, if I say, you don't seem to entertain any very perfect Notion of it yourself: However, I will endeavour to explain a Diversion to you, in which I spent three Evenings in the *Christmass* Holidays, and which I shall call a Trumpet; partly, in allusion to your Drum, and partly, as it was our chief Instrument of Music; tho' I do not find, you can give so good a Reason for the Name of your Assembly.

YOU must know then, that on the Day after *Christmass*, I dined at Sir *Thomas Hearty's*, where we had a great deal of good Company. There were present, Sir *Thomas* and my Lady, who are, you know, a very fond Couple,

---

[103] See above, p. 503 n. 96.
[104] For Miss Prue on the opera, see above, p. 505.
[105] On the 'Drum', see above, p. 504 and n. 97.

greatly happy in themselves, and very desirous of seeing every other Person so: the other Men were, Sir *Roger Fairfield*, Mr. *Woodly*, Mr. *Green*, Mr. *Jones*, Dr. *Gaylove, Jack Bonny*, and Sir *Thomas's* Chaplain: the Women were, besides her Ladyship of the House Old Lady *Cheerful*, Mrs. *Woodly*, Mrs. *Green*, Miss *Fairfield*, Miss *Cheerful*, Miss *Jenny Fairfield*, Miss *Betsy Fairfield*, and your humble Servant.

WHILE we were at our Tea, Sir *Thomas* came to us from the Men, and proposed a Diversion for the Evening, which was readily agreed to by the whole Company. This was a Trumpet, or, to explain it to you in a Term you are better acquainted with, it was to go a mumming.[106]

Two Hours were now spent in dressing ourselves, and, I do assure you, they were two very agreeable ones. My Lady *Cheerful*, who has, you know, all the Good-humour, without any of the Passions of Youth, was drest up for the Witch of *Endor*,[107] and made a Figure so ridiculous, that I can hardly help laughing, when I recollect it. Let me tell you, it is no little Indication of Good-sense and Good-nature too, in a Woman of any Age, to submit to make her Person disagreeable. Miss *Betty Fairfield* was drest as a Shepherdess, and made a most lovely Appearance. Your humble Servant consented to be a Nun, but remember it was only in jest.

AT Seven in the Evening, we were joined by the Men, who had likewise disguised themselves in various antic Dresses. Every Man chose his Woman, as well as he could guess, for we were all masqued. Sir *Thomas* fell to the share of the Witch, and your Friend the Nun became the Property of Friar *Jack Bonny*.

A WAGGON and Six now attended at the Gate, to which we were led by our several Partners; a Band of Music, with a Trumpet at their head, preceding.

SIR *Thomas* undertook to be Master of the Ceremonies, and the Waggon was ordered to drive to Mr. *Warmgrove's*, which is, you know, about three Miles distant from Sir *Thomas's*. It is almost impossible to describe the Pleasantness of our Ride; Music and Lights made the Gloom of the Night more delightful than the Day; and so much Good-humour, Mirth, and Wit too, I promise you, prevailed in our Waggon, that our Journey past almost in one continual Laugh. Perhaps there is not a more agreeable Creature upon Earth, than *Jack Bonny*.

---

[106] From medieval times, 'mumming' was a tradition in England at the Christmas season, when 'mummers', 'bands of men and women . . . dressed in fantastic clothes and wearing masks or disguised as animals, serenaded the people outside their houses, or joined in the revels within' (*EB*, s.v. 'mummers').

[107] See 1 Samuel 28: 7–25. In *Tom Jones* (I. xi), the fortune-hunting Captain Blifil is 'so passionately fond' of Squire Allworthy's estate he would have married it, 'had he been obliged to have taken the Witch of *Endor* into the Bargain' (p. 67).

WELL; when we arrived at Mr. *Warmgrove's*, we found a large Hall well lighted up with a swinging Fire prepared for us; for Sir *Thomas*, who has a great deal of true Politeness, without any of the Foppery which passes for it in some Places, had sent timely notice to his Friend of our Intention. We were received at the Gate, by Mr. *Warmgrove* and his Lady, and conducted into the Hall, where Wine and Cakes were immediately brought us. With these having regaled ourselves for some time, and some Scenes of Mirth having passed, on account of the Mistakes which were made in guesses at our several Persons, the Ball was begun by Mr. *Warmgrove* and Mrs. *Green*, who was drest in a Suit of Lady *Hearty's* Clothes, and past for her all the first Part of the Night. At Twelve we were conducted to a noble Supper, where we all unmask'd, and the Night concluded with so much Mirth and Jollity, that I believe no Set of Company ever past a pleasanter.

WE have since had two more Frolics of the same kind, of which I will not tire you with the Repetition; tho' Sir *Thomas*, who has shewn an excellent Taste for these Diversions, took care to give them a Variety, which greatly added to their Entertainment.

AND now, my Dear, what do you think was the Consequence of all this? Why, Sir *Roger* hath very honourably declared himself to Miss *Cheerful*, and Miss *Betty Fairfield* hath received a formal Visit from the Doctor; but, what is worst of all, I wish the poor Nun be not seduced by a wicked Friar to forsake the holy Veil. To be short, and to shew you, we Country Girls can sometimes own what we are not ashamed of, as well as you Town Ladies, if I write you after next *Thursday*, I shall sign my Letter by a strange Name.

IF you should laugh at all this, as Country Simplicity, or whatever else you please to call it, I shall have the Satisfaction of thinking, I have afforded you what the Town cannot; for, by your Letter, you do not seem to have laughed since you left us. If you meet with any thing more entertaining, I know you will readily communicate it to your Friends; if not, we shall have the Pleasure of expecting you the sooner, which, I do assure you, will be most acceptable to,

> *Dear* PRUE,
>> *Your sincere Friend,*
>> *And affectionate humble Servant,*
>> LUCY RURAL.

P.S. *Old* George *desires me to acquaint you, he has sent the Bacon, Cheese, Butter and Eggs, as ordered, by the Waggon; he has likewise sent a Hare, wild Fowl, Partridges, and other Game: the Beef and Mutton, Beer and Cyder will go the next time.* George *laughs, and says,* 'Sure, there is nothing good in that same London.'

LETTER XLIV.

VALENTINE *to* CYNTHIA.

[*At the* Bath.[108]

THOUGH ill-natured Accidents sometimes tear the Person of my dearest Creature from my Eyes, nothing can remove her, even for a Moment, from my Thoughts.

THIS I am certain she believes; and, unluckily for me, it is no Secret to the rest of my Acquaintance. Hence I become often the Mark of that Raillery with which all People are armed against Love; a Passion which no one will condescend to own: for such a Confession would reflect on the Modesty of your Sex, and Men consider it as no less an Imputation on their Understanding.

I MUST, however, do the Ladies the Justice to own, that many of them have Sense enough to despise this foolish Opinion, and are not ashamed of being known to love their Husbands: But I am afraid the Examples of such Sincerity on our side are much rarer: For I solemnly declare, tho' I know several who love their Wives with great Fondness, I scarce know one who is not ashamed of so doing.

THIS Treatment of a Passion to which I owe the sweetest Pleasures of my Life, always raises in me much Indignation; and I never fail on such Occasions of defending the injured Cause, and of becoming the Champion of Love;[109] though I generally meet with the Fate which attends all Opposers of vulgar Errors, and have the Reward of being laughed at.

I YESTERDAY encountered a large Company of both Sexes on this Subject; which I had introduced, by having drank your Health in a Bumper. I will not trouble you with the many Blasphemies (for so I call them) which were uttered against the divine Passion we both cultivate; but shall draw up my Argument into the Form of a Speech, and will leave it to your Judgment whether it could or could not be answered.

[108] In annotating this letter, Baker remarked that the city of Bath was, for HF personally, the appropriate setting for Valentine's theme of a husband's love for his wife, who lives in his thoughts 'though ill-natured Accidents sometimes tear the Person of my dearest Creature from my Eyes'. For it was at Bath in November 1734 that HF married Charlotte Cradock—'one from whom I draw all the solid Comfort of my Life', as he declared in the Preface to the *Miscellanies* (i, p. 13)—and it was at Bath that Charlotte died ten years later, in November 1744. In the heroines of his last novels, Sophia Western—'she resembled one whose Image never can depart from my Breast, and whom, if thou dost remember, thou hast then, my Friend, an adequate Idea of *Sophia*' (IV. ii, p. 156)—and Amelia Booth, he would keep her memory fresh.

[109] In the prefatory chapter to book VI of *Tom Jones*, 'Of Love', HF would act again as the 'Champion' of that 'Passion'.

SUPPOSE me then to have made the following Speech on the Occasion:

'I am surprized at nothing more, than that Love hath ever been reputed Folly, or that Men should use Words with such Impropriety, as to call it a Weakness of the Mind.

'THAT to pursue perfect Happiness, if we were capable of it, would be Wisdom, no one will, I believe, have the Confidence to deny; and if perfect Happiness be not attainable in this World, to acquire to yourself the highest Degree of human Happiness, must, I think, be esteemed the highest Degree of human Wisdom.

'NOW, in my Eye, Love appears alone capable of bestowing on us this highest Degree of human Felicity. I solemnly declare, when I am in possession of my Wife, (here was a great Laugh) my Happiness wants no Addition. I think I may aver, it could receive none. I conceive myself then to be the happiest of Mankind; I am sure I am as happy as it is possible for me to be.

'IT may be, perhaps, objected, that I have set myself up as the Standard of true Judgment: that though I should be sincere in what I say, yet this, which is so great a Blessing in my Estimation, may in the Opinion of another be a very slight and indifferent Matter; and that it appears otherwise to me, may be said to arise from that very Weakness of Mind of which I would avoid the Imputation.

'I SHALL endeavour therefore to evince by Reason, that Love, in the Mind which possesses it in the highest Degree, must create the highest Degree of human Happiness.

'FIRST, then, it seems to me, that the full Gratification of that Passion which is uppermost in our Minds, is the highest Happiness of which we are capable.[110]

'SECONDLY, it seems likewise, that one Man is capable of being happier than another, in proportion as the Passion by which he is possessed (if I may so express myself) is more or less capable of this full Gratification.

---

[110] A pervasive theme of *Amelia* is Booth's intellectual infatuation with the doctrine that every man acts of necessity from the impulse of an uppermost passion. With the present passage, cf. Booth's speech to Amelia (X. ix):

> I have often told you, my dear *Emily* . . . that all Men, as well the best as the worst, act alike from the Principle of Self-Love. Where Benevolence therefore is the uppermost Passion, Self-Love directs you to gratify it by doing good, and by relieving the Distresses of others; for they are then in Reality your own. But where Ambition, Avarice, Pride, or any other Passion governs the Man, and keeps his Benevolence down, the Miseries of all other Men affect him no more than they would a Stock or a Stone. (p. 451)

At the denouement, Booth is converted from this fatalistic philosophy by reading the sermons of Isaac Barrow (XII. v). For a discussion of this theme in the novel, see Battestin, 'The Problem of *Amelia*: Hume, Barrow, and the Conversion of Captain Booth', *ELH*, 41 (1974), pp. 613–41.

'LET us examine then by this Rule those two great Motives to the Actions of Men, which in modern Language are called Passions, Ambition and Avarice:[111] and if we can shew the Advantage which Love hath over these, it will be abundantly sufficient to found those Arguments which will effectually prove what we have undertaken to prove, *viz.* that Love is not Folly, nor ought any Man to be ashamed of its Possession and Influence.

'NOW when we consider the great Miseries which Ambition and Avarice produce to the World, we may, I think, reasonably expect, that they should at the same time make some amends by the Good which they convey to the Bosoms which they inhabit.

'WHETHER they do this or no, I shall not enter into a Common-place Inquiry; it is sufficient for my Purpose here, that neither of them are capable of a full Gratification: indeed, we may say, of any Gratification at all, since every Acquisition to them both brings Desire along with it: Desires which enlarge themselves in proportion to the Good obtained, and which exceed all Possibility of obtaining in the same Degree as what is already acquired hath exceeded Expectation. Instead of proving this from any trite known Stories, with which all Books, both of History and others, abound, I shall appeal for the Truth of it to common Experience, and to the secret Information of every Man's Breast, in which either of these Passions have any Place.

'IN LOVE it is far otherwise. This sweet Passion admits of instant complete Gratification. Every Good conferred on, and received from, the beloved Object, so fills the whole Mind with Pleasure, that it for a while leaves no Wish unsatisfied. And if, after its sweetest Satieties, new Desires arise, these are not, like those of Avarice and Ambition, restless uneasy Perturbation; but so sweet and pleasant, that they bring some Rewards along with them.

'IF LOVE then should appear more eligible than either Avarice or Ambition, as it is capable of receiving a fuller Gratification, we may likewise argue its Superiority, as it is capable of this Gratification two ways; either by giving or receiving Good; as it proposes a certain End; as this End is generally not only possible, but easy, safe, and innocent; seldom attended

---

[111] In the humanist tradition, ambition and avarice were regarded as the summarizing vices of human nature, complementary passions exemplifying positive and negative excess: e.g. Aristotle, *Politics*, II. vi. 19, and Horace, *Satires*, I. iv. 25–6. The motif recurs in HF's writings: e.g. *The Champion* (11 March 1740), p. 229; 'An Essay on Nothing', where they are 'our two greatest and noblest pursuits, one or the other of which engages almost every individual of the busy Part of Mankind' yet end in nothing (*Miscellanies* i, pp. 188–9); *Covent-Garden Journal*, No. 69 (4 November 1752), p. 364. In *Tom Jones* (VI. iv) the same passions define the villain Blifil: 'Avarice and Ambition . . . divided the Dominion of his Mind between them' (p. 284).

with Difficulty, Danger, or Crime to ourselves, or with any Mischief to others. In every one of which Lights it is preferable both to Ambition and Avarice.

'I AM aware, however, that I am here liable to an Objection not very different from what I have started above: for it may be said I am still arguing to others from myself, and making my own Sensations the Criterion of their Happiness. Nay, it may be said, that having admitted in my first Position, that the Happiness of Men consists in the Gratification of whatever Passion is uppermost in their Minds, my Doctrine can be only useful to such, whose highest Passion is Love; and not at all applicable to those Votaries of Ambition and Avarice, who have very weak, or perhaps no Traces of Love in their Minds.

'THIS I readily concede, insisting only on these two Points, that such Persons are less Capable of Happiness than the Lover, for the Reasons aforesaid; and that the Lover, who is clear of all the Impressions of Ambition and Avarice, hath full as good a Right to call all the Pursuits of Mankind which arise from those other Motives, Folly and Weakness of Mind, as the Slaves of those Passions have of imputing to such Folly and Weakness all the Energies of Love, merely because they never felt them.

'LIFE, to say the truth, without some strong Pursuit; without proposing to ourselves some principal End to which all our Labours tend, is wretchedly insipid; rising indeed very little above Vegetation. Why then am I to be thus insipid, or to become the Slave of Ambition and Avarice, contrary to my Inclination? Or why am I obliged to undergo all the Hardships which those severe Task-masters impose on their Servants, when I have no Relish for the pitiful Rewards which are by those two so niggardly bestowed upon them? Why am I not to become the Subject of Love, to whose Cause I am so well inclined, whose Labours are to me so easy, and whose Rewards so extremely delicious? Why must I be called a Fool, when I feel myself perfectly happy, and that by those who must, to themselves at least, acknowledge their own Misery?

'IN short, if Love be a Folly, it is so only in comparison of the Pursuits of those, who, disdaining the Imperfection, the Incertainty, and the transitory short Duration of worldly Happiness, fix their Attention on the perfect, certain, and durable Enjoyments of Futurity; and who think Heaven only worthy to be the great End of all their Actions. To such I shall only say, I think they might with great Safety take Love in their way: for surely, in my Sense of the Word, it would be so far from obstructing their Journey, that it would only serve to give them some Idea of the Blessings towards which they are travelling. But for the Slaves of Ambition and Avarice to give the Name of Folly to Love, is, in my opinion, a higher Degree of Insolence, than for a drunken Fellow over his nasty Porter[112] in an Alehouse to affect a Contempt for Gentlemen who are rioting over *Champaign*.'

THUS, my Dear, I have transcribed the Defence of this our favourite Passion. If I was not bless'd in the Knowledge of your Partiality to me, I should have some Apprehension that you might think me a weak Advocate in so good a Cause, which you yourself could, I am convinced, defend so much better; but you will pardon me when I say, if my Affection to, and Interest in every thing, did not exactly attend yours, you would be much more interested in a Defence of Love than myself; as I have so much better Excuse for the Violence of mine, in the singular Merit of its Object; but your Goodness will still force your Judgment to think those deserving who endeavour to be so.

OF this Inclination to please you, therefore, I will give you one Instance, by quitting a Subject which I could dwell on for ever, the delightful Contemplation of your Superiority; since it is the only one in which I am capable of giving offence to her who is the Delight of my Eyes, the Joy of my Heart, my Admiration, my Esteem, and my Glory.

I am
My SWEET
With a Tenderness inexpressible,
Your fond and faithful Husband,
VALENTINE.

---

[112] A kind of beer of a dark brown colour and bitterish taste—a favourite drink of porters and other labourers (*OED*, s.v. 'porter' sb.³).

8

THE JOURNAL OF A VOYAGE
TO LISBON (1755)

Most of what is useful to know about the circumstances and motives that led Fielding to undertake his voyage to Lisbon, and to enrol himself, as he put it, 'among the voyage writers' (p. 649), is set forth by Fielding himself in the Introduction to the *Journal*, or is apparent not only in the topics of his frequent digressions from the main narrative, but in his impatience with the people he must deal with—notably Richard Veale, Captain of the *Queen of Portugal*, Mrs Francis, the landlady at Ryde, and the watermen that overcharge. The voice one hears is that of a proud man suffering the debilitating effects of a hideous disease in the certain knowledge that he will never again see the homeland he loves—his tone at times melancholy, irascible, self-pitying, yet through it all courageous, even heroic. The last testament of Fielding's life, the *Journal* is the daily record of the events and feelings he experienced from his departure on 26 June 1754 from Fordhook, the estate he leased at Ealing to the west of London, to his arrival at Lisbon on 7 August. He died two months later, on 8 October, and was buried in an unmarked grave in a 'Burial Ground' which the English shared with the Dutch.

The voyage was a final, fruitless measure of many others he had taken in the hope of regaining his health over the course of five years and more. The steady decline in his health can be traced in his correspondence, beginning in December 1745 with complaints of the gout, which had 'imprisoned' him for a month.[1] From April to December 1748 the ravages of the gout are a recurrent theme in the letters he wrote as High Steward of the New Forest, Hants., to the Duke of Bedford and his agent; even as he pressed to finish *Tom Jones* in October of that year he informed his friend James Harris that 'a violent Fit of the Gout' had confined him 'not only to my Bed but to my Back, so that I was forced . . . to use an Amanuensis'. A year later, the *General Advertiser* (28 December 1749) reported that another painful attack

---

[1] See *Correspondence*, Letter 27, to James Harris.

of gout, exacerbated by a fever, threatened 'a Mortification in his Foot' that was prevented by the controversial Dr Thomas Thompson.

But the gout would return, and to its excruciating effects were added by 1753 the symptoms of what was called the 'dropsy'—the retention of fluid that grotesquely distended his belly—accompanied by jaundice and asthma (*Journal*, pp. 557–8). He was first 'tapped' to drain the water from his belly in early March 1754, when the notorious empiric Joshua 'Spot' Ward relieved him of fourteen quarts (pp. 561–2). The operation would be repeated four more times before he arrived at Lisbon.[2] Modern pathologists have diagnosed this dreadful illness as cirrhosis of the liver. And nothing could cure him: not any of the specifics or regimens he tried—the Duke of Portland's medicine, which in August 1753 he had taken 'near a year' (p. 554), Ward's 'pill and drop' (p. 561 n. 57), a 'milk diet' (p. 564), daily doses of tar-water recommended by Bishop Berkeley (p. 563); nor any of the four eminent physicians and surgeons he consulted—besides Ward, there were William Heberden (p. 565 n. 69), John Ranby (p. 554), and William Hunter (p. 577 and n. 108); nor even the warm, salubrious climate of Portugal—though for a time Fielding believed it had saved him.[3]

Though his health was the reason for the journey and ever first in his thoughts, and though in the Preface Fielding makes clear that he intended the *Journal* to elevate and define the genre of travel literature, he also regarded the work as yet another instrument in the programme of public service he had entered upon in his writings some five years earlier: this time he would take the opportunity to recommend reforms in 'the laws relating to our maritime affairs' (p. 554). This aspect of Fielding's career as an author is another context in which the *Journal* can be read; it is important enough to review here.

On Saturday 25 November 1752 Fielding brought *The Covent-Garden Journal* to an end with the seventy-second number, 'solemnly' declaring: 'unless in revising my former Works, I have at present no Intention to hold any further Correspondence with the gayer Muses' (p. 380). From January 1749, the publication of his masterpiece *Tom Jones* coinciding with his appointments to the magistracy, Fielding's sense of his true vocation had changed from fiction-writing to improving the social order. He had become

---

[2] In early May, Ward tapped him again (13 quarts), and again later that month (10 quarts). On 28 June at Gravesend HF's friend, the surgeon William Hunter, tapped him a fourth time (10 quarts); and at Torbay on 25 July another surgeon performed the operation (9 quarts).

[3] See HF's letter to John from Lisbon (Appendix C.3, Letter 3). The good news HF wrote his brother raised false hopes in London. On 16 October (eight days after his death) the *Public Advertiser* reported: 'Letters by the last Mail from Lisbon advise that Henry Fielding, Esq. is surprisingly recovered since his Arrival in that Climate. His Gout has entirely left him, and his Appetite returned.'

'court justice', the principal magistrate of the metropolis, whose chief concern would be the pursuit of remedies for the spreading evils of poverty and crime. The new direction in which he applied his impressive energies was manifest as early as July 1749, when, as Chairman of the Westminster Sessions, he published *A Charge delivered to the Grand Jury*, sending a copy to the Lord Chancellor accompanied by the draft of a 'Bill' (abortive as it proved) for the reformation of the police.[4] This new sense of purpose would also inform the darker mood of *Amelia*, which he began writing in that same inaugural year of his magistracy; after beginning with dour observations on the English 'Constitution', the first of the novel's four volumes opens in the courtroom of a corrupt justice and continues in the unwholesome setting of Newgate Prison. In the midst of writing the novel, the last of his works of mere fiction, Fielding paused to address the problem of crime in the streets of the capital in *An Enquiry into the Causes of the late Increase of Robbers* (January 1751).

By the time he put an end to *The Covent-Garden Journal*—a literary periodical of humour and satire, to be sure, but one also treating the moral and social themes that occupied him—Fielding, it appears, had come to accept the view of his 'graver Friends' that the work was a frivolous waste of his time: 'They have been pleased', he wrote in his farewel to the reader, 'to think it was below my Character, and . . . that I might employ my Pen much more to the Honour of myself, and to the Good of the Public' (p. 380). Indeed, he was even then engaged in writing *A Proposal for Making an Effectual Provision for the Poor*, which would be published in January 1753 with a dedication to Henry Pelham, the Prime Minister, at whose invitation he had undertaken the project.

In rehearsing the story of his personal affairs in the eleven trying months from August 1753 to the eve of his departure for Lisbon on 26 June 1754, Fielding in the Introduction to the *Journal* focuses on the two concerns that chiefly occupied him during that period. First, he considers the circumstances leading to the crowning achievement of his career as magistrate: the reorganization of the police on a firm and rational foundation, a reformation that, in the winter of 1753–4, resulted in the total suppression of street robberies. (Until recently, a society honouring Fielding as its founder flourished under the auspices of London's Metropolitan Police.) Having treated this subject, Fielding turns next to chronicling the gradual collapse of his health and the futility of every measure taken to restore it. Considering what he had accomplished and the cost to himself and family the effort

---

[4] For a transcript of the 'Bill', see *Life*, app. 1.

had exacted, he may be excused for having 'vanity enough', as he put it, 'to rank my self with those heroes who, of old times, became voluntary sacrifices to the good of the public' (p. 558).

He was not alone in this opinion. Saunders Welch, High Constable of the Holborn Division and chief of the so-called Bow-Street Runners, well knew the kind of man Fielding was, and in March 1754, as Fielding's illness worsened, Welch declared his hope that 'heaven [would] spare a life, invaluable to his friends and family, hazarded, I may say with truth, sacrificed to the public welfare, I mean a magistrate, whose good heart, and great abilities, justly entitle him to the affections of every worthy mind'. Welch paid this tribute in his pamphlet *Observations on the Office of Constable* (p. 46), which he dedicated to Fielding. When he left for Lisbon, Fielding would leave behind the draft of his own thoughts on the subject: 'A Treatise on the Office of Constable'.

The autobiographical Introduction to the *Journal* provides a personal context that deepens one's understanding of the narrative. But it does not stand at the very entrance to the work. For that place, Fielding reserved the Preface, whose function is purely literary: to redefine, and to elevate, the genre of travel literature. It seems fitting that his career as a writer of narratives should end as it began, with a Preface defining the elements of a new species of writing. The Preface to *Joseph Andrews* introduced to English letters the 'comic Epic-Poem in Prose' in a work that began the great tradition of the comic novel. In the judgement of Percy Adams, the historian of travel literature, who includes excerpts from the *Journal* in an anthology spanning the centuries from Herodotus to Henry James, Fielding's Preface has a comparable significance as the signal example of its kind: 'Prefaces to travel books in a way make up a whole body of literature in themselves, and a part of Fielding's preface must, in the present volume, represent them all.'[5] What is surprising about the comparison, however, is that now, in the Preface to the *Journal*, Fielding reverses his claim in *Joseph Andrews* (III. i) that, as mirrors of 'Truth', the best works of fiction are superior to the narratives of biased historians, who distort facts and are limited in their concern with a particular time and place:

is not [he asks] such a Book as that which records the Atchievements of the renowned *Don Quixotte*, more worthy the Name of a History than even *Mariana's* [author of the *General History of Spain*]; for whereas the latter is confined to a particular Period of Time, and to a particular Nation; the former is the History of the World in general, at least that Part which is polished by Laws, Arts and

---

[5] *Travel Literature through the Ages: An Anthology* (New York, 1988), p. 334.

Sciences; and of that from the time it was first polished to this day; nay and forwards, as long as it shall so remain. (p. 188)

In the Preface to *Joseph Andrews*, moreover, Fielding had declared Fénelon's *Telemachus*—a popular work of prose fiction whose theme is the education of a prince, that is, of Telemachus, son of Odysseus—to be 'of the Epic Kind, as well as the *Odyssey* of *Homer*'; and he distinguished such works as these from 'those voluminous Works commonly called *Romances* . . . which contain . . . very little Instruction or Entertainment' (pp. 3–4). Now, in the Preface to the *Journal* (pp. 548–9), Fielding denies any such distinction: 'But in reality, the Odyssy, the Telemachus, and all of that kind, are to the voyage-writing I here intend, what romance is to true history, the former being the confounder and corrupter of the latter.' And he concludes this remarkable paragraph with a sentence that reveals just how completely he had abandoned 'the gayer Muses':

For my part, I must confess I should have honoured and loved Homer more had he written a true history of his own times in humble prose, than those noble poems that have so justly collected the praise of all ages; for though I read these with more admiration and astonishment, I still read Herodotus, Thucydides and Xenophon, with more amusement and more satisfaction.

No more striking measure of the reordering of Fielding's literary and intellectual values could be hoped for than this wish to see Homer transformed into a progenitor of Bishop Burnet, author of the *History of His Own Time* (1724–34), whom Fielding in *Amelia* had called 'almost the only *English Historian* that is likely to be known to Posterity, by whom he will be most certainly ranked amongst the greatest Writers of Antiquity' (p. 571: 256.3).

If Fielding in the Preface to the *Journal* rejected the literary priorities he affirmed in *Joseph Andrews*, it is clear from the same source that, after recent attempts at reconciliation with Samuel Richardson, whom in 1741–2 he had offended by parodying *Pamela* in *Shamela* (above, pp. 133–95) and continuing the ridicule of Richardson's novel in *Joseph Andrews*, Fielding was once again mocking 'the great man' (p. 554). The change in attitude was likely provoked by Richardson's ill-disguised sneering at the alleged indecency of *Tom Jones* in the Postscript to *Sir Charles Grandison* (March 1754). This rebuff was his rival's response to the friendly overtures Fielding had been making since 1748, publicly in *The Jacobite's Journal*, Nos. 5 and 14 (2 January, 5 March 1748), privately in his famous letter of 15 October of the same year; and more recently in *The Covent-Garden Journal* (below, p. 553 n. 30). Now in the concluding paragraphs of the Preface he bristled and treated Richardson's vanity and moral posturing with a dose of sarcasm. This affront infuriated Richardson's friend Thomas Edwards, who, in May 1755, tried to soothe him by reviling Fielding and his works in a fulsome letter (below, Appendix C.3, Letter 11).

PUBLICATION

An account of the perplexing matter of the printing and publication of the *Journal*, as well as a discussion of the authority of the two editions posthumously published in 1755, will be found in Dr Amory's Textual Introduction. For reasons considered there, what the public first received was in fact the second, revised edition—commonly referred to as the 'Humphrys' edition after the (fictitious) name of the landlady at Ryde, in the Isle of Wight, who in the first edition is called 'Mrs. Francis', her actual name.

Exactly why this reversal in the order of publication occurred remains a vexed question. The usual explanation has been that, when Fielding's blind half-brother John became aware of the severity of the characterization both of the captain of the ship that carried Fielding to Lisbon and of Mrs Francis, he either revised the manuscript himself or instructed the publisher Andrew Millar to employ an editor for the purpose. Since Austin Dobson first called attention to the fact that two different versions of the *Journal* were published in 1755,[6] most scholars, despite the fact of John Fielding's blindness, have preferred the former alternative. Since, however, J. Paul de Castro, in a letter to Frederick S. Dickson in 1916, first called attention to the stylistic similarities between the 'Dedication to the Public' and Arthur Murphy's life of Fielding in his edition of the *Works* (1762), also published by Millar,[7] Fielding's biographers and editors have considered Murphy the most likely person to have written it. Amory, however, does not allow Murphy any part at all in the *Journal*, attributing to John both the Dedication and the editing. It does seem likely that—as the writer in *The Monthly Review* assumed[8]—the author of the Dedication was also editor of the work. But an argument can be made, more compelling in my opinion than any other to date, that Arthur Murphy, not Fielding's blind brother, was that person.[9]

The earliest notice of the *Journal* appeared in the *Public Advertiser*, the paper with which Fielding and John were closely affiliated, on Thursday

[6] Austin Dobson, *Fielding* (1883), p. 168 n. 1.
[7] Letter of 14 October 1916, Frederick S. Dickson Collection, Beinecke Rare Book and Manuscripts Library, Yale University.
[8] *Monthly Review*, 12 (March 1755), pp. 234–5.
[9] See Battestin, 'Who Edited Fielding's *Journal of a Voyage to Lisbon* (1755)? The Case for Arthur Murphy and a New Fielding Essay', *Studies in Bibliography*, 55 (2002 [for 2004]), pp. 215–33.

6 February 1755, the day when the bookseller Samuel Baker published the *Catalogue* of the sale of Fielding's library:

We can with Pleasure inform the Public, that they will soon be agreeably entertained with a posthumous Piece of the late Henry Fielding, Esq; entitled, A Journal of a Voyage to Lisbon; to which, we hear, will be added, a Fragment of his Answer to Lord Bolingbroke.[10]

A week later the same paper, as well as the *London Evening Post*, was more specific:

On Tuesday the 25th inst. will be published, | In One Volume Duodecimo, Price 3 s. bound, | *(Printed for the Benefit of his Wife and Children)* | THE JOURNAL of a Voyage to *Lisbon.* | By the late HENRY FIELDING, Esq; | To which is added, | A Fragment of his Answer to Lord Bolingbroke. | Sold by A. Millar in the Strand.[11]

But what, one wonders, had Millar done with the 'Francis' edition, which, as the ledgers of the printer William Strahan make clear (see below, pp. 538–9) is the first edition and therefore the copy-text for the present Wesleyan Edition? The notion has prevailed that Millar held it in storage for ten months, until news of the terrible Lisbon earthquake reached London on 25 November and public curiosity about all things concerning that stricken city was excited. The 'new' edition was announced in the *Public Advertiser* on Thursday 4 December:

This Day is published, | In one Volume Duodecimo, Price bound 3 s. or sewed 2 s. 6 d. | THE JOURNAL of a VOYAGE to LISBON. | By the late HENRY FIELDING, Esq; | To which is added, | A Fragment of a Comment on Lord Bolingbroke. | Printed for A. Millar, in the Strand.[12]

But is it likely that Millar, who could not foresee the Lisbon calamity, would do nothing to dispose of any of the 2,500 copies of this edition for so many months? The distinguished bibliographer A. W. Pollard long ago summed up the matter as follows:

What seems certain is that the whole case is so exceptional that the terms 'first edition', 'second edition', can only be used in connection with it at the risk of misunderstanding. We know that the small-type edition ['Francis'] was printed before the handsomer one ['Humphrys'], that the handsomer one was printed in the

---

[10] A similar notice appeared in the *London Evening Post* (4–6 February).

[11] *Public Advertiser* (Thursday 13 February 1755); preliminary notices were repeated in the *Public Advertiser* 14–15, 20–2, 24 February). Also in the *London Evening Post* (13–15, 15–18, 18–20, 20–2 February).

[12] The notice was carried in this paper four more times (5, 6, 8, 9 December); and in the *London Evening Post* for 2–4, 4–6, and 9–11 December.

same month [January], and that it was from a copy of the handsomer edition that a reviewer described the book in March, 1755 [*Monthly Review*]. Everything else is conjecture.[13]

RECEPTION

But to return to the first appearance of the book. The *Journal* was duly published, as announced, on Tuesday 25 February, with notices carried in both the *Public Advertiser* and *London Evening Post* until 1 March. The earliest of the reviews appeared in *The London Magazine* for February (24, pp. 54–6), which remarked that the work was 'far from doing discredit to [Fielding's] Memory' and echoed the appeal of the 'Dedication to the Public' to treat it generously for the sake of his family, who had been left with heavy debts to pay—it was with the same purpose at this time that John was writing his brother's friends to recommend the book.[14] In March favourable notices were published in both *The Monthly Review* and *The Gentleman's Magazine*. In the former, the reviewer drew his remarks chiefly from the Dedication—whose author, as mentioned above, he refers to as 'the editor' of the work. Repeating a compliment to Fielding that was by this time often heard, he observed that the 'reflections interspersed' in the *Journal* 'are worthy of a writer, than whom few, if any, have been more justly celebrated for a thorough insight into human nature' (12, pp. 234–5).

In *The Gentleman's Magazine* the reviewer, no doubt with the figures of the captain of the ship and the landlady 'Mrs Humphrys' in mind, assured readers that Fielding had drawn the characters 'with that humour in which he is confessed to have excelled every other writer of his age'. But the writer particularly valued 'the instruction' to be gained from Fielding's remarks 'upon many intollerable inconveniencies which arise either from the defect of our laws, or the ignorance of those by whom they should be executed': to illustrate the point he extracts Fielding's complaint about the dearness of fish in London, a hardship imposed upon the public by the greed of fishmongers (25, p. 129). Fielding's eloquence on the subject of the abundance of this delicious food, and therefore its potential for relieving the hunger of the poor (below, pp. 634–8), appears to have made an impression on readers, especially the editor of *The Gentleman's Magazine*, who some

---

[13] 'The Two 1755 Editions of Fielding's "Journal of a Voyage to Lisbon" ', *The Library*, 3rd ser., 8 (1917), p. 162. We may add that the extracts from the *Journal* quoted in *The London Magazine* 24 (February 1755), pp. 55–6, and by Matthew Maty in the *Journal Britannique* (March and April 1755), Article V, are also from the shorter 'Humphrys' version (Pollard's 'handsomer' edition).

[14] On 24 February, the day before publication, John wrote Thomas Birch: 'Dear Sir. I hope you will assist this little volume by your recommendation through the Beau Monde. | I am, Dear Sir, your affectionate Friend &c' (BL, Add. MS 4307, fo. 49).

months later published—'*not only as a Curiosity, but as a Confirmation of that important Truth advanced by Mr.* Fielding *in his Voyage to* Lisbon'—a list of the great variety of fish to be had in the west of England (26 [January 1756], p. 22).[15]

By far the most comprehensive of the reviews issued from The Hague in the Netherlands. In the *Journal Britannique* for March and April, the philomath Matthew Maty, who in a review three years earlier had come closer than any other critic to grasping the qualities of *Amelia*,[16] performed the same service for Fielding's *Journal of a Voyage to Lisbon*.[17] Maty surveys the work from the beginning, discussing the Dedication, which, like the reviewer of *The Monthly Review*, he attributes to 'the anonymous editor', and the Preface, there taking issue with Fielding's strictures against travel writers and his curious complaint that Homer had not written histories in prose instead of epic poems, and observing that Fielding's sarcasm against Richardson 'would not escape those who had read *Grandison*'. Though he wishes the Introduction had been four rather than twenty pages, he admires Fielding's selfless diligence in ridding the metropolis of 'brigands' at the expense of ruining his health, and he is moved by Fielding's submitting to repeated operations of the trochar and his humiliation at the mockery of the Thames watermen. As for the narrative of the *Journal* itself, Maty paraphrases some passages and translates others: he admires Fielding's characterization of Captain Veale and the innkeepers at Ryde ('Le morceau le plus travaillé'); and to illustrate the perils and pains of the voyage that help account for Fielding's peevish moods, he offers in full the account of the ship at the mercy of a storm (*Journal*, 19 July), a passage, he declares, worthy of 'the Author of the *Roman comique*', written by 'notre Scarron Anglais'.

Other than the testy reactions of Richardson's friends, notably Thomas Edwards and Margaret Collier (below, Appendix C.3, Letters 10–11, 13), references to the *Journal* in the correspondence of the period are scarce. Horace Walpole's only mention of it was terse and typically mischievous: on 27 March 1755 he alerted Richard Bentley, son of the eminent scholar, that he was sending him a parcel of books that included 'Fielding's travels, or rather an account how his dropsy was treated and teased by an innkeeper's wife in the Isle of Wight'.[18] And if what others particularly valued about the

---

[15] Years later a correspondent to the *Public Advertiser* (26 October 1767), signing himself 'Cogitator', applauded HF's facetious solution to the prohibitive cost of fish: 'I have ever thought with Henry Fielding, that the only Way to have Fish in Plenty, is to hang up all the Fishmongers.'

[16] *Journal Britannique*, 7 (February 1752), pp. 123–46; Paulson and Lockwood, No. 119.

[17] See below, Appendix C.5, pp. 777–83.

[18] *Yale Walpole*, xxxv, p. 214.

work was Fielding's panegyric on the fish of the sea, his cousin Lady Mary Wortley Montagu, in a letter of 22 September [1755] lamenting his death, preferred the anecdote of the kitten that was rescued from drowning only to suffocate in a feather bed (below, pp. 593–4, 643–4; Appendix C.3, Letter 12). To the end of the century, except for Arthur Murphy's remarks in his 'Essay on the Life and Genius' of Fielding (1762), no other comments on the *Journal* in English have come to light. An unauthorized edition was published in Dublin (1756), however, and it was translated into German (1764) and French (1783).

We might close this Introduction by recalling the coincidental circumstances that brought Fielding to Dr Johnson's thoughts in the last year of his life. Dying of a 'dropsy' and attended by William Heberden, the physician who had advised Fielding to seek a warmer climate (below, p. 565 n. 69), Johnson wrote to Boswell on 11 February 1784, and remembered the voyage to Lisbon:

My physicians try to make me hope, that much of my malady is the effect of cold, and that some degree at least of recovery is to be expected from vernal breezes and summer suns. If my life is prolonged to autumn, I should be glad to try a warmer climate; though how to travel with a diseased body, without a companion to conduct me, and with very little money, I do not well see. . . . Fielding was sent to Lisbon, where, indeed, he died; but he was, I believe, past hope when he went.[19]

ITINERARY OF THE VOYAGE

The narrative of the *Journal* is often interrupted by Fielding's digressions, which make it still more difficult to trace the rather tortuous course the journey is taking. The prevailing winds in the English Channel were south-westerlies, and they persisted during the voyage, forcing the *Queen of Portugal* to anchor at Deal (3 July), at Ryde (11 July), and in Torbay (21 July), and to remain anchored there until north-easterly or north-westerly winds released her. But the Fieldings' progress from the start of their forty-two-day journey from the little estate at Fordhook, Ealing, 6 miles west of London, to Lisbon and its suburb Junqueira is at times difficult to follow. A brief descriptive itinerary of its six principal stages should be helpful; these and intervening sites mentioned throughout the journey may be located on the accompanying map (below, Appendix C.1, p. 758).

[19] *The Letters of Samuel Johnson*, ed. Bruce Redford, 5 vols. (Princeton, 1992–4), iv, p. 285.

The Thames, 26 June–1 July

The party that accompanied Fielding to Lisbon included his second wife, Mary, *née* Daniel (1721–1802); Henrietta Eleanor, called Harriet (1743–66), the only surviving child by his first wife, Charlotte; Margaret Collier (1717–94), Harriet's governess; and two servants, Isabella Ash, called Belle, the family maidservant, and William Aldrit (d. 1800), whom Fielding refers to as his footman, but who may also have served as his amanuensis.[20] Accompanying the family as far as Gravesend were Margaret's sister the novelist Jane Collier (1715–1755?), and Saunders Welch, Fielding's close friend and chief of his new model police force. Left behind at Fordhook in the care of Mary's mother, Elizabeth Daniel, were the children William (1748–1820), Sophia (1750–1755?), and the newborn infant Allen (1754–1823). On 1 October, a week before Fielding died, Elizabeth Daniel would kill herself; Sophia died soon after her father.

The Fielding party and their companions embark on the *Queen of Portugal* at Rotherhithe (Surrey), across the Thames from Wapping and about a mile below the Tower of London. The ship is a 160-ton vessel built in the Thames in 1749.[21] The captain is Richard Veale (1686–1756), a skilled mariner of forty-six years, experience at sea, not only with commercial vessels, but also with privateers during the war with Spain and France (1739–48). Fielding must be hoisted aboard amidst the mockery of sailors and watermen. He will occupy a 'great chair' in the Captain's cabin, where from time to time he is hoisted on deck; Mary and their daughter, and Margaret Collier, will sleep (and suffer from seasickness) in a small adjoining cabin. Before sailing, Fielding sends for his friend the eminent surgeon William Hunter, to tap his belly of 10 quarts of water; but Mary can find no relief from an excruciating toothache.

Taking the tide to Gravesend (30 June), they are piloted past the docks at Deptford; the stately Royal Hospital at Greenwich, founded by Queen Mary in 1692 for the care of wounded seamen and designed by Christopher Wren; and the docks at Woolwich, where the *Royal Anne*, the grandest of warships, is nearing completion. These scenes are on the Kentish side of the river; on the Essex side are mostly mudflats and marshes. At Gravesend (Kent), as is the rule for all outward-bound ships, the *Queen of Portugal* drops anchor and submits to a search of the cargo by customs officers. Here Saunders Welch and Jane Collier take their leave and return to London by coach.

---

[20] See Tom Keymer, 'Fielding's Amanuensis', *N & Q*, NS 43 (1996), pp. 303–4.
[21] *Public Advertiser* (18 December 1756).

The Downs, 2–8 July

After setting sail, their progress is halted by contrary winds and they anchor in The Downs, off Deal (Kent), a favoured resort with shipping heading for London from abroad or departing for foreign ports (hence the London shipping news is dated from Deal). Here, rolling at anchor for a week, the women sick and no one to converse with, Fielding thinks of relieving the oppressive solitude by 'enroling myself among the voyage-writers' (p. 649).

Ryde (Isle of Wight), 11–18 July

Four days' sailing westward from Deal bring the *Queen of Portugal*, battling gale-force winds, to anchor on 'the Mother Bank on the Back of the Isle of Wight' (Fielding's letter to John of 12 July [Appendix C.3, Letter 1]). 'The ladies', who have enjoyed afternoon tea at Ryde, at the time a village of about thirty houses with a delightful prospect of the sea that takes in Portsmouth and Spithead to the north and St Helen's to the south-west, persuade Fielding to come ashore (13 July) and take lodgings at the only inn, the Nag's Head, kept by Mrs Ann Francis (d. 1758) and her husband, Jephtha (d. 1775); in the second edition their true name is concealed and they are called 'Humphrys'. Nearby is 'a neat little chapel'; and about 2 miles off, in the parish of St Helen's, is Appley House, where the widow Ann Roberts lives (she is not named in the *Journal*), a 'polite and good lady' who furnishes the Fieldings with produce from her garden and tea. The *Queen of Portugal* weighs anchor (18 July), but without a favourable wind is carried by the tide no farther than St Helen's.

Torbay (Devon), 21–7 July

The wind at last cooperating (19 July), the ship sails swiftly around the 'back' of the island, and westward along the coast of the mainland, passing Christchurch and the Isle of Portland (Dorset), and on 21 July to an anchor off Berry Head (Devon), at the point of the south shore of Torbay. There, the wind having shifted keeps the ship from proceeding on the voyage for a week. Though the delay is unwelcome, it enables Fielding to order presents of half-hogsheads of cider to be shipped to John, Saunders Welch, William Hunter, and his publisher Andrew Millar—and to savour and celebrate the wonders of the local fish. He also takes the opportunity to have his belly tapped for the fifth time by a local surgeon, who draws 9 quarts of water—a hopeful sign, Fielding believes, since 9 is 2 quarts less than the last operation.

On Saturday 27 July, twenty-six days since the voyage began at Gravesend, a favourable wind at last releases the *Queen of Portugal* from her confinement in the bay, and sailing freely for the most part they pass the westernmost point of Brittany and cross the Bay of Biscay, reaching the west coast of Portugal and proceeding down the coast until they reach the mouth of the Tagus (5 August), the great river that will carry Fielding to Lisbon.

The River Tagus (Portugal), 6–7 August

At Cape Roxent, as the English call the Cabo da Roca (the Rock of Lisbon), the *Queen of Portugal* picks up a pilot and sails up the Tagus, passing by the two forts that command the river and past a parched and uninviting landscape so unlike England's green and pleasant land. They anchor at the Torre de Belém (Fielding and others among the English Factory call it the Castle of Bellisle), a citadel honouring Vasco da Gama. There the ship is boarded by inspectors of customs and health, and Fielding's tobacco is seized. These ceremonies completed, at midnight they ride the tide 3 miles to Lisbon and cast anchor. The city, with its white buildings rising tier on tier up the hillsides, looks beautiful from a distance; but on entering it (Wednesday evening, 7 August), Fielding found it crude and revolting, its streets choked with filth.

Lisbon and Junqueira, 8 August–8 October

Though the *Journal* ends with the end of the voyage, Fielding's letters home to John and Millar make clear that the landing was inauspicious and the family's brief sojourn in this alien land marred by quarrelling (see Appendix C.3, Letters 3–5, 8). Upon arrival half the family came down with dysentery: Mary, Margaret Collier, and William were all stricken. The servants William and Belle defected, returning to England on Captain Veale's homeward voyage. Though their place was taken by 'a black Slave and his Wife', Fielding had to appeal to John to send him an amanuensis and a cook. And he found the cost of living in the city far beyond his means. He was saved by a wealthy English merchant, John Stubbs, who found him inexpensive lodgings in Junqueira, a suburb near Belém, which he called 'the Kensington of England'. Once there, except that Mary missed home and Margaret annoyed him by flirting with the chaplain of the English Factory, Fielding's mood brightened. His health seemed to be improving and he had found in the chaplain, the Revd Dr John Williamson, a clever companion. He dispatched chests of onions home, presents to John and six others. He wrote Millar that he had almost finished the *Journal*, which he thought 'the best of his performances'—the Preface and Introduction were written here—and he was planning a new work, nothing less ambitious, it seems, than a history of Portugal (Appendix C.3, Letter 8). But he was in fact no better, and he would write no more: two months after reaching Lisbon Fielding was dead.

Textual Introduction

The Authority of the Two Versions of Fielding's
Journal of a Voyage to Lisbon

Hugh Amory

Two versions of Fielding's *Journal* were published in 1755, but their textual differences were not publicly recognized until 1883, when Austin Dobson designated them the 'Humphrys' and 'Francis' versions from their names for Fielding's hosts at Ryde. Though he then knew the 'Francis' version only from its reprinting in Fielding's 1762 *Works*, he had questioned the authority of 'Humphrys' from the start, remarking that it 'seems to have been considerably edited'. In 1892, when he happened upon the 1755 edition of 'Francis' in the British Museum, these suspicions hardened: the 'Humphrys' version, he then concluded, 'was certainly considerably "manipulated" by the suppression of excision or a number of passages'.[1] He offered no evidence or even any explicit reason to support this conclusion, and indeed, as his collation of the two versions showed, 'Humphrys' contained additions to as well as 'excisions' from the 'Francis' text. Nevertheless, the surgery predominated, and the authenticity of the excised passages was not in doubt.

Dobson's *ipse dixit* has never been challenged, or even significantly corroborated, though F. S. Dickson and J. P. de Castro narrowed the range of questions and illuminated the stemmatic relationship of the two editions in 1917.[2] Dickson showed that they shared hundreds of occasional spellings

At the beginning of a recent article on the identity of the editor of Fielding's *Journal*, I called attention to Hugh Amory's 'The Authority of the Two Versions of Fielding's *Journal of a Voyage to Lisbon*': a 'masterly essay', in which Amory 'came close to solving the most perplexing textual problem in Fielding studies—as close, that is, as bibliographical analysis and circumstantial evidence allows' (below, n. 6). For granting permission to reprint this remarkable essay, which serves here as the Textual Introduction to the *Journal*, I wish to thank Judith Amory, and the members of the Bibliographical Society of Australia and New Zealand, who originally published the essay in *The Culture of the Book: Essays from Two Hemispheres in Honour of Wallace Kirsop*, edited by David Garrioch, Harold Love, Brian McMullin, Ian Morrison, and Meredith Sherlock (Melbourne, 1999), pp. 182–200. Except for parts of Amory's Appendix which detail textual matters fully treated by him in the textual apparatus to this edition, his essay and his notes are reprinted verbatim. Comments of the editor are included in square brackets. MCB

[1] Austin Dobson, *Fielding* (1883), p. 168 n.; HF's *The Journal of a Voyage to Lisbon*, ed. Dobson (1892), p. xi. The British Library *Catalogue of Printed Books* (1881–1900), pt. FET–FIK (1887) first distinguished the two editions.

[2] Frederick S. Dickson, 'The Early Editions of Fielding's *Voyage to Lisbon*', *The Library*, 3rd ser., 8 (1917), pp. 24–35; J. Paul de Castro, 'Henry Fielding's Last Voyage', ibid., pp. 145–59.

in the text they held in common, and he rightly argued that one must have been set from a marked-up copy of the other. The existence of two distinct autograph manuscripts was thereby ruled out. From a recently discovered Fielding letter, showing that the author's opinion of Captain Veale had soured in the course of composition, he concluded that the omission of many passages criticizing Veale in the 'Humphrys' text could not have represented Fielding's final intentions. Finally, and perhaps most persuasively, de Castro proved, from the Strahan ledgers, that the unabridged 'Francis' edition, though published later than 'Humphrys', was in fact printed before it. Apart from the alterations and deletions, in short, 'Humphrys' demonstrably descended from 'Francis'; and what authority could an editor have for these changes after Fielding's death? In the standard summary of and embroidery on these findings by W. L. Cross and F. S. Dickson (1918), Fielding's brother John had censored the 'Francis' text to remove personalities, disguising Fielding's hosts at Ryde under the name of 'Humphrys' and deleting the satire on Captain Veale, among other changes; and Fielding's publisher, Andrew Millar, temporarily 'suppressed' the first printing, only releasing it nine months later, when the Lisbon earthquake had opened up the market.[3]

Cross built upon what was, for its day, a spectacular piece of research, but it was inadequate for his purposes. As A. W. Pollard pointed out at the time, we know the order in which the two editions were printed and something of the order in which they were published; 'Everything else is conjecture'— a conclusion echoed by Martin Battestin in his recent authoritative biography.[4] The order of printing does not in itself settle the authorship of the revision in 'Humphrys' unless we also assume that the editor had no other resource for these alterations but himself, which is simply equivalent to assuming that they are not authoritative, bringing the argument full circle. On external evidence, the unflattering portrait of Veale in 'Francis' ought to be later, not earlier, than 'Humphrys'; internally, a number of passages unique to 'Humphrys', including two with excellent claims to Fielding's authorship, might point to the same conclusion (see Appendix B.5, 'First printed, second published edition, second issue', below). In point of fact, the only direct evidence for the authority of either version is the Dedication prefixed to both of them:

It was thought proper, by the friends of the deceased, that this little piece should come into your hands as it came from the hands of the author; it being judged that

[3] Cross, iii, pp. 83–92. F. S. Dickson provided Cross with most of this thesis; see Dickson's MS 'Index to The Journal of the Voyage to Lisbon', dated 15 November 1916, now in the Beinecke Library, Yale, Fielding Coll. K915dj.

[4] *Life*, p. 612.

you would be better pleased to have an opportunity of observing the faintest traces of a genius you have long admired, than have it patch'd by a different hand; By which means the marks of its true author might have been effac'd.

(*JVL*, p. 544)

This could not have been truly said of both versions, evidently—but was it meant to describe them both? A case could be made for either,[5] but Cross and Dickson chose to believe that it was written for 'Francis' and meant to disguise the editor's manipulations in 'Humphrys'. They also accepted the 'sage suggestion' of de Castro that Arthur Murphy had written the Dedication; the dedicator 'surely was not John Fielding, who almost certainly knew nothing of the statements made in the dedication', Cross pleaded, and rather than prove John's integrity, deprived him of his opportunity.[6]

Neither 'Francis' *nor* 'Humphrys', however, is what 'came from the hands of the author', entirely. Rather, as I shall argue, they represent two editorial views of the composition of a perplexed autograph manuscript—two clippings of the unedited 'rushes' of the same film, so to speak—by Andrew Millar, who owned the copyright, and by John Fielding, as the chief representative of Fielding's 'friends'. Cross's theory, moreover, assigns John a strangely contorted role. On one hand, 'John' drains the two apparently authentic additions in 'Humphrys' of their authority: the first is a paraphrase of Fielding's letter to John of 12 July 1754,[7] and the second recounts an anecdote of their brother Edmund;[8] both exhibit knowledge that only Fielding or an intimate member of his family could have supplied. On the other hand, many glaring errors survive in both editions that arguably attest the editors' fidelity—errors that Cross ignores in 'Francis' yet imputes to John's disability in 'Humphrys' ('as he was blind, the greater part necessarily escaped him') unless they can be assigned to 'the compositor's want of care'.[9] Editor 'John', it seems, is *capax editionis, nisi edidisset*.

Do we really need this busy cast of disadvantaged editors, publishers, dedicators, and compositors, each sufficiently unconscious of the others to

[5] See below, 'Printing and Publication', pp. 538–41.
[6] Cross, iii, p. 88; Dickson, 'Early Editions', p. 29; accepted in *Life*, p. 611. The identification of the dedicator rests chiefly (I believe solely) on an allusion to the Dedication in Murphy's 'Essay', prefixed to *Works* (i, p. 46, 4to). Murphy had no personal acquaintance with HF or his family. [Murphy, on the contrary, was HF's protégé and friend; and it is very likely that he was the dedicator and the editor of the *Journal*: see the Introduction above, p. 519 and n. 9, citing my article 'Who Edited Fielding's *Journal of a Voyage to Lisbon* (1755)?' MCB].
[7] See below, Appendix C.3, Letter 1.
[8] See below, Appendix B.4 (Historical Collation): citing pp. 621.24–622.41.
[9] Cross, iii, p. 92.

carry on the deception in all sincerity? I think not, because both versions may derive from a single, much revised manuscript. A correspondent of Samuel Richardson's visited Ryde shortly after the publication of the *Journal*, interviewed the Francises, and reported that Fielding had got it all wrong.[10] Clearly, Fielding had reshaped his actual experience of Ryde, and it seems likely that he never drew up a fair copy of his work, since he complained that decent pens and paper were unobtainable in Lisbon and appealed to John for an amanuensis.[11] In fact, the text of both editions preserves a number of false starts, corrections *currente calamo*, and lacunae that attest the presence of authorial revision and the fidelity of the compositors and editors (see Appendix B.5, 'Second printed, first published edition', below). Fielding's revisions were thus intermingled with the original text in a single manuscript, either interlinearly, on facing pages, or on inserted leaves. An editor might in all good faith have compiled a variant, authentic version from such a manuscript, and there is no need to suppose that most of the alterations in 'Humphrys' were his sole invention.

The numerous errors in both editions that I take as proof of fidelity, following the Dedication, Cross ascribes to the editor's blindness. His ingenious theory, however, will not account for the many small corrections of errors in 'Humphrys' that might readily have escaped John's notice yet are too important to ascribe to a compositor: for example, 'concession' for 'confession', 'hath' for 'has', or 'huts' for 'hats' (Appendix B.1)—to say nothing of improvements of capitalization (Perigord-pye, Christianity, Punic, Paradise, Methuen, Port) that run counter to the 'down' style of the compositors; most of these arguably return the text to what Fielding wrote. The dedicator, I suppose, made his declaration because he was only too aware how easily the editor might have corrected other errors, and he wished his readers to know that they had been intentionally left standing.

He had in mind readings so incongruous that modern editors regularly 'patch' them up, among them a number of blatant misdatings of the entries first noticed by Dobson and Dickson.[12] In both editions, the heading for

---

[10] First printed by J. P. de Castro, 'Fielding's Last Voyage', pp. 157–9; Richardson identified the writer as Margaret Collier, who travelled with Fielding to Lisbon, but his identification is no longer accepted. [See below, Appendix C.3, Letter 9.]

[11] See below, Appendix C.3, Letters 3 and 5. HF's manservant William Aldrit, who had returned to England in the first week of September, may also have acted as an amanuensis (Tom Keymer, 'Fielding's Amanuensis', *N & Q*, 241 [1996], pp. 303–4), though no hint remains of this employment either in the *Journal* or in HF's correspondence, and to judge by the result he did well to flee the scene.

[12] Dobson, 'Henry Fielding: Two Corrections', *N & Q*, 12th ser., 1 (1916), p. 284; with a reply by Dickson, *N & Q*, 12th ser., 2 (1916), p. 515. [See below, Appendix B.2 (Textual Notes): citing p. 619.5.]

each day's entry in the *Journal* gives the correct day of the week and month before 14–21 July, which are misdated '*Sunday, July 19*' to '*Sunday, July 26*' (what should have been '*July 25*' being misnumbered '*July 29*'); thereafter the heading gives only the day of the week. The new sequence is clearly authorial, as everyone since Dickson has agreed: though a '14' might perhaps be misread as a '19', it is unlikely that the compositor would repeat and even compound his error in seven further instances before abandoning the task, and even more unlikely that an editor who had no qualms about making larger 'improvements' would refrain from correcting such obvious mistakes. The 'Humphrys' edition, moreover, senselessly alters '*Wednesday*', 24 July to '*Wednesday* the 20th'. Since 'Humphrys' has been considered an entirely unauthoritative text, this alteration has not attracted comment, but editors do not make senseless changes, and compositors normally refrain from substantive alterations of their text. '*July* "19–26"' must descend directly from Fielding's autograph to both editions, and '*Wednesday* the 20th' must be mediated through an edited copy of 'Francis'.

As the dedicator suspected, these two sets of 'misdatings' and the incomplete series of calendar dates were not exactly errors, but 'marks of its true author'; they attest three stages of revision, corresponding to the three different and independent sequences of entries implied by their numbering. 'The first serious thought which I ever entertained of enroling myself among the voyage-writers', Fielding says, occurred to him 'in the Downs' (*JVL*, p. 649), where the *Queen of Portugal* arrived on the evening of 2 July and remained until the morning of the 8th. Composition of the *Journal* began on 5 July, since Fielding designated Wednesday 24 July 'the 20th'— i.e. the twentieth day of composition, uniquely preserved in 'Humphrys'. The original text is presumably signalled by the phrases 'This day' or 'This morning', etc., beginning on 1 July (*JVL*, p. 584)—so that the entries for 1–4 July would have been written retrospectively (for some later retrospective entries, cf. pp. 592 [for 7 July], 644 [20 July], 650 [30 July], and 651 [1 Aug]). In a letter of 12 July 1754 to John, Fielding remarked, 'Our Voyage hath proved fruitful in Adventures all which being to be written in the Book, you must postpone y^r Curiosity';[13] evidently Fielding was already contemplating publication, but a 'Book of Adventures' must have contained many 'merely common incidents' of personal or family interest, such as he recounted in his letters en route, but which he later abridged or remotivated (*JVL*, p. 552). One of these, still preserved in 'Humphrys', echoes his very letter to John, but was deleted in 'Francis'. Other deletions left lacunae in both editions related to Mrs Fielding: the cure of her toothache (2 July);

---

[13] See below, Appendix C.3, Letter 1.

some illustration of her goodness and gentleness (20 July); and her account of 'Axylus' and his habitation (26 July; see Appendix B.5, 'Second printed, first published edition', below). As in his letters from Ryde and Tor Bay and at various points still surviving in the 'Francis' text (*JVL*, pp. 577, 643–4), Fielding's attitude towards Veale was favourable, or at least tolerant of his failings.

The second stage of composition began 'at Lisbon', as noted in the Preface (*JVL*, p. 549 n.), written before Fielding's removal to Junqueira near the end of August. By 12 August, only five days after landing, he wrote Andrew Millar that he had 'almost finish'd the History of his Voyage',[14] and he marked this stage by renumbering the entries of the original 'Book', so that the entries for 14–21 July became numbers '19–26'—i.e. the nineteenth to the twenty-sixth day *of the entire voyage* since his departure from London on 26 June. A 'History' suggests a different narrative perspective from a mere 'Book of Adventures'—more judgemental, less immediate, and certainly less intimate. Besides adding the Preface and filling in events from London to the Downs, Fielding now deleted a number of purely personal incidents, dilating on others that provided an occasion for digressions on themes of 'public utility' (*JVL*, pp. 552–3). These 'observations', as they are generally called (*JVL*, pp. 546, 581, 590, 592, 607, 609, 634, 646–7), are sometimes delivered as though they occurred to the narrator at the moment of writing ('now', p. 585), but oftener they are introduced as commentary on a place in the text ('here', pp. 589, 591, 594, 609, 634, 648). The experience that Fielding had acquired en route now motivates the creation of a fictitious audience of naively uncritical readers (*JVL*, pp. 571, 573–4, 594, 603, 624–5, 642, 656), sometimes familiarly addressed as 'my friends' (pp. 575, 593, 651), sometimes slightly distanced as 'my fresh-water reader' (pp. 593, 651). In the Preface, Fielding defends this recasting of the historical record on Horatian grounds, balancing *utile* against *dulce*, the trivial morally uninstructive truths in the travels of scientists and explorers against the amusing but monstrous improbabilities of poets. His sentiments towards Veale remained unchanged before the first week in September, his health had steadily improved on the way down, and he had less reason to suppose, as he finally did, that his service to his country would cost him his life. For the moment, the *Journal* was only a semi-fictionalized 'History of his Voyage', not a plea to the public to take care of his family, much less a proposal for reform of the law.

Fielding's optimism crashed in September,[15] inaugurating a third stage of

[14] See below, Appendix C.3, Letter 8 (Thomas Birch to Philip Yorke, 7 September 1754).
[15] Amory, 'Fielding's Lisbon Letters', *Huntington Library Quarterly*, 35 (1971–2), pp. 65–83.

composition, in which he feared that he probably *had* lost his life serving the public (*JVL*, p. 636). In a new 'Introduction', he linked the progress of his disease since August 1753 to the triumph of his war against street robbers, synchronizing these accounts in a calendar dating that continued in the *Journal* down to 13 July. I suspect he also added two paragraphs at the end of his Preface, arguing that even if the reader found 'no sort of amusement' in the work, he should still prize its 'political reflections', the more so as it was no mere romance, but 'a work founded . . . on truth' (*JVL*, p. 554). This holds an authorial thumb on the Horatian scales, tilting them towards once contemptible truths, and the same emphasis continues in the 'Introduction', where Fielding 'relate[s] facts plainly and simply as they are' (*JVL*, p. 561) and declines to gild his 'anecdotes' for the amusement of his readers, contrary to the 'rule laid down in my preface' (p. 559). Whereas the chief characteristic of the 'reader' had previously been his or her parochial naivety and ignorance of matters maritime (*JVL*, pp. 546, 552, 571), the embattled narrator now implores the reader's 'candor' and 'kindness' (pp. 552–3) or defends himself against his outright hostility (pp. 553, 557), in the best manner of Fielding's novels. Thus Fielding transformed the *Journal* into an *apologia pro vita sua*, especially his career as a Westminster magistrate and his reform of the London police, to which his digressions on the reform of maritime law were now linked. Veale, he wrote John around 10 September, was a 'scoundrel',[16] and he inserted a number of passages in the *Journal* not only dubbing his captain a 'bashaw', but also recording instances of his idleness, deafness, and profanity. The revision closed with Fielding's death on 8 October, and presumably it was already faltering by the entry for 13 July. The sequence of entries imposed in the second stage of composition was never fully updated.

The Horatian tag at the end of the *Journal*—*hic Finish chartæq[ue] viæq[ue]*—now sagged into an epitaph; for Horace, as for Fielding, his 'Book' (*charta*) and his voyage (*via*) had once ended together, but in fact their lives (and revisions) continued, and Fielding's voyage ultimately became an allegorical vehicle for the pilgrimage of human life, beginning with 'the first traveller' Adam (*JVL*, p. 572). The narrator thus joins his readers in an appeal to 'our senates and our benches' (*JVL*, p. 585), 'our legislature' (p. 625), 'our governors' (p. 586, 590, 613), and 'our great men' (p. 610), which ultimately becomes an appeal to 'the Divine Love' and the 'dæmons' he has set over human life (p. 585) to remove the evils that perplex it and retard 'our' progress. Fielding is another Scheherazade, writing for his life, but allowed (or condemned) by 'Divine Love' to tell the same story

---

[16] See below, Appendix C.3, Letter 3.

over and over, reaching ever further back into the past in order to postpone
the inevitable ending—the *respice finem* that supersedes all other laws, the
blazing 'truth' whose trivial representatives had only done shadowy duty for
it in Fielding's narrative.

What has come down to us are most of stage 3—the 'Francis' version—
and an amalgam of stages 2 and 3—the 'Humphrys' version, which roughly
combines the text of the *Journal* at stage 2 with the 'Introduction' of stage 3.
I have described these stages as successive waves of change that swept
through the text in roughly the same chronological order as it was written
because the variation of the two editions is densest in the middle of the text,
and relatively negligible at the beginning and end. This model is only a
general inference, however: it does not exclude the possibility of some
editorial contamination in either edition, and the problems, as we might
expect, are heaviest in the middle. The chronology is also idealized, since
the same impulse that initiates a stage may have effects outside of it, so how
should we allocate particular revision among the three stages? and why, if
Fielding completed the second stage, does its numbering of the entries
end on 21 July? The survival of *'Wednesday* the 20th' was presumably an
accident, which Fielding may even have corrected, since the numbering is
absent in 'Francis'. After Tor Bay, the *Journal* entries merge into a more
or less continuous narrative, where weekdays are sometimes inserted in
square brackets (*JVL*, pp. 650, 653) or omitted altogether (p. 651), and
possibly they were never numbered, or numbered only with the day of
composition. Still it seems likely that the second-stage numbering continued some way past 21 July.

The names by which Dobson distinguished the two versions, ironically
enough, are among the more perplexing revisions. What stage do they
belong to? I doubt that an editor too honest to correct obvious mistakes in
the dating of the entries would have invented a pseudonymous identity for
two of Fielding's major characters, contrary to the policy stated in the
Dedication, and I suppose that the Francises' true name must also have
stood in the original 'Book of Adventures'. Fielding would have gilded his
hosts as 'Humphrys' in his first revision, wittily alluding to that proverbially
meagre diner Duke Humphry.[17] If he had changed their name at the final
stage, he could hardly have avoided noticing the discrepancy between
the calendar dates he was then using and the obsolete numbering of
July '19–26'. The revision need not have been uniform (cf. Mr Enderson/
Henderson/Anderson, the inept highwayman of *Tom Jones*!), and our

---

[17] *The Oxford Dictionary of English Proverbs*, 3rd edn., rev. F. P. Wilson (Oxford, 1970), p. 188a (Tilley
D 637).

present tidy distinction of the two versions may owe something to the 'extraordinary corrections' in 'Francis', for which Strahan charged 17*s*. In a 'Book of Adventures', indeed, jotted down extemporaneously with half an eye for Fielding's family and intimates, he presumably dispensed with the courteous flourishes that pepper his novels with appeals to the 'sagacious reader' and the like. We would not expect him to introduce his hostess to such an audience as 'Mrs Francis (for that was the name of the good woman of the house)' (*JVL*, p. 596); the slightly formal parenthesis belongs to 'Mrs Humphrys', just as in *Tom Jones* Tom's landlady enters the narrative as 'Mrs *Miller* (for so the Mistress of the House was called)' (xii. vi). It is one of the commonest formulas of Fielding's fiction, and he was fictionalizing his experience, but like Cross, the editors of both versions mistook the formula for sober fact, alternately deleting the parenthesis in 'Humphrys' and restoring the name of the Francises.[18]

Apart from the name of his hosts, and a few passages on 20 July, including a visit of Veale's nephew, the two versions of Fielding's stay at Ryde are substantially identical. The 'Humphrys' version of the nephew's visit preserves an anecdote of Fielding's brother Edmund—one of the rare occasions in which Fielding speaks openly of his family in print. Since the passage has only slight pretensions to 'public utility', we may assign it to an early stage of composition, and the relatively didactic 'Francis' version of the entry for 20 July to a later stage; we need not then suppose that Fielding ever returned to this section, and we can explain why an isolated sequence of second-stage numbers survived in it. The third stage, in short, proceeded serially, revising the 'Adventures' at Tor Bay (22–6 July) and deleting any obsolete numbering of the later entries before turning to the 'Introduction' and imposing calendar dates down to 13 July.

The 'Francis' account of the long episode at Tor Bay, where Fielding quarrels with Captain Veale and threatens to leave ship (23 July; *JVL*, pp. 639–42) is the most heavily revised section of the *Journal*. It was written 'not many hours ago' (*JVL*, p. 639), displays a positive attitude towards Veale (p. 642), and introduces an anecdote of an intimate friend of Fielding's as though this 'ingenious Peter Taylor' were generally known to the common reader, as he certainly was not. All of this material belongs in the earliest stage of composition, I believe. Nevertheless, Veale's pretended contempt for his passenger's 'pitiful thirty pounds' occasions a lengthy, but somewhat forced disquisition, including observations on the length and expense of the voyage (*JVL*, pp. 640–2) which assume the voyage has ended and which therefore belong to a later stage.

[18] On this formula in HF's fiction, see *New Essays*, p. 91 n. 68.

'Humphrys' omits most of this material, but leaves the anecdote of Peter Taylor untouched. Veale's intoxication, which served to explain why he lost his temper in 'Francis', becomes an occasion for social 'cheerfulness' in 'Humphrys', in which 'the ladies' join, 'being a little recovered from their sea-sickness'. Since their 'health and spirits' had already been 'restored' some three days earlier by 'very fine clouted cream and fresh bread and butter from the shore' (*JVL*, p. 624), this revision rings a decidedly false note. In a passage immediately following the episode, and retained in 'Humphrys', moreover, Fielding explains that Veale was 'one of the best-natured fellows alive'—'notwithstanding . . . the hasty impatience with which he rested any affront to his person or orders' (*JVL*, p. 643); and yet all trace of such 'hasty impatience' has vanished from 'Humphrys', rendering this concession meaningless. One can scarcely question the originality, 'truth', and indeed superior aesthetic merit of 'Francis' here, whereas 'Humphrys' condenses ten pages into a few lines that are slightly out of touch with the *données* of the narrative, both before and after. If this be not 'patchwork', where is patchwork to be found?

The motives behind these excisions and the levels to which they belong are not easily made out, however. A prudent regard for social propriety may explain the deletion of a few sarcastic swipes at the Duke of Newcastle (*JVL*, p. 555), but it is a less convincing motive for most of the other revisions in 'Humphrys'. The Francises and Captain Veale are rather small fry to be handled so tenderly, neither Veale nor his ship is ever explicitly named, and his portrait in the 'Francis' version of the Tor Bay incident is not even especially discreditable. In this comic scene, the normally docile author successfully rebels against his tipsy commander, with no hard feelings, apparently, on either side; the patience of both has been tested and found wanting. The real objection to the 'Humphrys' account is that it is maladroit—but that is scarcely a failing common in editors. Fielding, on the other hand, is perfectly capable of such revisions, as we see from the textual history of *The Wedding Day* (1743), *Tom Jones* (1749), and *Jonathan Wild* (1754); his native tendency to think two contradictory things at once was also accentuated by his illness, a more plausible explanation for the errors in the *Journal* than editorial blindness.[19] Various explanations of the two versions might be proposed that do not challenge their independent authority or conflict with the sequence of composition outlined above: the editor of 'Humphrys' may have selected an earlier stage that Fielding patched up to eliminate a 'merely common incident' of no 'public utility';

---

[19] *Miscellanies* ii, p. 165 n. 4 and p. 176 n. 9; iii, p. 166 n. 6 and p. 194 n. 2; H. Amory, 'The History of "The Adventures of a Foundling": revising *Tom Jones*', *Harvard Library Bulletin*, 27 (1979), pp. 277–303.

the editor of 'Francis' may rather have followed a revised account; Fielding himself may finally have restored parts of an earlier account, remotivating the whole with fresh reflections.

None of this contradicts the claim of the Dedication to present the text 'as it came from the hands of the author', for Fielding never finished his revision, even his latest intention can only be approximated, and for the most part what actually happened on the voyage still eludes us. The danger lies less in conjecture (which is inevitable) than in overgeneralizing from a few striking instances. Superior or necessary readings in 'Humphrys' may, of course, have been devised by an editor, but I think they deserve the benefit of the doubt. Where Cross sees censorial surgery, I would generally, but not invariably, infer an earlier, authentic stage of the manuscript. There will always be room for disagreement over individual readings, but an 'adulterated' version, as 'Humphrys' is often called, by definition contains some inconstant measure of truth—how much and where can only be determined case by case. The 'adulteration', such as it is, consists in a mixture of authentic stages of revision whose sequence is not always easy to make out, and it proceeds with an unusually scrupulous regard for Fielding's mistakes. Precisely in such evidence of 'a hand trembling almost in its latest hour', as the Dedication insists, lies the lurid confirmation both of Fielding's contested authorship and of the editor's integrity.

Dickson and his pupil Cross were undone by the cunning of history, which handed them their evidence in the wrong order. They did not learn that Fielding's opinion of Veale had changed for the worse until long after the leading scholar on Fielding had determined that 'Humphrys' was 'edited'; hence the discovery only reinforced their impression that 'Humphrys' was unauthorized, instead of demonstrating that it was earlier, and possibly genuine. The 'Francis' version, too, has always seemed 'truer' than 'Humphrys', in what Martin Battestin calls Fielding's 'unflattering characterization of Captain Veal . . . or his even harsher portrait of the landlady at Ryde, whom he explicitly identified'.[20] The exciting news that it had been 'suppressed' only encouraged this delusion, though the fictional elements of the *Journal* ought to have been obvious, and the assumption that the 'Francis' text preserves the narrative of the voyage *wie es eigentlich geschrieben* is clearly untenable. Indeed, the portraits of Captain Veale and Mrs Francis were indebted to a long line of sea-captains and landladies in his novels: the 'bashaws' of *Amelia* (1751) and *Jonathan Wild* (1754) were still fresh in his memory, and, like Veale, they regularly mourned the loss of a ship as for a beloved mistress; termagant landladies and their henpecked

---

[20] *Life*, p. 612.

husbands lay ready to hand in *Joseph Andrews* and *Tom Jones*. As in *Joseph Andrews*, Fielding was still committed to describing 'not an Individual, but a Species' (III. i), and though he 'explicitly identified' her proper name, Mrs Francis bears a distinct resemblance to Mrs Tow-wouse.[21] Her per capita charges recall those of Tom's sagacious landlady, the 'absolute Governess' of the inn where he recovers from the assault of Ensign Northerton (*Tom Jones*, VIII. vii). We do Mrs Humphrys wrong to call her by her 'true' name, being so majestical.

Over and above the unlucky timing of the evidence, which forced misleading implications on it, Dickson and Cross were hampered by the unquestioning acceptance of the view that authors pursue (and editors should realize) a single 'final intention', deviations from which are necessarily inauthentic. They therefore clung to 'Francis' like Hope leaning on her Anchor, instead of gathering the truth from its scattered witnesses. Fielding's *Journal of a Voyage to Lisbon* thus joins the little group of what Hershel Parker has called 'inherently problematical texts'.[22] The 'problem', such as it is, is 'inherent' in the nature of manuscript texts in an age of print, which promises—or seems to promise—all of them a 'second reading', an edition that the authors either were not yet ready for or may never have intended. Like our precursors in 1755 but without the benefit of Fielding's manuscript, we can only feel our way, variant by variant, towards truer, yet imperfect visions of Fielding's work. Both editions provide materials for this verdict on our author's Osirian *Nachlaß*.[23]

PRINTING AND PUBLICATION

In January 1755 William Strahan billed two editions of the *Journal of the Voyage to Lisbon* to Andrew Millar, each of 2,500 copies: a first edition in 10 sheets, charged at £1 15*s*. per sheet, and a 'second edition' in 12 sheets, at £1 13*s*. Neither the 1755 'Francis' editions, collating [A]⁴ B–L¹² M⁴ (M4 blank), nor the 'Humphrys' edition, collating [A]⁴ B–M¹² N⁶, both in

[21] *Miscellanies* iii, p. 160 n. 6; Charles L. Batten, Jr., *Pleasurable Instruction: Form and Convention in Eighteenth-Century Travel Literature* (Berkeley, 1978), p. 52.

[22] Herschel Parker, *Reading Billy Budd* (Evanston, Ill., 1990), pp. 173–8.

[23] Cf. Klaus Hurlebusch, ' "Relic" and "Tradition": Some Aspects of Editing Diaries', *Text: Transactions of the Society for Textual Scholarship*, 3 (1987), pp. 143–53; Siegfried Scheibe, 'Theoretical Problems of the Authorization and Constitution of Texts', in Hans Walter Gabler, G. Bornstein, and G. B. Pierce (eds.), *Contemporary German Editorial Theory* (Ann Arbor, 1995), pp. 171–91. Though Scheibe's approach is more 'documentary' than I can be wholly comfortable with, the misconstruction of the two versions of HF's *Journal* clearly stems from the ascription of unique authority to a single 'final intention', characteristic of Anglo-American textual criticism. Equally vital is the German criterion of coherence (*Textstufe*).

duodecimo, precisely corresponds in its number of sheets to Strahan's record, but 'Francis' must be the first edition: it has fewer sheets, and its smaller type regularly cost some 2s. more per sheet. Evidently, Strahan charged 20s. for the first 1,000 sheets of 'Francis', in small pica, but 18s. for 'Humphrys', in pica, with a charge of 5s. for every additional ream in either case.[24]

The slight discrepancy between the sheet-counts and Strahan's record is still unexplained, however. In both editions, sig. [A] was printed on the same paper from the same setting of type, but its paper matches that of the 'second edition' (i.e. the 'Humphrys') and we might tentatively assign both gatherings to it. Even so, Strahan's reckoning is imperfect: to complete them both, the first edition should have numbered $10\frac{1}{3}$ sheets (excluding [A]) and the 'second edition' $12(1/6)$ sheets (including two copies of [A]). In July 1756, moreover, Strahan recorded 500 copies of an additional half-sheet of the *Journal*. This charge corresponds to a reissue of 'Francis' with the first and last gatherings reset, collating a1, 2.3, B–L^{12}, M1, 2.3; copies of the reissue survive at Harvard, Cornell, and the University of Otago but have hitherto been mistaken for slightly imperfect copies of the first issue, wanting a half-title and final blank. Fewer than 2,500 copies of M^4 and 5,000 copies of [A]^4 must have been printed, then, and Strahan's records do not account for them. [25]

Both [A] and M were printed by half-sheet imposition: [A] on a Geneva paper, watermarked with a star in the centre of the sheet; M on the paper used for the 'Francis' editions, watermarked with a fleur-de-lis, off-centre, as usual.[26] Half of the star therefore appears centred on the edge of leaf [A]3, and half of the fleur-de-lis or no watermark, on the blank leaf M4. In both cases, there would have been a two-leaf cut-off that, together with the two signatures, should have raised Strahan's charges by one and half sheets, or a total of 39s. for 2,000 impressions. One reason for his omission of these charges may be that he shared the printing with Samuel Richardson, whose

[24] For this practice, used by Bowyer and Ackers, see K. I. D. Maslen, 'Printing Charges: Inference and Evidence', *Studies in Bibliography*, 24 (1971), pp. 91–8; and for the difference in type, I. G. Philip, *William Blackstone and the Reform of the Oxford University Press* (Oxford, 1957), p. 9.

[25] The Strahan entries (BL, Add. MS 48800, fos. 104^v [Jan. 1755] and 113^v [July 1756]) were accurately transcribed by J. Paul de Castro, 'The Printing of Fielding's Works', *The Library*, 4th ser., 1 (1921), p. 268. See also Patricia Hernlund, 'William Strahan's Ledgers: Standard Charges for Printing', *Studies in Bibliography*, 20 (1967), pp. 89–111, who concludes that Strahan 'usually' charged fractions of less than half a sheet exactly, 'occasionally' rounding them up to the next higher half-sheet, and 'rarely' made some intermediate charge. None of these practices precisely explains Strahan's charges for the *Journal*, however.

[26] A. W. Pollard, 'The Two 1755 Editions of Fielding's "Journal of a Voyage to Lisbon" ', *The Library*, 3rd ser., 8 (1917), pp. 75–7, first identified the paper and setting of sig. [A]; for the position of the watermark, see William B. Todd, 'Observations on the Incidence and Interpretation of Press Figures', *Studies in Bibliography*, 3 (1951), p. 197 n. 46.

ornaments appear on sigs. [A]–C of both editions;[27] Richardson, perhaps, billed Millar separately.

Leaving the two gatherings out of Strahan's reckoning, his record for 'Francis' is exact: B–L^{12} amounts to precisely 10 sheets. The record for 'Humphrys', however, is a half-sheet short: B–M^{12} N^6 is only 11½ sheets, and we must conjecture an A^6 half-sheet, imposed with N^6, to make up the account. This implies that [A]^4, containing half the Dedication, is a cancel gathering in 'Humphrys', and that it was printed after the completion of that version, at a moment when the publication of 'Francis' was suspended.[28] Cross's conclusion, that the Dedication 'had been prepared [i.e. printed] for the unedited version' (vol. iii, p. 88), is thus unwarranted. Whether the dedicator meant to disguise the existence of an alternative text, or sincerely accepted both versions as genuine, is a moot question, but if the editor 'knew nothing' of the Dedication, as Cross argued, we need not suppose that the dedicator knew anything of the editing, and he should not be heard on the sincerity of *either* version. In any case, no editor who had perpetrated the adulteries and castrations that Cross blithely ascribed to John Fielding would ever have confessed the shameful truth.

Most of the copies of 'Francis' that had left the warehouse by July 1756 were still, presumably, in the hands of booksellers, but these purchasers may have bought a pig in a poke, since copies of 'Humphrys' still surviving today outnumber its rival's by a factor of three.[29] The notices in the *London Magazine* (February 1755) and the *Monthly Review* (March 1755), indeed were of 'Humphrys' and the Dublin trade reprinted it in 1756; but if 'Humphrys' was therefore a kind of 'preferred issue' it could never have pre-empted the sale of 'Francis' for long. Cross supposed that Millar 'laid aside' or 'suppressed' the first edition and only released it when news of the Lisbon earthquake reached London in November 1755. The conjecture

---

[27] These will be authoritatively identified in the forthcoming inventory of Richardson's ornament stock by Keith Maslen, to whose assistance I am much indebted. [Amory was here looking forward to Maslen's article 'Fielding, Richardson and Strahan: A Bibliographical Puzzle', *Studies in Bibliography*, 53 (2000), pp. 227–40—an especially illuminating study on the puzzling subject of the printing of Fielding's *Journal*. Having considered a number of possible explanations as to how it happened that Richardson's press ornaments came to embellish the *Journal*, Maslen offers proof that these ornaments had been in Strahan's possession well before the printing of the book began: 'Richardson's collaboration in the printing of the *Journal* must therefore be ruled out as very unlikely' (p. 231). MCB]

[28] I assume that sig. M was already in type before production of 'Humphrys', but not yet run off, since the preliminaries, to be imposed with M, were still unwritten. When cancel preliminaries were run off together for both editions, M was reimposed as a half-sheet and printed separately. I do not know why Richardson did not print 5,000 copies of sig. [A] and 2,500 copies of sig. M together on a single sheet. [Maslen (above, n. 27), concluded that Richardson very likely had nothing at all to do with printing the *Journal*. MCB]

[29] [Based on *ESTC* as of March 2005: 73 copies of 'Humphrys'; 23 copies of 'Francis'; and 7 copies of the 1756 reissue.]

chimes with his suspicion that the 'Humphrys' version was 'edited' (i.e. censored), as we may see by his insinuation that 'but for an earthquake the chances are that we should not now have the unedited text' (vol. iii, p. 87).

Nevertheless, Fielding had evidently sold the manuscript of the *Voyage* to Millar outright—otherwise, the family would have edited it *before* it was printed[30]—and Millar had intended to publish 'Francis' from the first, when he ordered a supply of sigs. [A] and M for that purpose. With their bill coming due in six months, he could hardly have afforded to 'lay aside' 2,500 copies for longer, and while the Lisbon earthquake may have boosted sales, it was not the triggering factor. He released Fielding's satirical portraits of the Francises and Captain Veale during their lifetimes, and he canonized them in the 1762 *Works*, so that the milder version of 'Humphrys' vanished from public view for over a century. That someone on John's authority edited 'Humphrys' for the benefit of Fielding's family is plausible enough; equally, the family's view of Fielding's final intentions must have differed from Millar's (the cancelled preface to 'Humphrys' might have told us why); but John had no right to 'stay' publication, much less to pre-empt Millar's edition, and the shelf life of 'Humphrys' was too brief to silence his brother's 'frankness'. Such was Cross's scenario, however; not only the bibliographical facts, but also the freedom of the larger textual changes, the felicity of the smaller ones, the good faith that retained easily corrected errors, and the inefficacy and futility of any censorship, all tell against it.

---

[30] HF had made out a bond to Millar for £1,892 on 31 December 1753, on which John Fielding had paid £800, 28 January 1755—presumably the proceeds of the sale of Fordhook, 20 December 1754 (*Life*, pp. 581, 609–10). HF's only other major asset was his library, sold for about £364 (ibid., p. 610). The bond was last seen at the sale of the Bovet autograph collection by Charavay, Paris, 1885, and its details are unknown; still, HF could not have secured the balance of this debt except by mortgaging his future literary production.

THE
JOURNAL
OF A
VOYAGE to LISBON,

By the late

HENRY FIELDING, Esq;

LONDON:
Printed for A. MILLAR, in the Strand.
MDCCLV.

DEDICATION TO THE PUBLIC.[1]

YOUR candour[2] is desired on the perusal of the following sheets, as they are the product of a genius that has long been your delight and entertainment. It must be acknowledged that a lamp almost burnt out does not give so steady and uniform a light, as when it blazes in its full vigour; but yet it is well known that, by its wavering, as if struggling against its own dissolution, it sometimes darts a ray as bright as ever. In like manner, a strong and lively genius will, in its last struggles, sometimes mount aloft, and throw forth the most striking marks of its original lustre.

WHEREVER these are to be found, do you, the genuine patrons of extraordinary capacities, be as liberal in your applauses of him who is now no more, as you were of him whilst he was yet amongst you. And, on the other hand, if in this little work there should appear any traces of a weaken'd and decay'd life, let your own imaginations place before your eyes a true picture, in that of a hand trembling in almost its latest hour, of a body emaciated with pains, yet struggling for your entertainment; and let this affecting picture open each tender heart, and call forth a melting tear, to blot out whatever failings may be found in a work begun in pain, and finished almost at the same period with life.

IT was thought proper, by the friends of the deceased, that this little piece should come into your hands as it came from the hands of the author; it being judged that you would be better pleased to have an opportunity of observing the faintest traces of a genius you have long admired, than have it patch'd by a different hand; by which means the marks of its true author might have been effac'd.[3]

THAT the success of this last written, tho' first published volume, of the author's posthumous pieces,[4] may be attended with some convenience

---

[1] The Dedication was probably written by HF's young friend Arthur Murphy (1727–1805), who had begun his literary career as editor of *The Gray's-Inn Journal* (October 1752–September 1754), which he modelled on HF's *Covent-Garden Journal* (1752) and in which he became his most vocal admirer. In May 1759 Andrew Millar, HF's publisher, would employ Murphy to edit his *Works* (1762) and to write his biography. On the possibility that he also edited the *Journal*, see the Introduction, above, p. 519.

[2] 'candour': used throughout as 'sweetness of temper, kindness' (*OED*, s.v. 4).

[3] For the complex story of the two original editions of the *Journal*, see the Textual Introduction.

[4] In 1778, when the MS of HF's 'lost' comedy *The Fathers: or, The Good-Natured Man* was discovered and the play produced at Drury Lane by Garrick and Richard Brinsley Sheridan, Sir John Fielding, writing on 4 December to HF's friend the surgeon William Hunter (see below, p. 577 and n. 108), assured him that 'There are no other of his Works left unpublished.' Some forty years later, however, HF's grandson William Henry Fielding, referring to the Gordon Riots of 1780, told a collector that 'some Novels and other works, ready for the press, were in the House of *Sir John Fielding* when it was destroyed . . . and they thus fell a sacrifice to the flames' (*Life*, pp. 616–17). Fragments of HF's unfinished work on

to those innocents he hath left behind,[5] will, no doubt, be a motive to encourage its circulation through the kingdom, which will engage every future genius to exert itself for your pleasure.

THE principles and spirit which breathe in every line of the small fragment begun in answer to Lord Bolingbroke will unquestionably be a sufficient apology for its publication,[6] altho' vital strength was wanting to finish a work so happily begun and so well designed.

THE PREFACE.[7]

THERE would not, perhaps, be a more pleasant, or profitable study, among those which have their principal end in amusement, than that of travels or voyages, if they were writ, as they might be, and ought to be, with a joint view to the entertainment and information of mankind. If the conversation of travellers be so largely sought after as it is, we may believe their books will be still more agreeable company, as they will, in general, be more instructive and more entertaining.

BUT when I say the conversation of travellers is usually so welcome, I must be understood to mean that only of such as have had good sense enough to apply their peregrinations to a proper use, so as to acquire from them a real and valuable knowledge of men and things; both which are best known by comparison. If the customs and manners of men were every where the same, there would be no office so dull as that of a traveller: for the difference of hills, valleys, rivers; in short, the various views in which we may see the face of the earth, would scarce afford him a pleasure worthy of his labour; and surely it would give him very little opportunity of communicating any kind of entertainment or improvement to others.

Crown Law do survive, dispersed by the grandson during the period 1820–32 (see *Fielding's An Institute of the Pleas of the Crown*, ed. Hugh Amory [Cambridge, Mass., 1987], p. [iii]). But the only unpublished literary MSS that have come to light since HF's death are the two poems—the 'Cantos' and the 'Epistle to Lyttleton'—discovered by Isobel Grundy among the papers of Lady Mary Wortley Montagu, for which, see above, pp. 28 and 86.

[5] HF was survived by Mary, his widow, and four children: Henrietta Eleanor—or Harriet as she was called—a girl of 10 or 11 born of his marriage to his first wife, Charlotte; and by Mary, a daughter Sophia, 4 years old, who died within a year or two of HF; William, 6; and Allen, born in April 1754.

[6] For HF's *Fragment of a Comment on L. Bolingbroke's Essays*, appended to the original editions of the *Journal*, see below, pp. 665–80; also the Introduction, pp. 661–4. Murphy shared HF's indignation at Bolingbroke's religious scepticism, brazenly flaunted in his *Works*, posthumously published on 6 May 1754. In *The Gray's-Inn Journal* (25 May) Murphy sketched Bolingbroke's life story in the form of an oriental tale, deploring 'the baneful Influence' of his philosophy (1756 reprint, ii, p. 205).

[7] On the Preface, see the Introduction, above pp. 517–9.

To make a traveller an agreeable companion to a man of sense, it is necessary, not only that he should have seen much, but that he should have overlooked much of what he hath seen. Nature is not, any more than a great genius, always admirable in her productions, and therefore the traveller, who may be called her commentator, should not expect to find every where subjects worthy of his notice.

IT is certain, indeed, that one may be guilty of omission as well as of the opposite extreme: but a fault on that side will be more easily pardoned, as it is better to be hungry than surfeited, and to miss your dessert at the table of a man whose gardens abound with the choicest fruits, than to have your taste affronted with every sort of trash that can be pick'd up at the green-stall, or the wheel-barrow.

IF we should carry on the analogy between the traveller and the commen-tator, it is impossible to keep one's eye a moment off from the laborious much-read doctor Zachary Grey,[8] of whose redundant notes on Hudibras I shall only say, that it is, I am confident, the single book extant in which above five hundred authors are quoted, not one of which could be found in the collection of the late doctor Mead.[9]

AS there are few things which a traveller is to record, there are fewer on which he is to offer his observations: this is the office of the reader, and it is so pleasant a one, that he seldom chuses to have it taken from him, under the pretence of lending him assistance. Some occasions, indeed, there are, when proper observations are pertinent, and others when they are neces-sary; but good sense alone must point them out. I shall lay down only one general rule, which I believe to be of universal truth between relator and hearer, as it is between author and reader; this is, that the latter never forgive any observation of the former which doth not convey some knowledge that they are sensible they could not possibly have attained of themselves.

BUT all his pains in collecting knowledge, all his judgment in selecting,

---

[8] Zachary Grey LL D (1688–1766) editor in 1744 of Samuel Butler's burlesque epic *Hudibras*, with illustrations by Hogarth. A copy of this elaborate edition was in HF's library (Ribbles B65); to it was added in 1752 a supplement of *Critical, Historical and Explanatory Notes*. In the present passage, HF recalls the opinion of Grey he expressed in *The Covent-Garden Journal*, No. 24 (24 March 1752): 'the laborious, and all-read Dr. Zachary Grey, who to compile those wonderful Notes to his Hudibras, must have ransacked not only all the Stalls, but all the Trunks and Bandboxes in the World' (p. 156)—i.e. not only all the bookstalls, but all the receptacles of waste paper. In his note on the passage, Bertrand Goldgar remarks that, in the Preface to his edition of Shakespeare (1747), William Warburton had anticipated HF's complaint: 'I hardly think there ever appeared, in any *learned* Language, so execrable a heap of nonsense under the name of Commentaries.'

[9] Dr Richard Mead (1673–February 1754), personal physician to the King, was renowned as an antiquary and bibliophile. When the sale of his library began in November, *The Gentleman's Magazine* reported there were 10,000 volumes, 'among them whatever was curious, excellent, or scarce, besides a great number of *Greek*, *Latin*, and oriental manuscripts' (24, p. 514). The sale catalogue, to which HF refers in the journal entry for 27 June (below, p. 571 and n. 93), was published in July 1754.

and all his art in communicating it, will not suffice, unless he can make himself, in some degree, an agreeable, as well as an instructive companion. The highest instruction we can derive from the tedious tale of a dull fellow scarce ever pays us for our attention. There is nothing, I think, half so valuable as knowledge, and yet there is nothing which men will give themselves so little trouble to attain; unless it be, perhaps, that lowest degree of it which is the object of curiosity, and which hath therefore that active passion constantly employed in its service. This, indeed, it is in the power of every traveller to gratify; but it is the leading principle in weak minds only.

To render his relation agreeable to the man of sense, it is therefore necessary that the voyager should possess several eminent and rare talents; so rare, indeed, that it is almost wonderful to see them ever united in the same person.

AND if all these talents must concur in the relator, they are certainly in a more eminent degree necessary to the writer: for here the narration admits of higher ornaments of stile, and every fact and sentiments offers itself to the fullest and most deliberate examination.

IT would appear therefore, I think, somewhat strange, if such writers as these should be found extremely common; since nature hath been a most parsimonious distributer of her richest talents, and hath seldom bestowed many on the same person. But on the other hand, why there should scarce exist a single writer of this kind worthy our regard; and whilst there is no other branch of history (for this is history) which hath not exercised the greatest pens, why this alone should be overlooked by all men of great genius and erudition, and delivered up to the Goths and Vandals as their lawful property, is altogether as difficult to determine.

AND yet that this is the case, with some very few exceptions, is most manifest. Of these I shall willingly admit Burnet[10] and Addison;[11] if the

---

[10] Gilbert Burnet (1643–1715), Bishop of Salisbury, in religion a latitudinarian, in politics a Whig. HF greatly admired Burnet and was close to his son Sir Thomas Burnet, to whom he refers in the *Journal* as his 'ever honoured and beloved friend' (below, p. 560 and n. 53). HF's opinion of the Bishop's historical writings was extravagant: giving an account of the heroine's reading in the original edition of *Amelia* (VI. vii), he declares Burnet to be 'almost the only *English* Historian that is likely to be known to Posterity, by whom he will be most certainly ranked amongst the greatest Writers of Antiquity' (p. 256 and n. 2); indeed, later in this Preface, alluding to Burnet's *History of His Own Time* (published posthumously by his son Thomas in 1724), he goes so far as to 'confess' he would have 'honoured and loved Homer more had he written' such a history as Burnet's 'in humble prose' instead of his 'noble poems' (below, p. 549 and n. 16). The present reference, however, is to Burnet's *Travels thro' Switzerland, Italy, &c.* (1687), a copy of which was in HF's library, as indeed were the other works referred to above (Ribbles B56–9). In *A Serious Address to the People of Great Britain* (1745), HF quotes at some length Burnet's eyewitness account of the Catholics' persecution of the Protestants in France, referring to him as 'a learned and ingenious Writer' (*TP*, pp. 17–18).

[11] Joseph Addison (1672–1719), whose writings HF greatly admired. As early as the unfinished burlesque of *The Dunciad* (1729/30), Addison was 'immortal': 'Sense and Religion taught his Skilful Pen | The best of Criticks, and the best of Men' ('Cantos', above, p. 46 and n. 34). In the present context HF

former was not perhaps to be considered as a political essayist, and the latter as a commentator on the classics, rather than as a writer of travels; which last title perhaps they would both of them have been least ambitious to affect.

INDEED if these two, and two or three more, should be removed from the mass, there would remain such a heap of dulness behind, that the appellation of voyage-writer would not appear very desirable.

I AM not here unapprized that old Homer himself is by some considered as a voyage-writer; and indeed the beginning of his Odyssy may be urged to countenance that opinion, which I shall not controvert. But whatever species of writing the Odyssy is of, it is surely at the head of that species, as much as the Iliad is of another; and so far the excellent Longinus[12] would allow, I believe, at this day.

BUT, in reality, the Odyssy, the Telemachus,[13] and all of that kind, are to the voyage-writing I here intend, what romance is to true history, the former being the confounder and corrupter of the latter. I am far from supposing, that Homer, Hesiod,[14] and the other antient poets and mythologists, had any settled design to pervert and confuse the records of antiquity; but it is certain they have effected it;[15] and, for my part, I must confess I should have honoured and loved Homer more had he written a true history

refers to the Continent, commenting, as P. G. Adams notes, on 'politics, history, religion, architecture, literature, and the arts' (*Travel Literature and the Evolution of the Novel* [Lexington, Ky., 1983], p. 188). Earlier references to the *Remarks* occur in *The Craftsman*, No. 539 (30 October 1736; *New Essays*, p. 175) and in the heading to Letter XLI of Sarah Fielding's *Familiar Letters* (above, p. 491). A copy of the work was in HF's library (Ribbles A5).

[12] 'Longinus', the putative author of the first-century treatise *On the Sublime*, considered the *Odyssey* inferior to the *Iliad*, because 'reality is worsted by romance' in the *Odyssey*, which is 'a sort of comedy of character' (ix. 14–15). But there is no doubt of his admiration for both epics: 'in the *Odyssey* one may liken Homer to the setting sun; the grandeur [of the *Iliad*] remains without the intensity' (ix. 13). In *Tom Jones* (XI. i) HF placed Longinus in the company of Aristotle and Horace among the Ancients, 'those noble Critics, to whose Labours the learned World are so greatly indebted' (p. 569). In *The Covent-Garden Journal*, No. 10 (4 February 1752), attempting to define the elusive quality of 'Taste', he points to 'that inimitable Critic' Longinus, 'who of all Men seems most exquisitely to have possessed it' (p. 76).

[13] Referring to *Les Avantures de Télémaque fils d'Ulysse* (1699) by François de Salignac de La Mothe-Fénelon (1651–1715), Archbishop of Cambrai, a popular prose epic having as its theme the education of Telemachus, son of Odysseus. On the importance of this paragraph in the development of HF's views about the relative usefulness of fiction and history since the Preface to *Joseph Andrews* (1742), see the Introduction, above, p. 518.

[14] Hesiod (*fl. c.*700 BC). His *Theogony* is a mythological history and genealogy of the gods.

[15] HF shares the euhemerist persuasion that mythology is only 'the elaboration of ancient political and other historic events of great moment' (Frank E. Manuel, *The Eighteenth Century Confronts the Gods* [Cambridge, Mass., 1959], ch. 2); he was particularly influenced by the Abbé Antoine Banier's *Mythology and Fables of the Ancients, Explain'd from History* (1739–40), in his library (Ribbles B6): 'the most useful, instructive, and entertaining Book extant' (*JJ*, No. 9 [30 January 1748], p. 146).

of his own times[16] in humble prose, than those noble poems that have so justly collected the praise of all ages; for though I read these with more admiration and astonishment, I still read Herodotus, Thucydides and Xenophon,[17] with more amusement and more satisfaction.

THE original poets were not, however, without excuse. They found the limits of nature too strait for the immensity of their genius, which they had not room to exert, without extending fact by fiction; and that especially at a time when the manners of men were too simple to afford that variety, which they have since offered in vain to the choice of the meanest writers. In doing this, they are again excusable for the manner in which they have done it,

Ut speciosa dehinc miracula promant.[18]

They are not indeed so properly said to turn reality into fiction, as fiction into reality. Their paintings are so bold, their colours so strong, that every thing they touch seems to exist in the very manner they represent it: their portraits are so just, and their landscapes so beautiful, that we acknowledge the strokes of nature in both, without enquiring whether nature herself, or her journeyman the poet, formed the first pattern of the piece.

BUT other writers (I will put Pliny[19] at their head) have no such pretensions to indulgence: they ly for lying sake, or in order insolently to impose the most monstrous improbabilities and absurdities upon their readers on their own authority; treating them as some fathers treat children, and as other fathers do lay-men, exacting their belief of whatever they relate, on no other foundation than their own authority, without ever taking the pains of adapting their lies to human credulity, and of calculating them

---

[16] An implicit reference to *The History of His Own Time* by Bishop Burnet, HF's favourite English historian (above, p. 547 n. 10).

[17] Herodotus (*c.*484–425 BC), author of *Historia*, which relates the conflict between Greece and Asia from the time of Croesus to that of Xerxes (Ribbles H16). Thucydides (*c.*460–*c.*400 BC), author of the *History of the Peloponnesian War* (Ribbles T19). In *Tom Jones* (XIV. i) he is to Greek history-writing what Homer is to the epic and Aristotle to philosophy (p. 741); and in *Amelia* (IV. iii) Dr Harrison, HF's spokesman, quotes a passage from Thucydides, calling him 'my favourite *Greek* Historian' (p. 166). Xenophon (*c.*430–after 355 BC), author of the *Anabasis*, an account of the expedition of Cyrus against his brother Artaxerxes, and the *Hellenica*, which takes up the history of the Peloponnesian War at the point where Thucydides concludes; his works were also in HF's library (Ribbles X1).

[18] Horace, *Ars Poetica*, line 144: 'That then [they] may set forth striking and wondrous tales' (Loeb), describing the art of the *Odyssey*.

[19] Pliny the Elder (AD 23–79), author of the *Natural History*, a work replete with examples of unnatural phenomena and vulgar errors represented as fact; there were two editions in HF's library (Ribbles P28–9). In *Jonathan Wild*, HF intended Mrs Heartfree's narrative of her travels (IV. ix) as 'a Burlesque on the extravagant Accounts of Travellers' (*Miscellanies* i, p. 11), and he emphasized the point in the heading to the chapter: '*A very wonderful Chapter indeed; which, to those who have not read many Voyages, may seem incredible; and which the Reader may believe or not, as he pleases*' (*Miscellanies* iii, p. 162); in his note Goldgar refers to this paragraph in the *Journal*. In *The Covent-Garden Journal*, No. 12 (11 February 1752) HF quotes Pliny in a contrary light, complaining about '*the monstrous Lies*' of historians (p. 86).

for the meridian of a common understanding; but with as much weakness as wickedness, and with more impudence often than either, they assert facts contrary to the honour of God, to the visible order of the creation, to the known laws of nature, to the histories of former ages, and to the experience of our own, and which no man can at once understand and believe.

IF it should be objected (and it can no where be objected better than where I now write*, as there is no where more pomp of bigotry)[20] that whole nations have been firm believers in such most absurd suppositions;[21] I reply, the fact is not true. They have known nothing of the matter, and have believed they knew not what. It is, indeed, with me no matter of doubt, but that the pope and his clergy might teach any of those Christian Heterodoxies, the tenets of which are the most diametrically opposite to their own; nay, all the doctrines of Zoroaster, Confucius, and Mahomet,[22] not only with certain and immediate success, but without one catholick in a thousand knowing he had changed his religion.

WHAT motive a man can have to sit down, and to draw forth a list of stupid, senseless, incredible lies upon paper, would be difficult to determine, did not Vanity present herself so immediately as the adequate cause. The vanity of knowing more than other men is, perhaps, besides hunger, the only inducement to writing, at least to publishing, at all: why then should not the voyage-writer be inflamed with the glory of having seen what no man ever did or will see but himself? This is the true source of the wonderful, in the discourse and writings, and sometimes, I believe, in the actions of men. There is another fault of a kind directly opposite to this, to which

---

* At Lisbon.

---

[20] HF's animus against the Roman Catholic Church may have begun in childhood after his mother's death, with the rancorous proceedings of the custody suit brought against his father for marrying a Catholic; but it is evident throughout his writings—in his plays *The Old Debauchees* (1732) and *Pasquin* (1736), and in his anti-Jacobitical writings of 1745–8. His experience of Lisbon confirmed his prejudice. This was the city in which the Methodist George Whitefield, in horrified fascination, witnessed in Lent of 1754 the hooded penitential processions and idolatry that moved him to give thanks 'for the great Wonder of the Reformation' and England's deliverance in 1745–6 from the threat of the 'papist' Pretender to the throne (*A Brief Account of some Lent and other Extraordinary Processions and Ecclesiastical Entertainments seen last Year at Lisbon* [1755], pp. 2, 14). In June 1754, a few weeks before HF arrived in the city, the Inquisition, in the terrible ceremony of the auto-da-fé, had publicly burnt a Jew for relapsing from the faith (*Whitehall Evening Post*, 29 June–2 July). During his brief time in Lisbon there were other pompous spectacles of the Church: the funeral of Maria Anna, the pious dowager Queen, who died on 14 August; and during 4–7 September the installation of a new Cardinal Patriarch of the city, which was attended with 'festive peals of bells from his 40 parishes and 60 convents, besides those of the colleges and also churches, which continued for three successive days, while at night all the streets of the city were illuminated' (*Gazeta de Lisboa*, 12 September 1754; trans. Amory).

[21] 'suppositions': by implication false or mistaken beliefs (*OED*, s.v. 3); see also below, p. 594 n. 154.

[22] Zoroaster, or Zarathustra (*c.*628–551 BC), Kongfuzi (or Confucius, 551–479 BC), and Muhammad (or Mohammed, AD *c.*570–632)—founders, respectively, of Zoroastrianism, Confucianism, and Islam.

these writers are sometimes liable, when, instead of filling their pages with monsters which no body hath ever seen, and with adventures which never have nor could possibly have happened to them, waste their time and paper with recording things and facts of so common a kind, that they challenge no other right of being remembered, than as they had the honour of having happened to the author, to whom nothing seems trivial that in any manner happens to himself. Of such consequence do his own actions appear to one of this kind, that he would probably think himself guilty of infidelity, should he omit the minutest thing in the detail of his journal. That the fact is true, is sufficient to give it a place there, without any consideration whether it is capable of pleasing or surprising, of diverting or informing the reader.

I HAVE seen a play (if I mistake not, it is one of Mrs. Behn's, or of Mrs. Centlivre's)[23] where this vice in a voyage-writer is finely ridiculed. An ignorant pedant, to whose government, for I know not what reason, the conduct of a young nobleman in his travels is committed, and who is sent abroad to shew My Lord the world, of which he knows nothing himself, before his departure from a town, calls for his journal, to record the goodness of the wine and tobacco, with other articles of the same importance, which are to furnish the materials of a voyage at his return home.[24] The humour, it is true, is here carried very far; and yet, perhaps, very little beyond what is to be found in writers who profess no intention of dealing in humour at all.

OF one or other or both of these kinds are, I conceive, all that vast pile of books which pass under the names of voyages, travels, adventures, lives, memoirs, histories, &c. some of which a single traveller sends into the world in many volumes, and others are, by judicious booksellers,[25] collected into

---

[23] Aphra Behn (1640–89) and Susannah Centlivre (1669–1723). Cf. Behn's *The Feign'd Curtezans* (1679), in which Timothy Tickletext, tutor to Sir Signal Buffoon, having accompanied his charge to Italy, scoffs at the art and architecture of Rome while recording trivialities in a journal he intends to publish 'for the good of the Nation' (Keymer *Fielding's Journal*, p. xxi). Noting HF's uncertainty about the authorship of the play, Keymer suggests that he may also have had 'half an eye on *Mar-plot*' (1711), Centlivre's sequel to *The Busie-Body*. This is HF's only reference to Centlivre; Behn was earlier the target of a sarcasm directed at her novels (*Tom Jones* [x. ii, p. 530]).

[24] Cf. *Jonathan Wild* (i. vii), where HF ironically apologizes that his hero's travels abroad provided no adventure worth reporting; to supply the deficiency, 'we borrowed the Journals of several young Gentlemen who have lately made the Tour of *Europe*; but to our great Sorrow could not extract a single Incident strong enough to justify the Theft to our Consciences' (*Miscellanies* iii, p. 28). For a succinct survey of HF's satires of the vogue of the Grand Tour, which is a recurrent theme in his writings, see *The Craftsman*, No. 469 (28 June 1735), *New Essays*; pp. 74–5, 85 nn. 22–3.

[25] If HF had specific booksellers in mind, the brothers Awnsham and John Churchill 'fit' the allusion: their popular *Collection of Voyages and Travels* was first published in four folio volumes in 1704. In *The Covent-Garden Journal*, No. 67 (21 October 1752), p. 357, HF cites an episode from the collection. The curiously bitter tone of HF's remark may have something to do with the fact that Awnsham Churchill, who had been MP for Dorchester (1705–10), also bought estates in Dorset—among them in 1720 the farm at East Stour that was to have been the inheritance of HF and his siblings (*Life*, p. 19).

vast bodies in folio, and inscribed with their own names, as if they were indeed their own travels; thus unjustly attributing to themselves the merit of others.

Now from both these faults we have endeavoured to steer clear in the following narrative: which, however the contrary may be insinuated by ignorant, unlearned, and fresh-water critics, who have never travelled either in books or ships, I do solemnly declare doth, in my own impartial opinion, deviate less from truth than any other voyage extant; my lord Anson's alone being, perhaps, excepted.[26]

Some few embellishments must be allowed to every historian: for we are not to conceive that the speeches in Livy, Salust, or Thucidydes,[27] were literally spoken in the very words in which we now read them. It is sufficient that every fact hath its foundation in truth, as I do seriously aver is the case in the ensuing pages; and when it is so, a good critic will be so far from denying all kind of ornament of stile or diction, or even of circumstance to his author, that he would be rather sorry if he omitted it: for he could hence derive no other advantage than the loss of an additional pleasure in the perusal.

Again, if any merely common incident should appear in this journal, which will seldom, I apprehend, be the case, the candid reader will easily perceive it is not introduced for its own sake, but for some observations and reflections naturally resulting from it; and which, if but little to his amusement, tend directly to the instruction of the reader, or to the information of the public; to whom if I chuse to convey such instruction or information with an air of joke and laughter, none but the dullest of fellows will, I

---

[26] George Anson (1697–1762), Baron. *A Voyage round the World . . . by George Anson* (1748) was compiled from Anson's notes by Richard Walter, chaplain of his flagship, the *Centurion*, during a global cruise against the Spanish. In the Introduction, Walter states that he 'endeavoured, with my utmost care, to adhere strictly to truth in every article of the ensuing narration' (Keymer *Fielding's Journal*, p. 117 n. 10)—a claim supported by the verdict of *The Gentleman's Magazine* (18 [May 1748], p. 239): 'No Voyage was ever written with . . . more regard to truth.' See also below, p. 590 n. 146.

[27] Livy (Titus Livius) (59 BC–AD 17), whom HF called 'the greatest of all the *Roman* Historians' (*TP*, No. 2 [12 November 1745], p. 118). Sallust (Gaius Sallustius Crispus) (86–*c.*34 BC), Roman historian whose 'penetrating Genius' HF admired (*TP*, No. 17 [18–25 February 1746], p. 225). Copies of their works were in HF's library (Ribbles L21, S1). In *Jonathan Wild* (III. vi) HF, facetiously excusing the surprising eloquence of Wild's letter to Tishy, singles out Sallust as exemplifying the licence allowed in history-writing: 'it is sufficient if . . . the Historian adheres faithfully to the Matter, though he embellishes the Diction with some Flourishes of his own Eloquence, without which the excellent Speeches recorded in ancient Historians (particularly in *Sallust*) would have scarce been found in their Writings' (*Miscellanies* iii, p. 108). Thucydides (above, n. 17) provides explicit classical authority for this licence: his 'speeches are given in the language in which, as it seemed to me, the several speakers would express . . . the sentiments most befitting the occasion, though at the same time I have adhered as closely as possible to the general sense of what was actually said' (*Peloponnesian War*, I. xxii.1).

believe, censure it; but if they should, I have the authority of more than one passage in Horace to alledge in my defence.[28]

HAVING thus endeavoured to obviate some censures to which a man, without the gift or fore-sight, or any fear of the imputation of being a conjurer, might conceive this work would be liable, I might now undertake a more pleasing task, and fall at once to the direct and positive praises of the work itself; of which indeed I could say a thousand good things: but the task is so very pleasant that I shall leave it wholly to the reader; and it is all the task that I impose on him. A moderation for which he may think himself obliged to me, when he compares it with the conduct of authors, who often fill a whole sheet with their own praises, to which they sometimes set their own real names, and sometimes a fictitious one.[29] One hint, however, I must give the kind reader; which is, that if he should be able to find no sort of amusement in the book, he will be pleased to remember the public utility which will arise from it. If entertainment, as Mr. Richardson observes, be but a secondary consideration in a romance;[30] with which Mr. Addison I think agrees, affirming the use of the pastry-cook to be the first;[31] if this, I say, be true of a mere work of invention, sure it may well be so considered

[28] Cf. Horace, *Satires*, I. iv. 103–5: 'If I speak too jestingly, this bit of liberty you will indulgently grant me' (Loeb); also the motto of *The Champion* (26 January 1739/40). Cf. also HF's favourite lines in this context: *Satires* (I. i. 24–5), which he rendered in *Tom Jones* (XI. i), 'but surely a Man may speak Truth with a smiling Countenance' (p. 569); also cited in *The Covent-Garden Journal*, No. 10 (4 February 1752), p. 73; *Correspondence*, Letter 12, p. 18 and n. 10; and as the motto of *The Craftsman* No. 612 (1 April 1738): *New Essays*, p. 287.

[29] HF here revives the mockery of *Shamela* (above, p. 518), in which he caricatured Richardson's vanity in *Pamela* (1740), where, under the guise of editor, he filled the Preface with praise of his own work; and prefixed to the second edition (February 1741) twenty-four more pages of congratulatory letters and verse. On the renewal of strained relations between HF and Richardson at this time, see the Introduction, pp. 518–19.

[30] Richardson, referring to his novel in the Preface to *Clarissa* (December 1747): 'in all Works of This, and the Dramatic Kind, STORY, or AMUSEMENT, should be considered as little more than the *Vehicle* to the more necessary INSTRUCTION' (i, p. vi). In the revised Preface of the third edition (April 1751) he repeated this didactic principle: 'considerate Readers will not enter upon the perusal of the Piece before them, as if it were designed *only* to divert and amuse. It will probably be thought tedious to all such as *dip* into it, expecting a *light Novel*, or *transitory Romance*; and look upon Story in it . . . as its *sole end*, rather than as a vehicle of Instruction.' In *The Covent-Garden Journal*, No. 10 (4 February 1752) HF had cited with approval this same rule, which he now scorns: '*Pleasantry*, (as the ingenious Author of Clarissa says of a Story) *should be made only the Vehicle of Instruction*' (p. 73).

[31] Dobson was first to propose that HF was 'probably' alluding to *The Spectator*, No. 85 (7 June 1711), where Addison recalls finding a page of the Puritan divine Richard Baxter 'under a *Christmas* Pye'. Editors thereafter have followed, no doubt in desperation; for Addison nowhere explicitly declares that novels and romances are good for nothing but lining pie plates. HF anticipated this witticism in *Tom Jones* (IV. i), where he refers to 'those idle Romances which are filled with Monsters, the Productions, not of Nature, but of distempered Brains; and which have been therefore recommended by an eminent Critic to the sole Use of the Pastry-cook' (p. 150); for the suggestion that he may have confused two passages from Shaftesbury's *Characteristicks* (1711), see the note to the quoted passage.

in a work founded, like this, on truth; and where the political reflections form so distinguishing a part.

B UT perhaps I may hear, from some critic of the most saturnine complexion, that my vanity must have made a horrid dupe of my judgment, if it hath flattered me with an expectation of having any thing here seen in a grave light, or of conveying any useful instruction to the public, or to their guardians. I answer with the great man,[32] whom I just now quoted, that my purpose is to convey instruction in the vehicle of entertainment; and so to bring about at once, like the revolution in the Rehearsal,[33] a perfect reformation of the laws relating to our maritime affairs: an undertaking, I will not say more modest, but surely more feasible, than that of reforming a whole people, by making use of a vehicular story, to wheel in among them worse manners than their own.[34]

THE INTRODUCTION

IN the beginning of August, 1753, when I had taken the Duke of Portland's medicine,[35] as it is called, near a year, the effects of which had been the carrying off the symptoms of a lingering imperfect gout, I was persuaded by Mr. Ranby, the King's premier serjeant-surgeon,[36] and the

---

[32] 'the great man': i.e. Richardson, see above, n. 30.

[33] Having, sarcastically, referred to Richardson as 'the great man', HF perhaps recalled his own satire on 'the Instability of Human Greatness' in *The True Patriot*, No. 16 (11–18 February 1746), in which he offers Buckingham's 'inimitable' farce, *The Rehearsal* (1672), as 'the most striking Ridicule of all worldly Greatness drawn from its Instability . . . where [Act II, scene iv] the Gentleman Usher and Physician dethrone the two Kings of *Brentford* by a Whisper'. In the present context, readers who knew the play might detect an implicit application to the insecure 'greatness' of HF's rival: for at the approach of the true occupants of the chairs, the 'two Usurpers . . . *sneak off* as comically and as absurdly as they enter'd', the Gentleman Usher observing, 'No human Wit can ever bring Greatness to a more farcical End' (pp. 219–20). For HF's many references to *The Rehearsal*, see Ribbles B51.

[34] HF's sarcastic reference to 'a vehicular story' recalls the passage from the Preface to *Clarissa* (1747), which, as recently as *The Covent-Garden Journal*, No. 10, he had cited without irony (see above, n. 30): '*Pleasantry*, (as the ingenious Author of Clarissa says of a Story) *should be made only the Vehicle of Instruction*.' Keymer (*Fielding's Journal*, p. 118) also detects an allusion to the Postscript of the 1751 edition of *Clarissa*, where, after implicit gibes at the bad examples set by HF's heroes, Richardson deplores 'the general depravity' of 'all ranks and degrees of people', and pledges his novel 'towards introducing a Reformation so much wanted'. For the indignation expressed by Richardson and his friends at HF's sarcasms in these concluding paragraphs, see the Introduction, pp. 518–19.

[35] 'This celebrated powder, which obtained its name in consequence of being recommended by a duke of Portland, was long held as a specific in the cure of gout. It is composed of the roots of round birthwort and gentian, and of the tops and leaves of germander, ground pine and centaury, dried and reduced to powder' (Dobson, pp. 149–50, quoting William Watson's *Life* of HF [1807], p. 128 n.). It was said to have originated with Galen (*GM*, 23 [1753], p. 579).

[36] John Ranby (1703–73), HF's friend (a subscriber to the *Miscellanies* of 1743) had been appointed Principal Sergeant Surgeon to George II in 1742; he also acted as governor of the Company of Surgeons

ablest advice, I believe, in all branches of the physical profession, to go immediately to Bath. I accordingly writ that very night to Mrs. Bowden,[37] who, by the next post, informed me she had taken me a lodging for a month certain.

WITHIN a few days after this, whilst I was preparing for my journey, and when I was almost fatigued to death with several long examinations, relating to five different murders,[38] all committed within the space of a week, by different gangs of street robbers, I received a message from his Grace the Duke of Newcastle,[39] by Mr. Carrington, the King's messenger,[40] to attend his Grace the next morning, in Lincoln's-inn-fields, upon some business of importance; but I excused myself from complying with the message, as besides being lame, I was very ill with the great fatigues I had lately undergone, added to my distemper.

HIS Grace, however, sent Mr. Carrington, the very next morning, with another summons; with which, tho' in the utmost distress, I immediately complied; but the Duke happening, unfortunately for me, to be then particularly engaged, after I had waited some time, sent a gentleman to discourse with me on the best plan which could be invented for putting an

from its founding in 1745, the year in which HF, in his satire *The Charge to the Jury*, took Ranby's side in the medical controversy concerning the cause of Walpole's death (see *Champion*, pp. 601–17). HF compliments Ranby twice in *Tom Jones* (VIII. xiii, XVII. ix); and in *Amelia* (V. v) Ranby cures Colonel Bath of the wound he suffered in a duel, the narrator, in the first edition, calling him 'the most eminent Surgeon in the Kingdom, or perhaps in the World' (p. 211 and n. 3). After HF's death, Ranby helped relieve his family of a heavy debt by acquiring the lease of their farm at Fordhook, Ealing, for £800 (see below, p. 562 and n. 60).

[37] Mrs Dorothy Bowden (*née* Wingate), keeper of a fashionable lodging-house in Bath, frequented in the 1750s by, among others, HF's sister Sarah, Richardson's friend Lady Bradshaigh, and the poet Edward Young (*Correspondence*, Letter 84, pp. 131, 133 n. 3).

[38] On Saturday 22 September 1753 the *Public Advertiser* reported: 'This Week five several Persons have been examined before Justice Fielding for Murder.' On HF's exacting activities as a magistrate—activities which included his founding of the first metropolitan police force—during the months before his illness forced him in May 1754 to retire to the country, see *Life*, pp. 576–83.

[39] Thomas Pelham-Holles (1693–1768), first Duke of Newcastle and brother of Henry Pelham, the Prime Minister, was Secretary of State for the Northern Department and Lord Lieutenant of Middlesex, in which county HF served as principal magistrate. Newcastle House, the Duke's residence in town, was in Lincoln's Inn Fields. Though HF admired his brother (see below, p. 562 n. 58), he clearly disliked Newcastle, who treated him disdainfully. In July 1749 Newcastle discarded the 'bill' to reform the police that HF had submitted to the Lord Chancellor; in 1751 he ignored HF's recommendation of the honest constable William Pentlow for the office of Keeper of New Prison, Clerkenwell (though, in the event, the Middlesex justices chose Pentlow over the Duke's candidate); and in HF's correspondence of April 1753 his annoyance at Newcastle's repeated 'Commands' to produce evidence in the case of Elizabeth Canning that he did not have is obvious. On these three incidents, see *Correspondence*, Letters 53 n. 3, 63, 70–1. For HF's bitter allusion to his 'great patron', see below, p. 559 n. 50.

[40] Probably Nathan Carrington (d. 1777), whom Horace Walpole called 'the cleverest of all ministerial terriers' (Letter to Lord Hertford, 15 February 1764; *Yale Walpole*, xxxviii, p. 317 n. 1). The King's Messengers were employed by the Secretary of State to carry dispatches and to apprehend state prisoners (*OED*, s.v. 'messenger' 3).

immediate end to those murders and robberies which were every day committed in the streets; upon which, I promised to transmit my opinion, in writing, to his Grace, who, as the gentleman informed me, intended to lay it before the privy council.

THO' this visit cost me a severe cold, I, notwithstanding, set myself down to work, and in about four days sent the Duke as regular a plan as I could form, with all the reasons and arguments I could bring to support it, drawn out in several sheets of paper; and soon received a message from the Duke, by Mr. Carrington, acquainting me, that my plan was highly approved of, and that all the terms of it would be complied with.[41]

THE principal and most material of those terms was the immediately depositing 600 l. in my hands; at which small charge I undertook to demolish the then reigning gangs, and to put the civil policy into such order, that no such gangs should ever be able, for the future, to form themselves into bodies, or at least to remain any time formidable to the public.

I HAD delayed my Bath-journey for some time, contrary to the repeated advice of my physical acquaintance, and to the ardent desire of my warmest friends, tho' my distemper was now turned to a deep jaundice; in which case the Bath-waters are generally reputed to be almost infallible. But I had the most eager desire of demolishing this gang of villains and cut-throats, which I was sure of accomplishing the moment I was enabled to pay a fellow who had undertaken, for a small sum, to betray them into the hands of a set of thief-takers whom I had enlisted into the service, all men of known and approved fidelity and intrepidity.[42]

[41] Much simpler than his proposal for reforming the police set forth in the 'Bill' of July 1749 which Newcastle had quashed (for the full text, see *Life*, appendix 1), the plan HF now drew up refined and developed procedures he had adopted in the winter of 1749/50 soon after coming to Bow Street (*Life*, pp. 499–502); but this time the government approved the necessary funding. Announcements of the plan were published on the front page of the *Public Advertiser* beginning 20 November 1753, from which the elements of the scheme may be inferred: (1) magistrates, peace officers, and keepers of the turnpikes within 5 miles of London were to be (loosely) organized in order to encourage cooperation among them; (2) the public were urged to give immediate notice of crimes to HF, his brother John, or the turnpike keepers; (3) the expenses of those who prosecuted felons would be reimbursed; (4) the *Public Advertiser* would serve as the official organ for publicizing all matters relating to HF's campaign against crime, thereby facilitating communication between citizens and law enforcement officers; (5) gang members who turned informers would be rewarded and granted immunity from prosecution. On HF's plan and related topics, see John Fielding, *A Plan for preventing Robberies within Twenty Miles of London. With an Account of the Rise and Establishment of the real Thief-takers* (1755) and *An Account of the Original and Effects of a Police Set on Foot by His Grace the Duke of Newcastle in the Year 1753, upon a Plan presented to His Grace by the late Henry Fielding, Esq;* (1758); and HF's own 'Treatise on the Office of Constable', posthumously published in John's *Extracts from such of the Penal Laws, as particularly relate to the Peace and good Order of this Metropolis* (1761).

[42] The 'thief-takers' were the indispensable element in HF's plan. Led by Saunders Welch, High Constable of the Holborn Division (below, p. 568 n. 84), they were men such as William Pentlow (above, n. 39), chosen by HF from among constables of the metropolis who had proved their courage and

AFTER some weeks the money was paid at the Treasury, and within a few days after 200 l. of it had come to my hands the whole gang of cut-throats was entirely dispersed, seven of them were in actual custody, and the rest driven, some out of town, and others out of the kingdom.

THO' my health was now reduced to the last extremity, I continued to act with the utmost vigour against these villains; in examining whom, and in taking the depositions against them, I have often spent whole days, nay sometimes whole nights, especially when there was any difficulty in procuring sufficient evidence to convict them, which is a very common case in street-robberies, even when the guilt of the party is sufficiently apparent to satisfy the most tender conscience. But courts of justice know nothing of a cause more than what is told them on oath by a witness; and the most flagitious villain upon earth is tried in the same manner as a man of the best character, who is accused of the same crime.[43]

MEAN while, amidst all my fatigues and distresses, I had the satisfaction to find my endeavours had been attended with such success, that this hellish society were almost utterly extirpated, and that, instead of reading of murders and street-robberies in the news, almost every morning, there was, in the remaining part of the month of November, and in all December, not only no such thing as a murder, but not even a street-robbery committed. Some such, indeed, were mentioned in the public papers; but they were all found, on the strictest enquiry, to be false.

IN this entire freedom from street-robberies, during the dark months, no man will, I believe, scruple to acknowledge, that the winter of 1753 stands unrival'd, during a course of many years; and this may possibly appear the more extraordinary to those who recollect the outrages with which it began.

HAVING thus fully accomplished my undertaking, I went into the country in a very weak and deplorable condition, with no fewer or less diseases than a jaundice, a dropsy, and an asthma, altogether uniting their

---

integrity; acting on the principle of 'quick notice and sudden pursuit', as John Fielding called it, they came to be called 'the Bow Street Runners'. The particular case to which HF refers in these paragraphs was reported in the *Public Advertiser* during October 1753: one Thomas Preston was the informer who gave evidence against a vicious gang of thirteen 'villains and cut-throats', nine of whom were apprehended by HF's constables, who then pursued those who escaped into the country. Because of these thief-takers— HF's 'myrmidons' they were called—the winter of 1753/4 in the metropolis and its environs was virtually free of crime. Reports of their successes continued in the *Public Advertiser*, which on 14 December declared 'that since the apprehending the great Gang of Cut-throats, not one dangerous Blow, or Shot, or Wound has been given either in the Roads or Streets in or near this Town'. (*Life*, pp. 577–81).

[43] Cf. HF's *Enquiry into the Causes of the Late Increase of Robbers* (1751), section ix ('Of the Trial and Conviction of Felons'): 'The greatest and most known Villain in *England*, standing at the Bar equally *rectus in curia* with the Man of the highest Estimation, if they should be both accused of the same Crime' (p. 159).

forces in the destruction of a body so entirely emaciated, that it had lost all its muscular flesh.[44]

MINE was now no longer what is called a Bath case; nor, if it had been so, had I strength remaining sufficient to go thither, a ride of six miles only being attended with an intolerable fatigue. I now discharged my lodgings at Bath, which I had hitherto kept. I began, in earnest, to look on my case as desperate, and I had vanity enough to rank my self with those heroes who, of old times, became voluntary sacrifices to the good of the public.[45]

BUT, lest the reader should be too eager to catch at the word *vanity*, and should be unwilling to indulge me with so sublime a gratification, for I think he is not too apt to gratify me, I will take my key a pitch lower, and will frankly own that I had a stronger motive than the love of the public to push me on: I will therefore confess to him that my private affairs at the beginning of the winter had but a gloomy aspect;[46] for I had not plundered the public or the poor of those sums which men, who are always ready to plunder both as much as they can, have been pleased to suspect me of taking: on the contrary, by composing, instead of inflaming, the quarrels of porters and beggars (which I blush when I say hath not been universally practised) and by refusing to take a shilling from a man who most undoubtedly would not have had another left, I had reduced an income of about 500l.* a year of the dirtiest money upon earth, to little more than 300l; a considerable proportion of which remained with my clerk;[47] and indeed if the whole had done so, as it ought, he would be but ill paid for sitting almost sixteen hours in the twenty-four, in the most unwholesome, as

---

* A predecessor of mine[48] used to boast that he made 1000l. a year in his office: but how he did this

---

[44] HF's illness has been diagnosed as cirrhosis of the liver (*Life*, p. 577).

[45] HF repeats this reference to the self-sacrifice of Roman (and Spartan) patriots below (p. 560 and n. 53). In *The Champion* (8 January 1739/40) he cites on this subject the legendary examples of several 'ancient *Roman[s]*', among them Decius Mus, who gained a victory by rushing to his death; Marcus Curtius, who, to close a chasm that had opened in the Forum, leaped into it on his horse; and Horatius ('at the bridge') Cocles (p. 116).

[46] Despite what ought to have been ample income from various sources, HF on 31 December 1753 felt it necessary to borrow from his publisher Andrew Millar the extraordinary sum of £1,892 (Amory, 'Lisbon Letters', p. 80 n. 39).

[47] Sir Thomas DeVeil (c.1684–1746) preceded HF at Bow Street, Covent Garden, in the role of 'court justice', principal magistrate of the Liberty of Westminster, where in the courtroom of Justice Thrasher the opening scenes of *Amelia* (1751) are laid. Soon after he began sitting at Bow Street, HF was instrumental in purging the bench of one such magistrate, Henry Broadhead, a brewer by trade who used his office to extort money from prosecutors and accused alike; when he died in November 1754 he left an estate of £3,000 a year (*Life*, pp. 497–8, 675 nn. 110–11). For an account of DeVeil, see *Memoirs of the Life and Times of Sir Thomas Deveil* (1748); for DeVeil's own account of the corruptions associated with his office, see *Observations on the Practice of a Justice of the Peace* (1747); also *Enquiry*, pp. xix–xxi.

[48] On HF's clerk, see n. 49.

well as nauseous air in the universe, and which hath in his case corrupted a good constitution without contaminating his morals.

BUT, not to trouble the reader with anecdotes, contrary to my own rule laid down in my preface, I assure him I thought my family was very slenderly provided for; and that my health began to decline so fast, that I had very little more of life left to accomplish what I had thought of too late. I rejoiced therefore greatly in seeing an opportunity, as I apprehended, of gaining such merit in the eye of the public, that if my life were the sacrifice to it, my friends might think they did a popular act in putting my family at least beyond the reach of necessity, which I myself began to despair of

(if indeed he did it) is to me a secret. His clerk, now mine,[49] told me I had more business than he had ever known there; I am sure I had as much as any man could do. The truth is, the fees are so very low, when any are due, and so much is done for nothing, that if a single justice of peace had business enough to employ twenty clerks, neither he nor they would get much by their labour. The public will not therefore, I hope, think I betray a secret when I inform them, that I received from the government a yearly pension out of the public service-money; which I believe indeed would have been larger, had my great patron[50] been convinced of an error, which I have heard him utter more than once. That he could not indeed say, that the acting as a principal justice of the peace in Westminster was on all accounts very desirable, but that all the world knew it was a very lucrative office. Now to have shewn him plainly, that a man must be a rogue to make a very little this way, and that he could not make much by being as great a rogue as he could be, would have required more confidence than I believe he had in me, and more of his conversation than he chose to allow me; I therefore resigned the office, and the farther execution of my plan to my brother, who had long been my assistant.[51] And now, lest the case between me and the reader should be the same in both instances as it was between me and the great man, I will not add another word on the subject.

[49] When, in December 1748, HF took up residence in DeVeil's house in Bow Street, Joshua Brogden, DeVeil's clerk, continued in that capacity. HF thought so highly of Brogden that in July 1749 he recommended him to the Lord Chancellor for appointment to the magistracy. In the event, the commissioners rejected the nomination, noting contemptuously that Brogden was 'no better formerly than an Hackney Clerk married to Sr Thos Deveils maid' (*Correspondence*, Letter 53 and n. 4). HF, however, never wavered in his good opinion of Brogden, who later assisted him in *The Covent-Garden Journal* (1752), reporting on the cases brought before him at Bow Street. On one of these, Brogden commenting sympathetically on the plight of an unfortunate prostitute, HF interjected that Brogden, 'tho' he hath drawn so many thousand Commitments, is a Man of great Humanity' (p. 415).
[50] With one exception, editors of the *Journal*, remembering HF's fulsome acknowledgement in *Tom Jones* of the Duke of Bedford's 'princely Benefactions' (p. 5)—chiefly, the grant of property that enabled him to qualify for the Middlesex magistracy—have missed the irony in this account of HF's frustrating relationship with a scornful and indifferent 'great patron'. Keymer (*Fielding's Journal*, p. 119 n. 10) is certainly right in taking this as a sardonic reference to the Duke of Newcastle (see above, p. 555 n. 39), who as Secretary of State controlled funds paid out of 'the public service money'; moreover, since June 1751, when Bedford resigned his position as Secretary of State for the Southern Department, he was in opposition. The amount of the pension HF refers to was probably no less than £200 and no more than £400 (*Life*, pp. 459–60, 671 n. 5; also 614).
[51] HF was very close to his blind half-brother John (1721–80), who was appointed magistrate for Westminster in July 1751, nominated by the Duke of Bedford at HF's instance (*Correspondence*, Letters 64–6); he was commissioned magistrate for Middlesex in January 1754, thereby fully empowering him to act as HF's replacement at Bow Street (*Life*, p. 581). He was knighted in 1761.

doing.[52] And tho' I disclaim all pretence to that Spartan or Roman patriotism, which loved the public so well that it was always ready to become a voluntary sacrifice to the public good,[53] I do solemnly declare I have that love for my family.

AFTER this confession therefore, that the public was not the principal Deity to which my life was offered a sacrifice, and when it is farther considered what a poor sacrifice this was, being indeed no other than the giving up what I saw little likelihood of being able to hold much longer, and which, upon the terms I held it, nothing but the weakness of human nature could represent to me as worth holding at all; the world may, I believe, without envy allow me all the praise to which I have any title.

MY aim, in fact, was not praise, which is the last gift they care to bestow; at least this was not my aim as an end, but rather as a means, of purchasing some moderate provision for my family, which tho' it should exceed my merit, must fall infinitely short of my service, if I succeeded in my attempt.

TO say the truth, the public never act more wisely, than when they act most liberally in the distribution of their rewards; and here the good they receive is often more to be considered than the motive from which they receive it. Example alone is the end of all public punishments and rewards. Laws never inflict disgrace in resentment, nor confer honour from gratitude. For it is very hard, my lord, said a convicted felon at the bar to the late excellent judge Burner,[54] to hang a poor man for stealing a horse. You are not to be hanged, Sir, answered my ever-honoured and beloved friend, for stealing a horse, but you are to be hanged that horses may not be stolen. In like manner it might have been said to the late duke of Marlborough, when the parliament was so deservedly liberal to him, after the battle of Blenheim,[55] You receive not these honours and bounties on account of a victory past, but that other victories may be obtained.

---

[52] In concluding his *Proposal for Making an Effectual Provision for the Poor*, published in January 1753, HF declared a similar motive for writing it: 'Ambition or Avarice can no longer raise a Hope, or dictate any Scheme to me, who have no farther Design than to pass my short Remainder of life in some Degree of Ease, and barely to preserve my Family from being the objects of any such Laws as I have here proposed' (*Enquiry*, p. 277).

[53] Cf. above, p. 558 and n. 45.

[54] Sir Thomas Burnet (1694–1753), son of Gilbert, Bishop of Salisbury (above, p. 547 n. 10), whose posthumous *History of His Own Time* (1724–34) he edited; he was appointed King's Sergeant at Law in 1741 and was knighted in 1745. HF may well have been present in court when Burnet sentenced the horse thief to hang: in the summer of 1741 Burnet was one of two judges presiding at the assizes on the Western Circuit, which HF attended and where, at Bath, he and Burnet became dinner companions (*Life*, pp. 309–10, 311–2; *Correspondence*, Letter 10 and n. 7).

[55] John Churchill (1650–1722), first Duke of Marlborough, victorious commander of the British forces against France (1702–11). HF's compliment here to the great hero of the Whigs is the last of many that recur in his writings beginning with *The Universal Gallant* (1735). HF's father had served gallantly as a captain in the Duke's army at Blenheim (1704). As a reward for this great victory, Marlborough was

I WAS now, in the opinion of all men, dying of a complication of disorders; and, were I desirous of playing the advocate, I have an occasion fair enough: but I disdain such an attempt. I relate facts plainly and simply as they are; and let the world draw from them what conclusions they please, taking with them the following facts for their instruction. The one is, That the proclamation offering 100l. for the apprehending felons for certain felonies committed in certain places, which I prevented from being revived, had formerly cost the government several thousand pounds within a single year.[56] Secondly, that all such proclamations, instead of curing the evil, had actually encreased it; had multiplied the number of robberies; had propagated the worst and wickedest of perjuries; had laid snares for youth and ignorance; which, by the temptation of these rewards, had been sometimes drawn into guilt; and sometimes, which cannot be thought on without the highest horror, had destroyed them without it. Thirdly, That my plan had not put the government to more than 300l. expence, and had produced none of the ill consequences above-mentioned; but, lastly, Had actually suppressed the evil for a time, and had plainly pointed out the means of suppressing it for ever. This I would myself have undertaken, had my health permitted, at the annual expence of the abovementioned sum.

AFTER having stood the terrible six weeks which succeeded last Christmas, and put a lucky end, if they had known their own interests, to such numbers of aged and infirm valetudinarians, who might have gasped through two or three mild winters more, I returned to town in February, in a condition less despaired of by my self than by any of my friends. I now became the patient of Dr. Ward, who wished I had taken his advice earlier.[57]

---

awarded a dukedom, a palace, and other favours which Swift, a Tory, in his famous attack in *The Examiner* (23 November 1710), itemized at length, comparing the reward of a victorious Roman general (a formal triumph amounting to £1,000) to the prodigious bounty heaped on Marlborough (in all amounting, conservatively, to £540,000).

[56] HF underestimated the cost. In 1749 the statutory bounty of £40 for apprehending and prosecuting a robber to conviction was increased by £100 by royal proclamation, resulting in an annually burgeoning cost to the Treasury from £200 in 1748, the year HF began his magistracy to £6,500 in the period from 1751 to June 1752, when, acting on his advice, the Privy Council discontinued these supplements (*Life*, pp. 502, 577–8). On the abuse of the reward programme by corrupt thief-takers such as Stephen McDaniel and HF's role in ending the proclamations, see John Fielding, *A Plan for Preventing Robberies* (1755).

[57] Joshua 'Spot' Ward (1685–1761), a fashionable and kindly empiric, who claimed that his 'Pill and Drop' were universal nostrums (they were in fact virulent preparations of antimony and arsenic). He was a popular target for the satirists, such as Hogarth in plate V of the *Harlot's Progress* (1732) and Pope in the *Imitations of Horace*, II. i. 182 (1737), I. vi. 56 (1738); and in this facetious spirit HF's references to Ward and his cure begin in *The Craftsman*, No. 431 (5 October 1734; *New Essays*, p. 61) and recur in *Common Sense* (21 May 1737; *Champion*, p. 6), *The Champion* (28 February 1739/40, 26 August 1740), pp. 209, 437*, *A Journey from This World to the Next* (*Miscellanies* ii, p. 19), and *Tom Jones* (VIII. ix, p. 442). As the present passage makes clear, however, towards the end of his life HF turned to Ward as his illness worsened; in *Amelia* (VIII. ix, p. 346) he links together as remedies renowned for their efficacy both Ward's 'Pill' and the 'Powder' of his friend Dr Robert James (below, p. 604 and n. 183).

By his advice I was tapped, and fourteen quarts of water drawn from my belly. The sudden relaxation which this caused, added to my enervate, emaciated habit of body, so weakened me, that within two days I was thought to be falling into the agonies of death.

I was at the worst on that memorable day when the public lost Mr. Pelham.[58] From that day I began slowly, as it were, to draw my feet out of the grave; till in two months time I had again acquired some little degree of strength; but was again full of water.

During this whole time, I took Mr. Ward's medicines, which had seldom any perceptible operation. Those in particular of the diaphoretic kind,[59] the working of which is thought to require a great strength of constitution to support, had so little effect on me, that Mr. Ward declared it was as vain to attempt sweating me as a deal board.

In this situation I was tapped a second time. I had one quart of water less taken from me now than before; but I bore all the consequences of the operation much better. This I attributed greatly to a dose of laudanum prescribed by my surgeon. It first gave me the most delicious flow of spirits, and afterwards as comfortable a nap.

The month of May, which was now begun, it seemed reasonable to expect would introduce the spring, and drive off that winter which yet maintained its footing on the stage. I resolved therefore to visit a little house of mine in the country,[60] which stands at Ealing, in the county of Middlesex, in the best air, I believe, in the whole kingdom, and far superior to that of Kensington Gravel-Pits;[61] for the gravel is here much wider and deeper, the

---

[58] Henry Pelham (1695?–1754), Prime Minister, died on 6 March 1754; he was succeeded in office by his brother the Duke of Newcastle (above, p. 555 n. 39). HF's high regard for Pelham appears to date from the election campaign of 1747, when he emerged as the government's principal propagandist in *A Dialogue between a Gentleman of London, Agent for two Court Candidates, and an Honest Alderman of the Country Party*. He continued in that role in *A Proper Answer to a Late Scurrilous Libel* and in the *Jacobite's Journal*, where he lauds Pelham as not only 'one of the greatest Men now alive' (No. 31 [2 July 1748], p. 325), but also 'one of the best and worthiest Men in this Nation' (No. 43 [24 September 1748], p. 398). It is clear from a passage in *Tom Jones* (XI. ix, p. 612 and n. 1) that HF had enjoyed Pelham's hospitality at Esher Place, the Prime Minister's estate in Surrey. And it was to Pelham, who encouraged him to write the work, that HF dedicated *A Proposal to Make an Effectual Provision for the Poor* (1753).

[59] 'diaphoretic': having the property of inducing or promoting perspiration (*OED*).

[60] Some time in the latter half of 1752 HF began leasing a 44-acre farm at Fordhook, Ealing, about 6 miles west of town. It would be his final abode in England. Few would call the house 'little'; in the next century Lady Byron, the poet's wife, saw fit to reside there (*Life*, pp. 572, 584, 682 n. 338; below, Appendix C. 2).

[61] It was the salubrious air at the gravel pits that prompted William III to situate his palace, and Queen Mary her gardens, at Kensington soon after his accession in 1689. Samuel Garth in *The Dispensary* (1699) refers to the popularity of the place with the consumptive: 'The Sick to th'*Hundreds* in pale Throngs repair | And change the *Gravel-Pits* for *Kentish* Air' (iii. 235–6). HF's first wife, Charlotte, may have been among those who sought relief from the disease there in the winter of 1742–3 (*Life*, pp. 368–9).

place higher and more open towards the south, whilst it is guarded from the north wind by a ridge of hills, and from the smells and smoke of London by its distance; which last is not the fate of Kensington, when the wind blows from any corner of the east.

OBLIGATIONS to Mr. Ward I shall always confess; for I am convinced that he omitted no care in endeavouring to serve me, without any expectation or desire of fee or reward.

THE powers of Mr. Ward's remedies want indeed no unfair puffs of mine to give them credit; and tho' this distemper of the dropsy stands, I believe, first in the list of those over which he is always certain of triumphing; yet, possibly, there might be something particular in my case, capable of eluding that radical force which had healed so many thousands. The same distemper, in different constitutions, may possibly be attended with such different symptoms, that to find an infallible nostrum for the curing any one distemper in every patient, may be almost as difficult as to find a panacea for the cure of all.

BUT even such a panacea one of the greatest scholars and best of men did lately apprehend he had discovered. It is true, indeed, he was no physician; that is, he had not by the forms of his education acquired a right of applying his skill in the art of physic to his own private advantage; and yet, perhaps, it may be truly asserted, that no other modern hath contributed so much to make his physical skill useful to the public; at least, that none hath undergone the pains of communicating this discovery in writing to the world. The reader, I think, will scarce need to be informed that the writer I mean is the late bishop of Cloyne in Ireland, and the discovery, that of the virtues of tar-water.[62]

I THEN happened to recollect, upon a hint given me by the inimitable and shamefully distress'd author of the Female Quixote,[63] that I had many years before, from curiosity only, taken a cursory view of bishop Berkley's treatise on the virtues of tar-water, which I had formerly observed he

---

[62] The Revd Dr George Berkeley (1685–1753) recommended tar-water, an infusion of pine pitch used by the Narragansett Indians, in *Siris: A Chain of Philosophical Reflexions and Inquiries Concerning the Virtues of Tar-Water* (1744), a copy of which was in HF's library, bound in with Thomas Prior's *Authentic Narrative of the Success of Tar-water, in curing a great number and variety of Distempers* (Ribbles B19). A month before HF died in Lisbon, the *Public Advertiser* (9 September 1754) printed a letter of Berkeley's reporting the 'most remarkable Case' of a soldier who was cured of the dropsy by drinking 2 quarts of tar-water every day.

[63] Charlotte Lennox, *née* Ramsay (*c.*1729/30–1804). HF enthusiastically reviewed her novel *The Female Quixote* in *The Covent-Garden Journal*, No. 24 (24 March 1752), calling it 'a most extraordinary and most excellent Performance. . . . a Work of true Humour', and on some points preferring it to Cervantes' original (pp. 160–1). A copy of the work—and one of her first novel, *The Life of Harriot Stuart* (1751 [for 1750])—were in his library (Ribbles L11–12).

strongly contends to be that real panacea which Sydenham[64] supposes to
have an existence in nature, tho' it yet remains undiscovered, and, perhaps,
will always remain so.

UPON the re-perusal of this book I found the bishop only asserting his
opinion, that tar-water might be useful in the dropsy, since he had known it
to have a surprizing success in the cure of a most stubborn anasarca,[65] which
is indeed no other than, as the word implied, the dropsy of the flesh; and
this was, at that time, a large part of my complaint.

AFTER a short trial, therefore, of a milk diet, which I presently found
did not suit with my case, I betook myself to the bishop's prescription, and
dosed myself every morning and evening with half a pint of tar-water.[66]

IT was no more than three weeks since my last tapping, and my belly and
limbs were distended with water. This did not give me the worse opinion of
tar-water: for I never supposed there could be any such virtue in tar-water,
as immediately to carry off a quantity of water already collected. For my
delivery from this, I well knew I must be again obliged to the trochar;[67] and
that if the tar-water did me any good at all, it must be only by the slowest
degrees; and that if it should ever get the better of my distemper, it must be
by the tedious operation of undermining; and not by a sudden attack and
storm.

SOME visible effects, however, and far beyond what my most sanguine
hopes could with any modesty expect, I very soon experienced; the

[64] Thomas Sydenham (1624–89), 'the English Hippocrates', whose best-known work was *A Treatise of the Gout and Dropsy*, originally published in Latin in 1683 and translated by Dr John Pechey in Sydenham's *Whole Works* (1696), from which, in the ninth edition (1729), HF quotes in *The Champion* (3 May 1740, pp. 300–1) and *Tom Jones* (XIII. ii, p. 688). HF, who suffered from the gout and dropsy, admired 'the great *Sydenham*', as he calls him in *The True Patriot*, No. 1 (5 November 1745), where he is to 'Physic' as Shakespeare is to poetry, Handel to music, and Coke to law (pp. 104–5). HF may have in mind an ironic comment in Sydenham's dedication: 'whilst I was wholly absorbed in the grand operation of forging a Delphic sword in the shape of some *Methodus medendi* which should meet all cases [i.e. a panacea] . . . I made the following discovery, *viz.*, that I had opened my eyes only to get them filled with dust—no Olympic dust either' (*Works*, 2 vols., trans. R. G. Latham [1848–50], i, p. 4). Berkeley explains: 'by a panacea is not meant a medicine which cures all individuals (this consists not with mortality), but a medicine that cures or relieves all different species of distempers' (*Philosophical Writings*, ed. T. E. Jessop (1948–57), v, p. 175); specifically, 'In the modern practice, soap, opium and mercury bid fairest for Universal Medicines' (ibid., v, p. 54).
[65] 'anasarca': a dropsical affection of the subcutaneous cellular tissue of a limb or other large surface of the body, producing a very puffed appearance of the flesh (*OED*). Berkeley refers to 'a very bad anasarca in a person whose thirst, though very extraordinary, was in a short time removed by the drinking of tar-water' (*Works*, v. 33).
[66] An advertisement for tar-water in the *General Advertiser* (7 January 1748/9)—price '2s. 6d. the half-pint; 1s. 3d. the quartern'—gave Berkeley's directions as to dosage: 'Two large Tea-Spoonfuls in near a Gill [1/4 pint] of Water, may be taken Nights and Mornings, and an Hour before Dinner [the midday meal]'. Adjustments might be prescribed according 'to the several Degrees of Strength as the Stomach or Constitution requires'.
[67] 'trochar': 'A Cane, or Pipe made of Silver, or Steel, with a sharp-pointed End, us'd in tapping those who are troubled with the Dropsy' (*OED*, s.v. 'trocar' [1706]).

tar-water having, from the very first, lessened my illness, increased my appetite; and added, though in a very slow proportion, to my bodily strength.

BUT if my strength had encreased a little, my water daily encreased much more. So that, by the end of May, my belly became ripe for the trochar, and I was a third time tapped; upon which two very favourable symptoms appeared. I had three quarts of water taken from me less than had been taken the last time; and I bore the relaxation with much less (indeed with scarce any) faintness.

THOSE of my physical friends, on whose judgment I chiefly depended, seemed to think my only chance of life consisted in having the whole summer before me; in which I might hope to gather sufficient strength to encounter the inclemencies of the ensuing winter. But this chance began daily to lessen. I saw the summer mouldering away, or rather, indeed, the year passing away without intending to bring on any summer at all. In the whole month of May the sun scarce appeared three times. So that the early fruits came to the fulness of their growth, and to some appearance of ripeness, without acquiring any real maturity; having wanted the heat of the sun to soften and meliorate their juices. I saw the dropsy gaining rather than losing ground; the distance growing still shorter between the tappings. I saw the asthma likewise beginning again to become more troublesome. I saw the Midsummer quarter drawing towards a close. So that I conceived, if the Michaelmas quarter[68] should steal off in the same manner, as it was, in my opinion, very much to be apprehended it would, I should be delivered up to the attacks of winter, before I recruited my forces, so as to be any wise able to withstand them.

I NOW began to recall an intention, which from the first dawnings of my recovery I had conceiv'd, of removing to a warmer climate; and finding this to be approv'd of by a very eminent physician,[69] I resolved to put it into immediate execution.

AIX in Provence was the place first thought on; but the difficulties of getting thither were insuperable. The journey by land, beside the expence of it, was infinitely too long and fatiguing;[70] and I could hear of no ship

[68] In England the quarter-days dividing the year into four roughly equal parts are Lady Day (25 March), Midsummer Day (24 June), Michaelmas (29 September), and Christmas (25 December).

[69] Possibly Dr William Heberden (1710–1801), an eminent physician who later attended Samuel Johnson at the end of his life. In a letter to Philip Yorke of 20 October 1753, Thomas Birch reported that HF 'has been for some time in a very ill state of Health, which alarm'd his Friends, & induc'd him to call in Dr. Heberden, who has remov'd his Jaundice, but not yet restor'd his appetite' (*Life*, p. 580).

[70] The Aix waters were considered helpful in three of HF's ailments, gout, dropsy, and asthma. But the 'journey by land' from Paris in summer, as late as 1788, took five days by diligence, and the difficulties might well be called 'insuperable'. The cost of a place was 174 livres 16 sols = £7 5s., taking the livre at 10d., and the sol at ½d. (Dobson).

that was likely to set out from London, within any reasonable time for Marseilles, or any other port in that part of the Mediterranean.

LISBON was presently fixed on in its room. The air here, as it was near four degrees to the south of Aix, must be more mild and warm, and the winter shorter and less piercing.

IT was not difficult to find a ship bound to a place with which we carry on so immense a trade.[71] Accordingly, my brother soon informed me[72] of the excellent accommodations for passengers, which were to be found on board a ship that was obliged to sail for Lisbon in three days.

I EAGERLY embraced the offer, notwithstanding the shortness of the time; and having given my brother full power to contract for our passage, I began to prepare my family for the voyage with the utmost expedition.

BUT our great haste was needless; for the captain[73] having twice put off his sailing, I at length invited him to dinner with me at Fordhook, a full week after the time on which he had declared, and that with many asseverations, he must, and would, weigh anchor.

HE dined with me, according to his appointment; and when all matters were settled between us, left me with positive orders to be on board the Wednesday following; when he declared he would fall down the river to Gravesend; and would not stay a moment for the greatest man in the world.

HE advised me to go to Gravesend by land, and there wait the arrival of his ship; assigning many reasons for this, every one of which was, as I well remember, among those that had before determined me to go on board near the Tower.

---

[71] The Methuen Treaty of 1703 had given preferential treatment to British woollens and Portuguese wines and resulted in an immense imbalance of trade in England's favour (H. E. S. Fisher, *The Portuguese Trade* [London, 1971], p. 16).

[72] His brother John may have informed HF of the opportunity to sail on the *Queen of Portugal*, but it was their 'Neighbour', probably Peter Taylor (below, p. 638 n. 280), whom he thanks in his letter to John of 12 July (below, Appendix C.3, Letter 1) 'for recommending me to the Care of' Captain Richard Veale (below, n. 73).

[73] Richard Veale (1686–1756), from 1749 to 1755 Captain of the *Queen of Portugal* plying between London, Lisbon, and Madeira. He was a mariner, HF remarks (below, pp. 643–4), with forty-six years' experience at sea, not only sailing commercial vessels, but commanding privateers during the war with Spain and France, 1739–48. In the *Journal*, HF for the most part depicts him as blustering and imperious; in his letter of 12 July from Ryde he recognizes his masterly seamanship, calling him 'a most able and experienced Seaman to whom other Captains seem to pay such Deference that they attend and watch his Motions, and think themselves only safe when they act under his Direction and Example' (below, Appendix C.3, Letter 1). For an account of Veale's life and career, see Keymer, *Fielding's Journal*, app. II.

THE JOURNAL OF A VOYAGE TO LISBON.

Wednesday, June 26, 1754.

ON this day, the most melancholy sun I had ever beheld arose, and found me awake at my house at Fordhook. By the light of this sun, I was, in my own opinion, last to behold and take leave of some of those creatures on whom I doated with a mother-like fondness, guided by nature and passion, and uncured and unhardened by all the doctrine of that philosophical school where I had learnt to bear pains and to despise death.[74]

IN this situation, as I could not conquer nature, I submitted entirely to her, and she made as great a fool of me as she had ever done of any woman whatsoever:[75] under pretence of giving me leave to enjoy, she drew me in to suffer the company of my little ones,[76] during eight hours; and I doubt not whether, in that time, I did not undergo more than in all my distemper.

AT twelve precisely my coach was at the door, which was no sooner than told me than I kiss'd my children round, and went into it with some little resolution. My wife,[77] who behaved more like a heroine and philosopher, tho' at the same time the tenderest mother in the world, and my eldest daughter,[78] followed me; some friends went with us,[79] and others here took their leave; and I heard my behaviour applauded, with many murmurs and praises to which I well knew I had no title; as all other such philosophers may, if they have any modesty, confess on the like occasions.

---

[74] Earlier, on the occasion of the death of his daughter Charlotte (9 March 1742), HF had turned to the consolations of the Stoic philosophy and the Christian religion in his essay 'Of the Remedy of Affliction for the Loss of our Friends' (*Miscellanies* i); and when Charlotte, his wife, died (November 1744), he thanked James Harris in metaphor, for teaching him that same 'Philosophy' which had seen him arrive 'at the Head of this my School of Distress' (*Correspondence*, Letter 23, p. 47).

[75] Cf. HF's account, in his letter to Richardson, of being so moved when reading the plight of Clarissa that he wept: 'I then melt with Compassion, and find what is called an Effeminate Relief' (*Correspondence*, Letter 41, p. 70).

[76] When he left for Lisbon, HF left behind at Fordhook his three youngest children: Allen (1754–1823), 2 months old; Sophia (1750–*c.*1755), aged 4; and William (1748–1820), aged 6—committing them to the care of his mother-in-law, Elizabeth Daniel.

[77] Mary Daniel (1721–1802), his second wife, whom he married in November 1747.

[78] Henrietta Eleanor (1743–66), called Harriet, his only surviving child by Charlotte.

[79] Accompanying the Fieldings to Lisbon were William Aldrit (d. 1800), HF's manservant and, it appears, also his amenuensis (Keymer, *Fielding's Journal*); Isabella Ash (or Belle), maidservant, who had witnessed HF's will a week or two earlier; and Margaret Collier (1717–94), another witness to the will, who was a close family friend and acted as governess to Harriet. Accompanying the travellers as far as Gravesend were Margaret's sister the author Jane Collier (1715–55), a close friend of both HF and his sister Sarah; and Saunders Welch (below, p. 568 n. 84). Among those who bid HF farewell at Fordhook may well have been James Harris (1709–80) of Salisbury, perhaps HF's closest friend, whom he called 'the Man whom I esteem most of any psn in this World' (*Correspondence*, Letter 23, p. 42); on Harris's attendance at Fordhook on this occasion, see *Life*, pp. 585–6; below, Appendix C.4, p. 777.

IN two hours we arrive in Redriffe,[80] and immediately went on board, and were to have sailed the next morning; but as this was the king's proclamation-day,[81] and consequently a holiday at the Custom-house, the captain could not clear his vessel till the Thursday; for these holidays are as strictly observed as those in the popish calendar, and are almost as numerous. I might add, that both are opposite to the genius of trade, and consequently *contra bonum publicum*.[82]

To go on board the ship it was necessary first to go into a boat; a matter of no small difficulty, as I had no use of my limbs, and was to be carried by men, who tho' sufficiently strong for their burden, were, like Archimedes, puzzled to find a steady footing.[83] Of this, as few of my readers have not gone into wherries on the Thames, they will easily be able to form to themselves an idea. However, by the assistance of my friend Mr. Welch,[84] whom I never think or speak of but with love and esteem, I conquered this difficulty, as I did afterwards that of ascending the ship, into which I was hoisted with more ease by a chair lifted with pullies. I was soon seated in a great chair in the cabin, to refresh myself after a fatigue which had been more intolerable, in a quarter of a mile's passage from my coch to the ship, than I had before undergone in a land-journey of twelve miles, which I had travelled with the utmost expedition.

THIS latter fatigue was, perhaps, somewhat heightened by an indignation which I could not prevent arising in my mind. I think, upon my entrance into the boat, I presented a spectacle of the highest horror. The total loss of limbs was apparent to all who saw me, and my face contained marks of a most diseased state, if not of death itself. Indeed so ghastly was my countenance, that timorous women with child had abstained from my house, for fear of the ill consequences of looking at me.[85] In this condition,

[80] 'Redriffe': the colloquial, phonetic version of Rotherhithe (Surrey).

[81] George II acceded to the throne on 11 June and was proclaimed King of Great Britain on 15 June 1727 (OS), whose anniversary in 1754 fell on 26 June (NS).

[82] 'Contrary to the public good'.

[83] 'Give me a place to stand and I will move the earth', a saying attributed to Archimedes (c.287-212 BC). Cf. *Champion* (8 May 1740), p. 309 and n. 4.

[84] Saunders Welch (1711-84), High Constable for the Holborn Division and head of HF's new-model police force, the 'Bow-Street Runners', was HF's 'good Friend' (*Enquiry*, p. 108), as he later also became for Samuel Johnson. For Welch's part in quelling the riots of July 1749 HF, in his pamphlet on Bosavern Penlez, praised Welch as 'one of the best Officers who was ever concerned in the Execution of Justice, and to whose Care, Integrity and Bravery the Public hath . . . the highest Obligations (*Enquiry*, p. 57). In December 1753, thinking of the void his retirement as justice would cause, HF recommended Welch for appointment to the magistracy of Westminster and Middlesex; the fiat enacting the commissions was delayed, however, until March 1755. HF would remember Welch on his journey, sending him presents of cider from Devon and of onions from Lisbon (below, Appendix C.3, Letters 2-3); after HF's death, Welch would act as his widow's friend and protector.

[85] HF was so conscious of the horrid appearance of his countenance that, while at Ryde, Isle of Wight, he was said to have covered the looking glass in his room with a napkin (below, Appendix C.3, Letter 9).

I ran the gauntlope,[86] (so, I think I may justly call it) through rows of sailors and watermen, few of whom failed of paying their compliments to me, by all manner of insults and jests on my misery.[87] No man who knew me will think I conceived any personal resentment at this behaviour; but it was a lively picture of that cruelty and inhumanity, in the nature of men, which I have often contemplated with concern; and which leads the mind into a train of very uncomfortable and melancholy thoughts. It may be said, that this barbarous custom is peculiar to the English, and of them only to the lowest degree; that it is an excrescence of an uncontroul'd licentiousness mistaken for liberty,[88] and never shews itself in men who are polish'd and refin'd, in such manner as human nature requires, to produce that perfection of which it is susceptible, and to purge away that malevolence of disposition, of which, at our birth we partake in common with the savage creation.

THIS may be said, and this is all that can be said; and it is, I am afraid, but little satisfactory to account for the inhumanity of those, who, while they boast of being made after God's own image, seem to bear in their minds a resemblance of the vilest species of brutes; or rather, indeed, of our idea of devils: for I don't know that any brutes can be taxed with such malevolence.

[86] 'gauntlope': a form of the word *gantlope*. A military (occasionally also naval) punishment in which the culprit had to run between two rows of men who struck at him with a stick or knotted cord (*OED*, s.v., citing *Tom Jones* [VII. xi]: 'he deserved to run the Gauntlope' [p. 369]).

[87] On the behaviour of the seamen at Rotherhithe, cf. *The London and Westminster Guide* (1768): 'The seamen here are a generation differing from all the world. When one goes into Rotherhithe and Wapping, which places are chiefly inhabited by sailors, but that somewhat of the same language is spoken, a man would be apt to suspect himself to be in another country. Their manner of living, speaking, acting, dressing, and behaving, are so peculiar to themselves' (p. xv).

[88] Though ever an advocate of the vaunted right of Englishmen to liberty under the law, HF, especially during the period of his magistracy, repeatedly stressed the crucial distinction between liberty and licentiousness. When recommending enforcement of the vagrancy laws in *A Proposal for Making an Effectual Provision for the Poor* (1753), he encapsulated his view on the subject: 'I should scarce apprehend . . . that some Persons should represent the Restraint here laid on the lower People as derogatory from their Liberty. Such Notions are indeed of the enthusiastical Kind, and are inconsistent with all Order and all Government. They are the natural Parents of that Licentiousness which it is one main Intent of this whole Plan to cure; which is necessarily productive of most of the Evils of which the Public complains; of that Licentiousness, in a Word, which among the many Mischiefs introduced by it into every Society where it prevails, is sure at last to end in the Destruction of Liberty itself' (*Enquiry*, p. 267). Specifically relevant to the present context is a passage on the social necessity of 'Rules of good Breeding' from *The Covent-Garden Journal*, No. 55 (18 July 1752): HF declines to 'extend the Meaning of the Word Liberty, farther than I think it hath yet been carried, and will include in it not only an Exemption from all Restraint of municipal Laws, but likewise from all Restraint of those Rules of Behaviour which are expressed in the general Term of good Breeding. Laws which, tho' not written, are perhaps better understood, and tho' established by no coercive Power, much better obeyed within the Circle where they are received, than any of those Laws which are recorded in Books, or enforced by public Authority' (pp. 297–8). HF returns to the subject again in the entry for 16 July below (pp. 610–14). On the concept of liberty in his writings, see esp. Miller, *Essays*, pp. 94–103, and *CGJ*, pp. xl–xli.

A SURLOIN of beef was now placed on the table, for which, tho' little better than carrion, as much was charged by the master of the little paltry alehouse who dressed it, as would have been demanded for all the elegance of the King's Arms,[89] or any other polite tavern, or eating-house; for indeed the difference between the best house and the worst is, that at the former you pay largely for luxury, at the latter for nothing.

Thursday, June 27. THIS morning the captain, who lay on shore at his own house,[90] paid us a visit in the cabin; and behaved like an angry bashaw,[91] declaring, that had he known we were not to be pleased, he would not have carried us for 500 l. He added many asseverations that he was a gentleman, and despised money; not forgetting several hints of the presents which had been made him for his cabin, of 20, 30, and 40 guineas, by several gentlemen, over and above the sum for which they had contracted. This behaviour greatly surprised me, as I knew not how to account for it, nothing having happened since we parted from the captain the evening before in perfect good humour; and all this broke forth on the first moment of his arrival this morning. He did not, however, suffer my amazement to have any long continuance, before he clearly shewed me that all this was meant only as an apology to introduce another procrastination (being the fifth) of his weighing anchor; which was now postponed till Saturday, for such was his will and pleasure.

BESIDES the disagreeable situation in which we then lay, in the confines of Wapping and Redriffe, tasting a delicious mixture of the air of both these sweet places, and enjoying the concord of sweet sounds of seamen, watermen, fish-women, oyster-women, and of all the vociferous inhabitants of both shores, composing altogether a greater variety of harmony that Hogarth's imagination hath brought together in that print of his, which is enough to make a man deaf to look at;[92] I had a more urgent cause to press

---

[89] Probably the polite eating-place situated on the north side of Pall Mall, near the Haymarket, mentioned by HF in *The Jacobite's Journal*, No. 14 (5 March 1748), p. 186 and n. 3; it is also frequented by the characters in *Amelia* (esp. IV. v, p. 173 and n. 1).

[90] In Gainsford Street, parish of St John, Southwark (Keymer, *Fielding's Journal*, s.v. '*Thursday, June 27*', p. 123 n. 1).

[91] 'bashaw': earlier form of *pasha*, the Turkish title borne by officers of high rank, as military commanders, and governors of provinces; figuratively: a haughty, imperious man (*OED*).

[92] A reference to *The Enraged Musician* (1740) by William Hogarth (1697–1764), plate 88 in Jenny Uglow's biography, who well calls it 'his most sonorous print . . . Everything that can make noise seems to be here, while the desperate musician looks out his window'—his hands covering his ears, we might add— 'helpless against the barrage of the street's wild music' (*Hogarth: A Life and a World* [New York, 1997], p. 300). Hogarth, who provided the only authorized portrait of HF as the frontispiece for his *Works* (1762), was among his closest friends. From *The Champion* (10 June 1740), where, referring to Hogarth's *Rake's* and *Harlot's Progress*, HF calls him 'one of the most useful Satyrists any Age hath produced' (pp. 365–6), and the *Vernoniad* (1741), where he calls him 'my Friend *Hogarth*, the exactest Copier of Nature' (ibid., p. 563 n. [20]), compliments to him abound in HF's writings; indeed, in *Tom Jones* three

our departure, which was, that the dropsy, for which I had undergone three tappings, seemed to threaten me with a fourth discharge, before I should reach Lisbon, and when I should have no body on board capable of performing the operation; but I was obliged to hearken to the voice of reason, if I may use the captain's own words, and to rest myself contented. Indeed there was no alternative within my reach, but what would have cost me much too dear.

THERE are many evils in society, from which people of the highest rank are so entirely exempt, that they have not the least knowledge or idea of them; nor indeed of the characters which are formed by them. Such, for instance, is the conveyance of goods and passengers from one place to another. Now there is no such thing as any kind of knowledge contemptible in itself; and as the particular knowledge I here mean is entirely necessary to the well understanding and well enjoying this journal; and, lastly, as in this case the most ignorant will be those very readers whose amusement we chiefly consult, and to whom we wish to be supposed principally to write, we will here enter somewhat largely into the discussion of this matter; the rather, for that no antient or modern author (if we can trust the catalogue of Dr. Mead's library[93]) hath ever undertaken it; but that it seems (in the stile of Don Quixotte) a task reserved for my pen alone.[94]

WHEN I first conceived this intention, I began to entertain thoughts of enquiring into the antiquity of travelling; and, as many persons have performed in this way (I mean have travelled) at the expence of the public, I flattered myself that the spirit of improving arts and sciences, and of advancing useful and substantial learning, which so eminently distinguishes this age, and hath given rise to more speculative societies in Europe than I at present recollect the names of; perhaps indeed than I or any other besides their very near neighbours ever heard mentioned, would assist in promoting so curious a work. A work! begun with the same views,

characters, in their physical appearance—Bridget Allworthy (I. xi), Mrs Partridge (II. iii), and Thwackum (III. vi)—are specifically modelled on figures in Hogarth's prints (pp. 66, 82, 138). For a complete list of HF's allusions to Hogarth, see Ribbles H25, p. 167. For a succinct account of their personal and artistic relationship, and a bibliography, see *Companion*, p. 82.

[93] *Bibliotheca Meadiana*, published 10 July 1754 (*Public Advertiser*; which notes that 'Catalogues may be had at all the Chief Cities in Europe'). That HF might have received a copy of the catalogue in Lisbon is not unlikely, as he—and probably his brother, with whom he was corresponding—owned shares in the *Public Advertiser*, which served as a vehicle for notices relating to their magistracy (*CGJ*, p. lii). On Mead, see above, p. 546 and n. 9.

[94] At the close of the final chapter of *Don Quixote*, Cervantes' alter ego, Cid Hamet Benengeli, hangs up his pen with a warning to others who might presume to take it down, that 'this undertaking ... was reserved for me alone' (trans. Jarvis; though HF had certainly read *Don Quixote* earlier, the only copy of the work listed in the catalogue of his library is the second edition of Charles Jarvis's translation [1749]: Ribbles C18).

calculated for the same purposes, and fitted for the same uses with the labours which those right honourable societies have so cheerfully undertaken themselves, and encouraged in others; sometimes with the highest honours, even with admission into their colleges, and with inrolment among their members.

FROM these societies I promised myself all assistance in their power, particularly the communication of such valuable manuscripts and records as they must be supposed to have collected from those obscure ages of antiquity, when history yields us such imperfect accounts of the residence, and much more imperfect, of the travels of the human race; unless, perhaps, as a curious and learned member of the young society of antiquarians[95] is said to have hinted his conjectures, that their residence and their travels were one and the same; and this discovery (for such it seems to be) he is said to have owed to the lighting by accident on a book, which we shall have occasion to mention presently, the contents of which were then little known to the society.

THE King of Prussia, moreover, who from a degree of benevolence and taste, which in either case is a rare production in so northern a climate, is the great encourager of art and science,[96] I was well assured would promote so useful a design, and order his archives to be searched in my behalf.

BUT after well weighing all these advantages, and much meditation on the order of my work, my whole design was subverted in a moment by hearing of the discovery just mentioned to have been made by the young antiquarian, who from the most antient record in the world (tho' I don't find the society are all agreed in this point) one long preceding the date of the earliest modern collections, either of books or butterflies,[97] none of which pretend to go beyond the flood, shews us, that the first man was a

---

[95] The 'elder' Society of Antiquaries was founded in the reign of Elizabeth and expired in that of James I; a second Society, formally constituted in 1717, received a royal charter by George II on 2 November 1751 (Martin Folkes presiding) and in 1753 acquired the lease of a house in Chancery Lane (Joan Evans, *History of the Society of Antiquaries* [Oxford, 1956], pp. 10, 14, 50, 105, 112).

The identity of the 'curious and learned member' of the Society has eluded editors of the *Journal*—or perhaps they have considered the passage merely mischievous on HF's part and not deserving a note. It would be like him, however, to have had someone specific in mind. Though not named, the 'book' the unnamed antiquarian is said to have lighted on accidentally, the contents of which were 'little known to the society', will 'presently' (in the paragraph after the next) prove to be the book of Genesis, in which we learn that Adam and his family, expelled from Paradise, became the first travellers.

[96] Dobson (Notes, p. 161, re p. 32 line 14) made the likely suggestion that HF was here alluding to Hogarth's dedication of *The March to Finchley* (print 1750) to Frederick II (1712–86), King of Prussia, which reads: '*To His MAJESTY the KING of PRUSIA and Encourager of the ARTS and SCIENCES!*'—a gesture, according to a possibly apocryphal story, intended as a rebuke to George II, who, annoyed at the picture's burlesque of his soldiers, refused the honour (Paulson, ii, pp. 87–90).

[97] For HF and for Pope in *The Dunciad* (1743; iv. 421–36) butterfly collecting was a trivial pursuit that typified the folly of the 'virtuosi' (see below, p. 573 n. 98).

traveller, and that he and his family were scarce settled in Paradise before they disliked their own home, and became passengers to another place. Hence it appears, that the humour of travelling is as old as the human race, and that it was their curse from the beginning.

By this discovery my plan became much shortened, and I found it only necessary to treat of the conveyance of goods and passengers from place to place; which not being universally known, seemed proper to be explained, before we examined into its original. There are, indeed, two different ways of tracing all things, used by the historian and the antiquary; these are upwards and downwards. The former shews you how things are, and leaves to others to discover when they began to be so. The latter shews you how things were, and leaves their present existence to be examined by others. Hence the former is more useful, the latter more curious. The former receives the thanks of mankind, the latter of that valuable part, the virtuosi.[98]

In explaining, therefore, this mystery of carrying goods and passengers from one place to another, hitherto so profound a secret to the very best of our readers, we shall pursue the historical method, and endeavour to shew by what means it is at present performed, referring the more curious enquiry either to some other pen, or to some other opportunity.

Now there are two general ways of performing (if God permit) this conveyance; viz. by land and water, both of which have much variety; that by land being performed in different vehicles, such as coaches, caravans, waggons, &c. and that by water in ships, barges, and boats, of various sizes and denominations. But as all these methods of conveyance are formed on the same principles, they agree so well together, that it is fully sufficient to comprehend them all in the general view, without descending to such minute particulars, as would distinguish one method from another.

---

[98] 'virtuosi': this sentence is cited by the *OED* (s.v. 'virtuoso') as illustrating its neutral definition of the word: 'One who has a general interest in arts and sciences, or who pursues special investigations in one or more of these.' But elsewhere, and implicit throughout the present passage, HF's consistent attitude towards the virtuosi and the natural (or rather, in his opinion, unnatural) philosophers of the Royal Society was satiric and scornful, more suited as an illustration of the *OED*'s second definition: 'a student or collector of antiquities, natural curiosities or rarities, etc.; a connoisseur; freq. one who carries on such pursuits in a dilettante or trifling manner'. For this theme in his writings, see Miller, *Essays*, pp. 326–31. HF's objections to the virtuosi are conveniently summed up in *The Covent-Garden Journal*, No. 24 (24 March 1752): 'What but the utmost Impatience of Idleness, could prompt Men to employ great Pains and Trouble, and Expence too, in making large Collections of Butterflies, Pebbles, and such other wonderful Productions; while others from the same Impatience have been no less busy in hunting after Monsters of every Kind, as if they were at Enmity with Nature, and desirous of exposing all her Errors' (p. 157). See also Letter XL of *Familiar Letters* (above, pp. 484–5). HF's parodies of the *Philosophical Transactions* of the Royal Society include *The Champion* (16 August 1740), *Some Papers Proper to be Read before the R[oya]l Society* (*Miscellanies* i); and also, in the present editor's opinion, *An Attempt towards a Natural History of the Hanover Rat* (*Champion*).

COMMON to all of these is one general principle, that as the goods to be conveyed are usually the larger, so they are to be chiefly considered in the conveyance; the owner being indeed little more than an appendage to his trunk, or box, or bale, or at best a small part of his own baggage, very little care is to be taken in stowing or packing them up with convenience to himself: for the conveyance is not of passengers and goods, but of goods and passengers.[99]

SECONDLY, From this conveyance arises a new kind of relation, or rather of subjection in the society; by which the passenger becomes bound in allegiance to his conveyer. This allegiance is indeed only temporary and local, but the most absolute during its continuance, of any known in Great-Britain, and, to say truth, scarce consistent with the liberties of a free people; nor could it be reconciled with them, did it not move downwards, a circumstance universally apprehended to be incompatible to all kinds of slavery. For Aristotle, in his Politicks, hath proved abundantly to my satisfaction, that no men are born to be slaves, except barbarians; and these only to such as are not themselves barbarians:[100] and indeed Mr. Montesquieu hath carried it very little farther, in the case of the Africans;[101] the real truth being, that no man is born to be a slave, unless to him who is able to make him so.

THIRDLY, This subjection is absolute, and consists of a perfect resignation both of body and soul to the disposal of another; after which resignation, during a certain time, his subject retains no more power over his own will, than an Asiatic slave, or an English wife, by the laws of both countries, and by the customs of one of them. If I should mention the instance of a stage-coachman, many of my readers would recognize the truth of what I have here observed; all indeed, that ever have been under

---

[99] Cf. *Tom Jones* (XI. ix): 'in Stage-Coaches, where Passengers are properly considered as so much Luggage, the ingenious Coachman stows half a Dozen with perfect Ease into the Place of four' (p. 609).

[100] Cf. HF in *The Champion* (11 November 1740), citing Aristotle (*Politics*, 1. i. 4): patriotism distinguishes 'not only Man from the Brute-Creation, but the higher Order of Men, who breathe the pure Air of Liberty and Virtue, from the lower Class who drudge below in the dirty Bottoms of Vice and Slavery. This distinguish'd the *Greeks* and *Romans* from the *Barbarians*, and infused that Conceit into the Head of *Aristotle*, that some were born free and others Slaves by Nature' (p. 509). Also *The Jacobite's Journal*, No. 46 (15 October 1748), where HF archly inquires: 'Doth not *Aristotle* most excellently well prove, in the first Book of his *Politicks*, that all Mankind, except the *Grecians*, are by Nature Slaves?' (p. 410); and *Jonathan Wild* (1. viii; *Miscellanies* iii, p. 30 and n. 2).

[101] Charles-Louis de Secondat, Baron de Montesquieu (1689–1755) in *De l'esprit des loix* (1748). In book 15 Montesquieu discusses the laws of civil slavery in relation to climate; in chapter 5 ('On the slavery of Negroes') he rehearses, with consummate irony, the popular justifications for enslaving blacks (p. 250). In chapter 7 ('Another origin of the right of slavery') he rejects Aristotle's argument (*Politics*, 1. i [1254ᵃ17–1255ᵃ2]) 'that there are slaves by nature' (p. 252): *The Spirit of the Laws*, trans. A. M. Cohler, B. C. Miller, H. S. Stone (Cambridge, 1989). For another reference, in a facetious context, to Montesquieu, 'the ingenious Writer of *L'Esprit des Loix*', see *The Covent-Garden Journal*, No. 15 (22 February 1752), pp. 104–5.

the dominion of that tyrant, who, in this free country, is as absolute as a Turkish Bashaw. In two particulars only his power is defective; he cannot press you into his service, and if you enter yourself at one place, on condition of being discharged at a certain time at another, he is obliged to perform his agreement, if God permit: but all the intermediate time you are absolutely under his government; he carries you how he will, when he will, and whither he will, provided it be not much out of the road; you have nothing to eat, or to drink, but what, and when, and where he pleases. Nay, you cannot sleep, unless he pleases you should; for he will order you sometimes out of bed at midnight, and hurry you away at a moment's warning: indeed, if you can sleep in his vehicle, he cannot prevent it; nay, indeed, to give him his due, this he is ordinarily disposed to encourage; for the earlier he forces you to rise in the morning, the more time he will give you in the heat of the day, sometimes even six hours at an alehouse, or at their doors, where he always gives you the same indulgence which he allows himself; and for this he is generally very moderate in his demands. I have known a whole bundle of passengers charged no more than half a crown for being suffered to remain quiet at an alehouse door, for above a whole hour, and that even in the hottest day in summer.

BUT as this kind of tyranny, tho' it hath escaped our political writers, hath been, I think, touched by our dramatic,[102] and is more trite among the generality of readers; and as this and all other kinds of such subjection are alike unknown to my friends, I will quit the passengers by land, and treat of those who travel by water; for whatever is said on this subject is applicable to both alike, and we may bring them together as closely as they are brought in the liturgy, when they are recommended to the prayers of all Christian congregations; and (which I have often thought very remarkable) where they are joined with other miserable wretches, such as, women in labour, people in sickness, infants just born, prisoners and captives.[103]

GOODS and passengers are conveyed by water in divers vehicles, the principal of which being a ship, it shall suffice to mention that alone. Here the tyrant doth not derive his title, as the stage-coachman doth from the vehicle itself, in which he stows his goods and passengers, but he is called the captain; a word of such various use and uncertain signification, that it seems very difficult to fix any positive idea to it: if indeed there be any general meaning which may comprehend all its different uses, that of the

---

[102] Cf. Jolt the coachman in George Farquhar's farce *The Stage-Coach* (1704), who eats and drinks at the expense of the passengers and takes bribes from innkeepers to delay their journey.

[103] Cf. the Litany in the Book of Common Prayer: 'That it may please thee to preserve all that travel by land or by water, all women labouring of child, all sick persons, and young children; and to shew thy pity upon all prisoners and captives. | *We beseech thee to hear us, good Lord.*'

head, or chief, of any body of men, seems to be most capable of this comprehension; for whether they be a company of soldiers, a crew of sailors, or a gang of rogues, he who is at the head of them is always stiled the captain.

THE particular tyrant,[104] whose fortune it was to stow us aboard, laid a farther claim to this appellation than the bare command of a vehicle of conveyance. He had been the captain of a privateer, which he chose to call being in the king's service,[105] and thence derived a right of hoisting the military ornament of a cockade over the button of his hat. He likewise wore a sword of no ordinary length by his side, with which he swaggered in his cabin, among the wretches his passengers, whom he had stowed in cupboards on each side. He was a person of a very singular character. He had taken it into his head that he was a gentleman, from those very reasons that proved he was not one; and to shew himself a fine gentleman, by a behaviour which seemed to insinuate he had never seen one. He was, moreover, a man of gallantry; at the age of seventy he had the finicalness of Sir Courtly Nice, with the roughness of Surly;[106] and while he was deaf himself, had a voice capable of deafening all others.

NOW, as I saw myself in danger by the delays of the captain, who was, in reality, waiting for more freight, and as the wind had been long nested, as it were, in the south-west, where it constantly blew hurricanes, I began with great reason to apprehend that our voyage might be long, and that my belly, which began already to be much extended, would require the water to be let out at a time when no assistance was at hand; though, indeed, the captain comforted me with assurances, that he had a pretty young fellow on board, who acted as his surgeon, as I found he likewise did as steward, cook, butler, sailor. In short, he had as many offices as Scrub in the play,[107] and went

---

[104] Richard Veale, Captain of the *Queen of Portugal*: see above, p. 566 n. 73.

[105] In time of war captains of private merchant vessels were authorized by 'letters of marque and reprisal' to assault enemy ships that had allegedly done them injury. This in due course became a licence to fit out the vessel as a warship and to seize and plunder the merchant ships of the enemy (*OED*, s.v. 'marque'). Keymer (*Fielding's Journal*, p. 124 n. 10) quotes this contemporary definition of a privateer: 'a kind of a private man of war, though the commission be not reckoned very honourable . . . and some persons account those but one remove from pirates; who, without any respect to the cause, or having any immediate injury done them, or not being so much as hired for the service, spoil men and goods, and innocent traders, making a traffic of it, amidst the calamities of war' (M. Postlethwayt, *The Universal Dictionary of Trade and Commerce*, 2nd edn. [1757], ii, p. 549).

[106] In the list of characters for John Crowne's comedy *Sir Courtly Nice* (1685), Sir Courtly is described as 'A Fop, overcurious in his Diet and Dress' and Surly as 'A morose, ill-natur'd, negligent Fellow'. In *Tom Jones* (x. i) HF defines a critic of 'exquisite Judgment' as one who can 'note the Difference between Sir *Fopling Flutter* [in Etherege's *The Man of Mode* (1676)] and Sir *Courtly Nice*' (p. 525). HF quotes a line from this play by 'the comic Poet' Crowne in *Champion* (8 December 1739), p. 54.

[107] Scrub, the jack-of-all-trades in George Farquhar's comedy *The Beaux Stratagem* (1707; III. iii): 'Of a *Monday*, I drive the Coach; of a *Tuesday*, I drive the Plough; on *Wednesday*, I follow the Hounds; a *Thursday*, I dun the Tenants; on *Fryday*, I go to Market; on *Saturday*, I draw Warrants; and a *Sunday*, I draw Beer.'

through them all with great dexterity; this of surgeon, was, perhaps, the only one in which his skill was somewhat deficient, at least that branch of tapping for the dropsy; for he very ingenuously and modestly confessed, he had never seen the operation performed, nor was possessed of that chirurgical instrument with which it is performed.

Friday, June 28. By way of prevention, therefore, I this day sent for my friend Mr. Hunter, the great surgeon and anatomist of Covent-garden;[108] and, though my belly was not yet very full and tight, let out ten quarts of water, the young sea-surgeon attending the operation not as a performer, but as a student.

I WAS now eased of the greatest apprehension which I had from the length of the passage; and I told the captain, I was become indifferent as to the time of his sailing. He expressed much satisfaction in this declaration, and at hearing from me, that I found myself, since my tapping, much lighter and better. In this, I believe, he was sincere; for, he was, as we shall have occasion to observe more than once, a very good-natured man; and as he was a very brave one too, I found that the heroic constancy, with which I had born an operation that is attended with scarce any degree of pain, had not a little raised me in his esteem. That he might adhere, therefore, in the most religious and rigorous manner to his word, when he had no longer any temptation from interest to break it, as he had no longer any hopes of more goods or passengers, he ordered his ship to fall down to Gravesend on Sunday morning, and there to wait his arrival.

Sunday, June 30. NOTHING worth notice pass'd till that morning, when my poor wife, after passing a night in the utmost torments of the tooth-ach, resolved to have it drawn. I dispatched, therefore, a servant[109] into Wapping, to bring, in haste, the best toothdrawer he could find. He soon found out a female of great eminence in the art; but when he brought her to the boat, at the water-side, they were informed that the ship was gone; for, indeed, she had set out a few minutes after his quitting her; nor did the pilot, who well knew the errand on which I had sent my servant, think fit to wait a moment for his return, or to give me any notice of his setting out, though I had, very patiently, attended the delays of the captain four days, after many solemn promises of weighing anchor every one of the three last.

[108] William Hunter (1718–83), HF's near neighbour in Covent Garden and his 'old and sincere friend', as John Fielding later recalled when soliciting Hunter's help in promoting the posthumous production of HF's comedy *The Fathers* (1778; *Life*, p. 616). Hunter and HF were also Perpetual Governors of the Lying-in Hospital for Married Women, serving the 'industrious Poor'; and he is the likely author of articles concerning the Society of Naval Surgeons signed 'Benevolus' in HF's *Covent-Garden Journal*, Nos. 38 and 41 (*CGJ*, pp. xxxi, 251 n. 3). Later, from Torbay, HF would send him a present of Devon cider (below, Appendix C.3, Letter 2).
[109] William Aldrit (above, p. 567 n. 79).

BUT of all the petty bashaws, or turbulent tyrants I ever beheld, this soure-faced pilot was the worst tempered; for, during the time that he had the guidance of the ship, which was till we arrived in the Downs,[110] he complied with no one's desires, nor did he give a civil word, or, indeed, a civil look to any on board.

THE toothdrawer, who, as I said before, was one of great eminence among her neighbours, refused to follow the ship; so that my man made himself the best of his way, and, with some difficulty, came up with us before we were got under full sail; for, after that, as we had both wind and tide with us, he would have found it impossible to overtake the ship, till she was come to an anchor at Gravesend.

THE morning was fair and bright, and we had a passage thither, I think, as pleasant as can be conceived; for, take it with all its advantages, particularly the number of fine ships you are always sure of seeing by the way, there is nothing to equal it in all the rivers of the world. The yards of Deptford and of Woolwich are noble sights; and give us a just idea of the great perfection to which we are arrived in building those floating castles, and the figure which we may always make in Europe among the other maritime powers. That of Woolwich, at least, very strongly imprinted this idea on my mind; for, there was now on the stocks there the Royal Anne, supposed to be the largest ship ever built, and which contains ten carriage guns more than had ever yet equipped a first rate.[111]

IT is true, perhaps, that there is more of ostentation than of real utility, in ships of this vast and unwieldy burthen,[112] which are rarely capable of acting against an enemy; but if the building such contributes to preserve, among other nations, the notion of the British superiority in naval affairs, the expence, though very great, is well incurred, and the ostentation is laudable and truly political. Indeed I should be sorry to allow that Holland, France, or Spain, possessed a vessel larger and more beautiful than the largest and

[110] Keymer (*Fielding's Journal*, s.v. 'Sunday, June 30', p. 124 n. 1) cites Defoe's account of the Downs from the *Tour through the Whole Island of Great Britain*: 'the famous Road for Shipping, so well known all over the trading World by the Name of the *Downs*, and where almost all Ships which arrive from foreign Parts for *London*, or go from *London* to foreign Parts, and pass the Chanel, generally stop; the Homeward-bound, to dispatch Letters, send their Merchants and Owners the good News of their Arrival, and set their Passengers on Shore; and the Outward-bound, to take in fresh Provisions, to receive their last Orders, Letters, and Farewels, from Owners and Friends, &c.'

[111] The *Royal Anne* was of 2,047 tons' burthen, with 102 guns; it was laid down on 8 January 1746 and renamed the *Royal George* when it was launched, on 18 February 1756 (*London Magazine*, 25 [1756], p. 208). The first ship of the Royal Navy designed on 'scientific' French principles, it was 'at that time, deemed the paragon of beauty, and considered as the *ne plus ultra* of perfection in the science of marine architecture . . . Her force nominally exceeded that of any vessel then possessed either by France, Spain, or any other country in the universe' (John Charnock, *History of Marine Architecture*, 3 vols. [1800–2], iii, p. 138).

[112] 'burthen': the carrying capacity of a ship stated as a certain number of tons (*OED*, 'burden' I. 3).

most beautiful of ours; for this honour I would always administer to the pride of our sailors, who should challenge it from all their neighbours with truth and success. And sure I am that not our honest tars alone, but every inhabitant of this island, may exult in the comparison, when he considers the king of Great-Britain as a maritime prince, in opposition to any other prince in Europe; but I am not so certain that the same idea of superiority will result from comparing our land-forces with those of many other crowned heads. In numbers, they all far exceed us, and in the goodness and splendor of their troops, many nations, particularly, the Germans and French, and perhaps the Dutch, cast us at a distance; for, however we may flatter ourselves with the Edwards and Henrys of former ages,[113] the change of the whole art of war since those days, by which the advantage of personal strength is, in a manner, entirely lost, hath produced a change in military affairs to the advantage of our enemies. As for our successes in later days, if they were not entirely owing to the superior genius of our general, they were not a little due to the superior force of his money. Indeed, if we should arraign marshal Saxe of ostentation, when he shewed his army, drawn up, to our captive general, the day after the battle of La Val,[114] we cannot say that the ostentation was intirely vain; since he certainly shewed him an army, which had not been often equalled, either in the number or goodness of the troops, and which, in those respects, so far exceeded ours, that none can ever cast any reflection on the brave young prince[115] who could not reap

[113] Referring to the victories over the French of Edward III at Crécy (1346), his son Edward the Black Prince at Poitiers (1356), and Henry V at Agincourt (1415). Later in this paragraph, when referring to 'our successes in later days', HF will also implicitly include 'the superior genius' of Marlborough (above, p. 560 n. 55) and the 'glory' of 'the brave young Prince', the Duke of Cumberland (below, n. 115). Cf. *The Covent-Garden Journal*, No. 16 (25 February 1752), where, attributing Cumberland's defeat at Fontenoy (1745) to the cowardice of their Dutch allies, HF offers the same pantheon of English heroes: 'Had one of our Allies indeed been no more deficient in Bravery or Integrity at the great Action at Fontenoy, France had possibly felt the Force of English Valour on that fatal Day, with as bitter Lamentations as the Fields of Cressy or Agincourt, of Blenheim or Ramelie had ever occasioned; and our glorious General as he deserved no less, so would he have gathered no less Laurels, than the most successful of his Predecessors had been ever crowned with' (p. 113).

[114] In July 1747 at Lauffeld (or Val) in the Netherlands, Maurice, Comte de Saxe (1696–1750), Marshal of France, defeated the British and allied forces under Cumberland. During the battle General John Ligonier (1680–1770), leading a fierce cavalry charge, was taken prisoner when his horse was killed.

[115] William Augustus, Duke of Cumberland (1721–65), younger son of George II and Queen Caroline, commander of the British and allied forces at Lauffeld. In 1743, fighting beside his father in the victory over the French at Dettingen, he had proved his valour and skill. And in HF's view, even in defeat, at Lauffeld as earlier at Fontenoy, Cumberland had deprived the French of victory by his generalship in defeat, his 'Army . . . retreat[ing] in Order from the Attack, and which they durst not pursue' (*TP*, No. 6 [10 December 1745], p. 150). HF indeed never mentions Cumberland but in the most laudatory terms (see above, n. 113). In *Tom Jones* (VII. xi) he is 'the glorious Duke of *Cumberland*', whose cause Tom joins against the Jacobite rebels (p. 367). In *An Enquiry into the Causes of the Late Increase of Robbers* (1751), as in *The Covent-Garden Journal* (above, n. 113), HF includes Cumberland with Edward, Henry, and Marlborough in the ranks of the greatest British generals (p. 90). See also *Ovid's Art of Love*, above, p. 396 and n. 21.

the lawrels of conquest in that day; but his retreat will be always mentioned as an addition to his glory.

IN our marine the case is entirely the reverse, and it must be our own fault if it doth not continue so; for, continue so it will, as long as the flourishing state of our trade shall support it, and this support it can never want, till our legislature shall cease to give sufficient attention to the protection of our trade, and our magistrates want sufficient power, ability, and honesty to execute the laws: a circumstance not to be apprehended, as it cannot happen, till our senates and our benches shall be filled with the blindest ignorance, or with the blackest corruption.

BESIDES the ships in the docks, we saw many on the water: the yatchts are sights of great parade, and the king's body yatcht,[116] is, I believe, unequalled in any country, for convenience as well as magnificence; both which are consulted in building and equipping her with the most exquisite art and workmanship.

WE saw likewise several Indiamen[117] just returned from their voyage. These are, I believe, the largest and finest vessels which are any where employed in commercial affairs. The colliers,[118] likewise, which are very numerous, and even assemble in fleets, are ships of great bulk; and, if we descend to those used in the American, African, and European trades, and pass through those which visit our own coasts, to the small craft that ply between Chatham[119] and the Tower, the whole forms a most pleasing object to the eye, as well as highly warming to the heart of an Englishman, who has any degree of love for his country, or can recognize any effect of the patriot in his constitution.

LASTLY, the Royal Hospital of Greenwich,[120] which presents so delightful a front to the water, and doth such honour at once to its builder and the nation, to the great skill and ingenuity of the one, and to the no less sensible gratitude of the other, very properly closes the account of this scene; which may well appear romantic to those who have not themselves seen, that, in

[116] 'yatcht': variant spelling of *yacht* (*OED*). 'The royal yachts are commonly rigged as ketches, except the principal one reserved for the sovereign, which is equipped with three masts like a ship' (*OED*, s.v. 'yacht', quoting Falconer's *Dictionary Marine* [1769]; also s.v. 'body' VI. 29). HF probably saw 'the new *Caroline* yacht [with four masts], thought to be the handsomest ever built' (Phillips, *Thames*, p. 20, fig. 10).

[117] Large ships of 600 tons or more belonging to the East India Company, whose docks were at Deptford.

[118] Ships that carried coal from Newcastle and the north of England to London.

[119] Chatham, Kent, on the Medway: the principal naval base for operations on the North Sea.

[120] Founded in 1692 by Queen Mary, who was moved at the sight of the wounded who survived the victorious naval battle of La Hogue, the Naval Hospital at Greenwich was built on the site of a derelict palace. Its architect was Christopher Wren (1632–1723), who offered his services free, though occupied at the time supervising the building of St Paul's Cathedral and other churches in the City of London. Wren was assisted by Nicholas Hawksmoor, and he was succeeded by Sir John Vanbrugh. The hospital, though unfinished, began admitting seamen in 1705. In 1873 it became the Royal Naval College.

this one instance, truth and reality are capable, perhaps, of exceeding the power of fiction.

WHEN we had past by Greenwich, we saw only two or three gentlemen's houses, all of very moderate account, till we reached Gravesend; these are all on the Kentish shore, which affords a much drier, wholsomer and pleasanter situation than doth that of its opposite, Essex. This circumstance, I own, is somewhat surprising to me, when I reflect on the numerous villas that crowd the river, from Chelsea upwards as far as Shepperton,[121] where the narrower channel affords not half so noble a prospect, and where the continual succession of the small craft, like the frequent repetition of all things, which have nothing in them great, beautiful, or admirable, tire the eye, and give us distaste and aversion instead of pleasure. With some of these situations, such as Barnes,[122] Mortlake, &c. even the shore of Essex, might contend, not upon very unequal terms; but, on the Kentish borders, there are many spots to be chosen by the builder, which might justly claim the preference over almost the very finest of those in Middlesex and Surry.

HOW shall we account for this depravity in taste? for, surely, there are none so very mean and contemptible, as to bring the pleasure of seeing a number of little wherries, gliding along after one another, in competition with what we enjoy, in viewing a succession of ships, with all their sails expanded to the winds, bounding over the waves before us.

AND here I cannot pass by another observation on the deplorable want of taste in our enjoyments, which we shew by almost totally neglecting the pursuit of what seems to me the highest degree of amusement: this is, the sailing ourselves in little vessels of our own, contrived only for our ease and accommodation, to which such situations of our villas, as I have recommended, would be so convenient and even necessary.

THIS amusement, I confess, if enjoyed in any perfection, would be of the expensive kind; but such expence would not exceed the reach of a moderate fortune, and would fall very short of the prices which are daily paid for pleasures of a far inferior rate. The truth, I believe, is, that sailing in the manner I have just mentioned, is a pleasure rather unknown, or unthought of, than rejected by those who have experienced it; unless, perhaps, the apprehension of danger, or sea sickness, may be supposed, by the timorous and

---

[121] Cf. HF's Letter XLI in Sarah Fielding's *Familiar Letters between the Principal Characters in David Simple* (1747), where a French visitor remarks on the sights seen on a boat trip up the Thames from Whitehall to Putney: 'the Villas which border on both Sides this River [near Twickenham] . . . tend to give as magnificent an Idea of the Riches which flow in to these People by Trade, as the Shipping doth, which is to be seen below the Bridge of *London*' (see above, p. 493).

[122] A tradition, accepted by London County Council, has it that in the early 1750s, before he began leasing Fordhook in 1752, HF made his country residence at Milbourne House in Barnes, Surrey (*Life*, pp. 507, 676 n. 142).

delicate, to make too large deductions; insisting, that all their enjoyments shall come to them pure and unmixed, and being ever ready to cry out,

—*Nocet empta dolore voluptas.*[123]

THIS, however, was my present case; for the ease and lightness which I felt from my tapping, the gaiety of the morning, the pleasant sailing with wind and tide, and the many agreeable objects with which I was constantly entertained during the whole way, were all suppressed and overcome by the single consideration of my wife's pain, which continued incessantly to torment her till we came to an anchor, when I dispatched a messenger in great haste, for the best reputed operator in Gravesend. A surgeon of some eminence now appeared, who did not decline tooth-drawing, tho' he certainly would have been offended with the appellation of tooth drawer, no less than his brethren, the members of that venerable body, would be with that of barber, since the late separation between those long united companies,[124] by which, if the surgeons have gained much, the barbers are supposed to have lost very little.

THIS able and careful person (for so I sincerely believe he is) after examining the guilty tooth, declared, that it was such a rotten shell, and so placed at the very remotest end of the upper jaw, where it was, in a manner, covered and secured by a large, fine, firm tooth, that he despaired of his power of drawing it.

HE said, indeed, more to my wife, and used more rhetoric to dissuade her from having it drawn, than is generally employed to persuade young ladies, to prefer a pain of three moments to one of three months continuance; especially, if those young ladies happen to be past forty or fifty years of age,[125] when, by submitting to support a racking torment, the only good circumstance attending which is, 'tis so short, that scarce one in a thousand can cry out, I feel it, they are to do a violence to their charms, and lose one of those beautiful holders, with which alone Sir Courtly Nice declares, a lady can ever lay hold of his heart.[126]

HE said at last so much, and seemed to reason so justly, that I came over to his side, and assisted him in prevailing on my wife (for it was no easy

[123] Horace, *Epistles*, I. ii. 55: 'Pleasure bought with pain is harmful.'

[124] The barbers and surgeons of London had been united in one corporation since the time of Henry VIII. By Act of Parliament (18 Geo. II, c. 15), effective June 1745, this union was dissolved, the barbers and the surgeons becoming 'Two Separate and Distinct Corporations'. HF's friend John Ranby (above, p. 554 n. 36) was appointed governor of the new Company of Surgeons. In *Tom Jones* (VIII. vi) Partridge the barber laments 'that cruel Separation of the united Fraternities' (p. 424).

[125] Mary Fielding, however, was 33 at the time.

[126] Crowne's *Sir Courtly Nice* (1685), p. iv: 'Oh! there's nothing so charming as admirable Teeth. If a Lady fastens upon my Heart, it must be with her Teeth' (p. 37).

matter) to resolve on keeping her tooth a little longer, and to apply to palliatives only for relief. These were opium applied to the tooth, and blisters behind the ears.

WHILST we were at dinner this day, in the cabin, on a sudden the window on one side was beat into the room, with a crash, as if a twenty-pounder had been discharged among us. We were all alarmed at the suddenness of the accident, for which, however, we were soon able to account: for the sash, which was shivered all to pieces, was pursued into the middle of the cabin by the boltsprit[127] of a little ship, called a cod-smack, the master of which made us amends for running (carelessly at best) against us, and injuring the ship, in the sea-way; that is to say, by damning us all to hell, and uttering several pious wishes that it had done us much more mischief. All which were answered in their own kind and phrase by our men; between whom, and the other crew, a dialogue of oaths and scurrility was carried on, as long as they continued in each other's hearing.

IT is difficult, I think, to assign a satisfactory reason why sailors in general should, of all others, think themselves entirely discharged from the common bands of humanity, and should seem to glory in the language and behaviour of savages? They see more of the world, and have, most of them, a more erudite education, than is the portion of land-men of their degree. Nor do I believe that in any country they visit (Holland itself not excepted) they can ever find a parallel to what daily passes on the river Thames. Is it that they think true courage (for they are the bravest fellows upon earth) inconsistent with all the gentleness of a humane carriage, and that the contempt of civil order springs up in minds but little cultivated at the same time, and from the same principles, with the contempt of danger and death? Is it—? In short, it is so; and how it comes to be so, I leave to form a question in the Robin Hood society,[128] or to be

---

[127] 'boltsprit': a form of the word *bowsprit*, which HF later uses (below, p. 591). Keymer (*Fielding's Journal*, s.v. '*Sunday, June 30*', p. 125 n. 11) helpfully cites Johnson's definition ('Boltsprit'): 'A mast running out at the head of a ship, not standing upright, but aslope.'

[128] Goldgar in his commentary on HF's satires of the Robin Hood Society in *The Covent-Garden Journal*, Nos. 8 and 9 (28 January and 1 February 1752), offers the following account of its organization and the inflammatory nature of its meetings, attended chiefly by a crowd of freethinking bakers, cobblers, comedians, and other representatives of what HF called 'the Mobility': 'the Robin Hood Society [was] a debating club formed about 1747, which met every Monday evening at the Robin Hood in Butcher's Row to argue any questions the members chose to submit. Anyone who wished to attend and pay an entrance fee of sixpence had the right to speak for five minutes, at the end of which time the president [a wealthy baker named Caleb Jeacocke] rapped his hammer for silence.' Goldgar documents in some detail the contemporary attacks on the Society 'for religious heterodoxy and political disaffection' (*CGJ*, p. 60 n. 4). When Bolingbroke's posthumous *Works* appeared in March 1754, provoking HF to undertake his abortive *Fragment of a Comment* as an antidote to what he considered a poisonous farrago of blasphemy and irreligion (see below, pp. 661–3), the Robin Hood Society was debating the merits of the proposition: That Bolingbroke had done more than the Apostles to serve mankind (*Life*, pp. 582–3).

propounded for solution among the ænigmas in the Woman's Almanack for the next year.[129]

Monday, July 1. THIS day Mr. Welch[130] took his leave of me after dinner, as did a young lady of her sister,[131] who was proceeding with my wife to Lisbon. They both set out together in a post-chaise for London.

SOON after their departure, our cabin where my wife and I were sitting together, was visited by two ruffians, whose appearance greatly corresponded with that of the sheriff's, or rather the knight marshal's bailiffs.[132] One of these, especially, who seemed to affect a more than ordinary degree of rudeness and insolence, came in without any kind of ceremony, with a broad gold lace on his hat, which was cocked with much military fierceness on his head. An inkhorn at his button-hole,[133] and some papers in his hand, sufficiently assured me what he was, and I asked him if he and his companion were not custom-house officers; he answered with sufficient dignity, that they were, as an information which he seemed to conclude would strike the hearer with awe, and suppress all further enquiry; but, on the contrary I proceeded to ask of what rank he was in the Custom-house, and receiving an answer from his companion, as I remember, that the gentleman was a riding surveyor; I replied that he might be a riding surveyor, but could be no gentleman, for that none who had any title to that denomination, would break into the presence of a lady, without any apology, or even moving his hat. He then took his covering from his head, and laid it on the table, saying, he asked pardon, and blamed the mate, who should, he said, have informed him if any persons of distinction were below. I told him, he might guess by our appearance (which, perhaps, was rather more than could be said with the strictest adherence to truth) that he was before a gentleman and lady,

---

[129] *The Ladies' Diary: or, Woman's Almanac*, published since 1704, was edited by Robert Heath (1743–53) and by Thomas Simpson (1754–60) (E. G. R. Taylor, *The Mathematical Practitioners of Hanoverian England* [London, 1966], 'Biographies', nos. 271, 310). Around 1753, 30,000 copies were being printed annually (*N & Q*, 1st ser., 11 [1855], 441). One of its departments was a series of 'aenigmas', or puzzles, with answers published in the next year's almanac.

[130] See above, p. 568 n. 84.

[131] Jane and Margaret Collier (above, p. 567 n. 79). Jane, Sarah Fielding's close friend and collaborator, had recently praised HF's works in her novel *The Cry* (published March 1754). At Fordhook on the eve of his departure, HF returned the compliment, presenting her with a rare edition of his favourite Horace, inscribed 'as a Memorial (however poor) of the highest Esteem for an Understanding more than Female, mixed with virtues almost more than human' (*Life*, pp. 393, 587, 665 n. 219).

[132] 'knight marshal': an officer of the English royal household, who had judicial cognizance of transgressions 'within the king's house and verge', i.e. within a radius of 12 miles of the king's palace (*OED*); 'bailiff': a warrant officer.

[133] The badge of the exciseman or custom house officer. Dobson recalls Boswell's vignette of Johnson at the sale of Thrale's brewery: 'Johnson appeared bustling about, with an ink-horn and pen in his button-hole, like an exciseman' (*Life of Johnson*, ed. G. Birkbeck Hill and L. F. Powell [Oxford, 1934], iv, p. 87). At Gravesend, customs inspectors gave outward-bound ships a final clearance.

which should teach him to be very civil in his behaviour, tho' we should not happen to be of that number whom the world calls people of fashion and distinction. However, I said, that as he seemed sensible of his error, and had asked pardon, the lady would permit him to put his hat on again, if he chose it. This he refused with some degree of surliness, and failed not to convince me that, if I should condescend to become more gentle, he would soon grow more rude.

I NOW renewed a reflection, which I have often seen occasion to make, that there is nothing so incongruous in nature as any kind of power, with lowness of mind and of ability, and that there is nothing more deplorable than the want of truth in the whimsical notion of Plato; who tells us that 'Saturn, well knowing the state of human affairs, gave us kings and rulers, not of human, but divine original: for as we make not shepherds of sheep, nor oxherds of oxen, nor goatherds of goats; but place some of our own kind over all, as being better and fitter to govern them: in the same manner, were demons by the Divine Love, set over us, as a race of beings of a superior order to men, and who, with great ease to themselves, might regulate our affairs, and establish peace, modesty, freedom and justice. And totally destroying all sedition, might complete the happiness of the human race. So far, at least, may even now be said with truth, that in all states which are under the government of mere man, without any divine assistance, there is nothing but labour and misery to be found. From what I have said therefore, we may at least learn, with our utmost endeavours, to imitate the Saturnian institution; borrowing all assistance from our immortal part, while we pay to this the strictest obedience, we should form both our private oeconomy, and public policy, from its dictates. By this dispensation of our immortal minds, we are to establish a law, and to call it by that name. But if any government be in the hands of a single person, of the few, or of the many; and such governor or governors shall abandon himself or themselves to the unbridled pursuit of the wildest pleasures or desires, unable to restrain any passion, but possessed with an insatiable bad disease; if such shall attempt to govern; and at the same time to trample on all laws, there can be no means of preservation left for the wretched people.'*[134]

---

* Plato de Leg. lib 4. pp. 713c.–714, edit. Serrani.[134]

---

[134] Plato, *Laws*, iv. 713c–714a—Englished by HF from the standard edition of the Greek *Works* (Geneva, 1578), ed. Henri Estienne (or Stephanus), with Latin translation and notes by Jean de Serres (Serranus), 3 vols. A copy of this edition was in HF's library, Lot 481 of the Sale Catalogue (1755), described as in '2 tom.' (Ribbles P24); but advertised on the title-page of the Catalogue as in '3 vols'. In a letter to James Harris (24 November 1744) HF calls Plato (*c.*429–347 BC) 'my Godlike Master', who is to philosophy what Homer and Virgil are to poetry (*Correspondence*, Letter 23, p. 47).

IT is true that Plato is here treating of the highest or sovereign power in a state; but it is as true, that his observations are general, and may be applied to all inferior powers: and, indeed, every subordinate degree is immediately derived from the highest; and as it is equally protected by the same force, and sanctified by the same authority, is alike dangerous to the well-being of the subject.

OF all powers, perhaps, there is none so sanctified and protected, as this which is under our present consideration. So numerous, indeed, and strong are the sanctions given to it by many acts of parliament, that having once established the laws of customs on merchandize, it seems to have been the sole view of the legislature to strength the hands, and to protect the persons of the officers, who became established by those laws; many of whom are so far from bearing any resemblance to the Saturnian institution, and to be chosen from a degree of beings superior to the rest of human race, that they sometimes seem industriously picked out of the lowest and vilest orders of mankind.

THERE is, indeed, nothing so useful to man in general, nor so beneficial to particular societies and individuals, as trade. This is that *alma mater*,[135] at whose plentiful breast all mankind are nourished. It is true, like other parents, she is not always equally indulgent to all her children; but tho' she gives to her favourites a vast proportion of redundancy and superfluity, there are very few whom she refuses to supply with the conveniencies, and none with the necessaries of life.

SUCH a benefactress as this must naturally be beloved by mankind in general; it would be wonderful, therefore, if her interest was not considered by them, and protected from the fraud and violence of some of her rebellious offspring, who coveting more than their share, or more than she thinks proper to allow them, are daily employed in meditating mischief against her, and in endeavouring to steal from their brethren those shares which this great *alma mater* had allowed them.

AT length our Governor came on board, and about six in the evening we weighed anchor, and fell down to the Nore,[136] whither our passage was

---

[135] *'alma mater'*: nourishing mother. Commenting on HF's ambivalent attitude towards the effects of trade in society, as expressed in the Preface to the *Enquiry* (1751), Zirker calls this paragraph in the *Journal*, 'Fielding's most enthusiastic encomium on trade' (*Enquiry*, p. 70 n. 7). But HF is no less enthusiastic in the *Enquiry*: 'the Politician finds many Emoluments to compensate all the moral Evils introduced by Trade, by which the Grandeur and Power of the Nation is carried to a Pitch that it could never otherwise have reached; Arts and Sciences are improved, and human Life is embellished with every Ornament, and furnished with every Comfort which it is capable of tasting' (p. 70).

[136] 'the Nore': a sandbank (marked by a lightship since 1732) at the mouth of the Thames (Keymer, *Fielding's Journal*, s.v '*Monday, July 1*', p. 126 n. 7).

extremely pleasant, the evening being very delightful, the moon just past the full, and both wind and tide favourable to us.

Tuesday, July 2. THIS morning we again set sail under all the advantages we had enjoy'd the evening before: this day we left the shore of Essex, and coasted along Kent, passing by the pleasant island of Thanet, which is an island, and that of Sheppy, which is not an island,[137] and about three o'clock, the wind being now full in our teeth, we came to an anchor in the Downs, within two miles of Deal.[138] My wife, having suffered intolerable pain from her tooth, again renewed her resolution of having it drawn, and another surgeon was sent for from Deal, but with no better success than the former. He likewise declined the operation, for the same reason which had been assigned by the former: however, such was her resolution, backed with pain, that he was obliged to make the attempt, which concluded more in honour of his judgement, than of his operation; for having put my poor wife to inexpressible torment, he was obliged to leave her tooth *in statu quo;*[139] and she had now the comfortable prospect of a long fit of pain, which might have lasted her whole voyage, without any possibility of relief.

IN these pleasing sensations, of which I had my just share, nature, over-come with fatigue, about eight in the evening resign'd her to rest; a circum-stance which would have given me some happiness, could I have known how to employ those spirits which were raised by it: but unfortunately for me, I was left in a disposition of enjoying an agreeable hour, without the assistance of a companion, which has always appeared to me necessary to such enjoyment; my daughter and her companion[140] were both retired sea-sick to bed; the other passengers were a rude school-boy of fourteen years old, and an illiterate[141] Portuguese friar, who understood no language but his own, in which I had not the least smattering. The captain was the

---

[137] HF here reverses the order and characteristics of the Kent coast he passes. The Isle of Sheppey was separated from the mainland by a shallow strait, 'the Swale'. The Isle of Thanet, though isolated by two branches of the River Stour, was not an island, the sea passage behind it having closed up by the sixteenth century.

[138] Deal, a coastal town in east Kent, was the principal port of the Downs (above, p. 578 n. 110). 'Deal' is the dateline of all the shipping news from there reported at London in the *Public Advertiser* (Friday 5 July 1754): 'Deal, July 3, Came down and remain . . . Queen of Portugal, Veal, for [Lisbon]. . . . Wind S. W.' Subsequent reports in the *Public Advertiser* for Saturday 6 July, Monday 8 July, Tuesday 9 July, Wednesday 10 July confirm that contrary winds prevented the ship's departure until Monday 8 July, when 'all the Outward-bound' ships sailed (see below, pp. 592–3).

[139] '*in statu quo*': in the same state (as before).

[140] His daughter Harriet and Margaret Collier (above, p. 567 n. 79).

[141] 'illiterate': for educated persons of this period the word specifically signified those ignorant of Greek and Latin (*OED*, 1.a, citing Chesterfield's *Letters* [1748]). Cf. HF's *Amelia* (XI. ii), where Dr Harrison advises the Noble Lord that a certain colonel is uneducated: 'there is scarce a Foot Soldier in the Army who is more illiterate than the Colonel'. To which the Lord replies: 'Why as to Latin and Greek . . . they are not much requir'd in the Army' (pp. 458–9).

only person left, in whose conversation I might indulge myself; but unluckily, besides a total ignorance of every thing in the world but a ship, he had the misfortune of being so deaf, that to make him hear, I will not say understand, my words, I must run the risque of conveying them to the ears of my wife, who, tho' in another room (called, I think, the state-room; being indeed a most stately apartment capable of containing one human body in length, if not very tall, and three bodies in breadth) lay asleep within a yard of me. In this situation necessity and choice were one and the same thing; the captain and I sat down together to a small bowl of punch, over which we both soon fell fast asleep, and so concluded the evening.

Wednesday, July 3. THIS morning I awaked at four o'clock, for my distemper seldom suffered me to sleep later. I presently got up, and had the pleasure of enjoying the sight of a tempestuous sea for four hours before the captain was stirring; for he loved to indulge himself in morning slumbers, which were attended with a wind musick, much more agreeable to the performers than to the hearers, especially such as have, as I had, the privilege of sitting in the orchestra. At eight o'clock the captain rose, and sent his boat on shore. I ordered my man likewise to go in it, as my distemper was not of that kind which entirely deprives us of appetite. Now tho' the captain had well victualled his ship with all manner of salt provisions for the voyage, and had added great quantities of fresh stores, particularly of vegetables at Gravesend, such as beans and peas, which had been on board only two days, and had, possibly, not been gathered above two more, I apprehended I could provide better for myself at Deal, than the ship's ordinary seemed to promise. I accordingly sent for fresh provisions of all kinds from the shore, in order to put off the evil day of starving as long as possible. My man returned with most of the articles I sent for, and I now thought myself in a condition of living a week on my own provisions. I therefore ordered my own dinner, which I wanted nothing but a cook to dress, and a proper fire to dress it at; but those were not to be had, nor indeed any addition to my roast mutton, except the pleasure of the captain's company, with that of the other passengers; for my wife continued the whole day in a state of dozing, and my other females, whose sickness did not abate by the rolling of the ship at anchor, seemed more inclined to empty their stomachs than to fill them. Thus I pass'd the whole day (except about an hour at dinner) by myself, and the evening concluded with the captain as the preceding one had done; one comfortable piece of news he communicated to me, which was, that he had no doubt of a prosperous wind in the morning; but as he did not divulge the reasons of this confidence, and as I saw none myself besides the wind being directly opposite, my faith in this prophecy was not strong enough to build any great hopes upon.

Thursday, July 4. THIS morning, however the captain seem'd resolved to fulfil his own predictions, whether the wind would or no; he accordingly weighed anchor, and taking the advantage of the tide, when the wind was not very boisterous, he hoisted his sails, and, as if his power had been no less absolute over Æolus[142] than it was over Neptune, he forced the wind to blow him on in its own despight.

BUT as all men who have ever been at sea well know how weak such attempts are, and want no authorities of Scripture to prove,[143] that the most absolute power of a captain of a ship is very contemptible in the wind's eye, so did it befal our noble commander; who having struggled with the wind three or four hours, was obliged to give over, and lost, in a few minutes, all that he had been so long a gaining; in short, we returned to our former station, and once more cast anchor in the neighbourhood of Deal.

HERE, though we lay near the shore, that we might promise ourselves all the emolument which could be derived from it, we found ourselves deceived; and that we might with as much conveniency be out of the sight of land; for, except when the captain launch'd forth his own boat which he did always with great reluctance, we were incapable of procuring any thing from Deal, but at a price too exorbitant, and beyond the reach even of modern luxury; the fare of a boat from Deal, which lay at two miles distance, being at least three half crowns, and if we had been in any distress for it, as many half guineas; for these good people consider the sea as a large common, appendant to their mannor,[144] in which, when they find any of their fellow creatures impounded, they conclude, that they have a full right of making them pay at their own discretion for their deliverance: to say the truth, whether it be that men, who live on the sea-shore, are of an amphibious kind, and do not entirely partake of human nature, or whatever else may be the reason, they are so far from taking any share in the distresses of mankind, or of being moved with any compassion for them, that they look upon them as blessings shower'd down from above; and which the more they improve to their own use, the greater is their gratitude and piety. Thus at Gravesend, a sculler required a shilling for going less way than he would

---

[142] Æolus, god of the winds, who gave Odysseus a bag containing the contrary winds that would otherwise prevent his voyage.

[143] Cf. Acts 27, in which contrary winds impede and threaten the ship carrying Paul to Rome; ignoring Paul's warnings the master of the ship sails into the tempests and the ship is wrecked.

[144] The lord of a manor or his tenants may impound beasts of strangers that graze on their waste (i.e. uncultivated land) or 'common appendant', as security for the damage to the pasture (Sir William Blackstone, *Commentaries on the Law of England*, 4 vols., 5th edn. [1773], ii, p. 33; iii, pp. 12–13); an action technically known as a 'distress'. HF humorously applies the law to the 'distresses' of travellers, 'impounded' by watermen for damage to their 'waste', the sea. HA

row in London for three pence;[145] and, at Deal, a boat often brings more profit in a day, than it can produce in London in a week, or, perhaps, in a month; in both places, the owner of the boat founds his demand on the necessity and distress of one, who stands more or less in absolute want of his assistance; and with the urgency of these, always rises in the exorbitancy of his demand, without ever considering, that, from these very circumstances, the power or ease of gratifying such demand is in like proportion lessened. Now, as I am unwilling that some conclusions, which may be, I am aware, too justly drawn from these observations, should be imputed to human nature in general, I have endeavoured to account for them in a way more consistent with the goodness and dignity of that nature: however it be, it seems a little to reflect on the governors of such monsters, that they do not take some means to restrain these impositions, and prevent them from triumphing any longer in the miseries of those, who are, in many circumstances at least, their fellow-creatures, and considering the distresses of a wretched seaman, from his being wrecked to his being barely wind-bound, as a blessing sent among them from above, and calling it by that blasphemous name.

Friday, July 5. THIS day I sent a servant on board a man of war, that was stationed here, with my compliments to the captain, to represent to him the distress of the ladies, and to desire the favour of his long-boat to conduct us to Dover, at about seven miles distance; and, at the same time, presumed to make use of a great lady's name, the wife of the first lord commissioner of the admiralty;[146] who would, I told him, be pleased with any kindness shewn by him towards us in our miserable condition. And this I am convinced was true, from the humanity of the lady, though she was entirely unknown to me.

THE captain returned a verbal answer to a long letter; acquainting me, that what I desire could not be complied with, it being a favour not in his power to grant. This might be, and I suppose was true; but it is as true, that

---

[145] Rates for watermen on the Thames were fixed by the Lord Mayor and Aldermen of London. For 3*d.* a sculler could carry a passenger about a mile: e.g. from London Bridge to Wapping downriver, or to Westminster upriver, or any stairs between. A waterman demanding or taking more than this rate 'lies liable to pay forty Shillings, and suffer half a Year's Imprisonment' (*Universal Pocket Book* [1745], sect. xv); the same rates and conditions obtained as late as 1760.

[146] Lady Elizabeth Yorke (1725–60), daughter of the Earl of Hardwicke, Lord High Chancellor; in 1748 she married George, Baron Anson (above, p. 552 and n. 26), First Lord of the Admiralty. Though Lady Anson may not have known HF, HF was well acquainted with her father, whom he compliments often and extravagantly in his writings: notably in *The Champion* (9 September 1740), where 'our Law thrives under *Hardwick*' (p. 459), the earliest of HF's references to him; in *The True Patriot*, No. 33 (17 June 1746), where Hardwicke is 'that great and glorious Man' (p. 308); and *Tom Jones* (IV. vi), where, in his unfailing wisdom on the Bench, he is a figure for that 'active Principle' of conscience that guides the hero (pp. 172–3). In 1751 HF dedicated *An Enquiry into the Causes of the Late Increase of Robbers* to him.

if he was able to write, and had pen, ink and paper aboard, he might have sent a written answer, and that it was the part of a gentleman so to have done; but this is a character seldom maintained on the watery element, especially by those who exercise any power on it. Every commander of a vessel here seems to think himself entirely free from all those rules of decency and civility, which direct and restrain the conduct of the members of a society on shore; and each, claiming absolute dominion in his little wooden world, rules by his own laws and his own discretion. I do not, indeed, know so pregnant an instance of the dangerous consequences of absolute power, and its aptness to intoxicate the mind, as that of those petty tyrants, who become such in a moment, from very well-disposed and social members of that communion, in which they affect no superiority, but live in an orderly state of legal subjection with their fellow-citizens.

Saturday, July 6. THIS morning our commander, declaring he was sure the wind would change, took advantage of an ebbing tide, and weighed his anchor. His assurance, however, had the same completion, and his endeavours the same success, with his former trial; and he was soon obliged to return once more to his old quarters. Just before we let go our anchor, a small sloop, rather than submit to yield us an inch of way, ran foul of our ship, and carried off her bowsprit.[147] This obstinate frolic would have cost those aboard the sloop very dear, if our steersman had not been too generous to exert his superiority, the certain consequence of which would have been the immediate sinking of the other. This contention of the inferior, with a might capable of crushing it in an instant, may seem to argue no small share of folly or madness, as well as of impudence; but I am convinced there is very little danger in it: contempt is a port to which the pride of man submits to fly with reluctance, but those who are within it are always in a place of the most assured security; for whosoever throws away his sword, prefers, indeed, a less honourable, but much safer means of avoiding danger, than he who defends himself with it. And here we shall offer another distinction, of the truth of which much reading and experience have well convinced us, that as in the most absolute governments, there is a regular progression of slavery downwards, from the top to the bottom, the mischief of which is seldom felt with any great force and bitterness, but by the next immediate degree; so in the most dissolute and anarchical states, there is as regular an ascent of what is called rank or condition, which is always laying hold of the head of him, who is advanced but one step higher on the

---

[147] 'bowsprit': see above, p. 583 n. 127.

ladder,[148] who might, if he did not too much despise such efforts, kick his pursuer headlong to the bottom. We will conclude this digression with one general and short observation, which will, perhaps, set the whole matter in a clearer light than the longest and most laboured harangue. Whereas envy of all things most exposes us to danger from others; so, contempt of all things best secures us from them. And thus, while the dungcart and the sloop are always meditating mischief against the coach and the ship, and throwing themselves designedly in their way, the latter consider only their own security, and are not ashamed to break the road, and let the other pass by them.

Monday, July 8. HAVING past our Sunday without any thing remarkable, unless the catching a great number of whitings in the afternoon may be thought so; we now set sail on Monday at six o'clock, with a little variation of wind; but this was so very little, and the breeze itself so small, that the tide was our best, and indeed almost our only friend. This conducted us along the short remainder of the Kentish shore. Here we past that cliff of Dover, which makes so tremendous a figure in Shakespear,[149] and which, whoever reads without being giddy, must, according to Mr. Addison's observation, have either a very good head, or a very bad one; but, which, whoever contracts any such ideas from the sight of, must have, at least, a poetic, if not a Shakespearian genius. In truth, mountains, rivers, heroes and gods owe great part of their existence to the poets; and Greece and Italy do so plentifully abound in the former, because they furnished so glorious a number of the latter; who, while they bestowed immortality on every little hillock and blind[150] stream, left the noblest rivers and mountains in the world to share the same obscurity with the eastern and western poets, in which they are celebrated.

THIS evening we beat the sea[151] off Sussex, in sight of Dungeness, with much more pleasure than progress; for the weather was almost a perfect calm, and the moon, which was almost at the full, scarce suffered a single cloud to veil her from our sight.

Tuesday, Wednesday, July 9, 10. THESE two days we had much the same fine weather, and made much the same way; but, in the evening of the latter

---

[148] Cf. the digression dividing 'the human Species' into '*High* People and *Low* People' in *Joseph Andrews* (II. xiii), where HF surveys 'the Picture of Dependance, like a kind of Ladder' (p. 157).

[149] Edgar's description of the view from the cliff in *King Lear* (IV. vi. 11–23). Addison comments on the passage in *The Tatler*, No. 117 (7 January 1710): 'The Prospect from that Place is drawn with such proper Incidents, that whoever can read it without growing giddy, must have a good Head, or a very bad one.'

[150] 'blind': out of the way, obscure (*OED*, s.v. 8).

[151] 'beat the sea': to strive against contrary winds or currents at sea (*OED*, s.v. 'beat' 19).

day, a pretty fresh gale sprung up, at N. N. W. which brought us by the morning in sight of the Isle of Wight.

Thursday, July 11. THIS gale continued till towards noon; when the east end of the island bore but little a-head of us. The captain swaggered, and declared he would keep the sea; but the wind got the better of him, so that about three he gave up the victory, and, making a sudden tack, stood in for the shore, passed by Spithead and Portsmouth, and came to an anchor at a place called Ryde on the island.

A MOST tragical incident fell out this day at sea. While the ship was under sail, but making, as will appear, no great way, a kitten, one of four of the feline inhabitants of the cabin, fell from the window into the water: an alarm was immediately given to the captain, who was then upon deck, and received it with the utmost concern and many bitter oaths. He immediately gave orders to the steersman in favour of the poor thing, as he called it; the sails were instantly slackened, and all hands, as the phrase is, employed to recover the poor animal. I was, I own, extremely surprised at all this; less, indeed, at the captain's extreme tenderness, than at his conceiving any possibility of success; for, if puss had had nine thousand, instead of nine lives, I concluded they had been all lost. The boatswain, however, had more sanguine hopes; for, having stript himself of his jacket, breeches, and shirt, he leapt boldly into the water, and, to my great astonishment, in a few minutes, returned to the ship, bearing the motionless animal in his mouth. Nor was this, I observed a matter of such great difficulty as it appeared to my ignorance, and possibly may seem to that of my fresh-water reader: the kitten was now exposed to air and sun on the deck, where its life, of which it retained no symptoms, was despaired of by all.

THE captain's humanity, if I may so call it, did not so totally destroy his philosophy, as to make him yield himself up to affliction on this melancholy occasion. Having felt his loss like a man, he resolved to shew he could bear it like one;[152] and, having declared, he had rather have lost a cask of rum or brandy, betook himself to threshing at backgammon[153] with the Portuguese friar, in which innocent amusement they had passed about two thirds of their time.

---

[152] Cf. *Macbeth* (IV. iii. 219–21), where Macduff, lamenting the murder of his wife and children, replies to Malcolm's charge to 'Dispute it like a man': 'I shall do so; But I must also feel it as a man.' It was a favourite passage with HF, who has Joseph Andrews paraphrase it as here: '*Yes, I will bear my Sorrows like a Man, | But I must also feel them as a Man*' (III. xi, p. 267); HF also alludes to it in *The Jacobite's Journal*, No. 29 (18 June 1748), p. 312, and he parodies it in *Tom Jones* (XI. i, p. 568).

[153] 'threshing at backgammon': *OED*, s.v. 'thrash' B.2 [figurative]: *to thresh [thrash] straw*, to work at what is unproductive or unprofitable, citing Garrick's Prologue to Sheridan's *School for Scandal* (1777), i: 'All night at cards when threshing | Strong tea and scandal'.

BUT, as I have, perhaps, a little too wantonly endeavoured to raise the tender passions of my readers, in this narrative, I should think myself unpardonable if I concluded it, without giving them the satisfaction of hearing that the kitten at last recovered, to the great joy of the good captain; but to the great disappointment of some of the sailors, who asserted that the drowning a cat was the very surest way of raising a favourable wind: a supposition[154] of which, though we have heard several plausible accounts, we will not presume to assign the true original reason.

Friday, July 12. THIS day our ladies went a-shore at Ryde,[155] and drank their afternoon tea at an alehouse there with great satisfaction: here they were regaled with fresh cream, to which they had been strangers since they left the Downs.

Saturday, July 13. THE wind seeming likely to continue in the same corner, where it had been almost constantly for two months together, I was persuaded by my wife to go ashore, and stay at Ryde till we sailed. I approved the motion much; for, though I am a great lover of the sea, I now fancied there was more pleasure in breathing the fresh air of the land; but, how to get thither was the question: for, being really that dead luggage, which I considered all passengers to be in the beginning of this narrative,[156] and incapable of any bodily motion without external impulse, it was in vain to leave the ship, or to determine to do it, without the assistance of others. In one instance, perhaps, the living luggage is more difficult to be moved, or removed, than an equal or much superior weight of dead matter; which, if of the brittle kind, may indeed be liable to be broken through negligence; but this, by proper care, may be almost certainly prevented; whereas, the fractures to which the living lumps are exposed, are sometimes by no caution avoidable, and often by no art to be amended.

I WAS deliberating on the means of conveyance, not so much out of the ship to the boat, as out of a little tottering boat to the land. A matter which, as I had already experienced in the Thames, was not extremely easy, when

---

[154] 'supposition': see above, p. 550 n. 21. The sailors' superstition was in fact the opposite of what HF declares it to be: recorded as early as 1590 and well into the nineteenth century, their belief was that cats brought good luck and that drowning one, or losing one at sea, would immediately raise a storm and invite shipwreck. Captain Veale's concern for the kitten's safety, and the boatswain's heroics, may be attributed to less altruistic motives. (Radford's *Encyclopaedia of Superstitions* [New York, 1975], p. 87; *Dictionary of Superstitions*, ed. Iona Opie and Moira Tatem [Oxford, 1989], s.v. 'Cat: drowning at sea', where HF's remark contradicts all others; also, for the same superstition among French mariners, see Honoré de Mareville, 'Naval Folk Lore', *N & Q*, 10 245 [8 July 1845], 26).

[155] This day 'On board the Queen of Portugal . . . at anchor on the Mother Bank off Ryde', HF wrote John, asking him to assure his mother-in-law, who was looking after the children at Fordhook, that having safely weathered a storm during the night, he and his family had risen from breakfast 'in Health and Spirits', and grateful for the expert seamanship of Captain Veale (below, Appendix C.3, Letter 1).

[156] See pp. 573–4.

to be performed by any other limbs than your own. Whilst I weighed all that could suggest itself on this head, without strictly examining the merit of the several schemes which were advanced by the captain and sailors, and, indeed, giving no very deep attention even to my wife, who, as well as her friend and my daughter, were exerting their tender concern for my ease and safety; fortune, for I am convinced she had a hand in it, sent me a present of a buck;[157] a present, welcome enough of itself, but more welcome on account of the vessel in which it came, being a large hoy,[158] which in some places would pass for a ship, and many people would go some miles to see the sight. I was pretty easily conveyed on board this hoy, but to get from hence to the shore was not so easy a task; for, however strange it may appear, the water itself did not extend so far; an instance which seems to explain those lines of Ovid,

Omnia Pontus erant, deerant quoque littora Ponto,[159]

in a less tautological sense, than hath generally been imputed to them.

IN fact, between the sea and the shore, there was, at low water, an impassable gulf, if I may so call it, of deep mud, which could neither be traversed by walking nor swimming; so that for near one half of the twenty-four hours, Ryde was inaccessable by friend or foe. But as the magistrates of this place seemed more to desire the company of the former, than to fear that of the latter, they had begun to make a small causeway to the low water mark, so that foot passengers might land whenever they pleased; but as this work was of a publick kind, and would have cost a large sum of money, at least

---

[157] On 22 July from Torbay, Devon, HF would write John that he had 'got half a Buck from the New Forest, while we lay at the Isle of Wight, and the Pasty still sticks by us' (below, Appendix C.3, Letter 2). In March 1755, a month after the *Journal* was published, a visitor to Ryde wrote Samuel Richardson an uncomplimentary account of HF's sojourn there based on the report of his landlady Mrs Francis (Appendix C.3, Letter 9). According to this dubious authority, the pleasant barn HF describes was 'a fiction' and 'the circumstances . . . relating to the venison . . . were wholly misrepresented': far from the venison's being a present, HF had sent his servant to Southampton to purchase it for half a guinea, unlawfully, the deer being the king's property (Letter 9).

But there is no need to doubt the story as HF tells it. As an attorney riding the Western Circuit, and then from 1746 to 1749 as High Steward of the New Forest, serving the Warden, his patron the Duke of Bedford, HF had friends and connections in Hampshire—among them Richard Birt of Lymington, on the Hampshire coast across the Solent from the Isle of Wight. Birt, who is probably the Lymington lawyer whom Partridge in *Tom Jones* XVIII. vi) characterizes as 'a very good Sort of a Man, and . . . one of the merriest Gentlemen in *England*' (p. 937), was deputy Steward of the Forest, an office to which HF appointed him in 1746 and which he still held (on Birt, see *Life*, pp. 409, 432–4; *Correspondence*, Letter 32, p. 62 n. 1). Indeed, by 1751 HF had come to expect that Bedford's 'Goodness', as he called it, would provide him with just such a present during 'Venison Season' (see *Correspondence*, Letter 66 [18 June 1751]).

[158] 'hoy': a small vessel, usually rigged as a sloop [i.e. a single mast, fore-and-aft rigged], employed in carrying passengers and goods, particularly in short distances on the sea coast (*OED*).

[159] Ovid describing the Deluge: 'All is sea, and a sea without a shore' (*Metamorphoses*, i. 292).

ten pounds, and the magistrates, that is to say, the church-wardens, the overseers, constable and tithingman,[160] and the principal inhabitants, had every one of them some separate scheme of private interest to advance at the expence of the publick, they fell out among themselves; and after having thrown away one half of the requisite sum, resolved at least to save the other half, and rather be contented to sit down losers themselves, than to enjoy any benefit which might bring in a greater profit to another. Thus that unanimity which is so necessary in all publick affairs, became wanting, and every man, from the fear of being a bubble to another, was, in reality, a bubble[161] to himself.

HOWEVER, as there is scarce any difficulty, to which the strength of men, assisted with the cunning of art, is not equal, I was at last hoisted into a small boat, and being rowed pretty near the shore, was taken up by two sailors, who waded with me through the mud, and placed me in a chair on the land, whence they afterwards conveyed me a quarter of a mile farther, and brought me to a house, which seemed to bid the fairest for hospitality of any in Ryde.

WE brought with us our provisions from the ship, so that we wanted nothing but a fire to dress our dinner, and a room in which we might eat it. In neither of these had we any reason to apprehend a disappointment, our dinner consisting only of beans and bacon, and the worst apartment in his Majesty's dominions, either at home or abroad, being fully sufficient to answer our present ideas of delicacy.

UNLUCKILY, however, we were disappointed in both; for when we arrived about four at our inn, exulting in the hopes of immediately seeing our beans smoking on the table, we had the mortification of seeing them on the table indeed, but without that circumstance which would have made the sight agreeable, being in the same state in which we had dispatched them from our ship.

IN excuse for this delay, tho' we had exceeded, almost purposely, the time appointed, and our provision had arrived three hours before, the mistress of the house acquainted us, that it was not for want of time to dress them that they were not ready, but for fear of their being cold or over-done before we should come; which she assured us was much worse than waiting a few minutes for our dinner. An observation so very just, that it is impossible to find any objection in it; but indeed it was not altogether so proper at this time: for we had given the most absolute orders to have them ready at

---

[160] 'tithingman': a parish peace officer, or petty constable (*OED*).
[161] 'bubble': a dupe, a gull (*OED*, s.v. 'bubble' 5).

four, and had been ourselves, not without much care and difficulty, most exactly punctual in keeping to the very minute of our appointment. But tradesmen, inn-keepers, and servants never care to indulge us in matters contrary to our true interest, which they always know better than ourselves, nor can any bribes corrupt them to go out of their way, whilst they are consulting our good in our own despight.

OUR disappointment in the other particular, in defiance of our humility, as it was more extraordinary, was more provoking. In short, Mrs. Francis (for that was the name of the good woman of the house)[162] no sooner received the news of our intended arrival, than she considered more the gentility, than the humanity of her guests, and applied herself not to that which kindles, but to that which extinguishes fire, and forgetting to put on her pot, fell to washing her house.

As the messenger who had brought my venison was impatient to be dispatched, I ordered it to be brought and laid on the table, in the room where I was seated; and the table not being large enough, one side, and that a very bloody one, was laid on the brick floor. I then ordered Mrs. Francis to be called in, in order to give her instructions concerning it; in particular, what I would have roasted, and what baked; concluding that she would be highly pleased with the prospect of so much money being spent in her house, as she might have now reason to expect, if the wind continued only a few days longer to blow from the same points whence it had blown for several weeks past.

I SOON saw good cause, I must confess, to despise my own sagacity. Mrs. Francis having received her orders, without making any answer, snatched the side from the floor, which remained stained with blood, and bidding a servant take up that on the table, left the room with no pleasant countenance, muttering to herself, that had she known the litter which was to have been made, she would not have taken such pains to wash her house that morning. 'If this was gentility, much good may it do such gentlefolks, for her part she had no notion of it!'

FROM these murmurs I received two hints. The one, that it was not from a mistake of our inclination that the good woman had starved us, but from

---

[162] Mrs Ann Francis (d. 1758), keeper of the Nag's Head inn at Upper Ryde, and her husband, Jephtha (d. 1775), a farmer (*Life*, pp. 589 and 684 n. 382; for details about the family, see Keymer, *Fielding's Journal*, p. 128 n. 4). In the second edition of the *Journal* the name was changed to 'Humphrys', presumably to screen the living targets of HF's satire. Amory (see Textual Introduction, p. 534) considered that HF himself chose the name 'Humphrys' because it 'wittily' recalled the proverbial expression 'to dine with Duke Humphreys', meaning to go without dinner. If that was the intent behind the choice of the name, however, the joke is unlikely to have been HF's, unless one supposes he allowed both names to stand with equal authority in the MS.

wisely consulting her own dignity, or rather, perhaps, her vanity, to which our hunger was offered up as a sacrifice. The other, that I was now sitting in a damp room; a circumstance, tho' it had hitherto escaped my notice, from the colour of the bricks, which was by no means to be neglected in a valetudinary state.

MY wife, who, besides discharging excellently well her own, and all the tender offices becoming the female character; who besides being a faithful friend, an amiable companion, and a tender nurse, could likewise supply the wants of a decrepit husband, and occasionally perform his part, had, before this, discovered the immoderate attention to neatness in Mrs. Francis, and provided against its ill consequences. She had found, tho' not under the same roof, a very snug apartment belonging to Mr. Francis, and which had escaped the mop by his wife's being satisfied it could not possibly be visited by gentlefolks.

THIS was a dry, warm, oaken floored barn,[163] lined on both sides with wheaten straw, and opening at one end into a green field, and a beautiful prospect. Here, without hesitation, she ordered the cloth to be laid, and came hastily to snatch me from worse perils by water than the common dangers of the sea.

MRS. FRANCIS, who could not trust her own ears, or could not believe a footman in so extraordinary a phænomenon, followed my wife, and asked her if she had indeed ordered the cloth to be laid in the barn: she answered in the affirmative; upon which Mrs. Francis declared she would not dispute her pleasure, but it was the first time, she believed, that quality had ever preferred a barn to a house. She shewed at the same time the most pregnant marks of contempt, and again lamented the labour she had undergone, through her ignorance of the absurd taste of her guests.

AT length we were seated in one of the most pleasant spots, I believe, in the kingdom, and were regaled with our beans and bacon,[164] in which there was nothing deficient but the quantity. This defect was, however, so deplorable, that we had consumed our whole dish, before we had visibly lessened our hunger. We now waited with impatience the arrival of our second course, which necessity and not luxury had dictated. This was a joint of mutton which Mrs. Francis had been ordered to provide; but when being tired with expectation, we ordered our servants *to see for something*

---

[163] Richardson's correspondent of dubious authority declared HF's barn to be 'a fiction' (above, p. 595 n. 157).

[164] HF relished a meal of beans and bacon: in a facetious letter to James Harris, who was honeymooning at Dibden, Southampton Water, he promised to pay the couple a visit if tempted by 'some Bacon & Beans & a Bottle of Southampton Port' (*Correspondence*, Letter 24, p. 50). Harris indulged his friend's appetite by sending HF presents of chines of bacon (Letters 27 and 56).

else, were informed that there was nothing else; on which Mrs. Francis being summoned, declared there was no such thing as mutton to be had at Ryde. When I expressed some astonishment at their having no butcher in a village so situated, she answered they had a very good one, and one that killed all sorts of meat in season, beef two or three times a year, and mutton the whole year round; but that it being then beans and pease time, he killed no meat, by reason he was sure of not selling it. This she had not thought worthy of communication, any more than that there lived a fisherman at next door, who was then provided with plenty of soals, and whitings, and lobsters, far superior to those which adorn a city-feast. This discovery being made by accident, we completed the best, the pleasantest, and the merriest meal, with more appetite, more real, solid luxury, and more festivity, than was ever seen in an entertainment at White's.[165]

IT may be wondered at, perhaps, that Mrs. Francis should be so negligent of providing for her guests, as she may seem to be thus inattentive to her own interest: but this was not the case; for having clapt a poll-tax on our heads at our arrival, and determined at what price to discharge our bodies from her house, the less she suffered any other to share in the levy, the clearer it came into her own pocket; and it was better to get twelve pence in a shilling than ten-pence, which latter would be the case if she afforded us fish at any rate.

THUS we past a most agreeable day, owing to good appetites and good humour; two hearty feeders, which will devour with satisfaction whatever food you place before them: whereas without these, the elegance of St. James's, the charde, the perigord-pye, or the ortolan, the venison, the turtle, or the custard,[166] may titillate the throat, but will never convey happiness to the heart, or cheerfulness to the countenance.

As the wind appeared still immoveable, my wife proposed my lying on shore. I presently agreed, tho' in defiance of an act of parliament, by which persons wandering abroad, and lodging in alehouses, are decreed to be rogues and vagabonds; and this too after having been very singularly officious in putting that law in execution.[167]

---

[165] Founded in 1693, White's Chocolate House, in St James's Street near the Palace, was frequented by fashionable gamesters (Lillywhite, No. 1511). HF refers to it in a similar context in *Tom Jones* (XIII. vi, p. 710) and *Amelia* (III. x, p. 139; VIII. x, p. 346).

[166] HF names six dishes, three each associated with, first, the fashionable dining places of St James's in the West End: *charde* (or chard, the heart of artichoke), *perigord-pye* (a meat pie flavoured with truffles from France), and *ortolan* (a small bird considered a delicacy, as in *Tom Jones* [VII. vi, p. 346]); and next, the heartier fare favoured by aldermen of the City on such occasions as Lord Mayor's Day: *venison*, *turtle* from the West Indies, as in *Tom Jones* (I. i, p. 32 and nn. 1–2), and *custard*.

[167] HF refers to the Vagrant Act of 1744 (17 Geo. II, c. 4), entitled 'An Act to amend and make more effective the laws relating to rogues, vagabonds, and other idle and disorderly persons, and to houses of

MY wife, having reconnoitred the house, reported, that there was one
room in which were two beds. It was concluded, therefore, that she and
Harriet should occupy one, and myself take possession of the other. She
added likewise an ingenious recommendation of this room, to one who had
so long been in a cabin, which it exactly resembled, as it was sunk down
with age on one side, and was in the form of a ship with gunnels to.[168]

FOR my own part I make little doubt but this apartment was an ancient
temple, built with the materials of a wreck, and, probably, dedicated to
Neptune, in honour of THE BLESSING [169] sent by him to the inhabitants,
such blessings having, in all ages, been very common to them. The timber
employed in it confirms this opinion, being such as is seldom used by any
but ship-builders. I do not find, indeed, any mention of this matter in
Hern;[170] but, perhaps, its antiquity was too modern to deserve his notice.
Certain it is that this island of Wight was not an early convert to christianity;
nay, there is some reason to doubt whether it was ever entirely converted.[171]
But I have only time to touch slightly on things of this kind, which, luckily
for us, we have a society[172] whose peculiar profession it is to discuss and
develop.

Sunday, July 14.[173] THIS morning early I summoned Mrs. Francis, in
order to pay her the preceding day's account. As I could recollect only two
or three articles, I thought there was no necessity of pen and ink. In a single
instance only we had exceeded what the law allows gratis to a foot soldier
on his march, viz. vinegar, salt, &c. and dressing his meat. I found, however,
I was mistaken in my calculation; for when the good woman attended with
her bill, it contained as follows.

correction' (*Enquiry*, p. 137 n. 6). HF devotes section VI of the *Enquiry* to discussing the '*Laws relating to*
VAGABONDS', where (under article 12 of the 2nd 'Degree') Persons offending by 'Wandering abroad and
lodging in Ale-houses, Barns, Out-houses, or in the open Air, not giving a good Account of themselves . . .
are to be deemed Rogues and Vagabonds' (pp. 141–2); Zirker (*Enquiry*, p. 141 n. 6) cites the relevancy of
the present passage in the *Journal*. See also below, nn. 192 and 209.

[168] 'gunnels to': gunwale (or gunnel), the upper edge of a ship's side; the expression 'gunnels to' means
the gunwale is on a level with the water (*OED*, 'gunwale' b).

[169] See above, pp. 589–90.

[170] Thomas Hearne (1678–1735), Oxford antiquary. The auction catalogue of HF's library lists no
fewer than fifteen editions of Hearne's antiquarian chronicles (Ribbles, p. xix n. 34 and p. lii n. 36), among
the learned productions that earned him a place as the pedant 'Wormius' in Pope's *Dunciad* (1729),
iii. 184–90.

[171] Cf. Dr Harrison in *Amelia* (IX. v), who regrets that the adulterous Colonel James hadn't the benefit
of living 'in a Christian Society, which I no more esteem this Nation to be, than I do any Part of *Turky*'
(p. 375).

[172] i.e. the Society of Antiquaries (above, n. 95).

[173] On the curious inconsistencies of HF's dating of the journal entries from this point on, see the
Textual Notes (Appendix B.2, page 720: 600.19).

		l.	s.	d.
Bread and beer	—	0	2	4
Wind	—	0	2	0
Rum	—	0	2	0
Dressing dinner	—	0	3	0
Tea	—	0	1	6
Firing	—	0	1	0
Lodging	—	0	1	6
Servants lodging	—	0	0	6
	£	0	13	10

Now that four people,[174] and two servants should live a day and night at a public house for so small a sum, will appear incredible to any person in London above the degree of a chimney-sweeper; but more astonishing will it seem, that these people should remain so long at such a house, without tasting any other delicacy than bread, small beer, a tea cup full of milk called cream, a glass of rum converted into punch by their own materials, and one bottle of *wind*,[175] of which we only tasted a single glass, tho' possibly, indeed, our servants drank the remainder of the bottle.

THIS *wind* is a liquor of English manufacture, and its flavour is thought very delicious by the generality of the English, who drink it in great quantities. Every seventh year is thought to produce as much as the other six. It is then drank so plentifully, that the whole nation are in a manner intoxicated by it, and consequently, very little business is carried on at that season.[176]

IT resembles in colour the red wine, which is imported from Portugal,[177] as it doth in its intoxicating quality; hence, and from this agreement in the orthography, the one is often confounded with the other, tho' both are

---

[174] 'four': emended from 'five': the 'people' in HF's party were himself, his wife, his daughter Harriet, and Margaret Collier; the 'servants' were William Aldrit and Isabella Ash. Later, in a slightly less discriminatory spirit, he writes 'six persons, (two of them servants)' (p. 640).

[175] '*wind*': a strong liquor, probably rum or gin (Partridge). In Sarah Fielding's *Familiar Letters*, Letter XLI, HF's Frenchman devotes a paragraph to expressing his puzzlement over the nature of '*Wind*', which the English 'relish' (above, p. 495). And in *Amelia* (II. ix) the Keeper of Newgate boasts of the fine fare to be had in his prison for money: 'I shan't turn my Back to any of the Taverns for either eatables or Wind' (p. 95).

[176] By the Septennial Act of 1715 (1 Geo. II, 2 c. 38) general elections were to be held every seven years. HF would have had fresh in mind the drunken excesses of the election held in the spring of 1754, vividly depicted in plate 1 ('An Election Entertainment') of his friend Hogarth's series *An Election* (1754). On HF's treatment of the Septennial Act, see *New Essays*, pp. 3–7.

[177] In his letter of 22 July to John from Torbay, Devon, HF recalls that his brother is 'a Lover of [cider] when mixed with a Proper Number of Middx Turneps, as you are of Port-Wind well mixed likewise' (below, Appendix C.3, Letter 2).

seldom esteemed by the same person. It is to be had in every parish of the kingdom, and a pretty large quantity is consumed in the metropolis, where several taverns are set apart solely for the vendition of this liquor, the masters never dealing in any other.

THE disagreement in our computation produced some small remonstrance to Mrs. Francis on my side; but this received an immediate answer, 'She scorned to overcharge gentlemen: her house had been always frequented by the very best gentry of the island; and she had never had a bill found fault with in her life, tho' she had lived upwards of forty years in the house, and within that time the greatest gentry in Hampshire had been at it, and that Lawyer Willis[178] never went to any other, when he came to those parts. That for her part she did not get her livelihood by travellers, who were gone and away, and she never expected to see them more, but that her neighbours might come again; wherefore, to be sure, that had the only right to complain.'

SHE was proceeding thus, and from her volubility of tongue seemed likely to stretch the discourse to an immoderate length, when I suddenly cut all short by paying the bill.

THIS morning our ladies went to church, more, I fear, from curiosity than religion; they were attended by the captain in a most military attire, with his cockade in his hat, and his sword by his side. So unusual an appearance in this little chappel drew the attention of all present, and, probably, disconcerted the women, who were in dishabille,[179] and wished themselves drest, for the sake of the curate, who was the greatest of their beholders.

WHILE I was left alone I received a visit from Mr. Francis himself, who was much more considerable as a farmer, than as an innholder. Indeed he left the latter entirely to the care of his wife, and he acted wisely, I believe, in so doing.

AS nothing more remarkable past on this day, I will close it with the account of these two characters, as far as a few days residence could inform me of them. If they should appear as new to the reader as they did to me, he will not be displeased at finding them here.

---

[178] In colloquial use 'Lawyer' was often limited to attorneys and solicitors (*OED*, s.v. 'lawyer'); cf. 'Lawyer *Scout*' in *Joseph Andrews* (IV. iii), 'one of those Fellows, who without any Knowledge of the Law ... take upon them ... to act as Lawyers [i.e. attorneys] in the Country, and are called so' (p. 286); and 'Lawyer *Murphy*' in *Amelia* (XII. vi, p. 519). Hence HF is probably not, as Keymer suggests, (*Fielding's Journal*, s.v. '*Sunday, July 14*', p. 129, n. 3), referring to Sir John Willes (1685–1761), Chief Justice of Common Pleas, or his son Edward Willes, MP, KC, neither of them Hampshire gentry; more likely, perhaps, is James Willis of Ringwood, Hampshire, an attorney and one of the subscribers to HF's *Miscellanies* (*Miscellanies* iii, p. 349).

[179] 'dishabille': Anglicized form of French '*en déshabillé*', dressed in a negligent or careless style (*OED*).

THIS amiable couple seemed to border hard on their grand climacteric;[180] nor indeed were they shy of owning enough to fix their ages within a year or two of that time. They appeared to be rather proud of having employed their time well, than ashamed of having lived so long; the only reason which I could ever assign, why some fine ladies, and fine gentlemen too, should desire to be thought younger than they really are by the cotemporaries of their grand children. Some, indeed, who too hastily credit appearances, might doubt whether they had made so good a use of their time as I would insinuate, since there was no appearance of any thing but poverty, want, and wretchedness about their house; nor could they produce any thing to a customer in exchange for his money, but a few bottles of *wind*, and spirituous liquors, and some very bad ale, to drink; with rusty bacon and worse cheese to eat. But then it should be considered, on the other side, that whatever they received was almost as entirely clear profit as the blessing of a wreck itself; such an inn being the very reverse of a coffee-house: for here you can neither sit for nothing, nor have any thing for your money.

AGAIN, as many marks of want abounded every where, so were the marks of antiquity visible. Scarce any thing was to be seen which had not some scar upon it, made by the hand of time; not an utensil, it was manifest, had been purchased within a dozen years last past; so that whatever money had come into the house during that period, at least, must have remained in it, unless it had been sent abroad for food, or other perishable commodities; but these were supplied by a small portion of the fruits of the farm, in which the farmer allowed he had a very good bargain. In fact, it is inconceivable what sums may be collected by starving only, and how easy it is for a man to die rich, if he will but be contented to live miserable.

NOR is there in this kind of starving any thing so terrible as some apprehend. It neither wastes a man's flesh, nor robs him of his cheerfulness. The famous Cornaro's case[181] well proves the contrary, and so did farmer Francis, who was of a round stature, had a plump round face, with a kind of

---

[180] 'grand climacteric': the climacterics were thought to be critical stages of life occurring every seven or nine years. In HF's understanding, the former interval applied: in *Joseph Andrews* (IV. vii) girls 'the Age of fourteen or fifteen' have reached their 'second Climacteric' (p. 300); the 'grand Climacteric'—also referred to in *A Journey from This World to the Next* (I. xvi), where Julian as a foolish wise man reaches his 'grand Climacteric' (*Miscellanies* ii, p. 70)—occurred at age 63.

[181] Luigi Cornaro of Venice (1467–1566), author of *Trattato della vita sobria* (Padua, 1558), translated into English by W. Jones as *Sure and certain Methods of attaining a long and healthful Life* (1702; 2nd edn., 1711). Noting the attention paid the work by 'several Eminent Authors', Addison in *The Spectator*, No. 195 (13 October 1711), calls Cornaro's story 'the most remarkable Instance of the Efficacy of Temperance towards the procuring of long Life' (ed. Bond [Oxford, 1965], ii, pp. 266–7). The case of 'The famous LEWIS CORNARO', who 'liv'd 104 Years sound in Body and Mind by pure Regimen', is among those featured in the *History of Long Livers* (1722), translated from the French of Harcouet de Longeville (*c.*1660–1720), a copy of which was in HF's library (Ribbles H6).

smile on it, and seemed to borrow an air of wretchedness, rather from his coat's age, than from his own.

THE truth is, there is a certain diet which emaciates men more than any possible degree of abstinence; tho' I do not remember to have seen any caution against it, either in Cheney, Arbuthnot, or in any other modern writer on regimen.[182] Nay, the very name is not, I believe, in the learned Dr. James's dictionary;[183] all which is the more extraordinary, as it is a very common food in this kingdom, and the college themselves[184] were not long since very liberally entertained with it, by the present attorney and other eminent lawyers, in Lincoln's-inn hall, and were all made horribly sick by it.[185]

BUT though it should not be found among our English physical writers, we may be assured of meeting with it among the Greeks; for nothing considerable in nature escapes their notice; though many things considerable in them, it is to be feared, have escaped the notice of their readers. The Greeks then, to all such as feed too voraciously on this diet give the name of HEAUTOFAGI,[186] which our physicians will, I suppose, translate men that eat themselves.

As nothing is so destructive to the body as this kind of food, so nothing is so plentiful and cheap; but it was perhaps the only cheap thing the farmer

---

[182]   George Cheyne (1671–1743), physician of Bath and author of several treatises on regimen advocating an abstemious vegetarian diet. In *Tom Jones* (XI. viii, p. 605) HF alludes to his diatribe against punch in *An Essay on Health and Long Life* (1724; 10th edn., 1745). In *The Champion* (15 November 1739, 17 May, 12, 24 June 1740) Cheyne is tried for murdering the English language in his *Essay on Regimen* (1739). John Arbuthnot (1667–1735), physician to Queen Anne and, with Swift, Pope, and Gay, a member of the Scriblerus Club satirized by HF in his unfinished 'Cantos' (above, p. 59 n. 101). Here HF refers to Arbuthnot's *Essay concerning the Nature of Aliments, and the Choice of them, according to the different Constitutions of Human Bodies* (1731–2: with *Practical Rules of Diet*).

[183]   Robert James (1705–76), physician, whom HF, while puffing James's celebrated powder for the treatment of fevers in the first edition of *Amelia* (VIII. ix), calls 'my worthy and ingenious Friend' (p. 346). He was author of *A Medicinal Dictionary* (1743–5).

[184]   The Royal College of Physicians, founded in 1518 and situated in the eighteenth century in Warwick Lane.

[185]   In 1746 Dr Isaac Schomberg (1714–80; *Oxford DNB*) had applied for admission to the College of Physicians, but was denied on the grounds of his 'character' (he was a Jew), and for having made 'indecent' remarks. William Murray of Lincoln's Inn (1705–93) was appointed Attorney-General on 9 April 1754. Earlier, in 1751, as Solicitor-General and soon to become Lord Mansfield, Murray had presented Schomberg's appeal to the Lord Chancellor; but in Lincoln's Inn Hall, in July 1753, the Chancellor decided he had no jurisdiction over the case (William Browne, *A Vindication of the Royal College of Physicians* [1753]; *Daily Advertiser* [27 July 1753]). *The Battiad* (1750) by Moses Mendes (d. 1758), a mock-epic satire of the College of Physicians and William Battie in particular, attests to the notoriety of the dispute. Schomberg was finally admitted to the College in 1765. That he was Hogarth's close friend and physician may account for HF's sympathetic interest in the matter.

[186]   In Greek 'the self-eaters', HF's coinage, in this context a metaphor for those who are notable for consuming self-love and self-serving ambition. Perhaps inverting *Othello* (I. iii. 143–4) 'Cannibals that each other eat, | The Anthropophagi'. With the opening of the next paragraph—'nothing is so destructive to the body as this kind of food'—cf. *Julius Caesar* (I. ii. 194), the effect of pride and ambition on Cassius, who 'has a lean and hungry look'.

disliked. Probably living much on fish might produce this disgust; for Diodorus Siculus attributes the same aversion in a people of Æthiopia to the same cause: he calls them the fish-eaters; and asserts, that they cannot be brought to eat a single meal with the Heautofagi by any persuasion, threat, or violence whatever, not even though they should kill their children before their faces.[187]

WHAT hath puzzled our physicians, and prevented them from setting this matter in the clearest light, is possibly one simple mistake, arising from a very excusable ignorance; that the passions of men are capable of swallowing food as well as their appetites; that the former, in feeding resemble the state of those animals who chew the cud; and therefore, such men, in some sense, may be said to prey on themselves, and as it were, to devour their own entrails. And hence ensues a meagre aspect, and thin habit of body,[188] as surely as from what is called a consumption.

OUR farmer was one of these.[189] He had no more passion than an Ichthuofagus or Ethiopian fish-eater. He wished not for any thing, thought not of any thing; indeed he scarce did any thing, or said any thing. Here I cannot be understood strictly; for then I must describe a non-entity, whereas I would rob him of nothing but that free-agency which is the cause of all the corruption, and of all the misery of human nature. No man, indeed, ever did more than the farmer, for he was an absolute slave to labour all the week; but in truth, as my sagacious reader must have at first apprehended, when I said, he resigned the care of the house to his wife, I meant more than I then expressed; even the house and all that belonged to it; for he was really a farmer, only under the direction of his wife. In a word, so composed, so serene, so placid a countenance, I never saw; and he satisfied himself by answering to every question he was asked; 'I don't know any thing about it, Sir, I leaves all that to my wife.'

NOW as a couple of this kind would, like two vessels of oil, have made no composition in life, and for want of all savour must have palled every taste; nature, or fortune, or both of them, took care to provide a proper quantity of acid, in the materials that formed the wife, and to render her a perfect

---

[187] In *Bibliotheca Historica*, Diodorus Siculus (*fl.* *c.*60–21 BC) refers to the Ethiopians as 'fish-eaters' (*ichthyophagi*), whose characteristic was apathy: 'when at times their children or women were butchered before their eyes, they remained "insensible" in their attitudes, displaying no sign of anger or, on the other hand, of pity' (III. xv–xviii). HF frequently refers to Diodorus in *The Covent-Garden Journal*, where in No. 11 (8 February 1752) he calls him 'that great Penetrator into the Fogs of Antiquity' (p. 82), and in No. 66 (14 October 1752) offers another of Diodorus' illustrations of the insensibility of the Ethiopians (pp. 348–9). For HF's personal copy of the *Bibliotheca* in Greek and Latin (1604), see Ribbles D18.

[188] Cf. Cassius' 'lean and hungry look' (above, n. 186).

[189] 'one of these': 'these' here meaning 'the latter' (*OED*, 'these' B. I. 2), i.e. those who fed their 'appetites' not, like the 'Heautofagi', their 'passions'. The 'Humphrys' edition treats this as a misprint, emending to 'none of these'.

Help-mate[190] for so tranquil a husband. She abounded in whatsoever he was defective; that is to say, in almost every thing. She was indeed as vinegar to oil, or a brisk wind to a standing-pool, and preserved all from stagnation and corruption.

QUIN the player,[191] on taking a nice and severe survey of a fellow-comedian, burst forth into this exclamation, 'If that fellow be not a rogue, God Almighty doth not write a legible hand.' Whether he guessed right or no, is not worth my while to examine. Certain it is, that the latter having wrought his features into a proper harmony to become the characters of Iago, Shylock, and others of the same cast, gave a semblance of truth to the observation, that was sufficient to confirm the wit of it. Indeed, we may remark, in favour of the physiognomist, though the law hath made him a rogue and vagabond,[192] that nature is seldom curious in her works within; without employing some little pains on the outside;[193] and this more particularly in mischievous characters, in forming which, as Mr. Derham

---

[190] '*Help-mate*': perhaps italicized to emphasize the novelty of the word in the period (*OED* cites just two previous examples, 1715 and 1722), as a substitute for *helpmeet*, a term based on a misreading of Genesis 2: 18, where Eve is created as 'an help meet for' Adam.

[191] James Quin (1693–1766), the leading actor before the emergence of Garrick in 1741; he played Mondish in HF's *Universal Gallant* (1735). The two were good friends, and compliments to Quin appear in *The Champion* (9 September 1740), p. 455, where HF tried unsuccessfully to promote him for the position of manager at Drury Lane; in *Joseph Andrews* (III. x, p. 262), *Miscellanies* (i, pp. 53, 136), *The Jacobite's Journal*, No. 10 (6 February 1748), p. 153, and *The Covent-Garden Journal*, No 26 (31 March 1752), p. 167—in *CGJ*, No. 62 (16 September 1752), p. 336, HF recalls one of the witticisms for which his friend was known (see *Quin's Jests* [1766]).

In the present passage, the butt of Quin's wit was another of HF's theatrical chums, Charles Macklin (1697–1797), who acted in several of HF's plays. Macklin's '*good long, dismal, Mercy-begging Face*', as he himself called it in the Prologue to HF's *The Wedding Day* (1743; *Miscellanies* ii, p. 155), was a standing jest in theatrical circles, as witness the player in *Joseph Andrews* (III. x), for whom Macklin is an 'ill-looked Dog' (p. 262). In *Tom Jones* (VII. i, p. 329 and n. 1) HF obliquely alludes to a critical controversy in which Macklin's face, which everyone acknowledged was made for the role of Shylock, was deemed too ugly to allow him to play that of 'honest Iago'. In 1752 Macklin played HF in an entertainment called *Pasquin Turn'd Drawcansir*, a role in which he playfully celebrated HF's efforts as magistrate and author of *The Covent-Garden Journal* to extirpate the follies of the town. For another reference to Quin and Macklin, see below, pp. 634–5 and nn. 268, 270.

[192] Among those declared to be 'idle and disorderly' in the 2nd degree under the Vagrant Act of 1744 were 'Persons . . . Pretending to Physiognomy, or like crafty Science, &c.' See above, p. 599 n. 167.

[193] Among popular authors of the period, HF made the subject of physiognomy distinctively his own. From the Preface to the *Tragedy of Tragedies* (1731) to this present passage, it was a topic he returned to again and again, though he considered it most attentively in his 'Essay on the Knowledge of the Characters or Men': 'Nature doth really imprint sufficient Marks in the Countenance, to inform an accurate and discerning Eye' (*Miscellanies* i, p. 161). Cf. also *Joseph Andrews* (II. xvii): 'Nature generally imprints such a Portraiture of the Mind in the Countenance, that a skilful Physiognomist will rarely be deceived' (p. 182). For discussion of HF's interest in physiognomy, see *Essays*, pp. 192–4; Battestin, 'Four New Attributions', pp. 94–101, and '*Universal Spectator*', pp. 110–16, for two facetious essays on the topic attributed to HF.

observes,[194] in venomous insects, as the sting or saw of a wasp, she is some-times wonderfully industrious. Now, when she hath thus completely armed her hero, to carry on a war with man, she never fails of furnishing that innocent lambkin with some means of knowing his enemy, and foreseeing his designs. Thus she hath been observed to act in the case of a rattle-snake, which never meditates a human prey without giving warning of his approach.

THIS observation will, I am convinced, hold most true, if applied to the most venomous individuals of human insects. A tyrant, a trickster, and a bully, generally wear the marks of their several dispositions in their countenances; so do the vixen, the shrew, the scold, and all other females of the like kind. But, perhaps, nature had never afforded a stronger example of all this, than in the case of Mrs. Francis. She was a short, squat woman; her head was closely joined to her shoulders, where it was fixed somewhat awry; every feature of her countenance was sharp and pointed; her face was furrowed with the small-pox; and her complexion, which seemed to be able to turn milk to curds, not a little resembled in colour such milk as had already undergone that operation. She appeared indeed to have many symptoms of a deep jaundice in her look; but the strength and firmness of her voice over-balanced them all; the tone of this was a sharp treble at a distance, for, I seldom heard it on the same floor; but was usually waked with it in the morning, and entertained with it almost continually through the whole day.

THOUGH vocal be usually put in opposition to instrumental music; I question whether this might not be thought to partake of the nature of both; for she played on two instruments, which she seemed to keep for no other use from morning till night; these were two maids, or rather scolding-stocks, who, I suppose, by some means or other, earned their board, and she gave them their lodging gratis, or for no other service than to keep her lungs in constant exercise.

SHE differed, as I have said, in every particular from her husband; but very remarkably in this, that as it was impossible to displease him, so it was

---

[194] In his *Physico-Theology* (1713), a then well-known teleological argument for the being and attributes of God from the evidence of design in the creation, William Derham DD (1657–1735) wrote of the 'pretty Mechanism in the Sting' of wasps and bees (IV. xiv). Keymer notes (*Fielding's Journal*, s.v. 'Sunday, July 14', p. 131 n. 14) that HF has in mind Derham's argument that 'although the infinitely wise Creator hath put it in the Power of such vile Animals to chastise us, yet hath he shewed no less Wisdom and Kindness in ordering many, if not most of them so, as that it shall be in the Power of Man, and other Creatures to obviate or escape their Evils . . . Thus, for Instance, the *Rattle-Snake*, the most poisonous of any Serpent . . . involuntarily gives Warning by the Rattle in its Tail' (II. vi). Derham was represented in HF's library among the distinguished company of Boyle lecturers collected in *A Defence of natural and revealed Religion*, 3 vols (1739) (Ribbles D9). See also below, p. 636 n. 271.

as impossible to please her; and as no art could remove a smile from his countenance, so could no art carry it into hers. If her bills were remonstrated against, she was offended with the censure of her fair-dealing; if they were not, she seemed to regard it as a tacit sarcasm on her folly, which might have set down larger prices with the same success. On this latter hint she did indeed improve; for she daily raised some of her articles. A pennyworth of fire was to-day rated at a shilling, to-morrow at eighteen-pence; and if she drest us two dishes for two shillings on the Saturday, we paid half a crown for the cookery of one on the Sunday; and wherever she was paid, she never left the room without lamenting the small amount of her bill; saying, she knew not how it was that others got their money by gentlefolks, but for her part she had not the art of it. When she was asked, why she complained, when she was paid all she demanded, she answered, she could not deny that, nor did she know she omitted any thing, but that it was but a poor bill for gentlefolks to pay.

I ACCOUNTED for all this by her having heard, that it is a maxim with the principal innholders on the continent,[195] to levy considerable sums on their guests, who travel with many horses and servants, though such guests should eat little or nothing in their houses. The method being, I believe, in such cases, to lay a capitation on the horses, and not on their masters.[196] But she did not consider, that in most of these inns a very great degree of hunger, without any degree of delicacy, may be satisfied; and that in all such inns there is some appearance, at least, of provision, as well as of a man cook to dress it, one of the hostlers being always furnished with a cook's cap, waistecoat and apron, ready to attend gentlemen and ladies on their summons; that the case therefore of such inns differed from hers, where there was nothing to eat or to drink; and in reality no house to inhabit, no chair to sit upon, nor any bed to lie in; that one third or fourth part therefore of the levy imposed at inns was in truth a higher tax than the whole was when laid on in the other, where, in order to raise a small sum, a man is obliged to submit to pay as many various ways for the same thing as he doth to the government, for the light which enters through his own window[197] into his own house, from his own estate; such are the articles of bread and beer, firing, eating, and dressing dinner.

---

[195] On the likelihood that HF took advantage of his time at the University of Leiden in 1729 to tour France and Italy, see *Life*, pp. 73–6.

[196] Cf. *Tom Jones* (VIII. vii), where HF discloses 'some Maxims, which Publicans hold to be the grand Mysteries of their Trade', the last of which being: 'if any of their Guests call but for little, to make them pay a double Price for every Thing they have; so that the Amount by the Head may be much the same' (p. 429).

[197] By a statute of 1747 (20 Geo. II, c. 3) which revised the old law of 1696, a tax was levied on 'every Window or Light, in every Dwelling-house', the rates varying (6*d.*, 9*d.*, or 1*s.*) according to the number of windows. To avoid the heavier levy, 'Humphry Gubbins' in *The Jacobite's Journal*, No. 11 (13 February

THE foregoing is a very imperfect sketch of this extraordinary couple; for every thing is here lowered instead of being heightened. Those who would see them set forth in more lively colours, and with the proper ornaments, may read the descriptions of the furies in some of the classical poets, or of the stoic philosophers in the works of Lucian.[198]

Monday, July 15. THIS day nothing remarkable passed; Mrs. Francis levied a tax of fourteen shillings for the Sunday. We regaled ourselves at dinner with venison and good claret of our own; and, in the afternoon, the women, attended by the Captain, walked to see a delightful scene two miles distant, with the beauties of which they declared themselves most highly charmed at their return, as well as with the goodness of the lady of the mansion,[199] who had slipt out of the way, that my wife and her company might refresh themselves with the flowers and fruits with which her garden abounded.

Tuesday, July 16. THIS day, having paid our taxes of yesterday, we were permitted to regale ourselves with more venison. Some of this we would willingly have exchanged for mutton; but no such flesh was to be had nearer than Portsmouth, from whence it would have cost more to convey a joint to us, than the freight of a Portugal ham from Lisbon to London amounts to: for tho' the water-carriage be somewhat cheaper here than at Deal, yet can you find no waterman who will go on board his boat, unless by two or three hours rowing he can get drunk for the residue of the week.

AND here I have an opportunity which possibly may not offer again, of

1748) declares: 'I put out one haf of my Windows last Year, and if there comes another Ile put out t'other haf.—D—n me a Man may drink in the Dark' (pp. 157–8). In *Tom Jones* (VII. xiii) the landlady and her husband choose the same course: 'we have stopt up all we could; we have almost blinded the House I am sure' (p. 380). In 1748 this loophole was closed, however, by 21 Geo. II, c. 10.

[198] The avenging Furies figure notably in the *Oresteia* (458 BC) of Aeschylus; they later were called by the names Allecto, Megaera, and Tisiphone. Lucian of Samosata (*c.*120–180): among the number of his satirical dialogues ridiculing the presumption of philosophers are *Vitarum aucto* ('The Sale of Lives') and *Icaromenippus*. For HF, Lucian, 'the Father of true Humour', as he called him, together with Swift and Cervantes comprised the 'great Triumvirate' of comic authors who endeavoured 'to expose and extirpate those Follies and Vices which chiefly prevailed in their several Countries' (*Covent-Garden Journal*, No. 10 [4 February 1752], p. 74). See also Booth's panegyric on Lucian in *Amelia* (VIII. v). HF had in his library no fewer than nine editions and translations of Lucian (Ribbles L26–34); and in *The Covent-Garden Journal*, No. 52 (30 June 1752) he announced his intention (abortive as it proved) to collaborate with his friend the classicist William Young on a new translation: 'no Man', HF declared referring to himself, 'seems so likely to translate an Author well, as he who hath formed his Stile upon that very Author' (pp. 288–9). On HF and Lucian, see *Essays*, pp. 365–419.

[199] Ann Roberts (d. 1781), a widow, who lived with her two daughters at Great Appley in the parish of St Helens. Her seat was 'a small elegant place, situated about a quarter of a mile from Ride. From the house and garden, the road at Spithead and the town of Portsmouth appear to the greatest advantage' (Worsely, *History of the Isle of Wight* [1781], p. 200). When Margaret Collier settled at Ryde after returning from Lisbon, she wrote Samuel Richardson of her 'good friends at Appley ... Mrs. Roberts, and her amiable daughters' (3 October 1755, Richardson *Correspondence*, ed. A. L. Barbauld [1804], ii, p. 74). (Keymer [*Fielding's Journal*, s.v. '*Monday, July 15*, p. 131 n. 1; abridged].)

publishing some observations on that political oeconomy of this nation, which, as it concerns only the regulation of the mob,[200] is below the notice of our great men; tho', on the due regulation of this order depend many emoluments which the great men themselves, or, at least, many who tread close on their heels, may enjoy, as well as some dangers, which may some time or other arise from introducing a pure state of anarchy among them. I will represent the case as it appears to me very fairly and impartially between the mob and their betters.

THE whole mischief which infects this part of our oeconomy, arises from the vague and uncertain use of a word called Liberty,[201] of which, as scarce any two men with whom I have ever conversed, seem to have one and the same idea, I am inclined to doubt whether there be any simple universal notion represented by this word, or whether it conveys any clearer or more determinate idea, than some of those old punic compositions of syllables, preserved in one of the comedies of Plautus,[202] but at present, as I conceive, not supposed to be understood by any one.

BY liberty, however, I apprehend, is commonly understood the power of doing what we please: not absolutely; for then it would be inconsistent with law, by whose control the liberty of the freest people, except only the Hottentots and wild Indians,[203] must always be restrained.

BUT, indeed, however largely we extend, or however moderately we confine the sense of the word, no politician will, I presume, contend that it is to pervade in an equal degree, and be with the same extent enjoyed by every member of society; no such polity having been ever found, unless

---

[200] Historically the three Estates were the lords spiritual, the lords temporal, and the commons (*OED*, s.v. 'estate' 6). HF, however, repeating a definition he offered in *The Champion* (6 November 1740), pp. 503–4, remarks in *The Covent-Garden Journal*, No. 47 (13 June 1752), that the polity consisted of 'three Estates namely, King, Lords, and Commons', to which he adds another: 'that very large and powerful Body which form the fourth Estate . . . long dignified and distinguished by the Name of THE MOB' (p. 259 and n. 4). In *Tom Jones* (XII. i) he had defined them as 'the Poor . . . that large and venerable Body which, in *England* we call The Mob', of whom it is 'one of their established Maxims, to plunder and pillage their rich Neighbours' (p. 620).

[201] In *The Covent-Garden Journal*, No. 49 (20 June 1752) HF continued his remarks on the 'fourth Estate' (the mob), concluding with a promise that he would treat 'the mistaken Idea which some particular Persons have always entertained of the Word Liberty . . . in a future Paper' (p. 273). It was not, however, until this present discussion of 'a word called Liberty' that he kept that promise. See also above, p. 569 and n. 88.

[202] Plautus, Titus Maccius (*c.*254–184 BC): in his *Poenulus* (*The Little Carthaginian*), Act V, the hero speaks some unintelligible lines of Punic. The Delphin edition of Plautus' comedies (1679) was in HF's library (Ribbles P26).

[203] 'Hottentots': a primitive South African race who came to denote persons ignorant of the usages of civilized society (*OED*). Cf. *The Jacobite's Journal*, No. 16 (19 March 1748): that 'State of Nature which the *Hottentots*, and some other Nations [among whom, apparently, HF includes native Americans], live in at this Day; where every Man doeth what seemeth right in his own Eyes, and is at full Liberty to practise every Vice, and gratify all his Passions, without Disgrace or Controul' (p. 202); also *The Covent-Garden Journal*, No. 9 (1 February 1752), p. 67.

among those vile people just before commemorated. Among the Greeks and Romans, the servile and free conditions were opposed to each other; and no man who had the misfortune to be enrolled under the former, could lay any claim to liberty, 'till the right was conveyed to him by that master whose slave he was, either by the means of conquest, of purchase, or of birth.

THIS was the state of all the free nations in the world; and this, 'till very lately, was understood to be the case of our own.

I WILL not indeed say this is the case at present, the lowest class of our people having shaken off all the shackles of their superiors, and become not only as free, but even freer, than most of their superiors. I believe it cannot be doubted, tho' perhaps we have no recent instance of it, that the personal attendance of every man who hath 300 l. *per annum*, in parliament, is indispensably his duty;[204] and that, if the citizens and burgesses of any city or borough shall chuse such a one, however reluctant he appear, he may be obliged to attend, and be forcibly brought to his duty by the serjeant at arms.

AGAIN, there are numbers of subordinate offices, some of which are of burthen, and others of expence in the civil government: all of which, persons who are qualified, may be obliged to undertake and properly execute, notwithstanding any bodily labour, or even danger, to which they may subject themselves, under the penalty of fines and imprisonment; nay, and what may appear somewhat hard, may be compelled to satisfy the losses which are eventually incident to that of sheriff in particular,[205] out of their own private fortunes; and tho' this should prove the ruin of a family, yet the public, to whom the price is due, incurs no debt or obligation to preserve its officer harmless, let his innocence appear ever so clearly.

I PURPOSELY omit the mention of those military or militiary[206] duties, which our old constitution laid upon its greatest members.[207] These might,

---

[204] By 9 Anne, c. 5 (1710), MPs of cities, boroughs, or the Cinque Ports were required to have minimum incomes of £300 a year, and MPs of counties to have £600, excepting the eldest sons of peers and members for the two universities. HF next cites the procedure for enforcing attendance when the House was called (G[eorge] P[hilips], *Lex parliamentaria*, 2nd edn. [1734], p. 370). By two statutes, never repealed (5 Ric. II, 2, c. 4 [1382] and 6 Hen. VIII, c. 16 [1514–15]), absences were penalized.

[205] Blackstone, *Commentaries*, i, pp. 345–6; because of the expense, 'of late Years Persons of Great Fortune have declined this Office' (*TP*, No. 20 [18 March 1746], p. 241 and n. 6).

[206] 'militiary': HF's coinage. Since the Rebellion of the 'Forty-five', when a number of noblemen raised regiments of fencibles, there had been increased interest in a national militia, culminating in the Militia Act of 1757 (31 Geo. II, c. 26). See John R. Western, *The English Militia in the Eighteenth Century* (London, 1965), ch. 5; and *TP*, pp. xliv–xlv.

[207] Knight-service (Blackstone, *Commentaries*, ii, pp. 62–77), which with all its various feudal incidents was finally abolished by 12 Chas. II, c. 24 (1660). *The Champion* (12 April 1740), where HF alludes to the legal concept of 'Escuage' (p. 275), the accompanying note quoting Giles Jacon's *New Law Dictionary*: 'A kind of knight-service, called *service of the shield*, whereby the tenant was bound to follow his lord into the wars at his own charge' (p. 275 n. 4).

indeed, supply their posts with some other able-bodied men; but, if no such could have been found, the obligation nevertheless remained, and they were compellable to serve in their own proper persons.

THE only one, therefore, who is possessed of absolute liberty, is the lowest member of the society, who, if he prefers hunger or the wild product of the fields, hedges, lanes and rivers, with the indulgence of ease and laziness, to a food a little more delicate, but purchased at the expence of labour, may lay himself under a shade; nor can be forced to take the other alternative from that which he hath, I will not affirm whether wisely or foolishly, chosen.[208]

HERE I may, perhaps, be reminded of the last vagrant act,[209] where all such persons are compellable to work for the usual and accustomed wages allowed in the place; but this is a clause little known to the justices of the peace, and least likely to be executed by those who do know it, as they know likewise that it is formed on the antient power of the justices to fix and settle these wages every year, making proper allowances for the scarcity and plenty of the times, the cheapness and dearness of the place; and that *the usual and accustomed wages*, are words without any force or meaning, when there are no such;[210] but every man spunges and raps[211] whatever he can get; and will haggle as long and struggle as hard to cheat his employer of two pence in a day's labour, as an honest tradesman will to cheat his customers of the same sum in a yard of cloth or silk.

IT is a great pity then that this power, or rather this practice, was not revived; but this having been so long omitted, that it is become obsolete, will be best done by a new law,[212] in which this power, as well as the consequent power of forcing the poor to labour at a moderate and reasonable rate,

[208] In his *Proposal for Making an Effectual Provision for the Poor* (1753), HF recommended that magistrates be empowered to commit such idle persons to a 'County-House'—not the 'County-House of Correction', but a place he envisaged of such an enlightened design that he expected many of the unemployed to enter it voluntarily. The 'House' was to accommodate more than 3,000 men and 2,000 women, who were to be paid for producing certain 'Manufactures'. On HF's *Proposal*, see Malvin R. Zirker, *Fielding's Social Pamphlets* (Berkeley and Los Angeles, 1966), chs. III, VII; *Enquiry*, pp. lxxii–lxxvi; and *Life*, pp. 564–70.

[209] See above, p. 599 n. 167.

[210] By the Statute of Labourers (5 Eliz., c. 4, s. 11 [1562–3]), the County Quarter Sessions at Easter each year, 'respecting the Plentie or Scarcitie of the tyme, and other circumstances', were empowered to set wages; and by the Vagrancy Act of 1744 (above, p. 599 n. 167), persons refusing to work for 'the usual and common wages' were deemed vagrants (s. 1, slightly paraphrased in HF's text).

[211] 'spunges and raps': extorts and steals (*OED*, s.v. 'rap' v.³ obs.; citing this passage as its latest example).

[212] In the *Enquiry* (1751), HF remarked on the ineffectiveness of all previous legislative attempts to fix wages: 'so very faulty and remiss hath been the Execution of these Laws, that an incredulous Reader may almost doubt whether there are really any such existing. Particularly as to that which relates to the rating the Wages of Labourers; a Law which at first, it seems, was too carelessly executed, and which hath since grown into utter Neglect and Disuse' (p. 115 and n. 9).

should be well considered, and their execution facilitated: for gentlemen who give their time and labour gratis, and even voluntarily, to the public, have a right to expect that all their business be made as easy as possible; and to enact laws without doing this, is to fill our statute-books, much too full already, still fuller with dead letter, of no use but to the printer of the acts of parliament.[213]

THAT the evil which I have here pointed at is of itself worth redressing, is, I apprehend, no subject of dispute: for why should any persons in distress be deprived of the assistance of their fellow-subjects, when they are willing amply to reward them for their labour? or, why should the lowest of the people be permitted to exact ten times the value of their work? For those exactions encrease with the degrees of necessity in their object, insomuch that on the former side many are horribly imposed upon, and that often in no trifling matters. I was very well assured that at Deal no less than ten guineas was required, and paid by the supercargo[214] of an Indiaman, for carrying him on board two miles from the shore, when she was just ready to sail; so that his necessity, as his pillager well understood, was absolute. Again, many others who indignation will not submit to such plunder, are forced to refuse the assistance, tho' they are often great sufferers by so doing. On the latter side, the lowest of the people are encouraged in laziness and idleness; while they live by a twentieth part of the labour that ought to maintain them, which is diametrically opposite to the interest of the public; for that requires a great deal to be done, not to be paid, for a little. And moreover, they are confirm'd in habits of exaction, and are taught to consider the distresses of their superiors as their own fair emolument.

BUT enough of this matter, of which I at first intended only to convey a hint to those who are alone capable of applying the remedy, tho' they are the last to whom the notice of those evils would occur, without some such monitor as myself, who am forced to travel about the world in the form of a passenger. I cannot but say I heartily wish our governors would attentively consider this method of fixing the price of labour, and by that means of compelling the poor to work, since the due execution of such powers will, I apprehend, be found the true and only means of making them useful, and of advancing trade, from its present visibly declining state, to the height to

---

[213] Keymer (*Fielding's Journal*, s.v. '*Tuesday, July 16*, p. 132 n. 6) reads this, at first glance not implausibly, as 'another hit' at Samuel Richardson, printer of the *Journals of the House of Commons* and of individual bills—'the most lucrative branch of his business' (Eaves and Kimpel, p. 505). But HF refers to 'the printer of the acts of parliament'—i.e. printer of the *Statutes at Large*—who was Thomas Baskett (d. 1761), the King's Printer. Richardson did not acquire a share in this patent until 1760 (Eaves and Kimpel, p. 507).

[214] 'the supercargo': an officer on a merchant ship who superintends the cargo and commercial transactions of the voyage (*OED*, citing HF's *The Lottery* [1732]: 'as rich as a Supercargo').

which Sir William Petyt, in his Political Arithmetic,[215] thinks it capable of being carried.

IN the afternoon the lady of the above-mentioned mansion[216] called at our inn, and left her compliments to us with Mrs. Francis, with an assurance, that while we continued wind-bound in that place, where she feared we could be but indifferently accommodated, we were extremely welcome to the use of any thing which her garden or her house afforded. So polite a message convinced us, in spite of some arguments to the contrary, that we were not on the coast of Africa, or on some island where the few savage inhabitants have little of human in them besides their form.

AND here I mean nothing less than to derogate from the merit of this lady, who is not only extremely polite in her behaviour to strangers of her own rank, but so extremely good and charitable to all her poor neighbours, who stand in need of her assistance, that she hath the universal love and praises of all who live near her. But, in reality, how little doth the acquisition of so valuable a character, and the full indulgence of so worthy a disposition, cost those who possess it? Both are accomplished by the very offals which fall from a table moderately plentiful. That they are enjoyed therefore by so few, arises truly from there being so few who have any such disposition to gratify, or who aim at any such character.

Wednesday, July 17. THIS morning, after having been mulcted as usual, we dispatched a servant with proper acknowledgments of the lady's goodness; but confined our wants entirely to the productions of her garden. He soon returned, in company with the gardener, both richly laden with almost every particular which a garden at this most fruitful season of the year produces.

WHILE we were regaling ourselves with these, towards the close of our dinner, we received orders from our commander, who had dined that day with some inferior officers on board a man of war, to return instantly to the ship; for that the wind was become favourable, and he should weigh that evening. These orders were soon followed by the captain himself, who was still in the utmost hurry, tho' the occasion of it had long since ceased: for the wind had, indeed, a little shifted that afternoon, but was before this very quietly set down in its old quarters.

THIS last was a lucky hit for me: for, as the captain, to whose orders we resolved to pay no obedience, unless delivered by himself, did not return till

[215] Sir William Petty (1623–87), author of *Political Arithmetic* (1691), 'that excellent Work' as HF calls it in his *Proposal for Making an Effectual Provision for the Poor*, where he also confuses the surname of Petty, the 'famous' political economist, with that of William Petyt, the legal historian (*Enquiry*, p. 262 and nn. 8–9; also pp. 258 and 263). A copy of Petty's work was in HF's library (Ribbles P13).
[216] See above, p. 609 n. 199.

past six; so much time seemed requisite to put up the furniture of our bed-chamber or dining-room, for almost every article, even to some of the chairs, were either our own or the captain's property; so much more in conveying it as well as my self, as dead a luggage as any, to the shore, and thence to the ship, that the night threatened first to overtake us. A terrible circumstance to me, in my decayed condition; especially as very heavy showers of rain, attended with a high wind, continued to fall incessantly; the being carried through which two miles in the dark, in a wet and open boat, seemed little less than certain death.

HOWEVER, as my commander was absolute, his orders peremptory, and my obedience necessary, I resolved to avail myself of a philosophy which hath been of notable use to me in the latter part of my life, and which is contained in this hemistich of Virgil.

—Superanda omnis fortuna ferendo est.[217]

The meaning of which, if Virgil had any, I think I rightly understood and rightly applied.

As I was therefore to be entirely passive in my motion, I resolved to abandon myself to the conduct of those who were to carry me into a cart when it returned from unloading the goods.

BUT before this the captain perceiving what had happened in the clouds, and that the wind remained as much his enemy as ever, came up stairs to me, with a reprieve till the morning. This was, I own, very agreeable news, and I little regreted the trouble of refurnishing my apartment, by sending back for the goods.

MRS. Francis was not well pleased with this. As she understood the reprieve to be only till the morning, she saw nothing but lodging to be possibly added, out of which she was to deduct fire and candle, and the remainder, she thought, would scarce pay her for her trouble. She exerted therefore all the ill humour of which she was mistress, and did all she could to thwart and perplex every thing during the whole evening.

Thursday, July 18. EARLY in the morning the captain, who had remained on shore all night, came to visit us, and to press us to make haste on board. 'I am resolved,' says he, 'not to lose a moment, now the wind is coming about fair: for my own part, I never was surer of a wind in all my life.' I use his very words; nor will I presume to interpret or comment upon them farther, than by observing that they were spoke in the utmost hurry.

---

[217] 'All fortune is to be overcome by bearing' (*Aeneid*, v. 710).

WE promised to be ready as soon as breakfast was over; but this was not so soon as was expected: for in removing our goods the evening before, the tea–chest was unhappily lost.

EVERY place was immediately searched, and many where it was impossible for it to be; for this was a loss of much greater consequence than it may at first seem to many of my readers. Ladies and valetudinarians do not easily dispense with the use of this sovereign cordial, in a single instance; but to undertake a long voyage without any probability of being supplied with it the whole way, was above the reach of patience. And yet, dreadful as this calamity was, it seemed unavoidable. The whole town of Ryde could not supply a single leaf; for as to what Mrs. Francis and the shop called by that name, it was not of Chinese growth. It did not indeed in the least resemble tea, either in smell or taste, or in any particular, unless in being a leaf: for it was in truth no other than a tobacco of the mundungus[218] species. And as for the hopes of relief in any other port, they were not to be depended upon; for the captain had positively declared he was sure of a wind, and would let go his anchor no more till he arrived in the Tajo.[219]

WHEN a good deal of time had been spent, most of it indeed wasted on this occasion, a thought occurred, which every one wondered at its not having presented itself the first moment. This was to apply to the good lady, who could not fail of pitying and relieving such distress. A messenger was immediately dispatched, with an account of our misfortune, till whose return we employed ourselves in preparatives for our departure, that we might have nothing to do but to swallow our breakfast when it arrived. The tea–chest, tho' of no less consequence to us than the military chest to a general, was given up as lost, or rather as stolen; for tho' I would not, for the world, mention any particular name, it is certain we had suspicions, and all, I am afraid, fell on the same person.

THE man returned from the worthy lady with much expedition, and brought with him a canister of tea, dispatched with so true a generosity, as well as politeness, that if our voyage had been as long again, we should have incurred no danger of being brought to a short allowance in this most important article. At the very same instant likewise arrived William the footman, with our own tea–chest. It had been, indeed, left in the hoy, when the other goods were re-landed, as William, when he first heard it was missing, had suspected; and whence, had not the owner of the hoy been unluckily out of the way, he had retrieved it soon enough to have prevented our giving the lady an opportunity of displaying some part of her goodness.

---

[218] 'mundungus': bad-smelling tobacco (*OED*, s.v. 2).
[219] 'the Tajo': the river Tagus, at the mouth of which stands Lisbon.

TO search the hoy was, indeed, too natural a suggestion to have escaped any one, nor did it escape being mentioned by many of us; but we were dissuaded from it by my wife's maid, who perfectly well remembered she had left the chest in the bed-chamber; for that she had never given it out of her hand in her way to or from the hoy; but William, perhaps, knew the maid better, and best understood how far she was to be believed; for otherwise he would hardly of his own accord, after hearing her declarations, have hunted out the hoyman, with much pains and difficulty.

THUS ended this scene, which begun with such appearance of distress, and ended with becoming the subject of mirth and laughter.

NOTHING now remained but to pay our taxes, which were indeed laid with inconceivable severity. Lodging was raised six-pence, fire in the same proportion, and even candles, which had hitherto escaped, were charged with a wantonness of imposition, from the beginning, and placed under the stile of oversight. We were raised a whole pound, whereas we had only burnt ten, in five nights, and the pound consisted of twenty-four.

LASTLY, an attempt was made, which almost as far exceeds human credulity to believe, as it did human patience to submit to. This was to make us pay as much for existing an hour or two as for existing a whole day; and dressing dinner was introduced as an article, tho' we left the house before either pot or spit had approached the fire. Here I own my patience failed me, and I became an example of the truth of the observation, That all tyranny and oppression may be carried too far, and that a yoke may be made too intolerable for the neck of the tamest slave. When I remonstrated with some warmth against this grievance, Mrs. Francis have me a look, and left the room without making any answer. She returned in a minute, running to me with pen, ink, and paper in her hand, and desired me to make my own bill; for she hoped, she said, I did not expect that her house was to be dirtied, and her goods spoiled and consumed for nothing. 'The whole is but thirteen shillings. Can gentlefolks lie a whole night at a public house for less? If they can, I am sure it is time to give off being a landlady: but pay me what you please; I would have people know that I value money as little as other folks. But I was always a fool, as I says to my husband, and never knows which side my bread is buttered of. And yet to be sure your honour shall be my warning not to be bit so again. Some folks knows better than others some, how to make their bills. Candles! why, yes, to be sure; why should not travellers pay for candles? I am sure I pays for my candles, and the chandler pays the King's Majesty for them; and if he did not, I must, so as it comes to the same thing in the end. To be sure I am out of sixteens at present, but these burn as white and as clear, tho' not quite so large. I expects my chandler here soon, or I would send to Portsmouth, if your honour was to stay any time longer. But when folks stays only for a wind, you knows, there can be no dependence on such!' Here she put on a little slyness of aspect, and seemed willing to submit to interruption. I interrupted her, accordingly, by throwing down half a guinea, and declared I had no more English money, which was indeed true; and as she could not immediately change the thirty-six shilling pieces,[220] it put a final end to the dispute. Mrs. Francis soon left the room, and we soon after left the house; nor would this good woman see us, or wish us a good voyage.

I MUST not, however, quit this place, where we had been so ill-treated, without doing it impartial justice, and recording what may with the strictest truth be said in its favour.

FIRST then, as to its situation, it is, I think, most delightful, and in the most pleasant spot in the whole island. It is true it wants the advantage of that beautiful river,[221] which leads from Newport to Cowes: but the prospect here extending to the sea, and taking in Portsmouth, Spithead, and St. Helen's, would be more than a recompence for the loss of the Thames itself, even in the most delightful part of Berkshire or Buckinghamshire, tho' another Denham, or another Pope, should unite in celebrating it.[222] For my own part, I confess myself so entirely fond of a sea prospect, that I think nothing on the land can equal it; and if it be set off with shipping, I desire to borrow no ornament from the *terra firma*. A fleet of ships is, in my opinion, the noblest object which the art of man hath ever produced; and far beyond the power of those architects who deal in brick, in stone, or in marble.

WHEN the late Sir Robert Walpole, one of the best of men and of ministers,[223] used to equip us a yearly fleet at Spithead, his enemies of

---

[220] The 'thirty-six shilling pieces' were Portuguese coins called 'Joannes' (for John V, whose image they bear); the English called them 'Joes' (see J. P. C. Kent, 'The Circulation of Portuguese Coins in Great Britain', in *Actas do III Congresso Nacional de Numismatica* [Lisbon, 1985], pp. 397–9). In his letter of *c.*10–14 September HF would later inform his brother John that he had exhausted his supply of these coins (below, Appendix C.3, Letter 3).

[221] The River Medina.

[222] In *Windsor Forest* (1713), Alexander Pope (1688–1744) celebrated the beauty of that royal preserve in Berkshire, as in *Cooper's Hill* (1642), Sir John Denham (1615–69) had done for that site in Surrey (not Buckinghamshire). HF always admired *Windsor Forest*, which he praised even in his early attacks on Pope in the 'Cantos' (2. 15–16) and the 'Epistle to Lyttleton' (lines 58–9); see below, pp. 49, 93; for his only other reference to Denham, see 'Cantos' (line 177); below, p. 47.

[223] Sir Robert Walpole (1676–1745)—from 1742 first Earl of Orford—was Prime Minister from 1721 to 1742. HF's attitude towards Walpole, the 'Great Man' as he was called, was notably inconsistent. In his early writings (e.g. 'Cantos' [1729/30] and the 'Epistle to Lyttleton' [1733]: see below), and during his tenure as house playwright at Drury Lane (e.g. *The Modern Husband* and his contributions to *The Comedian* [1732]: see Appendix A. 1–2), he praised Walpole and sought his patronage. But from 1734 to 1740, whether in satires such as *Pasquin* (1736) and *The Historical Register* (1737) at the Haymarket Theatre, or in his contributions to such anti-ministerial journals as *The Craftsman*, *Common Sense*, and *The Champion*, he made Walpole the butt of ridicule. With the electioneering pamphlet *The Opposition: A Vision* (1741), however, it is the Prime Minister who appears as the generous champion of the nation against the attempts of power-seeking enemies to unseat him. Moreover, from 1747 to the end of his life HF was publicly aligned with Walpole's protégé and successor, Henry Pelham (above, p. 562 and

taste must have allowed that he, at least, treated the nation with a fine sight for their money.[224] A much finer, indeed, than the same expence in an encampment could have produced. For what, indeed, is the best idea which the prospect of a number of huts can furnish to the mind, but of a number of men forming themselves into a society, before the art of building more substantial houses was known. This, perhaps, would be agreeable enough; but in truth, there is a much worse idea ready to step in before it, and that is of a body of cut-throats, the supports of tyranny, the invaders of the just liberties and properties of mankind, the plunderers of the industrious, the ravishers of the chaste, the murderers of the innocent, and, in a word, the destroyers of the plenty, the peace, and the safety of their fellow-creatures.

AND what, it may be said, are these men of war, which seem so delightful an object to our eyes? Are they not alike the support of tyranny, and oppression of innocence, carrying with them desolation and ruin wherever their masters please to send them. This is indeed too true, and however the ship of war may, in its bulk and equipment, exceed the honest merchant-man, I heartily wish there was no necessity for it; for tho' I must own the superior beauty of the object on one side, I am more pleased with the superior excellence of the idea, which I can raise in my mind on the other; while I reflect on the art and industry of mankind, engaged in the daily improvements of commerce, to the mutual benefit of all countries, and to the establishment and happiness of social life.

THIS pleasant village is situated on a gentle ascent from the water, whence it affords that charming prospect I have above described. Its soil is a gravel, which assisted with its declivity, preserves it always so dry, that immediately after the most violent rain, a fine lady may walk without wetting her silken shoes. The fertility of the place is apparent from its extraordinary verdure, and it is so shaded with large and flourishing elms, that its narrow lanes are a natural grove or walk, which in the regularity of

---

n. 58). Despite these ambiguities in HF's political loyalties, modern editors of the *Journal*, holding to the notion that he was unwavering in his contempt of Walpole, have read the present compliment ('one of the best of men and of ministers') as ironic (see Pagliaro, Brooks, and Keymer); Dobson is the exception: 'Here [HF] returns to his first, and probably more genuine attitude of admiration.' Most scholars, including the late Sheridan Baker and Hugh Amory (*Miscellanies* iii, p. 21 n. 6), accept the compliment as sincere: e.g. Hollis Rinehart, 'The Role of Walpole in *Jonathan Wild*', *English Studies in Canada*, 5 (1979), p. 420; Brian McCrea, *Henry Fielding and the Politics of Mid-Eighteenth-Century England* (Athens, Ga., 1981), p. 196; Thomas R. Cleary, *Henry Fielding Political Writer* (Waterloo, Ont., 1984), p. 301; *Life*, p. 589; Frederick G. Ribble, 'Fielding's Rapprochement with Walpole in Late 1741', *PQ*, 80 (2001), p. 76 and n. 31.

[224] Spithead, a strait of the English Channel between the coast of Hampshire and the north-eastern coast of the Isle of Wight, opens into Portsmouth Harbour, the principal base of the British Navy. It was in HF's time, and long after, the scene of spectacular naval pageants.

its plantation vies with the power of art, and in its wanton exuberancy greatly exceeds it.

IN a field, in the ascent of this hill, about a quarter of a mile from the sea, stands a neat little chapel.[225] It is very small, but adequate to the number of inhabitants: for the parish doth not seem to contain above thirty houses.

AT about two miles distant from this parish, lives that polite and good lady to whose kindness we were so much obliged. It is placed on a hill, whose bottom is washed by the sea, and which, from its eminence at top, commands a view of great part of the island, as well as it does that of the opposite shore. This house was formerly built by one Boyce,[226] who from a blacksmith at Gosport, became possessed, by great success in smuggling, of 4000l. With part of this he purchased an estate here, and by chance, probably, fixed on this spot for building a large house. Perhaps the convenience of carrying on his business, to which it is so well adapted, might dictate the situation to him. We can hardly, at least, attribute it to the same taste with which he furnished his house, or at least his library, by sending an order to a bookseller in London, to pack him up 500 pounds, worth of his handsomest books. They tell here several almost incredible stories of the ignorance, the folly, and the pride which this poor man and his wife discovered during the short continuance of his prosperity; for he did not long escape the sharp eyes of the revenue-solicitors, and was by extents[227] from the Court of Exchequer, soon reduced below his original state, to that of confinement in the Fleet. All his effects were sold, and among the rest his books by an auction at Portsmouth, for a very small price; for the bookseller was now discovered to have been perfectly a master of his trade, and relying on Mr. Boyce's finding little time to read, had sent him not only the most lasting wares of his shop, but duplicates of the same, under different titles.

HIS estate and house were purchased by a gentleman of these parts,[228] whose widow now enjoys them, and who hath improved them, particularly her gardens, with so elegant a taste, that the painter who would assist his imagination in the composition of a most exquisite landscape, or the poet,

---

[225] Built by Thomas Player in 1719, and described in 1795 as 'a small neat chapel . . . now much too small for the inhabitants' (John Albin, *A New History of the Isle of Wight* [Newport, IoW, 1795], p. 508). Keymer (*Fielding's Journal*, s.v. '*Wednesday, July 17*', p. 133 n. 5).

[226] Daniel (or David) Boyce, who built Appley House in the 1720s, equipping it with vast cellars for contraband liquor. He was in the Fleet prison (for debts owed to the crown) by August 1732, and died there in 1740 (R. J. Hutchings, *Smugglers of the Isle of Wight* [Newport, 1985], pp. 9–10). Keymer (*Fielding's Journal*, s.v. '*Wednesday, July 17*', p. 133 n. 6).

[227] 'extents': a writ to recover debts due to the crown, under which the body, lands, and goods of the debtor may be seized (*OED*, s.v. 2, citing this passage from the *Journal*).

[228] John Roberts (d. 1741), whose widow, Ann Roberts, inherited Appley House (see above, p. 609 n. 199).

who would describe an earthly paradise, could no where furnish themselves with a richer pattern.

WE left this place about eleven in the morning, and were again conveyed with more sunshine than wind aboard our ship.

WHENCE our captain had acquired his power of prophecy, when he promised us and himself a prosperous wind, I will not determine; it is sufficient to observe that he was a false prophet, and that the weathercocks continued to point as before.

HE would not, however, so easily give up his skill in prediction. He persevered in asserting that the wind was changed, and having weighed his anchor fell down that afternoon to St. Helen's, which was at about the distance of five miles; and whither his friend the tide, in defiance of the wind, which was most manifestly against him, softly wafted him in as many hours.

HERE about seven in the evening, before which time we could not procure it, we sat down to regale ourselves with some roasted venison, which was much better drest than we imagined it would be, and an excellent cold pasty which my wife had made at Ryde, and which we had reserved uncut to eat on board our ship, whither we all chearfully exulted in being returned from the presence of Mrs. Francis, who, by the exact resemblance she bore to a fury, seemed to have been with no great propriety settled in paradise.

Friday, July 19. As we passed by Spithead on the preceding evening, we saw the two regiments of soldiers who were just returned from Gibraltar and Minorca; and this day a lieutenant belonging to one of them, who was the captain's nephew,[229] came to pay a visit to his uncle. He was what is called by some a very pretty fellow; indeed much too pretty a fellow at his years; for he was turned of thirty-four, though his address and conversation would have become him more before he had reached twenty. In his conversation, it is true, there was something military enough, as it consisted chiefly of oaths, and of the great actions and wise sayings of Jack, and Will, and Tom of our regiment, a phrase eternally in his mouth; and he seemed to conclude, that it conveyed to all the officers such a degree of public notoriety and importance, that it intitled him, like the head of a profession, or a first minister, to be the subject of conversation among those who had not the least personal acquaintance with him. This did not much surprize me, as I have seen several examples of the same; but the defects in his address, especially to the women, were so great, that they seemed absolutely inconsistent with the behaviour of a pretty fellow, much less of one in a red coat; and yet, besides having been eleven years in the army, he had had, as

---

[229] Samuel Buck Veale (d. 1766), Captain Veale's nephew, was from 1745 to 1755 a lieutenant in Colonel James Fleming's Regiment of Foot. Keymer (*Fielding's Journal*, s.v. '*Friday, July 19*', p. 133 n. 1).

his uncle informed me, an education in France. This, I own, would have appeared to have been absolutely thrown away, had not his animal spirits, which were likewise thrown away upon him in great abundance, born the visible stamp of the growth of that country. The character, to which he had an indisputable title, was that of a merry fellow; so very merry was he, that he laughed at every thing he said, and always before he spoke. Possibly, indeed, he often laughed at what he did not utter, for every speech begun with a laugh, tho' it did not always end with a jest. There was no great analogy between the characters of the uncle and the nephew, and yet they seem'd intirely to agree in enjoying the honour which the red-coat did to his family. This the uncle expressed with great pleasure in his countenance, and seemed desirous of shewing all present the honour which he had for his nephew, who, on his side, was at some pains to convince us of his concurring in this opinion, and, at the same time, of displaying the contempt he had for the parts, as well as the occupation of his uncle, which he seemed to think reflected some disgrace on himself, who was a member of that profession which makes every man a gentleman. Not that I would be understood to insinuate, that the nephew endeavoured to shake off or disown his uncle, or indeed, to keep him at any distance. On the contrary, he treated him with the utmost familiarity, often calling him Dick, and dear Dick, and old Dick, and frequently beginning an oration with D—n me, Dick.

ALL this condescension on the part of the young man, was received with suitable marks of complaisance and obligation by the old one; especially, when it was attended with evidences of the same familiarity with general officers, and other persons of rank; one of whom, in particular, I know to have the pride and insolence of the devil himself, and who, without some strong bias of interest, is no more liable to converse familiarly with a lieu-tenant, than of being mistaken in his judgment of a fool; which was not, perhaps, so certainly the case of the worthy lieutenant, who, in declaring to us the qualifications which recommended men to his countenance and con-versation, as well as what effectually set a bar to all hopes of that honour, exclaimed, 'No, Sir, by the D——, I hate all fools—No, d—n me, excuse me for that. That's a little too much, old Dick. There are two or three officers of our regiment, whom I know to be fools; but d—n me if I am ever seen in their company. If a man hath a fool of a relation, Dick, you know he can't help that, old boy.'

SUCH jokes as these the old man not only took in good part, but glibly gulped down the whole narrative of his nephew; nor did he, I am convinced, in the least doubt of our as readily swallowing the same. This made him so charmed with the lieutenant, that it is probable we should have been pestered with him the whole evening, had not the north-wind, dearer to our sea-captain, even than this glory of his family, sprung suddenly up, and called aloud to him to weigh his anchor.

WHILE this ceremony was performing, the sea-captain ordered out his boat to row the land-captain to shore; not indeed on an uninhabited island, but one which, in this part, looked but little better, not presenting us the view of a single house. Indeed, our old friend, when his boat returned on shore, perhaps being no longer able to stifle his envy of the superiority of his nephew, told us, with a smile, that the young man had a good five mile to walk, before he could be accommodated with a passage to Portsmouth.

IT appeared now, that the captain had been only mistaken in the date of his prediction, by placing the event a day earlier than it happened; for the wind which now arose, was not only favourable but brisk, and was no sooner in reach of our sails than it swept us away by the back of the Isle of Wight, and having in the night carried us by Christ-church and Peveral-point, brought us the next noon, *Saturday, July* 20, off the island of Portland, so famous for the smallness and sweetness of its mutton, of which a leg seldom weighs four pounds. We would have bought a sheep, but our captain would not permit it; though he needed not have been in such a hurry, for presently the wind, I will not positively assert in resentment of his surliness, shewed him a dog's trick, and slily slipt back again to his summer-house in the south-west.

THE captain now grew outrageous, and declaring open war with the wind, took a resolution, rather more bold than wise, of sailing in defiance of it, and in its teeth. He swore he would let go his anchor no more, but would beat the sea while he had either yard or sail left. He accordingly stood from the shore, and made so large a tack, that before night, though he seemed to advance but little on his way, he was got out of sight of land.

TOWARDS the evening, the wind began, in the captain's own language, to freshen; and indeed it freshned so much, that before ten it blew a perfect hurricane. The captain having got, as he supposed, to a safe distance, tacked again towards the English shore; and now the wind veered a point only in his favour, and continued to blow with such violence, that the ship ran above eight knots or miles an hour, during this whole day and tempestuous night, till bed-time. I was obliged to betake myself once more to my solitude; for my women were again all down in their sea-sickness, and the captain was busy on deck; for he began to grow uneasy, chiefly, I believe, because he did not well know where he was, and would, I am convinced, have been very glad to have been in Portland-road, eating some sheep's-head broth.

HAVING contracted no great degree of good-humour, by living a whole day alone, without a single soul to converse with, I took but ill physic to purge it off, by a bed-conversation with the captain; who, amongst many bitter lamentations of his fate, and protesting he had more patience than a Job, frequently intermixed summons to the commanding officer on the deck, who now happened to be one Morrison, a carpenter,[230] the only fellow that had either common sense or common civility in the ship. Of Morrison he enquired every quarter of an hour concerning the state of affairs; the wind, the care of the ship, and other matters of navigation. The frequency of these summons, as well as the solicitude with which they were made, sufficiently testified the state of the captain's mind; he endeavoured to conceal it, and would have given no small alarm to a man, who had either not learnt what it is to die, or known what it is to be miserable. And my dear wife and child must pardon me, if what I did not conceive to be any great evil to myself, I was not much terrified with the thoughts of happening to them: in truth, I have often thought they are both too good, and too gentle, to be trusted to the power of any man I know, to whom they could possibly be so trusted.

CAN I say then I had no fear; indeed I cannot, reader, I was afraid for thee, lest thou shouldst have been deprived of that pleasure thou art now enjoying; and that I should not live to draw out on paper, that military character which thou didst peruse in the journal of yesterday.

FROM all these fears we were relieved, at six in the morning, by the arrival of Mr. Morrison, who acquainted us that he was sure he beheld land very near; for he could not see half a mile, by reason of the haziness of the weather. This land, he said, was, he believed, the Berry-head, which forms one side of Torbay; the captain declared that it was impossible, and swore, on condition he was right, he would give him his mother for a maid.[231] A forfeit which became afterwards strictly due, and payable; for the captain whipping on his night-gown,[232] ran up, without his breeches, and within half an hour returning into the cabin, wished me joy of our lying safe at anchor in the bay.

Sunday, July 21. THINGS now began to put on an aspect very different from what they had lately worn: the news that the ship had almost lost its mizen,[233] and that we had procured very fine clouted cream and fresh bread and butter from the shore, restored health and spirits to our women, and we all sat down to a very chearful breakfast.

BUT however pleasant our stay promised to be here, we were all desirous

---

[230] Probably James Morrison, Veale's 'Mate', who had himself been master of a ship plying between London and Lisbon. Keymer (*Fielding's Journal*, s.v. '*Satuday, July 20*', p. 134 n. 3).

[231] 'give him his mother for a maid': 'Probably a fashionable catch-phrase', according to Eric Partridge, editor of Swift's *Polite Conversation* (London, 1963), where Tom Neverout speaks it to Miss Notable (p. 111).

[232] 'night-gown': a dressing gown (*OED*).

[233] 'mizen': a sail set on the after side of the mizzen mast (the aftermost mast of a three-masted ship) (*OED*).

it should be short: I resolved immediately to dispatch my man into the country, to purchase a present of cyder for my friends of that which is called Southam,[234] as well as to take with me a hogshead[235] of it to Lisbon; for it is, in my opinion, much more delicious than that which is the growth of Herefordshire. I purchased three hogsheads for five pounds ten shillings, all which I should have scarce thought worth mentioning, had I not believed it might be of equal service to the honest farmer who sold it me, and who is by the neighbouring gentlemen reputed to deal in the very best, and to the reader, who from ignorance of the means of providing better for himself, swallows at a dearer rate the juice of Middlesex turnip, instead of that *Vinum Pomonæ*,[236] which Mr. Giles Leverance of Cheeshurst,[237] near Dartmouth in Devon, will, at the price of forty shillings per hogshead, send in double casks[238] to any part of the world. Had the wind been very sudden in shifting, I had lost my cyder, by an attempt of a boatman to exact, according to custom. He required five shillings for conveying my man a mile and half to the shore, and four more if he staid to bring him back. This I thought to be such insufferable impudence, that I ordered him to be immediately chased from the ship, without any answer. Indeed, there are few inconveniences that I would not rather encounter than encourage the insolent demands of these wretches, at the expence of my own indignation, of which I own, they are not the only objects, but rather those who purchase a paultry convenience by encouraging them. But of this I have already spoken very largely. I shall conclude, therefore, with the leave which this fellow took of our ship; saying, he should know it again, and would not put off from the shore to relieve it in any distress whatever.

IT will, doubtless, surprize many of my readers to hear, that when we lay at anchor within a mile or two of a town, several days together, and even in the most temperate weather, we should frequently want fresh provisions and herbage, and other emoluments of the shore, as much as if we had been a hundred leagues from land. And this too, while numbers of boats were in our sight, whose owners get their livelihood by rowing people up and down,

[234] With HF's account of the virtues of Devon cider and the quality, variety, and cheapness of the local fish, here and in the *Journal* entry for 23 July, see the letter to his brother John from Torbay, 22 July (below, Appendix C.3, Letter 2).

[235] 'hogshead': a caskful of liquid containing 63 gallons (*OED*).

[236] 'Wine of Pomona', the Roman goddess of fruit.

[237] HF's letter of 21 July was directed (in another hand) to 'Mʳ Giles Lavorance at/Churston near Dartmouth/Devon': Ms Janice L. Wood, Archivist of the Devon Record Office, gives the surname as Laverance; Giles (b. 1698) or his son of the same name (b. 1733?) leased the demesne lands (or 'barton') attached to the manor of Churston Court from the squire John Yarde (d. 1773).

[238] 'double casks': presumably casks of extra strength for ocean shipment; staves were made in three thicknesses, 'slight', 'stout', and 'extra stout' (Kenneth Kilby, *The Cooper and his Trade* [Fresno, Calif., 1989], p. 29).

and could be at any time summoned by a signal to our assistance, and while the captain had a little boat of his own with men always ready to row it at his command.

THIS, however, hath been partly accounted for already, by the imposing[239] disposition of the people; who asked so much more than the proper price of their labour. And as to the usefulness of the captain's boat, it requires to be a little expatiated upon, as it will tend to lay open some of the grievances which demand the utmost regard of our legislature, as they affect the most valuable part of the king's subjects, those by whom the commerce of the nation is carried into execution.

OUR captain then, who was a very good and experienced seaman, having been above thirty years the master of a vessel, part of which he had served, so he phrased it, as commander of a privateer; and had discharged himself with great courage and conduct, and with as great success, discovered the utmost aversion to the sending his boat ashore, whenever we lay wind-bound in any of our harbours. This aversion did not arise from any fear of wearing out his boat by using it, but was, in truth, the result of experience, that it was easier to send his men on shore than to recall them. They acknowledged him to be their master while they remained on ship-board, but did not allow his power to extend to the shores, where they had no sooner set their foot, than every man became sui juris,[240] and thought himself at full liberty to return when he pleased. Now it is not any delight that these fellows have in the fresh air, or verdant fields on the land. Every one of them would prefer his ship and his hammock to all the sweets of Arabia the happy;[241] but unluckily for them, there are in every sea port in England certain houses, whose chief livelihood depends on providing entertainment for the gentlemen of the jacket. For this purpose, they are always well-furnished with those cordial liquors, which do immediately inspire the heart with gladness, banishing all careful thoughts, and indeed all others from the mind, and opening the mouth with songs of chearfulness and thanksgiving, for the many wonderful blessings with which a sea-faring life overflows.

FOR my own part, however whimsical it may appear, I confess, I have thought the strange story of Circe in the Odyssey,[242] no other than an

---

[239] 'imposing': using deception; practising imposture (*OED*, s.v. 3, citing this passage as its first instance).

[240] '*sui juris*': his own master.

[241] Arabia Felix (Yemen), fabled for spices in antiquity; according to Diodorus Siculus, 'the very earth itself is by its nature full of a vapour like sweet incense' *Bibliotheca Historica*, II. xlix. 4).

[242] Homer, *Odyssey*, x. 233–43; the story of Circe, who drugged the wine drunk by Odysseus' crew and turned them into swine, was already counted 'strange' in antiquity, 'a veritable dream of Zeus' (Longinus, *On the Sublime*, ix. 14).

ingenious allegory; in which Homer intended to convey to his countrymen the same kind of instruction, which we intend to communicate to our own in this digression. As teaching the art of war to the Greeks, was the plain design of the Iliad; so was teaching them the art of navigation the no less manifest intention of the Odyssey. For the improvement of this, their situation was most excellently adapted; and accordingly we find Thucydides, in the beginning of his history, considers the Greeks as a set of pirates, or privateers, plundering each other by sea.[243] This being probably the first institution of commerce before the Ars Cauponaria[244] was invented, and merchants, instead of robbing, began to cheat and outwit each other, and by degrees changed the Metabletic, the only kind of traffic allowed by Aristotle in his Politics, into the Chrematistic.[245]

BY this allegory then I suppose Ulysses to have been the captain of a merchant-ship, and Circe some good alewife, who made his crew drunk with the spirituous liquors of those days. With this the transformation into swine, as well as all other incidents of the fable, will notably agree; and thus a key will be found out for unlocking the whole mystery, and forging, at least, some meaning to a story which, at present, appears very strange and absurd.[246]

HENCE, moreover, will appear the very near resemblance between the sea-faring men of all ages and nations; and here perhaps may be established the truth and justice of that observation, which will occur oftener than once in this voyage, that all human flesh is not the same flesh, but that there is one kind of flesh of landmen, and another of seamen.

---

[243] Thucydides, *Peloponnesian War*, I. v. 1: 'in early times both the Hellenes and the Barbarians who dwell on the mainland near the sea . . . turned to piracy. . . . For this occupation did not as yet involve disgrace, but rather conferred something even of glory.'

[244] 'Ars Cauponaria': Greek *kapelikē*, the art of shopkeeping or trade (Aristotle, *Politics*, I. iii. 12 [1257ᵃ])—so translated by Denys Lambin in the Duval edition of *Aristotle's Opera, Greek & Latin* (Paris, 1629) in HF's library (Ribbles A23).

[245] Aristotle argues that the invention of money changed one sort of acquisition, carried out by barter (*allagē*) or exchange (*metabletikē*), into another 'that is specially called wealth-getting' (*chrematistikē*), aimed at unbridled profit (*Politics*, I. iii. 10–12 [1257]). The second sort of acquisition is an *ars cauponaria*, an unnatural and unnecessary way of 'getting wealth' (I. iii. 23 [1258ᵇ]). Cf. Dr Harrison in *Amelia* (IX. v): 'I am not the least versed in the *Chrematistic* Art ["The Art of getting Wealth" (HF's note)], as an old Friend of mine calls it. I know not how to get a Shilling, nor how to keep it in my Pocket if I had it' (p. 375). HA

[246] A comically euhemerist reading (see above, p. 548 n. 15), which, however, retains a traditional allegory. 'Circe indeed represents pleasure [*voluptas*], by which men are changed into monsters and filthy swine, according to what Xenophon reports that Socrates taught; Horace treats her as a harlot [*meretrix*]' (Charlese Estienne, *Dictionarium Historicum, Geographicum, Poeticum*, ed. Nicholas Lloyd [1686]; trans. Amory; in HF's library [Ribbles E9]). So Circe holds 'a voluptuous Court', from which only Ulysses' 'Prudence' (*moly*) extricates his companions; 'all the Transformations . . . this Princess wrought, were rather the Effects of her Charms and Beauty, than of her Magic, tho' *Horace* gives us plainly to understand it was the Potions she gave that brought about these Wonders' (Banier, *Mythology*, iv. 298–9). HA

PHILOSOPHERS, divines, and others, who have treated the gratification of human appetites with contempt, have, among other instances, insisted very strongly on that satiety which is so apt to overtake them, even in the very act of enjoyment. And here they more particularly deserve our attention, as most of them may be supposed to speak from their own experience; and very probably gave us their lessons with a full stomach. Thus hunger and thirst, whatever delight they may afford while we are eating and drinking, pass both away from us with the plate and the cup; and though we should imitate the Romans, if indeed they were such dull beasts, which I can scarce believe, to unload the belly like a dungpot, in order to fill it again with another load,[247] yet would the pleasure be so considerably lessened, that it would scarce repay us the trouble of purchasing it with swallowing a bason of camomile tea. A second haunch of venison, or a second dose of turtle, would hardly allure a city glutton with its smell. Even the celebrated Jew himself, when well filled with Calipash and Calipee, goes contentedly home to tell his money, and expects no more pleasure from his throat, during the next twenty-four hours.[248] Hence I suppose Dr. South took that elegant comparison of the joys of a speculative man to the solemn silence of an Archimedes over a problem, and those of a glutton to the stillness of a sow at her wash.[249] A simile, which, if it became the pulpit at all, could only become it in the afternoon.

---

[247] Cf. Seneca, *Ad Helviam Matrem* (*Dialogues*, XII), x. 3: Roman gourmets 'vomit that they may eat, they eat that they may vomit'; also Suetonius, *Lives of the Caesars* on Vitellius (xiii. 1) and Claudius (xxxiii. 1). In HF's library (Ribbles S15 and S74). For HF's amusement at such gourmandizing 'Knights of the Trencher', see *Champion* (15 April 1740), pp. 281–2—a passage anticipated by one 'Will Lovemeal' in an essay on '*Eating*' published in the *Universal Spectator*, Nos. 410–11 (14, 21 August 1736); attributed to HF by the present editor (see *New Essays*, Appendix B, pp. 525–30).

[248] If, as the definite article suggests, a particular person is meant, the most 'celebrated Jew' in England was Samson Gideon (1699–1762), the wealthiest and most important financier in the City, who was a close associate of Henry Pelham, the Prime Minister, and the government's chief financial adviser. Gideon figured prominently in satires of the period: in Arthur Murphy's 'Temple of Laverna' (1752, reprinted 1753), he is Caiphas, a Jewish broker with ties to the government; and in the satiric prints published in opposition to the Naturalization Act of 1753 he was depicted as the chief promoter of a measure he was in fact so strongly against that he severed his connection with the Sephardic Synagogue (see Thomas W. Perry, *Public Opinion, Propaganda, and Politics in Eighteenth-Century England: A Study of the Jew Bill of 1753* [Cambridge, Mass., 1962], pp. 9–10, 19–20, 110). Gideon, who married a Protestant and had his children baptized, was also lax in his observance of Jewish law. Though there is no report of his dining on turtle ('Calipash and Calipee' are the meat from the upper and lower shell, respectively, of the great green turtle, served at City feasts; see *Tom Jones*, I. i, p. 32), it is not unlikely that, with the majority of English Jews of the period, he observed the dietary laws (*kashrut*) 'casually or not at all' (Todd M. Endleman, *The Jews of Britain, 1656–2000* [Berkeley and Los Angeles, 2002], p. 55). For HF's interest in the laws of fasting in 'the *Jewish* Religion', see *Champion* (8 January 1740), p. 113.

That HF shared the anti-Semitic prejudices of most of his contemporaries is clear from his early satires of stockjobbers such as Zorobabel in *Miss Lucy in Town* (1742); that he was capable, as a magistrate, of acting with justice and humanity towards Jews is also clear from the case of Henry Simonds (*Life*, p. 528).

[249] Robert South (1634–1716), one of HF's favourite divines, in a sermon on wisdom, 'Her Ways are

WHEREAS, in those potations which the mind seems to enjoy, rather than the bodily appetite, there is happily no such satiety; but the more a man drinks the more he desires; as if, like Mark Anthony in Dryden, his appetite encreased with feeding,[250] and this to such an immoderate degree, *ut nullus sit desiderio aut pudor aut modus.*[251] Hence, as with the gang of Captain Ulysses, ensures so total a transformation, that the man no more continues what he was. Perhaps he ceases for a time to be at all; or, tho' he may retain the same outward form and figure he had before, yet is his nobler part, as we are taught to call it, so changed, that, instead of being the same man, he scarce remembers what he was a few hours before. And this transformation being once obtained, is so easily preserved by the same potations, which induce no satiety, that the captain in vain sends or goes in quest of his crew. They know him no longer; or, if they do, they acknowledge not his power, having indeed as entirely forgotten themselves as if they had taken a large draught of the river of Lethe.[252]

NOR is the captain always sure of even finding out the place to which Circe hath conveyed them. There are many of those houses in every port-town. Nay, there are some where the sorceress doth not trust only to her drugs; but hath instruments of a different kind to execute her purposes, by whose means the tar is effectually secreted from the knowledge and pursuit of his captain. This would, indeed, be very fatal, was it not for one circumstance; that the sailor is seldom provided with the proper bait for these harpies.[253] However, the contrary sometimes happens, as these harpies will

Ways of Pleasantness': 'How vastly disproportionate are the Pleasures of the Eating, and of the Thinking man? indeed as different as the silence of an *Archimedes* in the study of a Problem, and the stilness of a Sow at her wash' (*Twelve Sermons*, 2nd edn. [1697], i, pp. 19–20; the fifth edition [1722] was in HF's library [Ribbles S42]). In *The Champion* (20 May 1740) HF had quoted this same passage (p. 331); on the same topic and in the same humorous vein, he quoted South again in *Champion* (15 April 1740), p. 282, and *The Covent-Garden Journal*, No. 57 (1 August 1752), p. 308. In the latter journal, No. 18 (3 March 1752), HF declared: 'In the Sermons of [South], there is perhaps more Wit, than in the Comedies of Congreve' (p. 124).

[250] HF conflates Antony's speech in Dryden's *All for Love* (1678): 'There's no satiety of love in thee; | Enjoy'd, thou still art new' (III. i. 24–5); Enobarbus in Shakespeare's *Antony and Cleopatra*: 'Other women cloy | The appetite they feed, but she makes hungry | Where most she satisfies' (II. ii. 241–3); and *Hamlet*: 'As if increase of appetite had grown | By what it fed on' (I. ii. 144–5).

[251] Adapting Horace's lament to Virgil on the death of their friend Quintillius: 'Quis desiderio sit pudor aut modus | Tam cari capitis? (*Odes*, I. xxiv. 1–2), which Tom Jones quotes to Thwackum when Allworthy narrowly escapes death (V. ix) and which HF renders: 'What Modesty, or Measure, can set Bounds to our Desire of so dear a Friend!' commenting, 'The Word *Desiderium* here cannot be easily translated. It includes our Desire of enjoying our Friend again, and the Grief which attends that Desire' (p. 252). In the present context, he alters the passage to mean: 'there is neither shame nor measure to his thirst'.

[252] Cf. *A Journey from This World to the Next* (I. xxi), where Julian, before reincarnation, is 'forced to be dipped three Times in the River *Lethe*, to prevent my remembering' the horrors of his life (*Miscellanies* ii, p. 94).

[253] 'harpies': mythological birds of prey with the faces of women.

bite at almost any thing, and will snap at a pair of silver buttons or buckles, as surely as at the specie[254] itself. Nay, sometimes they are so voracious, that the very naked hook will go down, and the jolly young sailor is sacrificed for his own sake.

IN vain, at such a season as this, would the vows of a pious heathen have prevailed over Neptune, Æolus, or any other marine deity. In vain would the prayers of a Christian captain be attended with the like success. The wind may change, how it pleases, while all hands are on shore; the anchor would remain firm in the ground, and the ship would continue in durance, unless, like other forcible prison-breakers, it forcibly got loose for no good purpose.

NOW, as the favour of winds and courts, and such like, is always to be laid hold on at the very first motion, for within twenty-four hours all may be changed again; so, in the former case, the loss of a day may be the loss of a voyage: for, tho' it may appear to persons not well skilled in navigation, who see ships meet and sail by each other, that the wind blows sometimes east and west, north and south, backwards and forwards, at the same instant; yet, certain it is, that the land is so contrived, that even the same wind will not, like the same horse, always bring a man to the end of his journey; but, that the gale which the mariner prayed heartily for yesterday, he may as heartily deprecate to-morrow; while all use and benefit, which would have arisen to him from the westerly wind of to-morrow, may be totally lost and thrown away, by neglecting the offer of the easterly blast which blows today.

HENCE ensures grief and disreputation to the innocent captain, loss and disappointment to the worthy merchant, and not seldom great prejudice to the trade of a nation, whose manufactures are thus liable to lye unsold in a foreign warehouse, the market being forestall'd by some rival whose sailors are under a better discipline. To guard against these inconveniences, the prudent captain takes every precaution in his power: he makes the strongest contracts with his crew, and thereby binds them so firmly, that none but the greatest or least of men can break through them with impunity: but for one of these two reasons, which I will not determine, the sailor, like his brother fish the eel, is too slippery to be held, and plunges into his element with perfect impunity.

TO speak a plain truth, there is no trusting to any contract with one whom the wise citizens of London call a bad man;[255] for, with such a one, tho' your bond be ever so strong, it will prove in the end good for nothing.

---

[254] 'specie': coined money (*OED*, s.v. 6).

[255] 'a bad man': cf. *Champion* (26 January 1740): 'What is the Meaning of a good Man in the City, but a rich Man; or a bad Man, but a poor one?' (p. 144).

WHAT then is to be done in this case? What, indeed! but to call in the assistance of that tremendous magistrate, the justice of peace, who can, and often doth lay good and bad men in equal durance; and, tho' he seldom cares to stretch his bonds to what is great, never finds any thing too minute for their detention, but will hold the smallest reptile alive so fast in his noose, that he can never get out 'till he is let drop through it.

WHY, therefore, upon the breach of those contracts, should not an immediate application be made to the nearest magistrate of this order, who should be empower'd to convey the delinquent, either to ship or to prison, at the election of the captain, to be fettered by the leg in either place.

BUT, as the case now stands, the condition of this poor captain, without any commission, and of this absolute commander without any power, is much worse than we have hitherto shewn it to be; for notwithstanding all the aforesaid contracts to sail in the good ship the Elizabeth, if the sailor should, for better wages, find it more his interest to go on board the better ship, the Mary, either before their setting out, or on their speedy[256] meeting in some port, he may prefer the latter without any other danger, than that of 'doing what he ought not to have done,'[257] contrary to a rule which he is seldom Christian enough to have much at heart, while the captain is generally too good a Christian to punish a man out of revenge only, when he is to be at a considerable expence for so doing.[258] There are many other deficiencies in our laws, relating to maritime affairs, and which would probably have been long since corrected, had we any seamen in the House of Commons. Not that I would insinuate that the legislature wants a supply of many gentlemen in the sea-service: but, as these gentlemen are, by their attendance in the house, unfortunately prevented from ever going to sea, and there learning what they might communicate to their landed brethren, these latter remain as ignorant in that branch of knowledge, as they would be if none but courtiers and fox-hunters[259] had been elected into parliament, without a single fish[260] among them. The following seems to me to be an

[256] 'speedy': advantageous, expedient, helpful (*OED*, s.v. 1 obs.; latest citation 1449).

[257] From the Book of Common Prayer, the General Confession in the Order for Morning Prayer: 'We have left undone those things which we ought to have done, And we have done those things which we ought not to have done, And there is no health in us.'

[258] By 26 Geo. II, c. 5 (1753), a deserter forfeited two days' wages for every day of absence from his ship and was liable to be imprisoned at hard labour if he refused to return; all of which would have required the captain's attendance before a Justice of the Peace and the customary fees due to his clerk.

[259] 'courtiers and fox-hunters': i.e. Whigs and Tories, the Court and Country parties, respectively.

[260] 'without a single fish': a puzzling reading unchanged in the second edition. Amory suggests the compositor may have misread 'Jack' in the MS; but that word in HF's hand is unlikely to have been mistaken for 'fish'. His alternative suggestion is better: the compositor may have misread 'fish', by haplography, for 'fish-hunter'; something more, he remarks, seems necessary to point the parallel with 'fox-hunter', as in, e.g., 'sea-captain' and 'land-captain' (above, p. 623, lines 3–4).

effect of this kind, and it strikes me the stronger, as I remember the case to have happened, and remember it to have been dispunishable. A captain of a trading vessel, of which he was part-owner, took in a large freight of oats at Liverpool, consign'd to the market at Bear-key;[261] this he carried to a port in Hampshire, and there sold it as his own, and freighting his vessel with wheat for the port of Cadiz in Spain, dropt it at Oporto in his way, and there selling it for his own use, took in a lading of wine, with which he sailed again, and having converted it in the same manner, together with a large sum of money with which he was intrusted, for the benefit of certain merchants, sold the ship and cargo in another port, and then wisely sat down contented with the fortune he had made, and returned to London to enjoy the remainder of his days, with the fruits of his former labours and a good conscience.

THE sum he brought home with him, consisted of near six thousand pounds, all in specie, and most of it in that coin[262] which Portugal distributes so liberally over Europe.

HE was not yet old enough to be past all sense of pleasure, nor so puff'd up with the pride of his good fortune, as to overlook his old acquaintances the journeymen taylors, from among whom he had been formerly press'd into the sea-service,[263] and having there laid the foundation of his future success, by his shares in prizes, had afterwards become captain of a trading vessel, in which he purchased an interest, and had soon begun to trade in the honourable manner above-mentioned.

THE captain now took up his residence at an alehouse in Drury-lane,[264] where, having all his money by him in a trunk, he spent above five pounds a day among his old friends the gentlemen and ladies of those parts.

THE merchant of Liverpool having luckily had notice from a friend, during the blaze of his fortune, did, by the assistance of a justice of peace, without the assistance of the law, recover his whole loss. The captain, however, wisely chose to refund no more; but perceiving with what hasty strides envy was pursuing his fortune, he took speedy means to retire out of her reach, and to enjoy the rest of his wealth in an inglorious obscurity;

---

[261] 'Bear-key' (quay) on the Thames, just west of the Customs House and the Tower.

[262] Probably the 'Joannes' worth 36s. (above, p. 618 n. 220).

[263] The impressment of recruits for the Navy had been long practised in England; but in 1744 a new law (17 Geo. II, c. 15) empowered local authorities to conscript as soldiers or marines 'all such able-bodied Men' as are without 'lawful and sufficient Support and Maintenance'. HF presumably enjoyed the notion that the captain, formerly a tailor, had himself been 'press'd'.

[264] The Hundred of Drury was the most disreputable district of London: here were 'the Gates of Sodom . . . the Jakes of the Town' (Ned Ward, *A View of London and Westminster: or, The Town Spy* [1725], i, pp. 13–14; ii, p. 48).

nor could the same justice overtake him time enough to assist a second merchant, as he had done the first.

THIS was a very extraordinary case, and the more so, as the ingenious gentleman had steered entirely clear of all crimes in our law.

NOW, how it comes about that a robbery so very easy to be committed, and to which there is such immediate temptation always before the eyes of these fellows, should receive the encouragement of impunity, is to be accounted for only from the oversight of the legislature, as that oversight can only be, I think, derived from the reasons I have assigned for it.

BUT I will dwell no longer on this subject. If what I have here said should seem of sufficient consequence to engage the attention of any man in power, and should thus be the means of applying any remedy, to the most inveterate evils at least, I have obtained my whole desire, and shall have lain so long wind-bound in the ports of this kingdom to some purpose. I would indeed have this work, which, if I should live to finish it, a matter of no great certainty, if indeed of any great hope to me, will be probably the last I shall ever undertake, to produce some better end than the mere diversion of the reader.

Monday, July 22. THIS day our captain went ashore, to dine with a gentleman who lives in these parts, and who so exactly resembles the character given by Homer of Axylus,[265] that the only difference I can trace between them is, the one living by the highway, erected his hospitality chiefly in favour of land-travellers; and the other living by the water-side, gratifies his humanity by accommodating the wants of the mariner.

IN the evening our commander received a visit from a brother bashaw, who lay wind-bound in the same harbour. This latter captain was a Swiss. He was then master of a vessel bound to Guinea, and had formerly been a privateering, when our own hero was employed in the same laudable service. The honesty and freedom of the Switzer, his vivacity, in which he was in no respect inferior to his near neighbours the French, the aukward and affected politeness, which was likewise of French extraction, mixed with the brutal roughness of the English tar; for he had served under the colours of this nation, and his crew had been of the same, made such an odd variety, such a hotch-potch of character, that I should have been much diverted with him, had not his voice, which was as loud as a speaking trumpet, unfortunately made my head ach. The noise which he conveyed

[265] *Iliad*, vi. 12–19, where Axylus is described as 'a man rich in substance, that was beloved of all men; for he dwelt in a home by the high-road and was wont to give entertainment to all'. In *The Covent-Garden Journal* (Nos. 16, 20, 29), HF's essays on the virtues of good nature and benevolence are in the form of letters from 'Axylus'; and in *Amelia* (IX. viii) Dr Harrison applauds Homer for depicting a character of 'such extensive Benevolence' (p. 389). See also below, p. 646 n. 293.

into the deaf ears of his brother captain, who sat on one side of him, the soft addresses, with which, mixed with aukward bows, he saluted the ladies on the other, were so agreeably contrasted, that a man must not only have been void of all taste of humour, and insensible of mirth, but duller than Cibber is represented in the Dunciad,[266] who could be unentertained with him a little while: for, I confess, such entertainments should always be very short, as they are very liable to pall. But he suffered not this to happen at present. For having given us his company a quarter of an hour only, he retired, after many apologies for the shortness of his visit.

Tuesday, July 23. THE wind being less boisterous than it had hitherto been since our arrival here, several fishing boats, which the tempestuous weather yesterday had prevented from working, came on board us with fish. This was so fresh, so good in kind, and so very cheap, that we supplied ourselves in great numbers, among which were very large soals at four-pence a pair, and whitings, of almost a preposterous size, at nine-pence a score.

THE only fish which bore any price was a john dorée, as it is called.[267] I bought one of at least four pounds weight for as many shillings. It resembles a turbut in shape, but exceeds it in firmness and flavour. The price had the appearance of being considerable, when opposed to the extraordinary cheapness of others of value; but was, in truth, so very reasonable, when estimated by its goodness, that it left me under no other surprize, than how the gentlemen of this country, not greatly eminent for the delicacy of their taste, had discovered the preference of the dorée to all other fish: but I was informed that Mr. Quin,[268] whose distinguishing tooth hath been so justly

---

[266] Colley Cibber (1671–1757), comedian, playwright, and Poet Laureate. For twenty years Cibber had been the butt of HF's ridicule, but dullness—the fault for which Pope had made him hero of the *New Dunciad* (1742–3)—was never his characteristic, as HF protested in *The Jacobite's Journal*, No. 31 (2 July 1748): 'I have often thought Mr. *Pope's* Resentment hurried him too far, when he attempted to persuade the World that Mr. *Cibber* was a dull Fellow. Had he scrutinized very narrowly into his Works, he might possibly have found some Objection, which might have given my Friend more Trouble to refute; but when he was arraigned of Dulness, every Man of his Acquaintance was ready to bear Testimony on his Side, and the Accusation retorted all the Ridicule on the Accuser' (pp. 322–3).

[267] 'a john dorée': though HF represents this name for the delicious fish in question (*Zeus faber*) as generally used ('as it is called'), it appears to have been recently coined. The *OED* (s.v. 'John Dory') cites this passage as the earliest instance in print of prefixing the name *John* to *Dorée* or *Dory*, previously for 300 years the name of the fish. Otherwise 'John Dory', the captain of a French privateer, was the subject of a popular seventeenth-century song.

[268] On the actor James Quin, HF's friend, see above, p. 606 n. 191. Quin's fondness for 'John Dory dress'd in Bourdeaux wine' was well known. After retiring from the stage in 1751, he resided at Topsham, Devon, on the River Exe, and it is said he annually travelled to Plymouth 'to eat John Dory in perfection' (*Quin's Jests* [1766], pp. 88–9). HF's name for him—borrowed from the voluptuary Sir Epicure Mammon, of Ben Jonson's *Alchemist* (1612)—amused John Upton, who from Taunton, Somerset, on 30 August 1756 wrote James Harris: 'Sir Epicure Quin . . . has raisd the prize [*sic*] of John Dorys, a fish (as he calls it) of personal merit' (Burrows and Dunhill, p. 316).

celebrated, had lately visited Plymouth, and had done those honours to the dorée, which are so justly due to it from that sect of modern philosophers, who with Sir Epicure Mammon, or Sir Epicure Quin, their head, seem more to delight in a fish-pond than in a garden, as the old Epicureans are said to have done.[269]

UNFORTUNATELY for the fishmongers of London, the dorée resides only in those seas; for could any of this company but convey one to the temple of luxury under the Piazza, where Macklin the high priest daily serves up his rich offerings to that goddess,[270] great would be the reward of that fishmonger, in blessings poured down upon him from the goddess, as great would his merit be towards the high priest, who could never be thought to over-rate such valuable incense.

AND here having mentioned the extreme cheapness of fish in the Devonshire sea, and given some little hint of the extreme dearness with which this commodity is dispensed by those who deal in it in London, I cannot pass on without throwing forth an observation or two, with the same view with which I have scattered my several remarks through this voyage, sufficiently satisfied in having finished my life, as I have, probably, lost it, in the service of my country, from the best of motives, tho' it should be attended with the worst of success. Means are always in our power; ends are very seldom so.

OF all the animal foods with which man is furnished, there are none so plenty as fish. A little rivulet, that glides almost unperceived through a vast tract of rich land, will support more hundreds with the flesh of its inhabitants, than the meadow will nourish individuals. But if this be true of rivers, it is much truer of the sea shores, which abound with such immense variety of fish, that the curious fisherman, after he hath made his draught, often culls only the daintiest part, and leaves the rest of his prey to perish on the shore.

IF this be true, it would appear, I think, that there is nothing which might

[269] In *Tom Jones* (xv. i) HF distinguishes 'the antient *Epicureans*, who held . . . Wisdom to constitute the chief Good' from 'their Opposites, those modern *Epicures*, who place all Felicity in the abundant Gratification of every sensual Appetite' (p. 783). The school of the philosopher Epicurus (341–270 BC) was known as the 'Gardens', from the gardens in Athens where he taught.

[270] Charles Macklin (above, p. 606 n. 191) retired from the stage and in September 1753 leased chambers under the Grand Piazza next door to the playhouse in Covent Garden, for 'a magnificent Coffee-Room & a School of Oratory'. 'He was determined to cater to "the choice spirits of the age" ' and would take only silver, directing the waiters by a system of silent signals, 'imitated, he declared, from those invented by the Duke of York for use in the fleet'. The venture opened in March 1754 (for a description of the rooms, see *Public Advertiser* [11 March 1754]) and closed less than a year later, on 25 January 1755, with the bankruptcy of the proprietor. (William W. Appleton, *Charles Macklin* [Cambridge, Mass., 1961], pp. 98–107.)

be had in such abundance, and consequently so cheap, as fish, of which nature seems to have provided such inexhaustible stores with some peculiar design.[271] In the production of terrestrial animals, she proceeds with such slowness, that in the larger kind a single female seldom produces more than one a year, and this again requires three, four, or five years more to bring it to perfection. And tho' the lesser quadrupeds, those of the wild kind particularly, with the birds, do multiply much faster, yet can none of these bear any proportion with the aquatic animals, of whom every female matrix[272] is furnished with an annual offspring, almost exceeding the power of numbers, and which, in many instances at least, a single year is capable of bringing to some degree of maturity.

WHAT then ought in general to be so plentiful, what so cheap as fish? What then so properly the food of the poor? So in many places they are, and so might they always be in great cities which are always situated near the sea, or on the conflux of large rivers. How comes it then, to look no farther abroad for instances, that in our city of London the case is so far otherwise, that except that of sprats, there is no one poor palate in a hundred that knows the taste of fish.

IT is true, indeed, that this taste is generally of such excellent flavour, that it exceeds the power of French cookery to treat the palates of the rich with any thing more exquisitely delicate; so that was fish the common food of the poor, it might put them too much upon an equality with their betters, in the great article of eating, in which, at present, in the opinion of some, the great difference in happiness between man and man consists. But this argument I shall treat with the utmost disdain: for if ortolans[273] were as big as bustards,[274] and at the same time as plenty as sparrows, I should hold it yet reasonable to indulge the poor with the dainty, and that for this cause especially, that the rich would soon find a sparrow, if as scarce as an ortolan, to be much the greater, as it would certainly be the rarer, dainty of the two.

VANITY or scarcity will be always the favourite of luxury, but honest hunger will be satisfied with plenty. Not to search deeper into the cause of the evil, I shall think it abundantly sufficient to propose the remedies of it.

---

[271] Perhaps another allusion to William Derham's Boyle lectures (above, p. 607 and n. 194). Cf. *Physico-Theology* (II. vi) on 'The great Variety and Quantity of all things upon, and in the terraqueous Globe, provided for the Uses of the World': 'In the subaqueous Globe there are . . . so many Fishes . . . and other Creatures in the Waters . . . that there is nothing wanting to the Use of Man.'

[272] 'matrix': ovary (*OED*).

[273] 'ortolans': see above, p. 599 n. 166.

[274] 'bustards': the great bustard (*Otis tarda*), the largest European bird, now extinct in England (*OED*). In HF's *Miser* (III. iii) Lovegold cringes when his servant proposes to buy 'a Turkey, or rather a Bustard; which I believe, may be bought for a Guinea, or thereabouts'.

And, first, I humbly submit the absolute necessity of immediately hanging all the fishmongers within the bills of mortality;[275] and however it might have been some time ago the opinion of mild and temporizing men, that the evil complained of might be removed by gentler methods, I suppose at this day there are none who do not see the impossibility of using such with any effect. *Cuncta prius tentanda* might have been formerly urged with some plausibility, but *cuncta prius tentata* may now be replied:[276] for surely if a few monopolizing fishmongers could defeat that excellent scheme of the Westminster market,[277] to the erecting which so many justices of peace, as well as other wise and learned men, did so vehemently apply themselves, that they might be truely said not only to have laid the whole strength of their heads, but of their shoulders too, to the business, it would be a vain endeavour for any other body of men to attempt to remove so stubborn a nusance.

IF it should be doubted, whether we can bring this case within the letter of any capital law now subsisting? I am ashamed to own it cannot; for surely no crime better deserves such punishment; but the remedy may, nevertheless, be immediate, and if a law was made the beginning of next sessions, to take place immediately, by which the starving thousands of poor was declared to be felony, without benefit of clergy, the fishmongers would be hanged before the end of the sessions.

A SECOND method of filling the mouths of the poor, if not with loaves, at least with fishes,[278] is to desire the magistrates to carry into execution one, at least, out of near a hundred acts of parliament, for preserving the small

---

[275] Since 1592, when plague broke out, the Company of Parish Clerks had published weekly records of deaths (and later of births and baptisms) occurring in 109 parishes in and around London. HF's anger at the extortionate practices of the fishmongers was felt by many, including a correspondent to the *Public Advertiser* (26 October 1767) signing himself 'Cogitator': 'I have ever thought with Harry Fielding, that the only way to have Fish in Plenty, is to hang up all the Fishmongers.' See also below, n. 277.

[276] 'All other means have been already tried' for controlling the giants, Jupiter claims, before declaring war on them (Ovid, *Metamorphoses*, i. 190); Nicolaus Heinsius first adopted this variant reading in his epochal edition of Ovid (1658–61) and all other editors have followed since. *Cuncta prius tentanda*, the traditional reading, found in most manuscripts, would mean 'All other means must first be tried'; this was the reading HF followed in *The Jacobite's Journal*, No. 20 (16 April 1748), p. 240.

[277] The market was established in 1749 under 22 Geo. II, c. 49: 'An Act for Making a Free Market for the Sale of Fish in the City of *Westminster*; and for Preventing the Forestalling and Monopolizing of Fish'; it opened on 16 January 1750, below the new Westminster Bridge, the principal trustees being General James Oglethorpe, Viscount Trentham—MP for Westminster and brother-in-law of HF's patron, the Duke of Bedford—and another of his patrons, George Bubb Dodington. In its review of the *Journal*, *The Gentleman's Magazine*, 25 (March 1755) warmly endorsed HF's arguments on the subject (p. 129), perhaps helping to promote the Act of the following year (29 Geo. II, c. 39) intended to render the original measure 'more effectual'. The project, however, failed. See *The London Fishery Laid Open: or, The Arts of the Fishermen and Fishmongers Set in a True Light* (1759), by one of the Trustees; also Phillips, *Thames*, pp. 137, 213.

[278] Matthew 14: 17–21; Mark 6: 38–44; Luke 9: 13–17; John 6: 9–13.

fry of the river of Thames,[279] by which means as few fish would satisfy thousands, as may now be devoured by a small number of individuals. But while a fisherman can break through the strongest meshes of an act of parliament, we may be assured he will learn so to contrive his own meshes, that the smallest fry will not be able to swim thro' them.

OTHER methods may, we doubt not, be suggested by those who shall attentively consider the evil here hinted at; but we have dwelt too long on it already, and shall conclude with observing, that it is difficult to affirm, whether the atrocity of the evil itself, the facility of curing it, or the shameful neglect of the cure, be the more scandalous, or more astonishing.

AFTER having, however, gloriously regaled myself with this food, I was washing it down with some good claret, with my wife and her friend in the cabin, when the captain's valet de chambre, head cook, house and ship steward, footman in livery and out on't, secretary and fore-mast-man, all burst into the cabin at once, being indeed all but one person, and without saying, by your leave, began to pack half a hogshead of small beer in bottles, the necessary consequence of which must have been, either a total stop to conversation at that chearful season, when it is most agreeable, or the admitting that polyonymous officer aforesaid to the participation of it. I desired him, therefore, to delay his purpose a little longer, but he refused to grant my request; nor was he prevailed on to quit the room till he was threatened with having one bottle to pack more than his number, which then happened to stand empty within my reach.

WITH these menaces he retired at last, but not without muttering some menaces on his side, and which, to our great terror, he failed not to put into immediate execution.

OUR captain was gone to dinner this day with his Swiss brother; and tho' he was a very sober man, was a little elevated with some champaign, which, as it cost the Swiss little or nothing, he dispensed at his table more liberally than our hospitable English noblemen put about those bottles, which the ingenious Peter Taylor[280] teaches a led

---

[279] Again HF's remarks and their endorsement by *The Gentleman's Magazine* may have been influential. 'An Act for the more effectual Preservation and Improvement of the Spawn and Fry of Fish, in the River of *Thames* and Waters of *Medway*' was passed in 1757 (30 Geo. II, c. 21). Keymer (*Fielding's Journal*, s.v. '*Tuesday, July 23*', p. 137 n. 6).

[280] Peter Taylor (1714–77), a silversmith; he was later MP for Wells and Portsmouth (1765–6, 1774–7). Besides acting as HF's accountant (*Life*, p. 509), he was probably one of the proprietors of the Universal Register Office, the business venture which HF and his brother John launched in February 1750, located on the Strand across the way from Taylor's house (CGJ, p. xvii n. 4). From Lisbon, HF would send him a present of onions (below, Appendix C.3, Letter 3).

captain[281] to avoid by distinguishing by the name of that generous liquor, which all humble companions are taught to postpone to[282] the flavour of methuen,[283] or honest port.

WHILE our two captains were thus regaling themselves, and celebrating their own heroic exploits, with all the inspiration which the liquor, at least, of wit could afford them, the polyonymous officer arrived, and being saluted by the name of honest Tom, was ordered to sit down and take his glass before he delivered his message; for every sailor is by turns his captain's mate over a can, except only that captain bashaw who presides in a man of war, and who upon earth has no other mate, unless it be another of the same bashaws.

TOM had no sooner swallowed his draught, than he hastily began his narrative, and faithfully related what had happened on board our ship; we say faithfully, tho' from what happened it may be suspected that Tom chose to add, perhaps, only five or six immaterial circumstances, as is always, I believe, the case, and may possibly have been done by me in relating this very story, tho' it happened not many hours ago.

NO sooner was the captain informed of the interruption which had been given to his officer, and indeed to his orders, for he thought no time so convenient as that of his absence for causing any confusion in the cabin, than he leapt with such haste from his chair, that he had like to have broke his sword, with which he always begirt himself when he walked out of his ship, and sometimes when he walked about in it, at the same time grasping eagerly that other implement called a cockade, which modern soldiers wear on their helmets, with the same view as the antients did their crests, to terrify the enemy; he muttered something, but so inarticularly, that the word *damn* was only intelligible; he then hastily took leave of the Swiss captain, who was too well bred to press his stay on such an occasion, and

---

[281] 'a led captain': a sycophant or parasite (*OED*, s.v. 'led' 3). Cf. *Champion* (2 October 1740), where HF, after describing the bully behaviour of a military captain, relates how one can be pacified: 'Notwithstanding the great Fury of this Animal, I have observ'd, that by feeding it will become tame, and will *go led* by such its Feeders, on whom it will fawn in a very abject and submissive Manner; and, indeed, I have known few great Personages without one or more of these' (p. 470). Cf. also *Joseph Andrews* (II. xiv), pp. 165–6, and *Tom Jones* (XI. ix), p. 611.

[282] 'to postpone to': to put in an inferior position or rank (*OED*, s.v. 'postpone' 3).

[283] 'methuen': a jocular name for Portuguese wines imported under the favourable terms of the treaty of 1703 between England and Portugal negotiated by Paul Methuen, the English minister to Lisbon (*OED*; above, p. 566 n. 71). HF's syntax in this sentence is tortuous; but when unpacked, the meaning would seem to be as follows: his friend 'the ingenious Peter Taylor' teaches a toady at his table not to call for the expensive bottle of French champagne but to call instead for the cheaper bottle of port, the quality of which he has taught the toady to prefer to champagne. Cf. *True Patriot*, No. 13 (21–8 January 1746), where, in time of war with France, 'Sir *John*' offers 'no other Wine but that of *Portugal*', to which an affected young 'Bowe' retorts 'I had rather live under *French* Government, than be debarred from *French* Wine' (p. 203).

leapt first from the ship to his boat, and then from his boat to his own ship, with as much fierceness in his looks as he had ever express'd on boarding his defenceless prey, in the honourable calling of a privateer.

HAVING regained the middle deck, he paused a moment, while Tom and others loaded themselves with bottles, and then descending into the cabin exclaimed with a thundering voice, D—n me, why aren't the bottles stoed in, according to my orders?

I ANSWERED him very mildly, that I had prevented his man from doing it, as it was at an inconvenient time to me, and as in his absence, at least, I esteemed the cabin to be my own. 'Your cabin,' repeated he many times, 'no, d——me, 'tis my cabin. Your cabin! D——me! I have brought my hogs to a fair market.[284] I suppose, indeed, you think it your cabin, and your ship, by your commanding in it; but I will command in it, d—n me! I will shew the world I am the commander, and no body but I! Did you think I sold you the command of my ship for that pitiful thirty pounds? I wish I had not seen you nor your thirty pounds aboard of her.' He then repeated the words thirty pounds often, with great disdain, and with a contempt which, I own, the sum did not seem to deserve in my eye, either in itself, or on the present occasion; being, indeed, paid for the freight of ——weight of human flesh, which is above 50 per cent. dearer than the freight of any other luggage, whilst in reality it takes up less room, in fact, no room at all.

IN truth the sum was paid for nothing more, than for a liberty to six persons, (two of them servants) to stay on board a ship while she sails from one port to another, every shilling of which comes clear into the captain's pocket. Ignorant people may perhaps imagine, especially when they are told that the captain is obliged to sustain them, that their diet, at least, is worth something; which may probably be now and then so far the case, as to deduct a tenth part from the neat profits on this account; but it was otherwise at present: for when I had contracted with the captain at a price which I by no means thought moderate, I had some content in thinking I should have no more to pay for my voyage; but I was whispered that it was expected the passengers should find themselves in several things; such as tea, wine, and such-like; and particularly that gentlemen should stowe of the latter a much larger quantity than they could use, in order to leave the remainder as a present to the captain, at the end of the voyage; and it was expected, likewise, that gentlemen should put aboard some fresh stores, and the more of such things were put aboard, the welcomer they would be to the captain.

---

[284] 'You have brought your hogs to a fair market. Spoken in derision when a business hath sped ill' (J. Howell, *Proverbs or Old Sayed-Sawes and Adages in the English Tongue* [1659], p. 5). Keymer (*Fielding's Journal*, s.v. '*Tuesday, July 23*', p. 138 n. 11).

I WAS prevailed with by these hints, to follow the advice proposed, and accordingly, besides tea, and a large hamper of wine, with several hams and tongues, I caused a number of live chickens and sheep to be conveyed aboard; in truth, treble the quantity of provision which would have supported the persons I took with me, had the voyage continued three weeks, as it was supposed, with a bare possibility, it might.

INDEED it continued much longer; but, as this was occasioned by our being wind-bound in our own ports, it was by no means of any ill consequence to the captain, as the additional stores of fish, fresh meat, butter, bread, &c. which I constantly laid in, greatly exceeded the consumption, and went some way in maintaining the ship's crew. It is true, I was not obliged to do this; but it seemed to be expected; for the captain did not think himself obliged to do it; and, I can truly say, I soon ceased to expect it of him. He had, I confess, on board, a number of fowls and ducks sufficient for a West-India voyage: all of them, as he often said, 'Very fine birds, and of the largest breed.' This, I believe, was really the fact, and, I can add, that they were all arrived at the full perfection of their size. Nor was there, I am convinced, any want of provisions of a more substantial kind; such as dried beef, pork, and fish; so that the captain seemed ready to perform his contract, and amply to provide for his passengers. What I did then was not from necessity, but, perhaps, from a less excusable motive, and was, by no means, chargeable to the account of the captain.

BUT let the motive have been what it would, the consequence was still the same, and this was such, that I am firmly persuaded the whole pitiful 30 l. came pure and neat into the captain's pocket, and not only so, but attended with the value of 10 l. more in sundries, into the bargain. I must confess my self therefore at a loss how the epithet *pitiful* came to be annexed to the above sum: for not being a pitiful price for what it was given, I cannot conceive it to be pitiful in itself; nor do I believe it is so thought by the greatest men in the kingdom; none of whom would scruple to search for it in the dirtiest kennel,[285] where they had only a reasonable hope of success.

HOW, therefore, such a sum should acquire the idea of pitiful, in the eyes of the master of a ship, seems not easy to be accounted for; since it appears more likely to produce in him ideas of a different kind. Some men, perhaps, are no more sincere in the contempt for it which they express, than others in their contempt of money in general; and I am the rather inclined to this persuasion, as I have seldom heard of either, who have refused or refunded this their despised object. Besides, it is sometimes impossible to believe these professions, as every action of the man's life is a contradiction to it.

---

[285] 'kennel': the gutter of a street (*OED*).

Who can believe a tradesman, who says he would not tell his name for the profit he gets by the selling such a parcel of goods, when he hath told a thousand lies in order to get it?

PITIFUL, indeed, is often applied to an object, not absolutely, but comparatively with our expectations, or with a greater object: In which sense it is not easy to set any bounds to the use of the word. Thus, a handful of halfpence daily appear pitiful to a porter, and a handful of silver to a drawer. The latter, I am convinc'd, at a polite tavern, will not tell his name (for he will not give you any answer) under the price of gold. And, in this sense, 30 l. may be accounted pitiful by the lowest mechanic.

ONE difficulty only seems to occur, and that is this: How comes it that, if the profits of the meanest arts are so considerable, the professors of them are not richer than we generally see them? One answer to this shall suffice. Men do not become rich by what they get, but by what they keep. He who is worth no more than his annual wages or salary, spends the whole; he will be always a beggar, let his income be what it will; and so will be his family when he dies. This we see daily to be the case of ecclesiastics, who, during their lives, are extremely well provided for, only because they desire to maintain the honour of the cloth by living like gentlemen, which would, perhaps, be better maintained by living unlike them.

BUT, to return from so long a digression, to which the use of so improper an epithet gave occasion, and to which the novelty of the subject allured, I will make the reader amends by concisely telling him, that the captain poured forth such a torrent of abuse, that I very hastily, and very foolishly, resolved to quit the ship. I gave immediate orders to summons a hoy to carry me that evening to Dartmouth, without considering any consequence. Those orders I gave in no very low voice; so that those above stairs might possibly conceive there was more than one master in the cabin. In the same tone I likewise threatened the captain with that which, he afterwards said, he feared more than any rock or quick sand. Nor can we wonder at this, when we are told he had been twice obliged to bring to, and cast anchor there before, and had neither time escaped without the loss of almost his whole cargo.[286]

THE most distant sound of law thus frightened a man, who had often, I am convinced, heard numbers of cannon roar round him with intrepidity. Nor did he sooner see the hoy approaching the vessel, than he ran down again into the cabin, and, his rage being perfectly subsided, he tumbled on his knees, and a little too abjectly implored for mercy.

---

[286] Twice, after years of litigation, the courts had deprived Veale of the spoils from ships he had taken as a privateer (Keymer, *Fielding's Journal*, appendix II, p. 113).

I DID not suffer a brave man and an old man, to remain a moment in this posture; but I immediately forgave him.

AND here, that I may not be thought the sly trumpeter of my own praises, I do utterly disclaim all praise on the occasion. Neither did the greatness of my mind dictate, nor the force of my Christianity exact this forgiveness. To speak truth, I forgave him from a motive which would make men much more forgiving, if they were much wiser than they are; because it was convenient for me so to do.

Wednesday, July 24. THIS morning the captain drest himself in scarlet, in order to pay a visit to a Devonshire squire, to whom a captain of a ship is a guest of no ordinary consequence, as he is a stranger and a gentleman, who hath seen a great deal of the world in foreign parts, and knows all the news of the times.

THE squire, therefore, was to send his boat for the captain; but a most unfortunate accident happened: for, as the wind was extremely rough, and against the hoy, while this was endeavouring to avail itself of great sea-manship, in hawling up[287] against the wind, a sudden squall carried off sail and yard; or, at least, so disabled them, that they were no longer of any use, and unable to reach the ship; but the captain, from the deck, saw his hopes of venison disappointed, and was forced either to stay on board his ship, or to hoist forth his own long-boat, which he could not prevail with himself to think of, tho' the smell of the venison had had twenty times its attraction. He did, indeed, love his ship as his wife, and his boats as children, and never willingly trusted the latter, poor things! to the dangers of the seas.

TO say truth, notwithstanding the strict rigour with which he preserved the dignity of his station, and the hasty impatience with which he resented any affront to his person or orders, disobedience to which he could in no instance brook in any person on board, he was one of the best natur'd fellows alive. He acted the part of a father to his sailors; he expressed great tenderness for any of them when ill, and never suffered any, the least work of supererogation to go unrewarded by a glass of gin. He even extended his humanity, if I may so call it, to animals, and even his cats and kittens had large shares in his affections. An instance of which we saw this evening, when the cat, which had shewn it could not be drowned, was found suffocated under a feather-bed in the cabin. I will not endeavour to describe his lamentations with more prolixity than barely by saying, they were grievous, and seemed to have some mixture of the Irish howl in them. Nay, he carried his fondness even to inanimate objects, of which we have above set down a pregnant example in his demonstration of love and tenderness towards his

---

[287] 'hawling up': to trim the sails so as to sail nearer to the wind (*OED*, s.v. 'haul' 3).

boats and ship. He spoke of a ship which he had commanded formerly, and which was long since no more, which he had called the Princess of Brasil,[288] as a widower of a deceased wife. This ship, after having followed the honest business of carrying goods and passengers for hire many years, did at last take to evil courses and turn privateer, in which service, to use his own words, she received many dreadful wounds, which he himself had felt, as if they had been his own.

Thursday, July 25. As the wind did not yesterday discover any purpose of shifting, and the water in my belly grew troublesome, and rendered me short-breathed; I began a second time to have apprehensions of wanting the assistance of a trochar, when none was to be found: I therefore concluded to be tapped again, by way of precaution;[289] and accordingly I this morning summoned on board a surgeon from a neighbouring parish, one whom the captain greatly recommended, and who did indeed perform his office with much dexterity. He was, I believe likewise, a man of great judgment and knowledge in the profession; but of this I cannot speak with perfect certainty; for when he was going to open on the dropsy at large, and on the particular degree of the distemper under which I laboured, I was obliged to stop him short, for the wind was changed, and the captain in the utmost hurry to depart; and to desire him, instead of his opinion, to assist me with his execution.

I WAS now once more delivered from my burthen, which was not indeed so great as I had apprehended, wanting two quarts of what was let out at the last operation.

WHILE the surgeon was drawing away my water, the sailors were drawing up the anchor; both were finished at the same time, we unfurled our sails, and soon passed the Berry-head, which forms the mouth of the bay.

---

[288] Perhaps a false name; the ships Veale is known to have commanded before the *Queen of Portugal* were the *Saudades* (Portuguese meaning 'longing'), a commercial vessel, and the privateers the *Hunter*, the *Inspector*, and the *Dreadnaught* (Keymer, *Fielding's Journal*, appendix II, pp. 111–13). With this old mariner's affection for his ship, cf. the reaction of the seamen in *Jonathan Wild* (IV. viii) as they witnessed the wreck of their 'charming *Molly*': 'they beheld their Ship perish with the Tenderness of a Lover or a Parent, they spoke of her as the fondest Husband would of his Wife' (*Miscellanies* iii, p. 160); and also in *Amelia* (III. iv), the captain's fear for the safety of 'his dear *Lovely Peggy* . . . which he swore he loved as dearly as his own Soul' (p. 111).

[289] Cf. HF's letter to John from Junqueira (*c.* 10–14 September): 'With Regard to the principal Point, my Health . . . I was tapped again (being the 5th time) at Torbay partly indeed by way of anticipation, the Day before we sailed—wanting one [day] of three Weeks [actually four weeks: see above, "*Friday, June* 28"] since the operation in the Thames. Nine Quarts of Water were now taken away, and possibly here I left the Dropsy: for I have heard nothing of it since, and have now at almost 8 Weeks Distance not a Drop of Water in me to my Knowledge' (below, Appendix C.3, Letter 3). This sanguine report of his recovery in the more benign climate of Portugal raised false hopes in London, where on 16 October, eight days after his death, the *Public Advertiser* announced HF was well again: 'His Gout has entirely left him, and his Appetite returned.'

WE had not however sailed far, when the wind, which had, tho' with a slow pace, kept us company about six miles, suddenly turned about, and offered to conduct us back again: a favour, which, though sorely against the grain, we were obliged to accept.

NOTHING remarkable happened this day; for as to the firm persuasion of the captain that he was under the spell of witchcraft, I would not repeat it too often, tho' indeed he repeated it an hundred times every day; in truth, he talked of nothing else, and seemed not only to be satisfied in general of his being bewitched, but actually to have fixed, with good certainty, on the person of the witch, whom, had he lived in the days of Sir Matthew Hale,[290] he would have been infallibly indicted, and very possibly have hanged for the detestable sin of witchcraft; but that law, and the whole doctrine that supported it, are now out of fashion; and witches, as a learned divine once chose to express himself, are put down by act of parliament.[291] This witch, in the captain's opinion, was no other than Mrs. Francis of Ryde, who, as he insinuated, out of anger to me, for not spending more money in her house than she could produce any thing to exchange for, or any pretence to charge for, had laid this spell on his ship.[292]

THO' we were again got near our harbour by three in the afternoon, yet it seemed to require a full hour or more, before we could come to our former place of anchoring, or birth, as the captain called it. On this occasion we exemplified one of the few advantages, which the travellers by water have over the travellers by land. What would the latter often give for the sight of one of those hospitable mansions, where he is assured *that there is good entertainment for man and horse*; and where both may consequently promise themselves to assuage that hunger which exercise is so sure to raise in a healthy constitution.

AT their arrival at this mansion, how much happier is the state of the

---

[290] Sir Matthew Hale (1609–76), Chief Justice of the King's Bench. Hale was probably a more important source of HF's thinking about the common law than anyone but Sir Edward Coke (see *Enquiry*, pp. xxxi–xxxii and index); but HF nonetheless regretted Hale's enforcement of the laws against witchcraft passed in the reign of James I. In 1665 Hale presided at the trial of two women who were convicted of witchcraft and hanged (*A Tryal of Witches* [1682]); he expressed his belief in witchcraft in *A Meditation concerning the Mercy of God in Preserving Us from the Power and Malice of Evil Angels* (1693). See also below, p. 647 n. 296.

[291] The Witchcraft Act of 1604 (1 Jas. I, c. 12) was repealed in 1736 (9 Geo. II, c. 5), eliciting from HF, under the name of 'Rachel Foresight', a humorous contribution to *The Craftsman*, No. 503 (21 February 1736), in *New Essays*, pp. 127–38. (See also below, p. 647 n. 296.) In the present context, his reference to 'a learned divine' suggests Conyers Middleton (1683–1750), who, in *A Free Inquiry into the Miraculous Powers, Which Are Supposed to Have Subsisted in the Christian Church* (1749 [for 1748]), had declared that 'the belief of witches is now utterly extinct' (p. 223); the copy of this work in HF's library (Ribbles M18) appears to have been Middleton's own, purchased at the sale of his library (ibid., pp. xxxix and n. 103, 219).

[292] Cf. *Tom Jones* (XII. xi), where Partridge, like Veale, is convinced that an old woman whom Jones had failed to tip as they began their journey was a witch who had raised a storm against them (p. 662).

horse than that of the master? The former is immediately led to his repast, such as it is, and whatever it is, he falls to it with appetite. But the latter is in a much worse situation. His hunger, however violent, is always in some degree delicate, and his food must have some kind of ornament, or as the more usual phrase is, of dressing, to recommend it. Now all dressing requires time; and therefore, though perhaps, the sheep might be just killed before you came to the inn, yet in cutting him up, fetching the joint, which the landlord by mistake said he had in the house, from the butcher at two miles distance, and afterwards, warming it a little by the fire, two hours at least must be consumed, while hunger for want of better food, preys all the time on the vitals of the man.

How different was the case with us? we carried our provision, our kitchen, and our cook with us, and we were at one and the same time travelling on our road, and sitting down to a repast of fish, with which the greatest table in London can scarce at any rate be supplied.

Friday, July 26. As we were disappointed of our wind, and obliged to return back the preceding evening, we resolved to extract all the good we could out of our misfortune, and to add considerably to our fresh stores of meat and bread, with which we were very indifferently provided when we hurried away yesterday. By the captain's advice we likewise laid in some stores of butter, which we salted and potted ourselves, for our use at Lisbon, and we had great reason afterwards to thank him for his advice.

In the afternoon, I persuaded my wife, whom it was no easy matter for me to force from my side, to take a walk on shore, whither the gallant captain declared he was ready to attend her. Accordingly, the ladies set out, and left me to enjoy a sweet and comfortable nap after the operation of the preceding day.

Thus we enjoyed our separate pleasure full three hours, when we met again; and my wife gave the foregoing account of the gentleman, whom I have before compared to Axylus,[293] and of his habitation, to both which she had been introduced by the captain in the stile of an old friend and acquaintance, though this foundation of intimacy seemed to her to be no deeper laid than in an accidental dinner, eaten many years before, at this temple of hospitality, when the captain lay wind-bound in the same bay.

Saturday, July 27. Early this morning the wind seemed inclined to change in our favour. Our alert captain snatched its very first motion, and got under sail with so very gentle a breeze, that as the tide was against him, he recommended to a fishing-hoy to bring after him a vast salmon and some other provisions which lay ready for him on shore.

---

[293] See above, p. 633 n. 265.

Our anchor was up at six, and before nine in the morning we had doubled[294] the Berry-head, and were arrived off Dartmouth, having gone full three miles in as many hours, in direct opposition to the tide, which only befriended us out of our harbour; and though the wind was, perhaps our friend, it was so very silent, and exerted itself so little in our favour, that, like some cool partisans, it was difficult to say whether it was with us or against us.[295] The captain, however, declared the former to be the case, during the whole three hours; but at last he perceived his error; or rather, perhaps, this friend, which had hitherto wavered in chusing his side, became now more determined. The captain then suddenly tacked about, and asserting that he was bewitched, submitted to return to the place from whence he came. Now, though I am as free from superstition as any man breathing, and never did believe in witches, notwithstanding all the excellent arguments of my Lord Chief Justice Hale in their favour,[296] and long before they were put down by an act of parliament,[297] yet by what power a ship of burthen should sail three miles against both wind and tide, I cannot conceive; unless there was some supernatural interposition in the case: nay, could we admit that the wind stood neuter, the difficulty would still remain. So that we must of necessity conclude, that the ship was either bewinded or bewitched.

The captain, perhaps, had another meaning. He imagined himself, I believe, bewitched, because the wind, instead of persevering in it changed in his favour, for change it certainly did that morning, should suddenly return to its favourite station, and blow him back towards the bay. But if this was his opinion, he soon saw cause to alter; for he had not measured half the way back, when the wind again declared in his favour, and so loudly that there was no possibility of being mistaken.

The orders for the second tack were given, and obeyed with much more alacrity, than those had been for the first. We were all of us indeed in high spirits on the occasion; though some of us a little regretted the good things we were likely to leave behind us by the fisherman's neglect: I might give it a worse name, for he faithfully promised to execute the commission, which he had had abundant opportunity to do; but *Nautica fides* deserves as much

---

[294] 'doubled': to sail to the other side of (a cape or point), so that the ship's course is, as it were, doubled (*OED*, s.v. 'double' v. 9).

[295] Cf. Matthew 12: 30.

[296] On Hale, see above, p. 645 n. 290. Hale believed, 'That there were such Creatures as *Witches* he made no doubt at all; For *First*, the Scriptures had affirmed so much. *Secondly*, The wisdom of all Nations had provided Laws against such Persons, which is an Argument of their confidence of such a Crime' ('A Tryal of Witches', reprinted in Hale's *Short Treatise touching Sheriffs Accompts* [1716], p. 102). Cf. Parson Adams in *Joseph Andrews* (IV. xiv): 'he often asserted he believed in the Power of Witchcraft . . . and did not see how a Christian could deny it' (p. 335).

[297] See above, p. 645 n. 291.

to be proverbial, as ever *Punica fides* could formerly have done.[298] Nay, when we consider that the Carthaginians came from the Phenicians, who are supposed to have produced the first mariners, we may probably see the true reason of the adage, and it may open a field of very curious discoveries to the antiquarian.

WE were, however, too eager to pursue our voyage, to suffer any thing we left behind us to interrupt our happiness, which indeed many agreeable circumstances conspired to advance. The weather was inexpressibly pleasant, and we were all seated on the deck, when our canvas began to swell with the wind. We had likewise in our view above thirty other sail around us, all in the same situation.[299] Here an observation occurred to me which, perhaps, though extremely obvious, did not offer itself to every individual in our little fleet: when I perceived with what different success we proceeded, under the influence of a superior power, which while we lay almost idle ourselves, pushed us forward on our intended voyage, and compared this with the slow progress which we had made in the morning, of ourselves and without any such assistance, I could not help reflecting how often the greatest abilities lie wind-bound as it were in life; or if they venture out, and attempt to beat the seas, they struggle in vain against wind and tide, and if they had not sufficient prudence to put back, are most probably cast away on the rocks and quicksands, which are every day ready to devour them.

IT was now our fortune to set out *melioribus avibus*.[300] The wind freshned so briskly in our poop, that the shore appeared to move from us, as fast as we did from the shore. The captain declared he was sure of a wind, meaning its continuance; but he had disappointed us so often, that he had lost all credit. However, he kept his word a little better now, and we lost sight of our native land, as joyfully, at least, as it is usual to regain it.

Sunday, July 28. THE next morning, the captain told me he thought himself thirty miles to the westward of Plymouth, and before evening declared that the Lizard point, which is the extremity of Cornwall, bore several leagues to leewards. Nothing remarkable past this day, except the captain's devotion, who, in his own phrase, summoned all hands to prayers, which were read by a common sailor upon deck, with more devout force and address, than they are commonly read by a country curate, and received

[298] '*Punica fides*': 'Punic faith' (Sallust, *Jugurtha*, 108); Carthaginians were proverbial for treachery, as Greeks were for lying (*Graeca fides*). HF's coinage *Nautica fides* means 'seamen's faith'.
[299] The following notice appeared in the *Public Advertiser* (Thursday 1 August 1754), perhaps reporting news from a lost letter by HF: 'There are more outward-bound Ships detained in the Channel by contrary Winds, than is within the Memory of the oldest Man alive, at the same Time of the Year. The Number is computed at above 200; of which 30 are now in Torbay, Devon.'
[300] '*melioribus avibus*': with better omens (literally 'with better birds', by whose flight and song the Romans divined the future).

with more decency and attention by the sailors than are usually preserved in city congregations. I am indeed assured, that if any such affected disregard of the solemn office in which they were engaged, as I have seen practised by fine gentlemen and ladies, expressing a kind of apprehension lest they should be suspected of being really in earnest in their devotion, had been shewn here, they would have contracted the contempt of the whole audience. To say the truth, from what I observed in the behaviour of the sailors in this voyage, and on comparing it with what I have formerly seen of them at sea and on shore, I am convinced that on land there is nothing more idle and dissolute; in their own element, there are no persons near the level of their degree, who live in the constant practice of half so many good qualities. They are, for much the greater part, perfect masters of their business, and always extremely alert, and ready in executing it, without any regard to fatigue or hazard. The soldiers themselves are not better disciplined, nor more obedient to orders than these whilst aboard; they submit to every difficulty which attends their calling with chearfulness, and no less virtues than patience and fortitude are exercised by them every day of their lives.

ALL these good qualities, however, they always leave behind them on shipboard: the sailor out of the water is, indeed, as wretched an animal as the fish out of water; for tho' the former hath in common with amphibious animals the bare power of existing on the land, yet if he be kept there any time, he never fails to become a nuisance.

THE ship having had a good deal of motion since she was last under sail, our women returned to their sickness, and I to my solitude; having, for twenty-four hours together, scarce opened my lips to a single person. This circumstance of being shut up within the circumference of a few yards, with a score of human creatures, with not one of whom it was possible to converse, was perhaps so rare, as scarce ever to have happened before, nor could it ever happen to one who disliked it more than myself, or to myself at a season when I wanted more food for my social disposition, or could converse less wholsomely and happily with my own thoughts. To this accident, which fortune opened to me in the Downs, was owing the first serious thought which I ever entertained of enroling myself among the voyage-writers;[301] some of the most amusing pages, if indeed there be any which deserve that name, were possibly the production of the most disagreeable hours which ever haunted the author.

---

[301] The *Queen of Portugal* remained in the Downs from 2 to 8 July. Amory infers from the alteration of the heading 'Wednesday [24 July]' in the first edition to '*Wednesday* the 20th' in the second edition, which he takes to signify the twentieth day of composition, that HF began writing the *Journal* on 5 July (Textual Introduction, p. 531).

Monday, July 29. AT noon the captain took an observation, by which it appeared that Ushant[302] bore some leagues northward of us, and that we were just entering the bay of Biscay. We had advanced a very few miles in this bay before we were entirely becalmed; we furl'd our sails, as being of no use to us. While we lay in this most disagreeable situation, more detested by the sailors than the most violent tempest, we were alarmed with the loss of a fine piece of salt beef, which had been hung in the sea to freshen it; this being it seems, the strange property of saltwater. The thief was immediately suspected, and presently afterwards taken by the sailors. He was indeed no other than a huge shark, who, not knowing when he was well off, swallowed another piece of beef, together with a great iron crook on which it was hung, and by which he was dragged into the ship.

I SHOULD scarce have mentioned the catching this shark, though so exactly conformable to the rules and practice of voyage-writing, had it not been for a strange circumstance that attended it. This was the recovery of the stolen beef out of the shark's maw, where it lay unchewed and undigested, and whence being conveyed into the pot, the flesh, and the thief that had stoln it, joined together in furnishing variety to the ship's crew.

DURING this calm we likewise found the mast of a large vessel, which the captain thought had lain at least three years in the sea. It was stuck all over with a little shell-fish or reptile called a barnacle, and which probably are the prey of the rock-fish, as our captain calls it, asserting that it is the finest fish in the world; for which we are obliged to confide entirely in his taste; for, though he struck the fish with a kind of harping iron,[303] and wounded him, I am convinced, to death, yet he could not possess himself of his body; but the poor wretch escaped to linger out a few hours, with probably great torments.

IN the evening our wind returned and so briskly, that we ran upwards of twenty leagues before the next day's [*Tuesday's*] Observation, which brought us to Lat. 47°. 42′.[304] The captain promised us a very speedy passage through the bay, but he deceived us, or the wind deceived him, for it so slackened at sun-set, that it scarce carried us a mile in a hour during the whole succeeding night.

Wednesday, July 31. A GALE struck up a little after sun-rising, which carried us between three and four knots or miles an hour. We were this day at noon about the middle of the bay of Biscay, when the wind once more

---

[302] An island west of Brittany.

[303] 'harping iron': a harpoon.

[304] 'Lat. 47°. 42′: as the problem of determining longitude would not be solved until later in the century, the exact position of the ship cannot be fixed. For an approximation, showing it well into the Bay of Biscay and heading towards Lisbon, see the map, Appendix C.1, p. 758.

deserted us, and we were so entirely becalmed, that we did not advance a mile in many hours. My fresh-water reader will perhaps conceive no unpleasant idea from this calm; but it affected us much more than a storm could have done; for as the irascible passions of men are apt to swell with indignation long after the injury which first raised them is over, so fared it with the sea. It rose mountains high, and lifted our poor ship up and down, backwards and forwards, with so violent an emotion, that there was scarce a man in the ship better able to stand than myself. Every utensil in our cabin rolled up and down, as we should have rolled ourselves, had not our chairs been fast lashed to the floor. In this situation, with our tables likewise fastened by ropes, the captain and myself took our meal with some difficulty, and swallowed a little of our broth, for we spilt much the greater part. The remainder of our dinner being an old, lean, tame duck roasted, I regretted but little the loss of, my teeth not being good enough to have chewed it.

OUR women, who began to creep out of their holes in the morning, retired again within the cabin to their beds, and were no more heard of this day, in which my whole comfort was to find, by the captain's relation, that the swelling was sometimes much worse; he did, indeed, take this occasion to be more communicative than ever, and informed me of such misadventures that had befallen him within forty-six years at sea, as might frighten a very bold spirit from undertaking even the shortest voyage. Were these indeed but universally known, our matrons of quality would possibly be deterred from venturing their tender offspring at sea; by which means our navy would lose the honour of many a young commodore, who at twenty-two is better versed in maritime affairs than real seamen are made by experience at sixty.

AND this may, perhaps, appear the more extraordinary, as the education of both seems to be pretty much the same; neither of them having had their courage tried by Virgil's description of a storm,[305] in which, inspired as he was, I doubt whether our captain doth not exceed him.

IN the evening the wind, which continued in the N. W. again freshened, and that so briskly that cape Finister appeared by this day's observation[306] to bear a few miles to the southward. We now indeed sailed, or rather flew, near ten knots an hour; and the captain, in the redundancy of his good humour, declared he would go to church at Lisbon on Sunday next, for that he was sure of a wind; and indeed we all firmly believed him. But the event again contradicted him: for we were again visited by a calm in the evening.

---

[305] *Aeneid*, i. 81–156. See also below, p. 652 n. 308.
[306] In the sequence of days, 'Thursday' was overlooked.

BUT here, tho' our voyage was retarded, we were entertained with a scene which as no one can behold without going to sea, so no one can form an idea of any thing equal to it on shore. We were seated on the deck, women and all, in the serenest evening that can be imagined. Not a single cloud presented itself to our view, and the sun himself was the only object which engrossed our whole attention. He did indeed set with a majesty which is incapable of description, with which while the horizon was yet blazing with glory, our eyes were called off to the opposite part to survey the moon, which was then at full, and which in rising presented us with the second object that this world hath offered to our vision.[307] Compared to these the pageantry of theatres, or splendour of courts, are sights almost below the regard of children.

WE did not return from the deck till late in the evening: the weather being inexpressibly pleasant, and so warm, that even my old distemper perceived the alteration of the climate. There was indeed a swell, but nothing comparable to what we had felt before, and it affected us on the deck much less than in the cabin.

Friday, August 2. THE calm continued till sunrising, when the wind likewise arose; but unluckily for us, it came from a wrong quarter: it was S. S. E. which is that very wind which Juno would have solicited of Æolus, had Æneas been in our latitude bound for Lisbon.[308]

THE captain now put on his most melancholy aspect, and resumed his former opinion, that he was bewitched. He declared, with great solemnity, that this was worse and worse, for that a wind directly in his teeth was worse than no wind at all. Had we pursued the course which the wind persuaded us to take, we had gone directly for Newfoundland, if we had not fallen in with Ireland in our way. Two ways remained to avoid this; one was to put into a port of Galicia;[309] the other, to beat to the westward with as little sail as possible; and this was our captain's election.

AS for us, poor passengers, any port would have been welcome to us; especially, as not only our fresh provisions, except a great number of old ducks and fowls, but even our bread was come to an end, and nothing but sea biscuit remained, which I could not chew. So that now, for the first time in my life, I saw what it was to want a bit of bread.

THE wind, however, was not so unkind as we had apprehended; but

---

[307] Genesis 1: 16.

[308] *Aeneid*, i. 50–123: Juno, to prevent the founding of Rome, implores Æolus to raise a storm and wreck the Trojan ships: 'They swoop down upon the sea . . . East and South winds together, and the South-wester, thick with tempests' (i. 85–6).

[309] 'Galicia': a region above Portugal in north-west Spain bordering on the Bay of Biscay to the north and the Atlantic Ocean to the west.

having declined with the sun, it changed at the approach of the moon, and became again favourable to us; tho' so gentle, that the next day's observation carried us very little to the southward of cape Finister. This evening at six the wind, which had been very quiet all day, rose very high, and continuing in our favour, drove us seven knots an hour.

THIS day[310] we saw a sail, the only one, as I heard of, we had seen in our whole passage through the bay. I mention this on account of what appeared to me somewhat extraordinary. Tho' she was at such a distance that I could only perceive she was a ship, the sailors discovered she was a snow[311] bound to a port in Galicia.

Sunday, August 4. AFTER prayers, which our good captain read on the deck with an audible voice, and with but one mistake, of a lion for Elias, in the second lesson for this day,[312] we found ourselves far advanced in 42°, and the captain declared we should sup off Porte.[313] We had not much wind this day; but, as this was directly in our favour, we made it up with sail, of which we crowded all we had. We went only at the rate of four miles an hour, but with so uneasy a motion, continually rowling from side to side, that I suffered more than I had done in our whole voyage; my bowels being almost twisted out of my belly. However, the day was very serene and bright, and the captain, who was in high spirits, affirmed he had never passed a pleasanter at sea.

THE wind continued so brisk that we ran upwards of six knots an hour the whole night.

Monday, August 5. IN the morning, our captain concluded that he was got into lat. 40°, and was very little short of the Burlings,[314] as they are called in the charts. We came up with them at five in the afternoon, being the first land we had distinctly seen since we left Devonshire. They consist of abundance of little rocky islands, a little distant from the shore, three of them only shewing themselves above the water.

HERE the Portuguese maintain a kind of garrison, if we may allow it that name. It consists of malefactors, who are banished hither for a term, for divers small offences. A policy which they may have copied from the

---

[310] Saturday 3 August.
[311] 'snow': a small sailing-vessel resembling a brig, carrying a main- and foremast and a supplementary trysail mast close behind the mainmast; at this time often employed as a warship (*OED*).
[312] Two lessons are prescribed in the Book of Common Prayer for 4 August 1754 (the eighth Sunday after Trinity): for Morning Prayer, 1 Kings 13 (involving a lion); for Evening Prayer, 1 Kings 17 (involving Elijah). Curiously, HF uses the spelling 'Elias' as in the Roman Catholic Douay version, perhaps deliberately, so as to make the connection with 'lion' more obvious.
[313] 'Porte': presumably a typo for Porto, or Oporto, the Portuguese name (used by HF earlier, p. 632) for the port that was the centre of the wine trade.
[314] The Berlenga Islands, about 50 miles north of Lisbon.

Egyptians, as we may read in Diodorus Siculus.[315] That wise people, to prevent the corruption of good manners by evil communication,[316] built a town on the Red Sea, whither they transported a great number of their criminals, having first set an indelible mark on them, to prevent their returning and mixing with the sober part of their citizens.

THESE rocks lie about 15 leagues northwest of cape Roxent; or, as it is commonly called, the rock of Lisbon; which we past early the next morning.[317] The wind, indeed, would have carried us thither sooner; but the captain was not in a hurry, as he was to lose nothing by his delay. This is a very high mountain, situated on the northern side of the mouth of the river Tajo, which rising above Madrid, in Spain, and soon becoming navigable for small craft, empties itself, after a long course, into the sea, about four leagues below Lisbon.

ON the summit of the rock stands a hermitage, which is now in the possession of an Englishman,[318] who was formerly master of a vessel trading to Lisbon; and, having changed his religion and his manners, the latter of which, at least, were none of the best, betook himself to this place, in order to do penance for his sins. He is now very old, and hath inhabited this hermitage for a great number of years, during which he hath received some countenance from the royal family; and particularly from the present queen dowager,[319] whose piety refuses no trouble or expence by which she may make a proselyte; being used to say, that the saving one soul would repay all the endeavours of her life.

HERE we waited for the tide, and had the pleasure of surveying the face of the country, the soil of which, at this season, exactly resembles an old

---

[315] Actisanes, King of Ethiopia, conquered Egypt and banished thieves to a town not on the Red Sea, but on the Mediterranean near Gaza: 'he took all who had been judged guilty, and, cutting off their noses, settled them in a colony . . . called Rhinocolura [Nose-clipped] after the lot of its inhabitants' (Diodorus Siculus, *Bibliotheca Historica*, 1. lx. 4–5).

[316] In *The Covent-Garden Journal*, No. 10 (4 February 1752), HF provided the correct source of this proverb, which in *Tom Jones* (v. ii, p. 218) he had incorrectly attributed to Solomon: '*Evil Communications corrupt good Manners*, is a Quotation of St. Paul [1 Corinthians 15: 33] from Menander [*Thais*, Fragment 2]' (p. 77).

[317] The *Public Advertiser* (Thursday 29 August) confirmed the arrival at Lisbon of the *Queen of Portugal* on Tuesday 6 August.

[318] Not identified. The 'rock' in question was Cabo da Roca or the Rock of Lisbon, the westernmost point of the European continent, near the town of Cintra, a region of many hermitages. See Keymer's note (*Fielding's Journal*, s.v. '*Monday, Aug. 5*', p. 139 n. 3) for the impressions of contemporary tourists.

[319] Maria Anna of Austria (1689–1754), widow of John V (1689–1750). She died on 14 August, a week after HF arrived at Lisbon, the *Public Advertiser* (25 September 1754) carrying the following dispatch dated Lisbon, 21 August: 'The Remains of the late Queen Dowager have been interred with great Magnificence in the Church of the Barefooted German Carmelites, of which she was the Foundress, and to which she has left a Legacy of twenty thousand Pieces of Eight. Her Heart, it is said, will be carried to Vienna.'

brick kill,[320] or a field where the green-sward is pared up and set a-burning or rather a-smoaking, in little heaps, to manure the land. This sight will, perhaps, of all others, make an Englishman proud of and pleased with his own country, which in verdure excels, I believe, every other country. Another deficiency here, is the want of large trees, nothing above a shrub being here to be discovered in the circumference of many miles.

AT this place we took a pilot on board, who, being the first Portuguese we spoke to, gave us an instance of that religious observance which is paid by all nations to their laws: for, whereas it is here a capital offence to assist any person in going on shore from a foreign vessel, before it hath been examined, and every person in it viewed by the magistrates of health, as they are called, this worthy pilot, for a very small reward, rowed the Portuguese priest to shore at this place, beyond which he did not dare to advance; and in venturing whither he had given sufficient testimony of love for his native country.

WE did not enter the Tajo till noon, when after passing several old castles, and other buildings, which had greatly the aspect of ruins, we came to the castle of Bellisle,[321] where we had a full prospect of Lisbon, and were indeed within three miles of it.

HERE we were saluted with a gun, which was a signal to pass no farther, till we had complied with certain ceremonies, which the laws of this country require to be observed by all ships which arrive in this port. We were obliged then to cast anchor, and expect the arrival of the officers of the customs, without whose passport no ship must proceed farther than this place.

HERE likewise we received a visit from one of those magistrates of health before-mentioned. He refused to come on board the ship, till every person in her had been drawn up on deck, and personally viewed by him. This occasioned some delay on my part, as it was not the work of a minute to lift me from the cabin to the deck. The captain thought my particular case might have been excused from this ceremony; and that it would be abundantly sufficient if the magistrate, who was obliged afterwards to visit

---

[320] 'kill': kiln, pronounced 'kill' and therefore often spelled as here (*OED*). Portugal at this time was suffering from a severe drought, as reported in the *Public Advertiser* (26 August): '*Lisbon, Aug. 17*. The Heat and Drought are become intollerable in this Kingdom, particularly in the Province of Alemtejo, where the Cattle suffer greatly by the drying up of the Springs; and it is to be feared that the Heat of the Dog-Days will burn up their most fertile Pastures.'

[321] 'castle of Bellisle': the Tower of Belém, a citadel commanding the Tagus 2 miles west of Lisbon; others among the English there called it Bellisle (Rose Macaulay, *They Went to Portugal* [1946; Harmondsworth, 1988], p. 88). By mid-September HF had taken a villa in Junqueira, 'near Bellisle which is the Kensington of England, and where the Court now reside', in mourning for the Queen (below, Appendix C.3, Letter 3).

the cabin, surveyed me there. But this did not satisfy the magistrate's strict regard to his duty. When he was told of my lameness he called out with a voice of authority, 'Let him be brought up,' and his orders were presently complied with. He was indeed a person of great dignity, as well as of most exact fidelity in the discharge of his trust. Both which are the more admirable, as his salary is less than 30 l. English, *per annum*.

BEFORE a ship hath been visited by one of those magistrates, no person can lawfully go on board her; nor can any on board depart from her. This I saw exemplified in a remarkable instance. The young lad, whom I have mentioned as one of our passengers, was here met by his father, who, on the first news of the captain's arrival, came from Lisbon to Bellisle in a boat, being eager to embrace a son whom he had not seen for many years. But when he came along-side our ship, neither did the father dare ascend, nor the son descend, as the magistrate of health had not been yet on board.

SOME of my readers will, perhaps, admire the great caution of this policy, so nicely calculated for the preservation of this country from all pestilential distempers. Others will as probably regard it as too exact and formal to be constantly persisted in, in seasons of the utmost safety, as well as in times of danger. I will not decide either way; but will content myself with observing, that I never yet saw or heard of a place where a traveller had so much trouble given him at his landing as here. The only use of which, as all such matters begin and end in form only, is to put it into the power of low and mean fellows to be either rudely officious, or grossly corrupt, as they shall see occasion to prefer the gratification of their pride or of their avarice.

OF this kind, likewise, is that power which is lodged with other officers here, of taking away every grain of snuff, and every leaf of tobacco, brought hither from other countries,[322] tho' only for the temporary use of the person, during his residence here. This is executed with great insolence, and as it is in the hands of the dregs of the people, very scandalously: for, under pretence of searching for tobacco and snuff, they are sure to steal whatever they can find, insomuch that when they came on board, our sailors address'd us in the Covent-Garden language, 'Pray, gentlemen and ladies, take care of your swords and watches.' Indeed I never yet saw any thing equal to the contempt and hatred which our honest tars every moment express'd for these Portuguese officers.

---

[322] Tobacco was a Portuguese crown monopoly, rigorously enforced despite 'frequent foreign protests' (C. R. Boxer, *The Portuguese Seaborne Empire, 1415–1825* [Manchester, 1991], p. 321). HF would have found these restrictions particularly irksome: he was addicted to tobacco, which he sometimes chewed but more often took in the form of snuff—indeed, in his own caricature of himself in *The Champion* (27 May 1740) he has 'a great Quantity of Snuff on his Coat' (p. 345).

AT Bellisle lies buried Catharine of Arragon,[323] widow of Prince Arthur, eldest son of our Henry VII. afterwards married to, and divorced from, Henry VIII. Close by the church where her remains are deposited, is a large convent of Geronymites, one of the most beautiful piles of building in all Portugal.

IN the evening at twelve, our ship having received previous visits from all the necessary parties, took the advantage of the tide, and having sailed up to Lisbon, cast anchor there, in a calm, and a moonshiny night, which made the passage incredibly pleasant to the women, who remained three hours enjoying it, whilst I was left to the cooler transports of enjoying their pleasures at second-hand; and yet, cooler as they may be, whoever is totally ignorant of such sensation, is at the same time void of all ideas of friendship.

Wednesday, August 7. LISBON, before which we now lay at anchor, is said to be built on the same number of hills with old Rome; but these do not all appear to the water; on the contrary, one sees from thence one vast high hill and rock, with buildings arising above one another, and that in so steep and almost perpendicular a manner, that they all seem to have but one foundation.[324]

AS the houses, convents, churches, &c. are large, and all built with white stone, they look very beautiful at a distance, but as you approach nearer, and find them to want every kind of ornament, all idea of beauty vanishes at once. While I was surveying the prospect of this city, which bears so little resemblance to any other that I have ever seen, a reflection occurred to me, that if a man was suddenly to be removed from Palmyra[325] hither, and should take a view of no other city, in how glorious a light would the antient architecture appear to him? and what desolation and destruction of arts and

[323] HF confuses Catherine of Aragon, the first queen of Henry VIII, with Catherine of Braganza (1638–1705), daughter of John, King of Portugal, and queen of Charles II; after Charles's death (1685) and the 'Glorious Revolution' (1688–9), she returned to Portugal in 1692. On her death in December 1705 she was laid to rest in the chapel of the magnificent Jeronymite monastery at Belém; according to Charles Brockwell in 1726, the body was placed 'on the right Side of the High Altar enclosed in a Coffin of black Velvet, laced with a broad Gold Lace' (Keymer, *Fielding's Journal*).

[324] Cf. the impression of Lisbon, from much the same perspective, of the Welsh traveller Udal ap Rhys five years earlier: 'The City being built upon Seven Hills, some of them rise up above the rest; and some again are so interwoven and contrasted, that they form an agreeable Diversity of Hills and Vales: So that, from the opposite Sides of the *Tagus*, it looks like an immense Amphitheatre; which has all the Charms that can be produced by an infinite Variety of the most sumptuous Edifices, reflecting uncommon Beauties upon each other by the Happiness of their Situation' (*An Account of the Most Remarkable Places and Curiosities in Spain and Portugal* [1749], p. 241). Keymer (*Fielding's Journal* s.v. 'Wednesday, Aug. 7', p. 141 n. 1).

[325] The recent publication of Robert Wood's *The Ruins of Palmyra* (1753), with engravings from drawings by Giovanni Battisti Borra, may well have suggested the grandeur of that ancient Syrian city to serve in contrast with the 'desolation and destruction of arts and sciences' HF found in Lisbon. A copy of the first edition was in his library (Ribbles W20).

sciences would he conclude had happened between the several æra's of these cities?

I HAD now waited full three hours upon deck, for the return of my man, whom I had sent to bespeak a good dinner (a thing which had been long unknown to me) on shore, and then to bring a Lisbon chaise with him to the sea-shore; but, it seems, the impertinence of the providore[326] was not yet brought to a conclusion. At three o'clock, when I was from emptiness rather faint than hungry, my man returned, and told me, there was a new law lately made, that no passenger should set his foot on shore without a special order from the providore; and that he himself would have been sent to prison for disobeying it, had he not been protected as the servant of the captain. He informed me likewise, that the captain had been very industrious to get this order, but that it was then the providore's hour of sleep, a time when no man, except the King himself, durst disturb him.

TO avoid prolixity, tho' in a part of my narrative which may be more agreeable to my reader than it was to me, the providore having at last finished his nap, dispatched this absurd matter of form, and gave me leave to come, or rather to be carried, on shore.

WHAT it was that gave the first hint of this strange law is not easy to guess. Possibly, in the infancy of their defection,[327] and before their government could be well established, they were willing to guard against the bare possibility of surprize, of the success of which bare possibility the Trojan horse will remain for ever on record, as a great and memorable example. Now the Portuguese have no walls to secure them, and a vessel of two or three hundred tuns will contain a much larger body of troops than could be concealed in that famous machine, tho' Virgil tells us (somewhat hyperbolically, I believe) that it was as big as a mountain.[328]

ABOUT seven in the evening I got into a chaise on shore, and was driven through the nastiest city in the world, tho' at the same time one of the most populous, to a kind of coffee-house,[329] which is very pleasantly situated on

---

[326] 'providore': the chief customs officer.

[327] Probably referring not to the earliest phase of Portuguese independence but to the successful insurrection led in 1640 by the Duke of Branza (afterwards John IV) to end sixty years of Spanish rule. Keymer (*Fielding's Journal* s.v. '*Wednesday, Aug. 7*', p. 141 n. 3).

[328] *Aeneid*, ii. 15.

[329] Tradition has it that this was one of the inns on the Rua Sacramento à Lapa where Byron later stayed, in the district then known as Buenos Ayres—perhaps, as Keymer suggests (s.v. '*Wednesday, Aug. 7*', p. 141 n. 5), the same mentioned by Richard Twiss in 1772: 'On landing, I was conducted to an English inn, kept by one De War, on the hill of Buenos Ayres, where there is an ordinary every day frequented by Englishmen' (*Travels through Portugal and Spain, in 1772 and 1773* [1775], p. 1). It is pleasant, at least, to suppose this inn or 'coffee house' survived the great earthquake of 1755; if so, it would likely be the 'house of entertainment near the *English* burying ground [situated on the hill of Buenos Ayres]' kept by Joseph Morley in 1755 (*GM*, 25 [1755], p. 594).

the brow of a hill, about a mile from the city, and hath a very fine prospect of the river Tajo from Lisbon to the sea.

HERE we regaled ourselves with a good supper, for which we were as well charged, as if the bill had been made on the Bath road, between Newbury and London.

AND now we could joyfully say,

Egressi optata Troes potiuntur ærena. [330]

Therefore in the words of Horace,

—hic Finis chartæque viæque. [331]

---

[330] *Aeneid*, i. 172 slightly misquoted: *egressi optata potiuntur Troes harena* ('disembarking . . . the Trojans gain the welcome beach').

[331] Horace, *Satires*, 1. v. 104, adapted: 'this is the end of the story, and the journey'.

9

A FRAGMENT OF A COMMENT ON
L. BOLINGBROKE'S ESSAYS (1755)

WEDNESDAY 6 March 1754—'that memorable day', as Fielding recalled in
the Introduction to the *Journal of a Voyage to Lisbon* (above, p. 562 and
n. 58), 'when the public lost Mr. Pelham', the Prime Minister, and he was
himself 'at the worst' (p. 562)—was marked in his opinion by another
unwelcome event: the posthumous publication of *The Works of the late
Right Honorable Henry St. John, Lord Viscount Bolingbroke. In Five Volumes,
complete. Published by David Mallet, Esq;* and distributed by Andrew Millar.[1]
Garrick signalized this unhappy coincidence a week later in his 'Ode on the
Death of *Mr Pelham*':

> The same sad morn, to Church and State
> (So for our sins 'twas fix'd by fate,)
>   A double stroke was giv'n;
> Black as the whirlwinds of the North,
> St. John's fell genius issued forth,
>   And Pelham fled to heaven.

In his entry for this day in the biography, Boswell recorded his own and
Johnson's revulsion on the occasion:

The wild and pernicious ravings, under the name of 'Philosophy,' which were thus
ushered into the world, gave great offence to all well-principled men. Johnson,
hearing of their tendency, which nobody disputed, was roused with a just indignation, and pronounced this memorable sentence upon the noble authour and his
editor. 'Sir, he was a scoundrel, and a coward: a scoundrel, for charging a blunder-
buss against religion and morality; a coward, because he had not resolution to fire
it off himself, but left half a crown to a beggarly Scotchman, to draw the trigger
after his death!'[2]

---

[1] *Public Advertiser* (6 March 1754). The first printing, in quarto, was followed by two in octavo entitled
The Philosophical Works.
[2] *Boswell's Life of Johnson*, ed. G. B. Hill and L. F. Powell, 6 vols. (Oxford, 1934), i, p. 268.

Before the month was out the freethinking bakers, cobblers, and comedians of the Robin Hood Society were debating the proposition, That Bolingbroke had done more than the Apostles to serve mankind.[3]

Earlier, when Millar, soon after Bolingbroke's death in December 1751, began publishing his more openly heterodox writings with *Letters on the Study and Use of History* (March 1752), Fielding in *The Covent-Garden Journal* (Nos. 46 [9 June] and 69 [4 November]) had warned readers of the consequences to society if his religious scepticism became fashionable. Now, with the revision of *Jonathan Wild* (March 1754) behind him, his brother John fully qualified to relieve him of the burden of 'justice business', and in the ill-founded belief that he was beginning 'slowly, as it were, to draw my feet out of the grave', Fielding turned his attention to the eighty-one 'Fragments or Minutes of Essays' in which Bolingbroke uttered his thoughts. He began reading these fragments with 'a very high prejudice to the doctrines said to have been established in them', yet with 'the highest, and strongest prepossession, in favour of the abilities of the author.'[4] When he had finished reading, he found 'my prepossessions greatly abated, and my prejudices not in the least removed' (p. 667).

The price Fielding paid for this service to the public did not go unnoticed. On 18 April the *Evening Advertiser* paid him this tribute:

It must always be remembered to the honour of Mr. Fielding, that, while he is sinking under a complicated load of dangerous disorders, and is so near the verge of eternity, that at night there is but little probability of his surviving to the next day; he devotes the whole strength of his faculties to the honour of God, and the virtue and happiness of the human soul, in detecting the pernicious errors of the late Lord Bolingbroke; who, as long as his memory shall be transmitted to posterity, must be considered as the disgrace of his country, and the enemy of mankind.

Arthur Murphy—the likely author of the laudatory remarks on the *Fragment* that conclude the 'Dedication to the Public' prefixed to the *Journal*[5]— later attested to Fielding's serious commitment to this 'laborious' project. In his biography Murphy remarks on 'the preparation [Fielding] made for it of long extracts and arguments from the fathers and the most eminent

---

[3] See *The Connoisseur* (28 March 1754) and the notice signed John Hopkins in the *Public Advertiser* (17 April 1754).

[4] For an account of Bolingbroke's political career and influence, and of HF's early admiration of his qualities as an author and political theorist, see below, p. 667 n. 1; also above in *Familiar Letters*, p. 494 n. 61.

[5] See 'Who Edited Fielding's *Journal of a Voyage to Lisbon* (1755)? The Case for Arthur Murphy and a New Fielding Essay', *Studies in Bibliography*, 55 (2002 [for 2004]), pp. 215–33. In an allegorical leader of *The Gray's-Inn Journal* (25 May 1754) Murphy had himself decried the 'baneful Influence' of Bolingbroke's writings.

writers of controversy';[6] these papers, left in John Fielding's possession, were presumably lost when the house at Bow Street was burned in the Gordon Riots of 1780. That Fielding intended to produce a serious and substantial critique of the incoherent 'scraps' of philosophy Bolingbroke, in his own phrase, had 'thrown upon paper' for his friend Pope's edification[7] is confirmed by this passage in the *Fragment*:

The best way . . . of proceeding with so slippery a reasoner; the only way, indeed, in which I see any possibility of proceeding with him, is first to lay down some general rules, all of which will hereafter be proved out of his writings, and then pursuing him chapter by chapter, to extract the several proofs, however scattered and dispersed, which tend to establish both parts of the contradictions . . . (p. 675)

If this was the procedure Fielding intended to follow in the critique, however, circumstances prevented him.[8] To Bolingbroke's 'pernicious doctrines', as Fielding called them, the 'antidote' he left behind when the *Queen of Portugal* sailed for Lisbon was one more familiar to him: ridicule. He exposed his lordship's so-called 'philosophy' as a tissue of contradictions so contemptuously thrown together that it could only be meant in jest, as a kind of game indulging the author's mischievous penchant for sporting with the gravest subjects. Bolingbroke's life, Fielding declares, 'was one scene of the wonderful throughout':

That, as the temporal happiness, the civil liberties and properties of Europe, were the game of his earliest youth, there could be no sport so adequate to the entertainment of his advanced age, as the eternal and final happiness of all mankind. (p. 670)

RECEPTION

In March brief but complimentary notices of the *Fragment* found a place in reviews of the *Journal*. The writer in *The Gentleman's Magazine* (25, p. 129) assured readers that, 'however short', the piece 'will strongly incline every man who has a taste for wit, and a love of truth, to wish it was longer'. *The Monthly Review* (12, pp. 234–5) echoed this verdict, describing the *Fragment* as 'a small introductory sketch, of only twenty-seven pages;[9] in which

---

[6] *Works*, i, p. 98.

[7] Bolingbroke's *Works* (1754), v, p. [2].

[8] There is no evidence to support Cross's assertion (iii, p. 25) that Fielding meant to complete his commentary in Lisbon. Fielding makes no reference to it in the *Journal*, and if he had carried the five quarto volumes of Bolingbroke's *Works* to Lisbon, they would certainly have been confiscated by the censors of the Inquisition (see *Life*, pp. 583 and 684 n. 372).

[9] As first noted by Dobson (p. ix n. 1), the reviewer's reference to the number of pages occupied by the *Fragment* identifies the copy he used as the second ('Humphrys') edition.

the author shews himself in a new and advantageous light; so that we cannot but think it a misfortune to the public, that he did not live to prosecute and finish his design'. Matthew Maty, whose review of the work in the *Journal Britannique* (March and April 1755) is in general more comprehensive than any other, concludes with a full paragraph on Fielding's answer to Boling-broke, declaring as the others had done: 'the little fragment that has been saved suffices to make us regret that he did not live long enough to complete it' (see below, Appendix C.5, p. 783).

A

FRAGMENT

OF A

COMMENT

ON

L. BOLINGBROKE'S ESSAYS.

A FRAGMENT, &c.

I MUST confess myself to be one of those who brought with me to the perusal of the late published volumes of Lord Bolingbroke,[1] a very high prejudice to the doctrines said to have been established in them; but at the same time, can as truly assert, that I had the highest, and strongest prepossession, in favour of the abilities of the author. Such, indeed, was this prepossession, that it might, I think, be a sufficient warrant of a man's candour[2] against any prejudice whatever: and it is in the true spirit of this candour that I declare, upon the perusal, I have found my prepossessions greatly abated, and my prejudices not in the least removed.

COULD it therefore be supposed, that all mankind were alike able to try the cause of truth, and to form their judgment on the weight of argument and evidence only, I think there could be no danger in leaving the decision of this matter upon his lordship's own reasoning, without any attempt to answer him. But when we consider how very weak the abilities of mankind in general are, in disquisitions of this nature; how much weaker they are rendered for this purpose by want of due attention; and, lastly, how apt they are to carry any little partiality which they have pre-conceived before the examination of a cause, up to the final decision of it in their minds, it may possibly be very dangerous to the society to suffer such pernicious doctrines to stand unobjected to with so great a name at their head. Many, I am convinced, will think the authority of this name alone sufficient to establish their own belief upon, without any farther inquiry at all. Many others will imagine very little inquiry necessary, and, tho' they did not intirely acquiesce in taking his word, will be easily cajoled with his reasons, which,

---

[1] Henry St John (1678–1751), first Viscount Bolingbroke, statesman, political writer, and freethinker. Secretary of State in the Tory government under Queen Anne, he was dismissed by George I; he was impeached and attainted and fled to France at the Jacobite Rebellion of 1715 where he served the Pretender. He was pardoned and returned to England in 1723. Though barred from the House of Lords, he led the 'patriot' opposition to Walpole, in 1726 founding *The Craftsman*, the principal organ of that party. In 1733–4, in a series of lead articles, he published *A Dissertation on Parties*, which, together with his later treatise *The Idea of a Patriot King* (1738), articulated the political ideal of a disinterested patriotism that became the programme of anti-ministerial writers for years to come. As a political journalist, HF—in his pseudonymous contributions to *The Craftsman* (1734–9) and *Common Sense* (1737–8), and in his own periodical *The Champion* (1739–40)—openly promoted the political ideology Bolingbroke advocated. In the opening paragraph of the *Fragment*, HF's assurance that he brought to his reading of Bolingbroke's *Essays* (March 1754) 'the highest and strongest prepossession, in favour of the abilities of the author' is perfectly sincere. (On this topic, see *TP*, pp. lxxi–lxxiv). However, though he had come to admire Bolingbroke's 'Stile in Writing and Knowledge in Politics'—the qualities he mentions in the *True Patriot*, No. 1 (5 November 1745), the journal he wrote in support of the Hanoverian cause at the time of the rebellion— HF detested Bolingbroke's Jacobitism. And, as the *Fragment* abundantly attests, he considered Bolingbroke's impious effusions from beyond the grave pernicious in their possible effect on the social order.

[2] 'candour': freedom from mental bias, openness of mind (*OED*, s.v. 3).

however little they may have of substance, have much of the specious ornaments of wit and language, with all the allurements of novelty both of style and manner; and, finally, with an appearance, at least, of reading very singular and extensive.

FROM which last particular may arise a third sort very worthy of receiving some assistance on this occasion; such, I mean, as have not the least inclination to his lordship's doctrines, nor would, indeed, assent to them on the authority of any man breathing, who may yet have wanted leisure or opportunity sufficient to provide themselves with a proper fund of knowledge, to give a ready answer to various assertions which will occur in the works now under consideration, and which, tho' they have the worst of tendencies, have in reality themselves no better support (and not always so good a one) than some very weak and slender hypotheses, and are at other times built on the revival of old chimerical principles which have been confuted and exploded long ago.

NOW, to all these indifferent[3] constitutions, we shall endeavour to apply our several antidotes. And here, luckily for us, we are provided with an argument which must most effectually silence those who are the most difficult of all others to be usually dealt with in the way of reasoning: such are the persons I mentioned in the first class, who believe from authority only, and who have not yet, with the schools, given up the irresistible argument of, he Himself said it.[4]

THE force of this argument, however, even in the days when it flourished most, drew all its strength from a supposition that, if he himself said it, he himself believed it: for, if it could have been proved of Aristotle[5] that he had asserted *pro* and *con*, and had with the same clearness affirmed in one part of his works the same thing to be, and in another the same thing not to be, none of his scholars would have known which he believed, and all others would, perhaps, have thought that he had no belief at all in, nor indeed any knowledge of, the matter.

IF, therefore, his lordship shall appear to have made use of this duplicity

---

[3] 'indifferent': not particularly good; poor, inferior; rather bad (*OED*, s.v. 7b, citing Clarendon and Bishop Burnet).

[4] Referring to the authoritarian doctrine of *ipse dixit* (he himself [the master] said it) associated originally with the school of Pythagoras and later with the authority accorded Aristotle in the scholasticism of the Middle Ages. Cf. *Tom Jones* (v. i), where HF wishes 'To avoid . . . all Imputation of laying down a Rule for Posterity, founded only on the Authority of *ipse dixit*; for which to say the Truth, we have not the profoundest Veneration' (pp. 211–12). See also below, p. 675.

[5] At a time when the authority of Aristotle (384–322 BC) had been discredited by the empiricism of Bacon and Locke, HF held his writings in the highest esteem: the sales catalogue of his library lists numerous editions of Aristotle's works and of the commentaries on them (Ribbles A23–39). Referring to his *Politics*, *Rhetoric*, and *Nicomachean Ethics* in *The Covent-Garden Journal*, No. 70 (11 November 1752), HF declared, 'the merit of all which I think hath not been equalled' (p. 374).

of assertion, and that not in one or two, but in many instances, may we not draw the like conclusions? Luckily, perhaps, for his lordship, we may not be driven to the same absolute degree of uncertainty as must have resulted from the case of Aristotle, as I have put it above; since our noble author himself seems to have left us a kind of clue, which will sufficiently lead to the discovery of his meaning, and will shew us, as often as he is pleased to assert both sides of a contradiction, on which side we are to believe him.

AND here I shall premise two cautions; one of which I shall borrow from the rules established among writers; the reasonableness of the other I shall endeavour to evince, from a rule given us by one of the greatest lawyers whom this kingdom ever bred.[6]

THE first is, that of interpreting the sense of an author with the utmost candour, so as not to charge him with any gross and invidious meaning, when his words are susceptible of a much more benign and favourable sense.

THE second is, the observation formed upon the works of judge Littleton by lord chief justice Coke:[7] this is, that whenever that great lawyer is pleased to put down two opinions directly contradicting each other, that the latter opinion is always the best, and always his own.

To apply these to the present purpose, I first of all recommend to the candour of the reader, that whenever he shall find two assertions directly contrary to each other (and many such we do promise to produce to him) one of which directly tends to take away all religion whatever, and the other as directly to establish natural religion[8] at least, that he will be so kind, since it is impossible that my lord should have believed both, to imagine that he rather believed the latter; especially as this latter, from its contradicting the apparent purpose of the author, appears to have been last set down; and, consequently, will have my lord Coke's sanction in favour of the superior authority.

---

[6] Sir Edmund Coke (1552–1634), judge and authority on the law, who was for HF a 'great Writer' and a 'great Lawyer' (*Charge delivered to the Grand Jury* [*Enquiry*, pp. 8, 10]), indeed the very standard of his profession (*TP*, No. 1 [5 November 1745], p. 104). For his 'rule', see below, n. 7.

[7] Cf. the Preface to Coke's commentary (1628) on the *Tenures* of Sir Thomas Littleton (1402–81): 'Certaine it is, when he raiseth any question, and sheweth the reason on both sides, the latter opinion is his owne, and is consonant to Law' (*First Part of the Institutes of the Lawes of England* [1628], fo. [iii^v]); a copy of the work was in HF's library (Ribbles C38). In *Tom Jones* (III. iii), Thwackum is said to use 'the Scriptures and their Commentators, as the Lawyer doth his *Coke upon Lyttleton*, where the Comment is of equal Authority with the Text' (p. 126).

[8] Of the two sources of revelation of the being and attributes of God, nature, and Scripture, deists such as Bolingbroke accepted only 'natural religion', whereas Anglican theologians accepted both, as is evident in the title of the work the Ribbles find at 'the heart of Fielding's holdings in religion', the Boyle Lectures: *A Defence of Natural and Revealed Religion*, 3 vols. (1739). See Ribbles D9, and their discussion, pp. xxiv–xxvi.

LASTLY, if it should ever happen that his lordship's sentiments should be more clearly expressed in favour of the worse than of the better doctrine, we will endeavour all that in us lies to explain and illustrate those hints; by which, we trust, he will always assist a careful and accurate examiner in rescuing the esoteric purity of doctrines from that less amiable appearance in which their exoteric[9] garb represents them.

IN short, we doubt not but to make it appear as a fact beyond all contest, that his lordship was in jest through the whole work which we have undertaken to examine. If an inflamed zealot should in his warmth compare such jesting to his in the Psalmist;[10] or, if a cooler disposition should ask, how it was possible to jest with matters of such importance? I confess I have no defence against the accusation, nor can give any satisfactory answer to the question. To this, indeed, I could say, and it is all that I could say, that my lord Bolingbroke was a great genius, sent into the world for great and astonishing purposes. That the ends, as well as means of action in such personages, are above the comprehension of the vulgar. That his life was one scene of the wonderful throughout. That, as the temporal happiness, the civil liberties and properties of Europe, were the game of his earliest youth,[11] there could be no sport so adequate to the entertainment of his advanced age, as the eternal and final happiness of all mankind. That this is the noblest conservation of character,[12] and might, if perceived in himself,

---

[9] 'esoteric . . . exoteric': neo-Pythagorean terms referring, respectively, to abstruse doctrines intended only for the inner circle of initiated disciples, as opposed to doctrines intended for the general public. The terms were applied by HF's favourite, the satirist Lucian of Samosata, to the Peripatetic philosophers, who divided Aristotle's corpus into these two categories (*Vitarum Auctio*, 26) (Ted Honderich (ed.), *Oxford Companion to Philosophy* [Oxford, 1995], s.v. 'esoteric' and 'exoteric'). In the first three numbers of *The Jacobite's Journal* (5–19 December 1747), HF, in the guise of John Trott-plaid, Esq; divided 'the mysterious Doctrines of Jacobitism into Esoteric and Exoteric, in Imitation of the Doctrines of antient Philosophy, yet we do not imitate these Philosophers in revealing only the Exoteric to the Vulgar' (p. 103).

[10] Cf. the first verse of Psalms 14 and 53 on 'the corruption' and 'depravity of the natural man': 'THE fool hath said in his heart, *There is* no God.'

[11] A staunch Whig and admirer of Marlborough's success against the French in the War of the Spanish Succession (1702–13), HF no doubt alludes to the part Bolingbroke played as Secretary of State in the intrigues of the Tory administration under Harley (1710–14), particularly in secretly negotiating what HF called 'that detestable Treaty of *Utrecht* [1713] . . . by which *France* was again re-instated in almost every Thing she had lost, and relieved from all she had to fear from her victorious Enemies. To these destructive Schemes were sacrificed the Fruits of so much Blood and Treasure, and all those glorious Consequences which might have been drawn from the unparalell'd Successes of our Arms, under the Conduct of the Great, the Protestant, the Whig Duke of Marlborough' (*A Proper Answer to a Late Scurrilous Libel*, in *JJ*, p. 65).

[12] In *Tom Jones* (VIII. i) HF discusses 'what the dramatic Critics call Conservation of Character', a rule derived from Aristotle (*Poetics*, xv. 4) and Horace (*Ars Poetica*, 119–27), who stipulates that a character 'must be kept to the end even as it came forth at the first'. HF's phrase echoes Boileau: 'Conservez à chacun son propre caractère' (*L'Art poétique*, ed. D. N. Smith [Cambridge, 1931], iii, p. 112). Earlier, in much the same context as here, HF in *Jonathan Wild* (IV. xv) contrived the final act of the hero's life—Wild on the gallows picks the parson's pocket of a bottle-screw—'to shew the most admirable Conservation of Character' (*Miscellanies* iii, p. 188).

possibly lead our great genius to see the Supreme Being in the light of a dramatic poet, and that part of his works which we inhabit as a drama. 'The sensitive inhabitants of our globe,' says lord Bolingbroke, 'like the *dramatis personae*, have different characters, and are applied to different purposes of action in every scene. The several parts of the material world, like the machines of a threatre, were contrived not for the actors, but for the action: and the whole order and system of the drama would be disordered and spoiled, if any alteration was made in either. The nature of every creature, his manner of being, is adapted to his state here, to the place he is to inhabit, and, as we may say, to the part he is to act.'[13] It hath been, I think, too common with poets to aggrandize their profession with such kind of similes, and I have, somewhere in an English dramatic writer,[14] met with one so nearly resembling the above, that his lordship might be almost suspected to have read it likewise; but such conceits are inconsistent with any (even the least) pretence to philosophy. I recollect, indeed, a single instance, in the writings of Jordano Bruno[15] who was burnt at Rome for heresy, or, if we believe Scioppius,[16] for most horrid blasphemy, the latter end of the 15th century;[17] and who, from a want of a due correspondence between the passive powers of matter, and the active power of God, compares the Supreme Being to a fidler, who hath skill to play, but cannot for want of a fiddle.[18] This, it must be confessed, is going somewhat farther; as much

---

[13] Quoted verbatim from Bolingbroke's *Works* (1754), quarto, v, p. 377.

[14] Cf. Shakespeare, *As You Like It* (II. vii. 139–42): 'All the world's a stage, | And all the men and women merely players. | They have their exits and their entrances, | And one man in his time plays many parts.' In *The Craftsman*, No. 624 (24 June 1738), HF opens an essay on the characters of ministers by citing this passage. The trope of course was commonplace: cf. *Tom Jones* (VII. I), 'A Comparison between the World and the Stage'.

[15] Giordano Bruno (1548–1600), Italian pantheist philosopher and an outspoken critic of the institutions and doctrines of established religion: he denounced the monastic orders, dismissed miracles as magic tricks, scoffed at the mysteries of the faith, levelled the Jewish records with the Greek myths. A martyr to the cause of freedom of thought, he was condemned by the Inquisition at Rome to be burnt at the stake. His reputation in England in the eighteenth century may be illustrated by Eustace Budgell's leader in *The Spectator*, No. 389 (27 May 1712). The 'extravagant Price' paid at auction for a rare copy of Bruno's *Spaccio de la Bestia trionfante* ('Expulsion of the Triumphant Beast'; 1584) provoked Budgell into attacking those who placed such a value on the philosophy of 'a professed Atheist, with a design to depreciate Religion' (ed. Bond, iii, pp. 459–60). Budgel anticipated HF's strategy in the *Fragment* by choosing not to dignify the freethinkers by taking them seriously: 'the best way of dealing with them, is to retort their own Weapons upon them, which are those of Scorn and Mockery' (iii, p. 463).

[16] Caspar Schoppe (1576–1649), or Scioppius, German scholar and controversialist. He converted to Roman Catholicism *c*.1599 and witnessed Bruno's execution, of which he gave an account in a letter to Rittershusius, written in Latin. HF appears to have read the letter, which refers to the charge of blasphemy, as published in the deist John Toland's *Collection of Several Pieces*, 2 vols. (1726), i, pp. 305–11. HF owned the 1747 edition of this work (Ribbles T24); but, as Bertrand Goldgar has shown, he also knew the original edition (*Miscellanies*, ii, pp. 44–5 n. 3). See also below, n. 18.

[17] Both editions have this error: Bruno died in the first year of the seventeenth century.

[18] Immediately following the letter of Scioppius in Toland's *Collection of Several Pieces* (see above, n. 16), HF would have found 'An Account of Jordano Bruno's Book *Of the infinite Universe and*

farther, in reality, as to descend from the stage to the orchestra. This ludicrous treatment of the Being so universally (for half a dozen madmen must not be allowed to strip any opinion of universality) acknowledged to be the cause of all things, whilst it sounds so ill in the grave voice of reason, very well becomes the lips of a droll: for novelty, boldness, and even absurdity, as they all tend to surprize, do often give a poignancy to wit, and serve to enhance a jest. This affords a second reason why we may suspect his lordship was not over serious in the work before us.

3rdly, That his lordship never thought proper to revise this performance,[19] is a very strong argument that he could not be in earnest either in believing himself in his own doctriness, or in endeavouring to imprint such a belief on others. That he did not in fact revise his works is manifest, from the numerous contradictions that occur in them, and these often in the same page; so that, for the most part, they could not escape the dullest and bluntest degree of penetration: surely we cannot impute such repeated oversights to one who hath so explicitly asserted,[a][20] That to be liable to contradict yourself, is to be liable to one of the greatest of human imperfections![21] An author, in the first hurry of setting down his thoughts on a subject which warms him, may possibly, indeed, assert two opinions not

---

[a] Essays, p. 181.

---

innumerable Worlds: In five Dialogues' (an English translation of *De l'infinito, universo, e mundi*). In the fifth Dialogue, 'Albertinus' offers twelve objections 'in which consists all the force of the doctrine contrary to the plurality and multitude of Worlds' (i, p. 340): 'THE eighth objection is taken from the terminateness or finitude of natural things, and from their passive power which corresponds not to the Divine Efficacy and active Power: but here it is to be consider'd, how mighty inconveniently the first and most high Being is compar'd to a fidler, who has skill to play, but cannot for want of a fiddle; so that he is one that can do, but does not, because that thing which he can make cannot be made by him. This implies a more than manifest contradiction, which cannot but be seen, except onely by those who see nothing' (i, pp. 341–2).

[19] In the 'Advertisement' prefixed to volume V of the *Works*, Bolingbroke affected a certain insouciance about his philosophizing: 'THE foregoing Essays, if they may deserve even that name, and the Fragments or minutes that follow, were thrown upon paper in Mr. POPE's lifetime, and at his desire. They were all communicated to him in scraps, as they were occasionally writ. But the latter not having been connected and put together under different heads . . . I have contented myself to correct and extend them a little, and to leave them as Fragments, or minutes, in the form in which they appear.'

[20] *Works*, v, pp. 181–2: commenting on the Old Testament, where 'the all-perfect Being' is represented as approving and commanding 'on many particular occasions, the most abominable violations of the general laws of nature, which were his own', Bolingbroke remarks: 'As theists we cannot believe the all-perfect Being liable to one of the greatest of human imperfections, liable to contradict himself.'

[21] John Tillotson (1630–94), Archbishop of Canterbury and leader of the latitudinarian movement within the Anglican Church. Though the specific phrasing HF attributes to Tillotson has not been located, his sermons abound with essentially similar arguments such as those Allworthy in *Tom Jones* (II. ii) brings to bear against Captain Blifil, who quotes Scripture to prove that the sins of Tom's parents should be visited upon their bastard child (pp. 79–80 and n. 4). Among a number of complimentary references to Tillotson in HF's works, in *A Proposal for Making an Effectual Provision for the Poor* (1753), in order to make the point that religion alone is capable of correcting a bad mind, he quotes at length from a sermon by 'the excellent Archbishop *Tillotson* . . . this great Preacher' (*Enquiry*, pp. 269–70).

perfectly reconcilable with each other; nay, there are some writers from whom we can reasonably expect no less; since, as Archbishop Tillotson observes,[22] it is hard to contradict truth and nature, without contradicting one's self. But to expunge such mistakes is the office of revisal and correction; and therefore, a work in which these mistakes abound, is very justly called an incorrect performance. As this work therefore doth more than any which I ever saw, afford us instances of what his lordship calls the greatest human imperfection, charity shews me no more candid way of accounting for them than this which I have mentioned.

LASTLY, the very form and title, under which the noble lord hath thought proper to introduce his philosophy into the world, is a very strong evidence of the justice of all the foregoing observations. We may form, I think, one general precept from the trite story of Archimedes:[23] this is, not to undertake any great work without preconcerting such means as may be adequate to the execution. Now to turn the material world topsy-turvy, is a project scarce more difficult in appearance, than to perform the same notable exploit in the intellectual. And yet Archimedes might as judiciously have fixed his machine in vacuo, as his lordship hath chosen to argue against the best established systems in the intellectual world, in fragments[24] of essays. This method, not to mention the indignity it offers to the subject in dispute, is treating the whole body of the learned with more supercilious disrespect than nature seems yet to have qualified any member of that body to express towards the rest of his brethren; and which must appear to be wonderful, if serious, in one who expresses so modest an opinion of his own critical talents; tho', as to his modesty, it must indeed be confessed to be somewhat seasoned with a due mixture of contempt.

BUT whatever may lessen the idea of his lordship's modesty, there is only one way to lessen that of his absurdity; this is to conclude that he was in jest: nay there is one way to see this absurdity in an amiable light; for in such a light will he appear, if we suppose that he puts on the jack-pudding's coat[25]

---

[22] See above, n. 21.

[23] 'Give me a place to stand and I will move the earth.' In the *Journal* (p. 568 and n. 83) HF also alludes to this saying, attributed to Archimedes (*c*.287–212 BC).

[24] In his comment, HF was addressing volume V of Bolingbroke's *Works*, the contents of which are entitled 'Fragments or Minutes of Essays'. No doubt the choice of a title for his rebuttal ('A Fragment of a Comment' on the essays) was meant as a mocking allusion to the self-confessed inadequacy of his lordships arguments. He refers to these 'fragments' again on pp. 674–5.

[25] A clown, or merry-andrew, especially one attending on a mountebank (*OED*), citing HF in *The Covent-Garden Journal*, No. 10 (4 February 1752): 'Writers are not . . . to be considered as mere Jack-Puddings, whose Business is only to excite Laughter' (p. 73 and n. 1). As for the coat, cf. *The Covent-Garden Journal*, No. 18 (3 March 1752), 'Dulness . . . sometimes in Print, as well as on the Stage, disguises herself in a Jack-pudding Coat, and condescends to divert her good Friends with sundry Feats of Dexterity and Grimace' (p. 125); also *The Jacobite's Journal*, No. 38 (20 August 1748), pp. 372–4.

with the noble view of exposing and ridiculing those pernicious tenets which have lately been propagated with a zeal more difficult to be accounted for than its success.

THAT such an attempt of exposing any popular error would always prove victorious is, I think, extremely probable. My Lord Shaftsbury[26] hath been blamed for saying 'That ridicule is one of those principal lights or natural mediums by which things are to be viewed, in order to a thorough recognition: for that truth, it is supposed, may bear all lights[a].' Perhaps there may be some justice in this censure, as truth may by such a trial be subjected to misrepresentation, and become a more easy prey to the malice of its enemies; a flagrant instance of which we have in the case of Socrates.[27]

BUT whatever objection there may be against trying truth by ridicule, there can be none, I apprehend, of making use of its assistance in expelling and banishing all falshood and imposture, when once fairly convicted, out of society; and as this method is for this purpose very unexceptionable, so it is generally the most efficacious that can be invented; as will appear by some examples which will occur in the course of our comment on his lordship's essays, or fragments of essays, on which we shall now enter without further preface or apology.

SECT. I.

AND here, as a proof that we are as liable to be corrupted by our books as by our companions,[28] I am in danger of setting out with a contradiction.

---

[a] Essay on the freedom of wit and humour, part I. sect. I.

[26] Anthony Ashley Cooper (1671–1713), third Earl of Shaftesbury, author of *Characteristicks of Men, Manners, Opinions, Times* (1711), of which HF owned a copy of the sixth edition (1737–8) (Ribbles S18). Though rearranging the syntax, HF quotes from *Sensus Communis: An Essay on the Freedom of Wit and Humour* (1709), pt. I, sect. i: 'Truth, 'tis suppos'd, may bear *all* Lights: and *one* of those principal Lights or natural Mediums, by which Things are to be view'd, in order to a thorow Recognition, is *Ridicule* it-self'(*Characteristicks*, ed. Philip Ayres (Oxford, 1999), i, p. 38).

[27] In *Amelia* (X. iv) Dr Harrison shares HF's misgivings about not only the impropriety, but the danger to the social order, of acting upon Shaftesbury's famous axiom, adopted by the freethinkers, that ridicule is the surest test of truth, even the truth of religion: 'No Man is fonder of true Wit and Humour than myself,' Harrison assures Booth; 'but to profane sacred Things with Jest and Scoffing is a sure Sign of a weak and wicked Mind' (p. 425). In this, Harrison and his author side with John 'Estimate' Brown in his *Essays on the Characteristics* (1751), who, in the first essay ('On Ridicule as the Test of Truth') attacked Shaftesbury's rule. As early as the Dedication to *Don Quixote in England* (1734) HF had criticized Aristophanes for the 'destruction' of Socrates by satirizing him in *The Clouds*; more recently in *The Covent-Garden Journal*, No. 52 (30 June 1752) he denounced him for 'the base and barbarous Abuse of Socrates' (p. 286). In No. 10 (1 February 1752) HF had removed Aristophanes and Rabelais from their place in the pantheon of great comic authors he praised in *Tom Jones* (XIII. i), complaining that their 'Design' had been 'to ridicule all Sobriety, Modesty, Decency, Virtue and Religion out of the World' (p. 74). That HF once held Aristophanes in the highest esteem is clear from the Preface to *Plutus* (above, pp. 251–7).

[28] Cf. 1 Corinthians 15: 13, cited above, *Journal*, p. 654 n. 316.

Nay I must yet venture to do this in some degree with my eyes open, and must lay my defence on a distinction rather too nice, and which relies too much on the candour of my reader.

THE truth is, our noble author's chief strength lies in that very circumstance which I have before asserted to be of itself alone a sufficient argument of his weakness; whereas on the contrary his manner affords such a protection to his matter, that if he had designed to reserve to himself the sole privilege of answering his own doctrine, he could not have invented a more ingenious or effectual contrivance. It hath been alledged as a good reason for not answering certain books, that one must be obliged first to read them; but surely we shall find few men so very charitable, or so much our friends, to give them order and method with a view only of complimenting them with an answer.

THIS, however, I attempted, tho' I own with no great success; and that not so much, I apprehend, from want of sufficient matter to make out such colourable systems as may be expected in such a writer, as from a certain dark, cautious, and loose manner of expressing his sentiments, which must arise either from a writer's desire of not being very easily explained, or from an incapacity of making himself very clearly understood. The difficulties arising to the commentator on these fragments,[29] will appear to be assignable only to the former cause: for a very indifferent reader will be seldom at a loss in comprehending his lordship in his own works; but to transfer his doctrines with their authority (i.e. the *ipse dixit* of the author[30]) into another work, is often very difficult, and without long quotations, too apt to tire the reader, impossible. In this light a very fine thought of Mr. Pope's occurs to my memory.

> Tho' index-learning turns no student pale,
> It holds the eel of science by the tail.[31]

THE best way then of proceeding with so slippery a reasoner; the only way, indeed, in which I see any possibility of proceeding with him, is first to lay down some general rules, all of which will hereafter be proved out of his writings, and then pursuing him chapter by chapter, to extract the several proofs, however scattered and dispersed, which tend to establish both parts of the contradictions, which I shall now set down.

OUR noble author sets out in his first section, with a sly insinuation, that it is possible for the gravest of philosophers on the gravest of subjects, to

---

[29] See above, p. 673 n. 24.
[30] See above, p. 668 n. 4.
[31] Somewhat altered from *The Dunciad* (1728/9), i. 233–4; (1743), i. 279–80. Pope's lines begin 'How . . . | Yet . . .'.

advance propositions in jest. 'It is more probable,' says Lord B————,[32] 'and it is more candid to believe, that this philosopher (Descartes) was in earnest, than that he was in jest, when he advanced this proposition,[a] *concerning the immutability and eternity of certain mathematical truths.*'[33] I will add, that I believe that an idea of such jesting had never any footing in a human head, till it first found admission into that of this noble lord.

IN the same section, his lordship proceeds thus: 'The antients thought matter eternal, and assumed that the Demiurgus, or Divine Architect, composed the frame of the world with materials which were ready prepared, and independently on him, in a confused chaos. Much in the same manner such metaphysicians as the learned Cudworth[34] have imagined a sort of intellectual chaos, a chaos of eternal ideas, of incorporeal essences, independent on God, self-existent, and therefore co-eval with the supreme being, and therefore, anterior to all other natures. In this intellectual chaos God sees, and man must endeavour to see, the natures, the real essences of things: and thus the foundations of morality are laid higher than the existence of any moral agents, before there was any system of being from which the obligations to it could result, or to which they could be applied: just as the same philosophers suppose the incorporeal essences of white and black to have existed when there was no such thing as colour, and those of a square and circle, when there was neither form nor figure.[b]

HERE I am afraid the learned peer hath gone no farther for his erudition than the first or second pages of Ovid's Metamorphosis:[36] for could he be recalled from the dead, contrary to his own doctrine, as he hath recalled Descartes, and were asked whom he meant by the antients, he could not certainly answer in general, the antient philosophers, for then the whole tribe of athiests would be ready to testify against him. If he should answer,

---

[a] Essays, page 4.
[b] Ibid. page 6.[35]

---

[32] HF quotes verbatim from Bolingbroke's *Works*, v, p. 4.

[33] The italicized phrase paraphrases Bolingbroke's quotation attributed to René Descartes (1596–1650): 'I do not think that the essences of things, and those mathematical truths which can be known of them, are independent on God; but I think, however, that they are immutable and eternal, because God willed and ordered that they should be so' (ibid.).

[34] Ralph Cudworth (1617–88), Cambridge Platonist and author of *The True Intellectual System of the Universe* (1678), a critique of atheistical materialism directed in particular at Thomas Hobbes. A copy of the work was in HF's library (Ribbles C57).

[35] Except for the omission of 'for instance' after 'white and black' in the last sentence, as well as minor changes in the accidentals, HF quotes verbatim from Bolingbroke's *Works*, v, pp. 5–6.

[36] Ovid's *Metamorphoses* opens with an account of the creation of the world out of chaos.

that he meant the antient theists[37] only, and less he cannot be supposed to mean by those who are well-bred enough to suppose he meant any thing, he will be far from finding even among these an universal concurrence with his opinion. Thales,[38] the chief of the Grecian sages, and who is said to have first turned his thoughts to physiological enquiries, affirmed the independent pre-existence of God from all eternity. The words of Laertius[39] are remarkable, and I will render them with the most literal exactness in my power. He asserted, say Laertius, 'That God was the oldest of all beings, for he existed *without a previous cause* EVEN IN THE WAY OF GENERATION; that the world was the most beautiful of all things; for *it was* CREATED by God, &c.'[a] This notion of the creation Aristotle tells us, was agreeable to the concurrent voice of all antiquity; 'All,' says he, 'assert the creation of the world; but they differ in this, that some will have the world susceptible of dissolution, which others deny.'[b][40]

On this occasion Aristotle names Empedocles and Heraclitus, but, which is somewhat remarkable, never mentions Thales. The opinion itself is opposed by the Stagyrite;[41] and this opposition he was forced to maintain, or he must have given up the eternity of the world, which he very justly asserts to be inconsistent with any idea of its creation. But we will dismiss the antients from the bar, and see how his lordship will support his arraignment of the moderns. The charge against them is, that they have holden certain ideas, or incorporeal essences, to be self-existent. Concerning these doctrines his lordship thus harangues in the very same page[c],

---

[37] HF would have numbered Epicurus and his expositor Lucretius as atheists among the 'antient philosophers', and Socrates, Plato, and Cicero among the theists.

[a] Diog. Laert. Lib. I. sect. 35. where I submit to the learned reader the construction he will observe I have given to the different import of those terms, ἀγέννητον ποίημα; the first of which may be considered as a qualified, the latter as an absolute cause.

[b] Aristot. De cœlo, lib. I. cap. 10.[40]

[c] Essay, p. 6.

---

[38] Thales of Miletus (b. *c.*624 BC), considered the founder of Greek philosophy.

[39] Diogenes Laertius (*c.*AD 200–50), *Lives of Eminent Philosophers*, I. 35: 'Thales'. For comparison with HF's translation of the Greek, R. D. Hicks in the Loeb edition renders the two lines: 'Of all things that are, the most ancient is God, for he is the uncreated. | The most beautiful is the universe, for it is God's workmanship.' A copy of the 'elegant, and excellent' Greek and Latin edition (Amsterdam, 1692) was in HF's library (Ribbles D19).

[40] Aristotle, *On the Heavens*, I. x: 'All thinkers agree that [the world] has had a beginning, but some maintain that having begun it is everlasting, others that it is perishable . . . and others again that it alternates, being at one time as it is now, and at another time changing and perishing, and that this process continues unremittingly. Of this last opinion were Empedocles of Acragas and Heraclitus of Ephesus' (279[b] 13–17), referring to the philosophers Empedocles (*c.*490–430 BC), and Heraclitus (*c.*540–475 BC). In the next paragraph, Aristotle, who has argued that the world exists from all eternity and cannot change, admits that if one granted the possibility of change, which must be owing to some cause, 'then the thing which we said could not be otherwise *could* have been otherwise' (279[b] 22–6).

[41] Aristotle, who was born in Stagira, a town in the Greek province of Chalcidice.

'Mr. Lock observes, how impossible it is for us to conceive certain relations, habitudes, and connections, visibly included in some of our ideas, to be separable from them even by infinite power. Let us observe, on this occasion, how impossible, or, at least, how extremely difficult it is for us to separate the idea of eternity from certain moral and mathematical truths, as well as from such as are called necessary, and are self-evident on one hand: and, on the other, how impossible it is to conceive that truths should exist before the things to which they are relative; or particular natures and essences, before the system of universal nature, and when there was no being but the super-essential Beings.'

If I had any inclination to cavil, I might, with truth, assert that no such passage is to be found in Mr. Lock.[42] His words are: 'In some of our ideas there are certain relations, habitudes, and connections, so visibly included in the nature of the ideas themselves, that we cannot conceive them separable from them by any power whatsoever[a]'. It may be answered, perhaps, that the violence is done rather to the expression, than to the meaning of this truly great man; but if I should candidly admit that he seems, from the immediate context, to mean no less (I say, seems to mean: for, whoever will carefully compare what is said in another part of the same book[b],[44] of the powers of the mind in forming the archetypes of its complex ideas of mixed modes, may possibly think he sees sufficient reason for resolving what is here affirmed of arbitrary (not infinite) power, into the human mind only). I may yet reply, that such a violence even to the expression of such a writer on such a subject, is by no means void of blame, nor even of suspicion, when it is left without a reference to conceal itself in a large folio,[45] where it will not be easily detected by any but those who are pretty familiarly acquainted with the original.

---

[a] Essay on Human Understanding, I. 4. cap. 3. § 29.[43]
[b] Lock's Essay, I. 2 cap. 31.

---

[42] John Locke (1632–1704) in *An Essay concerning Human Understanding* (1690). HF is quoting from Locke's *Works*, 5th edn. (1751) in 3 vols. folio, a copy of which was in his library (Ribbles L22); of course he was familiar with the philosopher's writings much earlier. Later in the paragraph HF will call Locke 'this truly great man'. In the 'Paper War' he waged in *The Covent-Garden Journal*, No. 1 (4 January 1752) against hackney authors and illiterate critics, HF enlisted just two modern philosophers on his side: Francis Bacon, the founder and Locke, the greatest exponent of the new empiricism (p. 19).

[43] The reference is to Locke's *Works* (1751), book IV, ch. iii ('Of the Extent of Human Knowledge'), sect. 29; i, p. 263. HF does not exaggerate when he accuses Bolingbroke of distorting the meaning of the passage he pretends to quote: sect. 29 is long and dense.

[44] The passage referred to is the following from book II, ch. xxxi ('Of Adequate and Inadequate Ideas'), sect. 3: 'our complex ideas of modes, being voluntary collections of simple ideas, which the mind puts together, without reference to any real archetypes, or standing patterns, existing any where, are and cannot but be adequate ideas . . . archetypes [are] made by the mind' (i, p. 169).

[45] HF's copy of Locke's *Essay* is from the *Works* (1751), a 'large folio'.

BUT it is time to close this article, which, I think, seems to establish contradiction the first: for under what other terms shall we range the arguing *pro* and *con* in the same breath: for where is the force of the accusation, or, as a lawyer would call it, the gift of the indictment against poor Cudworth?[46] Is it not (to use my lord's own phrase) 'the laying the foundations of morality higher than the existence of any moral agents?'[47] And what says my lord to enforce the charge? Why, truly, he alleges in defence of the accused, that it was impossible for him to have done otherwise, and produces the authority of Mr. Locke to confirm this impossibility.

THE generosity of this sudden transition from accuser to advocate would convince all men on which side his lordship had here delivered his real sentiments, was it not somewhat controled by his having concealed from his readers, that the philosopher a little afterwards, in the same book[a] hath endeavoured to prove, and, I think, actually hath proved, that there is no absurdity in what my lord Bolingbroke objects, provided the doctrine be rightly understood, so as not to establish innate principles. That the actual existence of the subjects of mathematical or moral ideas is not in the least necessary to give us a sufficient evidence of the necessity of those ideas; and that, in the disputes of the mathematician as well as of the moralist, the existence of the subject-matter is rarely called in question; nor is it more necessary to their demonstrations and conclusions that it would be to prove the truth of Tully's Offices, to shew that there was some man who lived up

---

[a] Lib. 4. cap. 9.[48]

[46] Cudworth. See above, p. 676 n. 34.

[47] See the quotation from Bolingbroke, above p. 676.

[48] Locke's *Essay*, book IV, ch. ix ('Of our Knowledge of Existence'). In section 1 Locke maintains, empirically, that 'the essences of things . . . being only abstract ideas, and thereby removed in our thoughts from particular existence . . . gives [*sic*] us no knowledge of real existence at all'. In section 2 he distinguishes the modes of knowing existence: 'I say then, that we have the knowledge of our own existence by intuition; of the existence of God by demonstration' [a subject he treats at length in ch. x]; and of other things by sensation' (*Works* [1751], i, p. 293). In comparing the subjects of mathematics and morality, HF seems to have in mind *Essay*, IV. xii ('Of the Improvement of our Knowledge') sect. 8, where Locke remarks 'that morality is capable of demonstration, as well as mathematicks. For the ideas, that ethicks are conversant about, being all real essences, and such as I imagine have a discoverable connection and agreement one with another; so far as we can find their habitudes and relations, so far we shall be possessed of certain, real and general truths: and I doubt not, but if a right method were taken, a great part of morality might be made out with that clearness, that could leave, to a considering man, no more reason to doubt, than he could have to doubt of the truth of propositions in mathematicks, which have been demonstrated to him' (ibid. i, p. 306).

to that idea of perfect goodness, of which Tully hath given us a pattern.[49] There is somewhat very mysterious in all this; but we have not promised to explain contradictions farther than by shewing to which side his lordship's authority seems to incline. And surely it is better to decide in favour of possibility, and to lay the foundations of morality too high, than to give it no foundation at all.

Desunt caetera.[50]

---

[49] Marcus Tullius Cicero (106–43 BC), author of *De Officiis*, a treatise on the moral duties in the form of a letter addressed to his son. In 'Of the Remedy of Affliction for the Loss of Our Friends' HF, quoting a phrase from Cicero's *Tusculan Disputations*, recommends '*that exalted divine Philosophy*', which consists in 'acquiring solid lasting Habits of Virtue, and ingrafting them into our Character' (*Miscellanies* i, p. 212); and in *Tom Jones* (VIII. xv) Tom appears to echo Cicero on the same subject: 'as an excellent Writer observes, nothing should be esteemed as characteristical of a Species, but what is to be found among the best and most perfect Individuals of that Species' (p. 485).

[50] 'the rest is lacking'.

APPENDIX A

Writings Attributed to Fielding

NOTE: Included here are miscellaneous pieces that have been attributed to Fielding on the basis of circumstantial and internal evidence—on the evidence, that is, of notable parallels in words and phrases, ideas and metaphors, references to authors, and biographical details occurring between the text in question and corresponding features of Fielding's known writings.* In each case, the argument for Fielding's authorship is fully presented in the sources cited in the introduction to the text. In addition the pieces included have been selected because they are only to be found inconveniently in various scholarly publications.

Other writings attributed to Fielding since 1980—including forty-nine essays and the ballad 'The Norfolk Lanthorn'—are conveniently collected elsewhere in Battestin, *New Essays by Henry Fielding: His Contributions to The Craftsman (1734–1739) and Other Early Journalism*, with a stylometric analysis by Michael G. Farringdon (Charlottesville, Va., 1989; repr. 1993). In this collection the case for each individual attribution is fully presented.

In the texts that follow, footnote numbers enclosed in square brackets indicate Fielding's notes. In this Appendix editorial annotation is limited to the identification of persons referred to in the texts, which are fully annotated in the sources cited in the footnotes to the titles.

* A case for rejecting the attribution of these essays to Fielding is made by Thomas Lockwood, 'Did Fielding Write for the *Craftsman?*', forthcoming in *RES*. Advance Access to this article, published online on March 6, 2007, with implications for other attributions as well, is available through *The Review of English Studies*, doi:10.1093/res/hgl158.

THE

COMEDIAN,

OR

PHILOSOPHICAL

ENQUIRER.

NUMB. V.

AUGUST. 1732.

Sensum a cælesti demissam traximus Arce,
Cujus egent prona et Terram spectantia: Mundi
Principio indulsit communis Conditor illis
Tantum Animas, nobis Animum quoque.
Juvenal. Sat. 15.

LONDON:

Printed for J. ROBERTS, at the *Oxford-Arms,* in
Warwick-Lane, 1732.   (*Price Six Pence.*)

1. From *The Comedian, or Philosophical Enquirer*, No. 5 (August 1732)

i. Observations on Government, the Liberty of the Press, News-papers, Partys, and Party-writers (1732).[1]

AS Nature hath stamped on every Face Something particular, whereby it may be distinguished from those of all other Men, so hath she given to every Nation certain Characteristics different from one another. There is scarce a People on Earth who have not a particular Bent, which is as general among themselves as it is peculiar from that of the Rest of Mankind. Thus the general Cast of the *Dutch* is to Trade, that of the *Germans* to drinking, the *French* to dancing, the *Italians* to Music, and, I believe, the *English* may of all Nations be sayed to be most inclined to Politics; and the unbounded Liberty which we enjoy of speaking and writing our Thoughts is the Cause of the present flourishing State of Politics in this Kingdom.

I have often wondered within myself what Idea a Foreigner must conceive at his first Entrance into one of our celebrated Coffee-houses; every one of which resembles a Pamphlet-shop, or Register-office, especially on a Saturday, when, I believe, there are almost as many new Essays published in Journals in this City as are new Sermons preached in it the next Day. The *Spectator* was a great Enemy to these little Cabals, and inferiour Councils of State, and endeavoured to represent them as highly prejudicial to the retail Trade of the Kingdom: the Sale of three Hats have been sometimes lost by the reading one News-paper; and many Haberdashers have undone their Familys by their too great Zeal for the Good of the Nation. I must own that I cannot see the great Advantage which an Inferior Tradesman can reap from the Study of News-papers, unless it is from the Advertisements; which seem the Parts designed for his Perusal; and as they chiefly turn on buying and selling, I shall easily allow him the reading them: but of what Benefit those laborious political Essays which appear in the Front of our Journals, one of which I have seen employ a careful Reader a full Hour, can be to an honest Citizen I must confess I cannot understand: these weekly Venders of Sedition prejudice the State by raising strange Chimæras in the Brains of those who are not competent Judges of the Subject, yet are ready to acquiesce in every Assertion, tho it is seconded by no Colour of Proof; for Ignorance either believes every Thing, or it believes Nothing; it either leaps over Mountains, or stumbles at every Straw.

The Study of Politics is of that intricate Nature, and the secret Springs by which the Wheels of State move so difficult to be discerned, that it requires no slender Genius, nor a small Share of Knowledge, to gain an Insight into this Science; yet such is the foolish Forwardness of Mankind, especially of our Countrymen, that, tho you meet with thousands who will own their Ignorance in every other Way, you will scarce find one who is not in his own Opinion a tolerable Politician. This our

---

[1] See Battestin, 'Fielding's Contributions to *The Comedian* (1732)', *Studies in Bibliography*, 54 (2001), pp. 173–84.

epidemical Distemper the Enemys to our present happy Establishment have sufficiently nourished to their own Ends. I have been often diverted, tho with a Mixture of Concern, in seeing Half a Dozen of these mechanical *Machiavilians* shaking their Heads, as a Sort of Approbation of the Author and Dislike of the Government, at a flagrant Paragraph in one of the Papers against the Ministry, which some vociferous Member hath been reading aloud to the Table; whereas had the honest Board seen the Affair set in a true Light, they would not have wished to have had a Man of the Author's Principles for a Customer.

The *Dutch*, whose Wisdom in Government hath been the Theme of most of those whose Endeavours have been to depreciate our own, are extremely jealous of suffering their People to intermeddle in political Matters; nor indeed would such busy Heads, as our present Incendiarys, find Food for their Lucubrations, that wise State always prohibiting, with the strictest Severity, all Sorts of Libels, which are so many Firebrands, and have often raised Flames in a Commonwealth not to be extinguished without great Trouble, and often not without the Ruin of the State.

Tho I have been always an Advocate for every Branch of Liberty, and among others for that of the Press, yet I conceive that this, as well as all other good Institutions, may, for Want of some Regulation, be in the End attended with evil Effects. One of the Advantages arising from Liberty not abused is the Power of alarming the People when any Invasion on their Property is actually attempted, by producing to them the Fact or Facts by which the Attempt is evident; but to abuse in general Terms, to accuse without mentioning Particulars, and, in the vulgar Phrase, to call Names, savour more of the Licentiousness of *Billingsgate* than of the Liberty of the Press. I never yet heared it denied that a speaking Trumpet is of great Service to alarm a Turnpike, when a Robbery hath been committed on the Highroad; but should a Person take it into his Head, whenever an Express arrives from abroad, to cry out *stop Thief*, and thereby interrupt him who is employed in the national Busyness, I apprehend that some Stop should be put to that merry Gentleman's diverting himself at the Expence of the Public, and of the Character of the Person so employed: and I do not see, if a Stop was put to our present weekly Incendiarys in a legal Way, why the Liberty of *England* may not be sayed to stand on a very sound Bottom; however I would not be understood here to write against the Liberty of the Press, but the Abuse of it; and the great Men who have been most aspersed by the Abuse are most zealous for maintaining the Liberty of the Press; which will never fail while the present Ministry subsists.

My present Design is to caution such of my Fellow-countrymen, who cannot have had sufficient Opportunitys to improve in Politics, from giving too ready an Ear to the Voices of Envy and Revenge, and to advise them to rest contented under an Administration which hath hitherto defied their Enemys to make good any Charge against them; and whose chief Opponents have been the most flagitious and most approved Enemys of their Country: I would counsel them to be satisfied under the Blessings of Peace and Plenty tho they are not able to account for those Measures which have worked their Happyness.

Cicero, esteemed a wise man in his Time, has left a just Reproof behind him to these political Enquirers. Says he,[1] *when Men in the inferior Arts guide themselves by Methods of their own, must the wise and they who act in the more exalted Spheres of Life be obliged to govern themselves by the Directions of the Multitude, and proceed by Maxims only which are obvious to their Eyes?*[2]

ii. *An Epistle to* Mr. Ellys *the Painter* (1732)[3]

While *Jervass* lives in *Pope*'s admiring Song,[4]
And *Dandridge* borrows Fame from *B* ————*n*'s Tongue,[5]
Shall no impartial Muse, my *Ellys*, raise
A juster Trophy to thy Pencil's Praise?
To others while fictitious Charms they give,   5
Shall real Worth in thee neglected live?
Tho thou can'st need no Monument of mine,
Tho on thy Canvas best thy Beautys shine,
O! let this Verse an honest Tribute be,
Pay'd by a greater Friend to Truth than thee.   10
    When (the great Work of thine excelling Hand!)
We see the well-known Nymph or Hero stand,
Where thoughtful*[2] *Wager*[6] wakes to guard our Isle,
Where * *Albemarle*[7] enchants us with a Smile,
In * *Hoadley*[8] where, and * *Wake*'s[9] just Features, shine   15
All the great Symptoms of their Souls divine,
While skillful you each Passion's Mark unfold,
We gaze, nor ask whose Pictures we behold:
Nor is your Powr to these great Themes confin'd;
You know to paint each Passion of the Mind: 20

---

[1] An Tibicines, iique qui Fidibus utuntur, suo, non Multitudinis, Arbitrio, Cantus Numerosque moderantur, Vir sapiens, multò Arte majore præditus, non quid verissimum fit, sed quid velit Vulgus, exquiret? *Tusc. Quæst. Lib.* 5.
[2] Pictures drawn by Mr. *Ellys.*

---

[2] Though this passage from Cicero's *Tusculan Disputations* (v. xxxvi. 104) twice served HF as an epigraph—in *The True Patriot*, No. 19 (4–11 March 1746) and *The Jacobite's Journal*, No. 10 (6 February 1748)—it is possible that the concluding paragraph of this essay was added by HF's friend Thomas Cooke, editor of *The Comedian*. See the article cited in n. 1 above (p. 184 n. 48).

[3] This verse epistle to the painter John Ellys (1701–57) immediately follows the *Observations* (item 1 in this Appendix) in *The Comedian*, No. 5 (August 1732) and, according to the editor, Thomas Cooke, it was written by the same author. See Battestin, 'Fielding's Contributions to *The Comedian* (1732)', *Studies in Bibliography*, 54 (2001), pp. 173–89.

[4] Referring to Pope's verse epistle (1716) to the painter Charles Jervas (*c*.1675–1739).

[5] The painter Bartholomew Dandridge (1691–*c*.1755); and his patron Viscount Barrington (1717–93).

[6] Sir Charles Wager (1666–1743), admiral.

[7] Anne Lennox (1703–89), Countess of Albemarle.

[8] Benjamin Hoadly (1676–1761), Bishop of Salisbury.

[9] William Wake (1657–1737), Archbishop of Canterbury.

Behold th'undaunted *[3] Gladiator there;
How just his Posture! And how fierce his Air!
Behold his Looks impatient for the Fight;
Cowards would fly, *Argyle*[10] approve, the Sight!
    Equal with thine no other Art we view,   25
Who know'st decaying Nature to renew,
Can'st Death's lamented Triumphs render vain,
And bid departed Beauty live again.
Here the fond Parent of his Child bereft
May view at least the much lov'd Image left.   30
Leander here, when *Melesinda*'s coy,
Doats on the smiling Object of his Joy:
And far, alas! by cruel Fate remov'd,
(Too lovely Nymph! and O! too much belov'd!)
Here, in the slightest Sketch, I fondly trace   35
All the dear Sweetness of *Dorinda*'s |[4] Face:
Tho Parents, Fortune, and tho she, conspire
To keep far from me all my Soul's Desire,
Still shall my ravish'd Eyes their Darling see,
If not so beauteous, look more kind thro thee.   40
    O! let thine Art on future Times bestow
Those Beautys which our own to Nature owe:
Be no *Lourissa* on thy Canvas seen;
Nor draw the comic Phiz of *M*————[11]
How Nature errs let other Pencils tell;   45
Shew thine, more noble, how she can excel:
Shew *Richmond*'s[12] happy Pair in Love entwin'd,
Both grac'd alike in Person and in Mind;
Well will such Subjects all thy Powrs engage,
Honours to thee, and Glorys of their Age.   50
While Hope of Gain the venal Fancy warms,
The Painter often gives, not copys, Charms;
But thou such wretched Compliments refrain;
Who would paint *S*——*l*[13] lovely paints in vain.
Let perfect Art, like thine, those Subjects chuse   55
Where bounteous Nature hath been most profuse:
At *Chambers*[14] still thine Art incessant try,

[3] *Mr. *James Figg* [d. 1734; prize-fighter] drawn in the Posture of a Gladiator by Mr. *Ellys*.
[4] An unfinished Picture of Miss D. W. by Mr. *Ellys*.

[10] John Campbell (1680–1743), Duke of Argyll.
[11] Probably the quack Dr John Misaubin (d. 1734).
[12] Charles Lennox (1701–50), second Duke of Richmond, and his wife, Sarah (1706–51).
[13] Unidentified.
[14] Lady Mary Chambers (d. 1735).

At *Shaftsb'ry*'s[15] Mien, and *Wortley*'s[16] radiant Eye;
And, while some future *Dryden*[17] shall relate
What *Walpole*[18] was, how wise, humane, and great,   60
O! may the Patriot's mighty Image shine,
In future Ages, by no Hand but thine.

[15] Susanna Cooper (d. 1758), wife of the fourth Earl of Shaftesbury.
[16] Lady Mary Wortley Montagu (1689–1762).
[17] John Dryden (1631–1700), poet.
[18] Sir Robert Walpole (1676–1745), Prime Minister.

THE

HISTORY

OF OUR

OWN TIMES,

VIZ.

I. An Account of Foreign Tranſactions, from Time to Time, in an Hiſtorical Method, and on a regular Plan ; by which our Readers may de enabled to form a Judgment of the Intereſts and Meaſures of the ſeveral Potentates of *Europe*.

II. The preſent Hiſtory of *Great Britain*, ſubdivided into the following Sections : 1. The Hiſtory of the Great or Polite World ; in which will be contained an Account of the Pleaſures and Diverſions of the Town. 2. Of the Learned World ; in which we ſhall give an Account and Character of all new Books and Pamphlets in all Languages, wherever they are publiſh'd, (with Extracts from ſuch as merit it) and a conſtant Review of the political and other learned Controverſies which ſhall occur. We ſhall likewiſe preſent our Readers with ſeveral original Pieces both in Proſe and Verſe. 3. Of the three learned Profeſſions, . Divinity, Law, and Phyſic. 4. Mililary and Naval Affairs ; in which will be introduced an exact Journal of the Operations of the preſent War. 5. Of Mercantile Matters ; containing an Account of all Schemes advanced either for the Improvement or Hindrance of Trade ; the freſheſt Advices from our Ports, from *Exchange-Alley*, from *Bear-Key*, and the other moſt conſiderable Markets ; with the Prices of Goods at the ſaid Places.

III. Such new Parliamentary Speeches as may come to Hand.

No. II. From *January* 15 to 30.

To be continued regularly once a Fortnight.

By a SOCIETY of GENTLEMEN.

Printed for CHARLES CORBETT, at *Addiſon's Head*, againſt St. *Dunſtan*'s Church in *Fleet-Street*. 1741.

Price Four-pence.

2. From *The History of Our Own Times*
(January–February 1741)

NOTE: The case for Fielding's having assumed general editorial responsibility for this short-lived magazine, which consisted of four numbers only—No. 1 (1–15 January 1741), No. 2 (15–30 January), No. 3 (30 January–12 February), No. 4 (5 March)—was made by Thomas Lockwood, who also made the case for Fielding's authorship of the 'Introduction' in No. 1 and the essay 'Shame' in No. 2: see 'New Facts and Writings from an Unknown Magazine by Henry Fielding, *The History of Our Own Times*', *Review of English Studies*, NS 35 (1984), pp. 463–93. Lockwood subsequently published a 'facsimile reproduction' of the work (Scholar's Facsimiles & Reprints, New York, 1985), with an introduction and notes to the text, in which he also tentatively proposed ('Very possibly' or 'probably' [pp. 14, 53]) Fielding's authorship of the lead essay, 'The Vision of the Golden Tree', in No. 3. In the present editor's opinion the first two of these three essays are by Fielding; the third is less certainly by him.

i. Introduction

I BELIEVE it is a pretty just Observation, that most of us know more of former Ages than our own: Persons and Things generally appear in a truer Light to Posterity than to their Cotemporaries. *Wolsey, Buckingham,* and *Strafford,*[1] had, during their Lives, good Characters, with at least some Part (and perhaps a considerable) of their Countrymen; nor were *Walsingham* and *Clarendon*[2] without their Censurers and Revilers: And I much question whether several Persons now living, are universally beheld in the same Colours which future Ages will cast on them; Party and Prejudice constantly hold a false Glass before us, and misrepresent those Objects which indifferent and dispassionate Futurity will view with naked and disinterested Eyes.

Bishop *Burnet*[3] was so sensible of this, that, being resolved to deal pretty freely with Mankind, he reserved the Communication of what passed in HIS OWN TIMES, to those succeeding, and left the Publication of his History to his Executors.

But besides the Prejudice in Readers, there are likewise some few Faults in Writers themselves, which do not a little contribute to this Ignorance of what is acted by others, while we ourselves are on the Stage; and that notwithstanding the great Number of elaborate Historians now flourishing in this Kingdom, not perhaps to be equalled, either if we look back to former Times, or abroad into foreign

---

[1] '*Wolsey, Buckingham,* and *Strafford*': Thomas, Cardinal Wolsey (1475?–1530), Lord Chancellor under Henry VIII; George Villiers (1592–1628), first Duke of Buckingham and favourite of James I; Thomas Wentworth (1593–1641), first Earl of Strafford, Chief Adviser of Charles I (*HOOT*).

[2] '*Walsingham* and *Clarendon*': Sir Francis Walsingham (1530?–1990), Elizabeth's Secretary of State; Edward Hayde (1609–74), first Earl of Clarendon and Lord Chancellor under Charles II (*HOOT*).

[3] Gilbert Burnet (1643–1715), author of *The History of My Own Time* (1724–34): see above, *Journal of a Voyage to Lisbon*, p. 547 n. 10.

Countries. The chief of these Faults I shall endeavour to point out by and by, after I have enumerated the Historians in the best Order I can, and made some few Observations on their several Excellencies.

The *Craftsman*. This is a weekly Historian,[4] who began his History in the Year 1728: His first Page being sacred to political Essays, and his two last, with a Column of his second, appropriated to record the Works of eminent Men, in Writing, Physic, and the mechanic Arts, he hath but little Room for historical Matters.

Common Sense. An Author[5] whose History so nearly resembles the former, that we shall only note his first Beginning, which was in the Year 1737.

The *Englishman*. A History which began this present Year. It was first published three Times a Week, but now once only: This likewise communicates an Essay of the political Kind; but as it records fewer eminent Persons, so is the Body of the History much fuller than either of the foregoing.

The *Weekly Miscellany*, The *Universal Spectator*, *Applebee* and *Read's Journal*, weekly Historians likewise: The first of which places Religious, and the other Miscellaneous Essays, in the Front of their History.

At the Head of those Histories which appear three Times a Week in the Evening, I shall place the *Champion*,[6] as the only one, which presents an Essay to his Readers. These Essays are sometimes on political, and sometimes on miscellaneous Subjects, and are often writ with great Spirit, but mixed with a little too much of the Vinegar: The historical Part is likewise well chosen, and methodized in a new Manner; but in a Stile grave Men think rather too humourous for History.

The *London Evening Post*,[7] or, more commonly called, the *London Evening*, was first begun in the Year 1729. This History is generally esteemed for the great Dignity of its Stile, which is thought to be a Mixture of those of *Plutarch* and *Thucydides*; it likewise bears a near Resemblance to the Diligence of *Livy*, the Judgment of *Tacitus*, and the Penetration of *Sallust*; all which is the less to be wondered at, as its Authors are supposed to be Booksellers, who have long dealt in those Books.

The *St. James's* and *General Evening Posts*; whose Accounts are generally imagined to *come* from the Court-End of the Town.

The *Gazetteer* demands the first Place of the diurnal Historians, as it often contains curious Essays on political Subjects, of an entire new Kind; and in a Stile so perfectly easy and familiar, that it may justly be called *Sermoni propriore*. These Essays are built on the most perfect Christian Principles, teaching an absolute Submission to Governors, and attempting to *drive the Buyers and Sellers*, not only out of the Temple, but *the City too*. The historical Part is not very remarkable; but what most particularly recommends this History, is its Cheapness; it being to be had all over the Kingdom *gratis*.

---

[4] Nicholas Amhurst (1697–1742), editor.

[5] Charles Molloy (d. 1767), editor.

[6] Until recently HF edited *The Champion* under the pseudonym of 'Hercules Vinegar'; the paper was now chiefly conducted by his partner James Ralph (*c*.1705–1762).

[7] John Meres (1698–1761?), printer of the paper, is usually thought to have written it.

The *Daily Post*;[8] of which we shall say no more than that, it is in many Respects the Reverse of the former.

The *Daily Advertiser.* An Historian who, at his first Appearance, (in the Year 1730) applied himself almost entirely to celebrating the Excellencies of great Men, in the liberal and mechanical Arts; in recording empty Houses, and Stage-Coaches, lost Goods, and other such Particulars; but he hath since enriched his History with the most secret Councils of all the Princes of his Time, in such a Manner, that the Superstitious imagine him inspired; nay, it is generally thought that a Spirit, frequently mentioned in Scripture, is in him, or, according to others, begot him. It is certain he must deal with Some body more than human; for he *can* as *Shakespeare* says, *Look into the Seeds of Time, and tell which Grain will grow, and which will not.*[9] In other Words, he can peep into the Wheel of Fortune, and tell you not only whether your Ticket will be drawn a Blank or a Prize, but of what value the Prize will be. All wise Persons, who intend to buy Tickets in the Lottery, consult him whom to deal with, *i.e.* who sells those Tickets which are to be drawn Prizes; for none but *he* can tell.

The *London Daily Post.* The only Historian who records the ingenious Feats performed at the Theatres, from Time to Time; such as Tumbling, Rope-dancing, Dexterity of Hand, Foot, and Machine, &c.

Lastly, The *Farthing Post*; whose History might perhaps be of some Value, if it was printed so that it could be read, till when we shall say no more of it, but that is supposed to have good Friends among the Great, since it is the only Paper permitted to be published Duty-free.

Now the Merit of all these Historians is a little allayed by some few Faults; which prevent those good Effects they are so excellently calculated to produce.

First, Besides the Prejudice which Party Principles often introduce into the Mind, some of them are much suspected of a more blameable Influence; so that their Articles of History are properly to be received as Advertisements.

Secondly, The Matter of their Histories is so immethodically digested, that they distract the Mind of the Reader, who hath not Time to digest one Article, before another of a different Kind intrudes itself on him; by which Means his Understanding is confounded, and he is not much wiser, after he has gone through a whole Sheet of History, than he was when he began. For Instance: 'On *Tuesday* last, his Grace the Duke of, &c. arrived in Town from his Seat at, &c.' Here the Reader is at once delighted and instructed; he hath a Picture before his Eyes of a noble Parade through the Streets, a splendid Equipage, numerous Attendants; Tradesmen rejoicing as he passes, that their Bills will be paid in a few Days. Here perhaps he is led to meditate on true Nobility, and the Happiness it is for a great Mind to be endued with such profuse Power of doing good to Mankind. While the Reader is in this Temper what follows? Why, 'The same Day was committed to *Newgate*, by

---

[8] Also published by Meres.   [9] *Macbeth* (I. iii. 58–9).

Col. *Deveil*,[10] a Fellow named *Crookfinger'd Jack*, for being an Accomplice with *Bob Booty* in several Robberies.' Now all the Idea of Grandeur vanishes at once, or rather is so confounded with that of Meanness and Knavery, that one knows not which predominates. Palaces and *Newgate*, Coaches and Six and *Tyburn*, are all jumbled together, and perplex and distract, instead of instructing and entertaining.

Thirdly, I have heard it whispered that, notwithstanding their Insinuations, very few Prime Ministers communicate much to these Historians, or, indeed, maintain any great Intimacy with them; that they live in a total Ignorance of what is doing of Consequence in any Court of *Europe*; and that, like Beaus, they write Letters to themselves, which they pretend to receive from others, and with the same Truth.

Lastly, It is at present a pretty common Opinion, that many of their Articles are at the best but apocryphal: That they often say *we hear*, when in Truth *they do not hear*: That even in Matters of Moment, they indulge too much to Invention; as for Instance: 'Yesterday died in the 35th Year of her Age, Mrs. *Judith Huckleshark*, Wife to *John Huckleshark*, Esq; a Lady universally lamented by all those who had the Pleasure of her Acquaintance; and particularly the Poor, to whom she endear'd herself by her extensive Charity.–The same Day *Roger Redacre*, Esq; a Gentleman of a plentiful Estate in *Yorkshire*, was married to Miss *Nanny Smiler*, a young Lady of great Beauty, Merit, and a Fortune of 40,000 *l*.' Now, after all this, it is more than probable, not only that no such Persons are dead or married, but indeed that they were never yet born, and owe their Being, as well as their great Qualities, to the generous Historian.

To instruct our Cotemporaries therefore, a little better in the *History of their own Times*, this Pamphlet is instituted: Whether we shall avoid the Vices we here censure, we shall submit to the candid Opinion of our Reader; nor do we desire but the same Liberty which we have taken with others may be also taken with us. The Order into which we digest our History may be seen in our Title-Page; and as to the Truth of our Facts, as some of them are collected from no very faithful Historians, we shall always add to what is doubtful, the Authority from whence it is taken, with the following Abridgments. [Here is inserted a list of fourteen newspapers with the abbreviations to be used for each.]

The chief Favour we have to ask of our Reader, is, that he would content himself with conversing with us in this Manner (if he likes it) without enquiring who we are; by which Means no Censure or Applause will be bestowed on those who do not merit them.

ii. *An* ENQUIRY *whether the Fear of* SHAME *may not be turned to the* GOOD *of* SOCIETY.

If those who affect to mend the Manners of Mankind, instead of venting their Spleen in satyrical Invectives against general Passions, which are implanted in us by Nature, are common to all, and are (for aught we know to the contrary) as necessary

---

[10] Sir Thomas DeVeil (*c*.1684–1746), principal magistrate of the metropolis, was HF's predecessor at Bow Street, Covent Garden.

to the Composition of a Man as any of his Members are, would apply to what they condemn, the Assistance which they might borrow from them in their Work, would alone force them to confess the incomprehensible Wisdom of Providence, in giving us those very Passions which, to short-sighted and hasty Men, may appear condusive to Evil.

The Passion of Vanity seems, of all others, the most liable to this Question, *Cui Bono?* A short Experience and superficial Observation, will shew us many Instances of Men becoming ridiculous, absurd, and often wicked, as it appears from Vanity only; and yet if we search deeper, we must confess, that the Lawgiver hath been less beholden to all the other Passions than to this alone; which he can at the cheapest Rate either alarm or allure. Avarice is not only less general, and perhaps less powerful; it is likewise to be satisfied at a higher Price: It must be fed with the Riches, as Fear must with the Blood of the People.

But Vanity, as it costs the Politician little to allure it with the Rewards of Titles and Honours; so is it as clearly alarmed with Shame, which requires neither the Sacrifice of Lives or Limbs.

To omit therefore the former of these, I shall confine myself in this Essay, to the latter Method, which Lawgivers have taken to work on the Passion of Vanity; I mean by the Fear of Shame.

Shame, if I may venture to define it, is *the Disappointment of Vanity*; or rather, *the Uneasiness we feel from this Disappointment*. And the more affected the Mind is with Vanity, the more susceptible is it of Shame.

I would not be here understood to mean, that Self-condemnation which arises on the Conscience of those who are truly great and good, on the Reflexion of any Fault or Blemish; by Shame I intend only that Pain our Vanity feels from the publick Disapprobation of Mankind; and this as well when injuriously applied, as when directed with the utmost Justice.

The violent Effect which the Apprehension of this Evil works on our Minds, are [sic] evident in many Instances. Daily Experience shews us the numberless Triumphs which it gains over all our Passions, even those powerful Adversaries, Lust and Fear.

It may be questioned, whether Rods and Axes be so effectual a Support of the Magistrate's Power, as the Dread of Shame; which our own Ancestors seem to have been so sensible of, that it is one Part of most of our Punishments, and some of them consist in that only.

Seeing then that its Prevalence is so very great, and that it may be of such notable Use in our Laws, surely it is of the highest Consequence to prevent any Misapplication of this Punishment.

Tho' Shame be very well mixed with other Punishment, it should never be the sole Punishment of the Dregs of the People; and who are, perhaps not improperly, said to be below Shame; nay some of them feed their little and ill-guided Vanity with the Contempt of it. Thus Men have been seen standing in the Pillory, in the Stocks, and in a white Sheet, with an Air of uncommon Impudence, and sometimes of Triumph; nay, I am confident, great Numbers among the Vulgar may be found, who would undergo the Shame only of any of these for a Shilling. It follows, that some other Punishment should be allotted to these Persons, of which they might have a quicker Sensation, and higher Terror and Shame, should be only the Punishment of Persons, whose Birth and Station in Life, render them more afraid of, and more liable to be scurvily wounded by it.

If I am told our Laws punish Crimes without distinguishing the Person, I might perhaps confess, without approving this Disposition. Many wise Nations have punished the same Crime differently, according to the different Persons who committed it. The *Romans* particularly punished that with Death in a Slave, for which they only laid a pecuniary Mulct on a Freeman; and there was a Difference even among Freemen, between the Punishments of the highest and lowest People, for Crimes of the same Nature: Nay, among us, High-Treason is punished according to the Rank of the Offender, the lower Sort are hanged and quartered; whereas the higher have *only* their Heads struck off. The Reason of which Difference seems generally to be mistaken; for surely no one *with a Head on*, can imagine that to [be] beheaded on *Towrr-Hill* [*sic*], is less scandalous than to be hanged at *Tyburn*; but the Truth is, the Death is more shameful, though less painful since a great Man without a Head is the most opprobrious Spectacle in the whole World.

I am highly pleased with an Institution of *Artaxerxes*, who is said to have moderated the Severity of the antient Laws of *Persia*, where they had a very odd Custom of whipping their Nobility, and tearing off their Hair. Now he ordained, that for the future, those of the Nobility, who were convicted of any high Crime, should, instead of Whipping, as had been formally practised, be for the future *stripped only, and their Clothes whipped for them*; and instead of tearing off their Hair, they should for the future only *take off their Tiara*: A Punishment, which was probably as much more effectual, as less cruel than the former.[11]

Was I to institute a Society, I know no Law which I would more eagerly receive than this; and let us for Example's Sake (for I would be very unwillingly understood to presume to instruct my Superiors) suppose this Law had been to be found in the following Words, in one of our Statute Books.—'And be it enacted, that from and after &c. any Nobleman or Gentleman, who shall, in his own Right, or the Right of his Wife, be seized or possessed of an Estate in Land, of the clear Value of one thousand Pounds *per Annum*, or shall be seized or possess'd of any Office of Trust, ecclesiastical, civil, or military, which shall produce the neat Income of one thousand Pounds *per Annum*; or who shall be possessed of any Pension, &c. of like Value; or whose Estate in Land, Offices, and Pension, shall in the whole Produce, &c. or who shall be the Relation or Servant, or related to the Servant of the Prime M——r for the Time being; or who shall be the Brother, Son, or other near Relation, to the third Degree; or shall be Favourite or Dependent of any great Man, who shall happen to commit any Crime, for which the Vulgar are hanged, transported, or otherwise grievously punished, or shall commit any Crimes, for which they deserve to be hanged more than for any

---

[11] This story comes from Plutarch, *Moralia*, 173d. [Lockwood]

Crime which it is in the Power of the Vulgar to commit, shall have his best Suit of Clothes hung forth, and publickly brushed before his Door, for one whole Hour.

I have omitted the Stripping Part, which agreed better with the *Persian* Heat than it would either with our Climate, or the tender Constitutions of many of our Beaus, who might probably suffer a painful Death, by standing for a very few Minutes in the cold Air.

I have likewise forborn to mention any Ornaments, Ensigns, or Robes of Dignity, since by publickly whipping such, the Vulgar might abate of that high Veneration they now entertain for them; and since after his Clothes have been once well whipped, no Man will be ever capable of receiving any Honour or Respect from any outward Marks of Dignity whatever.

No Objections can be, I conceive, made to this Law, unless that it is new; for those who many imagine this Punishment too light for the Crimes to which it is allotted, may satisfy themselves by considering, that such Offenders are at present not punish'd at all, unless in Cases of High-Treason; and that the general Awe and Respect, as well as Tenderness for these Persons, which would make it intolerable to see corporal Punishments inflicted on them, might be well enough reconciled, to see the[i]r Coats brushed.

Perhaps it may be objected, that as great Numbers of such Persons, are intirely void of Shame, this Punishment will have no Effect on them; but this Objection proceeds, I apprehend, on a mistaken Foundation, and represents Men incapable of Shame, only because they differ in the Objects to which they apply it; for many of those who are not ashamed of doing what they should not do, would be highly ashamed of doing what they should, and though Breach of Trust, Cruelty, Treachery, Falshood, Avarice, and such like, may labour in vain to raise a single Blush, the least Instance of Poverty, Compassion, Love, Charity, or good Nature, would cover their Faces with Confusion. I could name a Place, where no Man, one would think, should be too infamous to appear, and yet I conceive, you cannot find one Person at this very Place, who would not be *ashamed of Patriotism*, or to own he had *any Love for his Country*. They have not therefore a Contempt, but a mistaken Notion of Shame, which would be remedied by this universal Consent. I might likewise add, that as many of our present great Men are Beaus and *Petit Maitres*; every Stroke which should hurt this Law or Embroidery, would go to their Hearts; nay, I much question, whether some of them would not give their Skins to save their Coats.

Another Objection may be perhaps raised among the fine-dressed People of the Age; *viz.* that it would occasion great Slovenliness, and no Man would care to appear in Company with a brushed Coat, for Fear of Suspicion; but this is of little Weight, since, when this Custom generally prevailed, I am convinced, no one, whose Coat had undergone the publick Ceremony, would have the Assurance to shew his Face, unless where it was infamous for Persons of a good Character to be seen.

In answering these few Cavils, which are all, I think, that can possibly be raised against this Law, I have incidentally mentioned some of its Advantages: There are many others, but as they are sufficiently obvious, I shall not take up the Reader's Time with them.

The second Part of this Law, which relates to the *Tiara*, I have reserved for the Ladies; but as so few Opportunities would offer to put this Law in Execution on them, I shall pass it by at present, without setting down any particular Form; I shall only mention one Case, in which it may be lawful to pull off the Hair itself, *viz.* when the Locks being false, the Hair is indeed no other than a Perriwig, and comes off at one Touch, together with the Cap. I must add, this is a Disgrace I should be very sorry to see inflicted on any of my pretty Countrywomen.

Thus, I think the Fear of Shame, and Vanity, on which it is grafted, may be made highly serviceable to the honest Law-giver in curbing and well ordering the Community; but if on the contrary, such a Handle to Mankind once fall into the Power of ill-disposed artful Men, this Passion may be very successfully applied to the entire Ruin and Subversion of all Virtue, Order, and of the Commonwealth itself; for by the Encouragement of Fashion, and by the Sanction of Numbers, Men may be taught to affect what they ought to detest, to seek for Honours in the Road of Infamy, and to be ashamed of nothing but of doing Good.

iii. *The Vision of the* GOLDEN TREE.

ACCORDING to the Notions of the divine *Homer*,[12] Dreams are of two Sorts; *viz.* such as *inform*, and such as *deceive*; to which perhaps may be added a Third, such as *amuse*; the Class under which I desire my Reader would range the following.

'Tis my Custom to read about half an Hour every Night, before I compose myself to sleep; as finding from Experience, that it effectually expunges the Impertinencies of the Day, and prepares the Mind for the sweet Approaches of Repose: To which End I am surrounded with a Variety of these mental Opiates; not all Drugs, but many of them such as lull like Music, and, to borrow of *Shakespeare*,[13] charm the Senses to Forgetfulness. Last Night I assigned this Province to that Glory of the *Roman* Poets, *Virgil*, and, having accidentally dipped into that Passage, where Æneas takes Possession of the wonderful *Golden Bough*,[14] set myself to unriddle the secret Meaning of that mysterious Passage; as likewise to explore the Virtues of a Plant, which even *Cerberus* and the *Furies* obeyed: But, before I could render my Conjectures in any Degree satisfactory, Sleep surprized me, and the Images yet dancing in my Brain produced the fantastic Scenes that ensue.

Methoughts I found myself in a large Area, listed round with a Fence resembling Lattice, or Chequer-work; in the Middle of which grew three large Trees; two close together, the Third at some Distance: All were surrounded with such vast Numbers of People, that 'twas with great Difficulty I made my Way thro', and procured an Opportunity of entering into the Particulars of the Scene before me. I, at last, however, got near enough to observe, that the single Tree was understood by the

---

[12] *Odyssey*, xix. 560–7 [annotations are from *HOOT*, p. 55]
[13] *2 Henry IV*, III. i. 8.
[14] *Aeneid*, vi. 190–211.

superstitious Herd to enclose a Deity; on which Account it was hung round with Garlands, Priests were appointed to offer solemn Sacrifices to it, and no body approached it without the profoundest Adorations. This, I was informed, was called the Tree of the EST'BL'SHM'NT: But, tho' it was thus highly revered, I soon perceived that this was but a necessary Ceremonial, which all were obliged to pay, who were passing on to the other two; and that the Moment they turned their Backs they thought of their Idol no more. These last seemed to be Twins, growing from the same Root, of the same Species, and producing the same Fruit. But it was not long before I was undeceived: One was entirely, Root, Branch, Fruit, and Leaf, vegetable Gold; the other, tho' looking to the full as splendid, only covered with a Golden Rind, and within arrant Mundic.[1] Underneath these extraordinary Trees, (the first of which was called the Tree of C'RR'PT"N, and the last the Tree of P'BL'c D'BTS) with one of his Harpy Feet on each, watched an ever-wakeful Dragon, who, while I yet looked on him, such is the Caprice of Fancy, started up in the Shape of a goodly *fat Man*,[15] with an insinuating Face, *French* Air, and persuasive Accent. He had a BILL in his Hand, and with a loud Voice proclaimed, that he was going to PRUNE; which was no sooner uttered, than the Crowd thickened ten-fold; every one pressed to be as near him as possible, and several officiously offered to take the *Bill* out of his Hand, by way of saving him the Labour: But their Services were somewhat peevishly refused, and he sat himself instantly to work with Might and Main, laying on his Blows with great Vigour and Dexterity; it being a Business he had been long accustomed to, and which he seemed to take a singular Pleasure in, tho' not a little fatiguing; especially in certain knotty Parts of the Tree, which, sometimes, almost wearied him out, and made him ready to drop his Instrument in Despair. All this Time every Body fastened their Eyes eagerly on the *Loppings*, and as many as could dexterously make off with a Bough, as they thought undiscover'd, seemed to have no Scruples of Conscience about Restitution. At length, having *done his Business*, he sat himself down on the Heap, the Croud prostrated themselves as Suppliants before him, and he began to distribute his Favours, not to those who deserved them, but to those who made it appear they were most at his Devotion; among the first of which were certain Cubs, said to be of his own Breed: To these succeeded three or four different Corps, in various Habits, and of various Professions, tho' ranked under one common Name of *Ayes* and *Noes*; and a mixed Multitude of Creatures, of all Ranks and Degrees, followed them, who received each a Branch, Sprig, Leaf, or Stalk, according to their different Claims. Now, tho' Numbers were served, yet greater Numbers were put off with Promises and Expectations only; and, except certain choice Twigs, which were laid by for *Rods*, and other precious Purposes, he affirmed, with great Confidence, that all was disposed of, and that he had nothing left but the *Sweepings* for his own Share.

It must be observed, that tho' the Soil, where these Trees grew, was naturally fertile, it looked like a Desart, dry, dusty, and incapable of Culture; they being of

---

[1] A splendid Mineral that in the Crucible evaporates.

[15] Sir Robert Walpole, the Prime Minister.

such a spungy Nature, that they exhausted all the natural Moisture round about, insomuch that the most hardy Weed could not take Root in their Neighbourhood: Nor was this natural Moisture sufficient, but once every Year there was a Necessity to load their Roots with a strange Compost of Soap, Coals, Candles, Salt, Leather, Spirits, Paper and Parchment, Cards, Dice, Mum, Malt, Beer, Ale, Perry, Cyder, Sweets, and ten thousand Things besides; which were carefully raked together by certain People called P'L'T'C'L SC'V'NG'RS, and, when gathered into a Heap, was laid on by certain Persons, under the absolute Command of the *fat Man* above mentioned, who claimed it as their Privilege, and boasted of it as an Honour, to be the sole Agents in this *dirty Work*; as a Consideration for which each of them claimed, and received his Proportion of the *Loppings*, above specified.

As the Husbandry of these People was of an extraordinary Nature, the Ceremony of *manuring* followed immediately that of *pruning*. Public Notice was first given for all the Parties concerned to attend, which was said to be the Will of the *Deity*, in whose Behalf the *fat Man*, above described, (who appeared likewise to be Chief Priest) made a long and earnest Speech, signifying in general, that the Tree of the C'NST'T"N, (for so it seems, in the sacred Language, the Tree of C'RR'PT"N is called) was above all Things dear to the *Deity*; that it faded for want of Nourishment; that the Season was come for *manuring*; that all imaginable *Ways* and *Means* must be thought of to collect a larger, and richer Quantity of *Compost* than ever; and that all Hands must labour Night and Day, till the Business was done, when they would be rewarded with the second *Prunings*, and might be at their own Disposal till the next Summons. This was no sooner uttered, but the Words *Gracious! Thanks! Unanimity!* &c. were shouted forth with great Vehemence, and the Task proposed was entered upon with all the Alacrity and Resolution imaginable.

It would be too tedious to give a Detail of all the Particulars of this strange Proceeding; it shall suffice therefore, to observe that the SC'V'NG'RS had Orders to discharge a full Fifth of their Load at the Root of the *Holy Tree*, which none failed to perform to a Tittle; and that on this Occasion I discovered what I had not observed before, *viz.* a strait fine *Sapling*, which grew from the Root of the *Holy Tree*, and depended for its Support on it; but which now seemed in a languishing Condition, the *fat Man* being a secret Enemy to it, and directing that it should be as little manured as possible, in hopes it would wither away for want of Nourishment.

The whole Posse was still hard at work, when a sudden Cry was raised, that the Enemy was at Hand; that they were all armed with new *Bills*, and they threatened to cut down the Tree forthwith; on which the *fat Man* set up a Horse-Laugh, as if he held their utmost Efforts in Contempt: But I could observe he was in a thorough Panic notwithstanding; which was farther witnessed by his mustering together his whole Corps upon the Spot, giving Instructions to some, Gratifications to others, and fair Speeches to all; insinuating, among other Things, that tho' the Enemy gave out they were coming to cut down the Tree, he had certain Intelligence their real Design was only to take Charge of it themselves; and tho' they pretended to make a Point of providing better for the *Sapling*, their real Intention was to cut down the *Holy Tree*, and destroy both Root and Branch.

He was heard with great Attention; but it appeared there was more Virtue in his Touch, than his Voice; for tho' many seemed in Suspence when he had done speaking, not a Man held out after he had taken him by the Hand; a Ceremony he was forced to go thro' with, even to the meanest Creature among them; and which was no sooner over, but the Air was rent with Acclamations; some vowing to preach for him, some plead for him, some write for him, some fight for him, and all vote for him. On this the Trumpets sounded a Charge, the whole Body began their March towards the Enemy, and the grand M————l[16] Standard was displayed, in which I could read distinctly, *Wot you not, that by this Craft we have our Living?*[17]

By this Time, those in the Opposition were likewise in Sight, and appeared far from being formidable in Point of Numbrs, but then they were followed almost by Millions, who, though unformed, and undisciplined, were ready enough to throw their Weight into the Scale; and, though they looked on, gave great Terror to the *Sc'v'ng'rs* and Comp. The Leaders of this Party were Persons of genuine Dignity; such as derived their Importance from their Merit and Capacity, not the false Glitter of Title and Ornament. The Motto in their Ensigns was, *The Tree that bringeth not forth good Fruit, shall be hewn down and cast into the Fire.*[18]

I now expected to be entertained with great Atchievements, such as would have ennobled History, and secured an Eternity of Fame to the Performers: But to my exceeding Surprise and Disappointment, all this Preparation ended in a *Parley*; and it was mutually agreed, that, according to antient Custom, all Differences should be determined by a *Plurality of Voices.*

A Succession of Speeches then followed, some of them such as would have done Honour to *Cicero* and *Demosthenes.* The Tree was proved to be no longer the Tree of the C'NST'T'T"N, as in the sacred Language it was falsly called, but a C'RR'PT"N Graft super-induced upon it, which had reversed its Nature to the very Root, and converted what was before balsamick in its Juices, to slow but infallible Poison. That the Tree of *p'bl'c D'bts* was originally but a *Sucker*, and never intended to be incorporated with the Tree of the *C'nst't't''n*; that Experience shewed it had attained to its present enormous Bulk, by the Negligence and Villany of those who had undertaken by Degrees to grub it up; and that unless both these pernicious Plants were destroy'd, they would in Time turn the whole Land into a Wilderness: That the *Holy Tree*, for which they had the highest Reverence, had no Manner of Relation to either of the others, nor would suffer the least Injury on their being removed; on the contrary, it would be restored, by that Means, to its original Significancy and Independancy, and would receive a more natural and kindly Nourishment from the Soil where it grew, than from all *forced Aids* whatever.

To all this was replied but two Words, *The Question! the Question!* Upon which the Suffrages on each Side were taken, and it was enroll'd as the Opinion of the Majority, *That whatever is, is right*; a Form of Words which I was assur'd had been constantly annex'd to whatever the *Fat Man* thought proper for almost twenty Years

---

[16] Ministerial.
[17] Cf. the proverb 'Craft against Craft makes no Living'. [18] Matthew 7: 19 (L).

together, and which signified the same with what, in other Countries, is understood by *'Tis such is our Pleasure*.

The Assembly then broke up, and the *Fat Man*, at the Head of his Band, march'd off in Triumph to the second *Pruning*: But who can paint the Horror he express'd, when it appear'd the whole Land was so exhausted, that the Compost fail'd both in Quantity and Quality: That the Tree had not produc'd above half its usual Shoots, and that the Demands, on the other hand, increased upon him every Moment? Resolv'd, however, to persevere to the End, he first lopp'd away all the Branches, to the last Sprig; next he undertook to strip off the Bark, and then proceeded to hew off large Slices of the main Body; and lastly, undertaking to rive the Root, his Strength fail'd him, the Tree closed suddenly, and, like *Milo*,[19] he was destroy'd by his own Experiment: Upon which the Spectators set up such a Shout, that I wak'd, as I thought, half stunn'd with the Noise, which proved to be one of his Majesty's Drums beating up for Voluntiers.

[19] The Olympic wrestling champion who fell prey to wolves when his hands caught in the trunk of a tree he was trying to split open.

3. From *The Gray's-Inn Journal*, No. 27 (Saturday 21 April 1753)

i. *On the Standards of modern Criticism.*[1]

Ingrediturque solo, & caput inter nubila condit.

VIRGIL.[2]

THERE are few Terms which are applied with greater Impropriety, than those characteristical Appellations, which Men usually bestow on their Acquaintance, or on others, in whose Company and Conversation they may at any Time have been casually engaged. Every Character, indeed, is formed by the Prevalence of some particular Passion, which influences the Temper, and gives a casting Weight to the Genius of the Person in whom it subsists. But no Rules that I know of, have been yet laid down, nor is there any certain Standard which should fix the Degree of Elevation, to which the ruling Passion must necessarily rise, before it can have Strength sufficient to determine the Character.

The Reader must, however, be informed, that I am not speaking of those moral Qualifications, or Endowments of the Heart, which speculative Writers have taken so much idle Pains to adorn and recommend; and which Men of Sense, or Men of the World, have unanimously agreed in rejecting, as unworthy of their serious Notice. The Qualities I mean are pure Virtues of the Head or Face; Properties, which enable the Possessor to assume a solemn Aspect at Incidents, which set the rest of the Table on a Roar; or to interrupt what is truly serious and grave, by impertinent Questions of Levity and Mirth; or lastly, to condemn and cavil, when all the World sees the highest Reasons for Applause and Admiration. The Effects which these Causes produce in Life, however various and complicated in their Appearance, may be reduced to the three general Sources of Wit, Humour, and Criticism, and as the Pretenders to these several Qualities are infinite in Number, I have determined on a certain Standard, in order to regulate and adjust their Claims. The Method I propose is, to decide their different Pretensions by the Height and Stature of the Body.

And lest this should be considered as a wild chimerical Design, I must beg Leave to assure my Reader, that the Theory I am forming is built upon the latest Discoveries, and most uncontroverted Principles of true Philosophy. It is possible however, that Persons of an over-refining Curiosity, may be able to raise some Objections to what I am going to advance, but as every Thing is liable to be called in Question by

---

[1] From Arthur Murphy's *Gray's-Inn Journal*, No. 27 (Saturday 21 April 1753), in the 1756 reprint, i, pp. 174–9; the title is from the list of Contents. See Battestin, 'Who Edited Fielding's *Journal of a Voyage to Lisbon* (1755)? The Case for Arthur Murphy and a New Fielding Essay', *Studies in Bibliography*, 55 (2002), pp. 215–33, esp. 224–33. The case for HF's authorship of this essay has been supported by Michael and Jill Farringdon using the cusum technique of computer-assisted analysis: see ibid., p. 224 n. 22.

[2] *Aeneid*, x. 767: the tyrant Mezentius 'walks the ground with head hidden in the clouds' (Loeb).

those who are disposed to cavil, they will give me but little Pain upon that Head. The plainest Truths have been disputed, and the most extravagant Opinions have been fortunate enough to meet with their Advocates and Admirers. Now, I would have such People recollect what are the general Apprehensions arising in the Mind, on the Sight of an uncommon Stature; and how favourable, withal, even the Notions of the Vulgar are to an unusual Height of Person. Is it not commonly supposed, that Men of this superior Eminence possess as superior Parts, and extraordinary Degrees of Merit. From this Principle, my little Friend of *Drury-Lane* is universally censured, as falling short of a true Hero, by near half a Foot;[3] whilst his more aspiring Antagonist is allowed to have all the necessary Dimensions, required both by ancient and modern Precedents, to constitute the heroic Character.

It is an Axiom in Philosophy, which few, I hope, will be so hardy as to deny, that the Soul is all and all in every Part. From hence it is obvious, that the Body which is a Covering only for the Ætherial Particle that is lodged within it, must necessarily receive its Dimensions from the Vigour of the Spirit, which actuates the exterior Frame. The greater Portion of Fire this Spirit is endued with, its elastic Qualities will be proportionably stronger; and the Dimensions of the Body will be protruded to a Size, exactly of the same Dimensions with the Soul which informs it. On this simple Hypothesis, which I imagine cannot be easily disproved, I proceed to settle the respective Qualifications of the different Pretenders, who have been mentioned above.

In the first Place, those who, with gentle *William* in the Play,[4] boast themselves not on Account of their Wisdom, but as they have a *pretty Wit*, do not exceed the lowest Degree of our appointed Standard. It is not in Nature, that such Persons can rise in their Stature, above the Height of five Feet and six Inches. For Wit, which is merely an Exercise of the Tongue, doth not require the same Bulk and Dimensions, which are essential to Qualifications of a superior Order. It is evidently a much less Exertion of the interior Faculties, than what are productive of that Talent which we call Humour. Hence we must advance a little in our Standard; and can admit no one to be a Man of real Humour, who does not come up to the full Height of five Feet and eight Inches; and this small Progression is the more allowable, as a considerable Part of Humour is frequently expressed by such Feats of Body, as require some little Degree of Size and Strength. Giving a Friend a violent and unexpected Slap on the Back, or the dexterous Leaping over Chairs and Tables, have been often regarded as so many undoubted Signs of genuine Humour; and are generally agreed to denote a most facetious Vein of Pleasantry, in the Authors of such exquisite Jokes. It will sometimes further happen, that these two Qualities may be blended in the same Person; as I doubt not but many of my Readers can recollect several of their Acquaintance, who are your only Men of Wit and Humour. Now, this Conjunction

---

[3] In *A Treatise on the Passions* (1747), Samuel Foote (1720–77) had complained that HF's close friend David Garrick (1717–79), rival to Spranger Barry at Covent Garden, was too small in stature to be effective in heroic roles.

[4] 'gentle *William* in the Play': referring to Fribble the fop, a part played by Garrick in his popular farce *Miss in Her Teens* (1747).

manifestly implies a much superior Energy of Soul; and consequently, a still higher Advancement in our Scale of characteristic Excellencies. These Candidates for Fame will accordingly rise two Inches above those who are mentioned last; and none are to pass under the Denomination for the future, but whose Height is five Feet ten. For these Qualities, when thus united, will frequently exert themselves in Strokes of Gallantry and Mirth, which are so much the more honourable as they are dangerous to the Person or the Purse of the ingenious Artist, who has the Courage or Curiosity to attempt the Experiment. The demolishing Windows, knocking down of Watchmen, bilking of Waiters at Places of Entertainment, with other Instances of the like Kind, are very laudable and convincing Proofs of these compound Qualities, residing together in the same Habitation. The last Quality, which greatly overtops the rest, and is indeed the Crown and Perfection of all, is the wonderful and most ingenious Faculty of modern Criticism. And as this is, in the most exalted Manner, the Gift of Nature, whoever has the Happiness to be born a true Critic, is at least six Feet complete. A Critic is the Master-piece and noblest Work of Nature; and may justly be expected to bear about him some distinguishing Tokens, which will enable a Spectator, at the first View, to acknowledge and revere his Merits. Hence she has bestowed on him a more than ordinary Portion of the *Daring* and *Tremendous;*[5] and these would appear to very little Effect in a Person of less Dimensions, than those which we have here assigned him. The Wit may be pert and sanguine; the Man of Humour confident or overbearing; but it is the Critic alone, who glares horribly terrific. His every Look freezes the young Author's Blood; and at the Sound of his Voice, the rooted Seats have been known to be torn from the Ground, and hurled violently through the Air, in furious and wild Commotion. Phænomena, like these, can only be produced by that iron Strength of Lungs, and brazen Audacity of Figure, which Nature has so liberally imparted to the modern Critic.

It will be necessary to obviate an Objection arising from popular Prejudice, that the Science of Criticism being to examine into the Merit of all Productions of Genius and Learning, it does not seem to demand the Size and Dimensions which I have made essential to the Character; but the Objectors, I apprehend, are mistaken in the End of modern Criticism; and have not perhaps duly reflected on the necessary Qualities to discharge the Province they are desirous of allotting it. To execute that Task, would require a moderate Portion of Sense, Taste and Judgment, under the Direction of Modesty and Candour; Talents so little practised by those who have taken up the Occupation of a a [*sic*] Critic, that they appear on all Occasions not to have the least Conception of them. Whoever will give himself Leave to consider, that the Character of a Critic, a Wit, and Man of Humour, in the present Estimation of the World, is supported wholly by Mechanical Operations, in which the Understanding has no Manner of Share, he will easily agree with me, that the

---

[5] 'the *Daring* and *Tremendous*': the terms characterizing the 'modern Critic', who 'glares horribly terrific' freezing 'the young Author's Blood', suggest Pope's characterization of John Dennis (1657–1734) in the *Essay on Criticism* (1711): '*Appius* reddens at each Word you speak, | And *stares, Tremendous!* with a *threatening Eye*, | Like some *fierce Tyrant* in *Old Tapestry*!' (lines 585–7).

surest Method to discover those Characters, must be taken from that Part which is principally concerned; and as we can truly judge from outward Appearances alone, I have shewn to a Demonstration that the Stature of a Person is the only infallible Criterion, by which we can decide, on the Justness of his Pretensions; and that no one for the future can have any Right to either of those Characters, but whose Dimensions will exactly tally with the Measures of this Standard.

APPENDIX B

The Texts

1. List of Emendations

NOTE: All alterations whether substantive or accidental to the copy-text of the first edition are listed here, with their immediate source, except for those specified in the Textual Introduction as silently made. Emendations credited to 'W' are not found in the copy-text. A few common conventions of notation are adopted here. The wavy dash ~ stands for the word provided in the lemma to the left of the bracket and is used exclusively in the notation of accidentals where it serves to call attention to the particular matter of the emendation. An inferior caret ‸ signifies the absence of punctuation when this is a point of variation. The vertical stroke | indicates the end of a line. An asterisk * preceding the page–line reference indicates the presence of a Textual Note (Appendix B. 2).

I. OCCASIONAL VERSE

NOTE: In Part I, only *The Masquerade* of the six poems published during HF's lifetime required a place in this section of Appendix B. As stipulated in the Textual Introduction to the Wesleyan Edition, certain modifications of format and the correction of obvious misprints in the copy-text were silently emended.

1. *The Masquerade* (1728)

NOTE: The second edition is a modernized reprint included by Millar in his posthumous collection of HF's *Dramatic Works* (1755). Throughout this edition, except for the Latin phrase at line 142, all italics were changed to roman, and capitals were reduced to lower-case except at the beginning of lines of verse and the names of persons and places. Not being authorial, these sophistications of the text were not adopted in the present Wesleyan Edition, with one exception at line 245.

SIGLA

The Masquerade (1728) = I
The Masquerade (1755) = II

245   Of ‸] II; ~, I

2. 'Cantos' (1729–30)

NOTE: In the special cases of the 'Cantos' and the 'Epistle to Lyttleton'—both of which are works in manuscript only, unpublished during HF's lifetime—footnotes to the texts, illustrating HF's revisions from earlier drafts, substitute for 'emendations'. See also the Textual Note appended to the Introduction to the 'Cantos'.

5. 'An Epistle to Mr. Lyttleton' (1733)

NOTE: See the note to the 'Cantos' above.

II. OCCASIONAL PROSE

1. *Shamela* (1741)

NOTE: Emendations credited to 'W' are not found in the two editions of 1741 (the first edition designated 'I' and the second 'II').

149. 7	like] II; alike I
151. 6	generally] W; genenerally I–II
152. 14	Favour] II; Honour I
*155. 22	Whole] W; whole I–II
159. 5	lie] II; lie lie I
159. 6	*Jewkes*] II; *Jervis* I
*159. 19	*Bailey*] II; *Baily* I
163. 5	*Williams*] W; *William* I–II
164. 9	are] W; are are I–II
164. 18	for,] W; ~ ‸ I–II
164. 18	shan't ‸] II; ~, I
165. 7	to-night] II; to Night I
165. 13	forbid,] II; ~ ‸ I
166. 17	you,] W; ~ ‸ I–II
166. 16	and ‸] II; ~, I
167. 23	Coarseness] II; Courseness I
167. 25	Tenant's] II; Tenants I
167. 25	Daughters,] II; ~ ‸ I
168. 1	what] II; what what I
172. 17	says] II; say I
174. 19	that;] II; ~, I
174. 20	the;] W; the the I–II
175. 8	hungry] II; hungty I
176. 15	*Revenge:*] II; ~ : I
176. 18	and] II; and and I

178. 13   Hussy,] II; ~ ˄ I
178. 25   LETTER ˄] II; ~, I
178. 26   HENRIETTA] II; HENRIETEA I
179. 29   How,] W; ~ ˄ I–II
180. 7   Mistress,] II; Mrs. I
181. 4   *A*] II; *a* I
182. 20   *Friend,*] II; ~ ˄ I
184. 24   Paduasoy] II; Paduosoy I
185. 35   her!] II; ~, I
188. 12   Penance,] II; ~ ˄ I
188. 17   two] W; too I–II
189. 11   answered,] W; ~ ˄ I–II
189. 13   vain,] W; ~ ˄ I–II
189. 20   I'fackins;] II; ~ ˄ I
190. 1   Aldermen] II; Alderman I
190. 17   left;] II; ~, I
191. 34   *Your*] II; *Yonr* I
191. 34   *Servant,*] W; ~ ˄ I–II
192. 2   me;] II; ~, I
192. 3   *Williams,*] II; ~ ;
*195. 4   favour'd] II; favour

2. *A Full Vindication of the Dutchess Dowager of Marlborough* (1742)

219. 23   he] W; she I–II
220. 12   Smiles] W; Smilies I–II
222. 10   Mistress?] W; ~. I–II
223. 9   Writers ˄] W; ~, I–II
225. 7   who] W; whom I–II
227. 12   Womankind] W; Woman kind I–II
231. 8   containing ˄] W; ~, I–II
235. 21   and] W; aud I–II

3. *Plutus, the God of Riches* (1742)

262. 15   *Girardus*] W; *Giraldus* I
265. 13   *Shoulder.*)] W; ~ ˄ I
293. 41   35] W; 85 I
314. 28   71] W; 7 I
328. 36   second] W; first I

4. Preface to *David Simple* (1744)

NOTE: W reverses italics and roman throughout the Preface.

5. *The Female Husband* (1746)

373. 25–6   bridegroom ˌ] W; ~, I
374. 5   acquainted] W; acqnainted I
374. 6   *Ivythorn*] W; *Jvythorn* I
*374. 18   ˌa] W; |a I

6. *Ovid's Art of Love Paraphrased* (1747)

NOTE: This record of emendations and the commentary that accompanies it was prepared by Dr Amory. As explained above in his Textual Introduction to the text ('Treatment of the Copy-Text', p. 393), Amory 'silently emended' the punctuation of the Latin, but recorded 'changes in spelling or wording' in an 'Apparatus Criticus', as below, where 'W' = the reading of the present Wesleyan Edition; 'I' = the first edition of 1747, which alone carries any authority; and '1756' = the first Dublin reprint. The section on the 'English Text' follows the record of emendations of the 'Latin Text'.

LATIN TEXT

Line:

11   *Achillem*] W; *Achillen* I
                     Some edns. (incl. Burmann's) *Achillen*, wrongly.
17, 21, 23, 30, 232 *Amor, –is*] W; *amor, –is* I
18, 204, 247, 442,   *deâ, –us, –o, –os*] W; *Deâ, –us, –o, –os* I
   562, 632, 637
21   *cedet*] W; *cedit* I
                     HF translates with the future ('so shall Love [submit] to me').
23   *fixit*] W; *finxit* I
                     HF translates both *finxit* and *ussit* in the present tense ('pierces . . . burns'); if he had meant to emend *fixit*, however, he would presumably have altered *ussit* to the present (*urit*) as well.
25   *mentiar*] W; *mentior* I
                     MSS divide; HF translates with the future ('I will tell no lyes').
53   *Andromedan*] W; *Andromedon* I
                     MSS divide; *Andromeden, –an, –on; Andromedon*, wrongly. Burmann prints *Andromedan*.
59   *Quot*] W; *Quod* I
72   *auctoris*] W; *autoris* I
                     The text uses both spellings; normalized. See also below, lines 654, 704.
77   *linigeræ*] W; *Linigeræ* I
79   *possit*] W; *posset* I

possit is the received reading, and HF's translation does not indicate that he departs from it.

94 *cum*] W; *dum* I
cum is the received reading, and HF's translation does not indicate that he departs from it.

97 *ruit*] W; *ruet* I
Some eds. *ruet*; HF translates with present ('swarm').
ad] Burmann; *in* I
Burmann notes, 'The early editions down to the latter Aldines all have *in*' (trans. HA), for which there is no MS authority; and cf. E. J. Kenney, *The Classical Text* (Berkeley, 1974), p. 68 n. 1. The difference of meaning is slight, but HF's '*to* the Theatres' may reflect Burmann's correction.

114 *repente*] Burmann; *petenda* I
The tradition is corrupt, as Burmann notes: 'I strongly question whether this can be good Latin: he should have said, *petendæ prædæ* ["but the meter forbids it"]. Hence, if any codex supported it, I would gladly read, *signa repente dedit* ["he *suddenly* gave a signal"]; or *Rex, populo prædæ signa petente, dedit* ["the king gave the people the signal for attack *they were seeking*"]' (trans. HA). HF translates 'on a sudden', following Burmann.

124 *manet . . . fugit*] Heinsius; *fugit . . . manet* I
MSS divide; HF translates 'one stands still, another endeavours to get out', with Heinsius.

133 *sollenia*] W; *solennia* I
['sollemnia' (Loeb)]

147 *eburnis*] W; *Eburnis* I
['ephebis' (Loeb)]

174 *Urbe*] W; *urbe* I
181 *ducem*] W; *ducum* I
211 *Qui*] Heinsius; *Quid* I
Though HF does not translate this line, he probably would have accepted Heinsius' emendation, proposed '*meo periculo*' ('I stake my life on it'); the sense is 'O Parthian, who fleest in order to conquer, why do you leave your conquests?' Heinsius would also have emended *victos* to *victo*, with an improved sense, but less necessarily.
vincas,] W; ~ ? I

232 *Amor*] W; *amor* I
235 *excutit*] W; *excudit* I
excudit ('forges') makes no sense; *excutit* is the received reading, and HF's translation ('if he happens to shake') supports it.

236   *et spargi . . . docet*] Burmann; *aspergi . . . nocet* I
        A difficult passage, literally, 'yet does it hurt even to be
        sprinkled on the breast with love' (Loeb)—*whose* breast not
        being named, though modern editors assume the lover's.
        HF's version ignores any damage ('he may possibly sprinkle
        the Bosom of your Mistress with Love'), following Burmann,
        who remarks, 'Can *nocet* really be right? So, Ovid, why are
        you teaching a noxious art? On the contrary, I think he *teaches*
        [*docet*] *the bosom* [to be sprinkled] *with love*. Cupid indeed can
        swiftly shake off the effects of wine; nevertheless wine teaches
        love to enter the bosom' (trans. HA).

246   *nocent*] Heinsius; *nocet* I
        MSS divide; the plural is called for.

248   Vincis] W; *vincis* I

253   *coetus*] W; *cœtus* I

254   *cedet*] W; *cedat* I
        cedet is the received reading, and HF's translation does not
        indicate that he departs from it.

267   *dociles*] Heinsius; *faciles* I
        MSS divide; HF's schoolmasterly translation, '*Mind all*'
        (= 'attend with docile minds', Loeb), follows Heinsius'
        preference.

268   *adeste*] Burmann; *adesto* I
        The MSS divide; the tense should parallel *advertite*.

272   *Maenalius*] W; *Menalius* I

293   *Cydoneæque*] W; *Sidoniæque* I
        MSS divide; *Sidoniadesque; Cydoniadesque* (Micyllus);
        Cydoneæque (Heinsius); HF '*Cydonian*'.

316   *decere*] Heinsius; *placere* I
        MSS divide; HF translates 'she is silly enough to think her
        Airs *become* her', with Heinsius.

328   *O*] W; *Ah* I
        HF translates 'O', and an expression of astonishment, not of
        sympathy, is called for.

336   *sanguinolenta*] W; *sangui nolenta* I

352   *molliet illa*] W; *molliat ille* I
        MSS divide; HF translates 'she will pave the way'.

377   *illa*] W; *illâ* I

378   *munus comparat*] Bersmann; *munnus teparat* I; *munus te parat*
        1756
        MSS divide: *temparat; te parat*. HF apparently understood
        comparat ('One thinks of *procuring* . . . Pleasures . . . for her
        Mistress'), with Gregor Bersmann, rather than *te parat* ('wins
        you', Loeb) with Heinsius and J. F. Gronovius.

408	*expositas*] Burmann; *ex positas* I
	MSS divide: *positas/expositas*. The typo seems to be the result of a MS insertion in the printer's copy.
472	*equi*] W; *æqui* I
486	*postmodo*] W; *post modo* I
510	*tempora*] W; *tempore* I
515	*ne*] W; *nec* I
524	*quærit*] W; *quæret* I
	quærit is the received reading, and HF's translation does not indicate that he departs from it.
542, 548	*satyri*] W; *Satyri* I
563	*Evoe!*] W; *Evæ*; I
569	*licentia ficto*] W; *latentia tecto* I; *latentia ficto* Bersmann; *licentia tecto* Burmann
	HF's translation combines Burmann's and Bersmann's emendations: 'by a fictitious Name' (*sermone ficto*) and 'a hundred amorous things' (*multa licentia*).
588	*bibenda*] Micyllus; *vivenda* I
	Micyllus glosses, 'the lover takes more cups than his instructions warrant' (trans. HA); HF translates 'pushing the Bottle further than is necessary'.
599	*dicas faciasve*] W; *dices faciesque* I
	HF's text has the indicative, with Heinsius ('whatever you do or say . . .', Loeb), but his translation preserves the subjunctive of 'the better manuscripts' ('If you should descend to Expressions . . .'), and their weaker logic, *Et* ('*for then* . . . it may be imputed' [trans. HA]), as against Heinsius' *Ut* ('*so that* . . . [it] may be put down', Loeb).
603	*discedet*] W; *discedit* I
	HF translates both *discedit* and *dabit* in the present tense ('When the Company *rises* to go away, there *is* always Confusion'), but presumably did not mean to emend *discedet*, the received reading.
604	‸*Ipsa . . . dabit.* ‸] W; (~ . . . ~ ‸) I
612	*Hæc*] Heinsius; *Hic* I
	MSS divide: *Hac/Hinc*; HF translates 'this Faith', with Heinsius.
616	*finxerat* ‸ *esse,*] W; ~, ~ ‸ I
628	*recondit*] W; *recondet* I
	MSS divide; HF translates in the present ('never displays').
634	*notos*] W; *Notos* I
654	*auctor*] W; *autor* I
665	Improbe!] W; *improbe*, I
674	*invitae*] W; *invitis* I

681   *Fabula*] 1756; *Fbaula* I
701   Mane!] W; *mane,* I
704   *Auctorem*] W; *Autorem* I
715   *flatus*] Heinsius; *fastus* I
               MSS divide; HF's translation ('immoderate Airs') follows
               Heinsius' preference.
735   *Attenuant*] W; *Attenuent* I
               MSS divide; HF translates in the indicative ('will bring this
               about').
740   *amicitia*] W; *amicitiæ* I
               Typo? the genitive is found in some eds. (e.g. Micyllus, 1549).
745   *Hermionam . . . amabat*] W; *Hermionem . . . amavit* I
               MSS divide: *Hermionem, –am, –en . . . amavit/amabat.*
               Hermionem is corrupt, and *amavit* implies either that their
               example is no longer relevant or that in fact they had once had
               a (brief) affair (as in line 285). Most modern edns. read *quo,*
               with Heinsius, but HF's translation does not clearly indicate
               his preference.
761   *leves*] W; *levis* I
762   *hirtus*] W; *hircus* I

                            ENGLISH TEXT

Page. line:
409. 1   ²a] W; *ital.* I
413. 9   out-runs] 1756; our-runs I
425. 24   perhaps ‸] W; ~, I
427. 11–12   *O . . . Note*] W; *no ital.* I
427. 17   *Sure*] W; sure I
437. 1   Deity).] W; ~: I
439. 22   *and all that*] W; *no ital.* I
439. 35   Stealth ‸] W; ~, I
441. 6   *Venus?*] W; ~. I
449. 17   *Naïs*] W; *Nais* I
451. 18   Dispositions] W; Disposition I

7. Preface and Letters XL–XLIV of *Familiar Letters* (1747)

NOTE. Except for those made silently, as explained in the Textual Introduction to
this Wesleyan Edition, the following is a complete record of emendations of the
copy-text, which is the Preface and Letters XL–XLIV of the first edition of Sarah
Fielding's *Familiar Letters between the Principal Characters in David Simple, and
Some Others,* 2 vols. (1747). The sigla: 'I' = the first-edition copy-text; 'II' = the
second edition (1752). According to the advertisement in HF's *Covent-Garden
Journal* (see the Introduction above, p. 470) the second edition was 'revised and

corrected'. Though collation of HF's Preface and the five letters he contributed shows that alterations to the text of the first edition were few and minor, they may well be authorial.

Page. line:

478. 22	capable ˄] II; ~, I
479. 17	Account] II; account I
495. 17	Bread] II; Bred I
497. 13	that] II; *om.* I
504. 19	not fine] II; not near fine I
510. 10	Eye] II; eye I
511. 18	others,] ~ ˄ I

8. *The Journal of a Voyage to Lisbon* (1755)

NOTE. Emendations credited to 'W' are not found in the two posthumous editions of 1755 (the first edition copy-text designated 'I' and the second edition 'II'); three emendations credited to 'M' are first found in the 'Murphy' edition of the *Works* (1762).

Page. line:

554. 9	Rehearsal] M; rehearsal I–II
*562. 7	months] II; month's I
568. 18	coach] M; couch I–II
571. 13	here] II; hear I
574. 26	stage-coachman ˄ doth,] II; ~ – ~, ~ ˄ I
580. 21	ply] W; ly I–II
*585. 33	people.'* | [*footnote*] *Plato de Leg. lib 4. pp. 713c.–714 edit. Serrani.] W; people,' ˄ | [*as text*] *Plato de Leg. lib* 4. *p.* 713. *c.* 714. *edit.* | *Serrani.* I–II
589. 5	Æolus] W; Eolus I–II
590. 13	to restrain] II; so restrain I
591. 10	its] II; it's I
*591. 37	heels] W; head I–II
599. 19	and] II; and that I
*600. 3	Harriet] W; Harriot I–II
*600. 19	14] W; 19 I–II
601. 10	four] W; five I–II
*605. 16	fish-eater] W; fisher I–II
606. 10	gave] II; gave us I
606. 12	hath] II; has I
*608. 3	censure] II; tacit censure I
609. 6	15] W; 20 I–II
609. 9	delightful] II; delighful I
609. 15	16] W; 21 I–II
611. 14	appear,] II; ~ ˄ I

611. 19   qualified ˄] II; ~, I
611. 26   appear] II; should appear I
614. 21   17] W; 22 I–II
615. 31   18] W; 23 I–II
*618. 5   thirty-six-shilling] W; ~ – ~ ˄ ~ I–II
*619. 4   huts] II; hats I
619. 4   mind,] II; ~? I
619. 6   known?] II; ~. I
620. 17   pounds]II; pound's I
621. 21   19] W; 24 I–II
623. 15   20,] W; 29. I–II
623. 28–9   to freshen;] II; *omit* I
624. 29   21] W; 26 I–II
625. 11   *Vinum Pomonæ*] W; *no italics* I–II
625. 22   encouraging] II; enouraging I
626. 21   *sui juris*] II; *no italics* I
627. 9   *Ars Cauponaria*] W; *no italics* I–II
630. 1   buttons] II; butttons I
633. 19   *Monday, July* 22.] W; *Monday.* I–II
634. 10   *Tuesday, July* 23.] W; *Tuesday.* I–II
635. 25   than] II; that I
640. 11   no,] W; ~ ˄ I
641. 15   as he] W; ashe I
641. 19   perform] M; perfom I
643. 9   *Wednesday, July* 24.] W; *Wednesday.* I; *Wednesday* the 20th. II
644. 8   *Thursday, July* 25.] W; *Thursday.* I–II
646. 16   *Friday, July* 26.] W; *Friday.* I–II
646. 35   *Saturday, July* 27.] W; *Saturday.* I–II
648. 28   *Sunday, July* 28.] W; *Sunday.* I–II
650. 1   *Monday, July* 29.] W; *Monday.* I–II
650. 5   us. While] W; ~, while I–II
650. 6   tempest,] W; ~; I–II
652. 18   *Friday, August* 2.] W; *Friday.* I–II
653. 11   *Sunday, August* 4.] W; *Sunday.* I–II
653. 24   *Monday, August* 5.] W; *Monday.* I–II
654. 9   hurry, . . . delay. *omit*] W; hurry, . . . delay. *Tuesday.* I; hurry. *omit* II
657. 13   *Wednesday, August* 7.] W; *Wednesday.* I–II
*657. 16   arising] II; aising I
659. 2   Tajo] II; Taio I
659. 9   *chartæque viæque*] W; *chartæq; viæq;* I–II

9. *A Fragment of a Comment on L. Bolingbroke's Essays* (1755)

673. 18   *in vacuo*] W; no italics I–II
*678. 1   'Mr. Lock . . . impossible ˄it is] W; ˄~ ~ . . . ~ 'it is I–II

2. Textual Notes

II. OCCASIONAL PROSE

1. *Shamela* (1741)

Page. line:

155. 22   Though, at 15. 22, both editions have lower case *w*, in HF's writing of that letter lower and upper case are often indistinguishable, and here the word occurs in the title of *The Whole Duty of Man* and is printed as such in *Joseph Andrews* (p. 24). At 175. 17 II has upper case 'W'.

159. 19   HF normally used the preferred spelling of 'Old Bailey', as in *Amelia* (p. 532) and *Tom Jones* (pp. 823, 932).

169. 31   Though II has 'Schollard', both forms are cited in the *OED* as vulgarisms (s.v. 'scholar').

174. 22   Though II has 'forever', the relatively recent form of the phrase 'for ever' (*OED* cites 1670 as the earliest example), HF preferred the phrase: C-H cites 66 instances in his fiction.

175. 9–10   Though II has 'Good-Humour', a form also found in HF's writings (as in 'An Essay on the Knowledge of the Characters of Men' [*Miscellanies* i, pp. 158–9]), C-H cites 38 instances of 'good Humour' in his fiction.

175. 21   See above, 155. 22.

184. 13   II alters to 'leap'd', but 'leapt' is the usual form in HF's fiction: C-H cites 27 instances.

184. 24   Though II has the more usual form 'Waistcoat', which HF usually preferred (C-H cites 10 instances in the fiction), 'Wastecoat' nevertheless occurs 3 times in *Jonathan Wild* (pp. 34, 144, 147) and once in *Tom Jones* (p. 266).

187. 27–8   II adds a hyphen ('good-humoured'). And in what C-H cites as the only other instance of the phrase in HF's fiction, so does the Wesleyan Edition of *Tom Jones* (p. 339. 22), emending, perhaps unwisely, the reading of all four editions published in HF's lifetime (see *Tom Jones*, ii, p. 995: 339. 22).

194. 12   Though II has 'Superiors', HF more often preferred 'Superiours', the spelling of the copy-text: C-H cites 27 instances in his fiction.

194. 22   Though II emends to 'persuade', which HF preferred (C-H cites 138 instances in the fiction), he at times used the spelling of the copy-text, 'perswade', as in *Tom Jones*, where it occurs four times (pp. 139, 735, 740, 853).

195. 4   'favour', the reading of the copy-text, occurs flush with the end of the line, and the past tense 'favour'd' of II would seem to be called for.

2. *A Full Vindication of the Dutchess Dowager of Marlborough* (1742)

227. 12   Womankind: The copy-text makes two words of this, which is one word both in *Remarks* (p. 33), which HF is here quoting, and in HF's usual practice (C-H has six examples).

5. *The Female Husband* (1746)

374. 18   A straight vertical bar the height of the line immediately before 'a' in all copies.

6. *Ovid's Art of Love Paraphrased* (1747)

NOTE: For Hugh Amory's commentary both on the Latin and English texts and on HF's footnotes, see his Textual Introduction to the work (immediately following the Introduction) as well as his 'Apparatus Criticus', provided in this Appendix, Section 1 (List of Emendations).

8. *The Journal of a Voyage to Lisbon* (1755)

Page. line:

562. 7   When denoting duration in this way, HF usually omitted the apostrophe: *e.g.* 'nine Months Lodging' (*Journey from This World to the Next, Miscellanies* ii, p. 2); 'three days Absence' (*Joseph Andrews* [II. iv, p. 115]); 'many Days March' (*Tom Jones* [VII. xiii, p. 383]); a 'Quarrel . . . of two Days standing' (*Amelia* [X. vii, p. 440]).

563. 28   Reflecting the English pronunciation (*kwiksot*) of the name of Cervantes' hero, still current today, 'Quixotte' is the spelling HF, as well as Smollett, preferred; for an example in his hand, see the copyright assignment of *Joseph Andrews* transcribed in the Wesleyan Edition (p. xxxi).

580. 21   Though both editions have 'the small craft that ly between Chatham and the Tower', Keymer's emendation of 'ply' for 'ly' makes better sense of the passage. See *OED*, 'ply' v.^{2} 7: 'Of a vessel or its master: To sail or go more or less regularly to and fro *between* certain places'.

585. 33   This citation was printed as text, perhaps because a footnote would have forced a page-break; the emendation normalizes it to HF's later citations. These are usually spaced out 5–6 mm., but may be solid with the text. The two lines of small pica here would have to squeeze into one line long primer. HF's cues are symbols (e.g.* †, etc.) in the *Journal*, but more often superscript letters in the 'Fragment'. HA

*591. 37   In the draft of his commentary on the text Amory remarks, HF 'obviously means "heels" '—or more likely I should say the singular 'heel', since a final 's' in the manuscript could not be mistaken for a 'd' ('head'); the *OED* ('heel' v.^{1} 3) gives the form of the locution: 'To catch or take by the heel'. Yet despite his certainty that the text preserves an error, Amory, with all previous editors, chose to allow the reading of the 1755 editions to stand because 'it is uncertain whether the mistake was compositorial or authorial'. In a case such as this, however, where an obvious error—certainly compositorial, the author being dead when the type was set—has escaped the proof-reader, the editor has not only the licence but the responsibility to emend the text. This was the opinion of Fredson Bowers and is also the view of David Vander Meulen, his successor as editor of *Studies in Bibliography*. The case for emending, moreover, is supported by HF's penchant for referring to 'heels' in his fiction and plays: C-H lists 44 instances, including from *Plutus* (IV. iii), 'The master . . . will lug him out by the heels' (above, p. 323); and *Tom Jones* (IV. viii), where Kate of the Mill, in falling, 'inverted the Order of Nature, and gave her Heels the Superiority to her Head' (p. 180).

600. 3 HF's daughter Henrietta was called 'Harriet' and HF was fond of the name, which he gave to Mrs Wilson in *Joseph Andrews* and to Mrs Fitzpatrick, Sophia's cousin, in *Tom Jones*; in both novels it is spelled with an 'e'.

600. 19 In the copy-text the headings for this entry, and for the seven succeeding entries, are misdated '*Sunday, July 19*' to '*Sunday, July 26*' (with Saturday in the sequence being '*July 29*' instead of 25 July). After this anomalous series the headings consist only of the names of the days of the week. In the second ('Humphrys') edition the only deviation from this peculiar pattern in the headings occurs with the entry for '*Wednesday, July 24*' which reads '*Wednesday* the 20th.' In the present edition the dates are corrected as shown in the List of Emendations (Appendix B.1).

Amory ('Two Versions of *Voyage to Lisbon*; pp. 184–5) accounts for these anomalies by supposing that HF, when revising the MS in Lisbon, wished to change the *numbering* of the headings for 14–21 July to 19–26 so as to reflect the number of days since he boarded the *Queen of Portugal* at Redriffe (Rotherhithe) on 26 June. The hypothesis does hold for the eight *numbers* in question, but raises the questions: Why, if this was his intent, did he not delete the references to the month? Why did he not alter the headings of the eighteen entries preceding those for these eight days so as to conform to the new system? and Why, after the entry for '*Sunday, July* 26 [i.e. 21]' did he abandon *both* numbering systems—both the calendar dates and the days of the journey? As for the anomalous '*Wednesday* the 20th' in the 'Humphrys' edition, Amory proposes, for this single instance, that HF had thought of yet a third numbering system: that this day marked the *twentieth* day of his keeping the *Journal*, which he therefore must have begun writing on 5 July. But, though HF later remarks that 'the first serious thought which I ever entertained of enroling myself among the voyage-writers' occurred to him 'in the Downs' (text p. 649 and n. 301 [Sunday 28 July]), and though he was aboard the *Queen of Portugal* anchored in the Downs on 5 July, yet he was also there every other day from 2 to 8 July; and this second hypothetical scheme, if it does reflect HF's intent, also declares his dissatisfaction with it, for he abandoned it at once.

601. 10   See the text, p. 601 n. 174.

605. 16   Though now an archaism, 'fisher' (for a fisherman) was not uncommon usage in the period (see *OED*). It is not, however, as the context requires, synonymous with 'Icthuofagus' and we have emended it accordingly.

608. 3   The correction in edition II restores the sense of the statement: remonstrating is a vocal activity, not at all tacit; in the following lines, not complaining about the bill could possibly be taken as 'a tacit sarcasm'.

618. 5   See the text, p. 618 n. 220.

619. 4   Most previous editors have followed Dobson in emending the first edition's 'hats' to the second edition's 'huts'. The emendation is supported by a letter of 30 September 1756 from Baron Fürstenberg, writing from an encampment of troops near Winchester, Hants., to James Harris at Salisbury: the Baron hoped that, 'before the breaking-up of our camp', Harris could enjoy a concert of music 'here in my hut' ['*ma cabane*'] (Burrows and Dunhill, p. 319).

657. 16   Except for Pagliaro, who has 'rising', all modern editors follow Murphy (who may indeed have made the original emendation) in taking the reading of edition II: 'arising'. For this now obsolete usage, see *OED*, s.v. 'arise' II. 11: To ascend, go or come higher.

9. *A Fragment of a Comment on L. Bolingbroke's Essays* (1755)

678. 1   By opening the quotation at 'it is for us . . .', both editions give the misleading impression that HF is quoting Locke's *Essay concerning Human Understanding*. The quotation, however, is entirely from Bolingbroke, beginning, 'Mr. LOCKE observes how impossible it is for us. . . .' (*Works*, v, p. 6). HF's footnote (†) is meant to direct the reader to the section of Locke's *Essay* that Bolingbroke is supposedly paraphrasing.

3. Word-Division

II. OCCASIONAL PROSE ONLY

End-of-the-Line Hyphenation in the Wesleyan Edition

NOTE: No hyphenation of a possible compound at the end of a line in the Wesleyan text is present in the first edition copy-text except for the following readings, which are hyphenated within the line in the first edition. Hyphenated compounds in which both elements are capitalized are excluded.

1. *Shamela* (1741)

Page. line:
188. 14–15   Wedding-night

2. *A Full Vindication of the Dutchess Dowager of Marlborough* (1742)

None

3. *Plutus, the God of Riches* (1742)

299. 9–10   Dropsy-legged.
334. 1–2   Well-baked Cake.

4. Preface to *David Simple* (1744)

None.

5. *The Female Husband* (1746)

370. 22–3   Cheese-monger.

6. *Ovid's Art of Love Paraphrased* (1747)

437. 3–4   new-ravished.
437. 24–5   Toast-maker.

7. Preface and Letters XL–XLIV of *Familiar Letters* (1747)

None.

8. *The Journal of a Voyage to Lisbon* (1755)

583. 5–6   twenty-pounder.
634. 14–15 four-pence.
649. 34–5   voyage-writers.

9. *A Fragment of a Comment on L. Bolingbroke's Essays* (1755)

None.

End-of-the-Line Hyphenation in the First Edition Copy-Text

NOTE: The following compounds, or possible compounds, are hyphenated at the end of the line in the first edition. The form in which they have been transcribed in the Wesleyan text, listed below, represents the general practice of the first edition as ascertained by other appearances or by parallels.

1. *Shamela* (1741)

154. 11	Coffee-house		165. 22	cross-legged
156. 19	Booksellers		179. 5	hereafter
159. 15	well-disposed		181. 16	Horseback
164. 16	Saucebox			
164. 31	Honeysuckle			
164. 32	Rosebud			
165. 22	Life-time			

2. *A Full Vindication of the Dutchess Dowager of Marlborough* (1742)

NOTE: No ambiguities appear.

3. *Plutus, the God of Riches* (1742)

252. 17	never-falling		313. 15	hereafter
253. 33	Pre-eminence		317. 24	House-keeping
275. 23	Sweetmeats		325. 4	well-shaped
288. 6	henceforward		329. 15	besprinkle
296. 21	Shoe-maker		331. 1	Heyday
305. 10	huzza-ing		331. 11	Hotchpotch
308. 26	Blear-eyedness			
309. 11	outstunk			

4. *Preface to David Simple* (1744)

NOTE: No ambiguities appear.

5. *The Female Husband* (1746)

369. 6	back-street	372. 1	both-sides

6. *Ovid's Art of Love Paraphrased* (1747)

405. 13	well-pointed		413. 9	Warlike
409. 23–4	Maidenhead		443. 17	sometimes
409. 25	likewise		443. 30	notwithstanding
411. 2	moreover		449. 13	Fox-hunter
411. 4	Aldermen			

7. Preface and Letters XL–XLIV of *Familiar Letters* (1747)

476. 1	After-ages	488. 11	over-looked
479. 17	over-balances	507. 13	Good-humour

8. *The Journal of a Voyage to Lisbon* (1755)

546. 12	wheel-barrow	614. 3	above-mentioned
556. 20	cut-throats	615. 2	dining-room
558. 24, 630. 12	twenty-four	616. 25	tea-chest
560. 23	ever-honoured	623. 3	sea-captain
563. 30	tar-water	626. 15, 641. 8	wind-bound
568. 3	Custom-house	626. 19	ship-board
578. 2	soure-faced	630. 10	prison-breakers
586. 5	well-being	630. 20	to-morrow
587. 25	school-boy	633. 34	hotchpotch
593. 19	boatswain	650. 8	salt-water
599. 10	city-feast	651. 21	forty-six
600. 12	ship-builders	652. 18	sun-rising
602. 7	overcharge	654. 6	north-west
603. 15	coffee-house	655. 27	before-mentioned
607. 16	small-pox	657. 8	moonshiny
607. 20	over-balanced		

9. *A Fragment of a Comment on L. Bolingbroke's Essays* (1755)

NOTE: No ambiguities appear.

4. Historical Collation

NOTE: These lists record all substantive variants from the edited text within other authorized editions or issues, including the *Works* of 1762. Thus the full history within these editions of all substantive alterations to the copy-text recorded in the List of Emendations is provided together with a complete history of all rejected substantive readings from these other specified editions. The lemma, or reading to the left of the bracket, is that of the Wesleyan text. Since only substantive variation from these readings is noted, the absence of the sigla for an edition or issue indicates that its reading is that of the Wesleyan text. A few so-called 'semi-substantive' readings have been recorded when accidentals variation, chiefly of punctuation, radically alters the meaning.

I. OCCASIONAL VERSE

NOTE: Except for *The Masquerade*, none of the poems qualifies for inclusion in this section of Appendix B as none was issued in a second edition or reprint during HF's lifetime or in the *Works* of 1762. Though posthumously published with *The Grub-Street Opera* in HF's *Dramatic Works* of 1755, *The Masquerade* there bears the date 1728 and is a true second edition.

1. *The Masquerade* (1728)

NOTE: References to the Dedication are to page and line; references to the poem are to line numbers. Though not strictly substantive, examples of variants in orthography and punctuation are included here for their general interest.

SIGLA

The Masquerade (1728) = I
The Masquerade (1755) = II

A2. 15	*here insisted on*] insisted on here II
A2. 22	*calls*] call II
15	Chymist] chemist II
16	search] seek II
51	inforce] enforce II
57	Laurel] laurels II
60	*Hay-Market*] Haymarket II
76	Milkmaids] milk-maids II
86	*Grubstreet*] Grub-street II
88	Laureat Brow] laureat-brow II
107	*Toupet*] toupee II
113	Ladys] ladies II
122	Sympathetick . . . Beaus] sympathetic . . . beaux II
127	ben't] been't II
131	changed] chang'd II
137, 253	cou'd] could II
137	Gizard] gizzard II
138	Vizard] vizzard II
139	Sir!] sir? II
143	humane] human II
150, 151	Magick] magic II
156	Hell.] hell, II
163	Magick-Art] magic art II
168	Sweet-meats] sweetmeats II
171	Inner-Room] inner room II
188	Others (rare Wits!)] ~, rare wits, II
190	Phrase—*Do you know me?*] phrase, 'Do you know me?' II

192	Wild-fowl] wild fowl II
193	Pocket] pockets II
242	through] thro' II
245	Of ₍ₐ₎] II; ~, I
267	*Beau-Monde*] beau monde II
290	hideous!] ~? II
353	wakes] awakes II
356	Ecstasie] ecstasy II

II. OCCASIONAL PROSE

1. *Shamela* (1741)

NOTE: This list records all substantive variants from the edited text within the first two editions. For the sigla employed in these collations, see the headnote to the List of Emendations, Appendix B.1.

149.7	like] II; alike I
151.6	generally] genenerally I–II
152.16	Favour] II; Honour I
155.22	Whole] whole I–II
159.5	lie] II; lie lie I
159. 6	*Jewkes*] II; *Jervis* I
163. 5	*Williams*] *William* I–II
164. 8	are] are are I–II
164. 18	shan't ₍ₐ₎] II; ~, I
167. 23	Coarseness] II; Courseness I
167. 25	Tenant's] II; Tenants I
168. 1	what] II; what what I
169. 31	*Scholard*] *Schollard* II
172. 17	says] II; say I
174. 19	that;] II; ~, I
174. 20	the;] the the I–II
174. 22	for ever] forever
175. 8	hungry] II; hungty I
175. 9–10	good Humour] Good-Humour II
175. 21	Whole] II; whole I
176. 11	mighty] might II
176. 18	and] II; and and I
178. 26	HENRIETTA] II; HENRIETEA I
179. 31	to me] me to II
180. 7	Mistress,] II; Mrs. I
180. 9	in] in in II

181. 4	*A*] II; *a* I
184. 13, 188.5	leapt] leap'd II
184. 24	Paduasoy] II; Paduosoy I
184. 24	Wastecoat] Waistcoat II
188. 17	two] too I–II
189. 11	answered,] ~ ˏ I–II
190. 1	Aldermen] II; Alderman I
191. 28	advised] advied II
191. 34	*Your*] II; *Yonr* I
192. 2	me;] II; ~, I
192. 5	*Williams,*] II; ~; I
194. 12	Superiours] Superiors II
194. 22	perswade] persuade II
194. 28	don't] don't II
195. 4	favour'd] II; favour I

2. *A Full Vindication of the Dutchess Dowager of Marlborough* (1742)

NOTE: The so-called second edition being a reprint of the first, the only variants recorded are emendations of the Wesleyan text. See Appendix B.1.

219. 23	he] she I–II
220. 12	Smiles] Smilies I–II
225. 7	who] whom I–II
235. 21	and] aud I–II

3. *Plutus, the God of Riches* (1742)

NOTE: As there was no second edition, the only variants recorded are emendations of the Wesleyan text. See Appendix B.1.

262. 15	*Girardus*] *Giraldus* I
293. 41	35] 85 I
314. 28	71] 7 I
328. 36	second] first I

4. Preface to *David Simple* (1744)

NOTE: HF's Preface was published in the second edition and the later issues are reprints of this text. There are, however, three substantive variants in Arthur Murphy's edition of the *Works* (1762).

348. 4	those who have conferred] those who conferred M
352. 16	their Reader] the reader M
353. 4	they are] they were M

5. *The Female Husband* (1746)

NOTE: The only variants from the first edition are the emendations in W of misprints and a briefly confusing comma.

373. 25   bridegroom $_\wedge$] ~, I

6. *Ovid's Art of Love Paraphrased* (1747)

NOTE: For Amory's emendations of the first and only authoritative edition, see this Appendix, B.1.

7. Preface and Letters XL–XLIV of *Familiar Letters* (1747)

495. 17   Bread] II; Bred I
497. 13   that] II; *om.* I
504. 19   not fine] II; not near fine I

8. *The Journal of a Voyage to Lisbon* (1755)

SIGLA

I = first edition (1755)
II = second edition (1755)
M = Murphy's *Works* (1762)

551. 3   they] *om.* I
554. 9   Rehearsal] M; rehearsal I–II
555. 10   the next morning . . . some time,] in Lincoln's-inn-fields, upon some business of importance; with which I immediately complied; when his Grace II
560. 5   confession] concession II
*562. 7   months] month's I
563. 27   and shamefully distress'd] *om.* II
568. 18   coach] M; couch I–II
570. 8–21   behaved . . . pleasure. [¶] BESIDES] after having express'd his concern at the impossibility of sailing so soon as he expected, hoped we would excuse delay, which he could not foresee, but assured us he would certainly fall down the river on Saturday. This indeed was no small mortification to me; for, besides II
571. 13   here] hear I
571. 20   Quixotte] Quixote II
576. 4   particular tyrant] captain II
576. 6   chose to call] looked upon as II
576. 7   thence] in this capacity he had gained great honour, having distinguished his bravery in some very warm engagements, for which he had justly received public thanks; and from hence he II

576. 8   hat. He likewise wore] ~, and of wearing II
576. 9   by his side . . . deafening all others.] *om.* II
576. 18–19   by the delays . . . freight,] from these unavoidable delays, II
577. 20–2   when he had . . . passengers,] *om.* II
577. 32–4   out, though I had . . . last.] out. *om.* II
*580. 21   ply] ly I–II
583. 27   Is it] It it II
585. 33   people.' | [*footnote*] *Plato de Leg. lib 4. pp. 713c.–714 edit.
                  Serrani.] people,' ₍ | [*as text*] *Plato de Leg. lib* 4. *p.* 713. *c.* 714.
                  edit. | *Serrani.* I–II
587. 17   her] her | her II
588. 1–2   unluckily, . . . ship,] ~ ₍ for me, besides his knowledge being
                  chiefly confined to his profession, II
588. 3–4   hear, . . . understand,] ~ ₍ *om.* II
588. 13   sight of] sight of what I thought II
590. 13   to restrain] so restrain I
590. 23–4   the wife . . . admiralty;] *om.* II
591. 14   sure] of opininion [*sic*] that II
591. 15   took] he took II
591. 16   assurance] hopes II
*591. 37   heel] head I–II
593. 4   captain ₍ swaggered, and] ~, being unwilling to come to anchor, II
593. 8   island.] ~; as did a great number of merchant ships, who
                  attended our commodore from the Downs, and watched his
                  motions so narrowly, that they seemed to think themselves
                  unsafe when they did not regulate their motions by his. II
593. 13   concern and many bitter oaths.] concern. *om.* II
593. 32–3   they had passed . . . time.] they passed their leisure hours. II
594. 18   dead] deed II
594. 27   art] tart II
596. 22   dominions, either . . . abroad,] ~ ₍ *om.* II
597. 8–9   Francis (for that . . .house)] Humphrys *om.* II
598. 3–4   tho' . . . bricks, which was] which, tho' . . . bricks, was II
599. 19   and] and that I
*600. 3   Harriet] Harriot I–II
*600. 19   14] 19 I–II
601. 10   four] five I–II
602. 1   of] in II
604. 7–8   dictionary; all which . . . kingdom,] ~. All which . . . ~. II
604. 8–11   and the college . . . sick by it.] *om.* II
605. 15   one] none II
*605. 16   fish-eater] fisher I–II
606. 6   If] If | if II
606. 7   God Almighty] the Creator II

*606. 10	gave] gave us I
606. 12	hath] has I
606. 15	within,] ~; I
*608. 3	censure] tacit censure I
608. 31–2	to the government . . . estate;] a taylor's bill, II
609. 6	15] 20 I–II
609. 15	16] 21 I–II
611. 14	appear] should appear I
610. 21	or] *om.* II
612. 1	there] their II
614. 21	17] 22 I–II
614. 29	inferior] *om.* II
615. 15	meaning] meading II
615. 15	understood] understand II
615. 31	18] 23 I–II
615. 31–2	captain, who . . . all night,] ~ ˄ *om.* II
617. 32	money] my money II
*618. 5	thirty-six-shilling] ~—~ ˄~ I–II
619. 4	huts] hats I
621. 25	19] 24 I–II
621. 24–622. 41	uncle. He was. . . . had not the north-wind,] uncle, and entertained the ladies with a description of those countries, the manners, dress, and diversions of the inhabitants of Minorca, to which he added an account of an officer's life in garrison, which, tho' it might be tolerable for three or four years, must, I think, be insupportable for a longer time. And I found, indeed, by his discourse, that the troops in general embarked from England to these garrisons, since they had been changed every third year, with the utmost chearfulness; but that, before this time, they looked upon going to Gibralter and Port Mahon in the light of banishment; which made many of them melancholy, and some of the soldiers, it is said, had such a strong desire of revisiting their native country, that they absolutely pined away, which I am much inclined to believe; for a brother of mine,[1] who was at Minorca about fourteen years ago, inform'd me that he came to England in the same ship with a soldier who shot himself thro' the hand, merely that he might be sent home, having been in that island for many years. But now the north wind, II

[1] Probably HF's younger brother Edmund (b. 1716, d. after 1755), who, like his father and namesake, General Edmund Fielding, was a career officer in the Army from age 17. In 1740–2 he served as ensign, then lieutenant in Colonel Blakeney's Regiment of Foot (*Life*, pp. 248, 652 nn. 443–4). Perhaps less likely is HF's half-brother William (1723–*c*.1778), also a career officer from 1740, when at age 16 he was commissioned second lieutenant in a newly raised regiment of Marines, to 1778 (*Life*, pp. 299, 657 n. 63).

623. 1   sea-captain, even than . . . his family,] captain ˄ even than the company of his nephew for whom he express'd the highest regard, II

623. 2–3   weigh his anchor. [¶] WHILE this ceremony . . . to shore;] ~ ~ ~. [*no* ¶] While this ceremony . . . to shore. [¶] II

623. 4–9   not indeed on an uninhabited island. . . . to Portsmouth.] *om.* II

623. 15   20,] 29. I–II

623. 18   not permit it; though] ~ ~ ~; for I must do him the justice to say, that whether the wind was fair or foul, he always made the most of it, for he never let go his anchor but with a manifest concern, and was generally out of humour for an hour or two upon these occasions, tho' II

623. 19   surliness] boldness II

623. 24   swore] declared II

623. 28–9   to freshen;] *om.* I

623. 36   deck; for he began . . . broth.] deck. *om.* II

624. 3–4   Morrison, a carpenter. . . . Of Morrison] ~, of whom II

624. 7–8   sufficiently . . . conceal it,] gave me to understand, that we were not totally free from danger, II

624. 15   any man I know . . . trusted.] any man. *om.* II

624. 18–19   enjoying; and that . . . yesterday.] ~. *om.* II

624. 23–7   declared . . . half an hour ˄] much surprized at this news, for he did not believe he was so near land, whipped on his night-gown, and regardless of every other dress, ran upon deck, saying, that if that was true he would give his mother for a maid, a forfeiture which afterwards became due, for within half an hour, he II

624. 29   21] 26 I–II

625. 19   inconveniences] inconveniencies II

625. 22   encouraging] enouraging I

626. 13   so he phrased it] as hath been before noticed II

630. 14   persons] some persons II

630. 28   inconveniences] inconveniencies II

633. 19   *Monday, July 22.*] *Monday.* I–II

633. 25   bashaw] captain II

634. 1   deaf] *om.* II

634. 10   *Tuesday, July 23.*] *Tuesday.* I–II

634. 14   in] with II

635. 20   Means . . . ends] Ends . . . means II

635. 25   than] that I

637. 15   capital] captital II

638. 14–30   captain's valet . . . sober man, was] captain returned from his visit II

638. 31   the Swiss] his Swiss brother II

639. 4–643. 8	WHILE . . . so to do.] HOWEVER, our commander being, as I observed, in great spirits, we spent the rest of this day with much chearfulness, the ladies being a little recovered from their sea-sickness. II
643. 9	*Wednesday, July* 24.] *Wednesday*. I; *Wednesday* the 20th. II
643. 35–7	cabin. I will not . . . in them.] ~, upon which occasion he exprest a concern which testified great goodness of heart. II
644. 8	*Thursday, July* 25.] *Thursday*. I–II
645. 5	firm] *om.* II
645. 7	tho' indeed . . . in truth,] lest any one should imagine, that he had real faith in witches: but the truth was, his patience, which he had before compared to that of Job, was wore out, tho' indeed II
645. 10	had he] if he had II
646. 16	*Friday, July* 26.] *Friday*. I–II
646. 32–4	acquaintance, though this foundation . . . the same bay.] acquaintance. *om.* II
646. 35	*Saturday, July* 27.] *Saturday*. I–II
648. 27	*Sunday, July* 28.] *Sunday*. I–II
649. 30	disposition, . . . thoughts.] ~. *om.* II
650. 1	*Monday, July* 29.] *Monday*. I–II
650. 5	us. While] ~, while I–II
650. 6	tempest,] ~; I–II
650. 20	thought] had thought II
650. 34	*Wednesday, July* 31.] *Wednesday*. I–II
650. 35	and] or II
652. 18	*Friday, August* 2.] *Friday*. I–II
653. 11	*Sunday, August* 4.] *Sunday*. I–II
653. 12	and with . . . day,] *om.* II
653. 24	*Monday, August* 5.] *Monday*. I–II
654. 9	hurry, as he was . . . delay.] ~. *om.* II
657. 6	evening] night II
657. 13	*Wednesday, August* 7] *Wednesday*. I–II
657. 16	arising] aising I
659. 2	Tajo] Taio I
659. 7	*optata . . . ærena.*] *optata . . . ærena* II
659. 9	*chartæque viæque.*] *chartæq; viæq*; I–II

9. *A Fragment of a Comment on L. Bolingbroke's Essays* (1755)

668. 16	indifferent] different II
677. 1	theists] atheists II
678. 1	'Mr. Lock . . . impossible ‸it is] W; ‸ ~ ~ . . . ~ 'it is I–II

5. Bibliographical Descriptions

NOTE: Except for the unpublished MSS, a facsimile of the title-page of the first edition introduces each text.

I. OCCASIONAL VERSE

1. *The Masquerade* (1728)

The First Edition (29 or 30 January 1728)

THE | MASQUERADE. | A | POEM. | INSCRIB'D TO | C—T
H---D---G---R. | [rule] | ———*Velut ægri somnia, vanæ* |———
Species——— Hor. Art. Poet. | [rule] | By *LEMUEL GULLIVER*, Poet
Laureat to the | King of *LILLIPUT*. | [rule] | *LONDON*, | Printed: and Sold by
J. Roberts in *Warwick-Lane*, and | *A. Dodd* at the *Peacock* without *Temple-Bar*. 1728.
| [Price Six Pence.]

Collation: 8°: A² B–C⁴, $1–2 (–A1), 10 leaves, pp. [i–iv], 1–15, 16

Contents: [i] title-page [ii] blank [iii] | [double rule] | THE | DEDICATION. |
ending on [iv], with the signature '*Lemuel Gulliver*.'; | [double rule] | THE |
MASQUERADE. | A | POEM. |, text ending on 15 with | [rule] | *finis.* | 16
blank.

Running Heads: A²ᵛ DEDICATION. | otherwise none.

Press figures: none

Catchwords variants: p. 3 Cardi- (Cardinals), p. 13 I (Her).

NOTE: [The following three copies were known to Baker; *ESTC* lists six others: see
Introduction, p. 8 n. 19.]: Yale, Fielding Collection, 728M; the National Trust
copy at Blickling Hall, Norwich, Norfolk, designated 'pamphlets 1724–28, 2'; and
the copy, Tract 269, in the Founders' Library, University of Wales, Lampeter
(Llanbedr Pont Stefan), Wales. It came with the gift of a collection in 1822 to the
newly founded St David's College, a collection made mostly by Thomas Bowdler II
(1661–1738) and given to the new college by Dr Thomas Bowdler (1754–1825),
editor of the famous sanitized *Family Shakespeare*. On the title-page of all copies,
the full stop after 'MASQUERADE' has slipped upward and the apparent full
stop after 'POEM' is a blurred comma, as the impression of type on the verso of
the Blickling Hall copy makes clear. I am indebted to Yvonne Lewis, Assistant
Libraries Adviser, the National Trust, and to David G. Selwyn, Conservator,
Founder's Library, for collating the Blickling and Wales copies against photocopies
of Yale's 728M.

SWB

The Second Edition ([1755])

THE | MASQUERADE, | A | POEM. | INSCRIBED TO | C — T
H – D – G – R. | [rule] | ———*Velut ægri somnia, vanæ* | ———*Species*
——— Hor. Art. Poet. | [rule] | By LEMUEL GULLIVER, | poet Laureat
to the King of LILLIPUT. | [rule] | [orn.] | [rule] | LONDON, | Printed, and
sold by J. ROBERTS, in Warwick-lane; | and A. DODD, at the Peacock, without
Temple-bar. | MDCCXXVIII. | [Price Six-pence.]

Collation: 8°: [E]⁴ F⁴, $1–2 (–[E] 1–2), 8 leaves, pp. [i–iv], [1], 2–11, [12]

Contents: [i] title-page [ii] blank [iii] | [orn.] | THE | DEDICATION. | ending
on [iv] with the signature 'LEMUEL GULLIVER'; [1] | [orn.] | THE |
MASQUERADE, | A | POEM. |, text, ending on 11 with | FINIS. | [orn.] |.

Running Heads: [none] | DEDICATION.; The MASQUERADE. | The
MASQUERADE.

Press figures: E3ᵛ—6 F2ᵛ—9

Catchwords: all match

NOTES: (1) This edition was printed as an addition to *The Grub-Street Opera*,
which bears the date of 1731 on its title-page but was actually not published until
1755 (see Introduction, pp. 8–10): | THE | GRUB-STREET | OPERA. |
As it is Acted at the | THEATRE in the HAY-MARKET. | [rule] | By
SCRIBLERUS SECUNDUS. | [rule] | Sing. Nom. *Hic, Hæc, Hoc.* | Gen.
Hujus. | Dat. *Huic.* | Accus. *Hunc, Hanc, Hoc.* | Voc. *Caret.* Lil. Gram. quod vid. |
[rule] | To which is added, | THE | MASQUERADE, | A | POEM. |
Printed in MDCCXXVIII. | [rule] | LONDON, | Printed, and sold by J.
ROBERTS, in Warwick-lane. | MDCCXXXI. [Price One Shilling and
Six-pence.]. *Collation*: 8°: A⁴ B–E⁸ F⁴ $1–4 (–A1, F3–4), 40 leaves, 80 pp.

(2) *The Masquerade*, with its separate title-page, begins on E5ʳ after the play's
ending on E4ᵛ, and page numbers begin anew, with the title-page on [i], though the
signatures continue through F4. Cross, in 1918, scanning Yale's holdings at that
time described this second edition as the first: Yale's 728mb, an extract from
the *Grub-Street Opera* volume with the Dedication missing, is bound separately.
Cross reproduces its title-page (opposite his i. 60) as that of the first edition.
Finding the Dedication in the *Grub-Street Opera* volume (Yale's 'Plays 791'), he
assumed that Fielding had added it in 1731 iii. 290). The ornament on the second
edition's title-page quickly distinguishes it from the unornamented title-page of the
first edition. 'INSCRIBED' is spelled out from the first edition's 'INSCRIB'D';
'H——D——G——R' is romanized; byline and publisher's imprint differ in
typography.

(3) Copies examined for this Wesleyan Edition: Yale, Fielding Collection, 728M,
728mb, Rare Book Room Plays 791; British Library, C.116.e.7, 643.h.19(4);
Harvard, EC7.F460.B755d; Huntington, 125937.

2. 'Cantos' (1729–30)

NOTE: HF's unfinished and untitled satire of Pope and the Scriblerians, written as a burlesque of *The Dunciad* in three 'Cantos', as well as what appears to be the final draft of a verse Epistle to his friend George Lyttelton, form part of volume LXXXI (folio measuring 34.8 mm. × 23.4 mm.) of the Harrowby MSS Trust, Sandon Hall, Stafford: 'Canto 2^d' and 'Canto 3^d' in fos. 172–80, '[Canto 1]' fos. 182–5; and the 'Epistle to Lyttleton', fos. 57–8, 64–5. The five leaves interrupting the Epistle contain wholly unrelated work by HF's cousin Lady Mary Wortley Montagu.

3. *Plain Truth* (*c.*1729–1730)

Title-page, Vol. v: A | COLLECTION | OF | POEMS | IN SIX VOLUMES, | BY | SEVERAL HANDS. | [orn.] | LONDON: Printed by J. HUGHS, | For R. and J. Dodsley, at Tully's-Head in Pall-Mall. | M DCC LVIII.

Collation, Vol. v: 8° π [i–iv] A–I⁸ K–U⁸ X⁸ $1–4 170 leaves 340 pp.

Contents: [i] half-title | [narrow line orn.] | VOL. V. | [narrow line orn.] | [ii] blank [iii] title [iv] blank *1* | [ornamental etching] | RURAL ELEGANCE: An ODE to the late Duchess of Somerset. | Written 1750. | By WILLIAM SHENSTONE, Esq; | text containing 28 more Shenstone poems followed by 25 poems by nine other poets, ending on 117; [narrow line orn.] | A LETTER to Sir ROBERT WALPOLE. | By the late HENRY FIELDING. | ending on 118; text of 54 poems ending on 301; 302 | [broad orn.] | PLAIN TRUTH. | By HENRY FIELDING, Esq; | ending on 305; text of 11 poems by others ending on 332 with | [rule] | ERRATA. | [4 items] |; 333 | INDEX to the Fifth Volume. | ending on 336 with | The END of VOL. V. |

4. *A Dialogue between a Beau's Head and His Heels* (1730)

Title-page: THE MUSICAL | MISCELLANY; | *Being a* COLLEC-TION *of* | CHOICE SONGS, | AND | LYRICK POEMS: | *With the* BASSES *to each* TUNE, *and* | *Transpos'd for the* FLUTE. | By the most Eminent MASTERS. | [rule] | [ornament] | [rule] | VOLUME *the* SIXTH. | [rule] | LONDON: | *Printed by and for* JOHN Watts, *at the* Printing- | Office *in* Wild-Court *near* Lincoln's-Inn Fields. | [rule] | M DCC XXXI.
NOTE: The only authoritative edition of HF's song is on pp. 170–3.

5. 'An Epistle to Mr. Lyttleton' (1733)

NOTE: Not published during HF's lifetime. For an account of the MS, see above, item 2, '*Cantos*'.

6. Epilogue to Theobald's *Orestes* (1731)

Title-page: ORESTES: | A | *DRAMATIC OPERA.* | As it is Acted at the | THEATRE-ROYAL | IN | LINCOLN'S-INN FIELDS. | [rule] | Written by

Mr. *THEOBALD*. | [rule] | *Pœnis agitatus Orestes*.   Virg. | [rule] | [orn.] | [rule] | *LONDON:* | Printed for JOHN WATTS at the Printing-Office | in *Wild-Court*, near *Lincoln's-Inn Fields*. | [short rule centred] | M DCC XXXI. | [Price One Shilling and Six-pence.]

Collation: 8°: A⁴ B–F⁸ $4(–A1, 3, 4) signed, 44 leaves, pp. *i–viii 1 2–77 78–80*

Contents: A1 title, verso blank; A2–3 'DEDICATION. | To the Right Honourable | *Sir* ROBERT WALPOLE.' Signed 'LEW THEOBALD.'; A4ʳ 'PROLOGUE; | Spoken by Mr. *WALKER*.'; A4ᵛ 'Dramatis Personæ'; B1 text, ending on F7ʳ with '*FINIS*.' | orn. [pp. [1]–77]; | F7ᵛ–8ʳ [orn.] 'EPILOGUE; | Written by *HENRY FIELDING*, Esq; | Spoken by Mrs. *YOUNGER*.'; F8ᵛ blank.

Copies collated: (no variants) British Library, 163.i.63; Michigan, PR/3729/.T5/06; Folger, PR/3729/T5/08/Cage; Harvard, EC7.T3426.7310; Yale (Beinecke) Tracts, 34; PLAYS 106; PLAYS 674.

7. Epilogue to 'Charles Bodens's' *The Modish Couple* (1732)

Title-page: THE | MODISH COUPLE | A | COMEDY. | As it is Acted at the | THEATRE-ROYAL | *In DRURY-LANE*. | By His MAJESTY's Servants. | [rule] | [orn.] | [rule] | *LONDON:* | Printed for J. WATTS at the Printing-Office in | *Wild-Court* near *Lincoln's-Inn Fields*. | [short rule centred] | M DCC XXXII. | [Price One Shilling and Six Pence.]

Collation: 8°: A⁴ B–F⁸ $4(–A1, 3, 4) signed, 44 leaves, pp. *i–viii 1 2–74 75–80*

Contents: A1 title, verso blank; A2–3 'DEDICATION. | To the Right Honourable | WILLIAM | Lord *HARRINGTON*.' Signed 'CHARLES BODENS'; A4ʳ 'PROLOGUE. | By a FRIEND.'; A4ᵛ 'Dramatis Personæ'; B1–F5ᵛ text; F6 [orn.] | 'EPILOGUE. | Spoken by Mrs. *CIBBER*. | Written by HENRY FIELDING, Esq;', ending on F6ᵛ with orn.; | F7–8 final two leaves Watts's advertisements.

NOTE: Listed in Watts's advertisements are seven plays by HF: *The Tragedy of Tragedy*, 2nd edn.; *The Lottery; The Coffee-House Politician; The Temple Beau; The Author's Farce* and *Pleasures of the Town; Love in Several Masques*; and *The Letter Writers*.

Copies collated: (no variants) British Library, 161.g.53; Michigan, PR/3324/.B5/M7 (wanting F7–8); Folger, PR/3324/B6/M7/Cage; Harvard, EC7.H4459.732m; Yale (Beinecke), Fielding Collection, 732Nd; 732Ne.

NOTE: A Dublin edition, 1732, 'Written by Mr. CHARLES BODENS.', and 'Printed by S. POWELL, | For G. RISK ... | G. EWING ..., and | W. SMITH' (Harvard EC7.H4459.732mb), reprints the London edition with no substantive variants.

8. Epilogue to Johnson's *Cælia* (1733)

Title-page: CÆLIA: | OR, THE | PERJUR´D LOVEr. | A | PLAY. | AS IT IS
ACTED AT THE THEATRE-ROYAL | in DRURY-LANE, | BY HIS MAJESTY'S
SERVANTS. | [RULE] |———*Tragicus plerumque dolet sermone pedestri.* Hor. |
[rule] | [orn.] | *LONDON:* | Printed for J. WATTS at the Printing-Office in |
Wild-Court near *Lincoln's-Inn Fields.* | [rule] | M DCC XXXIII. [Price 1 *s.* and
6 *d.*]

Collation: 8°: A⁴ a² B–E⁸ $4(–A2–4, a2 [3–4]) signed, 38 leaves, pp. *i–xii 1* 2–60 *61–
64*

Contents: A1 half-title, verso blank; A2 title, verso blank; A3 [orn.] Johnson's
'ADVERTISEMENT | TO THE | *READER.*'; A4 [orn.] 'PROLOGUE. |
Spoken by Mr. *THEOPH. CIBBER.*' ending with orn.; a1ʳ [orn.] | 'EPILOGUE.
| Written by *HENRY FIELDING*, Esq; | And Spoken by Miss RAFTOR.' | a1ᵛ
[orn.] | December 8, 1732. | [Watts's advertisement for vols. 7–8 of *Select Comedies
of Molière's Comedies*], continued on a2ʳ, ending with orn.; a2ᵛ 'Dramatis Personæ';
B1 = text, ending on E6ᵛ with '*FINIS*'; E7–8–4 pages of Watts's advertisements.

NOTE: Watts's concluding advertisement includes all HF's plays advertised in the
book of *The Modish Couple* with the exception of *The Lottery*; it adds to these *The
Modern Husband*, and *The Mock Doctor*.

Copies collated: (no variants) British Library, 161.d.58; Michigan, PR/3519/.J8/C2;
Yale, IK/J630/732C; Yale (Beinecke), PLAYS 681; Fielding Collection, 732C;
Harvard, EC7.J6307.733c.

9. Prologue to Lillo's *Fatal Curiosity* (1737)

Title-page: FATAL CURIOSITY: | A TRUE | TRAGEDY | OF |
THREE. ACTS. | As it is Acted at the | NEW THEATRE | IN THE |
HAY-MARKET. | By Mr. *LILLO.* | [orn.] | *LONDON:* | Printed for JOHN
GRAY at the *Cross-keys* in the | *Poultry* near *Cheapside.* M D CCXXXVII. | [Price
One Shilling.]

Collation: 4° (8° size): A–F⁴ $2(–A1) signed, 24 leaves, pp. *1–5* 6–47 *48*

Contents: A1 title, verso blank; A2ʳ 'PROLOGUE, | Written by *Henry Fielding*,
Esq; | Spoken by Mr. *Roberts.*'; A2ᵛ 'Dramatis Personæ'; A3 text, ending on F4ʳ
with '*FINIS.*'; F4ᵛ publisher's advertisement, 'Printed for *J. Gray* at the *Cross
Keys*'.

Copies collated: (no variants) British Library, 841.d.32 (9); Michigan, PR/3541/
.L5/F2; Folger, Bd.w./PR/3541/L5/E5/Cage.

NOTE: An Irish edition, 1737, 'DUBLIN. | Printed for *A. Bradley* at the *Two
Bibles* in *Dame-Street*, and also *J. Potts* Bookseller in *Belfast*' (Folger, Bd.w./PR/
3541/L5/F29/Cage), reprints the London edition.

II. OCCASIONAL PROSE

1. *Shamela* (1741)

The First Edition (2 April 1741), 8°

Title-page: AN | APOLOGY | FOR THE | LIFE | OF | Mrs. SHAMELA ANDREWS. | In which, the many notorious FALSHOODS and | MISREPRSEN-TATIONS of a Book called | *PAMELA*, | Are exposed and refuted; and all the matchless | ARTS of that young Politician, set in a true and | just Light. | Together with | A full Account of all that passed between her | and Parson *Arthur Williams*; whose Character | is represented in a manner something different | from what he bears in *PAMELA*. The | whole being exact Copies of authentick Papers | delivered to the Editor. | [*rule*] | Necessary to be had in all FAMILIES. | [*rule*] | By Mr. *CONNY KEYBER*. | [*rule*] | *LONDON:* | Printed for A. DODD, at the *Peacock*, without *Temple-bar*. | M. DCC. XLI.

Notes: 'FALSHOODS' is the usual form of the word until late in the century. The typo 'MISREPRSENTATIONS' remains in the second edition.

Collation: 8°: A–D^8 E^4 F^2, \$1–4 (–A1–2, E3–4, F2–4), 38 leaves, pp. *i–iv* v–xv *xvi* *1* 2–59 60

Contents: *i* half title *ii* blank *iii* title *iv* blank *v* [*dedication, headed by broad orn.*] | To Miss *Fanny*, &*c*. | MADAM, [*ending on* xii *with signature* Conny Keyber.] | ; xiii [*headed by broad orn.*] LETTERS | TO THE | EDITOR. | [*rule*] | [*ending on* xv *with orn.*]; *1* text [*headed by broad orn.*] AN | APOLOGY | For the LIFE of | Mrs. SHAMELA ANDREWS. | [*rule*] | [*text continues with two introductory letters, ending on* 8 *with orn.*]; 9 LETTER I. [*text continues, ending on* 59 *with FINIS. followed by orn.*]; *60* blank

Notes: (1) Copies collated: British Library, Cup.401.d.14[8]; Yale, Fielding Collection, 741a; Huntington Library, 124077. In addition to these three copies, the *ESTC* lists nine others plus four more 'unverified'. Not included in the list is the important copy once owned and annotated by the Fielding scholar J. Paul de Castro, acquired by Ximenes Rare Books in 1996 and sold to a private collector. (2) No press variants appear among the three copies collated, except that on the title-page colophon the 'e' in 'Printed' is dropped in the BL and Yale copies, but not the Huntington.

Running heads: DEDICATION. | DEDICATION.; SHAMELA. | SHAMELA.

Press figures: None

Catchword variants: p. v these (those); vii *Second- (Secondly)*; viii *Fourth- (Fourthly)*; 16 swered (swer'd); 18 How ⌃ (How,); 21 *Par- (Parson)*; 22 *Inge- (Ingenium)*; 28 imme- (immediately); 34 LETTER ⌃ (LETTER,); 42 who ⌃ (who,)

The Second Edition (31 October? 1741), 8°

Title-page: AN | APOLOGY | FOR THE | LIFE | OF | Mrs. SHAMELA ANDREWS. | In which, the many notorious FALSHOODS and | MISREPRSENTATIONS of a Book called | *PAMELA*, | Are exposed and refuted; and all the matchless | ARTS of that young Politician, set in a true and | just Light. | Together with | A full Account of all that passed between her | and Parson *Arthur Williams*; whose Character is | represented in a manner something different from | that which he bears in *PAMELA*. The | whole being exact Copies of authentick Papers | delivered to the Editor. | [*rule*] | Necessary to be had in all FAMILIES. | [*rule*] | By Mr. *CONNY KEYBER*. | [*double rule*] | *LONDON:* | Printed for A. DODD, at the *Peacock*, without *Temple-bar*. | M. DCC. XLI.

Notes: The typo 'MISREPRSENTATIONS' remains uncorrected. The first edition phrasing 'different | from what' is altered to 'different from | that which', resulting in an adjustment of three lines: in I, line 15 ends 'whose Character' > here this becomes 'whose Character is'; in I, line 16 ends 'something different' > here 'something different from'.

Collation: 8°: A–D⁸ E⁴, $1–4 (–A1–2, E3–4), 36 leaves, pp. *i–iv* v–xv *xvi 1* 2–56

Contents: *i* half title *ii* blank *iii* title *iv* blank v [*dedication, headed by broad orn., same as* I] | To Miss *Fanny*, &c. | MADAM, | [*ending on* xii, *with signature* Conny Keyber.]; xiii [*headed by broad orn., same as* I] | LETTERS | TO THE | EDITOR. | [*rule*] | [*ending on* xv *with orn., same as* I]; *1* text [*headed by broad orn., different from* I] | AN | APOLOGY | For the LIFE of | Mrs. SHAMELA ANDREWS. | [*rule*] | [*two introductory letters, ending on* 8 *with orn., same as* I]; 9 LETTER I. | text [*continuing and ending on* 56 *with FINIS*. | [*orn., same as* I]

Notes: (1) Copies collated: British Library, Cup.401.f.6; Yale, Fielding Collection, 741ab; William Andrews Clark Library, *PR3454.A61.1741a (see the reproduction, ed. Ian Watt, Augustan Reprint Society, No. 57, 1956); and Lewis Walpole Library, Farmington, Conn., 49/2474/6 (Horace Walpole's personal copy). In addition to these four copies, the *ESTC* lists eight others. Except that the BL copy lacks leaf A1 (half-title, verso blank), no variants appear in the copies collated. (2) The second edition was set from the standing type of the first, introducing corrections and, beginning at p. 18, closing spaces between paragraphs and moving lines from the following pages to occupy the space saved, a procedure enabling the elimination of the awkward final two-leaf F gathering.

Running heads: DEDICATION. | DEDICATION.; SHAMELA. | SHAMELA.

Press figures: None.

Catchword variants: p. vii *Second-* (*Secondly*,); viii *Fourth-* (*Fourthly*,); 16 swered (swer'd); 18 How ˄ (How,); 21 *Par-* (*Parson*); 48 Cor- (Corporation); 53 coun- (countenanced)

Dublin Edition (15 April 1741), 12°

Title-page: AN | APOLOGY | FOR THE | LIFE | OF | Mrs. SHAMELA
ANDREWS. | In which, the many notorious FALSHOODS | and MISREPRESEN-
TATIONS | of a Book called | *PAMELA*, | Are exposed and refuted; and all the |
matchless ARTS of that young Politician, | set in a true and just Light. | Together
with | A full Account of all that passed between her | and Parson *Arthur Williams*;
whose Character | is represented in a manner something different | from what he
bears in *PAMELA*. The whole being exact Copies of authentick Papers | delivered
to the Editor. | [*rule*] | Necessary to be had in all FAMILIES. | [*rule*] | By Mr.
CONNY KEYBER. | [*rule*] | *DUBLIN:* | Printed for OLI. NELSON, at *Milton's-
Head* in | *Skinner-Row*. M DCCXLI.

Collation: 12°: A⁵ B–F⁶ G¹ (=A6 [?]) $1–3 (–G1), 36 leaves, pp. *i–iv* v–x *1* 2–61 62

Contents: i half-title [lacking] *ii* blank [lacking] *iii* title *iv* blank *v* [*dedication, headed
by broad orn.*] | TO | Miss FANNY, &c. | MADAM, | [*ending on* viii, *with signature,*
CONNY KEYBER.] | ; ix [*broad orn.*] | LETTERS | TO THE | EDITOR. |
[*rule*] | [*ending on* x]; *1* text [*headed by broad orn.*] | AN | APOLOGY | For the
LIFE of | Mrs. SHAMELA ANDREWS. | [*rule*] | [*two introductory letters, ending on*
8]; 9 LETTER I. | text [*continuing until ending on* 61 *with FINIS.*]; 62 publisher's
advertisement

Notes: (1) This describes the British Library copy (Cup.401.b.4); the *ESTC*
lists only one other, at the William Andrews Clark Library, Los Angeles
(*PR3454.A61.1741). (2) Though the Dublin edition has no authority, its title-page
corrects the typo of the first edition by printing 'MISREPRESENTATIONS'; and
on p. 29 there is a misguided attempt to correct the malapropism '*Statue of
Lamentations*' (referring to the Statute of Limitations) by emending to '*Statute
of Lamentations*'.

Running heads: DEDICATION. | DEDICATION.; *SHAMELA*. | *SHAMELA*.

Press figures: None.

Catchword variants: 3 recon- (reconciled); 6 conse- (Consequences); 20 LET-
(LETTER); 21 LET- (LETTER); 35 LET- (LETTER); 40 Neigh-
(Neighbor)

2. *A Full Vindication of the Dutchess Dowager of Marlborough* (1742)

The First Edition (2 April 1742) 4° (8° size)

Title-page: A facsimile of the title-page introduces the text.
A FULL | VINDICATION | OF THE | DUTCHESS DOWAGER | OF |
MARLBOROUGH: | BOTH | With regard to the ACCOUNT lately | Published
by | HER GRACE, | AND TO | Her CHARACTER in general; | AGAINST |
The *base* and *malicious* Invectives contained | in a late *scurrilous* Pamphlet, entitled
| REMARKS on the Account, &c. | [rule] | In a Letter to the NOBLE AUTHOR |

of those *Remarks*. | [double rule] | *LONDON:* | Printed for J. ROBERTS, in *Warwick-Lane*. | M.DCC.XLII.

Collation: 4° (8° size): [A]² B–F⁴, $1–2, 22 leaves, pp. [i–iv], [1] 2–40

Contents: [A]1 half-title (verso blank), [A]2 title (verso blank), B1 text | [orn.] | *A full Vindication of her* | *Grace the Dutchess Dowager* | *of MARLBOROUGH.* | MY LORD, *ending on p.* 40 with | *Your Lordship's* | *most Obedient Humble Servant.* | [orn.]

Running heads: None

Press figures: B4ᵛ–3, F4ʳ–1

Catchword variant: 7 ‸*playing* ('∼')

Note: Copies collated: British Library, 292.i.12.(1), 113.c.4 (half-title wanting), 1202.h.1.(3), G14130(4); Harvard, *EC7.F460.742f; Huntington, 123333. In BL 292.i.12.(1), the *e* in the word *the* at the end of the first line of p. 32 is on the line, suggesting a copy early in the run, since this *e* has slipped progressively upward in the other copies examined: slightly in BL 113.c.4, G14130(4), and Harvard *EC7.F460.742f, and considerably more in BL 1202.h.1.(3) and Huntington 123333, as it has also in the three 'second edition' copies examined.

SWB

The Second Edition (4 May 1742) 4° (8° size)

Title-page: A FULL | VINDICATION | OF THE | DUTCHESS DOWAGER | OF | *MARLBOROUGH:* | BOTH | With regard to the ACCOUNT lately | Published by | HER GRACE, | AND TO | Her CHARACTER in general; | AGAINST | The *base* and *malicious* Invectives contained | in a late *scurrilous* Pamphlet, entitled | REMARKS on the Account, &c. | [rule] | In a Letter to the NOBLE AUTHOR | of those *Remarks*. | [rule] | The SECOND EDITION. | [double rule] | *LONDON;* | Printed for J. ROBERTS, in *Warwick-Lane*. | M.DCC.XLII.

Notes (1) This is, in all respects, a reprint of the first edition except for the title-page. All quirks of typography are those of the first edition, on the same paper watermarked with a fleur-de-lis. On the title-page the type remains undisturbed, except that the printer has moved up the two lines containing 'In a Letter . . . AUTHOR' in order to introduce a new single rule and the new line 'The SECOND EDITION.' (2) Copies collated against the first-edition text: London Library, 'HOOKE, CONDUCT OF DOWAGER DSS. OF MARLBOROUGH 1742/768'; Yale, Fielding Collection, 742fb; Illinois, x942.06.M343.aYf.1742a. No variants appear in any of the first- and second-edition copies examined. The *ESTC* lists eleven copies.

SWB

3. *Plutus, the God of Riches* (1742)

The First Edition (31 May 1742) 8°

Title-page: PLUTUS, / THE / GOD *of* RICHES. / A / COMEDY. / Translated from the Original *Greek* of / *ARISTOPHANES:* / With Large NOTES Explanatory and / Critical. / [rule] / By *HENRY FIELDING*, Esq; / AND / The Rev^d. Mr. *YOUNG*. / [double rule] / *LONDON:* / Printed for T. WALLER in the *Temple-Cloisters*. / [short rule] / M DCC XLII. [Price 2*s*.]

Collation: 8°: [A]² a⁸ B–H⁸, $1–4, 66 leaves, pp. [i–v] *i–v* vi–xv *xvi 1* 2–112 *113*

Contents: [Ai] half-title ([Aii] blank), [Aiii] title ([Aiv] blank); [i] dedication / [orn.] / To the Right Honourable the / LORD *TALBOT*. / MY LORD, ending on [iv] / [v] [orn.] / PREFACE. ending on xv; / [xvi] Dramatis Personæ, / [1] text [orn.] / PLUTUS, / *The* GOD *of* RICHES. ending on 112 with / *FINIS*. / [orn.] /

Running heads: DEDICATION. / DEDICATION. / PREFACE. / PREFACE. / *PLUTUS*, /. *The* GOD *of* RICHES. *PLUTUS*, &C. (P. 112)

Press figures: None.

Catchword variants: The text begins on p. [1] with footnotes separated by a rule. At the start the text catchword appears above the rule; the footnote catchword, at the bottom of the page. Departures from this format, however, are numerous. Beginning at page 3, the text catchword appears at the bottom of the page, replacing the footnote catchword in the following pages: 3, 11–14, 18, 21, 32, 37–40, 42–6, 49, 52–3, 55, 57, 59–61, 63, 67–69, 71, 74–81, 83–91, 94–89, 101, 103–104, 106, 108–109, 111.

Variants are as follows: Text = p. [1] Neces- (Necessity); p. 28 *Tan- (*Tantara-rara*); p. 73 super- (supernatural); Footnotes: = p. 4 veighs, ('veighs,); 6 the ('the); 9 pro- (probably); 27 Com- (Commentators); 49 *wicked (*Wicked*.).

Copies collated: British Library, 73.k.32 (half-title lacking) and 'Ashley' 3212; Harvard, *EC7.F460.742p; Huntington, 123348; Michigan, PR/3454/.Z4/A7p. All are identical. Paper watermarked with fleur-de-lis. The *ESTC* lists forty-three copies.

4. Preface to *David Simple* (1744)

The Second Edition (13 July 1744)

Title-page: THE / ADVENTURES / OF / *DAVID SIMPLE:* / Containing / An ACCOUNT of his TRAVELS / Through the / CITIES of *LONDON* and / *WESTMINSTER*, / In the Search of / A REAL FRIEND. / [rule] / By a LADY. / [rule] / IN TWO VOLUMES. / [rule] / VOL. I. / [rule] / THE SECOND EDITION, / *Revised and Corrected.* / With a PREFACE / *By* HENRY FIELDING *Esq*; / [double rule] / *LONDON:* / Printed for A. MILLAR, opposite *Katharine-* / street, in the *Strand*. / [short rule] / M. DCC. XLIV.

Collation: Vol. I. 12°: [A]¹ [A]²⁻¹⁰ B–M¹² N² (=A11–12) O⁶, \$1–6 (-A1, A6, N2 [3–6], O4–6), 150 leaves, pp. [i–iii] iv–xiii [xiv–xv] xvi–xvii [xviii] xix–xx [1] 2–137 [138] 139–278 [279–280]

Copies collated: British Library, 12611.ee.19; Michigan, PR 3459/.F3/A2/1744; Huntington, 371531; Illinois, x823/F465a/1744²; Harvard, *EC7. F460. A744f v. 1; Yale, Fielding Collection, 744a.

Notes: (1) All copies of volume I collated are identical, including a slightly slipped 'V' in the date on the title-page, the typographical error 'Friendshtp' (ix. 3), and other small idiosyncrasies. (2) In the *Works* (1762), both 4° and 8°, there are just three substantive variants of any significance: 'these who conferred' replaces HF's 'those who have conferred' (iii. 9–10); 'the reader' replaces 'their Reader' (xi. 4); and 'they were' substitutes for 'they are' (xi. 24). Arthur Murphy, who edited the *Works*, also lower-cases HF's initial capitals for nouns and words after a colon; he romanizes HF's italics for proper names, makes ''d' endings 'ed', changes 'tho' 'to 'though', etc.

                                                                          SWB

5. *The Female Husband* (1746)

The First Edition (12 November 1746)

Half-title: [orn.] / THE / *Female Husband:* / OR, THE / SURPRISING / HISTORY / OF / Mrs. *Mary*, alias Mr. *George Hamilton*. / [orn.] / (Price Six-pence.)

Title-page: THE / Female Husband: / OR, THE / SURPRISING / HISTORY / OF / Mrs. *MARY*, / ALIAS / Mʳ GEORGE HAMILTON, / Who was convicted of having married a YOUNG / WOMAN of *WELLS* and lived with her as / her HUSBAND. / TAKEN FROM / Her own MOUTH since her Confinement. / [rule] /————*Quodque id mirum magis esset in illo*; / *Fæmina natus erat. Monstri novitate moventur,* / *Quisquis adest: narretque rogant.*———— / OVID Metam. Lib. 12. / [double rule] / LONDON: / Printed for M. COOPER, at the Globe in Pater- / noster-Row. 1746.

Collation: 4°: [A]² B–D⁴, \$1–2, 14 leaves, pp. *i–iv 1* 2–23 *24*

Contents: [i] half-title [ii] blank [iii] title [iv] blank [1] / [orn.] / 'THE / Female Husband.' / text, *ending on 23 with 'FINIS'*. [24] blank

Running heads: None

Press figures: B4ʳ-2, C4ᵛ-2, D1ᵛ-2

Catchword variant: p. 20 dis- (discovery)

Copies collated: British Library, C.71.h.12; Bristol Public Libraries, GC 8443/ BL17B; Huntington, X70356; State University of Iowa Library, xPR3454.F4.

Note: No variants appear in the above copies; all are from the same printing. The Iowa copy lacks the half-title.

6. *Ovid's Art of Love Paraphrased* (1747)

The First Edition (25 February 1747)

Title-page: OVID'S | ART of LOVE | PARAPHRASED, | AND | ADAPTED to the Present Time. | With NOTES. | AND | A most CORRECT Edition of the Original. | [rule] | BOOK I. | [rule] | [orn.] | [double rule] | *LONDON:* | Printed for M. COOPER, in *Pater-Noster-Row*; | A. DODD, without *Temple-Bar*; and G. | WOODFALL, at *Charing-Cross*. (Price 2*s*.) | M.DCC.XLVII.

Collation: 8°: A⁴ B–F⁸ G⁴ $1–4 (–A1, 3, 4, G3, 4), 48 leaves, pp. [i–ii] iii–viii [1] 2–87 [88]

Contents: [i] Title [ii] blank iii | [*thick line of* orn.] | PREFACE. | *ending on* viii *with* orn.; [1] half-title | *OVID*'s | ART of LOVE | PARAPHRASED. | (2) | *line of* orn. | LIBER I. | [*Latin text on the left of every opening (verso of each leaf) ending on p.* 87 *with*] orn.; (3) | [line of orn.] | BOOK I. | [*English text on the right of every opening (recto of each leaf) ending on p.* 87 *with*] | FINIS. | [orn.]; [88] blank

Running heads: PREFACE. | PREFACE.; De Arte Amandi. Lib. I. | *The Art of Love Paraphrased.*

Press figures: B4ʳ–3 D6ʳ–3 F5ʳ–3

Catchword variants: Latin text on verso of each leaf carries catchword for the following verso leaf; as does the English text on each recto leaf for the following recto leaf. Latin (all verso): B1 *Nec* (*Phyllirides*), C8 *Quo* (*Quò*), E4 *Munditia* (*Munditiæ*), E6 *Impli-* (*Implicitamque*), F7 *Scilicet* (*Scilicet,*). English (all recto): B2 *School-* (*Schoolmaster*), Footnotes extending from the verso leaf to the following recto: B2ᵛ [*lacking*] (*gury*), E2ᵛ [*lacking*] (*Cydippe*).

Notes: (1) The first edition is the sole authoritative text. Copies collated: the John Rylands Library, Manchester (R67043; Yale, Fielding Collection, 747ab; Harvard, Houghton Library, *EC7 F460 7470); Princeton, Robert Taylor Collection. Other extant copies: Cambridge University, Trinity College, Rothschild 847; British Library, C192.a.81; Lincoln's Inn Library, London (Coxe's Tracts vol. 83). (2) The Latin text in the verso of each leaf is numbered in the right margin every fifth line, except that errors occur beginning p. 10, where line 69 is misnumbered 70, and continue accordingly until corrected on p. 24. The numbers for lines 315, 540, and 560 are omitted. The line numbers in the Wesleyan text have been silently rectified.

The Dublin Reprint (12 June 1756) 8°

Title-page: OVID's | ART of LOVE | PARAPHRASED, | AND | ADAPTED to the present TIME. | With NOTES. | AND | A most Correct EDITION of the ORIGINAL. | [rule] | BOOK I. | [rule] | By the late HENRY FIELDING, Esq; | [rule] | [space] | [double rule] | *LONDON*, Printed: | And *DUBLIN*, Re-printed, and sold by the Booksellers. | [short rule] | M DCC LVI.

Collation: 8°: A–M⁴ $1–2 (–M2; M3 missigned 'M2'), 48 leaves, pp. [i–ii] iii–viii [1] 2–42 [43] 44–87 [88] (43 misnumbered '45'; 45 correctly numbered).

Contents: [i] Title [ii] blank iii | [thick line of orn.] | PREFACE. | *ending on* viii | [1] half-title | *OVID*'s | ART of LOVE | PARAPHRASED. | 2 | [line of orn.] | LIBER I. | [*Latin text ending on p.* 86] | 3 | [line of orn.] | BOOK I. | [*English text ending on p.* 87 *with*] | FINIS. | [88] blank.

Running heads: PREFACE. | PREFACE.; De Arte Amandi. Lib. I. | *The Art of Love Paraphrased.*

Press figures: None

Catchword variants: Latin (all verso): 18 *Palliæ* (*Pallia*). English (all recto) None. Footnotes: 52 [*lacking*] (*Cydippe*).

Notes: (1) This describes Yale, Fielding Collection, 747ac. The likely publisher was George Faulkner, who published the only advertisements for it in his *Dublin Journal* for 12, 15, and 19 June 1756. (2) Reissued Dublin 1759, with cancel title-page: '[T]HE | LOVER's ASSISTANT[,] | OR, | New Year's Gift; | BEING, A | NEW ART of LOVE, | ADAPTED to the PRESENT TIMES. | [rule] | Translated from the LATIN, with NOT[ES] | BY the LATE INGENIOUS | HENRY FIELDIN[G, Esq;] | Of [FAC]ETIOUS MEMORY. | [rule] | [space] | [double rule] *LONDON*, Printed: | And *DUBLIN*, Re-printed, and sold by the Booksellers[.] | [short rule] | M DCC LIX. | [rule] | [Price a British Shilling.]'. This describes the British Library's apparently unique copy, with damaged title-page (11375.aaa.25), which is digitally available at Eighteenth Century Collection Online, Gale Group: <http://galenet.galegroup.com/servlet/ECCO>, document number CW3312207106. The *ESTC* lists another copy at the Royal Irish Academy, Dublin; shelfmark: Haliday Pamph 287 no. 4. (3) Reissued again in London, 1760, with cancel title-page reset to read, after 'ASSISTANT': 'OR, NEW | ART OF LOVE, | Adapted to the present Time. | For the Use of the Youth of both SEXES. | With NOTES. | By the late *HENRY FIELDING*, Esq; | Of facetious Memory. | *LONDON* Printed: | M. DCC. LX. | (Price One Shilling.)'. This describes the title-page of Yale, Fielding Collection, 747ad, copy 1, identical with the Yale 1756 and British Library 1759 except for the reworded title-page. Yale copy 2 lacks signature [A], with Preface; it begins with half-title on B1. For a modern reprint, see Claude E. Jones (ed.), Augustan Reprint Society, no. 89 (1961) and the review by William B. Coley, *PQ*, 41 (1962), pp. 587–8.

HA

7. Preface and Letters XL–XLIV of *Familiar Letters* (1747)

The First Edition (*10 April 1747*)

VOL. I. *Title-page*: FAMILIAR | LETTERS | BETWEEN THE | Principal Characters | IN | *DAVID SIMPLE*, | And SOME OTHERS. | To which is added, | A VISION. | [rule] | By the AUTHOR of | *DAVID SIMPLE*. | [rule] | IN

TWO VOLUMES. | [rule] | VOL. I. | [double rule] | *LONDON:* | Printed for the AUTHOR: | And Sold by A. MILLAR, opposite | *Katharine-Street* in the *Strand.* | M.DCC.XLVII.

Collation: 8°: A⁸ a³ b⁸ c⁴ B–I⁸ K–U⁸ $1–4 (–a3 c3–4), 175 leaves, pp. *i–ii iii–xlvi* (misnumbered 'xlviii') *47–350* (misnumbered '49–352')

Partial contents: i title iii | [double rule] | 'PREFACE: | *Written by a Friend of the* | *Author.'* | text, *ending on* xxii *with* orn.; xxiii | 'THE | LIST of SUBSCRIBERS.' | text, *ending on* xlvi (*misnumbered* xlviii) *with* orn.; 47 (*misnumbered* 49), text, *ending on* 350 (*misnumbered* 352), *with 'The* END *of the* FIRST VOLUME.'

Running heads (partial): The PREFACE. | the PREFACE.

Press figures: none.

Catchword variants: none.

VOL. II. *Title-page:* [Identical with that of volume I except 'IN TWO VOLUMES | [rule] | is omitted and 'VOL. II.' replaces 'VOL. I.']

Collation: π¹ A–U⁸ X–Z⁸ Aa⁸ Bb⁴ $1–4 (–S3–4* Bb3–4) 197 leaves, pp. *i–ii 1–276 277–278 279–284 285–286 287–392*

[* The signing of signature S is complicated by James Harris's two Dialogues and their title-pages, beginning on S3. Signatures are S, S2, S3 (unsigned), S4 (signed 'S3'), S5 (unsigned), S6 (unsigned), S7 (signed 'S3' again).]

Partial contents: i title 1 text, *continuing through* 'LETTER XXXVIII', *ending on* 275; (276) | [double rule] | 'LETTER XXXIX. | *From a Gentleman at London, to* | *his Friend in the Country.'* | *signed 'I am, &c.' with a footnote* 'These Dialogues were a kind Present to the Author by a Friend.'; (279) | [double rule] | 'MUCH ADO: | A | DIALOGUE.' | [rule] | text, *ending on* 284; (287) | [double rule] | 'FASHION: | A | DIALOGUE. | [rule] | text, *ending on* 293; (294) | [double rule] | 'Note' | [rule] | 'LETTER XL. | VALENTINE to DAVID SIMPLE.' | text, *ending on* 305 *with signature* 'VALENTINE.'; (306) | [double rule] | 'LETTER XLI. | *A LETTER from a* French | *Gentleman to his Friend at* Paris; | *in Imitation of* Horace, Addison, *and all other Writers of travelling Letters.* | text, *ending on* 324; (325) | [double rule] | 'LETTER XLII. | *From Miss* PRUDENTIA FLUTTER | *to Miss* LUCY RURAL.' | text, *ending on* 331 *with signature* 'PRUDENTIA FLUTTER'; (332) | [double rule] | LETTER XLIII. | *From Miss* LUCY RURAL *to Miss* | PRUDENTIA FLUTTER.' | text, *ending on* 339 *with signature* | LUCY RURAL. | P.S. *Old* George *desires me . . . in that same* London.'; (340) | [double rule] | 'LETTER XLIV. | VALENTINE *to* CYNTHIA.' | text, *ending on* 351 *with signature* 'VALENTINE.'; (352) | [double rule] | 'A VISION.' | text, *ending on* 392 *with* | '*FINIS.'* | [orn.]

Running heads (partial): LETTER XL. | LETTER XL. [etc., through 'XLIV.']; A VISION. | A VISION.

Press figures (partial): T6ʳ: 3 U5ᵛ: 3 X7ᵛ: 3 Y7ʳ: 1

Catchwords variant (partial): p. 295 And (AND)

Copies collated: British Library, 863.d.38; Huntington, 94253; Harvard, *EC7. F4605.747fa; Edinburgh University Library, V* 23.8. All are identical, except the BL copy of volume I binds the List of Subscribers (sigs. B8–c4 pp. xxiii–[xlvi]) at the end of the volume. An Irish reprint of 1747, 2 vols. 12°, bears the imprint: '*DUBLIN:* | Printed for E. and J. Exshaw, at the *Bible* on | *Cork-hill*, M,DC-C,XLVII.' It reproduces title-pages and text virtually verbatim.

The Second Edition (7 April 1752), volumes III and IV of a four-volume set,
12° [see the Introduction above, pp. 470–1.]

VOL. III *Title-page*: FAMILIAR | LETTERS | BETWEEN THE | Principal Characters | IN | *DAVID SIMPLE*, | And SOME OTHERS. | BEING | A Sequel to his Adventures. | To which is added, | A VISION. | [rule] | By the AUTHOR of | *DAVID SIMPLE*. | [rule] | The SECOND EDITION. | [rule] | VOL. III. | [double rule] | *LONDON*: | Printed for A. MILLAR, opposite *Katharine-* | *Street*, in the *Strand*. | M.DCC.LII.

Collation: Volume III 12m°: π¹ A⁶ B–I¹² K⁶, $1–6 (–A4–6, K4–6), 109 leaves, pp. *i–ii* iii–xiv *15–182* (misnumbered '25'–'192') *183–217* (misnumbered '169'–'203') *204* (actual 218 blank)

Partial contents: i title iii | [double rule] | 'PREFACE.' | *Written by a Friend of the Author.* | text, *ending on* xiv *with* orn.; (25) | [double rule] | Familiar Letters. | [rule] | 'LETTER I.' | text, *with successive letters ending on* '203' (actual 217), *with* | '*The* END *of the* THIRD VOLUME.'

Running heads: The PREFACE. | The PREFACE.; FAMILIAR LETTERS | *of* DAVID SIMPLE, &c.

Press figures (partial): A3ᵛ: 3

Catchwords variant (partial): iii Occa- (Occasions)

Note: Volume III misnumbers the first page of text, which follows preface-page xiv, '25' instead of '15', throwing the pagination off by 10. It also misnumbers signature I by beginning again with '169' following '192'. B3 is missigned 'B5'.

[VOL. IV] *Title-page*: [Identical with that of volume III, except for substituting 'VOL. IV.']

Collation: Volume IV 12°: π¹ B–L¹² M¹⁰ $1–6 (–M5,6), 131 leaves, pp. *i–ii* 1–179 *180–182 183–258 259–260*

Partial contents: i title 1 | [double rule] | Familiar Letters. | [rule] | VOL. II. | [rule] | 'LETTER XX.' | text, *continuing through* 193; 194 | [double rule] | 'Note.' | [rule] | 'LETTER XL.' | text, *followed by* Fielding's letters XLI–XLIV, *ending on* 231; 232 | [double rule] | A | VISION. | text, *ending on* 258 *with* 'FINIS.'; *259–260* | *publisher's advertisement*

Running heads: FAMILIAR LETTERS | *of* DAVID SIMPLE, &c.; *186–187* FAMILIAR LETTERS, &c. | [blank]; 234–258 A VISION. | A VISION.

Press figures (partial): K5ᵛ: 1 L11ᵛ: 2

Catchword variants (partial): p. 204 FROM (From); 219 Instru- (Instrument); 'Ambi- ('Ambition); 229 'disdain- ('disdaining)

Copies collated: (1) Copies of the second edition of *Familiar Letters* volumes III and IV collated against the first-edition copy-text and each other (no variants) are: British Library, 12611.ee.19; Michigan, PR3459/.F3/A2/1744; R. W. Woodruff Library of Advanced Studies, Emory University, Spec. Coll., PR3459/F 3A7/v. 3–4; Goucher College, 826.4/F 459Jf/v. 1–2; Yale, Ik/F 462/7446/v. 3–4; New York Public Library, NVC (Duyckinck Collection). (2) The five-volume sets that include Sarah Fielding's *David Simple* 'VOLUME THE LAST' (1753), with volumes bound as a set and marked on the spines from 'I' to 'V'—e.g. British Library 12611.ee.19 and Michigan PR 3459/.F3/A2/1744—incorporate the sheets of the only printing of the second edition. [*Note*: The University of Michigan set 'VOL. III.' omits A1–6, pp. *i–xiv*, containing HF's Preface.]

8. *The Journal of a Voyage to Lisbon* (1755)

with

9. *A Fragment of a Comment on L. Bolingbroke's Essays* (1755)

NOTE: The following bibliographical description of the *Journal* and the *Fragment* was prepared by Hugh Amory and reviewed by David Vander Meulen. The commentary is by Amory.

The First printed, second published edition, first issue (1755) = 1 ('Francis')

[facsimile]
THE | JOURNAL | OF A | VOYAGE TO LISBON, | By the late | HENRY FIELDING, Esq; | [orn. : Maslen R328] | *LONDON:* | Printed for A. MILLAR, in the Strand. | MDCCLV.

Collation: 12°: [A]⁴ B–L¹² M⁴ (M4 blank) [$1–6 signed (–L3, M3, and, in some copies, I1)] = 128 leaves, pp. [*4*] ᵖ[i] ii–iv; [i] ii–xv [xvi]; [17] 18–37 [38]; [39] 40–219 [220]; [221–222] 223–245 [246–248] (in some copies p. 176 is unnumbered).

Contents: [A]1 half-title (verso blank) 'THE | JOURNAL | OF A | VOYAGE TO LISBON.'; [A]2 title-page (verso blank); ᵖ[i]–iv '[orn.: Maslen RO67] | DEDICATION | TO THE | PUBLIC.'; [i]–xv '[orn.: Maslen RO68] | THE | PREFACE.' [xvi] blank; [17]–37 '[orn.: (Strahan)] | THE | INTRODUCTION.' [38] blank; [39]–219 '[orn.: (Strahan) RO47] | THE | JOURNAL | OF A | VOYAGE TO LISBON.' [220] blank; [221–222] divisional title-page. (verso blank) 'A | FRAGMENT | OF A | COMMENT | ON | L. BOLINGBROKE´S ESSAYS.'; 223–245 '[double rule] | A | FRAGMENT, &c.' [246–248] blank.

Running titles: The PREFACE. INTRODUCTION.; A VOYAGE | TO
LISBON.

Four formes may more or less dimly be made out by spacing and broken letters in
the running heads: 1. D(o), F(i), G(o), H(i), & K(o); 2. D(i), F(o), G(i), H(o), &
K(i); 3. E(o), & I(o)?; 4. E(i) & I(i)?

Paper: Sig. [A] is on Geneva demy (55.8 × 44.9 cm., uncut), watermarked with a star
centred on the sheet; the remainder of the volume is on a smaller demy watermarked with a fleur-de-lis/IV (cf. Heawood 1449, *c*.51.5 × 43 cm.).

Press figures:

B11ᵛ–3	E8ʳ–5	I5ᵛ–1
B12ᵛ–5	F1ᵛ–2	I7ʳ–6
C2ᵛ–5(inverted)/none	G1ᵛ–8	K6ᵛ–3
C12ʳ–8	G12ᵛ–6	K11ᵛ–5
D2ʳ–1	H1ᵛ–1	L7ʳ–2
D12ᵛ–2	H6ᵛ–5	L12ʳ–6
E2ᵛ–6		

Typography:

CONTENTS: *Type area*: 134 × 69 mm. *Dedication*: english (92 mm.) roman, set solid,
27 (±) lines to a page. *Pref., Introd., & Text*: pica (84 mm.) roman, set solid, 27–30
lines to a page (p. [176] is anomalous in length and numbering). *Footnotes*: long
primer (66 mm.) roman, set solid. MISE-EN-PAGE: 4–5-line Factotums + capitals
to open sections of the *Journal*; 2–3-line Initials + capitals to open sections of
the 'Fragment'. *Paragraphs* spaced, indented, with initial words in caps./sm. caps.
(–p. 231). ORNAMENTS (incl. factotums). Five of G1ᵛ eleven ornaments used in the
two London editions had recently been in the possession of Samuel Richardson;
see Keith Maslen, 'Fielding, Richardson, and William Strahan: A Bibliographical
Puzzle', *Studies in Bibliography*, 53 (2000), pp. 227–40, for a detailed discussion and
correction of the printing assignment of sigs. [A] and M that I made in Amory, 'Two
Versions of *Voyage to Lisbon*'.

Copies: L (–M4); CU (–M4), CSmH, CtY (Fielding Coll.), IaU (–M4), InU, MB,
MH (–M4), NIC (–M4), NjP (–M4), NNC (–M4), ViU (2); University of Otago,
Dunedin, NZ (–M4).

NOTE: Also issued as part of a three-volume set with the Dublin edition of
Fielding's *Miscellanies* (1743); the Dublin imprint is cancelled by a row of fleurons,
with '*LONDON*' stamped above it. The only copy seen, in Cambridge University
Library, wants volume I of the *Miscellanies*; its circulating library plate suggests an
issue date in the 1770s, and the stamped imprint is presumably false.

First printed, second published edition, second issue [1756]

[title-page as in I, reset: the *B* of 'By' is to the left of the *F* in 'FIELDING'.]

Collation: 12° a⁴ (–a4), B–L¹² M⁴ (–M4) [$1–6 signed (–L3 and, in some copies, I1)]

= 126 leaves, pp. [2] ᵖ[i] ii–iv; [i] ii–xv [xvi]; [17] 18–37 [38]; [39] 40–219 [220]; [221–222] 223–245.

NOTE: A reissue, with preliminary and final signatures reprinted (omitting the half-title); no substantive variants in sig. M were found.

Copies: MH, NIC; University of Otago, Dunedin, NZ.

Second printed, first published edition (1755) = 2 *('Humphrys')*
[title-page as in 'Francis']

Collation: [A]⁴ B–M¹² N⁶ [$1–6 signed (–N4–6)] = 142 leaves, pp. [4] ᵖ[i] ii–iv; [i] ii–xvii [xviii]; [19] 20–41 [42]; [43] 44–240 193–198; [199–200] 201–228 [= 276 pp.]

Contents: [A]1 half-title (verso blank) 'THE | JOURNAL | OF A | VOYAGE to LISBON.'; [A]2 title-page (verso blank); [i]–iv '[orn.: Maslen R067] | DEDICATION | TO THE | PUBLIC.'; [i]–xvii '[orn.: (Strahan)] | THE | PREFACE.' [xviii] blank; [19]–41 'orn.: (Strahan)] | THE | INTRODUC-TION.' [42] blank; [43]–240 193–198 '[orn.: Maslen R047] | THE | JOURNAL | OF A | VOYAGE to LISBON.'; [199–200] div. title-page (verso blank) 'A | FRAGMENT | OF A | COMMENT | ON L. BOLINGBROKE´S ESSAYS.'; 201–228 '[double rule] | A | FRAGMENT, &c.'

Running titles: The PREFACE.; INTRODUCTION.; A VOYAGE | TO LISBON.

Paper: Geneva demy, watermarked with a star centred on the sheet.

Press figures:

B1ᵛ–2	E5ᵛ–2	G8ʳ–2	K12ᵛ–2
B11ʳ–1	E12ᵛ–1	G11ʳ–1	L7ʳ–2
C2ᵛ–5	F2ᵛ–1/none	H8ʳ–8	L12ʳ–1
C5ᵛ–2	F5ᵛ–2	H12ᵛ–2	M2ʳ–5/none
D2ᵛ–5	F7ʳ–1	I7ᵛ–3	M7ʳ–8
D12ʳ–2	F10ʳ–2	I12ᵛ–7/5	N3ʳ–7
E4ᵛ–1	G3ᵛ–2	K7ᵛ–3	N4ᵛ–2

NOTE: The duplicate figuring of formes E(o), F(o/i), and G(i) is unusual and puzzling. Cf. W. B. Todd, *Studies in Bibliography*, 3 (1951), p. 156.

Typography:

CONTENTS: *Type area:* 130 × 70 mm. *Text:* english (92 mm.) roman, set solid, 24–7 lines to a page. *Footnotes:* small pica (73 mm.). MISE-EN-PAGE: as in 'Francis'. *Paragraphs*: spaced (except for the Preface and Introduction), indented, with initial words in caps./sm. caps. (except p. 112). ORNAMENTS: See note for previous edition.

Copies: L, C, CT (uncut); CSmH, CtY (Fielding Collection), IaU, MB, MH (2), MiU, NjP, NNC, ViU.

Dublin edition first issue (1756 [i.e. 1755?])

Title-page: A | JOURNAL | OF A | VOYAGE to *Lisbon*. | With a FRAGMENT of | A COMMENT | ON | Lord BOLINGBROKE´S ESSAYS. | By the late HENRY FIELDING, Esq. | [orn.: Mercury] | *DUBLIN:* | Printed by JAMES HOEY at the *Mercury* in | *Skinner-Row.* MDCCLVI.

Collation: 12° A–H¹² [$1–5 signed] = 96 leaves, pp. [i–iii] iv [v] vi–xvi; [17] 18–32; [33] 34–64 69 66–190; [191–192] (advts.).

NOTE: A reprinting of 'Humphrys'.

Copies: O; MH (uncut), TxU, InU

Dublin edition, second issue (1756)

Adds I⁶, pp. [1] 2–12, containing '[orn.] | An ACCOUNT of the | City of *LIS-BON*, | As it stood before the 1st of *Nov*. 1755. | And of the Customs, Manners, | &c. of the Inhabitants.'

Copies: C, DN (Joly Coll.).

NOTE: The Dublin editions have no authority, and are therefore degressively described.

The error in the paging of 'Humphrys' evidently resulted from casting off 'Francis' for reprinting. What is now sig. M in 'Humphrys'—indeed, the printing of 'Humphrys' itself—started on p. 193 with the assumption that the rest of the volume would fit into eight signatures, when in fact it ultimately occupied ten. On this assumption, the last two gatherings of 'Humphrys', containing pp. 193–7 of the *Journal* and the *Fragment* (pp. 198–228), would have been signed K¹² L⁶; the signatures, but not the paging, were ultimately revised to fit the earlier part of the volume.

This in turn suggests that the *Fragment* was added as an afterthought to the 'Francis' version, either by cancellation or by continuing composition. So far as they go (and they must be incomplete), Strahan's records favour the second hypothesis, but the collation of 'Francis' may once have been planned as [A]⁸ B–K¹² L⁴ (L3 advts., L4 blank, or something of the kind), in which sheet [A] | L was conjunct.[2]

The near coincidence of the number of signatures planned for the two editions may indicate that the editor had originally intended to print the text of 'Humphrys' in pica. If so, he changed his mind before printing began, for the *Fragment* is in english, and the Preface and Introduction of 'Humphrys', which would naturally have followed, omit all blank lines between paragraphs. Even had composition proceeded along these lines, the requisite 150 lines english could not be squeezed

---

[2] The conjecture that [A] is a cancel in 'Humphrys', which I proposed in Amory, 'Two Versions of *Voyage to Lisbon*', remains possible; cf. also Graham Pollard and A. Ehrman, *The Distribution of Books by Catalogue* (Cambridge, 1965), p. 176, who report a copy with an advertisement leaf. I have not succeeded in locating this copy.

into the 182 remaining pica spaces. Instead, more drastic changes were introduced, allowing a handsomer presentation at some cost to the text of the *Journal* proper.

Once he ordered the english format, the editor had good incentives for compacting the text, but the textual bearing of this bibliographical finding is obscure: the authority of these additions and deletions ultimately rests on subjective, 'internal' criteria.

Printing, Binding, and Marketing the *Journal*

Both London editions of the *Journal* were billed to Andrew Millar by William Strahan. In a small notebook s.d. 1 Jan. 1755, now in the American Philosophical Society, Philadelphia (B St. 83 no. 4), Strahan records under 'Work unfinished' that he had completed 2,500 copies of '7 Sheets @ £1:15' of the *Journal*—i.e. sigs. B–H of 'Francis'—and he charged Millar for both editions at the end of the month as follows (BL, Add. MS 48800, fo. 104ᵛ):

Voyage to Lisbon 10 Sheets No. 2500 @ 1:15	17	10—
Extraordinary Corrections in Do.		17—
Do. 2d Edition 12 Sheets No. 2500 @ 13:13:0	19	16—

Then in July 1756, for the reissue of 'Francis', we find (fo. 113ᵛ):

Fielding's Voyage to Lisbon ½ Sheet No 500, with Paper	—	16—

These charges amount to 20*s*. for printing the first 1,000 sheets of 'Francis' in pica, and 18*s*. for 'Humphrys' in english, respectively, with a charge of 5*s*. for every additional ream of 500 copies in either case, according to the trade's usual practices.[3]

As I have argued elsewhere, however, these records do not completely account for all the signatures of the two editions.[4] Sig. M of 'Francis' was probably once planned as part of a single sheet containing conjunct preliminaries, but as it worked out, it was printed as a half-sheet, closing the volume, and sig. [A] was also printed by half-sheet imposition, on a different paper. Thus some 4,500 copies of sig. [A], common to both editions, and 2,000 copies of sig. M appear to be unaccounted for, amounting to 4½ reams of Geneva demy and 2 reams of fleur-de-lis. These figures assume that the 1756 reprinting of the half-sheet a/M completed the warehouse's sets of both editions, but conceivably one or the other signature ran short. The exact division does not, however, greatly affect the overall picture, and I shall assume that only 4,000 copies of [A] were printed, 1,500 for 'Francis' and 2,500 for 'Humphrys'.

The cost of publishing the two editions may be estimated with some confidence from standard charges for paper and binding,[5] assuming of course that both of them

---

[3] Keith Maslen, 'Printing Charges: Inference and Evidence', *Studies in Bibliography*, 24 (1971), pp. 91–8; for composition charges, cf. I. G. Philip, *William Blackstone and the Reform of Oxford University Press in the Eighteenth Century* (Oxford, 1957), p. 30.

[4] Amory, 'Two Versions of *Voyage to Lisbon*', p. 197.

[5] For binding charges, see the lists edited by Mirjam Foot in *De Libris Compactis Miscellanea*, ed. Georges Colin (Brussels, 1984). The charge for print and paper of the reissue of 'Francis' implies that the Geneva demy cost 12*s*. a ream, and the fleur-de-lis demy is clearly of lower quality.

sold out at their advertised prices (which may have taken some years). 'Humphrys' was advertised at 3*s*. a copy 'bound' (*Public Advertiser*, 13 February 1755) and 'Francis' as 'bound 3s. or sewed 2s. 6d.' (*Public Advertiser*, 4 December 1755). What proportions of the edition were so sold is conjectural, but I have assumed that later issues were sewn (though I have never seen such a copy). Binding costs would be deferred to the time of sale, and this account must not be understood as a static picture. We have little or no information on sales, except that only a third as many copies of 'Francis' survive as those of 'Humphrys'. Each copy sold of 'Humphrys' realized about 1*s*. 11½*d*. profit, of 'Francis' about 1*s*. 4*d*.

HA

NOTE: To this analysis of the expense of printing the editions of the *Journal*, Amory attached this table (opposite).

T ABLE I

	Debit			Credit		
	£	s.	d.	£	s.	d.
Humphrys						
Print	19	16	0			
Paper (60R @ 12s.)	36	0	0			
Sig. [A] (2,500 copies)	2	5	7			
Advts., etc.	10	0	0			
Binding (2,500 copies @ 9d.)	93	15	7			
Total	161	6	7			
2,500 copies @ 3s.				375	0	0
Sig. [A]						
Print (4,000 copies)	1	8	0			
Paper (4R @ 12s.)	2	8	0			
Total	3	16	0			
To 'Humphrys'				2	5	7
To 'Francis'				1	10	5
Total				3	16	0
Francis (1755)						
Print and correction	18	7	0			
Paper (50R @ 10s.)	25	0	0			
Sig. M (2,000 copies)	1	0	0			
Sig. [A] (1,500 copies)	1	10	5			
Advts., etc.	5	0	0			
Binding 500 copies @ 8d.	16	13	4			
Folding and sewing 1,000 copies @ 2d./100 sheets	0	15	10			
Total	68	5	7			
500 copies @ 3s.				75	0	0
1,000 copies @ 2s. 6d.				125	0	0
Total				200	0	0
Francis (1756)						
Sig. a/M (print and paper)		15	0			
Folding and sewing 1,000 copies @ 2d./100 sheets	0	7	11			
Total	1	2	11			
500 copies @ 2s. 6d.				62	10	0

APPENDIX C

Documentary Supplement to

The Journal of a Voyage to Lisbon

1. Map of the Voyage

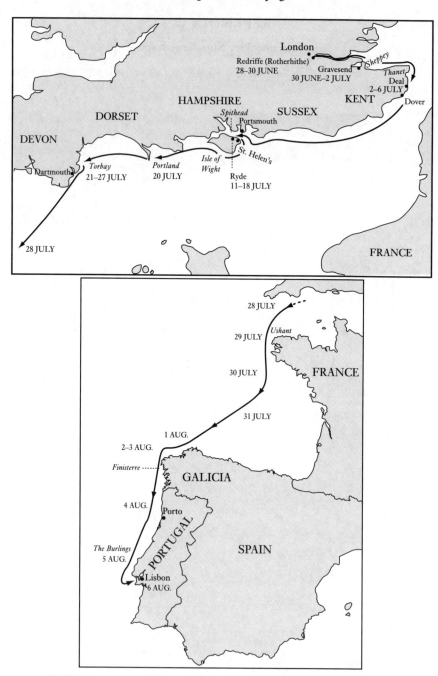

Fielding's voyage to Lisbon. Adapted by Amory from Bell and Varney's
edition (Oxford World's Classics), p. 121

2. Illustrations

Henry Fielding (*c.*1753), attributed to Sir Joshua Reynolds. From *Life*, plate 47

Sir John Fielding (1762), by Nathaniel Hone. From *Life*, plate 60

Fordhook, Fielding's house at Ealing, by Daniel Lyson. From *Life*, plate 61

Lisbon Harbour, after Clement Lempriere (*c*.1735). From *Life*, plate 64

3. Correspondence

NOTE: The following five letters from Henry Fielding to John Fielding reproduce the texts in *Correspondence*, Letters 73–7, omitting, however, the record of revisions in the manuscripts and adapting the notes to the present context.

1. *To* John Fielding[1] *On board the* Queen *of* Portugal, *off Ryde, I.o.W., 12 July 1754*

Dear Jack,

On board the Queen of Portugal Rich[d] Veal[2] at anchor on the Mother Bank off Ryde, to the Care of the Post Master of Portsmouth—This is my Date and y[r] Direction

July 12 1754

After receiving that agreeable Lr̃e from Mess[rs] Fielding & Co,[3] we weighed on Monday Morning[4] and sailed from Deal to the Westward Four Days long but inconceivably pleasant Passage brought us yesterday to an Anchor on the Mother Bank on the Back of the Isle of Wight, where we had last Night in Safety the Pleasure of hearing the Winds roar over our Heads in as violent a Tempest as I have known, and where my only Consideration were the Fears which must possess any Friend of ours, (if there is happily any such) who really makes our Well being the Object of his Concern especially if such Friend should be totally unexperienced in Sea Affairs. I therefore beg that on the Day you receive this M[rs] Daniel[5] may know that we are just risen from Breakfast in Health and Spirits this 12th Instant at 9 in the Morning. Our Voyage hath proved fruitful in Adventures all which being to be written in the Book,[6] you must postpone y[r] Curiosity—As the Incidents which fa<ll> under y[r] Cognizance will possibly be consigned to Ob<li>vion, do give them to us as they pass. Tell y[r] Neighbour[7] I am much obliged to him for recommending me to the Care of a most able and experienced Seaman to whom other Captains seem to pay such Deference that they attend and watch his Motions, and think

---

[1] HF's blind half-brother John (1721–80), who succeeded him as magistrate at Bow Street and was knighted in 1761.

[2] Richard Veale, Captain of the *Queen of Portugal*: see above, p. 566 n. 73.

[3] In February 1749/50 HF and his brother were chiefly responsible for founding the Universal Register Office—an ingenious, and under John's management a highly successful, business enterprise that combined the services of 'an employment agency, a financial institution, a real estate agency, a curiosity shop, and a travel bureau' (*CGJ*, pp. xv–xxii). The 'Company', as HF calls it, was made up of a 'Society of Gentlemen' who included Saunders Welch and (probably) Peter Taylor (see above, pp. 568 n. 84, 638 n. 280).

[4] i.e. 8 July.

[5] Elizabeth Daniel, HF's mother-in-law.

[6] *The Journal of a Voyage to Lisbon*, which HF began writing a week or so earlier.

[7] The helpful 'Neighbour' was probably Peter Taylor, who lived at the corner of Cecil Street and the Strand, directly opposite the Universal Register Office, where John resided until he replaced HF at Bow Street in June.

themselves only safe when they act under his Direction and Example. Our Ship in Truth seems to give Laws on the Water with as much Authority and Superiority as you dispense Laws to the Public and Examples to y^r Brethren in Commission.[8] Answer to me on Board as in the Date, if gone to be returned, and then send it by the Post and Pacquet to Lisbon to | y^r affec^t Brother

H Ffielding

Address: To | John Fielding Esqr at | his House in Bow Street | Cov^t Garden | London

Postmark: PORTS | MOUTH; *received at London* 15 July.

Text: ALS Harvard (fms Eng 870 (46)).

2. *To* John Fielding [*On board the* Queen of Portugal] *Tor Bay*, *Devon*, *22 July 1754*

Dear Jack   Torr Bay July 22 1754.

Soon after I had concluded my Letter of business to Welch yesterday,[1] we came to an Anchor in this Place, which our Capt says in the best Harbour in the World. I soon remembered the Country and that it was in the midst of the South hams a Place famous for Cyder[2] and I think the best in England, in great Preference to that of Herefordshire. Now as I recollect that you are a Lover of this Liquor when mixed with a Proper Number of Middx Turneps,[3] as you are of Port-Wind[4] well mixed likewise, I thought you might for the Sake of Variety be pleased with once tasting what is pure and genuine, I have therefore purchased and paid for 2 Hsĥds[5] of this Cyder where they will be delivered in double Casks to y^r Order transmitted by any Master of a Coasting Vessel that comes from London to these Parts. You must send the very Paper inclosed, that being the Token of the Delivery. The Freight of both by a Coaster of Devon or Cornwall will be 8 shillings only, which is I believe y^r whole Expence. They stand me within a few shillings at 4£, and the learned here are of Opinion they are the finest of their kind, one being of the rougher, the other of the sweeter Taste. Welch will easily find almost every Day one of these Coasters in London, which the Incertainty of our Stay here and the hurry which every Veering of the Wind puts us in prevents my providing here. It will be fit for drinking or bottling a Month after it hath lain in your Vault. I have consigned it in the following

---

[8] With his appointment to the Middlesex magistracy in January 1754, John had become fully qualified to assume HF's role as 'Court Justice'.

[1] On Saunders Welch, see above, p. 568 n. 84.

[2] With HF's account in this letter of the virtues of Devon cider and of the variety, quality, and cheapness of the local fish, cf. above, *Journal* (21 and 23 July).

[3] Cf. John Philips, *Cyder* (1708), ii, pp. 8–11: 'But this I warn Thee, and shall always warn, | No heterogeneous Mixtures use, as some | With watry Turneps have debas'd their Wines, | Too frugal.'

[4] Cf. HF's account of '*wind*' in the *Journal* (14 July), above, p. 601 and n. 175.

[5] Hogsheads: a measure containing 63 gallons.

manner. Half a Hȭd to yourself, half to Welch, half to Hunter[6] and half to Millar,[7] and I wish you all be merry over it.

In your last, there is only one Paragraph which I wish better explained. *If Boor*[8] *be Trusty*. Pray let me know any Shadow of a Doubt: for the very Supposition gives me much Uneasiness. If he is not trusty he is a Fool; but that is very possible for him to be, at least to catch at a lesser, and dishonest Profit, which is present and certain in Preference to what is in all Respects it[s] Reverse. Pray give me as perfect Ease as you can in this particular I begin to despair of letting my House this Summer. I hope the Sale of my Wine may be more depended on: for the almost miraculous Dilatoriness of our Voyage,[9] tho it hath added something to the Pleasure, hath added much more the Expence[10] of it. Insomuch that I wish Welch would send a 20£ Bill of Exch[a] by Perry[s11] Means immediately after me; Tho I fear Boor[s] Demands for Harvest Labourers have greatly emptied his hands, and I would not for good Reasons be too much a Debtor to the best of Friends. I hope at the same Time to see a particular Account of the State of Affairs at Fordhook, and the whole Sum of Payments to Boor from my leaving him to the Date of such Letter, <w>hen I presume the Harvest, as to Expence, will be pretty well over. I beg likewise an exact Account of the Price of Wheat *p* Load at Uxbridge.[12] I have no more of Business to say, nor do I know what else to write you: for even the Winds with us afford no Variety. I got half a Buck from the New Forest, while we lay at the Isle of Wight, and the Pasty still sticks by us. We have here the finest of Fish, Turbut, vast Soals and Whitings for less that you can eat Plaice in Middx. So that Lord Cromarty[s] Banishment from Scotland hither, was somewhat les cruel than that of Ovid from Rome to Pontus.[13] We may however say with him—Quam vicina est ultima Terra mihi![14] Ultima Terra you know is the Land[s] End[15] which a ten Hours Gale from North or East will carry us to, and where y[r] Health with all our Friends left behind us in England will be most cheerfully drunk by | y[r] affect[e] Brother.

H. Ffielding.

All our Loves to my Sister.[16]

Address: To | John Fielding Esq[r] | in Bow Street | Covent Garden | London

---

[6] The surgeon William Hunter: see the *Journal*, p. 577 and n. 108.

[7] Andrew Millar, HF's publisher.

[8] Richard Boor, HF's steward at Fordhook.

[9] Under favourable conditions the voyage to Lisbon would have taken a fortnight. It had been twenty-seven days since HF boarded the ship on 26 June; in all the passage would take forty-two days.

[10] The expense of the journey over and above the £30 Veale charged for carrying HF and his family to Lisbon is a topic he explores in the *Journal* (23 July).

[11] Probably Captain Perry, master of the *Prince of Wales*, who sailed regularly between London and Lisbon.

[12] Uxbridge, Middlesex, was one of the largest flour markets in England.

[13] After the rebellion of 1745, the Jacobite George Mackenzie, third Earl of Cromarty, was condemned to death but reprieved and banished to Layhill, Devon.

[14] Ovid, *Tristia*, III. iv. 52: 'how near to me is the margin of the world!'

[15] Land's End, Cornwall, the westernmost point of the English mainland.

[16] HF's sister-in-law, John's wife, Elizabeth.

[*Also in another hand*: To | Mr Giles Lavorance[17] at | Churston near Dartmouth | Devon]
Postmark: *received at London* 29 July
Text: ALS Huntington Library (HM 11615).

3. *To* John Fielding [*Junqueira, nr. Lisbon, c.10–14 Sept. 1754*][1]

I am willing to waste no Paper as you see,[2] nor to put you to the Expence of a double Letter as I write by the Packet,[3] by which I would have you write to me every Letter of Consequence, if it be a single sheet of Paper only it will not cost the more for being full, and perhaps you have not time even to fill one Sheet: for as I take it the idlest Man in the World writes now to the busiest, and that too at the Expence of the latter.

I have rec̃d here two Letters from you and one from Welch.[4] The Money I have tho' I was forced to discount the Note, it being drawn at 36 Days Sight upon a Portuguese, neither you nor Welch knew this, and it was the Imposition of the Drawer in London. Your Letter of Business I have not yet seen. Perhaps it is lost, as if it came by a Merchant' Ship, it easily may: for the Captains of these Ships pay no Regard to any but Merchants for which Reason I will have all my Goods even to the smallest Parcel consigned to John Stubbs Esqr[5] (as I mentioned before,[6] and hope will be done long before y° receive this) marked with the large red F——Pardon Repetition for abundans Cautela non nocet,[7] and tho I mentioned my orders, I did not give the Reason I believe either to y° or Welch, at least all my Reasons for there are several But this is the most worth y^r Notice. The Truth is these Captains are all ye greatest Scound<rels> in the World, but Veale is the greatest of them all. This I did not find out <ti>ll the Day before he sailed,[8] which will explain many things

---

[17] The purveyor of cider whom HF celebrates in the *Journal* (21 July).

[1] An approximate date for this letter and Letter 4 may be determined from HF's remark that Captain Allen of the *Boulter* 'sails next week': during HF's time there Captain Allen was in Lisbon for a fortnight only, arriving from London on 6 September and departing on Saturday, 21 September (see *Public Advertiser* [7, 14 October]).
[2] HF managed to squeeze the contents of this long letter within 'a single sheet' of paper folded in folio.
[3] HF wrote a 'single letter'—i.e. a letter written on one sheet of paper sealed. A single letter sent by the packet-boats that plied between Lisbon and Falmouth, Cornwall, once a week cost 1s. 6d., payable by the addressee.
[4] On Saunders Welch, see above, p. 568 n. 84.
[5] John Stubbs, one of the most prosperous members of the English Factory in Lisbon, had rescued HF and his family from financial ruin by finding them inexpensive lodgings in Junqueira (see below, p. 767 and n. 14).
[6] No earlier letter written by HF from Lisbon has survived, though two others, written to his publisher, Andrew Millar, were summarized by Thomas Birch in a letter of 7 September to Philip Yorke (see below, Letter 8).
[7] 'Abundant caution does no harm'—a legal maxim.
[8] On Captain Veale, see above, p. 566 n. 73.

when you see him <as per>haps you may for he is likewise a Madman, <which> I knew long before I reached Lis<bon> and he sailed a few Days ago. I shall not, after what I have said, thin<k him> worth my Notice, unless he should obiter fall in my Way <in this> Letter.

In answer to yours, if you can not answer it yourself, I will assure you once for all I highly approve and thank you, as I am convinced I always shall when yᵒ act for me, I desire therefore you will always exert unlimited Power on those Occasions.

With Regard to the principal Point, my Health, which I have not yet mentioned, I was tapped again (being the 5ᵗʰ time)[9] at Torbay partly indeed by way of anticipation, the Day before we sailed—wanting one [day] of three Weeks[10] since the operation in the Thames. Nine Quarts of Water were now taken away, and possibly here I left the Dropsy: for I have heard nothing of it since, and have now almost 8 Weeks Distance not a Drop of Water in me to my Knowledge.[11]

In short as we advanced to the South, it is incredible how my Health advanced with it, and I have no Doubt but that I should have perfectly recovered my Health at this Day, had it not been obstruc<ted> by every perverse Accident which Fortune could throw in my Way.

As soon <as> I landed my whole Family except myself Harriet and Bell fell s<ick> in which Condition William[12] continued the whole time he was here, being pulled down with a Flux occasioned by drinking too much Wine, and frightned with the Apprehensions of dying in a strange Country. In which Fright the miserable, cowardly Driveler, is returned to England with Veal, and Object too nasty and contemp[tible.]

In the next Place I found my self in the dearest City in the World and in the dearest House in that City. I could not for my Soul live for less than 2 Moidores[13] a day and saw my self likely to be left Pennyless 1000 Miles from home, where I had neither Acquaintance nor Credit among a Set of People who are tearing one anotherˢ Souls out for Money and ready to deposite Millions with Security but not a Farthing without. In this Condition moreover, I saw no Likelihood nor Possibility of changing my Situation. The House I was in being the cheapest of the Three in which alone I could get a Lodging <w>ithᵗ being poisoned.

Fortune now seemed to take Pity on me, and brought me by a strange Accident acquainted with one Mʳ Stubbs,[14] the greatest Merchant of this Place and the

---

[9] For the nature of HF's illness and its effects, see the General Introduction, pp. 514–15.

[10] HF means four, not three, weeks.

[11] This good news raised false hopes in London: see Introduction, p. 15 n. 3.

[12] On Harriet, HF's daughter, and the servants William Aldrit and Isabella Ash (Bell), see the Introduction, p. 524.

[13] A moidore was a gold coin worth 27s.

[14] Though HF attributed this 'strange Accident' to 'Fortune', his rival Richardson took credit for it. On 16 June 1755 Thomas Edwards wrote Daniel Wray complaining of HF's sarcasm against Richardson in the Preface to the *Journal*, a slur, he insisted, particularly reprehensible since 'the Good Man . . . by his correspondence at Lisbon had procured him accommodations which he could not otherwise have had' (Bodleian MS 1012, p. 212). Whether this was in fact the case is uncertain. Richardson's biographers comment: 'We know nothing more of Richardson's services to Fielding. He did have connections in Lisbon, and one hopes that he used them for Fielding. Edwards should have known: he must have had his information from Richardson, who is not likely to have lied outright' (Eaves and Kimpel, p. 305).

greatest Cornfactor in the World. He hath a little Kintor or Villa at a Place called Jonkera 2 Miles from Lisbon, and near Bellisle[15] which is the Kensington of England, and where the Court now reside.[16] Here he likewise got me a little House with^t any manner of Furniture not even a Shelf or a Kitchin Grate. For this I am to pay 9 Moidores a year, and h<i>ther I bold came with scarce suff^t Money to buy me the Necessari<es> of Life. My Furniture is as follows. 3 Table Cloths half a doz. Towells 10 ch>air>s a Tin Fish Kettle, Tea Kettle, Boiler and Saucepan, a Frying P<an a>nd Gridiron, a little china a few Glasses, and some Earthen Ware of the Manufacture he<re> cheap to an incredible Access.

When I was thus settled, my Money being all gone even to tapping the last 36<s> piece,[17] I recd y° Bill with which I discharged all Debts and about 9 Moidores remained in my Pocket.

The Tables were now turned My Expences were become moderate or rather indeed in the contrary Extreme to what they were before Instead of 2 Moidores a Day I now lived for Less than a Moidore *p* Week, and could not easily exceed it.

When then you will say was the Misfortune of all This? or what was there which could retard my Recovery, or shock a Philosophy so established as mine Which had triumphed over the Terrors of Death when I thought it both certain and near.

In Truth the worst, the whole is yet behind.[18] My Wife fell sick of a violent Flux which reduced her to almost the lowest Ebb of Life. She is, I thank God recovered; but so dispirited that she cries and sighs all Day to return to England. Is blind to the Good I have received so manifestly, and on which I receive daily Compliments as well from my Physical as from my other Acquaintance, insists upon it that the same, if it hath happened, would have happened in England, and that by returning thither I shall perfect my Recovery, that I want the Exercise of my Coach <&c> which nothing can supply, and that my children as well as Affairs can be by no <o>ther means preserved. The Part which another[19] acts on the Occasion is inconceivable, she is beco<m>e a fine young Lady of Portugal, a Toast of Lisbon, and is at the English Minister here in intimate Acquaintance of Millar^s[20] one Mr Williamson,[21] who is every Way the cleverest Fellow I ever saw, and is my chief Companion. He is smitten, and she would succeed, if I did not prevent it. She is indeed the most artful wicked B——in the world, blows the Coals of my Wife^s Folly, and is indeed the very Creature describe by Will[22] in the character of her

---

[15] i.e. Stubbs had a *quinta* at Junqueira, near Belém.

[16] On the death of the dowager Queen Maria Anna (she died on 14 August, a week after HF's arrival at Lisbon), the court went into mourning at Belém.

[17] One of the 'thirty-six-shilling pieces', called 'Joannes', to which HF refers in the *Journal* (above, p. 618 and n. 220).

[18] i.e. 'still to come' (*OED*, s.v. 'behind', 4).

[19] Margaret Collier, Harriet's governess.

[20] Andrew Millar, HF's publisher.

[21] John Williamson (*c.*1713–1763) of Balliol College, Oxford, Doctor of Divinity and Chaplain of the English Factory at Lisbon since 1749, in which year he was also elected FRS for his skill in mathematics.

[22] Not identified.

Sister.[23] By these means my Spirits which were at the Top of the House are thrown down into the Cellar.

I need, I think, say no more; but I desire you to act as follows for I really think my Life at Stake, and do support my self with the assured Hope of y^r Success.

First, shew this Letter to Mr Millar and desire him to write Mr Williamson the character of the B——what Obligations she and her Family have to me, who had an Execution taken out ag^t <m>e for 400£ for which I become Bail for her Brother, who took her starving in the Streets and nourished her in my own Bosom[24]—This he knows but perhaps you may instruct him somewhat in the Returns she has made to my Kindness.

2dly do procure as many Letters to be written to the Merch^{ts} and Ladies of Lisbon among the English of what character you and the Writers think I deserve as a Husband.

3dly Get me a conversible Man to be my Companion in an Evening, with as much of the Qualifications of Learning, Sense and Good humour, as y^o can find, who will <d>rink a moderate Glass in an Evening or will at least sit with me 'till one when I do.

4^{thly} send over <H> Jones[25] and Mrs Hussy.[26] I will pay their Passage hither, and will return them whenever they desire it and that not empty handed: for in Truth I ne<ver> was so likely to grow rich as <now nor was any> one ever more likely to recover his Health than my self. I have actually regained s<om>e Elasticity in my Limbs, get with^t Difficulty in and o<u>t of a <Ch>aise and when in it can ride a whole Day; but this w<i>ll be lost, and I shall be destroyed unless I can be reliev<ed> from the greatest Folly and the greatest Bitchery that ever w<er>e united in 2 Women by a 3^d who hath some Degree of Hon^r and Understanding at least shall have sense enough to see their own Int<e>rest and not form a Contempt of me as a good-natured Fool, shall lay such wild Schemes as to get me to send my Wife to England by Force, and to become the M^{rs} of my Family here under Colour of a Companion of my Daughter <I>shall only add that my Comfort is [,] as my Life absolutely depends <on> yr Success in what you attempt seems to me <alm>ost infallible.—If my male Friend understands Portuguese or Spanish, (which if he doth not, he may easily, if he hath the Latin Grammatical Rudiments, learn) he may put Money in his own, mine and the Great Millar^s Pockets. Note he must be my Amanuensi<s>.

I have sent by Veale 6 half chests Onions marked as you re<quest> for y^r self, Millar, Peter Taylor,[27] Welch and Mrs Daniel.[28] The sixth is for Dr Collier, whose

[23] Jane Collier, whom HF loved and admired as much as he had come to dislike her sister Margaret.

[24] On the financial crisis afflicting the Colliers, in which HF became embroiled in 1745, see *Life*, pp. 392–5.

[25] Not identified.

[26] Perhaps HF's friend, 'the celebrated Mrs. *Hussy*', whom he extols in *Tom Jones* (x. iii) as a 'Mantua-maker in the *Strand*, famous for setting off the Shapes of Women' (p. 538).

[27] On the 'ingenious' Peter Taylor, see above, p. 638 and n. 280.

[28] HF's mother-in-law.

very name I hate.[29] Tell Millar, there are 2 half hȡds of Calca<v>alla, one for himself, the other for Mr Rose[30] marked, I believe, M & R but ye Receipt is mislaid. I will in November which is the right season send you some Orange Trees as y^o desire, some Lemons and some Wine, Port or Lisbon, which y^o like best Y<ou> have half a dozen [ ] <by> Ca<p>t Allen of the Boulter who sails next Week.[31] Please send to m<e> . . . a Hamper of large Pars<n>ips and one of Nonpareils fro<m> . . . <like>wise from Welch 6 pound of . . . last <Michs> from . . . 2 half hdds. of sma . . . extraordinary, all . . . in a handsome . . . for the Winters here are short but cold. My old rug Wastecoat, and a dark blue Frock with a drest Sleeve. Desire Curtis[32] to make my Cloaths wider in the Shoulders. Let me have likewise my Tye and a new Major[33] Perriwig from Southampton Street, and a new Hat large in the Brim from my Hatter the Corner of Arundel Street. I have had a visit from a Portuguese Nobleman, and shall be visited by all as soon as my Kintor is in order. Bell follow Capt Veal to England where he hath promised to marry her, My family now consists in a black Slave and his Wife to which I desire you to add a very good perfect Cook, by the first Ship, but not by Veale. Scrape together all the Money of mine you can and do not pay a Farthing with^t my orders. My affairs will soon be in a fine Posture for I can live here, and even make a Figure for almost nothing. In Truth the Produce of the country is preposterously cheap. I bought three Days ago a Lease of Partridges for ab^t 14d English and this Day 5 young Fowls for half a Crown, What is imported from abroad is extravagantly dear, especially what comes from England as doth almost all the Furni<ture> of Lisbon. I must have from Fordhook likewise 4 Hams a very fine Hog fatted as soon as may be and being cut into Flitches sent me as likewise a young Hog made into Pork and salted and pickled in a Tub. A vast large cheshire cheese and one of Stilton if to be had good and mild. I thank Welch for this; but he was cheated:[34] God bless you and y^{rs}

H ffielding mil annos &c.[35]

In the World there is not such a Scoundrel as William, he cost me 8 Moidores bringing and sending him back; and not contented with that left me 3£. 12s. to pay his Nurse which he told me he had discharged and bid her not bring in till he was gone. He has my Draught on Bore[36] for ten Pound[;] bid Bore before he pays it Stop ye 3£ 12. and likewise take away his whole Livery. I would have some Act used to destroy the indorsing the Note which Bore may accomplish by getting him to strike out the words to order, or the Date of Lisbon before witnesses, or by paying him Part and getting ye word witness on the Back—in short an Attorney will shew him many ways, and there is <no> Punishment which

[29] Dr Arthur Collier (see n. 24 above).
[30] Perhaps John Rose, wine-cooper.
[31] Captain Allen sailed on 21 September (see n. 1 above).
[32] Not identified.
[33] A 'major' periwig was fashionable in 1750–70.
[34] In the second paragraph of this letter HF explains how Welch was 'cheated'.
[35] In Portuguese 'a thousand years, &c.' was the conventional complimentary close of a letter.
[36] Probably Richard Boor, who managed the financial affairs of the farm at Fordhook.

his Ingratitude doth not deserve; but Bell is only a Fool, and I wish she may be provided for at the Offer.[37] The Marks on y[e] chest are JF PT M W <R> C <Y>.[38]

Address: To | John Fielding Esq[r] | in Covent Garden | London | London | *p* the Lisbon Packet.
Postmark: received at London 5 Oct.
Text: ALS Huntington Library (HM 11616).

4. *To* John Fielding [*Junqueira, nr. Lisbon, c.20 Sept. 1754*][1]

Mr dear Jack.
An accident, which hath happened since I delivered my letter to Capt. Allen,[2] will explain more to you than I can by any other means, what is my situation here.

About a week ago I bought a parrot for Harriet and should have bought one for my sister[3] could I have found an easy way of sending it, but the Captains are too great to take money for such things and too little to take any trouble without it, so that what can't be called freight can not be sent as all, unless by their particular friends, amongst whom I have not the honour to be numbered.

I did not, however, think that water melons required much trouble to bring, and, accordingly, I ordered my black to buy me the six finest he could get for you. He brought them in whilst Mr. Stubbs[4] was sitting with me, who asked me jocosely whether I was to entertain the Court that day, being the day before yesterday. I told him they were for England by Capt. Allen who, as he had told me, was to sail in a day or two for England.[5] 'I thought,' said he, 'you did not know Captain Allen.' I told him I did not. 'Then I promise you,' said he, 'your water melons will stay behind,' This vexed me heartily, but my vexation lasted not long; on the contrary, my sister owes both her bird and her beast[6] to the accident; both of which were bought yesterday.

The one consigned by mamma is to the use of Billy, the other to Sophy.[7]

---

[37] The Universal Register Office, which served in part as an employment agency (see above, Letter 1 n. 3).
[38] As HF's explanation earlier in the letter makes clear the 'Marks' stand for John Fielding, Peter Taylor, Millar, Welch, Rose, and Collier. The final mark in the series should be a 'D' for Mrs Daniels, but isn't; it resembles a 'Y' (for HF's friend the Revd William Young?).

---

[1] The letter is undated, but it was probably written close to the time of Captain Allen's departure from Lisbon on 21 September.
[2] On Captain Allen of the *Boulter*, see above, Letter 3 and n. 1.
[3] i.e. HF's sister-in-law, John's wife, Elizabeth.
[4] On the wealthy merchant John Stubbs, see above, Letter 3 n. 5.
[5] Allen sailed for England on 21 September.
[6] Perhaps a monkey—the only exotic beast offered for sale when Fordhook was sold at auction in December 1754 (*Life*, pp. 609–10).
[7] William, aged 6, and Sophia, aged 4, HF's children by Mary, his second wife, remained behind at Fordhook.

This morning at breakfast Mr. Stubbs introduced Capt. Allen to me, whom you will find to a—captain of a ship. Harriet's parrot was on a stand by her chair; my sister's in the balconey, but neither Harriet nor Mamma in the room. 'If you send a parrott to England,' says Mr. Stubbs, 'let me advice you to send one more likely to live for I will not ensure that. Indeed it hath drooped these two days' (and I think it had). The mistake was soon rectified and they soon went away.

Now it happens that Harriet's parrott is the larger bird, for this is scarce full grown, and my wife, who doth not approve a preference of which she is jealous,[8] fancied (though the price was to a farthing the same) that Sophy was unfairly dealt with, having the smaller bird, and you will believe I did not interfere.

They came back into the room soon after my company left it. I whispered my wife what Stubbs had said. Harriet overheard imperfectly, or suspected, and fell into tears and declared she would not part with her parrott, for no notice had been taking of the drooping before by any but myself, nor was it agreed to now.

And now, Jack, what do you think? Why truly, mamma, suspecting my partiality discovered that I had laid a plot to deceive her. Mr.—— and Mrs.—— and Miss—— had all declared they liked Miss Harriet's parrott when first it was bought, and Mr. Stubbs would say anything I bid him. Here a crying bout between mother and daughter, both contending against themselves. . . . At last I condescended so low as to take the opinion of my black, for these blacks being the countrymen of the parrots are really good judges in them, but, so the devil ordained, my honest black knowing who was master, and desiring to please accordingly, declared against Mr. Stubbs and against me.

The matter was too ridiculous to be withstood. I called for my pipe and enjoyed it. Mamma went away in a rage vowing vengeance against poor Stubbs. B[9] is not at home.

Text: de Castro

Note: De Castro, who did not wish to be deemed 'wanting in good taste', reproduced in this modernized transcription 'about two-thirds' of HF's letter, explaining that the 'remainder' was 'of a confidential nature, written for the eye of John Fielding only'. The whereabouts of the original is unknown.

5. *To* John Fielding [*Junqueira, nr. Lisbon, late Sept. 1754*]

Dear Jack,

You must wait for an account of new wonders which every Day produces 'till the arrival of my amanuensis:[1] for there is no such thing as a Pen to be bought in all Lisbon, nor can I use their Paper or Ink with[t] Difficulty . . .

---

[8] Harriet, aged 11, was HF's only surviving child by his first wife, Charlotte.

[9] Margaret Collier: see above, Letter 3, where she is referred to as 'the most artful wicked B——in the world'.

---

[1] See above, Letter 3, p. 769.

Text: Solly.

Note: This six-line fragment of an autograph letter was first brought to the attention of scholars by Amory 'Lisbon Letters' and n. 4. It was purchased at auction by 'Cox', but it has not been traced.

6. *The Revd Thomas Birch to Philip Yorke*;
   20 October 1753 (fragment)
   [BL, Hardwicke Papers, Add. MS 35398, fo. 177; *Life*, p. 580.]

[Fielding] is at present fully employ'd in detecting the numerous Gangs of Banditti, who infest all the Roads about town, & is indefatigable in the Execution of his Office, tho' he has been for some time in a very ill state of Health, which alarm'd his Friends, & induc'd him to call in Dr. Heberden, who has remov'd his Jaundice, but not yet restor'd his appetite.

7. *The Revd Thomas Birch to Philip Yorke*;
   6 July 1754 (fragment)
   [BL, Hardwicke Papers, Add. MS 35398, fo. 182]

Mr. Fielding embark'd about a fortnight ago in the River for Lisbon to try the Success of that Climate upon a Constitution of Body which has twice supported tapping. His last Request to Mr. Millar, his Bookseller, was to take all Care, when he should hear of his Death, to prevent his Life from being undertaken by any of the Grubstreet Writers, who are so ready & officious on such Occasions.

8. *The Revd Thomas Birch to Philip Yorke*;
   7 Sept 1754 (fragment)
   [BL, Hardwicke Papers, Add. MS 35398, fo. 208^v; *Life*, p. 596]

Fielding arriv'd at Lisbon about a month ago, after a very tedious passage, the contrary Winds having kept him long in the Channel. I have seen two Letters from him to his Bookseller written with his usual Spirit & Vivacity, one from Torhay [*sic*] of the 25th of July, & the other from Lisbon of the 12th of August. He exclaims greatly against the extravagant price of every thing there, where the Expence of living is near thrice what it is in England. He has almost finish'd the History of his Voyage thither, which he offers to Millar as the best of his performances; & directs him to send him over all the Books which relate to Portugal for some other Work, which he has in view.

9. *Anonymous to Samuel Richardson*[1]
   '*Ryde in y*ᵉ *Isle of Wight March 31*ˢᵗ *1755.*'
   [J. Paul de Castro, 'Henry Fielding's Last Voyage', *The Library*, 3rd
   ser., 8 (April 1917), pp. 157–9; also Paulson and Lockwood, No. 155.]

We had the curiosity at this place to visit the landlord and landlady whom Mr. F.
has thought worthy so much of notice, and given so large a place to, in his late book,
and of whom he tells us, the description is lowered instead of being heightened,
recommending us to that of the Furies for an idea of the woman; but I must confess
the sight of her, having as he observes many symptoms of a deep jaundice in her
look, rais'd in my mind nothing but compassion; and in her behaviour we saw yet
less of the character of those infernal deities. We ask'd them if they remembred Mr.
F., they told us he had lodg'd with them, and had given them a great deal of trouble,
and that they thought Mr. F. the strangest man in the world, whom it was impossible to please: The chamber he lodged in here was the best I ever saw in a house of
the size and sort, nor did it want very sufficient and decent furniture, there were
two good beds in it, and a handsome looking-glass, which Mr. F. had a napkin put
over, that he might not be struck with his own figure, while he was exaggerating
that of others: in this room he cook'd his victuals, dressing as much as he could of it
by a chamber fire; and making the sauce himself. Here sending one day for the
landlord to keep him company, while his own were gone out, and he enquiring of his
health and expressing his wishes for the amendment of it, he saluted the stoic with
imprecations, bad him not talk of his health, but confine himself to the subject of
husbandry, which was what he wanted to talk to him about: now whatever means
Mr. F. had used to try the temper of the woman, whom he pronounced it impossible
to please, he certainly put to the proof that of the man, whom he honestly confesses
it impossible to displease. We found the circumstances of their dining in a barn a
fiction, there was no such barn with a pleasant view to the fields, nor dined they out
of the house. The venison so miraculously receiv'd on their coming to a place,
whither they were by accident driven; was not in fact so great a miracle as it appears
in the story, for Mr. F.'s servant was dispatch'd to Southampton to buy it, and paid
half a guinea for it, but whom it was bought of remains a secret to this day, and very

---

[1] On the basis of an inscription in a 'tremulous hand', presumably Richardson's, on the back of the
letter, it has been erroneously attributed to Margaret Collier ('Miss Peggy Collier'). But the letter cannot
be Margaret Collier's: whoever wrote it had not witnessed the scenes described as she had done (*Life*,
p. 684 n. 378). Keymer for this reason also rejects the ascription to Margaret (p. 108); however, he
suggests, cautiously to be sure, that Richardson (if indeed the tremulous hand is his) may have mistaken
Jane Collier for her sister, citing in support of the conjecture an affinity between the last paragraph of the
letter and the criticism of 'bad behaviour' in Jane's *Essay on the Art of Ingeniously Tormenting* (1753).
But everything we know about the long-standing relationship between Jane Collier and Fielding points
to its being one of mutual admiration and affection—and this is particularly clear at the time of his
departure for Lisbon (see *Life*, p. 587). As for Jane's *Essay on the Art of Ingeniously Tormenting*, there are
compliments in it to *Tom Jones* and *Jonathan Wild*, as well as to Fielding himself, whom she calls 'a good
ethical writer' (J. Paul de Castro, 'Fielding and the Collier Family', *N & Q*, 12th ser., 2 (5 August 1916),
pp. 104–6).

happily for the seller it does so. Fortune indeed must have been a very cunning goddess and attended very closely the steps of our author; to have found him at casting anchor with a present of a buck ready for his acceptance; the circumstances then relating to the venison we were convinced were wholly misrepresented.

As to the old woman, I believe she was naturally afflicted with too much gall, and now indeed was plainly dying under the overflowing of it, and consequently demanded great allowances on that score; but I am surprized that so great an observer of the humours of the lower class of people, had never discovered that the circumstance of paying them, will not always make them amends for the trouble you give them: I have seen those who have been very poor, and yet rather than be put out of their way would forego the profitts that would attend doing what they did not like, or were not used to: and Mr. F. was certainly under great obligations to any body that would admit him into their house, whom disease had render'd offensive to more senses than one: indeed our author appears under as great infirmities as the old woman, or any old woman whatever, and lays great claim from others of that charitable allowance, which a man of sound mind and body would have made for this poor creature. In this house he pass'd the last days he saw in his native land, in abusing the people to whom he was under some obligation, and yet not confining his invectives to them only—in ransacking every place for the means to gratify his depraved appetite, in tormenting himself, and all about him: afraid to see his own figure, unwilling to correct himself, he exposed that of others, and railed at their Faults.—

N.B. Tho' Mr. F. has printed the bills that were made him at the Inn, he paid them no more than he chose.—

10. *Thomas Edwards to Daniel Wray;*
    23 May 1755 (fragment)
    [Bodleian MS 1012, p. 212; Paulson and Lockwood, p. 393 n. 1]

Fielding's Voyage is the arrantest catch-penny that ever was published; I am amazed that a man who felt himself dying by inches could be so idly employed; but his insolenct censure of Mr. Richardson is unpardonable because it is highly unjust.

11. *Thomas Edwards to Samuel Richardson;*
    28 May 1755 (fragment)
    [Victoria and Albert Museum, Forster MS xii, fo. 141; Paulson and Lockwood, No. 156]

I have lately read over with much indignation Fielding's last piece, called his Voyage to Lisbon. That a man, who had led such a life as he had, should trifle in that manner when immediate death was before his eyes is amazing; but his impudence, in attributing that to your works which is the true character of his own which are the reverse of yours, is what puts me beyond all patience. It seems to me as if conscious that the world would not join with Warburton in transferring the palm from yours to his desertless head, he envied the reputation which you have so justly gained in that way of writing. From this book I am confirmed in what his other works had fully persuaded me of, that with all his parade of pretenses to virtuous and humane affections, the fellow had no heart. And so—his knell is knoll'd.

12. *Lady Mary Wortley Montagu to the Countess of Bute;*
    22 September [1755] (fragment)
    [*Complete Letters*, ed. R. Halsband (Oxford, 1965), iii, pp. 87–8]

I am sorry for H[enry] Fielding's Death, not only as I shall read no more of his writeings, but I believe he lost more than others, as no Man enjoy'd life more than he did, tho few had less reason to do so, the highest of his preferment being raking in the lowest sinks of vice and misery. I should think it a nobler and less nauseous employment to be one of the staff officers that conduct the Nocturnal Weddings. His happy Constitution (even when he had, with great pains, halfe demolish'd it) made him forget every thing when he was before a venison Pasty or over a Flask of champaign, and I am perswaded he has known more happy moments than any Prince upon Earth. His natural Spirits gave him Rapture with his Cookmaid, and chearfullness when he was Fluxing in a Garret. There was a great similitude between his character and that of Sir Richard Steele. He had the advantage both in Learning and, in my Opinion, Genius: They both agreed in wanting money in spite of all their Freinds, and would have wanted it if their Hereditary Lands had been as extensive as their Imagination, yet each of them so form'd for Happiness, it is pity they were not Immortal. . . .

. . . The most edifying part of the Journey to Lisbon is the history of the Kitten. I was the more touch'd by it, having a few days before found one in deplorable circumstances in a neighbouring Vineyard. I did not only releive her present wants with some excellent milk, but had her put into a clean Basket and brought to my own House, where she has liv'd ever since very comfortably.

I desire to have Fielding's posthumous works with his Memoirs of Jonathan Wild, and Journey to the Next World . . .

13. *Margaret Collier at Ryde, IoW, to Samuel Richardson*;
   3 October 1755 (fragment)
   [*Correspondence of Samuel Richardson*, ed. A. L. Barbauld, 6 vols.
   (London, 1804), ii, p. 77]

I was sadly vexed, at my first coming, at a report which had prevailed here, of my being the author of Mr. Fielding's last work, 'The Voyage to Lisbon:' the reason which was given for supposing it mine, was to the last degree mortifying, (viz. that it was so very bad a performance, and fell so far short of his other works, it must needs be the person *with him* who wrote it).

4. Anecdote of Fielding Facing Death

From James Harris, 'An Essay on the Life and Genius of Henry Fielding Esqr. Bath Feb. 5. 1758'

[Clive T. Probyn, *The Sociable Humanist: The Life and Works of James Harris (1709–1780)* (Oxford, 1991), app. III, pp. 312–13]

There is a fourth order of men, and those of no mean import, whose Wit and Humour keep pace with their condition. When Health and Fortune abound, then are Wit and Humour abundant also. If the Scene change, the Spring soon fails, and every attempt to exert themselves proves fruitless and vain. Nothing like this ever happened to our Author, whose Wit, though it might have had perhaps its intensions and remissions, yet never deserted him in his most unprosperous hours, nor even when Death itself openly lookt him in ye face.

Two Friends made him a visit in his last Illness on his leaving England, when his Constitution was so broken, that twas thought he could not survive a week. To explain to them his Indifference as to a protraction of Life, he with his usual humour related them the following story. A Man (sd. He) under condemnation at Newgate was just setting out for Tyburn, when there arrived a Reprieve. His Friends who recd. ye news with uncommon Joy, prest him instantly to be blooded; they were feard (they said) his Spirits on a change so unexpected must be agitated in the highest degree. Not in the least (replied the Hero) no agitation at all. If I am not hanged this Sessions, I know I shall ye next.

5. Matthew Maty's Review

NOTE: Of the four contemporary reviews of *The Journal of a Voyage to Lisbon* three—*London Magazine*, 24 (February 1755), pp. 54–6; *Gentleman's Magazine*, 25 (March 1755), p. 129; and *Monthly* Review, 12 (March 1755), pp. 234–5—are substantially available in Paulson and Lockwood, Nos. 151–3. By far the most comprehensive and thoughtful discussion of the work, however, is by Matthew Maty in the *Journal Britannique* (March–April 1755), Article V, 284–302. The following translation of Maty's review is by Professor Robert Denommé, University of Virginia.

This work has come from the same pen that gave us *Joseph Andrews*, *Tom Jones*, & *Amelia*, novels that have also appeared in other countries as well as in England. That alone would authorize me to include an excerpt here, for even the singularity of having been composed on a ship by a dying man, who preserved in the last moment of his life his good humour and love of humanity, would not in itself confer on this Voyage any claim to originality. That is what the anonymous editor of this post-humous work expresses:[1] *a lamp almost burnt out sometimes darts a ray as bright as ever. In like manner, a strong and lively genius will, in its last struggles, sometimes mount aloft, and throw forth the most striking marks of its original lustre.* [¶] *Wherever these are to be found, do you, the genuine patrons of extraordinary capacities, be as liberal in your applauses of him who is now no more, as you were of him whilst he was yet amongst you. And, on the other hand, if in this little work there should appear any traces of a weaken'd and decay'd life, let your own imaginations place before your eyes a true picture, in that of a hand trembling in almost its latest hour, of a body emaciated with pains, yet struggling for your entertainment; and let this affecting picture open each tender heart, (a)** and call forth a melting tear, to blot out whatever failings may be found in a work begun in pain, and finished almost at the same period with life.* [*Journal*, p. 544]

The preface by the Author himself follows the Editor's dedication. It appears to have been written at Lisbon, & must have only shortly preceded Mr. Fielding's death. He reflects on travellers in general and on the accounts of their travels. The desire to know men and the customs of different countries is, according to him, the only motive that can compel a reasonable man to leave his country; & only all that he has seen can render his conversation & his narratives interesting. If the way of thinking and of doing things were everywhere the same, nothing would be more boring than the occupation of a traveller: for the differences of mountains, of valleys, & of rivers, in a word, the different viewpoints offered by the earth's surfaces, would hardly suffice to provide him with pleasures proportionate to his efforts, & would give him but few opportunities to amuse or instruct others. This proves that Mr. Fielding, who had turned all his attention to the end of knowing mankind, was completely lacking in a taste for knowing nature, or antiquity. Other readers have other ideas. They find in the description of the wonders which the Creator has spread with as much variety as profusion in different countries, in the observations which allow us to focus on a site or facilitate access to it, in the remains, finally, of industry & the views of those who before us peopled the earth, objects worthy their attention. For them, Burnet, Addison, & two or three others, are not the only travellers who deserve to be read; and they take great care to place Tournefort, Labat, Sloane, Catesby, Ellis, Dampier, Feuillée, Frezier, Spon, Wheeler, Maillet, Shaw, Pococke & the travellers of Palmyra among those Goths

---

* (a) The sale of this work & of some other posthumous works of the same Author must comprise one of the principal resources of a young family deprived too soon of its Head. [Maty's note]

---

[1] In the review, passages quoted from the *Journal* ('Humphrys' edition) are translated in French and printed in italics.

and Vandals who, according to our Author, have claimed the exclusive privilege of writing Relations & Memoirs.

Mr. Fielding is certainly right in observing that, as everything a traveller sees is not worthy of being reported, everything he recounts should not commit him to preclude by his observations those of his readers. One needs to be selective & have a sense of taste, & these qualities, never very common, are found least, it seems, in a man who has seen many countries than in any other.

Homer himself (this is a new observation of my Author) is seen by some persons as a writer of voyages. The beginning of his *Odyssey* seems to favour this opinion, & Mr. Fielding does not undertake to challenge it. But to whichever kind of Writings the poem of the *Odyssey* belongs, it is surely the first, as the *Iliad* is at the head of another genre. That is what Longinus would acknowledge if he were here today. But the *Odyssey*, the *Telemachus*, & all the other works of this kind are to voyage-writing what the Romances are to histories. *I am far from supposing*, adds Mr. Fielding, *that Homer, Hesiod, and the other antient Poets and Mythologists, had any settled design to pervert and confuse the records of antiquity; but it is certain they have effected it;* (this appears no less certain to me) *and, for my part, I must confess I should have honoured and loved Homer more had he written a true history of his own times in humble prose, than those noble poems that have so justly collected the praise of all ages; for though I read these with more admiration and astonisment, I still read Herodotus, Thucydides and Xenophon, with more amusement and more satisfaction.* [*Journal*, pp. 548–9]. Here once again, Mr. Fielding reveals his simple taste, a laudable taste in a man close to death, but which will not induce others to follow him. As with matters of taste, talents are diversified; & instead of reducing them all to the same kind, even if that were the most excellent, it is better to ascribe them to those to whom they really belong, than to apply norms inappropriately to those who are not at all suited to them. Homer would not have maintained his pre-eminence if he had wished to be Herodotus, & a great Poet could have been a declaiming Historian, though one unreliable, or badly informed.

This is, more or less, what Mr. Fielding himself says to excuse Homer & the other original Poets. Nature, for them too limited, their times still too simple & too unvaried, would have encumbered their imagination; they were allowed to free themselves; & one can say that they changed realities into fictions much less than they converted fictions into realities. Their brush is so daring, & their colours so vivid, that everything they touch seems to exist in just the way they represent it. The exactness of their portraits, & the beauty of their landscapes, compel us to recognize in the one as in the other the elements of truth, & we do not ask if it is the effect of Nature, or her student the Poet who has furnished the design of the Piece.

But of all the Authors, those whom Mr. Fielding censures the most are those Writers who deliberately offer fables for truths, & thus trick the credulity of that kind of reader who lacks common sense enough to discern the deception. If our Author hadn't placed Pliny at the forefront of Writers of this kind, few persons would oppose what he says disparagingly about these fathers of lies or, I would say, these corruptors of reason.

[Fielding's critique of voyage-writing in these terms applies to the genre in general] *my lord Anson's alone being, perhaps, excepted* [because like Fielding's own work] *it deviates less from truth.* [Next is an italicized pastiche of paraphrased passages from the following two paragraphs (*Journal*, pp. 552–3), specifically these:] *Some few embellishments must be allowed to every historian . . . It is sufficient that every fact hath its foundation in truth . . . if any merely common incident should appear in this journal . . . the candid reader will easily perceive it is not introduced for its own sake, but for some observations and reflections . . . which, if but little to his amusement, tend directly to the instruction of the reader, or to the information of the public; to whom if I chuse to convey such instruction or information with an air of joke and laughter, none but the dullest of fellows will, I believe, censure it; but if they should, I have the authority of more than one passage in Horace to alledge in my defence.*

If one should reproach Mr. Fielding for having in effect taught nothing of importance to his country, he responds that his goal was to disguise the instruction under a veil of amusement, & thus to lead, all of a sudden, to a perfect reform in the laws relative to maritime affairs: *an undertaking, I will not say more modest, but surely more feasible, than that of reforming a whole people, by making use of a vehicular story, to wheel in among them worse manners than their own* [*Journal*, p. 554]. This small sarcasm [*trait de satyre*] would not escape those who have read [Richardson's] *Grandison* and recall his Italians.

At the head of the *Voyage* itself is another Introduction. It informs us of a few preliminaries which we cannot do without, but which should have taken up four pages instead of twenty. Mr. Fielding, much occupied in his duties as Justice of the peace with eradicating brigands, who to the shame of our police infest our streets and our highways, having ruined his health in this enterprise, & neglected for too long a case of hydropsy which finally resisted every remedy, & even those of Dr. Ward, resolved to try to regain his health in a warmer climate. The voyage to Lisbon was judged best suited to his affairs & his state of health. He prepared for the journey by undergoing the repeated tapping [of his belly], & he describes each of these operations with a detail excusable in a man who is speaking about himself, but which moreover do not produce any of those instructive & amusing observations that the Author promises us.

A Captain, formerly a Ship-owner, & actually in charge of a merchant vessel, negotiated terms for the voyage for Mr. Fielding as well as for his wife & and one of his daughters. After several delays, the 26th of June was absolutely set as the day of departure. The Author takes leave of his family on that day, gets into a carriage, gets into a long-boat, & in the midst of the inhuman mockery of the watermen, is brought to the ship, where he is hoisted aboard with precautions that he describes, & which could be useful to others in the same situation.

Here am I embarked with Mr. Fielding, but I do not care to follow him into all the places where he stops either willingly or against his will. I would fear that this voyage would appear as long to my readers as the contrary winds which delayed the ship for five weeks, to which our Author was subjected, on the coasts of England. His wit and gaiety never abandon him, but he is often reduced to seeing nothing;

confined to his cabin in the midst of a busy crew and a family either asleep or sick, he could relieve the boredom thus: in writing about little-nothings he works to keep his wits. Let us content ourselves then by giving an idea of his predicament.

Mr. Fielding had first of all proposed to place at the head of his work research on the antiquity of the art of travelling. He would promise himself assistance from the literary Societies of Europe, help from Manuscripts of all countries, & the protection of Kings who favoured the arts. But after having carefully considered his project & the scope of his work, he all of a sudden stood down upon learning of the discovery of a young member of the Society of Antiquairies. He proved (though up to this point the membership to which he belongs is not in complete agreement about his discovery) through monuments which precede by a great deal the date of the oldest modern collections of books or of butterflies, of which none goes back beyond the deluge, that the first man was a traveller, & that hardly had he & his family settled in paradise than displeased with their home, they set off for other places. From this, the result is that the urge to travel is as ancient as the human race, & constituted from the beginning man's torture.

Dispensing with this part of the story, which consists in representing what things had been, he limits himself to informing us what they are, as far as journeys are concerned, at least in England. Journeys by water or by land have two things in common: one, where luggage takes up most of the room, the least care is given to the passenger; the other, which the latter [the passenger] contracts upon setting off on the road, a new relationship, or rather subjugation, with the one who conveys him. Now, from the coachman up to the ship-Captain, there is no master whose authority is more despotic.

This tyranny is *scarce consistent with the liberties of a free people; nor could it be reconciled with them, did it not move downwards, a circumstance universally apprehended to be incompatible to all kinds of slavery. For Aristotle, in his Politicks, hath proved abundantly to my satisfaction, that no men are born to be slaves, except barbarians; and these only to such as are not themselves barbarians: and indeed Mr. Montesquieu hath carried it very little farther, in the case of the Africans; the real truth being, that no man is born to be a slave, unless to him who is able to make him so. [¶] This subjection is absolute, and consists of a perfect resignation both of body and soul to the disposal of another; after which resignation, during a certain time, his subject retains no more power over his own will, than an Asiatic slave, or an English wife [Journal*, p. 574]. Mr. Fielding wrote this in a brief moment of irritability, obliged to put up with the Captain's order, who called him on board two days before he intended to leave. For the rest, he justly credits the Captain's good qualities, his bravery, his humanity, his prudence, even his piety; but mocks, from time to time, some superstitious notions, from which few seamen are exempt, & his predictions of a favourable change in the wind, on which he had been mistaken twenty times, going by his own wishes twenty times. This last foible is equally applicable on land, & Mr. Fielding is not peeved with seamen alone. But one must read these details in the book itself, & appreciate the physical & mental condition of the one who writes them.

Here, for example, is a passage in which he portrays himself in a rather critical circumstance. Listen to him; the time is that of a storm. *The captain now grew outrageous, and declaring open war with the wind, took a resolution, rather more bold than wise, of sailing in defiance of it, and in its teeth. He declared he would let go his anchor no more, but would beat the sea while he had either yard or sail left. He accordingly stood from the shore, & made so large a tack, that before night, though he seemed to advance but little on his way, he was got out of sight of land. [¶] Towards the evening, the wind began, in the captain's own language, to freshen; and indeed it freshened so much, that before ten it blew a perfect hurricane. The captain having got, as he supposed, to a safe distance, tacked again towards the English shore; and now the wind veered a point only in his favour, and continued to blow with such violence, that the ship ran above eight knots or miles an hour, during this whole day and tempestuous night, till bed-time. I was obliged to betake myself once more to my solitude; for my women were again all down in their sea-sickness, and the captain was busy on deck. [¶] Having contracted no great degree of good humour, by living a whole day alone, without a single soul to converse with, I took but ill physic to purge it off, by a bed-conversation with the captain; who, amongst many bitter lamentations of his fate, and protesting he had more patience than a Job, frequently intermixed summons to the commanding-officer on the deck, . . . of whom he inquired every quarter of an hour concerning the state of affairs; the wind, the care of the ship, and other matters of navigation. The frequency of these summons, as well as the solicitude with which they were made, gave me to understand, that we were not totally free from danger, and would have given no small alarm to a man, who had either not learnt what it is to die, or known what it is to be miserable. And my dear wife and child must pardon me, if what I did not conceive to be any great evil to myself, I was not much terrified with the thoughts of happening to them . . . [¶] Can I say then I had no fear; indeed I cannot, reader, I was afraid for thee, lest thou shouldst have been deprived of the pleasure thou art now enjoying [Journal*, pp. 623–4]. This is worthy enough of the Author of the *Roman comique*, and our English Scarron says elsewhere [*Journal*, p. 649], that the thought of writing this narrative was the result of the impossible situation in which he found himself in the Downs, of exercising his sociable disposition, & that the most amusing pages of his book, if indeed there are any, were the result of the most disagreeable hours he experienced.

The best executed part of the work is the description he gives of an inn on the coast, & the portrait he sketches of the host and hostess. But I will not overcharge this article, which is becoming insensibly long.

His reflexions on the monopolies of the fishmongers who prevent the poor from nourishing themselves cheaply on seafood, on the tyranny of the coastal inhabitants who overcharge for the services they provide by ten times the value & on the disproportionate need to make use of them, on the transformation of the English sailors, obedient & industrious while on ship, undisciplined & independent as soon as they touch land, [all] indicate a man, even in his last days, concerned with exposing public abuses & reforming them.

The journey from the coasts of England to those of Portugal was short & uneventful. Mr. Fielding concludes his narration with a few words about the difficulty the strangers experienced on reaching Lisbon. It is a pity he did not live long enough to give us his observations on the country & on the inhabitants. What he does say about them leads us to believe he would not have been favourably inclined toward them.

A fragment, by the same hand, follows the narrative of the *Voyage*. It turns on the posthumous Works of my lord Bolingbroke. Mr. Fielding assures us that having undertaken the reading of these works with as much prejudice in the Author's favour as aversion toward his doctrine, he greatly diminished his esteem for the one without losing any of his contempt for the other. He had wanted to arm those whom a great reputation, an air of confidence, a brilliant imagination, an imposing style would scarcely fail to lead astray, against the illusion that a superficial reading of these famous Essays can produce. It is in juxtaposing the contradictions they contain one against the other that Mr. Fielding thought to execute his plan, & the little fragment that has been saved suffices to make us regret that he did not live long enough to complete it.

INDEX OF NAMES, PLACES, AND TOPICS

IN INTRODUCTIONS, TEXTS, AND NOTES

(Coverage of topics is selective; many titles in short form; page and note numbers in italics signify references or quotations within Fielding's text)